Rene Girard, Law, Literature, and Cinema

Eric M. Wilson

Rene Girard, Law, Literature, and Cinema

The Legal Drama of the Scapegoat

Springer

Eric M. Wilson
Independent Researcher
Pictou, NS, Canada

ISBN 978-981-97-1155-0 ISBN 978-981-97-1156-7 (eBook)
https://doi.org/10.1007/978-981-97-1156-7

This Springer imprint is published by the registered company Springer Nature Singapore Pte Ltd.
The registered company address is: 152 Beach Road, #21-01/04 Gateway East, Singapore 189721, Singapore

Paper in this product is recyclable.

A given dramatic performance constitutes a sort of rite, the shadowy similitude of the religious experience.—Rene Girard (Girard, 1977: 291).[1]

[1] Girard, R. (1977). *Violence and the sacred* (Gregory, P., Trans.). The Johns Hopkins Press.

To my three besties: Fresno, William, and Betty

Preface

It is an old joke within literary studies that Rene Girard (1923–2015) does not really need God because he already has Emile Durkheim. 'But I don't deal with theology. I deal with the anthropology of religion,' said Girard (Girard, 2020: 119), and he reiterated this in his interview with Thomas F. Bertonneau in 1987.

Beronneau: 'How far is your interest in religion, or indeed the religious element, responsible for the defensive attitude many people seem to take toward your theory?'

Girard: 'I would say ninety-eight-and-a-half per cent; maybe ninety-nine-and-a-half. The religious aspect wasn't there at the beginning, and maybe that's why some scholars can accept *Deceit, Desire and the Novel* (1961) but not *Violence and the Sacred*,[2] let alone *The Scapegoa*,[3] (Girard, 2020: 35).

At the heart of Girard's enterprise, which is in equal part literary and anthropological, is an overriding concern with the relationship between the religious and the judicial, both realms marked by an extreme ambiguity that results from both being rooted in the archaic phenomena of sacrificial violence. Expressed somewhat formulaically, Girard's position is that the anthropological directly anticipates, or 'mimics' in advance, the literary. This gives rise to the astonishing hypothesis, which is underappreciated by many readers of Girard, that the formal structure of literature itself enacts, or imitates, the social logic of prehistoric cultural formation, an inherently violent and chaotic process signified by a number of concepts that are central to Girard's lexicon: desire, mimesis, mimetic rivalry, *ressentiment*, the will-to-revenge, doubles, *meconnaissance* (or mis-recognition), sacrifice, myth, and the scapegoat. We are born without knowledge what to be or what to desire; therefore, we naturally acquire the desires and identities of others through imitation. But since we are purely mimetic beings, conflict and violence are unavoidable for we all cannot have exclusive possession of that which everyone else wants; identities become confused because everyone is claiming to be the true one and a systemic crisis of un-differentiation results. The cornerstone of cultural formation, as it turns out, is the therapeutic cure applied by both religion and law but which in their

[2] *La Violence et la sacre* (Paris: Editions Bernard Grasset 1972).

[3] *Le Bouc emissaire* (Paris: Editions Bernard Grasset 1982).

pre-civilizational form are two descending aspects of the primal reality of ritualistic sacrifice, the prehistoric foundation of cultural order, or *nomos*. 'In a world without judicial institutions, very small peasant communities, revenge, unleashed revenge, can destroy an entire community' (Girard, 2020: 23) making the curtailment, or de-escalation, of reciprocal violence the pre-eminent objective of primitive culture. And the means settled on, most likely the result of a series of not-so-happy accidents is the discovery, or invention, of the scapegoat: that member of the imitative crowd who is singled out from the others on the basis of some given criteria and then ceremoniously put to death as a means of expunging the collective violence of the group by means of a form of catharsis. With the expulsion of the collective violence of the crowd following the primal murder as if by magic, the slayers of the victim misinterpret the nature of the event and erroneously attribute to the scapegoated one a latent but now released supernatural power to restore peace and unify the community. And it is the legacy of the scapegoat, Girard argues, that conveys by encrypted means the revelation of the 'things hidden since the foundation of the world,' (Matthew 13:35) specifically the hitherto mis-recognized affinities of judicial and literary texts. Which explains why, jumping ahead several thousands of years, we can come to recognize that the 'legal' or 'courtroom drama' of both literature and cinema is the unconscious, or, in the alternative, the mis-recognized (*meconnaissance*) secular re-telling of the mythic and religious sacrificial drama of the sacred victim. The generic scapegoat may hold the interpretive key to the entirety of the canonical texts, literary and cinematic, of the academic field known as law-and-literature: within the domain of the legal drama the narrative and dramatic focus is invariably upon the validation of a victim, who almost inevitably turns out to be a moral and/or legal 'innocent' who has been subjected to persecutorial violence, physical and/or symbolic, as the result of an accusation that is false. In other words: a modern surrogate of the archaic scapegoat is the central object of the aesthetic and moral concern of the cultural representation of law.

The purpose of this volume, which is deliberately written as a polemic, is not merely to provide yet one more book on law-and-literature but to demonstrate the underappreciated relevance of Girard to the field. Both the methodological and moral imperatives of law-and-literature conform remarkably well to Girard's fundamental project which is also intensely normative: (i) the unmasking of the mimetic nature of desire insofar as the community is haunted by both the reality or eternal threat of violence; and (ii) the revelation of the innocence of the accused who is structurally homologous with the archaic scapegoat who is itself the primal source of the regenerative unanimity that is the foundation of the community, including that of the legal order itself. The demystification of the scapegoat is the moral heart of law-and-literature as well as Girard's 'fundamental anthropology', and both are nothing other than the exposure and abolition of *meconnaissance*. But in so doing I also wish to make a contribution to Girard studies by using law-and-literature to highlight what I perceive as a comparatively undertheorized aspect of Girard's work: the problem of the persistence of scapegoat mechanism in some occluded form following the formal suspension of the sacrificial society following the rise of Christianity and rabbinical Judaism in the first century CE.

The chapters herein are the expanded and greatly revised lecture notes that I first wrote for my course on law, literature, and cinema that I taught at the Faculty of Law, Monash University, Melbourne, Australia, from 2010 to 2015. Although I treat most of the established 'classics' or 'canonical texts' from both literature and film (exempting television for purposes of brevity), the reader will notice that virtually none of the works that I discuss are recent. There are two reasons for this. The first is that in order to ensure that my students obtained a functional literacy in law-and-literature I focused on those texts about which there is virtually no dispute over their canonical status. The second is related to the first by a rather indirect but disturbing route: although there is near unanimous consensus as to the classics prior to about 1995, there is noticeably less agreement concerning the canon after the millennium. The reason for this, I believe, is that the foundational and archetypal figure of the scapegoat has receded somewhat from legal drama. If I were to generalize grossly, I would argue that the current trend in legal drama is toward the political vindication of the accusing victim rather than the salvific defense of the wrongly accused. The reasons for this apparent shift are disturbing, to some at least, and I address them at full length in the final chapter where I arrive at a un-Girardian conclusion concerning the apparent return of scapegoating.

Pictou, Canada
Eric M. Wilson

Reference

Girard, R. (2020). *Conversations with Rene Girard: Prophet of Envy* (Haven, C. L., Ed.). Bloomsbury Academic.

Contents

1 **Rene Girard, Sophocles, *Oedipus Tyrannus*, and the Goat Song of *tragoidia*** 1
1.1 Sophocles, Scapegoating, and the Sacrificial Mechanism 2
1.1.1 Sophistry 9
1.1.2 Plague and Incest 15
1.1.3 Oracles and Meconnaissance 21
1.1.4 Oedipus the Foundling 28
1.2 Symbolization, Sacralization, and *Meconnaissance* 30
1.2.1 Mimesis and Desire 33
1.2.2 The Scapegoat and Evolution 39
1.2.3 Myth and Sacralization 47
1.3 Metaphysical Desire, Interdividual Psychology, and *Ressentiment* 53
1.4 Mimesis, Ethics, and Deconstruction 65
1.5 Law-and-Literature-and-Film as the Demystification of the Scapegoat 83
1.6 The Scapegoat as the Secret of Law-and-Literature 96
References 110

2 ***'El sueno de la razon produce monstruos'* or, 'The Dream of Reason Creates Monsters': Two Little Piggies Went to the Apocalypse in William Golding's *Lord of the Flies*** 115
2.1 *Lord of the Flies*, Fundamental Anthropology, and *Meconnaissance* 116
2.2 Social Contracting on the Beach: The Inadequacy of Secular Reason 123
2.3 From the State to Religion: Justice as Vengeance 126
2.4 'I'm the Reason Why It's No Go…": Rene Girard and Max Scheler on Mimesis and *Ressentiment* 130
2.5 'They Used to Call Me "Piggy"': *Meconnaissance*, Undifferentiation, and Censorship 135

2.6 'I'm not Going to Play Any Longer. Not with You.': The Parallels of Mimetic Crisis and Political Crisis 145
2.7 'Roger Sharpened a Stick at Both Ends': The Return of the Repressed 150
2.8 'Close, Close, Close!": The One Who Brings Existential Envy with Him 153
References 164

3 'Does Anybody Know Anything About the Law?': White Male Suburbanites in the Wilderness and Their Regression to the State of Nature in James Dickey's *Deliverance* 167
3.1 Thomas Hobbes in the Wilderness 168
3.1.1 Thomas Hobbes on the Family 170
3.2 'The World is Easily Lost': In the Country of the Nine-Fingered People 175
3.2.1 The Geographical: 'Savage Sacredness' 179
3.2.2 The Existential: 'Man-The-Hunter' 181
3.3 *Katabasis* 1: Dueling Banjos 185
3.4 'Why Do You Go on These Trips with Me, Ed?' 189
3.4.1 The Model 190
3.4.2 The Deer 191
3.4.3 Lewis (= Ed) 193
3.5 *Katabasis* 2: The Monstrous Doubles 199
3.6 'Well Now, How About This? Just...How *About* This?': The Primordial Epiphany of Sacralization and Sovereignty 203
3.7 Conclusion: 'Something or Other Was Being Made Good' 207
References 210

4 'A Little Law and Order Wouldn't Hurt Anybody Around Here': '*The Man Who Shot Liberty Valance*' and '*High Noon*' 213
4.1 Catharsis: The Western and Classical Mythology 213
4.2 I Kill Therefore I Am: Western Mythology and American History 218
4.2.1 The Westerner as Rugged Individualist 226
4.3 *The Man Who Shot Liberty Valance* (1962): The Murder-Crafted Garden 228
4.4 The Precarious Sovereignty of the Westerner: Carl Schmitt and the Friend-Enemy Distinction 236
4.4.1 Nomos: The Originating Violence of Everywhere 238
4.4.2 Das Feind: The Problem of Being Serious 241
4.4.3 The Death of Universalism: 'He Who Decides on the Decision of the Exception is the Sovereign' 245
4.4.4 The Deadly Reversal: Decisionism as Sovereignty 249

4.5 'Although You're Grievin', I Can't be Leavin', Until I Shoot Frank Miller Dead': *High Noon* (1952) or, the Tin Star of Decisionism 256
References 265

5 'A Woman Only Loves a Real Man': Metaphysical Desire and the Crisis of Undifferentiation in Akira Kurosawa's *Yojimbo* and *Rashomon* 269
5.1 The Archetypal Themes of the *Chambara* 270
5.2 *Chambara*, Mimetic Rivalry, and the Crisis of Undifferentiation 273
5.3 *Yojimbo*: Trauma and the Bodyguard 278
5.3.1 The Apocalypse of Mr. Mulberry Field 285
5.4 *Rashomon*, or Metaphysical Desire in a Grove of Bamboo 288
5.5 The Male Gaze and the Triangle of Desire 294
5.6 Psychological Time and the Grove of Internal Mediation 300
5.7 What Really Happened in the Grove: Metaphysical Desire and Saving Face 304
References 317

6 'I Just Want to Talk...': Liberalism, Generative Unanimity, and Post-sacrificial Scapegoating in *12 Angry Men* 319
6.1 The Law Movie as Genre 320
6.2 Law *Noir* 325
6.2.1 Sidney Lumet and 12 Angry Men: Preliminary Thoughts 328
6.3 Critical Legal Theory and Law *Noir* 332
6.4 *The Thin Blue Line*: Law *Noir* and Epistemological Undifferentiation 336
6.5 The Specter of the Scapegoat: A Girardian Reading of *12 Angry Men* 342
References 355

7 'You Must Always Point...': The Post-heroic Lawyer as Scapegoat and Scapegoater in *Presumed Innocent*, *The Verdict*, and *Cape Fear* 357
7.1 The Dramatic Peril of the Post-heroic Lawyer 358
7.2 'Is That You Here, Dear Rusty?' or, Rusty Sabich Who Art in Hell... 363
7.3 The Pernicious Legacy of Legal Realism: Legal Culture in Popular Culture 372
7.3.1 The Paradoxical Status of the Lawyer as Esoteric Knowledge-Worker 375
7.4 *The Verdict*: The Pathetic Case of Frank Gavin 380
7.4.1 Anti-heroic Lawyers: Virtue, Money, and Power 381
7.5 Frank Gavin as Post-heroic Lawyer 386

7.6 *Cape Fear* or, When the Client from Hell Returns 389
7.7 'You Sacrificed Me!': Sam Bowden Rediscovers the Scapegoat 396
References 408

8 The Telling of Lies and the Casting of Lots: Franz Kafka's *The Trial* and the Eternal Undecidability of the Scapegoat 411
8.1 'Someone Must Have Been Casting Lots About Josef K.': The Indeterminate 'Truth' of Franz Kafka 413
8.1.1 Girard's Interpretive Reading of the Book of Job 418
8.2 Nightmare/Profane 424
8.3 The Endless Undecidable 428
8.3.1 Justice-as-Organism 430
8.3.2 Justice-as-Desire 432
8.3.3 Justice-as-Desire = Law-as-Undecidable 434
8.4 Sacrificial/Sacred/Sacralizing 437
8.5 At the End There is a Window 456
References 460

9 '...Why do we, All of us, have to Keep Judging and Being Judged?': The Scapegoat and the Scapegoater in Albert Camus' *The Stranger* and *The Fall* 463
9.1 *L'absurde*: Fate Versus the Accident 463
9.2 The Facts of the Strange Case of M. Mersault (a.k.a. 'M. Death-Jump') 473
9.2.1 Katharsis/Pharmakos/Pharmakon/Katharma 478
9.3 Mersault as Tragic Hero, or the Accident Waiting to Happen 481
9.4 Jean-Baptiste Clamence: The Judge-Penitent as Universal Sacrifice 492
9.5 Jean-Baptiste Clamence Meets the Anti-Christ 499
References 505

10 'Out There': Monstrous Doubles and the *Folie a Deux* in Truman Capote's *In Cold Blood* 507
10.1 'The Odor of Windfall Apples Rotting Under the Apple Trees': Ghosts and Monsters 507
10.1.1 Alvin Dewey's Uncanny Encounter in the Graveyard 509
10.2 The Double-Monstrosity of Hickock-Smith: The Non-fiction Novel and the Techniques of Allegory 511
10.3 The *Folie a Deux*: Monstrous Doubles or Monsters Who are Brothers 519
10.4 'Of All the People in the World, the Clutters Were the Least Likely to Be Murdered': Herb Clutter and the Villagers of Holcomb 524
10.4.1 Herb Clutter and 'Tex' Smith 527

10.4.2 Herb Clutter and Perry Smith 528
10.4.3 Perry Smith and Truman Capote 529
10.5 'No Chicken-Hearted Jurors, They': The Brothers in the Breed of Cain 531
10.6 Mythic Un-Truth: The Sacred Murder of Nancy Clutter 537
References 541

11 The 'Good Murderer' Gary Gilmore: The Re-sacralization of the Scapegoat in the Age of Public Reason 543
11.1 Murder, Sacralization, and Apocalypse 544
11.2 Authenticity as Metaphysical Desire: John Rawls and the Violence of Neutrality 551
11.3 John Rawls and the Problem of Religion or, Isotropic Men of No Qualities 556
11.3.1 Objection I: The Un-Civil 'Friend or Foe' Distinction of Carl Schmitt 559
11.3.2 Objection II: Paul Dumouchel on the Violent Paradox of 'Those Who Exclude Themselves' 564
11.3.3 The Problem of Religion for Fundamentalist Neutralism 569
11.4 The Stumbling-Block of Public Reason: The Scandalizing Case of Gary Gilmore 572
11.4.1 The Visitations 580
11.4.2 Visitation One: Sacramento, Late 1946 583
11.4.3 Visitation Two: January 1, 1952, Salt Lake City 585
11.4.4 Visitation Three: Nevada, Summer 1946 585
11.5 The Violence of the Exclusion of Those Who Exclude Themselves by Refusing the Gift of Neutrality or, Scapegoating the Scapegoaters 587
11.5.1 The Just War of the Decent Peoples Against the Indecent Peoples of the World 590
11.5.2 Fundamentalist Neutralism and the Universal Crisis of Undifferentiation 593
11.6 Concluding Post-secularist Transcript 599
References 600

12 Spare a Thought for the Hangman: The Apocalypse of Rene Girard 603
12.1 Rene Girard and the Problem of *Meconnaissance* 604
12.1.1 'Sacrifice with a Bad Conscience': Modernity and De-sacralization 615
12.2 Political Religion: The Failed Substitute for the *Katechon* 617
12.3 The Persecution Society: Political Religion as *Skandalon* 622
12.4 From De-sacralization to the Neo-Sacralized Cult of the Victim 625

12.5 Victimology: The Sign of Citizenship in the Time of Globalized Undifferentiation 631
12.6 Sacrifice with a Good Conscience: The Super-Victimary Machine 637
12.7 Demystifying the Demystifiers: The *Skandalon* of Cancel Culture 647
References 660

Chapter 1
Rene Girard, Sophocles, *Oedipus Tyrannus*, and the Goat Song of *tragoidia*

Abstract The central thesis of this book is that Rene Girard's theory of the scapegoat provides an entirely new and original way of conceptualizing judicial modernity in a manner that is of enormous use and interest to the academic field of law-and-literature. This introductory chapter accomplishes three central tasks. The first is providing a concise definition of the most crucial terms within Girard's literary and anthropological theories. The second is performing a Girardian analysis of Sophocles' *Oedipus Tyrannus*, concluding that the primary role of law and legal culture in Girard's work has been under-appreciated. The third is advancing of my own argument that one of the great attractions of Girard's theory of mimesis and sacrificial violence is its under-appreciated relevance to the formal study of representations of law within cultural media of both literature and film. A concise definition of law-and-literature that includes law and film studies will also be provided. My general conclusion is that the ethical imperative of the legal drama is essentially identical to that of Girard's own enterprise: the demystification of the scapegoat and the scapegoating process.

Keywords Scapegoat · *Meconnaissance* · Undifferentiation · Double transference · Mimetic desire · Mimetic rivalry · Metaphysical desire · Acquisitive mimesis · Conflictual mimesis · Internal mediation · External mediation · Sacralization

There are two generally agreed upon definitions of the word *scapegoat*. The first, attributed to William Tynsdale, is taken from his vernacular translation of the Bible (1530) and is found in The Book of Leviticus 16: 5–10: 'one of the two goats that was chosen by lot to be sent alive into the wilderness, the sins of the people having been symbolically laid upon it.' The second is more general and ecumenical: the 'One who is blamed or punished for the sins of others' (Dawson, 2013: x). For literary critic and anthropologist Rene Girard (1923–2015) 'the most interesting meaning of the expression scapegoat, or, alternatively, the *surrogate victim* or *emissary victim*, lies in its relationship to the 'unconscious mechanism for the representation and acts of persecution" (Girard, 1986: 120), and he uses the concept of the scapegoat in an extraordinarily imperialistic fashion to construct a universalist 'fundamental anthropology'

E. M. Wilson, *Rene Girard, Law, Literature, and Cinema*,
https://doi.org/10.1007/978-981-97-1156-7_1

(McKenna, 1992) of the origins of religion, law, literature, and, not to be immodest about it, the entirety of each of the world's ostensibly diverse cultural orders. Civilization is ultimately derived from mythology, a series of carefully constructed lies, and the evolution of every mythological world-view 'is governed by the determination to eliminate any representation of violence' (Girard, 1986: 76) for the other great universal constant is that culture 'is predisposed to the permanent concealment of its origins in collective violence' (Girard, 1986: 100). The scapegoat is, in an anthropological sense, the All-Father of everything because violence and mythology are the twin pillars of social formation. But, as Girard repeatedly informs us, all of this is of the 'things hidden since the foundation of the world' for the scapegoat's role in the genesis of what became civilization has remained occluded, buried under sedimentary layers of partly intentional partly accidental acts of mis-recognition or *meconnaissance*. It is through texts that we must critically excavate, and our incisory diggings will be sited at those points where literature and law most clearly intersect. And an excellent place to begin the process of disinterment of culture's violent origins is with the playwrights of ancient Athens, for the original Greek word for Tragedy, *tragoidia* means '"goat song"'[1] although 'it might be better translated as "scapegoat song"' (Eagleton, 2020: 270). The question that confronts us is why Tragedy is called *tragoidia*, 'a word that seems to impose the animal on the development of high human civilization, the primitive and the grotesque on sublime literary creations' (Bremmer 2020: 130). It will not take us very long to come up with an answer. The essence of Tragedy, which is the sacrifice of an innocent and falsely accused victim, is identical to the essence of civilization, which is that no one understands what they are really doing.

1.1 Sophocles, Scapegoating, and the Sacrificial Mechanism

The great city (*polis*) of Thebes has a problem: everyone and everything is dying from something that appears to be a plague (*nosos*) that behaves as the destroyer of all things. Or so it is in Sophocles' goat song *Oedipus Tyrannus.*

The chorus:

'Our city—look around you, see with your own eyes—

Our ship pitches wildly, cannot lift her dead

From the depths, the red waves of death …

Thebes is dying. A blight on the fresh crops

And the rich pastures, cattle sicken and die,

And the women die in labor, children stillborn,

[1] Alternatively, the '"song at the sacrifice of a goat"' (Burkert, 2020: 133).

And the plague, the fiery god of fever hurls down

On the city, his lightning slashing through us—

Raging plague in all its vengeance, devastating

In the house of Cadmus! And black Death luxuriates

In the raw, wailing miseries of Thebes' (Sophocles, 1984: 160)

As Bernard Knox has commented.

> So far as the action is concerned [*Oedipus Tyrannus*] is the most relentlessly secular of the Sophoclean tragedies. Destiny, fate, and the will of the gods do indeed loom ominously behind the human action, but that action, far from suggesting primeval rituals and satanic [sic] divinities, reflects, at every point, contemporary realities familiar to the audience that first saw the play. (Knox, 1984: 134)

For, as everyone in that contemporary audience 'knows,' Oedipus murdered his father Laius and procreated with his mother Jocasta and Sigmund Freud created an entire secular mythology out of this difficult 'truth'. And the most critical of these contemporary realities is that of law as Michel Foucault argued: 'Oedipus—I mean *Oedipus Rex*—is, as you know, a foundational representation of law. Naturally, in saying this I am repeating a platitude and a truism' (Foucault, 2020: 329). Again, it is a matter of common knowledge.

> Everyone knows that in Greek tragedy, the theme of representing law—of the foundational representation of law—is essential. Whether it be Aeschylus through *Prometheus* or *Oresteia*, or Sophocles with *Antigone* and *Electra*, the problem of the confrontation of rights, the confrontation between the law of the family and the law of the city, the problem of the foundation of the law, the original institution of the tribunal, or the question of vengeance—all of this constitutes a theme which, if not universal, is at least constant throughout Greek tragedy. (Foucault, 2020: 330)

The Hellenic relationship between tragedy and law is in truth not dissimilar to 'the American Western which, after all, also presents a problem of law, of the confrontation of rights, of the confrontation of law and vengeance, of the right of conquest' (Foucault, 2020: 330),[2] and, as a result, we expect and receive dramatically intense sequences of personal rivalry and enmity. Oedipus, whose mandatory 'tragic flaw' is anger[3] (Girard, 1977: 68–71), is set against two 'enemies,' his 'brother-in-law' (and

---

[2] I discuss the American Western in Chap. 4, below. Foucault adds a further and equally fascinating thought, which this book, in part, directly responds to. 'One has the impression …that from the time of Greek theatre up to at least the end of the eighteenth century, one of the fictions … of theatre in European societies was to be the place or stage for debating the problem of law….It seems to me that there is an entire side to the institutions of representation—of the representative arts—in European societies that are organized around this question of the foundation of law and whose significance and meaning is to manifest, in one way or another, the fundamental problems of law' (Foucault, 2020: 330). The main thesis of this book is that the fundamental problem of law that literature-and-film most frequently, albeit semi-consciously, addresses is that of the scapegoat and sacrifice.

[3] 'Oedipus is typified by extreme susceptibility to suspicion and anger; he strikes back rashly against anything resembling a threat or an obstacle' (Girard, 2004: 64). It was anger and obstacle that led

maybe his 'uncle' as well) Creon and Tiresias the 'blind seer' over the assigning of the 'fault' of being the source of the plague. The rhetorical stratagems that unfold occur within a wider oratorical conflict concerning patricide and incest as to 'whether these crimes can be attributed to one particular protagonist, and to *one alone*' (Girard, 1977: 72) and the 'force exerted by the three men in the struggle corresponds to each man's illusion of superiority, his hubris' (Girard, 1977: 70). Sophocles, in this three-way contest concerning the twinned issues of guilt and innocence surreptitiously working against what everyone knows, re-stages the contest as the means for not establishing responsibility for the disaster but as a way of raising reasonable doubts about Oedipus' commonly accepted criminal guilt (Harshbarger, 2020). The first sticky issue concerns the number of the alleged killers of Laius.

> Creon: 'Well, he [Laius] was killed, and Apollo commands us now—he could not be more clear. "Pay the killers back—whoever is responsible"'.
> Oedipus: 'Where on earth are they? Where to find it now, the trail of the ancient guilt so hard to trace?' (Sophocles, 1984: 164–165).

The difficulty is that while Oedipus recollects killing all in the entourage of the man who attacked him earlier—'I killed them all, every mother's son!' (Sophocles, 1984: 206)— it appears that one of Laius' servants survived the slaughter.

> Creon: '…they were all killed but one. He escaped, terrified, he could tell us nothing clearly, nothing of what he saw—just one thing.'
> Oedipus: 'What's that? One thing could hold the key to all, a small beginning gives us grounds for hope.'
> Creon: 'He said thieves attacked them—a whole band, not single handed, cut King Laius down' (Sophocles, 1984: 165–166).[4]

This is a decisive moment and a narrative change introduced by Sophocles in order to subvert the common understanding of the past events that prove Oedipus' act of patricide, according to Sandor Goodhart.

> In the overall dramatic context … what is striking is not only that Oedipus may not be the murderer of Laius, but that there is a curious insistence in the play that the murderers of Laius may be many. The oracle, the witness as related by Creon … the Chorus (if we are to believe its information originates elsewhere), all the sources, that is, which are independent of Oedipus' own account, agree on at least one crucial detail. The multiplicity of the murderers was the 'one thing' about which the witness in Creon's report was 'certain' and the witness

Oedipus into killing the man who may have been his father, Laius: as he described it they 'were about to thrust me off the road—brute force—and the one shouldering me aside, the driver, I strike him in anger!—and the old man [Laius?], watching me coming up along his wheels—he brings down his prod, two prongs straight at my head! I paid him back with interest! … I killed them all, every mother's son!' (Sophocles, 1984: 206).

[4] This belief in multiple killers is repeated by the chorus: 'Laius was killed, they say, by certain travelers' (Sophocles 1984: 175). It is also reconfirmed by Jocasta, Oedipus' wife and possible mother: '…Laius, so the report goes at least, was killed by strangers, thieves, at a place where the three roads meet…', the 'place called Phocis', to which Oedipus replies: 'You said *thieves*—[the survivor] told you a whole band of them murdered Laius. So, if he holds to the same number, I cannot be the killer. One can't equal many' (Sophocles 1984: 201, 202, 208).

> testimony is corroborated independently, if we are to believe Creon, by the words of Apollo himself. (Goodhart, 1978: 59)

The Leader of the chorus:

'We asked Apollo… he sent his answer back:

"Relief from the plague can only come one way.

Uncover the murderers of Laius, put them to death or drive them into exile"' (Sophocles, 1984: 176). […].

> Oedipus: 'Now my curse on the murderer. Whoever he is, a lone man unknown in his crime or one man among many …' (Sophocles, 1984: 172).

There is an insinuation here of a political conspiracy against the tyrant: Creon, his rival, is the self-proclaimed mediator of the Delphic oracle and, therefore, controls both the flow of information and the 'correct' interpretation of its meaning. As only Creon has 'heard' the prophecy of Apollo, Oedipus cannot logically exclude the possibility that the content of the oracle has been altered in the course of its transmission by a covertly hostile intermediary, Creon and/or Tiresias.

> In reporting the oracle, Creon does not give the words of the priestess who received them from the god. Instead, he says *lego*, 'I say', so that he becomes the authority for what the oracle says, not the god or his priestess. He reports in his own words what Apollo's oracle has said and is hence responsible for its content and meaning. Oedipus never requests the exact words of the oracle. (Tyrell, 2020: 121 n 6)

Compounding this first blunder by the all too easily angered Oedipus is the tyrant's second, and even deadlier, mistake; 'By allowing discussion to take place before the elders [the chorus] and by granting Creon the initiative, Oedipus loses control of the search and the direction it will take' (Tyrell, 2020: 121 n 7) in the revelation of the culprit, the cause of the plague. Oedipus is at least implicitly aware of possible threats against his 'usurper's' rule being not the king but the 'strong man' (*tyrannus*) chosen by the community following the violent death of Laius.

Oedipus:

'But not to assist some distant kinsman,[5] no,

For my own sake I'll rid us of this corruption.

Whoever killed the king may decide to kill me too,

With the same violent hand—by avenging Laius.

I defend myself' (Sophocles, 1984: 167).[6]

---

[5] A reference to Laius whom Oedipus assumes at this point in the tragedy is the deceased husband of his wife Jocasta, not his own father.

[6] I am extrapolating here, but if, as Sophocles very slyly suggests, there may be a conspiratorial agreement between Creon and Tiresias to overthrow Oedipus out of envy, then it may be the case that Laius was attacked by a criminal gang who were in the employ of the same two conspirators. In

Chorus:

'People of Thebes, my countrymen, look on Oedipus.

He solved the famous riddle [of the Sphinx] with his brilliance,

He rose to power, a man beyond all power.

Who could behold his greatness without envy?' (Sophocles, 1984: 251).

A precarious situation rendered even more so, as he is an interloper, the 'foreign' (Corinthian, not Theban) husband of the widowed queen Jocasta, which, in the event of regicide, makes him an unlawful usurper, whereas Creon is Jocasta's brother, and the blind oracle Tiresias is the best soothsayer in the business.

> Oedipus: '... if the two of you had never put your heads together, we would never have heard about *my* killing Laius' (Sophocles, 1984: 192).

And this is Oedipus' more focused attack on Creon:

'O power—wealth and empire, skill outstripping skill,

In the heady rivalries of life,

What envy lurks inside you![7] Just for this,

The crown the city gave me—I never sought it,

They laid it in my hands—for this alone, Creon,

The soul of my trust, my loyal friend from the start.

Steals against me ... so hungry to overthrow me.

He sets the wizard [Tiresias] on me, this scheming quack,

This fortune-teller peddling lies, eyes peeled.

For his own profit—seer blind in his craft!' (Sophocles, 1984: 182).

And later Oedipus against Tiresias:

'Come here you pious fraud. Tell me,

When did you ever prove yourself a prophet?

When the Sphinx, that chanting fury kept her death-watch here,

Why silent then, not a word to set our people free?

There was a riddle, not for some passer-by to solve—

---

fact, Oedipus insinuates as much: '...now I see it all. You helped hatch the plot, you did the work, yes, short of killing him [Laius] with your own hands—and given eyes I'd say you did the killing single-handed!' (Sophocles, 1984: 178). One of many in-jokes in the play is that Tiresias is blind at this moment and Oedipus soon will be.

[7] For Creon's envy of Oedipus see Foucault, 2020: 343–345.

It cried out for a prophets. Where were you?

Did you rise to the crisis? Not a word,

You and your birds, your gods—nothing. No, but I came by, Oedipus the ignorant,

I stopped the Sphinx! With no help from birds,

The flight of my own intelligence hot the mark.

And this is the man you'd try to overthrow? (Sophocles, 1984: 182).

Within the 'contemporary realities' of Sophocles' audience that everybody knew was the tumultuous transition of only recently established Athenian democracy from *agonism* (constructive competition) as celebrated by Pindar to *antagonism* (destructive rivalry) as lamented by the anti-sophistic Socrates and which the ubiquitous chorus of citizens clearly denounces.[8]

'Pride breeds the tyrant,

Violent pride, gorging, crammed to bursting,

With all that is overripe and rich with ruin—clawing up to the heights, headlong pride.

Crashes down the abyss—sheer doom!

No footing helps, all foothold lost and gone.

But the healthy strife[9] that makes the city strong—

I pray that god will never end that wrestling:

God, my champion, I will never let you go' (Sophocles, 1984: 209).

The chorus on Tiresias:

'Here is the one who will convict him [the murderer], look,

They bring him on at last, the seer, the man of god.

The truth lives inside him, him alone' (Sophocles, 1984: 175).

Or so they say, for no sooner do the tyrant and the seer converse than they immediately begin to compete, substituting antagonism or agonism,[10] which culminates

---

[8] Consistent with its function; as the 'official college of citizens' the role of the chorus 'is to express through its fears, hopes, questions, and judgments the feelings of the spectators who make up the civic community' adding thereby to the juro-political subtext of tragic drama and underscoring the 'competitive' nature of the triangular exchange of Oedipus-Creon-Tiresias (Vernant and Vidal-Naquet 1990: 34).

[9] Competition, or *agonism*, was understood as healthy (*eris*) while antagonism was labelled *eris kake*, destructive rivalry (Vernant and Vidal-Naquet 1990: 335).

[10] The interchangeability of these terms appears to be fairly wide spread throughout European culture. Commenting on Girard's original essay, Mark R. Anspach notes that the 'word for "competitors" in the French text, *concurrents*, is nearly the same as the Latin *concurrentes*. The French

in Tiresias' ultimate comeback: '*You* are the curse, the corruption of the land!' (Sophocles, 1984: 179), as the chorus also makes clear.

'Zeus and Apollo know, they know, the great masters

Of all the dark and depth of human life.

But whether a mere man can know the truth,

Whether a seer can fathom more than I—

There is no test, no certain proof

Though matching skill for skill

A man can outstrip a rival. No, not until I see

These charges proved will I side with his [Oedipus'] accusers' (Sophocles, 1984: 187).

Oedipus attacks with 'Who primed you for this? Not your prophet's trade?' and Tiresias counters with 'You did, you forced me, twisted it out of me' (Sophocles, 1984: 179), along with the unforgettable 'This day will bring your birth and your destruction' (Sophocles, 1984: 184). Which, for Girard, is a pivotal moment in the tragedy that uncovers the real issue at stake behind the mutual, and escalating, accusations and counter-accusations: the three men are acting out a type of rivalry which, because it cannot be ended on the facts present to them at that moment in the tragedy, can only escalate with the result that each contestant comes to increasingly resemble the other.

> Oedipus and Tiresias each attempt to place the blame for the city's plight on the other; the accusations of patricide and incest are only especially striking contributions to a conventional exchange of incivilities. At this stage in the debate there is no reason to assume that either party is more guilty of any crime than the other. Both sides seem equally matched; neither seems able to gain the upper hand. (Girard, 1977: 72)

And it is the intensely personal nature of the rivalry that is the motivation that governs the flow of the action. Now that the possibility of conspiracy has been clearly, but quietly, raised, then all issues of truth, fact, and the gods can be subordinated to the wholly subjective displays of contending wills to power, the complete inversion of the proper relationship between means and ends, premise, and conclusion.

> If we take Tiresias's reply literally, the terrible charges of patricide and incest that he has just levelled at Oedipus did not stem from any supernatural source of information. The accusation is simply an act of reprisal arising from the hostile exchange of a tragic debate. Oedipus unintentionally initiates the process by forcing Tiresias to speak. He accuses Tiresias of having had a part in the murder of Laius; he prods Tiresias into reprisal, into hurling the accusation back at him. (Girard, 1977: 71)

---

verb *con-courir*, which literally means "to run together" is an ambivalent term, signifying either "to compete" or "to cooperate"' (Girard, 2004: n. 1, 122).

And, once again, the tragedy returns to the issue of law and legal reasoning, not only in the substance of the arguments which revolve around conflicting 'witness' testimony but with the structured nature of the emotionally violent exchanges.

> From the very start and throughout the play, the text contains a series of technical and precise judicial terms which were completely comprehensible for a Greek audience and which reveal that the play unfolds in the form of a trial. It is not, of course, a total and exhaustive representation of a trial, yet there is a perfectly clear judicial paradigm organized around the question of how to discover the guilty party whose crime has been established, but whose identity remains unknown. (Foucault, 2020: 331)

To cite just one example: Sophocles uses the term *menusis* when referencing Apollo's oracle, which, in legal terms, means a 'denunciation' that can only be made before a tribunal by a foreigner; 'So this is a case of a non-citizen who denounces a crime committed on the city's territory' (Foucault, 2020: 332); the 'general framework of the play is a procedural one that is easily recognizable.... It does not reproduce a trial exactly, but rather a judicial paradigm that would have been perfectly comprehensible and recognizable to a Greek audience and spectators' (Foucault, 2020: 334). Something which everyone would have known.

1.1.1 Sophistry

Tragedy developed in the sixth century BCE, preceding the emergence of philosophy, logic, and mathematical science but concurrent with the rise of the civic discursive practices of rhetoric, oratory, and sophistry. The latter was considered the most noxious by the logocentric philosophers of the Socratic era as sophistry was the formalization of both political and legal debate through the devices of affectivity and persuasion[11] and, therefore, excluded the strict binarism of the Socratic dialectic, 'according to which, given two contradictory propositions, if one is true the other must necessarily be false' (Vernant & Vidal-Naquet, 1990: 417 n 2). But, with sophistry—and to a lesser degree rhetoric and oratory—a proposition could be both true and false. So it was that 'Tragic man' found himself in a natural alliance with sophistry and

> ... appears to belong to a different logic, one that does not establish such a cut-and-dry cleavage between the true and the false. This is the logic of the orators and sophists that, during the actual years when tragedy was flourishing, still reserved a place for ambiguity since, in the questions it examined, it did not seek to demonstrate the validity of a single thesis but rather to construct *dissoi logoi*, double arguments that, in their opposition, countered but did not destroy each other. Since, at the will of the sophist and through the power of his words, each of the two conflicting arguments could be made in turn to dominate the other. (Vernant & Vidal-Naquet, 1990: 417–418 n 2)

---

[11] *Peitho*, which, in the wrong hands, could be equated with 'ideological mystification' (Vernant & Vidal-Naquet 1990: 336).

During the fifth century the sophists 'set themselves up as educators of the democracy' and 'claimed to be teaching an art or skill' (Vernant & Vidal-Naquet, 1990: 321). At the 'core of their art was the notion of *dissoi logoi*, "double speeches," which although formally dialectical (thesis versus antithesis but minus the synthesis) was generally disapproved of by the tragedians'; for them *dissoi logoi* 'is a speech of duplicity and ambiguity' that operated on 'the level of what we would call word play' being 'totally pervaded by ambiguity' (Vernant & Vidal-Naquet, 1990: 319). And since the quest for a stable foundation for democracy was at the heart of the Athenian political process, tragic playwrights deployed filled their dramas with 'double speeches' so as to draw a clear correlation between democracy, order, and 'single' or unitary speech.

> Through his participation in political life in which decisions were taken following open positivist, and secular debate, each citizen began to be aware of himself as an agent responsible for the conduct of affairs, more or less master, more or less in a position to direct the uncertain course of events by reason of his *gnome*, his powers of judgment, his *phronesis*, his intelligence. (Vernant & Vidal-Naquet, 1990:82)

And no less than the Socratic philosophers or the Protagorean sophists the Tragedians acted as the mid-wives of the development of Athenian political speech, discourse, and reasoning, albeit non-dialectical. Which is an important point: while the Tragedians engaged with the logic of sophistry, oratory, and rhetoric in a manner that was unlike the Socratic method, they nevertheless used the aesthetic discursive and performative techniques of drama to critique in a sub rosa manner the possible political and social dangers *dissoi logoi*.

> Through the tragic spectacle the city questioned itself. Both the heroes[12] and the chorus successively embodied now civic, now anti-civic values. In this way, tragedy introduced an interference between things that the city itself strove to keep separate, and that interference constituted one of the fundamental forms of tragic transgression. (Vernant and Vidal-Naquet, 1990: 320)

So that the grand unifying theme of Greek tragedy may be understood as the lethal danger of confusion, or, to use a more sophisticated term the *crisis of undifferentiation*, what Girard considers as the disastrous condition of 'mimetic multiplicity,' the catastrophic comingling of things which must be kept separate. And the one thing that above all others must remain uncontaminated by confusion is the sacred (*sacer*),

---

[12] On the most basic level, goat songs are dramatic adaptations of heroic legends, the subject of which is someone who is both a nobleman as well as a sacred, or quasi-religious figure, the bearer of some sort of supernatural power combined with elite social status, so that the political rule of any hero could easily equate with the perhaps too strong leadership of a single man, in constant tension with the 'rule of the *demos*,' or the people, which culminates in the hero undergoing a metaphorical portrayal of human sacrifice; 'if tragedy draws on heroic myth' it is because 'every hero has his cults, i.e., his sacrifices. The situation of the sacrifice may be just the point where heroic myth and Dionysiac *tragoidia* meet each other' (Burkert, 2020: 147).

so it is absolutely no surprise that what 'is essentially characteristic of the mythological quality of the sacred is its dual nature—it is both harmful and beneficial' (Girard, 1986: 1999).[13]

The sacred is the solution to the problem of undifferentiation for it is itself a kind of transcendental ambivalence. Greek tragedy is not, as Hegel thought, the dramatic conflict of irreconcilable absolutes, but, consistent with the cultural practices of sophistry and oratory, the destructive play of the irreducible ambiguity of words and meaning, alternatively interpreted as both objective and subjective 'truth'; 'The keystone of the tragic structure, the model that serves as matrix for its dramatic construction and language is reversal' (Vernant & Vidal-Naquet, 1990:120), which, by no coincidence, is a standard ploy of rhetoric.[14]

> All the Greek tragedians have recourse to ambiguity as a means of expression and as a modality of thought. But the double meaning takes on quite a different role depending on its place in the organization of the tragedy and the level of language at which the tragic poet is using it.... The dramatist plays on this to transmit his tragic vision of a world divided against itself and rent with contradictions. On the lips of different characters the same words take on different or opposed meanings because their semantic significance is not the same in religious, legal, political, and common parlance. (Vernant & Vidal-Naquet, 1990:113)

Oedipus, as the one who is to be scapegoated at the end of the play, bears all of the ambiguity of the scapegoat, the one who is the cause of and the solution for the crisis that is consuming Thebes; 'from the point of view of ambiguity, *Oedipus Rex*[15] is quite exceptional. This work can be taken as a model' (Vernant & Vidal-Naquet, 1990:113) for no 'literary genre of antiquity made such full use of the double entendre [*dissoi logoi*] as did tragedy and *Oedipus Rex* contains more than twice as many ambiguous expressions as Sophocles' other plays...' (Vernant and Vidal-Naquet, 1990:113). To take just one example which requires no comment.

---

[13] *Sacer* 'means cursed and blessed simultaneously. It means extreme violence and peace. It's really this ambivalence, and I really think it's a process through which human violence is transfigured' (Girard, 2020: 28).

[14] In this way, *Oedipus Tyrannus* stages a micro-spectacle of a wider pattern of Greek political developments: 'Justice (*dike*) was a challenge to the noble and tyrannical tradition, but it was as yet unestablished. Tragedy is constantly opposing one kind of *dike* to another and shows clearly how "justice" can shift and be transferred to its opposite'; here, 'the hero is both the investigator acting on behalf of the city and at the same time the very subject of that inquiry' (Vernant & Vidal-Naquet, 1990: 306). The name *Oidipous* is derived, in part from *oida*, 'to know' (Vernant & Vidal-Naquet, 1990: 323).

[15] More accurately, *Oedipus Tyrannus* or *The Tyrant Oedipus*. As with so much else, the character of king-tyrant is infused with ambiguity. 'On a religious level, Oedipus oscillates between the condition of divine being and that of *pharmakos*, the scapegoat that was expelled from Athens ... in order to purify the city. On a political level, Oedipus is a powerful statesman, a potential tyrant, a threat to which the fifth-century city responded through the purely secular institution of ostracism. It is abundantly clear that the two levels could easily merge' (Vernant & Vidal-Naquet, 1990: 349). I discuss the more particular Greek variant of the scapegoat, the *pharmakos* in Chap. 9, below. For Oedipus as *pharmakos* see Foley (2020).

Oedipus:

'Drive him out, each of you, from every home.

He is the plague, the heart of our corruption,

As Apollo's oracle has just revealed to me.

So I honor my obligations:

I fight for the god and for the murdered man.

Now my curse on the murderer. Whoever he is…

I curse myself as well … if by any chance

He proves to be an intimate of our house,

Here at my hearth, with my full knowledge, may the curse I just called down on him strike me!' (Sophocles, 1984: 172).

The archetypal model of Greek tragedy is 'not set out anywhere as a particular image, idea, or complex of feeling'; instead, the model assumes the form of a 'purely operational schema of reversal, a rule of ambiguous logic' but it happens that the tragedy 'gives content to this form….in the case of the face presented by Oedipus, the paradigm of the double man, the reversed man, the rule is embodied in the reversal that transforms the divine king into the scapegoat' (Vernant & Vidal-Naquet, 1990:139). The tragic-hero-sacrifice-victim is the dramatic site of what is known as *double transference* which serves as the sign of the scapegoat, the archaic belief that every medicine can double as a poison, so that anything that can cure can also contaminate.[16] But of more immediate concern is that the psychic power of double transference, a quintessentially affective notion, originates within the commonly mis-recognized operation of an even greater and more ambivalent power: *mimesis*, the desire to imitate and, ultimately, to 'become' another. For Girard, the central dramatic thread of *Oedipus Tyrannus* is the long and drawn out manner in which 'the dueling god-affected' come to resemble, to metaphorically 'become,' each other.

Tiresias: 'I pity you, flinging at me the very insults
Each man here will fling at you so soon' (Sophocles, 1984: 181).

Ironically, at one point it is Oedipus who attempts to scapegoat Creon as the cause of the plague (and ironically foretelling his own ultimate fate after losing the antagonistic context of counter-accusations), earning him a sharp rebuke from the Choir on the grounds of the mis-use of evidence.

Creon: 'Do you want proof? Go to Delphi yourself,

Examine the oracle and see if I've reported

The message word-for-word. This too:

[16] See below.

If you detect that I and the clairvoyant

Have plotted anything in common, arrest me,

And execute me. Not on the strength of one vote,

Two in this case, mine as well as yours.

But don't convict me on sheer unverified surmise.

How wrong it is to take the good for bad,

Purely at random, or take the bad for good' (Sophocles, 1984: 193–194). [...]

Chorus: 'Good advice, my lord, for anyone who wants to avoid disaster.

Those who jump to conclusions may go wrong.

Oedipus: 'When my enemy moves against me quickly,

Plots in secret, I move quickly too, I must,

I plot and pay him back. Relax my guard a moment, waiting his next move—he wins the objective,

I lose mine.'

Creon: 'What do you want? You want me banished?'

Oedipus: 'No, I want you dead' (Sophocles, 1984: 194). [...]

Creon: 'What if you're wholly wrong?'

Oedipus: 'No matter—I must rule' (Sophocles, 1984: 195) ....

Chorus: 'The man's your friend, your kin, he's under oath—

Don't cast him out, disgraced,

Branded with guilt on the strength of hearsay only.'

Oedipus: 'Know full well, if that is what you want

You want me dead or banished from the land....

Then let him go,

Even if it does lead to my ruin, my death

Or my disgrace, driven from Thebes for life.[17]

It's you, not him I pity—your words move me.

He, wherever he goes, my hate goes with him' (Sophocles, 1984: 215).

---

[17] As Girard remarks: 'If Oedipus does not destroy Creon, Creon will destroy him. All that is left are sacrificers and victims' (Girard, 2004: 86).

According to Girard one of the signs of the presence of mimesis is *skandalon*, or the 'stumbling-block': which 'designates a very common inability to walk away from mimetic rivalry which turns it into an addiction' meaning 'anything that attracts us in proportion to the suffering or irritation that it causes us' (Girard, 1996: 198). 'Derived from *skadzein*,' which means to limp, '*skandalon* designates the obstacle that both attracts and repels at the same time. The initial encounter with the stumbling block is so fascinating that one must always return to it, and each return becomes more fascinating' (Girard, 1986: 132), a concept derived from Hebrew Scripture but which not reasonably can be applied to the Hellenic goat song.

> The idea comes from the Bible and it means the obstacle against which one keeps stumbling. The Greek word appears first in the Greek Bible [the Septungiat] and it comes from a verb that signifies to limp.[18] The more we stumble against an obstacle, the easier it should be to avoid further stumbling but, frequently, the opposite happens: we stumble so much that we seem to be limping. (Girard, 1996: 198)

The explanation for this mis-recognition of our gait lies with *mimetic rivalry*.

> *Skandalon* designates the intersubjective process that results from a very general but not universal human failure to walk away from mimetic rivalry. *Skandalon* is the process through which we are attracted to whatever, or, rather, whoever treats us badly. *Skandalon* is destructive addiction of all kinds: drugs, sex, power, and, above all, morbid competitiveness—professional, political, intellectual, spiritual. *Skandalon* is the aching tooth that we cannot stop testing with our tongue, even though it hurts more. (Girard, 1996: 215)

In the case of Oedipus it hurt a lot. 'Oedipus's imminent fall has nothing to do with any heinous sin; rather, it should be regarded as the outcome of a tragic encounter in which Oedipus has met defeat' (Girard, 1977: 73) which leads to this shatteringly sophistic conclusion:

> At this point a strange and well-nigh fantastic thought suggests itself. If we eliminate the testimony brought against Oedipus in the second half of the tragedy, then the conclusion of the myth, far from seeming a sudden lightning flash of the truth, striking down the guilty party and illuminating all the mortal participants, seems nothing more than the camouflaged victory of one version of the story over the other, the polemical version over its rival—the community's formal acceptance of Tiresias's and Creon's version of the story, thereafter held to be the true and universal reason, the verity behind the myth itself. (Girard, 1977: 73)

The 'myth' of Oedipus, the original 'mythic' material that Sophocles was working with, and, therefore, was in a certain sense artistically bound by, held that the Delphic oracle of Apollo prophesized truthfully that the Theban king had committed both patricide and incest and therefore should be exiled whereas the Sophoclean 'tragedy' of Oedipus is that the king is a possible victim of a wholly secular process aimed to labeling him a scapegoat as the means of solving a crisis of community that has no obvious cause. The critical difference between the Oedipal myth and the Oedipal tragedy is that since 'no single individual is responsible for this general disaster, the investigation was bound to end by imputing guilt to a scapegoat' (Anspach,

[18] Which is a defining characteristic of Oedipus, presumably the result of having his feet pierced when exposed as a child as a sacrificial victim—allegedly.

2004: xxiii) which, 'tragically,' just happens to turn out to be Oedipus who, equally 'tragically,' just happens to be a tyrant within a culture that just happens to believe in oracular prophecies and blood sacrifices which everyone knows are infallible. 'Since any crisis affecting a kingdom is the king's responsibility, he functions by the very nature of things as an all-purpose culprit' (Anspach, 2004: xxv) and, following the affective reasoning of double transference, it follows that Oedipus may in fact be the sole source of the plague as his 'fatal(-ity) flaw' of anger would prove highly infectious; 'To be sure, it is Oedipus' anger which is *contagious*' (Girard, 2004: 70).[19] Sophocles' play, therefore, is not 'the dramatization of a myth...' (Anspach, 2004: xvi) for he 'never shows Oedipus killing his father or marrying his mother. Instead, he stages the process through which, in a time of crisis, everyone comes to *believe* that Oedipus killed his father and married his mother. In this sense, Sophocles' *Oedipus* is indeed "a play about the genesis of a myth"' (Anspach, 2004: xvi). Which is why Girard is so concerned with *Oedipus Tyrannus*, for Sophocles' 'tragedy is an exegesis of the myth, the most profound that we possess' (Girard, 2004: 54), because, as everyone knows, 'Fate' (*moirai*)[20] is 'the strictly mythical element' (Girard, 2004: 26) within the play that must be contested lest *dissoi logoi* prevail. What everyone doesn't know, however—including those contemporary audiences of Sophocles who had probably already forgotten this by then buried truth—is that 'tragedy, in Greek, is the ode of the goat' (Girard, 2004: 45) so that every tragedy, by definition, has a scapegoat as its protagonist meaning that, at least within the context of drama, a sacrificial outcome is 'fated'.

> The idea of the scapegoat provides us with perhaps the original meaning of animal sacrifice. The goat takes upon itself the sins of the fathers, of the sons, of the brothers, indeed of all the citizens. It carries away, into death or into the desert that closes around it, the seeds of those conflicts that the convergence of desires, which is to say the very unity of the culture, its internal cohesiveness, cannot fail to provoke. (Girard, 2004: 45)

And if there is any doubt, the dramatic triangulation among the three warring orators transparently duplicates, or mirrors, the operation of the scapegoating process: Creon-Tiresias as accuser/sacrifice/scapegoater and Oedipus as accused/sacrificed/scapegoated. And what unites them is the plague that they have mythically caused.

1.1.2 Plague and Incest

The plague is 'found everywhere in literature', and Girard claims, 'It is older than literature—much older, really, since it is present in myth and ritual in the entire world' (Girard, 1978: 136). And whenever Girard intones about a universal phenomenon he is invariably referencing an omnipresent but mis-recognized scapegoat mechanism of some kind, and his analysis of the literary history of contagions is no different. Hence, there is 'a strange uniformity to the various treatments of the plague,' from

[19] See below.

[20] Or, in the case of the tragic hero-victim, 'fatality'.

Daniel Defoe's *Journal of the Plague Year* to Antione Artaud's *Le Theatre et la peste*, 'not only literary and mythical but also scientific and non-scientific, of both past and present' (Girard, 1978: 136). The 'curious thing about these similarities is that they ultimately involve the very notion of the similar. The plague is universally presented as a process of undifferentiation, a destruction of specificities present' (Girard, 1978: 136). The Attic term for this loss of differences was *anomia*, 'a state of "confusion" in which everything is haphazardly confused and mixed up' (Vernant and Vidal-Naquet, 1990:439 n 135), so that the crisis of undifferentiation is actually the cause, and not the effect, of the 'plague', which is as much allegorical as it is bio-medical, physical destruction being 'often preceded by a reversal' within the cultural order (Girard, 1978: 136).

> Social hierarchies are first transgressed, then abolished.... The plague will turn the honest man into a thief, the virtuous man into a lecher, the prostitute into a saint. ...The plague makes all accumulated knowledge and all categories of judgment invalid. ...The distinctiveness of the plague is that it ultimately destroys all forms of distinctiveness present. (Girard, 1978: 136–137)

'The plague' is a symbol, like the 'flood' motif, of a universal violence, reciprocal, and escalatory, that is destroying the *polis* of Thebes through a collective and individual regression to warring bands of friends and enemies. The elimination of all signifying distinctions through a systemic undifferentiation mediated by reciprocating violence is the mimetic core of the 'plague motif' that Sophocles deploys with supreme artistry and which 'illuminates ... the collective character of the disaster, its universally contagious nature' (Girard, 1977: 76–77), the play making 'it clear that the infection and the onslaught of reciprocal violence are one and the same' (Girard, 1977: 76). For Girard 'Anarchy is a plague; in a sense, it is even more of a plague than the disease itself' (Girard, 1978: 138) and the 'mythic plague' of *Oedipus Tyrannus* is the dramatization of the 'passive contagion of desire and hatred which, spreading from one person to the next, shakes the very foundations of society' (Girard, 2004:43). But not only the foundations of the Greek city-state.

> In many parts of the world, the words we translate as 'plague' can be viewed as a generic label for a variety of ills that affect the community as a whole and threaten or seem to threaten the very existence of social life. It may be inferred from various signs that inter-human tensions and disturbances often play the principle role. (Girard, 1978: 138)

This becomes much more plausible when we reverse the subject predicate relationship, which double transference allows us to do, and recognize that literature's plague 'is a transparent metaphor for a certain reciprocal violence that spreads, literally, like the plague' (Girard, 1978: 139) so that, in purely aesthetic terms, there is nothing absurd about interpreting a physical disease as the effect of a cause that is wholly existential: the violence of mimetic rivalry.

> The appropriateness of the metaphor comes, obviously enough, from this contagious nature. The idea of contagiousness implies the presence of something harmful, which loses none of its virulence as it is rapidly transmitted from individual to individual. Such, of course, are bacteria in an epidemic; so is violence when it is *imitated*, either positively, whenever bad example makes the usual restraints inoperative, or negatively, when the efforts to stifle

> violence with violence achieve no more, ultimately, than an increase in the level of violence. Counter-violence turns out to be the same as violence. In cases of massive contamination, the victims are helpless not necessarily because they remain passive but because whatever they do proves ineffective or makes the situation worse. (Girard, 1978: 139)

However

> The epidemic that interrupts all the vital functions of the city is surely not unrelated to violence and the loss of distinctions. The oracle itself explains matters: it is the infectious presence of a *murderer* that has brought on the disaster.... In the myth, the fearful transgression of a single individual is substituted for the universal onslaught of reciprocal violence. Oedipus is responsible for the ills that have befallen his people. He has become a prime example of the human scapegoat. (Girard, 1977: 76, 77)

The murderer is the most terrible of transgressors, the one who crosses the most sacrosanct of boundaries, and the terrible truth of the scapegoat, as Girard has it, was most clearly announced by Caiaphas in the Gospel of John: '...it is better for you that one man should die instead of the people, so that the whole nation may not perish' (John 11:50).[21] But why is it that only *one* is selected?

If violence has become systemic ('From the depths, the red waves of death ...'), then guilt is universal which means that no true resolution is possible—everyone or no one must be punished. Which in the end solves nothing, for the entire problem is the contagion-like breakdown of social boundaries and identities (differences) within the community.[22] The advantage of a single victim is that it restricts retribution to a sufficiently safe and manageable number: a solitary individual. But on a more sinister, and vital, level, the collective accusation against a single perpetrator really does temporarily[23] solve the problem of escalatory violence because it acts to re-unify the citizens through the violent enforcement of a generally recognized difference[24] which

---

[21] The full passage, replete with Girardian innuendo, reads as follows: 'And one of them [of the Sanhedrin], Caiaphas, being high priest that year, said to them: "You know nothing at all, nor do you consider it expedient for us that one man should die for the people, and not that the whole nation should perish." Now this he did not say on his own authority; but being high priest that year he prophesied that Jesus would die for the nation, and not for that nation only, but also that He would gather together in one the children of God who were scattered abroad. Then, from that day on, they plotted to put him to death' (John 11: 49–53). This neatly unifies both the destructive and restorative aspects of the scapegoat: if Jesus is not killed (or 'sacrificed' as the Lamb of God) Israel will revolt and be destroyed by the Romans; as it turned out Israel revolted anyway and was destroyed by the Romans twice—which would have been the end of if not for the fact that the apostolic Church managed to gather into itself Jesus' followers, constituting the self-proclaimed successor to Judaism through the regenerative powers of Christ's death, interpreted as a deliberate sacrificial act after the fact. Meaning that Caiaphas' homicidal conspiracy did prove to be salvific but for completely different reasons. Or, at least, this is Girard's version.

[22] This brings to mind the famous apocryphal statement attributed to an anonymous member of the Engineering Department at Cal Tech: 'If a problem has been formulated in such a way as to be unsolvable the problem has been formulated incorrectly.' Which implies that Sophocles did not do his job correctly.

[23] Which in the midst of a fatal downward spiral of guaranteed mutual destruction is more than adequate.

[24] Girard's meaning of difference 'refers to the basic distinction arising from victimage and the beginning of culture (which of course may have taken place over hundreds of thousands of years).

in reality is actually a mis-recognition: the (falsely) guilty 'one' versus the (falsely) innocent crowd. And this *violent unanimity*, or the *generative unanimity of violence*, is itself the primal act that restores difference within the warring community: 'Oedipus is indeed the responsible party, so responsible that he frees the community from all accountability…It calls to mind the passivity of the 'patient' in the modern world of medicine. Everyone is sick. Nobody owes anybody anything by way of recompense or atonement—except, of course, Oedipus' (Girard, 1977: 77). But why Oedipus? Because he 'lost' the debate, meaning not merely that his crimes, hitherto unknown to him (and, therefore, unintentional, devoid of criminal intent), are uncovered, but, of truly tragic import, his actions objectively validate Tiresias' subjective accusation of Oedipus as the cause of the crisis of Thebes. And his crimes carry tremendous symbolic weight: killing the father and mating with the mother; 'The crimes of Oedipus signify the abolishment of differences, but because the nondifference is attributed to a particular individual, it is transformed into a new distinction, signifying the monstrosity of Oedipus's situation. The nondifference becomes the responsibility, not of society at large, but of a single individual' (Girard, 1977: 76). By the end, the 'dual disasters, incest and patricide, seem to be divorced from all context and visited on Oedipus alone either by pure chance or at the bidding of Destiny or some other sacred force' (Girard, 1977: 75–76) which is perhaps exactly what Creon-Tiresias intended. Jean-Pierre Vernant explicates the Hellenic belief in patricide and incest as the supreme destroyers of cultural and social prohibitions which is invariably 'expressed in terms of lost distinctions': both acts '"constitute … a direct violation of the game of draughts in which each piece stands, in relation to the others, at a specified place on the draught board of the city"' (Jean-Pierre Vernant qtd. Girard, 1977: 75 n 1),[25] a striking image that invokes the principle of sympathetic magic implicit within

The originary distinction is the one between the one between "here" or "us" by contrast to "it" or "that," the victim. This could have been originally a reflexive gesture or sign rather than spoken words. From this distinction all others stem: language, roles, institutions, etc.' (Girard, 1996: 289). See below.

[25] Incest as *anomia* also explains the strange form of the Sphinx's riddle which also implies that the real subject of the enigma was Oedipus himself, the contaminating source of the confusion: '"There is on earth a being with two, four, and three feet and with a single voice that, alone of all those that move on the earth, in the air and in the sea, changes its nature. But when it walks supported by the most feet, that is when its limbs are the least rigorous."' Although different versions were offered within the mythic tradition, what 'is notable in all the versions of the riddle, the normal chronological order is muddled, since the adult man (two feet) comes first, followed either by the old man (three feet), or the child (four feet)' (Vernant and Vidal-Naquet 1990: 468 n 20). And it is this 'muddle' that is the true answer of the riddle, an almost oracular prophecy of the crisis of undifferentiation to come. 'The Sphinx's question was: What is the creature with one voice that has two, three, and four legs? Confusing and mixing them up, it referred to the three successive ages of man that he can only know one after another: He is a child when he crawls on four legs, an adult when he stands on his two feet, and an old man leaning on his stick. By identifying himself simultaneously with his young children and his old father, Oedipus, the man standing on two feet, obliterates the barriers that ought to keep the father strictly separate from the sons and the grandfather so that each human generation occupies its appointed place both in the sequence of time in the order of the city' (Vernant & Vidal-Naquet, 1990: 138). But the riddle-muddle also predicts the tragic fate of Oedipus: as an adult (two legs) he realizes that he is the abandoned infant son (four legs) of Laius

double transference, occult 'action-at-a-distance' grounded on mimetic principles of identity 'in which, owing to a principle of similarity (*similia, similibus*), one thing is believed to be capable of acting on another at a distance' (Delcourt, 2020: 241 n 6). And at this point, 'We must return once again to the so-called crimes of the son of Laius' (Girard, 1977: 74).

In Girard's view, in Oedipus 'difference is so radically destroyed that all men shrink back in horror. And this shrinking back, this putting at a distance, is the restoration of the lost difference' (Girard, 2004: 85) through the selection of the 'one' who will be sacrificed in order to secure the preservation of the 'all'. The scapegoat is no ordinary victim; he or she is the one who is singled out as a proffered solution to the violence of the community that is both the cause and effect of undifferentiation and is, therefore, the restorer of differences, the differentiation that is maintained by entire series of distinctions (the un-mixed) and prohibitions (that which represses): the one and the many, the accused and the accusers, the guilty, the enemy and the friend, the foreigner and the citizen, the stranger and the neighbor, the strange and the normal, the sacrificed and the sacrifice, and the guilty and the innocent. And 'Once Oedipus is convicted of patricide and incest, he stands as the unique embodiment of violence and undifferentiation; a mythological difference is established' (Anspach, 2004: xxx). So toxic are Oedipus' transgressions that we understand why Sophocles found Oedipus an irresistible subject for a goat song: the sheer fatality of his pollution was the very thing required to effect such a salvific transformation of Thebes. Patricide 'represents the establishment of violent reciprocity between father and son, the reduction of the paternal relationship to "fraternal" revenge.... When it has succeeded in abolishing even the traditional father-son relationship, violent reciprocity is left in sole command of the battlefield' (Girard, 1977: 74). And from patricide it is only a small jump to regicide (and, after that, an equally small jump to deicide), the king being the 'father' to the community of children: 'The act of regicide is the exact equivalent, vis-à-vis the polis, of the act of patricide vis-à-vis the family. In both cases the criminal strikes at the most fundamental, essential, and inviolable distinction within the group. He becomes, literally, the slayer of distinctions' (Girard, 1977: 74). And incest, like patricide, is also 'a form of violence,' for in its 'power to confound distinctions, incest is akin to violence. Just as incest turns family members into doubles, violent conflict turns enemies into doubles' (Anspach, 2004: xiii). In truth, incest may be even more transgressive than patricide for 'it plays in consequence an extreme role in the destruction of differences.... Incestuous propagation leads to formless duplications, sinister repetitions, a dark mixture of unnamable things' (Girard, 1977: 74, 75) beautifully conveyed by Sophocles as '... a crowd of other horrors you'd never dream will level you with yourself and all your children' (Sophocles, 1984: 183).

---

and Jocasta, resulting in his blinding and banishment, both of which he navigates with the use of a staff (three legs). When Oedipus solves the riddle, he himself is the adult man with two feet, neither a child still nor an old, or hobbled, man yet. 'But his error ... is that, through solving the riddle ... he also returns to his place of origin, to his father's house and his mother's bed': which is where he was birthed as a child and died as an impaired exile (Vernant & Vidal-Naquet, 1990: 215).

> The equalization of Oedipus and his sons is expressed in a series of brutal images: the father has sown his children in the same place where he himself was sown; Jocasta is a wife: not wife but mother, whose furrows have yielded a double harvest of father and children; she has been sown, and from these same furrows, these 'equal' furrows, he has obtained his children. But it is left to Tiresias to endow this talk of equality with its true tragic weight when he addressed Oedipus in the following terms: Evil will befall you which 'will establish an equality between yourself and your children'. (Jean-Pierre Vernant qtd. Girard, 1977: 75 n 1)

And this being *tragoidia* it does not really matter whether or not Oedipus was guilty of his crimes: everyone knows that he is because the oracle says so (apparently) and the sacrifice can proceed and solve the problem of social violence/plague. But this is not quite good enough for Girard (although it appears to have been more than sufficient for the Thebans) and Sophocles' implicitly posed question remains: is it the revelation of Oedipus' crimes that identifies him as the scapegoat—a religious truth—or is it the contingency of the mere facts that he murdered his father and acquired knowledge of his mother that causes Oedipus to be labeled a scapegoat—a unanimous act of secular political will? Through an alleged act of incest, 'Oedipus is the man who abolishes every difference between father and sons, mother and wife, brothers and children' (Girard, 2004: 84), resulting in the birth of a monstrously weird city of 'doubles' in which everyone is, in reality, identical o everyone else now that all distinctions are lost in the vortex of the plague; 'If there is no longer any difference between men, that is because in truth there never was. The truth of the myth is absolute symmetry. There is no true father, and that indeed is the knowledge that the expulsion of the scapegoat obscures' (Girard, 2004: 78); between patricide and incest 'the violent abolition of all family differences is achieved. The process that links violence to the loss of distinctions will naturally perceive incest and patricide as its ultimate goals. No possibility of difference then remains; no aspect of life is immune from the onslaught of violence' (Girard, 1977: 74–75).[26]

Oedipus' oratorical duel with Tiresias mimetically imitates on the microscopic level the macroscopic catastrophe of the abolition of distinctions, which can only culminate in an accusation of responsibility for the plague that politically succeeds

---

[26] Which makes all that more revealing this comment by Jocasta to her husband-son: 'Many a man before you, in his dreams, has shared his mother's bed' (Sophocles, 1984: 21). One should not read this remark in an overly Freudian manner, however, as a political interpretation actually works better and is more historically accurate: among the ancient Greeks 'to dream of the union with one's mother—that is with the earth from which everything is born and to which everything returns—means sometimes death, sometimes taking possession of land, winning power. There is no trace in this symbolism of the anxiety and guilt that are peculiar to the Oedipus complex' of psycho-analysis (Vernant & Vidal-Naquet, 1990:111). Dreaming of sleeping with one's mother would be an oneiric commonplace for most Greek kings and tyrants as well as for certain commoners. Marie Delcourt makes this clear: 'A dream of sleeping with one's mother is apt to be a favourable sign, particularly for artisans, whose trade is called their "mother," as well as for public figures and all of those who aspire to power, for *the mother represents one's country*. Just as a man who follows the recepts of Aphrodite will have an obedient and happy partner, so too a leader who makes love to his mother in a dream can count on being respected and loved by his subjects' (Delcourt, 2020: 184–185). Oneiric incest proves a great leveler of social distinctions; 'Union with one's mother ... represents wither return to one's *native land* (favourable omen) or *burial* in its soil (fatal omen)' (Delcourt, 2020: 187).

in re-uniting the population in a violent unanimity, for within 'the domain of impure violence, any search for origins leads back to myth' (Girard, 1977: 69), and, as Tiresias asserts 'You are the king no doubt, but in one respect, at least, I am your equal: the right to reply' (Sophocles, 1984: 183) which reinforces the reciprocal nature of the verbal violence of threat.

> The only difference between the initial accusation [of guilt] and the counter-charge is the paradoxical quality of the latter. This quality, which could be a weakness, in fact becomes an added strength. Tiresias, not content to answer Oedipus's 'You are guilty,' by echoing 'You are guilty,' underlines what from his point of view is the most scandalous aspect of the accusation—a guilty man is levelling the charge: 'You pronounce me guilty and think yourself innocent whereas, O wondrous world, the guilty one is you. The criminal you pursue is none other than Oedipus'. (Girard, 1977: 71)

To accuse the other 'of Laius's murder is to attribute to him sole responsibility' for the plague even though 'everybody shares equal responsibility,' because 'everybody participates in the destruction of a cultural order' that is based upon the common recognition of differences. The 'blows exchanged…may not always land on their mark, but every one of them deals a staggering blow to monarchy and religion. Each party progresses rapidly in uncovering the truth about the other, without ever recognizing the truth about himself' (Girard, 1977: 71). Which culminates in a cascade of compounding acts of *meconnaissance.*

> In a series of replies Tiresias warns Oedipus of the purely reciprocal nature of the approaching tragedy; that is of the blows that each will inflict on the other. As far as I know, nobody has proposed a satisfactory interpretation of these lines. The very rhythm of the phrases, their symmetrical effects, anticipate and provoke the tragic debate. We see here violent reciprocity in action, canceling all distinctions between the two men.
>
> Enough. Let me go home now. If you follow my advice, we will both find it easier to bear our separate destinies….
>
> Ah! I see that your own words will fall wide of the mark; and I fear to have no better success with mine….
>
> I do not want to inflict pain on either of us….
>
> You reproach me for my stubbornness, but refuse to see the stubbornness that dwells within you; and therefore out of stubbornness cast blame on me…. (Girard, 1977: 71–72)

And there is only one possible ending for as tyrant Oedipus is the only member of the community who is of sufficient heroic grandeur to serve as an acceptable sacrifice. And, lest there be any nullifying doubt, at the end Oedipus does learn the 'truth' about himself which is his guilt.

1.1.3 Oracles and Meconnaissance

It is interesting that prior to the pseudo-conclusive determination of Oedipus as the scapegoat the chorus offers as the explanation for the plague the absence of proper worship of the gods as the enforcers and mediators of social differences (father/son, husband/wife). Deities are the guardians of the element of difference that 'materializes in the form of taboos, hierarchical distinctions and institutions that block the convergence of desires and eliminate the possibility of confrontation' (Girard, 2004: 73) which means that either the gods do not exist, the gods cannot stop the plague, or the gods will not stop the plague because something unknown is required by them.

Chorus:

'Never again will I go reverent to Delphi,

The inviolate heart of Earth

Or Apollo's ancient oracle at Abae

or Olympia of the fires—

unless these prophecies [concerning Oedipus] all come true

for all mankind to point toward in wonder.

King of kings, if you deserve your titles

Zeus, remember, never forget!

You and your deathless, everlasting reign.

They are dying, the old oracles sent to Laius,

Now our masters strike them off the rolls.

Nowhere Apollo's golden glory now—

The gods, the gods go down' (Sophocles, 1984: 210).

And if there is anything to the notion of a conspiracy against Oedipus, then this would explain the nature of the 'frame' that Creon and Tiresias attempt, both 'out for the big game of empire' as Oedipus calls it (Sophocles, 1984: 189): they massage the contested evidence against him based upon the somewhat ambiguous nature of the original prophecies,[27] and Oedipus, quite surprisingly, complies: 'Apollo told me once—it is my fate—I must make love with my own mother, shed my father's blood with my own hands' (Sophocles, 1984: 216). But the frame, if that is what it is, also doubles as an attempt to restore belief in the gods, underscored by Jocasta's apparently modern skepticism and her stated belief in the random nature of events, or chance; 'What should a man fear? It's all chance, Chance rules our lives. Not a man on earth can see a day ahead, groping through the dark. Better to live at random, best we can' (Sophocles, 1984: 215). Here, Sophocles challenges the 'contemporary reality' of the Athenians' reliance upon prophecy that Oedipus himself so clearly

[27] A view shared by Jocasta, who 'is fully aware of the difference between knowledge and hearsay' (Ahl, 2020: 427); 'Oedipus: "He [Cleon] says I murdered Laius—I am guilty"; Jocasta: 'How does he know? Some secret knowledge or simple hearsay?"; Oedipus: Oh, he sent his prophet in to do his dirty work. You know Creon, Creon keeps his own lips clean"' (Sophocles, 1984: 200).

exhibits, for two reasons. The first was the general climate of skepticism during the period he wrote, the late fifth century BCE.[28] The second reason, arising from the first, was the cultural, political, and moral doubt concerning the efficacy and ethical consequences of scapegoating. For, in truth it is by no means clear that Apollo demands retribution; rather, the god seems to be issuing a call for moral repentance which, perhaps, Creon and/or Tiresias, turn into the community's demand for the sacrifice of a designated victim. Note the exact words of Apollo at Delphi which are strongly suggestive of *metanoia*, the act of conversion, 'change of heart,' or the 'turning towards a new path', upon which Girard appropriates as the cornerstone of his entire theory of literary criticism.[29]

> Creon: 'Very well, I will tell you what I heard from the god.
> Apollo commands us—he was quite clear—
> "Drive the corruption[30] from the land,
> Don't harbor it any longer, past all cure,
> Don't nurse it on your soil—root it out!"'
> Oedipus: 'How can we cleanse ourselves—what rites? What's the source of the trouble?'

Girard is keen to point out that the 'verified oracle is not what it appeared to be; it brings not a curse but a blessing; it is not the sinister echo of an implacable destiny but the ambiguous sign of a hard-won salvation' (Girard, 2004: 54).[31] Yet, perversely, all three antagonists instinctively select victimization as the appropriate 'rite' for restoration. Mark now Creon's interpretation of Apollo's message.

> Creon: 'Banish the man, or pay back blood with blood.
> Murders set the plague-storm on the city.'

---

[28] The 'fifth century in Athens was an age of intellectual revolution.... belief in prophecy and with it belief in the religious tradition as a whole was under attack. Philosophers and sophists (the new professional teachers of rhetoric, political theory and a host of allied subjects) were examining all accepted ideas with a critical eye ... Among the younger intellectuals, prophecies, especially those peddled by self-appointed professional seers ... were viewed with skepticism if not scorn; inevitably some of the skepticism spread to embrace the more respectable oracular establishments [e.g., Delphi] that claimed to transmit divine instructions....the dictum of the sophist Protagoras—"the individual man is the measure of all things, of the existence of what exists and the non-existence of what does not"—subjected prophecy, and for that matter the gods themselves, to a harsh criterion and found them wanting' (Knox, 1984: 136).

[29] See below.

[30] This could also be a veiled reference to the replacement of *agonism* with *antagonism* within the public arena as exemplified by the triangulated rivalry among Oedipus, Creon, and Tiresias. Evidence of this is provided in the retort of the 'Leader' of the chorus to the King: 'I would suggest his [Tiresias'] words were spoken in anger, Oedipus ... yours' too, and it isn't what we need. The best solution to the oracle, the riddle posed by god—we should look for that' (Sophocles 1984: 182).

[31] Girard also recommends the interpretation put forward by the German poet Friedrich Hoelderin: '"Apply yourself, in general, to establishing clear, strict justice; maintain proper civil order."' To which Girard adds: 'Oedipus could avoid the worst, perhaps, by conducting himself prudently—that is, free from anger' and the reciprocal violence that it brings (Girard 2004: 47).

Oedipus: 'Whose murder? Whose fate does Apollo bring to light?'.
Creon: 'Our leader, my lord, was once a man named Laius, before you came and put us straight on course.'
Oedipus: 'I know—or so I've heard. I never saw the man myself' (Sophocles, 1984: 164).

Girard takes care to point out to us that this is the anti-thesis of one of the other great skeptical commentaries upon the scapegoat, the Old Testament Second Book Second Isaiah (53: 4–5): 'He bears our sins and suffers for us, yet we considered Him to be in pain, suffering, and ill-treatment. But He was wounded because of our lawlessness, and became sick because of our sins. The chastisement of our peace was upon Him, and by His bruise we are healed.' Girard's thesis, which is very much the expression of his Roman Catholicism, is that 'Any phenomenon associated with the acts of remembering, commemorating, and perpetuating a unanimity that springs from the murder of a surrogate victim can be termed "religious"' (Girard, 1977: 315) or, at least once the religious has been sufficiently comingled with the anthropological.

> The Songs of the Servant of Yahveh render fully explicit an identification with the scapegoat that we believe to be implicit in Sophocles. It does not define a superior form of religion, or something beyond religion, but rather a deepened relationship to religion. Before its religious meaning is revealed, the identification with the scapegoat looks like the ultimate in irreligiosity. This misconception concerning the victim, terrible but necessary, is an added ordeal to be undergone; it even ends up becoming the essential ordeal, the one that defines the essence of the prophetic condition. (Girard, 2004: 56)

The general conclusion is that the 'endless diversity of myths and rituals derive from the fact that they all seek to recollect and reproduce something they never succeed in comprehending' (Girard, 1977: 316), and it was impossible for them to do so. For how could myths convey truths? The modern word 'myth' is the translation of two archaic Greek words, *mythos* and *muthos*, which both mean 'a lie' for the Greeks knew this to be the truth.

> All religious rituals spring from the surrogate victim, and all the great institutions of mankind, both secular and religious, spring from ritual.... It could hardly be otherwise, for the working basis of human thought, the process of 'symbolization,' is rooted in the surrogate victim. Even if no example taken alone offers conclusive proof of my theory, their cumulative effect is overwhelming; all the more so because they coincide with archetypal myths that tell, in apparently 'naïve' fashion, how all man's religious, familial, economic, and social institutions grew out of the body of an original victim. (Girard, 1977: 306)

For Girard, as with Durkheim, both religion and myth are the universal foundations of every society throughout History, so that *mythos* is a by-product of functionality, the need to provide a coherent explanation for a social process that is consciously intended to produce certain foreseen and commonly agreed upon outcomes that enable the unification of society.

> Girard's conception of myth is clearly etiological in nature: for him, myth's deal fundamentally with cultural and social origins. Girard notes in support of his own views that the word 'etiological' itself comes from the Greek *attos, attitia*, whose first meaning in the dictionary is not 'cause' or 'origin' but 'culprit, guilty, accused, delinquent'. (Golsan, 2002: 62 n 4)

And this leads to a further disquieting possibility: could it be the case that the Greek goat songs, after they were translated into tragedy, represented an attempt, even if not wholly conscious, to undermine the scapegoating process centuries before what Girard takes as the coming of the greatest anti-sacrificial religions, Christianity and rabbinical (post-Second Temple) Judaism? Goodhart seems inclined to think so.

> …does Sophocles not compel us … to view the empirical issue [of who killed Laius] as less important than the universal matrix of scapegoat politics (in which all are identically "murderers of Laius") in terms of which it functions … and in retrospective relation to the arbitrary determination of a unique culprit for the plague to substitute? Shall we not begin, Sophocles demands of us, to examine the limits of our myths, the status of our mythic appropriations in context of the real social relations in which they exist, in context, that is, of the blindness and self-destructive violence that plagues identically Oedipus' world, Sophocles' world and our own?. (Goodhart, 1978: 67–68)

Expressed more formulaically, the proposition is that the Greek tragedians (Sophocles, Aeschylus, Euripides) all attempted in their respective ways to dismantle the scapegoat process, *Oedipus Tyrannus* arguably constituting the single most well-constructed yet still primitive demystification of the *muthos* of the scapegoat, which is the mis-recognized lie told about the victim, by way of a highly destructive dramatic revelation of the nature of the ungrounded theo-political assumptions underlying the selection and death of an innocent; as Oedipus puts it, 'I have a terrible fear the blind seer can see' (Sophocles, 1984: 203).

> Rather than an illustration of the myth, the play is a critique of mytho-genesis, an examination of the process by which one arbitrary fiction comes to assume the value of truth. Suspending the empirical foundation on which the myth is built [Oedipus' alleged crimes of patricide and incest], suggesting as arbitrary the political determination that Oedipus is alone is responsible for the 'numberless' plagues that is depopulating the Theban city, Sophocles undertakes an examination of the logic that assumes he is the unique culprit. Oedipus discovers he is guilty of parricide and incest … less by uncovering certain hitherto obscure empirical facts than by voluntarily appropriating an oracular logic which assumes he has always been guilty. At the genesis of Teiresian [sic] wisdom is an oracular idolatry which assumes he has always already been guilty…. Oedipus invests prophetic language with the power of truth…. Apollo is sufficient. (Goodhart, 1978: 67)

In Hellas oracles and prophesy formed the point of intersection between tyranny and sacred, or religious, power. (Delcourt, 2020). The reasons for this are the specific characteristics of Greek one-man rule: tyranny is an anti-democratic form of government consisting of a divinely favored 'hero' most frequently the male offspring of a deity and whose divine pedigree justifies his assumption of absolute power. Conversely, and by way of a double transference, the tyrant's supernatural origin is the very thing that enables the religiously prescribed means for determining the identity of a sacrificial victim to function, as happens with Oedipus after he fails to deflect the accusations directed against him by Creon-Tiresias and whose oratorical rivalry suggests a half-remembered ritualistic procedure for determining whether or not the tyrant requires undergoing scapegoating.[32] The very word religion, it must be

[32] A central component of primitive, or 'sacred kingship' was that the ruler would be sacrificed after a proscribed period of time or if there was a disaster of some kind, which everyone knew to be

fully remembered, is derived from the Latin *religio*, meaning "a sense of the presence of supernatural power, religious fear, awe… [or] religious feeling" (Warrior, 2006: 147). *Religio*, in turn, is derived from two earlier words, both of which imply sacrifice and community obligation and are thoroughly functionalist in nature: *religare*, 'to bind' the community through external religious rituals and practices (*superstitio*) and *relegare*, the binding of the community of men with the community of the gods through both public ceremonies and private acts of worship (*numena*) (Warrior, 2006). Marie Delcourt has usefully pointed out the potentially fatal peril of the *misleading portents* that were a stock-in-trade of both Greek drama and literature (Delcourt, 2020: 184–185), drawing attention to the ways in which texts, such as the goat songs of Euripides, that had been 'inspired by democratic ideas' weaponized this trope by 'malevolently ascribing to tyrants and kings the most disastrous errors and using them to show, first, that if oracles are wrongly interpreted, it is because those who consult them are arrogant and reckless, and, second, that the pretensions of despots are often thwarted just when they seem to be triumphing' (Delcourt, 2020: 191). But even more than politics, the problem is one of mimesis: Sophocles arranges it through his experimental foray into demystification of having the 'tragic' Oedipus of drama imitate the 'mythic' Oedipus of *mythos* through his otherwise difficult to explain willed act of compliance with the theo-political authority of institutionalized prophecy[33]; in other words, Oedipus becomes 'Oedipus' through an act of self-authorship but by way of the real author who is Sophocles. For, like most prophecies, this one is self-fulfilling, Sophocles being a Tragedian and not a Comedian like Aristophanes.[34]

---

of supernatural origin and which, everyone also knew, demanded a supernatural remedy (Girard, 1977: 104–108). This same issue of an only partially remembered ritualistic 'interrogation' of the scapegoat is touched upon in the biblical Book of Job. See Chap. 8, above.

[33] Consistent with tragedy's central role in the quest for democratic government 'the one thing never questioned by the chorus is the sovereignty of the oracle' (Vernant & Vidal-Naquet, 1990: 317); consistent because the failure to correctly question or challenge the meaning of the oracle, as Jocasta attempts to do, is the direct cause of the tragic outcome. 'Sophocles was dealing with matters that had urgent contemporary significance; prophecy was one of the great controversial questions of the day. It was in fact the key question, for the rationalist critique of the whole archaic religious tradition had concentrated its fire on this particular sector. Far more than prophecy was involved. For if the case for divine foreknowledge could be successfully demolished, the whole traditional religious edifice went down with it. If the gods did not know the future, they did not know any more than man' (Knox 1984: 137). Contra Girard, who sees Sophocles' task as the un-masking of the scapegoat, this interpretation would identify the author's concern as staging a highly self-reflexive discussion concerning the relevance of oracular prophecy to debate and decision-making in the public assembly. Girard, however, does take note of it: '…rationalism, ancient and modern, marks … the oblivion, in appearance definitive, of oracles…' (Girard 2004: 25), so that what 'is at stake is the sacred prestige of the priest [Creon] and thaumaturge [Tiresias]' (Girard 2004: 67).

[34] This goes straight to one of the common, but mistaken, perceptions of a central weakness of the play: once Oedipus and Jocasta interrogate the shepherd concerning his alleged acquisition of the infant Oedipus from Laius—apparently proving that Oedipus is the son of the dead king after all and that Jocasta is his mother—both entirely forget the all-important issue of the number of the killers of Oedipus' biological father. But when we read the play as a critique of the sacrifice and the sacred power upon which it relies, this plot hole vanishes. Oedipus' 'knowledge that he has indeed

> Even though the reasons adduced are quite mythical, the reality of the cure [an exorcism] may be a fact. Behind the entire myth there could be a real crisis, concluded by the collective expulsion or death of a victim. In this case the oracle would be truthful in part. What is true is not that there is, as a 'real culprit', a man who bears alone the entire responsibility for the plague. Such a man cannot exist, of course. The oracle [as interpreted by Creon] is really talking about a victim who is 'right', in the sense that against and around that victim everyone can unite. Oedipus may well be the right scapegoat in the sense that the accusation against him really 'sticks' and restores the unity of the community. This restoration is tantamount to a 'cure' if, as Sophocles himself appears to suggest, the plague is ... a crisis of mimetic violence. (Girard, 1978: 145)

The 'positive effect of such a transfer, the end of the crisis, must necessarily be interpreted as a confirmation of the "oracle", as absolute proof that the 'real culprit' has been identified. A faultless relationship of cause and effect appears to have been established' (Girard, 1978: 145–146). It is inevitable, then, that the 'process just described implies that the random victim must be perceived as a "real culprit", missing before and now identified and punished. This random victim, in other words, will never be perceived as random; the "cure" would not be operative if its beneficiaries realized the randomness[35] of the victim's selection' (Girard, 1978: 146). *Meconnaissance*, or mis-recognition, is key to the success of this violent but generative unanimity: 'This transfer will not appear as such, of course. Instead of truth, we will have the "crimes" of Oedipus, the "parricide and the incest" that are supposed to "contaminate" the entire city' (Girard, 1978: 146). And this, according to Girard, lies at very center of all of those unspeakable and nameless things hidden since the foundation of the world.

But why has all of this remained mis-recognized up to the time of Girard's heroic undertaking of disinterment?[36] The answer lies within the very thing that caused the collective absence of perception: *meconnaissance*. To know the truth that sets us free requires a deliberate act of demystification which in the case of the *meconnaissance* of sacrificial violence means the expectation of the absence of direct evidence.

> The theory of the surrogate victim is paradoxical in that it is based on facts whose empirical characteristics are not directly accessible. These facts can be drawn exclusively from texts that invariably offer distorted, fragmentary, or indirect testimony. We can only gain access to the generative event through constant reference to these enigmatic sources, which constitute at once the foreground in which our theory situates itself and the background against which its accuracy must be tested. (Girard, 1977: 309)

---

killed Laius is not directly established, but is inferred from the discovery of his origin and from the [resultant] discovery that he has fulfilled the half of the Delphic oracle that prophesied incest; ergo, his inference would run, presumably the other half that foretold patricide has been fulfilled, in view of his previous strong suspicions on this score' (Greene 2020: 369).

35 Following Jocasta, 'randomness' would mean the secular or profane nature of the selection, devoid of transcendental meaning, devoid of the gods. See Chaps. 8 and 9, below.

36 The single but very great exception, according to Girard, is none other than the 'anti-Christ' Friedrich Nietzsche and who, I will show, seems to operate as something of a double to Girard—or perhaps the relationship is reversed, the Dionysian Nietzsche being emulated in an inverted manner by the Christian Girard.

Sophocles, however, has provided us with one of many diverse and wholly unanticipated clues. It is a simple matter of correct interpretation, or reading.

1.1.4 Oedipus the Foundling

According to Girard, there is 'a unity that underlies not only all mythologies and rituals but the whole of human culture, and this unity of unities depends on a single mechanism, continually functioning because perpetually misunderstood—the mechanism that assures the community's spontaneous and unanimous outburst of opposition to the surrogate victim' (Girard, 1977: 299–300). This *victimary hypothesis* is central to Girard's project of a fundamental anthropology and is identical to the scapegoating dynamic assayed by Sophocles: 'foundlings' or 'exposed infants' such as Oedipus were understood to be surrogate or emissary victims, containers of great supernatural power who were offered up to the wilderness during times of social crisis (Delcourt, 2020: 191).

> The exposed child may be a reject to be got rid of, a misshapen monster or a humble slave. But he may also be a hero with an exceptional identity. Saved from death and victor in the trial imposed upon him at his birth, the exile reveals himself to be a chosen one invested with supernatural powers. Now that he has returned in triumph to the country that expelled him, he will live there not as an ordinary citizen but as its absolute master, reigning over his subject like a god set down in the midst of men. This is why the theme of the exposed child appears in almost all of the Greek legends about heroes. There is no doubt—the chorus imagines—because he is the son of some god, of the nymphs of Cithaeron, of Pan or Apollo, Hermes or Dionysus. (Vernant & Vidal-Naquet, 1990: 127)

Delcourt has remarked on the reversibility, or 'dual quality' of the exposed child (ordinarily deformed or 'marked' in some manner[37]) and the scapegoat properly understood.

> In both cases one encounters the same psychological components: fear in the face of the wrath of mysterious forces... anxiety in the face of an unknown transgression that is more or less explicitly conceived as the cause of the harm to the community; a desire to transfer this harm to an individual who can then be excluded from the community....Once exposed, these infants serve as a remedy by counteracting the harm of which they are a symptom and by preventing it from spreading. (Delcourt, 2020: 42)

Vitally, both the sacrificed child and the scapegoat are the site of a double transference of a meaning that allows them to be culturally transformed into a sacred being through the rituals of *sacralization*.[38]

> Their sacralization, in the event they were rescued [from the wilds], had the effect of bringing about a reversal of values, so that what had been seen as evil was now considered to be good.

---

[37] Redheads were almost certainly doomed to exposure. However, the 'dominant conception here is not ugliness, but strangeness. It is exactly this quality that governs the expulsion of newborns' (Delcourt, 2020: 43).

[38] See below.

> Similarly, a divine judgment, involving a trial from which the child emerges alive, ended not in acquittal pure and simple, but in the *preferment* of the accused and the *punishment* of the accuser.[39] And every exposure entailed a divine judgment. (Delcourt, 2020: 191)

Sacralization invests them with a positive value insofar as they were hero-saviors of the community, but their latent supernatural potency is what also made them dangerous, subject to the logic of double transference: their power to heal, if inverted, meant the power to kill, so that a dual nature and function is assigned to them, marking their existence under the sign of ambivalence.

> In many rituals the sacrificial act assumes two opposing aspects, appearing at times as a sacred obligation to be neglected at great peril, at other times as a sort of criminal activity entailing perils of equal gravity ... Because the victim is sacred, it is criminal to kill him—but the victim is sacred only because he is to be killed. Here is a circular line of reasoning that at a somewhat later date would be dignified by the sonorous term *ambivalence*...If sacrifice resembles critical violence, we may say that there is, inversely, hardly any form of violence that cannot be described in terms of sacrifice—as Greek tragedy clearly reveals ... but sacrifice and murder would not lend themselves to this game of reciprocal substitution if they were not in some way related. (Girard, 1977: 1; 256–273)[40]

Sophocles clarifies this point for us by presenting Oedipus as a wholly ambivalent figure, the one who first saves Thebes from the curse of the Sphinx, and then almost destroys it through his barrier blurring sins. And the Tragedian is able to do this supremely well because he is appropriating for his own purposes a vast reservoir of mythic meaning and signification.

> This mythical image of the hero exposed and saved, rejected and returning in triumph, is continued in the fifth century in a transposed form, in one particular representation of the *turannos*. Like the hero, the tyrant accedes to royalty via an indirect route, bypassing the legitimate line; like him, his qualifications for power are his actions and his exploits. He reigns by virtue not of his blood but of his own qualities; he is the son of his works and also *Tuche* [Chance; Fortune].[41] The supreme power that he has succeeded in winning outside the ordinary norms places him, for better or worse, above other men and above the law...the comparison of tyranny to the power of the gods—and the Greeks defined these as 'the most

---

[39] Laius exposes Oedipus and is later killed by him ... maybe.

[40] Anticipating Girard, Henri Hubert and Marcel Mauss clearly recognized the sacred duality of the scapegoat cause of and cure for the crisis of the community: 'What is pure and impure are not mutually exclusive opposites; they are two aspects of religious reality. The religious forces ... can be exerted for good as well as evil. ...Thus is explained the way in which the same mechanism of sacrifice can satisfy religious needs the difference between which is extreme. It bears the same ambiguity as the religious forces themselves. ...The victim represents death as well as life, illness as well as health, sin as well as virtue. ...It is the means of concentration of religious feeling; it expresses it, incarnates it, it carries it along. By acting upon the victim one acts upon religious feeling, directs it either by attracting and absorbing it, or by expelling and eliminating it' (Henri Hubert and Marcel Mauss qtd. Delcourt, 2020: 46).

[41] And it is the 'chancy' nature of the rise of the tyrant that signifies his ambiguous, or double-edged, relationship to the supernatural; 'Tyranny ... with the ambiguous meaning that it had in this period ... meant both the exercise of personal power by someone with the status of a hero and a privileged relationship with the gods that allowed him to give laws to the city; but tyranny as well—and this was the obverse side of the tyrant—as the man of excess who used his power beyond rule or measure' (Foucault, 2020: 347–348).

> strong,' 'the most powerful'—is a commonplace in the literature of the fourth and fifth centuries. Euripides and Plato both speak of the *turannos isotheos*, tyranny that is the equal of a god in that it is the absolute power to do as one wishes, to do anything one wants. (Vernant & Vidal-Naquet, 1990: 127)

And, of course, 'the absolute power to do as one wishes, to do anything one wants' can include patricide and incest, those crimes of special significance because they 'attack the very foundation of cultural order, the family and the hierarchical differences without which there would be no social order' (Girard, 1986: 15). As the entire point of the accusation against Oedipus, whether true or false, is to bridge 'the gap between the insignificance of the individual and the enormity of the social body' it is 'not enough for the social bond to be loosened; it must be totally destroyed' (Girard, 1986: 15). For if the scapegoat 'is to be capable of such a profound impact upon the entire community, his or her actions must reveal a degree of evil and destructiveness which far exceeds that of the average citizen. In effect, the scapegoat must "measure up" to the crisis he or she causes' (Golsan, 2002: 5). This explains the conceit of sympathetic magic that allows a single scapegoat to destroy an entire people; the scapegoat's 'sphere of individual action' magically corresponds to the 'consequences global consequences of an epidemic of the plague or any comparable disaster' (Girard, 1986: 15) raising the suspicion that scapegoats are not killed because they are magical but that they are assumed to be magical so that they may be killed. Which means that only a victim of tremendous supernatural power, such as a *turannos isotheos*, can be considered a viable candidate for scapegoating: Oedipus merits sacrifice precisely because of his ambivalence in both his identity and his meaning.

1.2 Symbolization, Sacralization, and *Meconnaissance*

Extrapolating from the clues provided by the Greek Tragedians, we are able to formulate a universal, or generic, linear sequence of scapegoating: (i) individual or group acts of escalating violence; (ii) crisis of social order; (iii) 'the victims are chosen not for the crimes they are accused of but for the victim's sins that they bear, for everything that suggests their guilty relationship with the crisis'; and (iv) 'the import of the operation is to lay the responsibility for the crisis on the victims and to exert an influence on it by destroying these victims or at least banishing them from the community they "pollute"' (Girard, 1986: 24). And concerning the case of the tyrant Oedipus this explains how the scapegoaters are able to invert the cause and effect relationship between biological plague and social disorder by having the latter the cause of the former, or, alternatively, interpreting the former as the sign of the latter, an escalating violence within the community that appears to have originated externally as a gift from the gods in the form of the *turannos isotheos*. And this inverted causality in which the sacred pollution of the cultural order can cause a catastrophic collapse of the natural order indicates that the phenomenon of the scapegoat is inseparable from the issue of magic which itself is 'a gigantic variation on the theme of the principle of causality' (Hubert and Mauss qtd. Girard, 1986: 52), the epitome of *meconnaissance.*

> The victim, in reality passive, becomes the only effective and omnipotent cause in the face of a group that believes itself to be entirely passive. If groups of people can, as a group, become sick for reasons that are objective or that concern only themselves, if the relationships at the heart of these groups can deteriorate and then be re-established by means if victims who are unanimously despised, obviously these groups will commemorate these social ills in conformance with the illusory belief that the scapegoat is omnipotent and facilitates the cure. The universal execration of the person who causes the sickness is replaced by universal veneration for the person who cures that same sickness. (Girard, 1986: 44)

Another paradox now presents itself: the 'crime' of the accused 'is always the imagination of the prosecutors' (Girard, 1986: 35) because the surrogate victim is interpreted as being sacred, a false and falsifiable premise that renders the entire scapegoating process one of mystification but of a self-validating kind.

> Admittedly scapegoats cure neither real epidemics nor droughts nor floods. But the main dimension of every crisis is the way in which it effects human relations. A process of bad reciprocity is its own initiator; it gains nourishment from itself and has no need of external causes in order to continue. As long as external causes exist, such as an epidemic of plague for example, scapegoats will have no efficacy. On the other hand, when these causes no longer exist, the first scapegoat to appear will bring an end to the crisis by eliminating all the interpersonal repercussions in the concentration of all evildoing in the person of one victim. The scapegoat is only effective when human relations have broken down in crisis, but he gives the impression of effecting external causes as well, such as plagues, droughts, and other objective calamities. (Girard, 1986: 43)

The sacrificial death of the scapegoat at the hands of the crowd is the very thing that transfigures him, permitting the sacred victim to be the thing that saves the community.

> If this victim can extend his benefits beyond death to those who have killed him, he must either be resuscitated or was not truly dead. The causality of the scapegoat is imposed with such force that even death cannot prevent it. In order not to renounce the victim's causality, he is brought back to life and immortalized, temporarily, and what we call the transcendental and supernatural are invented for that purpose. (Girard, 1986: 44)

Girard adopts 'the language of the ethologists' in asserting that 'a determined orientation toward natural causes gradually displaced man's immemorial preference for *significant causes on the level of social relations* which are also *the causes that are susceptible to corrective intervention,* in other words *victims*' (Girard, 1986: 96).

> We can trace in myths a system of representation of persecutions similar to our own but complicated by the effectiveness of the process of persecution. We are not willing that effectiveness because it scandalizes us on the level of both morality and intelligence. We are able to recognize the first evil transfiguration of the victim, which seems normal, but we cannot recognize the second beneficent transfiguration; it is inconceivable that it can unite with the first without destroying it, at least initially. (Girard, 1986: 44)

Although we no longer formally inhabit the mental landscape of either the magical or the mythological, we do possess religion in order to alleviate the epistemic trauma induced by the ambivalent duality of the victim who is both innocent and guilty, both the cause of and the cure for all of the community's ills. But even above and beyond religion, there are two other cultural artifacts that are of indispensable value in maintaining the mythic effect of the scapegoat. The first is law. The second is literature.

The surrogate-emissary scapegoat is the prehistoric cornerstone of what only recently came to be known as 'law' (as differentiated from everything 'non-law') because it is the artifact that enabled the creation of the generative unanimity necessary to establish, and then periodically regenerate, cultural order. The result is that there is 'a direct correlation between the elimination of sacrificial practices and the establishment of a judicial system'.

> [However] if it cannot be proven that the penal system owes its origin to generative violence, it might well be maintained that the judicial system is based on rational agreement, on a sort of social contract, and that men are indeed able to master their social environment in the direct and explicit way that rationalists conceive. Such a conclusion would flatly contradict my line of argument. (Girard, 1977: 297–298)

And the reason why humans are never in a position to enter into the rationality required for the social contract is because the true foundation of the human community is governed by processes that are inherently magical and irrational, or, at a minimum, contra-rational.[42] And if the scapegoat truly is the beginning of everything, the first cultural construction that enables all of the subsequent ones, then civilization itself is grounded upon a set of foundational beliefs that cannot be expressed in terms of orthodox representation; 'if the mechanism of the surrogate victim is simply another aspect of the original mechanism of the symbolic process, then there can be nothing in the whole range of human culture that is not rooted in violent unanimity—nothing that does not find its source in the surrogate victim' (Girard, 1977: 297). Quite literally, 'we' are all 'here' because our hominid ancestors survived the primordial cataclysm of undifferentiation through their invention of the scapegoat, echoed, and repeated through mythology, giving rise to more complex social structures that replicated the underlying dynamic of a cultural logic that is inherently sacrificial which requires a mystified mentality that elides expression through classical means of representation.[43] And this becomes even clearer when we shift our attention away from law and toward literature, for it is within the writing of fictions that 'the return of the repressed (scapegoat)' is experienced in the least mediated fashion that is culturally and psychologically possible. The scapegoating mechanism can only work by appropriating for its own purposes the very forces that are responsible for the pre-cultural plague-contagion of undifferentiation: these are mimesis, mimetic desire, mimetic rivalry, and, most destructive of all, *metaphysical desire*[44] which, as it turns out, are also the raw stuff of literature. But for Girard, the truth of literature is also the truth of anthropology: 'All desire is a desire for being' (Girard & Treguer, 2014: 12).

---

[42] See my discussion of *Lord of the Flies* in Chap. 2, below.

[43] See below.

[44] See below.

1.2.1 Mimesis and Desire

For Girard the potentially fatal dilemma of every cultural order is that the Self will model its relationship to the Other on the basis of imitation, or mimesis, that will not infrequently culminate in the Self attempting to either replace and/or destroy the Other, now a rival through a self-reinforcing pattern of mimetic conflict, an escalating rivalry over mimetic desire that eventually explodes into physical violence; as the passionately anti-Freudian psychoanalyst Mikkel Borch-Jacobsen put it in equally passionate terms: 'Desire is violence because it is a desire to be proper, a desire for propriation, and, as such, a hostile, murderous desire...Desire is a violent mimesis, then' (Mikkel Borch-Jacobsen, 1988: 90).

> Our hypothesis makes it logical to imagine that the rigorous symmetry between the mimetic partners ... the living obstacle[45] of the model that is automatically transformed into a rival ... must bring about two things among man's ancestors, little by little: the ability to look at the other person, the mimetic *double*, as an *alter ego* and the matching capacity to establish a *double* inside oneself, through processes like reflection and consciousness. (Girard et al., 2003: 284, 285)

And the phenomenological reality of this eternal homicidal predicament is not owing to something present, such as an activating instinct for violence and murder, but owing instead to something absent. Because our so-called human nature is profoundly under-determined we, quite literally, do not know what we want or know what we should want, which compels us to look to others for guidance which is the point of origin of the inevitable crisis of undifferentiation.

> Rivalry does not arise because of the fortuitous convergence of two desires on a single object; rather, *the subject desires the object because the rival desires it.* In desiring an object the rival alerts the subject to the desirability of the object. The rival, then, serves as the model for the subject, not only in regard to such secondary matters as style and opinions but also, and more essentially, in regard to desires. (Girard, 1977: 145)[46]

[45] Girard uses the word 'obstacle' in two different senses: (i) as short-hand for the external mediator, the person or thing that acts as a circuit-breaker of escalating mimetic rivalry; and (ii) the pathologized version (a 'mimetic paroxysm') of an 'ordinary' mimetic rivalry contaminated by metaphysical desire, in which mimetic rivalry 'increases to the point that the subject is no longer interested in anything but the rivalry itself'—which is psychosis. (Oughourlian, 2010: 12). Both senses will be used here.

[46] This touches upon one of the most common objections raised against Girard, namely that he has reduced all forms of desire to mimesis which, despite his occasional lapses into polemics, is incorrect; he makes it clear that neither 'appetite' nor 'need' are mimetic in nature, although both may acquire mimetic aspects in the event of intense interpersonal rivalry; 'For there to be desire according to our definition, the effects of mimesis must interfere, not directly with animal instincts and appetites, but in a terrain that has already been fundamentally modified by the process of hominization: in other words, the mimetic effects and a wholesale re-processing of symbols must develop in unison' (Girard et al., 2003: 283–284). So mimetic theory is in no way compromised by the disturbing truth that the 'more cruel and wild a society is, the more its violence is rooted in pure need. One must never exclude the possibility of violence that has nothing to do with mimetic desire but simply with scarcity. However, even at the level of basic needs, when rivalry begins and is related to an object, any kind of object, there's no doubt that it will soon become impregnated with

The rivalry that mimetic desire unleashes will, in the end, assume the most extreme and grotesque form of the violent, or *monstrous doubles* who are the micro-signifiers of the macro-crisis of the loss of distinctions: as the rivals intensify their mimetic struggle they effectively become identical, triggering a pathological crisis of identity which can only be resolved through an act of extreme violence, whether physical, emotional, or symbolic (Girard, 1977: 143–168).[47] Utilizing a series of anthropological assumptions (Oughourlian, 2010: 81–106, 2016: 3–31), Girard speculates that the logic of social formation is mirrored most perfectly by the logic of mythological narrative, *mythos* as the repository of *meconnaissance.* As mimetic rivalries are to be proscribed because of their ultimately violent consequences, the mimetic rivals must displace, or discharge, their common violence against a convenient surrogate victim that serves as the transference object of the violence—the scapegoat (Girard et al., 2003: 93).[48] Girard explains the ambivalent magical efficacy of the scapegoat by identifying two variants of mimetic desire: divisive *acquisitive mimesis,* which leads to or more individuals to desire the exact same object at the same moment in time,[49] and unifying *conflictual mimesis,* which induces all of the parties to the conflict to settle upon a common rivalry, or enemy, such restorative unanimity itself a by-product of mimetic desire. 'If *acquisitive mimesis* divides by leading two or more individuals to converge on one and the same object with a view to appropriating it, *conflictual mimesis* will inevitably unify by leading two or more individuals to converge on one and the same adversary that all wish to strike down' (Girard et al., 2003: 26). Mimesis, like the scapegoat itself, is both the cause and the cure of violence: mimetic desire creates mimetic rivalry but when humans scapegoat they mimetically imitate the desires of the others which is to kill or banish the 'one' as Sophocles demonstrated. 'Mimetic theory renders an account of sacrifice and archaic religion, to a purely natural force, human hyper-mimeticism' (Rene Girard qtd. Cowdell, 2014: 59) and mimesis is itself the site of a kind of double transference analogous to that of the scapegoat.[50] 'It is obvious that the same force that divides people by mimetic

mimesis. In these cases, there is always some social mediation at play' (Girard et al., 2008: 74). This also draws our attention to the importance of specific and localized material and environmental factors in regulating the intensity of mimetic conflict; 'One might say that any violent process that has any duration, any temporality, is bound to become mimetic' (Girard et al., 2008: 75).

[47] 'Violence is the process itself when two or more partners try to prevent one another from appropriating the object they all desire through physical or other means' (Girard qtd. Gallese 2011: 88).

[48] The preferred term of evolutionary psychologists is 'emissary victim'. The concept is identical (Reeve 2015: 179).

[49] 'If one individual imitates another when the latter appropriates some object, the result cannot fail to be rivalry or conflict. Such conflict is observable in animals; beyond a certain intensity of rivalry the antagonists tend to lose sight of their common object and focus on each other, engaging in so-called prestige rivalry. In human beings, the process rapidly tends toward interminable revenge, which should be defined in mimetic or imitative terms' (Girard 1987: vii).

[50] Girard's central contribution to mimetic theory is that he suspends any 'difference' between mimesis and mimetic desire. 'Mimesis is practically synonymous with mimetic desire. Mimesis evokes desire. Desire constitutes mimesis. Mimetic desire is a kind of unconscious imitation of others, but it is important to stress that the word "imitation" has to be joined with the adjective

rivalry also unites them by the mimetic unanimity of the scapegoat' (Girard, 1986: 196) so both division (acquisitive mimesis) and reconciliation (conflictual mimesis) are inherently ambivalent because the one possessed by mimetic desire migrates between the poles of a duality, destruction and restoration.

> Since the power of mimetic attraction multiplies with the number of those polarized, it is inevitable that at one moment the entire community will find itself unified against a single individual. Conflictual mimesis therefore creates a *de facto* allegiance against a common enemy, such that the conclusion of the crisis is nothing other than the reconciliation of the community. (Girard et al., 2003: 26)

Without exception the victim is 'held responsible for the renewed calm in the community and for the disorder that preceded this return. It is even believed to have brought about its own death' (Rene Girard qtd. McKenna, 1992: 15), and this, claims Girard, provides us with our first clue into the nature and universality of scapegoating: what has historically evolved into the divine is really the mythic re-telling of an archaic mis-recognized projection of a collective state of psychic anguish, the sacred as the 'externalization of human violence in relation to itself' (Dupuy, 2013: 109).

> The victim's death coincides with a moment of total unanimity and pure mystification. The sudden transition from all-out war to common peace is something so unforeseen that supernatural intervention seems the only explanation. Though the community deems the scapegoat a villain at his death, it must ultimately take him for 'divine,' believing he both willed and survived his own demise. (Dawson, 2013: 69)

But what this means in practice is that 'So long as the victim lives, he is part of the community; he can therefore participate in the unanimity forming against himself. The need for unanimity is the community's primary concern. There is no reason for him to be an exception. In fact, his assent is the most important of all' (Girard, 1987: 111) for there is no more infallible way of empirically proving the guilt of the scapegoat than having her implicitly confess her crimes by explicitly embracing her sacrificial death. And this assent, the scapegoat's voluntary acceptance of her fate, the cornerstone of a unanimous victimage, is indispensable in securing the introduction of the element of absolute difference that can resolve the crisis-of-confusion: the community must be divided in a completely totalizing manner between a completely innocent card and a thoroughly guilty accused; the restoration of 'the community is identical to the strengthening of socio-religious transcendence. But such reinforcement demands a flawless scapegoat mechanism, completely unanimous agreement that the victim is guilty' (Girard, 1987: 111).[51] And this almost ethological-like 'herd mentality' of scapegoating provides powerful but indirect evidence of the origin of religion and the sacred, the prehistoric corollary of law, as residing within a kind of deterministic naturalism.

> The sacred is thus a human agency, *though neither an invention nor a conscious discovery*; rather, it is the serendipitous chancing upon a viable form of life along the existing direction of

---

"appropriative" or "acquisitive" [or "emulative"]. Mimesis seeks to obtain that which the model desires. The function of culture is to control and channel this potential conflict over the object' (Girard 1996: 290).

[51] See Chaps. 8–10, above.

> evolution by natural selection. Reliable social order followed as the logic of this development is played out, with emerging culture sustained by the universal phenomena of prohibitions, myths, and rituals that moderns customarily group together under the label of religion. (Cowdell, 2014: 57)

But the cathartic,[52] or 'safety-valve', effect of the group's convergence upon a single victim can only work if human behavior, particularly in regard to its capacity for collective violence (the 'lynch-mob'), is intensely affective in its nature and mimetic in its operations, rendering all of us highly susceptible to the plague-contagion of the 'psychology of the crowd'; for Girard 'Mimetic attraction is bound to increase with the number of those who converge on one and the same antagonist' (Girard, 1996: 13), a phenomenon that is universal and which, mercifully, has now been demystified—by Girard.

> How can the scapegoat effect involve real belief? How can such an effect be generated without an objective cause, especially with the lightning speed that can often be observed in the case of the scapegoating mobs? The answer is that scapegoat effects are mimetic effects; they are generated by mimetic rivalry itself, when it reaches a certain degree of intensity. As an object becomes the focus of mimetic rivalry between two or more antagonists, other members of the group tend to join in, mimetically attracted by the presence of mimetic desire. (Girard, 1996: 12)

And through the prism of scapegoating, catharsis is 'nothing more than the vitalizing, binding sensation which the crowd feels at the sacrifice of the victim' (Golsan, 2002: 39).

> Mimesis is mimetically attractive, and we can assume that at certain stages, at least in the evolution of human communities, mimetic rivalry can spread to an entire group. This is what is suggested by the acute disorder phase with which many rituals begin. The community turns into a mob under the effect of mimetic rivalry. The phenomena that take place when a human group turns into a mob are identical to those produced by mimetic rivalry, and they can be defined as that loss of differentiation which is described in mythology and reenacted in ritua.l (Girard, 1996: 12)

Which is the precise mechanism, grounded upon anthropological phenomena, by which the scapegoat is established as the cornerstone of cultural order, an event that is repeated countless times by every culture that was able to survive the mimetic crisis of its origins and make the transition from the pre-historical to the historical.

> In order to understand primitive rules, prohibitions and rituals, one must postulate a mimetic crisis of such a duration and severity that the sudden resolution, at the expense of the single victim, has the effect of a miraculous deliverance. The experience of a supremely evil and then beneficent being, whose appearance and disappearance are punctuated by collective murder, cannot fail to be literally *gripping*. The community that was once so terribly stricken suddenly finds itself free of antagonism, completely delivered. (Girard, 1978: 28)

And because it has undergone the exorcism of mimetic conflict successfully, the delivered community is able to avoid the eternal threat of self-destruction. Girard is not merely providing an anthropology of the scapegoat but a phenomenology of it as

---

[52] See Chap. 9, above.

well but one which is supremely anti-modern, for archaic religious experience, which is literally nothing other than the sacrificial, is, in terms of subjective experience, indistinguishable from a state of possession.

> The hypothesis of the sacred reflects the human mind in its recognition that is surpassed and transcended by a force that appears to be exterior to it, since at any moment this force seems to exert its will on the entire community for reasons which, though they seem ultimately incomprehensible, seem nonetheless to be beneficent rather than malevolent. (Girard et al., 2003: 42)

Girard realizes that claims as sweeping as this require extensive empirical support and her have been considerable scientific advances in neurobiology that would appear to provide validation, or at least supplemental support, of the mimetic hypothesis, most notably research into the Mirror Neuron System (MNS).[53] I am speculating here, but other approaches that could provide partial support include the neuro-psychiatry of altered states of consciousness (ASC), neuro-anthropological work on incidents of collectively induced suggestion culminating in events of social contagion and communal religious experiences (McClenon, 1994), and, perhaps most fruitfully, the ethno-botany of entheogens. What unifies, and provides an intuitive plausibility to these diverse research paradigms is that they are all based on a unifying principle that is identical to the one that Girard has placed at the center of his fundamental anthropology: *meconnaissance*, the universality of mis-recognition, that gives rise to the inviolable rule that scapegoating 'becomes more and more effective as there is less and less knowledge, less awareness of it as a collective delusion' (Girard, 1987: 94).

> The archaic sacred is the necessary transcription of the scapegoaters' delusion. The victims are transfigured into all-powerful manipulators of disorder and order, founding ancestors, or divinities. Later on, the descendants of the scapegoaters will draw spiritual sustenance from their distorted recollections of the community's ordeal. The divinized victims become models of ritual performance and countermodels of prohibition. That is how religion and culture originate. (Girard, 2020: 58)

[53] The neurobiological lynchpin of mimetic theory, mirror neurons make up the neural circuitry that directly facilitates the pre-conscious phenomena of affectivity and empathy (Dupuy, 2011). 'The MNS for actions in humans is somatically organized, with distinct cortical regions within pre-motor and posterior parietal cortices being activated by the observation/execution of mouth-, hand-, and foot-related acts.' Although it sounds somewhat pedestrian, MNS is the neurocognitive foundation of our species' highly developed sense of sociability, the 'social,' of course, being the arena of imitation. 'Both the production and the perception of emotion-related facial expressions or body postures impinge upon common neural structures related to viscero-motor, somato-motor, and affective aspects of the emotion experience. It appears, therefore, that there is a "we-centric" dimension in the experience of a given emotional/affective state, and that it is underpinned by the activity of a common neural substrate. When we witness a given facial expression and comprehend that expression by a particular emotional state, we do not accomplish this type of comprehension through explicit inference from analogy. The other's emotion is first constituted and directly understood by means of embodied simulation producing an "as if" experience engendered by a shared body state. It is the body state shared by the observer and observed that enables direct understanding' (Gallese, 2011: 94, 95). Which proves that the determination of value, the desirability of an object or person, is always a 'group activity,' although we do not really require mirror neurons to validate this insight; 'all but the most die-hard reductionists would agree that the proposition "Man is a super-mimetic animal" is self-evidently true even if the biological mechanisms responsible for it remain unknown' (Dupuy, 2011: 194).

And to expand upon this point somewhat: apart from the problem of the false nature of magical causality (which may of course command the passionate belief of the scapegoaters), the other great and potentially fatal threat to the functional effectiveness of regenerative violence is the manner by which the scapegoat is actually chosen. This is the same problem that Sophocles touches upon; he raises reasonable doubt concerning Oedipus' guilt by providing us with a series of clues suggesting that the tyrant is the victim of a conspiracy; the epistemological upshot of this is not merely that Oedipus is really innocent but that the reason for selecting him is wholly random, subject not to supernatural authority but to the private motivations of the secular sacrificers.

> [The] scapegoat genesis requires an awareness of the unconscious dimension of scapegoating. The one thing we must not expect from a scapegoat-generated myth is a recognition that the victim is not a scapegoat … or, in other words, a recognition that the choice of the victim is arbitrary, that the causal link between the victim and whatever disaster is ascribed to him is not real. (Girard, 1987: 88)

Scapegoating's 'vitality as an institution depends on its ability to conceal the displacement upon which the rite is based' (Girard, 1977: 5) for an 'arbitrary victim would not reconcile a disturbed community if its members realized they are the dupes of a mimetic effect' (Girard, 1996: 14) which is another way of saying that that which must remained mis-recognized is that scapegoating is a profane political activity and not a sacred religious one. Which is why Girard identifies Luke 23: 34—'Father, forgive them, for they do not know what they do'— as the ultimate condemnation of scapegoating, for if self-awareness had kicked at that moment the execution would have been immediately halted.

> To scapegoat someone is to be unaware of what you are doing … This is the key role of the *meconnaissance* in the process[54]—it allows one to have the illusion that one is justly accusing someone who is *really* guilty and, therefore, *deserves* to be punished. In order to have a scapegoat, one must fail to perceive the truth, and therefore one cannot represent the victim as a *scapegoat*, but rather as a righteous victim, which is what mythology does. (Girard, 2020: 134)[55]

[54] Which, not surprisingly, is the most difficult part of Girard's theory for us to accept in Girard's own opinion: 'Scapegoating by others, scapegoating for which we feel no sympathy, appears to us an evil so stupid, so senseless, and nevertheless so widespread that it arouses our indignation. We cannot believe it as "sincere" and spontaneous. We cannot believe participants are really fooled by their own scapegoating, and we believe in foul play. Our understanding is blurred.' Which is why we moderns never scapegoat—we only persecute those who are *truly* guilty and 'Those we regard as scapegoat-makers, we are tempted to turn into …. Our own scapegoats' (Girard, 1987: 78). See Chap. 12, below.

[55] Girard never employs the term 'unconscious' in relation to scapegoating, given the neurocognitive aspects of the phenomenon as a purely social construction which would be antithetical to the psychoanalytical 'idea of *the* unconscious as a kind of "black box"'; 'I do not want to say *the* unconscious with the definite article because it implies a form of ontological essentialism that I distrust' or, more precisely, carries with it an undesirable 'Freudian connotation'. Contra Freud, Girard uses the epistemic *meconniassance* 'because there is no doubt that one must define the scapegoat mechanism as a form of misrecognition of its injustice, without ignoring who has been killed' (Girard, 2020: 135).

Scapegoating would never have been invented in the first place if all of the participants understood that what they were doing were setting up the conditions necessary to group administer a massive dose of catharsis. And so it came to pass that 'Mythology and religious cults forms systems of representation necessarily untrue to their own genesis. The episode of mimetic violence and reconciliation is always recollected and narrated, as well as re-enacted, from the perspective of its beneficiaries, who are also its puppets' (Girard, 1996: 14).The general rule of *meconnaissance* may be formulated this way: 'The efficacy of the mechanism and the richness of ritual production are inversely proportional to the community's aptitude at identifying this same mechanism in operation' (Guy Lefort qtd. Dupuy, 1988: 78). All humans are mimetically enslaved to the *scapegoat effect* which, crucially, is completely different from the modern, and wholly negative, sense of the term.

> The victim must be perceived as truly responsible for the troubles that come to an end when it is collectively put to death. The community could not be at peace with itself once more if it doubted the victim's enormous capacity for evil. The belief in this same victim's enormous capacity for doing good is a direct consequence of that first belief. The peace seems to be restored as well as destroyed by the scapegoat victim himself. (Girard, 1996: 14)

As soon as we begin to study the scapegoat 'we imagine a deliberate manipulation. We think of skillful strategists who are fully aware of the mechanisms of victimization and who knowingly sacrifice innocent victims in full awareness of the cause with Machiavellian ease' (Girard, 1986:40). But although factionalism among the scapegoaters may be possible, at least during the comparatively late stage of the cultural development of the mechanism such as the time of Greek tragedy, during the very first phases of social formation functionality would appear to have been the overriding and unifying concern.

> To understand human culture it is necessary to concede that only the damming of mimetic forces by means of the prohibition and the diversion of those forces in the direction of ritual are capable of spreading and perpetuating the reconciliatory effect of the surrogate victim. Religion is nothing other than this immense effort to keep the peace. *The sacred is violence*, but if religious man worships violence it is only insofar as the worship of violence is supposed to bring peace; religion is entirely concerned with peace, but the means it has of bringing it about are never free of sacrificial violence. (Girard et al., 2003: 32)[56]

And this ambivalence of the sacrificial violence of scapegoating is the true but mis-recognized source of everything human that came after it.

1.2.2 The Scapegoat and Evolution

Hominization itself is the by-product of the scapegoat mechanism for it is the thing that allowed early humans (hominids) to navigate the otherwise fatal consequences of the crises of violence that accompanied the development of self-awareness.

---

[56] For the integrative function of religion, see Dietrich et al. (2012).

> Mimetic rivalries are normally forbidden to men; primitive prohibitions ... are essentially concerned with these rivalries. In other words, forms of human sociality, unlike animal forms, cannot develop *directly* out of mimetic rivalries, but they do develop indirectly from them through the intermediary of the surrogate victim. (Girard et al., 2003: 93)

And Girard goes well beyond this, his fundamental anthropology reaching stratospheric heights.

> From an evolutionary perspective, language and the symbolic sphere could only be generated by a systematic 'catastrophe', which will act as a springboard for the emergence of culture ...There must be that upheaval there, which forced the change in behaviour. This upheaval is absolutely indispensable ... The only thing that can produce such a relational structure is *fear*, fear of death. If people are threatened, they withdraw from specific acts; otherwise chaotic appropriation [acquisitional mimesis] will dominate and violence will always increase. Prohibition is the first condition for social ties and the first cultural sign as well. Fear is essentially fear of mimetic violence; prohibition is protection from mimetic escalation. All these incredibly complex phenomena were triggered by the founding murder, by the scapegoat mechanism. (Girard et al., 2008: 109–110)[57]

The scapegoat mechanism is itself the mimetic-driven basis for the species transition from the pre-symbolic to the cultural, or the *pre-representational* to the *representational*: 'All human language, and other cultural institutions, in fact, originated in collective murder' (Girard, 1986: 193) and not only is this the case it cannot be anything other than this, the creation of 'the *symbolic* and the *imaginary*' a matter of necessity, not contingency (Girard, 1986: 196). 'In the founding mechanism reconciliation against and around the victim' with the result that 'at the most primitive levels the victimage mechanism is already at work and generates the most basic strata of meaning' which is *symbolization* (Girard et al., 2003: 102). And here is Girard's strongest claim: 'I believe that all human thinking, beginning with our ability to discriminate anything from anything else, is rooted in the victimage mechanism. It means that discrimination as a purely intellectual exercise is inseparable from discrimination as exclusion, expulsion, ostracization' (Rene Girard qtd. Golsan, 2002: 140). What he means literally is that every aspect of human thought is either sacrificial in essence or, at a minimum, possesses a latent sacrificial dimension, the mimetic repetitions of the primitive drawing and enforcement of differences constituting *Homo sapiens*' first experience of abstract thought.

> Because of the victim, in so far as it seems to emerge from the community and the community seems to emerge from it, for the first time there can be something like an inside and an outside, a before and after, a community and a sacred...the victim appears to be simultaneously good and evil, peaceable and violent, a life that brings death and a death that guarantees life. Every possible significant element seems to have its outline in the sacred and the same time to be transcended by it. In this sense the victim does seem to constitute a universal signifier. (Girard et al., 2003: 102)

---

[57] 'The mimetic theory provides the perfect bridge between the one-sidedness of ethological theories, which glibly assimilate animal culture to human culture, as if the symbolic nature of the latter were an unimportant supplement, and the one-sidedness of structural anthropologists *a la* Levi-Strauss, who see human culture as if, literally, it had fallen from heaven, completely disregarding the similarities between human and animal culture' (Girard, 2020: 61).

David Dawson states the obvious implication of this: 'A scrupulously naturalistic explanation is being ventured here, one that reduces the metaphysical character of the primitive sacred in the multiplicity of its expressions to the universality of a psychosocial event' mis-recognized as being of transcendental origins (Dawson, 2013:70). And, in Girard's defense, he has no small number of followers and fellow-travelers within the anthropological community, such as religious scholar Burton Mack who openly embraces the theory of the scapegoat as the universal master-sign of all significations: 'All systems that give structure to human society have been generated from [the scapegoat mechanism]: language, kinship systems, taboos, codes of etiquette, patterns of exchange, rites, and civil institutions. Thus, a theory of sacrifice has produced a comprehensive account of human social formation, religion, and culture' (Mack, 1987: 7).[58] Mythology, which is nothing other than *meconnaissance* embodied as the narrative structure of *mythos*, 'mediates' the sacrificial mechanism by transcribing the machine's constituent parts—the rites[59] and rituals[60]—into a comprehensive system of symbolized systems of meaning. 'Myths are the textual product of generative scapegoating' (Golsan, 2002: 169) yielding Durkheim's 'juxtaposition of real immanence, a force arising with the social order itself' with a '"transcendental power"' which, in this instance, is the supernatural power of the sacred victim (Girard, 2005: 100). And all 'religious rituals spring from the surrogate victim, and all the great institutions of mankind, both secular and religious, spring from ritual' and it 'could hardly be otherwise, for the working basis of human

[58] Once again this brings up the problem of evidence and once again Girard seeks justification in the epistemological wonders of inductive reasoning: 'It is sometimes argued that the scapegoat hypothesis cannot really be demonstrated, since it is never directly legible in a text. It describes a structuring process, and cannot be deduced directly from a single text. It is, in essence, comparative and hypothetical' (Girard, 1987: 31). Even if 'no example taken alone offers conclusive proof of my theory, their cumulative effect is overwhelming; all more so because they coincide with archetypal myths that tell, in apparently "naïve" fashion, how all man's religious, familial, economic, and social institutions grew out of the body of an original victim' (Girard, 1977: 306). Furthermore, 'There are just too many myths of this type and the only reasonable explanation for the traces of scapegoating they exhibit is that they truly originate in actual scapegoating' (Golsan, 2002: 169). Nevertheless, Girard does concede that there is 'nothing more difficult than detecting the structuring mechanism at work in the text. It is like looking for depth on a two-dimensional surface, the written text' (Girard, 1987: 31). Girard's strongest point is the *meconnaissance* of scapegoating, a process that is marked by the total absence of self-awareness, for if the crowd actually understood what it was doing the regenerative effect of the ritualistic death would be lost; therefore, no mythic text could ever afford to clearly reveal the truth of the mechanism and that the sacralized hero and/or god is really just a mutilated cadaver who gives ecstatic pleasure to the crowd immediately prior to its immolation.

[59] 'Rite' denotes 'a particular complete ritual act within a larger ritual' (Wright, 1993: 475).

[60] Rites are the 'constituent parts' of the scapegoating mechanism because they are the literal repetition of the originary physical actions that both killed the victim and regenerated the community and operate in an un-mediated manner; rites and sacrifice, by contrast (and the myths and rituals that they later gives rise to) are mediatory in that they provide an archaic pre-representational mental field within which the rites operate. 'Sacrifice stands in the same relationship to the ritual crisis [the need to murder the scapegoat] that precedes it as the death or expulsion of the hero to the undifferentiated chaos that prevails at the beginning of many myths. Real or symbolic, sacrifice … can happen only at the paroxysm of the ritual crisis' (Girard 1996: 11).

thought, the process of "symbolization," is rooted in the surrogate victim' (Girard, 1977: 306). Ritual, in turn 'gives way eventually to modern institutions, such as the judicial system, which take from it their own version of power and transcendence' (Cowdell, 2014:68), and this is the road that takes us back to law, for the 'things you must not do are called *prohibitions* and the things you must do are called *rituals*' (Girard, 1987: 93). Hence, Girard's radically anti-secularist proposition that religion is the true foundation of society (Girard, 1977; Kirwan, 2005: 43–50). Apart from his central concern with literature and the novel,[61] much of Girard's work constitutes a highly unorthodox form of legal anthropology, a hybridization of both Durkheim's Functionalist sociology of religion and Freud's psychoanalytic critique, yielding us the following general conclusion.

> The efficiency of our judicial system conceals the problem [of violence], and the elimination of the problem conceals from us the role played by religion. The air of mystery that primitive societies acquire for us is undoubtedly due in large part to this misunderstanding. It is undoubtedly responsible for our extreme views of these societies, our insistence on portraying them alternately as vastly superior or flagrantly inferior to our own. One factor alone might well be responsible for our oscillation between extremes, our radical evaluations: the absence in ['primitive'] societies of a judicial system…If we compare societies that adhere to a judicial system with societies that practice sacrificial rites, the difference between the two is such that we can indeed consider the absence or presence of these [judicial] institutions as a basis for distinguishing primitive societies from 'civilised' ones. (Girard, 1977: 18–19)[62]

But interwoven within this totalizing account of the origins of law is another, less expressly announced theory of the origin and nature of language. Girard makes much of the fact that symbolization, in its most primitive form, can only operate through the linguistic medium of the representational, the anti-realist model of speech and articulation that liberates consciousness from the confines of reductive or deterministic pre-representation, meaning that any 'one' thing may be substituted for any 'other' thing through a process of exchange of symbolizations: '… hunting, the domestication of animals, sexual prohibitions, etc., might all be described as the manipulation and differentiation of the sign constituted by victimage' (Girard et al., 2003: 103) because the 'one' victim of the sacrifice becomes symbolically inter-exchangeable with the 'one' victim of all future sacrifices, as though, by way of double transference, the sacred power of the sacred scapegoat eternally returns in order to be sacrificed and restore the community giving rise to an entire cosmological chain-of-signifiers expressed through *mythos*: 'The signifier is the victim. The signified constitutes all actual and potential meaning the community confers on to the victim and, through its intermediary, onto all things' (Girard et al., 2003: 103).

> The surrogate victim, as founder of the rite, appears as the ideal educator of humanity, in the etymological sense of *e-ducatio*, a leading out. The rite gradually leads men away from the sacred; it permits them to escape their own violence, removes them from violence, and

---

[61] See below.

[62] 'If a community is deprived of political and legal means to deal with internal divisions and agitations, there will be an irresistible tendency to pin the responsibility for whatever ails it on some individual or individuals close at hand' (Girard, 1978: 185). Which would mean some sort of vendetta, lynching, or pogrom.

> bestows on them all the institutions and beliefs that define their humanity. (Girard, 1977: 306)[63]

However, it proves impossible 'to resolve the problem of violence with the surrogate victim without at the same time elaborating a theory of the sign and signification' for the surrogate victim is itself the first cultural construct that marks the decisive transition of species consciousness toward abstraction and reification which is the primary enhancer of self-awareness and cognitive complexity—abstraction and reification—so that even the 'most elementary form of the victimage mechanism, prior to the emergence of the sign,' which is the scapegoat as properly constituted symbol, 'should be seen as an exceptionally powerful means of creating a new degree of attention, the first non-instinctual attention' (Girard et al., 2003: 99).

But there is an obvious problem in two parts, one that Girard never fully addresses: how long, exactly, is the sequence of sequence of causation that results in the transformation of pre-sacrificial hominids into fully constituted symbolizing scapegoaters? And by what means, precisely, did representational thought actually managed to evolve out of pre-representational thought, almost as though by means of a neurocognitive act of leap-frogging? Or, rather, might the reality be one less of discontinuity that continuity, so that, in an almost atavistic fashion, the representational 'recapitulates' the pre-representational within it at the most elemental levels of mimetic consciousness? For if the crisis of undifferentiation is the apocalyptic threat that always remains with us, both individually and collectively, we are always on the verge of sliding from representation to pre-representation, meaning that we have never truly left the latter behind.

> We are at the point of asking just how far back in human or pre-human history the victimage mechanism should be situated. If this mechanism is the foundation of everything that is human in man [sic], for humanity's most ancient institutions, such as hunting or the incest prohibition, the question then becomes the process of hominization, or in other words the transition from animal to man. (Girard et al., 2003: 84)

Given the enormity of his claims—and which, as we shall see, become even more enormous—the onus is on Girard to provide an at least approximate timeline and provide details concerning the relevant elements of 'deep time' but, really, the best he came up with was this: 'It is necessary to conceive of stages … which were perhaps the longest in human history, in which the signifying effects [of scapegoating] have still not truly taken shape' (Girard et al., 2003: 100). And then he re-states the problem but this time adding the useful supplement of the non-instinctive nature of most human behavior, at least post-hominid.

> We have to show that the intensification of mimetic rivalry, which is already very much in evidence at the level of primates, destroyed dominance patterns and gave rise to progressively more elaborate and humanized forms of culture through the intermediary of the surrogate victim. At the point when mimetic conflict becomes sufficiently intense to prohibit the direct

[63] 'The sacred is violence efficaciously removed from human communities, and violence is the sacred deviated from its divine position and creating havoc in the city' (Goodhart, 1988: 54–55).

> solutions that give rise to the forms of animal sociality[64] [e.g. 'dominance patterns'], the first 'crisis' or series of crises would then occur as the mechanism that produces the differentiated, symbolic, and human forms of culture Mimetic rivalries are normally forbidden to men; primitive prohibitions ... are essentially concerned with these rivalries. In other words, forms of human sociality, unlike animal forms, cannot develop *directly* out of mimetic rivalries, but they do develop indirectly from them through the intermediary of the surrogate victim. (Girard et al., 2003: 94)

However, this doesn't really get us anywhere because the fact remains that 'We have absolutely no idea what early[65] processes consist of, how they interlock with "natural" processes, and how they act on the latter to create more and more humanized forms' (Girard et al., 2003: 88). But he does provide at least partial explanation which, in fact, possesses a great deal of scientific merit: *neoteny* ('premature birth'), or the retention and extended development of infantile characteristics into the adult form of the species. Which, for primates, includes an upright posture and a disproportionate expansion of the size of the cranium, Girard correctly noting that 'Everyone today agrees in hypothesizing that the volume of the brain has grown too quickly to be attributed to a normal process of biological evolution' (Girard et al., 2003: 88).

> [Neoteny] is a factor of adaptation; it is no doubt responsible for the post-natal growth of the brain and thereby makes possible not only the power but also to extraordinary suppleness of human intelligence. Instead of being limited to instinctual patterns, we are capable of learning the most diverse lessons of culture. All of this contributes to the human being's superiority over other species. (Girard et al., 2003: 84–85)

The 'extraordinary suppleness' of the hominid brain is what allows for the remarkable evolutionary effect of mimesis and mimetic desire.

> In order for us to suppose that things did in fact happen this way it will be necessary and sufficient to show that mimetic power must increase not only during the process of hominization but even prior to its being set in motion, and to a degree great enough to set the process in motion. (Girard et al., 2003: 94)

Here Girard turns to geneticist (and atheist) Jacques Mond and his notion of 'the simulative function': 'It is the powerful development and intensive use of the simulative function that ... characterizes the unique properties of man's brain. And this is the most basic level of the cognitive functions, those on which language rests and which it probably reveals only completely' (Jacques Monod qtd. Girard et al., 2003: 94). The primacy of language also explains the reason why humans are so intensely mimetic: we largely lack the neurological 'hard-wiring' necessary for purely instinctual behavior which is a supremely ambivalent situation, for human desire 'consists of the grafting of mimesis on to instinctual patterns and the overactivation, aggravation, and disorganization of the latter' particularly in regard to sexuality, which has proven to be a wholly destabilizing force as the most intense form of mimetic rivalry possible (Girard et al., 2003: 95). The same holds true for violence in a wholly generic sense.

---

[64] These include 'dominance patterns' and 'instinctual inhibitions' on intra-species conflict (Girard et al., 2003: 86, 87).

[65] Again undefined.

> Human societies are obviously not based on [instinctual] dominance patterns, and we can see why: mimetic rivalry among human beings results easily in madness and murder. It would be a mistake, however, to attribute this increase in violence in human beings to an opaque, mute instinct; we would not only miss its real character but also ignore a more interesting explanation for it: it is part of the growth of mimetic rivalry linked to the increase in brain size. (Girard et al., 2003: 95)

'Reflexive imitation,' for Girard, 'was the primary thing' for representation 'as such is a late development. It may have taken hundreds of thousands of years, or longer, to reach the representational capacity of "humanity"' (Girard, 1996: 269). Which certainly fits with Monod's simulative function, but then Girard overreaches badly by asserting that mimesis is the cause, not the effect, of the 'premature birth' of the human brain, the central activating agent of a process of *direct selection.*

> There is reason to believe that the power and intensity of imitation increase with the volume of the brain along with the entire line that leads to *homo sapiens*. In the primates closer to man the brain is relatively more voluminous than in any other animal species. It must have been the increasing power of imitation that initiated the process of hominization, rather than the reverse, even if the process subsequently served to accelerate that growth ['the simulative function'] and made a prodigious contribution to the remarkable power of the human brain. (Girard et al., 2003: 94–95)

Contra Girard, there 'was *no direct selective pressure* to fix our ability to think symbolically—and, therefore, to self-reflect—in our genome' (Kastrup, 2021: 132). Self-awareness was the result of *indirect selection*, meaning a voluntary group action or learned behavior of some kind which may, of course, have included the cultural innovation of the sacrifice and related ritualistic behavior, such as hunting and warfare. This is the by far more persuasive approach adopted by Ian Tattersall, curator of the Hall of Human Origins of the American Museum of Natural History in his musings on the general origins of the human species.

> …as far as *Homo sapiens* is concerned it appears that the body form was one thing, while the symbolic cognitive system that distinguishes us so greatly from all other creatures was entirely another. The two were not acquired at the same time, and the earliest anatomical *Homo sapiens* appear right now to have been cognitively indistinguishable from Neanderthals and other contemporaries. (Tattersall, 2012: 185–186)

Neither was self-awareness 'a threshold effect of acquiring a greater brain volume over vast spans of time'; instead, 'it seems overwhelmingly likely that … our cognitive ability was acquired as a by-product of the hugely ramifying genetic accident that resulted in the appearance of *Homo sapiens*' meaning that, counter a strict and reductive adaptationism, the 'new potential it created then lay fallow for a substantial length of time, until its symbolic potential[66] was "discovered" by its owner' (Tattersall, 2012: 208–210) in response to an environmental need(s) of some sort, such as the imperative to reduce intra-group violence. 'The bottom-line is, *we currently have no natural explanation for our fall into self-reflection*' (Kastrup, 2021: 132), and it may have consisted of a number of different cultural innovations (sacrifice, hunting, entheogens) whose respective historical development and cross-fusions may remain

[66] Or, potential for symbolism.

permanently occluded. What matters is that it is possible 'to inscribe the genesis of human culture in nature and to relate it to a natural mechanism without depriving culture of what is specifically, exclusively, human' (Girard et al., 2003: 97) which is the primal act of the group attaining elemental awareness of itself in opposition to the one who is different from all others and whose death solves all problems for the time being.

> Up to now it was recognized that the rapid increase in brain size, as well as other phenomena, required an interaction between biological and cultural factors, but what has been missing is a model for the organizing and driving factor in the process, a motor for this strange machine. The victimage process gives us this motor. We can conceive of hominization as a series of steps that allow for the domestication of progressively increasing and intense mimetic effects, separated from one another by crises that would be catastrophic but also generative in that they would trigger the founding mechanism [sacrifice] and at each step provide for more rigorous prohibitions within the group, and for a more effective ritual canalization toward the outside.... One can also see that at each step more and more elaborate institutions would favour a new mimetic level, which would bring about a new crisis and thus continue on in a spiral movement that would progressively humanize the anthropoid. (Girard et al., 2003: 97)

The originary event of scapegoating 'should be viewed as an absolute beginning, signifying the passage from nonhuman to human, as well as a relative beginning for the societies in question' (Girard, 1977: 309) and even if 'innumerable intermediary stages exist between the spontaneous outbursts of violence and its religious imitations, even if it is only these imitations that come to our notice, I want to stress that these imitations had their origin in a real event' (Girard, 1977: 309). And as Tattersall insists that event became an originating action because the capacity for symbolization existed prior, and not subsequent, to the first act of sacrificial violence.

> Our ancestors made an almost unimaginable transition from a non-symbolic, non-linguistic way of processing and communicating information about the world to the symbolic and linguistic condition we enjoy today. It is a qualitative leap in cognitive state unparalleled in history. Indeed, ... the only reason we have for believing that such a leap *could* ever have been made, is that it *was* made. And it seems to have been made well *after* the acquisition of our species of its distinctive modern biological form. (Tattersall, 2012: 199)

The pre-representational symbolic logic and of sacrifice and substitution may have served as the trigger for the development of higher-order/representational social consciousness in hominids; development of self-awareness through the 'need' for the resolution of the problem of intra-group violence. Both scapegoating and its by-product double transference need to be critically understood at least as much through their epistemological relationship with the higher cognitive processes of abstraction and reification, the necessary pre-conditions for symbolization, as their 'erotic' dynamics of mimetic desire.

> Scapegoating, when it becomes unanimous, affects the whole community. The crisis has been long; it seems that the community is splitting and disintegrating. Then all of a sudden it's over, and it's over because of the scapegoat.[67] Who or what is responsible for ending the crisis? Who or what provoked the crisis? Here arises a problem that is the basis of what

[67] Which is the sign of double transference, but now understood in its cognitive dimension and not merely its 'libidinal' mimetic one: 'This disorder and order are the function of the *double*

> must become interpretation and representation, though in primitive or originary situations the crisis and its resolution are still pre-representational. (Girard, 1996: 269)

Representation is the socio-linguistic equivalent of that establishment of differences that is the demarcation between the archaic and the civilized. What is fairly clear in Girard's account is that the representational domain of self-stabilizing symbolization emerges out of the self-destruction of the pre-representational domain of the crisis of undifferentiation. But what is still needed is a very precise account of how, exactly, the species' exiting of the pre-representational was accomplished in the first place, appearing as though out of nothing as Paisley Livingston points out. And the fundamental problem remains: every time we enter the mimetic state of the undifferentiation we regress toward the pre-representational (ALL = ONE), and vice versa. Girard needs to posit some sort of jump in the cognitive evolution of the human species in order to establish the elemental significance of scapegoating which he can only partially explain, but for Livingston

> To the extent that one stresses the non-representational and non-intentional aspects of the primordial mimesis, a mechanical theory of hominid agency is embraced; yet this analysis is conjoined to a description, in "high" cognitive language, of the results of the scapegoat mechanism, results amounting to an ensemble of beliefs, attitudes, symbolic practices, and actions that are at once cultural and representational. (Livingston, 1992: 129)

The best answer may lie with the cultural artifacts that were developed so as to permit the sublimation of the pre-representational into the machineries of scapegoating by means of both mis-recognition and its performative twin *repetition*, the same artifacts that served as the cornerstones of culture, religion, and law.

1.2.3 Myth and Sacralization

For Delcourt, the correct definition of 'religious myth' is 'a story that reduces a mysterious reality, generally a rite, to a specific experience' and which 'were imagined solely in order to persuade someone to do something' (Delcourt, 2020: 216) which is both functionalism and mimesis unified through a wholly affective phenomenology.

> The explanation it gives has the effect of transforming an emotion that is common to all who accept the truth of the myth into a singular event, a personal experience. This experience, once it has undergone and internalized as an example to be followed, is colored by an *affectus* from which arises a dynamism capable of acting on all members of the group that accepts the myth. (Delcourt, 2020: 214)

And the mimetic-affective grounding of sociability proved to be highly cultivatable by the *long duree* forces of cultural formation precisely because *affectus* was so supremely well-suited to the mediation of symbolization and ritualism.

---

transference of the originary victimization: those involved in the collective violence transfer the disorder and the offenses producing it to the victim, but they transfer also their newly found peace to the victim, ascribing to him or her the power that brings it about' (Girard, 1996: 293).

> To the extent that a new type of attention is awakened, the [sacrificial] victim will be imbued with the emotions provoked by the crisis and its resolution.... There is no need to assume that the mechanism of awakening attention works right away; one can imagine that for a considerable period it produced nothing at all, or *next to nothing*. Nonetheless, even the most rudimentary signifying effects result from the necessity of controlling excessive mimesis; as soon as we grant these effects can be in the slightest degree cumulative, we will have recognized them as forerunners of human culture instinctual. (Girard et al., 2003: 100)

As Nietzsche knew all too well, the more 'cultured' early humans became the greater self-consciousness they attained, and with this heightened awareness-of-self came ever more existentially debilitating and illness-inducing forms of 'decadence' or inhibitory neuroses of the Nietzschean variety, the primary symptoms of which are an obsession with meaning and signification and incontrovertible proof that pre-representation has been left behind for good. The anthropological term for this phenomenological calamity that Nietzsche outlines is *sacralization*, the spatial localization of the manifestation of religious power ('sacred space'; 'sacred time') that is linked to the stereotypical ritualistic (liturgical) performances: 'In each case we are confronted by the same mysterious act—the manifestation of something of a wholly different order, a reality that does not belong to our world, in objects that are an integral part of our natural "profane" world' (Eliade, 1987: 11).

For Mircea Eliade *homo religios* cannot be understood outside of the sacred and 'the definition of the *sacred* is that it is *the opposite of the profane*' (Eliade, 1987: 10) for man is a creature of and for meaning—an object of desire, in truth— and the sacred 'reveals absolute reality and at the same time makes orientation possible; hence it *founds the world* in the sense that it fixes the limits and establishes the order of the world' (Eliade, 1987: 30).

> The *sacred* is equivalent to a *power*, and, in the last analysis, to *reality*. The sacred is saturated with *being*. Sacred power means reality and at the same rime enduringness and efficacity. The polarity sacred-profane is often expressed as an opposition between *real* and *unreal* or pseudo-real. ...Thus it is easy to understand that religious man deeply desires *to be*, to participate in *reality*, to be saturated with power. (Eliade, 1987: 12–13)

And it is through the supremely repetitive rituals of sacralization, '*the world becomes apprehensible as world, as cosmos, in the measure in which it reveals itself as a sacred world*' (Eliade, 1987: 64) and religious man's 'desire to live *in the sacred* is in fact equivalent to his desire to take up his abode in objective reality, not to let himself be paralyzed by the never-ceasing reality of purely subjective experiences, to live in a real and effective world, and not in an illusion' (Eliade, 1987: 28)—although of course it is, because, as already pointed out, the divine is nothing more than the 'externalization of human violence in relation to itself' (Dupuy, 2013: 109). This is sublimely Nietzschean as well as Girardian but for different reasons; for the former the issue is health and existential vitality (the opposite of decadence) while for the latter it is a problem of meaning and signification, which is the inevitable result of a scapegoating violence that must eventually be repudiated.

> This as much as to say that religious man can live only in a sacred world, because it is only in such a world that he participates in being, that he has a *real existence*. This religious need expresses an unquenchable ontological thirst. Religious man thirsts for *being*. His terror of

> the chaos that surrounds his inhabited world corresponds to his terror of nothingness. The unknown space that extends beyond his world—an uncosmicized because unconsecrated space, a mere amorphous extent into which no orientation has yet been projected, and hence in which no structure has yet arisen—foe religious man, this profane space represents absolute non-being. If, by some evil chance, he strays into it, he feels emptied of his ontic substance, as if he were dissolving in Chaos, and he finally dies. (Eliade, 1987: 64)

What Eliade is describing here is the crisis of undifferentiation as a cosmic phenomenon. The representational 'sign is the reconciliatory victim' and the symbolized scapegoat is the link, or point of interface, between nature and culture (Girard et al., 2003: 103), for in 'the founding mechanism' of sacrifice as a response to the post-instinctual mimetic 'chaos' of undifferentiation 'reconciliation is achieved against and around the victim' (Girard et al., 2003: 102). This means that 'the only thing an animal needs to become human is the surrogate victim' (Girard et al., 2003: 102), the preliminary step toward symbolization.

> The more intense mimesis becomes, the more the conflicts it provokes and their subsequent resolutions become 'contagious'. We can therefore suppose that as mimetic rivalries intensify they involve an increasing number of participants and that these are the ones eventually united around the sacralised victim and subjected to the double imperative of prohibition and ritual. The human community is nothing but such an assembly and can only exist as a function of it. (Girard et al., 2003: 98–99)

Girard's hypothesis literally 'refers to a set of real events, to a collection of actual victimages that really took place. A rigorously realist epistemology is inescapable here' (Dumouchel, 1988: 7).[68] Since ritual is performative repetition and its governing logic is mimetic *affectus*, the ritual is both a representation and a substitution for an earlier crisis of violence. Since 'sacrifice is always a question of substitution, it is always possible to make a new substitution and henceforth to sacrifice only a substitute of a substitute' (Girard et al., 2003: 53) it becomes impossible 'to resolve the problem of violence with the surrogate victim without at the same time elaborating a theory of the sign and signification' (Girard et al., 2003: 99). In Girard's case the vital ritualistic dimension of the sacrificial mechanism is the mimetic evocation of an earlier act of killing that was successful in resolving social crisis.

---

[68] 'The crisis and its resolution constitute, according to Girard, the common origin of all institutions as an independently repeated self-regulating mechanism that is always formally identical but whose precise circumstances vary from case to case. This hypothesis explains both resemblance and variety. It predicts that social and cultural institutions should share certain family resemblances; not that they should be identical, nor that any characteristic should be common to all sacrifices or rituals.' What is crucial is that the mechanism, independently discovered any number of times in pre-history, should operate blindly; the 'template is a social mechanism, one which arises from the composition of the actions of many agents … The reconciliation which follows the crisis is an unintended effect. That is why the mechanism is a self-regulating mechanism of violence. It rests solely on the unfolding of violence itself. In order to restore peace, it calls upon nothing but the murderous fury which moves the mimetic doubles … No one need design or will this order for it to exist; it is typically a spontaneous order. Like the invisible hand which transforms private interests into the common interest, or private vices into public benefits, the process of victimage diverts each individual's violence to the common peace and order' (Dumouchel, 1988: 16–17). Everything else is of secondary importance or a mere contingency.

> [T]he sacrificers...are striving to produce a replica, as faithful as possible in every detail, of a previous crisis that was resolved by means of a spontaneously unanimous victimization. All the dangers, real and imaginary, that threaten the community are subsumed in the most terrible danger that can confront a society: the sacrificial crisis. The rite is therefore a repetition of the original, spontaneous 'lynching' that restored order in the community by reestablishing, around the figure of the surrogate victim [the scapegoat], that sentiment of social accord that had been destroyed in the onslaught of reciprocal violence...In the scapegoat theme we should recognize the very real metamorphosis of reciprocal violence into restraining through the agency of unanimity. (Girard, 1977: 94–95, 96)

But the problem still remains, for *affectus* is pre-representational in its effects because through it all differences are abolished and any one thing can become everything. It is the *visceral* phenomenology of the rite that must never be underestimated; 'It is no exaggeration to say that as far as Girard is concerned, properly human representations and consciousness begin with in an illusion: the first "non-instinctual attention" ... is that excited by the vision of a victim killed by the rest of the group' (Livingston, 1988: 122). And it is this which is in perfect accord with Eliade, perhaps slightly more so than with Girard. Sacred time is generated through the mimetic repetition of sacrifice which itself becomes sacralized; 'religious man lives in two kinds of time, of which the more important, sacred time, appears under the paradoxical aspect of a circular time, reversible and recoverable, a sort of eternal mythical present that is periodically reintegrated by means of rites' (Eliade, 1987: 70). An 'eternal mythical present' is a pre-representational concept as every moment is experienced as identical to every other, which gives us the msytic icon of timelessness; 'It can be said of sacred time that it is always the same, that it is "a succession of eternities" (Henri Hubert and Marcel Mauss qtd. Eliade, 1987: 88) so that the apparent linear movement of Time is, in some sense, *meconnaissance*. Sacred Time 'is indefinitely recoverable, infinitely repeatable' (Eliade, 1987: 69); '*by its very nature sacred time is reversible* in the sense that, properly speaking, it is *a primordial mythical time made present*' (Eliade, 1987: 68) but it is the very thing through which rite, ritual, and prohibition can be formed and, more importantly, phenomenologically experienced as *affectus*. Every myth 'describes the various and sometimes dramatic irruptions of the sacred into the world' (Eliade, 1987: 97)—or, in an inverted manner, the collapse of the differentiated into the undifferentiated—and every ritual bears the traces of a double movement: the re-invocation of the past event and the projection of that earlier event's cathartic effect into future time. The 'prior event' that all ritual killings represent through mimetic substitution is a collective murder, an act of mob violence so that sacrifice 'then becomes a term that can be used to refer to the complex phenomenon of the collective killing of a human victim, its mythic rationalization, and its ritualization' (Mack, 1987: 8). The necessary pre-condition for the historical survival of the community is the successful exorcism of the unclean spirit of violence incarnated by the scapegoat. This is secured through the periodic enactment of the rituals of the machinery of sacrifice, which is itself the mimetic repetition of an earlier killing of a designated victim which successfully broke the cycle of retributive violence. And, although far from elegant, the endless return of the scapegoat may function as the solution to the problem of the transition from pre-representation to representation: the sheer act of endless repetition phenomenologically transforms the mimetic content of undifferentiation into the differentiated form of rites that, in turn, regulate the cultural evolution of symbolization.[69] As Jean-Pierre Dupuy has correctly pointed out, this should not be understood teleologically. 'The genesis of the scapegoating mechanism … was not invented by humankind *in order to* keep its violence in check. It constitutes one possible *attractor* of the dynamics of violence' (Dupuy, 2011: 208). By 'attractor' is meant 'a random procedure that takes on an aura of necessity,' in this case the empirically repeated—and *repeatable*—efficacy of the crowd's lynching of the scapegoat as the restoration of order, 'a condition of internal consistency' that reflects 'the correspondence between a priori beliefs and a posteriori results.' And mimetic contagion is an outstanding example of a non-teleological but beautifully self-validating attractor; the 'mimetic dynamic seems to be guided by an end that pre-exists it—and that is how it is experienced from the inside—but it is in reality the dynamic itself that brings forth its own end': the archaic triptych of conflict/sacrifice/reconciliation (Dupuy, 2011: 209).

Representation-as-differentiating-repetition-of-the-escape-from-undifferentiation would, of course, gain greater suasion if the hypothesis could, again, be framed more in terms of cognition than desire. An implied hidden continuity, as opposed to a decisive rupture, between the archaic (pre-representation) and the historical (representation) is, of course a classic trope of Freudian psychoanalysis. Yet, Girard largely eschews the Freudian theory of drive, or instinct (*Trieb*), claiming greater insight in the application of psychoanalysis to the collective (impersonal) dynamics of cultural formation[70]; in effect, the translation of Freud's late metapsychology into the referential terms of Durkheim's notion of function: 'The purpose of the sacrifice is to restore harmony to the community, to reinforce the social fabric. Everything else derives from that' (Girard, 1977: 8).[71] For Girard, the 'fundamental truth about violence' is that, 'if left unappeased, violence will accumulate until it overflows its

[69] To employ a 'rigorously realist' formulation of my own: the unintended outcome of multiple scapegoating incidents was to collectively train hominids, through learning and memory, to differentiate between the one and the many, from whom all could become a 'one'. But the species could no more leave behind pre-representation any more that it could leave behind the unconscious.

[70] Girard's mimetic theory 'differs from the Freudian unconscious in that there's no great treasure or mystery to be found in my unconscious. It is, you might say, a purely negative unconscious' whereas Freud 'wanted the unconscious to be some kind of storehouse or determinant' (Girard, 2020: 44, 45). In lieu of a metapsychological 'substance,' mimetic theory, 'because it's based on human relations,' locates the universal explanatory principle within wholly 'external structures that determine those relations over and above the individual psyche' (Girard, 2020: 99). So that we are condemned to be hyper-conformists by default, for 'Absence is a form of mediation' (Girard, 2020: 96).

[71] 'To affirm the mimetic nature of desire is to deny it any privileged object, whether a unique or well-determined object such as the mother in the Oedipus complex or else a class of objects as narrow or vast as might be supposed. It is equally necessary to renounce all psychic or biological entrenchments, including, of course, the pan-sexualism of psychoanalysis. We must renounce all entrenchments of desire in need. This does not imply a minimalization of sexuality or needs; quite the contrary, these are nearly always involved in the matter and can play the role, among others, of masking or obscuring mimesis. Mimetic desire is at times so inextricably mixed with other things that probably no kind of analysis can isolate it; it is nonetheless necessary to pose the other extreme

confines and floods the surrounding area. The role of sacrifice is to stem this rising tide of indiscriminate substitutions and redirect violence into "proper' channels'" (Girard, 1977: 10). Central to the success of the sacrificial mechanism is its status as ritual which is invariably a 're-enactment of a 'prior event' (Mack, 1987: 8). Since every ritual is a re-enactment, or a repetition, its governing logic is mimesis: the ritual is both a representation of and a substitution for an earlier crisis of violence. But this governing logic is itself in some way pre-representational: under the sign of substitution, all differences are abolished and any one thing can be traded for and replaced with any other thing, which is the precariously liminal moment of the in-between of differentiation and undifferentiation. The vital difference, which is introduced by representational systems of meanings which are themselves the signs of difference(s), is that pre-representational thinking is now safely ensconced within the psychic safety-net of ritualistic repetition. The essential point is that the ambivalence of the transition from pre-representation to representation constitutes a liminality that renders the two modes of thought and speech subject to reversal, as is recognized by mythological and religious thought which 'make the victim the vehicle and transforming agent of something sacred—mimesis—which is never conflictual or undifferentiated except in so far as it is spread throughout the community; its concentration in a victim makes it a pacifying and regulating force, the positive mimesis found in ritual' (Girard et al., 2003: 48). And as I will show in later chapters, the literary representation of the descent into the domain of undifferentiation and pre-representation is at the heart of every legal drama that is concerned with either the invention or the abolition of the scapegoat as the ground-zero of law. For to a degree largely unrecognized, the representation of law within both literature and cinema is taken up with the dramatization of the antecedent crisis of undifferentiation rather than with the regeneration of differentiation for what is most at issue is the moment and meaning of law's genesis.[72]

To summarize: the pre-human (the hominid) became the human (hominization) by re-directing the undifferentiating violence unleashed by mimetic conflict against a sacrificial victim who was the reified substitute of an original that is now absent. Which is how acts of repetition and substitution became archetypal forms of cultural praxis and how representational systems of symbolization can attain an approximate degree of stability through sacralization. But this also raises the possibility of an inverse meaning: if Girard is right that 'the only thing an animal needs to become human is the surrogate victim,' then is the abandonment of surrogate victimage the only thing the human needs to become an animal? In a certain sense Girard's answer is yes.[73] 'We must attempt ... to understand that at the most primitive levels

---

of need and appetites, a pole of desire itself, which, while both evident and mysterious, is not libido but mimesis' (Girard, 1978: 90).

[72] To cite a single example: in my discussion of Sidney Lumet's *12 Angry Men*, I argue that the narrative function of the protagonist, juror no. 8 (Henry Fonda) is to induce the transformation of the undifferentiated jurors—who are numbered, not named—into a differentiated community of distinct individuals capable of using representation in their deliberations, through the introduction of a substitute scapegoat for the accused. See Chap. 6, below.

[73] I discuss this cosmically pessimistic conclusion at full length in Chap. 12, below.

the victimage mechanism is already at work and generates the most basic strata of meaning' (Girard et al., 2003: 102), which is practically a mytho-poetic version of Original Sin and The Fall: the deliberate invention of the scapegoat was the means of acquiring the noumenal knowledge of Good and Evil that enables us to become as gods.

> Since we understand that human beings wish to remain reconciled after the conclusion of the crisis, we can also understand their penchant for reproducing the sign, or in other words of reproducing the language of the sacred by substituting, in ritual, new victims for the original victim, in order to assure the maintenance of that miraculous peace. The imperative of ritual is therefore never separate from the manipulation of signs and their constant multiplication, a process that generates new possibilities of cultural differentiation and enrichment.... There is no difficulty in explaining why ritual is repeated. Driven by sacred terror and wishing to continue life under the sign of the reconciliatory victim, men attempt to reproduce and represent this sign, this attempt consists first of all in the search for victims who seem capable of bringing about the primordial epiphany, and it is there that we find the first signifying activity that can always be defined, if one insists, in terms of language and writing. The moment arrives when the original victim, rather than being signified by new victims, will be signified by something other than a victim, by a variety of things that continue to signify the victim while at the same time progressively masking, disguising, and failing to recognize it. (Girard et al., 2003: 103)

Symbolization is perfected with sacralization's transcendental reification of the scapegoat, a visceral symbol. Girard's theory of myth can be broadly classified as Euhemeristic in that "the gods of myths were actual historical persons who have been deified"' (Golsan, 2002: 72 n 15). Which means that everyone of us can potentially become deified. And there is nothing in our neurological circuitry to prevent us from symbolizing this desire that is a form of death.

1.3 Metaphysical Desire, Interdividual Psychology, and *Ressentiment*

Against Freud, we did not invent civilization in order to prevent murder[74]—rather, we invented civilization in order to create the pre-conditions for a certain kind of murder: the sacrificial killing that postpones the apocalypse of unlimited undifferentiation, the ritualistic slaying that guarantees the victory of conflictual mimesis over acquisitive mimesis. 'This first murder basically changed the mode of being of human life' (Eliade, 1987: 101) making Girard's thesis not a theory of religion but a theory of the genesis of civilization that is grounded upon ritualistic human sacrifice; as Jean-Michel Oughourlian has observed, Girard's 'theory of religion is simply a particularly noteworthy aspect of a fundamental theory of mimetic relations' (Girard et al., 2003: 44) for it is in primitive societies that 'the mimetic crisis culminates in a phase of unbearable undifferentiation that is resolved by the violence of the sacrifice'

[74] Although Girard does concede that 'There is an element of truth to *Totem and Taboo*, and it consists in tracing humanity's origin to a collective murder' (Girard et al., 2003: 96).

(Girard & Treguer, 2014: 68). But this same mimetic process doubles as Girard's audacious theory of literature: every literary depiction of human drama, which is always a form of social phenomena, is ultimately about envy (Girard, 1965). For what else could it be about, as mimetic desire, or a desire that is specifically mimetic in nature,[75] is 'Desire according to the Other' (Girard, 1965: 5)? As with both Georges Bataille and Jean-Paul Sartre, the essence of the human dilemma is the absence of an essential self—anthropological *non-being*. 'The human subject does not really know what to desire, in the last resort' (Girard et al., 2003: 343); thus, the human subject 'desires *being*, something he himself lacks and which some other person [the 'model'] seems to possess. The subject thus looks to that other person to inform him of what he should desire in order to acquire that being' (Girard, 1977: 146). Girard conceptualizes this dynamic as *triangulation*: the impulse toward the object is ultimately an impulse toward the mediator' (Girard, 1965: 10) for the supremely simple reason that the 'mediator's prestige is imparted to the object of desire and confers upon it an illusory value. Triangular desire is the desire which transfigures its object' (Girard, 1965: 17) in the eye of the beholder who is the imitator of the model. The Self models its desire on the one that it has selected as its mediator between itself and the object of the model's own desire—which, logically (and obsessively) becomes the desire of the Self. Which, in turn, inevitably culminates in a mimetic 'crisis' of identity, or 'authenticity,' the crisis assuming the form of double, or reciprocal, mediation: 'where the desire to thwart rivals replaces desire for whatever constituted the original object of rivalry …' (Cowdell, 2014: 22).

> What is 'triangular,' or 'mimetic' desire? In simplest terms, Girard argues that our desires are not innate or autonomous. Instead, we copy them from others. If I desire a particular object, I do not covet it on its own merits but because I 'mimic,' or imitate the desire of someone I have chosen as a model. That person—whether real or imaginary, legendary or

[75] As opposed to mimicry that is more pedestrian in nature, such as the pedagogic: we imitate our driving instructor because we wish to learn how to drive and not because we wish to 'resemble' him or her (Livingston 1992). This is one of the critical weaknesses of Girard' s entire project: desire is either under-theorized and/or utilized in an inconsistent, incoherent, or contradictory way, consistent with the underlying pre-representational nature of sacrificial reason; 'one of the central and most explicit thrusts of Girard's thought is his rejection of myths of individual autonomy, rational control, personal lucidity, and so on: far from being a "philosophy of consciousness," his theory insists on the role of desire, and moreover, a type of desire that is a source of blindness, conflict, and delusion. Girard's theme is conation, not cognition: he explicitly claims that he wants to break with a philosophical tradition that conceives of mimesis as representation, and not as desire and interaction. Such an ambition leads him to employ expressions in which "desire" is made the determining condition of a very wide range of behavior' (Livingston, 1992: 24). A classic example of this is the following: 'If desire is the same for all of us, and if it is the key of relationships, there is no reason not to make it the real "subject" of the structure—a subject that comes back to mimesis in the end. I avoid saying "desiring subject" so as not to give the impression of relapsing into a psychology of the subject' (Girard et al., 2003: 303). The fact that all desire (the category) may not exhibit the characteristics of *mimetic* desire (the sub-category) does not invalidate Girard's thesis but it does restrict its operation to a narrower, but extraordinarily important, range of social-psychological phenomena.

> historical—becomes the mediator of my desire, and the relationship in which I am involved is essentially 'triangular'. (Golsan, 2002: 1)[76]

The archetypal example of double mediation is the pupil-teacher/master relationship, the social underpinning of an existential double-bind; here, 'Teacher' means not the professional pedagogue but any person who performs as the-one-who-mediates-the- 'true'-object-of-desire-which-is-authentic-Being. 'Everybody believes that someone else possesses the self he wants to acquire. That is why everybody experiences desire ... Since every desire seeks self-sufficiency, no one really possesses it' (Rene Girard qtd. Livingston, 1992: 9), so that the pupil's attraction to the teacher (or the teacher's seduction of the pupil) culminates in the psychic-existential double-bind of the self's pursuit of the mediatory Other who, in the final instance is mediating nothing; 'In short, desire relieves its subject of an intolerable knowledge,' that he is a 'no-one' meaning that he is not the true source of his own desires that define his sense of self (Girard et al., 2003: 303): '*Desire is always a reflection on desire*' (Girard et al., 2003: 328).[77]

> Desire aims to achieve shattering triumphs and pleasures that cannot be described. That is why it cannot hope to find them in ordinary experiences and relationships that can be brought under control. Desire will increasingly interpret the humiliation that it is made to suffer and the disdain that it is made to undergo in terms of the absolute superiority of the model—the mark of a blessed self-sufficiency that must necessarily be impenetrable to its own inadequacy. (Girard et al., 2003: 327)

The teacher-master-model is the *skandalon* in fleshy form because she not only incites imitation but she also works to ultimately sabotage her student's efforts at mimicry: 'The model indicates to his disciple the object he should desire and, in the same gesture, forbids him to proceed towards it' (Dumouchel, 1988: 5) for the more successful the model is at being the model, the more she has an interest in preventing her imitator from being wholly successful in her imitation lest she seize the 'place' of the model and turning the master into a no-one.[78] Mimeticism, therefore, is without exception a source of 'continual conflict': 'By making one man's desire into a replica of another man's desire, it invariably leads to rivalry; and rivalry in turn transforms desire into violence' (Girard, 1977: 169), although this violence may not assume a physical form for more often than not symbolic violence will suffice.

---

[76] Desire is deemed to be 'triangular' because 'its most basic structure involves at least three terms: the agent who desires, the object of the agent's desire, and the agent who serves as the "model" or "mediator" of the desire' (Livingston 1992: 1).

[77] 'If we grant the primordial error of desire' is its own mis-recognition that it rests upon a prior mis-recognition that it is always based upon the desires of the Other, a form of double-bind, 'we can say that desire gains nothing by getting to know itself better and better. On the contrary, the more this knowledge is extended and deepened, the more capable the subject becomes of causing his own unhappiness, since he carries to a further stage the consequences of the founding contradiction—the more he tightens the *double bind*' (Girard, et al., 2003: 329).

[78] 'The circle that viciously joins the Other as model and the Other as obstacle exists only because the Subject, or rather his "desire," interprets in terms of intentions and values what is merely the operation of a [mimetic] mechanism'—which, of course, remains mis-recognized (Dupuy, 1988: 78).

Which raises the difficult problem of explaining why, in any given circumstance, the subject has chosen a particular 'other' as their model. 'The key assumption would seem to be that people believe there are different kinds of people[79]; moreover, people believe there are hierarchical differences among these kinds' (Livingston, 1992: 46). Operating through the medium of *meconnaissance*, this would appear to constitute the wholesale importation of the dynamics of mis-recognition from the macro-level of the community to the micro-level of the interpersonal. 'Mimetic desire would then seem to be this fixation on a model whose desires are thought to manifest a hierarchical difference between self and other' (Livingston, 1992: 46) making possible the imitator's possession of the sacred difference of distinction that establishes one as the authenticating Self (Livingston, 1988); 'In other words, in any episode of mimetic desire, the imitator has both a real and an ideal conception of self and perceives someone else as corresponding to the ideal in some significant way. In respect to that ideal, the other's desire is deemed worthy of imitation' (Livingston, 1992: 66) which must be linked to a difference of some kind because difference is the sign of authentic individuality, the authentic sovereignty of the Self. Ergo, the emulative pupil, governed by acquisitive mimesis, 'imitates the desires of the rival thought to enjoy a hierarchical superiority. It is this belief in the hierarchical difference that essentially sustains and promotes the self's desires for the object desired by the other' (Livingston, 1992: 89).

There is a latently Nietzschean dimension to mimetic desire (superiority = Being) yielding a phenomenology of desire-for-being that is little more than a purely psychologistic variation of the will-to-power[80] mediated by the *meconnaissance* of individualism[81]; 'In Girard's analyses, it is often the case that the mediator is followed in primarily one sphere, that of romantic desire, yet this one sphere is firmly linked in the imitator's mind to a global conception of the self' (Livingston, 1992: 67). Desire 'transfigures' its object in an act (singular or multiple) of mis-recognition, which is the cruelest paradox of all: the deluded belief in the surplus of Being emanating from a mere object; in other words, idolatry.

> [This] process of transfiguration does not correspond to anything real, and yet it transforms the object into something that appears superabundantly real. Thus it could be described as metaphysical in character. We might well decide to use the word 'desire' only in circumstances where the misunderstood mechanism of mimetic rivalry has imbued what was previously just an appetite or need with this metaphysical dimension. (Girard et al., 2003: 296)

The 'self-concept' is the translation of the metaphysical notion of essence into the phenomenology of authenticity, and the belief in the genuineness of the Self 'must involve the agent's attempt to arrive at a reflective unification, not of the sum total of

[79] In the non-trivial sense that 'people do not consider themselves to belong to the kind they "would like to" and that they find themselves taking a special interest in those who do' (Livingston, 1992: 46). To paraphrase Borges, snobbery is the purest of all instincts.

[80] Which was itself Nietzsche's psychologistic bastardization of Schopenhauer's ontological conception of the Will.

[81] See below.

his or her experience, but of some privileged sub-set of the agent's beliefs, actions, and preferences. The self-concept … is an agent's momentary and perhaps deluded answer to the question "Who am I?"' (Livingston, 1992: 68). It is possible that 'we can say that a self-concept is a response, not to any and every possible question of the form "Who am I?" but to questions of that form motivated by a certain type of projection in relation to the self' (Livingston, 1992: 69). Which, in theory, will culminate in either an act of suicide and/or homicide: 'The desire that constitutes the self is itself modelled on, copied from, inspired by, and communicated by the other. It is the other's desire that causes the desire to appear that will engender the self' (Oughourlian, 2010: 98) so that at the bitter end the pupil must somehow kill the teacher.

The theory of mimeticism 'is intimately connected to a conceptualization of the predominant cultural and social institutions of the modern world' (Livingston, 1992: 73).

within which the existential 'self-concept' doubles as the

> [World] of acquisitive individualism and 'upward mobility,' a world where equality is held forth as the yardstick of all justice and legitimacy, indeed as the vey regulative ideal and vanishing point of social life, while at the same time a perpetual quest for personal distinction is the predominant emblem and lifetime burden of the successful and 'well-adapted' individual. (Livingston, 1992: 72)

We seem to have encountered a loop a mimetic repetition. The entirety of human desire, the erotic dimension of Humankind's social existence, is subsumed under mimesis—'desire itself is essentially mimetic, directed toward an object desired by the model' (Girard, 1977: 146), from which comes rivalry, 'the mimetic nature of conflict, which is to say the ultimate absence of any object proper to it' (Girard et al., 2003: 31). Rivalry, therefore, is the flip side of the crisis of undifferentiation, that potentially boundless state of existential anguish in which no one is anything in particular because all inhabit the universal space of absent identity, a hellish crisis of the collective of the loss of personal differences that triggers an avalanche of reciprocal and escalating violence between model and emulator: 'Sameness is the terrible war in which twins [or monstrous doubles] are personally engaged, right up until the moment when one manages to kill the other…When it spreads it becomes the famous war of all against all of which Hobbes spoke' (Girard, 2014a, 2014b: 104–105). The undifferentiated are devoid of being and the sameness of this undifferentiation continuously threatens to reduce society to the zero condition of originary chaos—a 'virtual' apocalypse of a un-reality of *meconnaissance*.

When everyone, both as individuals and as members of the community, reach this level of mimetic pathology we can know with certainty that mere (or controllable) mimetic desire has transmuted into the utterly lethal form of metaphysical desire, a notion that Girard appears somewhat embarrassed of: 'Words like "being" and "ontological" seem pompously philosophical in the context of flighty adolescents, yet they cannot be avoided. *Being* is what mimetic desire is really after …' (Girard, 1991: 43). He hastens to explain himself.

> By invoking the notion of metaphysical desire, I am not in any way giving in to metaphysics. To understand this notion, we have only to look at the kinship between the mimetic structure … and the part played by notions such as honor or prestige in certain types of rivalry that are regulated by society: duels, sporting competitions, etc. These notions are in fact created by rivalry; they have no tangible reality whatsoever. Yet the very fact that there is a rivalry involving them makes them appear to be more real than any real object. (Girard et al., 2003: 296–297)

Metaphysical desire is a kind of a delirium of mimesis because it is the state of the most extreme mis-recognition in which the representational logic of civilization has been replaced by the pre-representational logic of the archaic, that all things are as one and Self = Other. A totalizing 'indifference to difference' (McKenna, 1992: 30), pre-representation returns from the pre-sacrificial past and enables otherwise prosaic desire to transmute into delusion, or un-reality, the apotheosis of *meconnaissance*.

> The metaphysical threshold or, if we put it a different way, the point at which we reach desire properly speaking, is the threshold of the unreal. It can also be seen as the threshold of psychopathology. Yet we should insist upon this continuity, even the identity, between such a level of desire and everything that passes as completely normal because it is defined in terms sanctioned by society, such as the love of risk, thirst for the infinite, stirrings of the poetic soul, *amour fou*, and so on. (Girard et al., 2003: 297)

Which partially resolves the problem with Girard's terminology: 'real' desire (or desire 'properly speaking') is that desire which intrudes upon the domain of metaphysics herein conceptualized in terms of social psychology: the desire that deflects the anxiety of being no-one to being some-one or some-thing. The problem with this, of course, is that it implicitly denies the autonomy of all non-mimetic forms of desire which is the very issue in question. Girard's radical monism of desire would be at risk of constituting a circular argument: desire that is not metaphysical is not a true desire because all true desire is metaphysical. This may be true but it needs to be demonstrated either logically and/or empirically; it cannot be merely affirmed.

However, Jean-Michel Oughourlian, a psychoanalyst and a self-proclaimed devotee of Girard has had considerable success in translating his 'teacher's' mimeticist theories into the terms of metapsychology; the result is *Interdividual Psychology,* a post-Freudian innovation that owes as much to Marcel Proust as it does Girard (Wilson, 2019). To summarize: mimetic rivalry 'is always rooted in one of the two following claims: the claim of the self for the ownership of its own desire; and the claim of desire for its anteriority, its seniority over the other's desire, the other desire that has generated it, on which it is modelled' (Oughourlian, 1996: 43).[82] The failure of either claim reduces the Self to No-One; in truth, we are all 'Legion'.[83] Crucial is the temporal dimension of mimesis: mimetic rivalry, in both its latent and manifest form, is embedded within the structural parameters of psychological time, which is incommensurable with linear (non-reversible) physical time. Conflict follows a strict pattern of migration from two nodal points, *N* and *N'*:

[82] 'The desire that constitutes the self is itself modelled on, copied from, inspired by, and communicated by the other. It is the other's desire that causes the desire to appear that will engender the self' (Oughourlian, 2010: 98).

[83] The Gospel According to Saint Mark 5: 1–13.

> The constitution of the self in physical time can be summed up by a linear vector going from the past toward the future. Desire *D* [the model] mimetically elicits the birth of desire *d* [the subject], which, in turn, brings self *s* [the 'habitual self'; *habitus*] into existence. Such is the real sequence of events that unfold in physical time going from the past to the future. But this sequence has no meaning on the psychological level, for it unfolds completely without the knowledge of all the protagonists. (Oughourlian, 2016: 39)

The signature feature of nodal point *N* is 'the self's claim to the ownership of its desires' (Oughourlian, 2016: 38). Which is, of course, an illusion: 'Consciousness, like the self, is a function of the relation to otherness. The self as such is a mythic notion' (Oughourlian, 1991: 198). 'We' 'ourselves' are viscerally embodied fragments of *meconnaissance*, which borders on a kind of Gnosticism.

> The self, at point *N*, in the most banal and normal case, cannot survive unless it is persuaded that it is the owner of its desire. The simplest solution for the self consists in forgetting the otherness of the desire that constituted it and in considering that this desire truly belongs to it. In reality, it is not a matter of mere forgetting because if one forgets something, this implies that one once knew it. It is in fact a matter of active mis-recognition, though at this stage remaining peaceful and non-adversarial. (Oughourlian, 2016: 39)

Amnesia is our truth, just as it is for the gnostic. 'Forgetting preserves harmony in the self and keeps it in existence (Oughourlian, 2016: 74) ... Forgetting presides over the constitution of the self at the moment of its creation' (Oughourlian, 2016: 76); the new self *s* is always 'built on the overlooking of the otherness of desire' (Oughourlian, 2016: 74). In a perfect inversion of Jean-Paul Sartre, it is not the case that Man is condemned to be free—it is ten times worse than that. Man is condemned to eternally 'forget' (mis-recognize) that he is a slave (unconditionally un-free) precisely because the phenomenological basis of his sense of Being, his phenomenological Self, is the by-product of a set of processes, psychical and social, which are intrinsically mimetic in nature.[84] 'This otherness with which we are saturated and that constitutes us is the human condition; but it is very difficult to accept. Its mis-recognition is initial and necessary to the maintenance of the self in its existence' (Oughourlian, 2016: 45). Paradoxically, to the extent that we are real we are false, not truly of ourselves—which takes us directly into the domain of Saint Augustine and the true meaning of 'Original Sin' which is that we are depraved not because we are positively evil but because we are unable to (self-) author the Good. And, just to turn the screw one more time, the logic of mimetic relationships must necessarily lead to mimetic conflict or violence, physical and/or symbolic, which is clearly suggestive of the pre-determination of human actions that are the central dramatic trope of Greek tragedy. 'What is the clinical expression of mimetic desire? *Rivalry*. What I see every day in my practice is not mimicking, nor copying, nor learning; it is rivalry' (Oughourlian, 1996: 43). Why? When viewed in metapsychological terms, the relationship between model and subject is fraught with peril. Firstly, just as with language, desire is never private

[84] For 'mimesis to function in the constitution of the self in desire, it is essential that the desire gradually forget its mimetic origin, forget even as it comes from the other [Desire *D*] that it belongs to the other, in order, precisely, to feel itself autonomous, to exist as such, to constitute a self. Desire, as Hegel said, *negates* the desire of the other' (Oughourlian 1991: 232–233).

or personal, it is always public and collective: both language and desire partake, in equal degree, in 'Other-ness' (Oughourlian, 2010: 14).[85] The mis-named 'Self' is, in truth, the 'Collective self of a collective desire, which is to say of a purely mimetic, contagious, irresistibly attractive, violent, labile desire; plural somnambulism ... [a] merging of desires, mimetic hypertrophying, dissolution of each person's self—such is the crowd' (Oughourlian, 2016: 75).[86] Secondly, the model actively 'wishes to be copied' for a model with no imitators fails to qualify as a 'model,' just as Hegel's master 'needs' slaves; for the hierarchically subordinate subject, 'identifying with a model is consolation for not possessing all his or her belongings, since one [thereby] *becomes* that model' (Oughourlian, 2016: 47). But then so does everyone else—'Imitative desire is always a desire to be Another' (Girard, 1965: 83)—which is both intolerable and unsustainable, rendering every social relation inherently unstable. Compounding that toxic brew which is the community of unbridled mimesis is our own private 'hermeneutic of suspicion': at all times we are dimly aware that the model, vampire-like, establishes her being through the semi-voluntary alienation of our own—'The imitator often ... envies the model because the model is ...seeing his [the model's] role as a possession to be jealously guarded' so that 'While the model becomes circumfused with divine light, his follower sees himself relegated to the shadows, a mediocrity, abandoned and non-existent'—that is, a Nobody (Fornari, 2013: 38, 39). In other words, the Girardian constant of inter-individual relations is an *a-symmetrical reciprocity* with the result that the subject 'is torn between two opposite feelings toward his model—the most submissive reverence and the most intense malice. This is the passion we call *hatred* ... Only someone who prevents us from satisfying a desire that he himself has inspired in us is truly an object of hatred' (Girard, 1965: 10–11).[87]

The raw core of interdividual psychology is phenomenology (Oughourlian, 1991)—'it is desire that gradually brings the self into existence by constituting it as a *self-of-desire*' (Oughourlian, 2010: 98)[88]—and the critical factor is the subject's varying experiences of the incompatible modalities of Time: the irreparable dis-junction between the private psychological time of forgetting and the public physical time of un-Being, for it is within psychological time that 'self *s* declares itself the bearer and owner of desire *d* at nodal point *N* and desire *d* is [only later] scandalized to discover a desire *D* identical to itself and bearing on the same object, whose belatedness it will assert at nodal point *N*'' (Oughourlian, 2016: 39). (Note how this temporal dis-junction replicates perfectly the quantum-like temporality of

[85] The other of this other-ness is nothing other than the archaic victim; 'Human consciousness takes shape as attention is fixed on the other and particularly that special Other who is the scape-goat victim, the fountainhead of all signifiers, the transcendental signifier' (Oughourlian, 1991: 39).

[86] Here we are not far from a wholly phenomenological rendition of Marx's fetish of the commodity.

[87] Naturally, this mimetic a-symmetry of being reflects an *ontological* a-symmetry: the model (desire *D*) is more 'real', more replete with Being, in a manner in which self *s* (desire *d*) *never* is.

[88] This might be re-phrased as: 'I desire; therefore, I AM [THAT AM]'. The vital nexus of mimesis with psychosis lies with metaphysical desire; see above, n. 13. 'The focus [of metaphysical rivalry] becomes the business itself of the rivalry and antagonism between individuals vying for the unlimited good of more-potent-being or identity' (Reeve 2015: 163).

the Internet which is global instantaneity.[89]) Conversely, nodal point *N*', 'representing the self's claim to anteriority over the other's desire, which was responsible for inspiring and generating it' (Oughourlian, 2016: 38) is the spawning ground of both neurosis and psychosis, which for Oughourlian are quintessentially mimetic in nature. 'At nodal point *N'* … desire *d* will assert its anteriority [coming earlier in time] with respect to desire *D*. Such that self *s*, which is in [physical] reality the self-of-desire *d*, will lay claim loud and clear to the possession of the object of the two desires *d* and *D*' (Oughourlian, 2016: 39–40).[90] In the final analysis our mimetic '*illness of desire*' (Oughourlian, 2010: 104) is not orientated toward 'power' (pace Nietzsche) but toward Being, or 'psychological subjectivity' (Oughourlian, 2010: 101) along with its necessary attribute, autonomy, or 'self-grounding'. The neurotic/psychotic root of mimetic crisis, the ultimate ground of mimetic rivalry and violence, is the subjective awareness of self *s* that it is phenomenologically 'un-real,' that it does not really exist[91]: clinically, this uncannily resembles the classic definition of (what used to be known as) *hysteria*[92] and which presents us with an unsolvable double-bind. Without exception self *s* is alienated within psychological time: 'The whole psychological sequence will constitute a new time—psychological time, the time of memory, the only time that has any meaning for the subjectivity of human beings, the only one that appears true and in accord with reality' (Oughourlian, 2016: 40). Psychological time, within the unstable dynamics of mimetic relationships, operates as a kind of mystification.

> The physical time has no psychological reality although it is accessible to intelligence and therefore cognitive reality, but only when the first step toward wisdom is taken, that first step being the questioning or the recognition or the beginning of the recognition of the precedence [in physical time] of the other's desire, its priority over my desire, and therefore the non-ownership of 'my' desire. (Oughourlian, 2016: 40)[93]

---

[89] Somewhat unhelpfully, Oughourlian writes, 'It seems to me that memory … obeys the laws of quantum physics…' (Oughourlian, 2016: 41). He would have been more convincing if he had said that memory obeys the laws of Proustian narrative.

[90] All 'normal, neurotic, and psychotic phenomena exist in a continuum due to the gradual exacerbation of the mimetic mechanism … neurotic phenomena are essentially due to a claim at nodal point *N* and psychotic phenomena at a claim at nodal point *N'*, the two claims always being present…' (Oughourlian, 2016: 107).

[91] 'If one accepts the hypothesis of mimetic desire, it becomes clear that we must abandon the idea that the self is the source of desire. Rather, it is the movement of desire that gradually engenders in a subject a dynamic structure that is both changing and persisting and that can be designated as the "self"' (Oughourlian 2010: 98). And, because of the intolerable nature of its phenomenological 'prison' self *s* will have to rebel in order to establish the truthfulness of its sense of 'being a being': 'Self-individuation is a process originating from the necessity of disentangling the Self from the [Otherness] dimension in which it is originally and constitutively embedded' (Gallese 2011: 102).

[92] 'When the classical [nineteenth century] studies of hysteria said that the hysteric "suffers from memories," it was only the plural that was incorrect: it is a single, unique memory, always the same one essentially—the memory that brings back to the subject an awareness of the otherness of "his own" desire'—or lack of being (Oughourlian 2010: 108).

[93] Again, note the family resemblance to hysteria: 'Hysteria is one particular mode of [the] misunderstanding of interdividual relation and of the mimetic nature of desire' (Oughourlian, 2010: 109). For Oughourlian, hysteria is not an illness: rather 'it is a particular form of misunderstanding of

But to attain this wisdom the first thing that self *s* must do is to admit her total and complete absence of Being, which is tantamount to committing phenomenological 'suicide'.[94] A no-thing cannot become a some-thing simply by renouncing its nothingness which is its being. Or, as the saying goes: Everybody wants to go to Heaven, but nobody wants to die.[95] Hence

> Rivalry is recurrent, it repeats itself. The repetition syndrome identified by psycho-analysis is mimetic for two reasons: (1) because it is always the clinical expression of a rivalry and that rivalry is always mimetic; (2) because it reproduces itself, duplicates itself, imitating the circumstances of the first rivalry and always looking for an impossible victory. That victory is impossible, since it stems from a situation which mimics the circumstances of defeat. But those circumstances are the only ones of interest, since the only battle worth winning is the one that has every chance to be lost. (Oughourlian, 1996: 43)

Sisyphus had it easy. We have it much worse, as there are no externally mediating gods to impose the limit of the absolute upon us and to maintain the 'natural' relationship between Self and model. The fatal logic of substitution condemns us to eternal frustration. But it was not always so.

Marx famously said 'All that is solid melts into thin air' and Girard agrees: 'In a world where individuals are no longer defined by the place they occupy by virtue of their birth or some stable and arbitrary factor, the spirit of competition can never be appeased once and for all'; rather, 'everything gets increasingly inflamed; everything rests upon comparisons that are necessarily unstable and insecure, since there are no longer any fixed points of reference' (Girard et al., 2003: 307). Yeats is just as relevant as Marx here: the center cannot hold.

> [Our] society can unleash mimetic desire in a number of different domains without having to dread an irreversible escalation in the system, the runaway defined by cybernetics. It is because of this unprecedented capacity to promote competition within limits that always remain socially, if not individually acceptable that we have all the amazing achievements of the modern world…The price for all of this is perhaps not invariably the aggravation beyond all bounds, but certainly the democratization and vulgarization, what we call the neuroses, of what are always linked, I my view, to the reinforcement of mimetic competition and the 'metaphysical' aspect of the related tensions. (Girard et al., 2003: 307)

The theory of the scapegoat mechanism is Girard's mimeticist explanation for the eternal failure of the community to restrain the paroxysms of mimetic crisis and the epistemological key to the scapegoat is the logic of substitution: a new victim can be sacrificed as one member of an un-broken series of replicants of the original. But this some process of substitution which—that which re-introduces the

---

the interdividual relation, a certain type of reaction to mimetic conflict. It is a phenomenologically varied manifestation of a certain dialectic of desire, a multiform expression of desire's pretension to its own priority and anteriority' (Oughourlian, 1991: 183).

[94] Self-awareness of our mimetic condition 'requires us to re-think in the most fundamental way the notions of the subject and of desire and, despite all our shared beliefs, to renounce the glorious but mythic autonomy with which we have adorned humanity—to renounce, too, the pleasure we experience through being the playthings of those hidden mechanisms' (Oughourlian, 1991: 20).

[95] 'The vanishing of self *s*, the "habitual self," is equivalent to a "ritual death"' (Oughourlian, 2016: 196).

circuit breaking effect of differences and distinctions into the community through the binary opposition between crowd and scapegoat—is the same mechanism of political economy that drives *ressentiment*, the onto-phenomenological foundation of bourgeois morality and, therefore, of the politics of modernity. The *meconnaissance* of consumerism is that we can all replace each other through the accumulation of the external accruements of the Other. Tragically for the fetishizing consumer, 'Ressentiment is a symptom of internal mediation. It arises from the illusion of infinite freedom within a mimetic context. It is an invasive emotion that does not just affect private life, but also dominates the public sphere' (Tomelleri, 2015: 94); and 'it is in internal mediation that the profoundest meaning of the *modern* is found' (Girard, 1965: 92).

Although he cannot really be classified as a materialist, Girard does expressly correlate social structures with differences in patterns of mimetic behavior. *External mediation* signifies the regulation of mimesis and mimetic desires within hierarchical orders for which the classic examples are feudal Europe and the ancient regime. *Internal mediation* denotes the regulation of mimesis and mimetic desires within egalitarian cultural orders, the bourgeois societies that were spawned in the early nineteenth century and 'democracy is one vast middle-class court where the courtiers are everywhere and the king is nowhere ... *Men will become gods for each other*' (Girard, 1965: 119). Which is a potentially fatal problem. Just as there is a dis-junction between physical (objective) and psychological (subjective) time, so there is an equally powerful and parallel dis-junction between private and public desires: 'Society seems increasingly individualistic, but an analysis of mimetic *ressentiment* shows that an individualist mentality also arises from the logic that leads to *ressentiment*' (Tomelleri, 2015: 93). It is a question of *meconnaissance* again.

> People [imagine] realizing an individualist and authentic desire when in reality everything needs a mediator in order to find a new desire, a need that is increasingly exaggerated by the paradoxical combination between growing competition among equals and an equally arising social inequality. All are thus condemned to a fundamental dissatisfaction that leads to a desire that finds no rest. (Tomelleri, 2015: 93)

Receiving its classic contemporary expression in the eponymous work published by Max Scheler in 1912, *ressentiment* is 'a self-poisoning of the mind', the result of the long-term repression of otherwise normal emotional faculties whose denial lead to the obsessive (mimetic?) indulgence of 'certain kinds of value delusions and corresponding value judgments' which, like the Tenth Commandment, include but are not limited to 'revenge, hatred, malice, envy, the impulse to detract, and spite' (Scheler, 2010: 25). Broadly following Nietzsche (and Moses), Scheler views *ressentiment* as seeking natural expression through the anti-thesis of public reason, the 'spirit of revenge', the thing 'most suitable source for the formation of *ressentiment*. The nuances of language are precise. There is a progression of feeling which starts with revenge and runs via rancor, envy, and impulse to detract all the way to spite, coming close to *ressentiment*' (Scheler, 2010: 25).[96] In our era of Post-Human Capitalism

[96] The Mosaic linking of envy with both resentment and violence runs like a vein through Girardian scholarship. Compare Gil Bailie on this point: 'when I speak of ... mimetic desire ... the

and the abolition of all traditional forms of relationships of external mediation the specific form that revenge is most likely to assume will be envy; 'While each has the "right" to compare himself with everyone else, he cannot do so in fact. Quite independently of the character and experiences of individuals, a potent charge of *ressentiment* is here accumulated by the very *structure of society*' (Scheler, 2010: 28)—the 'system of free competition' as Scheler calls it but, in fact, a phenomenological version of Marx's notion of Capitalism as the substitution of contractual relationships for natural ones.[97]

Important to note here is that Scheler does not restrict envy to the frustrated coveting of 'objects' alone but extends it equally to the unbridled competition for social capital ('values') now wholly unregulated by external mediation, yielding the ultra-toxin of *existential envy*. Paradoxically, envy, owing to its existential rather than materialistic nature, operates to reduce the acquisitive impulse rather than strengthen to it precisely because of the intensely personal nature of the possible failure. Envy 'leads to *ressentiment* when the coveted values are such as cannot be acquired and lie in the sphere in which we compare ourselves to others. The most powerless envy is also the most terrible' so that '*existential envy*, which is directed against the other person's very *nature*, is the strongest source of *ressentiment*. It is as if it whispers continually: "I can forgive everything, but not that you *are*—that you are *what* you are—that I am not what you are—indeed that I am not *you*' (Scheler, 2010: 29, 30). Even worse, existential envy operates in a wholly mimetic fashion, a near-exact parallel of Girard's concept of violence-as-plague.

> Through its very origin, *ressentiment* is therefore chiefly confined to those who serve and are dominated at the moment, who fruitlessly resent the sting of authority. When it occurs elsewhere, it is either due to psychological contagion—and the spiritual venom of *ressentiment* is extremely contagious—or to the violent suppression of an impulse which subsequently revolts by 'embittering' and 'poisoning' the personality. (Scheler, 2010: 27)

Girard's relationship with Scheler is complex; although he critiques the latter for his failure to situate the elements of *ressentiment* into a social dynamic, he concedes that 'everything becomes clear, everything fits into a coherent structure if, in order to explain envy, we abandon the object of rivalry as a starting point and choose instead the rival himself, i.e., the mediator, as both a point of departure for our analysis and its conclusion' (Girard, 1965: 13). Why, then, is the will-to-revenge so central to human affairs? The answer, according to Girard, is that the sheer ferocity of violence, both physical and symbolic, is structurally embedded within the form of its transmission, which is best understood as a form of contagion.

> Why does the spirit of revenge, wherever it breaks out, constitute such an intolerable menace? Perhaps because the only satisfactory revenge for spilt blood is spilling the blood of the killer; and in the blood feud there is no clear distinction between the act for which the killer is being punished and the punishment itself. Vengeance professes to be an act of reprisal, and every

word "desire" means *the influence of others.*" ... the mimetic passions include jealousy, envy, covetousness, resentment, rivalry, contempt, and hatred' (Bailie, 1995: 112).

[97] Which is why Girard insists, in a somewhat conservative manner that a 'functional society is one which is dominated by external mediation' (Golsan, 2002: 136).

> reprisal calls for another reprisal. The crime to which the act of vengeance addresses itself is almost never an unprecedented offense; in almost every case it has been committed in revenge for some prior crime. (Girard, 1977: 15)

But what, precisely, is this 'prior crime'? It is nothing other than mimesis itself; the very thing that creates us (or, through which we are created) is, in a cosmically paradoxical fashion, the very thing that prevents us from ever becoming real. The loss of amnesia, the recovery of the memory of insufficiency, calls forth the demand for vengeance against the reality that condemns us to no-thingness. 'The infinite or absolute outcome of desire is tragic: to recognize that one can never fill in the gap between oneself [the un-real] and the model-rival [the real] is to realize that the model can never be reached; thus does it become an obstacle' (Oughourlian, 2016: 84). Historically, however, there has been a catch: a mimetic-rival is not precisely the same as a mimetic-obstacle, for the latter is governed by external mediation whereas the former is an object of a mediation that is wholly internal.

> Faced with the obstacle which is to say the rival who is always already there, who is so to speak insurmountable, the 'normal' attitude consists in renouncing competition with the other and in re-directing one's desire in a more constructive [agonistic?] direction, in accepting one's own limits as well as those imposed by social structure (for example, by the law). Renunciation is at the foundation of all hierarchical societies. This is because renunciation shows desire its impossibility. The obstacle is there, absolute. The mediator [of desire] is always external, even if he is right in front of you. (Oughourlian, 2016: 84–85)

However, within the era of universal internal mediation, the model-rival is the *skandalon* of modern civilization and scandal 'gratifies our craving for a sense of our own worth ... a moral rectitude that is fashioned over against its transgressors rather than requiring any foundation of its own' (Andrew J. McKenna qtd. Cowdell, 2014: 44). The one who has been thoroughly scandalized, like Dostoevskii, is both masochistic and suicidal in the final instance, a being who pitifully and tragically crashes into every obstacle on his path—like a moth drawn to the flame that consumes it ... *because they are more focused on removing the obstacle than on reaching the object* (Jean-Pierre Dupuy qtd. Cowdell, 2014: 148). And the threat of the war of all against all, or the universal and undifferentiating reciprocity of revenge, not only continues to threaten us, it has actually increased to the level of pathological intensity. So that the scapegoat, in some form, no matter how mis-recognized, remains with us still as the only viable solution to mimetic conflict.

1.4 Mimesis, Ethics, and Deconstruction

And so now we finally come to the single most audacious hypothesis within the plethora of Girard's scandalous suggestions: that literature mimics the mimetic and sacrificial logic of cultural formation. Girard argues nothing less than literature and fundamental anthropology are 'structurally isomorpohic' (Livingston, 1992: 105) and that the interpretive key to the history of Humankind may be found within the literary artifact known as the novel, which, when we stop to consider everything discussed so far, is a completely logical conclusion: 'What Rene Girard has discovered through literature is the mimetic dimension of human behaviour, its capacity to generate cultural forms. That is: the ability of mimesis to shape not only actions but also our perception of our actions' (Dumouchel, 1988: 8). But in order to prove his hypothesis, Girard needs to make a move that has been discredited by literary scholarship for the past fifty years: he needs to reassert the aesthetic primacy of the canon of 'great novels'.

> The great works to be considered range from Greek theatre to Dostoevkii and Proust, passing through Cervantes and Shakespeare. I am convinced that it is possible to extract from these works a unified theory of desire, and therefore a systematization of delirium,[98] through an essentially logical process the reality of which is verified by the sequence of great works. (Girard, 1978: 89)

He is extremely direct in his assertion, relating it to his own personal experience as a researcher of mimeticism; 'I started to read anthropology from the viewpoint of its drama' (Girard, 2020: 47) which provided him with the link to literature, for 'I had no formal intention of providing a universal explanation of cultural development, and, if that's what it provided to be, then I only recognized it after the fact' (Girard, 2020: 34).

> What desires 'imitates,' what it borrows from a 'model,' is desire itself, prior to gestures, attitudes, manners, and everything to which mimesis is usually reduced when it is understood only as representation. This mode of imitation operates with a quasiosmotic immediacy necessarily betrayed and lost in all the dualities of the modern problematics of desire, including the conscious and unconscious. This desire for the other's desire has nothing to do with the Hegelian desire for 'recognition.' Its existence is confirmed by cultural evidence of extraordinary richness that becomes more rare, more fragmentary as we approach the present and as the dogma of originality triumphs simultaneously with the complete banishment of mimesis. (Girard, 1978: 90)

The symbolic order of writing and speech is anthropologically and historically derived from a sacrificial arche that enabled Girard to hypothesize that the representational order of the Self is the outcome of the suspension of the crisis of undifferentiation through the erection of a cultural order of distinctions upon a sacrificial system of both ritual and meaning.

> We must remember that only in later situations, after the emergence of culture, can a belief in the victim's guilt actually motivate a unanimous turning of violence against one party: no such beliefs are at work in an unanimity generated by a non-representational mimesis. Beliefs in the victim's responsibility come later as a representational effect of this more mechanical form of mimesis. (Livingston, 1992: 129)[99]

---

[98] Metaphysical desire. Which accounts, in part, why so many novels that treat the theme of mimetic desire tend to adopt an 'hallucinatory' tone when dealing with the substance of mimetic conflict. Dostoevskii is the classic example of this.

[99] This passage draws our attention once again to the ambiguous nature of the species' movement from pre-representation to representation, here encapsulated as 'the representational effect of this more mechanical form of mimesis,' meaning that pre-representation has never truly been surpassed.

The much later cultural artifact of the novel recapitulates in textual form the evolutionary but highly ambiguous and liminal transition from non-representational to representational mimesis: the literary character's elemental mimetic desire, invariably acquisitive, undergoes a process of symbolic representation and psychological sublimation accompanied by a painfully heightened self-reflexivity. In this schema the acquisitive and conflictual varieties of mimetic desire that 'must be responsible for the functioning of the generative mechanism' of the scapegoat must, therefore, be equally responsible for the emergence of the literature which is revealed as possessing a hitherto functionalist dimension.

> These same motivational systems may also be operative in the cultural varieties of the dynamic of crisis and resolution, but here they may be supplemented and guided by the products of the mechanism's own history. Once we are in the historical context, sacred beliefs, notions about the cosmic order, knowledge of kinship ties, and so on, will play an important role in orienting the agent's actions. Violence itself, which in the genetic mechanism is but the product of the most mechanical agency, becomes invested with a cultural signification that in turn shapes the individual's motivational states and understandings of the possible and desirable courses of action. (Livingston, 1992: 106–107)

Desire 'is attracted to violence triumphant and strives desperately to incarnate this "irresistible" force. Desire clings to violence and stalks it like a shadow because violence is the signifier of the cherished being, the signifier of divinity' (Girard, 1977: 151). So that mimetic rivalry assumes, or anticipates, the narrative content of the novel, the tale of a protagonist who is undertaking some sort of action against an adversarial force or situation of some kind normally mediated by interpersonal rivalry. The next obvious question that needs answering is: what is literature?

It is no fault of Girard that we still do not have in our possession a universally satisfying definition of formal literary writing, but a number of proffered definitions are compatible with Girard's conception: literature is 'Any text worthy to be taught to students by teachers of literature, when these texts are not being taught to students in other departments of a school or university' (Hirsch, 2004: 50), or it is any 'literary discourse,' that is 'discourse that is either an imitation illocutionary act or distinctly above the norm in its ratio of implicit to explicit meaning' (Beardsley, 2004: 57)—defensible but partial accounts that fit well Girard's propensity for canonical writing. But as Girard has been rightly described as 'a perceptive phenomenologist of the novel …' (Weisberg, 1984: 76), the definition of literature that may be best suited and most useful for his enterprise is any literary work in which the author intends to 'invoke the literary response' so that the 'literary stance is defined by the expectation of (and consequently the attempt to identify) a certain type of value, i.e. literary aesthetic value, in the text in question' (Lamarque & Olsen, 2004: 59). And the essence of literary aesthetic value is the 'creative-imaginative aspect of literature' which is a type of complexity, because a 'literary text of any real value has far too complex a structure, and offers far too rich an experience, to be restated once and for all in a single sentence or paraphrase or book' (White : 420), so that the text always points to further experiential events that, in turn, further contribute to the aesthetic value of the original writing.

> Using the distinction between form and subject, we can say that the aesthetic value defined by the creative-imaginative aspect of the concept of literature is constituted by the imposition of form on a subject. Imposing form on a subject is to impose coherence on a complexity of elements: a manifold of elements is a construal both identified and recognized as forming a unity. An *expectation* of a complex and coherent form is thus one central element in the literary stance; and appreciation, the mode of apprehension defined by the literary stance, aims at identifying the complex and coherent form of a literary art. Coherence and complexity are not, however, values *sui generis* but acquire value through contributing, with the subject, to the definition of a *humanly interesting content*. (Lamarque & Olsen, 2004: 63–64)

And, of course, for Girard, 'humanly interesting content' would necessarily have to mean, and very frequently does mean, mimesis; 'An *expectation* of a humanly interesting content is thus the other central element in the literary stance, and the other central aim of appreciation is to identify such a content in a literary work' so that 'with the creative-imaginative aspect, the mimetic aspect is both a central and ineliminable facet of the concept of literature' (Lamarque & Olsen, 2004: 64). Literature 'has always been recognized as having what, for the sake of tradition and convenience, may be called a *mimetic* aspect. The interest which literature has for human beings, it has because it possesses a humanly interesting content, because what literature presents or says concerns readers as human beings', and it is the mimetic element that meets the 'need' for a humanly interesting content is the 'quality which gives literature its cultural prominence' (Lamarque & Olsen, 2004: 64). And here is the next great surprise that Girard springs on his reader: although we may never have really noticed it through mis-recognition, the basis of all great literature, the canon, which is always concerned with mimetic desire, is the 'conversion experience,' or the *metanoia*, of the author him- or herself. And thus does Girard break the second great taboo of literary criticism: he unreservedly abjures the 'death of the author.'[100] 'Literature clearly has a revelatory function' he somewhat prophetically tells us (Girard, 2020: 96) for he has learned this through a revelatory experience of his own while composing his first monograph, appropriately titled *Deceit, Desire and the Novel* (1961). Girard has, quite literally, lived his own theory for 'when I first started working with mimetic theory I noticed some pretty amazing effects. Quite suddenly, all these novels by Dostoevsky, Zola, and Flaubert made sense' (Girard, 2020: 34). And this sense was made through his own intellectual shift toward anthropology through the relative intellectual back channel of human mimeticism: 'I started to read anthropology from the viewpoint of its drama' (Girard, 2020: 47) even though 'I had no formal intention of providing a universal explanation of cultural development, and, if that's what it provided to be, then I only recognized it after the fact' (Girard, 2020: 34). Which is not nearly as extreme as it seems at first reading, for if we accept the phenomenological account of literature, then it becomes 'something of a critical truism that the meaning of a literary work is not in its message but in the experience

[100] In any event, Girard would appear to have dodged a bullet here concerning the superstition of presence for, taken by itself, the 'introduction of intention within the characterization of a literary work should not be taken as begging any question about an "intentional fallacy" in literary criticism for this characterization has no implications for the author's privileged position with regard to specific meanings assignable to elements in the work' (Lamarque and Olsen 2004: 64 n 1).

it offers its reader' in that any literary work 'defines an ideal reader whom it asks its audience to become, for the moment at least and in some sense forever' (White 1981–1982: 420, 429–430); 'forever' in the sense that the readers of a canonical novel will become the members of a literary community mediated by their common readership which is also experiential for, they too, will replicate the conversion experience of the author after the scales of *meconnaissance* fall from their eyes and they receive the revelatory knowledge that 'the death and resurrection symbolism at the conclusion of certain novels reflects a personal experience of "conversion," one that retrospectively transfigures the past of the author, finally enabling him [sic] to write the work he had always wanted to but never managed to write until then' (Golsan, 2002: 129) and which the readers will themselves imitate in the future.[101] 'Literature itself is a form of knowledge' (Dumouchel, 1988: 2), although we will not recognize it until we undergo our own *metanoia*, so that it is 'not the discarnate thought that interests us but the thought embodied in the novels' (Girard, 1997: 20); this 'victory over a self-centeredness which is other-centered, this renunciation of fascination and hatred, is the crowning moment of novelistic creation' (Girard, 1965: 299) which doubles as a form of spiritual experience, if not a formally religious one.

> Great novels always spring from an obsession that has been transcended. The hero sees himself [sic] in the rival he loathes; he renounces the 'differences' suggested by hatred. He learns, at the expense of his pride, this existence of the psychological circle [of mimesis]. The novelist's self-examination merges with the morbid attention he pays to his mediator. All the powers of a mind freed from its contradictions unite in one creative impulse. Don Quixote and Emma Bovary ... would not be so great were they not the result of a synthesis of the two halves of existence which pride usually succeeds in keeping separate. (Girard, 1965: 300)

For Girard the fictional 'universe of the novel is a universe of people possessed' (Girard, 1965: 307) and his approach 'involves what might be called "textual effectivity," the possibility for a text to intervene in the world' by inducing *metanoia*, although Girard's own word for it is 'truth' (Feldman, 2015: 56). The problem, though, is that 'in order to assert the effectivity of texts like the Bible or the novel, Girard had to restrict the range of effects to one trajectory alone: the revelation of truth' (Antonello and Webb, 2015: xxiv), Girard ascribing 'to Judeo-Christian Scripture a textual effectivity that in fact has no guarantee; he elides, in other words, the ungovernability of effects, an ungovernability that would be the true hallmark of a literary approach' (Feldman, 2015: 56).[102] Which is that religion has historically encouraged scapegoating as much as it has repudiated it.

---

[101] I discuss the importance of the notion of a community of readers for law-and-literature below.

[102] In defense of Girard he has pointed out that there is nothing specifically Christian about his reading of canonical novels as disguised confessionals concerning the repenting of mimetic desire. 'These observations emerge not only from theology, but from the phenomenology of the novel. I am not making any superficial attempt to "Christianize" novelists' citing the neo-Marxist literary scholar Lucien Goldmann in his defense: 'The final conversion of Don Quixote or Julien Sorel is not ...the attainment of authenticity or transcendence to a higher plane, but simply the recognition of the vanity and the degraded character of not only the previous quest, but also of any hope, of any possible quest' (Girard, 1978: 5). Julien Sorel is the mimetically contaminated anti-hero of Stendahl's *The Red and the Black* (1830).

> Novelistic conclusions are bound to be banal since they all quite literally repeat the same thing. This banality of novelistic conclusions is not the local and relative banality of what used to be considered 'original' and could again be given oblivion followed by a 'rediscovery' and a 'rehabilitation.' It is the absolute banality of what is essential in human civilization. The novelistic denouement is a reconciliation between the individual and the world, between man and the sacred. The multiple universe of passion decomposes and returns to simplicity. Novelistic conversion calls to mind the *analusis* of the Greeks and the Christian rebirth. In this final moment the novelist reaches the heights of Western literature; he merges with the great religious ethics and the most elevated forms of humanism, those which have chosen the least accessible part of man. (Girard, 1965: 308)

Girard assumes that 'the least accessible part of man' is the complex of mimetic impulses that express themselves through the sacrificial murder of the scapegoat, now revealed as an innocent victim of a sacrificial mechanism based on lies, but which can be dismantled by an anti-sacrificial process of revelation, conversion, and repentance, and it is this unifying concern with recognition and *metanoia* as substitutes for misrecognition and *meconnaissance* that infuses all aspects of Girard's interpretation of literature.

Which has not remained unchallenged. His is own critical 'meta-language' of mimetic theory 'purports to speak the "truth of the text' instead of recognizing its own role in the constitution of meaning' (Golsan, 2002: 111), and critics have found equally unconvincing Girard's 'insistence that his interpretations reveal the author's own understanding of mimesis' being 'commonly is viewed as the most flagrant sign of theoretical naivete' (Golsan, 2002: 111). And, clearly, there is a wholly reductive element in Girard's critical evaluation of the 'literary text to its referential pole' which is the negativity of mimetic desire; he invariably takes 'as his primary topic the degree to which a work accurately depicts, represents, and analyses "extraliterary" phenomena, [that are] ultimately, for Girard, the fundamental patterns of mimesis' (Golsan, 2002: 111), the exposure of which will prove the key to the existential rehabilitation of the reader who has somehow learned to overcome *meconnaissance*. Girard, however, remained unfazed through the onslaught of the critics.

> The elaboration of models and of a conceptual system that will finally do justice to the rigorous perception of a Doestoevskii is no less necessary to psychiatry than to literary studies. In my view, it is the only direction that can revitalize both and turn these disciplines into the allies that they should be. Only a pseudo-science runs counter to the greatest works of our literary heritage. A real science will justify their vision and confirm their superiority. (Girard, 1978: 78)

Combing the role of the author with the prophetic call for *metanoia* does accomplish one significant task: it suggests a somewhat eccentric way of circumventing the lingering problem of the death of the author by equating authorial presence with an ethical imperative. In this manner, the conversionary *telos* of the novel fulfills Michel Foucault's criterion for the 'author function,' *metanoia* serving as 'an initial directional role for the author' (Ward, 1995: 31).

> The author's name serves to characterize a certain mode of being of discourse: the fact that the discourse has the author's name, that one can say 'this was written by so-and-so' or 'so-and-so is the author', shows that this discourse is not ordinary everyday speech that merely

> comes and goes, not something that is immediately consumable. On the contrary, it is speech that must be received in a certain mode[103] and that, in a given culture, must receive a certain status. (Michel Foucault qtd. Ward, 1995: 30)

The author's conversion experience validates the author as a 'true' author vis-à-vis the canon,[104] enabling Girard to maintain an essentially realist approach to literary interpretation through the author function which is

> [C]haracteristic of the mode of existence, circulation, and functioning of certain discourses within society ... The manner in which they [the modes of circulation] are articulated according to social relationships can be more readily understood ... in the activity of the author-function and in its modifications, than in the themes or concepts that discourses set in motion. (Michel Foucault qtd. Ward, 1995: 31)

But the threat to the 'author function' is a principled anti-functionalist approach to literary interpretation in its entirety, for Girard is basing his critical evaluation of the novel on its performative utility for the somewhat non-literary cause of demystification which clearly suggests a wider and somewhat occluded political and social agenda.

> In Girard's approach, literature is deemed valuable only insofar as it can be granted an explanatory role, that is, insofar as it indeed serves as an agent of 'demystification'. The charge here is that this emphasis on the cognitive value of literature amounts to a betrayal of the specificity of literature which, if it is defined quite variously by Girard's critics, is commonly held by them not to consist of a 'transparent' or faithful representation of non-literary truths. (Golsan, 2002: 111)[105]

And Girard's implicit politicization of the canon has not gone unremarked by his critics: 'This linkage, coupled with Girard's claim that the Bible provides a means to demystify the misconceptions of modernity,[106] has led some to dismiss him as a reactionary religious fanatic or, worse, a secret admirer of the most extreme right-wing ideologies' (Golsan, 2002: 112). Girard's only viable response here is to artificially move the issue from the domain of the political to the realm of morality, as though there is ever an unambiguous difference between the two, and to subjugate critical resistance to the overriding ethical imperative to eliminate the possibility of scapegoating, which is anathema: 'It is very important to observe ... that the demystification of the quasi-mythical text, the text of mystified persecution, is inseparable from a certain ethical attitude. The only scientific reading of the text certainly coincides

---

[103] Which hints at a phenomenology of the 'experience of reading'.

[104] Gustav Flaubert backs up Girard on this point: 'The secret of a masterpiece lies in *the conformity between the subject matter and the author's nature*' (Gustave Flaubert qtd. Weisberg 1984: 88). As the great nineteenth century French literary critic Charles Augustin Sainte-Beuve observed, 'Flaubert seems to have believed that "it is proof of strength" to "appear inhuman in one's books," while remaining quite respectable in one's life' (Weisberg 1984: 93).

[105] Livingston makes a similar point: 'Girard complains that critics often fail to demonstrate, when they do not flatly betray, the cognitive value of literature and of literary research' (Livingston 1992: 175).

[106] Primarily that, with the Enlightenment, civilization has somehow managed to liberate itself from undifferentiation and the scapegoating mechanism.

with the fulfillment of an ethical exigency' (Girard, 1978: 192).[107] And Girard has found at least one stalwart champion in literary scholar Andrew J. McKenna who has argued, in the most robust manner conceivable, that all literary writing is considered with violence and, therefore, demands a wholly ethical response from the reader to the 'purely' literary work of the author.

McKenna's indispensable work *Violence and Difference: Girard, Derrida, and Deconstruction* (1992) is of considerable importance to me because he articulates how and why Girard's victimary hypothesis and its concurrent moral demand to demystify the scapegoat forms a vital nexus with law-and-literature, investing what might be otherwise dismissed as a rather sterile academic abstraction with an unbearable moral gravitas. 'In the human sciences, a theory is worth only the historical or institutional understanding it offers or the ethical insights its guarantees' (McKenna, 1992: 13), which, by definition, includes legal scholarship. Girard's fundamental anthropology 'lays claim to being a scientific hypothesis while asserting its source in the scriptural rehabilitation of the victim in Judaeo-Christian tradition' (McKenna, 1992: 23) culminating in its central moral insight that to 'sacralise the victim is to sacralise violence' (McKenna, 1992: 203) an act that is both immoral and hallucinatory. And as before, *meconnaissance* is the ultimate negativity of History.

> From a structural point of view, which is that of the community, the community originates in a sacred both exterior and prior to it … the sacred is not the origin itself but the origin that the community postulates for itself. Indeed, it is an imposture, for the community postulates an origin it itself has produced in the sacralization of the victim. The community has produced itself not by parthenogenesis but by retro-genesis, by attributing an origin it has produced. (McKenna, 1992: 16)

What culture denotes as the sacred 'is just this quid pro quo, which takes the effect of violence for its cause; the sacred is this misconstruction of its origin by the community' (McKenna, 1992: 15) which is fatally exposed to both intellectual and political dismantling.

> According to this deconstruction [sic] of events the sacred is nothing but the illusion that the community sustains itself about its (own) origin and that in turn sustains the community in ritual sacrifice. As long as it sacrifices to its divinity, its own violence will remain a *mysterium tremendum* to it; as long as it repeats this scenario it will achieve the unity necessary to its conservation. It places the origin of vits violence before its existence in time and outside its existence in space, whence notions of time and space as before and after and inside and outside accrue to experience. Otherwise stated, the sacred is a deluded *ex post facto* construct that accounts for the *de facto* pace and/in unanimity. This view may in every sense be labelled post-structural. (McKenna, 1992: 16)

---

[107] 'Girard never encourages us, in the name of a positivist value-neutrality, to treat social facts as mere things. Girard never loses sight of the fact that the ultimate goal of a "truly human" science is a knowledge that gives the lie to the "reasons" with which we justify our violence. The demystification of this spurious reason is a crucial activity, and in exhorting us to choose to abandon the gods of violence Girard is surely addressing himself, at least implicitly, to our potential for a more perfect reason, a reason that has as its goal a genuine freedom from violence and servitude' (Livingston 1988: 133).

McKenna argues that there is an unrecognized similitude between Girard's theory of *metanoia* and Jacques Derrida's revolutionary concept of deconstruction; both theorists are demystifiers motivated by an over-arching moral imperative and it is at their points of intersection that we can locate an opportunity 'to relate what appears to many to be a formalist critique, concerned only with texts, to real institutional practices and, accordingly, to substantive issues' (McKenna, 1992: 12).[108]

> When Rene Girard interrogates mythological texts he uncovers a scapegoat mechanism that he argues lies at the foundation of human culture. When Jacques Derrida interrogates philosophical texts he uncovers a systematic exclusion of writing [by philosophy], and he argues that this exclusion is necessary to the generation and stabilization of concepts. Notwithstanding the substantial difference between a discourse concerned with signifiers and one concerned with victims, there is a *formal* or *structural* resemblance in the processes of expulsion and mystification analysed by these two writers. (McKenna, 1992: 27)

The 'rigorous homology between Derrida's reading of the philosophical text and Girard's reading of culture' (McKenna, 1992: 28) comes down to the question of the relation of Being to differentiation and the two demystifiers concern with their respective objects of sacrificial desire: the scapegoat for Girard and writing for Derrida. The crucial issue is their respective formulation of the onto-political nature of the victim. For Derrida the archaic scapegoat is *not* a 'transcendental *signified*' which is understood to constitute '"*a concept signified in and of itself*, a concept simply present for that, independent of its relationship to language, that is of a relationship to a system of signifiers,"' and, therefore, '"would refer to no signifier"' (Jacques Derrida qtd. McKenna, 1992: 74); an *idios* or a 'dumb-thing' that speaks only of itself, signifying absolutely nothing other than itself as merely itself. Contra Derrida, for Girard the scapegoat *is* a 'transcendental *signifier*' in that the unified crowd, through *mesconnaissance*, collectively projects onto the physical corpse of the victim 'all actual and potential meaning of the community' and, 'through its intermediacy, on to all things' (Girard, 1978: 103). It is as a transcendental signifier that the 'sacred victim, who is a sign of contradiction (good and bad, desirable and taboo, mana of the structure, etc.) generates the play of differences' by way of liminality and ambivalence (McKenna, 1992: 195). The cadaver pre-historically acts as the orginary of culture which is the beginning of History so that, at all times, History itself is a stooge of *meconnaissance*, for it is unknowingly controlled at all times by a decomposed scapegoat. 'Social relations precede object relations and determine them' says McKenna (McKenna, 1992: 80), and the sacrificial victim has for incalculable millennia acted as 'the source of ambivalence' that which is 'the source of a properly human community' (McKenna, 1992: 80) a predicament that 'has not changed even today. What we identify as social tensions reflect institutional needs' that operate 'to channel ambivalence, mediate hostile rivalries, and succor victims,' while at the same time these self-same 'institutional needs just as inevitably generate hostility, and, indeed, produce victims' (McKenna, 1992: 80). But, under the eternal sign of ambivalence

[108] 'There are possibilities for real knowledge in deconstruction, which has to be redeemed from some of its formalist or nihilist temptations' (McKenna 1992: 12).

the scapegoat, as the embodiment of a 'sacred,' neither exists nor functions anywhere outside of the mob enforced mis-recognition of the nature of emissary victimage.

> If the etymology of *re-ligare* is to be believed, the ties that bind the community are double, issuing from a double bind that secures its foundational role. The sacred is nothing and nowhere, it is only the force of attraction and repulsion attending the object of a desire sufficiently intense to inspire another desire sufficiently intense to inspire another desire that in turn is sufficiently intense to render appropriation dangerous or dreadful. The object, the victim, becomes only a signifier of desire. The sacred is nothing but this mortal opposition, this resemblance of desires, which is why anything, any object, can represent the sacred: the sacred does not exist except as the signifier of desire's ambivalence. Thus, anything can represent the sacred .... (McKenna, 1992: 83)

According to McKenna the 'presence or appearing present of the victim in Girard's text depends entirely on abstinence or deferral' (McKenna, 1992: 72) because the body of the scapegoat signifies a no-thing, nothing other than itself which is an object devoid of any truth other than the physical violence of the crowd worked upon it; 'It is not ontological presence that is posited here, still less ontotheological presence, but its antithesis: a hallowed illusion, a quid pro quo by which abstinence constitutes presence. The only presence is that of the community to itself as mediated by the victim' (McKenna, 1992: 72). So that for Girard absolutely everything pertaining to civilization depends upon lies (*mythos*); the relation of the victim to the community is ambivalently 'active and passive: the community comes out of the victim no less than the victim comes out of the community' (McKenna, 1992: 73) presenting us with the conundrum of two no-things mutually giving birth to their non-selves. The scapegoat is transcendent but only in the sense that 'it is the matrix of differences and values (life/death, good/evil, and true/false as they depend on being in- or outside the community), which are in no wise antecedent to the power of attraction and repulsion emanating from the victim' but that exists nowhere outside of the mutilated cadaver (McKenna, 1992: 73). And this cultural-metaphysical dilemma is even worse in the case of Derrida, for Girard, in the end, stipulates that we can know the 'truth,' really, and that it will set us free, sort of, but Derrida cannot, and will not (truthfully) offer us any such assurances no matter how thin, for his metaphysical conceit is the same as Girard's: '"The substitute does not substitute itself for anything which has somehow existed before it"' (Jacques Derrida qt McKenna, 1992: 73). The only 'difference' between them is the (non-) identity of the sacrificial thing: for Girard it is the scapegoat, for Derrida it is writing, meaning literature, itself: 'Deconstruction originates as a critique of the sign and of difference that extends to the difference between the sign and the so-called thing itself. It is regularly shown that the difference between the thing and its sign may in fact be ambiguous, problematic, even undecidable' (McKenna, 1992: 144–145). And for Derrida, writing is the equivalent to Girard's scapegoat because the former, just like the latter, never attains the status of transcendental signifier, all appearances to the contrary. Writing 'symbolizes the origin of language as lacking an origin in the sense of an original world that it represents' (McKenna, 1992: 121) and since anything 'can represent the sacred, even writing' it follows that it is 'especially writing' that serves as 'the mark of an absence, of an abstinence prior to any awareness of presence or absence' just as the scapegoat does (McKenna, 1992:

83). 'The victim has no value; all values derive from its expulsion in the same way that ... all linguistic value, all meaning as representation, derives from its entombment or what its entombment represents: ob-literation of originary violence'—here, meaning philosophy's violent expulsion of writing from meaning, or Being (McKenna, 1992: 95).[109] But why does philosophy, Western culture's official censor of the intelligibility of truth-claims, insist upon sacrificing writing and transforming it into the scapegoat of the rule of reason, also known as logocentrism?

'The origin of the principle of reason ... is not rational' claims Derrida (Jacques Derrida qtd. McKenna, 1992: 154) which is why writing is the *skandalon* of philosophy: the historical 'rejection by philosophic tradition of a radical ambiguity or originary bivalence' accounts for the sacrificial expulsion of writing from *logos*, the dogmatic refusal to recognize philosophy—and, by implication, law—as a form of literature. Beginning with Plato, writing is 'invented as a supplement to speech, to presence of mind, to the origin as logos and logos as origin, and it is expelled for threatening to supplant it altogether' (McKenna, 1992: 28),[110] *supplement* for Derrida being 'what writing represents in our culture: a signifier in excess of an original meaning that it travestises or perverts' (McKenna, 1992: 75).[111] Language, or speech, is the supplement (substitution) to writing in the same way that writing is the supplement (substitution) to philosophy. This meshes beautifully well with

[109] For both Girard and Oughourlian the peoples of pre-history did not fear death; rather, they feared *the dead* who early humans did not regard 'so much as living beings as beings who have transcended life and death and have, for better or worse, become all powerful ...' (Girard, 1978: 83). 'The idea that humans less intelligent and courageous than ourselves invented religion in order not to face death in the naturalistic sense, death as the end of everything, period, is nonsense. Death as a purely natural event is obviously a very recent invention; early humanity never had to elude that kind of death because it never learned about it. Death first appeared as sacred power through the misunderstood scapegoat mechanism, which is the universal mechanism of human culture. Far from being a mask of our naturalistic concept of death, the awareness of which would have come first and be falsified only later by ad hoc religious myth, religion comes first, and it turns early man into a builder of tombs because religion is the mythological face of the misunderstood scapegoat mechanism' (Girard, 2007: 40). What is truly essential 'is the cadaver as talisman, as the bearer of life and fertility; culture always develops as a *tomb*. The tomb is nothing but the first human monument to be raised over the surrogate victim, the first and most elemental and fundamental matrix of meaning. There is no culture without a tomb and no tomb without a culture; in the end the tomb is the first and only cultural symbol. The above-ground tomb does not have to be invented. It is the pile of stones in which the victim of unanimous stoning is buried. It is the first pyramid' (Girard, 1978: 83). This also explains both the cultural and the biological juxtaposition of fertility with decomposition, life (regeneration) flowing from death (violence).

[110] A form of *ressentiment* in fact, for the Socratic interrogation of reality can all too easily double as a mis-recognized bid for superiority: '"skepticism's 'doubt' is motivated not by (not even where it is expressed as) a (misguided) intellectual scrupulousness but by a (displaced) denial, by a self-consuming disappointment that seeks world-consuming revenge"'—like every creature of *ressentiment*, philosophy cannot tolerate a rival (Stanley Cavell qtd. McKenna, 1992: 43).

[111] Which is why, to simplify the issue tremendously, there can never be an end or finality to either writing or speech because neither are ever in direct, or un-mediated, contact with any supposed 'real' that exists outside of their respective selves, both eternally resisting the 'illusions of full presence, immediacy, parousia' (McKenna, 1992: 11). Whenever one writes one thing one has, by that act alone, excluded the writing of an unlimited set of alternative things. Writing signifies the eternal absence, or lack, of Being (the real) precisely through its endless proliferation, the sign not

Girard's notion of the power of the scapegoat to introduce difference: each movement from speech to writing to philosophy constitutes a transition from undifferentiation to differentiation, each phase in the sequence marked by the introduction of a 'supplement of origin' that is itself a type of representation, a 'sensible marking' of difference.

> At issue in Derrida's critique is the capacity of language to refer to anything outside itself, to represent a 'reality' that is not always already a representation, indeed, a *supplement*, to writing. For writing is conceived in our culture, the most writerly, bookish culture of all, as a mere technical supplement to language, an arbitrary representation of representation that veils or distorts our access to reality, the thing itself; whereas for Derrida writing represents a 'supplement of origin' that replaces an origin, a presence that never took place. (Mckenna, 1992: 66–67)

For there is no 'real' presence that can ever 'take place'. The paradox is that Plato, the first philosopher to have actually written his own texts, must denigrate the ontological and cultural value of the very medium that he has appropriated: 'The emergence of the logos as the condition of truth, of the presence of the idea to itself, is thus traced to the expulsion of an otherness in which it originates' (McKenna, 1992: 32), but that, in turn, all 'subsequent cultural differentiations[112] ... derive from this inaugural expulsion, whose mistake, whose misprision, is essential to their maintenance and credibility' (McKenna, 1992: 32). Which is structurally homologous to the *meconnaissance* of the scapegoat: no one truly knows what they are doing when they are invoking Being which accounts for the violence that invariably flows from every invocation of transcendental meaning.[113] 'Philosophy is an institution like many another; if the origin of culture and cultural institutions is sacrificial, philosophy will not be immune to sacrificial mechanisms' (McKenna, 1992: 37). Provided that Luke 20:17 is neither a 'facile paradox' nor a 'cryptogram in a merely hermetic sense,' then 'The stone which the builders have rejected has become the cornerstone' serves as the epigraph to all of Derrida's texts 'in which writing is revealed as a *skandalon* to *logos*, a stumbling block to philosophy' (McKenna, 1992: 39).[114] McKenna labors to show that Derrida proved before him that 'it is not simply

---

of an overflowing excess, an unbounded surplus of creative power, but a negative excess-by-default-of-the-absence-of-Being. Nothing causes 'the many' to happen; rather, nothing causes 'the many' from *not* happening.

[112] In Derridean terminology, these 'cultural differentiations' are denoted as 'seriality' or 'systematicity' (McKenna, 1992: 32).

[113] Which perfectly mirrors one of Girard's central points: 'Today, all efforts of modern criticism could be said to focus upon the notion of Logos, which signifies human culture itself insofar as it is one with language. Contemporary criticism effectively reveals that Logos as a whole is coming unstuck and falling apart. This criticism can show more and more how meaning has been assembled and put together, the logical and structural flaws in even the most beautiful constructions of human culture. I fully agree with this criticism. I simply believe that it can be carried much further and that it is going to be carried to its logical end as the role of human violence in all cultural creation becomes more and more obvious' (Girard 2007: 47–48). The terminus of deconstruction is the mutilated remains of the scapegoat.

[114] In the same way and for the same reasons that *rhetoric* is the *skandalon* or stumbling block to law, as the history of critical legal studies clearly shows. Both law and philosophy share a logocentric

as representation, as sensible marking, that writing poses a threat; what makes it noxious is not its difference from the origin, from the self-same presence of the idea, but its indifference to origins, whence its paradoxical likeness to the origin it supplants' (McKenna, 1992: 28–29), or its mis-recognized doubling as the scapegoat. 'If truth were not repeatable, it would not be true. Because it is repeatable, its relation to another, bad repetition—writing—is problematic; it is undecidable, for the formal difference between memory and recollection ... between presence of mind and representation, is "hardly perceptible"' (McKenna, 1992: 29). This is the heart of the matter: writing is the scapegoat of philosophy for it constitutes philosophy's version of the primordial crisis of undifferentiation from which all difference, meaning, rites, rituals, prohibitions, and laws originate, which means that the process of genesis is intrinsically one of supreme violence. As though they were doubles, philosophy, like religion, 'installs order by marking the difference between a good and bad repetition,' for philosophy the 'bad repetition being that of the mark itself, that of writing' (McKenna, 1992: 31) whereas for religion the bad repetition being that of the *affectus* of the eternally returning scapegoat. Once again, the absence-of-presence, or the un-logos-of-logos, returns to haunt us, or taunt us, and we can never get away from the no-thing because it is the source(s) of every-thing. 'Far from being dominated by any oppositions, writing is the condition of the very possibility of opposition; it cannot be contained by any oppositions, but remains ever in excess of them. Writing is insubordinate in principle and, more importantly, of principle as such' (McKenna, 1992: 32). In reality, writing is 'not itself a harmful substance; it is harmful because it is not a substance, because it is not itself. Existing only as repetition, its identity is its non-identity, its difference is its indifference to difference, on which depends any notion, any formal or institutional possibility, of meaning, order, and structure' (McKenna, 1992: 30) which makes it the Derridean equivalent of metaphysical desire. The epistemologically bleak conclusion is that 'What is wrong with writing is that there is nothing wrong with it,' meaning that it is wholly undifferentiated, virtually 'orgiastic' or 'Dionysian'[115]; it 'merely represents the formal possibilities of representation, or mimesis—and that is what is wrong with it: "that the supplement itself can be 'typed,' replaced by its double," means that there is no limit to the contagion of mimesis, to the proliferation of doubles' (McKenna, 1992: 30). Which is identical to the pathological apex of metaphysical desire, the time of the monstrous doubles which must be pre-empted at all costs. 'Writing's capacity to represent anything derives from the fact that it represents nothing in particular' (McKenna, 1992: 31) just like monstrously identical twins do, for they bespeak of

preoccupation, resulting from its own *skandalon*, with un-mediated 'truth' that can be both perfectly known (intelligibility) and perfectly mediated, or conveyed (transparency) through its respective discourses. See below.

[115] 'The "Dionysiac" state of mind can and ... often does erase all manner of differences: familial, cultural, biological, and natural. The entire everyday world is caught up in a whirl, producing a hallucinatory state that is not a synthesis of elements, but a formless and grotesque mixture of things that are normally separate' (Girard, 1977: 160). The Dionysiac is the plague, the sovereignty of contagion under the aegis of undifferentiation as Sophocles clandestinely revealed in *Oedipus the Tyrant*.

the absence of that Being that is desired by both; therefore, writing is expelled by philosophy 'as a supplanter of origins' in the same way and for the same reason that a scapegoat 'such as Oedipus is expelled from the city: he represents mimetic fury. He is the inside turned out' which is the opening for sons to kill their fathers and take their mothers as lovers (McKenna, 1992: 31). McKenna drives this home.

> The victim is the matrix of difference for Girard for the same reason that writing is the matrix of difference for Derrida: both succumb to a mystified expulsion to which order and difference owe their origin, their institution ... The homology here is not merely formal or thematic: it is functional, operational, and pragmatic. It works. It produces philosophy along with other cultural institutions whose survival and credibility depend on concealing their violent origins. (McKenna, 1992: 33)

Despite all of their other differences[116] Girard and Derrida are doubles insofar as they both realize that the entirety of the cultural order is derived from repetitive acts of exclusion and that to 'deconstruct the sacred is to show this reversal of cause and effect, this co-implication of inside and outside, to show the origin of the structure in the victimary supplement' (McKenna, 1992: 18), the thing that cannot be accepted but must be rejected and that creates all other things in the wake of its expulsion-by-violence. 'The sacred is not theological or ontological in any way; it is not an entity of any kind, except according to our misconstruction of it' (McKenna, 1992: 176) and when 'conceived anthropologically,' the 'sacrificial scenario' remains 'no longer unknowable when traced to its institutional origin; its very unknowability is knowable as the mystification informing sacrificial substitution' (McKenna, 1992: 176). And as doubles, both monstrous in their own way, they share a cataclysmic view of world history based upon an equally astounding conception of the universal origin of civilization: The 'victim does seem to constitute a universal signifier' (Girard, 1978: 102) and if the sacred 'is not the origin of the cultural order, except as a misconstruction of violent agency, then the sacred and the cultural order are knowable once their mystified complicity is deconstructed' (McKenna, 1992: 176). To express this in prosaic terms: both Derrida and Girard have been able to conclusively demonstrate that civilization is based on the mis-recognition of reality, which is the moment of the apocalypse, the final and fatal unveiling of Truth. 'It is here, at the structural level, that the victimary hypotheses intersects with the deconstruction of speech as original presence of mind, which for Derrida is an origin that never takes place prior ... to the violent and mystified exclusion of writing' (McKenna, 1992: 16); the essential principle of writing is 'There is nothing outside of the text' (*Il n'y a pas de hors texte*) which McKenna translates as "There is no outwork"[117] that

[116] The preeminent and ultimately irreconcilable one being that Girard believes in Being whereas Derrida does not, although, as is always in the case of deconstruction, it is not clear whether Derrida argues against the existence of the real or merely its final, and exhaustive intelligibility; his situation is not unlike that of Wittgenstein who proclaimed that we must (for some reason) remain silent about that which we cannot 'truly' speak. An admonition that means nothing to a poet, surrealist or otherwise, but it may be of some applicability to a novelist who deals with mere prose which is always in some sense realist.

[117] Alternatively translated as 'there is no outside text,' meaning that 'there is nothing outside the game, no stable center to the structure, no transcendental signified that can anchor or arrest the

announces the immanency of the sacrifice brilliantly (McKenna, 1992: 24). Contra logocentric philosophy, the only 'reality' is that which can be expressed by writing which is itself an 'erasure' of differences, rendering the founding act of the *logos*—philosophy's expulsion of literature—one of mystification, a false and persecutory accusation made against writing in order to remove it from the *polis* and the domain of public reason that incorporates both law and politics. And in a truly world-historical irony, this act of Oedipus-like exile is the very thing that transfigures writing and literature into the supplement, or 'substitution,' of philosophy itself, the originary accuser. 'The victim, like writing, is a supplement of a supplement (speech), a stand-in, an arbitrary substitute for any and all members of a community that does not exist prior to the victim's expulsion' (McKenna, 1992: 16) so that philosophy, as the institutionalized gate-keeper of truth, creates the enemy armies of now 'irrational' pre-representation eternally arraigned against it.

> The deconstructive critique of metaphysics, logocentrism, ontotheology, essentialism, and the like, corresponds in its structure and dynamics to Girard's critique of sacrificial practices. The occlusions and exclusions to which writing ... are subjected correspond to the destiny of the sacrificial victim. It as if Derrida describes as happening to the linguistic signifier something that Girard describes as happening at the foundation of cultural institutions. (McKenna, 1992: 12)

According to 'the mimetic hypothesis, real knowledge of human affairs is massively accessible once we understand the unreality of desire' (McKenna, 1992: 22), and McKenna holds that this same demystifying impulse is present within deconstruction to an equal degree, the only difference here being that while Girard 'advances a theory of violence, Derrida is concerned with the violence of theory' (McKenna, 1992: 24).

> [Deconstruction] offers an explanatory potential for human affairs once it is yoked to an anthropological hypothesis. The [archaic] labyrinth, let us recall, originally houses a corpse—or a god.[118] The victimary hypothesis, as it explains the generation of the sacred, helps show this to be the same thing, for the immortality of the sacred, its transcendental, generative agency, masks the structural illusion of its violent origin; the before-and afterlife of the sacred constitute an objective allusion, a misconstruction of the victim's foundational and enduring role. (McKenna, 1992: 18)

And so is it with the case of both writing and language-speech itself, which can only establish, or 'ground' their being-as-the-real (logocentrism) through the tactical and utterly non-innocent sacrificial exclusion of all of that unspeakable undifferentiated stuff that it cannot subdue and incorporate within itself; 'There is no common measure in the fate of signifiers and of victims, but there is a common structure, or rather post-structure' (McKenna, 1992: 18), an 'a-structural homology between the supplement and the surrogate victim' (McKenna, 1992: 23) which is empirically verified by philosophy's scandalized eternal sacrifice of its own supplement. Which is the point that McKenna wants to lead us to for this is the opening in which he

---

substitution and displacement of signifiers'—that is, the unspeakable 'body' of primevally shapeless undifferentiation (McKenna, 1992: 101).

118 Same difference.

can prove (conclusively, he hopes) that the twinned projects of deconstruction and fundamental anthropology are both supremely ethical.

If philosophy's 'dedication to truth[119] issues from the sacrificial expulsion of writing, then the victimary hypothesis merges as the destiny of philosophy' (McKenna, 1992: 133) and the combination of the two opposites, recognition and mis-recognition, creates the necessity that the former annihilate (or sacrifice) the latter, the persecution of the persecutors in the name (or presence) of 'real' truth finally arrived at for real. The project of the demystification of the scapegoat is little less than a categorical imperative of universal action for if it were anything less than a mandatory obligation we would all forever be at risk of re-entering the primeval hell-swamp of pre-representational undifferentiation. The sequence leading to the final and irreversible demystification/deconstruction of the scapegoat is a fairly straightforward one and both approaches can be used together, for Girard manages to evade the deadly rays emanating from Derrida's deconstructive un-Being; the origin of all 'is born of mimesis, literally of re-petition: of mimetic seeking. Girard's theory thus survives the deconstruction of origins for it does not postulate presence but rather a mimetic abstinence and deferral at the origin of the species' (McKenna, 1992: 132), for what is denoted as the 'sacred' is 'but the name for the way that humanity misrecognizes human desire' (McKenna, 1992: 160). After that treacherous river has been crossed, Girard's fundamental anthropology makes 'explicit what is often only implicit in Derrida's interpretative activity' which is something supremely bloody and hideous but which provides the vital element to winning the war of universal demystification. 'What Girard does is thematize the moral impulse of deconstruction in its ever more subtle detections of unconscious violence. This is an impulse all too often ignored by both advocates and adversaries of deconstruction, which uncovers violence in texts only to concern itself thereafter with textuality and not with violence' (McKenna, 1992: 34), which is anything but a bloodless undertaking of subverting 'symbolic repression' when one considers how frequently 'mere' texts have been used as instruments of the most physically violent persecutions conceivable. 'For Girard, the victim is an effect in which the notion of causality originates in the same way that for Derrida the exclusion of writing … an effect on which the very notion of origin depends' (McKenna, 1992: 63). If the mis-recognition of the origin of violence can be empirically established it logically compels our identification with rather than alienation from the would-be expelled victim, indifference toward the victim now a way of 'being complicitous with the victimizers' (McKenna, 1992: 64). And it is not merely an issue of concern for the other but an equally robust, and correctly expressed, concern for the self. Girard's notion of the scapegoat as the source of all culture, and cultural differences, is 'rooted in the irreducible difference between victim and persecutor,' and it is this difference that 'has an indelible moral claim on our consciousness that we must reconcile our cognitive impulses to form a unified theory of culture' (McKenna, 1992: 62) for there is, quite literally, no margin for error, or allowance for *meconnaissance*: our only choice as a civilization

[119] Which can also be construed as a sacralization of a particular form of writing that renders profane all other forms.

is 'between total destruction and the total renunciation of violence' (Girard, 1977: 240). McKenna suggests,[120] by implication, nothing less than the eternal return of Hobbes' war of all against all unless we have made done with sacrificial persecution once and for all.

> No other form or norm of truth appears to remain or be desirable, because, among other things, our desire for truth is explained by our desire to escape victimization.[121] It is around the victim that our cognitive and moral impulses conjoin, that concern for fact and value cease to oppose each other.[122] The victimary hypothesis is an antidote, a true remedy to the cognitive nihilism that has recently beguiled as many theologians and philosophers as literary critics. It confides in the irreducible dichotomy of victim and persecutor, and no critique of difference, however bent on 'undecidability,' is proof against it, for indifference to that difference sanctions the persecution of all and threatens the survival of all. (McKenna, 1992: 135)

If it is true that it is 'only through identification with the victim that sacrificial practices, all persecutions and exploitations, are definitely renounced' (McKenna, 1992: 137) then it is clear that, more than any other institution of difference, it is law that acts as the vital point of interface between deconstruction's textual violence/violence-of-texts and the real-world massacre of the scapegoat. Roberto Calosso has made this brilliantly clear.

> It is significant that we talk about law *and* order—it's not enough to say just 'law' or just 'order.' Indeed, order does not repeat, does not embody the sense of law. Order is what law cannot achieve alone. Order is law plus sacrifice, the perpetual supplement, the perpetual extra[123] that has to be destroyed for order to exist. (Calasso, 2018: 159–160)

The victimary hypothesis privileges jurisprudence and judicial culture to a truly remarkable degree.

> [The] difference between a sign and a corpse, which, however mute and inert, may (by its marking, for instance) be a sign of criminal violence.[124] Whenever there is any dispute about the difference between a corpse and a sign, or the meaning of the signs on the corpse—about

[120] As does Girard. See Chap. 12, below.

[121] It merits noting that McKenna wrote these words in 1992, some time before Facebook, a tool of *meconnaissance*, conquered the world. Today we exist in a state that is McKenna's categorical imperative stood on its head: we all positively seek, or *emulate*, the victim as model, or, at least, the victim of a certain kind. I discuss the implications of this reversed-persecution process in Chaps. 11 and 12.

[122] Presumably David Hume's nefarious Is/Ought dichotomy is overcome by pragmatic self-interest (McKenna, 1992: 64). Which, against McKenna, raises the question whether enlightened self-interest (or even the pre-conscious fight-or-flight instinct) rises to the level of morality in its proper sense.

[123] All of that which cannot be assimilated into coherent and stable meanings of 'law' and/or 'reason' the two equated as essentially identical within the common-sense of 'public reason' as enunciated by John Rawls. See Chap. 11, below.

[124] Which is technically incorrect insofar as it references the dismemberment of the living body of the victim by the mimetically unified crowd that constituted the beginning of everything, meaning the genesis of law itself. No violence that precedes the law can be criminal for there is no law (nor judge, nor jury, nor accuser) to condemn it. This will be a topic of discussion in every chapter of this book.

the meaning, that is, of the corpse as a sign—the law intervenes, and it intervenes decisively with its restraint or its retribution. It is for the law as the supreme, unique arbiter of violence to arbitrate such differences as between a thing and a sign. This is in part the implication of Derrida's remark [that] concerning any debate on the scene of representation, "the police are always in the wings"'. (McKenna, 1992: 145–146)

Law is vulnerable to a totalizing demystification/deconstruction by fundamental anthropology not merely because it can be an instrument of exploitation and repression (Marx) or because it is imbricated by violence (Weber); instead, the moral obscenity of the law resides in its eternally mis-recognized complicity with both the creation and subsequent sacrifice of the scapegoat, who is an innocent. And, of course, any argument concerning the actual criminal or civil wrong-doing of the accused/defendant does nothing to dilute this anti-scapegoating moral judgment of the law. Throughout history the one chosen as the scapegoat could be a criminal or someone morally or socially noxious in some way; the real lie, the universal truth of Girard's apocalyptic demystification, is that the entirety of the scapegoat mechanism is devoted to the killing of the accused performed as an act of *meconnaissance* operating through an objectively false notion of causality: the physical elimination of the 'bad' will bring about the reign of the 'good' which is nothing other than the population of those not accused and then selected for sacrificial murder. And, when we frame our understanding of law and its relationship to two of its supplements of literature and cinema, we realize that there is absolutely nothing abstract or reified about the victimary hypothesis; rather, it is the visceral raw stuff of the judicial and political every day.

It is the difference between victim and persecutor, in the name of which the quest for truth as opposed to sacred or sacralised authority is decided. These decisions are being made every day in our institutions; in our schools, our law courts, and our councils of power these decisions are increasingly being called into question as the difference between good and bad victims becomes increasingly problematic in the face of revealing traces of violence that all disown—disown, that is, as one's own violence, for we are always prepared to confront another's violence as violently as you please. (McKenna, 1992: 99)

So it turns out that Derrida's *logique du supplement* 'is quite a discovery, and it's really an analysis of the mythical-victimage dimension in philosophical texts' (Golsan, 2002: 132).

I call mythical every text imprisoned in a system of representation structured by a hidden scapegoat. The question arises then, what is the relationship between myth and philosophy? Whereas the mythology of primitive religions expels real victims, has real scapegoats, philosophy expels these. The author: the same victims through mediation of the expulsion of religion. It expels the expellers in order not to see the expulsion.[125] It is *mythology blanche* as Derrida would say, an expression marvelously translated by Andrew McKenna as 'bleached out mythology'. (Golsan, 2002: 132)

[125] Meaning that philosophy is unable to recognize its own violence, or *meconnaissance* all over again.

The *logique du supplement* in mythology is 'simply the presence of the scapegoat which rebels against the deep-seated complicity of the text. Scapegoat representation is subjacent to all texts' (Golsan, 2002: 132–133). Which means that every text has a scapegoat: all that we need to do is to find it and *metanoia* will follow, for then we will no longer not understand what we are doing.

1.5 Law-and-Literature-and-Film as the Demystification of the Scapegoat

A central component of Girard's project is a highly unorthodox form of legal anthropology, the hybridization of both Durkheim's functionalist sociology of religion and Freud's cultural criticism (primarily *Totem and Taboo*) wherein every ritual bears the traces of a double transference: the re-invocation of the past event and the projection of that earlier event's cathartic effect into future time. The prior event that all ritual killings represent through mimetic substitution is a collective murder, an act of mob violence. '"Sacrifice" then becomes a term that can be used to refer to the complex phenomenon of the collective killing of a human victim, its mythic rationalization, and its ritualization' (Mack, 1987: 8). Collective murder mediated by ritual is the true beginning of human culture and the scapegoat is the first cultural artifact of human history (Girard, 1977). The necessary pre-condition for the historical survival of the community is the successful exorcism of the unclean spirit of revenge. This is secured through the periodic enactment of the rituals of the machinery of sacrifice, which is itself the mimetic repetition of an earlier killing of a designated victim, the scapegoat, which successfully broke the cycle of retributive violence.

But why is the will-to-revenge so central to human affairs? The answer, according to Girard, is that the sheer ferocity of social violence is structurally embedded within the form of its transmission, which is best understood as a form of contagion metaphorically represented by Sophocles as a plague.

> Why does the spirit of revenge, wherever it breaks out, constitute such an intolerable menace? Perhaps because the only satisfactory revenge for spilt blood is spilling the blood of the killer; and in the blood feud there is no clear distinction between the act for which the killer is being punished and the punishment itself. Vengeance professes to be an act of reprisal, and every reprisal calls for another reprisal. The crime to which the act of vengeance addresses itself is almost never an unprecedented offense; in almost every case it has been committed in revenge for some prior crime. Vengeance, then, is an interminable, infinitely repetitive process. Every time it turns up in some part of the community, it threatens to involve the whole social body. There is the risk that the act of vengeance will initiate a chain reaction whose consequences will quickly prove fatal to any society of modest size. The multiplication of reprisals instantaneously puts the very existence of a society in jeopardy and that is why it is universally proscribed. (Girard, 1977: 14–15)

But for us anti-scapegoating moderns the scapegoat mechanism has been effectively sublimated into the professedly anti-sacrificial juridical institutions of the rule of law and due process, things which are wholly representational in nature.

> Vengeance is a vicious circle whose effect on primitive societies can only be surmised. For us the circle has been broken. We owe our good fortune to one of our social institutions above all: our judicial system, which serves to deflect the menace of vengeance. The system does not repress vengeance; rather, it effectively limits it to a single act of reprisal, enacted by a sovereign authority specializing in this particular function. The decisions of the judiciary are invariably presented as the final word on vengeance. (Girard, 1977: 15)

At the heart of Girard's fundamental anthropology lies what is in effect a 'typology of cultures' formulated on the basis of competing taxonomies of legal systems, the sacrificial and post-sacrificial, that equate with legal institutions and practices that consciously scapegoat although mis-recognized as such, and those that scapegoat 'unconsciously' a double mis-recognition. Pre-modern legal systems do not know what they are doing; modern legal systems do not know that they do not know what they are doing but think that they are doing something else that is entirely different. And the vital thing that unifies them is the shared presence of the sacred and the sacralization of representational symbols and signs of meaning that constitute the anthropological foundations of religion.

It would seem to be an issue of atavism, the recapitulation of regressive traits within the more evolved organism that work to subversively undermine the presumed distinction between the advanced and the primitive. But as Girard would have it, even the civilized society of a post-sacrificial judiciary remains governed by *meconnaissance* for it has lost all awareness (by accident or design) of both its origin within the sacrificial as well as the subterranean survival of those same sacrificial praxis that proves, in fact, indispensable to the perpetuation of what we call 'law and order'. And the key to all of this is language, the names that we give to the actions we perform—rites, rituals, and prohibitions. This is most apparent in modern law's apparent success in demarcating the non-vengeful public justice (positive law) from vengeful private justice (natural law), the first denoting the secular the second signifying some order of the transcendental.

> Vocabulary is perhaps more revealing here than judicial theories. Once the concept of interminable revenge has been formally rejected, it is referred to as *private* vengeance. The term implies the existence of a *public* vengeance, a counterpart never made explicit. By definition, primitive societies have only private vengeance. Thus, public vengeance is the exclusive property of well-policed societies, and our society calls it the judicial system. (Girard, 1977: 15)

Which, if true, would render a Girardian critique, or, in the alternative, a thoroughly Derridean deconstruction of judicial modernity and its supplement the scapegoat both an intellectual and a moral imperative.

In terms of legal as opposed to literary scholarship a primary point of interface between deconstruction and jurisprudence is the law-and-literature movement which originated in North American law schools in the early 1980s as a sub-branch of a wider enterprise in progressive critique known as critical legal studies (CLS). Consisting of a number of different movements—feminist, critical race theory, neo-Marxist, queer studies—the dominant, and unifying, element of CLS was its deconstructionist approach to legal language and the nature of legal interpretation as a form of textuality: the rules regulating the construction of legal meaning(s) are themselves constructed meanings (Gordon, 1984). Law ordinarily adopts a representational theory of language operating as a form of objectivity (or 'objectivism') that constitutes its own form of mystification: as 'the ordinary language of all developed legal systems includes constant recourse to texts that authorize specific conduct' (Levinson, 1982: 374), the social and political legitimacy of law is guaranteed through its compliance with the representational requirements of language (i.e., 'right reasoning'). CLS, in contrast, substitutes an anti-representational, or pre-representational, model of language ('subjectivism') for the objectivist one, culminating in its central premise that 'Law *really is* Interpretative' (White). CLS therefore takes as its unofficial starting point a principled opposition to the classic statement of legal textual realism proffered by Christopher Columbus Langdell in his *A Selection of Cases on the Law of Contracts* (second edition, 1879):

> Law, considered as a science, consists of certain principles or doctrines. To have such a mastery of these as to be able to apply them with constant facility and certainty to the ever-tangled skein of human affairs is what constitutes a true lawyer ... [for] all of the materials of that science are contained in printed books. (Christopher Columbus Langdell qtd. Levinson, 1982: 373–374)

And because legal language, and the specifically legal form of objective reasoning it gave rise to, was both hierarchical and 'authoritarian' (or deferential to authority—or 'authoritative authors'—as the controlling element within legal interpretation), then CLS was also able to affirm an explicit correlation between law (the objective) and politics (the subjective). For Langdell law was 'essentially a literary enterprise, a science of extracting meaning from words that would enable one to believe in law as a process of submission to the commands of authoritative texts (the rule of law) rather than the creation of willful interpreters with submission concomitantly producing the rule of men' (Levinson, 1982:374). Law is politics ('the rule of men') because the political contains within it the extra-judicial structures that govern the selection of the language and linguistically grounded form of reasoning to be utilized in judicial decision-making (Weisberg, 1984) which accounts for the insuppressible truth that, at any given moment, every judge has a number of different rules that may be followed and/or precedents to be applied. Legal reasoning, which is the reasoning of the judge, proceeds by analogy which means that law is both inherently indeterminate and lacking self-grounding, the true ability to auto-interpret. And, as with Derrida's deconstruction of writing, any legal text is a wholly arbitrary system of meaning that is dependent upon the exclusion, expulsion, or sacrifice of all possible rival expressions of meaning. Legal reasoning, like writing itself, is potentially unlimited in principle but is censorious in operation and conforms to a sacrificial logic making the application of the tenets of literary theory and criticism a highly subversive way to deconstruct the 'common-sense' tyranny of law and legal interpretation.

Law-and-literature consists of two major components that invariably interpenetrate in good deconstructionist fashion: law-*as*-literature and law-*in*-literature. The first 'seeks to apply the techniques of literary criticism to legal texts' (Ward, 1995: 3) operating on the premise that the 'essence of "Law *as* Literature" is the suggestion that the techniques and methods of literary theory and analysis are appropriate to legal scholarship' (Ward, 1995: 16). Therefore any 'true' understanding of law will have to invoke the principles and methodologies of literary criticism, because law is nothing more than a text. And because law-and-literature, along with CLS, evolved entirely within academia and not the institutions of formal legal praxis, law-as-literature understands the nature of its endeavor as pedagogical: '"Novels about law" and particularly "procedural novels"[126] are the path to human understanding' within both legal education and legal practice (Richard Weisberg qtd. Ward, 1995: 9).[127]

> The point, institutionally, is not to replace LL.B.'s with joint degrees in law and literature but to get from the world of literature what we can by way of help toward a legal education. The point, intellectually, is not to pursue literary studies as an end in itself but, still operating in the interests of a basically traditional professional training, to use literature and literary theory as tools for gaining access to otherwise invisible or recalcitrant aspects of law. (Black, 1999: 113)[128]

But because 'Reading is a communal enterprise' (Ward, 1995: 52) that is centered upon the construction of 'community' either of readers and/or legal-political agents, law-and-literature cannot remain within the domain of intellectualization but must migrate toward the ethical.

> At the same time, while it may wish to stress the "ordinariness" of language, law *as* literature also wants to intellectualise legal study. It wishes to both widen and deepen. In other words, law *as* literature suggests that both teachers and students must be made aware of all the various 'isms' of literary theory, structuralism, post-structuralism, deconstructionism, and so on, which can then be used so that as lawyers we can better understand what a text means, both functionally and interpretively. (Ward, 1995: 15)

Everything depends on the validity of the assumed analogous relationship between law and literature as being reduced to a pragmatic textualism, so that the issue of social agency becomes unavoidable, as repeatedly explicated by James Boyd White.

> What is distinctive about legal and literary texts is that they seek to speak to a range of readers, not just one, and to operate across a spectrum of contexts. They seek to establish the meaning of terms not merely for one conversation, for the present moment, but for a class of conversations across time. Every legal and literary text implies a reader who will use it in circumstances that cannot now be known. (White, 1981–1982: 426)

---

[126] See below.

[127] 'The issue for the law-and-literature movement is not whether or not to provide students with a legal education but how to do it. It is of the greatest importance, in this connection, that legal scholarship, even as it borrows from or turns to literature, has the very constant and identifiable goal of education toward, or commentary upon, an existing professional regime. In other words, the law-and-literature approach represents a modification, but not an overturning, of an established order within which legal education is directly related to legal professionalism' (Black, 1999: 133). The only thing that should be added is that as law-and-literature, a fellow-traveler with CLS, is a 'progressive' movement, it seeks to modify legal education in such a manner as to realize outcomes, even if only restricted to professional training, that are broadly of the left.

[128] In the more jargoned words of law-and-literature scholar Marijane Camilleri, '"The law and literature movement proposes that the science of textual interpretation has interdisciplinary utility and that it is worthwhile to explore the congruous elements of literary and legal hermeneutics because the former is likely to illuminate the latter"' (Marijane Camilleri qtd. Black, 1999: 114).

It is a perhaps salvific truth that 'Writers produce texts, readers produce meaning. Thus, as with literary texts, the real "meaning" of a legal text "is not in its message but in the experience it offers its readers"' (James Boyd White qtd. Ward, 1995: 19) so that 'writing is never a merely the transfer of information, whether factual or conceptual, from one mind to another, as much as our talk about it assumes, but it is always a way of acting both upon the language, which the writer perpetually reconstitutes in his use of it, and upon the reader himself [sic]' (White, : 420). And this is remarkably close not only to the phenomenological notion of literature as the experience of reading but even more so to Girard's notion of *metanoia* which he identifies as the heart of the moral project of the novel. 'Action of this kind can never be wholly explained, and our talk about reading should reflect these facts' (White, : 420) because in this 'shared process readers maintain what might be called a culture of reading, a set of understandings and conceptions by which the process can go on. This is an interpretative culture rather like the culture of argument established by lawyers' (White, 1981, 1982: 415). The lawyer's reading of a legal text 'is by nature a communal activity, and he must always be alert to the readings that may be proposed by others' (White, 1981, 1982: 415) so that the lawyer can never read in isolation but is at all times embedded within larger networks of other actors which entails some form of 'pluriverse' of interpretations and meanings.

> Reading a legal text is often not so much reading for a single meaning as reading for a range of possible meanings. Law is in a full sense a language, for it is a way of reading and writing and speaking and, in doing these things, it is a way of maintaining a culture, largely a culture of argument, which has a character of its own. (White, 1981–1982: 434–436)

'Cultures of argument' directly corresponds to the 'legal community' which relies upon the replicability and repetition of legal speech and actions that it gives rise to, not forgetting, of course, that replication and repetition are hall-marks of the sacrificial mechanism which is also the creator of communities.

> Whenever we speak or write we define ourselves and another and a relation between us, and we do so in words that are necessarily made by others and modified by our use of them … Unlike any other conversation, it has an unlimited number of anonymous but necessarily individual partners, located in an unlimited set of cultural contexts. It offers its reader an experience of cultural reconstitution that can be repeated in the imagination at any place or time. In this sense it is a part of culture that transcends its own immediate location in space, time and social context. (White, 1984: 276, 280)

Every interpretative community is a sacrificial one because the defining boundaries that give rise to its existence require the exclusion of excess or deviant meanings. For White, and as against Derrida, this communal process is itself what establishes objective limits to the possibilities, or parameters, of textual interpretation in the same way that for Girard and McKenna the body of the scapegoat imposes an objective limit to the otherwise unbounded, and crisis of undifferentiation inducing, deconstruction of Derrida.

> The view that the community of readers creates the text by determining its meaning stands things on their head: for me it is the text that creates the community, rather than the other way round. It is with the text that meaning reading starts, or should start; and the different

> texts can be shown to create markedly different communities, both immediately, with their individual readers, and, more extensively, among those readers. (White, 1981–1982: 417)

The 'text that creates the community' is structurally homologous with the scapegoat that creates the community, both text and scapegoat flowing from an antecedent act of sacrifice. What unifies both is their causal efficacy in proving and maintaining generative unanimity; 'Law *as* literature seeks to do two things which, at first glance, seem paradoxical. In one sense it wishes to impress the necessity of our existence in language as a living force' (Ward, 1995: 15).

> Language is something which we can all use, and as such it is language which we can all design. Language is the construction of the community, and not some sort of transcendental force. It is this which makes language the essential medium for social change, and … gives law-and-literature its political, as well as educative value. (Ward, 1995: 15)

And just as *Oedipus the Tyrant* was a tragic representation of the community's creation of a scapegoat through the oratorical means of argument (or dueling words), so does law-as-literature adopt as its own the surprisingly simple but subversive truth that 'Rhetoric is important in law because many legal questions cannot be resolved by logical or empirical demonstration' (Posner, 1986: 1383). Central here is CLS's central premise that since law is language then law must necessarily conform to the formal structures of rhetoric given the adversarial nature of the common law system, an observation that constitutes an implicit political critique of jurisprudence. Rather than actually trying to resolve the paradox implied by the reduction of law to rhetoric law-and-literature scholars 'have tended to concentrate instead on resurrecting the art of rhetoric' which is the second thing that law-as-literature tries to do, and it is 'Perhaps the accommodation of this essential paradox in law-and-literature lies in the resurrection of rhetoric as a primary concern in the teaching of law' (Ward, 1995: 15).

> We should abandon the traditional search for the basis of legal argument because no such basis can be found, and we should replace such a search with a focus on legal arguments, in particular on its attempt to persuade. I suggest, in other words, that we look at legal argument as an example of rhetoric. (Frug, 1988: 872)

But what, exactly, is 'paradoxical' about this, as opposed, perhaps, to nihilistic? White provides us with the answer, and it is a political one: while law is clearly 'a branch of rhetoric' it is equally clear that the 'kind of rhetoric of which law is a species is most usefully seen not, as rhetoric usually is, either as a failed science or as the ignoble art of persuasion, but as the central art by which community and culture are established, maintained, and transformed' (White, 1985: 684). Meaning that there is an eternal risk that if law is mere rhetoric (or 'ignoble' speech which is merely persuasive, or demagogic) then, in principle, any kind of interpretive community may be formed which could be both politically and morally disastrous, at least in the interpretive frameworks of CLS academics.

Of all of the law-and-literature scholars, James Boyd White was arguably the most transparent concerning what was politically at stake here with his highly influential notion of *constitutive rhetoric*; for White, the most important aspect of legal rhetoric is its 'ethical or communal character, or its socially constitutive nature' (White, 1985: 690).

> What would be the effects of thinking of law in this literary and rhetorical way? … It should in the first place lead to a richer and more accurate understanding of and control over what we do. The law is something that lawyers themselves make all the time, whenever they act as lawyers, not something that is made by a political sovereign. From this point of view, the law can be defined as the culture that we remake whenever we speak as lawyers. (White, 1985: 696)

But, always, of course, toward an emancipatory outcome. This is quite consistent with both Girard and Sophocles, for it is painfully clear that *Oedipus Tyrannus* is a forensic study of rhetoric's potential for political malfeasance: the mis-recognized scapegoat under the sign *meconnaissance* is shown to be the indispensable element for that generative unanimity that is the salvation of the community. For Girard, to understand the true process of community formation it is necessary to dispense with *meconnaissance* and to recognize the scapegoat as the demystified transcendental signifier of social being. Typically, Girard expresses this in Christian terms: 'Myth is "satanic" because it is based on Satan's power of *accusation.* "Satan," in the Bible, means first and foremost the accuser, whereas the word "Paraclete" means the lawyer for the defense, the defender of victims' (Girard, 2020: 71) so that to come to the defense of the accused is to be on the side of the angels. But it is also painfully clear that Girard's eccentric preoccupation with literature as knowledge fits remarkably well with the field's paradigm of law *as* rhetoric that effectively reduces legal speech to a kind of functionalism, law-and-literature's focus on the 'active nature of literature' being centered upon 'the role of literature in reconstituting the community'. As with CLS it 'first it seeks to educate, and secondly it seeks to present a socio-political agenda. It is this very pragmatic ambition which demands a functionalist approach to literature, and which in turn then requires a reassessment of the discourse-forming role of the author-function as a determining factor in this use of texts' (Ward, 1995: 38) and, I would argue, is wholly compatible with Girard's commitment to the author function principle as setting objective limits to the interpretation of the text with the all-important *metanoia* experience of the author operating as a mis-recognized form of external mediation. For the political activist lawyer, what this means that if all else fails anyone can still choose to speak and to write 'differently' but in terms of Girard's fundamental anthropology this would express itself as the moral obligation of the author to enable the scapegoat to 'speak,' for as White powerfully argues, 'Both law and literature have as their essential object then, in George Eliot's phrase, "the extension of [our] sympathies"' for '"attention to what is apart from [our]selves"' is what '"may be called the raw material of moral sentiment"' (White, 1981–1982: 444–445). If law is rhetoric then law is persuasion institutionalized which places upon it the encumbrance of the moral absolute which is the recognition and defense of the powerless and the stranger, both of whom have historically performed the role of the scapegoat.

> To conceive of the law as a rhetorical and social system, a way in which we use an inherited language to talk to each other and to maintain a community, suggests in a new way that the

> heart of law is what we always knew it was: the open hearing in which one point of view, one construction of language and reality, is tested against another. The multiplicity of readings that the law permits is not its weakness, but its strength, for it is this that makes room for different voices, and gives a purchase by which a culture may be modified in response to the demands of circumstance. It is a method at once for the recognition of others, for the acknowledgement of ignorance, and for cultural change. So it is that fiction that gives voice to the voiceless. (White, 1981–1982: 444)

Both the methodological and moral imperatives of law-and-literature conform remarkably well to Girard's fundamental project which is also intensely normative: (i) the unmasking of the mimetic nature of desire insofar as the community is haunted by both the reality or threat of violence; and (ii) the revelation of the innocence of the accused who is structurally homologous with the archaic scapegoat that is itself the primal source of the generative unanimity that is the foundation of the community and that of the cultural and legal order itself: the demystification of legal textuality is identical to the exposure and abolition of *meconnaissance.*

This connection between law and politics through the 'back channel' of law as rhetoric is even more clearly discernible in the second component of law-and-literature, law-*in*-literature, which formally 'examines the possible relevance of literary texts, particularly those which present themselves as telling a legal story, as texts appropriate for study by legal scholars' (Ward, 1995: 3). Here, the focus is more on the myriad ways that literary texts and fictional or dramatic representations of the law and legal procedures act in problematizing outstanding issues in legal theory, or academic jurisprudence. On one level, this is simply an issue of selecting certain literary works that are concerned with the artistic representation of legal procedure and then reading them closely for their heuristic content; 'What [Kafka's] *The Trial*[129] and Camus' novels [*The Stranger*; *The Fall*[130]] actually do is to use the legal situation, and its peculiarly intense concern with motivation of the individual, to describe the wider human condition' (Ward, 1993: 70). But building directly upon the pedagogical and activist concerns of law-as-literature, law-in-literature appropriates literary works as the foundational texts of possible anti-logocentric and anti-representational forms of jurisprudence based upon a Derridean self-awareness of textuality and interpretation. Potentially far more radical, and subversive, than law-as-literature, law-in-literature constitutes 'a form of jurisprudence in its own right'.

> The most common, and it is suggested, the strongest [defense of law-and-literature] remains the fact that law is a part of life, and plays an integral role in the determination of the human condition. This condition is not, however, a purely legal condition. Once this is understood, and political, social and philosophical texts are introduced into jurisprudential discourse, there is no rational reason that narrative texts[131] should not also be included in the discourse. Once a narrative text is understood to be a piece of fiction…then the narrative can be understood as contributing in some part to the general debate on the nature of the human condition. At the same time, by presenting itself as a fiction, and as subject to the

[129] See Chap. 8, below.

[130] See Chap. 9, below.

[131] Both novels and films; see below.

> vicissitudes of interpretation, there is no requirement that it should present a determination of any concept.[132] It is for us to 'create' our interpretation, and in doing so to enjoin *a participatory dialogue.* (Ward, 1993: 79)

Through 'participatory dialogue' the 'meanings of a text are the "production" or "creation" of the individual reader; hence that there is no one "correct" meaning for all readers either of the linguistic parts or of the artistic whole of a text'; all reading, or consumption of texts takes place within *interpretive communities*, 'each of which is composed of members who share a particular "reading strategy" or "set of community assumptions" (Abrams, 1999: 257, 259). And this concern with 'community assumptions' generated a powerful critique of the political biases of law-in-literature by Robert M. Cover who argued for a fuller, and more truthful, recognition of the latent violence and sacrificial impulses inherent within the notion of the interpretive communities of participatory dialogue. 'The current academic interest in interpretation, the attention to community of meaning and commitment, is apologetic neither in its intent or effect. The trend is, by and large, an attempt to hold a worthy ideal before what we all would agree is an unredeemed reality' writes Cover (Cover, 1986: 1628), and he is in full accordance with both the anti-textuality and constitutive rhetoric of law-and-literature as both a moral and an intellectual good: 'The creation of legal meaning cannot take place in silence. But neither can it take place without the committed action that distinguishes law from literature' (Cover, 1983: 49). The potentially fatal flaw of law-and-literature is that the 'emergence of interpretation as a central motif does not, by itself, reflect upon the way in which the interpretative acts of judges are simultaneously performative utterances in an institutional setting for violent behavior' (Cover, 1986: 1611 n 24) with the result that within the humanist enterprise of law-and-literature '"the violent side of law and its connection to interpretation and rhetoric is systematically ignored or underplayed"' (Robert M. Cover qtd. Sarat, 1992: 259). The physical violence of law is incommensurable with the symbolic violence of textual interpretation; 'Taken by itself, the word "interpretation" may be misleading. "Interpretation" suggests a social construction of an interpersonal reality through language. But pain and death have quite other implications' (Cover, 1986: 1602) which signify a substrate domain of sacrificial meaning that remains mis-recognized.

> When [legal] interpreters have finished their work, they frequently leave behind victims whose lives have been torn apart by these organized, social practices of violence. Neither legal interpretation nor the violence it occasions may be properly understood apart from one another. This much is obvious, though the growing literature that argues for the centrality of interpretative practices in law blithely ignores it. (Cover, 1986: 1601)

It is precisely 'this embedding of an understanding of political text in institutional modes of action that distinguishes *legal* interpretation from the interpretation of literature, from political philosophy, and from constitutional criticism' (Cover, 1986: 1606). In reality, legal interpretation 'is (1) a practical activity,[133] (2) designed to

---

[132] The preferred approach is what might be called 'constructive indeterminacy'.

[133] Alternatively, 'a form of practical wisdom' (Cover, 1986: 1610).

generate credible threats and actual deeds of violence, (3) in an effective way' (Cover, 1986: 1610). Legal action is always preceded by words which means that we should begin.

> Not with what the judges say, but with what they do. The judges deal pain and death. That is not all they do. Perhaps that is not what they usually do. But they *do* deal death, and pain ... In this sense they are different from poets, from critics, from artists. It will not do to insist on the violence of strong poetry, and strong poets. Even the violence of weak judges is utterly real—a naïve but immediate reality, in need of no interpretation, no critic to reveal it. (Cover, 1986: 1609)[134]

Cover takes most of his empirical examples from the fields of constitutional law and criminal law, particularly those cases that involve capital punishment, the outermost extreme of legally sanctioned violence that clearly bear the visage of scapegoating. For Cover, no less than Girard, the violence of law acts as a force for State imposed unanimity that is intended to be 'generative'; 'Legal interpretation is either played out on the field of pain and death or it is something less (or more) than law' (Cover, 1986: 1606–1607) because 'legal interpretative acts signal and occasion the imposition of violence upon others' (Cover, 1986: 1601), for

> If legal interpretation entails action in a field of pain and death, we must expect, therefore, to find in the act of interpretation attention to the *conditions of effective domination*.[135] To the extent that effective domination is not present, either our understanding of the law will be adjusted so that it will require only that which can be reasonably be expected from people in conditions of reprisal, resistance, and revenge, or there will be a crisis of credibility. (Cover, 1986: 1616–1617)

For Cover, at least, it is 'enough that it is the case that where people care passionately about outcomes and are prepared to act on their own concern, the law officials of the nation state are willing and able to use either criminal or violent sanctions to

---

[134] The crippling weakness of much of the law-and-literature approach to legal textualism is that it is too frequently oblivious to the inherent violence of the State. 'According to an old and well-known line of thought law and force are regarded as opposite things. Force as such is put in opposition to law. In view of the extensive use of force, under the name of law, in the state organization, the contrast is, however, obviously false. Law as applied in real life includes a certain kind of force. It is organized, regulated force used against criminals, debtors and others according to patterns laid down by law-givers ... The real situation is that law ... consists chiefly of rules about force, rules which contain patterns of conduct for the exercise of force' (Karl Olivecrona qtd. Sarat 1992: 256 n 6). As Cover expresses it, the State only becomes central to legal interpretation because 'an act of commitment,' or enforcement of some kind, 'is a central aspect of legal meaning. And violence is one extremely powerful measure and test of commitment' (Cover, 1983: 4). Violence, in fact, is the most intense form of authenticity possible as illustrated by the case of the suicide bomber.

[135] Cover deploys this in a simple but effective materialist manner: any act of legal interpretation by the judge is relayed through complex and extended networks of judicial agencies and actors whose consent to the juridical 'word' is indispensable to its physical implementation, which invariably involves force or the threat of force. 'The judge's interpretive authorization of the "proper" sentence can be carried out as deed only because a system of social cooperation exists. That system guarantees the judge massive amounts of force—the conditions of effective domination—if necessary. It guarantees—or is supposed to—a relatively faithful adherence to the word of the judge in the deeds carried out against the prisoner' (Cover, 1986: 1619).

control behavior' (Cover, 1986: 1607 n 16); therefore, legal interpretation 'must be capable of transforming itself into action; it must be capable of overcoming inhibitions against violence in order to generate its requisite deeds; it must be capable of massing a sufficient degree of violence to deter reprisal and revenge' (Cover, 1986: 1617) which are the prohibited acts of violent resistance to the conduct of the court system and the physical implementation of judicial decisions. While it is true that coherent 'legal meaning is an element in legal interpretation' it is nevertheless 'an element potentially in tension with the need to generate effective action in a violent context' (Cover, 1986: 1617). But more ominous by far is the ineradicable fact that the 'coercive dimension of law is itself destructive of the possibility of interpretation' (Cover, 1983: 48)[136]; again like Girard, Cover sees law's force of violence as the ultimate source of the creation of systems of legal meanings which he situates within the deep interpretive context of the *nomos*, the ancient Greek notion of a law, or ritual, governed cultural order: 'We inhabit a *nomos*—a normative universe' (Cover, 1983: 4) not merely of laws but also of mores. But as 'No set of legal institutions or prescriptions exists apart from the narratives that locate it and give it meaning' (Cover, 1983: 4), and narratives are multiple because voices are multiple so that interpretive communities are multiple, *nomos* is constantly being threatened by an eternally recurrent pluralism that must, in the bitter end, be resisted by legal violence.

> To live in a nomos we need to know how to live. We need guidance, education, and commitment. We need shared meaning-making practices and a corpus of inherited texts. Out of these materials and practices we build institutions, paradigms for behavior, and patterns of discourse. We agree upon a shared repertoire of moves, 'a lexicon of normative action,' that we combine anew to meet the needs of our time. (Sherwin, 2001: 1524)

Contra White, the interpretation of a legal text is identical to the violent act of imposing of unanimity among rival interpretive communities that are overtly antagonistic.

> There is a radical dichotomy between the social organization of law as power and the organization of law as meaning. This dichotomy, manifest in folk and underground cultures in even the most authoritarian societies, is particularly open to view in a liberal society that disclaims control over narrative. The uncontrolled character of meaning exercises a destabilizing influence upon power. (Cover, 1983: 18)[137]

The pessimistic and peril-fraught conclusion is that if 'law's violence had any constructive purpose or possibility, it was to make possible a community that was

---

[136] Expressed poetically this would read: 'Confronting the luxuriant growth of a hundred legal traditions [judges] assert that *this one* is law and destroy or try to destroy the rest' (Cover, 1983: 53) which is tantamount to the sacrifice of everything that is legally 'deviant'.

[137] Pluralism would seem to be ineradicable, intrinsic to the very nature of the constitutive rhetoric that is community forming: 'The normative universe is held together by the force of interpretive commitments—some small and private, others immense and public. These commitments—of officials and of others—do determine what law means and shall mean. If there existed two legal orders with identical legal precepts and identical, predicable patterns of public force, they would nonetheless differ essentially in meaning, if, in one of the orders, the precepts were universally venerated while in the other they were regarded by many as fundamentally unjust' (Cover 1983: 7).

plural, diverse, and contentious in its articulation of normative ideals without, at the same time, being self-destructive' (Sarat, 1992: 265) which is most apparent in the domain of constitutional law and interpretation. Cover approvingly cites literary critic Kenneth Burke's observation that "'Constitutions are agonistic instruments. They involve an enemy, implicitly or explicitly"' (Kenneth Burke qtd. Cover, 1986: 816)[138] for what is at stake in the determination of the true, and universally enforceable, interpretation of any constitution 'is a conception of the possibility of a shared moral life' (Levinson, 1982: 374). Burke 'posited that constitutions not only are agonistic but that they establish a normative world on the basis of their opposition to other worlds' (Cover, 1986: 816) the reason for this being primarily socio-linguistic, if nothing else: 'For what a Constitution would do primarily is to *substantiate an ought* (to base a statement as to *what should be* upon a statement as to *what is*). And in our "agonistic" world, such substantiation derives point and poignancy by contrast with notions as to what should not be' (Kenneth Burke qtd. Cover, 1986: 816). And since there is legitimate skepticism that we can ever truly draw an 'ought' from an 'is,' every act of constitutional interpretation functions as an externalized form of the mediation of social consciousness while remaining embedded within the pluralistic agonism of the eternally unstable *nomos*.

> Burke's point about the agonistic element in constitutions is entirely consistent with a view of constitutional law as a 'culture of argument' or as operating within a 'community of interpretation.' It I also consistent with an understanding of the constitutional law of judges, which is far less benign. For while one dimension of the agonistic element of law may be argument, another and more important dimension is violence. While argument may be said to take place within a community, violence frequently marks the failure of community and the metaphors that evoke it. (Cover, 1986: 816–817)

Societies are partially stable conglomerations of diverse, and divergent, sub-communities each constantly reconstituting themselves through interpretative actions that frequently threaten the State's formal monopoly of both truth and power.

> In law to be an interpreter is to be a force, an actor who creates effects even through or in the face of violence. To stop short of suffering or imposing violence is to give law up to those who are willing to act. The state is organized to overcome scruple and fear. Its officials *will* so act. All others are merely petitioners if they will not fight back. (Cover, 1985, 1986: 833)

The latent, and ineradicable violence of law in both a physical and symbolic, or 'purely' textual sense, is the simplest and most obvious empirical evidence concerning the sacrificial nature of modern jurisprudence which is nowhere near as far removed from its pre-modern ancestry as the discourse of the Enlightenment would have all of us believe.

> So let us be explicit. If it seems a nasty thought that death and pain are at the center of legal interpretation, so be it. It would not be better were there only a community of argument, of readers and writers of texts, of interpreters. As long as death and pain are part of our political world, it is essential that they be at the center of law. The alternative is truly unacceptable—that they be within our polity but outside the discipline of the *collective* decision rules and the individual efforts to achieve outcomes through these rules. The fact that we require many

[138] Carl Schmitt believed the same thing; see Chap. 4, below.

> voices is not, then, an accident or peculiarity of our jurisdictional rules. It is intrinsic to whatever achievement is possible in domesticating violence. (Cover, 1986: 1628)

Cover aims to draw a clear distinction between legal interpretation as 'true' or physical violence, such as the case of capital punishment, and the 'precious' symbolic violence of constitutive rhetoric and participatory dialogue. However, if the victim, or the one to whom violence is done by law-as-legal-interpretation is conceptualized as a scapegoat, the transcendental signifier of the community, then law's two forms of violence may be unified through the 'body' (physical and symbolic) of that self-same victim. Alternatively, in order to unify legal interpretation's two forms of violence it will be sufficient to re-name law's victim as a scapegoat, those convicted of capital crimes being the paradigmatic example.[139] And if this can be shown to be true, then the member of the 'despised' interpretative community who is prosecuted by the State in the name of the ordering *nomos* may not implausibly be interpreted as a sacrificial victim of the regenerating mechanisms of political unanimity.

One way of going about proving the scapegoating dimension of law's violence would be by utilizing White's famous argument concerning legal narrative as an exercise in storytelling: White follows both Paul Ricoeur and Richard Rorty in 'stressing the "storytelling" function of narrative, and giving it a central role in the creation of "community"' (Ward, 1995: 7).[140]

> As narrative fiction presents itself as rhetoric, it also impresses upon us its unavoidable contingency, because it builds upon various contexts: social, historical, political, ethical, and so on. In turn, narrative texts, much more obviously than legal or political texts, present to us a greater sense of community. It is the peculiar nature of language which defines our relationship with others—and indeed, our relationship with the text. (Ward, 1995: 6–7)

For Ricoeur any 'story' or 'fable' is the equivalent of *muthos* that is the lie of myth that is the narrative of the scapegoat: 'Aristotle designates this verbal composition [of narrative] by use of the term *muthos*, a term that has been translated by "fable" or by "plot"' (Ricoeur, 1983: 179).[141] Which readily equates with law-and-literature's interpretation of conventional legal interpretation as pure textualism.

> A legal tradition … is part and parcel of a complex normative world. The tradition includes not only a corpus juris [body of law], but also a language and a mythos—narratives in

139 The preeminent example of this being Gary Gilmore. See Chap. 11, below.

140 'The use of "storytelling" in a jurisprudential tradition is clearly more popular in cultures which remain strongly tied to a theological basis' such as the Jewish and Islamic legal traditions which are the fruits of a broader culture that had its roots in sacrificial practices (Ward, 1995: 35).

141 'The codes that relate our normative system [*nomos*] to our social constructions of reality and to our visions of what the world might be are narrative. They very imposition of a normative force upon a state of affairs, real or imagined, is the act of creating narratively. The various genres of narrative—history, fiction, tragedy, comedy—are alike in their being the account of states of affairs affected by a normative force field. To live in a legal world requires that one know not only the precepts, but also their connections to possible and plausible states of affairs. It requires that one integrate not only the "is" and the "ought," but the "is," the "ought," and the "what might be." Narrative so integrates these domains. Narratives are models through which we study and experience transformations that result when a given simplified state of affairs is made to pass through the force field of a similarly simplified set of norms' (Cover, 1983: 4).

> which the corpus juris but also a language and a mythos—narratives in which the corpus juris is located by those whose wills act upon it. These myths establish the paradigms for behavior. They build relations between the normative and the material universe, between the constraints of reality and the demands of an ethic. These myths establish a repertoire of moves—a lexicon of normative action—that may be combined into 'the meaningful patterns culled from the meaningful patterns of the past'. (Cover, 1983: 9)

So if we were to argue by analogy—not unwarranted in this instance, I believe—then law can be interpreted as continuing the scapegoating process through its imitating, or repeating, of the repetition of the sacrificial mechanism which rests upon the strict equivalence of surrogate victims throughout time, 'the meaningful patterns culled from the meaningful patterns of the past'. And then only a small step is required to arrive at the much greater, and far more deadly conclusion that law's victim as scapegoat-as-transcendental signifier (a corpse that is the generator of all systems of meaning but now in the form of the de-sacralized executed one of death row) provides the wholly symbolic form of violence that saturates law-and-literature with an irresistible power of subversion and demystification. As Drucilla Cornell expressed it, albeit without using the word scapegoat.

> The Law of Law [the ethical imperative that] calls us to interpretation through an appeal to justice, and this process of interpretation also projects the good of the community, which is itself only an interpretation and not the last word on what the good of the community should be …Interpretation is transformation. Thus, we need to remember that we are responsible, as we interpret, for the direction of that transformation. We cannot escape our responsibility implicit in every act of interpretation. (Drucilla Cornell qtd. Ward, 1995: 55)

It all depends upon the legal-literary narrative being a myth-lie, a story that involves a scapegoat, literal or figurative, who is the innocent victim of violence and who, morally, must be exposed as such.

1.6 The Scapegoat as the Secret of Law-and-Literature

When I taught my introductory course on Law, Literature, and Cinema, I offered my students the extra bonus of learning from me the secret(s) of literature.[142] Working on the defensible premise that literature is any written work that instills a specifically aesthetic, or literary, response within the reader,[143] I identified at least three of literature's secrets, although I am today quite certain that there is a fourth. Somewhat to my surprise, I came to understand that all of the three secrets were central to the literary scholarship of Girard. The first secret is that literature is subversive; to paraphrase pulp novelist Jim Thompson, the first rule of writing is that 'nothing is what it seems' so that the act of both writing and reading literature must partake in the act of demystification, the recognition and subsequent repudiation of *meconnaissance*,

[142] The most brilliant exposition of this that I know of is Thomas McCarthy's appropriately titled *Tintin and the Secret of Literature* (McCarthy, 2008).

[143] See above.

often by means that are traumatic but transformative and salvific. In Girardian terms, the subversiveness of literature means bringing into the reader's consciousness that common-sense reality is a myth which is a lie which causes to remain hidden a truth that is unspeakable but capable of explaining everything: literature-as-subversion as-revelation-of-the scapegoat. The second secret is that literature's subversive power lies with the centrality of doubles to the narrative drama. The double may signify either the external (exoteric) relationship between the protagonist ('The Self') and one or more of the other characters (e.g., Joseph Conrad, *Heart of Darkness*; *The Secret Sharer*) or the internal (esoteric) relationship among the contending parts of the sub-divided, or 'split' personality of the protagonist (e.g., Dostoevskii, *Notes from the Underground; The Brothers Karamazov*), the '*double* inside oneself' created 'through processes like reflection and consciousness' (Girard et al., 2003: 284, 285). Here, literature is reflecting the social consciousness of early Hominids. And the third subversive secret is that at the heart of any novel—or, according to Girard, every 'great' novel consistent with the principle of literature as knowledge—is the subterranean presence of a controlling mimetic desire that invariably gives rise to some kind of mimetic conflict either between or within one or more characters. The Self will model its relationship to the Other/Double on the basis of imitation (mimetic desire) that will narratively culminate in the Self attempting to either replace and/or destroy the Double (mimetic rivalry), which, in turn, will give rise to an overflowing of *ressentiment* that will seek expression through an act of scapegoating of some kind.

Of the various texts on law-and-literature, one that I found most compelling and instructive was Richard Weisberg's *The Failure of the Word: The Protagonist as Lawyer in Modern Fiction* (1984) whose general approach was very similar to my own—up to a point. Weisberg's neo-Nietzschean reading of a number of the seminal literary texts of law-and-literature[144] is strongly influenced by Girard's foundational *Deceit, Desire, and the Novel* (Weisberg, 1984: 187 n 3[145]) and draws from it the

[144] These are: Dostoevskii, *Notes From the Underground*; *Crime and Punishment; The Brothers Karamazov*; Flaubert, *Salammbo, Sentimental Education;* Camus, *The Stranger*, *The Fall*; Herman Melville, *Billy Budd* and they all detail the spiritual malaise of Nietzschean nihilism which is expressed on the interpersonal level as *ressentiment*: 'In each of these texts, a central figure—usually the protagonist—employs complex narrative structures to avoid relatively simple central realities. These protagonists prefer the safety of wordiness to the risks of spontaneous human interaction. Highly formalized language mediates between them and the exigencies of life, protecting but also gradually distancing them from the sources of positive and creative action. They cannot accept love, because of its unpredictability and its non-verbal essence; nor can they fulfil the expectations of social responsibility thrust upon them by internal or external factors' (Weisberg, 1984: xi).

[145] The connection with Girard is most apparent in Weisberg's reading of the canonical texts as critiques of the delusion of romantic individualism or egoism: 'the "philosophers" in these books elevate to the status of narrative formulation an ethic of theoretical freedom from all structures, in order to disguise their inability to act positively in communal situations'—the hegemony of internal mediation has made the rites, rituals, and prohibitions of external mediation intellectually unintelligible and psychologically intolerable (Weisberg, 1984: 5). Hence, Dostoevskii's Underground Man 'having failed because of his overly self-conscious stance in every personal relationship he has encountered, attacks, through the medium of words, the essentially non-verbal approach to reality which brings fulfillment to others' (Weisberg, 1984: 6).

general hypothesis that 'One of the oldest literary paradigms, that of insult and revenge structures all of these highly modern texts' (Weisberg, 1984: xi).[146] The seminal texts of law-and-literature all have something to do with the will-to-revenge, or *ressentiment*, that which is 'essentially a prolonged sense of injury based on real or imagined insult,' in Weisberg's words, a 'full-blown intellectual malaise. It was this *ressentiment,* for example, which 'coloured the writings of Camus, whose hero from *The Fall*, the lawyer Clamence, Weisberg suggests is a literary companion to the French lawyer' (Ward, 1995: 8). But in truth we can detect the correlation between law-and-literature and revenge at least as far back as Shakespeare. 'Since *Hamlet*, literature has perceived the risk that eloquent language would be employed as a substitute for the inner strength to face reality as it is. Words tend to deflect, rather than reflect, the trained intuition (if it exists at all) of the articulate being' (Weisberg, 1988: 229) and Weisberg makes the intriguing argument that all of 'Hamlet's procedures are those of a lawyer, not an aristocrat or hero' setting up the cultural archetype of 'the protagonist as lawyer' who, 'with or without his *juris doctor*, became threatening precisely through his inability to take more than a formalized vengeance upon his perceived enemies' (Weisberg, 1984: 8), or a symbolic violence as per Cover. Weisberg goes on to articulate a powerful and seductive theory about nineteenth century literary realism wherein the 'mimetic artist took a step back and began to perceive law and legalistic reasoning all around him' (Weisberg, 1984: 7). And the reason for the cultural hegemony of 'legalistic reasoning,' even within cultural spheres that had no demonstrable connection with law, was the emergence of a new type of bourgeois anti-hero: *the verbalizer*, whose literary appearance signifies the very beginning of the ascendency of internal mediation within European culture. A creature possessed by both *ressentiment* and *meconnaissance*, the verbalizer was the collective sign of the middle-class individual's growing proclivity to determine the nature of reality and self through internally mediatory auto-narrative techniques.

> As the modern novel developed … authors explicitly set the values of the verbalizer into the framework of courts and lawyers. Recognizing that heroism and religious faith were dying absolutes,[147] writers sensed that legality was emerging as the controlling principle in modern society. But law, being no more than a relativistic *method* of ordering reality through language, exhibited the same stance toward spontaneous life as had the philosophical or priestly forms of earlier texts. The protagonist as lawyer, talking, writing, and ultimately reorganizing realities which would otherwise be both fascinating and threatening. (Weisberg, 1984: xii)[148]

---

146 'It is of the utmost importance to recognize that a single unresolved incident, when perceived by a complex sensitivity as a reproach to its existence, may well lead to a generalized vindictiveness which sees everything and everyone as potential sources of insult' (Weisberg 1984: 39). This is essentially equivalent to the triangulation of mimetic desire and the dangerous hyper-sensitivity of the pupil-teacher relationship (Weisberg 1984: 187 n 3 referencing Girard).

147 As cultural forms of external mediation.

148 Although he does not use the word, Weisberg established an unmistakable connection between the lawyer-verbalizer and *skandalon*: 'Ressentiment, unlike hatred, which can be resolved in a single decision or gesture, is a full-blown intellectual malaise, inclined to take institutional and formal, rather than personal and spontaneous revenge. It emerges only subtly and gradually from an unresolved sense of insult. The "insult"—real, imagined, or provoked by the desire to possess

This passage is saturated with Girardian meaning. *Ressentiment* and *meconnaissance* are attributes of the scapegoater; language especially in its representational form is the linguistic substance of the symbolization of sacrifice; and the lawyer, the one who applies violence to the accused, really is, or is the surrogate of, the scapegoater. Although he discusses mimetic desire and rivalry in only a very limited manner, Weisberg is infallible in his political decoding of the verbalizer, in both his lawyer and non-lawyer form: 'The lawyers in Flaubert, Dostoevski, Melville, Kafka, Faulkner, and Camus ... influence us to be sceptical *of the word*, precisely of the word as most effectively employed by clever, articulate beings in positions of institutional and cultural power' (Weisberg, 1988: 22).[149] Which is Cover's position on law's violence but now in combination with the phenomenology of the will-to-revenge.

> The rational outer forms of the law are shown to mask professional ambition, envy of the criminal, r*essentiment*, or powerlessness. This comment, self-consciously made by literary artists, may be less about law than about narrative endeavors generally. Thus lawyer-figures are created late in the novelists' oeuvre and are derivative of earlier priestly, philosophical, and intellectual characters sharing, more privately, the same resentments and distorting narrative proclivities. Articulate misinterpretations of various sorts take on the aura, more glaring than that of the alleged criminal act itself, of transgression. (Weisberg, 1988: 229)[150]

---

an inaccessible object or trait—grates on the intellect as much as on the emotions. The wounded party may eventually find himself thinking of little else, even wallowing in an exaggerated sense of injury. Perversely, though, he [sic] elevates the perpetrator of the "insult," who dominates his thought, to the level of an idol [the model]. The rage which should theoretically be directed against this figure he venomously misapplies to innocent third parties. If unchecked by a major effort of will, this process continues to pollute the victim's relationships until his values are overturned utterly. Existential envy of the perpetrator, which renders his presence a continuing necessity to the victim, and organic falsehood [*meconnaissance*], which flows from the vicissitudes in his personal and intellectual perspective, culminate the insidious process'—which is the invention of the 'rule of lawyers' (Weisberg, 1984: 19–20).

[149] Leaving us in no doubt as to his purpose, Weisberg explains that his book 'situates the source of modern literature's holocaustic predictions and postmortems in the futile wordiness of legalistic protagonists. Lacking spiritual substance, these figures exhibit all the characteristics of modern Western culture's own deepest malaise: perpetual rancor, or *ressentiment*' (Weisberg, 1984: xiii). For 'lacking in spiritual substance' Girard would read' we would read 'possessed by metaphysical desire'.

[150] Weisberg continues in this Nietzschean vein: 'As a chronic condition of lingering, unwanted dependence upon a person or a situation somehow seen as insulting, ressentiment finds fertile ground among reactive types with no firm sense of personal values. Envious of the graceful and harmonious existence of just individuals around him, the man of ressentiment at his most creative uses his gifts of pervasive observation and complex intellect to insinuate himself into power' (Weisberg, 1984: 14). And, of course, these underground-man-lawyers possess 'no firm sense of personal values' precisely because they are the embodiment of the mimetically destabilizing form of internal mediation. Weisberg makes this clear in his account of Dostoevskii's Underground Man which he borrows directly from Girard: 'The Underground Man represents a culture whose lack of coherent values makes it necessary to compare ourselves to others, to adopt rather than to create a personal world view. The *imitation Christi*, in other words, has degenerated into a relativistic pattern of *imitation alterorum*'—the imitation of others (Weisberg, 1984: 36). He cites Girard in *Deceit, Desire, and the Novel* in support (Weisberg, 1984: 189 n 20).

I would suggest that Weisberg is formulating his own version of Girard's notion of *metanoia* as a necessary part of the author function. Could the canonical texts of law-and-literature, most of which, as Weisberg notes, were 'created late in the novelists' oeuvre,' be the textual fruits of the author's fairly late conversion experience that was founded upon her or his 'revelation' that the modern judicial process is structurally homologous with pre-modern scapegoating? Or that the author himself is identical to his scapegoating lawyer-protagonists?And, if so, that the accused is, by that fact alone, is the literary substitute of the now de-sacralized scapegoat?

> The entire thrust of the legal procedure, and the task for which 'artistic legality' is eminently suited, is to recreate verbally, and thus to devalue, the existence of the spontaneous, vital individual who stands accused. Like the modern novelist, the lawyer employs his verbal gift to produce ironic or negative portraits of positive heroes. The personal problems of the examining and prosecuting lawyers (which in many cases fall under the category of ressentiment) become institutionalized in the *seemingly* rational procedures of criminal law. (Weisberg, 1984: 59)[151]

---

[151] A suspicion which is fully consistent with the inquisitorial nature of Continental jurisprudence, in sharp contrast to the adversarial nature of common law procedures: 'Far more than in the American system, Continental pretrial procedures aim to elicit a confession; hence the inquisitor's curiosity legally extends to every aspect of a suspect's personal life. All secret findings become a part of his dossier, for even if the suspect does confess, a full trial must still ensue to decide the measure of culpability and extent of punishment' (Weisberg, 1984: 47). And the great latitude of the inquisitor's investigative scope enables the author to equate the legal investigation with the aesthetic formalism of writing: 'As depicted by European novelists, the inquisitor possesses a degree of insight into others shared only by the literary artist himself. Endowed with clearly superior powers of observation and articulateness ... the inquisitor duplicates the methods and the creative deeds of the novelist. His professional duties frequently require that he direct at the subjects of his investigation the faculty of perception which is the novelist's primary power. Ultimately, his observations become a part of a written dossier which forms the backbone of the procurator's presentation at the trial. Thus, in both the inquisitor and the novelist, acuity of perception serves to uncover and to record reality in its fullness. The inquisitor (like the narrative-prone intellectual) embodies the author's proclivity' (Weisberg, 1984: 47). As the inquisitor-examining magistrate Porifiry Petrovich articulates it in *Crime and Punishment*, '"An inquisitor's ... business is, so to speak, some form of art"' (Weisberg, 1984: 48) and Weisberg proves it to be so: 'Like the perceptive novelist, Porfiry ferrets out the individual subject's [Raskolnikov's] deepest meaning, then uses his verbal skills to formulate a portrait which will further his own subjective goals. If the end of justice is to apply codified legal wisdom fairly in each particular case, the inquisitor's aim is to make of every case a generalized portrait' (Weisberg, 1984: 52). And the drawing of a representational 'generalized portrait' is essential in the production of a scapegoat: different enough to be strange but not so strange as to be completely different. This is at the heart of the issue with the Mersault in Camus' *The Stranger*; see Chap. 9, below. In any event, Dostoevskii does appear to be a primary example of Weisberg's *ressentiment* theory concerning the lawyer-protagonist: 'The process of legal investigation, for Dostoevski, displays subtly but insistently its own narrative standards, and it will have its way even if it must create falsehood to fit the individual suspect into its required patterns of behaviour,' for the 'legal investigator, like the novelist himself, is motivated by an essentially personalized vision of reality' as dictated by internal mediation that ultimately ends in existential if not juridical failure; in *The Brothers Karamazov*, the doubles of the brother Ivan and the procurator Ippolit Kirillovich both 'consciously attempt to mold reality into a preconceived form. Both fail to arrive at an ultimate vision of truth because truth refuses to submit to that form' (Weisberg, 1984: 58, 79). Which means that internal mediation can, in theory, deliver one over to the most psychotic forms of solipsism conceivable.

Which is how Weisberg brings the issue of mimesis in through the back door. The key to the entire process is that the lawyer 'raises his own confused reaction' to the non-mimetically infected accused 'to a level of seeming objective legality' (Weisberg, 1984: 63) which is exposed by the novelist as a sublimation of the will-to-revenge, or scapegoating. And, 'like a jury, the reader may all too often fall prey to the verbalizer's grandiose performance' (Weisberg, 1984: 65) taking the suspect lawyer's words at face value and becoming the one mystified by, rather than the demystifier of, *meconnaissance*, a passive accomplice to the act of scapegoating.[152]

The culmination of this literary development is the *procedural law novel* which invariably details a 'full-scale legal investigation,' constituting a sub-category of literary texts denoted as 'procedural narratives' wherein 'a structure is created that endorses a verifiable comprehension of anterior events at the same time as it questions a merely subjective, highly articulate, interpretation of those events' (Weisberg, 1988: 226). It is within the anterior position that *meconnaissance* dwells: 'The first part of the account—the first part of the structure—I call the anterior position' (Weisberg, 1988: 228), and it sets into play a novel-length exercise in mis-recognition deliberately and willfully manufactured.

> The procedural narrative (unlike the theatrical trial scene[153]) is less interested in conflict resolution than in the production of successive narrative versions of verifiable anterior events. The structure is not that of a 'whodunit' but that of a 'who said what': the spotlight is on the interpreter—the lawyer and the lawyer's narrative techniques—as much as or more than it is on the parties to the litigation. Thus the lawyer stands ready to take the narration of the matter to any possible venue, from the traditional forum of a pretrial hearing room to the conventional domain of the salon, the tavern, the brickyard, or even the boudoir. (Weisberg, 1988: 228)

As a fictional work, the procedural law novel forms the interstice of two non-literary phenomena. The first is European trial procedure, which, 'as some commentators have inferred, is no more than a representation in dramatic and legal form of the defendant created by the inquisitor from the data of the preliminary inquiry' (Weisberg, 1984: 122).[154] It is integral to authorial intent that the 'reader inevitably notices that the lawyer or lawyer-figure conducting the investigation, despite or because of his verbal facility, loses almost all sight of the anterior position,' which is the truth itself; 'Distortions, first minor, then catastrophic, filter into the lawyer's analysis,

[152] And lest we forget, 'Many techniques of the effective advocate ... involve the undermining of rational argument rather than its promotion: they include techniques for keeping relevant information out, for trapping or confusing witnesses, for "laundering" the facts, for diverting attention or interrupting the flow of argument, and for exploiting means of non-rational persuasion,' the substitution of pre-representation for representation which would be tantamount to the incitement of the lynch-mob (William Twinning qtd. Sherwin, 2000: 111).

[153] Literally indispensable to the cinematic sub-genre of the Law Film or the 'courtroom drama'. See Chaps. 6 and 7, below.

[154] It is also very morally satisfying in that the inquisitor-prosecutor-examining magistrate is able to assume of the characteristic of a theater director: '"the best courtroom stories, and therefore performances, are almost mythic in structure: good vs. evil, man vs. nature, big vs. small, innocence vs. deceit, etc."' (Avi J. Stachenfeld and Christopher M. Nicholson qtd. Sherwin, 2010: 255 n 65). And because mythic it is all a lie.

always artfully conveyed, usually in the form of prolix narrative statements that become metaphors for the writer's own enterprise. Error is not inevitable. But in modern fiction, the cleverer and more articulate the interpretation, the more likely the error' (Weisberg, 1988: 229). The procedural law novelist invariably sounds the clarion call concerning the political and the epistemological risks of subordinating culture to legalism.

> The structure of the procedural novel thus covertly reverses its overt admiration of the verbal mode. The text as a whole counsels us to avoid a self-gratifying dependence on language for its own sake, particularly in ourselves. We can avoid figurative transgression only through the most caring and careful attention to persons, texts, and events, which have a right to be indifferent to our idiosyncrasies. (Weisberg, 1988: 231)

The second is the ethics of the procedural narrative that is consistent with the Enlightenment's repudiation of religion and the de-sacralization of all that was once holy, including the scapegoat. The repudiation of *meconnaissance* is formative of, or even identical to, the moral repudiation of the scapegoating process, which is the occluded truth of the modern legal system suffering from the cultural pretension of secularization. But even more imperative is it to ensure the provision of 'the most caring and careful attention' to that which has 'a right to be indifferent to our idiosyncrasies', meaning the re-introduction of difference into the realm of the undifferentiated and rendering the unmediated lynch-mob impossible thereby. Another fascinating observation that Weisberg makes is that the (falsely) accused is almost always depicted as being animal-like and, therefore, symbolically akin to the scapegoat, an animal sacrifice, and the primary sign of his animality is an inability, or a resolute unwillingness, to speak, signifying the victim's sub-human existence within the realm of the undifferentiated. The archetypal plot of the procedural novel, therefore, is that 'a series of creative verbalizers organize criminal proceedings against a non-verbal defendant whose moral system differs from their own' (Weisberg, 1984: 133–134), meaning, by implication, the *nomos*. An outstanding example of this is the anti-hero Mersault from Camus' *The Stranger* (1942): 'Camus creates a protagonist whose basically nonverbal (*renferme*), sensual nature ... estranges him from the universe of legal reasoning' (Weisberg, 1984: 115–116) signifying that he is unable to represent and differentiate; Mersault is 'a working man, straightforward and mildly intelligent. His main defects are an inability to use words in a socially acceptable way and a concomitant susceptibility to purely naturalistic influences,' these being the sun, the sea, and women (Weisberg, 1984: 116). And so when Mersault is 'narratively' interrogated by the inquisitor[155] Camus the novelist working through the prosecutor 'exchanges his fluid and indefinable essence for a static portrayal as a hardened criminal' (Weisberg, 1984: 122).[156] The deconstructive hidden equation at work here is the verbalizer = speech = writing (the procedural novelist) = attempt

[155] I discuss Mersault as a scapegoat at much greater length in Chap. 9, but suffice it for now to note that his arrest and interrogation—that is, the State placing its 'hands' on him—allegorically suggests the Hebrew and Hittite rituals governing the seizing and presentation of the sacrificial victim (Wright, 1986).

[156] See Chap. 9, below.

to control undifferentiation through the introduction of difference, or 'the word,' into the primordial existential sea of undifferentiation. 'Clearly, the legal procedure's conclusion that the protagonist is a "moral monster"[157] derives from the deliberate exaggeration of incidents which were wholly unrelated to the actual crime and more or less innocuous in their original form'—which is delivered by the lawyer's speech and the novelist's writing (Weisberg, 1984: 122).

But Weisberg is far more existential than Cover (or White). His neo-Nietzschean bias leads him toward viewing the lawyer-protagonist's *ressentiment* as an amorphous phenomenological will-to-revenge toward the extremely undefined openness of 'life': 'the legalistic mode is revealed to be passionately self-interested and value-attuned, predicated on a combination of pseudo-moralism and imposed behaviourism, rejecting spontaneity and all that resists intellectualized formulation' (Weisberg, 1984: 115). Here is where the turn to Girard is necessary. Law-and-literature's concern with pre-representational language—a predilection shared by Girard—is how the field is able to subliminally introduce the principle of sacrifice and the sacrificial into its interpretative strategies for its demystification of the legal-literary text. And the greatest example of the accused's 'animality' that draws, or attracts, the attention of the vampire-like accuser-prosecutor-persecutor narratively represented as the protagonist-lawyer is Herman Melville's Billy Budd who, famously, stutters, rendering him incapable of formulating abstractions, or that which is differentiated and representational. Weisberg's analysis of *Billy Budd, Sailor* (1891) is excellent but crucially, and revealingly, he misses the central issue of mimesis and the triangulation of desire.

Weisberg begins: 'As in other great literary depictions of the legal process, the trial of Billy Budd parodies the seeming orderliness of criminal law by revealing it to be an instrument in the service of the "protectively secret" passion of the prosecuting authority' (Weisberg, 1984: 166). The verbalizer Captain Vere's scapegoating of the animal-like (un-verbal) Billy Budd is motivated by an existential envy that has attained the level of metaphysical desire. '*The Handsome Sailor*' is the naval model who is personified by Admiral Nelson while Vere's access to, or successful emulation of, the model is blocked by his more successful rival Billy Budd; 'Insofar as he emblematizes Nelson's heroic personality, Billy provides an avenue for Vere's frustrated vengeance' flowing from his failed mimesis. And Billy is unlawfully hanged as a result of Vere's dubious legal machinations 'because he unwittingly stands in place of the envied, magnificently overt Admiral Nelson' (Weisberg, 1984: 163). In other words, Vere is scandalized by Billy who is the unaware model-obstacle. Both Billy and Nelson are introduced as variations of the "Handsome Sailor," the type in which '"the moral nature was seldom out of keeping with the physical make". They are stamped by a consistent harmony of inner and outer man and an almost organic rejection of hypocrisy and covertness' (Weisberg, 1984: 167). So the issue is *ressentiment*-driven existential envy that has reached the heights (depths) of metaphysical desire by way of failed emulation, not as a result of an uncontainable out-pouring of the will-to-life; both the admiral and the foretopman occupy the place of authentic

[157] Meaning undifferentiated.

Being, the thing that Vere most covets since it is what he most lacks as per interdividual psychology. 'Each epitomizes the sailor's harmonic mode', and 'Melville's equation of Billy and Nelson' is 'meant to emphasize in addition that Nelson represents simplicity and sailor-like honesty on the highest level' (Weisberg, 1984: 167). Likewise, the reader learns that 'Billy was '"by no means of a satirical turn.... To deal in double meanings and insinuations of any sort was quite foreign to his nature"' (Weisberg, 1984: 212 n 6). Which is what links him to that other great scapegoat-sub-human-animal Mersault: 'Billy and Mersault, who tend to participate freely in unstructured reality, suddenly find themselves harnessed by legal forms totally alien to their non-verbal natures' (Weisberg, 1984: 135). The only thing that separates the two scapegoats is that Bill got to make it to the screen[158] while Mersault has been left eternally un-adapted. Which is too bad, really, because the scapegoat narrative, or 'drama,' is ideally suited for cinematic translation as Livingston knew full well.

> It is my contention that the Girardian critique of scapegoating works very well. It identifies with an unprecedented degree of precision some patterns of interaction and attitudes that appear across a wide range of contexts and domains. The bread and butter of the movie industry is a ritualistic fictional evocation of the resolution of a violent crisis by means of the heroic extermination of a monstrous scapegoat.[159] Similar fantasies also provide the scenarios for some of our most earnest political dramas. (Livingston, 1992: 174)

Film is very much the junior partner of law-and-literature but all of the tropes that are applied to the literary text may be equally applied to the visual text for the purposes of the critique of legal textualism. To address the obvious objection: law-and-literature films do qualify as 'texts' because they conform to the requisite forms of storytelling and *muthos*. Put simply, every film is a sequence of images arranged in a narrative structure: 'Film is part of the universe of meaning-making in which we all live. Film supplies at least some of the narratives and storytelling styles that situate our being in a normative world. It offers normative visions that may point us toward some possible future' (Sherwin, 2001: 1526). Which takes us directly to the issue of *nomos* and the violence of legal interpretation, this time enacted cinematically. Robert K. Sherwin persuasively argues this in 'Nomos and Cinema' (2001) making clear his reliance upon Cover.

> Law is more than a system of rules and the fear of predictable consequences. It is a world made up of meanings that are drawn from shared texts and practices. It is a normative world, which means that embodied within it is a moral point of view, a normative vision. In this sense, we may say, along with Cover, that law plots a trajectory from the present to the future. It is a bridge that crosses from the present moment to possible futures. Quoting Cover: 'A *nomos* is a present world constituted by a system of tension between reality and vision'. (Sherwin, 2001: 1526)

Law is '"a distinctive manner of imaging the real"' (Clifford Geertz qtd. Sherwin, 2001: 1526) and it is the 'function of art, poetry, and rhetoric alike to make particular

---

[158] The film version of the tale, *Billy Budd*, was released in 1962 by Rank Films and starred Peter Ustinov as Vere and Terence Stamp as Billy. It was also adopted as an opera by Benjamin Britten in 1951 (Weisberg, 1984: 207 n 11). Mersault never got to sing either.

[159] Although I present a different 'take' on this as the 'monstrous scapegoat' is most usually represented in the form of an innocent victim or a wrongly accused.

form of truth (and reason and justice) sufficiently compelling to lead the subject to a specific judgment or course of action in a particular context'; of these three, rhetoric is perhaps the most vital because, pace White, not only is the essence of the rhetorician's art 'to move the soul where he will' (Sherwin, 2001: 1540) it is also the essence of the lawyer's art. But this is not merely a matter of the practice of the law, it is also the core of law's pedagogy; legal education 'has a constant and identifiable telos' and, within the law-and-literature enterprise, is 'the *use* of film in the service of a *legal* goal' (Black, 1999: 133). However, 'a curious and somewhat disturbing asymmetry lurks in this apparent embrace' of legal education and the somewhat inchoate discipline of film studies (Black, 1999: 129).

> What we are invited to survey is a treatment of films as *legal texts*—and not, in any sense, legal texts, or law, *as film*. In other words, where law subordinates itself to *literature* (law and/in/*as* literature), film finds itself subordinated to law (film *as* legal text). This asymmetry may be expressed with the help of the mathematical 'is less than' notation: film < law < literature. In other words, law and literature are things 'as' which other things sometimes function. Film however, while it can function 'as' something else, cannot be functioned 'as'. (Black, 1999: 130)

The net result is that the 'primary flow of theoretical ideas is from literary to law and thence-perhaps—to film' (Black, 1999: 130).

Thus, there is 'no integral or necessary engagement with film history or the nature of film, but there is a pedagogical agenda' (Black, 1999: 123). I shall also be following this agenda in my treatment of law-in-film for the 'pedagogical' or heuristic purposes of Girardian critique, for *nomos* is not merely narrative *content* but narrative *style*, as 'much of what it means to say that we live in a narrative culture is that we live in a cinematic culture' (Black, 1999: 128). Philip N. Meyer makes this clear in his essential essay 'Law Students Go to the Movies' (1992).[160]

> [Cinema] is the predominant mode of narrative storytelling in contemporary culture. Law students, attorneys and law professors are a product of this culture.... Additionally ... when operating in the narrative mode of thought, in contrast to the paradigmatic or analytical mode of thought, we perceive—literally see—causality in relationships that properly may be characterized as 'cinematic'. (Meyer, 1992: 898)

And just as with the procedural law novels where the verbalizer-lawyer-protagonist emulates the theatrical techniques of the stage performer so too does the cinematic lawyer conform to the expectations of cinematic narration.

> I chose movies as texts because of the similarity between trial and movie storytelling. Many popular storytellers, particularly film-makers, have much to teach law students and valuable teaching themes are imbedded in popular movies. The aesthetic narrative constraints controlling the movie maker are akin to those controlling the trial attorney. Like the movie maker, the trial attorney is an oral cultural storyteller who tells fact-based narratives that convey a story and a particular vision of the world (Meyer, 1992: 896–897).

The 'trial attorney, like the movie director but *unlike* the novelist, describes the action in a shared external world' (Meyer, 1992: 897–898); however, 'Unlike a reader,

---

[160] See Chap. 7, below.

the audience at trial or at the cinema is unable to turn back the pages and revisit the past. The story is told at one speed and, to effectively communicate, must be shaped to conform to shared narrative expectations of the entire audience' (Meyer, 1992: 897–898). And, when examined closely, it becomes clear that the very nature of film narrative is ideal for the cinematic reproduction of the scapegoat; a central tenet, or rite, of screen-writing is that the scripted person's 'character traits have to be compressed and condensed. All non-essential character traits must be eliminated and then compacted—layered into a denser form' in order to conform to a model, or idealized figure, of some kind (Philip N. Meyer qtd. Black, 1999: 128).[161] And as with literature, cinema possesses its own form of the interpretive community and participatory dialogue; the 'reading' of the film as text invites a second-order level of communicative and interpretative behavior, an endless mirroring of the interpretations of interpretations.

But there is another reason why film is as essential as the novel for law-and-literature, even when subjected to a rather narrow mode of interpretation as 'text': the phenomenologically and psychological overpowering connection between visuality and affectivity (*affectus*) and, from that, to mimesis. 'Persuasiveness may come from a variety of discrete logics, including the associative logic in which one encounters the sudden power of an isolated phrase or image or cluster of novel juxtapositions of familiar mental representations' (Sherwin, 2000: 131); film is formidable in its 'powers of associative logic' and the only other human invention that can rival it is advertising which is, as we know, the offspring of rhetoric. As Judge Alex Kozinski explained while exalting the representational

> [The] moviemaker's art is not at all different from the lawyer's—especially the courtroom advocate's. Both must capture, in a very short space, a slice of human existence, and make the audience see a story from their particular perspective. Both have to know which facts to include and which ones to leave out; when to appeal to emotion and when to reason; what to spoon-feed the audience and what to make them work for themselves; when to do the expected and when the unexpected; when to script and when to improvise. (Kozinski, 1996: xi)

But it is far more than the useful (and revealing) fact that film editing operates rhetorically, for while words are the medium of representation, pictures, in a Jungian fashion, enable direct access to the non-rational domain of pre-representation and bring a more potent and dangerous form of mimesis in their wake; 'visual images may more effectively produce verisimilitude and thereby evoke more compelling, perceptual, cognitive, and emotional responses than words alone' (Sherwin, 2010) taking us into the realm of undifferentiation. It is only at the movies that 'we "feel

[161] This also casts light upon the eerie similitudes among scapegoating, screenwriting, and legal rhetoric: '"How far can a lawyer 'stretch' the facts to buttress a client's case without misrepresenting them? How can a lawyer (or anyone else) ever know what the 'truth' really was? In fact, once can ask if there's any such thing as 'truth' at all. These questions … are seldom, if ever, addressed in law school curricula"' (David Simon Sokolow qtd. Black, 1999: 124–125). What law-and-literature adds to the law school curricula is the insight that insofar as the lawyer resembles a screen-writer he or she is prepared to commit a sacrificial act: the expulsion of both truth and the representational capacity of speech.

ourselves feeling'" (Sherwin, 2010: 261), an indication of the enormity of the cultural shift that has resulted from the 'changes in our storytelling and mimetic practices from words alone to words mingled with sounds and moving images' (Sherwin, 2010: 247).

> We become 'not only the toucher but also the touched.' In short, it is through the sensorium of the body that the film viewer experiences what is in play on the screen. It is perhaps here that the senses become 'their own theoreticians.' Through mimesis, or mindfulness, we open up to the presence of objects and others before us and are led to appreciate the dynamic, open-ended process of *construction* through which we seek meaning. (Vivian Sobchack qtd. Sherwin, 2010: 261.

David F. Marks argues that what he calls '"Tactile epistemology"' is a form of consciousness that '"involves thinking with your skin ... Haptic cinema, appearing to us as an object with which we can interact rather than an illusion into which we enter, calls upon this sort of embodied and mimetic intelligence"' (David F. Marks qtd. Sherwin, 2010: 265 n 115). Which is where a supreme danger lies, for if we were to perceive law and legal events solely through the medium of the visual, or a tactile epistemology, then we have unwittingly entered the domain of undifferentiation: 'Uncritically viewed, visualizing reality under the auspices of law risks authorizing fleeting sensation, emotional regression, collective fantasy, and historical amnesia' (Sherwin, 2010: 264), the psychic concoction necessary for the rise of the crowd and the creation of the scapegoat precisely because a 'Tactile epistemology' would be supremely pre-representational, the sacrificed supplement of representation.[162]

Richard K. Sherwin provides us with the following 'fable' for our consideration. As the story goes, the very earliest classical representation of the goddess 'Justice' was that of a sword or scale bearing woman whose sight was both keen and unobstructed. However, by 1500 the representation of Justice began to change and the goddess was given an occluding blindfold. Cartesian objectivity and pre-Derridean logocentrism had attained cultural hegemony and under the rule of reason sight had become a despised sense to be sacrificed; 'Lust of the senses, the flesh of the eyes, and

[162] As it should be clear by now, there is simply no elegant, or even easy way, to negotiate the ambiguous liminality operating in-between pre-representation and representation. I would need to write another book to adequately treat this issue, but for now I would express it in these terms. The existence of the mirror-neuron network, along with other neuro-biological structures, predispose the human subject toward mimetic undifferentiation and cognitive pre-representation. At the same time, evidence for the very early evolution of the capacity for symbolic representation through indirect selection, invested hominids with a dual capacity that enabled the production of a differentiated mimesis and a representational mental landscape. Both sets of doubles are neurophenomenologically embedded within all of us. But as a species, the way in which we managed to achieve a specifically 'cultural' break-through into the hegemony of representation/differentiation was by the hyper-repetitive performance of rites, the primitive building blocks of later symbolized rituals, as the accidental means of unintentionally creating over time collective cognitive reorientation that has remained precariously superimposed upon the substrate of pre-representation/undifferentiation substrate, that which would serve as Girard's version of the non-Freudian unconscious. In a sense, this is not unlike Nietzsche's notion that the human capacity for memory was created through the deliberate infliction of pain: it is all a matter of training. The result is that we are more or less safe when we read and speak but we are imperilled every time we enter a movie theater.

the dangerous seductions of the image were, in this way, to be kept at bay' (Sherwin, 2010: 265), and we know this to be true for, historically, 'the fear of images' is the 'offshoot of a belief in unmediated reality' (Sherwin, 2010: 265 n 116) and unmediated, or perfect, knowledge had become the substitution for God; 'With the advent of modernity, the visual image gave way, as a source of authority, to the printed text. The word of law, it was thought, would avoid the false pretenses and blasphemy of the idolatrous image' (Sherwin, 2010: 265). But now deconstruction and the revelation of the scapegoat has reversed this reversal and the 'Cartesian foundation that undercut the once prominent role of rhetorical and ethical studies in the traditional, premodern knowledge base of the humanities, has now, in turn, entered a stage of decline' (Sherwin, 2010: 266). Our now truly 'perfect' knowledge instructs us that the 'human brain takes in visual information all at once' so that the mind is held, vise-like,' in the grip of moving images' and 'critical thinking is discouraged or effectively disabled; it is enough simply to keep up with the visual flow' with no psychic left-over, or surplus, available for consumption (Sherwin, 2010: 256, 257). Which may be the real explanation for why, pace Girard, the scapegoat is still very much with us, albeit in a disguised form and, again it has something to do with mimesis: 'cinematic narratives mimic the reality-distorting tendencies of the mind to simplify accounts and attribute blame in precisely these ways' (Sherwin, 2010: 257), the epistemic correlatives of pre-representation and undifferentiation. Scapegoating is simple, and therefore it is fast-moving and, even better, something that anybody can do, not just a crowd.[163] If it is the case that in 'our time, and for the foreseeable future, the world itself has become a picture' (Sherwin, 2010: 246), then the law film would supplement the law novel as the primary critical concern of law-and-literature[164] for visuality has become the new form of reading, one governed by a digitally 'flattened series of discrete and fleeting insights, impressions, relational possibilities, and affective intensities' (Sherwin, 2010: 266), the perfectly breeding ground for new forms of antagonistic groups or tribal identities. The elemental truth is that the 'way we respond to visual images is different, as a perceptual and cognitive matter, than the way we respond to words alone' (Sherwin, 2010: 255), enabling the wholesale cultural regression to pre-representational modes of thought.

> Law on screen privileges meaning making through associational logic that operates, in large part, subconsciously, through its emotional appeal. A viewer might be aware that an image is strongly linked to a particular emotional response without knowing or understanding just what the connections is. In this respect, then, visual images tend to capitalize on the power of people's intuitive, *gestalt* emotional responses to shape their judgments. These effects

[163] Which is the logical conclusion to be drawn from the critique of film made by Franz Kafka, himself an authority on scapegoating: the 'cinema disturbs one's vision. The speed of the movements and the rapid change of images force men to look continually from one to another. Sight does not master pictures, it is the pictures which master one's sight' (Franz Kafka qtd. Sherwin, 2010: 254). An undifferentiated crowd is the result.

[164] 'Understanding how visual representations are made and construed, how they generate meaning and move the will of the viewer—whether on the basis of explicit or implicit reasons, or on the strength of largely unconscious mental associations, moods, memories, and feelings—has now become an inescapable part of what it means to practice, teach, and theorize law in the digital age of audiovisual representation' (Sherwin, 2010: 243).

> operate beneath the radar of awareness and are thus less amenable to critical scrutiny and counterargument. (Sherwin, 2010: 255–256)

Or even elementary representation. Sophocles proved this to be the case with the chorus of concerned citizens in *Oedipus Tyrannus* with whom differences could no longer be recognized.[165]

Throughout this remainder of this book I will be making the following set of assumptions concerning the presence and role of the scapegoat in some of the canonical literary and cinematic texts of law-and-literature. The deliberate revisiting, or appropriation, of the pre-representational that pre-structures the scapegoat mechanism is how the novel, and in some cases the film, is able to narratively introduce the principle of sacrifice and its now unveiled correlations with mimesis and mimetic desire. That law is rhetoric and that the creation of the scapegoat is a rhetorical act of symbolic violence that warns the reader or viewer as to the latent violence of legal interpretation. That every legal drama is, on some level, about the regeneration, or even the creation, of a community through the capacity of the scapegoat, either sacralised or de-sacralized, to generate that unanimity which is the resolution of a crisis of undifferentiation. That the storytelling dimensions of both literature and film can be made out through an examination of the diverse ways that the narrative negotiates the issues of mimesis, *ressentiment,* mimetic rivalry, metaphysical desire, mediation, *muthos,* and sacrificial violence. That, consistent with Girard's fundamental anthropology, the overriding ethical imperative of both law novels and law films is the demystification of the scapegoat mechanism through the exposure of *meconnaissance* and the revelation of the innocence of the persecuted-prosecuted-accused-victim: the archaic scapegoat in contemporary form.

It is Girard's scapegoat that is the fourth and final secret of law, literature, and cinema.

---

[165] And in favor of the members of the chorus-crowd, it is equally possible that sufficiently powerful associational logic may induce the *metanoia* that is so critical to Girard's theory of the novel' 'a sudden insight, or *gestalt* might also occur as an act of *recognition* of that which is already known on a profound level by the viewer' (Sherwin, 2010: 256 n 69). Not infrequently '"the power of recognition—the moment of insight when one sees beyond what is already known—arises from the way it allows us to *glimpse something more, something new, yet nonetheless somehow known or true.* As a technology of showing, the camera thus brings an ontological charge far exceeding the verisimilitude of the 'realistic' likeness ..."' (Jennifer Deger qtd. Sherwin, 2010: 256 n 69). The problem with accounts like this, however, is that it is difficult if not impossible to decide between *knowing* and *feeling*: has one directly experienced the unmediated sublime or has one merely had a powerful emotional experience that is honestly mis-recognized as a transcendental encounter? The experience may be real qua experience but the referent is absent, thanks to deconstruction. However, if one is referencing a repressed or denied 'truth' concerning knowledge or purpose, as Girard does with his notion of conversion, then the experience may be said to be real because it is the sensation of mis-recognition being replaced by a new form of self-knowledge which interprets itself as such. And certainly many law films, such as Sidney Lumet's *12 Angry Men* function as cinematic narratives of *metanoia.* See Chap. 6, below.

References

Primary Sources

Sophocles. (1984). In: R. Fagles (trans). *The three Theban plays: antigone, Oedipus the King, Oedipus at colonus*. Penguin Books.

Secondary Sources

Abrams, M. H. (1999). *A glossary of literary terms*. Cornell University Press.
Ahl, Frederick. 2020. In M.R. Anspach (Ed.), *The Oedipus book: Reading Sophocles Oedipus the King* (pp. 421–452). Michigan State University Press.
Antonello, P., & Webb, H. (2015). Introduction. In P. Antonello & H. Webb (Eds.), *Mimesis, desire, and the novel: Rene Girard and literary criticism*, (pp. ix–liii). Michigan State University Press.
Anspach, M. R. (2004). Editor's introduction: Imitating Oedipus. In R. Girard & M.R. Anspach (Eds.), *Oedipus unbound: Selected writings on rivalry and desire* (pp. vii–liv). Stanford University Press.
Bailie, G. (1995). *Violence unveiled: Humanity at the crossroads*. The Crossroad Publishing Company.
Beardsley, M. (2004). The concept of literature. 2004. In E. John & D. Lopes (Eds.), *Philosophy of literature: Contemporary and classic readings: An anthology* (pp. 51–58). Blackwell.
Black, D. A. (1999). *Law in film: Resonance and representation*. University of Illinois Press.
Borch-Jacobsen, M. (1988). *The Freudian subject*. C. Porter (trans). Stanford University Press.
Bremmer, J. (2020). Scapegoat rituals in ancient Greece. In M. R. Anspach (Ed.), *The Oedipus book: Reading Sophocles Oedipus the King* (pp. 167–190). Michigan State University Press.
Burkert, W. (2020). Greek Tragedy and Sacrificial Ritual. In M. R. Anspach (Ed.), *The Oedipus Book: Reading Sophocles Oedipus the King* (pp. 129–166). Michigan State University Press.
Calasso, Roberto. 2018. *The Ruin of Kasch*. Trans. Richard Dixon. New York: Farrar, Strays and Giroux
Cover, R. M. (1985–1986). The bonds of constitutional interpretation: Of the word, the deed, and the role. *Georgia Law Review, 20*, 815–833
Cover, R. M. (1983). The Supreme Court 1982 term foreword: *Nomos* and narrative. *Harvard Law Review, 4*, 4–68.
Cover, R. M. (1986). Violence and the word. *Yale Law Journal, 95*, 1601–1629.
Cowdell, S. (2014). *Rene Girard and secular modernity: Christ, culture, and crisis*. University of Notre Dame Press.
Dawson, D. (2013). *Flesh becomes word: a lexicography of the scapegoat or, the history of an idea*. Michigan State University Press.
Delcourt, M. (2020). In M. DeBevoise (trans). *Oedipus; or, The Legend of a Conqueror*. Michigan State University Press.
Dietrich, O., Heun, M., Notroff, J., Schmidt, K., & Zarnkow, M. (2012). The role of cult and feasting in the emergence of neolithic communities: New evidence from Gobekli Tepe, South-Eastern Turkey. *Antiquity, 86*, 674–695.
Dumouchel, P. (1988). Introduction. In P. Dumouchel (Ed.), *Violence and truth: On the work of Rene Girard* (pp. 10–21). The Athlone Press.
Dupuy, J-P. (2013). In M.B. DeBevoise (trans.) *The mark of the sacred*. Stanford University Press.
Dupuy, J.-P. (2011). Naturalizing mimetic theory. In S. R. Garrels (Ed.), *Mimesis and science: Empirical research on imitation and the mimetic theory of culture and religion* (pp. 193–213). Michigan State University Press.

Dupuy, J.-P. (1988). Totalization and misrecognition. In P. Dumouchel (Ed.), *Violence and truth: On the work of Rene Girard* (pp. 75–100). The Athlone Press.

Eagleton, T. (2020). Excerpt from *Sweet Violence*. In M. R. Anspach (Ed.), *The Oedipus book: Reading Sophocles Oedipus the King* (pp. 269–278). Michigan State University Press.

Eliade, M. (1987). In W.R. Trask (trans.) *The sacred and the profane: The nature of religion*. Harcourt, Inc.

Feldman, K. S. (2015). On Girard's biblical realism. In P. Antonello & H. Webb (Eds.), *Mimesis, desire, and the novel: Rene Girard and literary criticism* (pp. 55–68). Michigan State University Press.

Foley, H. P. (2020). Oedipus as *Pharmakos*. In M. R. Anspach (Ed.), *The Oedipus book: Reading Sophocles Oedipus the King* (pp. 309–325). Michigan State University Press.

Fornari, G. (2013). In K. Buck (trans.) *A god torn to pieces: The Nietzsche case*. Michigan State University Press.

Foucault, M. (2020). Excerpt from *Wrong-Doing, Truth-Telling*. In M. R. Anspach (Ed.), *The Oedipus book: Reading Sophocles Oedipus the King* (pp. 329–361). Michigan State University Press.

Frug, J. (1988). Argument as character. *Stanford Law Review, 40*(4), 869–927.

Gallese, V. (2011). The two sides of mimesis: mimetic theory, embodied simulation, and social identification. In S. R. Garrels (Ed.), *Mimesis and science: Empirical research on imitation and the mimetic theory of culture and religion* (pp. 87–108). Michigan State University Press.

Girard, R. (2020). In C.L. Haven (Ed.), *Conversations with Rene Girard: prophet of envy*. Bloomsbury Academic.

Girard, R. (1965). In Y. Freccero (trans.) *Deceit, desire and the novel: Self and other in literary structure*. The Johns Hopkins University Press.

Girard, R. (2007). The evangelical subversion of myth. In R. Hamerton-Kelly (Ed.), *Politics & apocalypse* (pp. 29–49). Michigan State University Press.

Girard, R. (1987). Generative scapegoating. In R.G. Hamerton-Kelly (Ed.), *Violent origins: Walter Burkert, Rene Girard, and Jonathan Z. Smith on ritual killing and cultural formation* (pp. 73–146). Stanford University Press.

Girard, R. (1996). In J.G. Williams (Ed.), *The Girard reader*. The Crossroad Publishing Company.

Girard, R. 2005. In J.G. Willliams (trans.) *I see Satan Fall like lightning*. Orbis Books.

Girard, Rene. 2004. *Oedipus Unbound: Selected Writings on Rivalry and Desire*. Trans. Mark R. Anspach. Stanford: Stanford University Press

Girard, R. (2014). In M.B. DeBoise (trans.) *The one by whom scandal comes*. Michigan State University Press.

Girard, R. (1997). In J.G. Williams (trans.) *Resurrection from the underground: Feodor Dostoevsky*. Michigan State University Press.

Girard, R. (1986). In Y. Freccero (trans.) *The scapegoat*. Johns Hopkins University Press.

Girard, R. (1991). *A Theater of Envy: William Shakespeare*. St Augustine's Press.

Girard, R. (1978). *To double business bound: Essays on literature, mimesis, and anthropology*. The Johns Hopkins University Press.

Girard, R. (1977). In P. Gregory (trans.) *Violence and the sacred*. Baltimore: The Johns Hopkins Press

Girard, R., Antonello, P., Cezar, J., & de Castro, Rocha. (2008). *Evolution and conversion: Dialogues on the origins of culture*. Continuum.

Girard, R., Oughourlian, J.-M., & Lefort, G. (2003). In S. Bann & M. Metteer (trans.), *Things hidden since the foundation of the world*. Continuum.

Girard, R., & Michel, T. (2014). In T.C. Merrill (trans.) *When these things begin: Conversations with Michel Treguer*. East Lansing MI: Michigan State University Press.

Golsan, R. J. (2002). *Rene Girard and myth: An introduction*. Routledge.

Goodhart, S. (1988). 'I am Joseph': Rene Girard and the prophetic law. In P. Dumouchel (Ed.), *Violence and truth: On the work of Rene Girard* (pp. 53–74). The Athlone Press.

Goodhart, S. (1978). Oedipus and Lauis' Many Murderers. *Diacritics, 8*(1), 55–71.

Gordon, R. (1984). Critical legal histories. *Stanford Law Review, 36*, 57–125.
Greene, W. C. (2020). The murderers of Laius. In M. R. Anspach (Ed.), *The Oedipus book: Reading Sophocles Oedipus the King* (pp. 363–374). Michigan State University Press.
Harshbarger, K. (2020). Who Killed Laius? In M. R. Anspach (Ed.), *The Oedipus book: Reading Sophocles Oedipus the King* (pp. 381–392). Michigan State University Press.
Hirsch, E. D. (2004). What Isn't literature? In E. John & D. Lopes (Eds.), *Philosophy of literature: Contemporary and classic readings: An anthology* (pp. 46–50). Blackwell.
Kastrup, B. (2021). *Decoding Jung's metaphysics: The archetypal semantics of an experiential universe* (p. 2021). John Hunt Publishing.
Kirwan, M. (2005). *Discovering Girard*. A Cowley Publications Book.
Knox, B. (1984). Introduction and notes in Sophocles. In. R. Fagles (trans.) *The three Theban Plays: Antigone, Oedipus the King, Oedipus at Colonus*. Penguin Books.
Kozinski, A. (1996). Foreword. In P. Bergman, & M. Asimow (Eds.), *Reel justice: The courtroom goes to the movies* (pp. xi–xiii). A Universal Press Syndicate Company.
Lamarque, P., & Olsen, S. H. (2004). The concept of literature. In E. John & D. Lopes (Eds.), *Philosophy of literature: Contemporary and classic readings: an anthology* (pp. 59–64). Blackwell.
Levinson, S. (1982). Law as literature. *Texas Law Review, 60*(3), 373–403.
Livingston, P. (1988). Demystification and history in Girard and Durkheim. In P. Dumouchel (Ed.), *Violence and truth: On the work of Rene Girard* (pp. 113–133). The Athlone Press.
Livingston, P. (1992). *Models of Desire: Rene Girard and the psychology of mimesis*. The Johns Hopkins University Press.
Mack, B. (1987). Introduction: religion and ritual. In R.G. Hamerton-Kelly (Ed.), *Violent origins: Walter Burkert, Rene Girard, and Jonathan Z. Smith on ritual killing and cultural formation* (pp. 1–72). Stanford University Press.
McCarthy, T. (2008). *Tintin and the secret of literature*. Counterpoint.
McClenon, J. (1994). *Wondrous events: Foundations of religious belief*. University of Pennsylvania Press.
McKenna, A. J. (1992). *Violence and difference: Girard, Derrida, and deconstruction*. University of Illinois Press.
Meyer, P. N. (1992). Law students go to the movies. *Connecticut Law Review, 24*, 893–913.
Oughourlian, J.-M. (1996). Desire is mimetic: A clinical approach. *Contagion: Journal of Violence Mimesis, and Culture, 3*, 43–49.
Oughourlian, J.-M. (2010). In E. Webb (trans). *The genesis of desire*. Michigan State University Press.
Oughourlian, J.-M. (2016). In T.C. Merrill (trans.) *The mimetic brain*. Michigan State University Press.
Oughourlian, J.-M. (1991). In E. Webb (trans). *The puppet of desire: The psychology of hysteria, possession, and hypnosis*. Stanford University Press.
Posner, R. (1986). Law and literature: A relation re-argued. *Virginia Law Review, 72*(8), 1351–1392.
Reeve, Z. (2015). Mechanisms of internal cohesion: Scapegoating and parochial altruism. In P. Antonello & P. Gifford (Eds.), *How we became human: mimetic theory and the science of evolutionary origins* (pp. 161–186). Michigan State University Press.
Ricoeur, P. (1983). On interpretation. In A. Montefiore (Ed.), *Philosophy in France today* (pp. 175–197). Cambridge University Press.
Sarat, A. (1992). Robert cover on law and violence. In M. Minow, M. Ryan, & A. Sarat (Eds.), *Narrative, violence, and the law: The essays of Robert Cover* (pp. 255–276). The University of Michigan Press.
Scheler, M. (2010). In L.B. Coser & W.W. Holdheim (trans.) *Ressentiment*. Marquette University Press.
Sherwin, R. K. (2010). Imagining law as film (representation without reference?). In A. Sarat, M. Anderson, & C. O. Frank (Eds.), *Law and the humanities: An introduction* (pp. 241–268). Cambridge University Press.

Sherwin, R. K. (2001). Nomos and cinema. *UCLA Law Review, 48*, 1519–1543.
Sherwin, R. K. (2000). *When law goes pop: The vanishing line between law and popular culture.* The University of Chicago Press.
Tattersall, I. (2012). *Masters of the planet: The search for human origins.* St. Martin's Griffin.
Tomelleri, S. (2015). *Ressentiment: reflections on mimetic desire and society.* Michigan State University Press.
Tyrell, W. B. (trans). (2020). Oedipus Tyrannos. In M. R. Anspach (Ed.), *The Oedipus casebook: Reading Sophocles' Oedipus the King* (pp. 1–25). East Lansing MI: Michigan State University Press.
Vernant, J.-P., & Vidal-Naquet, P. (1990). In J. Lloyd (trans.) *Myth and tragedy in ancient Greece.* Zone Books.
Ward, I. (1993). Law and literature. *Law and Critique, 4*(1), 43–79.
Ward, I. (1995). *Law and literature: Possibilities and perspectives.* Cambridge University Press.
Warrior, V. M. (2006). *Roman religion.* Cambridge University Press.
Weisberg, R. H. (1984). *The failure of the word: The protagonist as lawyer in modern fiction.* Yale University Press.
Weisberg, R. (1988). Law in and as literature: Self-generated meaning in the "Procedural Novel." In C. Koelb & S. Nokes (Eds.), *The comparative perspective on literature: Approaches to theory and practice* (pp. 224–232). Cornell University Press.
White, J. B. (1981–1982). Law as language: Reading law and reading literature. *Texas Law Review, 60*, 415–445.
White, J. B. (1985). Law as rhetoric, rhetoric as law: The arts of cultural and communal life. *University of Chicago Law Review, 52*, 684–702.
White, J. B. (1984). *When words lose their meaning: Constitutions and reconstitutions of language, character, and community.* The University of Chicago Press.
Wilson, E. (2019). An Emoji for Rene Girard: Memes, mimesis, and the apocalypse of the eternally irrelevant. In A. Bown & D. Bristow (Eds.), *Post memes: Seizing the memes of production* (pp. 137–168). Punctum Books.
Wright, D. P. (1986). The gesture of hand placement in the Hebrew bible and in Hittite literature. *Journal of the American Oriental Society, 106*(3), 433–446.
Wright, D. P. (1993). Analogy in Biblical and Hittite Ritual. *Orbis Biblicus Et Orientalis, 29*, 473–507.

Chapter 2
'El sueno de la razon produce monstruos' or, 'The Dream of Reason Creates Monsters': Two Little Piggies Went to the Apocalypse in William Golding's *Lord of the Flies*

Abstract Operating on the assumption that William Golding's *Lord of the Flies* (1954) was written as a satire of Thomas Hobbes' *Leviathan* (1651), I use the novel as a means of offering an extended reflection upon Rene Girard's theory of the scapegoat. Contrary to the popular, and misleading, reading of the text, I argue that *Lord of the Flies* stands for the exact opposite proposition so frequently espoused by the moralist: rather than constituting a cautionary parable concerning the reversibility of the 'thin veneer of civilization,' what Golding really has the boys on the island doing is discovering for themselves the universal pattern of cultural formation: that the pre-representational logic of substitution and sacrifice provides the symbolic machinery necessary for cultural formation and abstract thought. The price to be paid lies with the murder of the scapegoat as the cornerstone of society. The unifying narrative arc of the tale imitates the evolution of sacrifice: from Simon to Piggy to Ralph and culminating in the establishment of Jack's theocracy and the cementing of ritualistic sacrifice as the foundation of social and political order, the endless replacement of the victim through the deliberate repetition of the original violence of generative unanimity. Which, as it turns out, was all the result of an accident caused by a very 'middling' sort of boy.

Keywords William Golding · Rene Girard · Thomas Hobbes · The commonwealth-by-institution · The commonwealth-by-acquisition · Existential envy

In Old English, the word 'God' possesses two meanings. The first one is the polite meaning that we can all chat about without anxiety: 'The One Who Comes When Called.' The second one leads to extreme unpleasantness: 'The One Who Eats the Sacrifice'.

E. M. Wilson, *Rene Girard, Law, Literature, and Cinema*,
https://doi.org/10.1007/978-981-97-1156-7_2

2.1 *Lord of the Flies*, Fundamental Anthropology, and *Meconnaissance*

Allegory may be concisely defined as 'a narrative, whether prose or verse, is allegorical when the agents and actions, and sometimes the setting as well, are contrived by the author to make coherent sense on the "literal", or primary level of signification, and, at the same time to signify a second, correlated order of significance.' There are two types of allegory: the historical or the political ('in which the characters and actions that are signified literally in their turn represent, or "allegorize", historical personages and events') and the sustained allegory of ideas wherein 'the literal characters represent concepts and the plot allegorizes an abstract doctrine or thesis...the central device is the *personification* of abstract entities such as virtues, vices, states of mind, modes of life, and types of character.' (Abrams, 1999: 5) *Lord of the Flies* (hereafter *Lord*) clearly falls under the latter category of 'sustained allegory of ideas' which was expressed by William Golding himself in this manner: 'The theme [of *Lord*] is an attempt to trace the defects of society back to the defects of human nature. The moral [sic] is that the shape of a society must depend on the ethical nature of the individual and not on any political system. ...The whole book is symbolic in nature' (William Golding qtd. Babb, 1970: 7). Despite my invocation of the author himself author, I believe that this is an incorrect albeit far from uncommon interpretation of the novel, one that Golding did much to encourage through almost incessant interviews (Hynes, 1988: 13–21). I would farther than merely dissent from the author's self-proclaimed interpretation; I would suggest that the majority of readers, along with Golding himself, is are suffering from a collective case of *meconnaissance* precisely because what *Lord* does so supremely well is to demystify the central foundation *mythos*-lie of civilization: that it originates within an act of rational and free consent rather than the extreme violence of collective enmity. Just as our historical ancestors have mis-recognized the truth of our origins to the same degree, and for similar reasons, have literary generations of readers of Goldings novel not understood what they were actually discussing within their respective interpretative communities.[1] In my own reading, based directly upon Girard's fundamental anthropology, rather than regressing toward barbarism, the boys, led by Jack Merridew, are in fact advancing toward civilization through their mis-recognized imitation of the anthropologically correct process of social formation: the establishment of a religious system predicated upon the ritualistic sacrifice of a formally designated scapegoat, the first one Simon, the second one Piggy, and then, almost, Ralph (Wilson, 2014). And my approach is implicitly validated by Paul Dumouchel's brilliant comment concerning the origin of cultural order in sacrificial violence: 'The difference between reason and violence, on which we would like to base the unanimous agreement of members of society, does not precede the action that establishes the political order, but flows from it' (Dumouchel: xvii). If we read *Lord* without the blinders of morality or

[1] See Chap. 1, above.

moralism, the intensely humanist and liberal interpretation that the boys have tragically regressed to barbarism stands in unrelieved tension to Golding's masterful depiction of the unnamed island as landscape-as-violence. The place lacking a name is a place that is undifferentiated, the island a space where violence not merely happens but where violence is the metaphysical foundation of Being itself. This is implied in the following lengthy passage:

> When Henry tired of his play and wandered off along the beach, Roger followed him, keeping beneath the palms and drifting casually in the same direction ... [Henry] went down the beach and busied himself at the water's edge. The great Pacific tide was coming in and every few seconds the relatively still water of the lagoon heaved forwards [sic] an inch. There were creatures that lived in this last fling of the sea, tiny transparencies that came questing in with the water over the hot, dry sand. ... Like a myriad of tiny teeth in a saw, the transparencies came scavenging over the beach. This was fascinating to Henry. He poked about with a bit of stick, that itself was wave-worn and whitened and a vagrant, and tried to control the motions of the scavengers. He made little runnels that the tide filled and tried to crowd them with creatures. He became absorbed beyond mere happiness as he felt himself exercising control over living things. He talked to them, urging them, ordering them. Driven back by the tide, his footprints became bays in which they were trapped and gave him the illusion of mastery. He squatted on his hams at the water's edge, bowed, with a shock of hair falling over his forehead and past his eyes, and the afternoon sun emptied down invisible arrows. Roger waited too. At first he had hidden behind a great palm bole; but Henry's absorption with the transparencies was so obvious that at last he stood out in full view. ... Roger stooped, picked up a stone, and threw it at Henry—and threw to miss. The stone, that token of preposterous time, bounced five yards to Henry's right and fell in the water. Roger gathered a handful of stones and began to throw them. Yet there was a space around Henry, perhaps six yards in diameter, into which he dare not throw. Here, invisible yet strong, was the taboo of the old life. Round the squatting child was the protection of parents and school and policemen and the law. Roger's arm was conditioned by a civilization that knew nothing of him and was in ruins. (Golding, 1954: 63–64)

In ruins for having just destroyed itself through limited nuclear warfare. Readers generally do not appreciate that the boys are imprisoned within parallel apocalyptic universes: the 'macro-apocalypse' of the outside world (World War Three) and the 'micro-apocalypse' of the undifferentiated island wherein the almost-too-obviously imitative 'civil war' between Ralph and Jack climaxes in a mirroring conflagration. But the invocation of Being-as-such, or the cosmos in general, throughout the novel has led Harold Bloom to accuse Golding of a deceptive moralizing.

> In many ways the book [*Lord*] is remarkably tendentious and too clearly has a program to urge us on. Overt moral allegory, even in a lively adventure story, may arouse our resentments, and I find it difficult to reread *Lord of the Flies* without a certain skepticism toward Golding's design on his reader. (Bloom, 2008: 7)

Geography counts for the real word is not isotropic.[2] Bloom knows this and he makes much of assumed cultural differences in order to draw sharply divisions between a hypothesized English versus American reading: 'I like to try the critical experiment of pretending to be Mark Twain as I read *Lord of the Flies*. How *would* Huck Finn' 'have reacted to the regressive saga of the English schoolboys of *Lord*

[2] See Chap. 3, below.

of the Flies?' (Bloom, 2008: 7) Why Twain? In part, it is a question of a perhaps unconscious case of mimesis; 'In some sense, the book [*Lord*] is Mark Twain turned upside down, and I mean the Mark Twain of *Roughing It* rather than of *Adventures of Huckleberry Finn*' (Bloom, 2008: 7). Truly—Huck and Tom would have little to say to either Ralph or Piggy, although Tom might be able to strike up a conversation with Jack. Nonetheless, 'We cannot find any trace of Huck in Ralph or Jack in Simon or in Piggy or in Roger. Golding, I think, would have been furious at my suggestion that this has something to do with Huck's being American and Golding's boys being British' (Bloom, 2008: 7). Why 'furious'? Because of the problem of universalism, which Bloom identifies as the central pillar of Golding's moralistic agenda to 'convert' his readers (Wilson, 2017).

> Original Sin is not a very American idea,[3] and the wonderful skepticism of Huck, at any age, would have preserved him from being either an implausible saint or a bestial hunter. This is hardly to suggest that we [Americans] are less savage or violence-prone than the British; Huck knows better, and we know better. But it may indicate some of the limitations of *Lord of the Flies*; as a grim fable, unrelieved in its rigor, it lacks all humor and is an involuntary parody of Twain's *Roughing It* or *Innocents Abroad*. (Bloom, 2008: 7)

Bloom's conclusion? Forgetfulness of geography, physical and cultural, is a type of mystification, or *meconnaissance*.

> I suspect that the issue comes down to the issue of universalism: Do the boys of *Lord of the Flies* represent the human condition, or do they reflect the traditions of the British schools with their restrictive structures, sometimes brutal discipline, and not always benign visions of human nature? Golding himself said that society, whether in life or in *Lord of the Flies*, plays only a minor role in bringing about human violence and depravity. But what about the one society his boys truly have known, the society of their schools? One can admire *Lord of the Flies* as a tale of adventure while wondering whether its moral fable was not more insular than Golding seems to have realized. (Bloom, 2008: 8)

Bloom is scandalized by the novel not because of morality but, as he says, in reaction to universalism whereas I argue that *Lord* apocalyptically reveals what we mis-recognize as regressive as the foundation of civilization, which is the central tenet of Girard's fundamental anthropology which is a supremely universalist project as he makes clear; according to Girard, there is 'a unity that underlies not only all mythologies and rituals but the whole of human culture, and this unity of unities depends on a single mechanism, continually functioning because perpetually misunderstood—the mechanism that assures the community's spontaneous and unanimous outburst of opposition to the surrogate victim' (Girard, 1977: 299–300). And, if this were not enough, Girard, no less than Golding, literally relies upon children as one of the primary sources of species behavior: 'I have often thought that, in order to understand myths, one has only to observe the behaviour of groups of children' (Girard et al., 1987: 123). The real problem of interpretation concerning *Lord* is that the universalism of Golding is mis-read as a moral one rather than as an anthropological one as Bloom has failed to do. As Golding subliminally conveys and as I shall laboriously

[3] So says the almost unimpeachable Bloom, although this would seemingly obviate the Puritan(-ical) Founding Fathers.

demonstrate, the totality of the totalizing class system of the English, or of that of any other intensely differentiated people (minus Huck Finn[4]), is wholly dependent upon diverse mediations of a sacrificial system as the means of postponing a terminal crisis of undifferentiation. Golding, then, had simply lied—the events described in the novel do not detail the collapse of civilization; rather, radically immersed within the state of nature and unknowingly following the social logic of community, the English schoolboys overthrow the foundations of a false model of social being and invent for themselves an original, and self-sustaining, aboriginal society. Golding appears to have been aware of the cultural reason of Jack Merridew's tribe of hunters, and he confessed *Lord* to be a repository of one of his consuming themes, the supremely anti-establishment 'off-campus history' which is the meta-narrative of the 'deep resentment handed down from generation to generation about a certain group or groups of people' (Bloom, 2008: 11)—in other words, the lurking presence of the seemingly eternal (and universal) phenomenon of *bellum omnia contra omnes.* In fact, Immanuel Kant's jibe concerning the 'unsocial sociability' of humankind (Dumouchel, 2015: 14) is the basis of what I argue is the only fully coherent interpretation of *Lord* possible: Golding's novel is a *satire* of Thomas Hobbes' theory of the state of nature and the social contract as the foundation of legal and political order ('Society') as outlined in his *Leviathan* (1651)—a supremely universalist text—and clandestinely expressed in the form of an allegorical novel. *Lord* is an act of literary mis-recognition about *meconnaissance.*

As I have shown elsewhere (Wilson, 2014), the relevance of Thomas Hobbes (1588–1679) to the novel is obvious: the 'constitutional crisis' faced by the boys is Golding's allegorical re-enactment of Hobbes' famous concept of the social contract and the resultant division between what appears at first glance as the democratic Commonwealth-by-Institution (represented by Ralph and Piggy) and the dictatorial Commonwealth-by-Acquisition (represented by Jack and Roger).[5] What is far less obvious is the manner in which the struggle over the political order of the island strictly parallels mimetic rivalry between the two boy-sovereigns, Ralph and Jack.[6] Doubling is one of the unappreciated strengths of the novel, the binary relationship of Self to Other signifying the esoteric union between exoteric opposites. Employing Girard's theory of mimetic rivalry as a supplementary reading to Hobbes' political

[4] Ironically it is none other than Jack who makes the boldest claim for the virtues of differentiation:

> 'I agree with Ralph. We've got to have rules and obey them. After all, we're not savages. We're English; and the English are the best at everything. So we've got to do the right things' (Golding, 1954: 42). Almost as ironically, the second boldest claim is made by the anonymous British naval officer when offering commentary on what Jack the Chief had wrought: "I should have thought,' said the officer as he visualized the search before him, 'I should have thought that a pack of British boys—you're all British aren't you?—would have been able to put up a better show than that—I mean—". (Golding, 1954: 224)

[5] See below.

[6] See below.

doubling of democratic with authoritarian rule, a much more challenging interpretation of *Lord* than that typically offered can be formulated: that the mimetic rivalry between the two boys replicates the mimetic dynamic between the competing forms of government that they each respectively signify, subverting any absolute distinction between liberal and dictatorial forms of the political state. In the calamitous end, the solution to the problem of secular democracy foisted on the boys at the beginning by the rhetorical ruses of Piggy, the voice of a 'common sense' that is in reality misrecognition, is a sacrificial Theocracy. In other words, Golding, like Girard, inverts the ideas of Ludwig Feuerbach in holding that religious consciousness is the foundation of social consciousness. The dramatic movement implied in Golding's book is a double arc: the migration from the utilitarian common-sense nature of language (Hobbes) to the transcendental language of religion (Girard) and the migration from Assembly and social contract apparently symbolized by the conch[7] to the sacrificial mechanism of the scapegoat signified by the signature pig's head impaled on a 'stick sharpened at both ends.'

The central question no becomes the meaning of the term 'civilization'? Among contending definitions, the one that is most useful to my argument is one that provided by Norbert Elias in *The Civilizing Process* (1939). For Elias, civilization is a collective exercise in impulse control; civilization is a by-product of complexity which both creates and depends upon chaotically emergent patterns of inter-dependence. The

> …libidinal energies which one encounters in any living human being are always already socially processed, they are, in other words, sociogenetically transformed in their function and structure, and can in no way be separated from the corresponding ego and super-ego structures. The more animalistic and automatic levels of people's personality are neither more nor less significant for the understanding of human conduct than their controls. What matters, what determines conduct, are the balances and conflicts between people's malleable drives and the built-in drive-controls. (Elias, 2000: 409)

The single most efficacious means of imposing impulse-control is through the monopolization of violence by means of a juridically robust state grounded in executive power. The boy's always potentially anarchic democratic Assembly will prove impossible to sustain in the long-term; as we know, in the end Jack will overthrow Ralph, his mimetic rival for the desired object of sovereignty in no small part because, for Elias the Commonwealth-by-Acquisition has certain built-in advantages over the Commonwealth-of-Institution.

> [The] peculiar stability of the apparatus of psychological self-restraint which emerges as a decisive trait built into the habitus of every 'civilized' human being, stands in the closest relationship to the monopolization of physical force and the growing stability of the central organs of society.[8]… When a monopoly of force is formed, pacified social spaces are created which are normally free from acts of violence.… Only with the formation of this kind of relatively stable monopoly institutions do societies acquire those characteristics as a result of which the individuals forming them get attuned, from infancy, to a highly regulated and differentiated pattern of self-restraint; only in conjunction with these monopolies does this

[7] I critique this lazy identification of the conch with what we call democracy below.

[8] For Elias, the 'ideal type' or 'model' State is Absolutist France (Elias, 2000: 387–414).

> kind of self-restraint require a higher degree of automaticity, does it become, as it were, 'second nature'. (Elias, 2000: 369)

Elias posits an explicit correlation between the processes of state formation (external landscape) and the reconfiguration of the psychic economy (internal landscape), one now founded upon rational calculation, self-denial, impulse control, and the self-censorship of violence—in two words, *common sense*—all of which are wondrously conveyed in Golding's mini-allegory of Roger's stalking of Henry on the beach, which could have been penned by Elias.

> The moderation of spontaneous emotions, the tempering of affects, the extension of mental space beyond the moment into the past and the future, the habit of connecting events in terms of chains of cause and effect—all these are different aspects of the same transformation of conduct which necessarily takes place with the monopolization of physical violence, and the lengthening of the chains of social action and inter-dependence. It is a 'civilizing' change of behavior. (Elias, 2000: 370)

Read superficially, the achievement of a stable, even if primitive, society is the pre-condition for the effective censorship of violence which is identical to that very movement of censorship from the exterior to the interior which will then yield a 'civilized' person at the end of a millennial-long process of incremental transformations. But read in a more penetrating manner, we can see that the effective 'domestication' of violence is the precondition for the primitive community. The catch, as Girard realized, is how could hominids successfully regulate violence *prior* to the development of effective institutions, for violence has to be quelled before institutions repressing violence via internalization can be 'invented'. Which is sort of the same problem that bedevils Hobbes: how can 'Man' practicably negotiate the social contract while he still inhabits the anarchic state of nature? Girard provides the answer which is the unifying narrative arc of *Lord*: the very thing that gives us peace is, paradoxically, grounded in violence, namely those self-same sacrificial rituals and practices binding us together (*religare*) that serve as a point of intersection between the social and the Absolute (*relegare*), yielding a self-stabilizing community which then be formally, or constitutionally, realized. We call the thing that is the violence-that-gives-us-peace-from-violence Religion (*religio*). But how exactly does it work? Or, to put it another way: why is it that on the nameless island of the boys who are lost does the common sense language of presentation fail in the face of the primitive form of pre-representation? The answer is that social being is a series of problems concerning imitation, undergirded by the 'unifying notion' of the 'mimetic cycle' (Palaver, 2013: vii); for Girard, 'mimetic theory is based in essence on the literary insight into man's unalterable religious nature' (Palaver, 2013: 27). And we can never be done with religion because we can never be done with the problem of envy.[9] 'The human subject does not really know what to desire, in the last resort' (Girard et al., 1987: 343); thus, the human subject 'desires *being*, something he himself lacks and which some other person [the 'model'] seems to possess. The subject thus looks to that other person to inform him of what he should desire in order to acquire that

---

[9] See Chap. 1, above.

being' (Girard, 1977: 146). The entirety of human desire, the libidinal dimension of humankind's social existence, is subsumed under mimesis—'desire itself is essentially mimetic, directed toward an object desired by the model,' (Girard, 1977: 146) from which comes rivalry, 'the mimetic nature of conflict, which is to say the ultimate absence of any object proper to it' (Girard et al., 1987: 31). Rivalry is the flip side of the crisis of distinctions, that potentially boundless state of existential anguish in which no one is anything in particular because all inhabit the universal space of absent identity, a hellish crisis of the collective of the loss of personal differences that triggers an avalanche of reciprocal and escalating violence; 'Sameness is the terrible war in which twins [or 'monstrous doubles'] are personally engaged, right up until the moment when one manages to kill the other. …When it spreads it becomes the famous war of all against all of which Hobbes spoke' (Girard, 2014: 104–105). Which is one of the primary reasons why I interpret *Lord* as a 'Hobbesian' novel.

There are two ways to mediate mimetic rivalry: external and internal. Historically, external mediation corresponds to class-based societies: 'As long as social difference or any other form of differentiation is present to channel mimetic desire, its conflictual dimension remains contained' (Palaver, 2013: 25). Internal mediation, however, is a sign of the egalitarian society in which mimetic conflict is resolved through the direct competition between the role model and the imitating/envious subject yielding an escalating violence, physical or symbolic (Palaver, 2013: 25), and '…it is in internal mediation that the profoundest meaning of the *modern* is found' (Girard, 1965: 92). The true catastrophe is when rigid social hierarchies begin to break down and give way to proliferating 'democratic' choices: as 'the metaphysical distance between desiring subject and model diminishes—the key component of internal mediation—the potential for rivalry and violence increases. The more negligible this distance becomes, the more probable it is that mimesis will end in rivalry and violence' (Palaver, 2013: 61). Girard

> …refers to this evolution of mimetic desire as internal mediation, where social differentiation has practically disappeared, and the power of mimesis is most destructive.… While the social distance between individuals gradually decreases, the mutual imitation of individual desires grows. In contemporary society, the transition from external mediation to internal mediation increases the person's illusion that he or she has a unique, autonomous, and individual desire, whereas actually differences among people are progressively disappearing. Everyone feels legitimated to compare him- or herself to others and to desire what the other has, independently of any distinction in terms of social role, job, or group of reference. (Tomelleri, 2015: 92–93)

Violence is the outcome not of the repression of desires but through their unrestrained expression; the collapse of social differences is 'a perquisite for the infectious spread of violent mimesis. The predominance of internal mediation must first be present within the community before mimesis can exert its contagious force. A stable social hierarchy, by contrast, prevents the spread of conflict and violence by restricting desire to external mediation' (Palaver, 2013: 141). Girard's mimetic cycle offers the true but hitherto concealed explanation of violence by 'showing quite simply that the disappearance of difference—physical or metaphysical—results in an increase in the frequency and intensity of conflict between both groups. Conflicts between equals have the greatest risk of turning violent, because the social limitations that normally prevent or channel mimetic desire are missing,' that is, the absence of external mediation (Palaver, 2013: 66). As mimetic rivalries are to be proscribed because of their ultimately violent consequences, the mimetic rivals must displace, or discharge, their common violence against a convenient surrogate victim that serves as the transference object of the violence—the scapegoat, the primordial instance of a 'form of differentiation present to channel mimetic desire' (Girard et al., 1987: 93). Girard explains the 'magical' efficacy of the scapegoat in terms of two sub-variants of mimetic desire: divisive acquisitive mimesis, which leads two or more individuals to desire the exact same object at the same moment in time, and unifying conflictual mimesis, which induces all of the parties to the conflict to settle upon a common rivalry, or enemy, whom they all wish to 'strike down' (Girard et al., 1987: 26). Historically, the ritualistic enshrinement of the scapegoat/sacrificial mechanism was the domain of religion (Girard et al., 1987: 48) which was founded upon the intermediary of the surrogate victim, the one who must die so that the community may live by being spared the 'apocalypse of the un-differentiated,' the master-sign of the mimetic collapse of distinctions. Girard's mimetic cycle, then, is not actually a theory of religion but one of social relations which are literally based upon victimage. As Jean-Michel Oughourlian has observed, Girard's 'theory of religion is simply a particularly noteworthy aspect of a fundamental theory of mimetic relations' (Girard et al., 1987: 44). It is in primitive societies that 'the mimetic crisis culminates in a phase of unbearable undifferentiation that is resolved by the violence of the sacrifice' (Girard & Treguer, 2014: 68), and it is religious thought that led early humankind to 'make the victim the vehicle and transforming agent of something sacred—mimesis—which is never conflictual or undifferentiated except in so far as it is spread throughout the community; its concentration in a victim makes it a pacifying and regulating force, the positive mimesis found in ritual' (Girard et al., 1987: 48). As Golding would put it: in order to survive, all hominids, even the pre-British ones, must sharpen a stick at both ends. For there was simply nothing else to do in the end at the very beginning.

2.2 Social Contracting on the Beach: The Inadequacy of Secular Reason

Arguably the single greatest work of British political philosophy, Thomas Hobbes' *Leviathan* takes its name from the allegorical sea-monster, or Beast, cited in The Book of Job. Very much like Golding was to do three hundred years later, Hobbes is meticulous in expressing his authorial intent.

> And thus I have brought to an end my Discourse of Civill and Ecclesiasticall Government, occasioned by the disorders of the present time [the Puritan Revolution], without partiality, without application, and without other designe, than to set before mens eyes the mutuall Relation between Protection and Obedience; of which the condition of Humane Nature, and

> the Laws Divine, (both Naturall and Positive) require an inviolable observation. (Hobbes, 1992: 491)

Although wide ranging in scope, almost the entirety of the text is ignored today; our contemporary interest is focused primarily upon Chaps. 13 and 14 of Book One ('Of Man') and Chap. 17 of Book Two ('Of Common-Wealth') where Hobbes provides the reader with what we take to be the core, and defining, elements of his theory of constitutionality. The first such expression is well known: 'Hereby it is manifest that during the time men live without a common power to keep them all in awe, they are in that condition that is called War, and such a war is of every men against every man' (Hobbes, 1992: 88). The second is even more famous.

> Whatsoever therefore is consequent to a time of War, where every man is enemy to every man; the same is consequent to the time wherein men live without other security, than what their own strength, and their invention shall furnish them with all. ... and [what] is worst of all [in such a condition], continual fear, and danger of violent death; and the life of man, solitary, poor, nasty, brutish, and short. (Hobbes, 1992: 89)

If I were to superimpose Hobbes' political treatise upon Golding's novel we would make the uncanny discovery that the latter is an almost point-for-point poetical embellishment of the former. Take, for example, the description of the original communal mingling of the Boys following their stranding upon the nameless island provided in Chapter One, 'The Sound of the Shell' (Golding, 1954: 1–29).

> Some [of the children] were naked and carrying their clothes; others half-naked, or more-or-less dressed, in school uniforms; grey, blue, fawn, jacketed or jerseyed. There were badges, mottoes even, stripes of color in stockings and pullovers. Their heads clustered above the trunks in the green shade; heads brown, fair, black, chestnut, sandy, mouse-colored; heads muttering, whispering, heads full of eyes that watched Ralph and speculated. Something was being done. (Golding, 1954: 14)

Peter Edgerly Firchow (2008: 90–94) has commented on the 'laboratory situation'-like nature of the novel (Firchow, 2008: 92–93), evidenced most clearly in its thoroughly implausible non-account of how it was that the boys became 'lost,' meaning, how they managed to arrive at the Island-of-Nameless-Things and the circumstances under which they arrived. For the entire narrative of the text hinges upon the state of affairs of pure absurdity that is the 'scattering': that all of the previously socialized groups of public-school boys manage to 'fall' (allegorically as well as physically) out of the sky and make landfall as total strangers who are physically isolated from each other. Firchow quite rightly notes that there is 'no discussion of why there are no injuries to the surviving children, or why some of them appear to be scattered over the island' (Firchow, 2008: 94) but manages to miss the point[10]: the 'scattering' of the boys mirrors the Hobbesian state of nature that narratively precedes the allegorically 'temporal' moment of the foundational act of

[10] Although he tries not to. Firchow's explanation is Golding's dated penchant for existentialism: 'Existentialism would account for the otherwise inexplicable way the boys 'drop in' on the island by analogy to the way we have all "dropped in" on life—also an inexplicable and even absurd event' (Firchow, 2008: 92).

the primeval Assembly that establishes the social contract of the common power that differentiates the contending sovereignties but with one crucial difference: the boys are already civilized which makes their mis-recognized regression into barbarism a collective display of mimetic performativity. It is not merely the case that the boys start out being wholly alienated from each other; Golding's double Hobbesian and pre-Girardian text absolutely requires that they be a population of utter strangers so that the proto-transactional analysis of *Leviathan* may be enacted, the true nature of the 'laboratory condition' that Firchow rightly identifies.

Note how the complex narrative of the Chap. 1 ('The Sound of the Shell') manages to both encapsulate Hobbes' foundational concerns and successfully anticipates, or foreshadows, all of the Hobbesian themes that will play themselves out to the homicidal end of the later chapters. And quite revealingly, it begins with the issue of language and representation, the text initially appearing to endorse the representational nature of language. The iconic conch serves as the literally 'natural' symbol of authority and reason as embedded within the landscape: 'Let him be the chief with the trumpet-thing' (Golding, 1954: 19). The second is that the state of nature is identical to the absence of the common power. The third is that the successful creation of the common power guarantees the elimination of that self-same state of nature. The first thing that the boys must do is to establish some rules—'That's why Ralph made a meeting. So as we can decide what to do' (Golding, 1954: 17)—including the maintenance of the all-important bonfire that will be used to perpetually generate a smoke-signal. To do so, and being well-mannered English schoolboys per Elias, they collectively and voluntarily subordinate themselves to the procedure of democratic Assembly and structured debate; both proto-rituals are signified by the holding of the conch, now taken as the master-sign of political reason and rational speech as per Hobbes. In short, all the boys voluntarily enter into a political compact premised upon the act of conveyance of their 'freedom' (isolation) toward the group, or, less charitably, the crowd which is for Hobbes the 'mutual transferring of Right is that which men call CONTRACT' (Hobbes, 1992: 94). As the boys discover for themselves, the entering into the social contract is the foundational act that creates the legal and political community; 'To *lay down* a man's *right* to anything, is to *divest* himself of the *liberty* of hindering another of his own right to the same' (Hobbes, 1992: 92). Matters are immediately complicated, however, by the intuitive realization that pure democracy is inadequate: the state of emergency—'We've got to decide about being rescued' (Golding, 1954: 18)—a life or death situation compounded by the absence of any grown-ups, or 'natural' leaders, the ones who stand in an unmediated relationship to the model of sovereignty, requires the self-selection of an executive power: a chief (Golding, 1954: 18–19).

> The only way to erect such a Common Power, as may be able to defend men from the invasion of foreigners and the injuries of one another…is *to confer all their power and strength upon one Man, or upon one Assembly of men, that may reduce all their own Wills by plurality of voices into one Will*; which is as much to say, to appoint one Man, or Assembly of men, to bear their Person; and every one to own, and acknowledge himself to be the author of whatsoever he that bears their Person, shall act, or cause to act, in those things which concern the common peace and safety; and therein to submit their Wills, everyone to his Will, and

their Judgments to his Judgment. This is more than consent or concordance; it is a real unity to them all, in one and the same person, made by the contract of every man with every man, in such a manner as if every man should say to every man, *I authorize and give up my right of governing myself to this man, or to this Assembly of men, on this condition, that you give up your right to him, and authorize all of his actions in like manner.* This done, the multitude so united in one person, is called a Commonwealth…This is the generation of that great LEVIATHAN, or…of that *Mortal God*. (Hobbes, 1992: 120)

For anyone who is familiar with *Leviathan*, or the great Beast from the Waters, the paradox at chthonic work in the novel is now in clear view: with Hobbes the completion of the social contract which is identical to the suspension of the state of nature constitutes the true beginning of civilizational ascent whereas with Golding it is the beginning of the (apparent) descent, colloquially known as 'the downward spiral into violence'. Read (somewhat didactically) from a law-and-literature perspective, *Lord* forces us to consider whether the contractarian theory of the foundation of law is adequate or whether 'something else' besides rational and self-interested contracting is necessary to explain the existence and nature of the State. As the saga of the boys goes on to show, both violence and non-rational forms of thought and speech cannot be suspended by the act of contract alone; it must be assimilated directly into the community by means of symbolic transference. And as the unruly protagonists learn for themselves, the successful completion of the legal and political order ('the State') can only come with the institutionalization of a mechanism of ritualistic sacrifice—or religion. The established Church of *religare* and *relegare* cannot, in the final instance, be separated from the State; rather, it must be collectively accepted as the true foundation of the community provided that the mystifying veil covering the originary act of foundational violence can remain tact.

And all of this because of a Beast which, like the island itself, remains unnamed.

2.3 From the State to Religion: Justice as Vengeance

The most remarkable feature of *Leviathan* was its uncompromising exclusion of Religion from political discourse; the social contract, as a self-grounding activity, is to be preserved from the contra-rational subjectivity of private faith; organized religion is to be understood solely as an instrument of government.

From this consolidation of the Right Politique, and Ecclesiastique in Christian Soveraigns, it is evident, they have all manner of Powers over their Subjects, that can be given to man, for the government of men's externall actions, both in Policy and Religion; and may make such Laws, as themselves shall judge fittest, for the government of their own Subjects, both as they are the Common-wealth, and as they are the Church: for both State, and Church are the same men. (Hobbes, 1992: 377–378; 375–379; 479–480)

Two of the four books of *Leviathan* are devoted to organized Religion and the Church[11]; yet in this text, unlike elsewhere in his writings, Hobbes' sole concern

[11] Book Three, 'Of a Christian Common-Wealth', 255–415, and Book Four, 'Of the Kingdome of Darknesse', or, more simply, Roman Catholicism (Hobbes, 1992: 417–482).

is with the relative value of *civil* Religion: not only the strict separation of private conscience from public speech, but the wholesale subordination of ecclesiastical institutions to secular power. Religious belief and its accompanying language are themselves devoid of persuasive value, the poetical expression of mere subjective opinion and unruly passion.[12] A problem for my reading of *Lord* emerges at this point: my interpretation accepts the text as an allegorical acting out of the political imaginary of the cultural logic of the social contract, culminating in Jack's establishment of the 'cult' of the Beast. We also know that religion formed an essential part of Golding's abiding concern as an author. How do we manage the ambiguities generated by Golding's (implicit) appropriation of an 'a-theistick' work for the purposes of a quasi-religious allegory?

An answer lies with juxtaposing Hobbes' revolutionary materialism with an equally challenging anthropological model of cultural formation that privileges religion as the source of society, specifically Girard's radically anti-secularist fundamental anthropology that posits religion is the true foundation of culture (Girard, 1977: 43–50; Kirwan, 2005). As I have already discussed in Chap. 1, Girard's hybridization of Durkheim's Functionalist sociology and Freud's psych-analytic critique of religion provides us with a highly original and unorthodox form of legal anthropology.

> The efficiency of our judicial system conceals the problem [of violence], and the elimination of the problem conceals from us the role played by religion The air of mystery that primitive societies acquire for us is undoubtedly due in large part to this misunderstanding. It is undoubtedly responsible for our extreme views of these societies, our insistence on portraying them alternately as vastly superior or flagrantly inferior to our own. One factor alone might well be responsible for our oscillation between extremes, our radical evaluations: the absence in ['primitive'] societies of a judicial system. … If we compare societies that adhere to a judicial system with societies that practice sacrificial rites, the difference between the two is such that we can indeed consider the absence or presence of these [judicial] institutions as a basis for distinguishing primitive societies from 'civilised' ones. (Girard, 1977: 18–19)

The foundational, but thoroughly mis-recognized, continuity between the modern and the archaic is of course a classic trope of Freudian psycho-analysis. Yet, Girard largely eschews the Freudian theory of drive, or instinct (*Trieb*), finding greater insight in the application of psycho-analysis to the collective (impersonal) dynamics of cultural formation; in effect, the translation of Freud's late metapsychology into the referential terms of Durkheim's notion of function: 'The purpose of the sacrifice is to restore harmony to the community, to reinforce the social fabric. Everything else derives from that' (Girard, 1977: 8). For Girard, the 'fundamental truth about violence' is that, 'if left unappeased, violence will accumulate until it overflows its confines and floods the surrounding area. The role of sacrifice is to stem this rising tide of indiscriminate substitutions and redirect violence into "proper" channels.' (Girard, 1977: 10). Key to the success of the sacrificial mechanism is its status as ritual which is invariably a 're-enactment of a "prior event"' (Mack, 1987: 8). Since every ritual

---

[12] See for example Chap. 31 of Book Three, 'Of the Kingdom of God By Nature', wherein Hobbes restricts proper religious speech to that uniformity of public worship governed directly by civil law (Hobbes, 1992: 245–254).

is a re-enactment, its governing logic is mimesis, the ritual is both a representation and a substitution for an earlier crisis of violence. But this governing logic is pre-representational: under the sign of substitution, all differences are abolished and any one thing can be traded for and replaced with any other thing. Since 'sacrifice is always a question of substitution, it is always possible to make a new substitution and henceforth to sacrifice only a substitute of a substitute' (Girard et al., 1987: 53). The vital ritualistic dimension of the sacrificial mechanism is the mimetic evocation of an earlier act of killing that was successful in resolving social crisis.

> [T]he sacrificers ... are striving to produce a replica, as faithful as possible in every detail, of a previous crisis that was resolved by means of a spontaneously unanimous victimization All the dangers, real and imaginary, that threaten the community are subsumed in the most terrible danger that can confront a society: the sacrificial crisis. The rite is therefore a repetition of the original, spontaneous 'lynching' that restored order in the community by reestablishing, around the figure of the surrogate victim [the scapegoat], that sentiment of social accord that had been destroyed in the onslaught of reciprocal violence. ... In the scapegoat theme we should recognize the very real metamorphosis of reciprocal violence into restraining through the agency of unanimity. (Girard, 1977: 94–95, 96)

In other words, the social value of scapegoating, as measured through its effectiveness in resolving the crisis of violence, would be sufficient in itself to force a reconsideration of the paramountcy of purely representational speech. Every ritual bears the traces of a double movement: the re-invocation of the past event and the projection of that earlier event's cathartic effect into future time. The 'prior event' that all ritual killings represent through mimetic substitution is a collective murder, an act of mob violence. '"Sacrifice" then becomes a term that can be used to refer to the complex phenomenon of the collective killing of a human victim, its mythic rationalization, and its ritualization' (Mack, 1987: 8). Collective murder mediated by ritual is the true beginning of human culture, and the scapegoat is the first cultural artifact of human history, the necessary precondition for the historical survival of the community is the successful exorcism of the unclean spirit of violence. This is secured through the periodic enactment of the rituals of the machinery of sacrifice, which is itself the mimetic repetition of an earlier killing of a designated victim (the scapegoat) which successfully broke the cycle of retributive violence. And, from this absolutely elementary chain of signifiers, grounded upon a langue of pre-representation, comes the panoply of early civilization: 'All systems that give structure to human society have been generated from [the scapegoat mechanism]: language, kinship systems, taboos, codes of etiquette, patterns of exchange, rites, and civil institutions. Thus a theory of sacrifice has produced a comprehensive account of human social formation, religion, and culture' (Mack, 1987: 7). Meaning that the entirety of the cultural logic of civilization itself is sacrificial.

The first of several obvious questions to be asked here is: why, exactly, is the will-to-violence so virulent?[13] Girard's answer is that the ferocity of social violence is structurally embedded within the form of its transmission, best understood as a form of contagion.

[13] See Chap. 1, above.

> Why does the spirit of revenge, wherever it breaks out, constitute such an intolerable menace? Perhaps because the only satisfactory revenge for spilt blood is spilling the blood of the killer; and in the blood feud there is no clear distinction between the act for which the killer is being punished and the punishment itself. Vengeance professes to be an act of reprisal, and every reprisal calls for another reprisal. The crime to which the act of vengeance addresses itself is almost never an unprecedented offense; in almost every case it has been committed in revenge for some prior crime. (Girard, 1977: 14)

Homo Sapiens, unlike other animals, is assumed by Girard to lack a genetically inscribed 'braking mechanism' for intra-group aggression: the dynamic of intra-community relationships leads automatically to a proliferating escalation of retribution. Violence within the human community can be nothing else other than endemic, or contagious; since the 'only answer to murder is another murder, cycles of reciprocal retaliation create unending series of revenge-killings. To bring the series to an end, a "final" killing is necessary. The final killing is achieved in the "mechanism of the surrogate victim"' (Mack, 1987: 8). On one level, this is nothing more than an exceptionally elegant and sophisticated restatement of the principle of vendetta, the primary retributive mechanism of 'primitive' justice (inclusive of the modern vigilante) recognized as a universal phenomenon by legal anthropology. Girard's true originality begins to emerge when he expands upon the first insight.

> Vengeance, then, is an interminable, infinitely repetitive process. Every time it turns up in some part of the community, it threatens to involve the whole social body. There is the risk that the act of vengeance will initiate a chain reaction whose consequences will quickly prove fatal to any society of modest size. The multiplication of reprisals instantaneously puts the very existence of a society in jeopardy, and that is why it is universally proscribed. (Girard, 1977: 14–15)

Language counts. The phrase 'interminable, infinitely repetitive process' directly evokes pre-representational language in which every action or event is taken as being in some sense identical to every other. And it was precisely the pre-representational mode of thought that permitted the scapegoat mechanism to emerge, facilitating the development of the religious praxis of what eventually came to be known as law. But the deeper, and mis-recognized, anthropological truth is that law could not evolve without the presence of violence as its double.

> Vengeance is a vicious circle whose effect on primitive societies can only be surmised. For us the circle has been broken. We owe our good fortune to one of our social institutions above all: our judicial system, which serves to deflect the menace of vengeance. The system does not suppress vengeance; rather, it effectively limits it to a single act of reprisal, enacted by a sovereign authority specializing in this particular function. The decisions of the judiciary are invariably presented as the final word on vengeance. (Girard, 1977: 15)

For us moderns, justice-as-revenge has been effectively superseded by, or, in less Hegelian terms, thoroughly sublimated into the universalist rule of law and the impersonal formalism of due process. I would expect the contemporary reader to tolerate Girard's assumptions concerning the archaic genealogy of judicial modernity, although our prejudice would be in favor of the irreversibility of the long progressive narrative of over-coming: any deviation from, or reversal of, the global course of universal secularization can be nothing other than barbarism.[14] But I also think that what the typical reader would unreservedly reject is Girard's valorization of the theological as the vital cultural mechanism at work in the human drama. Our common inclination to view religion as the master-sign of social dysfunction and cultural pathology would make such a notion secular heresy. It does sound uncannily like William Golding, however, for his faith was the same as Girard. Which is why that in the end it is Jack who wins and Ralph and Piggy who lose, for he is the only one who understands that religion works. Which means that he is the only one who understands that violence works.

2.4 'I'm the Reason Why It's No Go…": Rene Girard and Max Scheler on Mimesis and *Ressentiment*

For Girard, the plot, or drama, of the novel is driven by an escalating rivalry over mimetic desire that eventually explodes into full-scale mimetic conflict. For Girard, the archetypal plot of all literature is that the Self (protagonist) will model its relationship to the Other (double) on the basis of imitation (mimetic rivalry) that will narratively culminate in the Self attempting to either replace and/or destroy the double (mimetic conflict).

> Rivalry does not arise because of the fortuitous convergence of two desires on a single object; rather, *the subject desires the object because the rival desires it*. In desiring an object the rival alerts the subject to the desirability of the object. The rival, then, serves as the model for the subject, not only in regard to such secondary matters as style and opinions but also, and more essentially, in regard to desires. (Girard, 1977: 145)[15]

If this holds then it also holds that, for those concerned with mimesis as social force, there is something highly problematic about what we ordinarily take to be 'democracy,' usually reduced to a generic liberalism, a moderately flexible system of social relations punctuated by 'free elections'. For his part, Elias clearly has a problem with democracy, recognizing it as inseparable from a potentially all-encompassing crisis of the collapse of cultural distinctions, necessary components of the machinery of the civilizing process.

> It is one of the peculiarities of Western society that, in the course of its development, this contrast between the situation and the code of conduct of the upper and lower strata has decreased considerably. Lower-class characteristics are spreading to all classes. The fact that Western society as a whole has gradually become a society where every able person is expected to earn his living through a highly regulated type of work is a symptom of this: earlier, work was an attribute of the lower classes. And, at the same time, what used to be distinguishing features of the upper class are likewise spreading to society at large. … if the whole sweep of the movement over centuries is perceived, one can see that the sharp contrasts between the behaviour of different social groups—like the contracts and sudden

[14] See Chap. 11, below.

[15] See Chap. 1, above.

> switches within the behaviour of individuals—are steadily diminishing. … This reduction in the contrasts within society as within individuals, this peculiar commingling of patterns of conduct deriving from initially very different social levels, is highly characteristic of Western society. It is one of the most important peculiarities of the 'civilizing process'. (Elias, 2000: 383)

Cultural egalitarianism would seem to closely follow the collapse of spatial demarcations: as the economy of the eighteenth century incrementally converted to industrial capitalism, it became impossible for the Second Estate (the Nobility) to practically manage its materials affairs (i.e. avoiding bankruptcy) in social isolation from the increasingly rapacious burghers of the Third Estate (the middle-class). Form follows function.

> For the courtly nobility … the self-restraint imposed on them by their function and situation served at the same time as a prestige value, a means of distinguishing themselves from the lower groups harrying them, and they did everything within their power to prevent these differences from being effaced. … [However] Owing to the peculiar form of interdependence in which they lived, the court aristocracy could not prevent—indeed, through their contacts with rich bourgeois strata whom they needed for one reason or another, they assisted—the spreading of their manners, their customs, their tastes and their language to other classes. … Here too the force of the current of inter-weaving as a whole, the tensions and competition leading within it to ever-greater complexity and functional differentiation, to the individual's dependence on an ever-larger number of others, to the rise of broader and broader classes, proved stronger than the barricade which the nobility had been seeking to build around themselves. (Elias, 2000: 387)

But this entire line of argument is lifted wholesale by one of the truly great cultural analysts of the nineteenth century, Alexis de Tocqueville, who, in his masterpiece *Democracy in America* (1835–1840), accurately prophesizes that these USA will inevitably descend into increasingly catastrophic political conflict not because of an absence of democracy but because of a surplus of creeping egalitarianism.

> When all the privileges of birth and fortune are abolished, when all professions are accessible to all, and a man's own energies may place him at the top of any one of them, an easy and unbounded career seems open to his ambition and he will readily persuade himself that he is born to no common destinies. But this is an erroneous notion, which is corrected by daily experience. The same equality that allows every citizen to conceive these lofty hopes, renders all the citizens less able to realize them; it circumscribes their powers on every side, which gives freer scope to their desires. … They have swept away the privileges of some of their fellow-creatures which stood in their way, but they have opened the door to universal competition; the barrier has changed its shape rather than its position. (De Tocqueville, 1990: II 137–138)

And the rivalry, or 'universal competition,' that mimetic desire unleashes will, in the end, assume the most extreme and grotesque form of the violent, or 'monstrous' doubles who are the signifiers of the crisis of distinction: as the rivals intensify their mimetic struggle they effectively become identical, triggering a pathological crisis of identity which can only be resolved through an act of extreme violence, whether physical, emotional or symbolic (Girard, 1977: 143–168). Historically, the ritualistic enshrinement of the scapegoat, or sacrificial, mechanism was the domain of religion, which was anthropologically grounded upon the intermediary of the surrogate victim—the one who must die so that the community may live by being spared the 'apocalypse of the un-differentiated', the sign of the mimetic collapse of distinctions. 'Religious thought is…led to make the victim the vehicle and transforming agent of something sacred—mimesis—which is never conflictual or undifferentiated except in so far as it is spread throughout the community; its concentration in a victim makes it a pacifying and regulating force, the positive mimesis found in ritual' (Girard et al., 1987: 48). Therefore

> To understand human culture it is necessary to concede that only the damming of mimetic forces by means of the prohibition and the diversion of those forces in the direction of ritual are capable of spreading and perpetuating the reconciliatory effect of the surrogate victim. Religion is nothing other than this immense effort to keep the peace. *The sacred is violence*, but if religious man worships violence it is only insofar as the worship of violence is supposed to bring peace; religion is entirely concerned with peace, but the means it has of bringing it about are never free of sacrificial violence. (Girard et al., 1987: 32)[16]

But this insight is not just applicable to religion and literature—if true, then it can be directly applied to politics and, by implication, to law as well. And de Tocqueville recognized this as well, although perhaps for the wrong reasons, demonstrating that he too was a victim of *meconnaissance.*

> Men cannot abandon their religious faith without a kind of aberration of intellect and a sort of violent distortion of their true nature; they are invincibly brought back to more pious sentiments. Unbelief is an accident, and faith is the only permanent state of mankind. If we consider religious institutions merely from a human point of view, they may be said to derive an inexhaustible element of strength from man himself, since they belong to one of the constituent principles of human nature. (De Tocqueville, 1990: I 310)

That which may remain mis-recognized here is the erroneous substitution of human nature for human culture, or, at least, of social psychology.

As one part of his broader attempt to make Friedrich Nietzsche into a 'respectable' thinker, Max Scheler published his most memorable work *Ressentiment* in 1912, two years before the great pan-European settling of scores, or attempted resolution of intolerable rivalries. Clearly channeling the self-proclaimed 'anti-Christ,'[17] Scheler interprets *ressentiment*, the French word for 'revenge,' as nothing less than the phenomenological basis of the culture of 'bourgeois morality' and, therefore, of the social psychology of political modernity.

> *Ressentiment* is a self-poisoning of the mind which has quite definite causes and consequences. It is a lasting mental attitude, caused by the systematic repression of certain emotions and affects which, as such, are normal components of human nature. Their repression leads to the constant tendency to indulge in certain kinds of value delusions and corresponding value judgments. The emotions and affects primarily concerned are revenge, hatred, malice, envy, the impulse to detract, and spite. (Scheler, 2010: 25)

Scheler is in deadly earnestness about the literally psycho-somatic pathologies that *ressentiment* inflicts, likening it to a kind of psychic repression mechanism

---

[16] For the integrative function of Religion see Dietrich et al. (2012).

[17] See Chaps. 11 and 12, below.

conducive to emotional constipation or blockage culminating in a dual mechanism of both displacement and substitution wherein the psychically constipated middle-class person voluntarily erases their own identity as a means of relieving the intolerable pain of being eternally powerless.

> Revenge is distinguished by two essential characteristics. First of all, the immediate reactive impulse, with the accompanying emotions of anger and rage, is temporarily or at least momentarily checked and restrained, and the response is consequently postponed to a later time and more suitable occasion ('just wait till next time'[18]). This blockage is caused by the reflection that an immediate reaction would lead to defeat, and by the concomitant pronounced feeling of 'inability' and 'impotence'. Thus, even revenge as such, based as it is upon an experience of impotence, is always primarily a matter of those who are 'weak' in some respect. Furthermore, it is of the essence of revenge that it always constrains the *consciousness* of 'tit for tat,' so that it is never a mere emotional reaction. (Scheler, 2010: 25)

Ressentiment is a specific figure of mimetic desire that is typical of contemporary society, where the equality that is proclaimed at the level of values contrasts with striking inequalities of power and access to material resources. This dichotomy generates increasing tension between highly competitive and egalitarian mimetic desires and growing social inequalities which means that the only viable solution is the performance of some kind of retaliatory action: 'The desire for revenge disappears when vengeance has been taken, when the person against whom it was directed has been punished or has punished himself, or when one truly forgives him. In the same way, envy vanishes when the envied possession becomes ours' (Scheler, 2010: 26).

The relevance of Scheler's neo-Nietzschean working of revenge for mimetic theory are obvious; Girard's relationship with Scheler is complex, for although he critiques the latter for his failure to situate the elements of *ressentiment* into a social dynamic, he concedes that.

> The analysis is accurate and complete; it omits neither the envious person's self-deception with regard to the cause of his failure, nor the paralysis that accompanies envy. But these elements remain isolated; Scheler has not really perceived their relationship. On the other hand everything becomes clear, everything fits into a coherent structure if, in order to explain envy, we abandon the object of rivalry as a starting point and choose instead the rival himself, i.e., the mediator, as both a point of departure for our analysis and its conclusion. (Girard, 1965: 13)

The real gift that Scheler confers on Girard is the understanding that *ressentiment* provides the ideal means of providing if not a literally materialist base for mimetic theory then at least a kind of historical sociology grounded upon fluctuations in spatially and temporally specific fluctuations in class dynamics, permitting Girard to effectively dodge the bullet of a-historicism; 'everything becomes clear, everything fits into a coherent structure if, in order to explain envy, we abandon the object of rivalry as a starting point and choose instead the rival himself, i.e., the mediator, as both a point of departure for our analysis and its conclusion' (Girard, 1965: 13). Said

[18] I discuss the blinding relevance of this to Piggy below.

another way, everything becomes clear if we embed the mediator within a specific political and cultural landscape which provides a context for the specific operations of patterned mimetic relations without nullifying the underlying universalism of mimesis and mimetic desire as such. External mediation is nothing more than the mimetic economy of a hierarchical class system that aims to regulate the bright-line distinctions among and between divergent and amorphous social groupings. With de Tocqueville clearly in mind, Marc Ferro has suggested that a revolutionary change in the dynamics of mimetic relations occurred during the French Revolution (1789–1815): the 'political reason' of class struggle notwithstanding, the vital spark that ignited the conflagration that became the first truly modern war appears to have been the Second Estate's (the aristos) repeated attempts to pre-empt its imminent convergence with the 'bourgeois' Third Estate (the commoners) and the insufferable insults that these attempts spawned (Ferro, 2010: 21–31). For Robespierre, along with all of the other Jacobins, the political was deeply personal. But so too in the opposite of an absolutist society, the more economically innovate 'commercial republic' wherein mimetic conflict is resolved through the direct competition between the role model and the imitating/envious subject via internal mediation as the mimetic form of an approximately egalitarian class structure (Palaver, 2013: 59). The saving virtue of this plan is that free and open competition will reduce the political toxin of *ressentiment* by allowing everyone the opportunity to advance and acquire social recognition. The fatal flaw of this plan is that the anti-mimetic project of commercial republicanism is Sissyphean: there is no end point to be reached but all things are in eternally frustrated motion; 'As the metaphysical distance between desiring subject and model diminishes [...] the potential for rivalry and violence increases' (Palaver, 2013: 61)—this we already know. What is new is that internal mediation does not merely end in a generic and haphazard violence ('the riot' or 'the lynching'), but in a very unique and singularly destructive form of psychic pathology and mimetic contagion: the-eternal-recurrence-of-the-will-to-revenge. As Stefano Tomelleri powerfully expresses it.

> ...ressentiment is a symptom of internal mediation It arises from the illusion of infinite freedom within a mimetic context. It is an invasive emotion that does not just affect private life, but also dominates the public sphere (Tomelleri, 2015: 94).... Society seems increasingly individualistic, but an analysis of mimetic ressentiment shows that an individualist mentality also arises from the logic that leads to ressentiment. People imagine realizing an individualist and authentic desire when in reality everything needs a mediator in order to find a new desire, a need that is increasingly exaggerated by the paradoxical combination between growing competition among equals and an equally arising social inequality. All are thus condemned to a fundamental dissatisfaction that leads to a desire that finds no rest. (Tomelleri, 2015: 93)

But this is not the worst of it, not even remotely. It is bad enough that 'we covet what we see' (according to Hannibal Lecter); what is truly hideous is that we hate most passionately those who are closest to us, precisely because they are our immediate competitors, the only rival imitators of the model whom we can actually get our hands on and do violence to directly.[19] It is only when we are most up-close-and-personal that we really want to sink the axe into our neighbor. Yet one more pillar of liberal

[19] Although social media has changed this somewhat—homicidal mania at a distance.

humanitarianism needs to be torn down: the insufferable moralistic conceit that we only hate those whom we do not know.

> It is a misapprehension to assume that human bestialities require social distance or any depersonalization and dehumanization of victims. In Algeria, survivors in many cases recognized former neighbours, friends, and even relatives among their murderers. During the 'ethnic cleansing' in the former Yugoslavia, many of the incendiary murderers were particularly brutal with neighbours and co-workers from their villages. Proximity, not anonymity, brings about the most vicious atrocities; far from increasing the threshold of attack, it heightens the passion of violence. (Wolfgang Sofsky qtd. in Palaver, 2013: 63)

And if the 'grown-ups' cannot manage their affairs any better than this, then how are a group of pre-adolescent mainly upper-middle-class English public schoolboys to fare?

2.5 'They Used to Call Me "Piggy"': *Meconnaissance*, Undifferentiation, and Censorship

According to Girard, people 'can dispose of their violence more efficiently if they regard the process not as something emanating from within themselves, but as a necessity imposed from without, a divine decree whose least infraction calls down terrible punishment' (Girard, 1977: 14). From this it follows that when 'we minimize the dangers implicit in vengeance we risk losing sight of the true function of sacrifice' (Girard, 1977: 18). We need to examine with care that process Girard posits at the core of primitive religion as the circuit-breaker that pre-empts the contagion of violence spread through retributive acts of vengeance: the sacrificial machinery of the scapegoat. The internal cultural logic of the mechanism operates by means of the mimetic transference of collective violence toward a sacrificial substitute/surrogate (the 'surrogate victim') who is symbolically re-constituted as the contagious and contaminating source of all hatred and vengeance, that social dysfunction which Hobbes pointedly identified with 'Grief'.[20] This explains the most obvious, and well known, characteristic of the sacrificial victim: its impurity (pollution; stain) as a sin-bearing object.[21] Out of necessity, the scapegoat must always be socially marginal in some way, an expendable victim, human or animal, whose death will not

---

[20] See below.

[21] Which is one of the crucial demarcations between 'primitive' religions and the later Hellenistic paganisms and monotheistic faiths; for Girard the transformation of the status of the victim is the master-sign of a cultural revolution. In the 'primitive phase' of religion, the victim itself is impure or contaminated in some way, and purification, always communal, is achieved through the sacrifice/expulsion/destruction of the surrogate. But, beginning with Greek Tragedy and the later Hebrew prophets, such as in the Book of Job (the spawning ground of Leviathan), the victim becomes elevated through the reversal of the binary logic of impurity/purity: the victim, beloved of the god(s) is him or herself inherently pure but becomes an object of supernatural power and value (the original meaning of pollution, meaning a dangerous magic) by drawing unto themselves the collective impurity of the group (Girard, 1977). See Chap. 1, above.

cause violence to rebound because no one will bother to avenge them but which, for whatever reason, can serve as the focus of universal opprobrium.

> All our sacrificial victims, whether chosen from one of the human categories [slave; prisoner; captive] or...from the animal realm, are invariably distinguishable from the non-sacrificeable beings by one essential characteristic: between these victims and the community a crucial link is missing, so they can be exposed to violence without fear of reprisal. Their death does not automatically entail an act of vengeance. The considerable importance this freedom from reprisal has for the sacrificial process makes us understand that sacrifice is primarily an act of violence without risk of vengeance...The desire to commit an act of violence on those near us cannot be suppressed without a conflict; we must divert that impulse, therefore, toward the sacrificial victim, the creature we can strike down without fear of reprisal, since he lacks a champion. (Girard, 1977: 13)

On another level, one of unexpected depth, the scapegoat is always the object of a double transference: not only is the victim chosen to be the bearer of the collective sins of the community through some inherent but usually invisible flaw of its nature, but through the projection of sin into the alien object the community temporarily releases itself from its capacity for violence, which, because mimetic, remains eternally latent. The psychic price to be paid for this ritualistic transference is high: if sacrifice is the essence of religion and religion the essence of community, then the social body must constantly mis-recognize the violence of its own origins, precisely because, as Hobbes intuited, we adhere to the group precisely in order to subdue the violence within and to shield ourselves from the threat of violence from the outside. This collective act of *meconnaissance* usually seeks some sort of outlet through emotional or symbolic displacement, a process that is historically without end, because, in accordance with the logic of atavism, the recapitulation of undesirable 'primitive' traits within the more 'advanced' organism (biological or cultural) will always work to undermine the stable and stabilizing differences between the primitive and the advanced.

From a law-and-literature perspective, this dilemma is most evident in the liminality, or reversibility, that operates between both 'public' and 'private' justice and between natural law and positive law, as has been clearly recognized by Girard.-

> Vocabulary is perhaps more revealing here than judicial theories. Once the concept of interminable revenge has been formally rejected, it is referred to as *private* vengeance. The term implies the existence of a *public* vengeance, a counterpart never made explicit. By definition, primitive societies have only private vengeance. Thus, public vengeance is the exclusive property of well-policed societies, and our society calls it the judicial system. (Girard, 1977: 15)

It should now be obvious why Girard's highly original theory of mimesis serves as the philosophical antithesis of the contractual rationality of Hobbes' Commonwealth: words are radically disassociated from facts; therefore, the scapegoat is both profoundly true (subjective) and completely false (objective) at the same moment. Richard Tuck's excellent commentary upon Hobbes is very helpful on this point.

> The problem which exercised Hobbes, almost alone among the theorists of his time, was that even if men are basically self-protective and therefore in principle pacific towards one another, their independency of judgment about the world will lead to conflict. His proposed

> solution was therefore to eliminate independent judgment about most matters of fact. Natural man, he argued, would see the necessity for everyone to transfer their individual judgment in cases of uncertainty to a common-decision-maker, whose opinion about what constitutes a threat would be conclusive. (Tuck, 1992: xvii)

Hobbes is clearly situated within the classical episteme of the seventeenth century, signified by the onto-epistemological apparatus of the *camera obscura*: sensory data may be inherently unreliable but they can be assigned precise evidentiary value through the correct perception by and operation of an irreducible Mind that itself is devoid of constituent parts.[22] Technically Hobbes was a nominalist; like Descartes, he was extremely skeptical concerning the validity of sensory knowledge (Tuck, 1992: xiv, xv). However, as Tuck has pointed out, Hobbes, also like Descartes, was concerned to 'emphasise that a mind can know, without any doubt, whatever went on purely within itself. He put into this category all language—which he took to be the labelling of our internal experiences by terms intended to help us in recalling and organising them' (Hobbes, 1992: 31–37; Tuck, 1992: xv).If we take the time to read Book One of *Leviathan*, where Hobbes lays out his representational theory of knowledge (Hobbes, 1992: 13–115), we find that it is premised upon an equally robust representational theory of language consisting of three distinct propositions. The first, and most foundational, is a radical but simple Empiricism: sensation is the source of all human knowledge.

> The Originall of them all [the Thoughts of Men], is that which we call SENSE; (For if there is no conception in a man's mind, which hath not at first, totally, or by parts, been begotten upon organs of Sense). The rest are derived from the original...All which qualities called *Sensible*, are in the object that causeth them, but so many several notions of the matter, by which it presseth our organs diversely. (Hobbes, 1992: 13 and 14)

The second is an equally robust anti-Skepticism, tantamount to a form of Rationalism: the Self can be rendered transparent to itself for language is perfectible. Again as with Descartes, knowledge, mediated through correct language, can achieve self-validation, or self-grounding.

> For it is most true that *Cicero* sayth of [the Philosophers] somewhere; that there can be nothing so absurd, but may be found in the books of Philosophers. And the reason is manifest. For there is not one of them that begins his ratiocination from the Definitions, or Explications of the names they are to use; which is a method that hath been used onely in Geometry[23]; whose Conclusions have thereby been made indisputable. The first cause of Absurd conclusions I ascribe to the want of Method; in that they begin not their Ratiocination from Definitions; that is, from settled significations of their words: as if they could cast account, without knowing the value of the numerall words, *one, two, three*...By this it appears that Reason is not as Sense, and Memory, borne with us; nor gotten by Experience onely, as Prudence is; but attained by Industry; first in apt imposing of Names; and secondly by getting a good and orderly Method in proceeding from the Elements, which are Names, to Assertions made by

[22] 'Thus the *camera obscura* is inseparable from a certain metaphysics of interiority: it is a figure of both the observer who is a nominally free sovereign and a privatized subject confined in a quasi-domestic space, cut off from a public exterior world' (Crary, 1990: 39, 25–66).

[23] The fetishization of Geometry is a hallmark of dogmatic representation: Geometry 'is the onely Science that it hath pleased God hitherto to bestow upon Mankind' (Hobbes, 1992: 28).

> Connexion of one of them to another, till we come to a knowledge of all the Consequences of names appertaining to the subject in hand; and that is it, men call SCIENCE. (Hobbes, 1992: 34 and 35)

Third is Hobbes' signature contribution, as indicated by Tuck: the premise of the onto-political. Even if neither of the above were true (and it is vital to note the internal frisson, or tensions, that run throughout *Leviathan*), the political and social utility of the enforcement of standard(-ised) judgment makes objectivity and certainty indispensable, even if, perhaps, practically unattainable: the Sovereign is a beast of discourse, the censor of the process of naming (denotation), with the power of the regulation and guaranteeing of 'proper' speech the highest mark of Sovereignty.

> There being nothing simply and absolutely; nor any common Rule of Good and Evill, to be taken from the nature of the objects themselves[24]; but from the Person of the man (where there is no Common-Wealth) or, (in a Common-Wealth,) from the Person that representeth it; or from an Arbitrator or Judge, whom men disagreeing shall by consent set up, and make his sentence the Rule thereof (Hobbes, 1992: 39). ... [the multitude shall] therein ... submit their Wills, everyone to his Will, and their Judgments, to his Judgment. (Hobbes, 1992: 120)[25]

Therefore, the core of Girard's (and Golding's) challenge to Hobbes lies not so much with a pre-representational theory versus a representational one, but rather with the critical interrogation of *Leviathan*'s proclamation of success in attaining self-grounding: the social contract, while intelligible is ultimately impractical, for even if Hobbes succeeds in demonstrating the first and the second propositions (a very tall order) he must necessarily fail with the third. Hobbes' representational theory of knowledge is the foundation of his onto-political theory of the transference, or conveyance, of judgment of fact to a common decision-maker: an executive power that is as much epistemological as it is political. But Hobbes' move is undercut by Girard's theory of mimesis, a paramount instance of the pre-representational approach to language, for it is 'not possible to resolve the problem of violence with the surrogate victim without at the same time elaborating a theory of the sign and signification' (Girard et al., 1987: 99). The social functionality of the sacrificial mechanism depends upon the operation of a literally false but culturally and psychologically effective act of substitution, or *meconnaissance*; 'Violence and the sacred are inseparable. But the covert appropriation by sacrifice of certain properties of violence—particularly the capability of violence to move from one object to another—is hidden from sight by the awesome machinery of ritual' (Girard, 1977: 19). At the same time, the occluded machinery effects a second great transformation:

24 Invariably neutral 'in and of themselves'.

25 Although the term was not developed prior to David Hume in the mid-eighteenth Century, it is fairly clear that Hobbes' dilemma is essentially that of the Is versus Ought dichotomy: even if it were possible to self-ground Reason along the representational principles elucidated by Hobbes it does not follow, from that fact alone, that anyone is actually bound (contractually or otherwise) to follow them. Geometers may really speak the truth, but the vulgar crowd is still governed by its 'base passions'—only direct Executive Action will do the job of enforcing the uniform rules of correct speech and halting the spread of 'mis-information'.

the divinization of the selected victim, so that the 'low' is now rendered identical to, or the 'same thing' as, the 'high'.

> The death of the victim transforms relations within the community. The change from discord to harmony is not attributed to its actual cause, the unifying mimesis of collective violence, but to the victim itself. Religious thought tends to think of everything in terms of the victim, which becomes the focal point of all meaning; the actual principle in the return to order is never perceived. Religious thought conceives of a malevolent quasi-substance, the sacred, which becomes polarized around the victim and is transformed into a beneficent force through the accomplishment of the sacrifice and through the victim's expulsion from the community.
>
> Religious thought is thus led to make the victim the vehicle and transforming agent of something sacred—mimesis—which is never conflictual or undifferentiated except in so far as it is spread throughout the community; its concentration in a victim makes it a pacifying and regulating force, the positive mimesis found in ritual. (Girard et al., 1987: 48).

As Golding's readers knows full well, throughout *Lord* it is the hapless Piggy who serves as the Hobbesian monomaniacal eliminator of 'independent judgment about most matters of fact'. He acts as the 'reality principle' ('So now we can decide on what's what.' (Golding, 1954: 141)) to Ralph's dithering chief, bound by primitive democratic procedure. He is also the novel's paramount scapegoat and its most dramatic sacrificial victim[26]: his own name literally speaks his fate. *Lord* is the working through to the horrific end of the political consequences of a seemingly intractable crisis of representation, the solution of which demands the re-emergence of the religious imaginary that can only be provided by pre-representation, paradoxically resulting in the successful establishment of an indigenous community on a self-sustaining foundation: sacrificial murder.

The narrative spine of *Lord* is a logical sequence of three separate acts of murder (or attempted murder[27]), each one of ascending anthropological and jurisprudential significance, all of which mimetically repeat the co-evolution of religion, law, and

---

[26] The excruciating and prolonged set-up of Piggy's death by a politically incited mob, self-consciously manipulated by Jack and Roger, takes up almost the whole of Chap. 11, 'Castle Rock' (Golding, 1954: 187–202). It is also blackly comic: take, for example Piggy's 'asking for it' remark on page 189: 'I'm going to him [Jack] with this conch in my hands.' By contrast, Simon, the other significant sacrificial victim, is completely dismembered in less than one page at 168. Strikingly, the text spends far more time on the transmogrification of his mutilated carcass than on the actual moment of death which, because it is a spontaneous action by the crowd, is temporally compressed and 'muddled' as both sensation and memory—and denial. See below.

[27] With the exception of the appropriately nameless mulberry-faced boy, the announcer of the presence of the Beast (and, therefore, the author of the violence to come), the accidental victim of the contagion of violence via the conflagration/immolation mediated by the crowd, and the direct precursor of the parade of sacrificial victims to come. His catastrophic exit, an enforced disappearance in effect, encapsulates the entirety of the mimetic discourse of the text. 'The older boys first noticed the child when he resisted. There was a group of little boys urging him forward and he did not want to go. He was a shrimp of a boy, about six years old, and one side of his face was blotted out by a mulberry-coloured birthmark. He stood now, warped out of the perpendicular by the fierce light of publicity, and he bored into the course grass with one toe. He was muttering and about to cry.' He would be well advised to do so; as the anthropologically informed reader is immediately aware, the kid is doomed. And it is none other than Piggy, the pivotal victim of the sacrificial drama to unfold, who proclaims his extermination—perhaps out of an act of unconscious identification. 'The little'un—'gasped Piggy—'him with the mark on his face, I don't see him.

the state. The first victim is Simon, a key member of the Ralph-Piggy led Assembly, who serves as the archetype for the other two victims precisely because his manner of death is the simplest and the most primitive: the ignorant and blind (or arbitrary) violence of the crowd, classically known as *diasparagmos* (Girard, 1977: 131–132), the wholly spontaneous orgiastic or 'Dionysian assault' (Golding, 1954: 168–70). The tearing apart of Simon during the ritualistic frenzy of the crowd's celebration of the hunt is the act that, understandably mis-recognized by the boys as the violent event that temporarily exorcizes the Beast from the island and whom the reader is now aware is really the body of a jet-fighter pilot whose parachute has become entangled in the trees. As Simon is dismembered in frenzy after having been mistakenly identified as the Beast by the crowd,[28] the 'real' Beast undertakes his phantasmagoric migration to the deep waters of the Biblical Leviathan.

> Now a great wind blew the wind sideways, cascading the water from the forest trees. On the mountain-top the parachute filled and moved; the figure slid, rose to its feet, spun, swayed down through a vastness of wet air and trod with ungainly feet the tops of the high trees; falling, still falling, it sank towards the beach and the boys rushed screaming into the darkness. The parachute took the figure forward, furrowing the lagoon, and bumped it over the reef and out to sea. (Golding, 1954: 169)

Wholly consistent with Girard, the accidental victim, involuntarily butchered in Dionysian frenzy, is subsequently sacralized: the murder of the victim 'solves' the immediate crisis (the Beast leaves the island after the cathartic discharge of group violence), so that the victim whose death brings about the exorcism of the thing that is destroying the community is himself invested with supernatural power after the fact: the despised is now the divine and the most basic of all distinctions established. 'Dismemberment is emblematic of triumph and resurrection; it reflects the operation of the surrogate victim, the transformation of maleficent violence in beneficent violence,' (Girard, 1977: 286) so we need to be very precise in our understanding of the occluded nature of this foundational series of events: (i) Simon is murdered by the crowd in an act of collective *meconnaissance* (the victim = the Beast); (ii) the Beast is expelled from the island (temporarily), and; (iii) Simon's body is transfigured as a repository of sacred power. This last point is clearly elaborated in one of the most beautiful passages in the novel, where Simon's mutilated cadaver, submerged in the same waters that have just absorbed the Beast, is invested with the spectral luminosity of the micro-animals of the lagoon.

Where is he now?' The crowd was as silent as death…A tree exploded in the fire like a bomb. Tall swathes of creepers rose for a moment into view, agonized, and went down again The little boys screamed at them. … 'The little'un had a mark on his—face—where is—he now? I tell you I don't see him.' The boys looked at each other fearfully, unbelieving…Beneath them, on the unfriendly side of the mountain, the drum-roll continued' (Golding, 1954: 33–34, 46–47). Another example of text-book foreshadowing.

[28] An 'iconically' Girardian event, as the vulnerability of the selected victim is wholly dependent on the immediate situation of the group. 'If the crisis is moving toward a frenzy, a turbulence of Dionysiac proportions, there is less and less need for preferential signs' so the only thing that makes the boys select Simon is that he just happened to show up at that exact moment. 'When a mob is really frantic, the slightest incident will be interpreted as a sign of someone's guilt' (Girard, 1996: 271–272).

> The edge of the lagoon became a streak of phosphorescence which advanced minutely, as the great wave of the tide flowed. The clear water mirrored the clear sky and the angular bright constellations. … Along the shoreward edge of the shallows the advancing clearness was full of strange, moonbeam-bodied creatures with fiery eyes. … The tide swelled in over the rain-pitted sand and smoothed everything with a coat of pearls. Now it touched the first of the stains that seeped from the broken body and the creatures made a moving path of light as they gathered at the edge. The water rose further and dressed Simon's coarse hair with brightness. The line of his cheek silvered and the turn of his shoulder became sculptured marble. The strange, attendant creatures, with their fiery eyes and trailing vapors, busied themselves round his head. The body lifted a fraction of an inch from the sand and a bubble of air escaped from the mouth with a wet plop. Then it turned gently in the water.
>
> Somewhere over the darkened curve of the world the sun and moon were pulling; and the film of water on the earth planet was held, bulging slightly on one side while the solid core turned. The great wave of the tide moved further along the island and the water lifted. Softly, surrounded by a fringe of inquisitive bright creatures, itself a silver shape beneath the steadfast constellations, Simon's dead body moved out towards the open sea. (Golding, 1954: 169–170)[29]

But most important of all is that Simon is re-cast as a scapegoat only after his death; the 'fault' (sin) of the wrongful murder is retroactively attributed to the victim himself. This constitutes the core of the morning after conversation between Ralph and Piggy, who, as we should expect, is the one boy most in denial over the nature of the events of the night before.

He jumped to his feet and stood over Ralph.

'It was dark. There was that—bloody dance. There was lightning and thunder and rain We was scared!'

'I wasn't scared,' said Ralph slowly, 'I was—I don't know what I was.'

'We was scared!' said Piggy excitedly. 'Anything might have happened. It wasn't –what you said.'

He was gesticulating, searching for a formula.[30]

'Oh Piggy!.'

Ralph's voice, low and stricken, stopped Piggy's gestures. Ralph, cradling the conch rocked himself to and fro.

'Don't you understand Piggy? The things we did—.'…

Ralph continued to rock to and fro.

---

[29] The 'strange, attendant creatures' here invoke the multitude of Henry's 'tiny transparencies' (Golding 1954: 63–64). The presence of micro-organisms in both passages parallels the sub-text of Simon's transformation from victim to redeemer, the transition from profane violence to sacred violence.

[30] As is the wont of Geometers.

'It was an accident,' said Piggy suddenly, 'that's what it was. An accident.' His voice shrilled again 'Coming in the dark—he had no business crawling like that out of the dark. He was batty. He asked for it.' He gesticulated widely again.

'It was an accident—.'

'You didn't see what they did.'

'Look, Ralph. We got to forget this. We can't do no good thinking about it, see?'. (Golding, 1954: 173)

Pregnant with meaning, the dialogue is most notable for juxtaposing the ritualistic features of the *diasparagmos* with the beginning of the end of the Hobbesian political reason of representation: the conch which has been consciously understood by the boys as the sign of the power to invoke the Assembly is now revealed as a prop, or a fetish, leaned upon by Ralph in a clearly infantile manner. What announces itself in a steadily growing crescendo is that the un-nameable nature of the Beast—artificially created through a series of mis-recognitions and un-regulated speech—is the unassimilable thing that forces a fatal crisis of representation that is identical to the revolutionary political transformation of the island Common-Wealth by Jack. Golding's mixture of the political with the epistemic is the narrative motor of the second, and far more elaborate sacrificial act, the death of Piggy as a result of a self-consciously incited act of mob violence. At this point it is worthwhile to discuss Girard's theory of the scapegoat in a bit more detail.

> Strictly speaking, there is no essential difference between animal sacrifice and human sacrifice, and in many cases one is substituted for the other. Our tendency to insist on differences that have little reality when discussing the institution of sacrifice—our reluctance, for example, to equate animal with human sacrifice—is undoubtedly a factor in the extraordinary misunderstandings that still persist in that area of human culture…all victims, even the animal ones, bear a certain *resemblance* to the object they replace; otherwise the violent impulse would remain unsatisfied. (Girard, 1977: 10–11)

And what are the characteristics of the scapegoat that determines his/her identification and selection?

> From within the group, one person is separated out as victim. The selection is arbitrary and spontaneous, though there are requisites. The victim must be recognizable as a surrogate for the guilty party (or parties, and ultimately for the group itself); he must be vulnerable, unable to retaliate, without champions to continue the vengeful violence; and there must be unanimity within the group that he is the one at fault. When this unanimity is achieved the victim is treated as a criminal, killed, and expelled. This brings the violence to an end. The group has redirected its aggressions and its members are now able to cooperate. (Mack, 1987: 8)

The irony that is normally missed by those readers who advocate a moral reading of the novel, ordinarily the same ones who frequently mis-interpret Piggy as the allegorical personification of the salvific 'voice of Reason' or common sense—a kind of 'failed hero—is that it is precisely these characteristics that render him the ideal object of the scapegoating mechanism. His gory death in Chap. 11, 'Castle Rock' (Golding, 1954: 187–202), at the hands of the atavistic crowd as a sacrificial killing that doubles as a political assassination (Golding, 1954: 199–201) is the perfect allegorical expression of the radical insufficiency of representational political reason. As we have already seen, in Chap. 10 of the novel, 'The Shell and the Glasses' (Golding, 1954: 171–186), Piggy is depicted as the bearer of false consciousness because he is the one who most ferociously denies the logic of the sacrificial murder of Simon. Piggy's fatal error, for which everyone else pays a heavy price, is that he believes that the rationality underlying the original contract is adequate to guarantee the foundation of the community, beautifully expressed in perhaps the most famous passage of the novel: 'And in the middle of them, with filthy body, matted hair, and unwiped nose, Ralph wept for the end of innocence, the darkness of men's heart, and the fall through the air of the true, wise friend called Piggy' (Golding, 1954: 225). Therefore, his fall, which the by now thoroughly traumatised Ralph weeps over, is not just his literal fall to his physical death, but an allegorical fall: the revelation of Humankind as non-rational beings unable to conform to the representational ideal of the social contract. But the narrative groundwork for this apocalyptic moment is established much earlier, in Chap. 5, 'Beast from the Water' (Golding, 1954: 81–102), in which the community as a whole imperceptibly slides toward pre-representational thought, the epistemological sine qua non of the sacrificial mechanism. This is the moment of intractable political crisis which is the mirroring of an even more foundational crisis of knowledge: the failure to arrive at a final determination of the nature, or 'name,' of the Beast. As far as I am aware, no commentator has paid sufficient attention to the pivotal speech delivered to the Assembly by Maurice, a shadowy character like Jack's indecipherable lieutenant Roger but one who is vaguely within the Ralph-Piggy faction. The crucial chapter begins innocuously enough: as survival is the paramount function of the Hobbesian Sovereign Ralph calls an 'emergency session' of the Assembly in order to reaffirm the binding nature of democratic decision-making (Golding, 1954: 81–84). It also provides him with a wonderful Machiavellian opportunity to self-reflect upon the essentially discursive nature of Sovereignty: 'He was searching his mind for simple words so that even the littluns[31] would understand what the assembly was about. Later, perhaps, practiced debaters—Jack, Maurice, Piggy—would use their whole art to twist the meeting; but now at the beginning the subject of the debate must be laid out clearly' (Golding, 1954: 84). But once democracy is invoked everything turns to garbage[32] because everybody *wants* to talk about the Beast.

> He [Ralph] moved the conch gently, looking beyond them at nothing, remembering the beastie, the snake, the fire, the talk of fear.

[31] The fairly nameless boys of the lower forms.

[32] Literally. One of the reason why Ralph convenes the Assembly is to establish some new rules about public sanitation as the Boys have been using the gathering spot as a latrine: 'We've got to use the rocks again This place is getting dirty.' Golding, (1954: 86). It is widely underappreciated how scatological the *Lord* is; images of dirt, filth and blood populate the landscape. The constant referencing of the 'dirty' clearly signifies the latent violence of the community (impurity) which is unconsciously awaiting the collective cleansing effect (purification) of the ritualistic sacrifice. But I also believe that the scatological imagery also invokes the latent, and ultimately ineradicable violence of Nature itself, a cosmic tapestry of overlapping predator–prey relationships. For a discussion of the scatological in the novel see Dickson (1990: 51–52).

'Then people started getting frightened.'…

> We've got to talk about this fear and decide there's nothing in it. I'm frightened myself, sometimes; only that's nonsense! Like bogies. Then, when we've decided, we can start again and be careful about things like fire. (Golding, 1954: 87–88)

The Assembly scene is Golding's ultimate riposte to both the representational theory of language in general and to the Hobbes' prescriptive regime of the correct, or principled, use of speech in particular, as the elliptical grandeur of Maurice's rhetoric gloriously demonstrates.

Maurice spoke—so loudly that they jumped.

'Daddy said[33] they haven't found all the animals in the sea yet.'

Argument started again Ralph held out the glittering conch and Maurice took it obediently. The meeting subsided.

> I mean when Jack says you can be frightened because people are frightened anyway that's all right. But when he says there's only pigs on the island I expect he's right but he doesn't know, not really, not certainly I mean'—Maurice took a breath—'My daddy says there's things, what d'you call'em that make ink—squids—that are hundreds of yards long and eat whales whole.' He paused again and laughed gaily.' *I don't believe in the beast of course. As Piggy says, life's scientific, but we don't know, do we? Not certainly, I mean—*. (Golding, 1954: 94–95)[34]

The inherent namelessness of the island is coeval with its latent and ineradicable violence; naming is differentiation and the absence of naming is undifferentiation, as Hobbes shows in his brief disquisition on Adam and the naming of the animals.

> The first author of speech was *God* himself, that instructed *Adam* how to name such creatures as he presented to his sight … But this was sufficient to direct him to more names, as the experience and use of creatures should give him occasion; and to joyn them in such manner by degrees, as to make himself understood; and so by succession of time, so much language might be gotten, as he had found use for … (Hobbes, 1992: 24–25)

It is an inconvenient truth that the successful operation of the logic of exclusion is wholly contingent upon the completion of the system of knowledge being deployed. Maurice's epistemic and rhetorical slide is the true turning point of the political

[33] A nice patriarchal touch that makes Maurice's rhetorical subversion that much more fatal; he is invoking the model of the grown-ups which the boys should imitate.

[34] To introduce an uncouth materialist consideration here: the text does provide a possible representational identification of the Beastie, an amphibious snake-like thing with huge jaws. The novel strongly hints that the destination of the evacuees is the Southern Antipodes, either Australia or New Zealand; Firchow correctly points out that 'the island is somewhere in the Indian Ocean' as suggested by Golding's own 'intertextual reference to [Robert] Ballantyne's *Coral Island* [1858]' along with the fact that the boy's plane 'must have been flying in this direction, since it was said to have made two prior stops in Gibraltar and Addis Ababa' (Firchow, 2008: 93, 90). However, if the plane actually went down in the immediate vicinity of northern Australia (which would in part 'realistically' explain the *deus ex machina* materialization of the Royal Navy cutter at the end of the novel) then it may be tentatively suggested that the Beast that the littlun's claim to see is a real animal that would be probably be unknown to them and appear to them as a land traversing serpentine sea monster: a saltwater crocodile.

narrative: no one can agree upon the correct use of language leading to an act of secession based upon the nature of reality and the proper naming of things—the failure of censorship to maintain differences, resulting in the community's fall into undifferentiation and the pre-representational thought, the anti-thesis of Piggy.

Someone shouted.

'A squid couldn't come up out of the water!'

'Could.'

'Couldn't'.

> In a moment the platform was full of arguing, gesticulating shadows. To Ralph, seated, this seemed the breaking-up of sanity. Fear, beasts, no general agreement that the fire was all-important: and when one tried to get the thing straight the argument sheered off, bringing up fresh, unpleasant matter…The world, that understandable and lawful world, was slipping away. Once there was this and that; and now… (Golding, 1954: 95, 98)

The stage is now set for the irreversible descent into political violence—a crisis that can only be fully resolved through the elevation of the sacrificial mechanism raised to institutional practice with Ralph as the first fully 'realized' scapegoat.

2.6 'I'm not Going to Play Any Longer. Not with You.': The Parallels of Mimetic Crisis and Political Crisis

As Ralph himself memorably puts it, 'Things are breaking up. I don't understand why. We began well; we were happy. And then—' (Golding, 1954: 87) The lethal power struggle between Ralph and Jack that makes up the second half of the novel appears easy to understand in terms of my analysis so far: Ralph mis-recognizes the Beast because it is resistant to representation, whereas while Jack identifies the enemy correctly and establishes his chiefdom. The problem is that they are both wrong. The boys, like Hobbes, are focused upon external reality, the object of representational discourse; but as the Lord of the Flies herself (a sow) makes clear to Simon during his mystic or epileptic trance in Chap. 8, the fear of the Beast is nothing more than the symbol of the 'plague' of undifferentiation that calls forth the scapegoat as the antidote: 'You knew, didn't you? I'm part of you? Close, close, close! I'm the reason why it's no go? Why things are what they are?' (Golding, 1954: 158). And just in case we are any doubt as to whether or not the nameless island of violence is 'really' the domain of absolute undifferentiation, the talking pig's head throws this final taunt to the retreating Simon that demonstrates her supernatural immanence as being at one with both the island and with the violence that it generates: 'This is ridiculous! You know perfectly well that you'll only meet me down there—so don't try to escape!' (Golding, 1954: 158). The real question is why does 'the break up,' or the downward spiral into undifferentiation and violence, begin only after the social contract has been entered into and the answer is because the contract alone is inadequate to expel the latent violence from within the community. The unexpurgated remnant of violence forms the sinews of the novel's second narrative thread that entwines itself around the public procession of scapegoats which is the culmination of the mimetic rivalry between the two candidates for the chieftainship, Ralph and Jack.

> He [Ralph] argued unconvincingly that they would let him alone; perhaps even make an outlaw of him. But then the fatal unreasoning knowledge came to him again The breaking of the conch and the deaths of Piggy and Simon lay over the island like a vapor. These painted savages would go further and further. Then there was that indefinable connection between himself and Jack; who therefore would never let him alone; never. (Golding, 1954: 204)

In superficially political terms, Jack is read as the personification of the military power, which always rests upon the residual threat of and use of violence, that aspect of the Executive that is the most likely source of dictatorship. The need to hunt and kill the Beast provides the perfect rationalization for Jack to expand his 'emergency powers' at the expense of the democratic community. In contrast, Ralph is the personification of the principle of Assembly, democratic governance through consultation, debate, and the 'correct' use of political and legal speech, symbolized by his possession of the conch—the discovery of the conch having been shown in Chap. 1 to be identical to the invention of the community. On a deeper and more interesting level, though, both Jack and Ralph allegorically represent the two variant forms of the underlying substance of legal and political order; or, as Golding suggestively puts it, 'Jack and Ralph smiled at each other with shy liking'. (Golding, 1954: 19–20)

The reader must be made aware that in what follows I am deviating from Girard's theory of the novel as being based upon a strict triangulation of mimetic desire and rivalry.[35] Here, I am employing a binary model when discussing the mimetic conflict between Ralph and Jack, each boy the sign of a rival model of sovereignty, simplistically characterized in the secondary literature as 'democracy' and 'dictatorship'. Because of the narrative structure of *Lord*, it would be misleading to imagine both boys as competing for the single ideal-object of 'sovereignty' as such, with Ralph the mediator-obstacle and Jack the rapacious emulator. The advantage of reformulating the Girardian model of Ralph versus Jack as binary is that the absence of triangulation replicates one of the central problems of *Leviathan*: how is it possible for 'Man' to convene the Assembly that gives rise to the social contract at a moment of time that is represented as being prior to humankind's collective exiting of the anarchy of nature?[36] If Ralph and Jack existed within a triangle of desire, then the object of their desire, sovereignty, would not be in question; but that is the whole problem. Both Hobbes and Golding make it clear that before the Assembly sovereignty, as such, does not exist; the creation of power is the consequence, not the cause, of

[35] See Chap. 1, above.

[36] In a way, this is similar to the bootstrap-theory dimensions of Girard's less than complete account of the hominid's transition from pre-representational to representational language: hoe were early human's ever able to exist the archaic state of pre-representation since all of the artefacts of culture—the rites, rituals, and prohibitions of the transformative scapegoating process—constituted products of representation? See Chap. 1, above.

the Assembly.[37] Therefore, the competition between Ralph and Jack, while clearly mimetic, is not about an exclusive possession of an external good but, rather, the far more existential struggle over the affirmation of their respective forms of 'self' here re-configured as a rival types of political order: Ralph and Jack do not prevail because they successfully imitate sovereignty; rather, 'sovereignty' is the manner of the boy who merely happens to prevail. 'All desire is a desire for being'—sovereignty as a formal, or civilized, concept is a second-order denotation that names the outcome of an earlier elemental struggle over the 'real,' or being as such. The sovereign is he who is decided as the winner by the Assembly that is the mediator of the social contract; which means that on the unnamed island sovereignty is nothing other than the contingent actualization of the two models of boy-leader. Which is profoundly upsetting to that saccharine liberalism so despised by Golding.

Readers unfamiliar with *Leviathan* may be surprised to learn that Hobbes makes it clear that the two competing versions of the Commonwealth may be regarded with equal favor thanks to the thoroughly personalized nature of Hobbesian Sovereignty/Sovereign: 'And he that carries this Person [of the community] is called *Sovereign*, and said to have *Sovereign Power*; and everyone besides, his *Subject*' (Hobbes, 1992: 121). Even more surprising is the stance of strict neutrality that Hobbes himself assumes vis-à-vis both of them.

> The attaining to this Sovereign Power is by two ways. One, by natural force; as when a man makes his children to submit themselves, and their children [in turn], to his government, as being able to destroy them if they refuse; or by war subdues his enemies to his will, giving them their lives on that condition The other, is when men agree among themselves to submit to some Man, or Assembly of men, voluntarily, on confidence to be protected by him against all others. The later may be called a Political Commonwealth, or Commonwealth by *Institution*; and the former, a Commonwealth by *Acquisition*. (Hobbes, 1992: 121)

This passage does great 'violence' to our twenty-first century Human Rights-driven sensibilities: Hobbes is postulating a strict equivalence between the democratic and authoritarian forms of Sovereignty, in which dictatorship is the political equal of democracy provided that it was founded upon the social contract whereas we morally refuse to recognize the non-liberal State as a rightful Sovereign.[38] But on the island of undifferentiation this equivalence is scrupulously upheld, allegorically embodied by the rival boy-sovereigns, Ralph signifying Commonwealth-by-Institution and Jack Commonwealth-by-Acquisition.

On a strictly political reading of the novel, an obvious problem emerges: given their different political identities, both material and symbolic, should not Ralph and Jack be enemies? Instead, Golding insists upon their friendship and mutual admiration for each other.

[37] The symbolically elusive 'conch' (a sign if there ever was one) is a vital factor in the narrative but one, I think, that supports my view of Ralph and Jack as separate models in and of themselves rather than as competitors for a commonly agreed upon status object which can only be mediated by the social. See below.

[38] See Chap. 11, below.

> At the return Ralph found himself alone on a limb with Jack and they grinned at each other, sharing the burden. Once more, amid the breeze, the shouting, the slanting sunlight on the high mountain, was shed that glamour, that strange invisible light of friendship, adventure and content.

'Almost too heavy.'

Jack grinned back.

'Not for the two of us'. (Golding, 1954: 38–39)

Part of the answer is that Golding is ironically subverting the clear distinctions that we normally accept as separating democracy from dictatorship. As with Hobbes, Golding sees the relationship between the Assembly and the One Man as inherently fluid, as the individual's submitting to any form of political and legal structure necessarily involves the surrender of liberty, identical to the earlier act of conveyance of liberty to the Sovereign in exchange for protection from death. Golding, however, goes beyond Hobbes through his literary deployment of the cultural logic of ritualistic sacrifice: every form of political order requires the internalization and then outward projection of that mimetic violence based upon the eternal recurrence of rivalry and imitation. Nowhere in *Lord* is the logic of mimetic rivalry more clearly allegorized than with the narrative positioning of Ralph and Jack as doubles. Exempting the instinctual 'appetites' such as self-preservation or fear-of-death, Man, for Girard, 'is the creature who does not know what to desire, and he turns to others in order to make up his mind. We desire what others desire because we imitate their desires' (Girard, 1987: 122). Golding stages an almost point-for-point enactment of this in Chap. 1.

'Vote for a chief!'.

'Let's vote—'.

> This toy of voting was almost as pleasing as the conch. Jack started to protest but the clamor changed from the general wish for a chief to an election by acclaim of Ralph himself. None of the boys could have found good reason for this; what intelligence had been shown was traceable to Piggy while the most obvious leader was Jack. But there was a stillness about Ralph as he sat that marked him out: there was his size, and attractive appearance; and most obscurely, yet most powerfully, there was the conch. The being that had blown that, had sat waiting for them on the platform with the delicate thing balanced on his knees, was set apart. (Golding, 1954: 19)[39]

Almost predictably, Golding signals that Ralph has the superior claim to sovereignty because of his immediate, or un-mediated, proximity to the conch, the sign of nature and the signifier of Being. But the point being made here is a subtle one. In a Hobbesian manner the Assembly is not choosing democracy by choosing Ralph; rather, they are choosing Ralph who merely happens to be 'democratic' (thanks to Piggy) and who manages to establish the Commonwealth-by-Institution as a result of his successful but intensely personal rivalry with Jack. In a Girardian manner, Ralph is only now (not previously) the model and Jack the thwarted imitator; in

[39] I will re-visit this critical passage in the conclusion.

existential terms, it is Ralph who 'is' and Jack who 'is not'. This is decisive moment is pregnant with catastrophe because it raises the dreaded prospect of metaphysical desire, which is murderous. But again, the relationship between the two is binary rather than triangular because what we are witnessing is the unconventional action of the invention of the model rather than the recycling of a model that is pre-given. Which, I would argue, represents the continuation of the personal rivalry between the boys prior to the investiture of the conch with the symbolic meaning of Being.

> What are the consequences of imitation when, instead of patterning our desires according to the suggestion of some cultural model, we imitate one another in our choice of desirable objects? The model is anyone who suggests an object of desire to anyone else by desiring that object himself. The model and his imitator desire the *same* object, and they necessarily interfere with each other. (Girard, 1987: 122)[40]

The quasi-Hobbesian paradox at work here is that as soon as man enters into a community with others, desire will invariably 'mutate' into a condition of irrepressible mimetic rivalry between the 'doubles'. If Girard's theory of mimetic desire is correct, then the entrance into the Hobbesian social contract guarantees that violence will escalate precisely because inter-personal conflict is generated through the rivalry over possession of objects that are desired by the group.

> As I imitate the desire of my neighbour, I reach for the object he is already reaching for, and we prevent each other from appropriating this object. His relation to my desire parallels my relation to his, and the more we cross each other, the more stubbornly we imitate each other. My interference intensifies his desire, just as his interference intensifies mine. This process of positive feedback can only lead to physical and other forms of violence. Violence is the continuation of mimetic desire by violent means...Violence is a symmetrical, reciprocal process because it is mimetic. (Girard, 1987: 122–123)

Girard's concern with the mimetic nature of desire (the libidinal understood in a non-Freudian sense) closely matches Hobbes' abiding concern with the socially disruptive effects of the passion of envy, discussed at fair length in Chap. 13 ('Of the Naturall Condition of Mankind, as concerning their Felicity and Misery') where that particular vice is conceptualized as an essential part of the state of nature.

> From this [natural] equality of ability, arises equality of hope in the attainment of our objectives. And therefore if any two men desire the same thing, which nevertheless they cannot both enjoy, they become enemies; and in the way to their end, (which is principally their own conservation, and sometimes their delectation only), endeavor to destroy, or subdue one another. (Hobbes, 1992: 87)

Not only is envy unavoidable given the social existence of Man (necessary for self-preservation), but its ability to inflict misery is almost unrivalled among the passions.

> Again, men have no pleasure (but on the contrary a great deal of griefe) in keeping company where there is no power able to over-awe them all. For every man expects that his companion

---

[40] The obvious homoerotic allusions in Golding's text merely reinforces this vial point: 'Like violence, sexual desire tends to fasten upon surrogate objects if the object to which it was originally attracted remains inaccessible; it willingly accepts substitutes' (Girard 1977: 35).

> should value him at the same rate he sets upon himself: and upon all signs of contempt, or under-valuing, naturally endeavors, as far as he dares (which amongst them that have no power to keep them subdued, is far enough to make them destroy each other), to extort a greater value from his critics by gift; and from others, by the example. So that in the nature of man, we find three principall causes of quarrel. First, Competition; Secondly, Diffidence [Self-Assertion]; Thirdly, Glory. (Hobbes, 1992: 88)

Girard, as we know, proposes a grand solution to this eternal grief: the ritualistic sacrifice of the scapegoat.

> The real solution to the problem of vengeance must lie in the very unyielding intensity of mimetic rivalry. It must lie within murderous violence itself…The 'scapegoat' or unanimous-victimage hypothesis satisfies this requirement. When mimetic violence permeates an entire group and reaches a climatic intensity, it generates a form of collective victimage that tends toward unanimity precisely because of the participant's heightened mimetic susceptibility. (Girard, 1987: 125)

Ralph puts it well: "Then people started getting frightened" (Golding, 1954: 88). But Piggy puts it better: "…I know there isn't no fear…Unless we get frightened of people" (Golding, 1954: 90).

Here, Golding appears to follow Hobbes strictly in assuming that fear is the primary motive of social formation; however, Hobbes himself postulates envy as a universal constant of society, which renders fully consistent with both texts Girard's defining insight that the unavoidable escalation of unsustainable intra-community rivalry will seek a natural outlet through the re-direction of community wide violence toward the properly identified and named scapegoat. It is up not to Ralph but to Jack to make theory reality.

2.7 'Roger Sharpened a Stick at Both Ends': The Return of the Repressed

The final, and most ritualistically prescribed sacrificial murder, the one prepared for Ralph, is an inherently political and legal act. It establishes Jack's absolute (and unrivalled) leadership (Commonwealth-by-Acquisition) through the killing of his mimetic rival/double (Ralph/Commonwealth-by-Institution).[41] It is also the performance of the founding act of violence that will create the 'truer' community than

[41] Admittedly, Golding's narrative does some violence to the integrity of my close reading: as Girard makes clear, the rival himself can never act as the victim, for the killing of the rival will perpetuate the cycle of vengeance through retaliation (it will also appear too much like a 'mere' homicide); ordinarily another person, or, even better, an animal is substituted for the rival who is then only 'mimetically' killed. What I can rely on here is another of Girard's observations: that the animal-surrogate selected will always bear a physical resemblance to the original object. In Chap. 8, 'A Gift for the Darkness', Jack impales the head of the sow on a stick that is sharpened at both ends; the pig's head later mutates into the 'Lord of the Flies' while, of course, remaining a pig, which naturally reminds us of Piggy. The impaling of Ralph's head on the stick sharpened at both ends mimetically evokes Piggy, the bearer of the false consciousness of secular rationality and the archetypal victim. So, in effect, the by now fully ritualistic killing of Ralph will be the re-enactment

the one premised upon the false (and by now falsified) notion of the social contract. Most important of all, Jack's (and Roger's) tribal society self-consciously utilizes Religion and Theology, unlike Ralph's Assembly which was dominated by the tepid, superficial and common-sense rationalism of Piggy.

In the silence that followed each savage flinched away from his individual memory.

'No! How could we—kill—it?'.

Half-relieved, half-daunted by the implication of further terrors, the savages murmured again.

'So leave the mountain alone,' said the Chief, solemnly, 'and give [the Beast] the head if you go hunting again'...

'I expect the beast disguised itself.'

> 'Perhaps,' said the Chief. A *theological speculation* presented itself. 'We'd better keep on the right side of him, anyhow. You can't tell what he might do'. (Golding, 1954: 177–178)

As Jean-Pierre Dupuy usefully explains it.

> The history of humanity is the history of a kind of evolution peculiar to sacrificial systems, by which civilization made a dramatic advance in replacing the human victim by a stand-in—first an animal, then certain plants, and finally abstract symbolic entities. It is in this sense that the history of humanity is a story of symbolization. (Dupuy, 2013: 101)

While it is clear that the establishment of Jack's rule of One Man is concurrent with the creation of a native religion, it is frequently underappreciated that Jack and his hunters are the progenitors of a nativist culture, specifically a form of body-art, the (re-) discovery of which neatly recapitulates the onto-epistemological foundations of the pre-representational.

> Jack planned his new face. He made one cheek and one eye-socket white, then rubbed red over the other half of his face and slashed a black bar of charcoal across from right ear to left jaw. He looked in the mere for his reflection, but his breathing troubled the mirror...
>
> He knelt, holding the shell of water. A rounded patch of sunlight fell on his face and a brightness appeared in the depths of the water. He looked in astonishment, no longer at himself but at an awesome stranger. ... He began to dance and his laughter became a bloodthirsty snarling. He capered towards Bill and the mask was a thing on its own, behind which Jack hid, liberated from shame and self-consciousness. (Golding, 1954: 66–67)

---

of the foundational murder of Piggy/pig, with whom Ralph bears an almost fraternal similarity (Ralph = Piggy = pig) and who is now the stand-in for Jack's true enemy, the 'atheistick' social contract. And, of course, in the end all of Ralph's followers have deserted him, meaning that there is no one to avenge him; he becomes something of an obsolete rival. Strikingly, Golding inverts the historical progression here: the offering of human-surrogates for an original animal victim. The correct mimetic sequence should have been from Simon to Ralph to Piggy to the pig/Lord of the Flies, but this would have presented too many narrative difficulties and threatened the all-important moral interpretation of the novel as being about the regression to barbarism (Girard, 1977: 11).

Jack's impulsive act both represents and successfully solves Ralph's great political dilemma, which is exactly the same as Hobbes: monopolizing the act of judgment through the proper naming of things which is the representational process of differentiation.

> Ralph turned to the chief's seat. They had never had an assembly so late before. That was why the place looked so different. Normally the underside of the green roof was lit by a tangle of golden reflections, and their faces were lit upside down, like—thought Ralph, when you hold an electric torch in your hand. But now the sun was slanting in at one side, so that the shadows were where they ought to be. Again he fell into that strange mood of speculation that was so foreign to him. If faces were different when lit from above or below—what was a face? What was anything? (Golding, 1954: 83)

For what Jack proves is that there are no true faces insofar as every face is a mask which makes everyone different from the manner in which they are represented. But, then again, the same element of liminal ambiguity is also present in Ralph as established at the beginning of the novel: 'Piggy looked up to Ralph. All the shadows on Ralph's face were reversed; green above, bright below from the lagoon A blur of sunlight was crawling across his hair' (Golding, 1954: 10). This is the leader of a democracy meaning the defender of representation? Which is exactly what you get for trying to enforce the social contract on an island of pure undifferentiation or, where things do not objectively equate with the words we assign them.

> Strange things happened at midday. The glittering sea rose up, moved apart in planes of blatant impossibility; the coral reef and the few, stunted palms that clung to the more elevated parts would float up to the sky, would quiver, be plucked apart, run like rain-drops on a wire or be repeated as in an odd succession of mirrors. Sometimes land loomed where there was no land and flicked out like a bubble as the children watched. Piggy discounted all this learnedly as a 'mirage'; and since no boy could reach even the reef over the stretch of water where the snapped sharks waited, they grew accustomed to mysteries and ignored them, just as they ignored the miraculous throbbing stars. At midday the illusions merged into the sky and there the sun gazed down like an angry eye. (Golding, 1954: 60)

Now is the time to recall that Leviathan is the great Beast from the Waters, which means that the 'beastie' and everything that spawns it—including the pre-representational form of language and the mimetic logic of symbolic substitution—should all dwell together undifferentiated in the same 'glittering sea'.[42] But since the boys are unconsciously governed by the logic of mimetic substitution, nothing truly definitive about Nature can ever be said. As Hobbes expresses it, 'Naturall sense and imagination are not subject to absurdity. Nature it selfe cannot erre: and as men abound in copiousnesse of language; so they become more wise, or more mad than ordinary' (Hobbes, 1992: 28). Or as Golding conveys it through the poetic imagination that is immune to absurdity, 'A flurry of wind made the palms talk and the noise seemed very loud now that darkness and silence made it so noticeable. Two grey trunks rubbed each other with an evil squeaking that no one had noticed by the day' (Golding, 1954: 96–97).

[42] 'Glittering' suggests 'glamour' which is derived from the ancient concept of magically induced mis-recognition.

Silence is pregnant with Being. And to-***BE*** is what the pathology of mimetic rivalry is all about.

2.8 'Close, Close, Close!": The One Who Brings Existential Envy with Him

One of the greatest passages of modern English literature is on the one-hundredth page of Golding's masterwork.

'The trouble is: Are there ghosts, Piggy? Or beasts?'

'Course there aren't.'

'Why not?

'Cos things wouldn't make sense. Houses an' streets, an'—TV—they wouldn't work.'

The dancing, chanting Boys had worked themselves away till their sound was nothing but a wordless rhythm.

> But s'pose they don't make sense? Not here, on this island? Supposing things are watching and waiting? (Golding, 1954: 100)

So utterly prone is Piggy to *meconnaissance* and mystification, that his own creator had metaphorically given up hope on him. 'Piggy never gets anywhere near coping with anything on that island. He dismisses the beast ... says that there aren't such things as ghosts, not understanding that the whole of society is riddled with ghosts .... Piggy understands society less than almost anyone there at all' (William Golding qtd. Bloom, 2008: 66). Which is what makes him the most dangerous boy on the island of no names. The typical reading of *Lord* is very similar to any superficial reading of Sigmund Freud's *Civilization and Its Discontents*: without the rule of law, or the presence of the super-ego, 'Man' will naturally regress into savagery, or the domain of the Id. I have argued, however, that Golding's text, like those of Girard (and Hobbes) are decidedly un-Freudian. It is not the case that the boys regress; rather, they unconsciously act out the mimetic logic of cultural formation by transforming themselves into an indigenous but primitive society, collectively undergoing not a descent but a kind of profoundly contra-rational ascent. The Island-of-Undifferentiated-Things is transformed by their labor into a 'bubble' of *meconnaissance*, bounded by the infinite envelope of the irrational, acted out through the grown-up's waging of limited atomic war.

> A sliver of moon rose over the horizon, hardly large enough to make a path of light even when it sat right down on the water; but there were other lights in the sky, that moved fast, winked, or went out, though not even a faint popping came down from a battle fought at ten miles height. (Golding, 1954: 103)

The 'Beast' that descends, the dead fighter-pilot who, as Golding helpfully explains to us, represents the intrusion of History into the hermetically sealed world the Hobbes' rigorously a-contextual thought experiment (Firchow, 2007: 149), is perfectly real although, crucially, mis-named.

> But a sign came down from the world of grown-ups, though at the time there was no child awake to read it. There was a sudden bright explosion and a corkscrew trail across the sky; then darkness again and stars. There was a speck above the island, a figure dropping swiftly beneath a parachute, a figure that hung with dangling limbs. The changing winds of various altitudes took the figure where they would. Then, three miles up, the wind steadied it and bore it in a descending curve round the sky and swept it in a great arc in a great slant across the reef and the lagoon towards the mountain The figure fell and crumpled among the blue flowers of the mountain-side, but now there was a gentle breeze at this height too and the parachute flopped and banged and pulled. ... When the breeze blew the lines would strain taut and some accident of this pull lifted the head and chest upright so that the figure seemed to peer across the brow of the mountain Then, each time the wind dropped, the lines would slacken and the figure bow forward again, sinking its head between its knees. So as the stars moved across the sky, the figure sat on the mountain-top and bowed and sank and bowed again. (Golding, 1954: 103–104)

Which leads us directly to the 'tragic irony' of Piggy-the-scapegoat: the mimetic imitation of the grown-ups, the collective authors of nuclear war, yields the diametrically opposed outcome to the self-grounding secular society of the social contract of reason: the reinvention of religion and the successful establishment of the Commonwealth-by-Acquisition by Jack the theocrat-chief. The real reason why the boys are the prisoners (or victims) of History is due not to the weakness of civilization but to its central and defining paradox: the political economy of the modern is the atavistic descendant of the sacrificial economy of the archaic. And like all first-rate comedians, Golding saves his best joke for last.

> He [Ralph] staggered to his feet, tensed for more terrors, and looked up at a huge peaked cap. It was a white-topped cap, and above the green shade of the peak was a crown, an anchor, gold foliage. He saw white drill, epaulettes, a revolver, a row of gilt buttons down the front of a uniform.
>
> A naval officer stood on the sand, looking down at Ralph in wary astonishment. On the beach behind him was a cutter, her bows hauled up and held by two ratings. In the stern-sheets another rating held a sub-machine gun.
>
> The ululation faltered and died away. (Golding, 1954: 224)

The deus ex machina-style entrance of the Navy Officer constitutes the novel's ultimate mimetic substitution: not the resurrection of Piggy, which I will deal with shortly, but the trans-figuration of Jack. Ralph's encounter with the Man-in-Uniform (or 'Jack' as grown-up) on the beach reveals the truth of the historical and judicial line of succession from the 'primitive' to the 'modern' society, both premised upon the ritualistic deployment of sacrificial violence. The ululation stops because the arc of History has been completed. "Jolly good show," said the Man-in-Uniform (Golding, 1954: 224). Contra Piggy's incessant refrain throughout *Lord*, grown-ups might not be the best things to imitate, for now, after their rescue and their imminent return to an atomic bomb blasted landscape, the lives of the boys are guaranteed to be solitary, poor, nasty, brutish, and short.

An alleged crisis created by the absence of the grown-ups is frequently noted by the critics of *Lord* and just as frequently misunderstood. The problem is not that the boys lack appropriate role models, no matter how flawed, but that there is no superior power to enforce differences among them so that it is impossible to exit the state of undifferentiation by conventional means. Recall that the dramatic action of *Lord* begins with the boys' democratic selection of an executive; with no 'natural' leader they have to choose among themselves. But since the original act that forms the social contract is an egalitarian one, the political order of the island can be revoked by a counter-vailing democratic will, which is exactly what happens. The boys' first attempt at public reason, Ralph's and Piggy's democratic Assembly, is unable to maintain a political hierarchy and it descends into a hedonistic anarchy. In contrast, Jack's Commonwealth-by-Acquisition does provide political authority through the introduction of the sacrificial mechanism, which is founded directly upon the most primal distinction of all, that between the sacrificer and the sacrificed, or the community and the scapegoat, the very first Self and Other. If anything, *Lord* is even more relevant in 2024 than when it first appeared in 1954: Golding's re-working of R.G. Ballantyne's *The Coral Island* (1858) (Niemeyer, 1962) highlights like no other English novel the lethal finitude of public reason. Golding's satirical proto-deconstruction of Hobbes (intentional or otherwise) directly anticipates Girard's conception of the mimetic cycle as the onto-political 'remedy' for the eternal failure of the social contract to restrain the paroxysms of mimetic crisis. The epistemological key of the sacrificial mechanism, the logic of substitution, guarantees the triumph of the 'primitive mind' of the boys: a new victim can always be sacrificed as one member of an un-broken series of copies of the original, in their case Piggy. But this same process of substitution—that which re-introduces difference into the community through the binary opposition between crowd and scapegoat so as to restore all of the other externally mediated distinctions within the community—is the same mechanism of that drives *ressentiment*, the foundation of both 'middle-class morality' and the politics of modernity.

As we already know, Scheler views *ressentiment* as seeking natural expression through the antithesis of public reason, the 'spirit of revenge' (Scheler, 2010: 25). However, in our era of post-Fordist consumerism and the hyper-commodification of all forms of social and political relationships (the 'system of free competition' as Scheler calls it in an obvious steal from de Tocqueville), the specific psychic and social form that the spirit of revenge is most likely to assume will be *envy*.

> [R]*essentiment* must therefore be strongest in a society like ours, where approximately equal rights (political and otherwise) or formal social equality, publicly recognized, go hand in hand with wide factual differences in power, property, and education. While each has the 'right' to compare himself with everyone else, he cannot do so in fact. Quite independently of the character and experiences of individuals, a potent charge of *ressentiment* is here accumulated by the very *structure of society*. (Scheler, 2010: 28)

Scheler does not restrict envy to the frustrated coveting of objects (commodities) but extends it toward values as well, specifically the rigidly hierarchical values that govern the process of the creation and distribution of social capital. Which is doubly bad, for, as of the twenty-first century at least, the competition for the accumulation of social capital is now wholly unbridled, no longer regulated by external mediation, and throwing up from the undifferentiated Golding-esque sea of social exchanges the ultra-toxin of *existential envy.*

> Another source of *ressentiment* lies in *envy, jealousy*, and the *competitive urge*. '*Envy*,' as the term is understood in everyday usage, is due to a feeling of impotence which we experience when another person owns a good we covet. … Our factual inability to acquire a good is wrongly interpreted as a positive action *against* our desire—a delusion which diminishes the original tension … [Paradoxically] Envy does not strengthen our acquisitive urge; it weakens it. It leads to *ressentiment* when the coveted values are such as cannot be acquired and lie in the sphere in which we compare ourselves to others. The most powerless envy is also the most terrible. Therefore *existential envy*, which is directed against the other person's very *nature*, is the strongest source of *ressentiment*. … (Scheler, 2010: 29–30)

Even worse, existential envy operates in a wholly mimetic fashion, a near-exact parallel of Girard's concept of violence-as-contagion.

> Through its very origin, *ressentiment* is therefore chiefly confined to those who serve and are dominated at the moment, who fruitlessly resent the sting of authority. When it occurs elsewhere, it is either due to psychological contagion—and the spiritual venom of *ressentiment* is extremely contagious—or to the violent suppression of an impulse which subsequently revolts by 'embittering' and 'poisoning' the personality. (Scheler, 2010: 27)

I would suggest that *ressentiment* is most germane to *Lord* because it enables us to identify a hitherto over-looked set of doubles—one which, when identified, completely overturns every and any possible moralistic interpretation of the novel. With both Girard and Scheler in mind, ask yourself one simple question: of all of the undifferentiated boys on the island who is the one most vulnerable to existential envy and, therefore, the one most likely to be identified by the group as the source of *ressentiment*? Or, to put it another way—out of all of the boys, what is the name of the one most likely to be scapegoated?

We can exclude two of the most obvious suspects immediately, both Ralph and Jack. Although we are likely to identify them as the source of conflict precisely because they are in direct mimetic rivalry, the recollection of the mythology of the sacrificial mechanism corrects this erroneous conclusion: the scapegoat is the one who is identified as bringing harm to the community. Because of their pre-given elite status, the rivalry of these two boys is directed solely against each other as existential equals in a manner both narcissistic and homo-erotic; in Scheler's terminology, both of the warring sovereigns are '*noble persons*' who, as members of an intensely externally mediated 'class' of persons, enjoy 'a completely naïve and non-reflective awareness of his own value and of his fullness of being, an obscure conviction which enriches every conscious moment of his existence, as if he were autonomously rooted in the universe' (Scheler, 2010: 31). This is a disturbingly accurate description of the English upper class; it is also an insightful depiction of Ralph, who is also denoted as the 'being that had blown that [the conch], had sat waiting for them on the platform with the delicate thing balanced on his knees, was set apart' (Golding, 1954: 19). If Ralph is truly 'set apart,' (differentiated) then he is the opposite of 'common,' a circumstance replete with mimetic significance; the noble person 'experiences value *prior* to any comparison' whereas the common man experiences value '*in* and *through* a comparison. For the latter, the relation is the selective precondition for apprehending *any* value. Every value is a relative thing, "higher'" or "lower," "more" or "less" than his own. He arrives at value judgments by comparing himself to others and others to himself' (Scheler, 2010: 32). In a completely neo-liberal capitalist civilization such as ours *ressentiment* is nothing more than just this, 'a tendency to make comparisons between others and oneself' (Scheler, 2010: 30). Hence, the common person's denigration of value: it cannot be achieved—'Feelings of resentment … are irritated by the *unattainability* of positive values that others represent'(Frings, 2010: 6)— so the values of the noble persons (like hunters or members of the choir) are rejected in favor of the values that express the interest of the commoners, the purveyors of 'common-sense' (or the sense-of-the-common) which has now been weaponized in the *bellum omnia contra omnes* over access to social capital. Employing these criteria, the source of existential envy within the community, as externally symbolized as the Beast by Golding in a truly unforgettable scene, is the one who initiates the catastrophic leveling of internal mediation that abolishes the possibility of anti-mimetic external mediation and opening the floodgates to the toxic sludge of existential envy.

'There isn't anyone to help you. Only me. And I'm the Beast.'

Simon's mouth labored, brought forth audible words.

'Pig's head on a stick.'

> Fancy thinking the Beast was something you could hunt and kill!' said the head. … 'You knew, didn't you? I'm part of you? Close, close, close! I'm the reason why it's no go? Why things are the way they are? (Golding, 1954: 158)

So, the question may now be re-phrased as: of all of the boys, who is the one most common, or middle-class? The answer, just like Poe's purloined letter, is hiding in plain view.

'You told 'em. After what I said.'

His face flushed, his mouth trembled.

'After I said I didn't want—'.

'What on earth are you talking about?'

'About being called Piggy. I said I didn't care as long as they didn't call me Piggy; an' I said not to tell and then you went an' said straight out—'

Stillness descended on them. Ralph looking with more understanding at Piggy, saw that he was hurt and crushed. He hovered between the courses of apology or further insult.

> 'Better Piggy than Fatty,' he said at last, with the directness of genuine leadership. … (Golding, 1954: 21–22)

I dare say. During the original moment of decision over the social contract, Jack offers up his desire-to-be with these words: "I ought to be chief,' said Jack with simple arrogance, 'because I'm chapter chorister and head boy. I can sing C sharp" (Golding, 1954: 18).[43] What is difficult for the liberal (or the American which is the same thing) to come to terms with is that Jack is exactly right; if one applies Girard's cautionary admonitions concerning the existential implications of external mediation, Jack is the only one who is able to end the interminable crisis of distinctions. 'Fatty,' however, is an entirely different sort of boy from the natural leader of the choir. The 'common man' is he who 'can only experience his value and that of another if he relates the two, and he clearly perceives only those qualities which constitute possible differences' (Scheler, 2010: 32) and the name that Scheler assigns to such a middling sort of person is *arriviste*.

> The ultimate goal of the *arriviste*'s expectations is not to acquire a thing of value, but to be more highly esteemed than others. He merely uses the 'thing' as an indifferent occasion for overcoming the oppressive feeling of inferiority which results from his constant comparisons. If this type of value experience comes to dominate a whole society, then the 'system of free competition' will become the soul of this society. (Scheler, 2010: 32)

Consequently, the middle-class 'self-made' man is damned as the victim of eternal social frustration meaning that he will always be the bearer of revenge within the unmediated system of free competition, the type of social order that, for Scheler, is 'the most suitable source for the formation of *ressentiment* ….' (Scheler, 2010: 25).[44] The significantly 'nameless' Piggy is the only recognizably middle-class boy on the island, the solitary self-making *arriviste*. Internally, he is the one who introduces *ressentiment* into the community of boys who are relatively united through their non-middle class status. Externally, this means that he is an eternal loser within un-mediated game of social capital, and his lack of a proper name is not merely the signification of a sign but is the symbolic verification of his deficit of social status. Internally, he is 'blocked' or psychically constipated; the 'immediate reactive impulse, with the accompanying emotions of anger and rage, is temporarily or at least momentarily checked and restrained, and the response is consequently postponed to a later time and more suitable occasion' (Scheler, 2010: 25). Piggy's confessional outburst of 'just wait till next time'—which is also Scheler's (Scheler, 2010: 25)—is the signature refrain of the eternally impotent, and it is in 'Fatty's' speech patterns that both aspects of the *arriviste* converge in a singular existential victimage; according to Scheler, this 'blockage is caused by the reflection that an immediate reaction would lead to defeat, and by the concomitant pronounced feeling of 'inability' and 'impotence''(Scheler, 2010: 25)—or, in Piggy's case, 'ass-mar'(Golding, 1954: 8). Predictably, his *ressentiment* will assume the form of the inversion of values: common-sense and practical reason as monopolized by Piggy as the bearer of the island's sole pair of 'specs,' will be deployed as the (necessarily mis-recognized) means of self-validation. But it is not enough because it can never be enough; 'even revenge as such, based as it is upon an experience of impotence, is always primarily

[43] Which is a big deal in England—Huck Finn (and Harold Bloom) can't do that.

[44] See Gil Bailie on this point: 'when I speak of … mimetic desire … the word "desire" means *the influence of others*. … the mimetic passions include jealousy, envy, covetousness, resentment, rivalry, contempt, and hatred' (Bailie, 1995: 112).

a matter of those who are "weak" in some respect' (Scheler, 2010: 25) The solution? Simply this: 'The desire for revenge disappears when vengeance has been taken ... In the same way, envy vanishes when the envied possession becomes ours' (Scheler, 2010: 26). And what is the most envied possession on the island? Piggy shouts out the answer: 'I got the conch! ...Which is better—to be a pack of painted niggers like you are, or to be sensible like Ralph is? ... Which is better—to have rules and agree, or to hunt and kill? ... Which is better, law and rescue, or hunting and breaking things up?' (Golding, 1954: 199–200). As Scheler puts it, the 'formal structure of *ressentiment* expression is always the same: A is affirmed, valued, and praised not for its own intrinsic quality, but with the un-verbalized intention of denying, devaluating, and denigrating B. A is "played off" against B' (Scheler, 2010: 42) or Piggy plus A-Ralph against B-Jack. Throughout the novel, Piggy is always staging micro power plays and it is easily overlooked that it is he, and not Ralph, who is the one who ends the possibility of external mediation by pre-empting Jack's unconscious attempt to avoid the crisis of distinctions which is why, following Scheler ('The nuances of language are precise'), B-Jack denounces A-Ralph in very precise terms: 'He's like Piggy. He says things like Piggy. He isn't a proper chief' (Golding, 1954: 138). How right he is. Because the real problem that divides Ralph and Jack so badly, the two most clearly noble persons among the boys, is that Ralph is imitating a commoner who carries the plague of *ressentiment* with him.

Why does the reader learn the real name of 'Piggy'? The answer to this question would be to force the reader of *Lord* to endure that unveiling which is the apocalypse, or at least the end of the democratic faith in secular reason. The answer comes in two parts. The first part is that Piggy cannot have a name because he is the first 'proper' scapegoat, and the true scapegoat lives under the epistemic tyranny of the undifferentiated logic of substitution. 'Piggy' cannot have an alternate name designating his real self because every scapegoat is in some sense the exact replica of the others; 'sacrifice is always a question of substitution, it is always possible to make a new substitution and henceforth to sacrifice only a substitute of a substitute' (Girard et al., 1987: 53). But although Piggy cannot have a real name he can, and does, possess a real double.

On the Island-of-Nameless-Things there are in truth two little piggies, each one trying to solve the problem that he has caused: the first piggy proclaims the social contract, the second piggy unveils the scapegoat ritual. The alpha and the omega; the Commonwealth begins and ends with the conch which is the state of nature. Contrary to widespread and structurally embedded mis-cognition, the conch does not signify democracy and the rule of law; for if the conch were sovereignty properly so-called then Ralph's and Jack's rivalry would be triangular: Ralph as model-mediator would obstruct imitator Jack's approach toward the ideal-object of sovereignty. But, at the very most, the conch could only signify sovereignty in a secondary capacity; it is, rather, the localized manifestation of the state of nature, the thing, or state-of-being, that pre-exists all speech-acts (political or otherwise) and is itself the very thing that compels the Assembly to be called and the resultant common power to be formed, a common power which is eternally suspended between Sovereignty-by-Institution and Sovereignty-by-Acquisition. And it is as the state-of-nature and not its derivative democracy that the conch, whenever deployed, signifies directly, recalling the original moment of the contractual act, which at that very first moment which could have been for anything, rendering the substantive content of Commonwealth-by-Institution wholly accidental.Golding veritably screams it at us but we lack the ears to hear and the eyes to see.

'What's that?'

Ralph had stopped smiling and was pointing into the lagoon Something creamy lay among the ferny weeds.

'A stone.'

'No. A shell.'

Suddenly Piggy was a-bubble with decorous excitement.

> Sright. It's a shell! I seen one like that before. On someone's back wall. A conch he called it. He used to blow it and then his mum would come. It's ever so valuable—. (Golding, 1954: 10–11)

Mark Kinkead-Weekes and Ian Gregor do an important service to us when pointing out that the conch is 'made real to us in is context of salt water, brilliant fish, green weed; then in its own strange cream and rose spiral, emblossed by an art other than the human; finally in the harsh otherness of the noise which shatters the peace of the island and terrifies bird and beast' (Kinkead-Weekes & Gregor, 2008: 81). Although they never mention him by name both Kinkead-Weekes and Gregor reaffirm an insight worthy of Girard: what the conch really signifies is Being itself and the quest to possess the conch is an allegorical representation of the desire for un-mediated Being.

> Ralph ... hit the shell with air from his diaphragm. Immediately the thing sounded. A deep, harsh note boomed under the palms, spread through the intricacies of the forest and echoed back from the pink granite of the mountain Clouds of birds rose from the tree-tops, and something squealed and rain in the undergrowth.[45]

Ralph took the shell away from his lips.

'Gosh!'. (Golding, 1954: 12)

Mimetic rivalry 'is always rooted in one of the two following claims: the claim of the self for the ownership of its own desire; and the claim of desire for its anteriority, its seniority over the other's desire, the other desire that has generated it, on which it is modelled' (Oughourlian, 1996: 43). The failure of either claim reduces the Self to No-One; as the conch is the medium of the self-grounded will of the one who 'manfully' blows it—'the man-breath passes through the shell's spiral to emerge as signal'(Kinkead-Weekes & Gregor, 2008: 81)—this means that the one who is 'real' cannot be the commoner Piggy ('ass-mar') but must, out of existential necessity, be the noble Ralph.

---

45 Presumably a pig, the master-sign of the violence-that-leads-to-sacrifice latent within the Act of Creation.

> His ordinary voice sounded like a whisper after the harsh note of the conch. He laid the conch against his lips, took a deep breath and blew once more. The note boomed again: and then at his firmer pressure, the note boomed again: and then at his firmer pressure, the note, fluking up an octave, became a strident blare more penetrating than before. Piggy was shouting something, his faced pleased, his glasses flashing.[46] The birds cried, small animals scattered. Ralph's breath failed; the note dropped the octave, became a low wubber, was a rush of air. (Golding, 1954: 12–13)

More foreshadowing. Still, if you blow on it they will come.
Piggy exclaimed, 'there's one!'.

> A child had appeared among the palms, about a hundred yards along the beach. … The small boy squatted in front of Ralph, looking up brightly and vertically. As he received the reassurance of something purposeful being done he began to look satisfied, and his only clean digit, a pink thumb, slid into his mouth. (Golding, 1954: 13)

Needless to say all of this aural performativity evokes the interminable substitution of presence-for-absence-for-presence: is it the war of all against all, the pre-conscious motor driving the process of social formation, the presence of the will-to-violence, or the absence of protection which is the absence of the freedom from violent death? In either case, both are mediated by sovereignty which is the true being of the one who merely happens to be the real leader, the noble/set-apart/unique/inimitable possessor of 'man-sound'.

> But we must not translate the shell into the signal. What comes out is far from simple; and the human beings will be as taken aback as the animals and for the same reason. If we really look and listen, what we shall see and hear will be the harshness of human self-assertion as well as the signal of human sociability; will be the sound of irresponsibility and childishness as well as of forethought and intelligence; will be the fragility of order as well as the impulse toward it. As the sound penetrates the densest thickets, while clouds of birds fly and 'something squealed and ran in the undergrowth,' man-sound prefigures stuck pig and stuck Ralph squealing and running for their life, as well as the Assembly and the rules. (Kinkead-Weekes & Gregor, 2008: 81)

And just in case we forgot it: *Ralph = Being*. For how can 'Fatty' compete with existence? Even though Ralph is a mouth-piece for Piggy and the *arriviste* is just one step removed from Being,[47] that single step possesses the magnitude of the Himalayas. From which it also follows that the smashing of the conch is not only the mechanical cause of the death of Piggy, it also signifies the suspension of the Assembly. In truth, if the conch was the symbol of sovereignty, as most moralizing readers of *Lord* would have us believe, then the destruction of the conch would mean the end of sovereignty as such, not only of Ralph but of Jack as well. Yet, the very opposite happens: the obliteration of the thing-from-the-sea, which is the final destination of both Simon and Piggy, results in the solidification of Merridew's rule of One Man.[48] And, from this rather inconvenient narrative fact, we are able to

---

[46] The fetal stirrings of the embryo of political reason.

[47] 'Piggy paused for breath and stroked the glistening thing that lay in Ralphs hands' (Golding, 1954: 11).

[48] One of the events that buttresses my argument against the conch as the symbol of sovereignty is that in 'The Shell and the Glasses' Jack's tribe raids Ralph's camp not to seize the conch but to

construct a much more satisfying interpretation of the traumatic events constituting the fall of Piggy: the killing of the scapegoat is the 'same thing' as establishing the permanence of the sacrificial mechanism and the path to civilization.

Which brings me to the very last of my tiresome sets of doubles, or two sets actually: conch to pig's skull and Piggy to pig's-head. On cue, Golding screams the 'truth' at us and I have provided useful inserts just to make the point 'clear'.

> The pig's skull grinned [*like both Piggy*[49] *and Jack*] at him [*Ralph, the first possessor of the conch-of-Being*] from the top of a stick [*the sacrificial mechanism*]. He walked slowly into the middle of the clearing [*the platform of the Assembly*] and looked steadily at the skull that gleamed white as ever the conch had done and seemed to jeer at him cynically [*like Piggy wanted to do*]. An inquisitive ant was busy in one of the eye sockets but otherwise the thing was lifeless [*as Piggy now was*].
>
> Or was it? (Golding, 1954: 205)

No! For both of the little piggies yet live!! Ralph apocalyptically sees both of them no longer through a glass darkly but face to face: 'Little prickles of sensation ran up and down his back. He stood, the skull about on level with his face, and held up his hair with two hands. The teeth grinned, the empty sockets seemed to hold his gaze masterfully and without effort. What was it?'(Golding, 1954: 205) The 'it' that Ralph intuits is the sacrificial logic that unconsciously links Piggy with Simon and, by extension with the Beast/pilot: for the violent deaths of both at the hands of the mob provoke a magical transition of the victims from the status of strangers to the sacred, the detested to the divine, the low to the high. But Simon is a victim of the *diasparagmos*, which means that he will not resurrect, although in some obscure way he has been sacralized. Piggy, however, will definitely be able to return, albeit in a new form, as the first 'true' scapegoat fully conforming to the sacrificial mechanism, minus a few of the finishing rites intended for Ralph. And yet once again the missing object is hiding in plain view: what everyone seems to have forgotten is that Piggy's head gets smashed and all of his brains spill out, into the same undifferentiated water that accepted Simon and which, by a truly weird coincidence, is the same reservoir of sacred power that accepts the Beast after his exorcism, for Leviathan is the great Beast from the Waters. Again, my interpolations should prove useful—maybe. But as this passage is longer, I have divided it with exegesis attached.

'The rock struck Piggy a glancing *blow from chin to knee*; the conch exploded into a thousand white fragments and ceased to exist. Piggy, *saying nothing*, with no time even for a grunt, travelled through the air sideways from the rock, turning over as he went.'— Piggy falls from a great height after being allegorically 'thrown' off the cliff by the mob, a universal method of killing a scapegoat.

---

steal Piggy's specs in order to make a fire. Now that Jack has possessed Being without the conch the shell is meaningless; it signifies nothing except for the state of nature itself which has the boys have now completely exited under Jack's Commonwealth-by-Acquisition (Golding, 1954: 186).

[49] 'Ralph's lips parted in a delighted smile and Piggy, taking this smile to himself as a mark of recognition, laughed with pleasure' (Golding, 1954: 10). As befitting an *arriviste*, recognition is life. Which means that Piggy can never really be Ralph's 'true, wise friend'.

'Piggy fell forty feet and landed on his back across that square, red rock in the sea.'—a sacrificial altar.[50]

'His head opened and stuff came out and turned red. Piggy's arms and legs twitched a bit, like a pig's after it has been killed. Then the sea…'— the burial place of Simon and the receiver of the Beast; 'His head opened' subliminally suggests Piggy's head being forced open and the brains removed by a deliberately sacrificial act (the stone hammer of a sacred executioner); the twitching of limbs suggest both the resemblance to an animal (Dupuy, 2013: 101; Girard, 1977: 10–11) and a premeditated act of butchery.

'[the sea] breathed again in a long slow sigh, the water boiled white and pink over the rock; and when it went, sucking back again, the body of piggy was gone.'—like Simon and the Beast.

This time the silence was complete. Ralph's lips formed a word but no sound came out' (Golding, 1954: 200–201).

Which turns out alright in the end, for Ralph gets to converse with Piggy-mad-anew a short while later.

> *The skull regarded Ralph like one who knows all the answers and won't tell.* A sick fear and rage swept him. Fiercely he hit out at the filthy thing in front of him that *bobbed like a toy and came back*, still grinning into his face, so that he lashed and cried out in loathing. Then he was licking his bruised knuckles and looking at the bare stick, while the skull now lay in two pieces, its grin now six feet across. He wrenched the quivering stick from the crack and held it as a spear between him and the white pieces. Then he backed away, keeping his face to the skull that lay grinning at the sky. (Golding, 1954: 205–206)[51]

Simon disappears into the sea never to return in any form, a more primitive, unconsidered form of sacrifice. Piggy has returned from the waters, the dwelling-place of Leviathan, as the scapegoat fully considered—the dead man that is concealed within the god that is at the dark heart of the sacrificial machinery. The transmogrification of the *ressentiment* spawning commoner, the instigator of the crisis of undifferentiation through the invention of democracy reborn as the supernatural mediator of regenerative violence. The one who paves the way for the fully worked out rituals for the regulation of mimetic desire. The one who harms is now the one who heals who is also the one who eats the sacrifice. Neither through his speech nor his specs but through his magical sacrificial murder brought about by his own actions (say the boys in a collective act of mis-recognition) Piggy has achieved true sovereignty for it is only by becoming a sacralized victim that the commoner can become as a god.

The model *arriviste*.

---

[50] In Neolithic cultures flat rocks were used for sacrificial purposes.

[51] Emphases added.

References

Primary Sources

Golding, W. (1954). *Lord of the flies*. Faber and Faber.
Lord of the Flies. (2000). *The criterion collection*; directed by Peter Brook.

Secondary Sources

Abrams, M. H. (1999). *A glossary of literary terms*. Cornell University Press.
Babb, H. S. (1970). *The novels of William Golding*. The Ohio State University Press.
Bailie, G. (1995). *Violence unveiled: Humanity at the crossroads*. The Crossroad Publishing Company.
Bloom, H. (2008). Introduction. In H. Bloom (Ed.), *William Golding's lord of the flies* (New ed., pp. 7–8). Infobase Publishing.
Crary, J. (1990). *Techniques of the observer: On vision and modernity in the nineteenth century*. MIT Press.
De Tocqueville, A. (1990). *Democracy in America. Volumes One and Two* (H. Reeve, F. Bowen, & P. Bradley, Trans.). Vintage Books.
Dickson, L. L. (1990). *The modern allegories of William Golding*. University of South Florida Press.
Dietrich, O., Heun, M., Notroff, J., Schmidt, K., & Zarnkow, M. (2012). The role of cult and feasting in the emergence of neolithic communities: New evidence from Gobekli Tepe, South-Eastern Turkey. *Antiquity, 86*, 674–695.
Dumouchel, P. (2015). *The Barren sacrifice: An essay on political violence* (M. Baker, Trans.). Michigan State University Press.
Dupuy, J.-P. (2013). *The mark of the sacred*. (M. B. DeBevoise, Trans.). Stanford University Press.
Elias, N. (2000). *The civilizing process: Sociogenetic and psychogenetic investigations* (Revised Edition E. Dunnning, J. Goudsblom, & S. Mennell, Ed., E. Jephcott, Trans.). Blackwell Publishing.
Ferro, M. (2010). *Resentment in history*. (S. Rendall, Trans.). Polity Press.
Firchow, P. E. (2007). *Modern Utopian fictions: from H.G. Wells to Iris Murdoch*. The Catholic University of America Press.
Firchow, P. E. (2008). Peter Edgerly Firchow examines the implausible beginning and ending of *Lord of the Flies*. In H. Bloom (Ed.), *William Golding's Lord of the Flies New Edition* (pp. 90–94). Infobase Publishing.
Frings, M. F. (2010). Introduction. In M. Scheler (Eds.), *Ressentiment*, (Trans. L. B. Coser & W. W. Holdheim, pp. 1–18). Marquette University Press.
Girard, R. (1965). *Desire, deceit and the novel: Self and other in literary structure* (Y. Freccero, Trans.). The Johns Hopkins University Press.
Girard, R. (1977). *Violence and the sacred*. (P. Gregory, Trans.). The Johns Hopkins Press.
Girard, R. (1987). Generative scapegoating. In R. G. Hammerton-Kelly (Ed.), *Violent origins: Walter Burkert, Rene Girard, and Jonathan Z. Smith on ritual killing and cultural formation* (pp. 73–145). Stanford University Press
Girard, R. (1996). The Girard Reader. In J. G. Williams (Ed.), *René Girard: a biographical sketch*. New York: The Crossroad Publishing Company.
Girard, R. (2014). *The one by whom scandal comes*. (M. B. De Boise, Trans.). Michigan State University Press.
Girard, R., Oughourlian, J.-M., & Lefort, G. (1987). *Things hidden since the foundations of the world* (S. Bann & M. Metteer, Trans.). New York: Continuum.

Girard, R., & Treguer, M. (2014). *When these things begin: Conversations with Michel Treguer* (T. C. Merrill, Trans.). Michigan State University Press.

Hobbes, T. (1992). *Leviathan* fully corrected 1651 edition. Cambridge University Library, Syn3.65.1, ed. Richard Tuck. Cambridge University Press

Hynes, S. (1988). William Golding's *lord of the flies*. In J. R. Baker (Ed.), *Critical essays on William Golding* (pp. 13–22). G.K. Hall & Co.

Kinkead-Weekes, M. K., & Gregor, I. (2008). Mark Kinkead-Weekes and Ian Gregor address the symbolism of the conch. In H. Bloom (Ed.), *William Golding's lord of the flies New Edition* (pp. 79–82). Infobase Publishing.

Kirwan, M. (2005). *Discovering Girard*. A Cowley Publications Book.

Mack, B. (1987). Introduction: Religion and ritual. In R. G. Hammerton-Kelly *Violent origins: Walter Burkert, Rene Girard, and Jonathan Z. Smith on ritual killing and cultural formation* (pp. 1–72). Stanford University Press.

Niemeyer, C. (1962). The Coral Island revisited. *College English, 22*(4), 241–244.

Oughourlian, J.-M. (1996). Desire is mimetic: A clinical approach. *Contagion: Journal of Violence Mimesis, and Culture, 3*, 43–49.

Palaver, W. (2013). *Rene Girard's mimetic theory* (G. Borrud, Trans.). Michigan State University Press.

Scheler, M. (2010). *Ressentiment* (L. B. Coser & W. W. Holdheim, Trans.). Marquette University Press.

Tomelleri, S. (2015). *Ressentiment: Reflections on mimetic desire and society*. Michigan State University Press.

Tuck, R. (1992). Introduction. In T. Hobbes & R. Tuck (Eds.), *Leviathan* (pp. ix–xxvi). Cambridge University Press.

Wilson, E. (2017). "Pig's Head on a Stick": *Lord of the flies* as political and religious drama. In R. C. Evans & S. Fredericks (Eds.), *Critical insights: Lord of the flies* (pp. 226–245). Salem House.

Wilson, E. (2014). Warring sovereigns and mimetic rivals: On scapegoats and political crisis in William Golding's *lord of the flies*. *Law and Humanities, 8*(2), 147–173.

Chapter 3
'Does Anybody Know Anything About the Law?': White Male Suburbanites in the Wilderness and Their Regression to the State of Nature in James Dickey's *Deliverance*

Abstract This chapter is a close critical reading of the novel *Deliverance* (Dickey in Deliverance. Delta, 1970) by James Dickey from the perspective of law-and-literature. It employs the critical literary theory of Rene Girard in suggesting that *Deliverance* may be usefully understood as an interrogation, or even a satire, of the Hobbesian doctrine of the social contract. Whereas Hobbes raises the possibility, but then conspicuously fails to adequately theorize, the concept of the 'little Monarchy' or the private sovereignty of one man in the wilderness, *Deliverance* is premised upon both the feasibility and the desirability of man-the-hunter-as-sovereign-in-the-wilderness. A close reading of the novel reveals the employment of a number of critical notions of Girard—the crisis of undifferentiation, conflictual mimesis, the monstrous doubles—that collectively serve to undermine the facile assumption of the universality of the social contract as well as any clear demarcation between the realms of sovereignty and homicide, law and crime.

Keywords James Dickey · Crisis of undifferentiation · Conflictual mimesis · Monstrous doubles · *Katabasis*

To a degree commonly unrecognized, the primary concern of constitutional jurisprudence in the early seventeenth century, the era of Thomas Hobbes, was not with warfare between rival sovereigns but between the lawful sovereign and the unlawful contesters of that sovereignty within the territory of the Prince. The result was that the early development of social contract, which was in large part a reaction against the sectarianism of the Wars of Religion of the sixteenth century, theory was skewed toward the problem of the originary act, the prehistorical act of consent, the moment at which the sovereignty of the individual, or some smaller grouping such as the family or the clan, was permanently alienated. And from this it followed that one of the most contentious issues in early modern political philosophy was the right, if any, to a lawful revocation of consent and withdrawal from the legal order created by the contract. The general term employed to designate this highly liminal situation was secession, and the issue remains with us to this day. 'Secession is the revolutionary

E. M. Wilson, *Rene Girard, Law, Literature, and Cinema*,
https://doi.org/10.1007/978-981-97-1156-7_3

response to an order founded on consent or social contract. The return to foundational acts'—meaning that pregnant moment immediately prior to the entering into the contract—'can never be prevented or entirely domesticated' (Cover 1983–1984, pp. 23–24). Although not obvious at first glance, there is a Girardian dimension to secession: if mimetic desire has reached the pathological state of metaphysical desire, and the mimetically 'possessed' one is displaying their mimetic rivalry through the cultural channels of either law or politics, the model that such an emulator will naturally be drawn to would be that of sovereignty itself, requiring some kind of performative act to authenticate the imitator's success in overcoming the obstacle—the State—resulting in the physical creation of some kind of micro-sovereignty. Robert M. Cover, although apparently unfamiliar with Girard, was fully aware of the presence of desire in the act of secession: democracy and liberalism are never 'persuasive to a person sufficiently convinced of the destiny or providence that marks him or her as its agent' (Cover 1983–1984, pp. 23–24).

3.1 Thomas Hobbes in the Wilderness

In his seminal *Studies in Classic American Literature* (1923), D. H. Lawrence observed that the American novel served as so much 'hum-bug' to the English reader; the 'European moderns are all *trying* to be extreme. The great Americans I mention [Cooper, Hawthorne, Poe, Dana, Melville, Whitman] just were it. Which is why the world has funked them, and funks them today' (Lawrence, 1978, p. 5). For Lawrence, the two national literary traditions which refuse assimilation into the European tradition are the American and the Russian.[1] Even worse, from an American perspective, is the typical English readers' relegation of the great American novels to the status of what we today hygienically denote as 'young person's literature'.

> We like to think of the old-fashioned American classics as children's books. Just childishness, on our part. The old American art-speech contains an alien quality, which belongs to the American continent and to nowhere else. But, of course, so long as we insist on reading the books as children's tales, we miss all that ... It is hard to hear a new voice, as hard as it is to listen to an unknown language. We just don't listen There is a new voice in the old American classics. The world has declined to hear it, and has babbled about children's stories. (Lawrence, 1978, p. 7)

Lawrence's comment 'an alien quality, which belongs to the American continent and to nowhere else' is extremely interesting. I would suggest that this 'alien quality' of American novel, and the thing that enables it to serve as a 'twin' to the Russian, is the central importance placed upon that most un-English of phenomena, an unsettled frontier. In other words, American literature, most unlike its manifold European counterparts, radically problematizes the problem of geographical space through its signature motifs of both the hunt (*Moby Dick*) and the quest (*Huckleberry*

[1] 'Two bodies of modern literature seem to me to have come to a real verge: the Russian and the American....' Lawrence (1978), p. 5.

Finn; *The Great Gatsby*). From a law-and-literature perspective, such a dismissal is especially ironic as the subversive qualities of spatiality constitute one of the most destabilizing elements, or dangerous supplements, to the central text of British legal and political philosophy, *Leviathan* (1651) by Thomas Hobbes.[2] Having effectively reduced the problem of sovereignty to the effective exercise of consensual power within the community, encapsulated by the alternating constitutional systems of Common-wealth-by-Institution and Common-wealth-by-Acquisition, Hobbes is forced to confront the implications his own theory raises concerning the possibility of the establishment of lawful secessionist micro-sovereignties that exist outside of the effective control of the community—that is, on the frontier. Hobbes first approaches this threatening possibility in Chapter Twenty of Part Two, illustratively entitled 'On Dominion Paternall and Despoticall'.

> Covenants, without the Sword, are but Words, and of no strength to secure a man at all. Therefore notwithstanding the Lawes of Nature, (which every one hath then kept, when he has will to keep them, when he can do it safely,) if there be no Power erected, or not great enough for our security; every man will, and may lawfully rely upon his own strength and art, for caution against all other men (Hobbes, 1991, pp. 117–118).... For the Sovereign is absolute ... or else there is no Soveraignty at all; and so every man may Lawfully protect himselfe, if he can, with his own sword, which is the condition of war. (Hobbes, 1991, p. 142)

Although Hobbes' need to restrict the Common-wealth's potential for tyranny forces him to concede that the self-defense of the subject is an inalienable natural right, the notion of a wholly private form of sovereignty logically flows from the central premise of *Leviathan* itself. Hobbes frames the issue of self-defense this way: '...if there be no Power erected, or not great enough for our security; every man will, and may lawfully rely on his own strength and art, for caution against all other men' (Hobbes, 1991, p. 118). The use of the word 'lawful' here is most problematic, as the failure of the Common Power constitutes the failure of the Sovereign, the mortal god, that is the source of all law. So that if the private person can fall back upon what can be interpreted as a residual right, the implication would be that the individual's 'right' to use violence (as opposed to mere physical capacity to do so) had never been wholly alienated and the Leviathan's power less than complete. The robust positivism of the Hobbesian State leads us to conclude that the successful replication of the conditions of sovereignty on the personal or familial level could, prima facie, meet all of the criteria of the more widely recognized Common-wealth.

> By this it appears, that a great Family if it be not part of some Common-wealth, is of the self, as to the Rights of Soveraignty, a little Monarchy; whether the Family consist of a man and his children; or of a man and his servants; or of a man, and his children, and servants together: wherein the Father or Master is the Soveraign But yet a Family is not properly a Common-wealth; *unless it be of that power by its own number, or by other opportunities, as not be subdued without the hazard of war*. (Hobbes, 1991, p. 142)

Leviathan attempts to avoid the self-subverting implications of this wholly logical conclusion by a rather simplistic appeal to History—although the 'little Monarchy' is a theoretical possibility, it will never exist as a matter of fact.

---

[2] See Chap. 2, above.

> Nor is it the joyning together of a final number of men, that gives [men-in-society; the Multitude] this security; because in small numbers, small additions on the one side or the other, make the advantage of strength so great as is sufficient to carry the Victory; and therefore gives encouragement to an invasion The Multitude sufficient to confide in our Security, is not determined by any certain number, but by comparison with the Enemy we feare; and is then sufficient, when the odds of the Enemy is not of so visible and conspicuous moment, to determine the event of warre, as to move him to attempt. (Hobbes, 1991, p. 118)

But this can be made out to be a constitutional house of cards: all that the 'little Monarch,' or the 'micro-sovereign' need do to secure his rights is to physically prevail on the fields of combat. Which would make the frontier the perfect arena for a little war.

3.1.1 Thomas Hobbes on the Family

Sovereignty is always public in nature, never private, so that, employing contemporary terminology, there can be no such thing as a lawful micro-sovereignty or sub-state actor. The reason for this, however, has nothing to do with constitutional theory, but with the asymmetry among contending forces: any political association that is simply too small or weak to guarantee its own survival within the state of nature can never realize the material conditions of the commonwealth. Hobbes makes this clear in his brief consideration the family.

> For the Sovereign is absolute…or else there is no sovereignty at all; and so every man may Lawfully protect himself, if he can, with his own sword, which is the condition of war. By this it appears that a great Family [the private unit] if it be not part of one Commonwealth, is of itself, as to the Rights of Sovereignty, a little Monarchy…wherein the Father or Master is the Sovereign. But yet a Family is not properly a Commonwealth; unless it be of that power by its own number, or by other opportunities, as not to be subdued without the hazard of war. For where a number of men are manifestly too weak to defend themselves united, every one may use his own reason in time of danger, to save his own life, either by flight, or by submission to the enemy, as he shall think best…And this much shall suffice; concerning what I find by speculation, and deduction, of Sovereign Rights, from the nature, need, and designs of men, in erecting of Commonwealths, and putting themselves under Monarchs, or Assemblies, entrusted with power enough for their protection. (Hobbes, 1991, pp. 142–143)

An additional factor mitigating against the practical impossibility of a micro-commonwealth is Hobbes rather tortuous argument concerning the irrevocability of the social contract.

> First, because they [the People] Covenant,[3] it is to be understood, they are not obliged by former Covenant to anything repugnant hereunto. And consequently they that have already Instituted a Commonwealth, being thereby bound by Covenant, to own the Actions, and Judgments of one [the Sovereign], cannot lawfully make a new Covenant, amongst themselves, to be obedient to any other, in anything whatsoever, without his permission. And therefore, they that are subjects to a Monarch, cannot without his leave cast off Monarchy…nor transfer their Person from him, that bears it, to another Man, or other Assembly

[3] Meaning voluntarily enter into the social contract.

of men: for they are bound, every man to every man, to Own, and be reputed Author of all, that he that already is their Sovereign, shall do, and judge fit to be done: so that any one man dissenting, all the rest should break their Covenant made to that man, which is injustice: and they have also every man given the Sovereignty to him that bears their Person; and therefore if they depose him, they take from him that which is his own, and so again it is injustice. (Hobbes, 1991, pp. 121–122)

In marked contrast with his overall tone, Hobbes' tactical deployment of the seminal term '*injustice*' would seem to indicate supra-political moral considerations, which would take him dangerously close to an at least tacit concession to the principles of natural law. In a similar manner, Hobbes appears to assert the inalienability and indivisibility of the powers and prerogatives of the Sovereign that suggest the morality (or moralism) of contractual agreement: 'These are the Rights, which make the Essence of Sovereignty,[4] and which are the marks, whereby a man may discern in what Man, or Assembly of men, the Sovereign Power is placed, and resides. For these are incommunicable, and inseparable' (Hobbes, 1991, p. 127). The great paradox here is that although Leviathan is a thing of power—the Great Beast that emerges from the turbulence of the seas of politics—it seems to be imbibed with a moral nature, or, at the very least, appears to be some kind of thing to which we are obliged to show moral consideration for some reason. This is Hobbes on the Commonwealth-by-Institution: 'It is true that they that have Sovereign power may commit Iniquity; but not Injustice, or Injury in the proper signification' (Hobbes, 1991, p. 124). And this is Hobbes on The Commonwealth-by-Acquisition.

And this kind of Dominion, or Sovereignty, differs from Sovereignty by Institution, only in this, That men who choose their Sovereign, do it for fear of one another, and not of him whom they Institute: But in this case, they subject themselves to him [whom] they are afraid of. In both cases they do it for fear: which is to be noted by them, that hold all such Covenants, as proceed from fear of death, or violence, void: which if it were true, in any kind of Commonwealth, could be obliged to Obedience. It is true, that in a Commonwealth once Instituted, or acquired, Promises proceeding from fear of death, or violence, are no Covenants, nor obliging, when the thing promised is contrary to the Laws; But the reason is not, because it was made upon fear, but because he that promises has no right in the thing promised (Hobbes, 1991, pp. 138–139).

This is Hobbes contradicting himself twice: '*he that promises has no right in the thing promised*' logically imposes no binding obligation upon the 'Author of all' that is the source of everything social. The obvious question is why is it necessary for Hobbes to formulate such an absolute conception of sovereignty, one that is so excessive that he needs to make a sub rosa move in the direction of the normative rather than the descriptive. And the answer is that, on the basis of his own axiomatic assumptions, the sole alternative to absolute power is total chaos, the irreversible reversal to the state of nature which is the material condition of the crisis of undifferentiation[5]; in the event of secession from the social contract, the Commonwealth 'returns therefore to the Sword again; and every man recovers the right of protecting himself by his own strength, contrary to the design they had in the Institution (Hobbes,

[4] Hobbes (1991): Chapter XVIII, pp. 121–126.

[5] See Chap. 2, above.

1991, p. 123)…In those Nations, whose Commonwealths have been long-lived, and not been destroyed, but by foreign war, the Subjects never did dispute the Sovereign Power' (Hobbes, 1991, p. 145). But that still does not constitute an answer, or not a moral one, because if a group of citizens choose to defect from the Commonwealth, the prohibition against political catastrophe carries no moral weight within a world, and among a species, that is motivated by absolutely nothing other than self-interest. And Hobbes knows this perfectly well, which is why he is terrified. Because if there is any room for an objective 'moral right' in the Hobbesian universe it can only be this one, the self-same that gave rise to the birth of Leviathan at the beginning of History: 'And to every man remains, from the natural and necessary appetite of his own conservation, the *right* of protecting himself by his private strength, which is the condition of War; and contrary to the end for which every Commonwealth is instituted' (Hobbes, 1991, p. 126). This is the principle, the *right to survival*, that Hobbes cannot logically argue against because it is the existence of this 'right,' one which equals an absolute *need* ('natural and necessary appetite') dominating the realm of life or death, that is the true cause of the very thing that he proclaims: the mortall God.

Try as he might, Hobbes cannot deny the obvious: by reducing sovereignty to power coupled with assent he has introduced a perpetually de-stabilizing reversibility among diverse social groupings, both great and small. The intellectual paradox of Hobbes' legacy, what we laughably call the social contract—the quasi-mythic foundational or 'original act' of juridical order—is two-fold. There is the problem of what might be called inter-generational conveyance: that the social contract, to retain both its legitimacy and intelligibility, must necessarily be universal in time. No future defections, or secessions, are permissible because the original contract binds all future generations in their obedience to the lawful Common-wealth.[6] Just with time so too with space: in order to be sufficiently grounded so as to fulfill the vital need of collective security, the contract must bind all parties to it, even those who have exited the territorial borders of the site of the original act. For both these reasons, *Leviathan* is haunted by the specter of private sovereignty which yields us this question: is it ever possible, and, if so, under what circumstances, for the social contract to be freely revoked and a private sovereignty to be lawfully created within the space now vacated by the Common-wealth?

It is precisely this question that invests the American 'adventure novel' *Deliverance* (1970) by James Dickey (1923–1997), with its urgency.[7] In what follows, I will be developing my Girardian critique of Hobbesian social contract theory in Chap. 2 through a critical evaluation of *Deliverance*, which I consider to be one of the unacknowledged canonical texts of law-and-literature. I will treat this novel as a

[6] 'From that law of Nature, by which we are obliged to transferre to another, such Rights, as being retained, hinder the peace of Mankind, there followeth a Third; which is this, *That men performe their Covenants made*; without which, Covenants are in vain, and but Empty words; and the Right of all men to all things remaining, wee are still in the condition of Warre … But when a Covenant is made, then to break it is *Unjust*: And the definition of INJUSTICE, is no other than *the not Performance of Covenant*. And whatsoever is not Unjust, is *Just*' (Hobbes 1991, p. 100).

[7] For a much earlier version of this chapter see Wilson (2016).

complementary text to *Lord of the Flies* (1954) by William Golding, in that the adults undergo what deceptively appears to be a 'cultural regression' while on a journey into the wilderness of northern Georgia. As with lost boys on the nameless island, the same jurisprudential questions will be posed: is the social contract adequate to practically govern human behavior? Is it legally possible to validly revoke the contract if circumstances demand it? What unifies both texts are that they consist of an extended meditation on the foundations of both sovereignty and the law while doubling as a mimetic drama expressed through the homoerotic desires of the two, or twinned, protagonists. Which is what makes *Lord of the Flies* a veritable textbook of Girard's conceptualization of mimeticism.

> Our hypothesis makes it logical to imagine that the rigorous symmetry between the mimetic partners … the living obstacle of the model that is automatically transformed into a rival … must bring about two things among man's ancestors, little by little: the ability to look at the other person, the mimetic *double*, as an *alter ego* and the matching capacity to establish a *double* inside oneself, through processes like reflection and consciousness (Girard et al., 2003, pp. 284, 285).

In both Golding's novel and Brook's film the relationship between the two chief boys, Ralph and Jack, is strictly binary: they both serve as the model for a particular version of sovereignty (Institution versus Acquisition) and the monstrous doubles that they yield dramatically act out the triumph of one form of the Common-wealth ('one Will') at the expense of the other ('one Assembly'); 'The Greatest of humane Powers, is that which is compounded of the Powers of most men, united by consent, in one person, Naturall or Civill, that has the use of all their Powers depending on his will; such is the Power of a Common-wealth…' (Hobbes, 1991, p. 62) The mimetic relationship in *Deliverance*, however, is much more complex, with the rivalry between Ed Gentry and Lewis Medlock assuming the explicit form of the more mimetically charged triangle (Girard, 1965, pp. 1–52), specifically the triangulation of the master-disciple relationship.

> Mimesis cannot spread without becoming reciprocal; at every instant the rivals assume the roles of model and disciple. Mimetic desire always plays off a desire that is already mimetic. Desires attract, ape, and bind one another, creating antagonistic relationships that both parties seek to define in terms of difference. But, in reality, the relationship is undifferentiated. In fact, at every instance, mimesis engenders new reciprocities by a constant doubling of the same ruses, the same strategies, and the same mirror effects (Girard, 1978, p. 91).

And what makes the triangle so prone to psychic catastrophe is that it is founded upon metaphysical desire, the most dangerous form of rivalry and the one most conducive to the fostering of homicidal *ressentiment* and the birthing of monstrous doubles.

> The conflict of desires results automatically from their mimetic character. This mechanism necessarily determines the characteristics of what Nietzsche calls *ressentiment*. The re- of *ressentiment* is the resurgence of desire colliding with the obstacle of the model-desire. Necessarily opposed by the model, the disciple-desire returns toward its source to poison it. *Ressentiment* is only truly intelligible if we begin again with mimetic desire (Girard, 1978, p. 91).

The triangle is deadly because it can never be free from scandal: since the imitator (the disciple) can only approach the mimetic object through the intermediary presence of the model (the master), the imitator must undergo an interminable process of rejection and failure as the model will constantly seek his or her monopolization of access to that ideal which is Being. Ed, as hero-protagonist, is unconsciously antagonistic toward Lewis who is the model, and therefore both the mediator and the obstacle; that is, there is an ambivalence as to whether Lewis actually is the model that Ed strives to be or whether Lewis merely happens to occupy a position closer to the model that Ed reaches for, as Ed lets slip, 'Lewis was the only man I knew who could do with his life exactly what he wanted to' (Dickey, 1970, p. 6). But this leaves unresolved the issue as to whether Lewis is the 'real deal', the incarnation of the model itself, or is merely a superior imitator of it and, therefore, as possessed by mimetic desire (or metaphysical absence) as much as any other imitator-rival. Here is Dickey's own estimate of Lewis as though scripted by Girard.

> I think that we all yearn to be something other than what we are. I'm really very dissatisfied with what I am. This is the whole secret of Lewis, because he despises himself. Lewis is no more or less than an intellectual and physical counterpart of Charles Atlas, who was once a skinny, 97-pound weakling, but now can be proud of himself, because he's put all this time in on his body. He is a victim of a crushing inferiority complex, so he spends enormous amounts of time on himself, making himself impressive intellectually—physically first, and hopefully intellectually—with all his theories and mystiques, so that he can make other people feel inferior.' Or envy him; 'Ed is sort of taken in' (James Dickey qtd. Keesey, 1994, p. 204).

The plot of *Deliverance* re-enacts the transition from acquisitive mimesis—when the 'two mimetic rivals attempt to wrest from one another [the object] because they designate it as desirable to one another' (Girard et al., 2003, p. 15)—to conflictual mimesis, when the disguised death-struggle between the two is successfully resolved through a pair of sacrificial murders that serve as the foundational acts of the 'private' sovereignty of both of the sacrificers. What each novel makes clear in its own way—Golding's by use of the Biblical allegory of the Fall and the warring brothers, Dickey's by invoking the motifs of Greek and Celtic mythology—is that any literary dramatization of the foundational dilemmas of social contract theory must necessarily assume the form of a tale of mimetic rivalry within which the double form of sovereignty, public and private, is narratively twinned with the parallel doubles of the contending would-be sovereigns, or models.

Hobbes staked the entirety of *Leviathan* upon Man's overwhelming fear of death.[8] The question that *Deliverance* forces us to consider is whether the joy of killing, here symbolized by hunting, is capable of overcoming this primordial dread and seducing every 'Man' with the irresistible allure of the Covenant of the Sword, which would render the Common-wealth eternally unstable, a thing from which secession would always be possible and often realizable in fact. The libidinal economy of Ed and Lewis' 'little Monarchy' hinges on the answer to this question; if the answer is yes,

[8] This is the central premise of the whole of Chapter XVII, Part Two of *Leviathan*, 'Of the Causes, Generation, and Definition of a Common-Wealth' (Hobbes 1991, pp. 117–121).

then the social contract cannot bind absolutely. Dickey leaves us in no doubt as to what the answer and truly uncanny, then is the observation made by Fredric Jameson: '...an adventure story like Dickey's ... causes you to posit the need for Leviathan, or the authoritarian state, to hold the disorder and the anarchy of individual violence and of human nature in general in check' (Jameson, 1994, p. 53). This is backward: what Dickey's 'adventure story' demonstrates is that human nature will *always* seek the death of the 'mortall God'. Which in the case of *Deliverance* is none other than Lewis Medlock at the hands of his emulator Ed Lewis.

3.2 'The World is Easily Lost': In the Country of the Nine-Fingered People

Dickey's novel is a dual meditation on the inherent limitations of social contract theory, both geographical and existential, the social contract being portrayed as 'un-natural' because it is premised upon an inherently false notion of human nature that assumes an ontological dichotomy between society and nature.[9] According to Girard, the 'eternal return' (Girard & Treguer, 2014, p. 2) of mimetic rivalries explode the intelligibility of social contract doctrine and because Hobbes lacked an understanding of the scapegoat mechanism he falsely concluded that 'since violence looms...human beings are obliged to collaborate' (Girard & Treguer, 2014, p. 25). However, given the account of human nature that Hobbes himself provides in *Leviathan*, it is exceedingly implausible to conclude that 'Man' is actually capable of permanently adhering to the highly rationalistic terms of the social contract once entered into.

> For the Lawes of Nature (as *Justice, Equity, Modesty, Mercy* and in summe *doing to others, as wee would be done to,*[10]) of themselves, without the terrour of some Power, to cause them to be observed, are contrary to our natural Passions, that carry us to Partiality, Pride, Revenge, and the like. And Covenants, without the Sword, are but Words, and of no strength to secure a man at all (Hobbes, 1991, pp. 117–118).

As opposed to Hobbes' axiomatic reasoning, Girard argues that the community 'knows from experience that it is incapable of overcoming its divisions by its own means, incapable of patching together its own *social contract*, if you will. It thus turns once more to the scapegoat' (Girard & Treguer, 2014, p. 20).

The first of the novel's two epigraphs[11] is taken from Georges Bataille: '*Il existe a la base de la vie humaine, un principe d'insuffisance.*' I translate this (poorly) as

---

[9] Girard's frequent and direct appeals to ethology overcomes Hobbes' incoherent two-fold deployment of natural law: the objective (or environmental) condition of 'the state of nature' and natural reason which grounds the residual natural right of self-defence and survival. Girard resolves this messy situation by radically re-grounding Man-in-Nature: 'The strength of ethology lies in its ability to uncover indubitable resemblances between animal sociality and human sociality' (Girard et al., 2003, p. 91).

[10] Another example of Hobbes' evasive sliding towards natural law.

[11] I discuss the second epigraph below.

'The basis of human existence is insufficiency.' However, Girard's own translation might well read 'Imitative desire is always a desire to be Another' (Girard, 1965, p. 83). Girard and Bataille, in their very different ways, are philosophers of radical absence.[12] 'The human subject does not really know what to desire, in the last resort' (Girard et al., 2003, p. 343); thus, the human subject 'desires *being*, something he himself lacks and which some other person [the 'model'] seems to possess. The subject thus looks to that other person to inform him of what he should desire in order to acquire that being' (Girard, 1977, p. 146). The entirety of human desire, the libidinal dimension of social existence, is subsumed under mimesis; 'desire itself is essentially mimetic, directed toward an object desired by the model,' (Girard, 1977, p. 146) from which comes rivalry, 'the mimetic nature of conflict, which is to say the ultimate absence of any object proper to it' (Girard et al., 2003, p. 31). Rivalry is the flip side of the crisis of undifferentiation, that potentially boundless state of existential anguish in which no one is anything in particular because all inhabit the universal space of absent identity, a hellish crisis of the collective of the loss of personal differences that triggers an avalanche of reciprocal and escalating violence; 'Sameness is the terrible war in which twins [or 'monstrous doubles'] are personally engaged, right up until the moment when one manages to kill the other...When it spreads it becomes the famous war of all against all of which Hobbes spoke' (Girard, 2014, pp. 104–105).

Remarkably, Dickey places the crisis of undifferentiation at the very beginning of *Deliverance*, a novelistic enactment of a hideous convergence of two seemingly differentiated adults—Ed and Lewis—who are ultimately revealed to be doubles, or twins of mimetic desire. The second chapter contains a lengthy account of Ed and Lewis' drive from Atlanta to the remote mountain community of Oree, from which they, and their two companions, Bobby Trippe and Drew Ballinger, will begin a three-day canoe trip down the even more remote Cahulawassee River. A significant portion of the conversation between Ed and Lewis during this lengthy drive concerns Ed's notion of 'sliding,' a suggestive term that, on a superficial level, denotes moral and existential laziness as well as sexual impotence,[13] but that conceals within itself the latent potential for a crisis of identity, or difference.

> Ed: 'Do you know what sliding is?'
> Lewis: 'No. You want me to guess?'
> 'I'll tell you. Sliding is living anti-friction. Or, no, sliding is living *by* anti-friction. It is finding a modest thing you can do, and then greasing that thing. On both sides. It is grooving with comfort.'
> 'You don't believe in madness, eh?'
> 'I don't, at all. I know better than to fool with it.'...
> 'We'll see,' Lewis said, glancing at me as though he had me. 'We'll see. You've had all that office furniture in front of you, desks and bookcases and filing cabinets

[12] See Chap. 1, above.

[13] 'I knew that if I managed to get up, through the enormous weight of lassitude... [I would still suffer] a sense of being someone else, some poor fool who lives as unobserved and impotent as a ghost, going through the only motions it has' (Dickey, 1970, p. 18).

and the rest. You've been sitting in a chair that won't move. You've been steady. But when that river is under you, all that is going to change. There's nothing you do as vice-president of Emerson-Gentry that's going to make any difference at all, when the water starts to foam up. Then, it's not going to be what your title says you do, but what you end up doing. You know: *doing*.'

Then he waited, and I woke up fully,[14] where I had not been before (Dickey, 1970, p. 41).

At the heart of Lewis' apparently unanswerable retort is the direct invocation of the state of nature, the primitive condition 'where every man is enemy to every man...wherein men live without security, than what their own strength, and their invention shall furnish' (Hobbes, 1991, p. 89) which clearly invokes the re-establishment of differences among the competing enemy survivalists. For Hobbes all of this occurred earlier in time and has since been overcome by the original act of social contract, but Dickey subtly transposes the state of nature to an alien space within the present.

Lewis: 'I just believe,' he said, 'that the whole thing is going to be reduced to the human body, once and for all. I want to be ready.'
Ed: '*What* whole thing?'

'The human race thing. I think that the machines are going to fail, the political systems are going to fail, and a few men are going to take to the hills and start over.'

I looked at him...What kind of fantasy led to this? I asked myself. Did he have long dreams of atomic holocaust in which he had to raise himself and his family out of the debris of less strong folk and head toward the same blue hills we were approaching? (Dickey, 1970, p. 42)

... He pointed ahead, where the hills were moving from one side of the road to the other, and growing solid. 'That's where I'd go,' he said. 'Right where we're going. You could make something up there. You could make something and not have to build it on sand' (Dickey, 1970, p. 44).

The observant reader should realize immediately that Lewis' 'something not built on sand' passes the first test of Hobbes' definition of the little Monarchy.

And in all places, where men have lived by small families, to robbe and spoyle one another, has been a Trade, and so farre from being against the Law of Nature, that the greater spoyles they gained, the greater was their honour; and men observed no other Lawes therein, but the Laws of Honour; that is, to abstain from cruelty, leaving men to their lives, and instruments of husbandry. And as small Familyes did then; so now do Cities and Kingdomes which are but greater Familyes (for their own security) enlarge their Dominions, upon all pretences of danger, and fear of Invasion, or assistance that may be given to the Invaders, endeavour as much as they can, to subdue, or weaken their neighbours, by open force, and secret arts, for want of other Caution, justly; and are remembered for it in after ages with honour (Hobbes, 1991, p. 118).

What is less obvious, but becomes clearer when we apply Girard, is the manner in which Lewis' 'something' mimetically replicates not merely the little Monarchy

---

[14] A neat turn of phrase which we may identify as Ed's awakening from the 'slumber,' or the mystification, of liberalism.

of Hobbes but the entire libidinal economy of the nuclear family. Hobbes' perhaps accidental reversal of the relationship between family and Common-wealth parallels the un-grounded nature of all mimetic relationships which are always subject to an overriding reversibility.

> Ed: 'What could you make?'
> Lewis: 'If everything wasn't dead,[15] you could make a kind of life that wasn't out of touch with everything, with the other forms of life. Where the seasons would mean something, would mean everything. Where you could hunt as you needed to, and maybe do a little farming, and get along. You'd die early, and you'd suffer, and your children would suffer, but you'd be in touch' (Dickey, 1970, p. 44).

So Lewis' fantasized (meaning desired) little Monarchy of 'Lewis Medlock country' also passes the first test of what Girard called metaphysical desire, the desire to achieve an unmediated relationship with Being itself, the epitome of authenticity, the unassailable grounds of the true self-authoring of desire.

There is, of course, an obvious flaw in Lewis' conception of his authenticity-besotted survivalist State; as Robert Gordon has pointed out, any legal regime, no matter how primitive or small, 'consists less in the force that it can bring to bear against violators of its rules than in its capacity to persuade people that the world described in its images is the only attainable one in which a sane person would want to live' (Gordon, 1984, p. 109). Dickey has solved this problem, however, through his sub-textual deployment of the erotic; apart from all of the heavily encoded libidinal meanings associated with the family, of which Lewis' private sovereignty is a direct continuation, the seductive challenge of survivalism lies in its explicit valorization of metaphysical desire as a life-sustaining erotic force.

> Ed: 'You're ready, are you?'
> Lewis: 'I think I am,' he said. 'I sure am, psychologically. At times I get the feeling that I can't wait. Life is so fucked-up now, and so complicated, that I wouldn't mind if it came down, right quick, to the bare survival of who was ready to survive. You might say I've got the survival craze, the real bug. And to tell the truth I don't think most other people have. They might cry and tear their hair and be ready for some short hysterical violence or other, but I think most of them wouldn't be too unhappy to give down and get it over with' (Dickey, 1970, pp. 42–43).

---

[15] Lewis' use of the word 'dead' here is interesting, and crops up frequently in the writings of contemporary hunters when they attempt to justify their ritualistic predations within an increasingly sliding world. Consider this example from M. R. James: 'Despite our ever-changing, ever-indignant world with its growing ignorance of and indifference to the ways of the wild, I remain a predator, pitying those who revel in artificiality and synthetic success while regarding me and my kind [the Hunter] as relics of a time and place no longer valued or understood…Others around me may opt to eat only plants, nuts, and fruits. Still others may employ faceless strangers to procure their meats, their leathers, their feathers, and all those niceties and necessities of life. Such is their right, of course, and I wish them well. All I ask in return is that no one begrudge me—*and all of us who may answer the primordial stirrings within our hunter's souls*—my right to do some of these things for myself' (James, 1997, p. 107).

In other words, in order to overcome the crisis of undifferentiation, it is necessary to revoke the existing social contract which is premised on the absence of distinctions.[16] Lewis' challenge to the community, from a law-as-literature perspective is as simple as it is obvious: if sovereignty is nothing more than the effective operation of power then the successful resistance to that power subverts the universality of the social contract's rule of law and creates a space wherein the difference of subjective and authentic identity may be re-established. I have already discussed Hobbes' own solution to this apparently fatal flaw within the social contract: men may try to defect but the power of the State guarantees a general compliance (fear of death) which is enforced by punishment in the event of attempted secession. But as Lewis' 'seduction' of Ed reveals, the practical operation of sovereignty (and, therefore, its ultimate legitimacy) can be effectively opposed by two strategies of resistance. The first is the geographical: conceive of a space or area of habitation physically outside the effective operational parameters of the State. The second is existential: postulate a theory of human nature that is so inherently prone toward the will-to-secede that effective policing becomes physically and psychologically impossible. Ultimately, difference cannot be denied because the absence of difference is unbearable as Girard theorized.

3.2.1 The Geographical: 'Savage Sacredness'

The application of the academic discipline of geography to the interrogation of mainstream jurisprudence constitutes a little-known sub-category within Critical Legal Theory. An outstanding example of this approach is Wes Pue's article 'Wrestling with Law: (Geographical) Specificity vs. (Legal) Abstraction,' which is concerned with the case of *R v Dudley and Stephens* (1884), the most notorious incident of 'survival cannibalism' on the High Seas in the nineteenth century (Pue, 1990, pp. 567–568). According to Pue

> 'Law' is ... a profoundly anti-geographical faith. Judges are its high priests, courtrooms its sanctuaries, professional schools its seminaries. Its scriptures are 'authorities' passed down from generation to generation by appointed oracles. Its god is a de-contextualized, highly abstracted, and depersonalized 'rationality'. Contexts of all sorts—gender, class, religious, cultural, political, historical or spatial—are the enemies of Law. Law is the antithesis of region, locality, place, community (Pue, 1990, p. 566).

Law, by being radically de-spatialized, this a particular instance of a much wider process of de-contextualization, becomes a form of 'anti-geography' within which the 'entire world is transmuted into one vast isotropic surface'. Culturally hegemonic, law transmutes the 'subjects of Law' into undifferentiated and inter-exchangeable components; 'these are the men required by "justice" in John Rawl's original position [i.e., contemporary social contract theory].[17] Abstracted from social relations, they

[16] See Chap. 11, below.

[17] See Chap. 11, above.

know not who they are, where they are, from whence they came, or where they are going' (Pue, 1990, pp. 567–568). In short: there is no way to tell them apart. If law is isotropic, then it exhibits a lack of difference; in Girardian terms, law itself, and the legal order that it gives rise to, would suffer from a crisis of undifferentiation. It is, therefore, of consummate interest that as Dickey moves his doubled protagonists into the frontier his writing 'slides' increasingly toward the pre-representational reason of sacrifice. Both *Lord of the Flies* and *Deliverance* are embedded within a preternatural landscape, signifying, through poetic conceit, the pre-representational language that both invalidates the differentiation conventionally assumed by sovereignty and law and validates the logic of sacrificial surrogacy (Girard, 1977, pp. 250–273). As with Golding, Dickey forces the reader to confront an alien, and implicitly violent, landscape that doubles both as Hobbes' state of nature and as the externalized re-presentation of the pre-representational: the frontier is a 'strange' or 'violent' space where meanings begin to shift and anything can be exchanged for something else. Or, as Ed memorably puts it stealing from Gustav Mahler, 'The world is easily lost' (Dickey, 1970, p. 53).

> The trees and bushes where I was looking were connecting, becoming one solid thing; it was very hard to make out what the details were like ... I got squeamishly out into the water and held the canoe, the sliding cold around me full of the presence of night-creatures (Dickey, 1970, p. 82).

> I thought I heard Lewis holler to us, probably to slow down, but the voice, thinly floating through the boom of wall-sound, had no authority and very little being at all (Dickey, 1970, p. 140).

> But the sound was changing, getting deeper and more massively frantic and authoritative.[18] It was the old sound, but it was also new, it was a fuller one even than the reverberations off the walls, with their overtones and undertones; it was like a ground-bass that was made of all of the sounds of the river we'd heard since we'd been on it. God, God, I thought, I know what it is. If it's a falls we're gone (Dickey, 1970, p. 141).

And, of course, the catastrophic descent over the falls takes the hapless 'Suburbanites' as Ed calls them directly into the chthonic gorge that is the dramatic locus of the novel (Dickey, 1970, pp. 140–213).[19] This scene also highlights a rather peculiar personal characteristic of Ed, which is to self-consciously exploit the romantic conceit of the external landscape as the mirror of the internal Self.

> I was dead. I felt myself fading out into the unbelievable violence and brutality of the river, joining it. This is not such a bad way to go, I thought; maybe I'm already there...I got on my back and poured with the river, sliding over the stones like a creature I had always contained but never released (Dickey, 1970, p. 144).

The more time that Ed and Lewis spend along the frontier, the more their world is lost and the less feasible sliding becomes precisely because they are approaching their

[18] Note the substitution of a natural authority for a human one.

[19] It is within the gorge that Ed replaces the wounded Lewis as leader of the group, climbs the face of a cliff during a nocturnal ascent, and ambushes and kills the Mountain Man who presumably has fatally shot Drew and has been stalking the survivors. See below.

ideal which is authentic Being. At the same time, the beginning of Ed's transformation is nothing short of a direct encounter with the sacred which, as Girard knows perfectly well, carries with it its own subversive spatiality. No one cannot long exist if she either perpetually denies the transformative power of violence through the sacrificial mechanism or, paradoxically, if through mis-recognition imagines herself beyond the regenerative effects of sacred and sacralized violence.

> The complex and delicate nature of the community's dealings with the sacred, the ceaseless effort to arrive at the ordered and uninterrupted accord essential to the well-being of the community, can only be expressed, for want of the naked truth, in terms of optimum *distance*. If the community comes too near the sacred it risks being devoured by it; if, on the other hand, the community drifts too far away, out of range of the sacred's therapeutic threats and warnings, the effects of its fecund presence are lost (Girard, 1977, p. 268).

The a-theistick community of Hobbes must, in some sense, be a closed one; sovereignty-as-power requires finitude and the unambiguous demarcation of differences. However, the sacrificial mechanism requires not only the outside—the site of the infinitely dangerous sacred—it also demands periodic migrations, or regressions, toward it. In order to restored, the undistinguished normality of the everyday must be periodically abandoned, which forces an encounter with the Divine; 'Once the outer limits of the community have been crossed we enter the domain of savage sacredness, which recognizes neither boundaries nor limits. This is the realm not only of gods and supernatural creatures, of monsters and the dead, but also of nature itself…' (Girard, 1977, pp. 266–267). And this sliding across boundaries most often takes the form of an encounter with an animal.

3.2.2 *The Existential: 'Man-The-Hunter'*

Throughout his writings, Girard makes two fundamental anthropological assumptions concerning the shadowy process known as hominization. The first one is that the primal emergence of hominid society seems to parallel the supersession of the genetically prescribed 'dominance patterns' governing the less evolved groupings of apes. Unique among hominids, homo sapiens is the only species capable of truly acquisitive behavior as we lack the genetically inscribed dominance patterns 'canalizing desire in divergent directions and making acquisitive mimesis impossible' (Girard et al., 2003, p. 91). The second one is that the very early cultural adaptation of hunting, while clearly beneficial in its nutritional effects, was ultimately derived from even more archaic sacrificial practices.

> To understand what might have impelled human beings to set off in pursuit of the largest and most dangerous animals or to devise the strategies necessary for prehistoric hunting, it is necessary and sufficient to recognize that hunting, at first, was actively linked to sacrifice. The object of the hunt is seen as a substitute for the original victim in its monstrous and sacred aspects. What impelled men to hunt was the search for a reconciliatory victim. The ritual character of hunting is completely compatible with an activity demanding complex technique and the coordination of many individuals (Girard et al., 2003, p. 73).

Although he does not actually employ the term, Girard is an advocate of the 'hunting hypothesis', a radical theory of hominization first developed in the 1950s that views the need to engage in organized predation for nutritional purposes—the transition from a herbivorous to a carnivorous diet—as the primary motor of early cultural evolution; 'Our intellect, interests, emotions, and basic social life—all are evolutionary products of the success of the hunting adaptation' (Washburn & Lancaster, 1986, p. 293).[20] The hunting hypothesis is also essential to the work of a sometime collaborator of Girard, the German classicist Walter Burkert. In his monumental *Homo Necans: The Anthropology of Ancient Greek Sacrificial Ritual and Myth* (1983), Burkert speculated that hunting served as the pre-historic basis of social formation, underpinning an indissoluble link between culture and violence by serving as the biological-functional source of religion hunting requires the performance of rites that both incite and quell violence.[21] To a great degree, Burkert's work is a more anthropological exposition of the poetic insights of the Spanish philosopher Ortega y Gassett who wrote extensively on hunting; 'Life is a terrible conflict, a grandiose and atrocious influence. Hunting submerges man deliberately in that formidable mystery and therefore contains something of religious rite and emotion in which homage is paid to what is divine, transcendent, in the laws of Nature' (Ortega & Gasset, 1972, p. 112). And these rites, which are deeply ambivalent, serve as the basis for all Palaeolithic forms of mythology (Burkert, 1983, pp. 1–48).

> A basic fact established by ethology [animal behaviour] is the priority of ritual communication over language … What is it that makes ritual religion ritual? The simplest answer seems to be that it is the intervention of language and verbalized concepts, including names, to denote 'superior beings' … Hence an element of 'as if' is inherent in ritual from the start, creating some kind of void[22] to be filled out by mythical designations (Burkert, 1987, pp. 151, 153, 154).

Certain primitive peoples, such as the Ndembu, a matrilineal tribe in northern Zimbabwe that were extensively studied by Victor W. Turner, are exemplary in this regard. 'For the Ndembu…the hunt is more than a food quest; it is a religious activity. It is preceded and followed by the performance of rites and it is believed to be beset with perils of an ultra-human order' (Turner, 1967, p. 251). Following the successful performance of these rites, the hunter is 'assisted by the guardian spirit of a deceased hunter-kinsman and by the magical charms; he performs rites to propriate the spirits of the hunter-dead before he ventures into the bush, and he is believed to encounter there the inimical power of witches, sorcerers, ghosts, were-lions and persecuting ancestors' (Turner, 1967, p. 252).

Burkert's theory of religion-as-hunting-ritual is not merely pre-representational in form but actually pre-representational in content.[23] Because of its evolutionary

---

[20] For a general discussion, see Cartmill (1993), pp. 1–27, 225–245; Hill (1982), pp. 521–544.

[21] See below.

[22] In Bataille's terms, *un principe d'insuffisance.*

[23] The primal trauma of hunting itself created the need for a system of representation that, like the sacrificial, depended upon the logic of substitution; 'a theory of the ritualization of the hunt becomes a theory of the origin of religion…. [Burkert] proceeds…simply to describe how the hunting ritual

advantages, early hominids self-consciously organized themselves into hunting societies; this, however, created the uniquely human problem of 'intra-specific aggression'. Because we are not naturally predatory, homo sapiens lack the evolutionary adaptations of the 'natural' hunting species (the predators) that prevent members of the same species from killing each other. The cultural, or self-induced, transition to hunting catastrophically increased the levels of violence within primitive communities owing to the absence of genetic inhibitors.[24] Here, Burkert makes a direct appeal to Functionalism: in order to overcome this otherwise fatal problem primitive Man consciously invested his prey with symbolic and/or erotic significance so that the animal surrogate, and not the original human victim, could serve as the externalized locus of intra-specific aggression. At the same time, as Man is not a 'natural born killer', the objective nature of hunting, which is an act of killing and the shedding of blood, induces both individual and collective 'psychological shock' (horror; guilt) that creates the need for some sort of dramatic and symbolic reconciliation. The resulting rites of purification, culturally expressed through primitive myth, resolve the problem of sanguinary pollution by providing the cultural impetus for the evolution of organized religion and, thus, of a stable and self-stabilizing society of hunters. The terror induced by primitive myth mimetically replicates the horror of violence both inter- and intra-specific; 'With remarkable consistency, myths tell of the origins of man in a fall, a crime that is often a bloody act of violence' (Burkert, 1983, pp. 21–22). Religious rites guarantee the de-contamination of the bloodied hunter of violence through a cathartic purgation; rituals, therefore, 'consist in the paradox of transforming the conflictual disintegration of the community into social collaboration' (Girard et al., 2003, p. 20).[25] For Girard, no less than for Burkert, 'myth is nothing more than…the transfigured account of a real violence' (Girard et al., 2003, p. 109). Although Burkert is not explicitly concerned with the scapegoat as such, his work on hunting prioritizes the importance of mis-recognition, or *meconnaissance*, in a manner very close to Girard: the animal 'target' is deployed as the mimetic substitute for the now occluded human murder victim as a functionalist solution to the

gave rise to the full range of articulations that we understand to be mythic or symbolic, articulations characteristic of religion' (Mack, 1987, p. 26).

[24] 'One of the essential conditions for the organization of men in cooperative societies was the suppression of rage and of the uncontrolled drive for first place in the hierarchy of dominance' (Sherwood I. Washburn, cited in Girard et al., 2003, p. 86). Compare Girard on this same point. 'It is important to realize that extreme rage becomes centripetal once it has been given free rein; it is never naturally centrifugal. The more exasperated rage becomes, the more it tends to turn toward those who are closest and most cherished, those who are most protected in normal circumstances by the rule against violence' (Girard et al., 2003, 86). Girard, however, realizes that Washburn is facing the same problem that bedeviled Norbert Elias in Chap. 2: how can primitive man overcome rage and invent society prior to the invention of those cultural mechanisms that allowed for the effective suppression of rage. Washburn 'recognizes the necessity of mastering rage but he cannot tell us how or why rage was ever effectively mastered' (Girard et al., 2003, p. 86).

[25] On the relation between rites, rituals, and prohibitions, see Chap. 1, above.

problem created by Humanity's evolutionary lack with regard to the genetic prohibition against the infliction of indiscriminate violence and intra-specific aggression.[26] Thus, for both thinkers, '...we see the alpha and omega of human culture, when we understand the surrogate victim as the result of the mimetic process' (Girard et al., 2003, p. 63). This is most apparent in the almost obsessive element of repetition governing all forms of religious ritual. According to Girard.

> There is no difficulty in explaining why ritual is repeated. Driven by sacred terror and wishing to continue life under the sign of the reconciliatory victim, men attempt to reproduce and represent this sign; this attempt consists first of all in the search for victims who seem capable of bringing about the primordial epiphany, and it is there that we find the first signifying activity that can always be defined, if one insists, in terms of language or writing. The moment arrives when the original victim, rather than being signified by new victims, will be signified by something other than a victim, by a variety of things that continue to signify the victim while at the same time progressively masking, disguising, and failing to recognize it (Girard et al., 2003, p. 103).

Both Burkert's hunting rites and Girard's sacrificial mechanism lead to the same result: the restoration of social harmony, or a 'recovered unanimity,' through the initial ritualistic killing of a designated surrogate victim (human or animal) and the subsequent successful re-integration of the killer into the community through ceremonial purification.[27] Girard closely follows Durkheim in postulating a fundamental unity between religion and society that extends the boundaries of the community to include the realms of the Otherworld.

> All aspects of violence are assimilated to an individual ancestor or to the entire legion of the dead ... The worship of the dead, like the worship of the gods, represents an interpretation of the role of violence in the destiny of a community. In fact, it is the most transparent of all such interpretations, the closest to what actually occurred *the first time*—except, of course, that it has misconstrued, as always, the mechanism of recovered unanimity (Girard, 1977, p. 256).

The proof that 'human beings identify all death with the reconciliatory victim and the power of the sacred is what is called the *cult of the dead*, [which] unlike the naturalistic conception of death, appears to underlie all other forms of religion' (Girard et al., 2003, p. 81). Since 'every god, ultimately, conceals a dead man' (Girard et al., 2003, p. 82) Girard is able to determine that the apparitional manifestations of the Dead occur at the precise moments when the crisis of undifferentiation has reached its apogee.

---

[26] The difference between the two lies in the fact that Burkert understands the emergence of hunting within terms of evolutionary adaptation, primarily nutritional, which created all sorts of dis-equilibrium whereas Girard focuses upon the suspension of dominance patterns as opening the flood-gates to mimetic rivalry which required the acquisition of animal victims as sacrificial surrogates: that is, hunting.

[27] 'It is through common action that society becomes self-aware...the collective feelings and ideas that determine [society's] unity and character must be maintained and confirmed at regular intervals... [Religion constitutes] a unified system of beliefs and practices relative to sacred things...that unite into one single moral community ... all those who adhere to them' (Sosis & Alcorta, 2003, p. 265).

> In certain cultures, the gods are either absent or insignificant. In such cases mythic ancestors, or the dead, take the place of the missing divinities and are seen as the founders, guardians and, if need be, disruptors of the cultural order ... The crisis assumes the form of a loss of difference between the living and the dead, a casting down of barriers between two normally separate realms. We have here the proof that the dead incarnate violence; exterior and transcendent violence when order reigns, immanent violence when things turn bad and maleficent reciprocity walks abroad (Girard, 1977, p. 254).

It should come as no surprise, then, that Ed, Lewis, Bobby and Drew all undertake an odyssey into the Underworld—or, as Ed refers to the denizens of the liminal community of Oree, the Country of the Nine-Fingered People.[28]

3.3 *Katabasis* 1: Dueling Banjos

As Erling B. Holtsmark has pointed out, the theme or imaginary of *katabasis*—a term derived from Greek mythology meaning a 'going down or descent,' signifying the transition from the world of the living to the world of the dead—is a widely utilized but underappreciated motif in modern cinema (Holtsmark, 2001). And John Boorman's outstanding cinematic adaptation of *Deliverance* (1972; Warner Brothers) is an infamous example of the cinematic appropriation of the katabatic as icon. Like Golding in *Lord of the Flies*, Dickey mines classical mythology for literary devices for his aesthetic re-staging of the mythic journey away from the community and the social contract; the physical migration in the narrative parallels a psychic pilgrimage toward the sacred Underworld of the Land of the Dead. The narrative structure of *Deliverance* is governed by liminality (Turner, 1969, pp. 94–130), the migration from city to country paralleled by two concurrent migrations: that from Common-wealth to frontier and that from the profane to the sacred. In both readings, Girard's insight into the spatiality of the sacred underlies the twin convergences between religion and law and sacrifice and sovereignty.

While helpfully instructing us on how to recognize *katabasis* in cinema, Holtsmark provides a remarkably useful set of indices for the anthropologically savvy cinema-goer. When reading (or viewing) *Deliverance*, it is almost too easy to go through a kind of katabatic 'check list'—so easy in fact that there is no way to resist it. The first signifier of *katabasis* is: 'The lower world is generally dank and dark, and the journey usually takes place at dusk or during the night. The realm itself is inhabited by the wealthy king and queen of the dead and by the innumerable spirits of the dead, by monsters (e.g., Cerberus) and evil-doers (e.g., Tantalus)' (Holtsmark, 2001, pp. 25–66).[29] I do not believe that I am doing violence to the text in suggesting that the remote community of Oree itself is 'the Kingdom of the Dead', and its inhabitants 'the Dead'.

---

[28] So called because all of the inhabitants of Oree have lost at least one digit to farm machinery. In other words, they bear a mark that is both disfiguring and distinguishing, marking them as a 'special' class of sacred beings (Dickey, 1970, pp. 55–56).

[29] See Endel (1988) who links Dickey's use of *katabasis* with Dante's.

> When Lewis killed the engine, the air came alive and shook with insects, even in the centre of town, an in-and-out responding silence of noise … everything in Oree was sleepy and hookwormy and ugly, and most of all, inconsequential. Nobody worth a damn could ever come from such a place. It was nothing, like most places and people are nothing (Dickey, 1970, p. 55).

Here, the imaginary of the liminal is crucial to textual exegesis; according to Turner.

> The attributes of liminality or of liminal *personae* ('threshold people') are necessarily ambiguous, since this condition and these people elude or slip through the network of classifications that normally locate states and positions in cultural space. Liminal entities are neither here nor there; they are betwixt and between the positions assigned and arrayed by law, custom, convention, and ceremonial…liminality is frequently likened to death, to being in the womb, to invisibility, to darkness, to bisexuality, to the wilderness, and to an eclipse of the sun and moon (Turner, 1969, p. 95).

Turner provides an ironic reply to Pue, inverting the problematic relationship between law and identity. If Girard's theory of undifferentiation is valid, then it is the community, the thing that is governed by the recovered unanimity of sacrifice, which is the site of true identity or difference but, critically, one that requires the periodic regeneration of sacrificial violence. This is the exact opposite of law's isotropic pretence that Pue effectively critiques; instead, it is those spaces outside of the realms of law and community—the liminal—that can be truthfully categorized as isotropic precisely because are the spaces where the manifold crises of undifferentiation need to be acted out.[30] If my hypothesis is correct—that *Deliverance* is a literary dramatization of the violent encounters between sacrifice and sovereignty expressed through metaphysical desire—then it makes perfect poetic sense for Oree to symbolically serve as the threshold to be crossed in order to enter the Underworld and to confront the sacred so that regenerative violence may be performed. The presence of the 'infernal' is clearly conveyed in the description of the garage of the Griner Brothers.

> It was dark and iron-smelling, hot with the closed-in heat that brings the sweat out as though it had been waiting all over your body for the right signal … and through everything, out of the high roof, mostly, came this clanging hammering, meant to deafen and even blind. It was odd to be there, not yet seen, paining with the metal harshness in the half-dark (Dickey, 1970, p. 62).

---

30 Dissenting from Pue somewhat, I would frame the issue this way: it is not the case that law-within-community strips subjects of all particular identities; rather, it subordinates all subjective characteristics to the over-arching and a-contextual standard of the rational and contractual liberal Self. Difference is denied only to the degree that it interferes with the ability to contract. The liberal is 'a Man of no qualities' to the extent that all of his unique characteristics are 'trivial,' meaning that they do not practically impede transactional analysis. This is essentially the stratagem of John Rawls in excluding from the public domain all of the attributes of a given person that in the final analysis resist reconciliation with public reason. But the problem with Rawls is that the exclusion from the public domain is identical to the symbolic violence of ostracism, which is sacrificial. See Chap. 11, below.

And when we actually encounter the inhabitants, they all appear to be vacated of personality. Here is Dickey's description of the nameless 'Old man': 'His movements were very slow, like those of someone whose energies have been taken by some other thing than old age' (Dickey, 1970, p. 55); compare this with Dickey's account of the Lonnie, the 'albino boy':

> [The Old man] came back and behind him was an albino boy with pink eyes like a white rabbit's; one of them stared off at a furious and complicated angle. That was the eye he looked at us with, with his face set in another direction. The sane, rational eye was fixed on something that wasn't there, somewhere in the dust of the road (Dickey, 1970, p. 59).

As the reader is well aware, Drew's 'musical exchange' with Lonnie initiates the justifiably famous 'duelling banjos' sequence (Dickey, 1970, pp. 59–60), which achieved iconic status with the release of Boorman's film version. Not only does this represent the first of several encounters between the Suburbanites and the 'threshold people'—'[Lonnie] emphasized nothing, but through everything he played there was a lovely unimpeded flowing that seemed endless' (Dickey, 1970, p. 60)—it also re-establishes the mythic linkages between music and the Dead (Burkert, 1983, p. 39). As Lewis, an Odysseus-like figure who has traversed the two worlds on earlier occasions (Dickey, 1970, pp. 45–47 and 50–52), remarks, 'There's lots of music, it's practically coming out of the trees. Everybody plays something: the guitar, the banjo, the autoharp, the spoons, the dulcimer—or the dulimore, as they call it' (Dickey, 1970, p. 45). But, immediately afterward, he establishes a second, and even more ominous identification of the Nine-Fingered People with Death.

> 'These are good people, Ed. But they're awful clannish, they're set in their ways. They'll do what they want to do, no matter what. Every family I've ever met up here has at least one relative in the penitentiary. Some of them are in for the making of liquor or running it, but most of them are in for murder. They don't think a whole lot about killing people up here. They really don't' (Dickey, 1970, p. 45).

The second signifier of *katabasis* is that

> The entryway to the other world is often conceived as lying in caves or grottoes or other openings in the earth's crust into the nether regions, such as chasms or clefts. Further, since that other world lies beyond a boundary separating it from our realm, such natural topographical delimiters as rivers, bodies of water, or even mountain ranges may be the physical tokens of demarcation It is well known…that the underworld of classical mythology is penetrated by a number of rivers, most notably Styx and Acheron, which have to be crossed in a skiff punted along by the old ferryman Charon (Holtsmark, 2001, p. 25)

Mountains certainly dominate the landscape of the eternally shifting Community-on-the-Threshold: 'I looked off at the blue forms of the mountains, growing less transparent and cloudlike, shifting their positions, rolling from side to side off the road, coming back and centring our path, but strengthening all the time' (Dickey, 1970, p. 95). However, its mythic locus is the river, the fantastically remote Cahulawassee, that leads directly to the other-wordly gorge within which the final, and regenerative, ritualistic killing will be conducted. In Greek mythology, there are two great 'infernal' rivers that must be successfully crossed in order for the wandering soul (*psyche*) to reach its allotted place in the Underworld: Styx, the physical border of Hades, and Lethe, 'the river of forgetfulness,' whose waters bind the Dead to the Otherworld through amnesia. Although the river that the four Suburbanites travel exhibits the characteristics of both mythic streams, what is most striking is the sleep-inducing properties that the Cahulawassee seems to possess. There are, in fact, suspiciously numerous conjunctions between Ed and sleep (*Morpheus*) throughout the novel (Dickey, 1970, pp. 25, 73, 93, 102, 139, 144).

> There was something about me that usually kept me from dreaming, or maybe kept me from remembering what I had dreamed; I was either awake or dead, and I always came back slowly. I had the feeling that if it were perfectly quiet, if I could hear nothing, I would never wake up. Something in the world had to pull me back, for every night I went down deep, and if I had any sensation during sleep, it was of going deeper and deeper, trying to reach a point, a line or border (Dickey, 1970, p. 25).

However, while the regression into the unconscious seems to be one of Ed's defining characteristics (or neurotic symptoms), Dickey, no less that Girard, forbids us any overly easily psychoanalytical explanations: the novel makes it clear that it is the river itself that exerts an hypnotic influence over the 'hero'.

> A slow force took hold of us; the bank began to go backward. I felt the complicated urgency of the current, like a thing made of many threads being pulled, and with this came the feeling I always had at the moment of losing consciousness at night, going toward something unknown that I could not avoid, but from which I would return (Dickey, 1970, p. 73).

Girard has argued that mimetic desire, because it naturally assumes the form of endless repetition is identical to Freud's notion of the death instinct (Girard et al., 2003, p. 241).

> Mimetic desire makes you into the rival of your model: you fight with him over the object that he himself pointed out to you. This situation reinforces desire and increases the prestige of the obstacle as such. And the supreme obstacle, of course, is death, it's what can kill you. The death drive is the logical outcome of this mechanism (Girard & Treguer, 2014, p. 107).

In Greek mythology, Sleep (*Morpheus*) is the twin of Death (*Thanatos*), which, in at least one instance, Ed associates with Lewis; 'I was dead, and riding, which is a special kind of sleep not like any other, and I heard Lewis saying something that strove in and out of my consciousness' (Dickey, 1970, p. 103). Contrary to modern prejudice, primitive, or hunting, Man does not fear death—he fears the Dead; 'Far from being "innate", the naturalistic view of death is a relatively recent development that is alien to the greater part of humanity … We can account for this … if we recognize that the interpretation of death is determined by the victimage process; death is always intimately linked with life' (Girard et al., 2003, p. 80). The thanatological nature of Ed's desires naturally seek outlet through hunting, but, as Burkert has shown, this must also require Ed to make contact with either the rite-bound Cult of the Dead, or, in more extreme circumstances, with the Dead themselves—which is exactly what seems to transpire in *Deliverance*. Ed already has his traveling companions. All that he requires is a sacrificial victim.

3.4 'Why Do You Go on These Trips with Me, Ed?'

The third signifier of *katabasis* is: a 'journey is to obtain spiritual or material wealth...From the time of Odysseus' descent in the *Odyssey*, katabasis seems inevitably to entail at some level a search for identity. The journey is in some central, irreducible way a journey of self-discovery, a quest for a lost self' (Holtsmark, 2001, p. 26). It makes perfect literary sense that undistinguished Suburbanite Ed wants to die; that is, by means of the mimetic logic of the double, he wants to kill.[31]

> I was not much on theories myself. But I had a good feeling about this trip. After so much shooting at paper images of deer, it was exciting to think of encountering a real one...I knew that there was not much of a chance of our running into a bear or a hog; that was romance. But then, the idea of hunting, for me, was also a kind of romance. The death of a real deer at my hands was just a vaporous, remote presence that hovered over a figure of the paper deer forty-five yards away at target six of our archery range, as I tried to hit the heart-lung section marked out in heavy black (Dickey, 1970, pp. 6–7, 57).

The closer that Ed moves toward the object of his hunter's gaze, the more his desire is activated. The movement toward the animal victim is both erotic and perceptual, as his lethal action overcomes an intuitively perceived gap in his ideal versus actual self—in other words, a lack of Being:

> At first I didn't have any idea of really hunting. I had no firm notion of what I was doing, except walking forward carefully, away from the river and into more and more silence and blindness—for the fog was now coming up past me and thickening straight back into my face—and carrying a bow and a nocked arrow and three other arrows in one hand and fingering the bowstring with the other. It tingled like a wire in my right-hand fingers, giving off an electric current that came from the woods and the fog and the fact that hunting and pretending to hunt had come together and I could not now tell them apart (Dickey, 1970, p. 95).

In actual fact, this is an erotic phenomenon that is commonly experienced by hunters; 'You see the animal and it becomes a love object. There is a tremendous sexuality in this ... in the sense of wanting something deeply, in the sense of *eros*. All quests, all desires are ultimately the same.'[32] More interesting is that Ed's 'problem' turns on a far more complicated series of emotional crises regarding the correct regulation of the relationship between object and model that suggests a defect in his understanding of the process of substitution. Which is understandable given that he is a Suburbanite and is, therefore, bound to representation rather than pre-representation in which fantasy object and real object become one-and-the-same-thing. Consistent with his earlier meditation on targeting the outline image, or abstract representation,

---

[31] This is Dickey's own estimation of Ed Gentry, in many ways the author's own double: 'I wanted to implant in the reader's mind a couple of things. First, that the narrator, without his knowing it, has been a monster all his life, a born killer, as well as an "ordinary suburbanite."' Referring to a deleted scene in which Ed whips his wife Martha, Dickey states, '... this one chance episode ... gave him a chance to exercise to energize this hidden part of his personality [and] has, in a sense, freed him of it. His monstrousness may now take other forms; ones that are imaginary and harmless' (Hart, 2000, p. 443). Imaginary yes, harmless no.

[32] An anonymous hunter (Cartmill, 1993, p. 238).

of the deer as opposed to the 'real thing', Ed undergoes a series of what might be termed 'erotic crises' that appear to result from a failure in a mimetic rivalry of some kind.

3.4.1 *The Model*

As Ed makes clear, on one level hunting, and killing, simply serve as a remedy for boredom; 'The routine that I was used to pulled at me, but something in me rose daringly above it, full of fear and feeling, weak and incompetent but excited' (Dickey, 1970, p. 26). Even a pedestrian extra-marital affair is invested with metaphysical gravitas; while reflecting upon the first symbol of his sexual boredom, the woman, here almost too conveniently known only as 'The Model,' mutates into a free-floating signifier of the manifold associations between *eros* and *thanatos*. Most strikingly, the nameless woman is introduced to us in a scene that is a thinly disguised enactment of a sexual assault in the form of an advertising agency photo-shoot (Dickey, 1970, pp. 20–22).

> Inside the bright hardship of the lights was a peculiar blue, wholly painful, unmistakably man-made, unblinkable thing that I hated. It reminded me of prisons and interrogations, and the thought jumped straight at me. That was one side of it all right, and the other was pornography. I thought of those films at fraternity parties and in officer's clubs where you realize with terror that when the girl drops the towel the camera is not going to drop with it discreetly, as in old Hollywood films, following the bare feet until they hide behind a screen, but is going to stay and when the towel falls, move in; that it is going to destroy someone's womanhood by raping her secrecy; that there is going to be nothing left (Dickey, 1970, pp. 20–21).[33]

And when does 'the Model' stage her narrative return? During Ed's erotically charged nocturnal ascent of the gorge in preparation for the killing of the Mountain Man.

> Then I would begin to try to inch upward again, moving with the most intimate motions of my body, motions I had never dared use with Martha [Ed's wife], or with any other human woman.[34] Fear and a kind of enormous moon-blazing sexuality lifted me, millimetre by millimetre. And yet I held madly to the human I looked for a slice of gold like the model's in the river: some kind of freckle, something loveable, in the huge serpent-shape of light (Dickey, 1970, p. 176).

As we should expect, Ed's second object-model takes the form of an animal.

[33] For a Feminist critique of *Deliverance* see Heilburn (1994).

[34] The phrase 'any other human woman' remains tantalizingly unexplained but wondrously invocative.

3.4.2 *The Deer*

'The greatest and most moral homage we can pay to certain animals on certain occasions is to kill them with certain means and rituals' said Ortega y Gassett (Gassett, 1972, p. 110). For the hunter, 'stalking and pursuit of game ordinarily begins once the animal has been sighted' (Laughlin, 1986, p. 308), a clear correlation between erotic impulse and visual acquisition. Superficially, 'the game' is the woman, as passive object of the patriarchal male gaze, symbolically altered into the more 'acceptable' form of an animal victim. On a deeper level, however, a very different form of psychic substitution is underway. Note Ed's account to Lewis following Ed's failure to kill a deer.

'What about it, buddy?' Lewis said, looking at the two empty slots in the quiver.

'I got a shot'.

'You did?' Lewis said, straightening.

'I did. A spectacular miss at fifteen yards.'

'What happened? We could'a had meat' (Dickey, 1970, pp. 97–98).[35]

---

[35] A revealing comment that underscores Lewis' and Ed's separate status as a sub-group within the Suburbanites, set apart from Bobby and Drew. The notion of the hunter as a member of a dangerous elite is well attested to in anthropological scholarship. "Meat is a cause of quarrels" in two basic situations. In the first place, hunters often conceal from their fellow-villagers that they have made a kill, pleading doefully that they have had no luck. Meanwhile, they have divided the meat secretly among the members of their elementary family and personal friends, instead of the village matrilineage. If this is later discovered grudges (*yitela*) will develop, leading to the invocation of ghosts to kill the hunter, if the situation is not remedied. Such an invocation is known as *ku-shingana*, a "curse". In the second place, even when the meat is distributed in public, villagers tend to quarrel about the amount given them, e.g., a classificatory mother's brother will demand an equal share with a full mother's brother. Thus jealousy (of the hunter's prowess), envy over the distribution of the meat, hatred of the hunter by those who have been cheated, and quarrelling between individuals and factions over the amounts (quite a bunch of deadly sins, not to mention greed) are regularly associated with the hunter's role. One informant told me, "a hunter eats good meat while others starve, and they say that he ought to find bad luck because he does not give them meat." Another said that "hunting is sorcery (*wuloji*), for hunters have snake-familiars (*malomba*) which kill their relatives to increase their (the hunter's) power." For each tuft of their victim's [the relative's] hair the hunter is said to acquire the power (*ng'ovu*) to kill an animal. But far from feeling shame on account of their bad reputation, hunters, like big businessmen, seem often to rejoice in being known as "hard guys" and in song and invocation to hunter spirits refer to themselves by terms normally considered opprobrious, such as "adulterers who sleep with ten women a day" and "great thieves". They take pride in the envy directed against them for they say that only those who are successful are envied. To be "cursed" is part of what they term their "pride" or "dignity" or "self-praise of huntmanship" (*kudilemesha* or *kudivumbika kwaWuyang'a*). Yet there is ambivalence in Ndembu society's attitude towards the hunter for he is, when all is said and done, the provider of the most prized food of all' (Turner, 1967, pp. 255–256). The reader should note the frequent recurrence of the 'snake' or 'serpent' motif throughout *Deliverance* (Dickey, 1970, pp. 68, 101, 103, 120, 131, 174, 238).

As *Deliverance* is in part an extended poetic meditation on hunting,[36] Dickey frequently deploys sight and vision as metaphors for the will-to-death; as Ed confidently but cryptically declares, 'If there was one thing I felt reasonably certain about, it was my ability to get the elements of a layout into some kind of harmonious relationship' (Dickey, 1970, p. 18). Decoded, what Ed is referring to is the ability of his mimetic impulse, mediated through sight (as photographer) to reconstruct the thing sighted as a differentiated object—of desire. His Suburbanite non-life as an advertising executive and photographer serves as a perfect ironic commentary upon his always partially concealed murderous impulses: 'I pointed wherever I looked' (Dickey, 1970, p. 118).

> The effect of framing the target was a big advantage, at least for me, for it isolated what was being shot at, and brought it into an oddly intimate [erotic] relation with the archer. Nothing outside the orange frame existed, and what was inside it was there in a terribly vital and consequential way; it was as though the target were being created by the eye that watched it (Dickey, 1970, p. 32).

And since this is a mimetic 'relationship that we are observing then Ed's eye really does 'create' the target, re-constituting the mere object as an object of desire. Yet, oddly, when the physical deer comes into his field of vision, Ed seems unable to mentally shift from the representation to the real body.

> I stopped, and the fog rose exactly to my teeth...the ghost of a deer but a deer just the same...He was broadside to me; I had shot a thousand targets one-quarter his size at the same distance, and when I recalled this—when my eyes and hands got together—I knew I could kill him just as easily as I could hit his outline on cardboard. I raised the bow (Dickey, 1970, p. 96).

And misses. Throughout the novel Ed suffers from a chronic 'release problem,' in equal parts mimetic and katabatic in origin According to the Ndembu, hunters 'are afflicted with different kinds of bad luck in the chase by dead hunter kinsmen (patrilineal as well as matrilineal)' (Turner, 1967, p. 251). Therefore, they are required to undergo *Muteti*, an initiatory and transformative ritual process of affliction which is followed by fame in success in hunting (Turner, 1967, p. 267). 'Good luck [in hunting] depends on the favour of hunter ancestors, and they will withdraw their assistance from you' as a punitive measure that is also rehabilitative (Turner, 1967, p. 260).

> But this withdrawal, and even active persecution [by the spirit] is something more than merely punitive. For the Ndembu have the notion that affliction is also a sign of election. The afflicting ancestor spirit wishes to become 'your spirit' (*mukishi weyi*), in other words your guardian or patron spirit... 'If the spirit has been placated he will help you to kill many animals,' and so [will] contribute to your eventual fame as a great *'Mwima'* hunter. The motto of the Ndembu might well be 'you must suffer to succeed' (Turner, 1967, p. 260).

All is not lost, however.

Ed: 'What I was really thinking about up there was you.'

[36] Hunting is a recurrent theme throughout Dickey's work, both in his poetry and, most spectacularly, in his apocalyptic final novel *To the White Sea* (Dickey, 1993).

Lewis: 'Well, next time don't think about me. Think about the deer' (Dickey, 1970, pp. 98–99).
But Ed was already, for the deer is the surrogate of the 'real' object of his mimetic vision.

3.4.3 *Lewis (= Ed)*

Girard deems desire to be triangular[37] because 'its most basic structure involves at least three terms: the agent who desires, the object of the agent's desire, and the agent who serves as the "model" or "mediator" of the desire' (Livingston, 1992, p. 1).

> What is 'triangular,' or 'mimetic' desire? In simplest terms, Girard argues that our desires are not innate or autonomous. Instead, we copy them from others. If I desire a particular object, I do not covet it on its own merits but because I 'mimic,' or imitate the desire of someone I have chosen as a model. That person—whether real or imaginary, legendary or historical—becomes the mediator of my desire, and the relationship in which I am involved is essentially 'triangular' (Golsan, 2002, p. 1).

The archetypal example of double mediation is the pupil-teacher/master (or master-disciple) relationship, the social underpinning of an existential double-bind; here, 'master' means not the professional pedagogue but any person who performs as the-one-who-mediates-the-true-object-of-desire-which-is-authentic-Being. 'Everybody believes that someone else possesses the self he wants to acquire. That is why everybody experiences desire ... Since every desire seeks self-sufficiency, no one really possesses it' (Rene Girard qtd. Livingston, 1992, p. 9), so that the disciple's attraction to the master (or the master's seduction of the disciple) culminates in the psychic-existential double-bind of the self's pursuit of the mediatory Other who, in the final instance is mediating nothing; 'In short, desire relieves its subject of an intolerable knowledge' that he is a 'no-one' meaning that he is not the true source of his own desires that define his sense of self (Girard et al., 2003, p. 303): '*Desire is always a reflection on desire*' (Girard et al., 2003, p. 328).[38]

> Desire aims to achieve shattering triumphs and pleasures that cannot be described. That is why it cannot hope to find them in ordinary experiences and relationships that can be brought under control. Desire will increasingly interpret the humiliation that it is made to suffer and the disdain that it is made to undergo in terms of the absolute superiority of the model—the mark of a blessed self-sufficiency that must necessarily be impenetrable to its own inadequacy (Girard et al., 2003, p. 327).

---

[37] See Chap. 1, above.

[38] 'If we grant the primordial error of desire' is its own mis-recognition that it rests upon a prior mis'recognition that it is always based upon the desires of the model-Other, a form of double-bind, 'we can say that desire gains nothing by getting to know itself better and better. On the contrary, the more this knowledge is extended and deepened, the more capable the subject becomes of causing his own unhappiness, since he carries to a further stage the consequences of the founding contradiction—the more he tightens the *double bind*' (Girard et al., 2003, p. 329).

The master-disciple-model is the *skandalon* in fleshy form because she not only incites imitation but she also works to ultimately sabotage her student's efforts at mimicry: 'The model indicates to his disciple the object he should desire and, in the same gesture, forbids him to proceed towards it' (Dumouchel, 1988, p. 5) for the more successful the model is at being the model, the more she has an interest in preventing her imitator from being wholly successful in her imitation lest she seize the 'place' of the model and turning the master into a no-one.[39] Mimeticism, therefore, is without exception a source of 'continual conflict': 'By making one man's desire into a replica of another man's desire, it invariably leads to rivalry; and rivalry in turn transforms desire into violence' (Girard, 1977, p. 169), although this violence may not assume a physical form for more often than not the symbolic form will suffice. Which raises the difficult problem of explaining why, in any given circumstance, the subject has chosen a particular Other as their model. 'The key assumption would seem to be that people believe there are different kinds of people[40]; moreover, people believe there are hierarchical differences among these kinds' (Livingston, 1992, p. 46). Operating through the medium of *meconnaissance*, this would appear to constitute the wholesale importation of the dynamics of mis-recognition from the macro-level of the community to the micro-level of the inter-personal. 'Mimetic desire would then seem to be this fixation on a model whose desires are thought to manifest a hierarchical difference between self and other' (Livingston, 1992, p. 46) guaranteeing the sacred difference of distinction, the possession of which establishes one as the authentically original Self (Livingston, 1988); 'In other words, in any episode of mimetic desire, the imitator has both a real and an ideal conception of self and perceives someone else as corresponding to the ideal in some significant way. In respect to that ideal, the other's desire is deemed worthy of imitation' (Livingston, 1992, p. 66) which must be linked to a difference of some kind because difference is the sign of authentic individuality, the authentic sovereignty of the Self. Ergo, emulative disciple, governed by acquisitive mimesis, 'imitates the desires of the rival thought to enjoy a hierarchical superiority. It is this belief in the hierarchical difference that essentially sustains and promotes the self's desires for the object desired by the other' (Livingston, 1992, p. 89).

There is a latently Nietzschean dimension to mimetic desire (superiority = Being) yielding a phenomenology of desire-for-being that is little more than a purely psychologistic variation of the will-to-power[41] mediated by the romantic (egoistic) conceits of individualism; 'In Girard's analyses, it is often the case that the mediator [model] is followed in primarily one sphere, that of romantic desire, yet this

---

[39] 'The circle that viciously joins the Other as model and the Other as obstacle exists only because the Subject, or rather his "desire," interprets in terms of intentions and values what is merely the operation of a [mimetic] mechanism'—which, of course, remains mis-recognized (Dupuy, 1988, p. 78).

[40] In the non-trivial sense that 'people do not consider themselves to belong to the kind they "would like to" and that they find themselves taking a special interest in those who do' (Livingston, 1992, p. 46). To paraphrase Borges, snobbery is the purest of all instincts.

[41] Which was itself Nietzsche's psychologistic bastardization of Schopenhauer's ontological conception of the Will.

one sphere is firmly linked in the imitator's mind to a global conception of the self' (Livingston, 1992, p. 67). Desire 'transfigures' its object in an act (singular or multiple) of mis-recognition, which is the cruelest paradox of all: the deluded belief in the surplus of Being emanating from a mere object—in other words, idolatry.

> [This] process of transfiguration does not correspond to anything real, and yet it transforms the object into something that appears superabundantly real. Thus it could be described as metaphysical in character. We might well decide to use the word 'desire' only in circumstances where the misunderstood mechanism of mimetic rivalry has imbued what was previously just an appetite or need with this metaphysical dimension (Girard et al., 2003, p. 296).

The 'self-concept' is the translation of the metaphysical notion of essence into the phenomenology of authenticity, and the belief in the genuineness of the Self 'must involve the agent's attempt to arrive at a reflective unification, not of the sum total of his or her experience, but of some privileged sub-set of the agent's beliefs, actions, and preferences. The self-concept … is an agent's momentary and perhaps deluded answer to the question "Who am I?"' (Livingston, 1992, p. 68). It is possible that 'we can say that a self-concept is a response, not to any and every possible question of the form "Who am I?" but to questions of that form motivated by a certain type of projection in relation to the self' (Livingston, 1992, p. 69). Which, in theory, will culminate in either an act of suicide and/or homicide: 'The desire that constitutes the self is itself modelled on, copied from, inspired by, and communicated by the other. It is the other's desire that causes the desire to appear that will engender the self' (Oughourlian, 2010, p. 98) for at the bitter end the disciple must somehow kill the master.

The theory of mimeticism 'is intimately connected to a conceptualization of the predominant cultural and social institutions of the modern world' (Livingston, 1992, p. 73).

Within which the existential 'self-concept' doubles as the

> [World] of acquisitive individualism and 'upward mobility,' a world where equality is held forth as the yardstick of all justice and legitimacy, indeed as the vey regulative ideal and vanishing point of social life, while at the same time a perpetual quest for personal distinction is the predominant emblem and lifetime burden of the successful and 'well-adapted' individual (Livingston, 1992, p. 72).

This is the mis-recognized hell of internal mediation which is the eternal recycling of an existential lack: 'In a world where individuals are no longer defined by the place they occupy by virtue of their birth or some stable and arbitrary factor, the spirit of competition can never be appeased once and for all'; rather, 'everything gets increasingly inflamed; everything rests upon comparisons that are necessarily unstable and insecure, since there are no longer any fixed points of reference' (Girard et al., 2003, p. 307).

Throughout *Deliverance*, Ed is obsessed with his own image, frequently discussing himself as though observing himself in a mirror; in textbook mimetic fashion he is both radically self-directed and other-directed.

> I caught a glimpse of myself in the rear window. I was light green, a tall forest man, an explorer, guerilla, hunter. I liked the idea and the image, I must say. Even if this was just a game, a charade, I had let myself in for it, and I was here in the woods, where such people as I had gotten myself up as were supposed to be. Something or other was being made good. I touched the knife hilt at my side, and remembered that all men were once boys, and that boys were always looking for ways to become men Some of the ways are easy, too; all you have to do is be satisfied that it has happened (Dickey, 1970, p. 69).

Narcissistic obsession is not just central to Ed's sense of self; revealingly it is equally so to Lewis,' as the model-obstacle dutifully explains to the disciple concerning the fantasy life: 'That's all anybody has got. It depends on how strong your fantasy is, and whether you really—*really*—in your own mind, fit into your own fantasy, whether you measure up to what you've fantasized. I don't know what yours is, but I'll bet you don't come up to it' (Dickey, 1970, p. 49). According to Girard, contrary to what is stated by the Freudian theory of narcissism, 'desire never aspires to something that resembles it; it is always searching for something that it imagines to be most irreducibly *other*' (Girard et al., 2003, p. 338). In other words, narcissism is a symptom of an approaching crisis of undifferentiation: the more the Self comes to resemble the Other the more the former must violently affirm itself at the expense of the latter. The greatest importance, then, must be paid to Ed's reciprocating evaluation of Lewis.

> But Lewis and I were different [from other people], and were different from each other. I had nothing like his drives, or his obsessions. Lewis wanted to be immortal. He had everything that life could give, and he couldn't make it work. And he couldn't bear to give it up or see age take it away from him, either, because in the meantime he might be able to find what it was that he wanted, the thing that must be there, and that must be subject to his will … And yet he was the first also to take a chance, as though the burden of his own laborious immortality were too heavy to bear, and he wanted to get out of it by means of an accident, or what would appear to be an accident (Dickey, 1970, p. 9).

From this critical passage, we learn two things. The first is that Lewis, Ed's apparent 'model', is himself governed by an absence of being—that is, *lack*. The question now becomes: if Lewis is not the true model, then whom is he imitating? And the answer, as Lewis' lengthy disquisition to Ed during the drive to Oree clearly reveals, is Hobbes' 'Naturall' sovereign of the little Monarchy within the frontier.[42] This completely alters the nature of the mimetic dynamics between the two; in the place of a relatively stable binary relationship between model-imitator, we have a vicious triangulation, in which Lewis is himself the imitator of a commonly desired model, acting as an obstacle to Ed—a classic example of acquisitive mimesis. The second is that Lewis' desire must necessarily be homicidal; his controlling, if unconscious, impulse throughout *Deliverance* is to engineer a situation in which death 'appears' as a Hobbesian means of establishing his private sovereignty. The correct way of formulating the problem of Ed's narcissism should be: if Ed (the bearer of

---

[42] If we were to offer a literary exemplar for Lewis' model, then the two most likely candidates would be either Odysseus or Tarzan At numerous places in both the novel and the film a reference is made to Tarzan (Dickey, 1970, pp. 102, 103, 266).

thanatos) imitates Lewis, but Lewis is full of absence (merely another failed emulator, not a true model), then can Ed ever become anything 'real'?

For Ed, Lewis 'had the appearance of always leaping to meet something, of going forward with joy and anticipation I was tired of dragging; I felt a great deal lighter and more muscular when I was around Lewis' (Dickey, 1970, p. 34). The apparently narcissistic impulses unleashed within Ed by Lewis lead inexorably toward the more explicitly homo-erotic.[43]

I looked at him Lewis, for I have never seen him with his clothes off.

> Everything he had done for himself for years paid off as he stood there in his tracks, in the water. I could tell by the way he glanced at me; the payoff was in my eyes. I had never seen such a male body in my life, even in the pictures in the weight-lifting magazines, for most of those fellows are short, and Lewis was an even six feet. I'd say he weighed about 190. The muscles were bound up in him smoothly, and when he moved, the veins in the moving part would surface. If you looked at him that way, he seemed made out of well-matched red-brown chunks wrapped in blue wire (Dickey, 1970, pp. 102–103).

Because Girard strictly equates desire with mimesis, he places the libidinal squarely within the external realm of social relations. We can no more formulate a wholly private desire than we can fashion a completely private language; everyone is literally no 'one'. Therefore, he is robustly anti-Freudian in his approach to sexuality; 'human desire consists of the grafting of mimesis on to instinctual patterns and the over-activation, aggravation, and disorganization of the latter' (Girard et al., 2003, p. 95). What is important to Girard is not the universal essence of desire but that this 'essential link with mimesis assures that human sexuality will be even more conflictual than animal sexuality and makes sexuality itself incapable of being a factor of stability in human relations or even between sexual partners' (Girard et al., 2003, p. 95). Accordingly

> It is impossible to construct an adequate interpretation from the perspective of objects, whether it be the economic or the sexual object, as in Marxism or psychoanalysis; any such interpretation will be determined by an erroneous schematization of culture and will force one to discard as inessential phenomena that are entirely homologous with those that have been arbitrarily deemed essential (Girard et al., 2003, p. 75).

This causes him to somewhat question the veracity of homosexual desire, at least in the way that it is mediated by culture; 'the model and the rival, in the sexual domain, is an individual of the *same* sex, for the very reason that the object is heterosexual. All rivalry is thus structurally homosexual' (Girard et al., 2003, pp. 335, 336–388). What is vital is that homo-erotic desire is strategic in nature, the reflection of the particular position occupied by one or more participants within a wider field of acquisitive mimetic rivalry.

> Homosexuality corresponds to an 'advanced' stage of mimetic desire, but this stage can also correspond to a form of heterosexuality in which the partners play the roles of model and rival, as well as that of object, for one another. The metamorphosis of the heterosexual object

[43] It should be recalled that Turner identified bi-sexuality as one of the traits of 'threshold people'.

into a rival brings about effects very similar to the metamorphosis of the rival into an object (Girard et al., 2003, p. 337).[44]

Within literature, homosexuality 'is often the eroticizing of mimetic rivalry' (Girard et al., 2003, p. 346), and, literary critic that he is, Girard cheerfully concedes that the 'great writers' have described homo-eroticism 'much better than we could ever do. They alone are capable of seeing that the sexual side of the matter is far from being primary and must be subordinated to mimetism, which succeeds in obliterating differences all the more successfully as it seeks more greedily' (Girard et al., 2003, p. 338). This would certainly seem to apply in the case of Dickey. If homo-erotic desire is really heterosexual rivalry that has assumed an acquisitive form, then Ed's rivalry with Lewis becomes subject to the dynamics of the crisis of undifferentiation, with Lewis himself serving as the ultimate attractor for Ed's own smoldering will-to-murder. The narrative and mimetic logic of this relationship is that Ed must reveal or uncover Lewis' own lack (insufficiency) and either physically or symbolically kill him, thereby removing the obstacle that blocks his direct access to the model. The unifying resolution is a symbolic form of castration, inflicted upon the 'fake' Lewis by the all-controlling river itself.

After a minute or two Lewis came, doubled-up and broken-looking, one hand still holding his paddle and the other on his face, clasping something intolerable...He was writhing and twitching uselessly, caught by something that didn't have hold of me, something that seemed not present ... His bare legs were luminous, and the right leg of his drawers was lifted up to the groin I could tell by its outline that his thigh was broken. I reached down and felt of it very softly. Against the back of my hand his penis stirred with pain ... there was a great profound human swelling under my hand. It felt like a thing that was trying to open, to split, to let something out (Dickey, 1970, pp. 146–147, 149–150).[45]

Within the gorge, the epicenter of the sacred, a 'magical' transference from Lewis to Ed takes place.

From where we were the cliff looked something like a gigantic drive-in movie screen waiting for an epic film to begin. I listened for interim music, glancing now and again up the pale curved stone for Victor Mature's stupendous image, wondering where it would appear, or if the whole thing were not now already playing, and I hadn't yet managed to put it together (Dickey, 1970, p. 147).

Typical for the mimetically possessed, Ed confuses the face of 'god' with a cinema projection.

---

[44] An insight largely supported by Dickey; Ed's obsession with killing the second Mountain Man '"was not to be seen as any kind of *substitute* sexual longing at all...but is merely meant to show that a sense of unfulfillment [metaphysical desire] which gravitated, under Ed's ordinary, day-to-day circumstances, to sex, as such things will, has actually found a much more powerful and positive medium than his erstwhile sexual preoccupation." The more "powerful and positive medium," Dickey argued, was violence' (Hart, 2000, p. 473). But, of course, the move towards violence is the corollary of the move towards Lewis.

[45] Compare this passage with Ed's fond recollections forty pages earlier: 'Lewis' pectorals loomed up in my mind, and his leg, with the veins bulging out of the divided muscles of his thigh, his leg under water wavering small-ankled and massive as a centaur's. I would go with that' (Dickey, 1970, p. 110).

3.5 *Katabasis* 2: The Monstrous Doubles

The fourth signifier of *katabasis* is: 'The katabatic hero is often accompanied and helped by a companion (who may be female) or by a loyal retinue of retainers, some or all of whom may be lost in the course of the journey so that the protagonist returns alone' (Holtsmark, 2001, p. 26).

I held my breath.

'Kill him', Lewis said with the river.[46]

'I'll kill him if I can find him', I said.

'Well', he said, lying back, 'here we are, at the heart of the Lewis Medlock country.'

'Pure survival', I said.

'This is what it comes to', he said. 'I told you.'

'Yes. You told me' (Dickey, 1970, p. 160).

Dickey's re-presentation of Hobbes' state of nature—the war of all against all that historically proceeds the formation of the social contract—is interwoven perfectly with the logic of mimetic desire that descends into acquisitive rivalry: the imitator nominates himself as the substitute for the 'failed' model. Not only do Ed and Lewis stand in a mimetic relationship with each other, but also with the two (ambiguously named) 'Mountain Men', the monstrous doubles; as denizens of the Land of the Dead, they are monstrous in themselves, but their 'doubling' relationship to the protagonists mirrors the morally ambivalent status of the two hunting heroes; 'Two men stepped out of the woods, one of them trailing a shotgun by the barrel … "Escaped convicts" flashed up in my mind on one side, "Bootleggers" on the other. But they still could have been hunting' (Dickey, 1970, pp. 107, 108). The sudden appearance of a 'monster' (Dickey, 1970, pp. 107–117), a recurrent motif of Greek Mythology and Tragedy, serves as a projection in the form of an hallucination of the pathological intensification of the mimetic conflict of the twins/doubles; a fundamental principle of Hellenic *muthos* 'is that the double and monster are one and the same being … The unity and reciprocity that the enemy brothers have rejected in the benign form of brotherly love finally impose themselves, both from without and within, in the form of monstrous duality—the most disquieting and grotesque form imaginable' (Girard, 1977, pp. 160, 160–168). According to Girard, 'Under the heading *monstrous double* we shall group all the hallucinatory phenomena provoked at the height of the crisis by unrecognized reciprocity. The monstrous double is also to be found wherever we encounter an "I" and an "Other" caught up in a constant interchange of differences' (Girard, 1977, p. 164). But why do the two monsters appear at precisely this point in the story?

---

[46] The merging of Lewis and the river underscores the regenerative potential of the symbolic transferences of both phallus and sovereignty. It also symbolizes the extent of the regressive migration into the undifferentiated condition of the Netherworld.

'Every supernatural visitation is prompted by the spirit of revenge' according to Girard (Girard, 1977, p. 268). The answer, then, is that the mimetic rivalry between Ed and Lewis has reached its outermost limit, the twins suffering a complete loss of differentiation. Adding to the poetic device of the apparitional is the fact that that the loss of the singular identity of both Ed and Lewis, externally acted out through their homicidal encounters with the Mountain Men, takes place in the heart of the frontier, the zone of pure isotropic, and liminal, undifferentiation. The Mountain Men are the bearers of a double representation of radical Otherness: the geographical (isotropic space = lack of identity) and the existential, as outer manifestations of Ed's and Lewis' inner drive to murder and sovereignty. The sheer visceral nature of the monstrous doubles—materialized apparitions rather than mere hallucinations—allows the pathological intensity of the acquisitive mimesis of the twinned protagonists to be wholly uncovered, and, therefore, subject to exorcism. *Deliverance* 'doubles' back upon itself so that the ontological validation of one set of doubles guarantees the truth of the other. Or, to put it in mundane terms: the Mountain Men act out what Ed and Lewis have only been dreaming in a joint act of *meconnaissance*.

The first performative enactment focuses upon the homo-eroticism of the twins, particularly Ed's narcissistic mimeticism.

> There was no need to justify or rationalize anything; they were going to do what they wanted to … (Dickey, 1970, p. 114)

> I had never felt such brutality and carelessness of touch, or such disregard for another person's body. It was not the steel or the edge of the steel that was frightening; the man's fingernail, used in any gesture of his, would have been just as brutal; the knife only magnified his unconcern … (Dickey, 1970, p. 112)

> I had thought so long and hard about him to this day. I still believe I felt, in the moonlight, our minds fuse. It was not that I felt myself turning evil, but that an enormous physical indifference, as vast as the whole abyss of light at my feet, came to me: an indifference not only to the other man's body scrambling and kicking on the ground with an arrow through it, but also to mine. If Lewis had not shot his companion, he and I would have made a kind of love, painful and terrifying to me, in some dreadful way pleasurable to him, but we would have been together in the flesh, there on the floor of the woods, and it was strange to think of it. Who was he?[47] (Dickey, 1970, p. 180).

The second enactment is that of violence, the 'primordial epiphany' of the recovered unanimity of ritualistic sacrifice. At first glance, this would seem implausible, as the Mountain Men sexually assault Ed (Dickey, 1970, pp. 111–112, 115–116), rape Bobby (Dickey, 1970, pp. 113–115) and, slightly later, apparently murder Drew (Dickey, 1970, pp. 142–143), although both of the monstrous doubles are killed in turn by the self-authored 'justice' of both Lewis (Dickey, 1970, pp. 116–117) and Ed (Dickey, 1970, pp. 188–194), respectively. If the Mountain Men are meant to serve as the victim-surrogates they make remarkably poor ones, as they largely fail to comply with the criteria of the scapegoat.[48] It is here that I must make my boldest

[47] The answer is: 'he' was Lewis.

[48] One of the most important characteristics of scapegoats is that they are socially marginal, meaning that they have no family who are prepared to avenge their death, thereby intensifying reciprocal

leap, and follow the logic of my Girardian exegesis to its bitter end: if the twins of the monstrous doubles of the Mountain Men really are the two protagonists, then would this not signify that both Bobby and Drew are the intended but mis-recognized sacrificial/hunting victims of Ed and Lewis? The 'surrogate victim meets his death in the guise of the monstrous double' (Girard, 1977, p. 251); while Ed and Lewis commit no physical violence against either Bobby or Drew but they are trespassed against by the Mountain Men, and both of the Mountain Men are then subsequently killed by Lewis and Ed. The narrative structure would appear to be playing upon a set of symbolic substitutions operating upon two groupings of surrogates (Bobby-Drew/ Mountain Men) and monstrous doubles (Ed-Lewis/Mountain Men). The implication is that the unlikely presence of Bobby and Drew on the journey down the Cahulawassee is explained by the fact that they have been invited by Lewis and Ed under the former's unconscious intent to sacrifice them.[49] And Lewis, we know, has deliberately entered the frontier in order to engineer some sort of crisis of violence as the means of establishing his private sovereignty.

If we examine Bobby and Drew in more detail, we find that they both correspond remarkably well to the surrogate victim, much more clearly than do the two Mountain Men. Bobby bears an almost too obvious familiarity with another sacrificial victim in *Lord of the Flies*, the equally hapless and inept 'Piggy,'[50] a similitude that is highlighted in the film version when Bobby (Ned Beatty) is repeatedly ordered to 'squeal like a pig' while being 'corn-holed'; 'At last he [the Mountain Man] raised his face as though to howl with all his strength into the leaves and the sky, and quivered silently while the man with the gun looked on with an odd mixture of approval and sympathy. The whorl-faced man drew back, drew out…' (Dickey, 1970, p. 115). Of obvious significance is that the pig is a premier animal-victim of both the sacrifice and the hunt: 'Bobby took off his shorts like a boy undressing for the first time in a gym, and stood there plump and pink, his hairless thighs shaking, his legs close together'.[51] Girard has gone so far as to speculate that sacrifice was the origin of animal husbandry (Girard et al., 2003, pp. 68–73): 'All species of domesticated animals have been used or are still used as sacrificial victims. The process of domestication must have come about through the co-habitation of animals and human beings over many generations and would have had produced the effects of domestication in the species commonly used for sacrifice' (Girard et al., 2003, p. 70). So, by improbably inviting Bobby along with them for their sojourn in the woods, what Ed and Lewis are really doing

violence. The exact opposite is the case of the Mountain Men; the Suburbanites are terrified of suffering retribution at the hands of the relations of the Nine-Fingered People (Dickey, 1970, pp. 123–124).

[49] Consider in this light Drew's rather pathetic admonition to Ed concerning Lewis' plan to 'cover up' his murder of the first monstrous double: 'Think what you're doing, Ed, for God's sake…This self-hypnotized maniac is going to get us all in jail for life, if he doesn't get us killed' (Dickey, 1970, p. 130). Which, of course, he did.

[50] See Chap. 2, above.

[51] Dickey (1970), p. 113; Burkert (1983), pp. 256–264. See also Collins (2006) and Kolb (2008).

is bringing a sacrificial pig along with them into the wilderness.[52] As if to underscore the point of mis-recognized sacrificial intent, both Lewis and Ed direct a great deal of hostility toward Bobby throughout the novel.[53] Guy LeFort has indicated that 'good part of what we call politeness consists in self-effacement before another in order to avoid mimetic rivalry' (Girard et al., 2003, p. 9); this would mean that the twins' aggression toward Bobby enables the re-direction of violence away from each other, consistent with the surrogate victim as the attractor of the mimetic violence of the community. The case of Drew, involving not only sacrificial murder but magical transfiguration, is more complex but no less Girardian. Initially, Drew, the 'good' liberal of the Suburbanites, is unflatteringly described by Ed as 'the big-faced decent city man, the minor civic leader and hedge clipper'(Dickey, 1970, p. 60), yet, after having later discovered his body downstream, Ed laments: '"You were the best of us, Drew", I said loud enough for Bobby to hear; I wanted him to hear.[54] "The only decent one; the only sane one"' (Dickey, 1970, p. 220). This apparent inconsistency can be easily explained by Girard. 'We need to show that it is not possible to resolve the problem of violence with the surrogate victim without at the same time elaborating a theory of the sign and signification' (Girard et al., 2003, p. 99); accordingly, the signifier 'is the victim. The signified constitutes all actual and potential meaning the community confers on to the victim, and, through its intermediacy, on to all things. The sign is the reconciliatory victim' (Girard et al., 2003, p. 103). The victim, therefore, is always marked by the sign of ambivalence precisely because the original representation of the unifying effects of collective ritualized murder is 'determined by the violent reconciliation and the resulting sacralisation The victim is thus represented with all of the attributes and qualities of the sacred' (Girard et al., 2003, p. 111). The 'primordial victim' was hated by the community 'insofar as he polarized the as yet untransformed violence; he was revered insofar as he transformed the violence and set in motion the unifying mechanism of the surrogate victim' (Girard, 1977, p. 276). Bobby and Drew embody the ambivalent duality of the scapegoat who is always both the cause of and the remedy for violence. Bobby, as the animal victim who attracts displaced aggression, stands at the beginning of the sacrificial sequence, the sign of crisis, and is, therefore, 'low'. Drew, in contrast, personifies the 'high' magical victim who ends the crisis, and whose death, in a god-like fashion, releases the supernatural force (catharsis) that exorcizes the violence and brings about the generative unanimity that restores the community. How else to explain this utterly remarkable account of Drew's body which is a perfect literary representation of sacralization?

---

[52] This also opens the door to the possibility of a 'double doubling' of violence and sex on Dickey's part. Although Bobby is not physically killed he is raped and symbolically castrated by the Mountain Men who may be considered monstrous doubles of Ed and Lewis.

[53] 'I walked back and picked up the gun, and my craziness increased when I touched it. I sighted down the barrel and put the bead right in the middle of Bobby's chest. Do it, the dead [Mountain] man said. Do it; he's right there. But I got around the feeling…I didn't want to put the thing to my shoulder again; it had been close; very close' (Dickey, 1970, pp. 202, 99, 201). In the film version, Lewis (Burt Reynolds) is openly contemptuous of Bobby throughout (Boorman, 1972).

[54] An interesting detail, which can be explained by Ed establishing a clear difference between the sacrificial status of animal and sacred victim.

> Drew was sitting up, facing upstream, in a kind of rough natural chair made up of two stones where part of the river ran through, split off from the main current by a flat rock.[55] Though he was sitting, it was a very easy, careless—even carefree, position, partly on the base of his spine ... His eyelids were also kept propped open by the current, seeming to come out of the open water back up into the mountains, around all the curves of the river, infinitely ... the eyes... were blue and all-seeing and clear (Dickey, 1970, p. 216).[56]

The position of Drew's body also possesses a katabatic relevance, signifying the liminal demarcation between the worlds of the living and the dead that marks the crossing of the frontier, sacred and profane, back into community and the social contract. The regenerative effects of his death are so tremendous as to transform the nature of the river itself, from Death to Life. Exiting the gorge the Suburbanites' canoe is ejected by an almost supernatural force, an image of re-birth and violent eruption into the world.

> The river showed in front in a blinking leap, and we came shooting forward as though launched to take off into the air. We were going faster than I had ever been without an engine. The force of water around the paddle blade was stupendous; I felt as though I had dipped into some supernatural source of primal energy (Dickey, 1970, p. 224).

All that the remaining Suburbanites have to do now is to get away with murder in order to secure their sovereignty.

3.6 'Well Now, How About This? Just...How *About* This?': The Primordial Epiphany of Sacralization and Sovereignty

In the end all of law, all of politics, all of economics, all of warfare, all of law comes down to one very simple proposition: someone has to be sacrificed. Which is religion. The murder of the first Mountain Man and the lengthy debate over whether or not to conceal the 'crime' (Dickey, 1970, pp. 121–130) brings about a revealing change in Lewis: 'Another expression—a new colour—came into his eyes, a humorous conspiratorial craftiness, his look of calculated pleasure, his enthusiast's look' (Dickey, 1970, p. 126). This narrative conjunction between murder, cathartic purgation, and a 'debate' over the status of law is of central importance to the relevance of *Deliverance* to law-and-literature. Ed and Lewis can only overcome the crisis of acquisitive mimesis through an act of ritualistic sacrifice that exorcizes their escalating violence. However, in order to successfully execute their series of sacrificial murders, they must establish their own zone of private sovereignty within the frontier, which makes them the enemy of the Hobbesian 'Civill' Common-wealth of the social contract. The sacrificial function of the Mountain Men is revealed through

---

[55] In Neolithic cultures flat rocks were used for sacrificial purposes.

[56] This passage should be compared with Goldings' lyrical account of the mutilated body of Simon, another sacralized victim. See Chap. 2, above.

the invocation of the law as the stabilizing element of ambivalent difference that ultimately succeeds in resolving the increasingly pathological rivalry between Ed and Lewis: conflictual mimesis. The twins are reconciled through their mutual establishment of their micro-State; the murders expunge the violence and the performance of the sacrifice establishes (sanctifies?) the little Monarchy of the two. The rites of both hunting (Burkert) and the sacrificial mechanism (Girard) form the basis of religion but they also establish the parameters of the primitive State, the geographical space within which sovereign power may be exercised, as both a matter of power (*potestas*) and as a matter of right (*ius*).

Predictably, the two sides in the debate are Lewis the survivalist and Drew the liberal; the resolution of the dispute between 'anti-sliding' and 'the conventional point of view' hinges upon the isotropic nature of the law.

> Lewis: 'If we work this right, we'll never have to explain to anybody but ourselves' (Dickey, 1970, p. 218).[57] ... 'We just ought to wait a minute before we decide to be so all-fired boy scoutish and do the right thing. There's not any right thing.' 'You bet there is,' Drew said. 'There's only *one* thing' (Dickey, 1970, p. 123).

As Girard has pointed out, 'What permits us to conceive abstractly of an act of violence and to view it as an isolated crime is the power of a judicial institution that transcends all antagonists' (Girard et al., 2003, p. 12). As the liminal nature of the frontier doubles as the geographical limitation of the law (Pue) as well as the un-ambivalent differentiation of desire which is co-extensive with the community (Girard), the successful evasion of detection is tantamount to the establishment of the sovereign authority of the private self within a space which is legally empty which Hobbes understood perfectly. Ed's reflections on the chances of the success of the survivor's 'conspiratorial craftiness'—the secret burial of the two Mountain Men (Dickey, 1970, pp. 130–137, 196–209) and the cover story of Drew's death by drowning (Dickey, 1970, p. 219)—underscore the supremely subversive nature of any crime that remains invisible.

> I was pleased; I began to feel safer, for I was dreading going back to men and their questions and systems; I had been dreading it without knowing it (Dickey, 1970, p. 228) ... [Leaving the river] made me feel caught in the whole vast, inexorable web of modern communications. I was not sure that this was not the beginning of the enormous, unfathomable apparatus of crime detection, from which no one is entirely free: I could imagine stupendous filing systems, IBM machines tirelessly sorting punch cards, one thing being checked against another...Our story could not stand up against that, I was sure. And yet it might, even so (Dickey, 1970, p. 252).

The problem of the crime is solved through the formation of a 'private contract' which is itself a mimetic copy of the original or 'model' contract (Hobbes, 1991, p. 120) and that serves as the foundational act of the little Monarchy (Dickey, 1970, pp. 128–130, 232).

---

[57] See also Dickey (1970), pp. 227, 228, 235, 252, 268, 275.

> 'You see any law around here?' Lewis said. 'We're the law. What we decide is going to be the way things are done. So let's vote on it. I'll go along with a vote. And so will you, Drew. You've got no choice' (Dickey, 1970, p. 130)

Ed's response to this challenge is interesting.

> But I was ready to gamble. After all, I hadn't done anything but stand tied to a tree and nobody could prove anything else, no matter what it came to. I believed Lewis could get us out. If I went along with concealing the body and we got caught it could be made to seem a matter of necessity, of simply being outvoted (Dickey, 1970, p. 130).

True to form, Ed is the one to grasp that the basis of this dissenting social contract is not merely security-in-the-face-of-the-fear-of-death, but group complicity with a crime, or the violent unanimity of the crowd, which compels obedience to the Naturall Power of one man.

> The assurance with which Lewis had killed a man was desperately frightening to me, but the same quality was also calming, and I moved, without being completely aware of the movement, nearer to him. I would have liked nothing better than to touch that big relaxed forearm as he stood there, one hip raised until the leg made longer by the position bent gracefully at the knee. I would have followed him anywhere, and I realized that I was going to have to do just that (Dickey, 1970, pp. 128; 110, 130, 160, 174).

The mimetic triangle operating between Ed and Lewis raises the natural question as to whether Lewis' suggestion to conceal the crime is a true reflection of the state of nature or a cultural rationalization of his personal will-to-sovereignty.

> 'I did kill him.' Lewis said. 'But you're wrong when you say that there's nothing like a game connected with the position we're in now. It may be the most serious kind of game there is, but if you don't see it as a game, you're missing an important point' (Dickey, 1970, p. 126).

For Ed, the decision to follow Lewis is inseparable from his journey toward the regenerative heart of the river; Lewis 'had a point. I listened to the woods and the river to see if I could get an answer (Dickey, 1970, p. 124) ... The woods upstream became more mysterious than those downstream; the future opened only on that side' (Dickey, 1970, p. 129). The mimetic logic of the conspiracy is furthered strengthened when one recalls that all of the parties to the private contract are members of a hunting trip, the agency of sacred violence. Ed's description of his killing of the second Mountain Man constantly projects outward his inward double-ness, the fact of his undifferentiated civic life opposed to the model of the differentiated, and secessionist, hunter-killer.

> The river took me in, and I had the bow (Dickey, 1970, p. 143).... I was a killer. There were deaths involved: one certain murder and probably another...I could get there, in my mind. The whole thing focused, like an old movie that just barely held its own on the screen (Dickey, 1970, p. 173).... He got carefully down to his knees; blood poured when his mouth opened and seemed to splash up out of the ground, to have the force of something aiming out of the earth, a spring revealed when the right stone was moved. Die, I thought, my God, die, die (Dickey, 1970, p. 193).

And it is with Ed's murder of the second Mountain Man in imitation of Lewis' murder of the first, that *Deliverance* delivers its greatest and most profound surprise:

it is, in fact, *not* clear that Drew was actually shot (Dickey, 1970, pp. 142–143, 217–218) nor that the man that Ed kills was the shooter.[58] '"But listen Ed," [Bobby] said, and the pathetic human tone against the river-sound made me cringe, "you got to be sure" (Dickey, 1970, p. 152);[59] the problem is that the name of the Mountain Man that Ed kills is Stovall (Dickey, 1970, p. 203), but the name of the only local man who has been reported as missing, the presumed attacker of Ed and Bobby, is named Benson and he is/was the brother-in-law of Deputy Sheriff Queen of the town of Aintry, the point where the Suburbanites leave the river and cross back over into the community of representation (Dickey, 1970, pp. 262–263). Yet, as Ed seems to understand, absolutely none of this makes any difference as identities do not matter during the crisis of undifferentiation The logic of substitution governing the sacrificial mechanism guarantees that the identity of every surrogate-victim remains inherently indeterminate and inter-changeable; it is the ritualistic act of killing (hunting) itself that establishes identity and, therefore, of meaning: 'Since sacrifice is always a question of substitution, it is always possible to make a new substitution and henceforth to sacrifice only a substitute of a substitute' (Girard et al., 2003, p. 53). As Ortega y Gassett brilliantly expressed it.

> Death is essential because without it there is no authentic hunting: the killing of the animal is the natural end of the hunt and that goal of hunting itself, *not* of the hunter. The hunter seeks this death because it is no less than the sign of reality for the whole hunting process. To sum up, one does not hunt in order to kill; on the contrary, one kills in order to have hunted (Ortega y Gassett, 1972, pp. 110–111).[60]

A point not lost on Dickey.

> 'Look for deer,' Lewis said. 'When there's not much mast [foliage], they come down to the cornfields and along the roads.'... I looked, but I didn't see any, though at one curve in the road I thought I saw something dart back into the woods to the right. But the leaves where I thought it had gone were not moving, so probably it was my imagination (Dickey, 1970, p. 54). ... Something caught the tail of my left eye, and my stomach froze. I didn't turn my head at once, but slowly. I knew, though. I knew, and knew (Dickey, 1970, p. 188).

---

58 'He was dressed like the toothless man in the clearing; whether *exactly* like him I truthfully couldn't say, but very much like. He was about the same size, and he was thin and repulsive looking. And, though my time close to him in the clearing was burned in my mind, I had still seen him under those circumstances, which were a lot different from these; I believe that if I could have seen him move I would have known, one way or the other. But I didn't and I don't' (Dickey, 1970, p. 200). Meaning that the two inhabitants of the Underworld are undifferentiated and, therefore, exchangeable: killing one will be identical to killing the other in the land of pre-representation.

59 It is during this conversation with Bobby that Ed recalls the duelling banjos: 'I liked hearing the sound of my voice ... especially in the dark; it sounded like somebody who knew where he was and knew what he was doing. I thought of Drew and the albino boy picking and singing in the filling station' (Dickey, 1970, pp. 152–153).

60 Compare this with Girard: 'There is one and only one perspective capable of making lynching a positive action—since it sees the victim as a real threat that must be dealt with by any available means—and this is the perspective of the lynchers themselves, the perspective of the lynchers on their own lynching...The representation of lynching in myths is always found in a context that necessitates the inference of its reality, because only that inference can illuminate that myth as a whole and in all its details' (Girard et al., 2003, pp. 115, 119).

As M. R. James testified in his reflections on deer hunting, 'My first shot breaks the great buck's back' (James, 1997, p. 102). It should also be remembered that during the Neolithic period covenants were consecrated through the propitiatory blood of an animal sacrifice (Collins, 2006, p. 182).

3.7 Conclusion: 'Something or Other Was Being Made Good'

The fifth signifier of *katabasis* is: 'after his return, the hero sometimes assumes roles of increased responsibility and leadership (for instance, as a teacher or ruler) on the basis of his experience underground during his harrowing in hell' (Holtsmark, 2001, p. 26).[61] The unique 'One' who returns from the land of the Dead becomes the model for others.

'The world is easily lost' (Dickey, 1970, p. 11) laments Ed; the mythopoetic journey down the river, symbolizing the loss of both identity and the representational capacity of language, the imperceptibly 'slide' into the Netherworld that is revealed as the pre-representational site of the primeval unity of religion, difference, and sacrificial murder, enabling Ed to enter into an unmediated relationship with Being.

> Another odd thing happened. The river and everything that I remembered about it became a possession to me, a personal, private possession, as nothing else in my life ever had. Now it ran nowhere but in my head, but there it ran immortally. I could feel it—I can feel it—on different places of my body ... In me it still is, and will be until I die, green, rocky, deep, fast, slow, and beautiful beyond reality. I had a friend there who in a way had died for me, and my enemy was there (Dickey, 1970, p. 275).[62]

Deliverance operates on a 'double' level—the formation of the private contract narratively mirrors the resolution of the mimetic crisis—and its dramatic logic is resolved through the staging of a series of violent encounters among doubles: Ed

---

[61] What is most essential to *Deliverance*, according to Dickey, is the novel's mythical structure, its 'circular movement' from profane to sacred space and then back again '"What I really have in mind for the whole story … is an updated version of [Arnold] Van Gennep's *Rites de Passage*: "a separation from the world, a penetration to some source of power, and life-enhancing return" … *Deliverance* illustrates this for our time just as surely as *The Odyssey* did for its, or any other work at any other time which employs this theme. For my money, it is the most powerful theme in all of literature, all of mythology…' (Hart, 2000, p. 473; Guillory, 1976). Although the motif of 'rite of passage' is clearly evident throughout the novel, I have preferred to emphasize the katabatic elements. This is because rites exist on the level of representation, whereas Ed's transformation takes place on the river which is within the realm of the pre-representational, the originary space of the sacred. The Suburbanites do not actually undergo a ritual process; rather they re-enact the primordial Ur-event that gave birth to all subsequent rites (See Burkert, 1983; Van Gannep, 1960).

[62] Which underscores brilliantly D.H. Lawrence's point about the un-European nature of the American novel; '*Deliverance* is not an American *Heart of Darkness*. Unlike Marlow, the American hero does not beat a paranoiac retreat when he encounters the primitive aspects of his own psyche; rather, he approaches those manifestations, with trepidation perhaps, but also with fascination and a desire to understand their meaning and value' (Butterworth, 1996, p. 77).

versus Lewis; Ed/Lewis versus Bobby/Drew; the Mountain Men versus Bobby/Drew; Ed/Lewis versus the Mountain Men The novel accomplishes this remarkably complex task by re-capitulating the logic of the mimetic crisis as laid out by Girard; 'All desire is a desire for being' (Girard & Treguer, 2014, p. 12). The great obstacle, or stumbling block (*skandalon*) that the twin protagonists confront in their acquisitive rivalry for existence is the law: 'The object of desire is indeed forbidden. But it is not the "law" that forbids it, as Freud believes[63]—it is the person who designates the object to us as desirable by desiring it himself' (Girard, Oughourlian, and Lefort: 295).

Dickey has provided two epigraphs for his model. I have already discussed the first at the beginning of this chapter. I will now discuss the second, a notoriously ambiguous verse taken from the Old Testament that prophesizes the providential destruction of the descendants of Esau,[64] the Edomites, a violent and semi-nomadic hunting people who dwell in the mountains.

The pride of thine heart hath deceived thee,

Thou that dwelleth in the clefts of the rock,

Whose habitation is high; that saith in his heart, Who shall bring me down to the ground?

Obadiah, Verse 3

Ed provides the answer which reflects the reddened glint of metaphysical desire: 'I wanted to kill [the Mountain Man] exactly as Lewis had killed the other man: I wanted him to suspect nothing at all until the sudden terrible pain in his chest that showed an arrow through him from behind, come from anywhere' (Dickey, 1970, p. 174). By the end of *Deliverance*, Ed has overcome the *skandalon* and appropriated Lewis' place in proximity to the model. Both of the twins undergo the deliverance from the pathological violence of acquisitive mimesis.[65]

> Lewis limps over from his cabin now and then and we look at each other with intelligence, feeling the true weight and purpose of all water. He has changed, too, but not in obvious ways. He can die now; he knows that dying is better than immortality. He is a human being, and a good one. Sometimes he refers to me as 'U.C.', which means—to him and me—'Unorganized Crime,' and this has become a kind of minor conversation piece at parties, and at lunch in the city with strangers (Dickey, 1970, p. 277).

---

[63] Girard is a ferocious critic of Oedipal Theory: that the Law is really the symbolic projection of the psychic power of the castrating power of the Father exerted against the desire of the Son, society itself being nothing more than the replication of the triangulated psychic economy of the nuclear family. For an exhaustive critique of Freud, see Girard (1977), pp. 169–222 and Girard et al. (2003), pp. 283–392. See Chap. 1, above.

[64] The elder twin brother of Jacob, 'a cunning hunter, a man of the fields', both hairy and 'red all over'. In Genesis 27:41 Esau swears to kill Jacob, 'a plain man, dwelling in tents.' The *Elohim* ('angels') that Jacob periodically encounters in Genesis 28 to 33 are actually 'deified ancestors', signifying a proto-Israelite Cult of the Dead (Cooper & Goldstein, 1993).

[65] A possible objection might be raised that if Ed did not kill the 'right' Mountain Man but someone else then he has not really succeeded in supplanting Lewis. But this fails to take into account the undifferentiated reality of the Other Side: one Mountain Man is the same as any other. All that matters was a more successful, meaning a delivering, killing performed in superior imitation to Lewis'.

This ending is most satisfying from a Girardian perspective, as transference has shown to be identical to a reconciliation that still retains a lingering trace of hierarchy, or a reversed triangulation.

> Religious phenomena are essentially characterized by the double transference, the aggressive transference followed by the reconciliatory transference. The reconciliatory transference sacralises the victim and is the one most fragile, most easily lost, since to all evidence it does not occur until the mechanism has completely 'played itself out'. We remain capable, in other words, of hating our victims; we are no longer capable of worshipping them (Girard, 1977, p. 277).

It is with Girard that both the title of the novel and its primary narrative, a mythic lie of the establishment of the sovereignty of one man within the state of nature, makes the most sense. Through their homicidal-sacrificial foray into the wilderness, the twins have been delivered from the agony of their potentially fatal mimetic rivalry and their community, both private and the familial, has been regenerated through a generative unanimity. And, fortunately, the bodies of all three victims, Drew and the two Mountain Men, remain hidden, confined to the taboo space of the sacred.'Desire itself leads to madness and death if there is no victimage mechanism to guide it back to "reason" or to engender this "reason"' (Girard et al., 2003, p. 311) warns Girard; the 'surrogate victim dies so that the entire community, threatened by the same fate, can be reborn in a new or renewed cultural order' (Girard, 1977, p. 255). *Deliverance* proves, if a novel can ever be said to prove anything, that the outermost boundary of the law is nothing other than the extreme limit of mimetic rivalry that gives bloody birth to the Hobbesian power of death over life. Dickey has offered a notorious commentary on the ending that is germane for my own reading.

> It was self-defence. Knowing this, Ed can take even more of a kind of secret pride in what he's done because he's a peace-loving person. He's never had any record of any criminal activity, much less murder. It was forced upon him and he brought it off. He got away with it, and this is a kind of index of secret powers he never suspected he had. Now he knows what he is capable of doing (James Dickey qtd. Keesey, 1994, p. 205).

But given the nature of metaphysical desire it follows that Ed, this time as the model-obstacle, must do 'it' again. Which is why is he prophetically warned by Sheriff Bullard (played by James Dickey himself) 'And, buddy, let me tell you one thing. Don't ever do anything like this again. Don't come back up here' (John Boorman, *Deliverance*, 1972). If this is true, then the novel also proves that the mis-recognized double at the heart of law-and-literature is also its greatest secret.

Law is the monstrous double of crime.

References

Primary Sources

Deliverance (Warner Bros 1972; directed by John Boorman).
Dickey, J. (1970). *Deliverance*. Delta.
Dickey, J. (1993). *To the White Sea*. Houghton Mifflin.

Secondary Sources

Burkert, W. (1983). *Homo Necans: The anthropology of ancient Greek sacrificial ritual and myth*. Trans. Peter Bing. University of California Press.
Burkert, W. (1987). The problem of ritual killing. In R. G. Hamerton-Kelly (Ed.), *Violent origins: Walter burkert, rene girard, and Jonathan Z. Smith on ritual killing and cultural formation* (pp. 149–90). Stanford University Press.
Butterworth, K. (1996). The savage mind: James Dickey's 'deliverance.' *The Southern Literary Journal, 28*(2), 69–78.
Cartmill, M. (1993). *A view to death in the morning: Hunting and nature through history*. Harvard University Press.
Collins, B. J. (2006). Pigs at the gate: Hittite pig sacrifice in its Eastern Mediterranean context. *Journal of Ancient near Eastern Religions, 6*(1), 155–188.
Cooper, A., & Goldstein, B. R. (1993). The cult of the dead and the theme of entry into the land. *Biblical Interpretation, 1*(3), 285–303.
Cover, R. M. (1983–1984). The Supreme Court 1982 term foreword: Nomos and narrative. *Harvard Law Review, 4*, 4–68.
Dupuy, J.-P. (1988). Totalization and misrecognition. In P. Dumouchel (Ed.), *Violence and truth: On the work of Rene Girard* (pp. 75–100). London: The Athlone Press.
Endel, P. G. (1988). Dickey, dante, and the demonic: Reassessing *deliverance*. *American Literature, 60*(4), 611–624.
Gassett, O. (1972). *Meditations on hunting*. Trans. Howard B. Wescott. Charles Scribner's Sons.
Girard, R. (1965). *Desire, deceit and the novel: Self and other in literary structure*. Trans. Yvonne Freccero. The Johns Hopkins University Press.
Girard, R. (2014). *The one by whom scandal comes*. Trans. M.B. De Boise. Michigan State University Press.
Girard, R. (1978). *To double business bound: Essays on literature, mimesis, and anthropology*. The Johns Hopkins University Press.
Girard, R. (1977). *Violence and the sacred*. Trans. Patrick Gregory. The Johns Hopkins Press.
Girard, R., Oughourlian, J.-M., & Lefort, G. (2003). *Things hidden since the foundations of the world*. Trans. Stephen Bann and Michel Metteer. Continuum.
Girard, R., & Treguer, M. (2014). *When these things begin: Conversations with Michel Treguer*. Trans. Trevor Cribben Merrill. Michigan State University Press.
Golsan, R. J. (2002). *Rene gir̀ard and myth: An introduction*. New York: Routledge
Gordon, R. (1984). Critical legal histories. *Stanford Law Review, 36*, 57–125.
Guillory, D. L. (1976). Myth and meaning in James Dickey 1970's Deliverance. *College Literature, 3*(1), 56–62.
Hart, H. (2000). *James Dickey: The world as a lie*. Picador.
Heilburn, C. (1994). The masculine wilderness of the American novel. In R. Kirschten (Ed.), *Critical essays on James Dickey* (pp. 59–72). Maxwell Macmillan International.
Hill, K. (1982). Hunting and human evolution. *Journal of Human Education, 11*, 521–544.

Hobbes, T. (1991). *Leviathan* fully corrected 1651 edition, Cambridge University Library, Syn3.65.1 Edited by Richard Tuck. Cambridge University Press.

Holtsmark, E. B. (2001). The *Katabasis* theme in modern cinema. In M. M. Winkler (Ed.), *Classical myth and culture in the cinema* (pp. 23–50). Oxford University Press.

James, M. R. (1997). Dealing with death. In D. Petersen (Ed.), *A hunter's heart: Honest essays on blood sport* (pp. 102–107). Henry Holt Books.

Jameson, F. (1994). The great American hunter, or, ideological content in the novel. In R. Kirschten (Ed.), *Critical essay on James Dickey* (pp. 49–58). Maxwell Macmillan International.

Keesey, D. (1994). James Dickey and the Macho Persona. In R. Kirschten (Ed.), *Critical Essays on James Dickey* (pp. 204–212). Maxwell Macmillan International.

Kolb, M. J. (2008). Staple finance, ritual pig sacrifice, and ideological power in ancient Hawai'i. *Archaeological Papers of the American Anthropological Association, 9*(1), 89–107.

Lawrence, D. H. (1978). *Studies in classic American literature.* Penguin Books.

Laughlin, W. S. (1986). Hunting: An integrating bio-behaviour system and its evolutionary importance. In R. B. Lee & I. DeVore (Eds.), *Man the hunter* (pp. 304–320). Aldine Publishing Company.

Livingston, P. (1988). Demystification and History in Girard and Durkheim. In P. Dumouchel (Ed.), *Violence and truth: On the work of Rene Girard* (pp. 113–133). London: The Athlone Press.

Livingston, P. (1992). *Models of desire: Rene Girard and the psychology of mimesis.* Baltimore: The John Hopkins University Press.

Mack, B. (1987). Introduction: Religion and ritual. In R. G. Hamerton-Kelly (Ed.), *Violent origins: Walter Burkert, Rene Girard, and Jonathan Z. Smith on ritual killing and cultural formation* (pp. 1–72). Stanford University Press.

Oughourlian J.-M. (2010). *The genesis of desire.* Trans. Eugene Webb. East Lansing MI: Michigan State University Press.

Pue, W. (1990). Wrestling with law: (Geographical) specificity vs. (legal) abstraction. *Urban Geography* 11/6: 566–585.

Sosis, R., & Alcorta, C. (2003). Signaling, solidarity, and the sacred: The evolution of religious behavior. *Evolutionary Anthropology, 12*, 264–274.

Turner, V. W. (1967). Themes in the symbolism of Ndembu hunting ritual. In J. Middleton (Ed.), *Myth and cosmos: Readings in mythology and symbolism* (pp. 251–267). University of Texas Press.

Turner, V. W. (1969). *The ritual process: Structure and anti-structure.* Cornell University Press.

Washburn, S. L., & Lancaster, C. S. (1986). The evolution of hunting. In R. B. Lee & I. DeVore (Eds.), *Man the hunter* (pp. 293–303). Aldine Publishing Company.

Wilson, E. (2016). The ballad of Ed and Lewis; conflictual mimesis and the revocation of the social contract in James Dickey's *Deliverance. Law and Humanities*, 10/1: 115–160.

Chapter 4
'A Little Law and Order Wouldn't Hurt Anybody Around Here': '*The Man Who Shot Liberty Valance*' and '*High Noon*'

Abstract This chapter discusses the scapegoat as the historical artifact lying at the base of judicial order through a close reading of two classic but 'iconoclastic' Western films: John Ford's *The Man Who Shot Liberty Valance* (1962) and Fred Zimmerman's *High Noon* (1951). What links these two otherwise very different films is their unusually frank treatment of the central legal paradox of the Western which might be called originary violence: in order for the community-within-the-wilderness to be established and for the rule of law to be created, a foundational murder must be committed. Originary violence is central to Girard's notion of the scapegoat—the product of the violent unanimity of the group directed against a designated enemy—as not just an abstract but as a temporally concrete phenomenon; it also corresponds closely to the friend-enemy distinction of Carl Schmitt's theory of constitutional law. Schmitt's notion of the decision, that precise moment in time at which the identity of the enemy is named, allows the community (the friends) to emerge. The word 'decision' is etymologically derived from the Latin term *Decidere*, the initial incision into the body of the sacrificial victim; hence, the iconic plot of the Western—the war of the community against the outlaw—is dramatically identical to an act of scapegoating. The subversive genius of both films lies with their revealing of the sacrificial nature of the Western drama.

Keywords The Westerner · Originary violence · Catharsis · Carl Schmitt · *Nomos* · The friend-enemy distinction · The state of exception · Decisionism

4.1 Catharsis: The Western and Classical Mythology

Both the textual and film versions of *Lord of the Flies* and *Deliverance* establish the reversibility of, or the iterability between, 'the lawful' and the 'un-lawful' or 'outlawry'. In Hobbes' own conception of the social contract, the latent tension between Law and Crime arises from the original act of violence that gives rise to the Commonwealth, whether by Institution with Ralph and Piggy invoking the fear of death (the flip side of the promise of rescue) or by Acquisition with Jack and Lewis

E. M. Wilson, *Rene Girard, Law, Literature, and Cinema*,
https://doi.org/10.1007/978-981-97-1156-7_4

relying upon the direct application of physical force. The occluded and supremely anti-liberal truth present in both works is that as the community is the ritualistic expression of a social contract of some kind, it follows that the later innovation of the 'State' is dependent upon a foundational act of violence, death, or the threat of death being the thing that drives the process of contracting. In terms of film, the highest and most complex meditation upon this unspeakable truth is the genre[1] known as the *Western*, commonly regarded as the quintessentially American cinematic form[2] due to an elementary but signature dramatic device: 'The reason the Western has the classic showdown between hero and villain take place on the main street of town is that the matter at stake is not a merely personal but a public, a social matter' (Gilberto Geertz qtd. Gallagher, 1986: 22). Expressed another way, the '*naïve greatness*' of the Western is inseparable from the centrality of violence to its narrative technique (Bazin, 1971: 147).

> Why does the Western movie especially have such a hold on our imagination? Chiefly, I think, because it offers a serious orientation to the problem of violence such as can be found almost nowhere else in our culture. One of the well-known peculiarities of modern civilized opinion is its refusal to acknowledge the value of violence. This refusal is a virtue, but like many virtues it involves a certain willful blindness and it encourages hypocrisy. (Warshow, 1999: 46)

For Andre Bazin, the longevity of the Western, in many ways a 'juvenile' art form, can only be explained by the genre's ability to convey more serious concerns that are being expressed in a very specific sets of ways: 'The western must possess some greater secret than simply the secret of youthfulness. It must be a secret that somehow identifies it with the essence of cinema' (Bazin, 1971: 141). If Bazin is right that 'the western is cinema par excellence' and that the reflection upon violence is central to its greatness, then it follows that the essence of cinema is itself the *mythology of law* which is ultimately about the correct means of regulating violence. Interpreted from the critical perspective of Law-and-Literature, the Western operates on two premises. The first premise is the representational nature of language: that it is possible to unambiguously demarcate Law from Crime. Just as with *Deliverance* and *Lord of the Flies*, the Western invokes the existential intensity (if not metaphysical horror) of the overcoming of the state of nature.

> The relations between morality and law...were half [sic] a century ago the most vital thing confronting the youthful United States. Only strong, rough, and courageous men could tame these virgin lands. Everyone knows that familiarity with death does not keep alive the fear of hell, nor do scruples or moral debate. Policemen and judges are of most help to the weak. It was the force of this conquering humanity that constituted its weakness. Where individual morality is precarious it is only law that can impose the order of the good and the good of order. (Bazin, 1971: 145–146)

But the second premise exists in narrative and dramatic tension with the first and recalls the pre-representational notion: that the inherently violent nature of the

[1] Defined below.

[2] In the following discussion, the Western is understood in all of its myriad cultural forms although the emphasis will be upon the cinematic.

originating act of foundation—the dramatic event that is the 'specialty' of the Western hero and that serves as the narrative core of the Western film—always threatens to de-stabilize, or 'erase', this bright-line distinction between the lawful and the unlawful that the 'common sense' of public speech struggles to uphold. For the frontier communities of the West, like the hapless liberals up the river with no canoe in *Deliverance* and the boys without grown-ups on the Pacific island in *Lord of the Flies*, required an act of murder in order to set everything in order. Which means that, in the final instance Good Guy = Bad Guy. It is the lurking presence of this perpetual iterability between Law and Crime that creates the dramatic tension that invests the Western film with its exceptional moral seriousness. For Bazin the cinematic Western

> derives its real meaning only from the morality of a world in which social good and evil, in their simplicity and necessity, exist like two primary and basic elements. But good in its natal state engenders law in all its primitive rigor; epic becomes tragedy, on the appearance of the first conflict between the transcendence of social justice and the individual character of moral justice, between the categorical imperative of the law which guarantees the order of the future city, and the no less unshakeable order of the individual conscience. (Bazin, 1971: 147)

And in his seminal essay 'The Westerner', Robert Warshow points out the inconvenient truth that the filmic hero known as the Westerner is essentially the double of the cinematic Gangster; although commonly, and naively, assumed to be opposites, the Gangster and the Cowboy bear a more fundamental but occluded similarity through their respective relationships to violence:'The two most successful creations of American movies are the gangster and the Westerner: men with guns'(Warshow, 1999: 35).

> The truth is that the Westerner comes into the field of serious art only when his moral code, without ceasing to be compelling, is seen also to be imperfect. The Westerner at his best exhibits a moral ambiguity which darkens his image and saves him from absurdity; this ambiguity arises from the fact that, whatever his justifications, he is a killer of men. (Warshow, 1999: 39)

Just like those two great 'wannabes' from *Deliverance*, Lewis and Ed; as with the action-oriented but morally ambiguous anti-heroes of James Dickey, the Westerner bears many of the characteristics of the protagonists of classical mythology (Winkler, 1985), most specifically his role as an agent of *catharsis*, which complements perfectly Bazin's point concerning the Western as always a latently *tragic* art form.

> According to Aristotle, suffering and violence on the tragic stage arouse both pity and fear (*eleos* and *phobos*) in the spectator. These two powerful emotions accumulated within the audience during the play, are released at the drama's climax. Such draining of emotions Aristotle calls *catharsis*—'purification'. Catharsis leaves the spectator numb. If no purging like this occurred, the high-pitched emotions of pity and fear would have no outlet and would remain inside the spectator as harmful forces. Catharsis, then, is a psychological safety valve through which excessive emotions, including those of aggression and brutality, are neutralized and rendered harmless. (Winkler, 1985: 522)

The question now becomes: in what way is the Western cathartic? For Law-and-Literature the drama of the Westerner is the cinematic acting out of a very precise and extremely violent moment in the process of social formation that signifies the transition from the state of nature to the social contract, or from 'wilderness' to 'town'. The foundational violence performed by the Westerner on screen visually enacts the ritualistic (and dramatic) expurgation of violence-within-the-community that is the necessary precondition for the institution of the Commonwealth, allowing Robert B. Pippin, in his masterly *Hollywood Westerns and American Myth: The Importance of Howard Hawks and John Ford for Political Philosophy* (2010) to completely overturn John Rawls' apple-cart of transactional-analysis.

> It was certainly clear to the originators of the modern notion of contractual secular political authority that mere acknowledgement of the rationality of political contract was insufficient to account either for the mythical founding act itself or for the sustained allegiance, sacrifice, and civic cooperation necessary for a state to be and survive as a state. The fear of violent death, the powerful desire for a commodious and prosperous life, a natural sociability, and many other candidates for the role of decisive political passion entered the discussion. (Pippin, 2010: 70–71)

It is critical to always keep in mind that the Commonwealth that is inaugurated by the original violence of the Westerner is always the Commonwealth-by-Institution, never the Commonwealth-by-Acquisition. Why? Precisely because, pace both Harold Bloom and William Golding,[3] this is *American* history we are talking about, so that the possibility of the successful establishment of the Commonwealth-by-Acquisition has been ruled out in advance. More a question of history than moral virtue, America is unable to tolerate the notion of the Hobbesian of One Man, resulting in one of the defining elements of the Western genre: that the homicidal Westerner must always leave the community, or 'disappear' in some way, by the end of the story, which is both a closure and a cleansing.[4]

When considering the Western as a mythology of the Law, there are two essential terms of convenience: *myth* and *genre*. Here I am supplementing Girard's concept of *mythos* (the 'lie') with Claude Levi-Strauss' definition of myth, or the *mythic*, as 'a form of narrative mediation of culturally significant antagonisms' (Boehnke, 2001: 49) which means that the mythic is *diacritical*, or grounded upon a *binary* opposition that is a form of 'doubling'; similar in some ways to Girard, but different insofar as the doubling does not involve the scapegoat but some sort of parallel relationship between cosmic forces which are assumed, perhaps falsely, to be oppositional. The irreconcilable difference separating Girard from Levi-Strauss is that for Girard sacrificial killing is the foundation of mythology which is the mis-recognition of violent origins of the human, while for Levi-Strauss mythology is the foundation of sacrificial killing, meaning that scapegoating praxis is deterministically controlled by cultural archetypes, or universal structures of the human mind which operates

[3] Chapter 2, above.

[4] Perhaps the single greatest cinematic example of this is John Ford's *The Searchers* (1956) with Ethan Edwards (John Wayne) as the 'sacred executioner' who voluntarily undergoes the defilement of genocide necessary to restore the community but, as a result, is eternally exiled from his own people.

in a binary manner.[5] For the latter, the mythic is always foundational, providing an account for either the creation or destruction of an entire social order, so that mythic narrative will assume a very precise, and replicable, structural form, employing established tropes and stereotypes that give rise in turn to a highly patterned literary device known as *genre*, a primary category of literary classification. If the mythic gives rise to genre, and the Western is mythic in essence (and function as we shall see) then what are the idioms of the Western as genre? According to Jim Kitses, the Western-as-genre consists of four components: (a) History, invariably American; (b) Themes: 'expressed through a series of familiar character types and conflicts' (e.g., Cowboys versus Indians; Homesteaders versus Ranchers); (c) Archetypes: certain themes, situations or symbols that achieve a dominance within the genre on the basis of their 'elemental' (cathartic) relation to the audience; and (d) Icons: certain 'situations and actions can have an emblematic power... [and] a latent ritualistic meaning which can be brought to the surface and reflected. The quest, the journey, the confrontation, these can take on moral or allegorical overtones' (Kitses, 1969: 24–25). In cinematic terms, the icon is that thing or image that most simply, and most powerfully, connects the audience to an archetypal theme in purely emotional or cathartic ways.

> What holds all of these elements together (and in that sense provides the basic convention) is narrative and dramatic structure...However, with an art as popular as the western this must also mean a precise awareness of audience expectation with reference to a range of characters—pre-eminently hero and antagonist [binary]—and testing situations, conflicts, spectacle, landscape, physical action and violence. (Kitses, 1969: 25)

In response to the question what is the archetypal theme of the Western, the cathartic nexus between audience and myth as mediated by icons, the answer would be framed in terms of a legal mythology: The Western is the mythic story of the violent struggle over the creation of the Commonwealth-by-Acquisition within the state of nature which then gives way almost immediately to the social contract and the democratic Commonwealth-by-Institution. Instead of the primal, and irrevocable, Hobbesian choice of the Assembly, the Western plays with the allegedly 'exceptional' characteristics of American history and re-presents a secular (profane) process of political and social evolution in the form of a cinematic allegory (sacred). Not surprisingly, then the archetypal Western theme is paradoxical, for the Western as the mythic is nothing other than

> the conflict between two forms of the genesis of law. On the one hand law is seen as imposed upon society by an authority standing high above and issuing downwards its commands; on the other hand, law is regarded as developing within society, being spontaneous and growing upwards, independent of any dominant will. (Boehnke, 2001: 48)

Which automatically lends itself to thoroughly mythic treatment. Although Levi-Strauss's notion of the law 'establishing and justifying authority, as a mythical authority, avoids the question of the inherent violence of the law in [the] form of natural law, which assumes the justness of all natural causes' (Boehnke, 2001: 54),

---

[5] So that for Girard, Levi-Strauss's cardinal sin is that he eliminates physical violence from social origins, the very thing that Girard seeks to reverse. See below.

when translated into the historical particularities of the American Western as genre, law is always made to re-appear in the manner that Jacques Derrida said that it would: 'a power which one has granted, which is authorized, which is approved and justified, which is through its use justified or justified through use' (Boehnke, 2001: 55)—meaning that the 'justness of all natural causes' has in some way been delegated to the Westerner. And precisely because power must be justified, Law requires myth—or, more accurately, expression in in mythic form. Especially in America, the land of westward expansion.

4.2 I Kill Therefore I Am: Western Mythology and American History

The Western, then, is a *civilizational myth* or a narrative that mythologizes American civilization but in a manner that permits a universalized understanding.

> The Western, with its historical setting, its thematic emphasis on the establishment of law and order, and its resolution of the conflict between civilization and savagery on the frontier, was a kind of foundation ritual. It presented for our recurrent contemplation that epic moment when the frontier passed from the old way of life into the present. (Cawelti, 1999: 49)

Its primary icon is the Westerner,[6] an Americanized *homo sacer*, the out-law who is 'polluted' in a manner that is holy; in this instance, the sacred executioner, or designated *sacrificer*, the one who performs the 'special' murder that initiates the process of cultural transformation.

> The truth is that the Westerner comes into the field of serious art only when his moral code, without ceasing to be compelling, is seen also to be imperfect. The Westerner at his best exhibits a moral ambiguity which darkens his image and saves him from absurdity; this ambiguity arises from the fact that, whatever his justifications, he is a killer of men. (Warshow, 1999: 39)

With regards to (American) History, the term most commonly associated with the Western is the Frontier, which denotes 'a cultural zone or a civilizational struggle, a way of life: a semantic charge electrified by the terror and bloodshed that went along with settler expansion' (Grandin, 2019: 116). Richard Slotkin very broadly follows Levi-Strauss[7] in arguing that 'True myths are generated on a sub-literary level by the historical experience of a people and thus constitute part of that inner reality which the work of the artist draws on, illuminates and explains' (Slotkin, 1973: 4). Levi-Strauss, in turn, borrows from Ferdinand de Saussure in stipulating that all symbols, or concepts, are defined 'negatively by their relations with other terms of the system. Their most precise characteristic is in being what others are not' (Wright, 1975: 22).

> In societies that are still in the process of achieving a sense of identity, the establishment of a normative, characteristic image of the group's character is a psychological necessity; and

[6] See below.

[7] For a similarly structuralist approach see Wright (1975).

> the simplest means of defining or expressing the sense of such a norm is by rejecting some other group whose character is deemed to be the opposite. (Slotkin, 1973: 68)[8]

That which is mythic, therefore, is *mediatory* in both origin and 'intent,' an 'intellectual means for resolving a conceptual contradiction or duality in a particular society', in which the duality contains within it the grounds of its functional but perhaps unstable reconciliation: the 'structure of a myth establishes the terms of the duality and then "mediates" between them, thereby resolving the dilemma in the primitive [sic] mind' (Wright, 1975: 203). And what can the myth-generating meta-duality of the United States be other than the summation of all of the antinomies of settler-colonialism itself, the meta-types being the colonizer (the generic 'White') and colonized (the generic 'Indigenous')? The 'first colonists saw in America an opportunity to regenerate their fortunes, their spirits, and the power of their church[9] and nation[10]; but the means to that regeneration ultimately became the means of violence, and the myth of regeneration through violence became the structuring metaphor of the [Anglo-White] American experience' (Slotkin, 1973: 5) Slotkin broadly follows Frederick Jackson Turner in hypothesizing a double set of dualities ('Even at the source of the American myth there lies the fatal opposition, the hostility between two worlds, two races, two realms of thought and feeling' (Slotkin, 1973: 17), each of which requires its own mythic mediation through the meta-narrative device of the western landscape as site of an existential 'regeneration through violence' uncannily like Girard's concept of regenerative violence—which is sacrificial.

> In American mytho-genesis the founding fathers … were those who (to paraphrase Faulkner's *Absolom, Absolom!*) tore violently a nation from the implacable and opulent wilderness—the rogues, adventurers, and land-boomers; the Indian fighters, traders, missionaries, explorers, and hunters who killed and were killed until they had mastered the wilderness; the settlers who came after, suffering hardship and Indian warfare for the sake of a sacred mission or a simple desire for land; and the Indians themselves, both as they were and as they appeared to the settlers, for whom they were the special demonic personification of the American wilderness. Their concerns, their hopes, their terrors, their violence, and their justification of themselves, as expressed in literature, are the foundation stones of the mythology that informs our history. (Slotkin, 1973: 4; Wright, 1975: 16)

And as Art is a form of spectacle, the history of American westward expansion generated its own distinctive aesthetic forms pressed into the service of mythic necessity the (tragic) inevitability of violent conflict and conquest; 'Spectacles do all sorts of political work in every society but are especially useful in settler societies because they continue to redirect emotions, histories, and possibilities away from the means of societal and historical production—Indigenous dispossession, disenfranchisement, and containment' (Simpson, 2010: 206–207). Jean-Paul Sartre got it right.

---

[8] 'The characters in a myth represent fundamental social types.… a myth creates a conceptual model of important social types of people located in a complete social situation and taking significant [i.e., meaningful] social actions, actions that create social relationships. It is in this sense that a myth *explains* social interaction' (Wright, 1975: 129).

[9] Puritan.

[10] English (= Anglo-Saxon + Anglo-Celtic minus the Irish).

> They [the colonized] are cornered between our guns pointed at them and those terrifying compulsions, those desires for murder which spring from the depth of their spirits and which they do not always recognize; for at first it is not *their* violence, it is ours, which turns back on itself and rends them; and the first action of these oppressed creatures is to bury deep down that hidden anger which their and our moralities condemn and which is however only the last refuge of their humanity.... in the period of their helplessness, their mad impulse to murder is the expression of the native's collective unconsciousness. (Sartre, 1990: 16)

The first duality is materialist, labor versus capital, which can be reconciled through the violent act of colonization itself: masculinist 'virility' secures the Frontier which gives way to the settler-pastoralist ideology of the suspension of class conflict through a feminine homestead communitarianism (Slotkin, 1992: 145). This 'safety-valve' theory of American expansion would eventually resolve itself into Herman Melville's 'monster of a million minds' through the unregulated proliferation of republican micro-sovereignties throughout the unlimited empty spaces of the West, the Frontier having been identified as 'the terrain on which a proper ego formed, as well as the field on which an unrestrained id was let loose,' or, as Walter Weyl put it, the Frontier 'made the American mind a little sovereignty of its own, acknowledging no allegiances and but few obligations. It created an individualism, self-confident, short-sighted, lawless, doomed in the end to defeat itself, as the boundless opportunism which gave it birth became at last circumscribed' (Grandin, 2019: 76, 81, 56, 185, 169, 99, 85; Paul Foos qtd. Grandin, 2019: 98). It was also a supremely Hobbesian notion, the opportunity (or nightmare) of One Man 'rule' over the indivisible natural unit of the Family, the most primitive form of sovereignty within the state of nature that preceded the Assembly.

> The attaining to this Sovereign Power is by two ways. One, by natural force; as when a man makes his children to submit themselves, and their children [in turn], to his government, as being able to destroy them if they refuse; or by war subdues his enemies to his will, giving them their lives on that condition. The other, is when men agree among themselves to submit to some Man, or Assembly of men, voluntarily, on confidence to be protected by him against all others. The later may be called a Political Commonwealth, or Commonwealth by *Institution*; and the former, a Commonwealth by *Acquisition*. (Hobbes, 1991: 121)

The second duality is egalitarianism versus the 'end of the frontier,' or the exhaustion of the American project of settler-colonialism. Here D. H. Lawrence's mythic duality of mind-consciousness versus blood-consciousness comes into play in the political terms of social contract versus the right-to-self-defense, the first completely self-conscious political movement of poor White settlers.

> The anti-mythologists of the American Age of Reason believed in the imminence of a rational republic of yeomen farmers and enlightened leaders, living amicably in the light of natural law and the Constitution.[11] They were thereby left unprepared when the Jeffersonian republic was overcome by the Jacksonian Democracy of the western man-on-the-make, the speculator, and the wildcat banker; when racist irrationalism and a falsely conceived economics[12] prolonged and intensified slavery in the teeth of American democratic idealism; and when men like Davy Crockett became national heroes by defining national aspiration in terms of so many trees hacked down, so many Indians and Mexicans dead in the dust. (Slotkin, 1973: 5)

[11] The revealingly named 'machine that would go of itself'.

[12] The plantation mode of agrarian capitalism.

It was no coincidence that the concept of Frontier as a safety-valve first emerged during the presidency that coincided with the Steam Age which was all about re-directing pressure; not only would the western settler-colonies resolve the dilemma of the crisis of over-production, but, as America's version of Siberia, the Frontier would enable the internal ostracism and mass dumping of political undesirables: 'For over a century, from Andrew Jackson forward, the country's political leaders [Eastern elites] enjoyed the benefit of being able to throw its restless and angry citizens […] outward, into campaigns against Mexicans, Native Americans, Filipinos, and Nicaraguans, among other enemies' (Grandin, 2019: 255). The idea was that the management of the unruly forces of the interior (meaning the transfer of marginal Whites to the periphery) would stimulate an unceasing cascade of continental colonization—the Frontier. The complicating factor for Jacksonian democracy, however, was that the 'new type' of Western Man, or the *rugged individualist*, given both his natural attributes and, in some cases at least, his superior class origins 'back East,' is not a natural democrat but an instinctual aristocrat, the vanguard of 'progressivism' (Slotkin, 1992: 279–286),[13] an onto-existential paradox that neatly reproduces the political and economic paradox of the emergent regional hegemonies of Western corporate-capitalist and managerial interests all at the expense of Jefferson's yeomen-guardians-of-*demos*, or 'populism'(Slotkin, 1992: 19, 20). The unifying link of all of this was the Depression of 1873 and the Railroad Strike of 1877 which exacerbated labor tensions to such a degree that the popular culture industry was able to engineer a convincing popular discourse of a confederacy of 'murderous reds'—working-class radicals and racial savages both Red and Black—which, in turn, mandated emergency decision-making by exceptional but reliable exceptional White men (= rugged individualist + Outlaw/Vigilante); the 'substitution of the symbolism of "savage war" for that of "class war" shifts the ground of controversy […] to that of race war […] in which progress depends on the expulsion/extermination of a congenitally regressive type of humanity and on the aggrandizement of a privileged race of people.' It appears that a kind of Social Darwinism that applied equally to both Whites and non-Whites was a central component of America's 'progressive' form of colonialism, explaining 'the emergence of a new managerial ruling class and justifying its right

---

[13] Progressivism came in three waves: Roosevelt I (1901–1920), Roosevelt II (1933–1952), and Clinton-Bush II-Obama-Trump (1992–2020) with the construction of THE WALL along the U.S.-Mexico border deflecting endo-colonization inward towards the infinitely sub-divisible frontier of the ordo-liberal Self (Grandin, 2019: 244–247). As FDR put it: 'Our last frontier has long since been reached…. There is no safety valve in the form of a Western Prairie…. Our task is not the discovery or exploitation of natural resources…. It is the less dramatic business of administering resources and plants [?] already in hand … of distributing wealth and products equitably'—or regulation at gun-point. Slotkin's sub rosa substitution of the New Deal manager-leader for the traditional Vigilante-Outlaw Hero in no way invalidates the libertine-like qualities of the Westerner: his unconscious (sub-textual) motivation is the resolution of Frontier violence in order to pave the way for the next round of settlement = civilization/modernity (Slotkin, 1992: 257). However, to the degree that the 'progressivist' gun-fighter is an aristocrat and through the totality of his actions wages a war of possessive Whiteness he bears more than a passing resemblance to the equally iconic aristocrat of the 'Old South'; hence the subliminally sinister account of Warshow that 'The Westerner is *par excellence* a man of leisure' (Warshow, 1999: 37).

to subordinate lesser classes to its purposes' (Slotkin, 1992: 21, 22). Both short- and long-term trends in corporate governance meshed perfectly, permitting a nation-wide revival of Western mythology: the 'recognition of the "end of the frontier"—the end of that time when primitive individualists among the [White] lower orders can be allowed to roam at will and without control in search of fulfillment' (Slotkin, 1985: 487; 477–489). Here, pragmatic reconciliation is oblique as mythic operation, for the resolution of this duality is dependent upon an exclusively voluntarist re-affirmation of masculine performance as the guarantor of democratic civic virtue in the face of the inevitable disappearance of the Frontier itself,[14] pioneered by Owen Wister in his seminal novel *The Virginian* (1902) as 'the myth of the vigilante' (Slotkin, 1992: 156–193; for Wister Slotkin, 1992: 169–183).[15] Therefore, every Western implicitly carries within it both the alpha and the omega; ostensibly a narrative of Genesis, its corollary is either the Fall or the Apocalypse, as the creation of the Frontier is itself the act that establishes the insuperable *finitude* of the colonialist/civilizational project. What links the beginning with the end is rugged individualism. Mythic forms of regeneration require violence, either through act or through will by men who are either naturally violent or are fully capable of committing world-axial acts of violence when required to by circumstances, which reproduces the inherent ambivalence of performance: the naturally violent will perform the violent act, while the naturally non-violent man may be able to perform violence by volition but in both cases the external performance may equally signify a presence or an absence. Therein lies the masculinist dilemma—one can never exclude the possibility that one is a 'fake'.[16]

Levi-Strauss notwithstanding, the myths of the American West naturally invite, if not positively demand, a Girardian interpretation. Girard's apparent binary structure is clearly diacritical but wholly subject to the vital caveat that the *binary is itself* established upon an earlier act of violence: antagonism creates duality, it is never caused by it, which is the essential difference between Levi-Strauss and Girard.

[14] A classic exposition of this treacherous myth was provided in 1907 by John R. Commons, author of the Roosevelt-approved report *Races and Immigrants in America*: 'These are the basic qualities which underlie democracy—intelligence, manliness, cooperation If they are lacking, democracy is futile. Here is the problem of races, the fundamental division of mankind. Race differences are established in the very blood and physical constitution. They are most difficult to eradicate, and they yield only to the slow processes of the centuries. Races may change their religions, their forms of government, their mode of industry, and their languages, but underneath all these changes they may continue their physical, mental, and moral capacities and incapacities…' The ending of American settlement creates the conditions for an immanent 'reverse colonization', which, through multi-racialism and multi-culturalism, imperils democratic government (Slotkin, 1992: 190).

[15] 'Like [Theodore] Roosevelt, Wister sees the primary achievement of the Frontier as the creation of a new racial type, selected from among the Anglo-Saxon "democracy" and trained by the frontier experience in the skills and psychology of command. But Wiser goes further, to show that the hero—who represents a uniquely "American genius"—can succeed by taking a principled stand *against* democracy (in its traditional formulation) and becoming part of a class order whose power is greater in progressive [colonizing] potential than that of popular government' (Slotkin, 1992: 175).

[16] This is what separates Marshal Kane in *High Noon* from Ransom Stoddard in *The Man Who Shot Liberty Valance*. See below.

For the former the duality that is the basis of myth is embedded within the structures of the mind itself whereas for the latter it is the accidental invention of the scapegoat itself that creates the social consciousness of dualism so that, contra Levi-Strauss, it is History itself that produces 'mind': the resultant *muthos* of the sacrifice/scapegoat is always foundational but historically specific, providing an account for either the creation or destruction of a particular social order, obviating the need for the universal structure (and structuralizing) of an entirely hypothetical 'primitive mind'. The 'four fundamental oppositions' of the Western genre (outside-society/inside-society; good/bad; strong/weak; wilderness/civilization) all effortlessly devolve into the pre-historical *mythos*/lie of the primal sacrificer-scapegoat duality, all of which is kinematically encapsulated by the overpowering visual and dramatic imagery of the Frontier community under siege, or in some sort of unresolvable crisis: all frontier-settlers 'felt impelled to maintain traditions of religious order and social custom in the face of the psychological terrors of the wilderness. Later, the sons of these [westward] emigrants strove to justify their title to the land they took for their own' (Slotkin, 1973: 18). Through myth-making. Which is lying. Which is what murderers and thieves do to cover their tracks.

> 'The land was ours before we were the land's,' said Robert Frost. The process by which we [sic] came to feel an emotional title to the land was charged with a passionate and aspiring violence, and 'the deed of gift was many deeds of war.' Because of the nature of myth and the myth-making process (Slotkin, 1973: 1–14), it is a significant comment on our characteristic attitudes toward ourselves, our culture, our racial sub-groupings, and our land that tales of strife between Americans and interlopers, between dark races, and light, became the basis of our mythology and that the Indian fighter and hunter emerged as the first of our national heroes. (Slotkin, 1973: 17–18)

Which brings back to the Girardian insight that myth as *mythos* equals the lie which is itself the sacralization of a foundational killing of the Other (= scapegoat). If we were to interpret the safety-valve theory from Girard's perspective, we would conclude that Frontier society was 'created' in order to provide the pre-conditions necessary for a uniquely American kind of homicidal performance that was sacred, meaning generative.

> Any [artistic] work capable of attaining that unified and compelling vision [mythic] of the whole American experience would have to contain in its terms—narrative, character, imagery, values—the sum total of all of these experiences reduced to a basic and universal archetype of all the colonist's experiences, the one presenting the most vital psychological difficulties, and present its vision in terms appropriate to the historical experience of a wilderness people. (Slotkin, 1973: 19)

Which would be centered upon the ritualistic elimination of the savage Other through the sacrificial mechanism of scapegoating. The specter of sacrifice, paradoxically, becomes even more horrific as we collectively replace archaic myth (the anti-linear eternal-recurrence-of-the-same[17]) with 'History', wherein social consciousness shifts toward linear narrative. Unfortunately for us, the truth about History,

---

[17] 'Primitive societies [sic] ... rely on analogical mode of explanation where the reference is discontinuous, finite, and present to experience; that is, they explain themselves through an analogy to nature' (Wright, 1975: 204).

while post-myth and therefore 'scientific,' is that it is culturally embedded within an explanatory schema that reproduces in toto the social function of the mythic.

> Not only do stories demonstrate that experience *can* make sense [the linear succession of present over past], they also demonstrate *how* it makes sense, by showing that one important event causes another and by ignoring unimportant events.[18] Narrative *form*—the thing that makes a story a story and not a list of events[19]—is also the form which human consciousness imposes on real experience to give it meaning. (Wright, 1975: 193)[20]

Which is exactly mythic consciousness accomplishes: 'myth succeeds in making the past like the present [as] it also makes the present *like* the myth of the past' (Wright, 1975: 190).[21] If 'the West' is one part of the thing-that-is-History of what we call 'America' *and* that such a colonialist-settlement History has, culturally, attained the status of mythic ('The Western is a myth of contemporary American society' (Wright, 1975: 185)) then it follows that the Western functions, on at least some level, as 'a conceptual model for social action' (Wright, 1975: 198) for that is the essence of the lie: 'myths reconcile deep social conflicts through models of action: myths do this through their binary structure of images and their narrative structure of action' (Wright, 1975: 191). In other words, a specifically American form of *mimesis*, but one that is always culturally suspect and never historically innocent: 'myth uses the past as an "idealized example," in which "a heroic achievement in the past is linked to another in the future of which the reader [or viewer] is the potential hero"' (Slotkin, 1985: 19). For both Slotkin and Wright—and, by implication, Girard— the 'Western myth has taken the historical setting and shaped it into a model of the present, which states in concrete images the conceptual conflicts of modern America and resolves them through types of action' (Wright, 1975: 190). Which presents us with a second-order paradox: that the History-derived 'tradition' of the West is 'not based on the West itself but on the myth of the West' (Wright, 1975: 189). For at the heart of this tradition is a normative demand (repetition) to engage in a particular form of violent act (physical or symbolic) for a very specific purpose,[22] which is to first recognize and then to resolve a crisis within the community—namely, that of establishing a foundational order for the settlers-within-the-wilderness. 'The important point is that the hero is alone', as the bearer of a uniquely *sacred* form of violence, which provides a neat Girardian explanation for one of the signature features

[18] Such a 'decision' presupposing a whole array of prior decisions of inclusion–exclusion, conscious and unconscious (or ideological).

[19] 'Narratives explain change: they have a beginning, a middle, and end. A narrative is a temporal account of a sequence of events related by similarity of topic and by a relationship of explanation, or causality.... narratives resonate with human consciousness: one naturally by selecting events to fit the form, and one less naturally by forcing the form to fit all experience....Thus, the narrative form is maximally meaningful' (Wright, 1975: 19, 193).

[20] Which explains why modernity is wholly unconscious of its own mythic nature.

[21] Conversely, myths 'can use the setting of the past to create and resolve the conflicts of the present. Myths use the past to tell us how to act in the present' (Wright, 1975: 187).

[22] Narrative structure 'constitutes the myth just as the rules constitute the game. […] it is through the narrative action that the conceptual symbolism of the Western, or any myth, is understood and applied by its hearers (or viewers)' (Wright, 1975: 186).

of the Western hero, his capacity to kill 'righteously'. This is also the basis for the not unwarranted complaint about the intrinsically reactionary nature of the Western genre (independent of its revolutionary/transformational 'substance' as the thing that enables progress): the re-presentation of a 'private' sovereign power, Hobbes' Commonwealth-by-Acquisition, sublimated as the ethos of the rugged individualist. In the most primitive manner, the hero as the one who kills righteously is an only partially disguised One Man of the Commonwealth-by-Acquisition, who, like Jack in *Lord of the Flies*, is exempted from the *demos*, both by nature and choice, in order to meet the existential threat created by the 'cosmic' threat along the Frontier: the imminent triumph of wilderness (chaos) over civilization (order). 'Thus, in the classical Western we have an aristocratic tendency with a democratic bias. Under threatening circumstances, it is reasonable and proper to rely on a strong and elite group of men [or individual]; but when the danger has passed, they must become equal with everyone else, a requirement, in fact, they have been fighting to insure.' The myth of the Western Hero *is* the story of Horatio: 'If he maintained his position, the hero would change [society's] egalitarian nature and create a powerful and undemocratic elite'—which requires either the death, exile, or self-effacement of the Frontier's mythologized 'Founding Father' (Wright, 1975: 152 and 153).But the *mythos* of the Westerner also doubles as the 'lie' of Cain.

> Then Cain went out from the presence of the Lord and dwelt in the land of Nod opposite [to the east of] Eden. And Cain knew his wife, and she conceived and bore Enoch. And he [Cain] built a city and called the name of the city after the name of his son Enoch.[23]

The 'Founding Father' of the city (polis) is one and the same to the Father who invented murder. To make the Girardian point that both Slotkin and Wright are unwilling or maybe unable to: that which separates historical past from mythic memory is the existential imperative for action—or, more precisely, actions that can be successfully and endlessly *imitated*.

> Through history the past is postulated as the locus of an understanding of the present, but history alone cannot provide an understanding of the past as a ground for present action and involvement. This understanding must be created through historical myths, which establishes an analogy between past and present *in the same way* that primitive myths establish an analogy between nature and culture. (Wright, 1975: 208)

The duality, or mimetic ambiguity, of the Westerner is the perfect fusion of the historical and the mythic: the necessary reconciliation between nature and culture, city and wilderness, colonizer and colonized is achieved through the inversion of the relationship between the sacrificer and the sacrificed, both with their own narratives, each one subject to the mimetic logic of a generative violence that encompasses them.

---

[23] Genesis 4: 16–17.

4.2.1 The Westerner as Rugged Individualist

The Westerner is the anthropocentric representation of the intrusion of a life-restorative 'wilderness' (or 'savagism') into the primitive community in order to overcome the duality of civilization and wilderness, city and country, so that the historically localizable terms of existential combats along the Frontier are re-written as mythologically 'timeless' nature. But there's a catch: the overcoming of nature in favor of civilization requires the deployment of a kind of natural 'force' which is ambivalent in extremis.

> But the law is unjust to the extent that it pretends to guarantee a moral society but ignores the individual merits of those who constitute that society. If it is to be effective, this justice must be dispensed by men who are just as strong and just as daring as the criminals. These virtues … are in no way incompatible with virtue in the absolute sense. The sheriff is not always a better person than the man he hangs. This begets and establishes an inevitable and necessary contradiction. There is often little moral difference between the outlaw and the man who operates within the law. (Bazin, 1971: 146)

Another term for the ruggedly individualistic gun-fighter is *regulator*, suggesting an enforcer-of-finality: a supremely lethal 'Bad Man' who is invoked to cure the nascent community's affliction of other, less superior, 'Bad Men'. Consistent with the functionality of myth, the Westerner as giver-of-death is a figural of both performance and mimesis. All of his signature libertine attributes of perfect and total autonomy—repose, leisure, self-control, melancholy, loneliness, indifference to love and the feminine—are all 'sharply defined acquirements, giving to the figure of the Westerner an apparent moral clarity which corresponds to the clarity of his physical image against his bare landscape; initially, at any rate, the Western movie presents itself as being without mystery, its whole universe comprehended in what we see on the screen' (Warshow, 1999: 37). Transparency of image signifies clarity of vision which, through visualization, bespeaks of the self-grounded purity of the regulator's sovereign exercise of ultimate justice by way of theatrically staged and ritualistically prescribed executions. And it is this purity that guarantees both the efficacy and the moral righteousness of the gun-fighter's eliminationist violence. 'What he defends, at bottom, is the purity of his own image—in fact his "honor"'; therefore, the Westerner 'could not fulfill himself if the moment did not finally come when he can shoot his enemy down' (Warshow, 1999: 38)—the identity of the sacrificial victim revealed as the one targeted for killing through nothing other than his occupying the center of the annihilating gaze of the gun-fighter. And by the infallibility of his 'aim' the Westerner is revealed, in absolute truth, as the regulator of the equally 'true' victim. As Theodore Roosevelt explained it, a civilizing vigilantism would spontaneously emerge to guarantee the progressive incorporation of the West; 'Good' (White) Men would band 'themselves together as a regiment and put down the wicked with ruthless severity, by the exercise of lynch law, shooting and hanging the worst off-hand' (Grandin, 2019: 120). Contrary to first impressions, 'it is not violence at all which is the "point" of the Western movie, but a certain image of man, a style, which expresses itself most clearly in violence' (Warshow, 1999: 47) which, by being subject to emulation through later performance, guaranteed the perpetual re-generation of the American colonizer.

> And he has, after all, his own kind of relevance. He is there to remind us of the possibility of style in an age which has put on itself the burden of pretending that style has no meaning, and, in the midst of our anxieties over the problem of violence, to suggest that even in killing or being killed we are not freed from the necessity of establishing satisfactory modes of behavior. (Warshow, 1999: 47)

Although neither Warshow or Slotkin use these terms, their readings clearly indicate the lurking presence of two of the signature tropes of Girardian critique, sacred violence and catharsis. The former is subliminally embedded within a defining stereotype of the Western genre itself which is also one of its greatest perceived artistic shortcomings: its formulaic return, or repetition, of plot that invariably culminates in some kind of killing (the 'shoot-out'). Understood from a Girardian perspective, the repetition of narrative structure is itself evidence of the latently *sacred* nature of the Western's profane drama-of-violence (Tompkins, 1992: 29–45): the sacrificial mechanism is itself a thoroughly reactionary, and stereotyping, form of violence in which the myth/lie function—the supremely ritualized killing of the scapegoat and the regenerative suspension of conflict—depends upon the perfect imitation of a rigorously policed set of circumstances: 'timelessness', which means not the structural duality of human consciousness but the mimetic re-enactment of the generative violence that created the scapegoat. The latter trope flows from the former: since the killing/shoot-out restores the community by suspending its capacity for violence (as well as paving the way for a 'future') the decisive moment is both liberating and transformative: the mimetic and affective potency of the Westerner is identical to that cathartic 'release' of 'blocked' emotions (best understood here as a free-floating anxiety of the White spectator concerning the transition from 'settler' to 'citizen' concurrent with the open-ended struggle between 'eastern' progressivism and 'western' sovereignty) that traditionally has been identified as catharsis. The mimetic affectivity of the Western lies within an underlying continuity with pre-historical sacrificial violence, catharsis moving the genre from the interpretative domain of Slotkin's structural materialism to the *ur-grund* of classical (a-temporal) mythological and literary tropes.

But as Girard makes clear, for any lie to work, whether it concerns the conflict of natural forces or the self-exculpatory targeting of the scapegoat, the community needs to be blind to what it is actually doing. America and Americans are no different: to 'preserve our [neo-puritan] self-image it has been necessary to disguise the realities of these historical movements under the masks of moral purity and social redemption through violence' (Cawelti, 1999: 49, 47, 55).The conflict that myth is intended to address but which is papered over in the reconciliatory (and expedient) rhetoric of law-as-institution of Ralph's (and Piggy's) modern State is recovered and apocalyptically unveiled through the grand drama of the Westerner as the bearer of an all-consuming but life-giving naturalist justice.[24] The Western is 'the essence of

[24] For naturalism and natural law theory, see below.

cinema' (Bazin, 1971: 141), a universal cinematic form not only because of its manifest content (the supreme ease of its translation into visual and cinematic terms of reference) but also because of its latent content of a civilizational myth that operates *universally*; within the Western lies the mythic artifact necessary to make bearable the fact that ' the establishment of any legal order, of whatever doctrine, even liberal-democratic and humanist, must be illegal, violent, unjust, and brutal, and a society must find a way to represent that fact to itself as a national memory' (Pippin, 2010: 103). The political difficulty lies within the perilous gap between History and myth, or truth and lie, with 'life' (or Jack's tribe of hunters in *Lord of the Flies*) requiring only myth and lie in order to prevail. 'To see liberalism as an historical event means that one understands it as the inheritor and bearer not only of rights and freedoms but also of structures of power and domination, of colonial and class exploitations, of the hatred of, rather than the opposition to, the Other' (Strong, 2007: i-xix); but when America is presented mythically, the problem becomes the correct mode of the representation of 'the transition from the feudal patriarchal authority that arose in the pre-legal situation of the frontier to a more fraternal, modern form; and the [Western] films are about the psychic costs of such a transition' (Pippin, 2010: 22). Or, to put it another way, just as Melville found turning whaling into poetry as difficult as drawing tree sap with his bare hands, so too does settler-colonialism elide simple mythic transmogrification, for the *telos* of the whole enterprise is to achieve the blissfulness of an earlier and edenic anti-liberalism.

> [The] record of such an embourgeoisement is an incomplete and vexed one in the American experience, as the bourgeois virtues also seem to involve such a commitment to security, life, and peace that hypocrisy, self-deceit, and a prosaic form of life perhaps incapable of sustaining the required deep allegiance [to the Commonwealth] seem an inevitable consequence. (Pippin, 2010: 25)

The only possible way to effect mythic consciousness is to plumb the depths of the re-generative potential not of egalitarian democracy but aristocratic or ruggedly individualistic violence: the 'illusion of a full transition from the "frontier" and all that has come to signify is just that—an illusion—but the hiddeness and subtlety and to some extent internalized nature of bourgeois violence allow the luxury of a common representation of the frontier as overcome' (Pippin, 2010: 146–147). And the medium of this transition is art which, this being America, must be capable of being made into a movie. Which is exactly what John Ford tries to provide us.

4.3 *The Man Who Shot Liberty Valance* (1962): The Murder-Crafted Garden

The dominant form of legal theory during Antiquity (Greece and Rome) and the Middle Ages, down to the seventeenth Century (Machiavelli, Hobbes, Spinoza, Hume) Natural Law, or 'naturalism', very generally, stands for the proposition that an objectively true and universal jurisprudence is logically possible as it somehow equates with an equally universal form of natural reason; 'Natural law theories have traditionally asserted a metaphysical claim, a claim that metaphysical reality is such that human morality is grounded upon it' (Battaglia, 1980: 9). The seminal premises of Natural Law were stated by St. Thomas Aquinas—'We ought to act according to reason' (Battaglia, 1980: 15)—that yielded two essential corollaries: (a) That human moral reason is trustworthy because it is in touch with reality ('moral realism') and; (b) a generalizable moral imperative that may be formulated as 'We ought to act as we think we ought to act.' As a result, 'the stance toward morals we are speaking of does not commit us to a particular world view but rather to the seriousness of moral perception' (Battaglia, 1980: 16). Today, however, natural law commonly identified with the 'naturalistic fallacy', the highly contestable philosophical assumption that one cannot use a fact to deduce a moral principle; 'the "fallacy" is the assertion that goodness can be defined as a natural property of a thing or action' (Battaglia, 1980: 10). Historically derived from David Hume' *Is/Ought Distinction*—'the assertion that moral language is logically distinct from descriptive language, i.e. that there is no strictly logical connection between a description of a situation and what I ought to do in that situation' (Battaglia, 1980: 10)—positivism's wholesale rejection of natural law is imperiled by its superficial understanding of naturalist reasoning and the Hume's critique of it. John Finnis has argued that when formulating the dichotomy of Is and Ought, Hume is highlighting the objective condition that exists in 'real-world' situations where there is an objective difference, or 'gap', between knowledge of the good and the will to act on that knowledge. For Hume, knowledge of the good does not, by itself, compel an obligation to act in the normative sense; rather, any 'realistic' account of moral behavior must take into account both the knowledge of the good and the will, or 'inclination', to act on such knowledge which itself cannot be reduced to knowledge, as human agency is governed by a radical form of voluntarism. According to Hume.

> The moral obligation [is] the sentiment of right and wrong...No action can be required of as our duty, unless there be implanted in human nature some actuating passion or motive, capable of producing the action...Interest is the first obligation to performance of promises...Afterwards a sentiment of morals concurs with interest, and becomes a new obligation upon mankind'. (David Hume qtd. Finnis, 1980: 53–54)

The crucial point of the Humean critique of naturalism is that 'it is moral reason that is being referred to and thus bypasses the misreading of the traditional formulation [of natural law] which mistakenly says that there is some way of using ordinary descriptive language to automatically describe the right thing to do' (Battaglia, 1980: 23). The Thomistic directive 'We ought to act as we think we ought to act' is not tautological when examined closely; if the 'human mind can be trusted' on the basis of natural reason, then, in any given situation, the dictum constitutes both a knowledge of the moral reality (Is) and the duty or obligation to act on the basis of that reality (Ought). Given that 'the importance of this corollary is probably its statement of the freedom of the individual human conscience' (Battaglia, 1980: 23) which renders naturalism inseparable from voluntarism, the irreducible freedom of the will, the historical division of natural law theory into two major versions, the metaphysically 'thick' and the metaphysically 'thin', becomes much more intelligible as competing propositions concerning the autonomy of human agency. Naturalism as 'thick' metaphysics, is identified with the ontology of *essentialism* and has been historically linked to the Academy of Plato.

> Because of its divine character, natural law is absolutely binding and overrules all other laws. It precedes them in time, 'because it came into existence with the very creation of man as a rational being, nor does it vary in time but remains unchangeable.' [Natural law] also precedes [positive law] in dignity. 'Natural law absolutely prevails in dignity over customs and constitutions. Whatever has been recognized by usage, or laid down in writing, if it contradicts natural law, must be considered null and void'. (Gratian qtd. d'Entreves, 1970: 38)

Thus yielding the admittedly 'imperialistic' legal maxim that in the event of a direct and irreconcilable conflict between natural and positive law, natural law 'overrides' legislation. In contrast, the 'thinner' metaphysics of *nominalism* is historically derived from the School of Aristotle, signified by the key concepts of *telos, teleology,* and *habitus,* all of which indicate the search for manifestations of universals within the given particular under examination. Everything within the world will strive to realize its intrinsic nature over time; therefore, there will be a continual re-adjustment between that thing's 'good' and its correlative 'ends' on the basis of 'practical reasonableness'. That is, practical reasonableness operates within the domain of the human 'good', not the human 'end', or *telos,* which is reason, and it was this Aristotelian metaphysics that was seized upon with such gusto by St. Thomas Aquinas in the thirteenth century, resulting in the Thomist fusion of Theology with classical Philosophy known as 'Catholic Aristotelianism'.

> And so whatever is contrary to the order of reason is contrary to the nature of human beings as such; and what is reasonable is in accordance with human nature as such. *The good of the human being is being in accord with reason, and human evil is being outside the order of reasonableness*...So human virtue, which makes good both the human person and his works, is in accordance with human nature just in so far as it is in accordance with reason; and vice is contrary to human nature just in so far as it is contrary to the order of reasonableness. (Thomas Aquinas qtd. Finnis, 1980: 36)

So, in rather stark contrast to Platonic essentialism, the legal maxim of Aristotelian nominalism may be formulated in this way: an 'evil' Law may be correctly expressed as a Law in a formal and/or 'positive' way, but, because of its immoral nature, it lacks legitimacy and, therefore, the moral authority to demand compliance with it by those under its territorial jurisdiction; there is no moral obligation to obey it and, perhaps, a moral obligation to oppose it. And the key for determining the morality of any given law in the particular is the degree to which it succeeds in according to the objective requirements of *reasonableness,* which is a necessary property of homo sapiens as a 'rational animal'.

> Aquinas was a writer not on ethics alone but on the whole of theology. He was keen to show the relationship between his ethics of natural law and his general theory of metaphysics and the world-order. He wished to point out the analogies running through the whole order of being...The criterion of conformity with or contrariety to human nature is reasonableness. (Finnis, 1980: 35)

And according to Finnis

> ... for Aquinas, the way to discover what is morally right (virtue) and wrong (vice) is to ask, not what is in accordance with human nature, but what is reasonable. And this quest will eventually bring one back to the *un-derived* first principles of practical reasonableness, principles which make no reference at all to human nature, but only to human good. (Finnis, 1980: 36)

But embedded at the very heart of natural law doctrine is a horrendous paradox: if natural morality is that which is universally and eternally constant regardless of the positive law as expressed in any particular space and time, then, at any given instance, the private individual may, in theory, be eligible to make use of it outside of the domain of the state. And this disquieting possibility is the basis of the Western as a type of legal drama: 'A man who is always morally certain of the right thing to do must come to terms with the fact that the rule of law often not only permits but actually requires what such law would also prohibit' (Pippin, 2010: 96).

Aristotle defines tragedy as 'the story of the High being brought low', the hero ultimately undermined by the inexorable exercise of his own virtues until he reaches the point of self-destruction, that which happened to Oedipus.[25] In his suitably masterful study of one of Ford's most masterly works (*The Man Who Shot Liberty Valance* (directed by John Ford, Paramount, 2009), Sidney A. Pearson opines that *The Man Who Shot Liberty Valance* (1962) is a Greek tragedy 'in the sense that the qualities required to confront evil also prove to be the source of the hero's downfall' (Pearson, 2007: 24). The argument holds but only if we can make out that the main protagonist, Tom Doniphon or 'Death-Giver'—Latin *donum* + Greek *phontes*, a wholly appropriate moniker for the regulator of the first and final instance (Dienstag, 2012: 314 n 15)—begins the narrative as one of Tragedy's 'highs' who must be brought 'low' through his own virtues being turned into uncontrollable forces that nullify his (presumed) freedom of will and compel him to undergo a ritualistic death, a symbolic or physical *auto-sacrifice*. But how do we know that Doniphon is a superior man and, therefore, an eligible candidate for tragic hero? Simple: he is the only character in the film who is clearly The Westerner. The form of judicial theory that Doniphon embodies, his 'code' as the Westerner, is unambiguously natural law, and, in Platonic terms, Doniphon-the-Westerner, the rugged individualist's rugged individualist, is the 'rightly ordered soul' who effortlessly reflects objective and absolute moral virtue which is the stop-gap for a purely natural justice (*ius naturale*) in the absence of the state (Boehnke, 2001: 54–57; Livingstone, 2009). As John Locke pointed out, exercising extreme prejudice within the state of nature against those who need killing is no vice.

> In transgressing the law of nature [the inalienable right of all to self-preservation], the offender declares himself to live by another rule than that of reason and common equity, which is that measure God has set to the actions of men, for their mutual security; and so he becomes dangerous to mankind .... Which being a trespass against the whole species, and the peace and safety of it, provided for by the law of nature, every man upon this score, by the right he hath to preserve mankind in general, may restrain, or where it is necessary, destroy

[25] See Chap. 1, above.

> things noxious to them, and so may bring such evil on any one, who hath transgressed that [natural] law, as may make him repent the doing of it, and thereby deter him, and by his example others, from doing the like mischief. And in the case, and upon this ground, *every man hath a right to punish the offender, and be the executioner of the law of nature.* (John Locke qtd. Livingstone, 2009: 223)

And as the vigilante-like self-appointed regulator of natural justice it is Doniphon's identity as The Westerner that gives him the power to kill Liberty Valance, or 'Wild-Violence' = Liberty + Valance + Violence = Freedom (Dienstag, 2012: 315–316 n 20), the performance of the good deed which is the very action that destroys his Being.

> And because Shinbone is a town akin to a Hobbesian state of nature, even if Doniphon or someone else shot Valance before the opening of the movie, the town would still be ruled by the gun [i.e. *whoever* it was who shot Liberty Valance]. It would still be a jungle characterized by a Darwinist survival of the fittest. No doubt the fittest would be Doniphon, a sort of Platonic guardian without the formal education of the good behind him, but still, somehow, reflecting that good. The moral character of the toughest man in town may be essential in a state of nature, but in the city, we really do need the rule of law. Doniphon gives us a glimpse of the natural moral order behind law, properly understood, but from the perspective of the city. (Pearson, 2007: 28)

Although in many ways sympathetic to Joshua Dienstag's remarkable attempt to come up with a truly subversive theory of the origin of the Western (Dienstag, 2012), I am highly critical of his advocacy of the onto-politically mushy theory of 'democratic pessimism'. For Dienstag, Girard's foundational violence can be reconciled with a contemporary (American) liberal ethos provided that the original murder is in some way justifiable, which is managed by Ford through the 'erotic bonds' of community flowing through the love-triangle of Doniphon-Hattie-Stoddard, which, when examined closely, doubles as a kind of proto-liberal political conspiracy: this time it is the *Woman* who creates the Commonwealth through the sacrificial actions of her twinned lovers, one the sacred executioner (Tom Doniphon the true) the other the penitential but non-violent conjurer of Law-and-Order (Ransom Stoddard the false). To be absolutely clear about how it works: Hallie is the true controller of the 'action' (which is a ritualistic sacrifice) because her deliberate choosing of Ransom over Tom manipulates Tom's naturalist instincts (or virtues, now tragically turned against him as a 'flaw') in such a manner as to lead him into shooting Liberty so that Hallie can have both the man (Ransom) and the future (culture) that she wants which is the best of all possible worlds for everybody up until the moment that it no longer is (the destruction of existential intensity)—meaning that Doniphon, not Valance, is the true sacrificial victim for Hallie has made it come to pass that Tom ransomed himself for Ransom.[26] (Livingstone, 2009: 223, 226 n 38; Rohdie, 1975).

> [T]he lawgiver who instantiates a legal order where there was none [through murdering wild Liberty-Freedom]—is really both Doniphon and Stoddard, neither one of them sufficient

26 Which, in a weird way, kind of makes Ransom their 'son' as Hallie and Tom are the Mother and Father of the originary auto-sacrifice—Tom's life and Hallie's passion It also explains why Ransom and Hallie are childless; there are certain taboos which simply cannot be crossed in cinema (so far).

> to the task by themselves, both needing and acknowledging the other in the process of state formation.... What constitutes the state, then, is neither law nor power by themselves, but rather the erotic and narrative ties that create the relationship between them.... we are meant to be strengthened, if sobered, by the revelation that law is not self-generating or self-sustaining but requires a sacrifice to succeed. (Dienstag, 2012: 295)

Dienstag enticingly describes the cactus rose which 'has been used throughout the film to symbolize love' as a '"red colored triangular fruit"'; but for the flower to possess its sacrificial-inducing potency it is vital that it is not Stoddard but Doniphon who actually murders Valence—meaning that his performance reveals his essence.[27] As Dienstag puts it.

> Eros is always a particular attraction; it unites two or several but never all because it also excludes as it unites. But what it unites, it unites humanistically—it persuades without convincing and forces without violence—which is to say it shows how reason and power can be complementary elements of political attachment, and not always or only rival forms of social organization. (Dienstag, 2012: 317 n 33)

It turns out in the end that it is OK to murder Liberty because killing him is really an act of love, which almost sounds 'woke'. Dienstag's conclusion?

> We cannot undo the violence that has created and sustained the democracy we enjoy [sic], neither can we legalize it.... but perhaps we can *bear* to live with its memory if we come to believe that its origin was not selfish but shared and burdensome to those who perpetuated it. Not just an arbitrary decision to exclude [or 'decide against'] but a creative and collective action of union ... (Dienstag, 2012: 307, 309)

Which is exactly what every act of ritualistic annihilation of the scapegoat is, by definition. All that Dienstag is doing here is offering a series of dramatic (and narratively pleasing) 'buffers' between archaic origins and civilizing consequences, missing Girard's truly subversive point: the sacrificer does not 'really' decide the 'true' identity of the scapegoat (Doniphon kills Violence); rather, the scapegoat is the one who is killed in such a way that the community is brought into being, which is why lawyer Stoddard is assigned responsibility for the kill, not regulator Doniphon.[28] The sacrificial mechanism need not be based on truth in any sense (other than the affective-inducing performance of the killing itself), meaning that the liberal's big reveal of profane History is without effect: the only thing that matters is performance

[27] The giving and receiving of flowers can be a very dangerous business indeed, for they 'may signify both pain and pleasure, the death of childhood, and the awakening of sexuality' for the flower 'as sister of death and sex, the sign of infinity, has an amoral, "unimpeachable" quality, perhaps surpassing morality, and is thus full of fright and power' (Charlotte Nekola qtd. Brodey, 2009: 116 n 10). It is clear that poor Tom is doomed; he would have been better off bringing Hallie a pizza instead.

[28] This encapsulates the key un-decidable within Girardian theory: is the scapegoat the one whose death establishes/restores the community or is the scapegoat the one who is killed so that the community can be created/replenished? It all comes down to the degree to which the actors are aware of the nature and meaning of their actions. I address this problem in greater length in Chapter Eight on Kafka. Ford leaves us in little doubt that Hattie knows exactly what she is doing by choosing Stoddard over Doniphon—she is willing the 'garden' into existence and she is using two, and possibly three, male scapegoats to do it.

and mimesis, which periodically re-immerses us in reactionary mythic timelessness. This leads me to my central criticism of Dienstag: the erotic-conspiratorial triangle that sustains pessimistic democratic virtue (Hattie-as-enabler/Doniphon-as-sacred executioner/Stoddard-as-mythic-hero-liar) depends upon Doniphon, not Stoddard, as having shot Wild Violence. Yet, the only evidence we have that Doniphon was the 'real' shooter (historical, not mythic) is conveyed in a flash-back narrated by Doniphon to Stoddard, complete with occluding cigarette smoke and blurry/liquid transition shot (Pippin, 2010; Rohdie, 1975), on the verge of Stoddard abandoning the Territorial convention for statehood and going back East. In other words, at the *exact* moment when Hattie's erotically-grounded sacrificial-conspiratorial project is in jeopardy and in dire need of drastic action, Doniphon becomes the scapegoat for both Stoddard and Hattie as well as for the entire *demos*,[29] and if any one doubts my reading of this scene they would do well to remember Akira Kurosawa's transmogrifying *Rashomon* (1950)[30]: just because a scene has been shot on film does not mean that it is 'true'. But what is true is that every film genre needs all of its tropes (history, themes, archetypes, icons) to be artistically unified so that the Western must always approximately conform to American national experience, in this case the allegedly unifying narrative of Democracy. Therefore, Doniphon must be 'tragic' in both a classical Greek and in a contemporary American manner: not only does he 'fall' as a result of his own virtue, he must also necessarily *disappear* because his remaining imperils the very cause for which he was righteously sacrificed: democracy, which for Aristotle, was the 'rule of the poor'—although, in this instance, without vitalistic grandeur. In the film, this is achieved symbolically through Doniphon's 'vanishing' into the civilized landscape of the rule of law inaugurated by lawyer/liar Ransom Stoddard—or, even better, his self-induced decomposition within it.

So here is the really big problem of cosmic mythology that requires the American trope of the Western to solve: in order to create the rule of law within *profane* Time (History) a 'criminal' act must be performed. Therefore, a mythic device must be found that resolves the otherwise unbearable polarity between violence and community as well as between Crime and Law. On one level, Ford signals that the killing of Valence may be defended as an act of 'natural justice,' either of self-defense or coming to the aid of another. The problem is that the manner of the killing—shooting at a distance while standing in the dark[31]— prima facie violates the form of the Western genre and the 'code' of The Westerner; Valence's death results from neither a direct confrontation nor a personal challenge (the gun fight). A more promising strategy is to exploit the mimetic potential of doubling; 'Much of the film's complexity derives from the subtle development of similarities between Tom Doniphon and Liberty Valance, two men who appear totally opposite' (Luhr &

[29] A variation of the situation of Sophocles' anti-mythic Oedipus discussed in the Introduction; in this case Oedipus voluntarily but falsely confesses to murdering his father and sleeping with his mother for the purpose of providing Thebes with a salvific victim. See Introduction, above.

[30] See below, Chap. 5.

[31] Although Doniphon true-fake execution of Liberty in this manner enables him to stage-manage Stoddard's fake-true 'performance' as a gun-fighter.

Lehman, 1977: 80). Both are supremely competent and both are linked directly to nature ('pre-civilization'). Furthermore, they are always motivated by *private* motives as befitting the rugged individualist; Doniphon 'will not take Valence on principle, only when actually threatened' (Gallagher, 1986: 396) which means that Doniphon, like Valence, is an egoist in his motives; no matter how self-sacrificial they are thoroughly self-centered, flowing from his love for Hattie—and love, for the libertine, is just a matter of personal preference. The narrative tension generated by presenting Doniphon as Valence as doubles or mimetic twins provides the dramatic charge necessary to render affectively compelling the mirroring of primitive natural law and rational social contract theory as entwined rivals of political foundation: the mythic 'effect' of the Western is to emotionally compel the viewer to realize that both forms of law are inseparable from a foundational violence that is the source of everything. The vital, and saving, element of difference that Ford introduces so that the men in the audience do not become rabid vigilantes but mannered citizens is that Doniphon's personal motivation, because of his perfect embodiment of natural law and morality as the Westerner, will always compel him to act in the interest of the 'public good' which will later be codified as positive law with the rise of civilization, or the Age of Ransom (Stoddard). This is what makes him tragic, as exemplified by the Western archetype of the *retired gunfighter*.

> What he finds when he begins to live among the law-abiding and churchgoing is, to his great consternation, a profound need *for him*, for his skills in the way of violence. There is usually a crisis brewing, and the sheriff or marshal or all the townsfolk are not up to the task. A 'state of exception' always looms...This somewhat ironic twist—that the domestic world of commercial republics itself still contains, still relies on, must still deal with, but in many ways hides from itself, elements of disorder, injustice, and violence that the gunfighter is trying to escape and that only someone like him can cope with— 'completes' the Western narrative of founding and law in a way that itself seems to embody the weariness, disappointment, and final, stoic resignation of the gunfighter himself. (Gallagher, 1986: 145–146)

Therefore, no matter how 'right-wing' in context, sub-textually the Western is always revolutionary because it is invariably about the creation of a foundational order out of an ante-diluvian chaos; both protagonist and opponent are equally embedded within a primordial cinematic 'Nature' that doubles as the Hobbesian state of nature: the Westerner, just as with Girard's sacrificer, is an onto-political *middleman,* a mediating figure between the social ('townsfolk') and the natural (the Outlaw, the Indian, the Mexican) (Cawelti, 1999: 41–42). Which is the very heart of the paradox of Doniphon/Valence as doubles: it perfectly mirrors the wider paradox of both natural law and the wholly *mythic* social contract theory of political foundation for they are both inseparable from an originary violence. But unlike the mere outlaw who is wholly archaic, the Westerner, being mythic, mediates between past and future, meaning that he is the model for all future mimetic performances that, executed correctly, will culminate in the hoped-for cathartic surge of regeneration by means of violence. But for catharsis to work after the Frontier has died what kind of politics must prevail so that the cycle of existential restoration can be maintained in perpetuity? Post-Frontier politics must be of a kind in which the Westerner, or his contemporary incarnation, periodically needs to be summoned. Luckily for us, there is such a theory of politics—and law.

4.4 The Precarious Sovereignty of the Westerner: Carl Schmitt and the Friend-Enemy Distinction

According to Girard, the best way to make friends in a hostile world is to espouse the enmities and adopt the other's enemies. What is said to these others, on such occasion, varies very little: "we are all of the same clan, we form one and the same group inasmuch as we have the same scapegoat" (Girard, 1986: 154–155). For him 'the political thought of the modern Western world' (Girard, 1986: 115) is a secular derivative of the archaic sacredness of the scapegoating mechanism, itself the outcome of a crisis of undifferentiation that required for its resolution the violent reimposition of distinctions, or differences, upon an increasingly archaic community that had lost the capacity to detect and observe distinctions. In marked contrast to the Gospels

> The forces of this world are clearly divided into two non-symmetrical groups, on the one hand the constituted authorities and, on the other, the crowd. The former usually get the better of the latter, but in times of crisis the reverse is true. Not only does the crowd get the upper hand but it also becomes a kind of melting pot in which even authorities that seem unshakable eventually collapse. This process of fusion assures the reformation of the authorities through the mediation of the scapegoat, or in other words the sacred. The theory of mimesis throws light on a process that political science and the natural sciences have been unable to penetrate. (Girard, 1986: 115)

The 'most basic social practice that literally engenders society' is that thing that transfigures the crisis of undifferentiation 'in its most atomized form into the strongest social unity which is the unanimity of the original murder' (Girard, 1986: 182).

> In a crisis of mimetic conflict, the polarization on a single victim can become so powerful that all members of the group are forced to participate in his murder…. The persecutors all behave in the same way. Anyone who dreams of vengeance must take it from the whole collectivity. It as if the power of the state, non-existent in this type of society [paleolithic], comes into temporary but nevertheless real rather than symbolic existence in these violent forms of unanimity. (Girard, 1986: 177)

Mythology is not 'literally meaningless' but it does 'deals in extremes' consistent with the universal pattern of 'the polarization of persecution' (Girard, 1986: 32). '*The victim is a scapegoat.* Everyone has a clear understanding of this expression; no one has any hesitation about its meaning' (Girard, 1986: 39). 'Scapegoat indicates both the innocence of the victims, the collective polarization in opposition to them, and the collective end result of that polarization. The persecutors are caught up in the "logic" of the representation of persecution from a persecutor's standpoint, and they cannot break away' (Girard, 1986: 39) In truth the 'polarization exerts such a constraint on those polarized that the victims cannot prove their innocence' (Girard, 1986: 40)—which is the whole point for if the accused were able to prove their innocence they would disrupt the formation of the political community, the warring populations of enemies and friends. In fact, the word *mob* is derived from the Latin *mobile* and the word '*mobilization* reminds us of a military operation, against an already identified enemy or one soon to be identified by the mobilization of the crowd' (Girard, 1986: 16) signifying the crowd as the elementary substance of political being.

All of this is immediately suggestive of the radically illiberal constitutional theory of Carl Schmitt with whom an almost point-by-point comparison with Girard can be made, insofar as we are considering the world-historical role of the *mobile*. In fact, the comparisons are almost too easy: Girard's 'the crowd' and 'in times of crisis' equates with Schmitt's 'state of exception,' the crisis of undifferentiation is the double of 'the state of exception,' and the scapegoater is the shadow of the 'decider of the exception,' the one who controls the scapegoating process for the purpose of naming the 'enemy,' the existential threat to the community of 'friends'.[32] There is a near reversibility, or iteration, between the two: Girard's crowd assembles in order to identify and persecute the enemy, Schmitt's sovereign identifies and persecutes the enemy in order to assemble the crowd. And both recognize what is the central paradox of sovereignty 'consists in the fact that the sovereign is, at the same time, outside and inside the juridical order' (Giorgio Agamben qtd. Spinks, 2008: 123). For Schmitt the outstanding political problem is the disassociation between the legality and the legitimacy of the contemporary liberal state; within classical liberalism, 'legitimacy and legality cannot be the same; indeed, they stand in contradiction to each other' (Strong, 2007: xv). All political narratives are necessarily mythic because to be truly political they must invoke the existential intensity of the combat between perfectly opposed combatants, a moral dualism, which can only be realized within a situation of imminent death which *is* the *emergency*. Schmitt, when read closely, may be understood as engaging in a certain kind of mythologizing by formulating a comprehensive anti-liberal notion of statist modernity as 'modern bourgeois politics'; 'Schmitt is concerned with demonstrating the impossibility of understanding the legal order in exclusively rationalist terms, that is, as a self-sufficient, complete legal system of legal norms after the fashion of legal positivism' (Wolin, 1992: 431). Not for nothing has Schmitt been called the Martin Heidegger of political theory (Strong, 2007: ix–xxxi), arguing that neither the liberal state, nor its corollary the rule of law, can successfully achieve a form of self-grounding that is commensurate with their own professed first principles; 'Law cannot itself form a completely rational and lawful system; the analysis of the state must make reference to those agencies which have the capacity to decide on the state of exception[33] and not merely a formal plenitude of power' (Hirst, 1987: 21). Crucial to Schmitt's work is the notion that liberalism culminates in a self-serving strategy of de-politicization, or 'neutralization', in which the liberal state both creates and polices a kind of *meconnaissance* concerning the nature of the political: 'The systematic theory of liberalism concerns almost solely the internal struggle against the power of the State. For the purpose of protecting individual freedom and private property, liberalism provides a series of methods for hindering and controlling the State's and government's power' (Schmitt, 2007: 70) but wholly fails to address the existential imperative of struggles among

[32] See below.

[33] In the alternative, *the extreme state*: that is, the moment in real time that the formal recognition and naming of the enemy actually takes place, which is the auto-determination by the Sovereign that the conditions of 'the normal state' no longer prevail. See below.

the communities and sub-communities (not individuals) within the State. It is liberalism's mystifying reduction of politics to both Reason and speech that effects this colossal act of self-induced mass occlusion. Classical liberal democracy is 'rendered impotent by a rule-bound legalism, a rationalistic concept of political debate, and the desire that individual citizens enjoy a legally-guaranteed "private" sphere protected from the state,' constituting the single greatest crime against the true political nature of Man: 'The political is none of those things. Its essence is struggle' (Hirst, 1987: 16). Insofar as liberalism 'wishes to substitute procedure for the struggle' it 'will tend to undermine the possibility of the political' (Strong, 2007: xv). For Schmitt, the only way out of this interminable crisis of mis-recognition that spawns undifferentiation, which is in equal parts political and existential (as it is with Girard), is to induce the wholesale collapse of the public and private realms and to transpose in its entirety the existential tropes of authenticity (truth) and combat (violence) to the domestic realm of the State.

4.4.1 Nomos: The Originating Violence of Everywhere

Given the centrality of Heidegger to Schmitt's own thought (Derrida, 2005: 84–85), it would be worthwhile to frame the jurist's critique of the liberal state in terms of that ponderous metaphysician's political ontology. For Heidegger, the inherently political nature of the relationship between the political being of the state and political reason (*ratio*) springs from 'the essence of truth as correctness in the sense of the self-adjusting guarantee of the security of domination. The "taking as true" of *ratio*, of *reor*, becomes a far-reaching and anticipatory security. *Ratio* becomes counting, calculating, calculus. *Ratio* is self-adjustment to what is correct' (Heidegger, 1992: 50). Political 'truth' that equates with correctness is both delimited by a homologous discursive space and subjugated to the political will to domination; 'The essence of truth as *veritas* [i.e. correctness] is *without space* and without ground' (Heidegger, 1992: 50), signifying the un-reality of the heterologous, or the 'different'; 'The result is the *presence* of truth as self-evidence, or the presence of thought to itself in the manner of self-identity' within an exclusively homogenous discursive space (Bell, 2006: 28).[34] *Veritas* is the ground of western jurisprudence's conflation of law with reason, establishing an undifferentiated chain of signifiers delimiting the parameters of 'orthodox' or 'common' legal speech. Homology guarantees that whatever is not identical to *ratio* cannot constitute a portion of reality and, by political implication, cannot constitute an actual attribute of the 'true' state. Consequently, 'the idea of sovereignty, which clearly implies but one absolute power laying in the social order, with all relationships, all individuals…ultimately subject to it, has been the characteristic approach to the political community' (Nisbet, 1974: 386). It is not the least part of Schmitt's rhetorical genius that he takes Heidegger's exceptionally

[34] 'There is no space, no distance, between our true thoughts concerning a state of affairs in the world and that state of affairs: the two coincide' (Bell, 2006: 28).

reified concepts and changes them into myths: *ratio* and *veritas* are transformed into bloody, but heroic, acts of a dualistic appropriation and domination, signified through the erection of a series of impenetrable walls, both physical and metaphorical, that belie the foundational violence that lies at the very foundation of the State, including its degenerate nineteenth century liberal descendant. The central text of Schmitt's later career, *The Nomos of the Earth* (1950), undertakes a neo-Heideggerian exercise in constitutional foundationalism: both the political 'being' of the State (political ontology) and the heuristic apparatus of law are grounded on the terrestrial, or *telluric,* reality of the polity. 'In mythical language, the *earth* became known as the mother of law. This signifies a threefold root of law and justice' (Schmitt, 2003: 42): the planet 'Gaia' (Schmitt, 2003: 42), the land *Terra*, and, most interestingly, boundaries, or walls, or regulated frontiers. At the heart of *nomos* is a juridical construction of colonialism invested with the aesthetics of the sublime.

> First, the fertile earth contains within herself, within the womb of fecundity, an inner measure, because human toil and trouble, human planting and cultivation of the fruitful earth is rewarded justly by her with growth and harvest. Every farmer knows the inner measure of this justice.… Soil that is cleared and worked by human hands manifests firm lines whereby definite divisions become apparent. Through the demarcation of fields, pastures, and forests, these lines are engraved and embedded … the solid ground of the earth is delineated by fences, enclosures, boundaries, walls, houses, and other constructs. Then, the orders and orientations of human social life become apparent. Then, obviously, families, clans, tribes, estates, forms of ownership and human proximity, also forms of power and domination, become visible. (Schmitt, 2003: 42)

What the Crown-Jurist of the Third Reich accomplishes here is nothing short of revolutionary, for he has just provided a (more or less) workable way of translating frontier-colonialism into the terms of constitutionalism.

> First, we must not think of land-appropriation as a purely intellectual construct, but must consider it to be a legal fact, to be a great historical event, even if, historically, land-appropriation proceeded rather tumultuously, and, at times, the right of land arose from overflowing migrations of people and campaigns of conquest[35] and, at other times, from successful defence of a country against foreigners. (Schmitt, 2003: 46)

Colonization is land-appropriation and *nomos* is a fancy juridical term for primitive accumulation so that the co-existence of archaic/irrational and modern/rational economic structures can be shown to provide a binary foundation of the State which is itself dualist—and, therefore, in dire need of mythologizing, the stabilizing reconciliation of irreconcilable forces.

> Fence, enclosure, and border are deeply interwoven in the world formed by men, determining its concepts. The enclosure gave birth to the shrine by removing it from the ordinary, placing it under its own laws, and entrusting it to the divine.[36] The enclosing ring—the fence formed

[35] In German, *der Volkerwanderung*, or the 'wanderings of the peoples'; Schmitt's focus is upon *settlement*.

[36] It is widely agreed that Schmitt's political ontology, like Heidegger's, has its intellectual roots in German Catholicism; 'The juridic formulas of the omnipotence of the state are, in fact, only superficial secularizations of theological formulas for the omnipotence of God' (Schmitt, 2007: 42).

> by men's bodies, the man-ring—is a primeval form of ritual, legal, and political co-habitation. (Schmitt, 2003: 74)

Note how Schmitt elides the traditional alibi of terra nullius; all that matters is the ability of the vitalistic community to seize and hold its *territory*.

> *Nomos* is the *measure* by which the land in a particular order is divided and situated; it is also the form of the political, social, and religious order determined by this process. Here, measure, order, and form constitute a spatially concrete unity. The *nomos* by which a tribe, a retinue, or a people becomes settled, i.e., by which it becomes historically situated and turns part of the earth's surface into *a force-field*[37] of a particular order, becomes visible in the appropriation of land and in the founding of a city or a colony. (Schmitt, 2003: 70)

But because the community is inseparable from its wall—meaning that it is always situated along a 'Frontier' of some kind, physical and symbolic—it must, of necessity exist under the eternal threat of crisis, the threat of extinction. Schmitt authors an entire model of international public order (*ius publicum Europaeum*) premised upon a radically homogenous notion of the State that: (i) eternally exists in a condition of potential enmity with all other states; and (ii) unconditionally withholds recognition of the legal identity of any actor or entity that does not strictly conform to his model of the State.

> In this way, the earth is bound to law in three ways. She contains law within herself, as a reward for labor; she manifests law upon herself, as fixed boundaries; and she sustains law above herself, as a public sign of order. Law is bound to the earth and related to the earth. This what the poet[38] means when he speaks of the infinitely just earth: *justissima telus*. (Schmitt, 2003: 42)

Thus explaining the title of the text: *nomos* is the wall that signifies not only the establishment of boundaries (both material and epistemological) but the onto-political foundation of the polity itself.[39]

> This fundamental process of land-appropriation preceded the distinction between public and private law, public authority and private property, *imperium* and *dominium*. Land-appropriation thus is the archetype of a constitutive legal process externally (*vis-à-vis* other peoples) and internally (for the ordering of land and property within a country). It creates the most radical title, in the full and comprehensive sense of the term *radical title*. (Schmitt, 2003: 46–47)[40]

Hence Schmitt's overriding concern with the telluric: the reduction of the state to terrestrial 'walls' secures onto-political and judicial certainty by precluding recognition of both non-state political actors and all rival legal personalities.

---

[37] Or, a field-of-force, something that needs to be enforced.

[38] Virgil.

[39] 'In particular, *nomos* can be described as a wall, because, like a wall, it, too, is based on sacred orientations. The *nomos* can grow and multiply like land and property: all human *nomoi* are "nourished" by a single divine *nomos*' (Schmitt, 2003: 70-71).

[40] 'For our purposes, the term land-appropriation is better than land-division, because land-appropriation, both externally and internally, points clearly to the constitution of a radical title'—a title of exclusive possession that is good against all comers even if they were there 'first' (Schmitt, 2003: 81).

> The binding character of a comprehensive spatial order immediately is recognizable if the spatial order is conceived of as a *balance* (Schmitt, 2003: 188).… Only armed struggle between state sovereigns was war in the sense of international law, and only this type of struggle fulfilled the requirements of the concept of *justus hostis*. Everything else was criminal prosecution and suppression of robbers, rebels, and pirates.… To the essence of *hostis* belongs the *aequalitas*. Robbers, pirates, and rebels are not enemies, not *justi hostes*, but objects to be rendered harmless and prosecuted as criminals. (Schmitt, 2003: 153)

According to Schmitt, 'the term land-appropriation is better than land-division, because land-appropriation, both externally and internally, points clearly to the constitution of a radical title' (Schmitt, 2003: 81). The originating act of the appropriation of radical title is foundational in two ways: it secures the homogeneity, both political and ontological, of the resulting polity and it guarantees the epistemic regime that governs the juridical order.

> Thus, in some form, the constitutive process of a land-appropriation is found at the beginning of the history of every settled people, every commonwealth, every empire. This is true as well for the beginning of every historical epoch. Not only logically, but also historically, land-appropriation precedes the order that follows from it. It constitutes the original spatial order, the source of all further concrete order and all further law. It is the reproductive root in the normative order of history. All further property relations—communal or individual, public or private property, and all forms of possession and use in society and in international law—are derived from this radical title. All subsequent law and everything promulgated and enacted thereafter as decrees and commands are *nourished*, to use Heraclitus' word, by this source. (Schmitt, 2003: 48)

The importance of the telluric for the coherence of public order cannot be overestimated. It is the primary appropriation and secondary division/demarcation that infuses the *nomos* that validates both the objective legal identities of the actors within the order and the epistemic unity of the juridical system governing their actions, the 'bracketing' of war. Schmitt is able to conclude that land-appropriation 'precedes the distinction between private and public law; in general, it creates the conditions for this distinction. To this extent, from a legal perspective, one might say that land-appropriation has a categorical character' (Schmitt, 2003: 46). But it is precisely this apparently 'concrete' demarcation between public/private and legal/criminal that proves the most discursively unstable part of Schmitt's constitutional theory. For, just like that rugged individualist who is the Westerner, the sovereign is nobody else other than the one who can first articulate and then successfully defend his own properties. Which means that sovereignty is a vacant space that can be made into the possession of anyone who performs as a sovereign in the correct manner, which means successfully defending the walls of the community.

4.4.2 Das Feind: The Problem of Being Serious

The German word *Feind* encapsulates two categories that are formally distinct in English: *enemy*, in the sense of a rival or an opponent (*inimicus*), who is ordinarily the object of a 'private' conflict, and *foe*, the combatant or 'absolute enemy' (*hostis*), with whom the entire community engages in 'public' combat, or war, properly so-called; 'An enemy exists only when, at least potentially, one fighting collectivity of people confronts a similar collectivity' (Schmitt, 2007: 28). So that distinguishing 'the adversary as political and oneself as non-political (i.e., scientific, objective, neutral, etc.) is in actuality a typical and unusually intensive way of pursuing politics' (Schmitt, 2007: 21 n 2). Because all of politics is about the establishment of sovereignty through the existential 'peak experience' of combat.

> The beasts fight and kill in order to satisfy the lowest craving, which is for preservation. It belongs only to human beings to make war, not only to kill but to die, for a high cause and ultimately the highest cause, which is their faith. Schmitt can agree with those who have perceived the human record as a history of bloodshed, but far from interpreting the fact as a sign of God's neglect or punishment, he sees it as evidence of God's providence. By a dialectic of conflict, of 'ideals' that men take seriously enough to contend over, and not by any mere dialectic of reason, mankind is preserved from the lassitude of indifference that is the soul's death. (Cropsey, 1995: ix–x)

Schmitt was himself one of the supreme neo-Hobbesians of the twentieth century: 'In the background of [the] contractual ethic, an ethic of civil war always lurks' (Schmitt, 1999: 207) which follows directly from the fact that political unity 'is the highest unity—not because it is an omnipotent dictator, or because it levels out all other unities, but because it decides, and has the potential to prevent all other opposing groups from disassociating into a condition of extreme enmity—that is, into civil war' (Schmitt, 1999: 203). Hobbes' 'twinned' notions of both the absolute nature of Sovereignty and the universal nature of war[41] are closely mirrored in Schmitt's concept of the constancy of enmity in politics, which also presupposes unconditional obedience to the command of the Sovereign.

As Schmitt labors under the burden of providing a unifying normative schema within a universe of wholly anarchic (Hobbesian?) egoism he instinctively reaches for voluntarism (the Westerner's 'rugged individualism') to provide not only the self-justifying orientation of the will but the war-like existential intensity of self-realization to provide the visceral phenomenological spark to re-generate voluntarism into political *vitalism*.

> The state as the decisive political entity possesses an enormous power: the possibility of waging war and thereby publicly disposing of the lives of men. The *jus belli* contains such a disposition. It implies a double possibility: the right to demand from its own members the readiness to die and unhesitatingly to kill enemies. The endeavor of a normal state consists above all in assuring total peace within the state and its territory. To create tranquility, security, and order and thereby establish the normal situation is the prerequisite for legal norms to be valid. Every norm presupposes a normal situation, and no norm can be valid in an entirely abnormal situation. (Schmitt, 2007: 46)

Which takes Schmitt astonishingly close to Girard: at the heart of his account is both sacrifice and repetition. But beyond the mere political, there is the far more profound etymological: 'Everything touching the sacred is truly undecidable' (Girard, 1978: 105) says Girard, helpfully pointing out that '*Decidere*, in Latin,

---

[41] See Chaps. 2 and 3, above.

means to decide in our sense only because it first means to cut with a knife, to kill the sacrificial victim.' (Girard, 1978: 105). Which means that the originating act of foundation, the primeval seizing of land and the building and policing of walls 'has an aporetic relationship to time. The act of foundation conjoins past and present, in that it presupposes the past existence of what it also invents in the present…. Foundation is presupposition' (Ross, 2004: 51). And the foundation itself requires an even more elemental *decision:* the moment of the decision—or the *state of exception* which is Schmitt's version of the Unique understood as 'special' Time—is a sacrificial act, the establishing of the identity of the one who is the enemy (either symbolically or materially) who must be invested with the attributes of the scapegoat, the one who generates the unifying affectivity of the community seeking the death of a nameable Other.[42] For it is only when a community is in the psychic zone of righteous slaughter that it is able to do the thing that is necessary to preserve the community which is the re-staging of the act of foundation itself. But there is a bright spot—Schmitt made clear that the decision was fully compatible with *democracy*: 'Democracy begins with an event, a decision, an act, even a miracle' (Ross, 2004: 86). Which is the *crime* of the foundational establishment of *nomos* through a mythologized act of murder.

> In other words, what is indistinguishable is whether democracy begins with the originating crime or the originating miracle. The same event is describable in both terms. Democracy never begins 'democratically'. Law never begins 'legitimately'. If they cannot begin democratically or legally, then the fact that democracy or law can begin at all, if they ever do, is miraculous. As long as the foundational and presuppositional structure is necessary for the beginning of democracy, then this beginning is strictly impossible. And yet there are territories that call themselves democracies. In each case a miraculous fable, a myth, is involved. (Ross, 2004: 52–53)

So not merely politics in general, but democracy in particular, is counter-intuitively indistinguishable from a temporally prior, and originating, act of appropriation/possession/exclusion.

> The act does not inaugurate the rule of a people, because the act decides that there is a people, a 'we, the people'. Who could *become* democratic citizens. It decides that the people means *this* people *here*, not those people there. In short, it depends upon a decision about borders, which are never natural, nor neutral. Furthermore, the foundation is never *itself* a democratic act, and it can never follow a democratic method. This is not the same thing as saying that instituting democracy may not be popular. But unless there is a *way* of measuring that popularity and then translating that measurement into an official declarative act, how can the decision to inaugurate a democracy itself be democratic? And the means of measurement, and the threshold to be reached, would themselves be matters that must already have been

[42] An element of caution is required here. Although the religious scapegoat must be sacrificially murdered, the political (or political theological) scapegoat while an 'enemy' that must be opposed may not be destroyed in every circumstance, because 'such an enemy is central to one's own self-identity…. to destroy the one who defines you is, in the end, to destroy yourself or, at the very least to lose one's identity' (Grimshaw, 2013: xv). As Schmitt put it: 'The political enemy need not be morally evil, or aesthetically ugly; he need not appear as an economic competitor … But he is nevertheless, the other, the enemy…. The enemy is our own question given form' (Schmitt qtd. Taubes, 2013: 37).

> agreed upon in order to call such a decision democratic. And, before a democracy has begun, such agreement is obviously impossible in principle. (Ross, 2004: 86–87)

Which blows the whistle on the erotic-conspiratorial triangle in *The Man Who Shot Liberty Valance*: Hattie, Ransom, and Tom cannot go to the Assembly to plead the case for democracy because there is no Assembly there wherein to plead; instead they must 'pre-democratically' conspire privately (the plot of Three) in order to bring about the Assembly which is democratic. The 'violence' directed toward the Other for both the original foundation and the equally necessary periodic regeneration of the community is the specter that haunts liberalism (Mouffe, 2005): 'The issue is firstly one of justification of the distinction, a justification from power, that is, it is a classification inherently linked to the power of the one who makes the classification' (Grimshaw, 2013: xxviii). Schmitt's entire political theory constitutes an 'elaborate version of the old joke that a liberal is a person who cannot take his own side in an argument, that bourgeois liberal democracies are so oriented to debate and compromise that they will not be able to muster the collective will necessary to defend themselves from their true enemies' (Pippin, 2010: 69). My preferred version of this adage is that a liberal is someone who is passionate about neutrality. It was Schmitt who claimed that 'politics is a degree of intensity'; ergo, liberalism, properly understood, requires 'a denial of the cost others suffer by our being liberal'—identity is everything up to the moment that it signifies the real (Grimshaw, 2013: xxxi). Essential to political modernity is a wilful a-historicism, for in order for liberalism to function it can never be anything other than universalist, which means that it must eschew the local and the particular; 'liberals and liberalism in effect wish to stop humans from being time-located, historical humans in the name of idealism and the self-interest of liberals' (Grimshaw, 2013: xxxv). But it is also the existential dilemma of Tom Doniphon.

> If the certainty is not there at the inaugurating moment, which it can never be, then it is never finally certain…. And that is the violence of all foundation, a violence that necessarily hunts what it founds. Violence here does not necessarily refer to spilt blood. It is a matter of disrupting what preceded foundation…. This violence, this absence of legitimacy, does not mean that all democracies are illegitimate. But their legitimacy lies not in their past but in their future. As such, this legitimacy is never finally certain, never quite enough, and always in want of further confirmation. (Ross, 2004: 52)

Which requires enemies, the opposite of the liberal that can always be confronted and conveniently vanquished, usually through the relatively sanitized form of arguments over the meaning of citizenship. This friend-enemy distinction is the alpha and omega of politics after the The-Death-of-God-in-History, the Holy-Grail-of-the-Left: the abolition of the grounds of the possibility of meta-narratives; except, of course, of liberalism itself, the universality-of-nothing-in-particular. At all times one must remember that Schmitt does not formally reduce politics to the friend-enemy—the state of exception is primordial, and precedes every conceivable political configuration including the statist one, meaning that beyond the atomistic 'particle' of amity-enmity, there are no inherent limitations to political form; 'the nation-state, in other words, is only a political entity among other possible ones' (De Benoist, 2013:

99 n 244). In this way, friend-enemy is the ideal form of political decision-making along the Frontier because it is the ultimate act of political nostalgia, the performative re-enactment of the most elemental of political acts: Being-through-Hatred. 'The state of exception in jurisprudence is analogous to the miracle in theology' (Schmitt qtd. Taubes, 2013: 7); in the same way that violence is sovereignty, so is war politics as the naming of the outsider is the precondition for all other political acts.It is the alpha because it provides a compelling lie of the onto-political originary, one that is readily appreciative of the centrality of community violence to social formation akin to the scapegoat mechanism; the micro-self, no less than the macro-culture, owes its existence to the presence of the Other mediated through violence. And it is the omega because it is the only intelligible manner of conducting politics following the abolition of all and any form of transcendental signifier within public discourse: post-human politics, that-which-is after the unveiling of Modernity as the lie of *mythos*. Eternally warring *Gruppen* are the source of identity formation because the unbounded divisibility of sovereignty will always allow for, if not actively encourage, the eternal re-formation of combat units (*die Gruppierung*), even if only as a performative act of mimetic repetition. Combat-as-spectacle-as-nostalgia is the existential basis for the eternal divisibility of sovereignty; '*experiencing the other* is the basis of the community, even if it leads to conflict' (Maffesoli, 1996: 73). Despite the liberal categorical political imperative of 'blurring differences' ('*The entire political order is built on this*') it is 'possible to imagine that the bond holding a given entity together might in fact be constituted of that which divides. The tension between heterogeneities could be said to guarantee the solidity of the whole' (Maffesoli, 1996: 100).[43] All that is needed is to invest this onto-political 'unspeakable' with a constitutionalist form.

4.4.3 The Death of Universalism: 'He Who Decides on the Decision of the Exception is the Sovereign'

Telluric appropriation, along with the potential divisibility of the State (*nomos*), are the two necessary corollaries to Schmitt's signature constitutional notion: *the state of exception.* 'A definition of the political can be obtained only by discovering and defining the specifically political categories … The specific political distinction to which political actions and motives can be reduced is that between friend and enemy' (Schmitt, 2007: 26). This neo-Heideggerian re-conceptualization of the onto-political (and existential) basis of the State as the practical exercise of executive power effectively reduces sovereignty to *decisionism*; 'What always matters is the possibility of the extreme case taking place, the real war, and the decision whether this situation has or has not arrived' (Schmitt, 2007: 35). Political *existenz* as space coupled with force moves war to the center of life, yielding a radically Manichaean *weltanschaung*:

[43] 'While modernity has been obsessed with politics, it may be equally true that postmodernity is possessed of the idea of the clan, a phenomenon which is not without its effects on the relationship to the Other and, more specifically, to the stranger' (Maffesoli, 1996: 104).

'War as the most extreme political means discloses the possibility which underlines every political idea, namely, the distinction of friend or foe' (Schmitt, 2007: 35).[44] Of the greatest interest here is how Schmitt quite artfully blends two different sets of considerations into a single ontological postulate: (i) the political with the existential and (ii) the private with the public (both of which are formally separate in *nomos*, albeit deriving from the myth of telluric possession). 'The definition of the political suggested here neither favours war nor militarism, neither imperialism nor pacifism' (Schmitt, 2007: 33); what is essential, rather, is the demarcation of political space into a duality that is both the sign and the signifier of an authentic form of political commitment that is identical to 'truth'.

> Just as the term enemy, the word combat, too, is to be understood in its original existential sense ... The friend, enemy, and combat concepts receive their real meaning precisely because they refer to the real possibility of physical killing. War follows from enmity. War is the existential negation of the enemy. It is the most extreme consequence of enmity. It does not have to be common, normal, something ideal, or desirable. But it must nevertheless remain a real possibility for so long as the concept of the enemy remains valid. (Schmitt, 2007: 33)

And it is the etymological duality of the word *Feind* itself is what allows Schmitt to postulate an almost subliminal movement between public/*hostis* and private/*inimicus*: 'War is neither the aim nor the purpose nor even the very content of politics. But as an ever-present possibility it is the leading presupposition which determines in a characteristic way human action and thinking and thereby creates a specifically political behaviour' (Schmitt, 2007: 34) And politics itself is ultimately due to the uniqueness of the enemy[45] who, unsurprisingly, closely resembles the scapegoat: 'the other, the stranger; and it is sufficient for his nature that he is, in a specially intense way, existentially something different and alien, so that in the extreme conflicts with him are possible'(Schmitt, 2007: 27). Combat, therefore, which is identical to the moment of the decision—the identification of the enemy/other—is, to a perfectly inverse degree, *not* identical to war. Rather, war is both politically and existentially the most extreme form of combat, an apotheosis, combat serving as the onto-political *grund* of war, encapsulating both public and private systems of meaning: 'War, the readiness of combatants to die, the physical killing of human beings who belong on the side of the enemy—all this has no normative meaning, but an existential meaning

---

[44] It is vital to remember that Schmitt posits not a moral but a political concept of enmity: 'The enemy must ... be regarded politically: he must remain a *political* enemy, that is, an adversary that one must fight, certainly, but with whom one can one day make peace. ... And, as it is only with an enemy that one can make peace, that implies that the belligerents *mutually recognize one another*.' Alain de Benoist has therefore rightly critiqued attempts to collapse Schmittean agonism into the de-humanizing antagonism of warfare, such as the 'War on Terror'; the terrorist is a criminal/outlaw while the political 'enemy' is merely an opponent who never falls beneath the level of judicial and political actor; ergo, members of rival genders, sexualities, races, or classes may be enemies but they can never be criminalized, for to do so would be to invite the end-game of 'absolute war,' which, 'by attempting to eliminate the enemy ... eliminates the element which constitutes politics' (De Benoist, 2013: 22).

[45] 'The political consists not in war or armed conflict as such, but precisely in the relation of enmity: not competition but confrontation It is bound by no law: it is prior to law' (Hirst, 1987: 17).

only, particularly in a real combat situation with a real enemy' (Schmitt, 2007: 48–49). Schmitt's theory of combat-as-politics is not mere existentialism ('justice does not belong to the concept of war' (Schmitt, 2007: 49)), but a radicalized existentialism; by 'radical' I mean that both the truth and the value of the object (existent) in question is determined by an unconditional, and irreducible givenness that appears to the existentially inauthentic Self as an irruption by an alien Other.

> There exists no rational purpose, no norm no matter how true, no program no matter how exemplary, no social ideal no matter how beautiful, no legitimacy nor legality which could justify men in killing each other for this reason. If such physical destruction of human life is not motivated by an existential threat to one's way of life, then it cannot be justified. Just as little can war be justified by ethical and juristic norms. If there really are enemies in the existential sense as meant here, then it is justified, but only politically, to repel and fight them physically. (Schmitt, 2007: 49)[46]

Which means that myth is not merely useful, it is positively indispensable to *nomos*. And it is this iterability between war and combat, mediated through the act of recognition of the enemy that is the logical outcome of a decisionism that subverts the foundational liberal principle of the public/private distinction: the onto-political effects of the primordial decision is projected simultaneously into external and internal space.

> Political thought and political instinct prove themselves thematically and practically in the ability to distinguish friend and enemy. The high points of politics are simultaneously the moments in which the enemy is, in concrete clarity, recognized as the enemy (Schmitt, 2007: 67).... But also vice versa: everywhere in political history, in foreign as well as in domestic politics, the incapacity or the unwillingness to make this distinction is a symptom of the political end. (Schmitt, 2007: 68)

Most unnerving for the orthodox liberal is Schmitt's cold-blooded but completely logical conclusion that the sovereign as the executor of the decision is not itself reducible to (or exhausted by) law but acts as the sign of an inchoate extra-judicial 'space' of primordial order that is the true guarantor of 'law'. The State, as a supposedly 'legal personality' is not exhausted, or even explicable, in terms of the law; in order for it to exist as a lawful entity, it must necessarily invoke the presence of the extra-legal.

It is at precisely this juncture that the first of several dangerous supplements announce their presence within the Schmittean sub-text. By reducing sovereignty to decision—which is the logical corollary of the friend/self-enemy/other dichotomy—and by postulating combat (potentially a private act) as the originating ground for war (formally an exclusively public enterprise), Schmitt inadvertently admits to the possibility of the non-state actor as the sovereign; 'War has its own strategic, tactical,

---

[46] The deep irony of, and therefore the unsettling effect that this passage has on the liberal-bourgeois reader, is that the first sentence reads like a conventional argument in favor of pacificism: *nothing is worth the taking of human life*. As if life possessed its own sanctity. The 'alien' nature of Schmitt's thought is most clearly evidenced by the manner in which he re-deploys conventional anti-war rhetoric as justification for a more 'truthful' form of violence that is the sign of a 'sincere' form of politics.

and other rules and points of view, but they all presuppose that the political decision has already been made as to who the enemy is' (Schmitt, 2007: 34). The identity, or 'truth,' of the sovereign will stand revealed through the post facto 'concrete' deconstruction of this antecedent political decision. Schmitt acts as the surveyor of a crisis of an existential and not merely a political 'crisis of meaning'; the 'political unit is always, as long as it is present at all, the authoritative unit, total and sovereign. It is "total" first because every matter can be potentially political and therefore can be affected by the political decision; and second because man is totally and existentially grasped in political participation' (Schmitt qtd. Meier, 1995: 16). Schmitt's concern with political meaning as existential dilemma unmistakably marks him as a 'Germanic thinker,'[47] affirming 'the political because he sees in the threatened status of the political a threat to the seriousness of human life. The affirmation of the political is ultimately nothing other than the affirmation of the moral' (Strauss, 2007: 117). When it is said that 'the political is a basic characteristic of human life,' argues Leo Strauss, it means that 'man ceases to be man if he ceases to be political, this statement also, and precisely, means that man ceases to be human when he ceases to be political' (Strauss, 2007: 110).[48] For Schmitt, the 'distinction of friend and enemy denotes the utmost degree of intensity of a union or separation, of an association or disassociation' (Schmitt, 2007: 26); as a result, the 'greater the intensity the closer to the Truth we come.'[49] Conversely, were the friend-enemy distinction to vanish, 'then political life would vanish altogether. A people which exists in the political sphere cannot, despite entreating declarations to the contrary, escape from making this fateful distinction' (Schmitt, 2007: 51). For if a people 'no longer possesses the energy or will to maintain itself in the sphere of politics, the latter will not thereby vanish from the world. Only a weak people will disappear' (Schmitt, 2007: 53). Which should never happen to the rugged individualistic proto-citizens of the Frontier, provided that they are supplied with a steady stream of enemies who require killing in gun-fights; if not, then the enemy-less *existent* (existential subject) 'would lose its political being; it would purely and simply depoliticize itself' (Derrida, 2005: 77). And the absence, or final total elimination, of the enemy 'would be the death knell of the political as such. It would mark the beginning of depoliticization ... The beginning of the end of the political' (Derrida, 2005: 84). Because the bourgeois—or the fearful-of-death proto-citizens of Shinbone who cannot find it within themselves

[47] 'Since the end of the nineteenth century, longing for the realization of man's humanity has fuelled many of the most influential trends in German social criticism—so much so that there are few surer signs that a social critic has been educated in the German/continental philosophic tradition than complaints about dehumanization or demands that our autonomy be embodied in our institutions' (Yack, 1992: 365).

[48] See Meier (1995: 56–58) for the exchange between Schmitt and Strauss over the grounding of conflict/violence in 'human nature'.

[49] On the basis of this preoccupation with existential, Richard Wolin is able to situate Schmitt within the vitalist critique of rationalism, a defining feature of German revolutionary conservatism; 'one of the patented conceptual oppositions proper to the conservative revolutionary habitus was that between the "hero" (or "soldier") and the "bourgeois". Whereas the hero thrives on risk, danger, and uncertainty, the life of the bourgeois is devoted to petty calculations of utility and security' (Wolin, 1992: 427, 431).

to be done with Liberty Valance—is the antithesis of the heroic liberalism and its resultant political rationality can neither compel *nor explain* instances of *sacrifice*, either of the Self or of the Other.[50]

> A world in which the possibility of war is utterly eliminated, a completely pacified globe, would be a world without the distinction of friend and enemy, and hence a world without politics. It is conceivable that such a world might contain many very interesting antitheses and contrasts, competitions and intrigues of every kind, but there would not be a meaningful antithesis whereby men could be required to sacrifice life, authorized to shed blood, and kill other human beings. (Schmitt, 2007: 35)

From this follows the 'immorality' of liberalism that under 'no circumstances can anyone demand that any member of an economically determined society, whose order in the economic domain is based upon rational procedures, sacrifice his life in the interest of rational operations' (Schmitt, 2007: 48). Nothing could be more existentially hellish, or more un-ruggedly anti-individualistic, or more Ransom Stoddard-ish.

> The political entity cannot by its very nature be universal in the sense of embracing all of humanity and the entire world. If the different states, religions, classes, and other human groupings on earth should be so unified that a conflict among them is impossible and even inconceivable and if civil war should forever be foreclosed in a realm that embraces the globe, then the distinction of friend and enemy would also cease. What remains is neither politics nor State, but culture, civilization, economics, morality, law, art, entertainment, etc. (Schmitt, 2007: 53)

In other words, no *nomos*, the absence of which destroys the meaning of everything. But not to worry; this heady, and discursively unstable, onto-political admixture of the originating, the decision, and the authentic, however, is precisely what allows me to undertake a two-prong deconstruction of Schmitt's own inadvertently self-limiting concept of the political. The profound irony here is that it is Schmitt's own radically singular critique of the liberal state that facilitates the appropriation of his oeuvre by the Other.

4.4.4 The Deadly Reversal: Decisionism as Sovereignty

As Tracy B. Strong has rightly observed, 'Liberals are horrified at Schmitt because he offends against one of the deepest premises of liberalism: politics is necessary but it should not become too serious' (Strong, 2007: xxvi). As Schmitt forcibly reminds us, to see liberalism 'as an historical event means that one understands it as the inheritor and bearer not only of rights and freedoms but also of structures of power and domination, of colonial and class exploitations, of the hatred of, rather than

[50] 'The central task in the founding of a modern political order was to find a way to denigrate, contain, and de-emphasize the chief pre-modern mark of distinction, glory, with all the militaristic and violent and dangerous dimensions of the task, in favour of a more scientific view of the primacy of the fear of death and the desire for peace' (Albert O. Hirschmann qtd. Pippin, 2010: 25).

the opposition to, the Other' (Strong, 2007: xix). The true value of Schmitt's juro-political philosophy lies within his radical juxtaposition of liberalism with its own enemy: political violence and its ideological corollary 'extremism'. What 'primarily interests Schmitt ... is to complete the critique of liberalism' (Meier, 1995: 11), a goal achieved through his existential critique of liberalism's bad faith concerning the onto-political foundation of the primal decision concerning the enemy. In Schmitt's view it is the 'liberal state' itself that is the embodiment of a higher form of immorality: 'The concept of the state presupposes the concept of the political. According to modern linguistic usage, the state is the political status of an organized people in an enclosed territorial unit ... Vis-a-vis the many conceivable kinds of entities, it is in the decisive case the ultimate authority' (Schmitt, 2003: 19–20). Alternatively, in onto-political terms, the question is whether liberal society can 'really leave behind what it was' (Pippin, 2010: 24). For Schmitt, the essence of 'the definition of the bourgeois' is 'aspiring to life without political risk' (Schmitt, 2007: 51 n 22). Yet, with our awareness of the lurking presence of the decision, we know that the 'peaceful, legalistic, liberal bourgeoisie is sitting on a volcano and ignoring the facts. Their world depends on a relative stabilization of conflicts within the state and on the state's ability to keep at bay other potentially hostile states' (Hirst, 1987: 17). He writes that the 'problematic or unproblematic conception of man is decisive for the presupposition of every further political consideration, the answer to the question whether man is a dangerous being or not, a risky or a harmless creature' (Schmitt, 2007: 58). His answer: Men are Bad. Ergo

> [Liberalism] has produced a doctrine of the separation and balance of power, i.e., a system of checks and controls of state and government. This cannot be characterized as either a theory of state or a basic political principle. What remains is the remarkable and, for many, certainly disquieting diagnosis that all genuine political theories presuppose man to be evil, i.e., by no means an unproblematic but a dangerous and dynamic being. (Schmitt, 2007: 61)[51]

And, according to Schmitt's sometime correspondent Leo Strauss, 'In order to remove the smokescreen over reality that liberalism produces, the political must be made apparent as such and simply undeniable. The political must first be brought out of concealment into which liberalism has cast it, so that the question of the State can be seriously put' (Strauss, 2007: 100). The critique of liberalism, therefore, is we should have come to expect, not merely a political one but an existential one: 'what is at stake' in the act of commitment that is 'the decision' as to the identity of the enemy is 'indeed a phenomenalization as revelation, manifestation, unveiling' (Derrida, 2005: 131).

> This undecidable decision[52] bestows the force of unveiling. This deciding signification which unveils the kernel of things ... accrues to the decision. The unveiling of things, of the heart of things in the coming asunder of decision, is perhaps accomplished not in the act of war which bears death, but surely in the assundering possibility, of a killing, in this possibility

[51] 'A part of the theories and postulates which presuppose man to be good is liberal' (Schmitt, 2007: 60).

[52] Undecidable' in that the 'truth' of the enemy exists nowhere outside of the commitment to the friend-enemy distinction that is itself 'the decision'.

> *qua* real and present possibility. The latter can uncover the heart of things only in undressing the other, in uncovering the possibility of what Schmitt called … 'physical killing'. (Derrida, 2005: 128)

For Schmitt the Friend/Enemy distinction is the primordial ground of the emergence of what we call *'the concept of the political'*.

> The specific political distinction to which political actions and motives can be reduced is that between friend and enemy (Schmitt, 2007: 26) …The friend and enemy concepts are to be understood in their concrete and existential sense, not as metaphors or symbols…The enemy is not merely any competitor or just any partner of a conflict in general [i.e. competition; rivalry]. He is also not the private adversary whom one hates. An enemy exists only when, at least potentially, one fighting collectivity of people confronts a similar collectivity. (Schmitt, 2007: 27–28)

Thus, the moment in time at which the Friend-Enemy distinction is made ('enemy identification') is the exact point at which politics reaches its highest form, or zenith, which is the existential equivalent of warfare; 'The political is the most intense and extreme antagonism, and every concrete antagonism becomes that much more political the closer it approaches the most extreme point, that of the friend-enemy grouping' (Schmitt, 2007: 29). Three empirical requirements were needed to be made out in full before the moment of true politics could be established as the new, albeit temporary, historical reality. The first is that as the friend-enemy grouping is the essence of politics, then the 'Enemy' must necessarily be a *public actor*, for true combat could not take place within the private spaces; 'The enemy is solely the public enemy, because everything that has a relationship to such a collectivity of men, particularly to a whole nation, becomes public by virtue of such a relationship' (Schmitt, 2007: 28). From this it followed that a 'private person has no political enemies. Such a declaration can at most say that he would like to place himself outside the political community to which he belongs and continue to live as a private individual only' (Schmitt, 2007: 51).[53] The second is that during the 'peak experience' of the political, the public actors engaged in combat will openly seek to valorize warfare, formally acknowledging violence as the paramount instrument for the resolution political struggle.

> It would be ludicrous to believe that a defenseless people has nothing but friends, and it would be a deranged calculation that the enemy could perhaps be touched by the absence of a resistance…If a people no longer possesses the energy or the will to maintain itself in the sphere of politics, the latter will not thereby vanish from the world. Only a weak people will disappear. (Schmitt, 2007: 53)

[53] Although he first developed the notion of Friend/Enemy during the civil war era of the Weimar Republic (1918-1933), in his later writings which followed the destruction of the Third Reich and the Allied Occupation of Germany, Schmitt tended to replace the militaristic binary relationship of Friend-Enemy with the more existential 'twining' of Self/Other which permitted the universalization of the concept of the political to incorporate all forms of existentially intense combat, even those within the ostensibly sub-statist sphere, such as guerrilla warfare.

The third is that in times of normality, or 'peace'—which, for Schmitt, are merely the juridically sterile intervals between the explosive episodes of violent and radical creation—the 'symbolic order' is deemed vital for maintaining the potential for an emergency calling of the friend-enemy grouping; we recognize the State of peace that is waiting for war through its sponsoring (usually by means of funding) of the full panoply of the techniques of propaganda—which, today, would obviously include social media. All 'political concepts, images, and terms have a polemical meaning. They are focused on a specific conflict and are bound to a concrete situation; the result (which manifests itself in war or revolution) is a friend-enemy grouping, and they turn into empty and ghost-like abstractions when this situation disappears' but are then immediately replaced by an indefinite 'cold war' of sounds and images (Schmitt, 2007: 30). Although they sound harsh to us in our self-enforced naivete, Schmitt's words in fact describe very well the perpetual oscillation between administrative orderliness and chaotic street fighting that punctuated the Weimar Era; as his best friend and confident, World War One stormtrooper and hyper-modernist novelist Ernst Junger prophetically explained it 'We are approaching a state of affairs in which each person needs to be made aware within minutes of a news report, a warning, a threat. Hidden behind the face of entertainment promoted by the all-encompassing media, are special forms of discipline' (Ernst Junger qtd. Kaes, 1993: 115). And, as everyone knows, one of the premier and most memorable characteristics of the Third Reich (1933–1945) was its revolutionary utilization of filmic images and cinema for propaganda purposes. Which is the veritable antithesis of Liberalism, both political and judicial, which rest upon the wholly unproven assumption that 'legitimacy' stands in a necessary relationship to the 'symbolic negotiation' of violence. Robert Sherwin righteously calls all of us out on Liberalism's interminable pathology of onto-political denial.

> Deeper fears protect our willing delegation to the legitimate other, the state and its agents, of the right to use force. We need that legitimate other, just as we need the other's dark double, the one upon whom the force of law must operate. For, on a deep and hidden level within ourselves, we know that violence cannot be put off or denied. In this respect, the ancient Greeks were more honest with themselves than we tend to be about this state of affairs. They could admit that a horrible and terrifying fury *is* the steering force of the law (*'the utmost degree of intensity of a union or separation, of an association or disassociation'*), that such fury lies at the heart of law…. For us [liberals], this knowledge must be repressed. Law's violence must be sanitized, neutralized, denied. And when it cannot be, when public recognition of law's violence can no longer be concealed…at such times we witness law's legitimacy slipping. (Sherwin, 1994: 45)

As Peter Drexler points out in his remarkable essay, 'The German Courtroom Film during the Nazi Period' (2001), The Third Reich produced an unusually large number of 'law dramas' or law related films.

> Generally, many films of the Nazi period bespeak an immense preoccupation, in fact obsession, with questions of justice and legitimacy, and in this they mirror the perverted Nazi habit of justifying and legitimizing the most monstrous political measures…Representation of the law in film, as we have seen in the case of Weimar cinema, is rarely concerned with a realistic depiction of legal procedure or with a serious critique of existing laws. This is even more so with Nazi film, which uses the law in various functions: to demonstrate the

> 'humane' and 'benevolent' character of the political system, or to lead the erring individual back into the *Volksgemeinschaft* (folk community), to propagate the efficiency and security of the law system [sic], thus glossing over the actually existing perversion of the law, or by contrast, to denounce foreign law systems for propagandistic purposes. (Drexler, 2001: 71)

Of course it is almost too easy to re-define *'The perverted Nazi habit of justifying and legitimizing the most monstrous political measures'* as *moral judgment given the force of executive action.* But this is nothing more than the dark heart of legal positivism reworked into its most intense, or purest, form: if, as John Austin pontificated, 'Law is the command of the sovereign enforced by sanctions' on what grounds can the 'lawful' directives of executive power ever be legitimately resisted?

It is through his reduction of sovereignty to decisionism that Schmitt inadvertently subverts the longed-for totalizing unity of *nomos.* The truth of politics is violence (combat), which, through its own dynamic, escalates and multiplies itself over time through the proliferation of actors and entities, yielding a radical pluralization of the domain of legal persons. As Slavoj Zizek has opined, decisionism as the foundational principle of 'the rule of law ultimately hinges on an abyssal act of violence (violent imposition) which is grounded in itself; that is, every positive order to which this act refers, to legitimize itself, is self-referentially posited by this act itself' (Zizek, 1999: 18).

> According to Schmitt, it is not possible to pass directly from a pure normative order to the actuality of social life—the necessary mediator between the two is an act of Will, a decision, grounded only in itself, which *imposes* a certain order or legal hermeneutics (reading of abstract rules). Any normative order, taken in itself, remains stuck in abstract formalism, that is to say, it cannot bridge the gap that separates it from actual life. However—this is the core of Schmitt's argumentation—the decision which bridges this gap is not a decision for some concrete order, but primarily the decision for the formal principle of order as such. (Zizek, 1999: 18)

If we take Schmitt at his word—that the 'political is the most intense and extreme antagonism, and every concrete antagonism becomes that much more political the closer it approaches the most extreme point, that of the friend-enemy grouping' (Schmitt, 2007: 29)—then we have opened the doors to a limitless carnivalesque inversion of political and existential meanings: *any particular combat situation can serve as the grounds for the emergence of a new sovereignty.* If it is true that 'Sovereign is he who decides on the exception', then it is equally true that 'He who decides the exception is the sovereign' (or, rather, Sovereign is ***she***[54] who *succeeds in deciding the exception in the concrete instance*). The most self-subverting elements of Schmitt's political ontology is the extreme precariousness governing the relationship between the quasi-theological essentialism of the *nomos* and the radical nominalism underlying the friend-enemy distinction.

---

[54] Schmitt never appears to mention Women whose total absence in *Lord of the Flies* and partial absence in the Western genre speaks volumes—maybe. Because, after all, Hattie 'spoke' through her three scapegoats—Tom, Ransom, and Liberty.

> Only the actual participants can correctly recognize, understand, and judge the concrete situation and settle the extreme case of conflict. Each participant is in a position to judge whether the adversary intends to negate his opponent's way of life and therefore must be repulsed or fought in order to preserve one's own form of existence.... Thereby the inherently objective nature and autonomy of the political becomes evident by virtue of its being able to treat, distinguish, and comprehend the friend-enemy antithesis independently of other antitheses. (Schmitt, 2007: 27)

As Zizek has accurately observed

> Schmitt's notion of the exception is necessarily ambiguous: it stands simultaneously for the inversion of the Real (of the pure contingency ['the concrete situation'] which perturbs the universe of symbolic *automaton) and* for the gesture of the Sovereign who (violently, without foundation in the symbolic norm) imposes a symbolic normative order ... the Master-Signifier. (Zizek, 1999: 19)

Zizek's turn to the language of deconstruction is most welcome here: the successful performance of the act of recognition, or naming, of the enemy is the decision that signifies the presence of sovereignty and, therefore, of 'true' politics. Conversely, the constitutive act of such recognition is simultaneously the announcement of the friend, a non-identical 'self' with whom one does not exist in a state of combat. The enemy/other stands revealed not as a given fact (objective) but as a contingent construction (subjective) of the-will-of-the-decider. The act (or, temporally, the precise *time*) of the decision is the invocation of the presence of the enemy/other which is itself the signification of the *absence* of the friend/self. Enmity (the friend/self vs. enemy/other distinction) serves as the basis of real politics only because it enables the circulation of the master-sign of sovereignty, the ability to effect the command over perceptions that are reducible to the existential elemental of 'life and death'. The Sovereign not only decides, or commands, within the duration of the state of emergency, but also decides whether the state of emergency (which is identical to the naming of the enemy) has even been reached in the first instance. So conceived the decision is radically contingent, not self-grounding, as the ontological monism of *nomos* would seem to require.

> First, all political concepts, images, and terms have a polemical meaning. They are focused on a specific conflict and are bound to a concrete situation; the result (which manifests itself in a war or a revolution) is a friend-enemy grouping and they turn into empty and ghost-like abstractions when this situation disappears. (Schmitt, 2007: 30)

Intriguingly, Schmitt gives periodic indications that he seems aware of the radically contingent nature of sovereignty, which would render the decision more fully compatible with a divisible plurality; the 'concept of the political yields pluralistic consequences, but not in the sense that, *within one and the same political entity*; instead of decisive friend-and-enemy groupings, a pluralism could take its place without destroying the entity and the political itself' (Schmitt, 2007: 45). If Schmitt yields to the fragmenting of the primordial-mythic *nomos* then he must renounce his political ontology in toto; his solution, therefore, is to re-formulate the empirical instances of pluralism as errors, or 'enemy mis-identification'.

> For as long as a people exists in the political sphere, this people must, even if only in the most extreme case—and whether this point has been reached has to be decided by it—determine by itself the distinction of friend and enemy. … The justification of war does not reside in its being fought for ideas or norms of justice, but in its being fought against a real enemy. All confusions of this category of friend and enemy can be explained as results of *blendings* of some sort of abstractions or norms. (Schmitt, 2007: 49–50)

The employment of the term *blendings* here is interesting, suggesting as it does some sort of accidental spillage, or leakage, between normally sealed and separate contained spaces—meaning walls, the master-sign of the telluric settlements of the Frontier. Which jibes with Michel Maffesoli's own commentary on the City-as-sociality.

> Indeed, the *territory-myth* pair that is the organizing [telluric] principle of the city is both cause and effect of such a structure. That is, like a nest of Russian dolls, the city reveals other entities of the same type: neighborhoods, ethnic groups, associations, various tribes that will organize themselves around (real or symbolic) territory and common myths. These Hellenistic cities are founded essentially on the double polarity of cosmopolitanism and rootedness (which, as we know, was to produce a specific civilization). What does this say other than that all of these groups, strongly united by common sentiments, will structure a collective memory which in its very diversity is a founding structure. These groups may be of many types (ethnic; social); structurally, it is their very diversity that assures the *unicity* of the city.… it is the *tension* between these various groups that assures the durability of the whole. (Maffesoli, 1996: 124)

Apart from the fact that Schmitt clearly nominates the collectively deciding (but always potentially divisible) 'people' as the sovereign—an uncharacteristically 'democratic' move on his part—it is he himself who opens up the originating act to historical investigation and *destruktion*: if Schmitt declares that the decision exists nowhere outside of the concrete then the question must now be what are the particular set of events governing the process of naming the enemy in any specific situation? The aesthetic challenge that this philosophical dilemma poses to the scholar of Law and Literature is to reconceptualize the legal narrative—always imbibed with the mythological—so that Schmitt's a priori reasoning ('the sovereign is he who decides') may be replaced by a post-Schmittean, and supremely Girardian, a posteriori reasoning: who (or what) has empirically succeeded in deciding the concrete situation before us? Meaning who is the sacrificer and who is the scapegoat? Which is just another way of saying who is the friend and who is the enemy. Look to see what happens when a particular 'Other' is killed. Then, by their fruits you shall know them. And, as it turns out, there is a Western that proves that the gun fighter really will always be needed to separate the sheep from the goats—and who will come when called.

4.5 'Although You're Grievin', I Can't be Leavin', Until I Shoot Frank Miller Dead': *High Noon* (1952) or, the Tin Star of Decisionism

If we compare the *The Man Who Shot Liberty Valance* by the Catholic conservative John Ford with *High Noon* (1952)[55] by the para-Marxist Fred Zimmerman, we notice immediately that the narrative drama of each runs in opposite directions: Ford moves from the high to the low while Zimmerman moves from the low to the high. Which is not surprising when we consider that level of social development of the respective communities in the two films is radically different; Shinbone almost a frontier encampment, Hadleyville a 'proper' middle-class township, meaning that the social actors of the latter drama are the bourgeoisie from whom nothing good can ever come, at least according to Schmitt.

> The bourgeois is an individual who does not want to leave the a-political riskless private sphere. He rests in the possession of his private property, and under the justification of his possessive individualism he acts as an individual against the totality. He is a man who finds his compensation for his political nullity in the fruits of freedom and enrichment and above all in the total security of its use. Consequently he wants to be spared bravery and exempted from the danger of a violent death. (Schmitt, 2007: 62–63)

A cautionary tale of the 'fragile veneer of civilization' a la William Golding's *Lord of the Flies* through its not-so-subtle invocation of Custer's Last Stand (Slotkin, 1985: 1–47), Zimmerman's supreme 'anti-Western'[56] is a parody of Schmittean decisionism, anticipating Akira Kurosawa's equally seminal *Yojimbo* (1961)[57] by a decade: the un-Schmittean anomaly of an entire community being composed of nothing but enemies would mean that the state of exception would be tantamount to self-annihilation, the existential intensity of combat taken to the zero point of *reductio ad absurdum* with Teutonic fury. Even more than Ford, Zimmerman zooms in on the underlying social crisis that unconsciously fuels the conscious existential dimensions of the Westerner.

> For many great Westerns are indeed about the founding of modern bourgeois, law-abiding, property-owning, market-economy, technologically advanced societies in transition—in situations of, mostly, lawlessness (or corrupt and ineffective law) that border on classic 'state of nature' theories. The question often raised is that of how … the bourgeois virtues, especially the domestic virtues, can be said to get a psychological grip in an environment where the heroic and martial virtues are so important. (Pippin, 2010: 20)

---

[55] Pace Wright, the Westerns that he groups together under 'the Classic Plot' c. 1931–1955 (the solitary-gun-fighter-from-the-wilderness) most directly correlates to Schmitt's decisionism, although this is present in some form in all of the other types of Westerns, most notably *High Noon* (1952) which he excludes from the Classic Plot category. Even more bizarre is his failure to discuss the truly seminal film of the late American Western, *The Man Who Shot Liberty Valance*, a beautifully Schmittean Western, because of its failure at the box office (Wright, 1975: 32–59).

[56] *High Noon* (directed by Fred Zimmermann, Lionsgate, 2008).

[57] See below, Chap. 5.

While all Westerns are exercises in decisionism, the particular state of emergency that the genre refuses to contemplate is the very real possibility that the originating violence, ordinarily portrayed as a mythic event of timeless 'ordering', may, in fact, have to be periodically renewed—or mimetically repeated, for a new scapegoat must always be found in order to perform the sacred pseudo-magic of the sacrifice-of-restoration. The reasons for this lacuna are fairly obvious. The first is that if the sacrificial murder needs to be repeated it means that the sacrifice did not 'work' the first time which vitiates the mythic nature of the archetypal gun-fight. The second is that the structural logic of genre requires the Western to refuse the possibility of reverse colonization except in the situation of 'foreign' invasion which normally involved Indians; hence, the archetypal status of Custer whose spectacular death-by-incompetence was the nineteenth century version of Pearl Harbor. But what is not possible is the reversal of civilization through enemies who are situated within the properly founded communities of the now 'ex-Frontier'. Zimmerman's title signals his subversive intent: noon is the exact moment of transition from the early to the late day; the 'zenith' of the sun marking the passage from dawn to evening, or from youth to maturity. *High Noon* is the temporal expression of the exact moment of social transition and the passing of moral judgment upon the true nature of the community in a manner that totally flouts liberal consensus through the unexpected appearance of a true decider; 'law is regarded as developing within society, being spontaneous and growing upwards independent of any dominant will' (Boehnke, 2001: 48). Which is apocalyptically unveiled as idolatrous falsehood by the self-appointed exceptional citizen of Marshal Will Kane, the only rugged individualist in town. An added complication is the plot device of the transition between marshals: Kane's term has expired and the new marshal has not yet arrived. Therefore, in a sense the community is 'without' law, or is *liminally* governed by a revocation or absence of a prior state of the rule of law (re-) signified by the judge's flight from the community. We are in the state of nature, a form of 'bare life', at the center of the in-between-not-yet which requires emergency mediation. Which demands a middleman of exceptional qualities—the (re-)emergence of the true Westerner. But there is a problem, namely that the absence of the existential intensity of the pure politics that is now called for is not within the Westerner (Kane) but within *societas* itself: it is a collective of 'liminal people' so that the film title itself is the master-sign: 'noon' also signifies the liminality of the total environment, the motif of transition, in both time (morning to evening) and space (the Frontier between nature and civilization) reflecting perfectly the inherent moral (and legal) ambiguity of the underdeveloped community.

> The attributes of liminality or of liminal *personae* ('threshold people') are necessarily ambiguous, since this condition and these persons elude or slip through the networks of classifications that normally locate states and positions in cultural space. Liminal entities are neither here nor there; they are betwixt and between the positions assigned and arrayed by law, convention, and ceremonial. (Turner qtd. Pippin, 2010: 95)

The presence of legal authority is now absent and, minus the enforcing power of the State, the townspeople are now in a position to collectively renege on the social contract, which cataclysmically proclaims the re-emergence of the state of nature, the Hobbesian 'absence of a common power'. It is within this very precise and delicate space of 'judicial time' that the de-stabilizing 'trouble' manifests itself (Meyer, 2007–2008: 82) which is dramatically enacted as the temporal disruption of the continuity (inter-generational nature) of the social contract, but with the post-Hobbesian twist that *everybody* (minus two) has voluntarily deviated from the contract, reverting social space to the 'wilderness' (*bellum omnium contra omnes*) within which the community must be re-founded. In the meantime, all legal and moral identities are suspended; 'Symbolically, all attributes that distinguish categories and groups in the structured social order are here in abeyance; the neophytes are merely entities in transition, as yet without place or position' (Turner qtd. Pippin, 2010: 103), the liminal people serving as the dramatic background (or Hobbesian chorus?) to Kane's foregrounded ritualistic enactment of the genre role of the Westerner. The fact that Kane is legally no longer the marshal for the duration of the temporal crisis of liminality means that he is always acting within the state of nature; his own *personal status*, therefore, becomes of central dramatic importance, fulfilling a critical genre requirement of the iconic Westerner. If the rule of law is (temporarily) absent, then all of Kane's actions, although ultimately intended for the public good (the Commonwealth) are *private* in nature, the community having regressed to the state of nature. Yet it is not really persuasive to consider Kane as a naturalist Westerner in the sense that Doniphon is one; Shinbone, because it is primitive, directly reflects the 'natural' human instinct to socialize and to create a community out of pre-given human drives; Hadleyville, by contrast, exhibits all of the characteristics of the Hobbesian state as an artificial community, the atomistic egoists of the 'people' tending toward each other out of objective calculations of self-interest: there is no *telos* for Kane to either embody or protect. So we need to ask Gary Cooper the question that we asked John Wayne: if Marshal Kane is a Westerner, what kind of Westerner is he?

There are all kinds of possibilities. Jonathan Tillman has opted for Kane as an *Aristotelian* Westerner.

> In *High Noon* the character Kane represents the remnants of an Aristotelian political ideal…Hadleyville is a natural human community [sic], which, in Kane's mind, functions as the telos of value for the citizens whose various functions and virtues have meaning in terms of the goods of the city (Tillman, 2007: 40) … In addition, Kane believes that the townspeople will recognize the impending threat to their safety and will render aid on the basis of civic friendship. But all of these conclusions are mistaken. (Tillman, 2007: 42)

But as I have already indicated, the Law-and-Literature question that *High Noon* forces us to ask is: are the rational and egoistic calculations of the liberal-bourgeois Self adequate to maintain adherence to the social contract? Or are more elemental 'non-liberal' or even irrational *passions* required, passions which, if they are 'virtuous', are so only in effect not in origin? Tillman appears to concede this point: the townsfolk 'so stringently follow the notion of non-coercion that they can find no reasons to resist or compel anyone. The result is a lack of political will and a flabby sense of political obligation, which the film implies may be inherent liabilities in [liberal] theory' (Tillman, 2007: 44). A second, and at first glance more attractive possibility, is that the marshal is a *Kantian* Westerner, the cinematic incarnation of

Immanuel Kant's 'Formula of Universal Law', the proposition that the true moral agent should 'act only in accordance with that maxim through which you can at the same time will that it become a universal law' (Evans, 2010: 180). Applying this formula through his actions and speech, Kane's 'moral intuitions produce an obvious distinction between professional duties and moral ones. His professional duties are those of a marshal of Hadleyville, while his moral duties arise from his autonomy as a rational being who shows respect for the moral law' (Evans, 2010: 180). He is, in truth, the 'only person who gives himself the moral law such that he can will maxims that are universalizable [law and order = civilization = universal good]. The marshal's ability to be a moral agent is due to his autonomy, and his autonomy is due to his rational nature' (Evans, 2010: 181). The crucial phrase here is *gives himself the moral law* for it suggests less a detached contemplative act than a deeply personal volitional one. This is the exact point at which Nietzsche staged the demolition of Kantian ethics: the categorical imperative is not judgment but the *will-to-judgment* for it can only be exercised within the totality of a given and contingent situation—universalism is a reification, or, worse, false consciousness. For Kane to be a Kantian, lawlessness must be universally bad, but how do we know this as the 'good' citizens of Hadleyville seem not to know it themselves? Half of the town—the respectable burghers at the church—are not in favor of Frank Miller the outlaw but are against Marshal Kane on the basis of calculations of long-term profit; the other half, the disrespectable burghers at the saloon, are actively in favor of the bandit-chieftain out of non-calculated love for immediate gratification (fast money and sleazy pleasure) and viscerally hate the anti-hedonistic law-man (who is not only a kill-joy but the killer of joy). In other words, there is nothing wrong per se with anyone's cognitive abilities—rather, they 'Will' (!) different outcomes because they desire alternative kinds of goods on the basis of their desires. Meaning that Kane is never in a position where he actually has to convince or persuade anyone of anything; he merely needs to act in a manner that is more 'final' than anyone else's. The marshal is the one who names Frank Miller as the 'real' enemy of the community and he imposes his 'will' (= Will Kane/Cain/Kill) by actually going out and shooting Frank Miller dead before leavin' with his grieven' bride. The truth of his perception is validated only after the fact a posteriori, not before the fact a priori (as Kant would have it), and the absolute nature of his autonomy, the indispensable rugged individualism of the Westerner, is made real through the physical struggle to kill his enemy. In other words, the marshal is a Schmittean Westerner.

Although less stereotypically tragic than Doniphon who voluntarily undergoes auto-sacrifice, Kane, inhabiting a minoritarian space with the discursive field of the Western, relies upon the liminality of the noon-day sun to fulfill the requisite element of tragic status: 'Liminality implies that the high could not be high unless the low existed, and he who is high must experience what it is like to be low' (Turner qtd. Pippin, 2010: 97). Kane is 'in effect, a vigilante' although he wears a (tin) star of 'office' (Ryan, 1996: 38) and as an icon that is defined by marginality, Kane-as-Westerner may be reduced to merely one particular agent of violence, motivated by his adherence to 'the code' which, because of the weirdness of the situation, can only operate extra-judicially, meaning as a form of criminality. Under the stultifying normalities of legal positivism, law is the command of the sovereign enforced by sanctions; 'the sheriff's star must be seen as constituting a sacrament of justice, whose worth does not depend on the worthiness of the man who administers it' (Bazin, 1971: 146). But because it is noon, the norm, and all things normal, have been suspended for the brief duration of the in-between. Which is the phenomenological space of the exception and the exceptional. For Schmitt, only 'this definition can do justice to a borderline concept ... a borderline concept is not a vague concept, but one pertaining to the outermost sphere' (Schmitt, 2005: 5), so that the state of exception 'includes any kind of severe economic or political disturbance that requires the application of extraordinary measures' (Strong, 2007: v). Rugged individualism remains an eternal and universal constant.

> The norm requires a homogenous medium.... There exists no norm that is applicable to chaos. *For a legal order to make sense, a normal situation must exist, and he is sovereign who definitely decides whether this normal situation actually exists.... The decision parts here from the legal norm, and (to formulate it paradoxically) authority proves that to produce law it need not be based on law.* (Schmitt, 2005: 13)

He is sovereign who definitely decides whether this normal situation actually exists is a nice way of summarizing *High Noon*: if Ransom Stoddard's lament was 'What kind of community have I come to here?', Marshal Kane's lament is 'Who are you people?'[58] Kane is an even more performatively spectacular avatar of decisionism than is Doniphon precisely because he does not reflect the communal natural justice of the community (kill Valence) but signifies nothing other than the private/personal sovereignty of his own will which, in the event of victory in combat, will decide the issue of identity ('truth') for the to-be-regenerated town. But here is where everything turns to horse manure for those who are bourgeois-at-heart: 'For its institutions to claim legitimacy, a liberal democracy must be able to distinguish who is a member of the community and who is not—who is "inside" and who is "outside"' (Ryan, 1996: 29). But if, as in *Lord of the* Flies, liberal democracy fails at that very moment, either through absence of a generative unanimity or a factual error of identification (*meconnaissance*), political decision-making is thrown into crisis and the *demos* instantly reverts to the primitive, which is the beginning acted out all over again: *whose* definition of the enemy-other-out-law prevails? Or, as Golding's boys would have it: *what* is the Beastie?

If we construct the problem in the form of a Schmittean check-list, Kane receives a perfect score. For Schmitt, 'All law is "situational law"', meaning that law is never abstract or a-contextual but thoroughly grounded in the historical and the particular, effectively vitiating both the Aristotelian and Kantian conceptions of jurisprudence.

> It is precisely the exception that makes relevant the subject of sovereignty, that is, the whole question of sovereignty.... The decision on the exception is a decision in the true sense of the word. Because a general norm, as represented by an ordinary legal prescription, can never encompass a total decision, the decision that a real exception exists cannot therefore be entirely derived from the norm. (Schmitt, 2005: 6)

---

[58] Friend or enemy?

The issue is not consensus but anti-consensus: 'What matters for the reality of legal life is who decides' (Schmitt, 2005: 34). Law is always the result of the practical exercise of some kind of power against dissenting and competing actors as Robert M. Cover showed (Cover, 1986), which invokes the cultural imaginary of those hyper-masculine spaces occupied by the Westerner.

> If such action [the decision on the exception] is not subject to controls, if it is not hampered in some way by checks and balances, as is the case in a liberal constitution, then it is clear who the sovereign is. *He decides whether there is an extreme emergency as well as what must be done to eliminate it.* Although he stands outside the normally valid legal system, he nevertheless belongs to it, for it is he who must decide whether the constitution [the legal order] needs to be suspended in its entirety. (Schmitt, 2005: 7)

So it has come to pass that Law in its purest form is realized most perfectly through the unilateral action of the executive, or the will of the executor: '*Sovereign is he who decides on the exception*' (Schmitt, 2005: 5), which is understood as superseding all normal forms of institutional procedure and due process including the declaration that the normal no longer exists based upon the extra-normative action of the 'Will'.

Although frequently read as a 'leftist' film because of its presumed sub-textual critique of McCarthyism—the liminal people representing the universal absence of political resolve during the Hollywood blacklist[59]—*High Noon* is, when examined closely, radically anti-democratic; Kane's ambiguous and ironic 'victory' at the end is a manifestation of his personal sovereignty (= rugged individualism). The film ends with one of the most iconoclastic scenes in the history of the Western: the marshal drops his 'tin star', the totem of his public authority, into the street. Cheyney Ryan comments that it is 'natural, I think, to read this act as Kane's renouncing his job as marshal. But Kane has already done that—and nothing has licensed his taking it back. The badge that he rejects is one that no longer possesses legitimacy, a badge that has endowed him with only the appearance of legal authority' (Ryan, 1996: 38). Framing the adversary as political and oneself as non-political (i.e., scientific, objective, neutral, rational, liberal, etc.) is in reality a typical and underhanded way of pursuing post-existential politics (Schmitt, 2007: 21 n 2). Political philosophy may therefore be said to constitute the reification of the banal praxis of political psychology, for political theory is premised upon

> The question of what sort of soul is best suited for what sort of regime, and what sort of soul is likely to be produced by what sort of regime, as well as some position on the basic dynamics of the human soul, especially with regard to voluntary submission to some authority. This claim about the relevance of political psychology to political philosophy assumes that there is something amiss in addressing the political question as if human beings were exclusively rational calculators or creatures of pure practical reason. (Pippin, 2010: 12–13)

For liberalism's greatest sin is not its cowardice, its chronic inability to embrace decisionism; rather, it is its hypocrisy, for it intentionally veils the live-giving *potentia*

---

[59] Just on the off-chance that the author is not truly dead, there is no doubt the only thing in the mind of the screenwriter of *High Noon*, the black-listed former Communist Carl Foreman, was McCarthyism (Frankel, 2017). While this may be historically accurate, a narrowly biographical attempt at explanation totally ignores the transfiguring *mythic* dimension of the film 'text'.

of myth/*mythos*. Liberalism as a 'rational scheme is one thing; what it comes to mean in the actual lives of mortal, psychologically complex persons in some community at some time is another thing' (Pippin, 2010: 14).

> Moreover, at the first-order level [*Existenz*] of political life, for actual participants decisions are made, commitments affirmed, sacrifices made, and the like, all in a way that would appear to be much more decisively oriented from and grounded in one's experiences, sometimes crisis experiences of fear, humiliation, resentment, pride and so forth. (Pippin, 2010: 16)

The problem, therefore, is whether liberal society

> ...can really leave behind what it was. By this means leaving behind the mythic and largely feudal notion of nearly complete self-sufficiency and self-reliance, an honor code, the unavoidability of violence in establishing and maintaining proper status and order, a largely male and isolated world. (Pippin, 2010: 24)

Liberalism and political rationality can never compel sacrifice, but, even more importantly, neither can adequately explain sacrifice when it occurs voluntarily. So that if and when the salvific Decider-Westerner does announce himself and voluntarily exposes himself to Death (and Murder), the result is an apocalypse (the unveiling)—although it should not be so, for we should not have allowed ourselves to have become so decadent in the first place. The discarding of the tin star by the 'marshal,' now unveiled as the Decider, acquires a decidedly Schmittean significance. In a common but absurdly benign reading of the tin star, Kane is construed as a western Horatio, a mimetic figure who is complying with the genre's requirement that the too-powerful Westerner undertake voluntary exile in order to preserve the democratic republic of the limpid. In a slightly less unpersuasive interpretation, Kane's gesture is the public performance of moral contempt, the passing of private judgment upon the publicly liminal people for failing to keep faith with the strictures of a communal natural law whose *telos* it is for the exceptional citizen(s) to enforce. The truest reading is the Schmittean one: by throwing the hollow symbol (or the symbol of hollowness for tin doth not maketh the Man) into the horse manure of the town's streets, the marshal is proclaiming his own sovereignty, not merely as the decider of the state of exception but as the founder of a new micro-sovereignty, one that serves as the repository of an unmediated community of natural law: The Family. For it is only after Kane abandons both the tin star and the tin town[60] that he consummates his marriage to 'The Bride' Amy Fowler (Grace Kelly). Pippin has written convincingly on the vitalistic autonomy of the 'private bond' between Husband and Wife versus the anti-virile contractual nature of public relationships in *High Noon* (Pippin, 2010: 64–65), but the issue is of far greater onto-political significance than he imagines. (Graham, 1980) In fact, it takes us directly back to Hobbes' *Leviathan* and *Lord of the Flies*. Kane substitutes the naturalist family-unit for the artificial liberal-contractual commonwealth of the atomistic *demos*, the indeterminate and shapeless mass of liminal people who did not technically abandon the marshal but, far more damningly, collectively chose to *vote* against him in the Church assembly in favor of the enemy, Frank Miller, Kane's rival for sovereignty and, by implication,

60 'Tinsel' town?

an alternative 'Founding Father'. When the liminal people publicly vote against the formation of a posse—meaning that they fail to declare the state of exception, relying instead upon the *un*-grounded norms-of-the-normal—they implicitly elect Miller the de facto leader of the community, meaning that the only sovereignty available to the marshal as the Westerner is of his own kin (it also means that Miller has weirdly achieved the rule of One Man through an indirect version of Commonwealth-by-Institution—the *demos* voted for a tyrant). But Family is risky when public order is newly minted, for as Hobbes points out the micro-sovereignty of the Father-in-the-Wilderness only holds good until such time as he is overwhelmed by the larger and more organized forces of the public state; in other words, until he and his kith and kin are 'regulated'.[61] Riskier still is that the invocation of the Family as the true (natural) sovereignty invokes an equal, and possibly even greater, parallel movement toward the existential antithesis of the Westerner: the *feminine*.

High Noon's specular staging of the myth-performance of decisionism holds the key to one of the most commented upon aspects of the Westerner: his hyper-neurotic taciturnity. If my thesis of the Western hero as ritual sacrificer is correct then the inability of the Westerner to articulate (anything) is due to his sacrificial *telos*: his being is identical to the act that permits the development of the representational field itself[62] so that he cinematically inhabits the space–time of pre-re-presentation, although for narrative purposes he must a-chronologically mingle with those who historically come after him (he is symbolically prehistoric but cinematically walks around town carrying a six-gun). Ritualistic sacrifice of both Other and Self is the necessary supplement to Jane Tompkins' otherwise astute observation: 'The death of the heart, or, rather, its scarification and eventual sacrifice, is what the Western genre, more than anything else, is about. The numbing of the capacity to feel, which allows the hero to inflict pain on others, requires the sacrifice of his own heart, a sacrifice kept hidden under his toughness, which is inseparable from his heroic character' (Tompkins, 1992: 219). Both the feminine and the Female can form no 'vital' part of the Westerner precisely because the anti-vitalist domain of the social is the very thing that can only come into being subsequent to the Decider's required disappearance—or, in the case of Tom Doniphon, his (en-)forced decomposition. We also have to reconsider the other great trope of the Western: the emptiness of space ('the desert') as the romantic conceit of the gunfighter.

> Nature is the one transcendent thing, the one thing larger than man (and it is constantly portrayed as immense), the ideal toward which human nature strives.... The hero imitates the desert's fierceness ... and its silence in his frugal way with language.... the sayings of cowboy heroes, by their brevity, acknowledge as do the sayings of the desert fathers, the importance of things that cannot be said.... Not *imitatio Christi* but *imitatio naturae.*

[61] There is an uncomfortable invocation of this in the film which is almost subliminal. On their death march towards Kane, Frank Miller's younger brother Ben, on pure and unknowable impulse, smashes a storefront window and takes from it a bridal headdress, or bonnet (Graham, 1980: 249).

[62] To repeat Burton Mack's comment on Girard: 'All systems that give structure to human society have been generated from [the scapegoat mechanism]: language, kinship systems, taboos, codes of etiquette, patterns of exchange, rites, and civil institutions. Thus, a theory of sacrifice has produced a comprehensive account of human social formation, religion, and culture' (Mack, 1987: 7, 1–21).

As the inventor of generative sacrifice on the Frontier, the Westerner is also the (desert) 'Father' of culture and, therefore, must originate within a domain of emptiness that is not empty space but space-as-emptiness, the primal perfection of nothing(s). Again Tompkins is correct in asserting the centrality of the correlation between the natural and the 'pre-feminine' but she misses the sacrificial dimension of the conceit as she inadvertently admits: 'nature, which has played only a small role in the [women's] domestic novel where it is always pastoral and benign, dominates the Western, dwarfing the human figure with its majesty, the only divinity worshipped in this genre other than manhood itself' (Tompkins, 1992: 37–38, 84, 44, 47, 72, 39). The sacrificial is interwoven into Tompkins' account of the Westerner but only in its erotic aspect, not the metaphysical. For the metaphysical is the part that is now missing, meaning that all we have left after the marshal has been subjugated to the domestic rule/role of Woman is the feminine stuff which is the detritus of the foundational act of murder. If we dwell within the rhetorical spaces of the Western genre it means that when we say 'Woman' we mean weak which means the absence of 'Man' which is the presence of the real, the desire for Being realized. The proof of the pudding of decisionism is in the killing, so now new dramatic possibilities emerge. What if the Westerner, performatively fecund with the power of the gun, for decisionism is just a fancy word for sex, reveals himself and nothing happens; meaning that he has, somehow, been 'feminized'. What if no foundational ritual is possible at all—meaning that he, somehow, has been symbolically (or otherwise) castrated. For that genre-busting possibility, tantamount to the death of the Western, an entirely different narrative form, or genre, is required, one that is explicitly grounded, preferably in a manner combining hysteria and paranoia, on the antinomy of the Western—that in the absence of the Frontier, restorative decisionism is no longer conceivable let alone practical and has at its dramatic center the problematic feminization of the male. The time is permanently out of joint, for the community is populated exclusively by liminal people perpetually threatened with the destruction of civilization and the return to the state of nature, the predetermined outcome of the catastrophic and claustrophobic collapse of the post-Frontier upon itself, the Big Nowhere suspended under the opposite of noon which is midnight. Evermore. Which is another genre in its own right: *Noir*.

In one of the greatest books ever written on popular culture in Cold War America Peter Biskind firmly placed *High Noon* within the *radical* tradition of the 'Fifties film': it simultaneously rejects both liberal consensus (*Twelve Angry Men*) and conservative reaction (*On the Waterfront*) focusing instead on the dramatic foregrounding of the liminal people who signify the uncertainty of identity, which is an archetypal characteristic of *noir*, resulting in the creation of a new and hybrid sub-genre: the *noir Western* (Biskind, 1983: 1–6, 44–49). Which all turns upon the tricks of the art of narration. Stephen King said that the horror film is a fairy-tale for teenagers, meaning that even if you follow all of the rules you *may* still die in the end. *Noir*, by contrast, is a fairy-tale for adults, meaning that even if you follow all of the rules you are *guaranteed* to die in the end; the real problem is that even if you break all of the rules you are *also* guaranteed to die in the end, but this time as the result of being buried alive in the infernal cesspit of the interminably liminal people, a.k.a. the Big Nowhere. The City-of-*Noir*, the suspension of meaning, is what happens after liberalism has eliminated all forms of community-regenerating violence. Death signifies nothing and nobody. *Noir* signifies the absence of exit. It is the post-public private eternal now of unruggedly post-individualistic males who no longer own their own 'six-gun'. Contemporary man wants to be the Westerner but just can't. It is the end of the Frontier. It is Hadleyville *sub specie aeternitas*. It is Hollywood.

For Kane is the re-builder of cities.

And he has left with his Bride.

References

Primary Texts

High Noon (Lionsgate 2008; directed by Fred Zimmermann).
The Man Who Shot Liberty Valance (Paramount 2009; directed by John Ford).

Secondary Texts

Battaglia, A. (1980). *Toward a formulation of natural law*. Seabury Press.
Bazin, A. (1971). *What is cinema? Volume II*. (H. Gray, Trans.). University of California Press.
Bell, J. A. (2006). *Philosophy at the edge of Chaos: Gilles Deleuze and the philosophy of difference*. University of Toronto Press.
Biskind, P. (1983). *Seeing is believing: How Hollywood taught us to stop worrying and love the fifties*. Pluto Press.
Boehnke, M. (2001). Myth and law in the films of John Ford. *Journal of Law and Society, 28*(1), 47–63.
Brodey, I. S. (2009). Cactus roses and camellias: Flowers, action, and masculinity in "Sanjuro" and "the man who shot liberty valance'. *Japan Women's Journal, 36*, 92–116.
Cawelti, J. G. (1999). *The six-gun mystique sequel*. Bowling Green State University Popular Press.
Cover, R. M. (1986). Violence and the word. *Yale Law Journal., 95*, 1601–1629.
Cropsey, J. (1995). Foreword. In H. Meier (Ed.), *Carl Schmitt and Leo Strauss: The hidden dialogue*. (J. H. Lomax, Trans., pp. ix–xii). Chicago University Press.
D'Entreves, A. P. (1970). *Natural law: An introduction to legal philosophy*. Hutchinson University Library.
De Benoist, A. (2013). *Carl Schmitt today: Terrorism, 'just' war, and the state of emergency*. ARKTOS.
Derrida, J. (2005). *The politics of friendship* (G. Collins, Trans.). Verso.
Dienstag, J. F. (2012). A storied shooting: Liberty valance and the paradox of sovereignty. *Political Theory, 40*(3), 290–318.
Drexler, P. (2001). The German courtroom film during the Nazi period: Ideology, aesthetics, historical context. *Journal of Law and Society, 28*(1), 64–78.
Evans, D.-N. (2010). The duty of reason: Kantian ethics in *High Noon*. In J. L. McMahon & B. S. Csaki (Eds.), *The philosophy of the Western* (pp. 171–183). The University Press of Kentucky.

Finnis, J. (1980). *Natural law and natural rights*. Clarendon Press.
Frankel, G. (2017). *High noon: The Hollywood blacklist and the making of an American classic*. Bloomsbury.
Gallagher, T. (1986). *John Ford: The man and his films*. University of California Press.
Girard, R. (1978). *To double business bound: Essays on literature, mimesis, and anthropology*. The Johns Hopkins University Press.
Girard, R. (1986). *The Scapegoat* (Y. Freccero, Trans.). The Johns Hopkins University Press.
Graham, D. (1980). The women of "high noon": A revisionist view. *Rocky Mountain Review of Language and Literature, 34*(4), 243–251.
Grandin, G. (2019). *The end of the myth: From the frontier to the border wall in the mind of America*. Metropolitan Books.
Grimshaw, M. (2013). Introduction. In J. Taubes (Ed.), *To Carl Schmitt: Letters and reflections* (K. Tribe, Trans., pp. ix–xliii). Columbia University Press.
Heidegger, M. (1992). *Parmenides* (A. Schuwer and R. Rojcewicz, Trans.). Indiana University Press.
Hirst, P. (1987). Carl Schmitt's decisionism. *Telos, 72*, 15–26.
Hobbes, T. (1991). *Leviathan*. Fully corrected 1651 edition, Cambridge University Library, Syn.3.65.1 Edited by Richard Tuck. Cambridge University Press.
Kaes, A. (1993). The cold Gaze: Notes on mobilization and modernity. *New German Critique, 59*, 105–117.
Kitses, J. (1969). *Horizons West: Anthony Mann, Budd Boetticher, Sam Peckinpah: Studies of authorship within the Western*. Indiana University Press.
Livingstone, D. W. (2009). Spiritedness, reason, and the founding of law and order: John Ford's the man who shot liberty valance. *Perspectives on Political Science, 38*(4), 217–227.
Luhr, W., & Lehman, P. (1977). *Authorship and narrative in the cinema: Issues in contemporary aesthetics and criticism*. Capricorn Books.
Mack, B. (1987). Introduction: Religion and ritual. In R. G. Hammerton-Kelly (Ed.), *Violent origins: Walter Burkert, Rene Girard, and Jonathan Z. Smith on ritual killing and cultural formation* (pp. 1–72). Stanford University Press.
Maffesoli, M. (1996). *The time of the tribes: The decline of individualism in mass society* (D. Smith, Trans.). Sage Publications.
Meier, H. (1995). *Carl Schmitt and Leo Strauss: The hidden dialogue* (J. H. Lomax, Trans.). Chicago University Press.
Meyer, P. N. (2007–2008). Why are the characters in a death penalty brief like the characters in a movie? *Vermont Law Review, 32*, 877–917.
Mouffe, C. (2005). *On the political*. Routledge.
Nisbet, R. (1974). *The social philosophers: Community and conflict in Western thought*. Heinneman.
Pearson, S. A. (2007). It is tough to be the second toughest guy in a tough town: Ask the man who shot liberty valance. *Perspectives on Political Science, 36*(1), 23–28.
Pippin, R. B. (2010). *Hollywood Westerns and American myth: The importance of Howard Hawks and John Ford for political philosophy*. Yale University Press.
Rohdie, S. (1975). Who shot liberty valance? *Salgamundi., 29*, 159–171.
Ross, D. (2004). *Violent democracy*. Cambridge University Press.
Ryan, C. (1996). Print the legend: Violence and recognition in *the man who shot liberty valance*. In J. Denvir (Ed.), *Legal reelism: Movies as legal texts* (pp. 23–43). University of Illinois Press.
Sartre, J.-P. (1990). Preface. In F. Fanon (Ed.), *The wretched of the earth* (C. Farrington, Trans., pp. 7–26). Penguin Books.
Schmitt, C. (1999). Ethic of state and pluralistic state. In C. Mouffe (Ed.), *The challenge of Carl Schmitt* (D. Dyzenhaus, Trans., pp. 195–208). Verso.
Schmitt, C. (2003). *The nomos of the earth in the international law of the Jus Publicum Europaeum* (G. L. Ulmen, Trans.). Telos Press Publishing.
Schmitt, C. (2005). *Political theology: Four chapters on the concept of sovereignty* (G. Schwab, Trans.). University of Chicago.

Schmitt, C. (2007). *The concept of the political* (G. Schwab, Trans.). University of Chicago Press.

Sherwin, R. C. (1994). Law frames: Historical truth and narrative necessity in a criminal case. *Stanford Law Review, 47*(1), 39–83.

Simpson, A. (2010). Settlement's secret. *Cultural Anthropology, 26*(2), 205–217.

Slotkin, R. (1973). *Regeneration through violence: The mythology of the American frontier*. Wesleyan University Press.

Slotkin, R. (1985). *The fatal environment: The myth of the frontier in the age of industrialization, 1800–1890*. Atheneum.

Slotkin, R. (1992). *Gunfighter nation: The myth of the frontier in twentieth-century America*. University of Oklahoma Press.

Spinks, L. (2008). Except for law: Raymond Chandler, James Ellroy, and the politics of exception. *South Atlantic Quarterly, 107*(1), 121–143.

Strauss, L. (2007). Notes on Carl Schmitt. In C. Schmitt (Ed.), *The concept of the political* (G. Schwab, Trans., pp. 117–129). University of Chicago Press.

Strong, T. B. (2007). Foreword: Dimensions of the new debate around Carl Schmitt. In C. Schmitt (Ed.), *The concept of the political* (G. Schwab, Trans., pp. i–xxxix). University of Chicago Press.

Taubes, J. (2013). *To Carl Schmitt: Letters and reflections* (K. Tribe, Trans.). Columbia University Press.

Tillman, J. (2007). *High noon* and the problems of American political obligation. *Perspectives on Political Science, 36*(1), 39–45.

Tompkins, J. (1992). *West of everything: The inner life of Westerns*. Oxford University Press.

Warshow, R. (1999). Movie chronicle: The Westerner. In J. Kitses & G. Rickman (Eds.), *The Western reader* (pp. 35–48). Limelight Editions.

Winkler, M. M. (1985). Classical mythology and the Western film. *Comparative Literature Studies, 22*(4), 516–540.

Wolin, R. (1992). Carl Schmitt the conservative revolutionary: Habitus and the aesthetics of horror. *Political Theory, 20*(3), 424–447.

Wright, W. (1975). *Six guns and society: A structural study of the Western*. University of California Press.

Yack, B. (1992). *The longing for total revolution: Philosophic sources of social discontent from Rousseau to Marx and Nietzsche*. University of California Press.

Zizek, S. (1999). Carl Schmitt in the age of post-politics. In C. Mouffe (Ed.), *The challenge of Carl Schmitt* (pp. 18–37). Verso.

Chapter 5
'A Woman Only Loves a Real Man': Metaphysical Desire and the Crisis of Undifferentiation in Akira Kurosawa's *Yojimbo* and *Rashomon*

Abstract This chapter continues the discussion of the themes dealt with in Chap. 4 but in relation to two classic 'Eastern' or samurai films, *Yojimbo* (1961) and *Rashomon* (1950), both directed by Akira Kurosawa. Both films are concerned with the relationship between the mimetic crisis of undifferentiation ('the war of all against all') and legal reasoning as a variant of the scapegoat mechanism. *Yojimbo* examines the ways in which the restoration of justice cannot be successfully achieved in the absence of the use of armed force, but in a manner that spectacularly parodies the Girardian and Schmittean themes of the Westerns: here it is the lone swordsman who must scapegoat the community in order to expel the Enemy which turns out to be everybody, necessitating the apocalypse. *Rashomon*, a much more complex film, draws our attention to the centrality of existential envy and metaphysical desire to violence. Superficially a 'hybrid' of the samurai and legal thriller film, *Rashomon* is a meditation on the tension between external and internal mediations, which Girard identifies as latently inhabiting every relationship between the model and his or her imitator. External mediation, which is a by-product of social hierarchy, works to reduce mimetic rivalry by establishing the 'correct' social spaces between model and imitator; internal mediation, in contrast, is the unstable bourgeois counterpart of 'the ego and its own'. Few societies were as hierarchical as pre-modern Japan; there, external mediation was invested with the status of a categorical imperative. And it is precisely here that Kurosawa stages his two homicidal dramas of mimetic rivalry. The key to solving the mystery of what really happened in the grove of bamboo lies with correctly situating all four protagonists within their respective internal or 'private' mimetic crisis. Frequently, and absurdly, mis-read as a post-modern meditation on the relativity of truth, *Rashomon* is much better understood as a Japanese social drama about mimesis. All of the witnesses must lie because to tell the truth would be to admit the truly unbearable which is their failure to convincingly imitate their respective models that are the entirety of their being: an honest woodcutter who robs the dead, a noblewoman who wants to kill her husband, a samurai who is afraid to die, and a bandit who is afraid to kill. Each witness is not merely a failure in the emulation of their respective model, and they are the exact opposite of it, meaning that they are devoid of a true existence.

E. M. Wilson, *Rene Girard, Law, Literature, and Cinema*,
https://doi.org/10.1007/978-981-97-1156-7_5

Keywords *Sengoku-jidai* · *Jidai-geki* · *Ken-geki* · *Chambara* · *Ninjo* · *Giri* · The male gaze

5.1 The Archetypal Themes of the *Chambara*

The other great cinematic genre besides the Western that portrays law as a form of mythology is 'the Eastern', or the Samurai film, also known as the *chambara* (sword film), *Jidai-geki* ('period film'[1]), or *Ken-geki* ('sword-theatre').[2] And, as a type of cinematic genre, the *Ken-geki*, no less than the gunfighter film, must comply with the perquisites of encoded imagery and dialogue that are necessary to convey a mythic view of the world that is specific to that genre.[3]

> Genres are formal systems for transforming the world in which we actually live into self-contained, coherent and controllable structures of meaning. Genres can thus be considered to function in a way that a language system does—offering a vocabulary and a set of rules which allow us to 'shape' reality, thus making it appear less random and disordered (Greenfield et al., 2001, p. 18).

And as a genre of its own, *chambara* must be situated within a defining History, in this case Japanese. The Eastern most commonly takes place in one of two periods of Japanese history: the middle or late phase of the Tokugawa Shogunate (*Edo-jidai*; c.1600–1868) that arose after the *Sengoku-jidai* Wars or 'The Warring States Period' (1467–1600) following the collapse of the Ashikaga Shogunate, or the very early part of the Meiji Restoration (*Sugato Sanshiro*; 1868–1912) which marked the commencement of the 'Westernization' of Japan. Apart from extreme levels of violence and social disruption, what unites both of these periods is their status as eras of liminality: the *Sengoku-jidai* was the near-genocidal transition under Oda Nobunaga from political chaos to the rigid hierarchical stability of the of Tokugawa shogunate which ended with an equally socially destabilizing shift towards the Westernization of the Meiji. This meant that both of these time frames were extremely a-typical of Japanese history wherein social identities and conventional moral codes of conduct were in a high degree of flux and uncertainty. In Girardian terms, they are the two periods in Japanese history that witnessed the most naked struggles for cultural hegemony between the two primary mechanisms for regulating mimetic rivalry, external mediation, and internal mediation. The historical stipulations of the genre signify, therefore, a fundamental difference between the Western and the Eastern: the Western is about the act of foundation, the cinematic enactment of the mythology of the 'frontier society'. From the American mythological perspective.

[1] Always set sometime before 1868, the beginning of the Meiji Period (Galloway, 2005, p. 214).

[2] Leading examples of sword theatre include: *Seven Samurai* (1954)*; The Hidden Fortress* (1958)*; Throne of Blood* (1957)*; Sanjuro* (1962)*; Kagemusha* (1980)*; Ran* (1985)*; Hara-Kiri* (1962)*; Samurai Rebellion* (1967)*; Sword of Doom* (1966)*; The Twilight Samurai* (2002)*; The Hidden Blade* (2004)*; Three Outlaw Samurai* (1964).

[3] See Chap. 4, above.

> Every nation's principal myths are about starting out, meeting the wilderness head-on and taming it, breaking the spirit of indigenous enemies and declaring the land and the inhabitants the food of this new collective self. Myth is a sort of family history, an account of a migration to a new world, and who the heroes were in the great struggle to make a home on someone else's property. Myths don't look for justification; the great thrust of each is the boldness and aggression needed to turn strange, unknown territory into a collective self (Paul Christensen qtd. Brodey, 2009, pp. 116–118).

The Eastern, in marked contrast, is more about the act of restoration of a previous state of cultural order, or *nomos*.[4] Just as the Western is always 'progressive' no matter how 'conservative' on the superficial level, so is the Eastern always 'reactionary,' although in the best possible way; its violence is always restorative rather than creative because what is at issue is the recovery of the life-sustaining past, the realm of Being, rather than the creation of a future that is nihilistically devoid of certainty and transparency, wherein images no longer correspond to realities: *meconnaissance*. Therefore, mimesis and mimetic desire, the successful emulation of the model as the answer to the question of 'To be or not to be,' operate under an extreme level of Schmitt-like existential intensity.

> Post-war Japan [1945–1952] also needed a new myth to explain its most recent re-founding. Japan's post-war new beginning echoed the drastic reformation of society during the Meiji Restoration, when Western ways were explicitly adopted and the samurai class lost nearly all its earlier power and privilege. Interestingly, each round of westernization resulted in a direct loss of power for the Japanese military. The importance of samurai films in the post-war years also helps us understand Japan's ambivalent response (and mixed success with) the process of democratization and demilitarization (Brodey, 2009, pp. 98–99).[5]

Which bears directly upon the archetypal themes of the Eastern, those situations or symbols that achieve a dominance within the genre on the basis of their 'elemental' relation to the audience; 'violence is its key component' of the *chambira*, deployed for the purpose of recovering a lost past rather than establishing a new world, 'expressed through a series of familiar character types and conflicts' (Silver, 1977, p. 35). The Eastern version of The Westerner (or gun-fighter[6]) is the *Swordsman*, who may appear as a *samurai* (a swordsman pledged to a master, or *daimyo*), a *ronin* (a 'masterless' swordsman, or 'hired sword'), or more infrequently a *kyokaku* (a commoner entitled to carry a sword[7]). With the swordsman

---

[4] See Chap. 1, above.

[5] Which is central to the film work of Akira Kurosawa: 'Above all, it is necessary to emphasize Kurosawa's work as a project, as a specific undertaking influenced by an immediate social challenge (i.e., the cataclysm of the second world war and the general cultural upheavals that it precipitated)' (Price, 1999, p. XV).

[6] The Japanese appropriation of the icons of the Western and then re-exported as a 'Westernized' version of *chambara* is an old chestnut of film criticism often associated with the West's embrace of Kurosawa: '…his affection for detectives, doctors, and samurai as characters—all have endeared him to Western audiences and have helped make his work comprehensible in relation to Hollywood movies, especially if gunfighters are imaginatively substituted for samurai' (Prince, 1999, p. x), which, however, can only be taken so far. See below.

[7] The rarest of the three archetypal heroes, the most outstanding example is Toshiro Mifune as Kikuchiyo in Akira Kurosawa's *Seven Samurai*.

as the archetypal character embedded within the genre-based historical landscape of feudal or pre-Meiji Japan, the 'archetypal plot' of *chambara* is the protagonists' internal struggle with two competing principles: *giri* ('the notion of duty or fealty which each warrior owes to his master') and *ninjo* ('natural conscience…or proper judgment') (Silver, 1977, p. 22) which provides the narrative framework of a drama that depicts the struggle between external behavior and internal inclination.

> Obviously, if the warrior…trusts in his own *ninjo*, then any discrepancy between what he sees as correct action, and what *giri* requires him to do—for instance, to participate in what appears to him an unjust feud with a rival clan—might induce schizophrenia; and this…type of interior conflict is a mainstay of dramatic structure in the samurai film (Silver, 1977, p. 22).[8]

And as with the Western, there is a direct correspondence bewteen the archetypal theme and the icon, that thing or image that most simply, and most powerfully, emotionally connects the audience with the genre-defining themes and characters. Instead of the gun, the central icon that visually signifies the *Ken-geki* film is, not surprising, the sword itself, which can come in one or more of three variants:[9] the 'long sword' (*katana; daito; tachi*), the 'short sword' (*wakizashi*), and the 'dagger' (*tanto*), the last proving central to the reconstruction of the 'truth of the events' in *Rashomon.* As samurai film expert Alain Silver incisively remarks.

> The primary *genre* expectation of *chambara* is quite obviously the swordsman. Whether this character is developed as a hero or an anti-hero [*Yojimbo*; *Rashomon*], his physical introduction into the scene and the viewer's apprehension of him as the potential dramatic center are basic to all samurai films. While this character does not need to be a true samurai…he must, even if a *ronin* or *kyokaku*, be armed. In this manner, the sword may be seen as *chambara*'s fundamental icon and the whole *genre* as a manifestation of that ideal which regarded the swordsman and his weapon as one (Silver, 1977, p. 35).

'*While this character does not need to be a true samurai*' takes us to the heart of the sword-theatre genre and exposes the mimetic heart of the dramatic struggle between *giri* and *ninjo*: the attempt to determine who is the 'true' samurai, or the 'real thing', meaning that identities and the ability to establish oneself as possessing a defining truth have been put into basic doubt, which, in Japanese terms, would constitute a form of psycho-social trauma.[10] Expressed in Girardian terms, this would imply a possibly interminable conflict between external and internal forms of mediation, raising the serious possibility that the establishment of the final, or defining, truth of any social actor may not be possible. Just as with Oedipus, the protagonist of the *Ken-geki* may be confronting the 'plague' of undifferentiation.[11]

---

[8] Possibly the greatest, and certainly the purest, example of this genre defining plot is Masaki Kobayashi's *Samurai Rebellion.*

[9] It is permissible for the samurai to carry more than one bladed weapon, because the word means 'the two-sword men'.

[10] From the perspective of 'warring absolutes', a strong case can be made that the two greatest *chambara* films ever made were *Samurai Rebellion* and *Har-Kiri.* In the former, the 'rebel' samurai is actually the 'true' one, while in the latter, all of the 'real' ones were really 'un-real'.

[11] See Chap. 1, above.

5.2 *Chambara*, Mimetic Rivalry, and the Crisis of Undifferentiation

If we look at the films of Akira Kurosawa (1910–1998), one of the most important and, in his own way, subversive of the *chambara* directors,we notice that,some what uncharacteristically, they do not 'dramatize a "timeless" Japan, an unchanging national essence, but rather the traumas of historical transition' (Prince, 1999, p. 136). The clearest evidence of 'Kurosawa's avoidance of portrayals of a timeless Japan' is the fact that his 'narratives tend to take place during moments of historical transition, as the old order crumbles and the new has not yet appeared' (Prince, 1999, pp. 380–383), so that, as with Sophocles' *Oedipus Tyrannus*, his dramas unfold within environs that are contaminated by the 'plague' of undifferentiation,[12] which are very generally those that marked the *Sengoku- jidai*, political and cultural chaos that resulted in the breakdown of firm demarcations of social identity. Although *Rashomon* (1950) is set in the late Heian period and *Yojimbo* (1961) takes place at the very end of the Edo era, the majority of Kurosawa's sword-theatres, and many of the films that he is most well-known for—*The Seven Samurai* (1954), *Throne of Blood* (1957); *The Hidden Fortress* (1958); *Kagemusha* (1980); *Ran* (1985)—are set during the time of the Warring States.

> The Sengoku period has been characterized as an age of change, a time when the Japanese world had turned 'upside down' as the boundaries of class or vassalage became unstuck as 'persons in inferior positions challenged those in authority and often took mastery over them' (Neil McMullin qtd. Prince, 1999, p. 204). Kurosawa is attracted by these fluid class boundaries and the new potentials for human realization they offer, as well as to the social and economic changes characterizing the era. 'The troubled times of Japan's civil wars provided the lower classes with both the occasion for independence and the opportunities for self-advancement. While the feudal wars brought destruction and turmoil, they served also to encourage social mobility and widespread economic growth' (John Whitney Hall qtd. Prince, 1999, p. 204). The changes of the sixteenth century have been compared with the Meiji period in terms of a comparable release of cultural energies and restructuring of society (Prince, 1999, p. 204).

Kurosawa stated "I think I'm the only one who has ever made films about the sixteenth-century civil wars" (Prince, 1999, p. 205), and there is a good reason for this: it was difficult, perhaps impossible, to assimilate a tale of the *Sengoku-jidai* into the prescribed form of the samurai genre.

> I think that there's a misunderstanding not only on the part of Westerners, but on the part of younger-generation Japanese as to what a Samurai is. In fact, the profession of the warrior began around the eleventh or twelfth century and most of the films that you and I see are set in the seventeenth or eighteenth century, a period of peace when the professional warrior had an entirely different code of ethics and way of behaving. This was imposed by the Tokugawa Shogunate of that time and its atmosphere is entirely different from that period I'm much more interested in, which is the late sixteenth century.... The warrior class had much more

[12] See Chap. 1, above. I discuss the plague motif in greater detail below.

freedom at that time; a peasant could still become a warrior then (Akira Kurosawa qtd. Prince, 1999, pp. 205–206).[13]

Girard argues that, historically, there are two ways to mediate mimetic rivalry: external and internal. Historically, external mediation corresponds to class-based societies; 'As long as social difference or any other form of differentiation is present to channel mimetic desire, its conflictual dimension remains contained' (Oughourlian, 2010, p. 20). When external mediation prevails, the model operates as an obstacle to the proliferating mimetic desires of the subject by precluding the possibility of true rivalry, for a serf can never be 'like' a knight. And to take world literature's single greatest example of this, we can say with total confidence that the impoverished gentry Don Quixote can directly imitate his chosen model of Amadis of Gaul, but that the hedonistic peasant Sancho Panza cannot because the social space between the real peasant and the delusional knight-errant supremo is too great; socially, Quixote more nearly approximates the ideal; therefore, he can base his actions directly upon the model. Similarly, Quixote can never enter into mimetic rivalry with Amadis (as opposed to mere non-acquisitive imitation) because the latter's insurmountable status as the 'ideal' enables 'him' to act as an external mediator: Amadis is the supreme 'real' although he is totally non-existent (Oughourlian, 2010, pp. 20–21). Cervantes brilliantly demonstrates that the affective power of the mediator stands in an inverted relationship to his ontological status—the less real he is as the 'Ideal', the more mimetically powerful he becomes as the model. What Cervantes presents us with is a double-edged Girardian practical joke: in a manner that prefigures the drama of the enactment of his dis-order which is the 'quest,' Quixote's original error lies in mis-recognizing the false for the real (*meconnaissance*): he 'reads' interprets the chivalric romances of Amadis as historical accounts, causing the undifferentiation of truth and fable. Alfred Schutz has described this epistemological manoeuvre brilliantly.

> Let us look first at Don Quixote's world of chivalry…. Again and again the ingenious knight refutes any doubt on the part of outsiders that the heroes of whom the books of chivalry give an account have ever lived and that their adventures occurred as described in the books. He has good arguments to proffer. The institution of knights errant, he explains … is universally acknowledged and authenticated. The story of Fierrabras took place in the time of Charlemagne, the deeds of King Arthur are recorded in the histories and annals in England, in the King's armory in Madrid Roland's horn can be seen even to this day. Furthermore, the books which deal with the life and history of the knights describe in all details the family, time, place, action of this or that knight day by day. Based on these reports, Don Quixote can describe Amadis of Gaul with all of his features, characteristics and actions so that he may say he has seen him with his own eyes. He calls this an 'evidence infallible' for their existence. In addition, is it thinkable that books printed by royal license lie? And how can one possibly doubt that giants existed in reality? In the island of Sicily shinbones and shoulder blades have been discovered of a size which show their owners were giants as tall as towers. Also the Holy Scriptures, which cannot depart from the truth by so much as

[13] The classic exposition of this last point is the character of Kikichiyo (Toshiro Mifune), 'the farmer who becomes a warrior in *Seven Samurai*', the 'ideal type' of entrepreneurial commoner 'symptomatic of the fluid class boundaries of that period, a fluidity that fascinated Kurosawa' (Prince, 1999, p. 352).

> an inch, know giants such as Goliath. If we examine why, within the reality of our natural attitude, we believe in historical events we can only refer to arguments similar to those of Don Quixote: to documents, monuments, authenticated accounts by witnesses and uninterrupted tradition (Schutz, 1967, p. 137).

Ergo, when Quixote imitates the un-real (fictitious) model, he does not technically suffer a delusion. Rather, in an act of pre-representational thinking, he substitutes the world-view of the un-real but all-powerful mediator for the perceptual consensus of the everyday and then behaves accordingly ('They might be giants'), indicating that he has entered into the realm of un-mediated undifferentiation: 'Generalized imitation has the power to create worlds that are perfectly disconnected from reality; at once orderly, stable, and totally illusory' (Dupuy, 2011, p. 209). Quixote's problem is not cognitive but libidinal; with Quixote/Amadis, we are moving away from 'ordinary' mimesis to a state more akin to possession, which Girard understands as 'an extreme form of alienation in which the subject totally absorbs the desires of another' (Girard, 1977, p. 165) which is the deadly domain of metaphysical desire and monstrous doubles.[14] In contrast, internal mediation is a sign of the egalitarian society which, in principle, is devoid of scandals or obstacles, and mimetic conflict is resolved through the direct competition between the model and the imitating/envious subject, spawning interminable violence, physical and symbolic (Palaver, 2013, p. 25). Crucially, the efficacy of external mediation rests upon the absence of direct and immediate communication, both spatial and temporal, among social actors. The true catastrophe is when rigid social hierarchies begin to break down and give way to proliferating 'democratic' or 'anarchic' choices: as 'the metaphysical distance between desiring subject and model diminishes—the key component of internal mediation—the potential for rivalry and violence increases. The more negligible this distance becomes, the more probable it is that mimesis will end in rivalry and violence' (Palaver, 2013, p. 61). Commenting on Girard, Stefano Tomelleri writes that 'where social differentiation has practically disappeared [there] the power of mimesis is most destructive'. Hence

> While the social distance between individuals gradually decreases, the mutual imitation of individual desires grows. In contemporary society, the transition from external mediation to internal mediation increases the person's illusion that he or she has a unique, autonomous, and individual desire, whereas actually differences among people are progressively disappearing. Everyone feels legitimated to compare him- or herself to others and to desire what the other has, independently of any distinction in terms of social role, job or group of reference (Tomelleri, 2015, pp. 92–93).

So it is tempting to equate a strict correlation between the Western and the Eastern, because both genres are cinematically depicting an empty landscape in cultural flux. This, however, is simplistic, because in truth the 'generic codes of Westerns and samurai films do not freely circulate from one genre to the other' (Prince, 1999, p. 17). Instead of direct imitation, the issue of aesthetic similitude seems to be one of translation, as Kurosawa himself pointed out: '"Westerns have been done over and over again and in the process a kind of grammar has evolved. I have learned from this

[14] See Chap. 1, above.

grammar of the Western"' (Akira Kurosawa qtd. Prince, 1999, p. 17). And what is this grammar? One part of it is immediately noticeable, especially in the *chambara* films produced following the American Occupation (1945–1952).

> Many samurai films deal with samurai who are in the employ of their lords and many others deal with the ronin, or unemployed, samurai; but in either case samurai behaviour is clearly prescribed by custom and constrained by the class hierarchy. Even when a samurai has fallen from his respected position in society, an implicit comparison with the prescribed codes of class might be made: much of the humor of [the Kurosawa films] *Yojimbo* and *Sanjuro* depends on the distance between [Toshiro] Mifune's shaggy, dirty, self-interested ronin and the warrior ideal (Prince, 1999, p. 15).

Which means that the *Ken-geki* does not, in the final analysis, strictly corresponds to the Western; sword theatre '"deals with myth in a way which the American Westerns cannot attempt because of different national needs, conventions and historical film traditions"' (Stuart Kaminsky qtd. Prince, 1999, p. 14). The myth of The Eastern is not the creation of the new but the exceedingly improbable restoration of the old in the face of traumatic social conflict and cultural transformation, which means that it is 'really' all about *class*, a word that Girard is somewhat reluctant to employ.

> Class identity, relations, and conflict are all central to the samurai film while being quite peripheral to the Western … Historically and socially, the gunfighter-peasant relationship is not the same as the samurai-farmer relationship. … unlike the samurai film, 'there is no distinction in the rank of characters who appear in Westerns. The sheriff, outlaw, cowboy, farmer, etc., are more or less on an equal social footing.' The samurai belonged to a distinct space in the social hierarchy that marked him off from such other classes as the farmers or the aristocracy (Prince, 1999, p. 15).

Which means that the cinematic 'myth' of the samurai cannot really work any more. The structuralist purpose of myth is to reconcile otherwise irreconcilable absolutes whereas the historical reality of Japan is one of absolute undifferentiation, and the *chambara*, as a genre of 'period' filmmaking (*Jidai-geki*) is bound to reflect this: 'If one looks at the films and reconstructs their signs … then abundant evidence emerges of an aesthetic sensibility that prizes discontinuity, shock, and the apocalyptic … narratives abound of social collapse, of psychic crisis, of worlds shaken by social, cultural, and economic conflicts' (Prince, 1999, p. 24). And more than any other director working within the genre of *Jidai-geki*, it was Kurosawa who realizes this the most clearly precisely because, as an *auteur*, his overriding and unifying theme is the traumatic suffering inflicted by cultural revolution; 'In a culture that emphasizes *giri*, or obligation, and ties of joint responsibility linking members of a group, Kurosawa has repeatedly broken with tradition to challenge the social determinants structuring the individual' (Prince, 1999, p. 3). Which Kurosaw freely admits to having done within the governing contours of contemporary Japanese history: during the Edo period of the Tokugawa shogunate, Japan was 'a very closed society; then in the Meiji era everything came rushing in from abroad at an incredible rate. We all tried to absorb this as quickly as possible—western literature, painting, music, art. So it's all part of my make-up and comes to the surface very naturally' (Akira Kurosawa qtd. Prince, 1999, p. 21). No more than John Ford, one of his favorite filmmakers, can Kurosawa avoid the strictures of the historical setting mandated by the genre.

> Kurosawa's cinema addresses the themes of modernity in the Japanese experience. His films convert them into felt challenges of individual conscience by telling stories of strong protagonists grappling with the social ills of a developing nation and the modern order: poverty, disease, industrial and political corruption, fear of the bomb. As [Marius B.] Jansen has pointed out, these dilemmas 'combine to make more complex the search for autonomy of personality and freedom of choice.' Kurosawa's cinema is powerfully resonant because it clarifies the stakes of this search and so directly, and poignantly, exhibits the probability of its failure (Prince, 1999, p. 25).

Herein lies the kernel of truth within the general assumption that '"Without the American cinema, there would be no Kurosawa"' (Joseph Andersson qtd. Prince, 1999, p. 14): the gunfighter has not absorbed the two-sword man, and he has displaced him precisely because after 1945 the global model of class relations is the American myth-lie of no class relations: unbridled, unlicensed, unlimited, and unconditional internal mediation. And in terms of cinema, the American myth (or the lie of America) is mediated by the Western.[15]

> ...the mythological appeal of the American West was precisely its supposed classlessness: it was the region where failed Easterners or oppressed Europeans could find the space and the opportunity to build a new society free of the political and economic corruptions of the old world. Drawing on this mythology, Westerns are implicit celebrations of the building of civilization, dramatizing a future full of promise and optimism...or they dramatize the collapse of the myth, the closing of the land and of the opportunities that it promised.... Westerns portray society as embodying the progressive unfolding of history, or they bitterly attack it for failing to do better. The logic of these portrayals depends on the gunfighter as a catalyst, a character free of ties to the past, obligated to no one, and thereby able to help usher in the golden future or, because of his 'pure' isolation, able to bring down violently the old order (Prince, 1999, pp. 15–16).

It is for this reason that 'Nihilism is rarely the Western's reply to history and society' opines Stephen Prince (Prince, 1999, p. 16).[16] It is very much the opposite in Japanese Easterns, particularly those of Kurosawa.[17] Despite their apparent similarities, the gunfighter and the samurai films are in reality perfect inversions of each other: the myth-lie of the Western is that there are no 'real' class differences even though there are while the myth-lie of the Eastern is that there are 'real' class differences even though there are not. Oedipus' plague of undifferentiation is the result.

---

[15] See Chap. 4, above.

[16] Here, as in so many other things, the great exception is Sergio Leone, the intensely Americanized product of the oldest culture of the Old World, but with a twist: 'Only in Sergio Leone Westerns, and in those he inspired, has a nihilist response been evident, but Leone derived his cycle of films from Japanese samurai films, specifically Kurosawa's *Yojimbo*' (Prince, 1999, p. 16).

[17] To be fair, there were other outstanding examples: 'The nihilism of a film like *Hara-Kiri* [Shochiku Ofuna, directed by Masaki Kobayashi, 1962] is the response to unyielding historical and cultural patterns' (Prince, 1999, p. 16), said patterns being the Americanized form of internally mediated modernization wherein anyone may be anything so that all are no one, or everybody is a double of someone else who is really the same.

5.3 *Yojimbo*: Trauma and the Bodyguard

Japanese film scholar Tadao Sato has pointed out that every nation's 'cinema is especially sensitive to the cross-currents of an era' (Prince, 1999, p. 25).

> Japan had cast off feudalism to embrace modernism with such haste and vigor that repercussions of the battle between old and new were being felt at all levels of society. However, as the movements in the film world have been the most active and lively, it is through film that we will witness the clearest tremors of the battle (Tadao Sato qtd. Prince, 1999, pp. 25–26).

But what this means is that on the level of the particular, the predicament of the 'activist' or 'engaged' Japanese film-maker after 1945 was not dissimilar to that of the German: the overriding need to excoriate the native culture for its responsibility in fostering the spirit of militarism, Fascism, and genocidal imperialism.[18]

> In Edo [Tokugawa] society one could not observe any emerging freedom of the individual based on the rising power of the people from the bottom. There was lacking among the people any strong critical spirit or thought pattern based on respect for individual worth (Takeo Yazaki qtd. Prince, 1999, p. 27).[19]

Accordingly, Kurosawa believed in the post-war era that 'for Japan to recover it was necessary to place a high value on the self' (Prince, 1999, p. 29);[20] even worse, the Japanese 'see self-assertion as immoral and self-sacrifice as the sensible course to take in life. We are accustomed to this teaching and had never thought to question it. I felt that without the establishment of the self as a positive value there could be no freedom and no democracy' (Kurosawa, 1983, p. 146). Like other Japanese film-makers,[21] Kurosawa was tasked with "'making films whose themes and subjects could be seen to be appropriate propaganda for the United States' desire to de-militarize and de-feudalize Japanese attitudes,'" making the adaptation of "'Western modes in a deliberate manner so as to explore the nature of Western ideals as they impact upon Japan'" (David Desser qtd. Prince, 1999, p. 72) the unifying theme of his journeyman work. His earliest films 'constitute a series of responses to the particularly sensitive dilemma of how and where the autonomous individual may be

[18] 'The wave of political repression and assassinations in the 1930s, when a virulent form of militarism cowed intellectuals and the Left with violent dreams of expanding empire and service unto death in honor of emperor and nation, demonstrated for Kurosawa the need for such a [cinematic] experiment at cross-cultural fertilization' (Prince, 1999, p. 29).

[19] Reconfirmed with the Showa-era 'Fundamentals of Our National Polity' published by the Ministry of Education in 1937: "When people determinedly count themselves as masters and assert their egos, there is nothing but contradictions and the setting of one against the other" (Prince, 1999, p. 68).

[20] It was "not until the end of the Second World War that the modernization of the country as a whole became once again one of the major concerns of Japanese intellectuals and writers. As in the Meiji period, modernization is again identified with Westernization, or more accurately … with Americanization" (Shuichi Kato qtd Prince, 1999, p. 70).

[21] During the American Occupation, Japanese studios 'were subject to firm guidelines specifying what kinds of subjects would be tolerated. Generally, films were to extoll individual freedoms and be critical of militarism and feudalism' (Prince, 1999, p. 71).

positioned in relation to more traditional cultural norms' (Prince, 1999, p. 200); as he later explained it.

> The freedom and democracy of the post-war era were not things I had fought for and won, they were granted to me by powers beyond my own. As a result, I felt it was all the more essential for me to approach them with an earnest and humble desire to learn, and to make them my own (Kurosawa, 1983, p. 145).

It follows that 'Kurosawa's radical gesture is to substitute a variant ideological conception of the self as an independent consciousness, bounded by its own imperatives, heedless, even defiant, of outward role demands'—a wholly unmediated internal mediation, albeit one that exists in permanent dramatic tension with the prevailing forces of traditional external mediation (Prince, 1999, p. 30). The revolutionary effect of this, at least in cinematic terms, becomes clearer when we consider just how 'interactionist' Japanese society was and in many ways still continues to be, albeit in increasingly weakened form, if the nihilistic mega-gore-fest films of Shinya Tsukamoto and Takashi Miike are anything to go by. Historically, the Japanese regarded 'outward role demands as "the really important center of the self" (Christine Kiefer qtd. Prince, 1999, p. 30), so that "A person is invariably identified as acting in some kind of human relationship, never autonomously" and both "self and other can be expressed only in relational terms" (Robert J. Smith qtd. Prince, 1999, p. 30). The result is a kind of slowly accumulating psychic trauma: "The unrestrained pursuit of one's own interest at the expense of another's goes against the norm of sociability. Concerned with his own interest, the individual will find the imperative of sociability and harmony oppressive" (Takie Sugiyama Lebra qtd. Prince, 1999, p. 111). The cinematic imperative was to formulate some specifically Japanese aesthetic tradition that could ameliorate the necessary mediation of the psychic and cultural trauma created by the 'foreign' (modernizing) contagion of undifferentiation and internal mediation, forcing a parallel concern with problematizing the issue of 'individualism'. In a sense, the issue was one of revisiting (and re-vitalizing) the archetypal conflict between *giri* and *ninjo*. 'loyalty' now represented by its darker aspect of conformist obedience, and 'proper judgment' portrayed as the will-to-freedom.

> While the formal organization of Japanese society and the official norms of social behaviour have been rigidly hierarchical and authoritarian, there has paradoxically always been a tacit acceptance, or sometimes even an open idealization, of certain trends which were in apparent opposition to the official norm. Thus, in Japanese social history there has been a tradition of glorifying such trends as the defense of their own rights by dissident groups, defiance of authority, individual action, and open personal achievement (Kazua Kawai qtd. Prince, 1999, p. 29).

The result was that by the Taisho Era (1912–1926) the 'Meiji ideals of public dedication and self-sacrifice had to accommodate a new ethic of success that honoured the individual, that valorized "the pursuit of the self alone in the private interest, a self no longer limited by concerns for family name or honouring one's native place"' (H.D. Harootunian qtd. Prince, 1999, p. 29).

> The design of Kurosawa's cinema, and its response to felt problems of cultural identity, needs to be regarded as a dynamic one: as a process marked by tensions, by achievements

> and setbacks, rather than as a consistent, and therefore static, system of themes and forms. Organized by a social conception that accords great value to the autonomous individual, these forms are charged with ideological value. The narrative design of the films and the unfolding of their visual codes are shaped by a central, organizing problematic. Kurosawa's films form a series of inquiries on the place and the possibilities of the autonomous self within a culture whose social relations stress group ties and obligations (Prince, 1999, p. 27).

It is possible to summarize the unifying meta-narrative of Kurosawa's filmic oeuvre as the following: the quest for the means of successfully reconciling the antithetical operations of external and internal mediation in such a manner as to create the conditions for a vital individualism without opening the doors to Nietzsche's 'uncanniest of guests,' nihilism.

> … Kurosawa frequently codes human relationships in terms of hierarchy of status and ability: master and pupil, hero and masses. Implicit within this coding are social relations and obligations prevailing among its constituents. Likes the ties that bound the warrior to his lord, the pupil demonstrates allegiance to the master, and the hero discovers it is incumbent upon him or her to protect the welfare of the masses. The tension within this coding is between the impulse toward individual autonomy and a countervailing recognition of the obligations of the interactionist self (Prince, 1999, p. 52).

The only problem with this project is that it is doomed to disastrous failure, for reasons which Girard knew all too well. According to Stephen Prince

> What lends the films their richness and constitutes their historical value is that Kurosawa's attempt at a cultural synthesis did not succeed, and that failure is significant because, in addition to being full of pathos, it clarifies the limitations of a particular kind of political filmmaking and, more generally, the dilemma of the artist who seeks to use art to make history (Prince, 1999, p. 31).

But it also 'clarifies' the dark magic of mimetic desire, which, in the final, and most bitter instance, renders it psychically impossible for any human being to constitute themselves as a true individual; even worse, and extraordinarily 'un-Japanese' if we think in terms of myth, the 'interactionist self' turns out to be the perfect spawning ground for mimesis in its most destructive form, metaphysical desire.

Unlike the two Westerns that I discussed in Chap. 4, both of the Easterns that I deal with here are concerned with the issue of trauma, which, consistent with their respective historical settings, are both concerned with the violent recovery and forcible re-imposition of an earlier state of order governed by external mediation. And on this basis, I would have to classify both *Yojimbo* and *Rashomon* as films that are deliberately subversive of the *chambara* genre, either as parody or as satire. Bearing both a Girardian text and a Schmittean sub-text, Kurosawa's *Yojimbo* [*The Bodyguard*] (1961), is focused on the community itself and externalizes the trauma of the collapse of mimetic mediation through public behavior and action, yielding an 'apocalyptic landscape' governed by violent individualism and the Hobbesian fear of death. Tellingly, the dean of western Japanese film scholarship Donald Richie describes that the semi-deserted nameless town of *Yojimbo* "is very much like one of those god-forsaken places in the middle of nowhere remembered from the films of [John] Ford" (Prince, 1999, p. 13; Richie, 1984, p. 147). And, up to a point, *Yojimbo* does constitute an instance of 'cinematic invasion,' the deliberate hybridization of competing genres: in this case, both the supremely American Western and Gangster film superficially re-staged as an Eastern, *Yojimbo* being, in fact, an adaptation of the classic Dashiell Hammett *noir* novel *Red Harvest* (1929) in which the equally nameless and semi-deserted American mining town has been devastated by the incessant warfare of two rival, and equally amoral, criminal gangs which are, cinematically and mimetically, essentially undifferentiated. Not only is the swordsman protagonist legally 'master-less,' symbolically existing outside of domain of external mediation, intriguingly he, like the town, is literally nameless as well, *Sanjuro* or 'Mr. Mulberry Field' (another way of saying 'The-Man-with-No-Name') the alias taken by the utterly un-identifiable *ronin*.

The character of the Bodyguard is the cinematic site of a complex two-level negotiation of the archetypal themes of *ninjo* and *giri*. As Sanjuro is only a ronin, and not a samurai he is not as bound by *giri* as he is by *ninjo* ('natural conscience…or proper judgment'); however, as each of the warring sides within the community is equally bad, every order he receives is immoral ('kill my enemies'); therefore, his every lethal action, which involves multiple instances of betrayal, is the free operation of his *ninjo* not balanced by *giri*, meaning that the inability of the film to resolve the conflict between the two is the sign of a world that is off-kilter, precisely because the required aesthetic norms of the genre cannot be complied with. And, contrary to viewer's (and critic's) expectations, although Sanjuro is always 'false,' he is never schizophrenic. *Yojimbo* is a perfect inversion of *High Noon* (1952): here, the violence of the only just man in the town is directed inward against the community in order to destroy it rather than to save it, so that an actual apocalypse is offered up in lieu of a potentially restorative act of generative unanimity. Kurosawa has said as much in his autobiographical appraisal of the film.

> For a long time, I'd wanted to make a really interesting film. It finally turned into this picture. The story is so ideally interesting that it's surprising no one else ever thought of it [sic]. The idea is about rivalry on both sides, and both sides are equally bad. We all know what that is like. Here we are, weakly caught in the middle, and it is impossible to choose between evils. Myself, I have always wanted to somehow or other stop these senseless battles of bad against bad, but we're all more or less weak—I've never been able to. And that is why the hero of this picture is different from us. He is able to stand squarely in the middle and stop the fight. And it is this—him—that I thought of first. That was the beginning of the film in my mind (Kurosawa, 1983, p. 97).[22]

This duplicates the existential crisis that Kurosawa felt immediately after 1945: as resistance from within was impossible, the only chance for the restoration of the Japanese community was the staging of Ground Zero and the introduction of a social

[22] While it is not inaccurate to say that Kurosawa plagiarized Hammett, it is equally true that Kurosawa was plagiarized by Sergio Leone, when Leone unofficially remade *Yojimbo* as *A Fistful of Dollars* (1964), the first of the archetypal movies of the sub-genre of the fiercely nihilistic 'Spaghetti Western'.

contract of some sort by a foreign, and invading, power that was unparalleled in its violence and unstoppable in its force—like the Bodyguard.[23]

From a strictly law-and-film perspective, the central importance of *Yojimbo* is as a satire of the Schmittean assumptions of the classic Western: if the identification (or 'naming') of the Enemy is the foundational act of Society, then civil war is the necessary result of politics, because the naming process is inherently contestable. As I have already discussed in Chap. 4 on the relationship between Schmitt and the Western, for its 'institutions to claim legitimacy, a liberal democracy must be able to distinguish who is a member of the community and who is not—who is "inside" and who is "outside"' (Ryan, 1996, p. 29). Meaning that Sanjuro, no less than Marshal Kane, is a Schmittean character, for he too is the decider of the Enemy within the state-of-exception that is the cultural vacuum of undifferentiation. Kurosawa would appear to be cinematically 'reasoning' along the same lines as Schmitt did jurisprudentially, proffering the view that 'All law is "situational law"' (Schmitt, 2005, p. 13), so that, contra both Aristotle and Kant, law is never abstract or a-contextual, and that at the end of the day, or at the moment that the body count has been completed, 'What matters for the reality of legal life is who decides' (Schmitt, 2005, p. 34). Law is always the result of the practical exercise of some kind of power, in this case practical exercised at the point of a sword. As '*Sovereign is he who decides on the exception*' (Schmitt, 2005, p. 5), the successful exercise of decision-making constitutes law in its most elemental form; 'In the context of Schmitt's work, a state of exception includes any kind of severe economic or political disturbance that requires the application of extraordinary measures' (Strong, 2007, p. 7) and only 'this definition can do justice to a borderline concept' not a 'vague concept, but one pertaining to the outermost sphere' (Strong, 2007, p. 5). The term 'borderline concept' invokes, as it did with both *High Noon* and *The Man Who Shot Liberty Valance*, the seminal notion of liminality which, for Kurosawa, also doubles as both a cultural and a legal state of being: the super-normalized but undifferentiating criminality of the gangster (*yakuza*) town in *Yojimbo* is the cinematic representation of the late Tokugawa shogunal trauma of the mimetic crisis that inaugurated the collapse of civil society of the Meiji Restoration, a quintessentially Schmittean predicament.

---

[23] Pace Kurosawa, who tended to avoid direct representations of class struggles, Prince has argued that a neo-Marxist interpretation of *The Bodyguard* may be made out on the basis of a feudal reaction against capitalism: '*Yojimbo* presents the apocalypse of the business class, the incarnation of every traditionalist's most fervent dream, and …. Its drama of samurai against merchant, its portrayal of a world rent by greed, controlled by thugs, but brought down by Sanjuro's sword, constructs a fable about the end of capitalism…. Sanjuro is explicitly offered as a wish-fulfilling figure, as a formal conceit necessary for the imaginary destruction of the business class, which, from an ideological perspective, incarnated a set of values contrary to the ideals of samurai life…. The merchants are destroyed by a member of the class they ultimately made extinct, as Kurosawa permits himself an outcome that the actual development of events did not allow' (Price, 1999, p. 223). But as capitalism, at least in its industrial rather than mercantile form, was a 'foreign import' in Japan, the film could just as easily be read as a nativist protest against alien cultural influence. Whatever the historical mechanism of the delivery of mimetic crisis, apocalyptic civil war or alienating foreign importation, the thing that really matters is the breakdown of the systems of external mediation—both military conflict and class struggle will suffice as far as phenomenology is concerned.

> It is precisely the exception that makes relevant the subject of sovereignty, that is, the whole question of sovereignty…The decision on the exception is a decision in the true sense of the word. Because a general norm, as represented by an ordinary legal prescription, can never encompass a total decision, the decision that a real exception exists cannot therefore be entirely derived from the norm (Schmitt, 2005, p. 6).

Since the 'state of the normal' has been temporarily suspended within the emergency that calls forth the decision, unanimity is no longer possible for the duration of the crisis, so that there is a collective sense of crisis of social and moral certainty: any one can be named as any 'thing' and language, intensely representational in its everyday or common-sense usage, is taken to the threshold of pre-representation, the master-sign of undifferentiation.

> The norm requires a homogenous medium…There exists no norm that is applicable to chaos. *For a legal order to make sense, a normal situation must exist, and he is sovereign who definitely decides whether this normal situation actually exists…The decision parts here from the legal norm, and (to formulate it paradoxically) authority proves that to produce law it need not be based on law* (Schmitt, 2005, p. 13).

Which is why it is providential that it is a master-less and name-less *ronin* who is the best swordsman in town, for it is precisely because he is the perfect fusion of liminality of identity and the potency 'to decide' that he is able to prevail within the chaos of the state-of-exception unencumbered by the moral and epistemological constraints of normalcy. To put it in cinematic terms: Sanjuro is the only one who knows exactly what 'needs' to be done. If we were to draw a direct narrative parallels between *Yojimbo* and *High Noon*, then the town that Yojimbo wanders into is Hadleyville after Frank Miller's gang has re-assumed control over it; the traumatized town in *Yojimbo* is an X-ray of Hadleyville which requires decisionism in its purest form in order to, hopefully, serve as a restorative act of generative unanimity.

> If such action [the decision on the exception] is not subject to controls, if it is not hampered in some way by checks and balances, as is the case in a liberal constitution, then it is clear who the sovereign is. *He decides whether there is an extreme emergency as well as what must be done to eliminate it.* Although he stands outside the normally valid legal system, he nevertheless belongs to it, for it is he who must decide whether the constitution [the legal order] needs to be suspended in its entirety (Schmitt, 2005, p. 7).

But here is where useful comparisons between *Yojimbo* and *High Noon* utterly break down. The question is: what is the essence of the decision? And the answer is: the naming and enforcing of the distinction between the Friend and the Enemy. For in politics 'What always matters is only the possibility of conflict' (Schmitt, 1996, p. 39) and 'to the enemy concept belongs the ever-present possibility of combat' (Schmitt, 1996, p. 32) which is what makes 'politics' an hygienic metaphor for 'war' which, as General Sherman reminded us, 'means killing': 'The specific political distinction to which political actions and motives can be reduced is that between friend and enemy…The distinction of friend and enemy denotes the utmost degree of intensity of a union or separation; of an association or disassociation' (Schmitt, 1996, p. 26). The absolutely central concept of Schmitt's theory of jurisprudence is that the existence of any State depends in the very final instance on the state of exception which is nothing other than that exact moment in time (or History) in which a unifying identification of the Enemy has been made. In a sense Marshal Kane had it easy in *High Noon*, for the enemy was easy to name (the Frank Miller gang), and he had one clear friend: his 'natural' ally, his wife Amy Fowler.[24] Sanjuro does not have it so easy, for the unprecedented paradox that Kurosawa throws at us is that the community is nothing other than an entire population of enemies, everyone minus a handful of civilians a member or affiliate of one of two warring *yakuza* clans. To repeat Kurosawa: 'The idea is about rivalry on both sides, and both sides are equally bad. We all know what that is like'—because this is nothing other than a crisis of undifferentiation. If everyone is 'equally bad' (or, in the alternative, no one is better than anyone else), then the act of the decision becomes, in a sense, arbitrary: the successful application of power does not bring about the objectively right outcome, but merely represents the subjective will of the successful enforcer of the decision, which, nihilistically, is his own. Which, although not violating the spirit of Carl Schmit does stretch the genre of sword-theatre to its breaking point: is the 'right' or the 'good' (which we hope somehow equates with the law) that which the Sovereign commands or is it rather nothing more than whatever the Sovereign merely happens to choose to command under the circumstances of the particular and contingent moment of the perceived state of exception? If it is the latter—and in the non-cinematic universe of reality it might very well be the case—then, any representation of the Schmittean decision would necessarily have to transgress against the genre's archetypal clash of moral principles (*giri* and *ninjo*) that invests the *Ken-geki* genre with both cultural intelligibility and moral seriousness.[25] And, as this is post-War (or post-trauma) Japan that we are talking about, *Yojimbo* must conform to the regenerative imperatives of *chambara* for the film to make any 'sense' to its target audience. If the Bodyguard cannot be situated within any conventional framework of legal value (positivist, naturalist, Aristotelian, Kantian) even if in a satirical or self-parodying form and portrayed as something at least slightly different from Schmitt's enforcer of the decision, then his destruction of the Enemy, which is literally almost everybody in town, is void of any self-grounding moral or political meaning, nothing more than the accidental outcome of the triumph of the subjective but will of the successful enforcer of his own decision who prevails by, quite literally, scapegoating the entire population of the community—with the sword. But there is, in fact, a way to save *Yojimbo* for the sake of the preservation of the genre integrity of sword-theatre: a Girardian sub-text that would permit the dramatic conflict of *ninjo* and *giri* to be represented in an entirely novel manner.

---

[24] See Chap. 4, above.

[25] Sergio Leone was able to get away with this in *A Fistful of Dollars* but only because there is nothing genre-bending about moral nihilism in European film.

5.3.1 The Apocalypse of Mr. Mulberry Field

If we examine *Yojimbo* closely, we can make out that Sanjuro's public heroic striving as a self-authored righteous Schmittean decider (executor) of the state of exception is doubled by his private mimesis-driven imperative to establish his separateness from the undifferentiated *yakuza* gangs of the anarchic post-community of crypto-Hobbesian criminality. As I have already discussed, for Girard, the archetypal plot of all literature is that the Self (protagonist) will model its relationship to the Other (double) on the basis of imitation that will narratively culminate in the Self attempting to either replace and/or destroy the double (mimetic rivalry).[26]

> Rivalry does not arise because of the fortuitous convergence of two desires on a single object; rather, *the subject desires the object because the rival desires it.* In desiring an object the rival alerts the subject to the desirability of the object. The rival, then, serves as the model for the subject, not only in regard to such secondary matters as style and opinions but also, and more essentially, in regard to desires (Girard, 1977, p. 145).

But this same process doubles as Girard's theory of literature: every literary representation of human drama, which is always a form of social phenomena, is ultimately about envy (Girard, 1965). As for both Georges Bataille and Jean-Paul Sartre, the essence of the human dilemma is the absence of an essential self—anthropological *non-being*. 'The human subject does not really know what to desire, in the last resort' (Girard et al., 1978, p. 343); the human subject 'desires *being*, something he himself lacks and which some other person [the 'model'] seems to possess. The subject thus looks to that other person to inform him of what he should desire in order to acquire that being' (Girard, 1977, p. 146). The entirety of human desire, the libidinal dimension of our social existence, is subsumed under mimesis because 'desire itself is essentially mimetic, directed toward an object desired by the model' (Girard, 1977, p. 146), from which comes rivalry, 'the mimetic nature of conflict, which is to say the ultimate absence of any object proper to it' (Girard et al., 1978, p. 31).

To summarize: mimetic rivalry 'is always rooted in one of the two following claims: the claim of the self for the ownership of its own desire; and the claim of desire for its anteriority, its seniority over the other's desire, the other desire that has generated it, on which it is modelled' (Oughourlian, 1996, p. 43).[27] The failure of either claim reduces the Self to No-One; existentially and phenomenologically we are all perfectly equal in being nobodies. Crucial then is the temporal (or historical) dimension of mimesis: mimetic rivalry, in both its latent and manifest form, is embedded within the structural parameters of psychological time, which is incommensurable with linear (non-reversible) physical time. Conflict follows a strict pattern of migration from two nodal points, *N* and *N'*:

> The constitution of the self in physical time can be summed up by a linear vector going from the past toward the future. Desire *D* [the model] mimetically elicits the birth of desire *d* [the

[26] See Chap. 1, above.

[27] 'The desire that constitutes the self is itself modelled on, copied from, inspired by, and communicated by the other. It is the other's desire that causes the desire to appear that will engender the self' (Oughourlian, 2010, p. 98).

> subject], which, in turn, brings self *s* [the 'habitual self'; *habitus*] into existence. Such is the real sequence of events that unfold in physical time going from the past to the future. But this sequence has no meaning on the psychological level, for it unfolds completely without the knowledge of all the protagonists (Oughourlian, 2016, p. 39).

The signature feature of nodal point *N* is 'the self's claim to the ownership of its desires' (Oughourlian, 2016, p. 38), which is, of course, an illusion, for 'Consciousness, like the self, is a function of the relation to otherness. The self as such is a mythic notion' (Oughourlian, 1991, p. 198). A truth so brutal that no one who is sane can ever fully admit it (Wilson, 2019).

> The self, at point *N*, in the most banal and normal case, cannot survive unless it is persuaded that it is the owner of its desire. The simplest solution for the self consists in forgetting the otherness of the desire that constituted it and in considering that this desire truly belongs to it. In reality, it is not a matter of mere forgetting because if one forgets something, this implies that one once knew it. It is in fact a matter of active mis-recognition, though at this stage remaining peaceful and non-adversarial (Oughourlian, 2016, p. 39).

Amnesia, the fruit of *meconnaissance*, is our salvation for a while. 'Forgetting preserves harmony in the self and keeps it in existence (Oughourlian, 2016, p. 74) … Forgetting presides over the constitution of the self at the moment of its creation' (Oughourlian, 2016, p. 76); the new self *s* is always 'built on the overlooking of the otherness of desire' (Oughourlian, 2016, p. 74). In a perfect inversion of Jean-Paul Sartre, it is not the case that Man is condemned to be free—it is ten times worse than that. Man is condemned to eternally 'forget' (mis-recognize) that he is a slave (unconditionally un-free) precisely because the phenomenological basis of his sense of Being—his Self—is the by-product of a set of processes, psychical and social, that are intrinsically mimetic in nature but which subject at all times to an all-controlling *meconnaissance*. 'This otherness with which we are saturated and that constitutes us is the human condition; but it is very difficult to accept. Its mis-recognition is initial and necessary to the maintenance of the self in its existence' (Oughourlian, 2016, p. 45). Paradoxically, to the extent that we are 'real' we are false, not truly of ourselves, because for mimesis to function in the 'constitution of the self in desire, it is essential that the desire gradually forget its mimetic origin, forget even as it comes from the other that it belongs to the other, in order, precisely, to feel itself autonomous, to exist as such, to constitute a self' (Oughourlian, 1991, pp. 232–233). And, just to turn the screw one more time, the logic of mimetic relationships must *necessarily* lead to mimetic conflict, or violence, physical and/or symbolic. 'What is the clinical expression of mimetic desire? *Rivalry*. What I see every day in my practice is not mimicking, nor copying, nor learning; it is rivalry' (Oughourlian, 1996, p. 43). When viewed in meta-psychological terms, the relationship between model and subject is fraught with peril. In other words, the Girardian constant of inter-individual relations is an *a-symmetrical reciprocity* with the result that the subject 'is torn between two opposite feelings toward his model—the most submissive reverence and the most intense malice. This is the passion we call *hatred* … Only someone who prevents us from satisfying a desire that he himself has inspired in us is truly an object of hatred' (Girard, 1965, pp. 10–11). Rivalry, therefore, is the flip side of the crisis of undifferentiation, that potentially boundless state of existential anguish in which no one is anything in particular because all inhabit the universal space of absent identity, a hellish crisis of the collective of the loss of personal differences that triggers an avalanche of reciprocal and escalating violence; 'Sameness is the terrible war in which twins are personally engaged, right up until the moment when one manages to kill the other…When it spreads it becomes the famous war of all against all of which Hobbes spoke' (Girard, 2014, pp. 104–105). The undifferentiated are devoid of being and the sameness of this undifferentiation reduces society to the zero condition of chaos, a 'virtual' apocalypse.

> The rivalry that mimetic desire unleashes will, in the end, assume the most extreme and grotesque form of the violent, or 'monstrous' doubles who are the signifiers of the crisis of undifferentiation: as the rivals intensify their mimetic struggle they effectively become identical, triggering a pathological crisis of identity which can only be resolved through an act of extreme violence, whether physical, emotional or symbolic (Girard, 1977, pp. 143–168).[28]

The relevance of this to the alternative (and salvific) reading of *Yojimbo* should be obvious: consistent with the genre requirements of *chambara*, the externalization of the dramatic narrative of *ninjo* and *giri* is achieved through the public spectacle of the repeated blood-soaked enactment of *Ken-geki* sword-theatre in the streets: Sanjuro is the 'real thing' ('the hero of this picture is different from us. He is able to stand squarely in the middle and stop the fight') and everyone else is a 'fake': they are all indistinguishable from each other and have experienced a traumatizing collective fail of mimetic emulation. But this should also give rise to a more nuanced reading, because it raises the possibility that we are looking at an outstanding example of what we might very tentatively consider to be a specifically Japanese form of an *'interactionist'* mimesis: the real issue is precisely not to be truly something, but to act as though one really is that some-thing in a manner that is nothing short of perfect. As I have already mentioned, the Japanese, in a manner quite different from Europeans,[29] regarded 'outward role demands as "the really important center of the self"' (Christine Kiefer qtd. Prince, 1999, p. 30), so that '"A person is invariably identified as acting in some kind of human relationship, never autonomously"' and both '"self and other can be expressed only in relational terms"' (Robert J. Smith qtd. Prince, 1999, p. 30). The Japanese 'content' of *Yojimbo* partially dilutes the nihilistic implications of the ambiguous nature of the Schmittean decision: it really does not matter what one is truly because the one true thing that possesses social value is how one actually behaves, which acting in strict conformity with a pre-determined social role, a cultural stereotype. Sanjuro is the decider of the exception not because he really is the decider but he makes and enforces the decision while acting in perfect conformity with the prescribed behavior of that social class designated to restore difference and the hierarchy of distinctions: the samurai. It might even be possible to express this

[28] 'Violence is the process itself when two or more partners try to prevent one another from appropriating the object they all desire through physical or other means' (Girard qtd Gallese, 2011, p. 88).

[29] With the outstanding exception of the English whose culture is highly performative and, therefore, intensely interactionist.

negatively: Sanjuro is the only one who successfully differentiates himself from the Hell-of-the-Same of the others not because he is a genuine samurai but because he is the only one who does not behave as a genuine *yakuza* in an interactional manner. It is by focusing exclusively on his external behavior in compliance with the samurai role while ignoring his own internal preferences (or 'state of mind'), that Kurosawa is able to successfully represent the Bodyguard as the perfect embodiment of the naturalism of *ninjo* that allows *Yojimbo* to be integrated into the genre of sword-theatre.[30] *Yojimbo* really is, then, the inversion of *High Noon*: it is not the case that Sanjuro's 'final' decision of the exception makes him the true swordsman; it is because he is able to perfectly replicate the true swordsman that he is able to decide the exception. The Bodyguard's natural virtue is signified by his proper, albeit brutal, performance of civic duty: the total violence that clears the way for the possibility of authentic restoration of that Japanese order that equals meaning, or at least the differentiated truth of individual identities. So we have a perfect inversion of the Western: the power of the decider-enforcer comes not from the inner virtue flowing outward, as with Tom Doniphon and Marshal Kane, but from perfectly correct behavior flowing inward. The problem that remains, however, is that Kurosawa has still not resolved the cultural trauma of internal mediation which renders impossible interactionist social relations. Sanjuro may be spared the agony of metaphysical desire because he is able to completely vacate his interior in favor of his exterior and, therefore, behave perfectly. But this might not always be so easy for other protagonists in a Kurosawan *Jidai-geki*. And it is metaphysical desire, as I shall show, that is the key to arguably the greatest Japanese film ever made, also by Kurosawa.

5.4 *Rashomon*, or Metaphysical Desire in a Grove of Bamboo

Although considered wildly different types of films, there is a great deal of thematic bridging between the *Yojimbo* and *Rashomon*, the unnoticed similitudes mainly consisting of slightly divergent approaches to the problematic and destructive nature of mimetic desire and internal mediation. In *Yojimbo*, everyone is clearly posited as equally bad (including, perhaps, Sanjuro himself, the killer of the killers). In *Rashomon*, we have lost all ground for making moral evaluations or identifications of any kind but in a manner that far surpasses the later film; not merely might it be the case (strongly hinted at) that everyone is equally bad (although in different ways), but that it is ultimately impossible to decide whether anyone is objectively bad or good. Here, undifferentiation has reached its absolute form.

Admittedly, there is a very strong objection that can be made to my thesis of the mimetic themes off *Ken-geki*: *Rashomon*, which I consider to be a samurai film, is set in neither of the virtually mandatory of eras of *Senguko* or early Meiji. Instead,

---

[30] Kurosawa plays this same trick a second time in his sequel to *Yojimbo*, the appropriately titled *Sanjuro* (1962) although there the emphasis is slanted more toward *giri*, or loyalty.

the action takes place in the late Heian Era (794–1185), an unusual fact signaled to the cinematically aware audience (Japanese) by the fact that the samurai is of the pre-classical variety, being equipped with bow and arrow along with the iconic *katana* and *tanto*. But these matters are of secondary importance, Kurosawa opting for the comparatively under-utilized settings of the Heian as a result of being bound by his source material, two acclaimed but narratively dissimilar short stories by Ryunosuke Akutagawa (1982–1927), 'Rashomon'[31] or 'The Demon Gate' (1915), essentially a ghost story set in the twelfth century (Akutagawa, 2006, pp. 3–9), and 'In a Grove' (1921), a 'locked-room' mystery re-played as a legal drama (Akutagawa, 2006, pp. 10–19). Although Akutagawa, like Kurosawa, does not explicitly stipulate the historical frames of the action, he clearly indicates social collapse through warfare and famine, hinting that both fables, which themselves are based on chronicle materials from the twelfth century, take place during the fall of the Heian government and the country's descent into a new round of ultra-violent civil war.[32] A liminal zone of undifferentiation within whose nihilistic spaces a garden of pathological delights, notably internal mediation and metaphysical desire, has been allowed to bloom. But the real solution to the problem of genre lies with Kurosawa's decision to adopt both stories and to combine them into a single cinematic text; Kurosawa splices together these two quite different narratives in order to create a domain of nihilistic anarchy to act as the arena within which the contending mechanisms of external and internal mediation can wage their own civil war, *Rashomon*'s de-populated Kyoto directly anticipating the gangster village of *Yojimbo*, and the genre's imperative of restoration raised to the level of existential intensity, for *Rashomon*, even more than in *Yojimbo*, is a drama about being versus non-being.

> Based on a twelfth-century tale,[33] Akutagawa's retold story ['Rashomon'] is set at the decaying end of the [Heian] era, when power had largely shifted from the courtiers to the warlords who would dominate the coming centuries—and much of the city—like the gate itself—lay in ruins. Despite its title, Kurosawa Akira's celebrated film, *Rashomon* (1950), owes little to this tale—perhaps only the scruffy servant, whose cynical view of human nature the film ultimately rejects, and the setting beneath the gates where Kurosawa's characters

---

[31] 'The "rashomon" was the largest gate in Kyoto, the ancient capital of Japan. It was 106 feet wide and 26 feet deep, and was topped with a ridge-pole; its stone-wall rose 75 feet high. This gate was constructed in 789 when the then capital of Japan was transferred to Kyoto. With the decline of West Kyoto, the gate fell into bad repair, cracking and crumbling in many places, and became a hide-out for thieves and robbers and a place for abandoning unclaimed corpses' (Akutagawa, 1970, p. 34); '"Mon" means "gate". The Rashomon (originally, Rajomon: outer gate) was the great southern entrance to Kyoto during the golden age of the imperial court, the Heian period. Massive pillars supported a cavernous chamber topped by a sloping roof, with stone steps leading into and out of its towering archway. In its heyday, all its wooden surfaces wore a coat of vermilion lacquer. The broad Suzaku Avenue running north from the Rashomon led straight to the gate of the Imperial Palace, where lived the tiny, aesthetically refined fraction of the population depicted in the country's greatest literary monument, Murasaki Shikibu's *The Tale of Genji*' (Akutagawa, 2006, p. 237).

[32] The Genpei/Jisho-Juei War (1180–1185) between the Minomata-Genji and Taira-Heike clan alliances ending in the establishment of the Minomato Kamakura shogunate (1185–1333).

[33] The original tales mined by Akutagawa for 'Rashomon' (1917) and 'In a Grove' (1922) were both in the twelfth-century collection *Konjaku monogatari*, or *Tales of Times Now Past* (Akutagawa, 2006, p. 238).

wait out the rain and tell the famous story reflecting multiple angles on truth ['In a Grove'] (Akutagawa, 2006, pp. 236–237).

If we take the corpus of Akutagawa in its entirety, we notice immediately that metaphysical desire comprises one of his signature aesthetic concerns, which is what we should expect given that Akutagawa's overriding concern is with the 'modernization' of Japanese literature (or the importation of Western literary modernism) in order to keep cultural pace with the socially emergent anti-feudal national bourgeoisie during the Meiji Period.[34] It is easy to understand why Akutagawa was a natural draw for Kurosawa, whose films "begin with an acute awareness of a fragmented world" (Keiko McDonald qtd. Prince, 1999, p. 24). It is also no surprise that the violent collapse of Heian was Akutagawa's favorite period of Japanese history, 'who identified it with *fin-de-siecle* Europe, and he symbolized the decay with the image of the crumbling Rashomon gate that dominates his story' (Rubin, 2006, p. xlii); he also deployed the Demon Gate as a way of establishing a connection between the advanced decomposition of the late Heian and the city of Kyoto, technically *Heian-kyo*, 'Capital of Peace and Tranquility,' the very things that are missing and, therefore, that which cries out for restoration (Akutagawa, 2006, p. xli). Both Akutagawa's literary fiction and Kurosawa's film invoke the apocalyptic Buddhist prophecy of "the end of the law," the eschatological era wherein 'human life would fall to its point of greatest degeneracy' (Prince, 1999, p. 128).

> … Kyoto had been struck by one calamity after another in recent years—earthquakes, whirlwinds, fires, famine—leading to the capital's extraordinary decline. Old records tell us that people would smash Buddhist statues and other devotional gear, place the pieces by the roadside with flecks of paint and gold and silver foil still clinging to them, and sell them as firewood. With the whole city in such turmoil, no one bothered to maintain the Rashomon. Foxes and badgers[35] came to live in the dilapidated structure, and they were soon joined by thieves. Finally, it became the custom to abandon unclaimed corpses in the upper story of the gate, which made the neighborhood an eerie place everyone avoided after the sun went down (Akutagawa, 2006, p. 3).

If, however, the film is not really about 'multiple angles on truth' as so commonly alleged by Western film critics and scholars,[36] but the psychological pathology of mimetic crisis, then Kurosawa's *Rashomon* owes a great deal to Akutagawa's tale of nocturnal malfeasance.

---

[34] The list includes but cannot be restricted to: 'Absorbed in Letters' (Akutagawa, 1964), 'Yam Gruel', 'The Martyr', 'Kesa and Morito' (Akutagawa, 1970), 'Loyalty', 'Horse Legs', 'Daidoji Shinsuke: The Early Years', 'The Life of a Stupid Man', and, most unforgettably, 'Spinning Gears' (Akutagawa, 2006).

[35] Two of the four 'supernatural' animal species of Japan, the other two being toads and crows (or ravens). Both make an appearance, deployed by Akutagawa as secular signifiers of an occult presence: 'Crows … flocked here in great numbers. During the day they would always be cawing and circling above the gate turned red after sunset, the crows stood out against it like scattering of sesame seeds. They came to the upper chamber of the gate to peck the flesh of the dead.'; the spectral old woman pulling the hairs out of the cadavers 'mumbled and croaked like a toad' (Akutagawa, 2006, pp. 3–4, 8).

[36] See below.

> Kurosawa's *Rashomon* is based primarily on this story, set in the late Heian Period.... While this story [like Akutagawa's 'Rashomon'] is based on a twelfth-century tale ... the place names are real, and most relate to the steep hills that line the ancient capital of Kyoto's eastern flank. Yamashina ... was a village lying just beyond the hills. Situated in the foothills on the city side, Toribe Temple was connected with a burial ground toward the south. Kiyomizu Temple is still a major site of popular worship. Awataguchi was a familiar northeasterly point of entry from the hills. Wakasa Province would have been several days' journey on foot to the northeast of Kyoto. The "Magistrate" (*Keibiishi*, literally "Examiner of Misdeeds," also translated "Police Commissioner") to whom the characters speak was a Kyoto city official who exercised both police and judicial authority. In the original [twelfth-century] tale, the highwayman has no name; Akutagawa seems to have borrowed "Tajomaru" from another story about a "famous bandit" in the same collection of [Heian Period] tales' from which he drew on for 'Rashomon' (Akutagawa, 2006, p. 238).

In *Rashomon*, the trauma driving the main plot device--the unmediated juxtaposition of incompatable narratives—is of a wholly internal and subjective nature, but the thing that completely controls all of the Conradian unreliable narrators of whom there are six, those of: 'a Woodcutter', 'a Traveling Priest', 'a Policeman', 'an Old Woman' (the mother of the wife of the samurai), 'Tajomaru' (the bandit), the 'Penitent Confession of a Woman in the Kiyozimu Temple' (the wife), and 'The Testimony of the Dead Man's Spirit Told Through a Medium' (the samurai).[37] So deft and so audacious is his use of the very un-Japanese importation of the quintessentially modernist[38] narrator-who-is-unreliable, that Kurosawa (and Akutagawa) was able to create a *nom d'arte* for legal practice and education: the dilemma of objectively incompatible testimonies of otherwise reliable and truthful eye-witnesses. For the professionally trained legal advocate.

> The inevitable impulse, at first sight, is to speculate on which of those who claim guilt is really guilty of the warrior's death. But whatever conclusion to be tentatively reached, what eventually slops back into the spectator's mind and possesses it, is the traumatic violence of the basic pattern: that violence which is the heart of the enigma...But is not the heart of the confusion *within the event itself?* Is this happening not one so frightfully destructive of human poise and ethical custom that it breeds its own ambiguity and that this ambiguity infects the minds of these people?... Three lives have been irretrievably altered after being reduced to

[37] There is some speculation in the critical literature that Akutagawa was influenced by Ambrose Bierce's 'The Moonlit Road' (1907) which features the apparently truthful testimony of a murder victim speaking through a medium that corrects the accounts provided by the other two witnesses to the murder. If Akutagawa borrowed from Bierce, then this would provide indirect support to the essential, but incomplete, truthfulness, of the dead man's account. Bierce's tale also touches upon the theme of mimesis in multiple places, such as the confession provided by the first narrator, the son of the murderer (father) and his victim (mother): 'I am the most unfortunate of men. Rich, respected, fairly well educated and of sound health—with many other advantages usually valued by those having them and coveted by those who have them not—I sometimes think that I should be less happy if they had been denied me, for then the contrast between my outer and my inner life would not be continually demanding a painful attention' (Bierce, 1988, p. 417). Which we might consider the lament of the samurai.

[38] 'Akutagawa's devotion to modernism, or, more exactly, his commitment to reconciling western modernism with traditional Japanese literary forms acquires that much greater significance as his text served as the template for a declared belief in a universally shared 'epistemic crisis' in both Art and Law' (Murakami, 2006, p. xxxiv).

> the most primitive condition imaginable.[39]… Regardless of what literally took place in the forest's depths that mild summer day, each participant is justified in reconstructing it in a manner to redeem the prestige of moral sense, which, consciously or not, is a civilized person's most precious possession (Tyler, 1967, p. 39).

And strictly in terms of legal practice, *Rashomon* presents us with the judge's and jury's worst nightmare: nobody's testimony can be believed because, literally, everyone is lying about some things, but not the same things, and in different ways.

> Ironically enough, *confession* has become a sin. What seems significant to the whole is the collective nature of the liars: they literally outnumber the truth-teller (whichever he [or she]) may be. The 'sin' involved has gone beyond individual performance and exists objectively as would a natural cataclysm such as a volcanic eruption. That each participant assumes guilt, including the dead man, reveals the comprehensiveness and irresistibility of the disorder. A lie, then, actually becomes the symbol of the operation by which these people mutually regain their moral identities. These identities having been destroyed as though by an objective force beyond anyone's control, any means seems fair to regain them (Tyler, 1967, pp. 40–41).

'These identities having been destroyed as though by an objective force beyond anyone's control, any means seems fair to regain them' is a concise summary of the film, but it fails to specify the exact nature of the annihilating 'objective force' which, of course, is internal mediation. In Girardian terms, what is at issue is not lying per se but the metaphysics of desire, which gives rise to a very special kind of mis-recognition: everybody lies not merely because the 'an objective force beyond anyone's control' has destroyed the commonly assumed correlation between their private and public selves (or *persona*, Attic Greek for 'mask' which is a false face), but that the destruction wreaked by the violence (rape and murder) has revealed that everyone's true self—the psychic holding pen of their mimetic desires—is, in 'truth' the exact opposite of their public performances and, even worse, is not truly their own. It is not a question of mere disillusion; it is, rather, a matter of social extinction or survival; the apocalyptic revelation of the absolute gap between desire and actualization admits of no mediation because the gap itself is the signifier of the metaphysical nature of the desire, the life-or-death imperative to validate oneself as both the owner and creator of one's own identity, as outlined by Oughourlian. All of which would even be more unbearable if one is Japanese, for what is at stake is the revelation of their external inability to behave in accordance with interactional relations; the mimetic desires of the four protagonists have emerged into full view, preventing each of them from truly expressing themselves in those exclusively relational terms which are externally mediated.

With *Rashomon*, we have gone far beyond mere deceit and hypocrisy into the extreme realms of negation and extinction, but we have also, weirdly, managed to remain within the conventions of sword-theatre, albeit at the outermost edge. As I have already established, a central component of the plot of many *Ken-geki* films is a dramatic struggle over who can most successfully imitate the 'ideal' form of the samurai, so much so that the archetypal dilemma of *giri* versus *ninjo* can be easily translated into the terms of mimetic crisis: what, exactly, is the ideal pattern to be

---

[39] The undifferentiation of 'the state of nature' as with *Lord of the Flies* and *Deliverance*.

followed? However, both *Yojimbo* and *Rashomon* upset the viewer's expectations through their respective re-working of the archetypal swordsman with his iconic sword. The difference between the two films, again, is the public/external/objective and the private/internal/subjective. *Yojimbo* operates primarily within the realm of the 'objective'/interactional and is, therefore, the more conventional *chambara* than *Rashomon*, although highly eccentric because of its cinematic flirting with nihilism. In contrast, *Rashomon*, from an epistemological perspective, is the more challenging film, as the mimetic tensions at the heart of the drama are manifested through all of the characters failing to comply with their relational roles, which are the bases of their respective self-images that are staked, in turn, upon the metaphysical nature of their desires. Cinematically, the supremely subversive, and ironical, act that Kurosawa undertook was to 'tell' lies on screen, meaning filming a false version of events in exactly the same manner as a 'true' event, which, as everyone in the audience knows, is a fiction. Which is basically how Kurosawa described what he was doing, highly aware at all times that the word 'lie' necessarily invokes the notion of 'Truth'. He sounds exactly like Oughourlian.

> Human beings are unable to be honest with themselves about themselves. They cannot talk about themselves without embellishing. The script portrays such human beings—the kind who cannot survive without lies to make them feel they are better people than they really are. It even shows this sinful need for flattering falsehood going beyond the grave—even the character who dies cannot give up his lies when he speaks to the living through a medium. Egoism is a sin the human being carries with him from birth; it is the most difficult to redeem (Kurosawa, 1983, p. 183).

The Buddhist sin of Egoism is the correlative of the Christian sin of Pride, and Donald Richie makes much out of it in his moralistic synopsis of the film.

> One can now assign various reasons for the five [characters] having seen and heard the things that they thought they saw and heard. All the stories have in common one single element—pride. Tajomaru is proud to have raped and killed; the wife is proud to have (perhaps) killed [sic]; the husband (for now there is every reason to believe that the dead talk) is proud to have killed himself; and the woodcutter is proud to have seen and robbed [sic]. They are proud of these actions and we know because they insist upon them. One confesses only what one is openly or secretly proud of, which is the reason that contrition is rarely sincere...Each is proud of what he [and she] did, because as he [or she] might tell you: 'It is just the sort of thing that I would do' (Richie, 1984, p. 75).

The problem with this account, just like the problems with moralizing readings of *Lord of the Flies*,[40] is that they fail to come to grips with both mimesis and the utter a-morality of metaphysical desire. Richie is clearly wrong in concluding that the wife is 'proud to have (perhaps) killed' and the woodcutter 'is proud to have seen and robbed'. Quite the opposite is true: on pain of existential extinction, the wife must disavow any homicidal action (or desire) against her samurai husband, and the woodcutter will move heaven and earth in order to deny that he is 'really' a thief—which he does quite literally by taking an oath near the end of the film to give the 'true' account of what 'really' happened in the grove, but still comes up

[40] See Chap. 2, above.

with a second mis-direction that is a lie in part, although true overall (he also totally violates universal cinematic expectation that when an accused finally promises to confess the honest-to-God truth at the end of the picture, she will actually do so—it doesn't happen here). It is striking that the two errors that Richie makes relate to the tales of the wife and woodcutter, for, as I will show, their respective stories are narratively symmetrical, meaning that the approximate truth of the woodcutter's second tale objectively disproves the truth of the wife's single testimony. The better explanation lies with viewing *Rashomon* as a study of the crisis of undifferentiation occurring on the private level as opposed to the public crisis of mimetic catastrophe of universalized desire in *Yojimbo*. All of the characters are united (or rendered existentially identical) through their 'separate' acts of lying which in fact constitute a single act of *meconnaissance*: their utterly failed attempts to re-establish their 'proper' identity through their correct imitation of their respective mimetic models, in this case, 'honest' (but poor) laborer, 'proper' wife, 'correct' samurai, 'real' (or 'serious') bandit. The trauma of *Rashomon* is the collapse of social identity through the irruption of mimetic desire, which on the surface level of the text, assumes an erotic form: the multiple divergences among the incompatible narratives all flow from what happened immediately after the rape of the samurai's wife by the bandit, which leads to a very big problem.

5.5 The Male Gaze and the Triangle of Desire

Richie relates the interesting but uncomfortable anecdote that 'Once asked why he [Kurosawa] thought that *Rashomon* had become so popular, both in Japan and abroad, he answered: "Well, you see…it's about this rape" Everyone laughed…' (Richie, 1984, p. 75). Which, while indelicate, is useful in illustrating the centrality of mimetic triangle to the film, a triangulated economy of mimetic desire as both the foreground to the murder of the samurai and as the interpretative key to the issue of the truth of identity and the metaphysics of desire. *Male/Female* was the name given to the original script of *Rashomon* by screen-writer Shinobu Hashimotu; although conventional academic commentary has focused on the epistemological ('cognitive dissonance') and jurisprudential (fallibility of eye-witness testimony) aspects of the film, an underappreciated aspect of the narrative is its relations to Feminism and the mimetic dimensions of the *male gaze*, a quintessential term of film scholarship attributed to Laura Mulvey and her seminal essay 'Visual Pleasure and Narrative Cinema' (1975): 'The cinema satisfies a primordial wish for pleasurable looking, but also goes further, developing scopophilia in its narcissistic aspect' (Mulvey, 1975, p. 9). One of the most important and influential essays of film criticism ever written, Mulvey's text draws heavily on the post-Freudian psychoanalytical theories of Jacques Lacan and his equally seminal concept of the 'mirror phase': once the child realizes that its reflection in the mirror is identical to his/her own self, the child is able to enter into the realm of the symbolic. That is, the child constructs an image of itself through mental projection that is considerably greater, or more 'ideal', than the real or actual self and this idealized self-projection becomes, in turn, the basis of self-love, or narcissism. And cinema has become our culture's primary repository of the narcissistic imagination through its total reliance upon the visual (the image) and its manipulation of desire for fun and profit. The vital addition that Mulvey adds to the Lacanian schema is the Feminist political critique of gender relationships.

> The magic of the Hollywood style at its best (and of all the cinema which fell within its sphere of influence) arose, not exclusively, but in one important aspect, from its skilled and satisfying manipulation of visual pleasure. Unchallenged, mainstream film coded the erotic into the language of the dominant patriarchal order (Mulvey, 1975, p. 8).

Which explains why the cinematic representation of women is especially problematic: 'Traditionally, the woman displayed,' or 'projected' oneirically onto the movie screen, 'has functioned on two levels: as erotic object for the characters within the screen story, and as erotic object for the spectator within the auditorium [sic], with a shifting tension between the looks on either side of the screen' (Mulvey, 1975, pp. 11–12). In film, the woman is always presented as the object of male desire, denoted as the neo-narcissistic male gaze, so that the value and nature of the object are constituted through its observation by a male who invests that object with his own libidinal imagination. A classic literary example of this is provided us by James Dickey in his very male (or phallo-) centric account of Ed Gentry's erotic meditations on the 'golden-eyed girl' at the end of the novel *Deliverance*.[41]

> Because of the associations she had for me, I looked up the girl in the Kitt'n Britches ad and took her out to dinner a couple of times. I still loved the way she looked, but her golden-halved eye had lost its fascination. Its place was in the night river, in the land of impossibility. That's where its magic was for me. I left it there, though I would have liked to see her hold her breast once more, in a small space full of men. I see her every now and then, and the studio uses her. She is a pleasant part of the world, but minor. She is imaginary (Dickey, 1970, p. 277).

The real danger for the male is that Woman as an object of desire doubles as a source of anxiety. For Freud and Lacan what defines Woman-as-Woman (her 'essence') is that she is 'Not-Man'; that is, she lacks the phallus (=castration), so that her being is signified by a 'minus'. Translated into the language of Marxism, 'the ruling symbols of any society are the symbols of the ruling gender,' so that the Feminist definition of patriarchy, or 'the rule of men,' is premised upon the all-controlling influence of phallo-centrism, the totalizing ideological system wherein the male penis is re-worked as the foundation of the symbolic order. Because the Woman lacks the phallus, it is suspect for her to serve as the object of desire of the male, for the male is attracted to that which represents his potential 'un-making,' or symbolic castration, which un-does the patriarchal operation of power by eternally threatening the man with transformation (through an act of reduction) into a non-man/wo-man. Within the specific terms of cinema, 'castration anxiety' (the feminization of the male through the operational medium of the gaze) operates on two levels: (a) mimesis, where the viewer one strives to imitate the object of one's love (erotic desire), as mediated

[41] See Chap. 3, above.

by the screen, and (b) the 'inversion of the gaze' which occurs whenever the film makes the woman-object an active personality and prioritizing *her* gaze as against the male reducing the man to a passive object, a kind of 'counter-feminization' that equals symbolic castration. The patriarchal solution to this phallocentric dilemma of woman-on-screen is the effective 'silencing' of the dangerous Woman/Un-Man, by extensively encoding her with complex cinematic symbols and images: her meaning is determined for her through the film that is the vehicle for the male gaze, so that, for any movie to work within a patriarchal social order, the woman-on-screen can never be allowed to exist outside of the coding mechanisms of passivity.

> Woman then stands in patriarchal culture as signifier for the male other, bound by a symbolic order in which man can live out his phantasies and obsessions through linguistic [or 'visual'] command by imposing them on the silent image of woman still tied to her place as bearer of meaning, not maker of meaning…the psychoanalytic background [is] that woman as representation signifies castration, inducing voyeuristic or fetishistic mechanisms to circumvent her threat (Mulvey, 1975, pp. 7, 17).

Mulvey breaks cinematic voyeurism-narcissism into three component parts: (a) the camera; (b) the audience; and (c) the characters within the film; each component is replicating the voyeuristic logic of the other two: 'The conventions of narrative film deny [or disguise the presence of] the first two and subordinate them to the third, the conscious aim being always to eliminate intrusive camera presence and prevent a distancing awareness in the audience' (Mulvey, 1975, p. 17). But this is where mimetic theory comes into play: Lacan's notion of scopophilia and the male gaze closely follow the logic of mimesis, so that 'castration anxiety' can be read as flowing from mimetic desire, or, more accurately, a desire that is mimetic in nature, which Girard encapsulates within the all-important triangle of mimetic mediation: 'The infinite or absolute outcome of desire is tragic: to recognize that one can never fill in the gap between oneself and the model-rival is to realize that the model can never be reached; thus does it become an obstacle' (Oughourlian, 2016, p. 84). Historically, however, there has been a catch: a mimetic-rival is not simply the same as a mimetic-obstacle, for the latter is governed by an external mediation of some kind.

> Faced with the obstacle, which is to say the rival who is always already there, who is so to speak insurmountable, the 'normal' attitude consists in renouncing competition with the other and in re-directing one's desire in a more constructive direction, in accepting one's own limits as well as those imposed by social structure (for example, by the law). Renunciation is at the foundation of all hierarchical societies. This is because renunciation shows desire its impossibility. The obstacle is there, absolute. The mediator is always external, even if he is right in front of you (Oughourlian, 2016, pp. 84–85).

Just as with language, desire is never private or personal, it is always public and collective; both language and desire partake, in equal degree, in 'Other-ness' (Oughourlian, 2010, p. 14).[42] The mis-named 'Self' is, in truth, the 'Collective self of

[42] The other of this other-ness is the archaic victim; 'Human consciousness takes shape as attention is fixed on the other and particularly that special Other who is the scape-goat victim, the fountainhead of all signifiers, the transcendental signifier' (Oughourlian, 1991, p. 39).

a collective desire, which is to say of a purely mimetic, contagious, irresistibly attractive, violent, labile desire; plural somnambulism … [a] merging of desires, mimetic hypertrophying, dissolution of each person's self—such is the crowd' (Oughourlian, 2016, p. 75). Secondly, the model actively 'wishes to be copied' for a model with no imitators fails to qualify as a 'model' (just as the master 'needs' slaves); for the hierarchically subordinate subject, 'identifying with a model is consolation for not possessing all his or her belongings, since one *becomes* that model' (Oughourlian, 2016, p. 47). But then so does everyone else—'Imitative desire is always a desire to be Another' (Girard, 1965, p. 83)—which is both intolerable and unsustainable, rendering every social relation inherently unstable. Compounding the toxic brew which is community is our own private 'hermeneutic of suspicion': at all times we are dimly aware that the model, vampire-like, establishes her being through the semi-voluntary alienation of our own—'The imitator often … envies the model because the model is …seeing his [the model's] role as a possession to be jealously guarded' (Fornari, 2013, p. 38). In other words, the Girardian constant of inter-individual relations is an *a-symmetrical reciprocity* with the result that the subject 'is torn between two opposite feelings toward his model—the most submissive reverence and the most intense malice. This is the passion we call *hatred* … Only someone who prevents us from satisfying a desire that he himself has inspired in us is truly an object of hatred' (Girard, 1965, pp. 10–11). Which explains the homicidal dilemma of *Rashomon* very well: the bandit clearly does want to rape the noblewoman, but he wants to kill the samurai even more, which means that the rape of the female is only an unsatisfactory and temporary substitution for the physical extermination of the (rival) male.

Rashomon very self-consciously manipulates the unconscious operation(s) of the male gaze but in a way that is not specifically Feminist because the real title of the film should not have been *Male/Female* but *Male/Male* (or *Pupil/Teacher*): the relationships between the bandit and the samurai are negotiated by and through their respective gazing at the Woman. Tajomaru the bandit is portrayed by both Kurosawa and, even more clearly by Akutagawa, as being the puppet of a mimetic rivalry: to become as the samurai through the possession of 'the master's' Woman. Compare these two extracts, the first from the film script, and the second from the original text of the short story. Important to remember is that the film adaptation has Tajomaru (Toshiro Mifune again) lying on the ground looking up to the woman who is above him, on horseback: 'Just for a glimpse…then she was gone. I thought I'd seen an angel. I decided I'd take her…even if I had to kill the man. But if I could do it without the killing—all the better' (Kamir, 2000, p. 47). Contrast this with these lines of dialogue to the original short story, 'In a Grove'.

> I met the couple yesterday, a little after noon. The second I saw them, a puff of wind lifted her veil and I caught a peek at her. Just a peek: that's maybe why she looked so perfect to

me—an absolute bodhisattva[43] of a woman. I made up my mind right then to take her even if I had to kill the man (Akutagawa, 2006, p. 13).

Which means that the killing of the samurai, the symbolic equivalent of assuming his place, is the governing passion of the bandit; the 'sex' is merely incidental, or of secondary importance. Tajomaru's 'testimony' is the longest in the tale (three pages) and the more he talks, which is considerable, the more he allows to slip out the mimetic nature of his allegedly sexual motivation.

Oh come on, killing a man is not as big a thing as people like you [the High Police Commissioner] seem to think. If you're going to take somebody's woman, a man has to die. When *I* kill a man, I do it with my sword, but people like you don't use swords. You gentleman kill with your power, with your money, and sometimes just with your words: you tell people you're doing them a favor. True, no blood flows, the man is still alive, but you've killed him just the same.[44] I don't know whose sin is greater—your or mine (A sarcastic smile).

Of course, if you can take the woman without killing the man, all the better. Which is exactly what I was hoping to do yesterday (Akutagawa, 2006, p. 13).

But, suspiciously, it does not turn out that way, even though Tajomaru had managed to bind the samurai with ropes after deceitfully leading him into the bamboo grove under the hackneyed pretense of recovering a lost treasure. So how does it come about? Because the wife wants Tajomaru to externally validate *his* relational identity as a true man, meaning the real swordsman, through allowing her to maintain her honor after her violation at his hands. In effect, the bandit's account of the wife's behavior provides the alibi needed as cover for Tajomaru's un-confessable desire to kill his rival, and, therefore to become the samurai.

Still, I *am* Tajomaru…. And so I was able to make the woman mine without taking her husband's life.

Yes, you heard me: without taking her husband's life. I wasn't planning to kill him on top of everything else. The woman was on the ground crying, and I was getting ready to run out of the grove and leave her there when all of a sudden she grabbed my arm like some kind of crazy person. And then I heard what she was shouting between sobs. She could hardly catch her breath: 'Either you die or my husband dies. It has to be one of you. It's worse than death for me to have two men see my shame. I want to stay with the one left alive, whether it's you or him." This gave me a wild desire to kill her husband (Sullen excitement) (Akutagawa, 2006, pp. 14–15).

Which means that, in accordance with the mimetic nature of his desire, Tajomaru is committed to the narrative that has him killing the samurai with his sword, preferably in a way that confirms his real status as a swordsman and, therefore, proving his existence as the self-grounded author of his own being.

---

[43] A *bodhisattva* or 'saint' is a popular figure from later Mahayana Buddhism, who is a human being who achieves enlightenment but refuses migration into Nirvana in order to return to the world in order to aid Humankind and who, more often than not, is a woman, establishing a link between the woman an object of veneration and the symbolic Feminine as a metaphysical absolute or ideal (Akutagawa, 2006, p. 238).

[44] An uncharacteristically direct political accusation which bespeaks of the possibility of the bandit being driven by class envy or *ressentiment*.

> When I say this, you probably think I'm crueller than you are. But that's because you didn't see the look on her face—and especially, you never swathe way her eyes were burning at that moment. When those eyes met mine, I knew I wanted to make her my wife. Let the thunder god kill me, I'd make her my wife—that was the only thought in my head.[45] And no, not just for lust. I know that's what you gentleman are thinking. If lust was all I felt for her, I'd already taken care of that. I could've just kicked her down and gotten out of there. And the man wouldn't have stained my sword with his blood. But the moment my eyes locked into hers in that dark grove, I knew I couldn't leave there until I had killed him (Akutagawa, 2006, p. 15).

So they fight a duel, even though there is no real need to, for all that the bandit has to do is execute the helpless samurai. But that would be in violation of the samurai's code of chivalry (*bushido*[46]), which would not normally be binding upon a bandit, unless the bandit, like Don Quixote, dreamed of being a knight, which bespeaks here of the absolute absence of external mediation. Naturally, the issue is not in doubt.

> Still, I didn't want to kill him I a cowardly way. I untied him and challenged him to a swordfight.... The man looked furious as he drew his big sword, and without a word he sprang at me in a rage. I don't have to tell you the outcome of the fight. My sword pierced his breast n the twenty-third thrust. Not till the twenty-third: I want you to keep that in mind. I still admire him for that. He's only the only man who ever lasted even twenty thrusts with me (Cheerful grin.) (Akutagawa, 2006, p. 15).

The pain of Tajomaru is that he has to admit that this is what he really wants because it is what he really does not have. But he can make real his reputation as the toughest bandit slightly northeast of twelfth century Kyoto by claiming personal credit for a fictitious event that is validated by the censor of truth, the legal system: 'So that's my confession. I always knew my head would end up hanging in the tree outside the prison someday, so let me have the ultimate punishment'—which he truly merits (Akutagawa, 2006, pp. 15–16).

One of the things that Tajomaru is counting on in being able to get away with his narrative misdirection(s) away from the metaphysical nature of his desires is that he, along with the other three on-scene witnesses (woodcutter, wife, samurai), is assuming that because the rape and murder both occurred within an occluded space—a grove of bamboo which is a plant ideally suited for camouflage—the true nature of their private actions and motives can never be recovered; in truth, it bears more than a passing resemblance to the Cahulawassee River in *Deliverance*.[47] Unfortunately for all of them, mimetic theory enables us to reconstruct the most plausible (or least implausible) chain of events and it has nothing to do with space but everything to do with time. It is true that the Heian dynasty is collapsing, Kyoto is in a state of semi-ruin, and that with political and social anarchy comes the Sophoclean plague of

---

[45] Unfortunately for the bandit she runs away after the alleged 'fight' begins; what 'real' noblewoman would want to be stuck with a commoner? (Akutagawa, 2006, p. 15).

[46] The Japanese version of chivalry that 'emphasized courage, integrity, fortitude and fealty' (Prince, 1999, p. 118), *bushido*, or the 'way of the samurai', was a development of the Edo Period (*Edo-jidai*; c.1600–1868) but was often implicitly referenced by film-makers whenever working on a *Jidai-geki* ('period film') of any era.

[47] See Chap. 3, above.

undifferentiation, meaning that a bandit really can become a samurai (or a commoner a lord) by the simple thrust of a sword. It is also true that the grove is a separate or hidden space; there is no interactionist 'external' gaze, so agency can become uninhibited and escape the bonds of a no longer enforceable external mediation. But it is also true, again, that because the grove is outside of external mediation and space (social and physical), it is, by those facts alone, outside of time (social and physical) as well. Because the grove is an enclosed space wherein the dynamics of external mediation no longer operate, the counter-veiling forces of internal mediation are no longer held in check and all of the actors (or the mimetically possessed) can give unmediated expression of their desire for authentic Being. The name of the 'objective force beyond anyone's control' that has destroyed all identities is the crisis of undifferentiation: since there is nothing in place to block internal mediation, everyone in the segregated micro-space of unmediated immediacy (timelessness) is able to all want the same thing at the exact same moment, which results in someone dying.

5.6 Psychological Time and the Grove of Internal Mediation

As I have already discussed in Chap. 1, for Jean-Michel Oughourlian, 'it is desire that gradually brings the self into existence by constituting it as a *self-of-desire*' (Oughourlian, 2010, p. 98) which might be re-phrased as the biblical sounding 'I desire; therefore, I AM THAT AM'. The vital nexus of mimesis with psychosis lies with metaphysical desire; 'The focus [of metaphysical rivalry] becomes the business itself of the rivalry and antagonism between individuals vying for the unlimited good of more-potent-being or identity' (Reeve, 2015, p. 163). This mimetic a-symmetry in turn reflects an ontological a-symmetry: the model (desire *D*) is more 'real,' more replete with Being, in a manner in which the emulating self *s* (desire *d*) never is. And since the real object of emulation, or intense mimetic desire, is nothing other than the usurpation of the 'space' of being occupied by the rival, then the potential for psychosis remains latent within any model-imitator situation, constituting a highly dangerous form of the everyday; '...all normal, neurotic, and psychotic phenomena exist in a continuum due to the gradual exacerbation of the mimetic mechanism ... neurotic phenomena are essentially due to a claim at nodal point *N* and psychotic phenomena at a claim at nodal point *N'*, the two claims always being present...' (Oughourlian, 2016, p. 107). And the critical factor is the subject's varying experiences of the incompatible modalities of time. There is an irreperable dis-junction between the private non-relational psychological time of forgetting and the public relational physical time of un-Being, for it is only within anti-interactionist psychological time that 'self *s* declares itself the bearer and owner of desire *d* at nodal point *N* and desire *d* is [only later] scandalized to discover a desire *D* identical to itself and bearing on the same object, whose belatedness it will assert at nodal point *N*''

(Oughourlian, 2016, p. 39). Conversely, nodal point *N'*, 'representing the self's claim to anteriority over the other's desire, which was responsible for inspiring and generating it' (Oughourlian, 2016, p. 38), is the spawning ground of both neurosis and psychosis, which for Oughourlian are quintessentially mimetic in nature. 'At nodal point *N'* … desire *d* will assert its anteriority [coming earlier in time] with respect to desire *D*. Such that self *s*, which is in [physical] reality the self-of-desire *d*, will lay claim loud and clear to the possession of the object of the two desires *d* and *D*' (Oughourlian, 2016, pp. 39–40). In the final analysis our mimetic '*illness of desire*' (Oughourlian, 2010, p. 104) is not orientated toward 'power' (pace Nietzsche) or 'sex' (pace Freud, Lacan, and Mulvey) but toward Being, or 'psychological subjectivity' (Oughourlian, 2010, p. 101) along with its necessary attribute, autonomy ('self-grounding') all of which are denied by relational interactionism of Japanese society. The neurotic/psychotic root of mimetic crisis, the ultimate ground of mimetic rivalry and violence, is the subjective awareness of self *s* that it is phenomenologically 'un-real,' that it does not really exist. 'If one accepts the hypothesis of mimetic desire, it becomes clear that we must abandon the idea that the self is the source of desire. Rather, it is the movement of desire that gradually engenders in a subject a dynamic structure that is both changing and persisting and that can be designated as the "self"' (Oughourlian, 2016, p. 107). And, because of the intolerable nature of its phenomenological prison self *s* will have to rebel in order to establish the truthfulness of its sense of 'being a being': 'Self-individuation is a process originating from the necessity of disentangling the Self from the [Otherness] dimension in which it is originally and constitutively embedded' (Gallese, 2011, p. 102). Or, very possibly, the self must rebel in order to prove that she is not psychotic. Clinically, this uncannily resembles the classic definition of what used to be known as *hysteria*[48] and which presents us with an unsolvable double-bind. Without exception self *s* is alienated within psychological time: 'The whole psychological sequence will constitute a new time—psychological time, the time of memory, the only time that has any meaning for the subjectivity of human beings, the only one that appears true and in accord with reality' (Oughourlian, 2016, p. 40). Psychological time, within the unstable dynamics of mimetic relationships, operates as a kind of mystification.

> The physical time has no psychological reality although it is accessible to intelligence and therefore cognitive reality, but only when the first step toward wisdom is taken, that first step being the questioning or the recognition or the beginning of the recognition of the precedence [in physical time] of the other's desire, its priority over my desire, and therefore the non-ownership of 'my' desire (Oughourlian, 2016, p. 40).[49]

---

[48] 'When the classical [nineteenth century] studies of hysteria said that the hysteric "suffers from memories," it was only the plural that was incorrect: it is a single, unique memory, always the same one essentially—the memory that brings back to the subject an awareness of the otherness of "his own" desire'—or lack of being (Oughourlian, 2010, p. 108).

[49] Again, note the family resemblance to hysteria: 'Hysteria is one particular mode of [the] misunderstanding of interindividual relation and of the mimetic nature of desire' (Oughourlian, 2010, p. 109). For Oughourlian, hysteria is not an illness; rather 'it is a particular form of misunderstanding of the interindividual relation, a certain type of reaction to mimetic conflict. It is a phenomenologically varied manifestation of a certain dialectic of desire, a multiform expression of desire's pretension to its own priority and anteriority' (Oughourlian, 1991, p. 183).

But to attain this wisdom the first thing that self *s* must do is to admit her total and complete un-reality which is tantamount to committing phenomenological 'suicide'. *Metanoia*, or the revelatory self-awareness of our mimetic condition compels the one who undergoes conversion to 're-think in the most fundamental way the notions of the subject and of desire and, despite all our shared beliefs, to renounce the glorious but mythic autonomy with which we have adorned humanity—to renounce, too, the pleasure we experience through being the playthings of those hidden mechanisms' (Oughourlian, 1991, p. 20). But the impediment to conversion is that a no-thing cannot become a some-thing simply by renouncing its nothingness which is its true being. Or, as the saying goes: everybody wants to go to Heaven, but nobody wants to die; the 'vanishing of self *s*, the "habitual self," is equivalent to a "ritual death"' (Oughourlian, 2016, p. 196). As a result

> Rivalry is recurrent, it repeats itself. The repetition syndrome identified by psycho-analysis is mimetic for two reasons: (1) because it is always the clinical expression of a rivalry and that rivalry is always mimetic; (2) because it reproduces itself, duplicates itself, imitating the circumstances of the first rivalry and always looking for an impossible victory. That victory is impossible, since it stems from a situation which mimics the circumstances of defeat. But those circumstances are the only ones of interest, since the only battle worth winning is the one that has every chance to be lost (Oughourlian, 1996, p. 43).

The events that took place within the purely physical time of the grove, the antecedent time of the genesis of desire, occurred because the four witnesses had been removed from the illusory psychological time of externally mediated society that is governed by memory, making the 'time' in the grove a 'loss of memory,' a kind of amnesia. And only afterward, having been re-immersed into the world of external mediation through being forced to testify in that courtroom which constitutes the return to the *nomos* of psychological time, do they seek to 'restore' themselves through inconsistent lies and incommensurable testimonies ('any means seems fair'). Therefore, the act(s) of restoration at stake in *Rashomon* are not only thoroughly private in nature, but they are driven wholly by external factors: four different attempts (woodcutter, bandit, wife, samurai) to re-establish their earlier position within the symbolic order of external mediation after having accidently *recognized*, or become consciously aware of, their lack of being within the hermetically sealed grove. Which is why all of their lies make perfect sense when read through the interpretive lens of mimetic theory: the truth of each one is not merely that they are failed imitators, and their truth is that they are the *exact opposite* of their respective models. In order to undergo that remembering which is the restoration, they have to conform to the most idealized version possible of their externally mediated models; they cannot admit to their desire for true autonomy because that would be tantamount to their confessing their lack of that very thing which would double as their exposure as a 'fake'. And so they all reject the possibility of *metanoia* that their physical time in the grove offered them.[50] If they cannot manage to be the true 'real thing' in their fake 'truth'

[50] Although the ending of the film, which has been criticized for sentimentality, suggests that the woodcutter may have begun down the path toward conversion when he decides to take in an infant that had been abandoned at Demon's Gate.

as master they can be the fake 'real thing' in their real 'truth' as pupil, each one the perfect performer of their pre-assigned and externally mediated roles which are only 'real' within the memory-bound psychological space that exists outside of the grove. This takes us to the outermost liminal boundaries of lie and fantasy; as Joshua Oppenheimer commented on the in-famous and mis-directional 're-enactments' of fictitious events in Errol Morris's *The Thin Blue Line* (1988),[51] the post-modern bits were not proper re-enactments but 'dramatizations of our self-deceptive fantasies', fantasies being 'the prism of a dreamscape of lies' (Morris, 2005). But that is not where the heart is, as Kurosawa knew full well.[52]

So what is the 'moral' of *Rashomon*? In terms of the Japanese cultural vocabulary of the interactionist self, the film is a moral fable about egoism as moral evil, that self-affirmation that yields nothing but '"contradictions and the setting of one against the other"' (Prince, 1999, p. 68).

> *Rashomon* is a cinematically straightforward presentation of the sins of egoism. The ambiguity within the film—the question of the reliability of the various stories—is psychological in nature, issuing from the characters and the reasons they may have for lying. It is not an [modernist] ambiguity of form, located in the visual and aural organization of the film. As Kurosawa said, the paradoxes in the film are those of the human heart. They are not those of the image itself (Prince, 1999, p. 131).

But the vital caveat that must be added is that the profoundly 'un-Japanese' egoism on display is the universal dynamic of mimetic desire. Even in hyper-mimetic Japan the regression to the 'state of nature' (the grove) triggers (or allows for) the unmediated free play of metaphysical desire and mimetic rivalries that distort the perception of reality itself, the non-space and non-time of 'no one is really who they think they are' which is the green jungle hell of undifferentiation and which makes restoration impossible in the absence of a two-sword samurai/ronin like Sanjuro. The "inner relationship" between world and reality is denied', consistent with a culture regarded where 'outward role demands' function as "the really important center of the self" (Christine Kiefer qtd. Prince, 1999, p. 30), allowing us to properly frame the meaning of the grove: 'This communicative disjunction is viewed in the film in ontological terms as a space wherein human sin and evil originate. The failure of language to grasp the world of events is a story about the human fall from the grace into a world deformed by heterodoxy and multiplicity' (Price, 1999, p. 134). And this moral provides us with the means of reconstructing the 'truth'. Kurosawa himself tells us so.

> This film is like a strange picture scroll that is unrolled and displayed by the ego. You say that you can't understand this script at all, but that is because the human heart itself is impossible to understand. If you focus on the impossibility of truly understanding human psychology

[51] See Chap. 6, below.

[52] 'What has made *Rashomon* a tantalizing film is its refusal to validate any of the witnesses' stories as a true account. There is simply no way to know who is telling the truth. In this ambiguity Kurosawa has found a narrative expression for his own pessimism about what Conrad referred to as the human heart of darkness' (Prince, 1999, p. 130)—or, more accurately, the impossibility of reconciling external with internal mediation.

and read the script one more time, I think that you will get the point of it (Kurosawa, 1983, p. 183).

Truthfully.

5.7 What Really Happened in the Grove: Metaphysical Desire and Saving Face

Jean-Luc Godard unconditionally rejected 'the conventions of narrative cinema entirely' (Prince, 1999, p. 135). Why? It was because of 'His awareness of the "magical" properties of photographic images, their power to demand a reading as the real objects they represent rather than as signifiers, and of the moral and political ramifications of this confusion' (Prince, 1999, p. 135). Kurosawa's elder brother Heigo, possibly the director's private model and the real-life exemplar for the master-pupil relationships that occurs so frequently in his films, shared Goddard's sentiments, spending much of his youth working as a *Katsuben*, the theatre-appointed narrator for silent films.

> At the time [the late 1920s] my brother had taken a great step. He was no longer simply writing program notes for films as a great fan of the movies, he had become a professional silent-film narrator. The narrators not only recounted the plot of the films, they enhanced the emotional voices and sound effects and providing evocative descriptions of the events and images on the screen—much like the narrators of the Bunraku puppet theatre (Kurosawa, 1983, p. 74).

Which meant that the controlling voice-over narration was not really controlling; in principle, it could be wholly disassociated with what was being projected on the screen so that the audience could pick and choose which version of the filmic reality (which was all fiction, both the director's and the narrator's) they preferred—and which, when broken down completely, meant that the viewer could conclude, perhaps even unconsciously, that she was seeing a 'lie' projected as a moving image while hearing the 'truth' from the voice. The implications of this, a modernist appropriation and re-deployment of the pre-modern artefact of the puppet theatre, must not be underestimated, especially since Kurosawa wanted his adaptation of 'In a Grove' to incorporate the aesthetic tropes of silent film.

> I like silent pictures and always have. They are often so much more beautiful than sound pictures. Perhaps they have to be. At any rate, I wanted to restore some of this beauty. I thought of it, I remember, this way: one of the techniques of modern painting is simplification, I must therefore simplify this film (Akira Kurosawa qtd. Prince, 1999, p. 132)

He elaborates upon his nostalgic affection for silent film at considerable length in his *Something Like an Autobiography* (1975).

> Since the advent of the tallies in the 1930s, I felt, we had misplaced and forgotten what was so wonderful about the old silent movies. I was aware of the aesthetic loss as a constant irritation. I sensed a need to go back to the origins of the motion picture to find this particular

> beauty again; I had to go back into the past.... *Rashomon* would be my testing ground ... To provide the symbolic background atmosphere, I decided to use the Akutagawa 'In a Grove' story, which goes into the depths of the human heart as if with a surgeon's scalpel, laying bare its dark complexities and bizarre twists. These strange impulses of the human heart would be expressed through the use of an elaborately fashioned play of light and shadow (Kurosawa, 1983, p. 182).

Or black and white, just like in the silent films.

> In light of Kurosawa's intent to recapture the silent film aesthetic in *Rashomon*, Joseph Anderson's remarks about the function of the katsuben, the narrator of a silent film for Japanese audiences, are provocative, in that they suggest that *Rashomon* has internalized the voice(s) of the katsuben as the competing discourses of narrative, image, and character: 'The dominance and apparent reality of the images on the screen were readily deconstructed by the katsuben's words and demeanor. Indeed, the katsuben attacked the ontological status of the film. Was truth in the photographic images or in what the katsuben said? Which was unreliable?' (Joseph Anderson qtd. Prince, 1999, pp. 379–378).

Both were. The second version of the events in the grove told by the woodcutter is not in the original short story; it was penned by Kurosawa in order to provide the necessary clue to enable the audience to decipher what really happened in physical, not psychological, space and time. Since the events within the grove occurred within physical time, and outside of the all-enveloping *meconnaissance* of the psychological time of the law court where the testimonies were heard, it really is possible to recover the truth through the act of representation. The 'solution' offered to the audience on a platter is an iron-clad necessity of cinematic convention but it also but bespeaks of a commitment to a realist, or representational, epistemological framework consistent with the status of the film as a social drama of a specifically Japanese kind: the sensation of un-reality created by the film flows from its concern with the nature of human lies, not multiple universes. Or perhaps I should say *Rashomon* allows the Japanese audience to actively decipher what happened, because they understand what it means to 'save face,' making them the antithesis of the internally mediated Western audiences who are obsessed with epistemological relativism.[53] *Rashomon* is decidedly not a post-metaphysical post-modern *jouissance* of parallel realities and irreconcilable interpretative worlds[54] but an existentially intense Japanese social drama wherein

---

[53] When *Rashomon* was shown at the 1951 Venice Film Festival, it 'seemed mystically [sic] in synch with the existentialism of European culture, and it added a new proof to the epistemological and moral relativism of that era' (Prince, 1999, pp. 340–341). There is no need to labor the point that if *Rashomon* is a folklore-like account about *lying*, then the film is not an exercise in epistemological relativism but, rather, epistemological realism.

[54] The phrase 'the Rashomon Effect' is a cliché of both legal education and practice applied heuristically to the the hard-to-decipher situation wherein multiple witness testimonies concerning the 'same event' are not only contradictory but objectively irreconcilable; in extra-legal terms, the phrase 'has come to refer to any instance where people perceive the same phenomenon and come away with different ideas and memories about what happened,' which is really nothing more than problematizing the mundane reality of interpretation, which seems to constitute a serious epistemological threat to many (Fassano, 2010, p. 811). In a non-banal sense, the Rashomon Effect—which, as I will show, has absolutely no relevance to the eponymous film whatsoever—does point to a recurrent problem concerning the methodology of social scientific research, the divide between the

everyone has an all-controlling need to lie no matter what lest their hidden truth of nothingness be publicly exhumed. The dramatic subject of the film is metaphysical desire and the primary narrative work is performed by the body of the slain samurai which acts as a referent that, in a manner that is wholly anti-deconstructionist, sets objective limits to the process of interpretive reading. As I have already shown in Chap. 1, the scapegoat, for Girard and in opposition to Derrida, operates as a transcendental signifier in that the unified crowd, through *meconnaissance*, collectively transfers onto the physical remains of the victim 'all actual and potential meaning of the community' and 'through its intermediacy, on to all things' (Girard et al., 1978, p. 103). All of the major participants in the events in the grove are linked to the cadaver as the transcendental signifier of mimetic desire: the bandit/masculinity, the wife/femininity, the woodcutter/wealth, the channelled spirit of the samurai/self as the corporeal locus of his own metaphysical desire to-be-samurai. 'Social relations precede object relations and determine them' says Andrew J. McKenna (McKenna, 1992, p. 80) and the victim has for incalculable millennia acted as 'the source of ambivalence' which is 'the source of a properly human community' (McKenna, 1992, p. 80). But within medieval (and post-medieval) Japan 'a properly human community' means absolute deference to the institutions of external mediation, signifying an extreme mimetic crisis generated through a totalizing political imperative to restore social norms. So 'what really happened in the grove' is not a metaphysical puzzle but a tragic melodrama about metaphysical desires and their signifying doubles—that is, no one is truly identical to their own selves and they have, in private, all failed miserably to maintain the face of their respective public selves. Following Akutagawa, what Kurosawa presents the viewer with is an 'honest' woodcutter who is a thief, a 'noblewoman' who is a whore, a 'samurai' who is afraid of death, and a 'bandit' who is afraid of murder. In all five lies are told.[55] The first lie is the first tale of the woodcutter; he is apparently the first person to have discovered the body of the samurai, slain by some kind of blade, and his representation of the cadaver establishes the human remains as the phenomenological core of the narrative that unites all of the other fake narratives and, therefore, remains as the constant and objective truth that external mediates the limitations to myth-making, or the *muthos*-lie of the differing and contradictory fables.[56]

positivist and the interpretivist approaches. 'The *positivist* approach maintains that a true explanation or cause of an event or social pattern can be found and tested by scientific standards of verification. The *interpretivist* approach does not seek an objective truth so much as to unravel patterns of subjective understanding. The latter assumes that all versions of the truth are shaped by the viewer's perceptions and understanding of their world. In the case of a contested or event with many different versions, the analyst's job is to uncover what these versions reveal about the people who tell them, their positions in the social structure of their communities, and their cultural understandings' (Roth and Mehta, 2002, p. 132). It goes without saying that Kurosawa's film is interpreted as an icon of the interpretivist approach whereas, in objective reality, it is a milestone of deductive reasoning.

[55] The priest's tale is unproblematic and provides proof of both the samurai and his wife as being present in the grove, and the constable's account of his having arrested Tajomaru is perfunctory. The film version leaves out the tale told by the noblewoman's mother.

[56] See Chap. 1, above.

> The body was in a bamboo grove on the other side of the mountain.... He had only one stab wound, but it was right in the middle of his chest; the bamboo leaves around the body were soaked with dark red blood.... Did I see a sword or anything? No Sir, not a thing.... Just the rope and comb is all. But the weeds and the bamboo leaves on the ground were pretty trampled down: he must have put up a tremendous fight before they killed him (Akutagawa, 2006, p. 10).

The second lie is that told by Tajomaru the bandit who claims to have made passionate love with the samurai's wife and then killed her husband after a heroic swordfight which lasted for twenty-three strokes. The third lie is that of the wife who claims that she was raped by the bandit and then killed her husband with the dagger as a way of sparing him from shame of being powerless to prevent her from being violated (and after having allowed himself to be placed into humiliating bondage by Tajomaru, a commoner). The fourth lie is impressively told by the deceased spirit of the samurai being channeled by a medium: in this fable, the samurai kills himself with the *tanto*[57] after claiming that his wife urged the bandit to kill him. The samurai's tale is the most interesting of the four provided by Akutagawa because he provides an account of the theft of the *tanto* that is highly compelling; it is also the ending of 'In a Grove'.

> Lying there, I was enveloped in a deep silence. Then, someone crept up to me. I tried to see who it was. But darkness had already been gathering around me. Someone ... that someone drew the small sword softly out of my breast in its invisible hand. At the same time once more blood flowed into my mouth. And once and for all I sank down into the darkness of space (Akutagawa, 1970, pp. 32–33).

It is also the only lie that shows the samurai's death on-screen. In his testimony Tajomaru has the samurai die at the end of a prolonged swordfight, but the fatal twenty-third stroke is off-screen[58] and, in the wife's tale, we see her in a profiled close up, moving from left to right, with the *tanto* extended before her; she exits the screen and all that we see is a dark space, while the samurai's death remains invisible and silent. What is most intriguing about this montage is that it is partially reproduced in the woodcutter's second lie, the one penned by Kurosawa, but this time with Tajomaru who is extending his *katana* in front of him, slightly raised almost in the form of a spear, as he advances to the right but is shaking and sweating noticeably which clearly indicates the commoner's profound fear of the enormity of his would-be act which is to kill a nobleman who is, again, lying on the ground, off-screen. The symmetry between the two 'death' scenes creates the subliminal impression that we are witnessing 'unreal events' in both of them. But that is nothing compared to what comes immediately before this highly suspect moment: lying prone on the ground and cornered by Tajomaru, the samurai utters the phrase that is anathema to

---

[57] There is some uncertainty concerning the identity of this weapon, for the text literally reads that the wife 'drew a small sword'. Although it is unlikely that a woman would be carrying a small sword (*wakizashi*), the usage of the term suggests that *tanto*, a dagger, is what is meant, although the two items could be used interchangeably (Akutagawa, 1970, p. 25).

[58] At the moment that the death stroke is delivered, we see only Tajormaru standing over the samurai who is obscured by the bushes laying on the ground; the camera does a medium close-up of the bandit and we never actually see the nobleman die.

any hero of a *Ken-geki*: *'I don't want to die!'* Under the laws of *bushido*, the penalty for cowardice, which is dis-honor, is ritualistic suicide, by a blade. Meaning that the nobleman has the perfect reason for committing suicide, one fully consistent with his mimetic desire to-be samurai.

I would suggest that of the five lies the one that is closest to the truth is the woodcutter's second fable: in essence this is the 'true' account of what really happened in the grove except for the assertion that the bandit killed the samurai; this is an interpolation by the woodcutter in his last-ditch effort to maintain the concealment of his mimetic failure, the existential danger of losing face for having stolen the short sword by withdrawing it from the dead man's corpse, as was recounted by the warrior's ghost and which the woodcutter needs to refute. And I make this assumption on the grounds that not only is metaphysical desire the prime motivator of all of the character's actions, but that the *meconnaissance* of psychological time is itself the interpretive key to reconstructing the true sequence of events that took place during the representational physical time spent in the grove: to reconstruct the crime, we have to read the respective tales for the mimetic desire that is revealed through the nature of the lie that is being told. To solve the mystery of the grove ask the question: what is it that each character finds the most unbearable to admit about themselves? What is the precise form that their respective metaphysical desire assumes?

The wife's lie is the easiest one to dismiss on a priori grounds precisely because the nature of her behavior revealed by the approximately truthful second tale of Kurosawa's woodcutter is so extreme that the noblesse oblige behavior that she clams for herself in her own story is too transparently crafted under the rubric of feminine perfection. In other words, she, more than anyone else, is revealed as the perfect opposite, a pure double, in the narrative incompatibility of her lie and the woodcutter's second fable. She is also outweighed by the other three witnesses: the samurai and the bandit the first time and the woodcutter the second time, meaning that the samurai was either killed by the bandit or committed suicide and that either the bandit or the samurai is telling the true, or truer, account. But if we watch the film closely, Kurosawa would appear to tip the scales almost, but not completely, in the favor of the samurai. The woodcutter's second fable is the least implausible of the five and explains everything except for the actual death of the samurai which, as testified to by the dead man, was suicide. And although Tajomaru makes the point of informing the High Police Commissioner that 'I got rid of the sword before coming to Kyoto, though' (Akutagawa, 2006, p. 15), suggesting that he was actually in possession of the samurai's *katana* after taking it as a prize, the important point is that he makes no mention of the *tanto*. And the thing that none of the versions can account for is the disappearance of the *tanto*, other than the samurai testifying that it had been removed from his body. The woodcutter's reaction to the testimony channeled by the medium—the turning of his head in the direction of the possessed woman, a small but significant gesture in a culture that requires absolute stillness during public ritual—bears out the basic but incomplete truth of the dead man's testimony. The samurai's penultimate words are: 'Then stealthy footsteps came up to me. I tried to see who it was, but the darkness had closed in all around me. Someone—that someone gently pulled the dagger from my chest with an invisible hand' (Akutagawa, 2006, p. 19), which is where Akutagawa ends the fable. As both the wife and the bandit have fled by this point, and as Akutagawa would have committed an unpardonable literary sin in introducing an unknown character at the very end, especially in a locked-room type of mystery, then the thief with hands that were invisible could only have been the woodcutter.[59] Which is why he had to omit it in his second tale and continue with the lie of the bandit killing the samurai; everything else, because it did directly concern him, could be related truthfully. Whatever else did nor did not happen, two things must be true: (a) that the woodcutter stole the knife and (b) that the knife was inside the samurai, meaning that the dagger (*tanto*) and not the sword (*katana*) were the instrument of his death.[60] The *tanto*'s placement within the body of the samurai and its having been withdrawn by the woodcutter precludes the possibility of the warrior having been killed in a duel with Tajomaru and invalidates the bandit's tale of heroic swordplay leaving only the samurai's story and the second version of the woodcutter, which is where the probable truth lies for it alone unifies almost all aspects of the different versions once we realize that each tale is governed by the logic of metaphysical desire.

The woodcutter's second and unofficial testimony constitutes one of the greatest of rarities in cinema: the filming of a lie. The depiction of the bandit fictitiously 'killing' the samurai off-screen visually imitates the wife's equally fictitious act of the killing of her equally off-screen husband and the strict parallelism between the wife's clearly false tale and the woodcutter's incomplete second tale indicates that both are lying, but in different ways and to varying degrees. Here, the wife very aggressively (and dangerously) assumes command of the two men by appropriating the logic of phallocentrism and then reversing the male gaze back against itself and deploying it as weapon for symbolic castration. She is also correct in her anti-phallic assessment: neither the bandit nor the samurai are 'real' men, meaning that both are afraid of death. Which explains the sheer harlot-like extremity of her speech; this is the moment of the woman's capture and redirection of the male gaze against the men in the audience, or the interpretive community of masculinist film-viewers (Mulvey, 1975) as visually conveyed by the masterful expressions of boyish shame and phallic embarrassment expressed by both samurai and bandit.

> 'It's not me! It's you [Men] who are weak! If you're my husband, why don't you kill this man? Then you can tell me to kill myself…like a real man would. But you aren't a real man. That's why I was crying! I'm tired. I'm tired of this farce. I thought that Tajomaru might find some way out. I thought…if he'd only really save me I'd do anything for him. But he's not a man either. He's just like my husband [Spitting in Tajomaru's face, laughing, she adds:] Just remember…a woman only loves a real man. And when she loves—she loves madly, forgetting all else. But a woman can only be won with the strength of swords (Kamir, 2000, p. 54).

---

[59] An additional fact in support of this is that by telling the second tale, the woodcutter confesses to having been present at the time of the events in the grove but secreted.

[60] Forensics helps. Although this is pre-scientific the twelfth-century, the Japanese of the time would have been experts at identifying sword and knife wounds and recognizing the differences among them.

Recall that Kurosawa's working title of the film was *Male/Female*; if there is a mimetic triangle (samurai-wife-bandit) present in the narrative—and the 'cutting of certain sections of *Rashomon*' highlight the manner wherein 'angular compositions visualize the three corner relationships among the bandit, samurai, and noblewoman' (Prince, 1999, p. 56) indicates that there is—then it is dramatically appropriate for the woman to flee at the end, leaving the men to engage in their pantomime of the pseudo-battle of dueling cowards. And Kurosawa's cinematic re-presentation of triangular desire neatly replicates Akutagawa's literary narration, most especially in the samurai's account of the conspiracy of the wife to murder her husband after deciding to abandon him for Tajomaru.

> And that was not her only crime against me. If that were all she did, I would not be suffering so here in the darkness. With him leading her by the hand, she was stepping out of the bamboo grove as if in a dream,[61] when suddenly the color drained from her face and she pointed back at me. 'Kill him!' she screamed. 'Kill him! I can't be with you as long as he is alive!' Again and again she screamed, as if she had lost her mind, 'Kill him!' even now her words like a windstorm threaten to blow me headlong into the darkest depths. Have such hateful words ever come from the mouth of a human being before? Have such damnable damnable words ever reached the ears of a human being before? Have such—(An explosion of derisive laughter.) Even the bandit went pale when he heard her (Akutagawa, 2006, p. 18).

Castration with a vengeance.

'Have such hateful words ever come from the mouth of a human being before?' the disembodied voice rhetorically asks. Sure they have: in Akutagawa's 'The Robbers' published in 1917, the same year as 'Rashomon' and which, like its sister tale, re-presents Kyoto as the dilapidated arena for internal mediation to run amok (Akutagawa, 1964, pp. 53–126). In fact, so advanced is the decomposition of Kyoto and its attendant regression into undifferentiation, that the city, like the grove, would appear to be in the thrall of physical time; Akutagawa also casually references a certain bandit named 'Tajomaru' as a member of one of the criminal gangs that exercise nocturnal control over the disintegrating *polis* (Akutagawa, 1964, p. 94).

> Though often she [the Old Woman/Obaba of Inokuma] had passed that way, when she now compared her own younger self of years ago in these surroundings, everywhere she showed change beyond belief. She reflected how at one time she had been a kitchen maid in an aristocratic house, and had been wooed by a man of higher station and had at length born Shakin; compared with that time, except in its name, the Capital bore few vestiges of the old times.
>
> In those times there had been roads by which oxcarts had come and gone, where now only the thistles bloomed desolately in the sunny spots between the half-fallen fences, and now there were fig trees with their unripe fruit, and flocks of crows, unheeded by anyone, gathered at the waterless ponds even by day…. Yet, even to steal and to kill had become as household tasks; perhaps it was that her heart had grown wild like the highways and byways overgrown with weeds, and no longer did such things distress her (Akutagawa, 1964, p. 60).[62]

---

[61] The signifying of psychological time.

[62] Admittedly this passage presents an apparent problem for my mimetic reading of the text, as the reveries of the 'old woman' are less suggestive of mediation than iterability, the good citizens of Kyoto migrating between the polar opposites of law and crime, each one the double of the other:

This passage is reminiscent of a 'plague narrative' and, as we have already seen with *Oedipus Tyrannus*,[63] that any major 'social upheaval can bring about conditions favourable to an outbreak of the plague' (Girard et al., 1978, p. 136). The plague 'is universally presented as a process of undifferentiation, a destruction of specificities' (Girard et al., 1978, p. 136) and the great 'levelling' of the resultant mega-death is actually the cause, and not the effect, of the 'plague,' which is as much allegorical as it is bio-medical, for the 'destruction is often preceded by a reversal' which is the undifferentiation attendant upon the breakdown of external mediation (Girard et al., 1978, p. 136).

> Social hierarchies are first transgressed, then abolished.... The plague will turn the honest man into a thief, the virtuous man into a lecher, the prostitute into a saint.... The plague makes all accumulated knowledge and all categories of judgment invalid.... The distinctiveness of the plague is that it ultimately destroys all forms of distinctiveness present (Girard et al., 1978, pp. 136–137).

'Anarchy,' the abolition of cultural distinctions, is itself kind of plague; 'in a sense, it is even more of a plague than the disease itself' (Girard et al., 1978, p. 138) since the plague is 'a transparent metaphor for a certain reciprocal violence that spreads, literally, like the plague' (Girard et al., 1978, p. 139).

> In many parts of the world, the words we translate as 'plague' can be viewed as a generic label for a variety of ills that affect the community as a whole and threaten or seem to threaten the very existence of social life. It may be inferred from various signs that inter-human tensions and disturbances often play the principle role (Girard et al., 1978, p. 138).

Also noteworthy is that one of the three principal characters of 'The Robbers' is the 'failed' samurai Taro, who, thanks to the capital's descent into mimetic crisis, is unable to maintain the persona of a proper knight but who has thrived as a bandit in the new city of unlimited equal opportunity: 'In looking back at the time when I was a low-grade official ... I did not forget to respect the Three Treasures [Buddha, scriptures, priesthood]; nor did I neglect to follow the Imperial Laws. Now I thieve; I

'So, everything was changed, and yet in another sense all was the same as it had always been; what her daughter was doing now, and what she herself had done in old times were unexpectedly similar. And, too, what Taro and Jiro were doing, and what her husband had done in his time, would not be so much different. In this way the people of all times would do over the same things. So, if she thought of it in that way, here still was the old Capital, and even she herself was her old self.' To which there are two responses. The first is that as a passionate advocate of the modernist conceit of the unreliable narrator, the ruminations of every character of Akutagawa should be treated with the maximum degree of scepticism, reason always held suspect as rationalization and confession revealed as self-exculpation: 'In the heart of Obaba of Inokuma, such thoughts came vaguely fleeting ... suddenly the old woman contorted her wrinkled face into a spirited grin, and began to enliven her face and the frog's leg stick she carried. But there was nothing unusual in that.' The second is that the deterministic influence of the urban wasteland, described in the neutral and omniscient third-person voice of the narrator, oppressively imposes itself upon the imagination of the reader as the all-controlling environment of a pre-civilizational chaos, the Hobbesian state of nature reborn, that all are at war with all—which means that everyone is operating within a closed world of true equality and unlicensed desire (Akutagawa, 1964, p. 60).

[63] See Chap. 1, above.

sometimes commit arson; and not only two or three times have I murdered' (Akutagawa, 1964, p. 68), but by the end of his spiral descent into fratricidal fantasy, Taro is reinstated as a samurai in the service of the law enforcing Governor of Tango—the perfect ending, for as Taro explains it, "After all—everybody is a beast" (Akutagawa, 1964, p. 92). But most relevant of all is that, directly anticipating 'In a Grove' (1922), 'The Robbers' also portrays a triangulation of erotic desire as the façade of a metaphysical form of mimetic rivalry: Taro the model, fallen samurai turned bandit, his younger brother Jiro the imitator, wannabe samurai turned wannabe bandit, and Shakin, the bandit-queen/femme fatale/Catwoman of post-apocalyptic *Heian-kyo*, 'Capital of Peace and Tranquility' who 'mediates' between the two brothers and whose 'deportment served only to enshroud her with a mysterious halo, and ... aroused not the least feeling of vulgarity' (Akutagawa, 1964, p. 69).

> She was a woman of twenty-five or twenty-six years of age, of medium stature, and she moved her limbs as lithely as would a cat. Her face was a mixture of an awful wildness and extraordinary beauty. Narrow forehead and tender cheeks, fresh teeth and sensual lips, sharp eyes and arrogant eyebrows—all these cannot be expected in one person, but strangely she had them all. There was not the slightest flaw; most wonderful was the hair falling over her shoulders; as the sunlight shone bright blue on black, we might say that her hair was no different from the feathers of a bird. [Jiro] felt the never-ending fascination of this woman to be rather distasteful (Akutagawa, 1964, p. 79).

Here is the model-obstacle Taro, the samurai as bandit, on his kid brother Jiro the emulator.

> Since he was a child, Jiro has regarded me as his idol; I believe that Jiro will not yield to the temptation [of possessing Shakin], but will at least have that much discretion. Yet ... it would be ill-judged for me to place too much confidence in my brother. No, as for overestimating my younger brother—it would be a mistake to underestimate Shakin's flattering technique. It is not only Jiro; the number of men ruined by that woman's one glance is more numerous than the swallows flying about in the scorching sky. For instance, even I, after I first met that woman, have been gradually degrading myself ... (Akutagawa, 1964, p. 67).

But Shakin, as the model of mimetic desire, makes Taro do it, meaning that he is imitating her.

> Since I had committed a crime,[64] my living honestly or my leading a precarious life would be the same thing in the eyes of the law. If I were to die, at least I would live on as long as I could. With this in mind, at last I became obedient to Shakin; together with my brother I entered the fraternity of thieves. From that time on I burned, I murdered. There are no evil deeds that I have not done, though, at first, of course, I acted unwillingly; but after I had committed such acts there was no longer any inhibition. I began to believe the doing of evil is natural for human beings ... (Akutagawa, 1964, p. 72).

Hence, the 'more crimes I committed, one after another, the more I became attracted to Shakin. My killing and stealing—all was because of that woman' (Akutagawa, 1964, pp. 72–73) just as it was with Tajomaru in the grove of internal mediation and physical time.

[64] The murder of a prison guard at Shakin's instigation.

> I had already known that I was not the only man who had made Shakin do his bidding; even Shakin herself had proudly told me many times the names of the Court nobles and priests with whom she had had relationships. I felt that this woman's flesh was known to many men, but that the woman's heart was occupied only by me. True—woman's chastity was not of the body; believing this, I suppressed my jealousy (Akutagawa, 1964, p. 70).

Everything is different with the baby brother, however; 'But he and his younger brother were no longer as they had been in those far-off days' of idyllic fishing trips in their youth (Akutagawa, 1964, p. 71). Jiro, as the emulator, is bound by the logic of metaphysical desire to slay his brother and to assume his place of unmediated access to the model.

> Now I must face the fact that Shakin is being stolen from me by my brother; she is being stolen by Jiro whom I helped at the risk of my life. It is not clear to me whether she *will be* seized or *has been* seized from me. I, who did not doubt Shakin's heart, allowed her relationship with other men for the sake of carrying out our evil deeds ... But with Jiro her relationship is different. My younger brother and I seem different in character, but we are not really so. As for facial features—the smallpox of seven or eight years ago marked me heavily and my younger brother lightly—his features being as they were when he was born, Jiro has become handsome, while I, having lost an eye on account of the smallpox, have become unnatural and deformed. If I, so ugly and one-eyed, have until now captivated Shakin's heart—even though this might be self-conceit—I am sure it must have been by the power of my soul (Akutagawa, 1964, p. 73).

Everything really does come down to sex.

> And even my younger brother, born of the same parents, has the same spirit as I.... But my brother, compared with me, is handsome in everybody's eyes; it is reasonable that Shakin is attracted by such a man as Jiro. Besides, in comparing him with me, I doubt he could resist her allurement. Yes, I am always ashamed of my ugly face; almost always in love affairs I am modest. Even such as I have loved Shakin to distraction; and Jiro, who is handsome, could not but fall foul of her flattery. When I think of it, it is reasonable that they should come together. But because it is not unreasonable—just for that alone do I suffer. My younger brother will take Shakin from me; he will take all of Shakin from me; at some time he will surely do so. Ah—but my loss is not only for Shakin alone; I shall lose my brother, too. And instead, I shall have an enemy called Jiro; and I give no mercy to mine enemies. Nor would my enemy give me any mercy. That being so, I know well the place we will go from here. Would I kill my younger brother, or would I be killed ...? (Akutagawa, 1964, pp. 73–74).[65]

And here is Jiro on Shakin whose attitude toward her anticipates Tajomaru's attitude toward the noblewoman in the grove and her fixation upon 'the strength of swords'.

---

[65] Just to make certain that we do not miss the mimetic rivalry between the brother-doubles, Akutagawa provides this remarkable passage following Taro's reverie that clearly references the woodcutter's fake first account of discovering the samurai's body in the grove: 'The smell of death, striking his nose, frightened Taro; the death in his heart had no odor. Looking around .... He found that there lay naked under the wide fence the decomposed bodies of two children, dumped one athwart the other. Perhaps because they had been beaten upon by the fierce sun, some parts of the discoloured skin protruded glutinous flesh, and on them both blue flies—countless—had settled. Nor was that all, for under one of the children who lay face downwards, the swift ants had already attached themselves. Taro felt that before his eyes there was revealed to him his own future' (Akutagawa, 1964, p. 74). And the decomposing bodies of the children are transcendental signifiers no less than the body of the samurai: the phenomenological constant of both texts is death.

> I myself love Shakin; at the same time I hate her. It angers me only to think of that woman's fickle character. Besides, she's a ceaseless liar; furthermore, even when my elder brother and I myself would seem to hesitate [during a 'job'], she will commit a cruel murder indifferently. Sometimes I stare at her wanton sleeping figure, and puzzle as to why I might have been attracted to such a woman, especially when I find she has given herself to men she barely knows; I feel even as though I might kill her with my own hands. So much do I hate Shakin. Yet, looking into her eyes, I feel still more fascination. There is no other like her possessing such an ugly soul and beautiful flesh (Akutagawa, 1964, p. 77).

Shakin makes Jiro do it just like she made Taro do it, both brothers being possessed by mimetic rivalry: 'Jino felt Shatkin's eyes keen like a wild cat's peering at him, and in those eyes there was a fearful strength, and gradually his own will power seemed to be crippled … The two of them, alone together, their hands clasped, felt the awful will to agree' (Akutagawa, 1964, pp. 82, 83). For how could Jiro refuse the model who is authentic Being since a desire that is metaphysical is the sign of an absence, the lack of presence, within the imitator?

> My brother seems not to know of my hate. My brother, by nature, does not seem like me to hate her bestial mind. For instance, when observing the relationship between her and other men, my brother's outlook is entirely different from mine. My brother keeps his silence when seeing her with anybody else.[66] He seems to permit her such whims as though they were passing fancies; but I myself cannot do so. To me the fact of Shakin soiling her body is the same thing as Shakin soiling her mind; I cannot permit her to turn her mind towards other men; it is still more painful that she has given her naked body to other men. Because of that I am jealous also of my brother; in my feeling of sorrow there is jealousy. In this way of thinking would there be much difference in our outlook if I compare my elder brother's outlook and my own? And this very difference would worsen our relationship… (Akutagawa, 1964, pp. 77–78).

Taro resolves to kill Jiro; Shakin convinces Jiro to murder Taro[67]; Shakin connives with a third party (the nameless 'samurai at Judge To's mansion') to liquidate Jiro (Akutagawa, 1964, pp. 82, 100, 79); however, both brothers unite to murder Shakin instead and are reconciled over the corpse of their 'real' enemy, the woman (Akutagawa, 1964, pp. 124–125) which, according to the samurai's testimony, is almost what occurred in the grove. Not long afterward, both brothers re-enter the ranks of the samurai and are re-integrated into the now restored, and restoring, machinery of external mediation. Ten years after the killing of Shaki, her housemaid and sole witness to the homicide, Akogi

> Saw a man renowned for his bravery pass by; he was one of the escorts of the Governor of Tango, and she said he was Taro. Indeed, the man did have thin pockmarks and only one eye…. but whether it were Taro or whether it were not, *that* nobody knew. Known only was the fact that the man in question had a younger brother who was reputed to serve the same master; that much was discreetly rumored (Akutagawa, 1964, pp. 125–126).

Because both brothers, as reconstituted samurai, are under the aegis of external mediation, both may stand in an externally mediated hierarchical relationship to the

---

[66] The name for this is 'voyeurism'.

[67] Employing the admittedly impressive logic that '"If it's all right to kill Taro, it will be all right to kill any of our companions"' (Akutagawa, 1964, p. 82).

model (the Governor of Tango) free of the pathology of mimetic rivalry—unlike with the femme-fatale of the Kyoto underworld. Within the new 'over-world' of demarcated hierarchies, the samurai brothers are now the doubles of the bandits who were previously the doubles of the samurai during crisis era of undifferentiation.

'In the Grove' recapitulates all of the essentials of the triangulation of 'The Robbers' as Tajomaru's response to the wife's impassioned request for the murder of her husband indicates—or, at least, this is how the husband tells it.

> Even the bandit went pale when he heard her. She clung to his arm and screamed again, 'Kill him!'. The bandit stared at her, saying neither that he would kill me nor that he would not. The next thing I knew, however, he sent my wife sprawling on the bamboo leaves with a single kick (another explosion of derisive laughter.) The bandit calmly folded his arms and turned to look at me.
>
> 'What do you want me wo do with her?' he asked. 'Kill her or let her go? Just nod to answer. Kill her?' For this if for nothing else, I am ready to forgive the bandit his crimes (Akutagawa, 2006, p. 18).

Conversely, when the samurai confronts the bandit in three of the versions (none of them his own), he is doubly castrated; he is overcome by a commoner (bound and gagged and then sexually insulted by being forced to watch the rape-seduction of his wife by the bandit) *and* he loses the sword fight, which also violates the rules of the *Ken-ge*. Which is where Akutagawa ends. But not Kurosawa. Provided that we can essentially discount both the wife's and the bandit's versions, the samurai's tale permits two conclusions. The first is that the samurai was killed by his own hand with the *tanto* as a result of the revelation of the failure of his metaphysical desire to conform to the model of the samurai in his humiliating display of a fear of death, the antithesis of *bushido*. The second is that when the woodcutter gives his second version of what 'really' happened in the grove, the commoner rightly accuses him of lying *still* for the one thing that the fabulist cannot admit to is his theft of the *tanto* and his defilement of the samurai's body.

Kurosawa's *Rashomon*, as I have already indicated, is a fusion of two Akutagawa tales, 'In a Grove' and 'Rashomon,' and the director pulls this off cinematically by positioning three characters standing under the Demon Gate during a *King Lear*-like rainstorm and whose discussions frame the action of the film: the woodcutter and the priest from 'In a Grove' and a third man who resembles 'the lowly servant' from the short story of 'Rashomon'; it should be remembered here that as the lowly servant was not present at the trial, then all of these recountings of the unreliable testimonies of the ones who were in the grove are the recountings of earlier recountings that are suspect. The priest is a witness but only for testifying to having seen the samurai and his wife traveling in the direction of the grove; of the three, only the woodcutter was present at the murder scene, falsely claiming that he arrived sometime after the killing. So why does Kurosawa place these three at the Demon Gate? They could have been anywhere: outside the courtroom, at a tavern, sitting along the side of the road. And why all of the rain? Because Akutagawa's 'Rashomon' is all about a lowly servant consciously deciding to become a thief.

> Rather than say that the servant was 'waiting for the rain to end,' it would be more appropriate to write that 'a lowly servant trapped by the rain had no place to go and no idea what to do.' ... He was determined to find a way to keep himself alive for one more day—that is, a way to do something about a situation for which there was nothing to be done.
>
> The rain carried a host of roaring sounds from afar as it came to envelop the Rashomon. The evening darkness brought the sky ever lower until the roof of the gate was supporting dark, heavy clouds on the ridge of its jutting tiles.
>
> To do something when there was nothing to be done, he would have to be prepared to do anything at all (Akutagawa, 2006, p. 4).

And so the great transformation, or the serious failure of mimesis, takes place. After stopping an old woman from removing the top hairs from a pile of cadavers in order to make a wig, the lowly servant is filed with righteous indignation.

> The servant had no idea why the crone was pulling out the dead person's hair, and thus could not rationally call the deed either good or evil. But for him, the very act of plucking hair from a corpse on this rainy night up here in the Rashomon was itself an unpardonable evil. Naturally he no longer recalled that, only moments before, he himself had been planning to become a thief (Akutagawa, 2006, p. 7).

But all of this rapidly changes after the crone provides the reason for her weird nocturnal behavior: '"I can't help it. If I don't do it, I'll starve to death"' (Akutagawa, 2006, p. 8). The servant now has a new model to emulate, and it is not a member of the respectable cultured elite of the externally mediated 'Capital of Peace and Tranquility'.

> As he listened a new kind of courage began to germinate in his heart—a courage he had lacked earlier beneath the gate: one that was moving in a direction opposite to the courage that had impelled him to seize the old woman. He was no longer torn between starving to death or becoming a thief. In his current state of mind, the very thought of starving to death was nearly banished from his consciousness that it became all but unthinkable for him (Akutagawa, 2006, p. 8).

And why does Kurosawa go so far as to actually title his film after 'Rashomon' when it should have been 'In a Grove,' the adaptation of which takes up ninety percent of the movie? Because Akutagawa's 'Rashomon' signifies becoming-a-thief, which is what Kurosawa makes the woodcutter become because it is the only way that a coherent explanation for what happened in the grove can be provided: the samurai had to have a *tanto* embedded in his corpse and the woodcutter must have removed it, forcing him to lie twice. The second version of events told by the woodcutter is correct *except* for the bandit's killing of the samurai; the bandit was too afraid to kill and it was necessary for the woodcutter to falsely claim that the dagger was not present. And the accounts provided of the real behavior of wife (whore), bandit (incompetent), and samurai (coward) are all so perfectly antithetical to their externally mediated performances that they all undergo not merely the social trauma of the loss of face ('I am not what I try to be') but the life-negating catastrophe of the defeat of metaphysical desire ('I am nothing'). Each one has been equally revealed and then un-made having left the psychological time of the community for the physical time and the internally mediated space of the grove. But Tajomaru, at least, can still dream, just like Quixote.

All that he has to do is to act the part of a murderer.

References

Primary Sources

Akutagawa, R. (1964). *The beautiful and the grotesque.* Trans. Takashi Kojima and John McVittie. Liveright.

Akutagawa, R. (1970). *Rashomon and other stories.* Trans. Takashi Kojima. Liveright.

Akutagawa, R. (2006). *Rashomon and seventeen other stories.* Trans. Jay Rubin. Penguin Books.

Dickey, J. (1970). *Deliverance.* Delta.

Kurosawa, A. (1983). *Something like an autobiography.* Trans. Audie E. Bock. Vintage Books.

Rashomon (The Criterion Collection 2002; directed by Akira Kurosawa).

The Thin Blue Line (MGM 2005; directed by Errol Morris).

Yojimbo (The Criterion Collection 1999; directed by Akira Kurosawa).

Secondary Resources

Bierce, A. (1988). The moonlit road. In C. Fadiman (Ed.), *The collected writings of Ambrose Bierce* (pp. 417–426). Pan Books.

Brodey, I. S. (2009). Cactus Roses and Camellias: Flowers, action, and masculinity in 'Sanjuro' and 'the man who shot liberty valance.' *Japan Women's Journal, 36*, 92–116.

Dupuy, J.-P. (2011). Naturalizing mimetic theory. In S. R. Garrels (Ed.), *Mimesis and science: Empirical research on imitation and the mimetic theory of culture and religion* (pp. 193–213). Michigan State University Press.

Fassano, A. (2010). The Rashomon effect, jury instructions, and peremptory challenges: Rethinking *Hernandez v. New York. Rutgers Law Journal, 41*, 783–816.

Gallese, V. (2011). The two sides of mimesis: Mimetic theory, embodied simulation, and social identification. In S. R. Garrels (Ed.), *Mimesis and science: Empirical research on imitation and the mimetic theory of culture and religion* (pp. 87–108). Michigan State University Press.

Galloway, P. (2005). *Stray dogs and lone wolves: The samurai film handbook.* Stone Bridge Press.

Girard, R. (1965). *Deceit, desire and the novel: Self and other in literary structure.* Trans. Yvonne Freccero. The Johns Hopkins University Press.

Girard, R., Oughourlian, J.-M., & Lefort, G. (1978). *Things hidden since the foundation of the world.* Trans. Stephen Bann and Michael Metteer. Continuum.

Greenfield, S., Osborn, G., & Robson, P. (2001). *Film and the law.* Cavendish Publishing Limited.

Kamir, O. (2000). Judgment by film: Socio-legal functions of *Rashomon. Yale Journal of Law and Humanities, 12*, 39–88.

McKenna, A. J. (1992). *Violence and difference: Girard, Derrida, and deconstruction.* University of Illinois Press.

Murakami, H. (2006). Introduction. In R. Akutagawa (Ed.), *Rashomon and seventeen other stories.* Trans. Jay Rubin, xix-xxxvii. Penguin Books.

Mulvey, L. (1975). Visual pleasure and narrative cinema. *Screen, 16*(3), 6–18.

Oughourlian, J.-M. (1996). Desire is mimetic: A clinical approach. *3 Contagion: Journal of Violence Mimesis, and Culture, 3*, 43–49.

Oughourlian, J.-M. (2010). *The genesis of desire.* Trans. Eugene Webb. Michigan State University Press.

Oughourlian, J.-M. (2016). *The mimetic brain.* Trans. Trevor Cribben Merrill. Michigan State University Press.

Oughourlian, J.-M. (1991). *The puppet of desire: The psychology of hysteria, possession, and hypnosis.* Trans. Eugene Webb. Stanford University Press.

Palaver, W. (2013). *Rene girard's mimetic theory.* Trans G. Borrud. Michigan State University Press.

Prince, S. (1999). *The Warrior's camera: The cinema of Akira Kurosawa.* Revised and Expanded Edition. Princeton University Press.

Reeve, Z. (2015). Mechanisms of internal cohesion: Scapegoating and Parochial Altruism. In P. Antonello & P. Gifford (Eds.), *How we became human: Mimetic theory and the science of evolutionary origins* (pp. 161–186). Michigan State University Press.

Roth, W. D., & Mehta, J. D. (2002). The *Rashomon* effect: Combining positivist and interpretivist approaches in the analysis of contested events. *Sociological Methods and Research, 31*(2), 131–173.

Richie, D. (1984). *The films of Akira Kurosawa.* Revised edition. University of California Press.

Rubin, J. (2006). Translator's note. In R. Akutagawa (Ed.), *Rashomon and seventeen other stories.* Trans. Jay Rubin, xli-li. Penguin Books.

Ryan, C. (1996). Print the legend: Violence and recognition in *The man who shot liberty valance.* In J. Denvir (Ed.), *Legal reelism: Movies as legal texts* (pp. 23–43). University of Illinois Press.

Schmitt, C. (1996). *The concept of the political.* Trans. George Schwab. University of Chicago Press.

Schmitt, C. (2005). *Political theology: Four chapters on the concept of sovereignty*, Trans. George Schwab. University of Chicago.

Schutz, A. (1967). Don quixote and the problem of reality. In A. Schutz (Ed.), *Collected papers II: Studies in social theory* (pp. 135–158). Martinus Nijhoff.

Silver, A. (1977). *The samurai film.* A.S. Barnes and Company.

Strong, T. B. (2007). Foreword: Dimensions of the new debate around Carl Schmitt. In C. Schmitt (Ed.), *The concept of the political.* Trans. George Schwab, i-xix. University of Chicago Press.

Tomelleri, S. (2015). *Ressentiment: Reflections on mimetic desire and society.* Michigan State University Press.

Tyler, P. (1967). *The three faces of film: The art, the dream, the cult.* A.S. Barnes and Co.

Wilson, E. (2019). An Emoji for Rene Girard: Memes, mimesis, and the apocalypse of the eternally irrelevant. In A. Bown & D. Bristow (Eds.), *Post memes: Seizing the memes of production* (pp. 137–168). Punctum Books.

Chapter 6
'I Just Want to Talk…': Liberalism, Generative Unanimity, and Post-sacrificial Scapegoating in *12 Angry Men*

Abstract Sydney Lumet's film *12 Angry Men* (1957), arguably the greatest legal drama ever made, is deceptively simple, a colossal exercise in cinematic misrecognition. Predictably, the film ends with an unconditional affirmation of the secular liberal State as a post-sacrificial society through the jury's unanimous verdict to acquit the accused. Examined more closely, however, the film possesses an added depth of meaning: the control of the scapegoat mechanism is the primary means of determining the nature of social order. *12 Angry Men* expressly portrays scapegoating as not merely a necessary but a sufficient condition for the creation of generative unanimity. It is the decision not to scapegoat, or condemn to death, that is the transformative event that causes all members of the jurors to undergo the conversionary experience of *metanoia* and reassemble as an interpretive community of readers empowered to secure the foundations of a liberal, secular, and apparently anti-sacrificial *nomos*. Here I follow closely the short but brilliant exposition of the film provided by Peter Biskind who views it as a microcosm of the wider debate among liberal, conservative, and radical approaches to social issues in the American films of the 1950s. Biskind's insights are only strengthened with the realization that virtually all of Juror Number Eight's arguments for the innocence of the accused are factually erroneous and legally invalid. What matters to Lumet is the jurors' conversion to liberalism as the only legitimate form of constitutive rhetoric which, ironically, rests upon the sacrificial expulsion of all speech that is illiberal. *12 Angry Men* transcends its banal status as an anti-capital punishment film and in a truly subversive act unveils the scapegoat as the master sign of political ontology within an ostensibly post-sacrificial secular *nomos*.

Keywords Legal realism · Critical legal realism · Law *Noir* · The strong attorney · The weak judge · Pluralism

In 2008 Ron Perlstein published one of the truly great books about contemporary American politics entitled *Nixonland: The Rise of a President and the Fracturing of America* that detailed the conversion of the Executive Branch to a proto-Schmittean

E. M. Wilson, *Rene Girard, Law, Literature, and Cinema*,
https://doi.org/10.1007/978-981-97-1156-7_6

decisionism a la Gary Cooper in *High Noon*[1] and the parallel transmogrification of the progressive liberal neo-Keynesian New Deal into the neo-conservatism of neo-liberalism.

> I have written of the rise, between the years 1965 and 1972, of a nation that had believed itself to be at consensus instead becoming one of incommensurate visions of apocalypse: two loosely defined congeries of Americans, each convinced that should the other triumph, everything decent and true and worth preserving would *end*. […]
>
> I have written of a cult of "American consensus" that rose up among the punditocracy and reached its apogee with the landslide defeat of Barry Goldwater[2] [in 1964]—their fervent imagining, alongside Lyndon Johnson's, that "these are the most hopeful times since Christ was born in Bethlehem," that America was united and at peace and would forever be, if only "extremists" stopped stirring up the pot. And I have written about the type of intellectual self-suppression it took to believe this: that the demonic furies of race and war were gathering even as the words were written, that America has always been divided and will always be. It is not too much to suggest that the rages that accompanied the crumbling of this myth of consensus, as the furies of the 1960s advanced, would not have been so rageful—would not have been so literally murderous—had the false rhetoric of American unity not been so glibly enforced in the years that preceded it: that some of the 1960s anger and violence was a return of what America had repressed. […]
>
> Do Americans not hate each other enough to fantasize about killing one another, in cold blood, over political and cultural disagreements? It would be hard to argue they do not.
>
> How did Nixonland end? It has not ended yet. (Perlstein, 2008: 747, 748)

What is truly at stake in *12 Angry Men* is not the innocence (or guilt) of the accused; rather, it is whether or not Juror no. 8, will be able to convert all of the other angry male members of the jury to liberalism. And from this collective *metanoia* the 'correct' verdict of innocence will naturally flow, enabling the restored community which is the America of the New Deal and the New Society to prevent Nixonland's apocalypse of reaction and racism, a politicized version of Girard's crisis of undifferentiation but one apparently bereft of the restorative scapegoat. All of which is liberalism's signature form of *meconnaissance.*

6.1 The Law Movie as Genre

The justification for the academic sub-discipline of 'Law-and-Film Studies' is ordinarily based upon its practical application to advocacy training, specifically as visual and auditory training manuals for developing the narrative-saturated 'story senses' of lawyers (Posner, 1986). Successful trial lawyers are invariably a '*fact-based story-teller*,' and that 'upper-level law students rediscover their creative and imaginative

[1] See Chap. 4, above.

[2] In November 1964, Lyndon Johnson's re-election was the greatest landslide in American History up until that time, being outdone by Republican Ronald Reagan's revanchist victory over Democrat Walter Mondale in 1984.

story senses is imperative. They must learn to listen to and trust their instincts and their emotions in addition to categorical analytical functions' (Philip N. Meyer qtd. Greenfield et al., 2001: 9). Philip N. Meyer has made the law-and-literature reform movement of legal education his personal crusade.

> Like the movie-maker the trial attorney is an oral cultural storyteller who tells fact-based narratives that convey a story and a particular vision of the world. The principles of narrative ordination for a trial storyteller are like the aesthetic structures that compel movie directors to craft stories along a tightly ordered narrative spine. Severe restraints are placed on narrative subjectivity by certain storytelling conventions, such as rules of evidence. (Philip Meyer qtd. Greenfield et al., 2001: 10)

Understood this way, the generic *Law Film*, or *the courtroom drama*, may best be literally understood as penumbra, or the 'shadow' of the law as a substantive discipline and practice; 'Law films, then, are not really about what might be described as the substance of the law or the detail of the law; rather they are concerned with the penumbra of law, the places of law and the people of law' (Greenfield et al., 2001: 21). Which means that the Law Film constitutes a type of cinematic genre in that it provides an encoded imagery and dialogue that conveys a mythic understanding of the world.[3]

> Genres are formal systems for transforming the world in which we actually live into self-contained, coherent and controllable structures of meaning. Genres can thus be considered to function in a way that a language system does—offering a vocabulary and a set of rules which allow us to 'shape' reality, thus making it appear less random and disordered. (Greenfield et al., 2001: 18)

And, like the Western, in many ways the dark twin of the Law Film, the overwhelmingly, the dramatically (and commercially) successful courtroom drama is American, a telling and highly revealing fact not lost upon the European student of the Law Film.

> What came to amaze us was the striking uniformity of the legal procedures that are portrayed in movies: predominantly criminal procedures. We discovered that American procedure has provided the foundation for almost all cinematic legal procedures...There are a number of reasons for the dominance of American legal procedure in movies: not only do American films enjoy international box office success, but American legal procedure is structurally more suitable for a film than is the so-called inquisitorial procedure found in civil law systems, such as we find on the Continent. American courtroom films have created a manner of portraying legal procedure which has been followed in courtroom films set in other countries and other legal systems. (Machura et al., 2000: 123)

And of course, the reason why the inquisitorial courtroom does not lend itself easily to cinematic adaptation is precisely because it is mediatory, not confrontational. Here, we are revisiting Andre Bazin's classic insight into the Western as the 'essence' of cinema[4] for both genres derive their 'real meaning only from the morality of a world in which social good and evil, in their simplicity and necessity, exist like two primary and basic elements' (Bazin, 1971: 147). Which means that the all-important

---

[3] See Chap. 4, above.

[4] See Chap. 4, above.

(meaning box-office) 'entertainment value theory' of the Western applies equally well to the courtroom drama: consistent with Carl Schmitt, the genre's rich dramaturgy of combat (the adversarial system) makes the courtroom the secular sacred site of the enactment of the *decision.*

> American legal procedure seems more suitable for movies because it is more hospitable to scenes of intense drama, featuring classical confrontations between two antagonists between good and evil which have to be resolved…In American procedure the parties wrestle to establish their individual version of the facts of the case as well as their legal views. Where the courtroom is seen as a battleground, fierce conflict becomes the norm. (Machura et al., 2000: 124–125)

Which is utterly Schmittean, for the added dimension of the American Law Film is that not only the formalist categories of guilt versus innocence is at play but the existential categories of Being versus non-Being (or 'truth' vs. 'lie'); as Alan M. Derschowitz memorably put it, 'The truth is that most criminal defendants are, in fact, guilty. Prosecutors, therefore, generally have the *ultimate* truth on their side. But since prosecution witnesses often lie about some facts, defense attorneys have *intermediate* truth on their side. Not surprisingly, both sides emphasize the kind of truth they have more of' (Kuzina, 2000: 94). And which 'kind of truth'[5] prevails carries with it a surcharge of doubled existential intensity precisely because this is the USA that we are talking about: which 'kind of truth' can be literally a life or death issue because capital punishment is a frequent possibility,[6] just as in the Western we know that somebody will be killed in the shoot-out. And because the threat of death is always so theatrically staged and publicly displayed, the Law Film, again like the Western, doubles as a meditation upon the complex relationship between rule-governed 'democracy' and passion-fueled 'populism'; for here too 'there is a link with ancient Greek drama if one looks at the jury as a replacement for the chorus' (Machura et al., 2000: 126)[7] meaning that the iconic law-hero, like Marshal Kane in *High Noon* (1952), must make the 'long walk' toward nemesis. However, although the protagonist of the legal drama stands in a binary relationship with his enemy, unlike the Westerner and the Outlaw, the combatants (or rival deciders) are not doubles: the protagonist and opponent are thoroughly oppositional. The enemy is most often not the rival attorney but the *Weak Judge* whose unpredictability and susceptibility to persuasion on both the personal and professional level carries within him the constant threat of the thwarting of the process of resolution: 'Basically the judge in the American legal system has the job of controlling procedure [the interpretation and application of the law]. This weak role strengthens the positions of the prosecution and the defense, and thereby facilitates greater emphasis on conflict' (Machura et al., 2000: 127). But because all of the roles of the courtroom actors are so highly scripted—America having left the wild streets of Shinbone following the pre-judicial execution of Liberty Valance—the Weak Judge remains thoroughly passive, an agent of reaction to the lawyer-icon hero who is almost

[5] Which, interpreted another way, reads as 'sort of real'.

[6] Which implies that European trials where execution is not an option are cinematically boring.

[7] Something that Sophocles does in *Oedipus Tyrannus*; see Chap. 1, above.

always the sole instigator of action (or advocacy): the *Strong Attorney*, the personal and personalized bearer of the central themes of the Law Film genre 'expressed through a series of familiar character types and conflicts': 'good vs. evil, right vs. wrong, justice vs. injustice, and protagonist vs. antagonist'. And again, because this is the USA, the indispensable ideological sub-text, or myth,[8] of the textual drama is liberal democracy. Attorneys 'almost always stand for liberalism. In the political life of the USA, mistrust toward government organizations and the fight for civil rights have traditionally had important roles. The lawyer sometimes appears as defender of individual rights against the state, which is often regarded ambivalently' (Machura et al., 2000: 128). Conversely, a popular lawyer-icon variant of the Strong Attorney, the *Crusading Prosecutor*, may be depicted as utilizing the power and the legitimacy of the courts to reform vestigial illiberal elements within Society (racism, organized crime, poverty). And it is the courtroom drama's preoccupation with the political sub-text (as with the Western's) that two of the other defining tropes of the genre emerge into clear view: an implicit invocation of the US constitution as a universally palliative sacred-text and the staging of the action under the rubric of the *social issue drama*: 'Beneath the surface, this sub-genre is about the problem of the congruence between official action and declared rule which is worth striving for and which constitutes what is called "the internal morality of the law". Factual social-issue courtroom dramas often demonstrate how the principles of legality have been shattered' (Kuzina, 2000: 82). And, of course, how the principles of legality can be restored through some kind of act of generative unanimity; the Western is in some sense a Levi-Straussian myth of cosmic conflict, so it follows that the courtroom drama must also serve as the locus of the regeneration of the world, or at least the only part of the world that really counts the USA. For as a genre the Law Film, no less than the Western or the Eastern,[9] must be fitted into an historical context and this must be American (and not Japanese) which means that the genre must operate on some level, even if only heuristically or pedagogically, as a commentary upon the evolution and operations of American legal culture. And it is no coincidence that the genre first emerged in the early 1930s (about the same time as the Gangster film) which, the invention of sound technology (an indispensable requisite for courtroom drama) notwithstanding, was the era of The New Deal and an almost revolutionary transformation of the American system of government and law: Keynesianism, centralized planning, the new Federalism, 'Activist Courts', public policy rulings, and, most importantly, '*the sociological movement in jurisprudence*,' epitomized by the Roosevelt appointed Supreme Court justices Benjamin N. Cardozo and Louis D. Brandeis, after whom the sociologically intensive 'Brandeis Brief' was named. If the 'ideology' of the sociological movement in jurisprudence can be summarized in a single sentence, it is this: whatever can be established as the correct public policy must, by legal interpretation, be transformed into law. Law Films were ideal candidates for the translation of public policy concerns into social issue dramas because the American

[8] See Chap. 4, above. Richard Slotkin clearly sees myth as a form of ideology whose purpose is to reconcile otherwise irresolvable political and social tensions, or contradictions.

[9] See above, Chap. 5.

State during the New Deal had become both interventionist and bureaucratic to an unprecedented degree: 'The sociological movement in jurisprudence is a movement for pragmatism as a philosophy of law…the adjustment of principles and doctrines to the human conditions they are to govern rather than to assumed first principles' (Roscoe Pound qtd. Purcell, 1973: 77), so that it is only by 'studying the social impact of legal principles and rules could men know whether the law in fact brought about the administration of real justice' (Purcell, 1973: 77). But because the Weak Judge is the guardian of the conservative (pre-New Deal) legal establishment of ensconced and unassailable proceduralism and the Strong Attorney is the harbinger of the activist subordination of legal rulings to social progress, the Law Film could emerge as an appropriately genre-mythic form of drama, for its necessary *archetype*, that defining theme that existed in an 'elemental' relation to the audience could be expressed formulaically: the Manichaean contest between *Law versus Justice* (or procedures versus outcomes). Which means that the law-hero is not that far removed from the Westerner in that, although non-violent (at least physically if not always symbolically), the Strong Attorney must at some point allegorically abandon the law in order to safeguard the even more elemental thing that is the true foundation of the legal order: justice. The genre's 'key concept is probably the relationship between law and justice, and a recurring theme through law films is the delivery of justice at the expense of formal legal rules…Law is often portrayed as a barrier to justice and lawyers have to step outside of legal procedures to ensure the end result is just' (Greenfield et al., 2001: 23) so that the following generalization holds true.

> We suggest that law films are always concerned with the enforcement of justice in some shape or form and that this is a crucial starting point. Films may then be divided into a number of sub-categories of films that share the relevant characteristics—rookie lawyer wins through; lawyer on the skids redeems himself [*The Verdict*]; last-minute evidence or witness saves the day [*The Verdict*]; unpopular cause or defendant is proved to be meritorious [*To Kill a Mockingbird*; *Philadelphia*]. (Greenfield et al., 2001: 24)

Extrapolating from this, we can detect 'two factors that may be applied to the question of justice: formal and informal enforcement, though these may exist separately or co-terminously'; 'For example, with vigilante films [*A Time To Kill*] the emphasis is solely on an informal subjective method and system of the enforcement of justice. At the other end of the scale is the formal process of law, though often there will be an element of informal or improper justice…' (Greenfield et al., 2001: 24). The *generic* definition of the law film may be expressed this way: a *self-reflective cinematic meditation on, and mediation of, two concepts of justice simultaneously and equally applicable to both public and private spaces, which are temporarily in conflict with each other*—the cosmic struggle that the civilizational myth of law must prove itself capable of resolving, for otherwise there is simply no point to it all. For the dramatic purposes of the genre the public space of justice is the 'law' itself, defined in exclusively and excluding formal terms; the private space is the far more liminal realm of 'private justice' which, while morally defensible, constitutes no part of the civilizing form of law, although it is indispensable to the state of nature that is the spatial domain of The Western as Tom Doniphon demonstrated. This mythic duality becomes most clear when we are treating the most common and popular form of the courtroom drama, the criminal trial film, the type that is the most dramatic, entertaining, and existentially intense, because what is at stake is what Hemingway called 'the last serious thing': Death. Again, almost but not quite the same as The Western, 'Criminal trial films set up a tension between two sorts of law: immutable natural law or justice on the one hand [private] and fallible man-made law [public] on the other' (Rafter, 2001: 10). And this, in turn, yields the most interesting and most important sub-genre of the courtroom drama which established the unassailable global hegemony of the American variant of the Law Film: *Law Noir*.

6.2 Law *Noir*

In terms of 'inter-genre' comparisons, the type of movie that the Law Film most closely resembles is the *Crime Film* which is the cinematic manifestation of that reversibility, or iterability, between law and crime at the heart of the mythic content of both the Western and Eastern film genres. As Nicole Rafter beautifully expressed it in her *Shots in the Mirror: Crime Films and Society* (Second edition 2006), the structural coherence of the crime genre depends upon a strict dialectical relationship with its narrative 'twin,' the *Detective Film*, the 'basic pattern' of which is 'that of the search.'

> These tales have… 'goal-oriented plots,' patterns of action to which investigation is key. Mysteries and detective films often mete out clues in small, progressive portions, so that the viewer's process of discovery parallels the investigator's. Sometimes…they conceal the object of the search, such as the villain's identity, as long as possible…At other times the goal of the search is clear from the start, and the investigator's job is to find the thing that is missing. (Rafter, 2006: 190)

And more often than not 'the thing that is missing' is meaning itself, the detective a collector and sorter of hermeneutical clues to a revelatory ending that is both legal and moral. Suffice it to say that the Detective Film is wholly bound to an utterly representational theory of language, which means that the premium narrative tropes are of reason and objectivity.

> [The detective] reassures us of an ultimate rationality, 'a benevolent and knowable universe,' 'a world that can be interpreted by human reason, embodied in the superior intellect of the detective…The detective's skill is precisely the ability to code 'seemingly unrelated data into a coherent system of signs, a text identifying the malefactor'. (Tony Hilfer qtd. Sherwin, 1994: 48)

The detective's actions assume the guise of both a crusade and the inquisitorial examination of the conscience of the assorted suspects; 'The function of the detective hero is to guarantee the readers' absolution from guilt. This is basic to the genres' wish fulfillment…What matters is the detective's revelation, not the murders' punishment, for in this myth of rationality truth takes priority over justice' (Tony Hilfer qtd. Sherwin, 1994: 52 n 49). No surprise then that the genres' paired double, the

Crime Film, constitutes the antithesis of the detective's super-rationalist thesis of the transparency, or representational nature, of the world.

> 'The central and defining feature of the crime novel [or film] is that in it self and world, guilt and innocence are problematic. The world of the crime novel is *constituted* by what is problematic in it'…. A crime novel maneuvers its reader into various forms of complicity, managing to subvert the reassurances of the detective novel by 'put[ting] the signification process into doubt or even exploit[ing] the gap between socially accepted signification and ultimate reality'. (Tony Hilfer qtd. Sherwin, 1994: 52 n 50)

And consistent with its oppositional stance the Crime Film is both pre-representational in its approach to language and meaning, and therefore (or because of), it is committed to an aesthetic of ontological deviation: 'To the degree the crime novel puts the signification process into doubt or even exploits the gap between socially accepted signification and ultimate reality, it subverts the reassurances of the detective novel' (Tony Hilfer qtd. Sherwin, 1994: 48).

The early development of the Law *Noir*, which took place at approximately the same time as Hollywood's more general turn to all things *noir*-ish following the Second World War, represented the genre's approach to artistically diversify itself (and increase profitability) by assimilating key tropes of the Crime Film into a genre that should have been exclusively concerned with the moral drama and conceits of the Detective tale.[10] Central to the process of appropriation, or 'cinematic invasion,' were changes to dramatic and moral representation and placing greater emphasis upon the identity and motivations of 'the client who, more often than not, carried within them a "shadow of doubt"'; Law *Noirs* present a 'baleful view of lawyers' and 'portray people, some entirely innocent and others not-so-innocent, trapped in a highly fallible legal system' (Norman Rosenberg qtd. Rafter, 2001: 13–14). The other great change effected, at times almost undetectable, was with the sub-genre's treatment of the defining icon of the Law Film, the *courtroom* itself. Icons, as we know, are certain 'situations and actions can have an emblematic power… [and] a latent ritualistic meaning which can be brought to the surface and reflected. The quest, the journey, the confrontation, these can take on moral or allegorical overtones' (Kitses, 1969: 24–25) and the courtroom was the theater of combat within which the highly stylized rituals were to take place, a setting both secular as part of the judicial branch of government, and sacred, an allegory of the 'Final Judgment' which is literally true in the case of capital crimes. The genre's symbolic representation of an allegedly isomorphic 'law space' (Pue, 1990) meets all of the requirements necessary to stage the obligatory appearance of the iconic.

> In order to qualify as a law film the following characteristic(s) must be present in some shape or form: the geography of law, the language and dress of law, legal personnel and the authority of the law. This excludes films where 'justice' is enforced outside of any legal

[10] Two of the greatest examples are both by Alfred Hitchcock, *Witness for the Prosecution* (1958) and *The Paradine Case* (1948), the latter starring Gregory Peck who played two other famous lawyer-heroes, the morally pristine Atticus Finch in *To Kill a Mockingbird* (1963) and the somewhat compromised Sam Bowden in the original *Cape Fear* (1961), but nowhere near as compromised as Nick Nolte was in the Scorsese re-make. See Chap. 7, below.

framework for example, war films, social dramas and family sagas. (Greenfield et al., 2001: 24)

And while true, what is frequently under-emphasized is that whatever the precise icons of the law film, what they all signify in common is the post-foundational suspension of 'the state of nature,' which presents to the audience the cinematic allegory of modern law having permanently exited the pre-historic domain of the will-to-revenge, scapegoating, and the sacrificial mechanism. And to make this perfectly clear in wholly secular, meaning non-archaic terms, the filmic depiction of the courthouse and the courtroom will visually emphasize the pronouncedly neo-classical nature of the architecture of both. If mythic religion can no longer provide guidance to legal truth, Hellenic philosophy will have to do.

American adversary procedure is in some ways reminiscent of ancient drama. Even the outward appearance of the courtroom is similar to the architecture of the classical Athenian theater. The 'scene', where the action in Greek tragedy takes place, is similar to the space in front of the bench where opposing counsel act, plead, and question witnesses. The 'orchestra', where the chorus sings and dances, has its functional equivalent in the jury box. The 'theatron', where the audience sits, is also present in the courtroom. The dialectic structure of the adversary procedure—thesis of the prosecution, antithesis of the defense and synthesis of the verdict—also uses classical structure elements such as one finds in Sophocles' *Antigone*, which is about the conflict between two opposing positions, each partially right.[11] This structure is also found in courtroom films like *Philadelphia* which portray an ambivalent conflict unfolding before the judge. (Machura et al., 2000: 125)

The role of architecture within the genre cannot be over-emphasized.

There is good reason why the courtroom drama has been categorized and recognized as a distinct type. One of the most important elements is the setting: the architecture of the building and, in particular, the courtroom itself. Whilst American courtrooms are more functional and lack the theatrical pageantry of their British counterparts, there is still a common and accepted layout which is instantly recognizable. (Greenfield et al., 2001: 22)

That 'common and accepted layout' that is 'instantly recognizable' is a fusion of the Greek theater and the Roman forum mediated by American democracy. Nowhere was this made more visually compelling than in the authentically iconic opening shot of Sidney Lumet's 1957 *12 Angry Men* (1957).

We are presented with a shot of the massive façade of the Supreme Court Building in New York's Square. The camera slowly crawls up the stone columns to the pediment above. Carved across it in bold letters are the words: 'The administration of justice is the firmest pillar of good government.' Ninety minutes later we will have seen justice served, and know that in the United States, government is indeed good. The Supreme Court Building is a monument, like the Lincoln and Jefferson memorials that are 'quoted' in so many films, and as we look up with the camera at the majestic inscription over our heads, we realize that this is a film that legitimates an American institution: the criminal justice system. (Biskind, 1983: 10)

And it should come as no surprise that the almost evangelical Juror no. 8 in *12 Angry Men*, Henry Fonda, should reveal himself to be an architect by profession, for what he is doing is overseeing the design of a liberal legal order, or *nomos*, that is predicated upon the rejection of scapegoating as I shall discuss shortly.

[11] As per Alan M. Derschowitz.

6.2.1 *Sidney Lumet and 12 Angry Men: Preliminary Thoughts*

So all-controlling is the iconography of the sacred majesty of allegedly post-religious America that, unusual for a film genre, the icon itself achieved a measure of cultural force and began re-shaping the dramatic representation of the major protagonists that are now a triune: Strong Attorney, Weak Judge, and 'Uncertain' or 'Shadowy' Client. As Peter Biskind makes clear in his seminal work *Seeing is Believing: How Hollywood Taught Us to Stop Worrying and Love the Fifties* (1983), the single greatest change induced by the transformative icon was with the hero, the Strong Attorney, now increasingly vulnerable to the narrative machinations of the *noir* sub-genre. Biskind provides a brilliant taxonomy of 'Fifties films' that is of decisive importance to the historical development of the law film: *pluralist*, *conservative*, and *radical*. The pluralist film is centered upon the inherently heroic activities and beliefs of *'Cold War Liberals'*, the dominant, or hegemonic, political/ideological faction within post-1945 US political culture.

> Pluralists believed that America was composed of a diversity of interest groups which competed on a more or less equal basis for a piece of the pie. Like the various blocs of jurors in *12 Angry Men*, they could adjust their differences by reasoning together, if they would only avoid ideologizing their conflicts…. In other words, if labor accepted the capitalist framework, capital reciprocated by agreeing to play by the rules of the game that had been laid down by the New Deal. (Biskind, 1983: 16, 15)

All that was needed for liberalism to succeed was a mediator. Pluralism as a political-cinematic discourse emerged at the same time that 'sociological jurisprudence' achieved dominance over the US legal system and the strict parallel movement between law and politics toward technocracy and social engineering was made clear by Arthur Schlesinger: 'The thrust of the democratic faith is away from fanaticism; it is towards compromise, persuasion, and consent in politics, towards tolerance and diversity in society' (Biskind, 1983: 16). The second grouping, *conservative*, treats its target audience in a similar matter. Conservatives were in basic alignment with liberals/pluralists and were committed to the New Deal (the Welfare State) and the Cold War 'military industrial complex' (Eisenhower) but here pluralists and conservatives 'parted company. They disagreed on how to conduct affairs at home. Conservatives…put their faith in the law, and therefore conservative films dramatized the breakdown of order' (Biskind, 1983: 35–36). The third group of films, the *radical*, attacked 'both centrist models of the community: the federally enforced, top-down model favored by corporate liberals and the more bottom-up, populist model favored by the conservatives' (Biskind, 1983: 47). As evidence for his thesis, Biskind puts forward no less a formidable work of cinematic grandeur than Fred Zimmerman's clearly radical *High Noon* (1952).[12] Herein

> Consensus is bankrupt, the refuge of fools, knaves, and cowards, and values exist only outside it. Whereas pluralists applauded themselves for their 'idealistic' pragmatism and ridiculed

[12] See Chap. 4, above.

> extremists for their preoccupation with fundamental questions of right and wrong, which they considered irrelevant and even obstacles to the smooth operation of democracy, *High Noon* does the opposite. The center is ridiculed for its obsession with mean, trivial, business-as-usual affairs, while [Marshal] Kane is applauded for his life-and-death confrontation with the Millers. Moreover, Kane can't transform consensus, redeem society, as [Henry] Fonda did in *12 Angry Men*. Rather, he just gives up and walks away from it. And, of course, once consensus is repudiated, the question who holds authority within the center is irrelevant. Both corporate liberals and conservatives are bad. (Biskind, 1983: 46–47)

Biskind is correct in his instinct to juxtapose *High Noon* to *12 Angry Men*, as the latter is a masterly critique, both explicit and implicit, of the populist logic at work in jury deliberations, rendering it an iconic representation of the liberal form of the Law Film.[13] I would add this caveat, however: while *12 Angry Men* displays both the language and politics of neutrality, or the almost fine liberal art of appearing to be neutral in a manner that borders on both the pretentious and the absurd, it is, in fact, a Law *Noir* masquerading as a pluralist Law Film. For what is really at stake in this cinematic text is the unsolvable problem of the scapegoat, although this is by no means apparent at first glance.

What is apparent at first glance, however, is the presence of the director Sidney Lumet as an *auteur* and the overall conformity of this film, along with most of his others, with *auteur theory*, a term 'applied to film directors that was popularized by French film critics (Bazin, 1971) and refers to film directors with their own distinctive styles' (Pramaggiore & Wallis, 2011: 451). The general consensus is that Lumet qualified (as did Akira Kurosawa and John Ford) as an *auteur* in a manner that politically marked him as a maker of liberal films[14]: Lumet's signature thematic concern with the dynamics of family and social life; the importance of a rational, personal responsibility for the existence of a humane social order; humankind's propensity for self-delusion and flight from its own best self; and the ubiquity of meaningful suffering that lies at the heart of life (Cunningham, 1991: 108). And it was the ultra-pluralist *12 Angry Men* that cemented Lumet's reputation as a filmic 'author'.

> *12 Angry Men*...reflects a strain of persistent liberalism in Lumet that is out of fashion among many of today's academic intellectuals and critical writers...Lumet's films are much like the basic theme in this film: the evidence is to be respected: theory is less trustworthy than the particularity of each instance of reality as the characters perceive it (Cunningham, 1991: 120).

However, as Nancy S. Marder has pointed out in 'Why *12 Angry Men* (1957): The Transformative Power of Jury Deliberations' (2006), there are a set of unresolved tensions latent within the common straight liberal reading of the film as an exemplary instance of pluralist cinema, consistent with both Lumet as *auteur* and the objective

---

[13] As does the other film discussed at length in this chapter, Errol Morris' *The Thin Blue Line* (2005); employing Biskind's taxonomy, we would place it within the radical tradition.

[14] *Unlike* Akira Kurosawa and John Ford who were both conservatives employing Biskind's taxonomy.

nature of correct legal procedure and reasoning. Formally marketed as an entertainment, Lumet provides the viewer with a model for civic virtue to emulate, meaning that *12 Angry Men* is designed to perform a mimetic function.

> The movie serves a didactic function: it makes clear which behaviors we ought to emulate and which we ought to avoid when we serve as jurors. [Henry] Fonda is the hero of this movie. He is fair-minded, articulate, and persevering. We admire him and hope that were we to serve on a jury, we would approach the role of juror as he does. (Marder, 2006: 166)

The conservative or radical catch, however, is that 'unanimity cannot be achieved until all of the jurors understand that their role demands impartiality, and that anger interferes with impartiality and inhibits the dispensation of justice' (Marder, 2006: 163). But as this is Lumet's movie and as he is an *auteur*, in the end the juror's seemingly unanimous 'judgment is consistent with a fundamental precept of our criminal justice system: it is preferable to allow a guilty man to go free than to convict an innocent man mistakenly' (Marder, 2006: 166). Read as a pluralist film, Fonda's character of Juror no. 8 is both: (a) a Detective, the one who solves the case, in this instance actually proving the innocence, or disproving the guilt of the accused, which, in terms of genre, would appear to situate this film within the Detective rather than the Crime/Noir category, and (b) a Strong Attorney, so strong, in fact, that 'Fonda is willing to ask questions that were not even raised by the defendant's attorney' (Marder, 2006: 163). As Marder intuits, the 'really big problem' with *12 Angry Men* is that as a Law Film, it is a total fantasy.[15] From a law practitioner's point of view, the first inconvenient truth is that Lumet stages the dramatic action as a verdict-driven deliberation, 'one in which there is an early, public vote that typically leads

[15] Arguably the most spectacular instance of this is Henry Fonda's 'miraculous' (or gimmicky) production of a switchblade that is identical to, or indistinguishable from, the one that the son allegedly used to kill his father but which the prosecution, relying upon the fallible police, insisted was incredibly rare even though it wasn't, apparently, for Juror no. 8 had found such a knife while talking a walk through the immediate vicinity of the rime-scene and then, after concealing it in his jacket pocket, brought it with him into the sequestered jury room and presented it as un-entered 'evidence'. 'This is fabulous theatre but incontrovertible misconduct' at the very least (Weisselberg, 2007: 723) and is completely wrong on a number of levels. 'Juror #8's unsanctioned stroll through the defendant's neighbourhood, his search to find a similar knife, and, finally, his production of the knife in the jury room were highly inappropriate behaviors. Indeed, it is likely the judge admonished the jurors to avoid such conduct. If discovered before the verdict, the conduct would have resulted in a mistrial.' And this is the hindmost part of it. 'But put this substantial legal problem aside. Is it not a strange [improbable] coincidence that some other assailant would use a knife identical to the one the defendant admitted he bought earlier that evening [of the murder] following the fight with his father? Although the knife may not have been unique as the prosecution contended, it appears to have been an unusual knife. Indeed, the evidence suggests it was at least rare. What is the probability that the murderer would have gone to the father's apartment and attacked him with a knife identical to the one the defendant bought *and* "lost" that very night?' (Vidmar et al., 2007: 695). But as Biskind would mischievously point out, what is the strict enforcement of due process and the rules of evidence compared to the ethical concern of safe-guarding the victory of pluralism over conservatism? 'In one fell swoop, the Fonda juror exposes the carelessness with which the police investigated the murder. It is doubtful that anyone comes out of the theatre after seeing *12 Angry Men* thinking that the Fonda character should have been discharged from the jury for misconduct' (Abramson, 2007: 604 n 57). See below.

to adversarial factions preoccupied with winning the point and silencing dissenters' (Marder, 2006: 159). In an eleven-to-one situation, it is virtually impossible to reverse the majority and avoiding a 'hung jury' and a formal declaration of a mis-trial, so Juror no. 8 being able to 'turn it around' in favor of the morally mandatory liberal outcome is not merely unlikely but, given the narrative set-up (vote first, deliberate later) is virtually impossible. But this first inconvenient truth pales into insignificance compared to the second inconvenient truth which is the cultural bias ideological sub-text of the film, the trace of the hidden presence of the off-screen director as *auteur*. Biskind cuts through this.

> What is at issue in *12 Angry Men* is not only what really happened, but how we find out what really happened, and whom we listen to. The answer, of course, is the corporate liberals themselves. Getting at the truth is a strenuous operation, requiring the intervention of a dispassionate, rational consciousness, which is why the jurors have to be tutored in the language of reality by [Henry] Fonda...The cult of complexity [i.e. 'social engineering'] implied that experts—intellectuals, scientists, and technocrats—were the only ones who could understand[16] and therefore run society...Like Fonda, they are well suited to deal with reality because they have the correct ideology, which is no ideology. (Biskind, 1983: 17–18)

According to Karl Jaspers, ideology is best understood as a 'complex of thoughts or ideas, which for the thinker represents as absolute truth an understanding of the world and his/her situation therein that is really a self-deception, a stratagem to justify, disguise and evade, one way or another, to his/her present advantage' (Karl Jaspers qtd. Kuzina, 2000: 83 n 15). To the liberal there is 'no ideology' in *12 Angry Men* because pluralism is simply the unmediated 'truth' as is the case with science: it is always the Enemy-Other who is ideological, ideology being the breeding ground of extremism (= non-liberalism) which is ideological, or at least on the basis of Jasper's definition. Both the character of Juror no. 8, an architect, the sort of person who designs neo-classical-style court houses, and the dramatic function that he performs can only be made intelligible within the totality of the political landscape of pluralism; his 'objectivity' and 'neutrality' are actually manifestations of a very particular historical context in which the technocrat/expert has usurped the prerogative of privileged speech and is therefore empowered to monopolize the process of establishing the difference between the objectively true and the objectively false. Cunningly, the political bias of the film's *auteur* is effectively disguised through the dramatic technique of aiming for a narrative closure (the solution of the Detective) that simultaneously affirms the legitimacy of legal orthodoxy; 'Put simply, films such as *12 Angry Men*...first highlight a court trial as a means for providing *relatively* assured and authoritative "closure to narrative," and second represent a courtroom as a special, public forum in which potentially troubling cultural questions about the specialized discourses of legal professionals can be laid to rest' (Rosenberg, 1994: 344). And as Lumet is eager to show us, the legal process 'provides a unique forum for overcoming both individual passions and interpretative difficulties' (Rosenberg, 1994: 346).

[16] Today we might phrase this as 'the only ones who are capable of detecting mis-information'.

The obsolete relics of leftist theory notwithstanding—ideological mystification and false consciousness—the serious narrative problem of placing the Strong Attorney within a pluralist/liberal film, as opposed to the conservative or radical film, where she might be quite well-suited, is that neither legal language nor legal reasoning is grounded, or self-validating. Thanks to the *noir*-ish nature of the pre-representational language, the Strong Attorney will always be able to properly function as a Detective in the manner prescribed by genre. On one level this is another instance of legal practice contaminating the artistic purity of the Law Film; the primary function of any attorney is to persuade, which means that she is committed to a pre-selected outcome; the true, and effective, a lawyer must always be the antithesis of the detached, impersonal, and wholly 'objectivist' solver of crimes being of the same sort as the corporate liberal. On another level, the problem is of a philosophical nature: the lurking and periodic irruption of the contra-rational incoherence of law itself.

> Like any closed model of rationality, the 'black letter' tradition is shot through with contradictions, omissions and absurdities, which generations of judges and jurists have sought to repress. For instance, the notion of law as resting upon an objective body of principle founders when we consider that the quest for underlying principles must evolve a selection from the sum of principles and thus has a strong evaluative element. (David Sugarman qtd. Osborn, 2001: 166)

Meconnaissance is always strongest when it is wholly unconscious of itself, for that is when it manifests as 'common sense'.

6.3 Critical Legal Theory and Law *Noir*

The also uniquely American philosophical correlate to the rise of the sociological movement in jurisprudence was *legal realism*, a view of law that takes the political nature of jurisprudence into account while simultaneously obsfucating its own ideological bias under the guise of scientific objectivity. A classic exposition of New Deal legal thought was 'Transcendental Nonsense and the Functional Approach' by Cohen (1960) that demonstrated the radically non-self-grounding nature of Law in a manner that was compatible with the operative pragmatism of activist and interventionist jurisprudence.

> [In] every field of law we should find the same habit of ignoring practical questions of value or of positive fact and taking refuge in 'legal problems' which can always be answered by manipulating legal concepts in certain approved ways. In every field of law we should find peculiar concepts which are not defined either in terms of empirical fact or in terms of ethics but which are used to answer empirical and ethical questions alike, and thus bar the way to intelligent investigation of social fact and social policy…Legal arguments couched in these terms are necessarily circular, since these terms are themselves creations of law…. (Cohen, 1960: 45)

But legal realism also constitutes the ideological mystification of pluralism that serves as the mis-recognized foundation of Lumet's cinematic jury deliberations in *12 Angry Men.* For Cohen every 'judicial decision is a social event…Behind the decision are *social forces* that play upon it to give a resultant momentum and direction; beyond the decision are human activities affected by it' (Cohen, 1960: 70). However, since no verdict is ever arrived at through pure formalism, every decision is the reflection of the moral, social, or political bias of the judge, the premier interpreter of legal texts; 'Legal systems, principles, rules, institutions, concepts, and decisions can be understood only as functions of human behavior' (Cohen, 1960: 72). Cohen, therefore, advocates a particularly rigorous kind of anti-formalism which he designates as 'Anti-Euclideanism': 'A legal decision is thus conceived as a logical deduction from fixed principles. Its meaning is expressed only in terms of its logical consequences. A legal system, thus viewed, is as far removed from temporal activity as a system of pure geometry' (Cohen, 1960: 72). Which means that law's general preference for deductive logic, the move from general first principles toward the particular item of fact, is to be replaced by an equally binding passion for inductive logic, the movement from the particular fact(s) to the formulation of a conditional general rule, as was first expounded by none other than Justice Oliver Wendell Holmes who

> …departed entirely from the subject-predicate form of logic, and employed a logic of relations. He did not try to show how a legal entity possesses certain inherent properties. What he was trying everywhere to bring out is: If a certain group of facts is true of a person, then the person will receive a certain group of consequences attached by the law to that group of facts… [this constitutes] an inductive science of law. For both the antecedent and the consequent are to be proved and ascertained empirically. (John C. H. Wu qtd. Cohen, 1960: 54)

As all 'correct' judicial decisions are to be arrived at upon strictly empirical-inductive grounds, then there is an implicit normative imperative for the judge to base her ruling upon explicit considerations of public policy or social consequences and this, in turn, requires the observance of the Is-Ought dichotomy: that it is logically impossible to derive a general normative rule from any given set of facts, so that law is morally neutral in terms of universal principles but is highly attentive in practice to the factual details of the immediate case under consideration. Which means that the judge both can and 'should'[17] invent a rule and/or value exclusively on the basis of the particular, not the general.

> Intellectual clarity requires that we carefully distinguish between the two problems of (1) objective description, and (2) critical judgment, which classical jurisprudence lumps under the same phrase. Such a distinction realistic jurisprudence offers with the double-barreled thesis: (1) that every legal rule or concept is simply a function of judicial decision to which all questions of value are irrelevant, and (2) that the problem of the judge is not whether a legal rule or concept actually exists but whether it *ought* to exist. Clarity on two fronts is the result. Description of legal facts becomes more objective, and legal criticism becomes more critical'. (Cohen, 1960: 68)

[17] Which in itself indicates a perhaps 'unconscious' or sub-rosa moral imperative. Another way of expressing this is that what Cohen dismisses as 'Euclidean' jurisprudence is a form of Realism (words stand to things in an objective manner), while Anti-Euclidean legal realism is Nominalism (that there is no objective relationship between words and they things they denote).

And since under the mystifying effect of the antiquated and pre-scientific Aristotelian logic of deduction legal thinking 'necessarily proceeded from arbitrarily selected postulates' because 'every judge had to select his first premise, or rule of the case, in a way that was logically wholly indeterminate and therefore arbitrary,' so that all judicial decisions in reality 'had to be the result of some unacknowledged inductive process, which could only mean the subjective way that the judge evaluated the probable social results of his decision' (Purcell, 1973: 90). From all of this, it follows that every time a judge decides, even if wholly unconscious of it, she is engaged in a moral act, the value of which is to be established by the practical effects upon outcomes that the ruling actually has and, which, in principle, should always be amenable to quantitative and statistical analysis; hence the Brandeis Brief that inaugurated the age, the tyranny, of the 'expert' and 'expert testimony'. So what is Cohen's general conclusion but the nature of legal reasoning about the particular? 'It is the great disservice of the classical conception of the law that it hides from judicial eyes the ethical character of every judicial question, and thus serves to perpetuate class prejudices and uncritical moral assumptions which could not survive the sunlight of free ethical controversy' (Cohen, 1960: 67). Which means that whenever the judge (or jury) reasons from universal and de-contextualized axioms, a kind of pre-representational thinking, then they are doing nothing other than rationalizing their cultural biases, which is subjective, prejudicial, and un-scientific, resulting in an unsupported and intolerable state of juridical undifferentiation: the single = the universal, the one = the all, the particular = the general.

Which may or may not sound great in theory—and legal realism really was 'all the rage' for the duration of New Deal America (c.1932–c.1980) until Nixonland—but, unfortunately for its pluralist partisans, it possesses at least one fatal ideological flaw of its own which is the subjective particularity of the judge herself: the abolition of a deductive theory of ethics reduces the legal decision to the will-to-decide of the judge herself, with nothing binding the power of the court other than the operation of a counter-veiling force of some kind which, under the terms of legal realism, is always unable to provide a normative account of itself. For super legal realist Karl Llewellyn, 'What these officials do about disputes is, to my mind, the law itself' (Purcell, 1973: 82), effectively reducing law to nothing more than social engineering, a continuation of politics by other means; 'The most fruitful thinking about law has run steadily toward regarding law as an engine (a heterogeneous multitude of engines) having purposes, not values in itself' (Purcell, 1973: 82). Which, as should be clear, is potentially anti-democratic *in extremis*, or, at the very least, insufferably dismissive of all other contending variables that motivate actual human beings to turn to the law in seeking within the resolution of a given dispute the means for publicly expressing those passions which raise political struggle to the level of existential intensity: a thoroughly anti-liberal 'fact situation' as Carl Schmitt pointed out (Schmitt, 2006). Which may be the hidden key to the entire problem of legal realism: it was intended to remove passion from both law and politics, which would certainly explain the weird otherworldliness of architect Juror no. 8 that is central to the Lumet's pluralist plot: in *12 Angry Men* Henry Fonda as the designated technocratic corporate liberal stages an 'anti-passion' (or 'anti-populist') coup, announcing, perhaps unintentionally, that deference to the legal reasoning of pluralism is *not* really politically neutral but, in truth, aggressively anti-democratic. Legal realism rests upon an extraordinarily naïve view of the ability to retrieve and constitute facts, including the fact of existentially intense political and social struggle; it therefore fails to adequately problematize the nature of the production of legal and social scientific knowledge. As New Deal liberals, the legal realists 'were especially sympathetic to the new social science because they shared many of its assumptions. They were wholly naturalistic in their approach to the problems of knowledge, and they continually emphasized the empirical nature of all human knowledge' (Purcell, 1973: 87), which explains Cohen's revealing blindness to the contestability of every judicial decision.

> If we conceive of legal rules and concepts as functions of judicial decisions, it is convenient, for purposes of this analysis, to think of these decisions as hard and simple facts. Just as every physical object may be analyzed as a complex of positive and negative electrons, so every legal institution, every legal rule or concept may be analyzed as a complex of plaintiff decisions and defendant decisions. But simplicity is relative to the level of analysis. For the chemist, the atom is the lowest term of analysis. But the physicist cannot stop the process of analysis with the atom or the electron. It would be heresy to the faith of science to endow either with final simplicity and perpetual immunity from further analysis. (Cohen, 1960: 69–70)

Not only is legal knowledge, no less than its mimetic model scientific knowledge, ultimately and eternally incomplete and undetermined (a situation brilliantly exposited by Donald Rumsfeld as 'unknown unknowns') but the very nature of the law itself is altered through its own mis-recognitions, including its various media representations that flow directly into the reservoir of variables that determine the social consciousness of a particular culture and that culture's perhaps temporary conception of both the 'true' and the 'good'. James B. Twitchell made this point regarding American literary culture: 'What characterizes the condition of culture since World War II is…that now we have more signs than [referents], more images than meanings that can be attached to them. The machinery of communication often communicates little except itself—signs just refer to each other, creating a "simulacrum" of reality' (James B. Twitchell qtd. Sherwin, 1994: 64 n 111). And as law, whatever its true nature, it is certainly a cultural artifact of some kind, wholly subject to the temporal emergence of new social forces: 'Over-communication, a surplus of images, a popular culture with more signs than referents, and an increasingly mass-mediated reality are cultural phenomena that lawyers and legal scholars cannot ignore' (Sherwin, 1994: 64). Which calls into serious doubt two of the central issues concerning the liberal-pluralist approach to legal reasoning: (a) can the social forces that legal realism postulates as ultimately governing legal reasoning ever actually be uncovered and correctly re-presented in a manner that is capable of yielding authentic certainty?; (b) even if we can obtain objective knowledge of these social forces in terms of their functionality, is the social force, once it is discovered, in reality a thing-in-itself or yet another construction of the ideological bias of the knower, which may be the real social force that never reveals itself as *meconnaissance*? As concerning law, then, and totally against Cohen, it 'is in an increasingly incongruous position:

it vainly attempts to isolate the real in an era in which reality is becoming rapidly indistinguishable from its fictional representations' (Roseanne Kennedy qtd. Rosenberg, 1994: 343 n 7)—an epistemological form of undifferentiation—and today it is fairly safe to conclude that we have collectively evacuated the realm of legal realism for the successor-state of *critical legal realism*, generically known as 'critical legal theory' or CLS. The implication of this being true is that any Law Film produced within such a culture would have to be a *noir* for what unifies film and praxis is a common commitment to pre-representational forms of understanding, Rosenberg clearly 'suggesting that, in a number of ways, the filmic discourses in law noirs seem to parallel those found in certain modes of critical legal realism' (Rosenberg, 1994: 347 n 18). He would seem to be right.

6.4 *The Thin Blue Line*: Law *Noir* and Epistemological Undifferentiation

In many ways that are almost too good to be true, Errol Morris' 1988 documentary *The Thin Blue Line* (MGM, 2005) serves as the perfect critical legal realist foil to Lumet's legal realist masterwork *12 Angry Men.*

> 'The Thin Blue Line' is more than just a sterling investigative documentary about a miscarriage of justice; in expanding into a uniquely perceptive film about the limits and distortions of perception, 'The Thin Blue Line' is one of film's few works of epistemological reach. It's not only a brilliant detective story, but an even more brilliant evocation of the ultimate tension between chaos and order tugging at every atom in the universe. (Jay Carr qtd. Sherwin, 1994: 53 n 52)

Here Jay Carr is accidently invoking Felix S. Cohen in relation to 'the ultimate tension between chaos and order tugging at every atom in the universe'; Cohen's pretentious deployment of sub-atomic physics as a model for scientific legal reasoning is brilliantly lampooned by director Morris' pop culture subversion of the epistemological naiveté of the social scientific certainty of 'facts.' Each interview (or talking head) in the film 'invariably creates more questions than it answers. And the more maps, diagrams and key details the director assembles, the more frighteningly the truth slips away' (Janet Maslin qtd. Sherwin, 1994: 53 n 52). All of this compounded by Morris' scandalizing transgressions against the central icon of the genre: the comparative absence of courtroom imagery from *The Thin Blue Line* signifies like nothing else that the purpose of the Morris film is to *de*-legitimate the criminal justice system. We are facing the Law *Noir* taken to its maximal degree of artistic (and existential) intensity, for at stake is nothing other than the false imprisonment of an innocent man on Death Row. According to Morris, 'On one level, [the film is] the story of a miscarriage of justice. On another level—at least I like to think of it as such—it's a story about self-delusion and fantasy' (Sherwin, 1994: 53 n 52). Morris' evocation of 'self-delusion' and 'fantasy' is particularly effective as it completely relativizes legal realism's complacent mis-understanding of ideology:

namely that it really is possible to 'exit' a prejudiced point of view, enabling one to be governed by a reality in-itself and in an un-mediated manner. According to Hans-Georg Gadamer 'Prejudice certainly does not necessarily mean a false judgment, but part of the idea is that it can have either a positive or negative value…The prejudices of the individual, far more than his judgments, constitute the historical reality of his being…' (Hans-Georg Gadamer qtd. Sherwin, 1994: 63 n 109). And Jean Baudrillard agrees: 'Illusion is not false, for it doesn't use false signs; it uses senseless signs, signs that point nowhere. This is why it deceives and disappoints our demand for meaning., but does so enchantingly' (Jean Baudrillard qtd. Sherwin, 1994: 64 n 111).

A case in point is the contrasting cinematic styles of *12 Angry Men* and *The Thin Blue Line*, most notably the all-important *mis-en-scene*: the physical staging of 'a scene through the artful arrangement of actors, scenery, lighting, and props—everything that the audience sees' (Pramaggiore & Wallis, 2011: 92). In the first film, the pronounced emphasis upon *mis-en-scene*, coupled with a comparatively 'static' camera style, reveals Lumet's ideological commitment to the politics of pluralism, an objectivity that is both moral and epistemological, the political corollary of legal realism. The unusually lengthy opening scene that ends with our witnessing the jurors filing out of the courtroom and toward the jury room is an outstanding example of this.

> By his formal composition and intra-shot montage, Lumet suggests a tone of almost classical stateliness and rationality for the forthcoming action. The extraordinarily leisurely camera movements, featuring but one cut in almost four minutes and ending in a slow tracking shot to the outside of the courtroom where the boy's trial is being conducted, imply that the course of human justice is glacially slow and that only the classical values of ordered, reasoned, meditative inquiry will possibly defeat the irrational prejudice that we are soon to see dominating the jury room. (Cunningham, 1991: 112)

In contrast, Morris adopts a diametrically opposed camera style, with absolute minimal staging and scenery, in order to convey the 'anti-realist' nature of the 'judicial fact finding' under examination.

> If Morris wanted to tell a purely linear tale [like *12 Angry Men*], he certainly would have proceeded differently. Consider, for example, the film's failure to provide captions identifying who is speaking. Why this blatant defiance of the conventional documentary style? Instead of telling us how to take the words of the speaker in terms of his or her social and legal status,[18] we are left with the words themselves, and perhaps also with the felt need to know the speaker's status in order to know how to take what he or she is saying. This technique of non-disclosure provokes a feeling of disorientation. And this disorientation is only the beginning. Morris goes much further to knock us out of the standard causal-linear loop. (Sherwin, 1994: 61)

In fact, the epistemological strategy of Morris is the exact opposite of that of Lumet concerning the same issue, that of *reasonable doubt* as Robert W. Sherwin brilliantly elucidates: law's 'demand for truth and justice can clash with the modern mind's demand for closure and certainty. When truth defies certainty and becomes

[18] Cohen's 'expert'.

complex, justice requires difficult decisions on the basis of that doubt' (Sherwin, 1994: 41). Truth, however, at all times 'requires a reasonable basis for certainty, and justice requires a reasonable basis for assigning responsibility' (Sherwin, 1994: 62) meaning that we need to 'feel sure enough in our reasonable doubt' (Sherwin, 1994: 42) that the objective doubt can be persuasively considered to meet the threshold criteria of reasonable. The really big problem with *The Thin Blue Line*, however, is that director 'sells out' on exactly this point, for it turns out that in Morris' film 'the truth is knowable' (David Denby qtd. Sherwin, 1994: 53 n 53) after all, which blatantly violates the anti-realism of its central premise: the impossibility of the law to achieve certainty.

> But on an allegorical level, the film depicts a battle that rages back and forth, moment by moment, across a thin blue line of representational order. It is a battle against chaos, fate, and deception, forces that could easily destroy human agency and makes individual responsibility impossible. Metaphorically, the film asks a fundamental and daring question: Who (or what) polices meaning? It is a daring question that Morris does not quite see through. For in the end, the counterplot does not take hold'. (Sherwin, 1994: 64)

The cinematic 'tension' within the film that Sherwin rightly identifies is that incommensurability between the Detective film and the Crime film that forms the heart of the suspect counterplot of the film; the surface text of *The Thin Blue Line* is the detective story, while the submerged sub-text is the *noir* tale of criminality. The film's

> … parodic, post-modern, self-conscious images are eventually overwhelmed by the linear detective plot. The viewer resists the invitation to find problems in the film's linear plot. We refuse to entertain the possibility that the purported 'documentary' nature of the film is itself merely another dramatic re-enactment. We reject the parody and prefer to play it straight. (Sherwin, 1994: 70)[19]

Just as Lumet cheats in the way he 'frames' the jury deliberations, Morris similarly cheats by opting for a documentary film style rather than a far less pretentious 'theatrical re-enactment'; the epistemological and political prejudice, or mystification, of the documentary form is that it is inherently truthful, for the documentary style is implicitly premised, like the Detective film, on the representational nature of language and reality, for, otherwise, there would be never be any point in making any documentary in the place of cinematic 'fictions'.

[19] In fact 'there are two tales here, and one subverts the other. When framed as causal-linear documentary and detective story, Morris's film employs conventional wisdom (including schemata, scripts, and stereotypes) about lying, madness, official corruption, local prejudice, and psychological trauma. It takes us along a straight path of meaning: from mystery (why is this main in jail?) to resolution (because he was framed!). Within this frame, we know that human nature and the world operate according to causal-linear principles. Things make sense, and judgments are not difficult. When the film is framed as a non-linear composite of symbols, however, we find ourselves in a universe of fate and fortune, circularity and irresolution.' But where we are instead is within the realm of 'the mythic narratives of ancient Western cultures,' specifically 'the classical culture of Sophocles and Aeschylus, with their vast interjaculating array of non-rational forces' that 'are also (perhaps always have been) shaping our world' (Sherwin, 2000: 155, 116). And the gifts that Sophocles and Aeschylus bore us were Sophocles and Orestes, the mythic entities of lies, *meconnaissance*, and sacrifice.

> A documentary film is shot with three cameras: (1) the camera in the technical sense; (2) the filmmakers' mind; and (3) the generic patterns of the documentary film, which are founded on the expectations of the audience that patronizes it. For this reason one cannot simply say that the documentary film portrays facts. It photographs isolated facts and assembles from them a coherent set of facts according to the divergent schema. All remaining possible facts and factual contexts are excluded. The naïve treatment of documentation therefore provides a unique opportunity to concoct fables. In and of itself, the documentary is no more realistic than the feature film'. (Alexander Kluge qtd. Greenfield & Osborn, 1994–1995: 1197)

So that quite weirdly Morris as documentary film-maker comes to occupy the same moral-cognitive-political role of the Lawyer-Detective that Juror no. 8 does in *12 Angry Men*: he appears to be revealing the truth through controlling the process of narrative which is exposed as an artful construction.

> It's common sense. In a world of official corruption, greed, cynical self-interest, madness, local prejudice, and profound psychological trauma, these things happen. Innocent outsiders get framed, and local sociopaths go free. It makes sense. Randall Dale Adams should never have been in prison at all. The film sets the record straight. Justice miscarried, but truth will out in the end. The causal-linear metaphysics of common sense triumphs. Morris' expose allows us to rest easy: Error can be corrected, order can be re-imposed, and, above all, our belief in the ultimate triumph of justice can be confirmed. (Sherwin, 1994: 59)

So why, exactly, does the representational text overwhelm the pre-representational sub-text? The answer, not surprisingly, lies with morality, or, more precisely, the unnerving nihilistic immorality, or a-morality, of anti-realism (or post-modernism) in general and of the Law *noir* in particular: for the real-world issue at stake is execution or clemency, law's surrogate for Schmitt's existential intensity. In *The Thin Blue Line* Randall Adams is unambiguously portrayed as innocent, yet as a critical legal realist documentary film maker Morris cannot arrive at such a determinative conclusion of guilt or innocence or even reasonable doubt because all of the necessary onto-epistemological devices (truth, objectivity, reason, transparency, intelligibility) are either absent or obsolete within the realm of critical legal realism to which his film is a cinematic monument. So what makes the formally guilty party truly innocent? It is that the film's counterplot of 'What is Truth?'

> …fails in the same way that skeptical post-modernism is likely to fail in law and lawyering generally. In a legal context, the reality that it portrays is aesthetically and psychologically untenable. In matters of life and death, whether it be the execution of the accused or the possibility of his killing again, we instinctively reject the message of skeptical post-modernism. Human traits like prejudice, deceit, greed, abuse of power, and the reality of a deliberate frame-up are things we can understand. But mystification, time's circularity, fate, and coincidence defeat the practical demands of human judgment. (Sherwin, 1994: 70)

'*Practical demands*' meaning, of course, moral certainty if not factual exactitude. Notice how Sherwin conflates the metaphysical with the ethical in the above passage. Any representation of reality (metaphysics) that renders certainty impossible is an objectively bad thing (ethics) because it would mean that too many people would suffer, which is universally unacceptable owing to an unspoken principle that has somehow managed to withstand the onslaught of post-realist relativism.

> Chaos is disorienting and unpleasant, especially in matters of life and death. Decisions of such consequence are no time for epistemological conundrums or aesthetic musings. Thus, once nestled in the sobering frame of a criminal trial, storytelling fictions such as Morris' self-consciously cartoonish images and their playful interference with the linear documentary have a boomerang effect. These caricatures of reality only send us running back to the 'truer' reality, the reality that the linear plot alone is able to provide. Faced with untenable disorder on the one hand, and a meaningful drama on the other, there is no choice. (Sherwin, 1994: 71)

Although in terms of social forces while it may be the case that we will always opt for the existential intensity of the Schmittean decision out of an equally existential terror of eternal in-decision, as a matter of cinematic aesthetics it is a matter of cultural fact that the genre-conforming law-film-as-detective-story constitutes an *ethical* rejoinder to amoral-and-relativistic Law *Noir*: '*The Thin Blue Line*'s aesthetic and psychological failures offer a cautionary lesson about the art of persuasive legal story-telling: The law has little use for the kind of skeptical, radically subversive post-modernism that has been featured of late in some legal and much non-legal scholarship' (Sherwin, 1994: 71) for the social consequences of epistemological nihilism is that we 'become strangers in a strange and incomprehensible land' wherein the 'unified self and human agency come to be seen as illusory' and 'no normative stance seems worthy of commitment' (Sherwin, 2000: 129). Even the accused who is presented as innocent may in reality be guilty because his speaking truth to power sounds fake; which is why documentary film-maker Joshua Oppenheimer described Randall Dale Adams as a 'man who has already honed his performance,' a 'performance of righteous indignation' (MGM, 2005).

Here are the facts as we 'know' them. Two white males, 28-year-old Adams and 16-year-old David Ray Harris,[20] were arrested and charged with the November 1975 murder of Dallas Police officer Robert W. Wood who had been fatally shot during a routine car search. The prosecution alleged that the vehicle was stolen by Harris, but it was possible that both Harris and Adams were in car and Adams as the driver. Although Harris originally claimed to being a cop killer when talking with friends after Wood's murder, at trial he changed his testimony and claimed that he witnessed Adams perform the shooting. Adams' story was that on the evening of the shooting he and Harris, who had met for the very first time earlier that day, spent the day drinking beer and smoking marijuana and later went to a local drive-in to see two 'beer-drinking movies' (*Student Body* and *Swinging Cheerleaders*). Adams did not care for the second feature: 'an R-rated cheerleader type of thing…I didn't know what it was,' telling Harris that 'I don't really care to sit here and watch this.' Leaving early, both returned to Adam's residence (The Comfort Motel) which Adams shared with his unnamed brother and who was present in the motel room for the entire night. Adams asked his brother if Harris could stay for the night, but the off-screen sibling objected; as Harris described it, the 'brother don't like to do that, or something'. It is a matter of no small concern that Adam's brother is never named, never described

[20] Harris was a minor and ineligible for the death penalty; one of the main contentions of both Morris and the film is that Adams was fingered for Harris' crime because the latter could not be executed.

in any manner, and never interviewed, which is a real shame as he may be the only one capable of establishing the true facts pertaining to the following crucial event. According to Adams, Harris left immediately after the brother's cryptic demurral; after a short discussion with the 16-year old in the parking lot about something unspecified Adams then returned to the room, and watched 'The Carol Burnett Show' at 9:00 pm and the first half of The Ten o'clock news, going to bed (alone) by 11:00 pm. Harris, however, originally testified that he slept overnight in his car in the parking lot of the Comfort Motel and then returned to Vidor, Texas early in the morning. In an immunity agreement, however, Harris testified at Adams' trial that he and Adams left The Comfort Motel in his car with Randall driving, claiming that it was Adams who shot Officer Woods. Adams' brother was apparently present at the motel room for the entire evening, but in his original testimony provided to the prosecutor during a pre-trial interview, which contradicted Adams, was that the two of them watched a wrestling match all evening. The brother then later decided not to testify as a witness for the defense, allegedly out of fear of committing perjury, suggesting that Adams was not present in the motel room at the time of the shooting, depriving Randall of an alibi.[21] If the brother was lying about Randall being at the motel, the most likely scenario would seem to be that Adams and Harris returned to the Comfort Motel to spend the night together; after the brother refused to allow the teenager to stay, both men return to the car and left in order to have a tryst somewhere else, possibly in the car itself. If so, then both Harris and Adams may have been in the car when it was pulled over by Officer Woods; Adams may or may not have been the driver, but Harris was most likely the shooter, as he possessed both a gun and a serious criminal history, including having receiving the death-sentence for an unrelated murder in 1985. But even if Adams was not the shooter, he was, at the very least, an accomplice, guilty of the first-degree murder of a Dallas police officer. The brother may well be the verifier of what 'really happened,' but the ability to retrieve or uncover the truth is not possible because he is missing, for whatever reason, from Morris' film which is premised upon the inherent unreliability of conflicting narrators, essentially in the same manner as Kurosawa's *Rashomon*.[22]

The 'moral', then, is that the life-or-death nature of the American criminal justice system is too morally important, and existentially intense, to allow for cinematic

[21] Sherwin makes the same observation as I do. 'But why didn't Adams brother confirm Adam's story, or at least verify one of Harris's versions of events at the trial? If Harris made it all up, why such detail? The climax of the movie comes when Harris mysteriously proclaims that Adams might only be in jail because "he didn't have no place for somebody to stay that helped him that night. ... That might be the only, total reason why he's where he's at today." Consider the ambiguity of this statement. It might mean that had Adam's brother agreed to let Harris stay over, the shooting would not have occurred' (Sherwin, 2000: 121–122).

[22] See Chap. 5, above. If Morris had some choice in the matter, and if the brother could testify to a same-sex liaison between Adams and the under-age Harris, then Randall would not only be physically present at the shooting, but he would also have possessed sufficient motive to kill a police officer: the avoidance of the charge of pedophilia within a solidly conservative state of Texas in the 1980s. And if this is true, then the moral bias of the audience and, therefore, the legal and moral rightness of Adam's release from prison would depend completely on the identity of the accused, a member of an historically persecuted (and prosecuted) minority.

subversion of the Law Film genre past a certain, but undefinable, point. So, although I believe that Sherwin is correct on the question of 'fact'—moral seriousness demands public declaration of loyalty to representation and objectivity—I believe that he is wrong on the substance of the normative imperative he invokes. For if there is something objectively immoral and unacceptable about Law *Noir*, it has nothing to do with modernity's construction of Enlightenment objectivity; to the contrary, it has everything to do with the 'return of the repressed,' for what critical legal realism and the Law *Noir* both signify is the re-summoning of the archaic scapegoat now re-normalized and re-vitalized as 'social justice'. If the epistemological foundation of post-realism is the pre-representational theory of language wherein anything or word can be substituted for any other allowing for a wholly arbitrary system of classification, then this would be sacrificial in nature. The innocence and guilt of the accused would never be a question of fact but a matter of interpretation or communal reading governed by processses which could never be considered wholly rational and controlled at all times by the group's desire for exclusion.

It must never be forgotten that the foundation of the pagan Hellenism that the neo-classical architecture of the courtroom-as-icon eternally signifies was the sacrificial mechanism. And this takes us to what I believe the true message of *12 Angry Men* really is in all of its Girardian signification: that the 'masses apparently need someone to hate, if they are to learn not to hate' (Hay, 2007: 852) so 'that law will never escape its origins in ritual sacrifice; the most one can hope to do is substitute allegorical bloodlettings for real ones' (Hay, 2007: 680). Which is a truly universal message that can be applied equally well to conservative, radical and, above all, to the pluralist. As I will show, both Lumet and Morris (and Girard) share the same stumbling-block: the scandalous error of regarding truth itself as a moral value.

6.5 The Specter of the Scapegoat: A Girardian Reading of *12 Angry Men*

What narratively unites *12 Angry Men* and *The Thin Blue Line* is that the social triumph of liberalism—causality, linearity, reason, rationality, representation, nego-tiation, mediation, objectivity— is an absolute moral good that must be obtained at all cost, including willful and knowing mis-recognition, for the racist and/or stupid jurors of Lumet are the mimetic doubles of Morris' corrupt persecutors and unreliable witnesses. And what Lumet unconditionally denounces as heretical Morris tepidly holds as heterodoxical: epistemological undifferentiation makes the resurrection of the scapegoat possible and perhaps necessary. "'First principle: any explanation is better than none'" said Nietzsche (Sherwin, 2000: 283 n 25) and, as anthropology proves, the institutionalized mis-recognition of the un-reality of the scapegoat can be as, or even more, affectively binding than any providentially revealed truth, provided, according to Girard, that *meconnaissance* controls speech and perception; 'For uncer-tainty by itself, is highly volatile. It is a state that cannot be maintained. Jurors in its grip will seek relief elsewhere, in any respite of meaning, grasping for a way to tolerate the difficult responsibility of deciding whether to acquit for condemn' (Sherwin, 2000: 117). And Sherwin's admonition that 'even the criminal defense attorney, who deliberately sets out to activate uncertainty in order to establish that the state has failed to carry its burden of proving guilt beyond a reasonable doubt, may go too far' (Sherwin, 2000: 117) seems to suggest the rhetorical machinations of Juror no.8; is it really unreasonable to interpret the decision of the others to acquit less a matter of rational conviction than an overpowering desire to release themselves from an intolerable state of cognitive anxiety? It appears an immutable truth that we '"never say precisely what wish to say or mean precisely what we say. Our discourse always tends to slip away from our data towards the structures of consciousness with which we are trying to grasp them"' (Hayden White qtd. Sherwin, 2000: 281 n 12).[23] This is the condition of pre-representation, and, thanks to it, the freakish and unpredictable appearance of the scapegoat-of-the-double-transference remains an eternal possibility: '"Fateful accidents are the reality of our life, because as human beings we are always 'entangled in stories"' which means that interpretation is never and cannot be foreclosed (Odo Marquard qtd. Sherwin, 2000: 282 n 18). Liberal Juror no. 8 told his story and then symbolically scapegoated illiberal Juror no. 3; the Dallas prosecutor told his story and physically scapegoated Randall Dale Adams; Randall Dale Adams told his story to Errol Morris (who then told everybody) and then physically scapegoated David Harris, maybe.

> We believe that truth travels a straight line and deceit curves. We believe justice will out in the end because the law's machinery, once set in motion, ensures that it must, and because the narrative demands of the story promise that it will. Yet, we can also tolerate a non-linear tale, as long as it appears to be serving truth's straightforward ends. Just as we can tolerate the justice in factual ambiguity, in reasonable doubt, as long as we locate it in a tale that lets us feel certain about something—even if it is only the certainty that we are heroic in resisting the temptation to yield a false certainty. (Sherwin, 1994: 71)

Contra Sherwin, however, the cultural truth of the scapegoat is that he signifies the reality of both guilt and innocence—and the moral values attached to both—as cultural constructs rather than epistemological axioms. Which means, paradoxically, that the scapegoat is true in the sense that it is false, a mis-recognized object that generates socially transformative effects which are completely real. Which leads to a second paradox: while Morris starts with post-modernism but has to migrate toward some sort of realism, Lumet starts out as a realist but winds up telling a tale that is at least partially anti-realist in its implications. The real issue at stake in *12 Angry Men* is not the acquittal of the accused but the conversion of the jurors from the sacrificial to the post-sacrificial, from pre-representation to representation; an exercise in conflictual mimesis synonymous with a liberalism that is premised upon the innocent of the accused member of a minority group as well as the inherent

---

[23] Wittgenstein put it this way: '"I did not get my picture of the world by satisfying myself of its correctness; nor do I have it because I am satisfied with its correctness. No: it is the inherited background against which I distinguish between true and false"' (Ludwig Wittgenstein qtd. Sherwin, 2000: 117).

wrongness of a certain type of citizen. Representational language is inherently anti-scapegoating for it prevents the undifferentiation of desire which Lumet clearly trumpets with the iconic Juror no. 8. This much is clear using Girard's terminology. But what is not so clear—what is in fact quite occluded—is that the film possesses a sub-textual scapegoating counterplot through the surface but mis-recognized plot to redirect the scapegoating desire of the crowd toward the new minority of the despised: the would-be but now failed scapegoaters who are Biskind's conservatives as cinematically portrayed by Lumet.

Liberalism is the *meconnaissance* of the post-sacrificial *nomos* of modernity that requires the creation of an interpretive community of anti-sacrificial readers[24] that do not, however, actually disavow scapegoating but invert the dynamic: the symbolic or 'un-bloody' scapegoating of the scapegoaters, the symbolic persecution of the physical persecutors, who, in this instance, are Juror nos. 3 and 10. And the architect, or model-mediator, of this community will be the one who stands in the closest relationship to the object of emulation, the idealized liberal Juror no. 8: Henry Fonda. Juror no. 8, or Mr. Davis, is not merely an architect, but he is the answer to the prayers of Ron Perlstein who seeks a secular saviour to lead the American demos out of the thrall of anti-pluralistic Nixonland.

> I have written of these liberal's simple faiths […] compared them to the drama staged by the Henry Fonda character in *12 Angry Men*: the belief that if only Nixon's people could truly see *reason*, grasp "the responsible literature in the field," their prejudices would melt away, their true interests would be recognized—and they would end up liberals too. (Perlstein, 2008: 747)

And no. 8 the messiah leads the jurors to liberalism (and out of Nixonland) because he bestows upon the newly converted readers (*metanoia*) a unifying language, or constitutive rhetoric; for James Boyd White, the most important aspect of legal rhetoric is its 'ethical or communal character, or its socially constitutive nature' (White, 1985: 690)[25] and it is the speech of Juror no. 8 that instigates 'the transformation of twelve men into apostles of something called "reasonable doubt"' (Hay, 2007: 813). What 'the deliberation achieves is the emergence of their *common* sense' (Burns, 2007: 648) which is a double-entendre for regenerative violence: everyone possesses the common sense of right reasoning and general truth but that the possession, and demonstration, of such commonality-of-sense is the signification of an identity-in-common, the generative unanimity of the *nomos* of pluralism.[26]

---

[24] See Chap. 1, above.

[25] See Chap. 1, above.

[26] And indeed, so totally (and totalizing) has liberalism become the exclusionary sign of the *nomos* of American civic virtue that, in an almost Kafka-esque fashion, Juror no. 8's dissenting heroism has undergone a complete inversion into its perfect opposite: irrational and immoral deviancy. 'With the passage of time since *12 Angry Men* played in the theatres, the holdout juror has lost his hold on the popular imagination. Instead of the hero, the holdout has become a villain … Instead of the embodiment of reasonable doubt, the holdout is variously described as "unreasonable," "unreachable," "eccentric and disengaged." Instead of focusing a runaway jury to deliberate, the holdout is pictured as "disengaged" and "un-deliberative." Instead of rational argument, the holdout invokes "religious scruples" and "God's will"' (Abramson, 2007: 595). In short, a conservative.

And, in fact, Lumet provides a cinematic solution to both Robert M. Cover's difficulty with pluralism and Biskind's quest for unassailable consensus: as liberals, the rhetorically constituted community is committed to a form of tolerance that proceeds in a wholly uniform, and unifying fashion, the requisite generative unanimity provided by the convert's emulation of Christ/God: Jesus-like Juror no. 8[27] and God-like advanced senior citizen Juror no. 9 (who are also the only two jurors whose names we learn: Davis and McCardle) are the only ones who are wholly distinct, or differentiated. In truth, Juror no. 8 is guilty as charged by ultra-cynic Juror no. 7: 'Fonda *is* a salesman,' the purveyor of the 'soft sell' technique of advertising (Hay, 2007: 848), although, of course, he is really selling the truth of the *metanoia* that is pluralism by his playing his adult version of the childish games of the other jurors: charades (Hay, 2007). But this requires *meconnaissance* in order to work, for 'That's the thing about the soft sell: when it's done right, people don't know it's happening,' and, as Lumet intended, 'If this film is done right, audiences will love it without fully knowing why' (Hay, 2007: 860). Politically, everyone will love being a liberal without fully knowing why, and so 'Henry Fonda's character finds that he needs to play tricks, set traps, break the law, smuggle in evidence, build factions, provoke enemies, flatter, cajole, and shout, all in the service of ferreting out the truth' (Abramson, 2007: 592) but which he may very well have succeeded in re-interning, albeit for the higher cause of an ethical concern of the pluralist variety. As Jeffry Abramson convincingly demonstrates, *12 Angry Men* is a highly idiosyncratic legal drama that 'brings to the fore the distinctive feature of an institution where power can ultimately flow to the persuasive, rather than the numerous' (Abramson, 2007: 592), which is the essence of rhetoric in its debased form of advertising, and Juror no. 8's forte is constitutive rhetoric, a kind of an inverted Creon or Tiresias[28] who uses suasion to turn a guilty man into an innocent one. It is most fitting that in a trial that is all about patricide that the two 'architects' (one literal, one allegorical) of the reintroduction of difference are both 'Fathers'. According to Austin Sarat, who has totally bought into the ethical concern of Lumet's *auteur* filmmaking, *12 Angry Men* being the 'celebration of civic virtue and the seeming triumph of reason over passion

[27] In addition to building a stellar career out of portraying Jesus surrogates, he also got to play a very lethally violent 'lawman' (or gun-fighter) in 1946 in another John Ford epic, *My Darling Clementine* (Landsman, 2007: 751) who, while not very Christ-like, was exceptionally effective in 'confounding' those sinning against the true community of the righteous. It is quite reasonable to suggest that *12 Angry Men* is a 'talkie' Western set back East in New York City with Juror no. 8 as a verbose Westerner re-located. And it was none other than the *auteur grand* of French cinema Francois Truffaut, like Andre Bazin a lover of Westerns, who highlighted the manner in which *12 Angry Men* is an action film which, while unfolding in slow motion, is performing the same dramatic work of a John Ford gunfighter movie: '"[We] experience intensely the feeling, not of something done, but of something being done"'—which, is to say, a film 'about a process,' the creation of a new community in the same manner of the iconic scene of the raising of the church roof in Ford's *My Darling Clementine*, starring Henry Fonda. And after the raising a dance, the coming together of the now unified many. And so it is in *12 Angry Men*: Henry Fonda's Mr. Davis the architect constructs a courthouse that is the sacrificial center of the now self-stabilizing *nomos* that excludes and silences instead of crucifying, electrocuting, or shooting.

[28] See Chap. 1, above.

and prejudice' (Sarat, 2007: 863), the 'film's heroic Juror #8' earns the 'admiration of the film's imagined audience by enacting another kind of fatherhood as well as by scrupulously and unquestioningly adhering to law's existing rules and conventions and submitting to them the image of a good judge as one who separates public and private,' reason from emotion' (Sarat, 2007: 864), as does the liberal. Which raises the question of whether or not jurors nos. 8 and 9 managed to restore difference through regenerating patriarchy, or at least a benevolent form of paternalism, which is fully compatible with corporate liberalism and techno-cratic statist interventionism.[29] So naturally we see throughout *12 Angry Men* Fonda 'patiently and calmly' teaching everybody else 'as a father would teach his children' about 'deliberation, reason, good judgment, about the virtues that law would claim for itself, leading them toward self-awareness and social responsibility,' the existential type of adulthood that doubles as mimetic difference (Sarat, 2007: 882). Which makes *12 Angry Men* a veritable parable for Girard's theory of the scapegoat for what is being enacted before us is the differentiation of previously undifferentiated 'angry' men through the substitution of representation for pre-representation as mediated by a scapegoat.

> We must remember that only in later situations, after the emergence of culture, can a belief in the victim's guilt actually motivate a unanimous turning of violence against one party: no such beliefs are at work in an unanimity generated by a non-representational mimesis. Beliefs in the victim's responsibility come later as a representational effect of this more mechanical form of mimesis. (Livingston, 1992: 129)

The question here is to what extent does Lumet predetermine this outcome by opting for a verdict-driven deliberation rather than an evidence-driven deliberation? I have discussed the narrative implausibility of a juror of 1–11 ever flipping over to 12–0 as a legal fantasy, but there is a more sinister aspect of the *auteur*'s maneuver, because the verdict-driven deliberation is 'one in which there is an early, public vote that typically leads to adversarial factions preoccupied with winning the point and silencing dissenters' (Marder, 2006: 159), an act of exclusion that is sacrificial.

> Verdict-driven deliberations are more likely to lead to the creation of coalitions and a more adversarial style of discussion because each side is intent upon winning the point and stifling dissenters. In contrast, evidence-driven deliberations are more likely to encourage the participation of jurors because the emphasis is on story construction and recollection of facts and evidence without individual jurors having to align themselves with a particular position. (Marder, 2007: 890 n 11)

---

29 '"Lumet interweaves … a motif of fathering that becomes an important visual correlative to the theme of the necessity for personal responsibility in an increasingly depersonalized, bureaucratized world"' in which, of course, all distinctions are inexorably abolished (Frank Cunningham qtd. Sarat, 2007: 864 n 7).

Lumet has set it up (or stacked the deck) so that the unifying model of mimetic attraction may manifest itself and a collective *metanoia* result.[30] It would be visually impossible to film a conversion event with an evidence-driven narrative of anti-drama but even more vital is that Juror no. 8 be given the opportunity to speak, because liberal-pluralist technocrats are the only ones who can know with certainty which particular group objectively merits 'sacrifice,' which, in 1957 New York, means exclusion, disempowerment, and permanent minority status.[31] And here are two of the most outstanding rhetorical mis-directions of Henry Fonda.

---

[30] This may represent real artistic cunning on Lumet's part, for it plays upon the ambivalence of the true meaning of reasonable doubt. In general, 'jurors show they understand that the prosecution bears the burden of proving the defendant guilty beyond a reasonable doubt, but by the end of the deliberations, the ever-increasing number of defecting jurors voting for acquittal tends to speak of their conviction that the defendant is "innocent"' (Burns, 2007: 647 n 22; Weisselberg, 2007: 724). If Lumet is set upon dismantling the scapegoat mechanism through the generative unanimity engineered by Juror no. 8, then the surest way of achieving the *nomos* of anti-sacrificial pluralism is by presenting not merely reasonable doubt concerning guilt but positive evidence of innocence, the most morally powerful form of demystification possible and one that makes the conservative jurors even more deserving of ostracism, for they were not merely trying to prove the accused's guilt, they were actively conspiring to murder an innocent boy.

[31] Vidmar et al. discuss a real-life case that uncannily mimics Lumet's legal fantasy although the jury divide was never 11–1. In the case of the trial of Manuelo Rojas for the murder of the Morenos, a Hispanic couple in New York City, the initial majority that wanted to convict were gradually overcome by a 'highly-educated member of the jury who favored acquittal' and who 'provided leadership for the other jurors who favored acquittal' in the face of the powerful evidence against the accused. For just like 'Henry Fonda in *12 Angry Men*, this juror became an amateur defense attorney, unrestrained by law or the lack of evidence. He argued as fact things that, at best, were speculation.' The result was that 'unable to match the highly articulate leader of the group of jurors arguing for acquittal, the majority of jurors who initially favored conviction eventually subscribed to his logic and voted not guilty' (Vidmar et al., 2007: 699, 700). Commenting on this apparently skewed result, Richard Ulliver argued that the verdict was a false acquittal for the very same thing that sunk the twelve angry men: 'It was their disregard for the corroborating evidence' that led both juries to ignore 'a substantial body of circumstantial evidence' that indicated the accused's guilt (Richard Uberville qtd. Vidmar et al., 2007: 700). As far as *12 Angry Men* is concerned, apart from Juror no. 8's false miracle of the switchblade, the two most egregious examples of amateur (or thespian) defense lawyering 'unrestrained by law or lack of evidence' are the un-expert 're-staging' of the elderly but hobbled witnesses' 'rush' to the door of his apartment and the incontrovertible proof that the female witness could not have seen what she claimed to have saw because she wore glasses as indicated by the 'marks on her nose'—which could have been the indentations made by reading glasses. Just to make things worse (or better if one is a liberal-technocrat-architect), the jurors 'engaged in untested speculation about [the old man's] need to feel important, constructing a scenario that because he was old and poor he must have designed his testimony to take advantage of this being the first time in his life he was the center of attention' (Vidmar et al., 2007: 697) with everyone, film viewers and critics alike, missing the in-your-face joke that the one who works hardest to invent this scenario is none other than Juror no. 9 (Mr. McCardle who claims 20/20 vision), by far the eldest member of the twelve and openly identified by the others as an 'old man,' raising the strong suspicion that when destroying the witness he is really describing himself, with lengthy monologue and in extended close-up, just as he does when 'attacking' the vision of the lady-with-the-marks-of-maybe-non-reading-glasses-on-her-nose. The obvious rejoinder concerning the female witness is that the twelve men 'never considered the likelihood that regular wearers of glasses keep their

'I haven't got anything brilliant. I only know as much as you do' (Marder, 2007: 894 n 28)—which is a blatant lie, considering that he has illegally bought and brought an exact double of the accused's incredibly 'rare' switchblade knife into the jury room with him, concealed in his jacket pocket in anticipation of the pre-planned moment of truth.

'It's very hard to keep personal prejudice out of a thing like this. And no matter where you run into it, prejudice obscures the truth' (Marder, 2007: 892 n 22)—which knowingly conceals the fact that the evidence against the accused is, in fact, very strong, which means that, in this case at least, prejudice does not obscure the truth, which is guilt. And, reasoning backwards from the apparent to the hidden, we know that the real purpose, or *telos*, of the film is the engineering of an interpretive community of liberals who resolutely adhere to 'the faith known as "reasonable doubt"' (Hay, 2007: 854) wholly independent of the actual guilt or innocence of the accused, for the simple reason that the 19-year old Puerto Rican patricidal youth, the denier of distinctions, is almost certainly guilty. Bruce L. Hay, who is one of the very few commentators on *12 Angry Men* who recognizes it as a religious allegory, conveys this brilliantly within the context of Biskind's trope of Eisenhower-era pluralist film-making.

> Suppose you are a filmmaker (or team of filmmakers) trying to give a boost to the values of legal liberalism[32]—the rule of law and not of men, respect for due process, tolerance of

---

glasses handy on a bedside table and automatically put them on before looking anywhere' including at real-time murders (Vidmar et al., 2007: 697). And as Charles D. Weisselberg helpfully reminds us, 'When jurors conduct experiments in the jury room that are not under conditions described in the trial testimony, they are also functionally considering extraneous and untested evidence' (Weisselberg, 2007: 728). And the reason why he reminds us of this is because, for him, it is a matter not merely of dramatic license but ethical concern of the formalist variety: 'our justice system fosters (and is unable to question seriously) the gospel that juries return reliable verdicts. Our system depends on selling [sic] this concept. If we want citizens to accept and respect jury verdicts, which is of paramount importance, people must believe in the jury as a reliable trier of fact. It is no overstatement to say that in the criminal justice system, the jury is an American idol' (Weisselberg, 2007: 731). Or model. The conclusion is as painful to as it is undeniable for the liberal: Lumet's 'jury deconstructed the evidence in a biased way. Led by Juror #8, they systematically dismantled inculpatory evidence without the plausibility of the deconstruction. Motives of eyewitnesses were manufactured from whole cloth, but the plausibility of the defendant's story was not tested for internal consistency or against circumstantial evidence pointing to guilt' (Vidmar et al., 2007: 697). Tellingly, the incorrigible pluralists among us would not accept any part of the revelation of Juror no. 8's mis-recognized soft sell; the liberal interpretation of Juror no. 8 is that there 'was no *undue* or *improper* influence. Fonda "managed to convert his peers through a series of rational and persuasive arguments concerning the quality of the state's evidence"' (Saul M. Kassin and Lawrence S. Wrightman qtd. Weisselberg, 2007: 720).

[32] Which marks *12 Angry Men* as a 'cold war film,' as Fifties Hollywood had 'committed itself to an effort to produce patriotic fare' and one of 'the favorite themes in that effort was the dramatization of ways in which the United States as different from and superior to the Soviet Union' (Landsman, 2007: 750). Although seemingly counter-intuitive—a lynch-mob in the form of a jury of hyper-aggressive white males would not serve as a good soft sell for the American Way—this observation fits in well with Biskind's account of pluralist cinema. '*12 Angry Men* offers the jury as a foil to the prevailing McCarthyism of the 1950s. The conformist politics roiling the national sage are presented in miniature; far from being an exception to the contagions of group thinking, the jury at first seems

> dissent, equality under the law, the responsibility of citizenship, a healthy skepticism instead of dogmatism,[33] and so on.[34] … One possible strategy might be this: Devise a carefully orchestrated advertising campaign to give legal liberalism an aura it otherwise lacks. Send in a top salesman, preferably one with experience playing Christ figures.[35] Suggest that those whom he reaches have been touched by the hand of God. Make the Constitution a sacred covenant, equate courts with churches, conflate reasoned deliberation with religious conversion. (Hay, 2007: 848. 849)

However, the sacrificial mechanism has in no wise been completely dismantled, just as is the case in the non-cinematic world; rather, there has been an occluded act of substitution engineered by the architect Juror no. 8: the collective violence of the 12 'angry' (white) men has been re-directed towards the two new surrogate victims standing in for the formally accused—the two irredeemable conservatives (as per Biskind), jurors no. 10 and, more importantly no. 3, the one angry man who 'seems to think that the accused is his own son' (Hay, 2007: 837)[36] which bespeaks of a

---

to be the epitome of it. And yet, in the end the jury alone triumphs over the prejudices that make witch hunts possible' (Abramson, 2007: 593). The geo-political implications are that American pluralism-liberalism is itself the infallible antidote to any democracy's subversion by conservatism and radicalism, surface appearances to the contrary, making Juror no. 8's triumph of constitutive rhetoric that much more imperative.

[33] Biskind would say conservatism or radicalism.

[34] And, of course, the 'bad' or violently angry jurors are re-presented as caricatures of conservative models, most prominently Juror no. 3 as Joseph McCarthy. And the most McCarthy-like thing about him is that he refuses the multi-layered common-sense of pluralism in a manner morally and intellectually wrong and emotionally hysterical, as one possessed by the spirit of the primitive: 'Excitable! You bet I'm excitable. We're trying to put a guilty man into the chair where he belongs and all of a sudden somebody's telling us fairy tales … and we're listening!' (Burns, 2007: 657). Of course, if Henry Fonda really is pushing the soft sell, Lee J. Cobb's Juror no. 3 is the only one whose primitive instincts and passions are sufficient to allow him to see through the charade of liberal mis-recognition. Which means that he is the one who must be sacrificed—for speaking the truth.

[35] Fonda played the very Christ-like Tom Joad in *The Grapes of Wrath* (1940) and then went on to make a career of it, saintliness plus sagacity. 'During his fabled career, Fonda played other legends, including the young Abraham Lincoln [in John Ford's magisterial *Young Mr. Lincoln* (1939)] … the President of the United States (twice), Admiral Chester Nimitz (twice), "Mr. Roberts," and two celebrated Clarences of the law—Clarence Darrow and Clarence Earl Gideon. Who can resist Fonda as still another heroic figure, doggedly pursuing the truth? The late actor radiated honesty and integrity. His face was an affidavit.' Is it any wonder that the American Film Institute 'rates Fonda's Juror #8 as fifteenth on its list of the greatest fifty movie heroes of all time?' (Weisselberg, 2007: 717).

[36] So that when no 3 finally breaks down and cries out 'not guilty!' between his convulsive sobs, he is declaring his belief in the innocence of both boys, one a literal father-slayer, the other a symbolic one: patricidal 'monstrous doubles' who are both possessed by the same metaphysical desire. Or, so may it be read. Sarat did just that: no. 3 is "'the juror most in need of fathering and most irresponsible in terms of his ability to exercise rational judgment in an issue that calls up dimly realized personal associations for him that are highly charged with subliminal energy" (Frank Cunningham qtd. Sarat, 2007: 882 n 84). In more practical terms, this comes down to convincing the sacrificer that the scapegoat in front of him is not really the same 'one' that first appeared in the time of Genesis.

total regression to the atavism of possessory pre-representational thought, the master-sign of ultra-conservatism.[37] They are the most clearly reactionary of the yet-to-be-converted and they both undergo a mild (liberal) form of symbolic death, tantamount to exile or non-violent exclusion, by succumbing out of a kind of epistemological anguish to the psychological and social terrors of ostracism and shaming by the newly converted 'majority'[38] that is, really, the properly constituted community which can itself be interpreted as a counter anti-conservative lynch-mob of liberals[39]; this is expressed in the most naked terms by the recently converted ex-conservative Juror no. 4 to the still unconverted racist Juror no. 10: 'If you open your mouth again I'm going to split your skull' (Burns, 2007: 659) which is extremely exclusionary to say the least.[40] But it is right and just that it be so and convincing everyone of this is Henry-Jesus-Fonda-Christ's single greatest act of *meconnaissance* for the purpose of conversion.

> This whole 'trial' has been a parade of con artists,[41] which the men themselves are unwittingly marching in. As they step into the jury room, these 'jurors' are unable to judge anything, and the 'verdict' they are ready to deliver has nothing to do with speaking the truth. They don't know that they've been part of a theatrical production in which they pay the part of the deluded multitude, desperately in need of someone to awaken them to something called 'reasonable doubt'. (Hay, 2007: 815–816)

As it ever was, the undifferentiated are undifferentiating, possessed of a mimetic desire that is purely pre-representational ('This Puerto Rican is every Puerto Rican';

---

[37] Hay indicates that the desires of both of the 'right wing extremists,' racism for 10, patriarchy and masculinism for 3, are metaphysical by likening their more-or-less enforced conversion as symbolically equivalent to a casting out of unclean, or contagious, spirits: 'The demons that have possessed poor Jurors #3 and #10, causing them to shriek and rant, are exorcised' (Hay, 2007: 841). And we have been cued that of all the jurors these are the two the most in thrall to the crisis of loss of distinctions for they are the only ones to speak in terms of totalizing identities; for no. 10 it is the 'Them' of Puerto Ricans and for no. 3 it is 'kids' for all young males everywhere.

[38] 'How often does one holdout juror the other eleven around? Well, almost never … Holding out in these circumstances requires more courage and tenacity that most of us can muster. Indeed, the end of the movie illustrates this well, as the final holdout jurors crumble, not because they are convinced the defendant should be acquitted but because of the social pressure to give in to the emerging consensus (Astimow, 2007: 712). Which is the point: truth does not really matter, all appearances to the contrary, what really matters is the correct form of generative unanimity. For his part, Michael Astimow believes that 'the defendant should have been found guilty' (Astimow, 2007: 712). But then he qualifies this: *12 Angry Men* 'is an inspiring tribute to a common man holding out against lynch mob mentality' (Astimow, 2007: 716) excepting that Juror no. 8 is anything but common.

[39] Hay is clear that part of the mis-recognized soft sell of Lumet is the occluded message. But then Hay also points out that one of the 'messages' of *12 Angry Men* is that the 'masses apparently need someone to hate, if they are to learn not to hate,' which can be applied equally well to liberal, conservative, and radical (Hay, 2007: 852).

[40] It is also the only time that physical violence is actually threatened, the other two times predictably made by the McCarthyite Juror no. 3 to the Christ-surrogate Juror no. 8, the 'obvious' difference being is that the former's violence is good whereas the latter's is bad. Lumet makes it clear that he regards Juror no. 4's threat of bodily harm to juror no. 10 as a moral denouement.

[41] Whose ranks include the trial judge, the prosecutor, the public defender attorney, both of the witnesses, and the entire NYPD.

'This kid is every kid'). The introduction of difference seemingly from the inside (profane) but really from the outside (sacred) is possible and does in fact happen as if by miracle, but only if the precise conditions required for the intervening agent to manifest are met, which is that of a mis-recognized sacralization.

> A key part of that role ... is that it must be misunderstood by everyone. No one comprehends that this man is laying down his life; nor does anyone see why he is doing it. Everyone thinks it's the kid who's on trial here, that he's the one who's in jeopardy. How deluded these men are. They have no clue that *they* are the ones on trial, that *they* are the ones in the most terrible danger. They have no idea how false their sense of security is.... Fonda is not here to save the *kid*, for heaven's sake. He's here to save *them.* (Hay, 2007: 837–838)

Why exactly are the 12 men angry?[42] The defendant is accused of the crime of patricide which is not only an act of revolt against men of authority but it is also, along with incest, the transgression that is most closely linked to the crisis of undifferentiation, as Sophocles showed in *Oedipus Tyrannus*.[43] It also explains why we (almost) never learn anyone's name; instead of signs of difference all bear the mark of sameness which is a (serial) number. And, as with any such crisis, the solution is the reintroduction of difference through an act of exclusion—scapegoating— for we know that the jurors have a potentially violence inducing problem with difference; 'The difficulty is that the jurors, with the exception of Fonda, fail to distinguish between the ordinary and the extraordinary; they allow their ordinary concerns to predominate in an extraordinary situation,' 'ordinary' doubling here as undifferentiated (Marder, 2007: 894). Marder approvingly quotes Hannah Arendt on the possibility, and morality, of a purely epistemic form of differentiation: '"thinking's chief characteristic ... is that it interrupts all doing, all ordinary activities no matter what they happen to be"' (Hannah Arendt qtd. Marder, 2007: 894).[44] And so it is that the reverse is equally true; what Marder likes so much about *12 Angry Men* is the same thing that Arendt, the author of *Eichmann in Jerusalem: A Report on the Banality of Evil* (1963), would also presumably like so much.

> [The film's] depiction of everyday [undifferentiated] acts by ordinary [numbered] men have the potential to lead to unspeakable evil. The lesson is made more poignant by the setting: our [American] legal system. My intent is to show how indifference, whether through haste, bias, or boredom, of individuals can so easily allow the machinery of the state to murder a boy[45] and how only a keen sense of individual responsibility can keep such evil at bay. (Marder, 2007: 888)

---

[42] And angry to a self-parodying degree. 'The movie *12 Angry Men* starts by showing lay participation at its worst. The discussion is cursory. The jurors exchange insults and put-downs. The comments about the trial and the defendant reflect snap judgments and prejudice. In short, the men ae really bad jurors' (Hans, 2007: 585).

[43] Lumet also replicates Sophocles' symbolization of the unlimited violence of monstrous doubles by way of a natural calamity, only this time the plague is a heat wave: '"I phoned up for the weather this morning. This is the hottest day of the year. ... You'd think they'd at least air condition the place"' (Marder, 2007: 888).

[44] Which is perfectly consistent with the liberal's undying belief that the conservative is inherently stupid, or 'un-thinking' in some elemental manner.

[45] And the fact that the accused may very well be guilty is irrelevant here if the real evil being treated is systemic carelessness in the conduct of capital offence cases.

'Readers' equate with the paying of attention to material evidence through an act of reading, an epistemic action that is identical to differentiation.[46] Which is not as un-realistic as it sounds for it is quite consistent with the 'story model' of jury deliberations.

> [The] decision-making process consists of three stages: developing stories (or "narratives') from the trial evidence; considering the verdict alternatives from the legal instructions provided by the judge (such as guilty versus not guilty); and, finally, matching the various stories to these verdict categories. The verdict is derived from the best fit between narrative and verdict category. (Vidmar et al., 2007: 693)

And differentiation is the raw stuff of pluralism which would seem to equate with morality in the face of a lynch-bob, or, rather, a lynch-mob that is striving to kill the wrong victim. So we are in no doubt as to what the *auteur* considers to be the best fit between the narrative (which he has written) and the verdict (which he has engineered): whatever that maximizes pluralist outcomes, which would be a truly (meaning falsely) secular differentiation.

And this takes us back to the question of the controlling ethical concern of the *auteur*: do the jurors prove the innocence of the accused or merely arrive at the legal verdict of not guilty on the grounds of reasonable doubt which is epistemologically different from and morally less compelling than true innocence of both law and fact proven, either by objectively exonerating evidence and/or the correct interpretive reading of the evidence in the event of ambiguity?[47] Concerning *The Thin Blue Line*, in order to arrive at the moral conclusion that Morris so clearly wants—the acquittal of the accused, in mimicry of his presumed model Henry Fonda—he has to re-invoke the entirety of the epistemic-normative apparatus that he has already thrown out by way of his hyper-hip post-modern anti-realist subliminal editorializing posturing, epitomized by the recurrent flying milkshake of dubious reliability. But Lumet does not need to tie himself into such aesthetic knots; his mimetic desire for liberalism is so intense that he can operate within the cinematic strictures of realism and still produce a self-subverting work that is conducive to *metanoia*, perhaps the very kind that Morris was longing for. Lumet's difficulty, though, is this: in order to save the corporate liberal *nomos* he has to destroy it, for it is only by undermining the foundational pillars of the rule of law and due process that he is able to perform the ritual of exorcism

---

[46] At the beginning the jurors are un-differentiated (numbered) and do not 'strike us as a very diverse group. To start with, it's all men and includes no black jurors. Yet within this sameness, distinctions and differences emerge' as they incrementally undergo conversion. *12 Angry Men*, apparently, '"powerfully communicates the ideal of jury diversity. It is one of its central messages."' True only up to a point, because there is nothing natural or inevitable about the process of differentiation; it can only occur as the result of the *deus ex machina* of a new model who induces *metanoia* by redirecting the crowd's attention to an alternative candidate for scapegoat: the conservative. '"Each juror has a distinctive point of view, and each makes a different contribution, often based on his own experience. Once the case discussion gets going in earnest, the men's comments derived from their divergent perspectives enrich the deliberation and cause other jurors to rethink some of their original assumptions"' (Phoebe Ellsworth qtd. Hans, 2007: 586–587). If not for Henry Fonda …

[47] For the existentially unsatisfying nature of an acquittal on the basis of reasonable doubt, which is psychologically tantamount to the 'not proven' issue of both the accused's guilt and innocence, see Chap. 7, below.

necessary to purge pluralist order of all the anti-pluralist forces that, as Cover labored to demonstrate, liberalism will have to destroy in the end.[48] Stephan Landsman is perfectly correct in making these, and other mystifying gestures, absolutely central to the *auteur*-architects' grand design of securing the foundations of the American *nomos* of post-sacrifice, in a manner quite different than the formalist Cover argued for.[49]

> If the [jury] proceedings are going to be saved, it is only by the exertions of someone who chooses to work outside the law. That is exactly what Juror #8 does. He transgresses the rules; conducts his own search for evidence; brings that new, untested, evidence before his fellow jurors; and with it seizes control of the deliberations. The lesson seems to be that a vigilante for justice may use any means to get the 'right' result. Such a lesson runs counter to the core ethos of jury trial—that fair procedure in open court should serve as the sole basis for a decision by twelve disinterested citizens. (Landsman, 2007: 752)

In a sense, both Lumet and Morris face the same problem which is potentially fatal to the ethical concern of those who are committed to modernity's allegedly post-sacrificial *nomos*: the extreme ambivalence of the relationship between *meconnaissance* and the judicial, for the post-sacrificial legal order, cannot do without mis-recognition no less than the sacrificial one.[50] Echoing Sherwin's comments on *The Thin Blue Line*, Sanford Levinson makes this clear in his damning account of law's necessary relation to *meconnaissance*: 'It is not surprising that judges are ultimately limited in their skepticisms' concerning the objective meaning of law, normally understood as a realist form of textualism, 'at least so long as they continue to engage in their responsible tasks of judging. Academics, being irresponsible (and often socially marginal), are freer to follow ideas out to their most destructive limits' (Levinson, 1982: 379n 18). The disquieting truth is that the Derrideans of law-and-literature scholarship may prevail in the end (like Richard H. Weisberg), all textual meanings may be deconstructed (like the killing of Officer Robert W. Wood), and all of the accused may be revealed to be scapegoats (like all Puerto Rican kids) and yet, in the final instance, this may prove to have absolutely no effect on judicial praxis whatsoever.[51] For neither truth is any manner practically useful to the ordinary business of the courts which is the mediated of law as an instrument of social order, the product of an anterior generative unanimity that is grounded in the sacrificial. In a certain sense, then, law need never really require some sort of relationship to truth and Owen Fiss explained it to us.

> In what ways is the interpretation of the judge uniquely authoritative? There are two answers to this question.... [First, a] judicial interpretation is authoritative in the sense that it legitimates the use of force against those who refuse to accept or otherwise give effect to the

[48] See Chap. 1, above.

[49] See Chap. 1, above.

[50] This same truth, if not fatal, is a serious challenge for Girard as well. See Chap. 12, below.

[51] As David Black pointedly but painfully points out in, 'If, indeed, "literature can prepare the lawyer to respond to diverse perspectives, such as those of feminists, by stimulating open dialogue about where the law is unjust," we nonetheless might question how often this is likely to happen in so straightforward a manner and, if exposure to narratives of injustice were all that were required to liberalize anti-feminists, why it had not happened already' (Black, 1999: 115).

> meaning embodies in that interpretation. The second sense of authoritativeness … stresses not the use of state power, but an ethical claim to obedience.—a claim that an individual has a moral duty to obey a judicial interpretation, not because of its particular intellectual authority … but because the judge is part of an authority structure that is good to preserve. (Owen Fiss qtd. Cover, 1983: 43)

That '*the judge is part of an authority structure that is good to preserve'* is the controlling thought and the greatest truth, but one that is supremely ambivalent for it is not simply a matter of mis-recognition—and, since it is not, demystifying mystification can only have a limited effect, because the pragmatic necessity of exclusion, persecution, and sacrifice (albeit not overly 'bloody') remains as the indispensable but undifferentiated workings of the banal reproduction of the *nomos*, any *nomos*, by means of generative unanimity that do seem to be inherently sacrificial. Marder and Arendt are only half right because when they discuss murder as 'evil,' they are describing a state of exception, whereas sacrifice is the stuff of normality and the prerogative pragmatism of legal order, any legal order, has made it so. The angry jurors are not potentially evil because evil is banal; rather, the jurors are banal in the potentiality of their evil because sacrifice, even in its most symbolic and abstracted form, is the onto-political force of legal and political order that is the time of the normality of the norm, the opposite of the differentiated state of exception. Carl Schmitt proved this, calling it the friend-enemy distinction, that which is difference.[52] And even the community of liberal friends can perform sacrifices that are good provided that conservatives and radicals are the victims. This has all of the blinding clarities of revelation when we recall the biblical concept of murder, as Girard would want us to do.

What must be reckoned as murder, and as breaches of this [The Sixth] commandment?

Besides direct murder, by whatever means, the same sin may be committed in the following, and in similar cases:

1. When a judge *condemns* a prisoner whom he knows to be *innocent*.
2. When any one *conceals* or *sets free a murderer*, and so gives him opportunity for fresh crime (St. Philaret, 2020: 283–284).

No matter how secular we are the sacred continues to present itself to us as our double, our *skandalon*. So, the real ethical concern of the pluralist legal drama of the twelve white men who were angry is simply this: we can prove that the correct liberal verdict is to expel the conservatives and vote to let the guilty man go free if sparing the accused one saves the lives of the pluralist many, which is an act of murder.

[52] See Chap. 4, above.

References

Primary Resources

12 Angry Men (MGM 2008; directed by Sidney Lumet).
The Thin Blue Line (MGM 2005; directed by Errol Morris).
The Verdict (20th Century Fox 2007; directed by Sidney Lumet).

Secondary Resources

Abramson, J. (2007). Anger at angry jurors. *Chicago-Kent Law Review, 82*(2), 591–611.

Astimow, M. (2007). 12 angry men: A revisionist view. *Chicago-Kent Law Review, 82*(2), 711–716.

Bazin, A. (1971). *What is cinema? Volume II* (H. Gray, trans.). University of California Press.

Biskind, P. (1983). *Seeing is believing: How hollywood taught us to stop worrying and love the fifties*. Pluto Press.

Black, D. A. (1999). *Law in film: Resonance and representation*. University of Illinois Press.

Burns, R. P. (2007). A jury between fact and norm. *Chicago-Kent Law Review, 82*(2), 643–660.

Cohen, F. S. (1960). *Legal conscience: Selected papers of Felix S. Cohen*. Yale University Press.

Cover, R. M. (1983). The Supreme Court 1982 term foreword: *Nomos* and narrative. *Harvard Law Review, 4*, 4–68.

Cunningham, F. R. (1991). *Sidney Lumet: Film and literary vision*. The University Press of Kentucky.

Greenfield, S., & Osborn, G. (1994–1995). The living law: popular film as legal text. *Law Teacher, 28–29*, 33–42.

Greenfield, S., Osborn, G., & Robson, P. (2001). *Film and the law*. Cavendish Publishing Limited.

Hans, V. P. (2007). Deliberation and dissent: 12 angry men versus the empirical reality of juries. *Chicago-Kent Law Review, 82*(2), 579–589.

Hay, R. L. (2007). Charades: Religious allegory in 12 angry men. *Chicago-Kent Law Review, 82*(2), 811–861.

Kitses, J. (1969). *Horizons west: Anthony Mann, Budd Boetticher, Sam Peckinpah: Studies of authorship within the Western*. Indiana University Press.

Kuzina, M. (2000). The social issue courtroom drama as an expression of American popular culture. *Journal of Law and Society, 28*(1), 79–96.

Landsman, S. (2007). Mad about 12 angry men. *Chicago-Kent Law Review, 82*(2), 749–758.

Levinson, S. (1982). Law as literature. *Texas Law Review, 60*(3), 373–403.

Livingston, P. (1992). *Models of desire: Rene Girard and the psychology of mimesis*. The Johns Hopkins University Press.

Machura, S., Nevins, S., Ulbrich, F. M., & Behling, N. (2000). Law in film: Globalizing the Hollywood courtroom drama. *Journal of Law and Society, 28*(1), 117–132.

Marder, N. S. (2007). The banality of evil: A portrayal in 12 angry men. *Chicago-Kent Law Review, 82*(2), 887–899.

Marder, N. S. (2006). Why *12 Angry* Men? (1957): The transformative power of jury deliberations. In R. Strickland, T. E. Foster, & T. L. Banks (Eds.), *Screening justice—The cinema of law: Significant films of law, order and social justice* (pp. 157–169). William S. Hein & Company.

Osborn, G. (2001). Borders and boundaries: Locating the law in film. *Journal of Law and Society, 28*(1), 164–178.

Perlstein, R. (2008). *Nixonland: The rise of a president and the fracturing of America*. Scribner.

Posner, R. A. (1986). Law and literature: A relation reargued. *Virginia Law Review, 72*(8), 1351–1392.

Pramaggiore, M., & Wallis, T. (2011). *Film: A critical introduction* (3rd ed.). Laurence King Publishing.

Pue, W. (1990). Wrestling with law: (Geographical) specificity vs. (legal) abstraction. *Urban Geography, 11*(6), 566–585.

Purcell, E. A. (1973). *The crisis of democratic theory: Scientific naturalism & the problem of value*. The University of Kentucky Press.

Rafter, N. (2001). American criminal trial films: An overview of their development, 1930–2000. *Journal of Law and Society, 28*(1), 9–24.

Rafter, N. (2006). *Shots in the mirror: Crime films and society* (2nd ed.). Oxford University Press.

Rosenberg, N. (1994). Hollywood on trials: Courts and films, 1930–1960. *Law and History Review, 12*(2), 341–367.

Saint Philaret of Moscow (2020). The longer catechism of the Eastern Orthodox Church. In R.W. Blackmore (trans.), J. Scooping (Ed.) *The holy standards. The creeds, confessions of faith, and catechisms of the Eastern Orthodox Church* (pp. 107–297). St. Theophan the Recluse Press

Sarat, A. (2007). Fathers in law: Violence and reason in 12 angry men. *Chicago-Kent Law Review, 82*(2), 863–886.

Schmitt, C. (2006). *Political theology: Four chapters on the concept of sovereignty* (G. Schwab, trans.). University of Chicago.

Sherwin, R. K. (1994). Law frames: Historical truth and narrative necessity in a criminal Cass. *Stanford Law Review, 47*(1), 39–83.

Sherwin, R. K. (2000). *When law goes pop: The vanishing line between law and popular culture*. The University of Chicago Press.

Vidmar, N., Beale, S. S., Chemerinsky, E., & Coleman Jr, J. E. (2007). Was he guilty as charged—an alternative narrative based on the circumstantial evidence from 12 angry men. *Chicago-Kent Law Review, 82*(2), 691–710.

Weisselberg, C. D. (2007). Good film, Bad Jury. *Chicago-Kent Law Review, 82*(2), 717–731.

White, J. B. (1985). Law as Rhetoric, Rhetoric as law: the arts of communal and cultural life. *University of Chicago Law Review, 52*, 684–702.

Chapter 7
'You Must Always Point...': The Post-heroic Lawyer as Scapegoat and Scapegoater in *Presumed Innocent*, *The Verdict*, and *Cape Fear*

Abstract This chapter develops the argument in Chap. 6 regarding the scapegoat by analyzing the way in which three films and two novels—*Presumed Innocent*, *The Verdict*, and *Cape Fear*—widen the category of the scapegoat to include not only the accused-criminal but the accuser-lawyer. These three texts make up a series of counter-intuitive lawyer dramas that undermine the reader's *meconnaissance* of the similitudes between criminal prosecution, which is a profane activity, and the scapegoat, which signifies the sacred. In the first two texts discussed—*Presumed Innocent* and *The Verdict*—the lawyer-accuser is himself subjected to the scapegoat mechanism by assuming the ritually prescribed role of martyr, or the one who performs an act of auto-sacrifice in pursuit of a sacred objective. In both cases, the sacred cause is the redemption of law itself; both texts frame the drama of the scapegoat in terms of professional practice and the schizophrenic divergences between the nature of legal knowledge and professionalism (esotericism) and its largely negative representations within popular culture (exotericism) that corrode the legitimacy of the justice system. Both Rusty Sabich and Frank Gavin sacrifice themselves in order to mediate the rift between the two conceptual frames by effecting a dramatic reconciliation between law and justice. In sharp contrast, Sam Bowden in *Cape Fear* enacts an antithetical drama of his own within the private crypto-legal spaces of the lynch-mob: if Sabich and Gavin embrace their 'inner Christ' Bowden responds by embracing his 'inner pagan' with equal enthusiasm, effecting an even stronger act of mediation between law and justice by apocalyptically revealing the true identity of the lawyer as the fully self-aware executioner of scapegoats, in his case serial rapist Max Cady, his double.

Keywords The lawyer film · Esoteric knowledge · Exoteric knowledge · The heroic lawyer · The anti-heroic lawyer · The lawless lawyer · The post-heroic lawyer

E. M. Wilson, *Rene Girard, Law, Literature, and Cinema*,
https://doi.org/10.1007/978-981-97-1156-7_7

7.1 The Dramatic Peril of the Post-heroic Lawyer

A reasonably accurate generic definition of the Law Film would be: a self-reflective cinematic meditation on, and mediation of, two concepts of justice, public and private, which are in depicted as being conflict with each other. While clear and concise in the abstract, in the visceral realities of popular film, it runs afoul of Alfred Hitchcock's notorious First Rule of moving-making: audience interest (that is 'suspense') is generated by the calculated upsetting of the viewer's expectations. In terms of the Law Film, conformity to the First Rule has thrown up an interesting (dangerous) mutation that, just like Akira Kurosawa's internally mediated two-sword men, poses the dramatic risk of vacating virtually all of the icons and archetypal themes of the genre: the *post-Heroic* Lawyer (a more precise variation of the *anti-Heroic* Lawyer), a highly liminal character that has given rise to a sub-genre of his/her own, the *Lawyer Film.* The three lawyer-protagonists that I will be discussing in this chapter—'Rusty' Sabich (*Presumed Innocent*), Frank Gavin (*The Verdict*), and Sam Bowden (*Cape Fear*)—all succeed in scandalizing the viewer/reader's expectations through the symbolic violence they inflict upon the archetypal Strong Attorney, the vanguard character of the liberalism-pluralism tradition of courtroom cinema. As I will show, the post-Heroic Lawyer variant of the Lawyer Film drama is the cinematic enactment of the unveiling of the scapegoat mechanism within secular law, with the morally liminal lawyer himself as the possible scapegoat. Within this triptych, Frank Gavin is the embodiment of pathos, Sam Bowden the almost righteous avatar of vigilantism, and Rusty Sabich the poster-boy of the gray a-morality of legal technicalities: he fails to actually prove his innocence under either law or fact but in a realistic albeit wholly uninspiring manner is found by the court to be 'not guilty' by way of a mis-trial.

In what follows, it is important to remember that "legal technicalities" substitute for a more substantive explanation of the seeming ability of many criminals to escape punishment while their victims suffer' (Corcos, 1997: 137), so I will begin my discussion with both the novel and the film of *Presumed Innocent* as one of popular culture's most sophisticated meditations upon this inconvenient, and frequently unbearable, truth.

> Does [*Presumed Innocent*] illustrate the continuing tension between two images of the goal of law: one the impression that non-lawyers have, that the goal of law is to achieve justice, and the other the opinion that lawyers have, that the goal of law is to preserve the processes of fairness?... *Presumed Innocent* presents us with both models of the relationship between law and justice and rejects them because of a fatal flaw in both. Using one of the fundamental fictions upon which our legal system is based, the film [and novel] reveals that neither model deals successfully with the very real possibility that it can end in failure. (Corcos, 1997: 131)

That *Presumed Innocent* ultimately hinges on a collective act of failure—the absence of a positive determination of guilt—fundamentally subverts the entire narrative and ideological structure of the courtroom drama and casts the lawyer-protagonist unquestionably within the post-heroic mode because the technocratic mantra of legal realism—the infallibility of the result of correct application of legal reasoning and procedure—has been so spectacularly exploded in this naked deviation from pluralist consensus.

> *Presumed Innocent* is a different case. We obtain no public resolution, no "truth," in the filmic trial, because the jury never returns a verdict. Rather, along with Rusty, we obtain a private resolution—we learn "truth" in a way that leaves permanently unresolved the basic questions that the legal system is designed to answer. Further, we who have knowledge from both inside and outside the courtroom can create a story that resolves the primary question about Rusty's innocence. But that resolution forces us to consider more deeply the question of another kind of guilt or innocence: the guilt or innocence of the legal system in creating or allowing the circumstances of Rusty's arrest and trial. (Corcos, 1997: 133)

There are two fatal flaw(s) of the fundamental fiction of the presumption of innocence. The first one is formal, which is law's procedural separation of law from truth, so that what is true or false in 'law-world' may not correspond to what is true or false in 'real-world'. The film of *Presumed Innocent* (2010) begins and ends with a shot of an empty courtroom, coupled with Rusty's (Harrison Ford's) voice-over narration wherein 'Rusty explains the jury's role, which is to find the truth, to convict the guilty and to exonerate the innocent. The jury's role in fact is to interpret the evidence which the judge allows it to hear and to judge its persuasiveness, which may or may not have anything to do with truth' (Corcos, 1997: 145 n 28). The second fatal flaw is substantive, but it flows directly from the formal flaw: nobody actually believes in the presumption of innocence; a prosecutor 'can never presume an accused innocent, because to do so would violate the canons of legal ethics applicable to prosecutors' (Corcos, 1997: 145). Although on one hand general disbelief in the presumption of innocence may simply be the perception that the court is 'biased' and, therefore, fails to comply with its own rules, the real problem is much deeper than that and goes directly to the legitimacy of the law as such.

> [For lawyers] process is all; thus 'legal technicalities' preserve that process. Such technicalities are not evidence of failure but of success. Thus Rusty's story ought to validate the process. Yet, for them, the outcome is unsatisfactory as well. The system whose substance is process ought to provide judicial if not actual certainty. Rusty is either innocent or guilty; the ideal process would result in acquittal or conviction. (Corcos, 1997: 135)

For the layperson, however, 'the substance of the legal system, to preserve and mete out justice, is often subordinated to the necessity to preserve its form. Thus, injustice is often the inevitable outcome of law' (Corcos, 1997: 135–136). In actual fact, readers/viewers 'with limited knowledge [of the law] who believe in Rusty's [factual] innocence will be dissatisfied with the dismissal, since it seems equivalent to the Scottish verdict of "not proven"' (Corcos, 1997: 134 n 9). Rusty is post-heroic protagonist, then, because his dramatic predicament is one of inconclusive ambiguity rather than the familiar certainty demanded and created by the dominant cinematic form of liberalism-pluralism; *Presumed Innocent*, precisely because it turns on the declaration of a mis-trial as a result of missing evidence, is narratively premised on a kind of absence, so that the dominant tone of the text, both novel and film, is ironic (Corcos, 1997: 142–145), which, in certain circumstances, can provide a sense of *jouissance* to the lay reader/viewer. In part Rusty is a victim of popular entertainment: as the unparalleled example of Perry Masson incontrovertibly demonstrates, the viewer's pleasure in the courtroom drama is inseparable from the centrality of the courtroom confession to the resolution of the mystery which is dramatically enacted as the accused's public admission of guilt.

> If one considers the law to include not solely the operations of the judiciary, but its dissemination in the cultural imagination—and I suspect that more people's attitudes toward the legal system are shaped by courtroom dramas and mystery novels than by knowledge of that system itself—dramatized representations of the law provide only the most explicit indications of how our culture has internalized notions of judgment and wrongdoing. The effects of such internalization are presumably to be located less in the constraints placed on our overt criminal behavior than in more finely nuanced concerns about transgression, exposure, and punishment. Such issues are most fortrightly staged by courtroom drama in the confrontation between avenger and murderer and most satisfyingly capped by the criminal's impassioned confession—a confession compelled by motives that subtly threaten to bring confusion to the system of law it serves. (Sokolsky, 1989: 189)

Roland Barthes definition of *jouissance* as the reading of 'texts', both literary and 'pop', as aesthetic pleasure operating under the guise of cultural seriousness raises an extremely important problem of practical application: how to explain the *jouissance* of the texts of certain cultural forms, such as Horror or Crime, that should not be the sources of pleasure? With regards to the Law Film, the answer is fairly obvious.

> In courtroom dramas, the manner in which the confession is compelled is less intriguing than why self-betrayal is so compulsive…Indeed, given the alacrity with which such criminals, and in particular murderers, blurt out the manner and motive of their crimes when confronted with damning (but not, perhaps, irrefutable) evidence, wantonly refusing to take the Fifth [Amendment] prior to copping a plea, it would seem that that moment of release more than compensates for, even perhaps motives, their strenuous risks in apprehension of unspecified—and so in some measure absolute—punishment. (Silbey, 2000: 190)

One of the most striking of the 'reverses' of *Presumed Innocent* is precisely how the lawyer-protagonist, who is the criminally accused (i.e., the 'guilty party'), does not hesitate to 'plead the Fifth' which, within the aesthetics of the courtroom drama, is stereotypically read as a sign of guilt. Rusty makes this vital point clear to us.

> If I took five and refused to testify, as I had every right to do, it would probably never reach the papers, but every lawyer in the PA's office would know and through them half the others on the street…Tommy Molto [prosecutor] refused to accept any substitute for my assertion of the privilege and so one bleak afternoon in May, I , like so many others I had often ridiculed, snuck into the grand-jury room, a little windowless chamber that looks something like a small theater, and repeated in response to thirty-six different questions, 'On the advice of my attorney, I will decline to answer because it may tend to incriminate me.'
>
> 'So,' says Sandy Stern [defence lawyer and Strong Attorney]. 'How do you enjoy seeing the world from the other side?'. (Turrow, 1988: 157–58)

'*A little windowless chamber that looks something like a small theater*' encapsulates perfectly the theatrical nature of the confessional act which doubles as both a legal and narrative rituals.

> One might attribute the audience's fascination with this scenario to the unfathomable inertia of the mind in relation to its most banal fantasies; or to a devotion to the inexorable workings of justice; or to a vindictive and abject delight at the collapse of insolence in face of a more ruthless sadism. What it is not is a tribute to the judicial system. For one thing, it's hard to

> imagine that a mass audience would be sufficiently apprehensive or enamored of that system *per se* to crave its ritual celebration; for another, these dramatic representations generally betray a strong skepticism about the prosecutor's legal maneuvers. Confession works in fact to forestall judicial miscarriage by a shortsighted and pigheaded prosecution. If the interest is not solely in these psychological projections nor in a formal apprenticeship to the hazards of the legal system, the scenario of confession, I will argue, exercises its greatest power as the site of a fantasy about how agency is constituted under the law. (Silbey, 2000: 191)

'*Agency is constituted under the law*' through the rhetorical and forensic utilization of State power, a political act encoded as theater that invokes a secularized version of a sacred ritual.

> Now, like ore deposits, the harder stuff of duty and obligation has settled in the veins where those softer feelings moved. I have a job to do. It is not that I have grown uncaring. Believe me. But this business of accusing, judging, punishing has gone on always; it is one of the great wheels turning beneath everything we do. I play my part. I am a functionary of our only universally recognized system of telling wrong from right, a bureaucrat of good and evil. This must be prohibited; not that. One would expect that after all these years of making changes, trying cases, watching defendants come and go, it might have all become a jumble. Somehow, it has not. (Turrow, 1988: 8)

'*I am a functionary of our only universally recognized system of telling wrong from right, a bureaucrat of good and evil*' means that within this 'aesthetic game,' the 'moral function of the lawyer as a representative of society is to recast the murderer's sense of compulsion as an issue of ethical responsibility' (Silbey, 2000: 193). The irony at work in *Presumed Innocent* is that the 'hero' must become the subject of his own disciplinary mechanisms, which means that the sacrificer, the namer of scapegoats, may himself be sacrificed after being revealed as the true scapegoat. Rusty also explains this to us.

This is how I always start:

'I am the prosecutor.

I represent the state. I am here to present to you the evidence of a crime. Together you will weigh this evidence. You will deliberate upon it. You will decide if it proves the defendant's guilt.

This man—And here I point.

You must always point, Rusty, I was told by John White...If you don't have the courage to point, John White whispered, you can't expect them to have the courage to convict.

And so I point. I extend my hand across the courtroom. I hold one finger straight. I seek the defendant's eye. I say:

This man has been accused' (Turrow, 1988: 7).[1]

[1] Rusty's ritualistically performative act of pointing allegorically suggests the Hebrew and Hittite rituals governing the seizing and presentation of the sacrificial victim (Wright, 1986).

The existential significance of the courtroom confession, the very thing that never actually occurs in *Presumed Innocent*, is the primary site of the re-constitution of the legal subject.

> Detective and murderer turn out to share a belief in the notion of a self whose responsibility as an agent consists in acting out who he or she must be as though there were a choice involved…For the murderer almost never confesses at the point when it could be he and only he who committed murder. In fact, the apparently remorseless logic which isolates the culprit also pricks his remorse precisely toward the structure which affirms the inexorability of his identity as a murderer, of being who he must be; he bursts forth with a confession before being in fact compelled to, but with the air of compulsion, as though to rectify any potential flaw in the system that would allow him to slip through its cracks. Murderer and detective collude in engendering the compulsive nature of the confession. The scandalous thrill of the true confession thus resides not so much in the revelation of truth as in the fact that the moment when the law triumphs demands the mobilization of an heretical ideology in order to reassert the primacy of the belief that one can choose one's compulsions. (Silbey, 2000: 194)

It is significant that Sabich's highly stereotyped address to the jury at the beginning of the novel obfuscates precisely this revelation of inner motive.

> Let me remind you. There was a real crime. No one will dispute that. There was a real victim. Real pain. You do not have to tell us why it happened. People's motives, after all, may be forever locked inside them. But you must, at least, try to determine what actually occurred. If you cannot, we will not know if this man deserves to be freed—or punished. We will have no idea who to blame. If we cannot find the truth, what is our hope for justice?. (Turrow, 1988: 8)

Central to this process of truth-finding/justice-creation is the quasi-inquisitorial cross-examination. Although narratively and dramatically central to the courtroom drama in 'law-world,' the archetypal requirements of the cinematic genre represents the cross-examination in a wholly anti-realist manner.

> The legal process of examination, cross examination and re-examination can hardly be rated high as an instrument for ascertaining the facts of past history, at least no scientist would expect to extract the truth from opposite distortions…No one can fail to be struck by the contrast between the high degree of sophistication attained by forensic science in the detection of crime and the pre-scientific character of the trial process itself. (Brian Wootton qtd. Greenfield & Osborn, 1995: 117–118)

Pre-scientific because law did not ultimately originate with science but with religion. Hence the laity's increasing demand for forensic evidence to be introduced in order to resolve the difficulties of 'correct' forms of legal reasoning, as mythically enacted by Juror no. 8 in *12 Angry Men*[2]; in the USA at least 'juries tend to believe so-called scientific evidence, and more and more they tend to disregard all other evidence. Too often, if the prosecution can't show that prints were found on the murder weapon, the jury will refuse to believe that the accused could possibly have used it to commit the crime' (Robert Daley qtd. Stark, 1987–1988: 283). The ideological mystification (or uncritical techno-philia) at work in the jury's over-reliance

[2] See Chap. 6, above.

upon forensics obviates the existential uncertainty at stake in the assignment of guilt, such 'fear and trembling' a direct carry over from the archaic function of the law as a direct appeal to the supernatural. For no less than the courtroom confession does the religious act of confession serve as the primary site of the re-constitution of the penitent, the two confessional rituals veritable doubles. And such doubling of sacred and secular is also true for the scape-goat. In order for the sacrificial mechanism to work, the one who is to be sacrificed must be truly guilty, otherwise the sacrifice will fail and 'We will have no idea who to blame,' which, if Girard is to be believed, is tantamount to the end of civilization. For what is truly at stake for Rusty Sabich is not whether he is innocent or guilty; rather, it is whether he will be sacrificed or not, proving that at the most elemental level, the legal drama is a religious drama and all of the signs 'point' to Rusty's guilt as one who merits scapegoating. The suspense is unbearable.

7.2 'Is That You Here, Dear Rusty?' or, Rusty Sabich Who Art in Hell...

Prima facie Rusty merits scapegoating—meaning being made subject to persecution—because he is the bearer of the plague of mimetic desire and undifferentiation, and Scott Turrow makes no bones in letting us know this, for he presents the fictional locale of *Presumed Innocent* 'Kindle City' (in reality, Chicago or Cook County) as an allegorical representation of Hell which is the terminus of undifferentiation, the point at which the loss of distinctions becomes absolute. In fact, he frequently goes beyond the allegorical and suggests Hell is an objectively physical condition, witnessed by his description of The Grace Street projects.

> The small balconies at the rear of each apartment have been curtained off with chicken wire to end the rain of suicides, infants, drunks, and persons pushed, who, over the first five years, became a sauce upon the pavement below...It is not Sunday school, was Lionel Kenneally's favorite phrase. And he was right; it was not. But it was more than cheap irony or even rabid racism could comprehend. This was a war zone, akin to what was described by the guys I knew who came back from Nam. It was a land where there was no future—a place where there was little sense of cause and effect. Blood and fury. Hot and cold. Those were terms that had some meaning. But you could not ask anybody to do anything that involved some purchase on what might happen next year, even next week. At times when I listened to my witnesses describe the daily events of project life in the disconnected way most of them had of doing that, I would wonder if they were hallucinating. (Turrow, 1988: 350–351)

For Dante, the essence of Hell is a condition of eternal frustration; the damned are 'looped' into endlessly repetitive acts that are incapable of completion, signifying the perversion of the human will and intellect. Therefore, Hell is, more than anything else, a place of meaninglessness. And the outward manifestations of senselessness equate with the spiritual desolation of the interior of the damned; damnation as the total absence of God, the eternal lack of the *telos* of Being. The aspect of Hell as an existential state is repeatedly mapped out in Rusty's frequent internal dialogues.

> I finally leave the building. The heat is intense; the sun is blinding. I feel instantly unsteady on my feet. Compulsively, I try to calculate the one thousand subtle impacts on the trial of Raymond's testimony and his evident hostility to me, but that soon gives way. Ideas come and go erratically. I see my father's face. I cannot make things connect. After all these weeks, after all of this, I feel that I am finally going to pieces, and I find, stunningly, that as I turn about in the street, I am praying, a habit of my childhood, when I would try to cover my bets with a God in whom I knew I did not much believe.
>
> And now, dear God, I think, dear God in whom I do not believe, I pray to you to stop this, for I am deathly frightened. Dear God, I smell my fear, with an odor as distinct as ozone on the air after a lightning flash. I feel fear so palpably it has a color, an oozing fiery red, and I feel it pitifully in my bones, which ache. My pain is so extreme that I can barely move down this hot avenue, and for a moment cannot, as my backbone bows with fear, as if a smelted rod, red-hot and livid, had been laid there. Dear God, dear God, I am in agony and fear, and whatever I may have done to make you bring this down upon me, release me, I pray, release me. Release me. Dear God, in whom I do not believe, dear God, let me go free. (Turrow, 1988: 197)

And just to complete the cohesiveness of this allegorizing secularist appropriation of the sacred, within the un-religious inferno of Kindle County, penal incarceration serves as the substitution for damnation which is shown to be the state of undifferentiation.

> If I am convicted, they will take me away from [his son Nat]. Even Larren Lyttle [the District Attorney] will send me to prison for many years, and the thought of missing the remainder of his young life shatters me, breaks me into pieces. Oddly, I feel little conscious fear of prison itself. I dread the exile and the separation. The thought of confinement can make me ill at ease. But the actual physical horrors I am sure to suffer are seldom in my mind, even when I pierce myself with the thought of the extreme consequences that I face.
>
> And yet I know. I have spent days at Rudyard, the state pen, where every murderer is sent. I have been there usually to interview a witness, but the sights are chilling. The bars are heavy iron slats…and behind them are all these bastards who now—now it strikes you—are so much the same. The black guys chattering their manic raging stuff. The white guys in their rolled-up stocking caps. The Latinos who look out with pointy-eyed rage. They are collectively every man you have avoided in a hallway or a bus station, every kid you picked out in high school as destined to be a bum. They are the ones who always wore their deficits like scars, headed here almost as certainly as a skyward-shot arrow plunging back to earth.
>
> About this group it is no longer possible to harbor any kind of sentiment. (Turrow, 1988: 223–224)

As though all of this were not enough, Turrow, for good effect, throws in Rusty's son Nat as the dramatically obligatory vehicle of 'grace', the loss, or exile from which, constitutes true damnation as true absence of Being.

> As I watch Nat sleep, the weirdness of science overcomes me: I think of atoms and molecules, skin and veins, muscles and bones. I try to comprehend my son for an instant as a compilation of parts. But that fails. We cannot ever enlarge the realm of our final understanding. I know Nathaniel as the hot mass of my feelings for him; I behold him as something no smaller or more finite or reducible than my passions. He will not piece or parse. He is my boy, gentle and beautiful in sleep, and I am grateful, grateful so that my heart is sore and breaking, that in this rough life I have felt such tenderness. (Turrow, 1988: 223)

And, of course, within Kindle County-as-Inferno the courthouse, the visual center of legal geography in the courtroom drama, is really the gateway to Hell. Again, the landscape is suggestive of a crisis brought about by the loss of distinctions.

> It is here that crime always seemed most real, the air quivering with a struggling agony at the brink of finding a voice.
>
> In the hallway outside two enormous central courtrooms, there is a churning mass, like my imaginings of the crushed poor in the steerage bowels of the old oceangoing vessels. Mothers and girlfriends and brothers are here weeping and crying out over the young men detained in the granite lockup that abuts the courtroom. Lawyers of a kind move about hustling clients in the subverted tones of scalpers, while the state defenders shout out the names of persons whom they have never met and whom they will be defending in a moment. The prosecutors are shouting, too, searching for each of the arresting officers on a dozen cases, hoping to enhance the slender knowledge provided by police reports prepared in a deliberately elliptical fashion, the better to hinder cross-examination.
>
> Inside the vaulted courtroom, with its red marble pillars and oaken buttresses and straight-backed pews, the tumult continues, a persistent din. Situated closer to the front so they will not fail to hear their cases called, prosecutors and defense lawyers haggle amiably over prospective plea bargains...And far to one side of the courtroom, there is a continuing clamor from the lockup, where defendants in custody await their appearance, one or two of them inevitably shouting obscenities at the bailiffs or their attorneys, complaining about the cramped conditions back there and the indecent odors from the commode. The rest moan occasionally or bang on the bars. (Turrow, 1988: 55)

So the question that the Dantesque symbolism that *Presumed Innocent* forces us to ask is: if Rusty Sabich really is in the allegorical 'Inferno' of the legal system, then to what part of it has he been assigned? The theological answer that Girard would supply is: the second circle, the sin of Lust.

In Dante's topography of Hell, the torments of the second circle are milder than in the lower circles, because of all the deadly Sins, Lust is the one closest to one of the greatest Virtues: Love. And Dante's primary exposition on lust as the perversion of love occurs in Canto Five, centered upon the tale of the doomed lustful youths Paolo Malatesta and Francesca da Rimini, who bear an uncanny resemblance to none other than Don Quixote, the cause of their fall into damnation being the metaphysical desire to emulate the characters in (another) book, the Arthurian romance of Lancelot and Guinevere. And, with unerring instinct, Girard makes much of the mimetic implications of this fable. A love which is not yet lustful 'advances in their souls in step with their own progress through the book. The written word exercises a veritable fascination. It impels the two young lovers to act as if determined by fate; it is a mirror in which they gaze, discovering in themselves the semblances of their brilliant models' (Girard, 1978: 2). This is the fodder of Girard's uncompromising antipathy to romanticism,[3] the sign of the bourgeois culture of individualism and internal mediation. And, again like Quixote, the mimetic crisis that the two enter into two is akin to the state of possession, the unbearable trauma of the eternal failure of metaphysical desire which is an unconditional demand for un-reality and the result is their murder at the hands of Francesca's unappealing husband Giovanni

[3] See Chap. 1, above.

Malatesta, aka Gianciotto, 'crippled John' (Lansing, 2010: 409). Which is what they deserve for having selected a literary text for their model of being.

> Thus Paolo and Francesca never achieve, even on earth, the coupled solipsism that is the definition of absolute passion; the Other, the book, the model, is present from the beginning; it is the model that originates their future self-absorption. The romantic and individualist reader fails to perceive the role played by bookish imitation precisely because he too believes in absolute passion. Draw the attention of such a reader to the fact of the book and he will reply that it is an unimportant detail; reading it, for him, does no more than uncover desire that existed beforehand. (Girard, 1978: 2)

But Girard is quick to point out that Dante himself signals the book as the culprit, having Francesca, an 'imitator of imitators,' confirm to him while sojourning through Hell that 'Galeotto was both the book and its author', Galeotto being an evil knight opposed to Arthur 'who sows the seeds of passion in the hearts of Lancelot and Guinevere' that ignites the civil war that destroys the kingdom. Girard then draws the obvious conclusion: Dante is illustrating that whether 'written or oral, it has to be some person's word that suggests desire. The book occupies in Francesca's fate the place of the Word in the Fourth Gospel: the Word of man becomes the Word of the devil if it usurps the place of the divine Word in our souls' (Girard, 1978: 3, 4). The result is that Paolo and Francesca are 'the dupes' of Lancelot and Guinevere 'who are themselves the dupes of Galleot' and so all of 'the romantic readers, in their turn, are dupes of Paolo and Francesca' (Girard, 1978: 2) who have all conned themselves into believing that their desires are actually their own, a sign of their individuality and authenticity.[4] And this allows Girard to return to his central passion: the existential need for *metanoia* and the renunciation of metaphysical desire which is foundation of alienation; 'The individualist is not unaware that there exists a second, and derivative, form of passion, but it is never, for him, "true passion," that is to say, his own or his models' (Girard, 1978: 3). Individualism is an illusion created by mimetic desire and mimesis is the short and easy path to the Inferno (or courthouse) of undifferentiation which Girard believes is one of the universal secrets of literature.[5] 'One must read the great work of fiction as a single entity, a totality. The individual and collective history of secondhand desire always moves toward nothingness and death. A faithful description would elucidate a dynamic structure in the form of a descending spiral' (Girard, 1978: 4). And since it is Christianity that 'has handed on to us horror of fetishism in all its forms' (Girard, 1978: 6), it is no accident that.

> In the light of this metamorphosis, worldly existence, the spiral descent, appears as a *descent into Hell*, that is, as a necessary ordeal on the way to final revelation. The descending movement finishes by transforming itself into an ascending movement, without there being any going back. It is obvious, I believe, that this forms the structure of *The Divine Comedy*. And doubtless we must look back further still to define the archetype of the novel form—back to the *Confessions* of Saint Augustine, the first work whose genesis is truly inscribed in its form. (Girard, 1978: 5)

---

[4] The Lord of La Mancha was a dupe as well. 'Don Quixote, in his imitation of a chivalric model, courts the same quasi-divinity as Paolo and Francesca. Like them, he spreads the evil of which he is a victim' which is metaphysical desire (Girard, 1978: 3).

[5] See Chap. 1, above.

Or 'Every man carries a circle of hell around his head like a halo...Every man has to go through hell to reach his paradise' as Robert De Niro's Max Cady puts it in Martin Scorses's version of *Cape Fear* (1991), speaking from experience.[6]

Theologically, Lust is the 'purest' perversion of one of the highest goods. But following legal realism, there are no such things as true goods,[7] so that expressed in secular terms love-perverted-into-lust translates as first-degree-homicide-as-act-of-sexual violence; although, when Turrow re-translates the secular into the allegorical frame of the sacred, Sabich's attraction to murder victim Carolyn Polhemus then becomes a debasement of the will-to-love, the knife-edged transition from virtue to sin.

> She was herself someone who had suffered vastly—and who claimed in every visible aspect of her being, to have triumphed over it all. That was not true. She could no more leave the horrible weight of her past behind than those Greek heroes could fly close to the sun. But does that mean it is impossible for all of us?
>
> I reached for Carol. In a part of me, I knew my gesture was ill-fated. I must have recognized her troubled vanity, the poverty of feeling that reduced her soul. I must have known that what she offered was only the grandest of illusions. But still I fell for that legend she had made up about herself. The glory. The glamour. The courage. All her determined grace. (Turrow, 1988: 423)

The '*grandest of* illusions' that Carolyn offers is that she stands in an unmediated relationship to Being, that she is the true model for authenticity. So why does Dante envision the Second Circle as a vast, abominable, subterranean wind-tunnel? It symbolizes the overcoming of the freedom of the self by debased passion.

> The souls punished here are those of the lustful. Like all the souls consigned to the first five circles of Hell (Cantos I-VIII) their sin—in a concept derived from Aristotle—arises from incontinence, or lack of restraint, which is intellectual as much as physical. Dante seems concerned with their reason mastered by desire, as is embodied by their situation buffeted helplessly by the wind, rather than simply with their sexual behavior itself. Reason, in the Augustinian moral system, is not mere logic-chopping but the quality of mind capable of perceiving truth. Ideally, reason's perceptions guide and anchor desire, which in itself can be as wild and aimless as the whirlwind. (Pinsky, 1994: 385)

Within the Augustinian tradition, which Dante draws heavily on, the sins of incontinence are equated to what, in post-theistic terms we would categorize as addictions—the cravings that can never be filled— so that it is quite important that Anita Sokolsky places the issue of addiction at the center of her discussion of the jouissance of confession in the legal drama.

> [At] the moment when detective or therapist forces a true confession, murderer or patient is compelled to reveal that his or her guilt consists not only in an act of literal or psychic violence but also in a secret belief in the necessity, not just the circumstance, of having been oneself. The murderer is accused of and condemned for the immoral ruthlessness of believing that his imperative desires must be acted upon. One must not merely be oneself, but must also be addicted to being oneself, in order to become a murderer. (Sokolsky, 1989: 193)

---

[6] See below.

[7] See Chap. 6, above.

'The necessity … of having been oneself' is a very forensic description of metaphysical desire. And Turrow furthers the Dante connection by parodying the poetic conceit of signifying *eros* by the metaphor of flight as Aligheri did in Canto Five.

> To fly about this obscure world of anguish, this black universe of pain! For me there will always be that struggle to escape the darkness. I reached for Carolyn. I adored her, as the faith healer is adored by the halt and lame. But I wanted with wild, wild abandon, with a surging, defiant, emboldened desire, I wanted the extreme—the exultation, the passion and the moment, the fire, the light. I reached for Carolyn. In hope. Hope. Everlasting hope. (Turrow, 1988: 423)

And Hope, of course, is the one thing in Hell that you can never have for Carolyn will always manage to fly away from you, as Francesca did with Paolo, for she is the master-obstacle and Rusty the mere pupil-imitator. And the absence of Hope for the lustful explains one of the striking things about Dante's discussion of the Second Circle in Canto V: the exceptionally visceral language and imagery he employs, with the Lustful suffering constant chaotic motion.

> And now I can hear the notes of agony
>
> In sad crescendo beginning to reach my ear;
>
> Now I am where the noise of lamentation
>
> Comes at me in blasts of sorrow. I am where
>
> All light is mute, with a bellowing like the ocean
>
> Turbulent in a storm of warring winds,
>
> The hurricane of Hell in perpetual motion
>
> Sweeping the ravaged spirits as it rends,
>
> Twists, and torments them. Driven as if to land,
>
> They reach the ruin: groaning, tears, laments,
>
> And cursing the power of Heaven.
>
> (Pinsky, 1994: 85)

Strikingly, Rusty privately experiences a similarly 'chaotic motion' when meditating upon the tension that imbibes the implicitly mimetic erotic rivalry between his two women, his mistress Carolyn and his wife Barbara which, as we should expect, constitutes a form of triangulation, the mimetic signature of the metaphysically deficient.[8]

> The physicists call it Brownian movement, the action of molecules coursing against one another in the air. This activity produces a kind of hum, a high-pitched, almost screeching sound at a frequency level on the margins of human audibility. As a child I could hear this tone, if I chose to, at virtually any moment. Most often, I would ignore it, but every now and

[8] See Chap. 1, above.

> then my will eroded and I would let the pitch rise inside my ears to the point where it was almost blaring.
>
> Apparently at puberty the bones in the inner ear harden so that the Brownian ringing can no longer be heard. Which is just as well. Because by then there are other distractions. For me, during most of my married life, the allure of other women has been like that daily hum which I willfully ignored, and when I started working around Carolyn that resolve went weak, and the pitch rose, vibrated, *sang*. (Turrow, 1988: 37)

Note how the highly modeled erotic play-acting between Rusty and Carolyn quickly assumes the form of violence, both physical and psychological.

> At first I did not understand what it was she wanted. But she bumped her behind against me until I realized that was what I was being offered, a marble peach.
>
> No, I said.
>
> Try it. She looked over her shoulder. Please.
>
> I came up close behind her.
>
> Just easy, she said. Just a little.
>
> I went in too fast.
>
> Not that much, she said.
>
> She said, Oh.
>
> I pressed in, remained, pumped. She arched, clearly in some pain.
>
> And I found, suddenly, that I was thrilled.
>
> Her head lolled back. Her eyes held tears. Then she opened them and looked at me directly. Her face was radiant.
>
> Does Barbara? She whispered, does Barbara do this for you? (Turrow, 1988: 115).

For Dante, the transition from lechery to violence marks the descent into the lowest regions of Hell. Circles Seven through Nine—the Sins of Violence (Seven), the sins of Fraud (Eight) and the sins of Betrayal (Nine)—all correspond to the Deadly Sin of Wrath, or Anger. Predictably, Rusty's meditation upon his and Carolyn's lust culminates in his surveying the murder-scene, a place of graphic sexual violence.

> Even in death, she retains her erotic bearing. But, I slowly recognize, other experiences must influence this response. Because what is actually here is horrible…She is drawn back in an ugly tormented bow and her face is ghastly; her eyes, with the hyperthyroid look of an attempted strangulation, are enormous and protruding and her mouth is fixed in a silent scream. I watch, I study. Her look holds the same wild, disbelieving, desperate thing that so frightens me when I find the courage to let my glance fix on the wide black eye of a landed fish dying on a pier. I take it in now in the same reverential, awestruck, uncomprehending way. And, worst of all, when all the dirt is scraped off the treasure box there is rising within, unhindered by shame, or even fear, a bubble of something light enough that I must eventually recognize it as satisfaction, and no lecture to myself about the baseness of my nature can quite discourage me. Carolyn Polhemus, that tower of grace and fortitude, lies here in my

line of sight with a look she never had in life. I see it finally now. She wants my pity. She needs my help. (Turrow, 1988: 32–33)

Which means that Carolyn is not the true model but just one more fake mediator for the one who can access Being has no need for pity. And, of course, the photographic reproductions of Carolyn's death scene are the visual projection of Rusty's homicidal impulse; 'my reasons are sufficiently personal as to lie within the realm of the unspoken, even the unspeakable' (Turrow, 1988: 48). The love-lust of/for the Woman-who-is-now-a-Corpse is mediated by Rusty and his fellow damned souls through the language and imagery of misogyny.

My friend Dan Lipranzer looks at me. 'I think you killed her…I figure you cracked her in anger. The rest was just to make it look good. There wouldn't be much point in sayin' you were sorry once she was dead.'

'And why was I so pissed off?'

'I don't know. Who knows? She dumped you, right? For Raymond. That's enough to be pissed off about'. (Turrow, 1988: 411)

The irony of *Presumed Innocent* is that two corrupt officers of the law, a detective and a Judge, serendipitously collaborate to exonerate an innocent man; the exact opposite of what, we presume, occurred in the O.J. Simpson case, that the LAPD conspired to frame a guilty man.

What makes Hell 'Hell'? The undifferentiation of damnation is the universality of guilt, which, in an unnerving manner, mirrors perfectly the nature of legal practice, as Alan M. Derschowitz reminds us: 'The truth is that most criminal defendants are, in fact, guilty. Prosecutors, therefore, generally have the *ultimate* truth on their side. But since prosecution witnesses often lie about some facts, defense attorneys have *intermediate* truth on their side. Not surprisingly, both sides emphasize the kind of truth they have more of' (Alan M. Derschowitz qtd. Kuzina, 2000: 94). Which seals Rusty's fate as a scapegoat in the making: the evidence overwhelmingly points to Rusty's guilt (even though the damning semen traces from the condom turns out to have been planted by a third party, so the morally guilty man is really legally innocent although guilty of something else), but he must plead innocence, because the one who is selected as the scapegoat truly is innocent even though he cannot be in reality because, owing to mis-recognition, his selection as scapegoat is incontrovertible proof of guilt.[9]

And now, on sudden impulse, I finally bring myself to say what vestigial pride has so long prevented: 'Sandy, I'm innocent.'

Stern reaches over and, as only he could do, pats me on the hand. He has a look of deep, if practiced, sadness. And as I meet this brown-eyed spaniel expression I realize that Alejandro Stern, one of this town's finest defense lawyers, has heard these ardent proclamations of innocence too many times before. (Turrow, 1988: 173)

[9] I discuss the epistemological paradox of the innocent/guilty scapegoat in Chaps. 8 and 9, below.

But this would be the lament of any sacrificer; 'Nearly everyone in *Presumed Innocent* is guilty of something, although only a few are punished' (Corcos, 1997: 164) which is that very undifferentiation of damnation that Rusty's ritualistic sacrifice is meant to exorcize. If guilt is universal, but punishment is selective, then the determination of either 'guilt' or 'innocence'—the presumed essence of justice—appears wholly capricious, just like the chaotic fluctuations of Hell or the Brownian motion of the infernal regions of Carolyn Polhemus' bedroom and the chthonic wind-tunnel of the lustful.

> We must postulate that the elaborate mechanisms of legal procedure, those 'legal technicalities,' will result more often than not in the freeing of the innocent and sometimes the conviction of the guilty. If we do not begin with that assumption, we miss much of the film's ironic message, as it forces us to question the seemingly arbitrary and byzantine twists of fate that Rusty undergoes. (Corcos, 1997: 141)

But the ironical effect of *Presumed Innocent* depends completely upon our collective adherence to the representational language that underlines the technocratic operations of legal realism; that the act of legal naming (guilty, innocent, sinner, penitent) objectively corresponds to both fact and truth, which is the very thing that the novel denies: it is not the case that one goes to Hell because one is guilty, but that one is guilty because one goes to Hell, meaning one becomes the same as everybody else because everyone already is the same as everybody else. And the final turn of the screw is simply this: that the arbitrariness of damnation/guilt and non-damnation/innocence (one cannot truly say 'salvation' in Kindle County) is itself the logical outcome of legal realism methodically applied: we can know the guilty one (the scapegoat) in advance because he or she is a member of a category of persons whom the law always treats as guilty, the ones who are undifferentiated from the other members of the homogenous criminal class. Which means that what Rusty Sabich 'really' is or is not, literally does not matter; what does matter, in terms of the sociology of jurisprudence,[10] is how the designated object of the law is treated by those mechanisms and procedure that we know through past behavior pragmatically constitute the law. Meaning that Rusty is completely out of luck, because he escaped Hell/undifferentiation on the basis of a legal technicality, which signifies nothing existential or moral, but everything technocratic and mechanical.

> A game that I play with myself is called What Is the Worst Part? So many things seem trivial. I do not care much now about the way the women gape at me when I walk around in the village center. I do not worry about my reputation, or the fact that for the rest of my life, even if the charges are dropped tomorrow, many people will cringe reflexively whenever they hear my name. I do not worry about how hard it will be for me to find work as an attorney if I am acquitted. But the steady emotional erosion, the sleeplessness, the manic anxiety I cannot pretend about or minimize. What is worst are these midnight wakings and the instants before I can gather myself, when I am sure that the terror is never going to end. It is like groping for the switch plate in the dark, but I am never certain—and here the terror is the worst—I am never sure that I will find it. As the search becomes more and more prolonged, the little bit of sense that holds forth in me erodes, gives way, bubbles off like a tablet dropped into water, and the wild blackness of some limitless and everlasting panic begins to swallow me. (Turrow, 1988: 223)

[10] See Chap. 6, above.

But what has been taken can be given, or 'returned'. Just like God and Job, Sabich is restored to his previous condition—minus his murderess wife Barbara who, by killing Carolyn and framing Rusty reveals herself as the true model of Being—by means that are as arbitrary as the ones who sent him to the phenomenological Inferno of lost distinctions. And, further still, he has been granted even more! Not only does Rusty the Fallen get restored as the acting District Attorney, but he then goes on to elected a county judge. Girard said that the scapegoat transmogrifies after its sacrifice, which is how we can identify the identity of the scapegoat after the fact—look at the one who has been glorified and then magically transformed, becoming the new source of generative unanimity that ends the crises of missing difference. It makes for great entertainment. It also explains why people universally hate lawyers.

7.3 The Pernicious Legacy of Legal Realism: Legal Culture in Popular Culture

Any general survey of both popular opinion about the law and lawyers as well as representations of lawyers and the legal system within popular culture reveal two highly interesting sets of polarizing results. The first is that public trust in the justice system is considerably higher than public trust in the lawyers themselves (Asimow, 1999, 2000).

> In 1999, the ABA [American Bar Association] published results of a follow-up poll…It revealed that while 30% of respondents were extremely or very confident of the United States justice system, only 14% were extremely or very confident of lawyers. In contrast, 27% had slight or no confidence in the justice system but 42% had little or no confidence in lawyers. Lawyers were soundly beaten by state legislatures, prison systems, and the United States Congress; only the media came in behind lawyers. Thus, the public seems to have moderate confidence in its justice system but almost none in the lawyers who make that system function. The same survey also asked about public satisfaction with particular lawyer services they had purchased in the last five years. The satisfaction levels with transactional attorneys (real estate, contracts, or estate planning) were much higher than the satisfaction levels with litigating attorneys (family law, civil, or criminal disputes)'. (Asimow,1999, 2000: 539)

The second is that

> The public opinion of lawyers is inversely proportional to education; the more education people have, the more unethical they think lawyers are (Asimow1999, 2000: 540)…People with post-graduate degrees have more confidence in the justice system than people who went to college or have a high school diploma or less education; but people with post-graduate degrees have less confidence in lawyers than people with a high school diploma or less education. People with college degrees have less confidence in lawyers than either of the other groups. (Asimow1999, 2000: 540 n 36)

Prima facie, these results are counter-intuitive; why the sharp discrepancy between the perceived legitimacy of the courts and the stereotypical assertion of the unacceptable behavior of lawyers? The answer seems to lie within American political culture, which is itself contradictory: within the US national experience, the courts have traditionally been seen as protectors, or even the enhancer of constitutional rights; popular culture 'does not label "undemocratic" an institution that guards rights or expands them…the "legitimacy" of law and legal institutions, for us, is understood and assessed by what these institutions *do*' (Friedman, 1989: 1604). But yet, at the same time, the workers within the institution that guards and expands rights are viewed negatively by the better educated, for the equally counter-intuitive reason that the lawyer who applies her expertise within an adversarial context is the mirror-image of American rights-minded and privacy-minded consumer-capitalist culture: meaning, that to members of the social elites, the adversarial lawyer as an expert technician is capable of thwarting the elites' access to what they consider an entitlement, the vigorous enforcement and inflationary expansion of their 'rights' (Post, 1987).

> Americans have always had ambivalent feelings about lawyers. Almost every generation has expressed its distaste for this profession which lives by subtlety and conflict, but each generation has put its most important public and private affairs into the hands of persons trained to the law. This fact is true whether one looks to positions of private or public power. (Greenfield, 2000: 27)

Expressed brutally, the better educated realize that the lawyer is an enemy elitist: 'Freedom and democracy, in the minds of lawyers, in contrast to the public at large, tend to be conceived in largely *procedural* terms. Lawyers are taught and trained to regard "due process" as the very essence of fairness and the rule of law' (Friedman, 1989: 1603), which means that legal outcomes that are viewed by the laity as constituting moral or cultural goods are instrumentalized by the legal expert as the value-neutral product of a technical procedure, resulting in a professional 'dis-interest' in the inherent rightness or wrongness of the 'product'. And since the American legal system is both adversarial and largely privatized, the technocratic neutralism of lawyers can be easily weaponized in the pursuit of a special or partisan interest that is hostile to the self-interest of the layman who is seeking the morally and legally right outcome which invariably corresponds to their own self-interest or world-view. Lawyers, and especially the litigating attorney, therefore,

> …are especially disliked because they manipulate the legal system in the interests of their particular clients, without regard to the common, universal values of right and wrong. But recall also that lawyers are praised because their first priority is to the private perspective of their client [the transactional lawyer]. Lawyers, in other words, bestride the following cultural contradiction: we both want and in some respects have a universal, common culture, and we simultaneously want the culture to be malleable and responsive to the particular and often incompatible interests of individual groups and citizens. We expect lawyers to fulfill both desires, and so they are a constant irritating reminder that we are neither a peaceable kingdom of harmony and order, nor a land of undiluted individual autonomy, but somewhere disorientingly in between. Lawyers, in the very exercise of their profession, are the necessary bearers of that bleak winter's tale, and we hate them for it. (Post, 1987: 386)

Which suggests that pluralism might be a form of secular mythology founded upon sacrificial, or exclusionary and antagonistic acts of decision-making. But it also suggests something far more profound. If the lawyer is the one who may be identified as the source of conflict within the community, meaning the absence of unanimity, then the lawyer will come to be invested with at least some of the attributes of the scapegoat.

> We hate them, that is, because they are own dark reflection. We use lawyers both to express our longing for a common good, and to express our distaste for collective discipline. When we recognize that the ambivalence is our own, and that the lawyer is merely our agent, we use the insight as yet another club with which to beat the profession. For then we dismiss the lawyer as a mere 'hired gun,' or 'paid…tool,' or, worse yet, as an inveterate liar. The charge of insincerity strikes a particular tender nerve in the modern sensibility, because as a culture we are in a state of such uncertainty concerning the meaning of authenticity. (Chase, 1987: 386)

Which comes as no surprise to Girard because the individualist society of internal mediation is, by definition, suffering from a collective anxiety over the uncertainty of the meaning of authenticity; hence, the plague of metaphysical desire. And this free-floating anxiety over authenticity and individualism is exacerbated by the adversarial nature of the American legal system, adversarialism, an institutionalized form of trial-by-combat, acting as the primary cause of the cultural schizophrenia concerning legal culture: within the common law tradition, truth is secondary to winning and, under a certain reading of legal realism, winning is how truth is created.

The adversary dynamic bleeds like electrical wires into two other outstanding, but largely unconscious, anxieties about the bureaucratic technocracy that is law. Adversarialism proves, conclusively, that the nature of legal speech is wholly, if not entirely, a form of rhetoric.[11] 'Rhetoric is important in law because many legal questions cannot be resolved by logical or empirical demonstration' (Posner, 1986: 1383), says no less a luminary than Richard A. Posner, resulting in the mass-manufacture of 'Judicial opinions' that are 'unavoidably rhetorical' (Posner, 1988: 372). And the essential rhetorical nature of both legal speech and legal reason takes the profession not into the rudimentary domain of 'the lie' as is so simple-mindedly reiterated by the multitudinous lay critics of law but by the vastly more disquieting epistemological shadowland of the nature of reality itself. The nightmare of Kurosawa's *Rashomon*[12] may very well lie at the very foundation of jurisprudence, a vastly greater problem than the one laid out by Robert C. Post in his brilliant excursus not on the widely presumed similarity between the lawyer and the actor but on the fundamental dissimilarity between the lawyer and the actor, which is far worse.

> Actors…lie directly: we all know that [Laurence] Olivier is only pretending to be King Lear, and that it is just a performance. But consider, in this light, the trial lawyer making a summary to the jury. In that case we know both (1) that the lawyer must be representing the interests of his client, so that his speech does not sincerely represent his 'personal' views; and (2) that if the lawyer distinguishes between his personal views and those of his client, his client will suffer, so that the lawyer can perform his job only if he 'appears' to be and in fact convinces us that he is sincere. Unlike the actor, then, the lawyer's job requires that he totally conceal his performance. And he must do this about issues of public importance, where the integrity of the self as a constituted member of the community is most at stake…the lawyer must

[11] See Chap. 1, above.

[12] See Chap. 5, above.

> convince us that he is an orator, exercising his highest function as a citizen, when in reality he is simply a secret actor, 'lost' in the identity of his client. (Chase, 1987: 385)

If lawyers really were more like actors than they actually are, then it might be possible to avoid the existential horror of being unable to separate the authentic from the inauthentic and to know with certainty what reality is, even though we might still vary in our normative evaluations of it. But they are not and cannot be for so long as the legal system is adversarial, legal speech is rhetorical, and the lawyer is an expert-for-hire. So the great terror of law and lawyers will always be with us which is bad news all round, except in Hollywood, where it is devoured as manna.

7.3.1 The Paradoxical Status of the Lawyer as Esoteric Knowledge-Worker

One of the central problems of law-and-film studies is the methodological difficulty in both measuring (quantitatively) and describing (qualitatively) the social effect that cinematic representations of lawyers in popular culture actually have on: (a) wider perceptions of the law and the legal culture; and (b) the practical conduct of legal practice. Legal culture can be easily defined as the 'ideas, attitudes, values, and opinions about law held by people in a society' (Friedman, 1989: 1579) whereas popular culture

> ...refers first, and more generally, to the norms and values held by ordinary people, or at any rate, by non-intellectuals, as opposed to high culture, the culture of intellectuals and the intelligentsia...Second, and more narrowly, it refers to "culture" in the sense of books, songs, movies, plays, television shows and the like; but specifically to those works of imagination whose intended audience is the public as a whole, rather than the intelligentsia. (Friedman, 1989: 1579)

To a large extent, one's willingness to ascribe causal importance to popular culture in the evolution of legal culture depends upon what degree one is committed to the traditional or formalist conception of the law, the notion that the primary function of law 'is to provide a mechanism for the settlement of disputes in the light of broadly conceived principles on whose soundness, it must be assumed, there is a general consensus among us' (Grant Gilmore qtd. Macaulay, 1989: 1545). From the perspective of legal realism,[13] the formalist notion of the law is always inherently a-political, exemplified by Felix S. Cohen's 'Euclidean' form of sociological jurisprudence (Cohen, 1960); it regards law as autonomous of wider social and historical condition and, therefore, finds the exercise of judicial decision-making unproblematic. An 'autonomous legal system' is 'one that is independent of other sources of power and authority in social life' (Friedman, 1989: 1581 n 5), which, although good to think if one is committed to the eternal neutrality of objectivism, soon runs afoul of the countervailing critical legal notion of the *social theory of law*.

[13] As does critical legal studies but from an intellectual and political position that is diametrically opposite. See Chap. 6, above.

> By social theories of law, [is meant] theories of law whose premises deny, altogether or in large part, any notion of legal 'autonomy'. That is, these theories try to explain legal phenomena by searching for causes and causal factors 'outside' the legal system. They treat law as a dependent variable, and assign a leading role in molding the shape of legal institutions and legal arrangements to systems or sub-systems that society defines as 'non-legal,' that is, as economic, social, cultural, or political. Social theories assume some sort of meaningful boundary—conceptual and analytical—between law and not-law; between the legal and the social; but these theories also conceive of this boundary as wholly or largely porous, a kind of network or meshwork through which energy easily flows, rather than as a tough, tight skin. (Friedman, 1989: 1580)

Just as the social theory of law has had a stronger influence within the USA because of the rise of the sociological jurisprudence of legal realism and the New Deal, so too does American legal culture self-consciously understand itself as reflecting wider social and political movements to a greater degree than other jurisdictions with their own, and often quite different, legal cultures. An outstanding historical example of this was the apogee of the New Deal, The Civil Rights Act (1964), which was both the cause and the effect of American political and legal pluralism; it is also outstanding proof, if any were actually needed, that the American social (dis-) order is governed exclusively by internal mediation.

> Civil rights norms also affect popular culture in deeper, more subtle ways. The civil rights *idea* is broader than the actual categories that make up the *law* of civil rights. It is, in its expanded form, nothing less than expressive individualism itself: the notion that each individual is unique, that the central task of a human being is to somehow constitute a self, to *choose* a way of life. (Friedman, 1989: 1590)

So political freedom as personal choice can be interpreted as a constitutional basis for mimetic rivalry and metaphysical desire, guaranteeing the eternal recurrence of undifferentiation within a society of rugged individualists. And the connection between legal outcome and social value—internal mediation and 'self-actualization' as the *summum bonum* of both the individual and society—so clearly on display with The Civil Rights Act is an excellent example of symbolic anthropologist Clifford Geertz's categorization of aw as nothing more, or less, than a cultural form of activity. The antithesis of a legal realist, Geertz holds that law 'is not a bounded set of norms, rules, principles, values, or whatever from which jural responses to distilled events can be drawn, but part of a distinctive manner of imagining the real' (Clifford Geertz qtd. Macaulay, 1989: 1545). From an anthropological perspective, all manner of thought is 'a traffic in…significant symbols…used to impose meaning upon experience' (Clifford Geertz qtd. Macaulay, 1989: 1547), so that all mental processes are governed by what Geertz calls *culture patterns*: 'Culture patterns—religious, philosophical, aesthetic, scientific, ideological—are "programs"; they provide a template or blueprint for the organization of social and psychological processes' (Clifford Geertz qtd. Macaulay, 1989: 1547), and law, as a specific sub-set of culture pattern, constitutes a 'complex of characterizations and imaginings, stories about events cast in imagery about principles' (Clifford Geertz qtd. Macaulay, 1989: 1546). All of which means law as narrative. Employing deductive reasoning, it follows that if law meets all of the criteria of a culture pattern, then depictions of law and lawyers within popular culture must necessarily have some genuine cognitive effect, on both the collective and the individual level. The cultural dissemination through mass media of the lawyer-icon, which is itself a symbolic construct, a part of the 'template', reflects perfectly the inherently symbol-manipulation nature of legal practice: rhetoric, oratory, and theatrical performance.

But I can take Geertz's central insight even farther than this. What truly reveals law to be anthropology's culture pattern is by subjecting to anthropological treatment the absolute core element of law fetishized by both the legal realists and the legal formalists: the lawyer's monopolization of expert knowledge. Cohen's non-Euclidean technocracy (Cohen, 1960) can be revealed as a modernized version of an archaic cultural residue that continues to govern our social consciousness through modernity's toxic enforcing of collective mis-recognition: what Pierre Bourdieu has described as the 'juridical field' of symbolic power.

> Law is the quintessential form of the symbolic power of naming that creates the things named, and creates social groups in particular. It confers upon the reality which arises from its classificatory operations the maximum permanence that any social entity has the power to confer upon another, the permanence which we attribute to objects. (Bourdieu, 1987: 838)

Which at first glance sounds like legal realism, but it doesn't really when one stops to think about it, for legal culture that is premised upon a naively positivist epistemology in which the legal expert is able to know and manipulate the definition of reality, whereas, for the anthropologist, the lawyer is just another post-archaic manipulator of symbols and legal realism's public policy a carefully stage-managed superstition. Bourdieu's point is strengthened greatly by Lawrence Friedman's observation concerning the binary nature of legal culture, premised upon a 'division of symbolic labor' between two interpretive communities: 'the external [exoteric] legal culture is the general population; the internal [esoteric] legal culture is the legal culture of those members of society who perform specialized tasks' (Friedman, 1989: 1580 n 4). And we know this to be true because it is the esoteric experts who bill the exoteric laymen and not the other way round. The operation of symbolic power is always constrained by the wider cognitive frames of the community as a whole; the perpetual re-creation of truth through symbolic power, an eternal *meconnaissance*, always reflects some wider, or exoteric, conception of reality from which the esoteric community derives its cultural legitimacy and professional status, which are the sources of the billing.

> Symbolic acts of naming achieve their power of creative utterance to the extent, and only to the extent, that they propose principles of vision and division objectively adapted to the pre-existing divisions of which they are products… the specific symbolic effect of the representations, which are produced according to schemas adapted to the structures of the world which produce them, is to confirm the established order…. Such an act is a veritable act of creation which, by proclaiming orthodoxy in the name of and to everyone, confers upon it the practical universality of that which is *official*. (Bourdieu, 1987: 839)

From this, I can formulate two hypotheses concerning law as a symbolic system. The first is that, from the perspective of the social theory of law, the highly stereotypical manner in which lawyers are portrayed in popular culture, primarily film and television, is the sign of the operation of 'symbolic acts of naming' that directly affect the cognitive structures that control legal culture and judicial practice. This hypothesis attains greater force when we consider mass media itself as a culture pattern,[14] which explains the hegemonic nature of both the visual and the cinematic within contemporary culture. David Mamet explained the universality of 'the filmic consciousness' this way: 'If you listen to the way that people tell stories, you will hear that they tell them cinematically. They jump from one thing to the next, and the story is moved along by the juxtaposition of images—which is to say by the *cut*' (David Mamet qtd. Meyer, 1992: 897 n 11). Collectively

> …we exist in a post-literate story-telling culture and the dominant and most influential form of story-telling is, I believe, that of the popular cinema. Jurors, and attorneys, are products of this culture and their ways of understanding and meaning making are deeply rooted in the folk psychology and schematic patterns of the popular cinema, as well as in the specifics and cultural vocabulary created by the cinematic stories themselves. (Meyer, 2000: 134)

If so, then it follows that as with the exoteric laity for the esoteric in-training law students what 'they see *is* what they think' (Meyer, 1993: 86); it is necessary for us to consider popular culture as one of the primary mechanisms of a reverse transmission through which exoteric symbolic power exerts a material influence over esoteric cognition. And there are clear parallels between the film-maker and the trial lawyer as post-literate story-tellers.

> The aesthetic narrative constraints controlling the movie-maker are akin to those controlling the trial attorney. Like the movie-maker, the trial attorney is an oral cultural story-teller who tells fact-based narratives that convey a story and a particular vision of the world. The principles of narrative ordination for a trial story-teller are like the aesthetic structures that compel movie directors to craft stories along a tightly ordered narrative spine [the 'script']. Severe constraints are placed on narrative subjectivity by certain story-telling conventions, such as the rules of evidence. (Meyer, 1992: 896–897)

My second hypothesis is that if legal argument is essentially narrative, then it follows that all forms of courtroom representation must strictly conform to the relevant culture patterns.

> Lawyers tell imagistic narratives constructed upon aesthetic principles that are closely akin to the structural principles that control the formulation of plot-structure in commercial cinema. We tell stories with hard driving plot-lines and clear themes that are readily distilled. We shoot our films from the fixed perspective of protagonist-clients. We are simple realists who construct our stories to hook the sympathy and capture the imagination of audiences who think in pictures. We sequence shots on imaginal storyboards until we establish the patterns that ultimately suit our purposes. We speak and think filmically. (Meyer, 1993: 91)

In similar terms, Friedman argues that the wider exoteric culture that ensconces the esoteric professional culture of law is inherently individualist and anti-authoritarian, spawning horizontal forms of culture patterns.

---

[14] In terms of both form and substance, as Marshall McLuhan famously put it, 'the medium is the message'.

> The trend toward suspicion of authority is of course another reflex of our special brand of individualism—a form of consciousness which *literally* stresses the individual, and which is distrustful of whatever is large-scale, organized, governmental; not to mention what comes clothed in traditional trappings of authority. Twentieth-century authority, unlike earlier versions, is what we might call *horizontal*, rather than vertical. It is oriented toward peers and equals. (Friedman, 1989: 1592)

And, of course, an egalitarian friendly culture pattern of 'peers and equals' privileges democratic participation and the populist expectations of the wholly internally mediated.

> A free society means a society in which matters are so arranged that the system produces what people consider right *results*; the opportunities, choices, and social goods they find desirable, for whatever reason. In modern times, it is likely that wide segments of the public think of a free society as a society of guarantees and entitlements; a society which, moreover, allows or provides a wealth of options and leeways. It is a society with fences and assurances protecting freedom, privacy, and other social goods; the protections make the choices and opportunities real. A free society, in other words, is built on and supported by a tough, resilient scaffolding of *rights*. (Friedman, 1989: 1604)

Consider how closely Friedman's 'legal culture of rights' is aligned with a capitalist market economy; rights equal choice, which can be reduced to the (unlimited) public right to (private) consumption (or 'preference'), which is Girard's anthropological notion of internal mediation expressed through the terms of a reductive materialism, which is itself a culture pattern. The result is that 'in this society at least, the "legitimacy" of judicial review, or judicial activism, or the cult of the living constitution, is a question of public opinion—or, more accurately, of popular legal culture' (Friedman, 1989: 1604). So all instances of both judicial and political activism really are nothing more than real-life examples of a cultural reason that is economic in essence—choice. America's post-New Deal culture is

> result-oriented and, by virtue of its boundless adherence to the spirit of modern individualism, it is also rights-minded and privacy-minded. In any event, clues to the legitimacy of courts, and other agencies of law, insofar as we consider this a social and empirical question, are not to be found in the structure of doctrine, or in the formal texts of jurists ['an autonomous legal system'], but in the broad messages travelling back and forth between the public and the organs of popular culture. (Friedman, 1989: 1605)

Or along the open cultural channels between the exoteric and esoteric sections of the population. It is no coincidence that the USA, in addition to the sociology of jurisprudence, is also the homeland of two of the most powerful transmission mechanisms of popular culture: the film industry and the advertising industry. And Hollywood intuitively sensed the dramatic gold that could be extracted from the subliminal sets of associations between the otherwise antithetical hedonism of exoteric advertising and asceticism of esoteric professionalism and then turned into the cinematic fodder of a new form of Law *Noir*.

> Wall Street lawyers [esoteric] thought of themselves as gentlemen; they kept a low profile, and above all kept their names out of the newspapers. The loud, flamboyant lawyers [exoteric], the ones who preened and paraded before the public, the ones who shouted their names and promoted themselves, were a lesser breed. They were lawyers who lacked permanent clients.

> Their work was personal injuries divorce, criminal law—work with 'one-shot' clients. These were the lawyers who were in and of mass culture; they needed mass culture; they needed word of mouth, publicity, newspapers; and the upper echelons of the bar despised them, snubbed them, fought them professionally. (Friedman, 1989: 1601)

The exoteric lawyer has a name. It's Frank Gavin.

7.4 *The Verdict*: The Pathetic Case of Frank Gavin

Within the Hollywood orthodoxy of prescribed cultural patterning, the lawyer signals her status as an icon by acting as the primary bearer of the narrative drama of the Law Film. However, this deceptively simple maxim generates complex outcomes, raising the problem of the sub-genre. When attempting a precise definition of the Law Film, or any kind of film, as a genre, it is vital to avoid the pitfalls of determinism and reductionism, for the reality is that it is always possible to identify several distinct sub-genres within any given genre. Nicole Rafter has provided a good example of this with her discussion of the nebulous nature of the Crime Film, the first cousin to Law *Noir*

> Crime films do not constitute a genre (a group of films with similar themes, settings and characters) as Westerns and war films do. Rather, crime films constitute a *category* that encompasses a number of genres—detective movies, gangster films, cop and prison movies, courtroom dramas, and the many offerings for which there may be no better generic label than, simply, crime stories. Like the terms *dramas* and *romances, crime film* is an umbrella term that covers several smaller and more coherent groups. (Rafter, 2007: 5)

As I have already suggested, the generic definition of the Law Film is its archetypal theme: a self-reflective cinematic meditation on, and mediation of, two concepts of justice, public and private, that are in active conflict with each other. But under this rubric are a number of several smaller and more coherent groups, of which the two most prominent are the Courtroom Drama/the Trial Film and the Lawyer Film. What provisionally separates the genre from the sub-genre is the relationship between the archetypal them and the icons: if a film evidences the archetypal theme, then it is within the Law Film genre but the presence or absence, and subsequent employment, of certain icons will enable that film to conform to one or more varieties of sub-genre. And the two icons most in play are the courtroom and the lawyer himself. The courtroom drama, of which there are a large number of examples (*The Parradine Case; To Inherit the Wind; Compulsion; A Few Good Men*) I have already dealt with in another way in my discussion of *12 Angry Men.*[15] The issue here is the definition of the Lawyer Film and its kinship to its twin sub-genre, the Law *Noir.*

If we can follow Stephen King in defining a Horror Film as any movie that has a monster in it, then I would define that the Lawyer Film as any Law Film that has as its main protagonist a lawyer, but that treats the lawyer in a prescribed or stereotypical sort of way reflecting the conscious understanding that the lawyer is

---

[15] See Chap. 6, above.

an icon, so that more often than not a degree of self-referentiality or even parody is present. What also needs to be understood is that the lawyer as cinematic icon tends to be represented within a very rigid structure of binary oppositions which replicate in a striking way the binary relationship between the esoteric and the exoteric.

> A key, [and] as yet unresolved dimension, to the study of cinematic portrayals of law and lawyers, has been the causal link between what the public sees (the cultural representation) and the effect of such representation. One of the apparent contradictions is between a historically generally positive screen image of lawyers and a general lay [exoteric] dislike for the activities of the profession [esoteric], most crudely indicated by the range of (anti-) lawyer jokes. (Greenfield, 2000: 26)

Again, the schizophrenic or split-minded nature of the representation of the lawyer within popular culture is a direct manifestation of the schizoid nature of the attitude of the lay client toward the services provided by the profession; 'Often…such contradictions are fault lines leading right to the heart of a culture's vision' (Chase, 1987: 380). As a result, and consistent with Girard's theory of mimesis and scapegoating, we can detect within the culturally patterned cinematic representation of the lawyer-as-icon a recurrent series of doubles which invariably point to the lurking presence of sacrifice. And as the exemplar of Rusty Stabich illustrates, the lawyer as icon doubles as the icon of the scapegoat, the member of the detested class who, if eliminated, would produce the generative unanimity necessary to solve the crisis of authenticity.

7.4.1 *Anti-heroic Lawyers: Virtue, Money, and Power*

I would summarize what follows in these terms: the Strong Attorney of the genre strictly correlates with the *Heroic Lawyer* of the Lawyer Film sub-genre, but as the real dramatic essence of the Lawyer Film is that of the Law *Noir*, the Heroic Lawyer is as likely to manifest herself as either the *anti-Heroic Lawyer* or as the *post-Heroic Lawyer*. It is relatively easy to define and identify the Heroic Lawyer: it is the Strong Attorney transplanted to the Lawyer film, which means that changes have been made to either her own character and/or to the environment of the courtroom.

> The representation of an unpopular defendant is often a key moral issue that the cinematic lawyer must embrace in order to distinguish him from other, more mortal lawyers…Representing the unpopular puts the lawyer outside and above the local community, especially given that the crime at stake is almost inevitably murder. There are two elements here, which often cross over, first the right to representation and secondly the sanctity of the rule of law. This latter point is concerned with the relationship between lawyers and the legal process. The due process of law is legitimized and raised to an important level, supported by lawyers. (Greenfield, 2000: 29)

Cinematic short-hand for the Heroic Lawyer is the *Friend of Liberty*, which definitely suggests Henry Fonda's Juror no. 8 from *12 Angry Men*.

> The 'archetypal positive image of the virtuous lawyer in the United States' is very much grounded on the libertarian elements of the Constitution, which 'doubles' as the foundational

> document of both the legal culture and the political culture; 'a protector who stands with his or her client against all the world no matter what the odds; indeed, no matter what the attorney's personal political views or estimate of the client's 'guilt' or 'innocence,' a matter left to judge and jury. (Chase, 1987: 282)

But once *noir*-ized the Heroic Lawyer transforms into her evil twin, the anti-Heroic Lawyer, whose predictable cinematic short-hand is the *Enemy of Liberty*. This villainous and derivative icon comes in two forms: (a) the 'interloper', or the 'foreigner', the anti-social cynic, the personal injury (PI) lawyer, 'the ambulance-chaser,' or 'the shyster', and; (b) the slightly more complex character of the 'trouble-maker'; 'this negative image is more an overtly political, relatively recent counter-image to [the] manifestation of the positive lawyer as 'friend of liberty' archetype…The characterization of the defense attorney as one who dangerously subjects the community to grave risk (by getting thugs and crazies "off") has become increasingly significant' (Chase, 1987: 287), as the almost cliched nature of the 'polarization' of American political culture proves highly amenable to the framing of all 'unacceptable' verdicts, especially those of criminal trials (O.J. Simpson, Kyle Rittenhouse) in terms of Carl Schmitt's Friend-Enemy distinction.[16]

The second set of doubles concerns the all-important issue of money and private wealth; within American legal practice, which is ordinarily based upon some kind of business model, it is notoriously difficult to discursively separate the lawyer from money, but not solely for pecuniary concerns; more vitally, lawyers cannot remain outside of the ambit of cash because economic power is one of the central pillars of political power, and politics, as both legal realism and critical legal theory instruct us in their different ways, is the primary motor of legal culture. Expressed cinematically.

> While the relation of lawyers to *power* is seen primarily through the optic of [lawyerly] indifference to mere economic competition and scrambling…in relation to *money*, lawyers are seen as the key to prosperity or bankruptcy—the professionals who know where the dollars are hidden and how to climb the financial tree. (Chase, 1987: 291)

Under the rubric of economics = politics = power, the Heroic Lawyer performs as the *Lawyer-as-Professional*: 'The positive image of lawyers in relation to power often presents attorneys as ethically superior to the dog-eat-dog values of a competitive business system as well as economically "market proof"—as thoroughgoing professionals who are the beneficiaries of a genteel security' (Chase, 1987: 293). And as if by cue, the anti-Heroic Lawyer can also transform into the much-beloved *Lawyer-as-Shark*, the cinematic meme of lawyerly negativity: 'The negative image of lawyer-as-shark, with the smell of money replacing the smell of blood, clearly undercuts the positive presentation of lawyers as individuals whose power is reflected in their indifference to cool cash' (Chase, 1987: 293). There is no end to the cultural schizophrenia. In 1986 the *National Law Journal* undertook a national survey of popular attitudes toward lawyers; when asked 'what were the most positive aspects of lawyers, far and away the most popular responses were that their "first priority is to their clients' (38%), and that they 'know how to cut through red tape"' (Chase,

[16] See Chap. 4, above.

1987: 315), which bodes well for the cultural vitality of the Lawyer-as-Professional. However, when asked in the same survey what were the most negative characteristics of lawyers, 'By far the largest proportion, 32%, disapproved of lawyers because "[t]hey are too interested in money"'; the second and third reasons 'were that lawyers "manipulate the legal system without any concern for right or wrong" (22%), and that they "file too many unnecessary lawsuits' (20%)"' (Chase, 1987: 380), which would seem to be a win for the symbolic potency of the Lawyer-as-Shark.

> In other words, lawyers are applauded for following their client's wishes and bending the rules to satisfy those wishes; and they are at the very same time condemned for using the legal system to satisfy their client's desires by bringing lawsuits at their client's behest and using the legal system to get what their clients want, rather than to uphold the right and denounce the wrong. (Chase, 1987: 380)

Which is what you would expect in a culture of unbridled internal mediation where, by definition, no one can ever be in the wrong according to themselves and the disunity of society is due to the partisan preferences of others who are all alike. But how could it be otherwise? Even the sacred cow of due process cannot escape the schizoid zig-zagging. Here, the Heroic Lawyer enacts the part of the *Lawyer-as-Defender-of-Due-Process*, the classic case being Henry Fonda as the eponymous lead in John Ford's *Young Mr. Lincoln* (1939); as with all things 'Lincoln' Fonda is a veritable one-man 'mass culture archetype: the lawyer who intervenes to impose (or re-impose) sanity and civilization' (Chase, 1987: 296). Not to be outdone, the anti-Heroic Lawyer puts in an appearance as the difficult to conceptualize *Lawyer-as-Agent-of-Legal-Order-as-Nightmare*, the only cinematic exemplars at hand being Errol Morris' true-fiction documentary *The Thin Blue Line* (MGM, 2005)[17] and Orson Welles' adaptation of Franz Kafka's *The Trial* (1962).[18] Another strong contender here is Alfred Hitchcock's *The Wrong Man* (1957; also with Henry Fonda), which is a mare courtroom-based variation of Hitchcock's *auteur* theme of the falsely accused innocent man with no obvious means of proving his innocence short of getting the guilty one to confess somehow—and definitely not by raising a 'reasonable doubt' or relying upon a legal technicality. Hitchcock scholar Donald Spoto may have defined this tortuous sub-genre best in his discussion of the borderline supernatural thriller *The Birds* (1963): 'a dark, lyric poem about the fragility of our supposedly ordered world, and the chaos which is ready to burst and shatter our expectations' (Donald Spoto qtd. Chase, 1987: 298), which is what we talk about when we talk about the Kafkaesque.[19] And this takes us to the most interesting variant of the lawyer-icon and the one template that might conceivably act to reconcile the apparently irreconcilable presentations of the lawyer within popular culture: an ingenious fusion of the Heroic and anti-Heroic into the hyper-liminal lawyer who 'operates outside of the system' in the guise of the good/bad *legal vigilante* or the *Lawless Lawyer*. One who embodies a radical and eccentric form of naturalism, who breaks the rules of the court (or even the laws themselves) in order to achieve

---

[17] See Chap. 6, above.

[18] See Chap. 8, below.

[19] See Chap. 8, below.

the true good, meaning the verdict that is 'right,' the superior sort of pluralist even though technically deviant, who knowingly departs from the law only when doing so is necessary to secure that justice that saves the law: in other words, Henry Fonda's lawless juror no. from Sidney Lumet's *12 Angry Men* but this time with an actual law degree.

> When lawyers as a profession are negatively associated with lawlessness, the thrust of the accusation is something different. It is not that all lawyers are actual criminals, literally breaking the law, it is rather that the concept of 'law' itself has assumed a double meaning. Law is on the one hand the positive enactments of the state. Law in this sense is technical, ambiguous, and complex. It can almost always be circumvented…by ascertaining its 'legal limits' and escaping through its 'loop-holes'. But by dealing in this strict if dubious legality, lawyers stand accused of breaking a different kind of law, the law which is associated with justice and with our values as a community. (Post, 1987: 382–383)

As always, we turn to Art to reconcile ourselves with Truth; aesthetics is the opium of the critically hip.

> In point of plain fact, however, the lawyer's betrayal is most often not a matter of corruption or ill will. It comes instead from the unpleasant fact that we do not live in a society ordered by a spontaneous, coherent system of values, but instead in a wildly pluralistic culture, in which individuals constantly struggle to achieve recognition for the legitimacy of their private perspectives. We have organized our legal system so that lawyers speak for the specific and particular sides of this struggle. Most commonly, when a lawyer argues for one interpretation of a law rather than another, she is arguing for one ordering of values, rather than another. (Post, 1987: 385–386)

The Lawless Lawyer is perhaps best understood as the Heroic Lawyer infected by a morally dubious paradox; in the history of the Lawyer Film, many of the most cinematically powerful representations of the icon are based upon the lawyer 'breaking the rules and behaving lawlessly'; the populist-leaning 'heroic' (or 'good') lawyer is the one who temporarily suspends due process and the rule of law in order to obtain justice.

> The issue here is the role of the hero-lawyer in the delivery of justice. More fundamentally it concerns the leeway, given to the central figure, to ignore the procedures of law where he feels it necessary to reach the 'right' result. In essence this is part of the subjective core of the lawyer's function…The emphasis here is on the relationship between the lawyer, the court, and the client and whether procedural rules and ethical requirements can be ignored in order to achieve a higher ideal. This has implications for the sanctity and probity of the legal profession, the relationship between law and justice, and the fundamental question of to whom does a lawyer owe a duty. (Greenfield, 2000: 34)

Admittedly, the lawlessness of the Heroic Lawyer is a direct expression of an essentially populist demand for democracy and direct justice, which is radically anti-lawyer, anti-professional, and anti-formalist in nature; however, as Jessica Silbey persuasively argues in her essay 'Patterns of Courtroom Justice' (2000), the populist sentiments of the sub-genre are more apparent than real. In her analysis of five leading 'trial films' (*And Justice For All*, *Class Action*, *12 Angry Men*, *The Verdict*, *A Few Good Men*) the protagonist-hero/anti-hero Lawless Lawyer manages to both legally prevail (esoteric) and prove his moral superiority (exoteric) by actually violating due process and breaching the rule of law, a perversion of his esoteric knowledge. For Silbey, the sub-genre's staged antagonism between legal function and dramatic success (which can be construed as an extension of the esoteric/exoteric dichotomy) actually serves the cultural patterning purposes of the dominant liberal-pluralist representation of the legal system and is, therefore, considerably less subversive than it appears at first glance. The trial itself 'is a ritualistic aspect of the law that is often overlooked (and, in fact, a stage in the litigation process that is rarely reached) but that is crucial to the law's binding of its practice with its ideals in [popular] culture. I would dare to say that the trial, for many people, is the symbol of law in action' (Silbey, 2000: 97). The liberal nature of the political system, premised upon the secular sacredness of individual rights, naturally yields a representation of law within popular culture that both rationalizes and is rationalized by a liberal, rights-based individualism, wholly consistent with a social order of internal mediation.

> The trial film's viewer-subject mirrors the concept of the liberal legal subject (the subject of legal liberalism) and his central role in the pursuit of justice [which does not strictly correspond with the Law]. In a three-stage [narrative] process, the trial film encourages its viewer-subject both to believe in his crucial contribution to the law's success and to critique the law's all-encompassing constitutive capabilities. Normally (that is, generically), this critical position is incorporated into the films story of law and results in an affirmation of both law's capacity to include those who dissent from it [pluralism] and film's capacity to incorporate its viewers in its world-making...In other words, the viewer-subject of trial films, as constituted by the discursive strategies of film and law, is encouraged to expect justice through law by virtue of his unique contribution to the system (the filmic system of meaning and the legal system of justice), and yet also to insist that justice resides apart from the law's institutionalized processes. (Silbey, 2000: 98)

For Silbey, the key to the cinematic portrayal of the virtuous lawlessness of the hero-lawyer is the reduction of legal action to moral choice, which is a supremely private matter for the internally mediated individualist—which means that the Lawless Lawyer can be interpreted as an extension of the even more archetypal cinematic icon of The Westerner.[20] It also explains why the 'framing patterns and courtroom shots that are consistent in so many of these films serve not to make complex the relationship between the legal subject and his desire for justice through the process of law, but to simplify that relationship as an individual's decision between right or wrong, truth or falsehood' (Silbey, 2000: 111). In the sub-genre of the Lawyer Film, there are two common conclusions toward which the above mapped framing patterns and courtroom scenes eventually lead. The first is that 'trial law helps to uncover a long-kept secret and fit it, like a puzzle piece, into its proper place [the trial-lawyer as detective], thus perpetuating law's reputation as a means toward the whole truth and its resultant justice'; the second is that trial law is a process through which 'law extends its authority and power, despite what the viewer knows to be the facts of the case, perpetuating law's reputation as an ever-present social organizer—not because the law is always right, but because it is always the law, the last sanctioned force, the foundation upon which everyone has dared to stand' (Silbey, 2000: 111–112) which closely corresponds to Bourdieu's notion of the juridical field of symbolic power.

[20] See Chap. 4, above.

What Silbey declines to point out, however, is that there is another name besides trial law for that thing which serves as 'the foundation upon which everyone has dared to stand'. That thing is also called the scapegoat.

7.5 Frank Gavin as Post-heroic Lawyer

From our very first views of him in Sidney Lumet's *The Verdict* (1982), Frank Gavin (Paul Newman) appears to be the very embodiment of the anti-Heroic Lawyer, the epitome of the ambulance-chasing, PI shark of the interloper—the certified practitioner of the esoteric knowledge of law but one deserves no place within the august company of the masters of the occult art of jurisprudence. He is the stereotypical 'foreigner,' the 'stranger' (and alcoholic) who, being devoid of 'friends' is, by default, to be considered as an 'enemy,' making him within the terms of reference of the Lawyer Film the 'enemy of liberty', untrustworthy, unprincipled, and worst of all, incompetent as well: the 'shyster'. But these same character flaws also denote him as something else: a scapegoat. Not only is he antithetical to everything that the Heroic Lawyer is supposed to symbolize, being friendless means that there is no one to avenge him if and when he is sacrificed, an indispensable requirement for scapegoat status (Girard, 1977).[21] Such an anathema is Frank Gavin that, according to screenwriter William Goldman, the character's nakedly outlier status caused a great deal of problems with the casting of the lead role; '[Robert] Redford is still interested in doing a movie about medical malpractice—but the main role, that of the lawyer, Gavin, that's the problem. He's a boozer and a womanizer and Zanuck and Brown [the producers] hear that Redford thinks that the character could be bad for his image' (William Goldman qtd. Greenfield, 2000: 35 n 35). As Goldman later ruminated

> Here is one of the basic lessons a screenwriter must learn and live with: Stars will not play weak and they will not play blemished, and you better know that now. Sure, Brando and Pacino will play Mafia chieftains. They're only warring on bad mafia guys and crooked cops; they're only trying to hold the family business together. Try asking a major star to play a real mafia head, a man who makes his living off whores and child pornography, heroin and blood; sorry folks those parts go to the character actors or the has-beens (William Goldman qtd. Greenfield & Osborn, 1994, 1995: 113)

But as with *12 Angry Men*, we are in Sidney Lumet country again, and *The Verdict* exemplifies Lumet's status as an *auteur* of pluralist film whose signatures were 'Lumet's consistent thematic concern with the dynamics of family and social life; the importance of a rational, personal responsibility for the existence of a humane social order; humankind's propensity for self-delusion and flight from its own best self; and the ubiquity of meaningful suffering that lies at the heart of life' (Cunningham, 1991:

[21] The scapegoat must always be socially marginal in some way; an 'expendable victim, human or animal, whose death will not cause violence to rebound because no one will bother to avenge them' (Girard, 2011: x).

108). So it was natural that Lumet would be attracted to a Lawyer Film in which the bright protagonist of the Heroic Lawyer was placed under the *noir*-ification process necessary to mutate him into his double. *The Verdict* is very much centered upon the personal moral redemption, or *meatanoia*, of the protagonist himself; hence the dramatic centrality of the epiphany in the hospital ward when he is taking photographs of the comatose victim. The real problem with Frank Gavin, meaning the question of the narrative integrity of his conversion experience after actually seeing up close and personal the brain-dead victim of medical malfeasance, is that he does not formally equate to any of the iconic characteristics of the Heroic-Lawyer. Cinematically he is so clearly an anti-Heroic Lawyer that there is no dramatically plausible way for him to be harboring the reservoir of repressed moral integrity necessary for him to make an authentic repentance, the proverbial act of redemption. If we go through the sub-genre checklist of the attributes of the Heroic Lawyer (even a post-redemptionist one) Gavin crashes out on all of them. Is he The Friend of Liberty? Not even remotely: Gavin does not represent an unpopular client and does not concern himself with issues of criminal conviction, constitutional protection or civil rights; at stake in *The Verdict* is a civil suit for personal injury which, historically, has not been the subject matter of heroic lawyerly action. Does he qualify as The Lawyer-as-Professional? No way. Gavin is incompetent, unconscionably failing to consult with his client or to provide adequate representation of their interests; even worse, he fails to make certain that the testimony of his key witness is admissible. Does he make it as The Lawyer-as-Defender-of-Due-Process? Not a chance. Nothing in this case affects due process or wider issues of the rule of law; in fact, all of the participants (plaintiff counsel, defendant counsel, the bench) all violate due process in some manner, so there are only competing forms of uncleanliness within this courtroom. But the problem remains the same as before: Lumet-as-*auteur* has to bring his film to a very particular, and very liberal-pluralist, moral conclusion, just as he did in *12 Angry Men*.[22]

The only thing that Lumet has left in his bag of directorial tricks is to pullout the least used, most morally ambiguous, exceedingly unattractive, and perhaps overly complex lawyer-icon there is: The *post-Heroic Lawyer*. Difficult to define, the best way that I can put it is in terms of secularized religious allegory: the post-Heroic Lawyer is the Heroic Lawyer, essentially, who through primarily external circumstances (usually some sort of an 'attack' from the outside[23]) 'falls' into the Rusty Sabich-esque depths of the anti-Heroic Lawyer but who, because of her innate moral virtue—the love of justice which usually means going lawless at the critical moment—is able to bring about the morally correct verdict, usually due to nothing that she has accomplished on her own but because of those same set of external forces that caused her to fall in the first place now working in the opposite direction in order to secure her restoration to righteousness and professional success as a now recognized esoteric knowledge worker. Expressed a bit more concisely, the

[22] See Chap. 6, above.

[23] The Greeks most commonly identified this outside hostile force as Fate or *moirai*. I discuss this more fully in Chaps. 8, 9, 10, and 11, below.

post-Heroic Lawyer is the Lawless Lawyer who is weighed down by the narrative burden of patho*s*, the quality that incites a sense of catharsi*s*, or release of emotional tension, within the audience: we witness the agony of the one who suffers, apparently unfairly like Job, and we rejoice at the end when he is restored.

There are three reasons why we can know with certainty that Gavin is the post-Heroic Lawyer properly defined. The first is that within the film's depiction of the legal culture, the conventional heroism of the Heroic Lawyer is an utter impossibility; *The Verdict* is simply too realistic a portrayal of legal and lived trauma to allow juror no. 8 to exercise his architectural esotericism; '[W]isdom has rotted into calculation, justice into deal-making. The lawyer today is forced to face all manner of complex problems confusing his moral authority: matters economic, racial, sexual, political. The magic circle is broken' (T. Appelo qtd. Greenfield, 2000: 27). The second reason is the inversion of the first: as the courtroom is irredeemably corrupt and Gavin is hopelessly incompetent, the only rhetorical move open to him is by appealing directly to the exoteric citizen-jurors in an esoteric attempt to make them experience a sense of both awe and pity. Which means that Gavin must both theatrically and truthfully reduce himself to the level of an object of pure pity, which he does in his closing remarks to the jury which is the moral denouement of the film and which will, hopefully, like Henry Fonda did in *12 Angry Men*, cause a sequestered jury to collectively undergo *metanoia*.

> So much of the time we're just lost. We say, Please God, tell us what is right, what is true. When there is no justice, the rich win and the poor are powerless. We become tired of hearing people lie. We think of ourselves as victims. We become victims, we become weak, we doubt ourselves, we doubt our beliefs, we doubt our institutions. We doubt the law.

We doubt the law.

> We doubt the law, but today you are the law. [Today the law is] not some book, not a marble statue or the trappings of the court. Those are just symbols of our desire to be just. They are in fact a prayer, a fervent and frightened prayer. In my religion, they say 'Act as if ye have faith, and faith will be given to you'. If we are to have faith in justice, we need only to believe in ourselves and act as if there is justice.

The Verdict subverts the orthodox form of the Law Film through its failure to ground the resolution of the problem within the proper exercise of legal machinery, so that the Lawless-Lawyer leaves the system only temporarily in order to ultimately come back to it. Here, Lumet discards this genre norm altogether: *The Verdict*'s post-Heroic-lawyer must actually take the jury and the audience along with him into temporarily abandoning the prescribed formalities of the legal system altogether and implement the moral rejuvenation of the law through their combined moral (or populist) will by subordinating the esoteric courtroom to the exoteric exigencies of justice. Which means that, technically, Gavin did not win the case—the jury won it for him, by responding in a cathartic manner to the spectacle of his self-induced pathos, in a manner not at all dissimilar to the similarly scapegoated but equally helpless Rusty Sabich who 'wins' on a legal technicality brought about through the unsolicited evidence tampering by an investigator friend of his. The third, and most important reason, is the natural extension of the second: as the conversion of the lawyer is central to the film's dramatic narrative, the symbolic resurrection of Gavin dramatically complements the 'legal resurrection' of the physically destroyed victim, so that we can frame *The Verdict* as a religious narrative allegorized through the secularized conceit of the Lawyer Film. And if *The Verdict* is all about Frank Gavin bringing himself 'back to life' and symbolically 'healing' the harm done to the victim-client (or, in a more exorcist-like manner, casting out the evil that has been done to her) by reducing himself to a state of nothing in the sight of the jury, then there is no doubt that Frank qualifies as a scapegoat. His address to the jury is actually a prayer; specifically a prayer of auto- or self-sacrifice in which Gavin offers himself (along with his intended professional comeback to the legal order) as a sacrifice whose acceptance will heal the 'real-world' rift between law (what we do) and justice (what we ought to do).[24] At the same time, and very much consistent with the restorative powers of the scapegoat, Gavin overcomes as well as the symbolic rift within the cultural patterning of the esoteric minority and the exoteric majority undergirding the schizoid fragmentation of how lawyers actually behave as opposed to what it is that we want them to do. So that it is all about the problem of mimesis: the solution of the problem of the love-hate of lawyers lies with the mediation of the esoteric technicians of a certain kind of model, that of a Lawless Lawyer who is supremely effective at what she does, although, in truth (or fiction), the ideal Lawless Lawyer will correspond most closely to the post-Heroic type. Rusty Sabich and Frank Gavin are both post-Heroic-Lawless-Lawyers, but they were both nudged into becoming so, Stabich by the actions of others, Gavin by his own freewill. Sam Bowden, in contrast, seized the opportunity to become lawless with both bloodied hands.

7.6 *Cape Fear* or, When the Client from Hell Returns

There are two types of people in the world: those who think that the Martin Scorsese version of *Cape Fear* (1991) is superior than J. Lee Thompson's original black and white version, and those who think the opposite.[25] Even though Thompson's *Cape Fear* was released in 1962 in many ways, it can be considered a Fifties film; that is, it is a 'study in paranoia' focusing on hyper-normal Family unit facing an abnormal threat from the Outside. If we accept that *Cape Fear* is a Lawyer Film *noir*-ized to an unusually intense degree and that the apparently Heroic lawyer Sam Bowden is really a Lawless Lawyer taken to the maximal degree possible,[26] and if we were to apply the typology supplied by Peter Biskind (1983), then we would label the

[24] An intensely cinematic resolution of the Is-Ought dichotomy.

[25] I am in the latter category.

[26] Here, of course there is an objective degree of difference between the moral-seriousness-that-kills (literally) of Gregory Peck in the Thompson film and the slowly degenerating moral insanity of Nick Nolte in the Scorsese version, but the real point is the meaning of the two performances within their respective time-frames, the Fifties versus the Nineties: both actors are taking their roles to the absolute limit of the sub-genre of Lawless Lawyer within the confines of their own *nomos*.

film as conservative and decidedly anti-pluralist. In Biskind's model, conservatives were in basic alignment with liberal-pluralists and are committed to the New Deal (the Welfare State) and the Cold War 'military industrial complex' (Eisenhower), but 'here they parted company. They disagreed on how to conduct affairs at home. Conservatives...put their faith in the law, and therefore conservative films dramatized the breakdown of order' (Biskind, 1983: 35–36).[27] Thompson's *Cape Fear* is a protracted study of the 'breakdown of order,' but with an added novelty: the notion that law and order is powerless to deter truly extremist threats, which creates the de facto need for anticipatory self-defense. Vitally, however, the pre-emptive strike must ultimately be strictly subordinate the Rule of Law: the entire rationale, both legal and moral, for the first strike is the ultimate restoration of the law-governed state of normalcy. In this way, the film is able to subliminally raise the issue of Carl Schmitt's state of exception as the moment of departure from the norm without invoking all of the subversive implications that come with it concerning the foundational relationship between law and violence that were so central to both The Western and The Eastern.[28] And what is clearly carried over from those two genres is the existentially intense enmity between Friend and Enemy.

> The specific political distinction to which political actions and motives can be reduced is between friend and enemy...The distinction of friend and enemy denotes the utmost degree of intensity of a union or separation, of an association or disassociation...[The Enemy is] the other, the stranger; and it is sufficient for his nature that he is, in a specially intense way, existentially something different and alien, so that in the extreme case conflicts with him are possible. (Schmitt, 2007: 26–27)

If we read *Cape Fear* as a conservative Lawyer Film, then the 'moral' would seem to be that necessary deviations from liberalism, the 'normal, are wholly acceptable provided that: (a) the threat is 'real' and cannot be reasoned or negotiated with on the basis of pluralistic consensus because the threat is the Enemy; and (b) the protectors of liberalism are so thoroughly liberal (i.e., 'moral') themselves that they are safe and can be trusted to suspend the state of exception after the Enemy has been dealt with. Which goes straight to the in-joke at the heart of *Cape Fear*: the lawless Sam Bowden is portrayed by Gregory Peck, the same actor who delivered the unforgettable performance of the superhumanly moral Atticus Finch in *To Kill a Mockingbird* (1963). So, since Sam Bowden is really Gregory Peck, just like juror no. 8 was really Henry Fonda, the seasoned American moviegoer is basically accepting of everything that Bowden does because Peck is always true to type. But this cinematic voyeurism carries within it a powerfully Schmittean message.

> Deeper fears protect our willing delegation to the legitimate other, the state and its agents, of the right to use force. We need that legitimate other [The Friend], just as we need the other's dark double [The Enemy], the one upon whom the force of law must operate. For, on a deep and hidden level within ourselves, we know that violence cannot be put off or denied. In this respect, the ancient Greeks were more honest with themselves than we tend to be about this state of affairs. They could admit that a horrible and terrifying fury *is* the steering force

[27] See Chap. 6, above.

[28] See Chaps. 4 and 5, above.

> of the law (*'the utmost degree of intensity of a union or separation, of an association or disassociation'*), that such fury lies at the heart of law. (Sherwin, 1994: 1045)

In their respective discussions of the two film versions of *Cape Fear*, both Richard K. Sherwin (1994) and Thain (2001) make much of the 'cultural differences' between the 1950s and the 1990s. In Biskind's terminology, these wider cultural changes signify the displacement of the conservative movie by the radical film that attacked 'both centrist models of the community: the federally enforced, top-down model favored by corporate liberals and the more bottom-up, populist model favored by the conservatives' (Biskind, 1983: 47). Sherwin's commentary on Thompson's version is especially illuminating.

> The film's message is not hard to decipher: even the most upstanding citizen, a dutiful attorney committed to the lawful demands of due process [a Hero-Lawyer], beloved by wife and daughter [a patriarch[29]], a well-respected member of his community [a Republican], can be driven toward unrestrained, unlawful violence [a member of the NRA]. All of us, the film seems to be telling us, are capable of such fury under the right circumstances. Yet, in the end the film leaves us with a significant assurance: even when such fury is provoked, it can be checked by reason, and the law can take its proper course. We do not have to act on our rage; we do not have to kill. Like Sam Bowden, we can depend on law to do the work of retribution without the need for self-help. In this way, law appears to be properly calibrated to meet our felt need for punishment in proportion to the menace and outright violence perpetrated by the likes of Max Cady.
>
> In short, the original 1962 version of *Cape Fear* presents a picture of violent rage and the law's inability to stave off violent threat. Law clearly has its limitations; it cannot insulate us completely from the risk of anti-social violence. But it can do justice when such violence ultimately erupts. (Sherwin, 1994: 1025)

Which is Carl Schmitt for Americans. But this also means, according to Sherwin who is in the pro-Scorsese camp, that Thompson's version is hindered by a cultural and moral naiveté. The real appeal of Scorse's stunner (with Robert de Niro as Max Cady) is that it speaks directly to the permanent absence of the legitimacy of the law, an absence signified by the law's failure to truly perform the foundational Schmittean task of objectively discerning between Enemy and Friend. The way that Scorsese, predictably, tells it, Sam Bowden is as morally compromised as Max Cady so that there is a strict equivalence of a-morality between the two.

> None of these assurances survive the ensuing twenty-nine years from Thompson's original *Cape Fear* to Martin Scorsese's brilliant and far more unsettling remake. The world has changed radically from what it was: for now, neither law, nor family, nor the virtues of individual character, nor even justice itself can be trusted to prevail in the face of irrational violence. The force of corruption has grown pervasive. And the shadow world from which Max Cady emerges has now become a place to which none of us can claim to be a stranger. According to Scorsese's vision, we are all living at least partly submerged in the shadow of violence, guilt, and denial. (Sherwin, 1994: 1025)

---

[29] It is notable that the two sons in John D. MacDonald's original novel are missing from both film versions, presumably so that the father may possess unmediated access to both the daughter and the wife. See below.

Although Sherwin does not employ Biskind's terminology, he clearly has the radical film in mind when he classifies the Scorsese version as post-modern. Here, he means primarily two things, hyper-reality and montage. Hyper-reality is a 'post-modern sense of the real that accounts for our loss of certainty in being able to distinguish clearly and hierarchically between reality and its representation, and in being able to distinguish clearly and hierarchically between the modes of its representation' (John Fiske qtd. Sherwin, 1994: 1037 n 10) which is the pre-representational episteme that signifies the crisis of undifferentiation. The essence of the hyper-real is the Nietzschean insight that Being consists of nothing more than the sum total of its representations; the only thing that we can know with certainty is the content of the representation as the substitute for Reality which is now inaccessible and resistant to mediation. The hyper-real nature of Scorsese's remake thus subverts or deconstructs law by reducing it to a series of illusions/gestures/signs that all signify law-justice but never actually provide it, precisely because the 'Real' is the very thing that is missing. Montage, deployed by Scorsese in a powerfully arresting and confronting manner, is one of the most visually striking and innovative elements of the re-make. Sherwin basically follows the Sergei Eisenstein's famous account of montage theory or Soviet montage in his discussion of Scorsese.

> *Representation* A and *Representation* B must be so selected from all possible features within the theme that is being developed, must be so sought for, that their *juxtaposition*—the juxtaposition of *those very elements* and not of alternative ones—shall evoke in the perception and feelings of the spectator the most complete *image of the theme itself*'. (Sergei Eisenstein qtd. Meyer, 1992: 897 n 10)

At the 'heart of Eisenstein's montage theory is the cut or juxtaposition of contrasting "shots." The ordering and selection of these shots is compelled by a "theme." This theme is not an intellectual abstraction, but a reflection of the film's internal emotional logic—an artistic vision—revealed to and shared with its audience' (Meyer, 1992: 897 n 10). So that the Scorsese version, in principled opposition to the conservative/naive representationalism of the Thompson film, is a radical exercise in pre-representation, so that the remake's truly stunning, and montage-saturated, visuals work to undermine the archetypal theme of the Law Film genre itself: that Lawyer and Criminal are presented as opposites when in 'truth' they are one and the same. They are undifferentiated and, like the citizens of Thebes in Sophocles *Oedipus Tyrannus*, have become doubles.[30]

Although I believe that Sherwin is essentially correct in everything that he says about the Scorsese version, especially his treatment of montage as the visual cue of undifferentiation, he fails to take into consideration what everyone else who has written about the 1991 film has also collectively ignored: as a child of the Sixties Scorsese is naturally prejudiced against the Fifties without apparently realizing, or failing to openly acknowledging, that the original novel by pulp fictio' writer John D. MacDonald is far more radical, and pre-representational, than anything Scorsese has ever thrown up on the screen. The property that was to become both films called *Cape Fear* was a pulp novel titled *The Executioners* and first published in 1957.

[30] See Chap. 1, above.

If the original book is read carefully, or even just read at all, two things become immediately apparent. One is that virtually all of Scorsese's alleged improvements on Thompson's black-and-white film are the result of him going back to the MacDonald novel, which is from the 1950s, an inconvenient truth that largely undercuts Sherwin's implicit assumption concerning the naivete of pre-postmodern culture. Two is that *The Executioners* is actually far more radical than both of the film adaptations, because, read in a particular way, MacDonald's text makes clear what the radical merely takes for granted, that reality is absent. The truth about reality is that it is never absent; it is, however, literally unspeakable, which takes us away from post-modernism and toward the machinations of Akira Kurosawa in the multiple concealments of an unbearable truth in *Rashomon* (1950).[31] Everything hinges on the one thread of objective truth that Scorsese took from MacDonald: that the Lawless Lawyer Same Bowden and the criminal's criminal Max Cady are doubles.

All great works of literature, according to Girard, operate on the basis of a series of parallel doublings; in the case of *The Executioners* (which is a truly great work within the tradition of pulp fiction), we can make out three sets of binary pairings: Sam Bowden/Max Cady; Law/Crime; and Public/Private justice. But the considerable dramatic power of the novel becomes clear when juxtaposed with its two relatively anemic film adaptations. Thompson tried to salvage Bowden's Lawless Lawyer by making him safe for liberalism (an Heroic Lawyer who deviates temporarily by the need to protect his family, consistent with his status as patriarch), while Scorsese attempted to radically deconstruct him as part of the cool post-modern affectivity of the Nineties, whereas MacDonald, the true radical of the three, utterly demolishes the *noir*-ized lawyer-icon by immersing him into an acid bath of an annihilating moral nihilism. For MacDonald's strategy conforms almost perfectly to Girard's notion of *monstrous doubles* by framing Bowden and Cady as converging on a single but overarching object of desire, the exclusive possession of which would authenticate the being of the holder of the prize and mandating the physical destruction of the rival.[32]

> Our hypothesis makes it logical to imagine that the rigorous symmetry between the mimetic partners ... the living obstacle of the model that is automatically transformed into a rival ... must bring about two things among man's ancestors, little by little: the ability to look at the other person, the mimetic *double*, as an *alter ego* and the matching capacity to establish a *double* inside oneself, through processes like reflection and consciousness. (Girard et al., 2003: 284, 285)

Girard uses the word 'obstacle' in two different senses: (a) as short-hand for the external mediator, the person or thing that acts as a circuit-breaker of escalating mimetic rivalry; and (b) the pathologized version, a 'mimetic paroxysm,' of an ordinary mimetic rivalry contaminated by metaphysical desire in which mimetic rivalry 'increases to the point that the subject is no longer interested in anything but the rivalry itself'—which is psychosis. (Oughourlian, 2010: 12). The archetypal plot of all literature is that the Self (protagonist) will model its relationship to the Other

---

[31] See Chap. 5, above.

[32] See Chap. 1, above.

(double) on the basis of imitation (mimetic rivalry) that will narratively culminate in the Self attempting to either replace and/or destroy the double (mimetic conflict).

> Rivalry does not arise because of the fortuitous convergence of two desires on a single object; rather, *the subject desires the object because the rival desires it.* In desiring an object the rival alerts the subject to the desirability of the object. The rival, then, serves as the model for the subject, not only in regard to such secondary matters as style and opinions but also, and more essentially, in regard to desires. (Girard, 1977: 145)

The rivalry that mimetic desire unleashes will, in the end, assume the most extreme and grotesque form of the violent, or monstrous doubles who are the signifiers of the crisis of undifferentiation: as the rivals intensify their mimetic struggle, they effectively become identical, triggering a pathological crisis of identity which can only be resolved through an act of extreme violence, whether physical, emotional, or symbolic. (Girard, 1977: 143–168). 'Violence is the process itself when two or more partners try to prevent one another from appropriating the object they all desire through physical or other means' (Rene Girard qtd. Gallese, 2011: 88) and *The Executioners*, as if by cue, walks the reader through the whole of Girard's menagerie of mimesis: pre-representation, doubles, mimetic crisis, the crisis of undifferentiation, monstrous doubles, murder/sacrifice/scapegoat. The narrative pivot is that Bowden and Cady reciprocally descend into the pathological extremity of mimetic and homicidal rivalry, announcing their co-joined identity as monstrous doubles, or doubles who are monstrous. 'Under the heading *monstrous double* we shall group all of the hallucinatory phenomena provoked at the height of the crisis by un-recognized reciprocity. The monstrous double is also to be found wherever we encounter an "I" and an "Other" caught up in a constant interchange of differences' (Girard, 1977: 164). And for Sam and Max, this 'interchange of differences' orbits around their claim of possession of a very particular woman—Sam's daughter Nancy.

> There is no monster who does not tend to duplicate himself or to 'marry' another monster, no double who does not yield a monstrous aspect upon close scrutiny … The nature of the relationship between monster and double, stubbornly denied by the antagonists, is ultimately imposed on them in the course of the shifting of differences—but it is imposed *in the form of hallucination.* The unity and reciprocity that the enemy brothers have rejected in the benign form of brotherly love finally impose themselves, both from without and within, in the form of monstrous duality—the most disquieting and grotesque form imaginable. (Girard, 1977: 160)

The 'form of the hallucination' assumed in *The Executioners* is that because Bowden is a lawyer and Cady is a criminal, they are polar opposites, whereas, in fact, they are virtually the same person, psychically enslaved by the patriarchal prerogative of incest. 'There will never be a connection between you and Max Cady!' Sam Bowden (Nick Nolte) bellows at his daughter Nancy (Juliette Lewis), unaware that the 'nature of the relationship between monster and double' will always be 'stubbornly denied by the antagonists.' And because they are really the same—meaning that their desires are their own and not the by-product of their imitation of the other—each one must kill the other in order to continue the hallucination of existing as the 'Real'. Bowden and Cady unconsciously act out the mimetic logic of the crisis of undifferentiation that culminates in the creation and destruction of the expiatory scapegoat which, like the Law itself, is 'the last sanctioned force, the foundation upon which everyone has dared to stand' (Silbey, 2000: 111–112). For Girard, the scapegoat and its psychic and ritualistic mechanisms are nothing less than the Alpha and the Omega, because its deployment of language for the purposes of pre-representation as a means of creating an infinite series of substitutions—one sacrifice after another—is the primal thing 'hidden since the foundation of the world'.

> All systems that give structure to human society have been generated from [the scapegoat mechanism]: language, kinship systems, taboos, codes of etiquette, patterns of exchange, rites, and civil institutions. Thus a theory of sacrifice has produced a comprehensive account of human social formation, religion, and culture'. (Mack, 1987: 7)

And at the original center of every-thing is law, the sum total of the rites, rituals, and prohibitions by which the community designates and prepares the scapegoat for sacrifice in order to postpone the final reckoning of the loss of distinctions and the collapse of external mediation. And the loss of distinctions is a matter of paramount importance, because as Sophocles showed in the case of Oedipus, incest, along with patricide, is the transgression most certain to effect a cataclysm of undifferentiation.[33]

Scapegoating is law's ancient *telos* today mis-recognized; ergo, if the law is not able to perform its purpose adequately, the lawyer, as the agent of the law which is supposed to be identical to justice, is rightfully empowered to undertake scapegoating on his own initiative, a salvific act of private justice that proves restorative for the public community. MacDonald grasps this completely and shows that he has by having Sam explain to his wife Carol 'I'm trying to say that I'm one of the boys. And the boys take care of their own' (MacDonald, 2007: 10). Sam Bowden, then, is the antithesis of Frank Gavin, who is definitely not one of the boys and for whom no one takes care of; MacDonald's Lawless Lawyer sacrifices not himself but Max Cady the other who is the enemy not only of the public domain but the private domain of the family, which is Bowden's. And, in the end, everything is okay, because the Bowden's clan premeditated murder of Cady in cold blood accomplishes two vital tasks of mimesis, one private, one public, but both interchangeable. It resolves the private crisis of undifferentiation between Sam and Cady, whose mimetic desires had converged on early teen-age daughter Nancy and permitted the re-stabilization of the family unit by terminating with extreme prejudice the outsider's threat to the exclusivity of paternal rights to the daughter. It also restored the anti-mimetic of external mediation by deploying the true telos of the Law in a lawless manner in order to obtain the right outcome that legal formalism would not permit: the extra-legal enforcement of difference through a private act of execution, justifiable for having been applied against a true scapegoat, the cause of mimetic tension within the group. To prove my point, I am going to undertake a 'close' reading of *The Executioners*, interspersed with references to Sherwin's extended discussion of the 1991 Scorsese version with Robert DeNiro (Cady) and Nick Nolte (Bowden).

---

[33] See Chap. 1, above.

7.7 'You Sacrificed Me!': Sam Bowden Rediscovers the Scapegoat

The obvious place to begin is with potential for paternal incest as a sign of the micro-sovereignty of nuclear patriarchy as was implicitly signaled by Thomas Hobbes in *Leviathan* (1651).[34]

> By this it appears, that a great Family if it be not part of some Common-wealth, is of the self, as to the Rights of Soveraignty, a little Monarchy; whether the Family consist of a man and his children; or of a man and his servants; or of a man, and his children, and servants together: wherein the Father or Master is the Soveraign But yet a Family is not properly a Common-wealth; *unless it be of that power by its own number, or by other opportunities, as not be subdued without the hazard of war*. (Hobbes, 1992: 142)

Threats from the intrusive outsider are premium and elicit the most violent action, or, failing that, the most intense introspection.

> Like Oedipus [!], Sam Bowden unknowingly confronts a riddle together with its solution. His family life will soon unravel, and the agent of destruction is sitting right there in front of him [in the movie theater]. For Oedipus, that agent was himself. For Sam Bowden, you might say it's his double. The scene is now set for impending violence. (Sherwin, 1994: 1031)

But Sam soon discovers for himself the Hobbesian intensity of imminent combat with the intruder: 'But it makes me feel a little ineffectual. I'm the king of this little tribe. I should be able to put the fear of God in Cady. But I don't see how I could. Not with this office-type physique. He [Cady] looks like he's got muscles they haven't named yet' (MacDonald, 2007: 26). Just so that we do not miss it, MacDonald has Bowden, the Dan Draper of 1950s Savannah, spend a great deal of time looking his daughter. Although the novel's accounts of Nancy are objective descriptions of her physical beauty, making her the target of Cady's sexual-homicidal violence through which he can supplant his obstacle, all of these observations are conveyed through the constitutive gaze of Sam Bowden/Father, highly suggestive of Laura Mulvey's seminal comments on the male gaze (Mulvey, 1975).

> They watched the boys go into the water. Nancy and her friend stood up. She waived at her parents. She tucked her dark hair into her cap as she walked to the stern of the *Sweet Sioux*. Sam looked at her and felt sad and ancient as he saw how quickly her slim figure was maturing. And, as always, he thanked private gods that Nancy took after her mother. The boys took after him. Sandy-red hair, knobbly bone structure, pale-blue eyes, freckles, oversized teeth. It was evident that at maturity both boys would be like their father, incurably lean, shambling, stringy, tall men of physical indolence and ropy toughness. It would have been tragic if he had willed his only daughter such a fate (MacDonald, 2007: 6-7)…. As they stepped into the water, Nancy was clambering up over the stern of the *Sweet Sioux*. Water droplets sparkled on her bare shoulders. Her hips, so recently lanky, had begun to swell into woman-lines. (MacDonald, 2007: 12)

But it doesn't stop there. Male voyeurism is as endlessly repetitive as the mechanisms of sacrifice: 'He [Sam] looked at the doorway through which she had gone.

---

[34] See Chap. 3, above.

Such a precious and precocious age. Half child and half woman. And when she was all woman, she was going to be extraordinarily lovely. And that would create its own special set of problems' (MacDonald, 2007: 22). What kind of problems exactly? Look and see.

> As they talked, Sam looked idly at his family...Nancy wore very short red shorts, old and faded, and a yellow linen halter. Her legs were long and brown and slim, beautifully shaped. She worked the sanding block with both hands, turning lithely at the waist. The smooth young muscles bunched and lengthened under the sheen and texture of her back. (MacDonald, 2007: 51)[35]

Shortly afterward we get MacDonald's account of Sam's observation at a voyeuristic distance of the interaction between Nancy and Tommy Kent, her alternate or 'second' boyfriend.

> Sam was glad to see how well she handled him. No melting looks. No tinges of adoration. She was brusque with him, fencing with him in pert confidence and the sure-footedness of self-respect, quietly aware of her own attractiveness. Sam was surprised that her young weapons were so professionally edged and were wielded with such an air of long practice...She was as careful as if she was dancing...Young man [Sam thought], she just sank the hook. She's keeping the rod tip up, and she's got the drag set perfectly. And when the time comes, she's going to be just as expert with the net, and you will flap in the bottom of the boat, eyes rolling and gill covers trembling. Pike Foster never had a chance, and now she's ready for bigger game. (MacDonald, 2007: 59)

We call this foreshadowing, for Nancy is the hook that Bowden will sink into the pedophiliac flesh of Cady, the source of a rival male gaze, and, therefore, the double of the father who mediates access to the daughter: the *skandalon* of Max Cady. But there is also mimetic rivalry between Cady and Bowden as Husband, for Wife Carol, no less than Daughter Nancy, is constituted by the male gaze.

> When he [Sam] looked at her [Carol] it was as though she had suddenly, tragically become an older woman. At thirty-seven she had taken great pride in her agelessness, at the way she could look a consistent thirty and, at special times, a gay and miraculous twenty-five. Now, with shoulder slumped, and face all bones and gauntness, he saw for the very first time how she would look when she became very old. (MacDonald, 2007: 60)

Sherwin notes the 'unconscious alliance' between Leigh Bowden (whom Scorsese re-named) and Max Cady, the would-be rapist of Nancy and murderer of Sam.

> We shall now see that the violence at work here is not that of Max Cady alone, nor is the spirit of vengeance Cady's alone. For the Bowdens are up to their necks in barely repressed, and at times irrepressible violence. And strangely, Max Cady, feared and hated as he is, is also a vehicle of vengeance for Leigh Bowden...her rage toward her husband, justifiably perhaps, makes her complicit, at least sub-consciously, in Cady's criminality, in his rage for vengeance against Sam. (Sherwin, 1994: 1031)[36]

---

[35] Scorsese omits this scene but he references it beautifully with this sharp exchange between Sam and Nancy (Juliette Lewis): 'Put some clothes on! You're not a kid anymore!' (Sherwin, 1994: 1035–1036).

[36] A situation complicated somewhat, I admit. By Leigh's repressed and unacknowledged aggression towards Danielle, who might be Sam's illegitimate daughter: 'The child can't be mine' (Sherwin, 1994: 1028–1029).

By now there is no doubt that Max Cady fulfills all of the literary, and mimetic, requisites to qualify as the true double of Sam Bowden.

> He [Sam] remembered how the sergeant had looked in court. Like an animal. Sullen, vicious and dangerous. And physically powerful. Sam looked at him and knew how lucky [Bowden's] punch had been. Cady had looked across the court at Sam as though he would have dearly enjoyed killing him with his own hands. Dark hair grew low on his forehead. Heavy mouth and jaw. Small brown eyes set in deep and simian sockets. Sam could tell what Cady was thinking. A nice clean non-combat lieutenant. A meddler in a pretty uniform who'd never heard a shot fired in anger. So the pretty lieutenant should have backed right out of the alley and gone on his way and left a real soldier alone. (MacDonald, 2007: 5)[37]

As Sherwin comments, 'Cady fully and openly expresses the kind of self-serving manipulation of power that we suspect lies, less openly perhaps, within the legal profession and the law itself. Cady, then, can be seen as embodying both Sam Bowden's and the law's dark underside. He is their barely repressed double' (Sherwin, 1994: 1036). And in *The Executioners*, the law, the juridical field of symbols meant to channel a wholly sanitized form of physical and social violence through a series of acts of creating naming, is often metaphorically referenced in terms of the imagery of the male body.

> 'I wouldn't have recognized him [Cady]. He's about five nine, wide and thick set. He's more than half bald and deeply tanned, and he looks as though you couldn't hurt him with an ax. The eyes are the same and the jaw and the mouth are the same, but that's all.'
>
> 'Did he threaten you?'
>
> 'Not in any explicit way. He had control of the situation. He was enjoying himself'. (MacDonald, 2007: 7)

At this point Sherwin opts for the somewhat hackneyed notion of the return of the repressed, meaning that Cady is the externalized manifestation of Bowden's unconscious.

> Yet, when the civilizing effect of law is inverted, when we willfully defy law and its procedures[38] [i.e. suppressing evidence], its principles of fairness and due process, even when the particular circumstances may seem to warrant our defiance [the 'trade mark' of the Hero-Lawyer], that same fury is let loose again in the world, it is torn free from law's civilizing constraints. From this viewpoint, then, we might say that Scorsese's is, at heart, a *conservative* message. Beware the dark forces within. Beware the return of the repressed. Beware the loss of the reality principle when confronted with the chthonic potent agencies of desire, fantasy, and magical thinking. (Sherwin, 1994: 1041)

But by following Scorsese a little too closely Sherwin commits the same error as the director in reducing Cady's dramatic essence to the external projection of

[37] This references Sam's disruption of Cady's attempted rape of a teen-age girl by landing a knock-out blow to the assailant, but MacDonald only uses this as the gimmick needed to set up the mimetic triangle.

[38] A very interesting innovation of Scorsese's film is that he has Cady seeking revenge against Bowden, his former defense attorney, for having violating his professional oath by supressing the report of the sexual history of Cady's rape victim and setting up Max's incarceration. In other words, Cady is seeking revenge against a Lawless Lawyer.

Bowden's own incestuous desires: 'The small deep-set brown eyes changed, but the smile still exposed the cheap white teeth. "We started pretty near even back there in forty-three, Lieutenant. You had a fancy education and a commission with little gold bars, but we both had a wife and a kid. Did you know that?"' (MacDonald, 2007: 53). So the mimetic rivalry migrates from 'kid' to 'wife' as a forbidden sexual drama.

> He patted her hand. 'Now brace yourself, Carol-bug…I had a lot of chances to observe him. And the more I listened, the more a little warning bell rang, louder and louder. You don't have to be a trained psychoanalyst. Somehow, when a person is different, you know it. I suppose we all run in a pack, in a sense. And there are always little clues to the rogue beast. I don't think Cady is sane.'
>
> 'My God!'. (MacDonald, 2007: 8)

Like Bowden, Cady likes male-gazing at Nancy which means that incest establishes the mimetic nature of his desire, given that back in 1943 the two were essentially equals.

> [Sam] went over and put the sandwich and thermos on the sawhorse. As he was unbuttoning his shirt, he had his back to Nancy. He stopped, motionless, his finger touching the third button. Max Cady sat on a low pile of timbers twenty feet away. He had a can of beer and a cigar. He wore a yellow knit sports shirt and a pair of sharply creased slacks in a shade of cheap electric blue. He was smiling at Sam (MacDonald, 2007: 52) … 'That's a real stacked kid, Lieutenant. Almost as juicy as your wife' (MacDonald, 2007: 56) … There he told [Carol] about Max Cady. 'Here!' she said, her eyes wide and round. 'Right here?' 'Right here, watching Nancy, when I got back. And when I looked at Nancy I seemed to see her the way he was seeing her and she'd never looked more undressed, even in that Bikini thing you let her wear only when we're on the island without guests'. (MacDonald, 2007: 60)

Cady's earlier rape of the girl in Melbourne, resulting in his court martialing after Bowden testifies for the prosecution, doubles as the mimetic enactment of Bowden's sexual aggression against both daughter and wife

> The great stone city [Melbourne] with its wide, deserted streets, just a few lights burning. The sound of his [Sam's] heels echoing coin sounds from the empty walls…And then he stopped and stared without comprehension at the pale tumbled legs, the brutal rhythm of the attacker, and heard the animal whining, heard the meaty crack of his fist against her face. With comprehension had come a high-wild anger…The girl was fourteen, big for her age and very plain-looking (MacDonald, 2007: 4–5) … [Sam] could hear a faint mewling sound [Nancy], a hopeless sound of fright and pain and heartbreak so like the unforgettable sound he had heard so long ago in a Melbourne alley that it seemed to him his heart would stop. (MacDonald, 2007: 167)[39]

Sherwin, again, makes the predictable Freudian move, here, correlating Cady's psychopathy with Bowden's Id; 'Scorsese's *Cape Fear* might be read as an updated version of Freud's *Civilization and Its Discontents.* If we do not challenge the unquenchable claim of instinct ("where it [the id] was there *I* [the ego] will be!"), we shall leave civilization in shambles' (Sherwin, 1994: 1041). Or as private detective Sievers puts it in the novel

---

[39] A theme also touched on by Scorsese with Bowden placing a noticeably aggressive headlock on Nancy outside the cinema where the entire family encounters Cady for the first time (Sherwin, 1994: 1032).

> 'He's one of the wild ones. They don't think the way people do. He was headed for jail whether he got caught on that rape charge or not. People like that have no comprehension of right and wrong. Their only thought is whether or not they'll be caught. Anything you can get away with is worth doing.'
>
> 'Isn't there a word for that?'
>
> 'Psychopathic personality. They make us learn the terms. But that's a classification where they put people they don't know what else to call'. (MacDonald, 2007: 89)

The word 'they' use when 'they don't know what else to call it' is 'it' reiterated as Id, which is the inexpressible repressed of the unconscious, although, as Sherwin points out, the repressed cannot be restricted to the sexual unconscious alone; it can be deployed to signify the morally and socially unspeakable as well.

> Cady's fateful mission of justice reflects a curious, and potent blend of diverse cultural forces. It was nurtured under the influence of Friedrich Nietzsche, whose *Will to Power* stands prominently on Cady's prison book shelf, right beside the Bible and the law books. It's a mission nurtured as well before the gaze of Robert E. Lee and Stalin whose photos adorn Cady's prison wall. It as if Cady has come to embody the dark underside of Western culture, a force that has a historical and intellectual as well as an artistic dimension. (Sherwin, 1994: 1039)

And Max's 'fateful mission of justice' is the legal equivalent to morality's incest taboo: vengeance as an act of extra-legal but perhaps a naturally justified, and psychologically pleasurable, private justice. In marked contrast to both film versions, Bowden's novelistic trespass against Cady involves neither an upholding (testimony) nor a breaching (suppression of evidence) of the law; rather, it consists of a private act of physical violence.

> He had wrested the soldier away from [the fourteen-year-old girl] and, as the man [Cady] had scrambled up, had struck wildly and with all his strength and had hit the hard shelf of jaw. The man had grappled with him weakly, then slid down, rolled unto his back and, to Sam's astonishment, had begun to snore. He ran out [of the alley] and a few moments later hailed a Shore Patrol jeep. (MacDonald, 2007: 4–5)

'You get one sucker punch in a lifetime, Lieutenant. You've had yours' (MacDonald, 2007: 56), Cady tells him, initiating the sequences of private retribution that, through escalating mimetic rivalry, culminates in Cady's attempted supplanting of Bowden as patriarch: the resolution of the crisis of undifferentiation through the physical obliteration of the monstrous double. Which means that the Freudian gimmicks that Girard despised aside, *The Executioners* is really a legal drama which leads inexorably to the foundational problem of the scapegoat. Bowden reveals his *meconnaissance* of the law through two pivotal conversations in *The Executioners*, the first with police chief Dutton, who relates to the lawyer-naif the history of a 'negotiated truce' between the rival forces of police and mafia.

> 'If it doesn't work out, Captain, couldn't you still force someone to leave town?'
>
> Dutton nodded. 'We've done it, not frequently. The last time was three years ago. This is a fairly clean town. Cleanest of its size in the state. That doesn't mean spotlessly clean, Mr. Bowden. But it means that we've kept the syndicate type of operation out. We let a

few small-time operators stay in business, because there's always a certain level of demand. When they try to get too big, or when they try to move on legitimate enterprise or rough up the taxpayers, we crack down quick and hard. When a syndicate operation tries to move in, we give our small-time operators protection. In return they contribute to both political parties and to the Police Benevolent Fund, and they keep us advised on any floaters who come to town and start looking around for a score. I'm speaking frankly and off the record...The Christer set continually tries to nail us for playing footsie with our tame rascals. We keep the little devil we know in business and keep out the big devil we don't'. (MacDonald, 2007: 71)

Edifying stuff to be sure, but in terms of the raw power of disillusionment it pales in comparison with Sam's chat with senior law partner Bill Stetch concerning the un-ethical practices of Bowden's firm. This is Scorsese's version.

Ah, just another day in the life of a modern attorney. No longer do we see the lawyer's virtuous concern for his client's desperate financial need—as in the tort case Sam Bowden handled nearly thirty years before. Gone, too, is the attorney's virtuous concern for the well-being of an elderly witness. Now we have legal maneuverings, private investigations to counter deceptions, S & Ls—the familiar landscape of social corruption and private scandal. Indeed, soon we'll see Sam's law partner try to persuade Sam to undertake some unspecified, but clearly unethical, perhaps illegal, action in the divorce case that Sam is handling. "No, that's bull-shit, and I'm not doing it," we'll hear Sam say. (Sherwin, 1994: 1029)

But in the novel, Bowden learns, to his chagrin, that the only reason why he was hired by his firm was largely to provide them with a 'front' of respectability; we can see that 'bullshit' has been substituted for 'I'll be damned'.

'I'll be damned if I ever see myself going to the police and politely asking them to do something unlawful.' [i.e. 'leaning' on Max Cady]

Stetch chuckled. 'That old glamour girl holding those scales [of Justice] and taking a peek every little once in a while under her blindfold. And Samuel Bowden is her most avid worshipper. A lot of kids feel that way about it, but it's a damn rare man that can...continue that infatuation.'

Sam felt that he was being patronized, and it annoyed him. 'What do you mean?'

'Don't get indignant Sammy. Hell, when it was just Dorrity and Stetch, I knew we needed some noble motives around here, so we could retain our sanctimonious manner...Mike Dorrity and I are a pair of licensed pirates. We needed a balanced wheel. One with starry eyes'. (MacDonald, 2007: 74–75)

It is interesting to speculate whether Scorsese was making a back-handed referenc to this portion of MacDonald's text in Nick Nolte's 'No, that's bull-shit, and I'm not doing it,' scene.

'You're a partner [Sam]. You do a hell of a fine job. You more than hold up your end. We're damn pleased we took you in. It was a smart move. But there's some parts of this business you can't handle, and we don't give you a chance to handle. Mike and I dirty our hands with that. It's the loophole division. We're well paid to find the loophole, regardless of the equities of the matter at hand.'

'Like that Morris option last year?'

> 'Just like that Morris option last year.'
>
> 'I thought that stank.'
>
> 'And it did, boy. That's why I took it away from you before you lost us a client. And handled it myself'. (MacDonald, 2007: 75)

Bowden's idealism in fact impairs his ability as a lawyer, especially since the firm's clientele are borderline criminals, with the result that the Hero-Lawyer beings to acquire self-awareness of his own unacknowledged liminality.

> 'You make me feel like a damn neophyte.'
>
> Bill shook his head. 'You're not. You're a smart attorney, Sammy. And you are a very rare article. You are a good man who believes in what he is doing. Every law firm ought to have at least one in the shop. Too few do. So pay no attention to a cynical old bandit. We don't actually steal. Sometimes we show other people how they can steal, but it doesn't happen too often. Keep your regard for the lady with the scales. But don't get too appalled at yourself when you ask the police for an extra-legal favor. Life is a continual process of compromise, Sammy. The idea is to come out the other end still clutching a few shreds of self-respect'. (MacDonald, 2007: 76)

Expressed in Giardian terms, this is the moment when the spectral figure of the scapegoat, just as with Bowden's repressed sexual deviancy, begins to emerge from the depths not of the erotic but the cultural unconscious. Sherwin gets this exactly right.

> By film's end we come to realize that Sam's imperious act of vigilantism, his decision to assume the role of judge, condemning his client when he should have been the client's most zealous advocate, has unleashed an even more violent form of vigilantism. He has triggered the vengeful fury of Max Cady. And in this too we see an inversion of Thompson's original *Cape Fear*. Indeed, Scorsese's film plays out as an inversion of Aeschylus' great tale of law and vengeance in the *Eumenides*. In that classic tale, the hideous fury of retribution was tamed, it was brought *into* the law. In that process of containment furious vengeance was civilized; thus was the trial and its procedures born and handed down to us, borne through the ages to our own day. (Sherwin, 1994: 1041)

But what Sherwin fails to recognize is that all of those classic Greek tragedies that he references are myths about the scapegoat enacted theatrically. If we omit consideration of scapegoating as the true return of the repressed, then, in very superficial terms, the decidedly un-heroic Bowden would appear to conform to the positive version of the Lawless-Lawyer icon, as he is facing a dilemma that can only be solved by obviating traditional legal mechanisms and remedies: 'Stop bleeding, Bowden. You're all grown up. Stop marching around and waving your little flags. Cady shoots your kids while you cry onto your diploma and look through all the dusty books for a way to slap his wrist legally' (MacDonald, 2007: 76). The problem is that the only alternative mechanism available to solve the problem of Max Cady's lethal threat to Sam Bowden's micro-patriarchy by way of the doubling of monsters is vigilantism, in this case first-degree (pre-meditated) homicide, which, narratively, cannot be rationalized away by the reader/viewer as a morally justifiable departure from 'mere' legal procedure. Unless…

> 'I want to kill Cady…That was not a figure of speech. I mean that I want to plan it all out and lay a trap and kill him and dispose of the body. I want to commit murder, and I think I know how it can be done.'
>
> She [Carol] stared at him for what seemed a long time. And then she looked away, as though in shyness. 'Not murder. Execution.'
>
> 'Don't help me rationalize. Murder. And it may go wrong, but not if we're careful. Have you got the guts to help me?'. (MacDonald, 2007: 89)

And the word execution is pivotal: one murders an enemy, but one executes a scapegoat, because the killing of he or she that meets the criteria of lawful scapegoat can be made subject to a process that while extra-judicial is, nonetheless, morally acceptable in a naturalist sense, provided that everyone is certain about their respective identities. So it is quite possible to read *The Executioners* almost in terms of a rite of passage tale, or fable, in which Sam re-covers the culturally repressed memory of the scapegoat mechanism. It begins when Captain Dutton refuses assistance to Bowden in his request to drive Cady out of town on the basis that there is no self-interest for police department to do so.

> 'This is something that, as a lawyer, you can understand. It would set a curious precedent. We used extralegal methods and a lot of time. And manpower to avert a definite threat to the whole city, not just to one individual. Were we to do this, there would be questions asked. If he [Cady] should employ the right shyster—forgive the term—it could get damn hot around here. The men I would assign would be very curious about this extra duty. You are not a resident of this city. You pay no city taxes. Your firm does, but this is not the business of your firm. As an individual, you pay no fractional part of my salary'. (MacDonald, 2007: 73)

In an interesting and significant deviation from both film versions, MacDonald has Bowden going to the private detective Sievers first, well before he makes any contact with the police.

> 'I'm sorry, Sievers. Maybe it's a weakness in me, but…I can't operate outside the law. The law is my business. I believe in due process.'
>
> Sievers stood up. 'It's your money. A type like that is an animal. So you fight like an animal. Anyway, I would. If you change your mind, we can have a private talk. This wouldn't be through the agency'. (MacDonald, 2007: 30)

So the narrative movement is from a wholly illicit act of private justice, which would in effect be an imitation of Cady's behavior, toward an illegal act of public justice but morally salvageable by being performed and therefore sanctioned by the police, to a radically different but in fact archaic form of natural justice that is outside the norms of legal modernity yet remains intelligible in its purpose and structure. As a result of these two 'private talks', an appropriately 'unnamable' type of agency is put in the employment of a private justice that is completely justifiable if we were to remember the original purpose of scapegoating: the restoration of the community by sacrificial violence. And if both Bowden are Cady are a threat to the community for being carriers of the plague of undifferentiation, then the sacrificial murder of one of the monstrous doubles is wholly justified.

> To Sam the situation was curiously unreal. He had not thought such a conversation possible in his office…Sievers took on the look of a man thinking back across the years. 'It used to be easier long ago, in other places. You take Chicago or Kansas City or Atlanta or Birmingham in thirty-three or thirty-four. The rates were cheap. Ten bucks for a broken leg. And a top of two hundred if you wanted somebody killed and they weren't important. There's only a handful of killers for hire now in the whole country and they're on retainer for the syndicate. Even if you could contact them, the price would be up in the clouds. A hopped-up kid can be bought for less, but the job would be bungled. The pros do a clean job. Come in by plane with a good cover story. Two or three of them. Rent a legitimate car. Stay in a good hotel. Pick the time and place and do it fast and clean and then get out. An amateur always gets caught and always sucks in the guy who hired him'. (MacDonald, 2007: 99)

As a literary character, it is necessary that Sam Bowden undergoes a personal transformation, or conversion, of some kind as Girard argued. In his case, the movement is centered upon his demystification of the nature of both law and justice, but demystification of a very special kind, namely that modern law is the result of the collective forgetting of the eternal but lurking presence of the scapegoat mechanism. Doubly significant is it when Bowden identifies private justice with 'primitive times'.

> You have the best reason in the world to be upset, honey. I know how you feel. And I know you've got cause for complaint. I provide food, clothing, shelter. Very civilized. It would be a hell of a lot easier to handle Cady during more primitive times, or in a more primitive part of the world. I am a member of a social complex. He is the outsider. I would rally my gang and we would kill him. I would very much like to kill him. I might even be able to manage it. You [Carol] are re-acting on a primitive level. That is actually what your instinct tells you I should do. But your logic will tell you how impossible that is. I would be sent to prison. (MacDonald, 2007: 36–37)

The problem with Bowden's smugly liberal speech, of course, is precisely that Carol, along with everyone else in the novel, is miles ahead of him. Bowden's *metanoia* is, in a sense, his dim recognition of the eternal verity, and practical relevance, of the 'primitive' which is identical to the lynching of the scapegoat, the true enemy of the good. Which is, of course, the very opposite of what Girard meant to describe, which is the renunciation of mimetic desire and imitation. The essential turning point is the moment that Bowden consciously recognizes the incommensurability of the demands of the allegedly neutral public space of the law and the ultra-subjective psychological dynamic of the private space which is the Family that doubles as the locus of Bowden's own incestuous longing. And it is the exact moment that the scapegoat-as-the-It-that-is-repressed finally returns.

> The night was empty. His four incredibly precious hostages to fortune were in deep sleep. The earth turned and the stars were high. All this, he told himself, was reality. Night, earth, stars and the slumber of his family. And the other thing that had seemed so valuable [the law] was just a dusty and archaic code which enabled men to live closely together in reasonable peace and safety. In olden times the village elders punished those who broke the taboos. And all of the law was a vast, top-heavy super-structure built on the basic idea of the group enforcing the punishment of the non-conformist. It was a tribal rite, with white wigs, robes, and oaths. It just did not happen to apply to his own situation. Yet two thousand years ago he could have sat in council with the elders and explained his peril and gained the support of the village, and the predator would be stoned to death. So this action was a supplement to the law. Thus it was right. Yet, when he got back into bed, he still could not accept his rationalization. (MacDonald, 2007: 80–81)

'*So this action was a supplement to the law. Thus it was right*' is the big take-away from MacDonald's pulp masterpiece which is a hymn to the restorative powers of lynching in solving crises of undifferentiation: Bowden as the lawful instigator of the lynch-mob is justified through the community's recognition of him as the Friend who is the enemy of the Enemy. In *The Verdict*, Frank Gavin is post-heroic because the normative consensus guaranteeing the truth of legal speech has evaporated. Scorsese adopts a similar line, deconstructing the complacent metaphysics of liberal pluralism through a cinematic presentation of pre-representation.

> Once upon a time, one might have said that there is a natural law, a form of justice that could intervene in human history to set straight the crooked course of human affairs. Once perhaps, but no longer. Nietzsche and the Romantics of the late nineteenth century have already mourned the death of God and the flight of the gods. Indeed, much of twentieth century art, literature, and philosophy has been taken up with the de-sacralization of nature and the secularization of society…In the early 1960s, perhaps we could be assured. Law would do its job in the end. But today we are not. Today, we must depend upon a wind, a current—something more in keeping with a theory of chaos than of divine or natural law. (Sherwin, 1994: 1042)

In *The Executioners,* however, Sam Bowden is equally post-heroic but for radically different reasons: he acts on the now revealed objective truth of the law that Scorsese muddled through his post-modern montage posturing: the objective and universal truth of the law is that it is the symbolic ritualization of the violence of the scapegoat mechanism. Bowden explains it this way: 'I was idealizing my profession, and leaning on it too heavily. Now I know it's just a tool. You use it like any other tool. Use it wisely and it can help you. And when it's of no use to you, you take a course of action that will be of use' (MacDonald, 2007: 181) which is killing the Enemy. Sam Bowden, the supremely Lawless Lawyer, goes to the absolute extremity of lawlessness and directly encounters the unmediated figure of the scapegoat. He thereby reverses the only apparently restorative work of Rusty Sabich and Frank Gavin; instead of allowing himself to be sacrificed by his monstrous double the criminal, the real (esoteric) lawyer willingly assumes the guise of the sacrifice and, by this transmogrifying action, re-establishes law on its eternal and universal foundations of scapegoating. If Rusty and Frank or Christ-like in their enactments of *Imitatio Christi*, then Sam is the anti-Christ in his *Imitatio Nietzsche*, the one who invokes the archaic gods of the primitive blood sacrifice as the only 'course of action that will be of use'. *The Executioners* is an apocalyptic novel: law is revealed as violence and justice is unveiled as revenge and both are governed by rites and mimetic crises. And consistent with this logic of the Lawless-Lawyer ad extremis Bowden succeeds in murdering Cady through the use of his private gang of executioners, or his personal lynch-mob: his Family. And it is as a Family, the most primitive of social groupings, that the executioners arrange the sacrificial murder of the scapegoat in a manner that is suitably primitive.

> 'Can't keep your family hid out forever.'
>
> 'I know that [Sievers]. I've thought of that. But what else can I do? Do you have any ideas?'

> 'The only one I got I'm not proud of, Mr. Bowden. Think of him like he's a tiger. You want to get him in out of the brush. So you stake out a goat and you hide in a tree'. (MacDonald, 2007: 139)

And since the Family is the executioners, the logic of patriarchy demands that the Wife should be the first in line to assist: as voyeuristic sexual bait, meaning that Sam affirms Max's identity as monstrous double at the very moment that he kills him.

> 'Yes, Sam. I can help you and you can depend on me and there won't be any going to pieces, either. Waiting is what ruined me. Action won't.'
>
> 'That's what I hoped. Your part is harder than mine.'
>
> 'Tell me,' she said. She was leaning forward, dark eyes frowningly intent, tanned arms crossed and resting on her knees. He looked at her and thought how good her legs were, and how all of her was truly compact and vibrant…It was, to him, a moment of curious significance, of a dramatic unreality. This, he thought, cannot be Sam and Carol, man and wife. He had thought he knew this woman and knew himself. But this was a time of change. There was a new quality of tension and excitement between them, but there was an unhealthiness about it, a tinge of rot. (MacDonald, 2007: 152)

This 'tinge of rot' is also known as 'good sex' which is ordinarily linked to some kind of violence (even if only as 'excitation' or mimetic 'role play,' which is exactly what is going on) but in classical literary terms we call it catharsis, 'the descriptive term for clarifying, separating out, and getting centered upon the *right* emotion' (Richard Kuhns qtd. Sherwin, 1994: 1044), 'right' meaning aesthetically appropriate to the unfolding of the narrative. MacDonald's description of Bowden's sacrificial elation is a perfect satire of 1950s American white sub-urban masculinism.

> Sam looked at the body as they rolled it back onto the stretcher. A blade of grass was pasted to his lips. He had killed this man. He had turned this elemental and merciless force into clay, into dissolution. He searched through himself, looking for guilt, for a sense of shame.
>
> And found only a sense of savage satisfaction, a feeling of strong and primitive fulfillment. All the neat and careful layers of civilized instincts and behavior were peeled back to reveal an intense exultation over the death of an enemy…
>
> It was Bowden [who] did it.
>
> Sam Bowden, who had wanted to throw his head back and yell at the sky, who had wanted to dance around the body and chant the defeat of the enemy.
>
> When he felt strong enough he plodded up the stairs to wait there until Carol awoke, and then he would tell her, and then he would sleep, and then he would drive down to get the kids (MacDonald, 2007: 176–177).

Naturally, the return of the returned repressed to repression, or the termination of the crisis of undifferentiation of the monstrous doubles, allows for the immediate resumption of Bowden's displaced incest fantasies, this time the erotically recharged Wife employed as surrogate for Daughter in an almost-but-not-quite knowing manner.

> [Carol] grunted in a sleepy way and rolled over and craned her arms back and unhooked the bra part of the two-piece suit and said, 'Baste me, ole friend.'

> He put the beer can down, rested his cigarette on top of it, uncorked the lotion bottle, poured it warm into the palm of his hand, and stroked it into the long, clean brown lines of her back. One of the rarest of women, he thought. Woman of grace and spirit, pride and delicacy. And once again he thought of the nightmare thing that had so nearly happened to her. A duller spirit[40] might have survived the crime without too much emotional damage, but Carol never. It would have broken her utterly and forever. When he thought of the narrowness of the escape, it made his eyes sting, and it blurred the shape and pattern of her (MacDonald, 2007: 178).

And then

> They walked down to the water hand in hand. Suburban husband and suburban wife. A handsome, mild and civilized couple, with no visible taint of violence, no lingering marks of a dreadful fear.
>
> He swam out with her, stopped and smiled lovingly at her, ducked her unexpectedly and violently, then swam for his life toward the stern of the boat, while the kids yelled for her to catch him. (MacDonald, 2007: 182)

If Sabich and Gavin have embraced their 'inner Christ' which secures their moral victory, Bowden (along with Carol) embrace with even greater enthusiasm their 'inner pagan' which is what makes the sex so good.[41] MacDonald's magnificent pulp fiction fable provides the solution to the seemingly interminable problem of the legitimacy not only of the law but of lawyers themselves by reminding us of the eternal recurrence of that lawfully lawless violence that is scapegoating, the foundational IT that is the figural to all that universally flows from it. Bowden assumes the burden of the necessary execution of Cady by voluntarily undergoing a process of cultural regression to the archaic condition of the foundational scapegoater, the inventor of sacrificial killing. And, as Sherwin quite rightly remarks on behalf of all liberal-pluralists everywhere, 'For us, this knowledge must be repressed. Law's violence must be sanitized, neutralized, denied. And when it cannot be, when public recognition of law's violence can no longer be concealed...at such times we witness law's legitimacy slipping' (Sherwin, 1994: 1045). Sherwin claims that the legitimacy of law is threatened if and when *meconnaissance* is neutralized. But pace the ultimately groundless conceits of law's secularism and liberalism, the successful recovery of the scapegoat will prove to be the infallible solution to the problem of its legitimacy, precisely because law is really all about the identity of the breaker of the law, conventionally known as the criminal but who is modernity's surrogate for the scapegoat. As the veritable (anti-) Father of post-modernism himself, Jacques Derrida, unforgettably expressed it

> Law has an 'interest in a monopoly of violence.' This monopoly doesn't strive to protect any given just and legal ends but law itself...The admiring fascination exerted on the people by 'the figure of the "great" criminal,' can be explained as follows: it is not someone who has

[40] That fourteen-year-old plain girl in Melbourne?

[41] There must be something about the name 'Carol', because by the end of *The Executioners*, Carol Bowden has entered into an inter-textual mimetic rivalry with the equally erotically a-moral Carolyn Polhemus from *Presumed Innocent* both women, in marked contrast with men, depicted as possible model-mediators of Being.

committed this or that crime for which one feels a secret admiration; it is someone who, in defying the law, lays bare the violence of the legal system, the juridical order itself. (Jacques Derrida qtd. Sherwin, 1994: 1043)

All that we require in order to proceed with the generative restoration of the law through scapegoating is the name of this 'great criminal'.

References

Primary Sources

Cape Fear (Universal Studios 2003; directed by J. Lee Thompson)
Cape Fear (Universal Studios Home Entertainment 2009; directed by Martin Scorsese)
MacDonald, J. D. (2007). *Cape fear*. Fawcett Rei Miti edition.
Presumed Innocent (Warner Home Video, 2010; directed by Alan J. Paluka)
The Verdict (Twentieth Century Fox 1982; directed by Sidney Lumet)
The Thin Blue Line (MGM 2005; directed by Errol Morris).
Turrow, S. (1988). *Presumed innocent*. Penguin Books.

Secondary Sources

Asimow, M. (1999–2000). Bad lawyers in the movies. *Nova Law Review, 24*, 533–591.
Biskind, P. (1983). *Seeing is believing: How Hollywood taught us to stop worrying and love the fifties*. Pluto Press.
Bourdieu, P. (1987). The force of law: Toward a sociology of the juridical field. *Hastings Law Journal, 38*, 805–853.
Chase, A. (1987). Lawyers and popular culture: A review of mass media portrayals of American attorneys. *American Bar Foundation Research Journal, 11*(2), 281–300.
Cohen, F. S. (1960). *Legal conscience: Selected papers of Felix S. Cohen*. Yale University Press.
Corcos, C. A. (1997). Presuming innocence: Alan Pakula and Scott Thurow take on the great American legal fiction. *Oklahoma City University Law Review, 22*, 129–166.
Cunningham, F. R. (1991). *Sidney Lumet: Film and literary vision*. The University Press of Kentucky.
Friedman, L. M. (1989). Law, lawyers, and popular culture. *The Yale Law Journal, 98*(8), 1579–1606.
Gallese, V. (2011). The two sides of mimesis: mimetic theory, embodied simulation, and social identification. In S. R. Garrels (Ed.) *Mimesis and science: Empirical research on imitation and the mimetic theory of culture and religion* (pp. 87–108). East Lansing MI: Michigan State University Press.
Girard, R. (2011). *Sacrifice* (M. Pattillo, & D. Dawson, trans.). Michigan State University Press.
Girard, R. (1978). *To double business bound: Essays on literature, mimesis, and anthropology*. The Johns Hopkins University Press.
Girard, R. (1977). *Violence and the sacred* (P. Gregory, trans.). The Johns Hopkins Press.
Girard, R., Oughourlian, J.-M., & Lefort, G. (2003). *Things hidden since the foundation of the world* (S. Bann, & M. Metteer, trans.). Continuum.
Greenfield, S. (2000). Hero or villain? Cinematic lawyers and the delivery of justice. *Journal of Law and Society., 28*(1), 25–39.

Greenfield, S., & G. Osborn. (1994–1995). The living law: popular film as legal text. *Law Teacher, 28–29*, 33–42.

Greenfield, S., & Osborn, G. (1995). Where cultures collide: The characterization of law and lawyers in film. *International Journal of the Sociology of Law, 23*, 107–130.

Hobbes, T. (1992). *Leviathan* fully corrected 1651 edition. Cambridge University Library, Syn3.65.1, ed. Richard Tuck. Cambridge University Press

Kuzina, M. (2000). The social issue courtroom drama as an expression of American popular culture. *Journal of Law and Society, 28*(1), 79–96.

Lansing, R. (2010). *The Dante encyclopedia* (R. Lansing, Ed.). Routledge.

MacAulay, S. (1989). Popular legal culture: An introduction. *The Yale Law Journal, 98*(8), 1545–1558.

Mack, B. (1987). Introduction: Religion and ritual. In R. G. Hamerton-Kelly (Ed.) *Violent origins: Walter Burkert, Rene Girard, and Jonathan Z. Smith on ritual killing and cultural formation* (pp. 1–72). Stanford University Press.

Meyer, P. N. (1992). Law students go to the movies. *Connecticut Law Review, 24*, 893–913.

Meyer, P. N. (1993). Visual literacy and the legal culture: Reading film as text in the law school setting. *Legal Studies Forum, 17*(1), 73–93.

Meyer, P. N. (2000). Why a jury trial is more like a movie than a novel. *Journal of Law and Society, 28*(1), 133–146.

Mulvey, L. (1975). Visual pleasure and narrative cinema. *Screen, 16*(3), 6–18.

Oughourlian, J.-M. (2010). *The genesis of desire* (E. Webb, trans.). East Lansing MI: Michigan State University Press.

Pinsky, R. (1994). *The inferno of Dante. A new verse translation by Robert Pinsky*. Farrar, Straus & Giroux.

Posner, R. (1986). Law and literature: A relation re-argued. *Virginia Law Review, 72*(8), 1351–1392.

Posner, R. (1988). *Law and literature: A misunderstood relation.* Harvard University Press.

Post, R. C. (1987). On the popular image of the lawyer: Reflections in a dark glass. *California Law Review, 75*(1), 379–389.

Rafter, N. (2007). *Shots in the mirror: Crime films and society* (2nd ed.). Oxford University Press.

Schmitt, C. (2007). *The concept of the political* (G. Schwab, trans.). University of Chicago Press.

Sherwin, R. K. (1994). Cape fear: Law's inversion and cathartic justice. *University of San Francisco Law Review, 30*, 1023–1045.

Silbey, J. (2000). Patterns of courtroom justice. *Journal of Law and Society, 28*(1), 97–116.

Sokolsky, A. (1989). The case of the juridical junkie: *Perry Mason* and the dilemma of confession. *Yale Journal of Law and the Humanities, 2*, 189–199.

Stark, S. D. (1987–1988). Perry Mason Meets Sonny Crockett: The history of lawyers and the police as television heroes. *University of Miami Law Review, 42*, 229–283

Thain, G. J. (2001). 'Cape fear': Two versions and two visions separated by thirty years. *Journal of Law and Society, 28*(1), 40–46.

Wright, D. P. (1986). The gesture of hand placement in the Hebrew Bible and in Hittite literature. *Journal of the American Oriental Society, 106*(3), 433–446.

Chapter 8
The Telling of Lies and the Casting of Lots: Franz Kafka's *The Trial* and the Eternal Undecidability of the Scapegoat

Abstract This chapter continues the discussion of the accused as scapegoat through an examination of one of the greatest texts in law-and-literature, Fran Kafka's *The Trial*. The drama of Josef K. can be understood as the demystification of legal process as a mechanism of scapegoating in which the violence of the community is directed at a ritualistically selected sacrificial victim. What Kafka, or 'Franz K.,' did so supremely well is to undertake this deconstruction of the law exclusively from the perspective of the scapegoat: the novel is a running commentary on the inherent arbitrariness, or 'undecidability', of the pre-representational logic of sacrificial substitution told from the point of view of the sacrificial goat from the Book of Leviticus. But I also argue, following Elias Canetti, that *The Trial* doubles as a real-time commentary on the 'trial' underwent by Franz K. following the collapse of his engagement to Felicia Bauer. Josef K. and Franz K. are 'double doubles,' both with each other and with the two sacrificial offerings to the Lord in the Book of Leviticus, the goat for Azazel and the goat of the sin offering. What undermines the facile contemporary interpretation of Franz K. as persecuted but innocent neurotic are the clear parallels between his own predicament and that of his textual double Josef K. Both really are guilty, but not of the unspecified accusation of some kind of visible legalistic transgression; rather, it is the mis-recognized mimetic 'sin' of metaphysical desire and *ressentiment*.

Keywords Emissary victim · *Katharma* · *Pharmakon* · Sacralization · Cyclical time · Eternal return

In what follows, I will be relying upon the following definition of the scapegoat, or, in more technical terms, the *emissary victim*: 'Taken from the Vulgate *caper emissarius*, a very broad interpretation of the Greek *apopompaios* "one who wards off illnesses." The Greek term is a translation of the Septuagint, which is itself an equally broad translation of the Hebrew, which means "destined to Azazel"' and expelled into the wilderness (Girard et al., 2003: 131) as opposed to its double, the 'the goat of the sin offering' which is ritually slain. The issue of Girard's use of the term 'scapegoat,' a specifically Hebrew concept, for the more universal construct of the emissary, or

E. M. Wilson, *Rene Girard, Law, Literature, and Cinema*,
https://doi.org/10.1007/978-981-97-1156-7_8

surrogate, victim has given rise to no small amount of criticism; among others, Mary Douglas has argued that when Girard incorrectly deploys the term scapegoat, he really means the Greek notion of the *pharmakos* which, in popular usage, has been conflated with its Jewish counterpart; "when talking about scapegoats in everyday parlance we are drawing upon Greek rituals to rid the city of scum, discarded elements, useless and dirty people" (Dawson, 2013: xi). David Dawson, however, has come to Girard's defense, arguing that the term scapegoat, as it has evolved lexically and etymologically since the Reformation, more adequately conveys the double or ambiguous meaning of the victim as both a destroyer and a restorer, originally of the community and, following the rise of Christianity, the whole of Creation. To make an extremely long story very short, by the sixteenth century, the two Levitical goats had been theologically combined into a single *typon*, or an alleged Old Testament pre-configuration of Christ. The immolation of the goat for the sin offering became the symbol of Christ's visible physical death and the exile of the goat 'destined to Azazel' into the wilderness read as the symbol of Christ's invisible redemption of souls, beginning with the cosmic liberation achieved through the 'Harrowing of Hell' that culminated in the Resurrection. The Puritan Henry Burton expressed the Mosaic typology this way: "figuring the humanity the slaine Goate, and the divinity of Christ, the scape Goate: or the slaine Goate the death of Christ; and the Scape Goate his resurrection" (Dawson, 2013: 59). In fact, the scapegoat as *typon* was established as early as the third century CE; 'Tertullian suggested that the two goats represent Jesus. He says, "The two goats, which were offered at the Fast, are not these also figures of Christ's two activities?" The goats have to be alike, because both represent Christ. According to Tertullian, the goat "driven into perdition" (a clear reference to the goat for Azazel) marks the Lord's suffering: he was "cursed and spit upon and pulled about and pierced." The other goat [of the sin offering] symbolizes Christ's offering for sin' (Pinker, 2008: 13–14). Once this signifying act had been accomplished, the suffering of 'innocents' now re-configured as the mimetic stand-ins for Christ becomes a moral abomination and the West begins its long transition toward a fully developed 'victimology' centered upon the fusion of Christ with both absolute sacredness and total innocence. The cosmically transfigurative Lamb of God, a term that became symbolically and discursively interchangeable with scapegoat, comes to imply 'the substitution of one victim for the others but replaces all the distasteful and loathsome connotations of the goat with the positive associations of the lamb. It indicates more clearly the innocence of this victim, the injustice of the condemnation, and the causelessness of the hatred of which it is the object' (Girard, 1986: 117). In the end it seems to have come down to the historical accident that the novel term scapegoat 'was coined by translators of the King James Bible because they did not know how to translate the Hebrew term Azazel' (Pinker, 2008: 2, n 1).[1]

---

[1] For discussion of the *pharmakon*, see Chap. 9, below.

8.1 'Someone Must Have Been Casting Lots About Josef K.': The Indeterminate 'Truth' of Franz Kafka

Franz Kafka is at the forefront of that most hallowed body of writers (Orwell, Hemingway, Dosteoevskii) whose surname has come to be deployed as an adjective: *Kafkaesque*,[2] Kafka's unique literary affect achieved by way of a Modernist re-deployment of Yiddish folkloric motifs that have been infected by a cosmic nihilism, or in the case of certain works, such as 'A Country Doctor' (Kafka, 1952: 148–156), cosmic horror. And of all of the novels that I discuss, with none of them, except perhaps *In Cold Blood* by Truman Capote,[3] is the relationship of the person and personality of the author as central to critical interpretation as Kafka's *The Trial* or *Der Prozess* (1925), with its accidentally-on-purpose quasi-confessional opening line that is almost universally misunderstood: 'Somebody must have made a false accusation against Josef K., for he was arrested one morning without having done anything wrong' (Kafka, 1994: 1). Against Roland Barthes' imperious declaration of the 'death of the author', Kafka held that '...writing means revealing oneself to excess...' (Kafka qtd. Canetti, 1974: 37), so that it is to be expected that 'Kafka's fiction was but a more or less heavily disguised autobiography' (Friedlander, 2013: 10). But this to a degree that is virtually unparalleled in modern fiction, for, as I shall show, he managed to transform the raw phenomenological life-stuff of his own day-to-day as the occultic fuel of his greatest aesthetic accomplishment: the-narrative-that-never-ends, which is the novel-of-the-eternal-return. For Kafka, writing was a supremely therapeutic action, and, as he confessed it, 'Each of us has his own way of emerging from the underworld, mine is by writing. That's the only way that I can keep going, if at all, by writing, not through rest and sleep' (Franz Kafka qtd. Parry, 1994: xiv). Which means that Kafka is always returning to...some-thing which remains elusive, or unnamable.

> 'How everything can be said, how for everything, for the strangest fantasies, there waits a great fire in which they perish and rise up again.' Of course, [Kafka] means transformation, writing as a phoenix from the flames. [The] night gave him both assurance and fear, typical of the tension which dogged him through life and was the stuff of those 'strange fantasies' he wanted to transform into art. The creative burst proved that in the right circumstances he could shape his own reality into literary form. Allied to this was fear that unspecified forces might compromise the purity of his effort. 'Only *in this way* can writing be done, only with such coherence, with such a complete opening out of the body and the soul.' For Kafka the only viable condition was that which encouraged transformation of self into literature. Nothing must disturb productive coherence...He must write or die. 'My life consists, and basically always has consisted, of attempts at writing, mostly unsuccessful. But when I didn't write, I was at once flat on the floor, fit for the dustbin. My energies have always been pitifully weak... (Parry, 1994: x–xi)

---

[2] Which has become a catch-all phrase for the unsettling influences of apparently hostile but occluded control: discussing *The Thin Blue Line*, Robert K. Sherwin comments that when Randall Adams 'talks about a nightmare from which he cannot awaken, we tend to agree. Yes. That's what oppression must feel like. It's Kafkaesque' (Sherwin, 2000: 118). See Chap. 6, above.

[3] See Chap. 10, below.

We see similar sentiments expressed in his diary entry for January 27, 1922.

> The strange, mysterious, perhaps dangerous, perhaps saving comfort there is in writing…A higher kind of observation is created, a higher, not a keener type and the higher it is…the more independent it becomes, the more obedient to its own law of motion, the more incalculable, the more joyful, the more ascendant its course. (Friedlander, 2013: 147)

If we employed the terminology Girard deployed in his account of the sacrificial mechanism, the two concepts that Kafka evidences a longing for are *katharma* and *pharmakon*, two archaic types of radical but necessary medicinal cure that double as supremely destructive metaphysical dangers. *Katharma*, or 'catharsis' in the English, is a term taken from ancient Hellenic magical practices, in which the victim of an ailment was cured through the supernatural extraction from his/her body of a 'foreign object' that was the source of illness; 'The extracted object had no place in the human organism and no right to be there. It was something brought in by outside forces' (Girard, 1977: 287) and therefore it is 'strange' and unclassifiable. *Pharmakos* possessed two meanings: (a) originally, the 'strange object' removed from the victim; (b) a *ritualistic human sacrificial victim* that was mimetically 'substituted' for the generic 'strange object' that was the cause of suffering; 'The Greek term for an evil object extracted by means of a [dramatic-magical] ritual is *katharma.* This term was also used as a variant of *pharmakos* to designate a sacrificial human victim' (Girard, 1977: 286). By the time of Socrates, *pharmakos* gave way to *pharmakon*, denoting a more general notion of both 'poison' and 'remedy': the person or thing that can absorb all of the illnesses of the community (remedy; cure) can also serve as the source of re-contamination (poison) if not handled properly (ritual). 'The *pharmakon* is thus a magic drug or volatile elixir, whose administration had best be left by ordinary men in the hands of those who enjoy special knowledge and exceptional powers—priests, magicians, shamans, doctors, and so on' (Girard, 1977: 95), this 'and so on' including tragic playwrights and modernist novelists. In a June 1913 letter to his long-suffering crypto-fiancé Felice Bauer,[4] Kafka wrote

> All I possess are certain powers which, at a depth almost inaccessible under normal conditions, shape themselves into literature, powers to which, however, in my present professional as well as physical state, I dare not commit myself, because for every inner exhortation of these powers there are as many, if not more inner warnings. Could I but commit myself to them they would undoubtedly, of this I am convinced, lift me out of my misery in an instant. (Friedlander, 2013: 118)

And what, exactly, is the source of Kafka's misery? On the level of the sublime it is that he suffers from an acute case of *metaphysical desire* as evidenced by this comment in his predictably unsent missive to his 'dearest' Father: '…I could not be certain of anything…I needed new validation of my existence with every passing second…' (Kafka, 2010: 65). On the level of the banal it is that it is psychically impossible for Franz to co-exist peacefully with the Family, the originating Oedipal community. On October 18, 1914, he wrote in his diary

[4] See below.

> Baldly put—hence with a harshness that doesn't quite correspond to the truth—my position is about as follows: I, who for the most part have been a dependent creature, have an infinite yearning for independence and freedom in all things. Rather put on blinkers and go my way to the limit rather than have the familiar pack mill around me and distract my gaze. For that reason it is easy for every word I say to my parents and they to me to become a stumbling block under my feet.[5] Every relationship that I don't create or conquer by myself, even though it be in part to my own detriment, is worthless, it hinders my walking, I hate it or am close to hating it. The way is long, my strength is little, there is abundant reason for such hatred. However, I am descended from my parents, am linked to them and my sisters by blood, am sensible of it neither in my everyday affairs nor, as a result of their inevitable familiarity to me, in my special concerns, but at bottom have more respect for it than I realize. Sometimes this bond of blood too is the target of my hatred; the sight of the double bed at home, the used sheets, the nightshirts carefully laid out, can exasperate me to the point of nausea, can turn me inside out; it is as if I had not been definitely born, were continually born anew into the world out of the stale life in that stale room, had constantly to seek confirmation of myself there, were indissolubly joined with all that loathsomeness, in part even if not entirely, at least it still clogs my feet which want to run, they are still stuck fast in the original shapeless pulp. That is how it sometimes is. (Kafka, 1976: 371)

Because Kafka hides in his room, he is never seen, and, therefore, he never truly 'is' (*sein*). Yet Kafka was not merely a malcontent at large; his—let us call it this—hatred was generated by somewhat more specific causes than the Oedipus complex or cosmic strife; 'I have been betrayed by [my parents], but I cannot defy the laws of nature without going mad—hence more hatred and nothing but hatred' (Kafka, 2010: 97). What was this 'betrayal'?

In his indispensable work of 'Kafka Studies' *Kafka's Other Trial* (1974) Elias Canetti argues that Kafka's greatest period of creativity of 1912–1914 ('which included The Judgment', 'The Metamorphosis', and *The Trial*) was the literary excrescence of the psychic trauma occasioned over and over again by Kafka's disastrous and probably insincere plans to marry Felice Bauer; that 'Kafka had a genius for complicating what was already inextricably confused, and so turning it into a source of guilt' (Parry, 1994: xiii–xiv) is one of the all-time great understatements. The hellish downward spiral into the eternal recurrence of the traumatic-sameness began, as far as we can reconstruct the sequence of events, on June 1, 1914, with the commencement of Kafka's official engagement with Felice in the Bauer household in Berlin. But just six weeks later, on July 12, 1914, we note the beginning of some weirdly hobbled together intra-family 'tribunal' assembled in response to Kafka's apparent intent to break the engagement. Canetti deduces straightforward cause-and-effect: 'It can be shown that the emotional substance of both events entered directly into *The Trial*, which Kafka began to write in August. The engagement becomes the arrest in the first chapter; the "tribunal" appears as the execution in the last' (Canetti, 1974: 63). Furthermore, the composition of the nightmarish short-story 'The Judgment' (Kafka, 1952: 3–19) immediately preceded, or perhaps even occurred simultaneously with, the writing of what became 'officially' recognized as the 'last' chapter

[5] *Skandolon*: the object that thwarts mimetic desire but which cannot be abandoned but eternally returned to precisely because it is the obstacle. See Chaps. 1 and 3, above.

of the otherwise literally endless novel known as *The Trial*, meaning that Kafka had started at the end.

Two clear indicators, or traces, of authorial presence within *The Trial*, or *Der Prozess* in German, can be gleaned from extraneous but contemporaneous texts. The first one is that in both his letters and diary Kafka referred to the hotel in Berlin (the Askanische Hof) where the last-ditch attempt at mediation between the two families was undertaken as an informally, or privately, convened *Gerichtshof*, a 'tribunal' or 'Court of Justice'. During those 'sessions,' Kafka was subjected to what he felt to be an almost legal examination and passing of official judgment upon his character by self-appointed private persons behaving in a self-parodying imitation of formal legal procedure devoid of substantive meaning but psychically invested with moralistic fervor: a micro-mob in search of a scapegoat. The second is that he wrote *The Trial* while living at home with his parents. The entire 'topography' of the apartment scenes in the novel appear to have been taken from life, coupled with all of the psychic overtones of imminent emotional collapse.

> Kafka, coming up to thirty, slept and worked and wrote his letters to Felice sandwiched between his parent's bedroom and their living-room, with access from both, so that it served as passageway as well as living quarters. At night, his favourite time for writing, he could hear the snores and nocturnal heavings of his large, powerful father, the successful and uncomplicated man he admired and feared. The law can only be a wall's width away. (Parry, 1994: xii)

Compare this observation with the insight provided by Gilles Deleuze and Felix Guattari on the aestheticized claustrophobia that permeates the text: whatever happens in the novel always occurs 'in the office next door…always an office next door, always the contiguous room' (Deleuze & Guattari, 1986: 50, 51). And because the workings of the law is, without exception, always occurring outside of the unmediated immediacy of the physical presence of the formally, or merely suspected, accused, the resolution of the issue can never be brought to a procedurally final and existentially meaningful end so that the dramatic narrative of the novel perfectly evokes the workings of an occluded deliberation, a some-thing that generates a *meconnaissance* that literally envelops everything, an aesthetic impulse executed so flawlessly as to make any unifying and coherent interpretation of the Kafkian text a virtual impossibility. Contradictions, reversals, and mis-directions abound; the relationship between the spatially segregated actor and the 'process' is so perfectly mimetic that both are condemned to a totality-of-the-interminable, an eternal turning toward proliferating inward spirals. Kafka's best friend and literary executor Max Brod has told us as much.

> Franz regarded the novel as unfinished. Before the final chapter given here ['End'] a few more stages of the mysterious trial were to have been described. But as the trial, according to the author's own statement made by word of mouth, was never to get as far as the highest Court, in a certain sense the novel could never be terminated—that is to say, it could be prolonged to infinity. (Brod, 1995: 75)

And because the structural homologies between the processes of the fake court of the Askanische Hof are so great and numerous with the Kafkaesque peregrinations of *The Trial*, the fictional 'Josef K.' of the novel takes on the role of the mimetic double of the author, whom I feel free to refer to as 'Franz K.', underscoring the twined realities of both as *doppelgangers*.

I identify what we might call 'three shades of the Kafkaesque'; *The Trial* is a supremely allegorical novel, and operates simultaneously, or in a migratory manner, among at least three different levels of meaning: the *nightmare/profane*, the *endless/undecidable* and the *sacrificial/sacred*. I base my discussion upon a dichotomy that I establish between Deleuze and Guattari's 'post-modernist' saturated *Kafka: Toward a Minor Literature* (1986) and Girard's theory of the scapegoat which I use to detect a series of binary relationships within *The Trial*: desire versus revenge, the 'endlessness' of the sacrificial mechanism versus the erotized eternal return of the same; the inherent undecidability of the scapegoat versus the law-as-organism; positivism versus naturalism; and, as un-veiled most apocalyptically in Kafka's supplemental text, *Dearest Father* (2010), that represents the patriarch as the site of the interminable repetition of the un-grounded oscillation between positivist and natural law. The 'interminable' for Franz K. is the endless suspension of judgment, an epistemological problem that equates with the jural delay, or postponement, of the reconciliatory moment of decision-of-finality which, in turn, doubles as the profane postponement of the sacrificial act of the consummating sacred. The occluded 'thing' that unifies these perpetual delays as a coherent literary device (the novel that is *The Trial*) is the objective indeterminacy/undecidability of the willed construction of the scapegoat itself. Deleuze and Guattari's celebration of eternal recurrence in a pseudo-Dionysian manner constitutes an objective (intentional?) mis-recognition of the repetitive nature of sacrificial violence.[6] By following Nietzsche-the-faux-anti-Christ so slavishly (!) both authors of *Kafka* unwittingly eternalize, or re-sacralize, *ressentiment*, the antithesis of Dionysian 'liberation'. Here, I follow Mircea Eliade's definition of *sacralization* as sacrificial ritual embedded, or encoded, within a *cyclical conception of Time*: sacralization as the temporal repetition of sacrifice as the ritualistic symbolization of the eternal-will-to-revenge is revealed as conforming to the psycho-logic of *ressentiment* (Eliade, 1988). Contra Deleuze and Guattari, Girard argues that the true abolisher of the will-to-revenge is the New Testament Gospel, which eliminates the circularity of time (eternal return) through its 'heretical' suspension of the sacrificial mechanism with the eschatological narrative of Christ/God-as-scapegoat. Neither Josef K.'s nor Franz K.'s 'story' ever progresses in a linear fashion but instead constitutes an eternal turning back upon itself because, as a scapegoat in the Mosaic sense, both are bound by the circularity of Time that is sacrificial. Josef K. as an Old Testament scapegoat is never 'finally' invested with the salvific redemption of transmogrification of scapegoat-as-innocent-victim, although he does hold out his arms in supplication of an anticipated recognition by the Divine in the 'End' of the 'last' chapter. Suspiciously like a major figure from the Old Testament.

[6] For an effective dismissal of their central work, *Anti-Oedipus: Capitalism and Schizophrenia* (1972), see Girard, 1978: 84–120.

8.1.1 Girard's Interpretive Reading of the Book of Job

Girard, as we know, makes *meconnaissance* the indispensable requirement for scapegoating because in order for the generative unanimity of sacrifice to occur, it is essential to prevent the cathartic crowd from realizing that the selection of the victim is wholly arbitrary, meaning of profane origin; instead, the mob is led to believe that the scapegoat's selection is pre-ordained, meaning of sacred origin, which is achieved through the mis-directed rituals of sacralization. The twin pillars of sacrificial misrecognition are: (i) the victim is the unique and singular cause of the entirety of the life-threatening disorder; (ii) his or her death will trigger a supernatural effect that will regenerate the community and transform disorder into order, undifferentiation into differentiation. And although Girard mines the Jewish Torah for the theological material needed to formulate his own conception of the scapegoat, his main concern is not so much with the Book of Leviticus, wherein the scapegoat receives its archetypal expression, but in the later and radically different Book of Job which ostensibly has no discernible connection with sacrifice. Here Girard is repeating the same maneuver he performed with *Oedipus Tyrannus*[7]: a text which does not exhibit an overt concern with the sacrificial, or does so in only a limited way, is revealed to be forensically depicting, through a mis-direction of its own, the ritualistic steps undertaken in the occluded 'manufacture' of a scapegoat—which, for the sake of my argument, can be metaphorically conceived as occult discussions held 'in the office next door'. And what Girard brilliantly illustrates for us in *Job: The Victim of His People* (1987) is that the Greek tragedy and the Hebraic scripture share an identical dramatic structure: both texts consist of a rhetorical exchange, or duel, over the protagonist's hidden identity as a sacrificial victim so that Job speaks as the double of Oedipus.

Though I think myself right, his mouth may condemn me;

Though I count myself innocent, it may declare me a hypocrite.

But am I innocent after all? Not even I know that… (Girard, 1987: 127).[8]

For Girard the central, and original portion of Job, 'The Dialogues,' is the poetic dramatization, unparalleled in classical literature, of a designated scapegoat protesting his innocence against the unified front of his ritualistic accusers (the 'Three Friends'[9])—which, in the process of Franz K., could be taken as stand-ins for his family and his almost in-laws.

---

[7] See Chap. 1, above.

[8] This passage is Job 9: 20–22. Because the book has been notoriously difficult to translate, Girard relies exclusively upon *The Jerusalem Bible* translation, that being the one, he freely admits, most 'friendly' to the interpretation of Job as the innocent victim of a scapegoating process.

[9] Eliphaz the Temanite king, Bildad the Shuhite ruler, and Zophar the Nammathite king (Job 2: 16). They are all Gentiles, the Book of Job probably originating, as a Mesopotamian text.

> The process of choosing one surrogate victim eliminates everyone's antagonism in one move by focusing on a common adversary, and then eliminating[10] the victim. It re-establishes peace, as it were miraculously, and the effect it achieves is magnified by the fact that the suddenly regained unity appears to be the result of the intervention of a supernatural power. (Girard, 1987: 69)

Which meant that in July 1914 the Askanische Hof/*Gerichtshof* in Berlin was the site of a re-enactment of the scapegoating ritual, the 'materialization' of the spirit of Job in fleshy form of Franz K., now the reborn substitutional, or emissary 'victim of his people'. The similitude is simply too good to be true.

Job:

And now ill will drives me to distraction,

And a whole host molests me,

Rising, like some witness for the prosecution,

To utter slander to my very face.

In tearing fury it pursues me,

With gnashing teeth.

My enemies whet their eyes on me,

And open gaping jaws.

Their insults strike like slaps in my face,

And all set on me together (Girard, 1987: 5).

Which, as Girard is keen to point out, is 'That is all a myth is—an absolute faith in the victim's total power of evil that liberates the persecutors from reciprocal recriminations and, therefore, is identical to an absolute faith in the total power of good' (Girard, 1987: 34).

> The victim's role that Job claims is bound to be significant within a collection of texts like the Bible where victims, always and everywhere, are prominent. On further reflection, it becomes apparent that the reason for the astonishing similarity between Job's discourse and what we call the penitential Psalms can be found in the perspective common to victims surrounded by numerous enemies. (Girard, 1987: 8)

An outstanding example of this is Psalms 31: 11–13:

To every one of my oppressors

I am contemptible,

Loathsome to my neighbors,

To my friends a thing of fear.

[10] Or expelling into the wilderness, like a scapegoat.

Those who see me in the street

Hurry past me;

I am forgotten, as good as dead in their hearts,

Something discarded.

I hear their endless slanders,

Threats from every quarter,

As they combine against me,

Plotting to take my life (Girard, 1987: 9).

So it is the case that 'One must begin with the crowd phenomena described in Job in order to understand rituals. What Job is describing should be recognized as the original mould of all rituals. The proximity of that origin endows the Dialogues with their extraordinary symbolic radiance' (Girard, 1987: 87). For what Job is describing is having to endure a state of absolute and unconditional ostracism,[11] the 'singling out' of the enemy-scapegoat immediately prior to their being lynched by the mob which is now imminent, having been deprived of any possible avenger to come forth and exact revenge in the aftermath of his immolation.[12]

Job:

My brothers stand aloof from me,

And my relations take care to void me.

My kindred and friends have all gone away,

And the guests in my house have forgotten me.

The serving maids look on me as a foreigner,

A stranger, never seen before.

My servant does not answer when I call him,

I am reduced to entreating him.

To my wife my breath is unbearable,

For my own brothers I am a thing corrupt.

Even the children look down on me,

Ever ready with a gibe when I appear.

All my dearest friends recoil from me in horror:

Those I loved best have turned against me (Girard, 1987: 4).

---

[11] Not dissimilar to that of Jurors nos. 3 and 10 in *12 Angry Men*. See Chap. 6, above.

[12] See below.

For who would avenge the lynching of one with whom there is no longer any bond? 'The sacred lie,' or *meconnaissance*, of 'the friends is contrasted with the true realism of Job' (Girard, 1987: 32), so that the justly named Dialogues 'present the two visions in counterpoint. The true revelations of the persecuted alternate with the untruthful sacralised speeches of the persecutors' (Girard, 1987: 32). One of the three not-so-friends Bildad the Shuhite ruler really lays it on thick.

His memory fades from the land,

His name is forgotten in his homeland.

Driven from light to darkness,

He is an exile from the earth,

Without issue or posterity among his own people,

None to live on where he has lived.

His tragic end appals the West,

And he fills the East with terror.

A fate like his awaits every sinful house,

The home of every man who knows not God (Girard, 1987: 118).

Of all 'the revelatory details offered by the Book of Job the most extraordinary remains the counterpoint of the two perspectives, made possible by the dialogue format; it resembles a theatrical production,[13] the object of which is not catharsis but the disappearance of all catharsis' (Girard, 1987: 32) enabling Girard to provisionally identify the beginning of civilization's long march toward the demystification of scapegoating with this very text.

> All this would hardly have helped Western civilization and its literature. Catharsis would lose its efficacy and all forms of the sublime would decompose.[14] The great form of tragedy, the highest of all forms, would lose its balance. It would forfeit its acceptable conclusion.[15] We see this clearly today in the demise of this form. The sacrificial subterfuges are exhausted. But it has taken a long time to reach this stage. (Girard, 1987: 46)

Which explains the late appearance of the youthful interloper Elihu[16] who 'became furious; and he was very angry with Job, because he declared himself to be righteous [innocent] before the Lord. He was also very angry with Job's three friends, because they found no answer to Job, and yet affirmed he was an ungodly man' (Job 32: 2–3). He informs Job (as though the intended scapegoat did not already know) that God, in a manner that decidedly violates due process

[13] Like *Oedipus Tyrannus* with the absolutely vital distinction that Oedipus comes to voluntarily accept his status as a guilty victim while Job steadfastly refuses to admit his 'true' guilt throughout.

[14] Meaning that the transcendence-spawning sacrificial mechanism could no longer operate.

[15] Which is premised upon the tragic hero-victim voluntarily reconciling himself to his fate which is divinely ordinance Fate, or Destiny. I discuss this at greater length in Chap. 9, below.

[16] The son of Barachel the Buzite, of the family of Ram, of the country of Ausitis. Another Gentile.

Smashes great men's power without inquiry

And sets up others in their places.

He knows well enough what they are about,

And one fine night he throws them down for men to trample on

He strikes them down for their wickedness,

And makes them prisoners for all to see (Girard, 1987: 17).

Translated, this means that what appears to us as injustice is not, really, because the 'disaster' was actively willed by God, meaning that all of the death, destruction, and pain is sacred, or 'divine' justice. And since Job is 'incapable of directly confronting the notion that God is destroying him, here resorts to the weapon of the weak: he protests' (Girard, 1987: 133). Yet precisely because Elihu's theodicy of just retribution is clearly a cheap example of a debased, and debasing, *meconnaissance*, Job is able to reply to his accusatory 'friends' that 'As for you, you are only charlatans, physicians in your own estimation' (Girard, 1987: 80).[17] Which returns us to Girard's central ethical concern: the need to identify and then cast out the unclean spirit of *meconnnaissance* is essential if the eternally repetitive violence of sacrificial mechanism is to be permanently suspended.[18] And the key to this counter-sacrificial movement is to enable the scapegoat to actually speak, to cross-examine and interrogate his accusers, and to establish his own contrarian identity as a true innocent. As we know, the restoration of 'the community is identical to the strengthening of socio-religious transcendence. But such reinforcement demands a flawless scapegoat mechanism, completely unanimous agreement that the victim is guilty' (Girard, 1987: 111). But what this means in practice is that 'So long as the victim lives, he is part of the community; he can therefore participate in the unanimity forming against himself. The need for unanimity is the community's primary concern. There is no reason for him to be an exception. In fact, his assent is the most important of all' (Girard, 1987: 111). Which is why a scapegoat who actually protests is so supremely subversive: by transgressing against the ritualistic prescriptions in such a confrontational manner the victim who refuses to comply with his own death is poised to be able to explode the entire machinery of unjust elimination. 'The system consists of whitening the community by blackening the scapegoat; to consolidate it, the belief in this mythic blackness must be strengthened. The most effective means, obviously, is the victim's confession, in due and proper form. Job must publicly admit his infamy, proclaiming it loudly and convincingly' (Girard, 1987: 112). Which is the very thing that Job refuses to do—indeed, it is why the Dialogues is the central (and probably original) section of the text because it is precisely where the rupture in the façade of *meconnaissance* takes place. Hence the supremely dramatic nature of the scripture

[17] 'The friends regard the sacrifice of Job as socially therapeutic. It is not so much a question of curing certain individuals as of watching over the well-being of the entire community. This is reminiscent of the shamans, of all the *medicine men* who operate by purifications and eliminations' (Girard, 1987: 79).

[18] See Chap. 1, above.

which rivals anything in Hellenic tragedy; 'The three friends try to obtain Job's assent to the verdict that condemns him. That is the true purpose of their mission, since the efficacy of the scapegoat mechanism depends on it. This is no abstract discussion of the question of Evil' (Girard, 1987: 111). Eliphaz of Teman makes what is at stake terrifyingly clear.

And will you still follow the ancient trail

Trodden by the wicked?

Those men who were borne off before their time,

With rivers swamping their foundations,

Because they said to God, 'Go away!

What can **Shaddai** do to us?'

Yet he himself had filled their houses with good things while these wicked men shut him out of their counsels.

At the sign of their ruin, good men rejoice,

And the innocent deride them:

'See how their greatness is brought to nothing!

See how their wealth has perished in the flames!'. (Girard, 1987: 14)

The ones who are about to be sacrificed 'must recognize that they have sinned and that all their suffering is justified' (Girard, 1987: 115), and in the last analysis 'the unfortunate man is asked to confess that he has been struck by an infallible god rather than by fallible men. He is asked to confirm the sacred union of the unanimous lynching' (Girard, 1987: 117). This is exactly what the three accusers demand of the victim (Girard, 1987: 116), and it is why the speeches of the friends 'give off a waft of primitive liturgy that prompts our recognition of a kind of ritual in this process' for not only 'do they represent the community, but they are fulfilling a social and religious function. They are there to watch over the successful operation of the scapegoat mechanism' (Girard, 1987: 76).[19] Girard describes the anthropological dimension of the literary text of Job as a thinly veiled disquisition on *sacrificial preparation* and just as with the tragic choruses of Sophocles 'the rhythmic clamour of the three series of speeches reminds us of ritual recitations intended to excite participants to a religious fury. The receptive quality of these incantations mimics the movement and shouts of a crowd as it begins to polarize itself in opposition to a victim' (Girard, 1987: 76). More clinically, this is the ritualistic channeling of the double transference of mimetic desire, each away from each other and all in the direction of the 'divinely' designated one, said designation having taken place behind

[19] 'The scapegoat mechanism was pure spontaneity. From the point at which it is programmed from beginning to end, it ceases inevitably to be itself. Ritual imitation is the exact opposite of spontaneity. The greater its triumph, the more the ritual becomes the pure mechanical, sterile and dead activity we call rite' (Girard, 1987: 90).

the doors the metaphorical 'other room'. Which bespeaks of *meconnaissance* yet again, but this time infecting the somewhat stage-managing sacrificers themselves: 'Persecutors do not know why this mechanism has such a beneficial effect on their mutual relationships and the entire community, but they are aware of is operation and are very receptive to it' (Girard, 1987: 76). Because that is where the precious substance of generative unanimity can be found, for 'Once the victim is designated, he no longer counts as an individual. His only value is to serve to polarize any errant violence in the community' (Girard, 1987: 76). And what the Three Friends perform in microcosm so do the rite-invested priests perform in macrocosm through the ritualistically prescribed devices of sacralizing the public spectacles of sacrifice.

> It consists of stirring up the participants, usually the entire community, to the point of effervescence, at which time the necessary violence will be so spontaneous that it will seem that the mechanism has been set in motion of its own accord. The final immolation must be made to look as much as possible like the natural orgasm of collective violence, the final paroxysm of a mob soon to be incited. In order to prevent this compressed violence from spreading dangerously and being unleashed elsewhere than on the victim, ritual vigilance surrounds the process with all sorts of precautions. (Girard, 1987: 71)

In what follows I will be presuming that *Der Prozess* is both a parody of the ritualistic prescriptions of the scapegoat mechanism as outlined in the Book of Job as well as the attempts by both of the K.'s to demystify the 'primitive liturgy' of their respective accusers, corporeal and textual. Not unlike Sophocles' tragic Oedipus, rhetorical response is the authors' the way of raising a reasonable doubt as to his occluded 'guilt' and his stratagem, formally literary and informally quasi-legal, is the universalization of uncertainty, the undecidability of the act of sacrifice and the demystification of the lie of the sacred nature of the selection process, an early twentieth century instance in metaphorical form of the archaic casting of lots. But all of this, ultimately, is to no avail. The dilemma of both Josef K. and Franz K. is identical to that of Job: the unjustly accused is permitted no type of defense but is mandated to voluntarily comply with the process of sacrificial preparation in atonement for the disorder that he has created. Meaning that not merely has he have no defense to offer, he does not even have the right to reply.

8.2 Nightmare/Profane

Although the accusation against him is never explained, Josef K. appears to intuit that it his moral character that is being subjected to some sort of inquisitorial proceeding. He is clearly of 'two minds' about the whole thing, or, he expresses himself in two inconsistent voices; the first 'mind', or persona, assumes innocence while the second implies an obscured guilt; the first voice is legalistic, the second voice is moralistic. The first:

> Thoughts about his case never left him now. Several times he had considered whether it would not be advisable to prepare a written document in his defence and lodge it with the court. His idea was to present a short account of his life and, in the case of each relatively

> important event, explain the reasons for his action, say whether he now thought that course of action should be condemned or approved, and give his reasons for this judgment. (Kafka, 1994: 89)

The second: 'Please don't ask for names but get rid of your failings. You can't defend yourself against this court; you have to acknowledge your guilt. Acknowledge your guilt at the first opportunity. Only then are you given the possibility of escape, only then' (Kafka, 1994: 85–86). Which sounds like the predicament of Job and the 'guilt' here appears to be an informally moral one, not a formally legal one. The guilt of the accused of the second persona is the presence of a truthfully guilty conscience but one that, crucially, remains unconscious: '"... its characteristic of this judicial system that a man is condemned not only when he's innocent but also in ignorance." "It's like that," said the woman, who had not understood him properly' (Kafka, 1994: 39). Now compare this brief exchange from the novel with this entry from Kafka's diary, September 21, 1917, concerning a recent visit from Felice Bauer.

> F. was here, travelled thirty hours to see me; I should have prevented her. As I see it, she is suffering the utmost misery and the guilt is essentially mine. I myself am unable to take hold of myself, am as helpless as I am unfeeling, think of the disturbance of a few of my comforts, and, as my only concession, condescend to act my part. *In single details she is wrong, wrong in defending what she calls—or what really are—her rights,* but taken altogether, she is an innocent person condemned to extreme torture; I am guilty of the wrong for which she is being tortured, and am in addition the torturer[20]—With her departure...and a headache (the last trace in me of my acting), the day ends. (Kafka, 1976: 385)

Note that Kafka and his ambivalence ('*what she calls—or what really are—her rights*') is simultaneously the bearer of the will-to-violence and the will-to-expiation. Franz K. has effectively doubled his internal Self of dual voices/minds in the perfect imitation of the scapegoat, whose defining characteristic is also ambivalence as both the cause of the ills of the community and the source of its future restoration following the ritualistic murder. Canetti also recognizes this unstable, and quite dangerous, admixture of latent violence and professed expiation, but he fails to call Franz K.'s 'thing' by its proper name, so I will: *grooming*, a term that we would not ordinarily identify with the largely self-negating Franz K. But therein lies the solution to the puzzle: metaphysical desire is at work: 'The image he had had of Felice...was unbearable to him, and he devoted himself to the Herculean task of changing it' (Canetti, 1974: 103). With mixed success, as is the case of most would-be controllers.

---

[20] Both torture and sadomasochism figure prominently in Kafka's sexual fantasy life (Friedlander, 2013: 88–93). In a letter to Milena Jesenska, he wrote: 'Yes, torturing is extremely important to me, I am preoccupied with nothing but being tortured or torturing...' (Kafka qtd.. Friedlander, 2013: 88). One of the recurrent moral failings of Kafka's protagonists is their withdrawal from scenes of extreme violence and the abandonment of the torture victim to his or her fate (Kafka, 1994: 92–93 and 111–112). In *The Trial*, this is most clearly on display in Chap. 5, 'The Whipper' and in Chap. 8, 'Block the Merchant; Dismissal of the Lawyer'; see also 'A Country Doctor'. Interestingly, in the latter chapter, the S-M victim Block is likened to a dog, which establishes a strict correlation between K and Block as doubles, K famously dying 'like a dog' at the conclusion of the novel. See below.

> In due course, what began as a desire to influence Felice [the 'chain' of his epistles] becomes a regular campaign, and it is clear what the real issue is. He wants to rid her of her bourgeois traits, so to speak, to move the furniture out of her, which, to his mind, embodies the most terrifying and odious aspect of bourgeois marriage. She is to learn how little significance should be attached to office work and family, as corollaries of selfishness; and he contrasts these with the humble activity of helping in a home for refugee children. But the parsonical overbearingness with which he harries her is something of which one would not have thought him capable. He asks her about every step that brings her closer to the [Jewish People's Home in Berlin], and then about every detail of her activity there, once she has been accepted. There is one letter in which he puts twenty questions to her about her work; his voracity increases, and he becomes insatiable for news about it. He spurs her on, criticizes her, collaborates in the writing of a talk that she is to give at the Home…He hunts for books for the children in the Home, even sends her from Prague several works edited for young people which he considers especially suitable, keeps referring to them in his letters with a meticulousness that is tantamount to pedantry, asks for photographs of Felice among the children, whom he wants to know by precise observation from a distance. He showers praises upon Felice when he is pleased with her, and this praise is so intense that she must have thought it a sign of love—and it comes whenever she follows his instructions. Gradually it does come to be a sort of subordination and obedience that he expects from her. The reification of her image, the changing of her character, without which he cannot conceive of living with her in the future, turns into control of her. (Canetti, 1974: 104–105)

Canetti admonishes us to 'keep in mind Kafka's deeper intent during the first period of this correspondence [with Felice]: he was establishing a connection, a channel of communication, between her efficiency and health and his own indecisiveness and weakness. Across the distance between Prague and Berlin he wishes to hold fast to her robustness' (Canetti, 1974: 12). On the other hand (or mind), 'As long as he was circling her from a distance he idolized and tormented her…The love that she turned upon him flowed through his heart like blood, so he declared in one letter, and he had no other blood' (Canetti, 1974: 31). But as the Sicilians say 'Blood washes blood,' and Franz K. is no stranger in truth to the lurking presence of *ressentiment* that haunts every occult corner of his unexpiated self, spiritualized resentment being but the obverse of metaphysical desire. This even comes through in their depleting discussions of marriage arrangements which, with a 'normal' person—meaning one who is not the bearer of a mimetic pathology—should be a source of rejuvenation; instead, 'One has the impression that Felice has now set them both a goal, and that she is trying to infuse into Kafka the power to reach a decision' (Canetti, 1974: 42). Even one such as Canetti, a world-weary cynic of the first order, is impressed by the mimetic spectacle of it all.

> His insight into his own sensibility and nature is pitiless and terrifying…he says that fear and indifference combined make up his deepest feeling toward human beings…This would explain the uniqueness of his work, in which emotions hardly appear, though literature otherwise swarms with them, volubly, and chaotically. If one thinks about it with a little courage, our world has indeed become one in which fear and indifference predominate. Expressing his own reality without indulgence, Kafka was the first to present the image of *this* world. (Canetti, 1974: 47–48)

And 'this' world is the world of *ressentiment* having achieved full self-awareness. Both Canetti and Saul Friedlander argue that Franz K.'s lack of the knowledge of the law ('ignorance') is his alienation from the morality of law, which is based upon natural reason's axiomatic logic concerning the equality of all human beings as rational and moral agents, so no surprise then that 'some of the major issues to which he kept returning' in his repetition-obsessed writings are 'a shameful absence of moral feelings and moral responsibility'. (Friedlander, 2013: 97–98)

> This [natural] Law demands that all men accept each other as equals regardless of social rank or position—something none of the characters in *The Trial* can do. Asserting his innocence to the unsympathetic Priest [the chapter entitled 'In the Cathedral' in Kafka, 1994: 154–173], Josef K. himself, by now totally confused by his plight, inadvertently states the Law he is guilty of violating: 'How can a human being ever be guilty? We are all human beings here after all, each the same as the other.' ['That is right,' said the priest, 'but everyone who is guilty always talks like that' Kafka, 1994: 164]. In Josef K.'s relationship with his colleagues, it is this Law that he most persistently violates. Assertion of the self over the others is the law by which bourgeois society thrives, but it also alienates us from other human beings, and this is why…Josef K. seems to be such an inadequate human being….at times stridently assertive, at others passively acquiescent, and always cold and emotionally detached from his surroundings. (Mellon, 1970: 298, 296)

Der Prozess as the moral process (-ing) of Josef K.'s guilty but repressed conscience ('ignorance') explains one of the most curious aspects of the narrative: his repetitive inability to refuse to obey the orders of the Court; 'K.'s only possibility of avoiding the frustration of liberating himself is to ignore the arrest altogether as he could well have. The simplest manner of escaping the Court would be to disregard it. This…however, is a fallacious argument, for being K. [morally guilty but in 'ignorance' of the fact] simply means "impossibility of ignoring the Court"' (Deinert, 1964: 196, n 6). Which means, of course, that to Josef K. the Court is a *skandalon*, something that constantly thwarts him but that he cannot help returning to—endlessly. Now, of course, is the time to avoid the pseudo-intellectual pitfall of an overly easy identification of author and character.

> Kafka might[21] have been plagued by guilt-consciousness; K. is not, that is the decisive difference [between them] …if *The Trial* is really a reflection of Kafka's situation, could it not be that it is precisely Kafka's own incomprehensible and paralyzing guilt consciousness which appears as the incomprehensible and destructive 'accusation' in *The Trial*? In other words, *The Trial* might express Kafka's secret belief that his own guilt feelings were just as unwarranted as K.'s arrest. Thus *The Trial* would be a subtle kind of self-liberation. (Deinert, 1964: 198, n 9)

The fact that so many of the law offices of the Court are situated in attics would seem to constitute a cheap metaphor of Freud's theory of the super-ego. But Kafka, whatever his other proclivities, such as repressed pedophilia (Friedlander, 2013), was never cheap. The recurrence of the images of attics, sealed rooms, small corridors, and claustrophobic but strictly segregated micro-spaces of all kinds (including innumerable bedrooms) points to an alternative, and more Girardian, reading.

---

[21] Given what we have already read of Franz K.'s diary entries concerning Felice, 'might' really would seem to be the operative word here.

8.3 The Endless Undecidable

A standard cautionary tale, or parable, of legal culture is the *noir* drama of the false accusation, or, in the alternative form, the wrongful conviction. In Chap. 7 I briefly discussed the *Lawyer-as-Agent-of-Legal-Order-as-Nightmare* as one of the tropes of the anti-Heroic Lawyer—briefly, owing to the paucity of examples of the sub-type but, fortunately, quite germane to my discussion of Kafka, as the only cinematic exemplars at hand within American film are Errol Morris' intensely Kafkaesque true-fiction documentary *The Thin Blue Line* (MGM, 2005)[22] and Orson Welles' obviously more self-consciously Kafkaesque adaptation of *The Trial* (2003). Both the novelistic and filmic incarnations of *The Trial* have become cultural signifiers of the private trauma of undergoing both false accusation and wrongful conviction. In terms of popular understanding, *The Trial* is a reflection of the laity's view that the judicial system is both inherently deficient and implacable in its operations once initiated, so that the moniker Kafkaesque is frequently applied to 'legal nightmares' of the sort detailed in *The Thin Blue Line* and, in a similarly nightmarish way, in Scott Turrow's *Presumed Innocent*.[23] In the latter work 'We obtain no public resolution, no "truth," in the filmic trial, because the jury never returns a verdict' just as Josef K.'s case never makes it to the highest Court.

> Rather, along with Rusty, we obtain a private resolution—we learn 'truth' in a way that leaves permanently unresolved the basic questions that the legal system is designed to answer ['Guilt' or 'Innocence']. Further, we who have knowledge from both inside and outside the courtroom can create a story that resolves the primary question about Rusty's innocence. But that question forces us to consider more deeply the question of another kind of guilt or innocence: the guilt or innocence of the legal system in creating or allowing the circumstances of Rusty's arrest and trial...Using one of the fundamental fictions upon which our legal system is based [the presumption of innocence], the film reveals that neither model [justice nor due process] deals successfully with the very real possibility that it can end in failure....Through the story of Rusty Sabich, we see the presumption of innocence release a genuinely innocent person from formal accusation while failing to liberate him from informal suspicion. (Corcos, 1998: 133, 131)

But formally denoting *Presumed Innocent* as Kafkaesque is more misleading than revealing, because the central narrative mechanism of *The Trial* is the indeterminism—meaning the eternal but inherent undecidability—of legal and/or moral 'guilt' which manifests as an uninterrupted and open-ended process of being judged.

> Rusty Sabich metamorphoses from one role to another [prosecuting attorney to criminally accused] so frighteningly, and so quickly, both in our minds and in the minds of his friends and associates, that we begin to understand how tenuous and incidental freedom is for anyone not caught by the legal system, and how easy are capture, arrest, trial, and possible conviction. (Corcos, 1998: 146)

But with this crucial distinction: in Rusty's case a final verdict is possible; it merely so happens that the case is thrown out because of a seemingly fortuitous technicality.

---

[22] See Chap. 6, above.

[23] See Chap. 7, above.

The entire point of Josef K.'s 'nightmare', in contrast, is that *Der Prozess* can never end because the decider of the issue (the Court) is never in possession of the moral certainty (or objective knowledge) required in order to arrive at a final (terminating) verdict. In a way, Welles, who should have known better,[24] falls for the too easy moral interpretation of the Kafkaesque tale by framing the film through the genre stereotype of the moralistic *parable* of 'legal nightmare'.

> For Welles the writer-director begins his film with a version of that parable ['Before the Law']—so that the ensuing drama seems like its enactment—then appears near the end to reprise the parable. He stands there, large, commanding, himself owning the screen where the parable unfolds like a movie. In Kafka, there is never any ultimate authority. But Welles cannot resist the egoistical gratification of awarding himself that role. (Thomson, 1996: 370)

David Thompson's juxtaposition of 'ultimate authority' with 'egoistical gratification' is an interesting one and reveals more than he intended, for the egoistical impulse that seeks gratification through the finality of unappealable authority[25] is nothing other than 'the spirit of revenge' itself, indicating that Josef K.'s plight will 'unfold' as nothing other than a series of (literally) tortuous exercises ostensibly intended to establish his guilt with certainty but operating in such a way that K. must always be re-called before the court. The nightmare is a form of eternal return that reflects the mimetic replicability of the scapegoat that itself mimics the eternal recurrence of the will-to-revenge that is the phenomenological core of sacrifice, for the very 'word "sacrifice"—sacri-fice—means making sacred, producing the sacred' which will always return to maintain the cycle that restores all things until the next cycle.

> Sacrifice takes place when sacred violence takes charge of the victim; it is the death that produces life, just as life produces, in the uninterrupted circle of eternal recurrence common to all the great theological views that are grafted upon sacrificial practices—those that do not acknowledge the demystifying effect of the Judaeo-Christian tradition. It is not by chance that Western philosophy begins, and up to a certain point ends, in the "intuition" of the Eternal Recurrence that the pre-Socratics and Nietzsche hold in common. This is the sacrificial intuition *par excellence.* (Girard et al., 2003: 226)

The same thing was intuited by fellow Nietzsche aficionado Leo Strauss but with the residual element of *ressentiment* predictably elided: 'The eternal return is discovered in the search for a strong and courage-producing myth.…It is asserted convulsively by Nietzsche only because he had to wean us and himself from millennia-old pampering (softening) due to belief in creation and providence' (Leo Strauss qtd. Ranieri, 2008: 164). God may be dead but, fortunately, judgment and revenge remain.

[24] Apparently, Welles did not want to accept Dino De Laurentis' assignment to film *The Trial*; his preference was for *The Castle*.

[25] 'Unappealable' meaning not subject to future review.

8.3.1 Justice-as-Organism

In much of what follows I will be engaging in a running critique of a central work of Kafka criticism, Deleuze and Guattari's *Kafka: Toward a Minor Literature*, wherein we find this gem: 'The law is written in a porno book' (Deleuze & Guattari, 1986: 49). In a sense, this sentence summarizes the entirety of the Deleuzian reading of Kafka, which is centered upon the description of the 'law books' of the examining magistrate.

> They were old, well-worn books; one cover had almost disintegrated in the middle, the sections hung together by the threads. 'How dirty everything is here,' said K., shaking his head, and before he could reach for the books the woman wiped the dust off with her apron, superficially at least. K. opened the top book, to reveal an indecent picture. A man and a woman were sitting naked on a sofa; the artist's vulgar intention was clear enough, but his incompetence was so great that in fact all that could be seen was a man and a woman projecting their gross physique out of the picture, sitting rigidly upright and, because of false perspective, finding the greatest difficulty in turning towards each other. K. looked no further but merely opened the second book at the title page. It was a novel called *The Torments Grete Had to Suffer from Her Husband Hans*. 'So these are the law books studied here,' said K. 'It's by people like this I'm supposed to be judged'. (Kafka, 1994: 41)

The single greatest puzzle of *The Trial* is also its most Kafkaesque feature is: *Why exactly* does Josef K. continually *return* to the Court especially as it seems to possess no legitimate authority outside of the robotic machinations of its tin-pot officers? Or, to put it in more Girardian terms, why is it that the Court becomes the *skandalon* for Josef K.?[26] For Deleuze and Guattari, the answer lies with a pun: 'Trial' in German is *Der Process,* so that literally, the 'whole of this operation is to be called a Process, one that is precisely interminable' (Deleuze & Guattari, 1986: 48). Picking up on the machinic undertones of the text's master-sign, Deleuze and Guattari deploy Kafka's novel as a literary exemplification before the fact of their revolutionary pluralistic notion of Being-as-multiplicity, or 'desire machines'.

> *Where one believed that there was law, there is in fact desire and desire alone.* Justice is desire and not law. Everyone in fact is a functionary of justice—not only the spectators, not only the priest and the painter, but also the equivocal young women and the perverse little girls who take up so much space in *The Trial*…It is not a stable will but a moving desire… 'The court asks nothing of you. It receives you when you come and it releases you when you go' (Kafka, 1994: 173)…Repression doesn't belong to justice unless it is also desire itself—desire in the one who is repressed as well as in the one who represses. (Deleuze & Guattari, 1986: 49)

In the uncanny case of Josef K. law is reconstituted as a form of 'anti-desire' signifying the occluded nature of law as a type of a desire machine, or a Deleuzian

[26] Of course, if I were to adopt an exclusively biogeographical approach, the answer would be simple and banal: it is because the 'Court' is the self-parodying *Gerichtshof* assembled by Franz K.'s own family and that of his would-be in-laws. There is no way that he could not answer, or 'appear before' them, and he would have every reason to resist the accusations of, shall we say, 'moral turpitude' at every occasion. The situation of the wholly literary Josef K., however, is considerably more complex and compelling.

form of an organism, the hierarchy-saturated producer of overdetermined meanings ('Thou shalt not'), devoid of the 'smooth spaces' of the under-determination of meaning ('I will') which is the genuinely free (anarchic) play of the pure *eros*, the anti-thesis of a Freudian rule governed desire, a kind of *delirium* that is absolute and inexhaustible and, for both reasons, ultimately indescribable.[27] In *The Trial*, the law is

> examined in terms of its connection to the parties that the different commentators belong to. But politically, the important things are always taking place elsewhere, in the hallways of the congress, behind-the-scenes of the meeting, where people confront the real, immanent problems of desire and of power—the real problem of justice. (Deleuze & Guattari, 1986: 50)

And as if by an occult agreement, Kafka provides us with this marvelously Deleuzian interpretation of the Court. Or is it the other way round?

> The hierarchical structure of the court was endless and beyond the comprehension even of the initiated. Court proceedings were in general kept secret from the minor officials, so they could hardly ever follow later developments in the matters they were dealing with; legal business simply appeared in their orbit and they did not know where it had come from, then it passed on, and they were not told where it was going...Even if it were possible to rectify certain details—but that was just a senseless delusion—the best one could hope for would be to achieve something for the benefit of future cases, but that would be at the expense of doing oneself immeasurable harm through attracting the particular attention of a bureaucracy which was always vengeful. Just never attract attention! One had to keep quiet, even when this went against the grain! And try to see that this great legal organism was always in a state of equilibrium, so to speak, and that anyone who independently made an alteration in his own area would be cutting the ground from under his feet and could come crashing down, while the great organism itself compensated for the slight disturbance by easily producing a replacement at another point—everything after all was connected—and remained unchanged, assuming it did not become (this was probable) even more secretive, even more observant, even more malevolent. (Kafka, 1994: 93–95)

In summation: 'law as machine can never be the object of desire precisely because it is anti-erotic; however, justice can form a proper object of desire precisely because, as we have already seen in multiple instances, an underdefined and free-floating justice is frequently placed in an antagonistic relationship to the law which, in the popular culture of the Law Film and the Law Novel is ordinarily reduced to a mechanical formalism—which, in the case of Josef K, has proliferated to the nightmarish dimensions of 'out of control''. Deleuze and Guattari explain it this way: 'If justice doesn't let itself be represented, that is because it is desire' (Deleuze & Guattari, 1986: 50). Translating law-as-organism in terms of law-and-literature, I would say that formalism in opposition to 'just outcome' creates a domain of violence that invokes the erotic-libidinal 'drama' of resistance, struggle and combat. Which means that it has something to do with sex.

---

[27] To make an incredibly long, complex, and difficult story as short, simple, and easy as possible: the 'big idea' of Deleuze and Guattari was to provide a revolutionary alternative to the Frankfurt School's ultimately failed attempt to convert psycho-analysis to the case of social revolution (Herbert Marcuse et al.), by substituting a Nietzschean will-to-power (Dionysus) for the Freudian unconscious (Moses): the transcendental vanguard replaced with an anarchy of pure immanence.

8.3.2 *Justice-as-Desire*

Franz K. repeatedly asserts in an almost obsessive compulsive manner the radical liminality of the 'secret' court that proliferates endlessly, nullifying the objective demarcation between public and private law and legal agency: 'K. examined the court usher's civilian jacket which displayed, as sole indication of official rank, two gilt buttons, along with several ordinary ones, gilt buttons which seemed to have been detached from an old military greatcoat' (Kafka, 1994: 48). The 'fake' or 'private' nature of the Court—the parodic reworking of the *Gerichtshof* at the Askanische Hof where the bourgeois tragedy of Felice Bauer was played out—is a perfect satirical device for representing nepotism and judicial corruption as integral to a 'shadow' legal system emanating directly from a mimetic universe of second-rate fakery: 'K. was now met by a guard, recognizable as such mainly by his sabre, whose scabbard, to judge by its colour, was made of aluminium' (Kafka, 1994: 51). The 'Court' seems to constitute a parallel, or even a private body that is concerned with moral rather than legal formal judgment. Which is exactly how the Kafka and the Bauer families were carrying on.

> The defence was in fact not really sanctioned by the law but merely tolerated, and even whether toleration could be read into the relevant clause of the law was a matter of dispute. So, strictly speaking, there were no advocates recognized as such by the court; all those who appeared before this court as advocates were basically only back-street lawyers...But nevertheless the most important thing was the advocate's personal connections, this was where the main value of defence counsel lay...True value was to be found only in respectable personal connections, and indeed with higher officials—by which he [the Advocate] meant only higher officials of the lower grade...No, K. himself had seen how officials, and among them really high ones, came of their own volition, willingly gave information which was unambiguous or at least easily interpreted, discussed the next stage in the proceedings, indeed even in some individual cases allowed themselves to be won over and gladly accepted the outsider's opinion. (Kafka, 1994: 91–93)

Two conclusions can be drawn: (a) the private nature of the agency of the Court symbolizes its concern with the moral conscience of the accused who appear before it and; (b) the Court's apparent prurience is a reflection of its focus upon sexual desire, which is why K.'s (semi-) public denunciation of the 'corrupt' nature of the Court operates as an ironic commentary upon the private/moral/sexual nature of K.'s actual 'guilt'.

> There is no doubt that behind all the utterances of this court, and therefore my arrest and today's examination, there stands a great organization. An organization which not only employs corrupt warders and fatuous supervisors and examining magistrates...but also supports a judiciary of the highest rank with its inevitable vast retinue of servants, secretaries, police officers and other assistants, perhaps even executioners—I don't shrink from the word. And the purpose of this great organization, gentlemen? To arrest innocent persons and start proceedings against them which are pointless and mostly, as in my case, inconclusive. When the whole organization is as pointless as this, how can gross corruption among the officials be avoided? (Kafka, 1994: 36)

On the one hand, the Court really does seem to operate as a kind of extortion racket, with the famous 'arrest scene' at the beginning of the novel assuming the form of an implied threat that immediately precedes a shake-down.

> But the warder merely said in an indifferent manner: 'You'll soon come up against it.' Franz intervened and said: 'See, Willem, he admits he doesn't know the law and says at the same time he's innocent.' 'You're quite right, but you can't make him understand anything,' said the other. (Kafka, 1994: 5)

Notice how the gangster-like banter of the two warders effectively doubles as an ironic commentary on Josef K.'s bad conscience and failure to perceive naturalist moral law, for as the issue of the examining magistrate's 'law books' (Kafka, 1994: 41) signifies, the truth of Josef K.'s guilt, and the main object of concern with the Court to which he is summoned, appears to be located within his sexual desires. This underscores the double-bind nature of the Court and its proceedings: as both Josef K.'s and Franz K.'s sexuality (-ies) is/are objectively deviant,[28] any declaration of innocence doubles as an implied confession of guilt. The continual struggle between Josef K.'s sexual drives and his highly imperfect self-awareness is re-enacted through stage-managed acts of externalized doubling as a competition between eros (sex) and sophia (wisdom): whenever he approaches some sort of understanding with the law or the courts, Josef K. is immediately 'seduced' by a woman (Kafka, 1994: 41–47). The exemplary female here is Leni, the Advocate's nurse-maid but really a succubus,[29] who disrupts K.'s possibly salvific meeting with his lawyer, his uncle, and, most importantly, the 'director of the court offices'. Leni's stratagems start off with a bang: "I threw a plate against the wall to bring you out [of the conference]". In his embarrassment K. said: "I was thinking of you too." "All the better,' said the nurse. Come on" (Kafka, 1994: 84). They become more intimate.

> 'Has [your girlfriend] any physical defect?' 'A physical defect?' K. asked. 'Yes,' said Leni. 'You see, I have a little one—look.' She stretched the middle and ring fingers of her right hand apart and revealed a connecting membrane of skin reaching nearly to the topmost joints of the stubby fingers. In the darkness K. did not immediately realize what she was trying to show him, so she moved his hand there to feel it. 'What a freak of nature!' said K, and he added when he had examined the whole hand: 'What a pretty claw!'. (Kafka, 1994: 85)

And with her bestowal of an unworldly, if not supernatural, gesture of approval, Leni's accursed work is done.

> 'Boy!' he [K.'s Uncle] cried. 'How could you do it? You've done a terrible injury to your cause which was going well. You sneak off with a filthy little creature who is obviously the advocate's mistress, and you stay away for hours. You don't even make an excuse, you hide nothing, no, you're quite open, you run to her and you stay with her. And in the meantime there we are sitting together, your uncle who is doing his best for you, the advocate who must be won over to your side, and above all the director, this important man who has virtual control of your case at its present stage. We were going to discuss how you can best be helped...Instead of that, you stay away...We sat there minute after minute without a word, listening to see if you would come at last. All in vain'. (Kafka, 1994: 88–89)

---

[28] See Chap. 3, 'Love, Sex and Fantasies' in Friedlander, 2013: 66–88 for Kafka's 'transgressive' sexuality: homoeroticism and presumably repressed paedophilia.

[29] See below.

But then as the nameless Priest adequately sums up near the end of the otherwise endless process, "You look for too much outside help," said the priest disapprovingly, "and especially from women. Don't you see it is not true help?" (Kafka, 1994: 164). Not truly helpful for being all too revealing.

8.3.3 Justice-as-Desire = Law-as-Undecidable

As two seminal 'post-modernists', both Deleuze and Guattari advance a radically pre-representational theory of language. Throughout, *The Trial* presents 'the law as pure and empty form without content, the object of which remains unknowable: thus, the law can be expressed only through a sentence, and the sentence can only be learned through a punishment. No one knows the law's interior' (Deleuze & Guattari, 1986: 43). This is nicely conveyed by Franz K. by having his fictitious double 'examine' the portrait of the (original) examining magistrate hanging in the Advocate's apartment.

> He [K.] was especially struck by a large picture which hung to the right of the door. He leaned forward to see it better. It showed a man in the robes of a judge. He was sitting on a high throne-like chair whose gilding stood out prominently in the picture. The unusual thing about it was that this judge was not sitting in tranquil dignity but was pressing his left arm hard against the back and side of the chair and had his right arm completely free and just held the other arm of the chair with this hand as if his intention was to spring up at the next moment with a violent and perhaps outraged gesture to utter something decisive or even pronounce judgment. The defendant had to be imagined at the foot of the steps, whose upper ones, covered in yellow carpet, were visible in the picture. 'Perhaps that is my judge,' said K., and he pointed his finger at the picture. (Kafka, 1994: 85)

The pre-representational nature of language renders the meaning of the law perpetually indeterminate which Josef K. subjectively experiences in terms of a spatial distance from the senior levels of the Court as the center of decision-making and, therefore, the assignment of the correct interpretation of the law that equals truth; "'Again, only an examining magistrate,' said K. in disappointment, 'the top officials keep out of sight. But he's sitting in a judge's chair.' 'That's just make-believe,' said Leni, bending her face over K.'s hand, 'actually he's sitting on a kitchen chair with an old horse-blanket thrown over it'" (Kafka, 1994: 85). However, as Deleuze and Guattari point out, law is never a statement of Truth governed by

> the demands of a hidden transcendence; it is almost the exact opposite: it is the statement, the enunciation, that constructs the law in the name of an immanent power of the one who announces it—the law is confused with that which the guardian utters, and the writings precede the law, rather than being the necessary and derived expression of it. (Deleuze & Guattari, 1986: 45)

In a certain way this is not far from the anti-formalism of the legal realists such as Felix Cohen and his notion of law as 'Transcendental Nonsense'.[30]

---

[30] See Chap. 6, above.

> Intellectual clarity requires that we carefully distinguish between the two problems of (1) objective description, and (2) critical judgment, which classical jurisprudence lumps under the same phrase. Such a distinction realistic jurisprudence offers with the double-barrelled thesis: (1) that every legal rule or concept is simply a function of judicial decision to which all questions of value are irrelevant, and (2) that the problem of the judge is not whether a legal rule or concept actually exists but whether it *ought* to exist. (Cohen, 1960: 68)

Which raises the problem of the self-validation, or the grounding of legal reasoning. Since

> deduction necessarily proceeded from arbitrarily selected postulates, then every judge had to select his first premise, or rule of the case, in a way that was logically wholly indeterminate and therefore arbitrary...Judicial decisions, then, had to be the result of some unacknowledged inductive process, which could only mean the subjective way that the judge evaluated the probable social results of his decision. (Purcell, 1973: 90)

The result of this ineradicable indeterminacy is that legal reason fragments into two irreconcilable paradigms: positivism, which carries within it the threat of reducing law to the arbitrary (meaning incontestable) will-of-the-Sovereign, and naturalism, which for contemporary post-theistic jurists is fatally marred by the absence of the self-grounded transcendence of either natural reason or natural justice ('God is dead'). However, positivism and naturalism do prove to be unified sub rosa through their mutual acceptance of the principle of necessity, either secular (sovereignty) or transcendental (metaphysics), so that both juridical world-views threaten to reduce law in the final instance to the wholly arbitrary and unpredictable exercise of power: God = the Father = Truth. This, of course, raises the apocalyptic specter of law as being nothing more than the perpetration of a certain kind of violence by clandestine means. Canetti clearly picks up on law's unspeakable twinning with both power and violence, each a sign of an onto-political arbitrariness, in his account of the *Gerichtshof*: when 'describing Kafka's relationship with Felice', it is 'appropriate to show how filled his mind was with the very phenomenon that has become most pressing and terrible, above all others, in our epoch. Of all writers, Kafka is the greatest expert on power. He experienced it in all its aspects, and he gave shape to this experience' (Canetti, 1974: 80). And, as proof of this, Canetti offers the epistolary records Kafka himself provides that trace the nature of his pseudo-juridical relationship with Felice, and which unintentionally provide incontrovertible of his moral and mimetic guilt.

> In a letter to Felice he coins the appalling phrase 'the terror of standing upright'....Standing upright signifies the power of man over beast; but precisely in this most obvious attitude man is exposed, visible, vulnerable. For this power is also guilt, and only on the ground, lying among the animals, can one see the stars, which free one from this terrifying power of man. (Canetti, 1974: 88)

Simply put, Justice-as-Desire equates with the will-to-violence because the latter is a sub-set of metaphysical desire wherein violence, even when ritualistically expressed as combat, constitutes proof of existence, being hard-won in the face of an annihilating judgment. Josef K.'s will-to-violence is expressed as resistance to the law as a way to 'win' from it the recognition of his being; but as a metaphysical desire mediated through the rituals of combat his resistance is not restricted just to the Court, but operates in a free-floating manner throughout *The Trial*; 'From the beginning, Kafka sided with the humiliated…what issues from above and spreads among the ordinary people is humiliation at the hands of the superiors' (Canetti, 1974: 83). This is beautifully demonstrated in a fragment excised from the published version of the novel, the 'Struggle with the vice president' of the bank (Kafka, 1998: 254–258).

> The vice president must not be left with the impression that K. had been disposed of; he musn't be allowed to sit quietly in his office under that impression, he had to be disturbed, he had to be made aware as often as possible that K. was alive, and that, like all living things, he might one day show surprising new capabilities, no matter how harmless he appeared at the moment. (Kafka, 1998: 256)

But unfortunately for Josef K. the logical corollary to his own will-to-combat-as-proof-of-life is the Court-as-Justice-as-Organism, that thing whose summons he is always weirdly compelled to respond to, that is itself the signifier of the occluded essence of the law which is an unpredictable and undecipherable will to manufacture endlessly new interpretations that eternalize guilt. This is established in magnificently indeterminate Kafkaesque fashion in Josef K.'s discussion of the unfinished portrait of an anonymous (naturally) judge of the Court by the 'official' painter of the Court, Titorelli, a portrait of a judicial officer that uncannily doubles as a semi-occluded representation of the Nike, the goddess of victory—or vengeance.

> 'It's a portrait. Good piece of work but not quite finished yet.' This was a fortunate chance for K.; it presented him with an opportunity to speak about the court, for it was obviously a portrait of a judge. It was also strikingly familiar to the picture in the advocate's study. This was clearly a different judge [from the examining magistrate], a stout man with a bushy black beard far up his cheeks on both sides; also, the other picture was in oils, this was sketched lightly and indistinctly in pastel colours. But everything else was similar; here too the judge was in the act of rising in a menacing way from his chair, whose arms he was gripping. 'That's a judge of course,' K. had almost blurted out, but he restrained himself for a moment and went up to the picture as if he wanted to study the details. He was not able to make out a large figure in the middle behind the back of the chair and asked the painter about it. 'That still needs a bit of work,' answered the painter and he took a pastel from a side-table and sketched with it round the edges of the figure, but K. found it no clearer. 'It's Justice,' said the painter at last. 'Ah, now I recognize it,' said K., 'here's the bandage [sic] over the eyes and these are the scales. But aren't these wings on the ankles and isn't the figure running?' 'Yes,' said the painter, 'I was commissioned to paint it like that. Actually it is Justice and the goddess of Victory in one.' 'That's hardly a good combination,' said K. with a smile. 'Justice has to be motionless or the scales will waver and there's no possibility of a correct judgment.' 'I'm only following the instructions of the person who commissioned me,' said the painter. 'Yes, of course,' said K., who had not wished to cause offence with his remark. 'You have painted the figure exactly as it's really situated on the chair?' 'No,' said the painter, 'I've seen neither the figure nor the chair, all that's invention. I was simply told what I had to paint.' 'What?' asked K., deliberately pretending not to understand the painter. 'But it is a judge and he is sitting on a judge's chair.' 'Yes,' said the painter, 'but it's not a senior judge and he has never sat on an official chair like that.'…The sight of the picture seemed to have stimulated a desire to work; [Titorelli] rolled up his sleeves and selected some pastels, and K. watched as under the moving tips of the pastels a reddish shadow took shape by the judge's head and tapered off in rays toward the edge of the picture. Gradually this play of shadow surrounded the head like an embellishment or a high mark of distinction. But around the figure of Justice everything stayed bright, apart from a slight tinting; in this brightness the

figure seemed to be positively thrusting forward, it was scarcely reminiscent of the goddess of Justice any more, nor of the goddess of Victory either; now it looked exactly like the goddess of the Hunt. (Kafka, 1994: 114–115)

Without pushing it too hard, I would suggest that this passage directly touches upon one of the central issues of James Dickey's *Deliverance*: as the identities of the enemies/victims are inherently ambiguous pursuant to pre-representational language, then it is the pre-representational ritualistic act of hunting/killing that itself provides the grounds of identity and, therefore, of Being (Dickey, 1970).[31] 'It was just here one could see the disadvantage inherent in a judicial organization which at its very beginnings created a secret court. Contact between officials and the public at large was non-existent...' (Kafka, 1994: 93). But this is Josef K. speaking in his highly selective and self-serving voice as a rationalist innocent, which he is not, truly. Or perhaps, more accurately, in the voice of the scapegoat, who is beginning to recognize exactly what it is that is confronting him and with which he, like Job, must engage in repeated metaphysical combat: the Court resembles nothing so much as a roaming, nomadic crowd that repetitively occupies liminal spaces (attics, basements, abandoned apartments, or closets) meaning that Deleuze and Guattari's autistic organismic producer of overdeterministic meanings is, indeed, a machine, but of an entirely different kind of desire: it is the machine, or mechanism, of ritualistic sacrifice, whose *telos* is the manufacture of sacrificial victims, the mass production of scapegoats.

Once the higher powers have chosen their victim, they will follow his every step on the road to perdition...The ominous surveillance usually takes place in the midst of a larger crowd either staring at or surrounding the main character, never in a friendly way. The ever-present 'other's gaze,' is a repeated fixture in Kafka's texts...Somehow, 'the others' are always there in Kafka's texts. 'LÉnfer, cést les autres'—Hell is other people—Sartre has one of his characters say in *Huis-Clos*. Kafka had preceded him by twenty years. (Friedlander, 2013: 115, 116)

And the fact that '*the others are always there*' is the vital clue that we need to prove that both Josef K. and Franz K. are scapegoats, entrapped within an interminable drama that is decidedly anti-postmodernist and quintessentially Girardian.

8.4 Sacrificial/Sacred/Sacralizing

An inherently liminal text, the forum of the perpetual 'sliding' of meanings and identities centered upon the literary representation of liminal or border spaces (attics, doorways, hallways, staircases, corridors, basements, closets), *The Trial* neatly doubles as a religious allegory, one of the great scholars of Jewish mysticism, Gershom Scholem, opining that 'divine judgment was the one and only theme in all of Kafka's writings' (Leavitt, 2007: 117), an issue that I will discuss in greater detail below. Although a number of literary scholars have attempted to situate Kafka directly within the

[31] See Chap. 3, above.

esoteric tradition of Jewish mysticism (Leavitt, 2007),[32] Franz K. was too much of a modernist and a skeptic to be interested in the Qabbalah in the naïve manner. Both Canetti and Friedlander are critical of the theory of Kafka-as-Gnostic; his primary concern was with Yiddish folklore motifs as a 'ready-made' form of metaphysical symbolism deployed for purely literary effect; it is mere artistic convenience that 'the notion of an evil demiurge fits Kafka's view of the human predicament' (Friedlander, 2013: 127). What is more convincing is that he used Jewish occultism as a source of aesthetic tropes but also as an almost subliminal invocation of the sacrificial mechanism as theorized by Girard and signified by one of the novel's most striking characteristics: the periodic but unpredictable interfacing with the unbearably profane central actors with a series of supernatural entities disguised in the camouflage of the secular or the profane.[33] And one of the most subversive techniques of the novel is Kafka's almost surreal deployment and description of spaces that are astonishingly liminal; the pseudo-public offices of the Court inter-phase with, and merge imperceptibly into, private domains. This signifies both esoteric knowledge (suggestive of that of the out-of-view decisions taking place behind the closed doors of other rooms) as well as the more free-floating paranormal notion of parallel realities.

> It was a long passageway with crudely made doors leading to various compartments in the attic. Although there was no direct source of daylight the place was not entirely dark, for some of the compartments had on the corridor side instead of solid wooden walls wooden grilles which reached up to the ceiling and through which some light penetrated and through which also some official could be seen writing at desks or standing by the grille and watching people in the corridor through the gaps. (Kafka, 1994: 49–50)

The Trial is full of allusions to rank (low versus high officials in a parody of celestial hierarchies) and esoteric knowledge (which doubles as satire of 'professional language'), which signify a Qabbalistic system of magical power and authority.[34] Titorelli the painter clearly hints at this.

> I inherited this connection. My father before me was painter to the court. It's a post always handed down by inheritance. New people can't be employed. You see, there are so many complicated and above all secret regulations about how the different grades of officials are to be painted that they just can't be known outside certain families. For example, there in the drawer I've got my father's notes, which I never show to anybody. But only the person familiar with these is qualified to paint judges. And even if I were to lose them, I would still retain in my head so many rules inaccessible to others that no one could dispute my position. After all, every judge wants to be painted just like the great old judges were painted, and I'm the only one who can do that. (Kafka, 1994: 119)

[32] The issue of Kafka's involvement in esotericism is highly contentious, but there seems to be a tacit consensus that he was passionate about Yiddish theatre and folklore, causing him to become a serious student of Jewish folk beliefs and the Yiddish language, along with both classical and modern Hebrew (Leavitt, 2007: 109–114).

[33] See below.

[34] Compare the secular Friedlander on this point: 'A complex hierarchy of higher and lower officials seem to be set in motion by the force at the center of the mysterious spiderweb, down to the emissaries who watch the victim at each turn of the twisted path leading to his downfall'—or immolating sacrifice (Friedlander, 2013: 114).

Many of the characters affiliated with the Court have been given attributes of minor supernatural beings; Titorelli's 'girls' are clearly meant to suggest as spirits, or imps (Kafka, 1994: 111–129).

> 'Does a painter called Titorelli live here?' The girl, hardly thirteen years old and a bit of a hunchback, nudged him with her elbow and looked up at him with her head on one side. Neither youth nor physical deformity had saved her from utter depravity. She did not even smile but looked at K. gravely with a sharp intelligence. (Kafka, 1994: 111)

There is also the recurrent motif of the nocturnal visitation, the non-arrest/arrest at the beginning more than a little suggestive of an alien intrusion, Titorelli's studio, the locus of the production of the images or representations of the judges, appearing to serve as the hub of interfaces between the material and spiritual orders.

> Now K. saw the little door in the wall for the first time. 'Of course this place is far too small for a studio,' said the painter as if he wanted to forestall K.'s criticism. 'I had to arrange things as best I could. The bed in front of the door [that leads to the Court] is of course in a very bad position. To give you an example: the judge I'm painting just now always comes in through that door by the bed; I've given him a key to the door too so that he can wait for me in the studio if I'm not at home. But he usually comes early in the morning when I'm still asleep. Of course I'm dragged out of even the deepest sleep when the door is opened here next to the beds'. (Kafka, 1994: 112)

The occult imagery is most pronounced in K.'s encounter with the 'director of the court offices' in yet another bedroom, this time the Advocate's.

> 'I am at this moment enjoying a visit from a dear friend.' And [Dr. Huld] pointed to a dark corner of the room. 'Where is he?' asked K. almost rudely in the first shock of surprise. He looked around the room uncertainly. The light from the tiny candle fell far short of the opposite wall. And something began to stir there in the corner. By the light of the candle which the uncle was now holding on high an elderly gentleman became visible, sitting there at a small table. He could not have been breathing, to be unnoticed for so long. Now he stood up ceremoniously, obviously not at all pleased that attention had been drawn to him. It was as if he wanted to fend off with his hands, which he moved like abbreviated wings, all introductions and greetings, as if he had no wish to disturb the others in any way by his presence, and asked only to be returned to the darkness where his presence might be forgotten. But that could not be granted now. 'You took us by surprise, you see,' said the advocate by way of explanation, encouraging the gentleman with a gesture to come nearer, and he this he did, slowly and looking around hesitantly, yet with a certain dignity. (Kafka, 1994: 82)

The esoteric backdrop, whatever Kafka's personal religious views notwithstanding, do much to buttress my central thesis that *Der Prozess*, along with much of the author's other work, are paradoxical and self-contradictory accounts of the sacrificial mechanism told from the perspective of the scapegoat, a perspective markedly devoid of self-understanding.

> 'Our authorities, as far as I know them, and I know only the lowest grades, do not go in search of guilt in the population but are, as it says in the law, drawn to guilt and must send us warders out. That is the law. Where could there be a mistake in that?' 'This law is unknown to me,' said K. 'All the worse for you,' said the warder. (Kafka, 1994: 5)

The transcendental dilemma of both law and the scapegoat is the radical undecidability of the law itself, which can be encapsulated by the divide between foundational positivism (Sovereign) and naturalism (God); which means that the signature trademark of the Kafkaesque scapegoat is a (self-subverting) conviction of his or her real innocence. The occluded and liminal features of the process signify private justice/natural law as the 'dangerous supplement' to public justice/positivism—just as the *Gerichtshof* was an absurd simulacrum of the eternally occluded Courthouse—and it is this permanent absence of certainty, the ability to determine with finality, that ultimately dooms Josef K. The source or cause of his guilt is immaterial; what is material is the absolute 'givenness' of his guilt, the sign of his identity, or truth, as scapegoat. It is of the greatest resemblance that in Kafka's other great work written 'In the Time of Felice' (1912–1914), *The Metamorphosis*, Gregor Samsa is described as an *ungeheures Ungeziefer*, or a 'monstrous vermin'; '*Ungeziefer* derives (as Kafka probably knew) from the late Middle High German word originally meaning "the unclean animal not suited for sacrifice"' (Stanley Corngold qtd. Friedlander, 2013: 35), which is why Gregor is merely cast into exile by being locked up in his room, a form of internal exile. But Josef K.'s dilemma, from a juridical perspective, is far more profound (and worked out) than that of Samsa, because Josef K.'s 'being' as scapegoat, like the law itself, remains eternally undecided, a 'mystery', which mirrors perfectly the rhetorical oscillations between positivism and naturalism. Either the scapegoat is guilty (i.e., he/she really is the scapegoat) for no reason other than it has been decided that he/she is the scapegoat, which is positivism, or the identity of the scapegoat is established on the basis of a metaphysical truth which can neither be expressed nor explained by natural reason; instead, the very best that we can do is to 'read the signs' correctly and invoke power. And, according to Girard, it is the 'reading' of these signs that is the basis of, literally, everything; as 'the symbolic order is born of the scapegoat mechanism, that is of a collective violence that is always at the mercy of reciprocal violence' (Girard, 1978: 111) it is unfortunately the case for scapegoats everywhere that 'the metamorphosis [!] of a community into a blind and demented mob constitutes the necessary precondition of all mythical and ritual creation' (Girard, 1978: 103). Girard re-conceptualizes the sacrificial machinery, or *process*, that is the core of primitive religion as the 'circuit-breaker' that pre-empts the escalation of violence through retributive acts of vengeance; the 'fundamental truth about violence' is that 'if left unappeased, violence will accumulate until it overflows its confines and floods the surrounding area. The role of sacrifice is to stem this rising tide of indiscriminate substitutions and redirect violence into "proper" channels' (Girard, 1977: 10). On this everything depends because hominids can only physically survive the process of cultural evolution if they invent an adequate means for dealing with revenge, the generic term for all-consuming reciprocal violence.[35]

> Why does the spirit of revenge, wherever it breaks out, constitute such an intolerable menace? Perhaps because the only satisfactory revenge for spilt blood is spilling the blood of the killer; and in the blood feud there is no clear distinction between the act for which the killer is being punished and the punishment itself. Vengeance professes to be an act of reprisal, and every

[35] See Chap. 1, above.

> reprisal calls for another reprisal. The time crime to which the act of vengeance addresses itself is almost never an unprecedented offense; in almost every case it has been committed in revenge for some prior crime. (Girard, 1977: 15)

And the problem of reciprocal and escalatory violence not only governs the process of social formation, it also controls the archaic notion of time which is cyclical, for it is the contaminating possession and transformative exorcism of the community of violence that constitutes the most primal experience of eternal return.

> Vengeance, then, is an interminable, infinitely repetitive process. Every time it turns up in some part of the community, it threatens to involve the whole social body. There is the risk that the act of vengeance will initiate a chain reaction whose consequences will quickly prove fatal to any society of modest size. The multiplication of reprisals instantaneously puts the very existence of a society in jeopardy, and that is why is universally proscribed. (Girard, 1977: 14–15)

For pre-modern cultures Time is circular because the foundation of social order is a series of endlessly repetitive events: the community is peaceful; mimetic rivalry intensifies; the community erupts into reciprocal violence; the designated god appears to name the one responsible for the mimetic violence; the scapegoat is murdered; the community is peaceful—ad infinitum (or, as Kurt Vonnegut would say, 'And so it goes'). Girard holds that when 'we minimize the dangers implicit in vengeance we risk losing sight of the true function of sacrifice' (Girard, 1977: 18) which is the sum total of all ritualistic procedures required to effect the mimetic transference of reciprocal-collective violence toward a sacrificial substitute, the emissary victim, who is symbolically reconstituted as the source of all hatred and vengeance, the generic scapegoat. So the cyclical nature of archaic time, which lies under the aegis of the cultural construction of emissary victimage, is a double one: the eruption of interpersonal violence (symbolized by the scapegoat) and the corresponding enactment of ritualistic sacrifice (also symbolized by the scapegoat). The Hellenes, especially the pre-Socratic philosophers, understood all of this perfectly. Girard is surely right to offer generative violence as the key to the meaning of the haunting and only direct quotation that we have from Anaximander: 'Where things are born, there too they must perish; for each in turn metes out punishment and expiation for its wickedness, each in the allotted time' (Girard, 1977: 308). And 'Where things are born' denotes the plurality of ritually inscribed sacralized spaces, the designated locales and liturgical calendrical 'allotted time' wherein the sacrificial act of generative violence was to take place, which is where they 'perish'.

> There is reason to believe that these symbolic sites of unification gave birth to all religious forms; it was there that the various cults were established, spatial relationships fixed, the clock of history set in motion, and the beginnings of a social life plotted out...There everything begins; from there everything emanates; there everything returns when discord breaks out. (Girard, 1977: 307)

And, even more fatal for modernity, this is 'why violence'—and not 'desire' as Deleuze and Guattari cartoonishly express it—'can always stage a stunning, catastrophic comeback' (Girard, 1977: 307): the insuperable power of violent unanimity has forced upon us a universal amnesia, resulting in an equally global false consciousness. 'In the evolution from ritual to secular institutions men gradually draw away from violence and eventually lose sight of it; but an actual break with violence never takes place'; this is why the 'possibility of such an occurrence'—an apocalyptical irruption of violence encased within the symbolic form of the hackneyed 'return of the repressed'[36]—invariably 'conforms to the dire predictions of divine vengeance that are to be found in every religious system' (Girard, 1977: 307). Contra Deleuze and Guattari, the 'endlessness' of *The Trial* is not due to the inexhaustible nature of justice as anarchic desire that always rises in rebellion against the organism of the law but rather to the eternal recurrence of the will-to-revenge that necessarily brings forth an emissary victim that must be despatched all over again; for Deleuze, Justice-as-Desire forces Josef K. into endless confrontations with the Court-as-the-super-organism-of-the law but for Girard the mimetic crisis of community compels the eternal repetition of a series of sacrificial 'ones' such as Josef K.; 'Since sacrifice is always a question of substitution, it is always possible to make a new substitution and henceforth to sacrifice only a substitute of a substitute' (Girard et al., 2003: 53). And the history of the civilizing process begins at precisely the moment that scapegoating gives rise to a formalized indigenous system that we can correctly classify as law.

> Vengeance is a vicious circle whose effect on primitive societies can only be surmised. For us the circle has been broken. We owe our good fortune to one of our social institutions above all: our judicial system, which serves to deflect the menace of vengeance. The system does not suppress vengeance; rather, it effectively limits it to a single act of reprisal, enacted by a sovereign authority specializing in this particular function. The decisions of the judiciary are invariably presented as the final word on vengeance. (Girard, 1977: 15)

Which explains why Girard proposes a global 'typology of cultures' on the basis of their legal systems.

> The efficiency of our judicial system conceals the problem [of violence], and the elimination of the problem conceals from us the role played by religion. The air of mystery that primitive societies acquire for us is undoubtedly due in large part to this misunderstanding. It is undoubtedly responsible for our extreme views of these societies, our insistence on portraying them alternately as vastly superior or flagrantly inferior to our own. One factor alone might well be responsible for our oscillation between extremes, our radical evaluations: the absence in ['primitive'] societies of a judicial system...If we compare societies that adhere to a judicial system with societies that practice sacrificial rites, the difference between the two is such that we can indeed consider the absence or presence of these [judicial] institutions as a basis for distinguishing primitive societies from 'civilized' ones. (Girard, 1977: 18–19)

There is, however, an outstanding problem with employing legal anthropology as the basis for a universal cultural schema: atavism, the reappearance of primitive characteristics within a more 'advanced' organism, erases the teleological distinction between pre-modern and modern. This is especially evident in the liminality, or reversibility, that operates between public and private justice, and between natural law and positive law.

---

[36] To say nothing of its even more puerile twin, 'cognitive dissonance,' a very pale imitation of the far more ontological *meconnaissance*.

> Vocabulary is perhaps more revealing here than judicial theories. Once the concept is interminable revenge has been formally rejected, it is referred to as *private* vengeance. The term implies the existence of a *public* vengeance, a counterpart never made explicit. By definition, primitive societies have only private vengeance. Thus, public vengeance is the exclusive property of well-policed societies, and our society calls it the judicial system. (Girard, 1977: 15)

What Girard describes here is the entire dilemma of Josef K. who has been surreptitiously ensnared by an atavistic private judicial system in early 20th Prague. So, either the schema is wrong and a typology of cultures based on legal anthropology is fatally flawed or there is something embedded within the cultural landscape of fin de siecle Austro-Hungary that is highly conducive to the re-production of the spirit of revenge. It is the latter. As Franz K. makes clear, there is something radically 'wrong' about the world of Josef K.: there is a universal moral guilt shared by all of the novel's characters that is derived from their psychological alienation from each other and their respective ignorance of authentic (or natural) morality, yielding a society of petty rivalry and nasty snobbery that can only culminate in mimetic envy and *ressentiment* which lead to the utter pathology of metaphysical desire. If we read *The Trial* closely, we detect numerous signs of what we might call a free-floating violence. This is expressed most clearly in Chap. 5, 'The Whipper', the action of which, predictably enough, takes place behind the closed doors of an empty room away from Josef K.'s office, and which also doubles as a deflected re-examination of Josef K.'s sexuality.

> 'We are only being punished because you [Josef K.] reported us. Otherwise nothing would have happened to us, even if they had found out what we had done [stolen the linen]. Can that be called justice?'...The scream uttered by Franz rose up in one unchanging note; it did not seem to come from a man but from a tortured instrument. The whole corridor rang with it, and it must surely be audible throughout the whole building. (Kafka, 1994: 69)

True to his alienated nature (absence of conscience), Josef K.'s sense of social propriety (and superiority) impedes his ability to perform a genuinely moral action.

> He was really anxious to have the warders let off. Having begun his battle against the corruption of this judicial system, it was natural he should intervene from this quarter too. But as soon as Franz began to scream, everything of course was at an end. K. could not allow the clerks and possibly all kinds of other people to come and surprise him in his dealings with the crew in the lumber-room. Nobody could expect K. to make this sacrifice. If he had thought of doing that, it would almost have been simpler to take his own clothes and offer himself to the whipper as a substitute for the warders.[37] (Kafka, 1994: 70)

The endlessness of the process is the narrative enactment of the corresponding endlessness of the process of substitution underlying emissary victimage, a chain of parallel signs and significations that are deployed in the manufacture of the required

---

[37] Meaning that Josef K. is incapable of self-sacrifice. It is interesting that, traditionally, the scapegoat never voluntarily offers him or herself up to the crowd. The pagan notion of the scapegoat underwent a revolutionary transformation with Christianity, and later Islam, with the transformative self-sacrificing figure of the martyr, who is a type of anti-scapegoat through willful submission to the Divine. See Chap. 12, below.

scapegoat through a ritualistic performance of a type of sacred reading, or divination. And a religious world-view premised upon the providential provision of salvific 'substitute of a substitute' can only conceive of, and be conceivable within, a universe that is holly repetitive in nature, consistent with both the cause (violence) and the effect (sacrifice) that punctuates the life-cycle of the community.

> Since ritual is, by definition, a re-enactment of a 'prior event', it must be investigated under two aspects: (1) the way in which the ritual 'represents' or 'substitutes for' the prior event and (2) the way in which both the ritual and prior event interpret the act of killing. In Girard's view, the 'prior event' that all ritual killings rationalize and represent in various 'substitutions' is a collective murder, an act of mob violence. 'Sacrifice' then becomes a term that can be used to refer to the complex phenomenon of the collective killing of a human victim, its mythic rationalization, and its ritualization. To understand how a collective murder could stand at the beginning of human culture, how an act of violence could possibly define both the problem and the solution for social formation, Girard suggests the following scenario. Humans have no braking mechanism for intra-specific aggression. This means that rivalries and conflicts, once unleashed, cannot stop short of manslaughter. Violence, therefore, is endemic. Since the only answer to murder is another murder, cycles of reciprocal retaliation create unending series of revenge-killings. To bring the series to an end, a 'final' killing is necessary. The final killing is achieved in the 'mechanism of the surrogate victim'. (Mack, 1987: 8)

What are the characteristics of the scapegoat that determines his/her identification and subsequent selection as the emissary-surrogate? Unfortunately—and this really is the 'mystery' of religion—no one knows. 'Everything touching the sacred is truly undecidable' (Girard, 1978: 105) Girard reminds us, and he makes much out of the fact that '*Decidere*, in Latin, means to decide in our sense only because it first means to cut with a knife, to kill the sacrificial victim.' (Girard, 1978: 105).[38] We know how things work from the outside, the domain of exoteric knowledge.

> From within the group, one person is separated out as victim. The selection is arbitrary and spontaneous, though there are requisites. The victim must be recognizable as a surrogate for the guilty party (or parties, and ultimately for the group itself); he must be vulnerable, unable to retaliate, without champions to continue the vengeful violence; and there must be unanimity within the group that he is the one at fault. When this unanimity is achieved the victim is treated as a criminal, killed, and expelled. This brings the violence to an end. The group has redirected its aggressions and its members are now able to cooperate. (Mack, 1987: 8)

But there is no certainty within the domain of esoteric knowledge; nobody, not even the Three Friends of Job, knows what it is that validates the correctness of the selection process that can tolerate no error, meaning that the scapegoat, being the one whose death is necessary to resolve the crisis of violence through the release of transformative magic (*pharmakon*), must, as the source of the contagion, be impure in essence; but essence, by definition, is something that is invisible. And even if some sort of mark can be detected such as the external feature of social isolation or emotional alienation, it is statistically unlikely to be wholly unique; social isolation is a necessary but not a sufficient condition of the scapegoat, so there must be a 'something else' which cannot be seen.

---

[38] See Chap. 4, above.

> Violence belongs to all men, and thus to no one in particular. All the actors have the same role, with the exception of the surrogate victim. But anybody can play the part of the surrogate victim. It is futile to look for the secret of the redemptive process in distinctions between the surrogate victim and the other members of the community. *The crucial fact is that the choice of the victim is arbitrary.* The religious interpretations...are at fault precisely because they attribute the beneficial results of the sacrifice to the superhuman nature of the victim or of the other participants, insofar as any of these appears to incarnate the supreme violence. (Girard, 1977: 257)

Not all is lost, however; 'The selection is arbitrary and spontaneous, though there are requisites' (Mack, 1987: 8). It is possible to draw up a provisional list of external characteristics of the scapegoat 'pool' forming a universal victimology which operates largely on the principled application of deductive logic and inferential reasoning. The question for Kafka now becomes: applying the universal taxonomy of the sacrificial victim as a sort of check-list, how high does Josef K. score? The answer is: extremely high.

Like many other commentators, it is easy for me to identify Josef K. as a paramount 'existential hero', very much like Mersault in Albert Camus' *The Stranger*.[39] Where I would depart from the conventional modernist reading of *The Trial*, would be in understanding Josef K.'s 'existential' character as being sacrificial in nature—his 'alienation', or radical 'aloneness', is indicative of his suitability for sacrifice, not as some kind of anti-hero of Romantic revolt.

> All our sacrificial victims, whether chosen from one of the human categories [slave; prisoner; captive] or...from the animal realm, are invariably distinguishable from the non-sacrificeable beings by one essential characteristic: between these victims and the community a crucial link is missing, so they can be exposed to violence without fear of reprisal. Their death does not automatically entail an act of vengeance. The considerable importance this freedom from reprisal has for the sacrificial process makes us understand that sacrifice is primarily an act of violence without risk of vengeance...The desire to commit an act of violence on those near us cannot be suppressed without a conflict; we must divert that impulse, therefore, toward the sacrificial victim, the creature we can strike down without fear of reprisal, since he lacks a champion [or an Advocate]. (Girard, 1977: 13)

But again we have the same problem: Josef K. is hardly the only one who is alienated—everybody in the novel seems to be to some degree, although K. may be so more than the others. But there is still the stop-gap that can be relied upon to guarantee the correctness of the selection (or the arrest) and, therefore, the restorative power of the sacrifice: there are many who are alone, but the special one who is the emissary victim will be the one chosen by a process of 'chance' that really represents a higher order of control which, being esoteric, we ultimately cannot understand. The classic formulation of this, and one which Franz K. was no doubt painfully familiar with, is to be found in the Book of Leviticus, the third book of the Torah.

And Aaron shall cast lots upon the two goats; one lot for the LORD, and the other lot for Azazel[40] [...].

---

[39] See Chap. 9, below.

[40] The under-defined 'demon of the wilderness,' possibly a pre-Mosaic Canaanite demon that was incorporated in early Judaism and was 'connected with the chthonian power expressed in goats'

And Aaron shall present the goat upon which the lot fell for the LORD, and offer him for a sin offering.

The casting of lots for the purposes of determining the identity of the victim operates on two levels. The first one is chance: since all of the prospective victims do, in fact, appear similar, there is no human agency that can make a determinative ruling; ergo, the selection process is made at random. This element of arbitrariness in the victim-selection process accords uncannily well with the opening line of the novel: 'Somebody must have made a false accusation against Josef K., for he was arrested one morning without having done anything wrong' (Kafka, 1994: 1).[41] Which conveys to us the meaning that Josef K. has been pre-determined to be guilty even though he probably is not.[42]

The second level is that of authority, the invisible source or agency (or both) that possesses infallible occult knowledge; in other words, a decision that is of supernatural origins. In pre-modern societies, there is no such thing as chance, randomness, or accident; all socially significant occurrences are the result of intention, either human or super-human. Therefore, when one is casting lots as part of a sacred process, the entity being invoked to oversee the selection process will manipulate the lots on the basis of his/her/its magical knowledge; the god will esoterically know who the true scapegoat is, although to the finite mortal participant this decision may exoterically appear arbitrary. Although it isn't—not 'really'. It should be obvious

(Pinker, 2008: 9) which would imply that the cast out goat "is in reality returning evil to its source, the netherworld" (Jacob Milgrom qtd. Dawson, 2013: 147, n 44), the wilderness serving as generic symbol of the underworld (Pinker, 2008: 9). *Ez* appears to denote 'goat' and '*azal*' means 'to go away,' so the total meaning is '"the goat that goes" or departs is removed and so (e)scapes' (Dawson, 2013: 1). And once (e)scaped it was never seen again; "The scapegoat must remain in the wilderness, dead or alive; under no circumstances is it permitted to return to the human society that has sent it out. Later generations saw to it that the scapegoat was guaranteed not to return; they had a non-Jew, if possible, push the animal into a ravine, where it broke its neck" (Erhard Gerstenberger qtd. Dawson, 2013: 147, n 47).

[41] The original German is '*Jemand musste Josef K. verleumdet haben, den ohne das ser etwas Boses getan hatte, wurde er eines Morgens verhaftet*' (Mitchell, 1998: xvii). This has been translated in the milder form of 'Someone must have been telling lies about Joseph K., for without having done anything wrong he was arrested one fine morning' (Kafka, 1968: 1). But, alternatively, we can get the more unsettling 'Someone must have slandered Josef K., for one morning, without having done anything wrong, he was arrested.' (Kafka, 1998: 3). But the real element of menace lies with *den ohne das ser etwas Boses getan hatte* which, more literally may mean 'without having done anything evil,' or, perhaps, 'without having done any evils' which figuratively screams out the sacrificial motivation of the arrest. Because if Josef K. really is 'free' from evil than he is less of a scapegoat and more of a Lamb of God.

[42] Girard makes the ontological gravitas of the lottery clear; 'If the choice of the victim is left to the calculation of the sacrificers, there is always risk of discord. It must therefore be left to chance, a pattern that is familiar to those who sacrifice in spontaneous gatherings, thereby constituting the real phenomenon of the scapegoat, and the ideal model of the perfectly achieved sacrifice' (Girard, 1987: 78). My problem with this is that in pre-modern societies that believe in the normality of providential interventions, there can be no such thing as genuine chance; even the most apparently random event is the product of a supernatural or occult 'will' of some kind. Furthermore, given the world-annihilating evil of the to-be-scapegoated, God would take immaculate care in making certain that the 'right one' is chosen. See Chap. 9, below.

that what we might call the onto-judicial paradox of the scapegoat reflects perfectly the onto-political undecidability of the law itself, which is yet another re-staging of the wider problem of the incommensurability of positivism and naturalism. In terms of the political, the positivist notion of law-as-power may lack legitimacy in terms of self-validation, but may prove, in any particular instance, to be unanswerable; in contrast, the naturalist conceit of law-as-truth (as a moral good sufficient unto itself), may be eternal, but may also prove itself ineffectual in any particular instance if countermanded by secular power, or, at the very least, be manifested in an unsatisfactory manner, meaning that its truth can never be conclusively validated. With regards to the ontological, exoteric Law-as-Power and esoteric Law-as-Truth are equally contingent in their appearance (representation) to the 'merely' Human who are the laity who are the majority: power is always reversible, and truth is unobtainable unless we possess an utterly infallible means of knowing it. And, yes, Freud notwithstanding, there is a patriarchal element to this dilemma; in Kafka's *Dearest Father* the undecidability of the law is re-written, point for point, in terms of an apparently Oedipal conflict and rivalry; 'My writing was about you, all I did there was to lament what I could not lament on your shoulder' (Kafka, 2010: 63) he claims to his conveniently absent old man, which, if truthful, meant that one some level all of Franz K.'s texts were 'letters' to his Father. As Canetti has argued, although not using the vocabulary of Girard, this is Franz K. taking up the Court's scandalous blocking of Josef K.'s metaphysical desire in the real world; 'Kafka's sovereign perspective on psycho-analysis ought to have helped critics to detach from its constricting domain his own person at least. His struggle with his father was essentially never anything but a struggle against superior power as such' (Canetti, 1974: 86), which bespeaks of metaphysical desire, this superior power being the stumbling-block to the recognition of the imitator's existence. But the Son continues bantering with the Father: '[M]y sense of guilt actually originates in you and is so imbued with its own uniqueness; indeed, this sense of uniqueness is an integral part of its agonising nature, that any replication of it is unthinkable' (Kafka, 2010: 81). Franz K. therapeutically, or cathartically, frames the singularity of his guilt through the literary device of re-writing his rivalry for Being with the Father through an extended meditation on the indeterminate relationship between law and violence-power through the medium of a religious allegory about the scapegoat—which means that the nature of the rivalry is Girardian rather than Freudian. He deploys legal positivism as a trope to construct an image of the Father-Obstacle-God as an exoteric object.

> You [Father] had reached such heights, solely by your own efforts, that you had unbounded confidence in your own opinions…In fact, your self-confidence was so great that you did not even have to be at all consistent, and could still never be wrong…You took on, for me, that enigmatic quality of all tyrants whose right to rule is founded on their identity rather than on reason. At least, it seemed that way to me. (Kafka, 2010: 25)

But hermeneutically he utilizes the transcendental imaginary of naturalism as a way to disclose the esoteric truth of the obstacle that is blocking the Son's unmediated access to Being: Father is God who cannot be successfully imitated but can always be the object of rebellion or combat.

For me as a child...everything you barked at me was as good as God's law, I never forgot it, it remained for me the most important means for judging the world, above all for judging you, and there you failed completely...Please understand me correctly, Father, [my examples] would in themselves have been utterly insignificant details, they only came to depress me because they meant that you, a figure of such tremendous authority for me, did not yourself abide by the commandments you imposed. Hence there were for me three worlds, one where I lived, a slave under laws that had been invented solely for me and, moreover, with which I could never fully comply (I did not know why), then another world, infinitely distant from mine, in which you dwelt, busy with ruling, issuing orders and being angry when they were not obeyed, and finally a third realm where everybody else lived happily, free from orders and obligations. I was forever in disgrace, either I obeyed your orders, which was a disgrace for they applied, after all, only to me; or I was defiant, that was also a disgrace, for how dare I presume to defy you, or my reason for failing to obey was that I lacked, for example, your strength, your appetite, your aptitude, although you expected it of me as a matter of course, that was, in fact, the greatest disgrace of all. That was not how I thought as a child, but rather how I felt. (Kafka, 2010: 28–30)

Compare this with Kafka's diary entry on November 3, 1911: 'I say: "I am doing my utmost to hold back," and sense in Father, as always in such intense moments, an underlying wisdom of which I can only catch the slightest pulse' (Kafka, 2010: 91). The esoteric wisdom that Kafka is conveying is that Father-Obstacle-God is both truly omniscient and wholly unknowable, so that the truth is 'out there' but it incessantly demands an act of faith on the part of the recipient of the decree (think of Abraham and Isaac), which is guaranteed to prove unsatisfactory to the scapegoat who literally cannot understand his dilemma which is esoteric origin.[43]

Throughout the novel Josef K. is being examined for 'signs' of some sort of 'special status', which, in a certain way, is surprising, although entertaining. The lots have already been cast against Josef K., and they have announced (or lied) that

[43] An unbearable situation both oedipal and theological, for what Franz K. seemed to most intensely resent about his patriarch was the arbitrary way that he exercised his will, especially in regards to punishment. In his unsent letter to his father, ostensibly written in response to the patriarch's query as to why Franz claimed to be afraid of him, his son recounted this incident as incontrovertible proof of the rationality of his fear: 'There is only one episode from those early years [of childhood] that I remember directly, perhaps you remember it too. I was whining persistently for water one night, certainly not because I was thirsty, but in all probability partly to be annoying, partly to amuse myself. After a number of fierce threats failed, you lifted me out of my bed, carried me out onto the pavlatche [balcony] and left me awhile all alone, standing outside the locked door in my nightshirt. I do not mean to say that this was wrong of you, perhaps at that time there really was no other way of having a peaceful night, but I mention it as a characteristic example of the way you brought me up and the effect it had on me. This incident almost certainly made me obedient for a time, but it damaged me on the inside. I was by nature unable to reconcile this simple act (as it seemed to me) of casually asking for water with the utter horror of being carried outside.' The final sentence conveys the theological sub-text of the account: 'Years later it still tormented me that this giant man, my father, the ultimate authority, could enter my room at any time and, almost unprovoked, carry me from my bed out unto the pavlatche, and that I meant so little to him' (Kafka, 2010: 22–23). Which, to a young child, is both god-like and unreasonable and, therefore, unpredictable, insofar as the penalty does not seem to accord with the trespass; admittedly, though, Kafka does slide somewhat in his phrasing 'almost unprovoked'. Which is the theological heart of the matter: there is a provocation of some kind, but the time, and nature, of divine retribution is unknowable, other than the certainty that there will be one.

he is impure; the issue of guilt has been decided before the novel (or the process) even begins. Nevertheless, the exoteric impulse to re-validate the esoteric decision a posteriori will remain strong, even if only as a means of gratifying a ghoulish voyeurism, or, better yet, a vengeful cruelty. After all, if every goat looks pretty much the same as every other, at least within the aggregate spread, and none are exhibiting severe deviations of miniscule statistical probability (four horns, two heads, three eyes, five legs, all which empirically demonstrate an 'impurity' or 'transgression' of some kind even if only in the chromosomes), then the sheer exoteric mediocrity of the chosen one as signifier of all evil is bound to raise doubts as to the infallibility of esoteric knowledge; could it be that there are no such things as real experts? Hence the unfathomable mystery of Josef K.'s lips (Kafka, 1994: 63, 136). The merchant Block, the Advocate's other client of whom I will speak more about later, tries to explain this to Josef.

> 'One of the superstitions [concerning the accused], for instance, is that, according to many people, the outcome of a case can be seen in the accused man's face and particularly in the line of his lips. And these people said that, judging by your lips, you are sure to be convicted, and soon… 'My lips?' asked K., taking out a pocket mirror and examining himself. 'I can't see anything peculiar about my lips, can you?' 'Neither can I,' said the merchant, 'not at all.' 'How superstitious those people are,' K. cried. 'Didn't I tell you?' asked the merchant. (Kafka, 1994: 136)

Josef's landlady Fraulein Montag conducts herself in the prescribed manner: "'What is there to say!'" answered K. who was tired of seeing Fraulein Montag staring at his lips all the time. 'She was trying by these means to assume control of whatever he might say' (Kafka, 1994: 63). But, as we should expect, the death blow is administered by the Advocates' spooky house-servant and comforter, Leni-the-succubus.

> Leni has one idiosyncrasy…this idiosyncrasy is that she finds nearly all accused men handsome. She is attracted to them all, loves them all, and seems to be loved by them too. To amuse me she sometimes tells me about these affairs, when I let her. I am not as amazed about all of this as you seem to be. When you've got the proper eye for it, accused men do often appear handsome. This is a remarkable, you might even call it scientific, phenomenon. Of course, there's no clear and exactly definable change in their appearance because of the accusation. After all, it's not like in other legal cases; most of these men continue their normal way of life and if they have a good advocate to look after them they're not much impeded by the proceedings. Yet those with experience in these matters can pick out the accused men, every single one of them, in the largest mass of people. How do they do this, you might ask. My answer will not satisfy you. The accused men are simply the most handsome. It can't be guilt which makes them handsome because—at least in my opinion as an advocate—not all are guilty; neither can it be future punishment which makes them handsome in advance, for not all are punished; so it can only be an attribute of the proceedings instituted against them. Of course, among the handsome ones a few are especially conspicuous. But all are handsome, even Block, that miserable worm. (Kafka, 1994: 43–44)

Meaning that if a female sex-demon 'wants' you it can only be because, as a supernatural creature, she can see/smell/taste/touch/hear whatever 'it' was that the thing that controlled the casting of the lots could. And, of course, if Josef K. is the true scapegoat, then the reactions of the other characters to him starts to make complete sense, subject to the internal logic of the ritualistic prescriptions of scapegoating and ritualistic sacrifice laid out in the Book of Job. And as he can no longer deny his special status, Josef K. does begin to consciously take on the attributes of the chosen on, which, in a perverse way, satiates his metaphysical desire for recognition.

> 'So you don't believe me?' asked K., and, unconsciously provoked to it by the man's humble demeanor, he seized him by the arms as if to compel him to believe. But he did not want to hurt him and had only gripped him gently, yet in spite of that the man shrieked as if K. had taken hold of him not with two fingers but with glowing hot pincers. (Kafka, 1994: 51)

And consistent with his true identity as scapegoat (the lips), Josef K. is often looked at for signs of some sort of 'transformation,' the collective expectation of the manifestation of the magical power of the *pharmakon* that will be restorative in its effects, most notably at the very end of 'The End': 'But the hands[44] of one of the gentlemen were at K.'s throat while the other drove the knife into his heart and turned it there twice. With his failing sight K. could still see the gentlemen right in front of his face, cheek pressed against cheek, as they observed the decisive moment' (Kafka, 1994: 178); or the moment of *Decidere*, the cutting with the knife that changes everything (Mckenna, 1992). The image of the knife as a sacrificial instrument was very much on Franz K.'s mind during and after the process of the Askanische Hof; his diary entry for September 16, 1915 reads, in part: 'Between throat and chin would seem the most rewarding place to stab. Lift the chin and stick into the tensed muscles. But this spot is probably rewarding only in one's imagination. You expect to see a magnificent gush of blood and a network of sinews and little bones like you find in a roast turkey' (Kafka, 1976: 342). But given that Franz K. had been having such fantasies for quite some time—his diary entry on November 2, 1911, almost three years prior to the *Gerichtshof*, commences with 'This morning, for or the first time in a long time, the joy again of imagining a knife twisted in my heart' (Kafka, 1976: 101)—would suggest that he had psychically internalized the model of the scapegoat as his own from the very commencement of his writing period. Clearly, the author was not lying when he famously declared that 'it seemed as though the shame was to outlive him.' This final scene is the most intensely Girardian point of contact between *Prozess* and Father-God-Rival, as Kafka makes clear in his all-or-nothing letter to his 'Dearest' one: 'I had lost my self-confidence whenever I was in your presence, had exchanged it for a boundless sense of guilt (I was thinking of this boundlessness when I once summed it up perfectly in relation to someone else: "He is afraid that his shame will outlive him")' (Kafka, 2010: 55). See below.[45] So here Franz K. is actually referencing his fictional doppelganger Josef K., these being the final words of *The Trial*: '… it seemed as though the shame was to outlive him' (Kafka, 1998: 231).[46] Even more intriguing is that, according to Josef K., of all of his Father's recurrent threats the one that he found most terrifying as a child

---

[44] The placing of the hands upon the victim is a direct reference to Leviticus, although here Kafka is combining the image of both the goat for Azazel and the goat of the sin offering.

[45] See below.

[46] *The Trial* was written intermittently from 1914 to 1915, and the letter was written sometime in 1919 (Kafka, 2010: 9).

was, "I'll gut you like a fish" (Kafka, 2010: 33). Which leads us to an astonishing conclusion: the thing that makes Josef K. such an utterly unique literary creation is that the model-object of his metaphysical desire is to be nothing other than the scapegoat itself, the complying sacrificial victim of the obstacle-accuser. Or, more precisely, he has as his model the goat of the sin offering, 'the goat upon which the lot fell for the LORD' and is accepted by God following its sacralized death. And, if this is correct, then the interminable nature of *The Trial* becomes even easier to explain: just as Franz K. was superficially complying with the hand-made ritualistic prescriptions of the familial tribunal and its sacrificial demand for unanimity, Josef K., was narratively complying, with more sincerity but less self-awareness, with the textual Court of scapegoating as a means of acquiring unmediated access to Being.[47]

But there is a problem here for my theory of Josef K. as emissary victim; according to Leviticus, the scapegoat properly so-called is not ritualistically killed, but is driven into the wilderness, as a propitiatory offering/gift to Azazel.

> And Aaron shall lay both his hands[48] upon the head of the live goat, and confess over him all of the iniquities of the children of Israel, and all their transgressions, even all their sins; and he shall put them upon the head of the goat, and shall send him away by the hand of a man that is in readiness into the wilderness.
>
> And the goat shall bear upon him all their iniquities into a solitary land: and he shall let go the goat into the wilderness...
>
> Rather, it is 'the goat of the sin offering' that is physically slain.
>
> Then shall [Aaron] kill the goat of the sin offering, that is for the people, and bring his blood within the veil...and sprinkle it upon the mercy-seat, and before the mercy-seat.

In other words, the sacrificial goats are double*s*. From this it follows that, Josef K. is really 'the goat of the sin offering' which has serious implications concerning the

---

[47] It should be noted that throughout *The Trial*, Josef K. is quite sardonic, even insolent, in his attitude toward the Court and its unofficial officials, almost as though he is goading them into inflicting violence upon him. Which may be part of the prescribed expectations; it could also be an attempt to fulfill is metaphysical desire for the validation of his self as sacrificial victim.

[48] The fact that Aaron places both hands rather than one on Azazel's goat is significant, for 'the placement of the sins is effected by both the hand placement gesture which designates where the sins re to rest *and* the spoken confession which concretizes the sins which then fall on the head of the goat' (Wright, 1986: 436) thereby publicly announcing that the animal is not to be killed but 'eliminated' (expelled). By contrast, only one hand is placed upon the goat of the sin offering which announces the death of the victim; the single hand placement signifies the offerer's ownership of the animal guaranteeing 'that the benefits accruing from it will return to him' which can only be effected through immolation (Wright, 1986: 436). 'Demystified' what this tells us is that Josef K. is not only meant to be killed but that his death will 'benefit' some unknown party. The text does not really help us, but if the trial of Josef K. was the double of *der Prozess* of Franz K., then we can only assume that the beneficiaries of Kafka's symbolically sacrificial ordeal would have been his own family through the regaining of their honor following the cancellation of the marriage with Felice. As Franz K. expressed this thought in relation to his father, 'I could conceive of another Abraham for myself—he certainly would never have gotten to be a patriarch or even an old-clothes dealer—who was prepared to satisfy the demand for a sacrifice immediately, with the promptness of a waiter...' (Franz Kafka qtd. Sarat, 2007: 865, n 14).

nature of his impurity, metaphysical desire and *ressentiment*. Compare the elaborate ritualistic process that Josef K. is submitted to in both the introductory and concluding (or twinned) chapters, 'The Arrest' (Kafka, 1994: 1–24) and 'The End' (Kafka, 1994: 174–178). Josef K. is physically escorted to the outskirts of town, the allegory of the Levitical camp ('the goat of the sin offering, whose blood was brought in to make atonement in the holy place, shall be carried forth without the camp') and taken to a quarry, a kind of wasteland, where he is bound to an altar-like boulder as a sacrificial offering.

> In order not to leave K. standing motionless, exposed to the rather chilly night air, he [one of the sacrificers of the Court] took him by the arm and walked back and forth with him a little, while the other man searched for some suitable spot in the quarry.[49] When he had found it, he waved, and the other gentleman led K. over to it. It was near the quarry wall, where a loose block of stone was lying. The men sat K. down on the ground, propped him up against the stone, and laid his head down on it. In spite of all their efforts, and in spite of the cooperation K. gave them, his posture was still quite forced and implausible. So one of the men asked the other to let him work on positioning K. on his own for a while but that didn't improve things either. Finally they left K. in a position that wasn't even the best of those they had already tried. (Kafka, 1998: 230)

In a frequently overlooked detail of the sacred execution, Josef K. is expected to commit ritualistic suicide, by plunging the knife into his own heart, a deliberate act of self-sacrifice, the same demand that was made, in effect on Job. And like Job, Josef K. demurs.

> Then one man opened his frock coat and, from a sheath on a belt that encircled his vest, drew forth a long, thin, double-edged butcher knife, held it up, and tested its sharpness in the light. Once more the nauseating courtesies began, one of them passed the knife across K. to the other, who passed it back over K. K. knew clearly now that it was his duty to seize the knife as it floated from hand to hand above him and plunge it into himself. But he didn't do so; instead he twisted his still-free neck and looked about him. He could not rise entirely to the occasion; he could not relieve the authorities of all their work; the responsibility for this final failure lay with whoever had denied him of the remnant of strength necessary to do so. (Kafka, 1998: 230)

Lev Gillett (a.k.a. 'a Monk of the Eastern Church') has offered a very useful commentary on the auto-sacrificial nature of repentance, especially in regards to the Christian Easter which is the Jewish Passover, the *pessah* or 'passage' that is fulfilled by the offering of the Passover goat as a blood sacrifice (Gillet, 1980: 162, n 4).

> The Eucharist, before it becomes the presence of Christ in us, is the sacrifice of Christ for us. At this feast of Holy Thursday [the Last Supper, an enactment of the Passover meal], it is particularly important to remember the link which our lord wanted to establish between the meal in the upper room and the Jewish Passover, and between this same meal and the Passion. Every Eucharist is a sacrificial meal. Each time that we make our communion with the body of Christ that has been broken and with his blood that has been shed, we are in

---

[49] There is an interesting aside that Kafka provides here concerning the preparation of Josef K.: the servants of the court remove his upper clothing, adding that the executioner 'folded the clothes carefully, as if they would be needed again, though not in the immediate future' (Kafka, 1998: 229). Leviticus: 'And he that burneth [the sin offering] shall wash his clothes, and bathe his flesh in water, and afterward he shall come into the camp...'.

> communion with his Passion, and take part in his sacrifice. We ought to break and offer our own selves, our selfish desires, our will: we should plunge the knife of the sacrificer into our own hearts. (Gillet, 1980: 152)

A literal reading and a purely moral interpretation of the 'The End' from the perspective of the accuser and consistent with the prescribed behavior of the scapegoat would indicate that Josef K. is a mimetic failure. His refusal, like Job, to conform to the cultural model of expiation—'Nobody could expect K. to make this sacrifice' (Kafka, 1994: 70)—would signify to the sacrificer the unconfessed nature of his sin which is *ressentiment*: his continual refusal to respect the dictates of the Court, right up to the literal last-minute resistance to positioning himself on the altar in the proper manner, are all indicators of a wider resistance to examine his own conscience and consider the possibility of moral guilt which is the final proof of his absence of remorse. So if Josef K. is really the goat of the sin offering and the sacrificial victims in Leviticus are doubled, then who is the true scapegoat? It is Block the Merchant, who is the double to Josef K.: both Block and Josef K. are the only two expressly accused men in the novel, they both have Dr. Huld as their advocate, and, most crucially, they are engaged in both mimetic desire and mimetic rivalry vis-a-vis Leni the Succubus, who finds both of them to be marked and, therefore, irresistible.

> 'Kneel or crawl on all fours, do what you like, it won't bother me.' But Block still had some feelings of self-respect, for he advanced on K., threatening him with his fists, and shouted as loudly as he dared in the proximity of the advocate: 'You can't talk to me like that, it's not right. Why are you insulting me? And here in the presence of the Herr Advocate too, where both of us, you as well as I, are tolerated only out of compassion? You are no better than I am, you too are a defendant, you have a case pending against you. If in spite of everything you are still a gentleman, then I'm a gentleman too, if not a better one. But if you think you are privileged just because you are allowed to sit here and listen while I crawl on all fours, as you put it, then I'll remind you of the old legal maxim: For a man under suspicion movement is better than rest, for the man who is at rest can always, without knowing it, be on the scales being weighed together with his sins. (Kafka, 1994: 149–150)

A conventionally moral reading of *The Trial* is that the Kafkaesque nature of the process of perpetual judgment lies within the structuring in-determinability of Josef K.'s relationship with the Court, delicately posed between guilt or innocence, accusation or guilt; an eternal-recurrence-of-the-same premised upon the infinite postponement of Josef K's realization/confession of his guilt (his self-incriminating refusal to recognize the rights of the other), itself a symptom of a un-exorcised will-to-violence (*ressentiment*) which denotes Josef K. as the goat of the sin offering, making him a candidate for execution. On such a superficial reading, the fact that Block takes his predicament seriously, whereas Josef K. continually defies the court and sabotages his own defense, signifies that Block's moral self-awareness is less impaired and, therefore, he deserves the lesser punishment of exile to death as the scapegoat of the community; it also means that he is the more suitable of the two goats for assuming the sacred weight of the collective sins (unpurged violence) of the community. On a deeper level, however, K.'s eternally passive aggressive acts of resistance, denying while always returning, goes directly to the nature of his sin and it is this that qualifies him as the offering to the Lord, which is Father, model, rival, and obstacle all rolled into one. *Ressentiment* is merely a by-product and hardly singles out K. as unique as everyone in *The Trial* is infected with the contagion creating a state of undifferentiation; rather, the sin of Josef K. who is the literary double of Franz K., as the offering to God alone and not, as with the scapegoat, on behalf of the sins of the community (Block being the acceptable offering as the bearer of *ressentiment*) is metaphysical desire itself: the only way that either K. can establish their existence is to actually replace the Father-God who is the exclusive and excluding possessor of Being.

The very last line of *The Trial* has created enormous problems of interpretation: '"Like a Dog!" he [K.] said. It was if the shame would outlast him' (Kafka, 1994: 178). But just as with the equally indecipherable ending of Camus, *The Stranger* which is an extravagant re-staging/un-veiling of the mechanism of catharsis,[50] the last lines make perfect sense when we situate Josef K. within the sacrificial mechanism. "Only *in this way* can writing be done, only with such coherence, with such a complete opening out of the body and the soul" Kafka tells us (Kafka qtd. Parry, 1994: x–xi), and it also so happens that the body and soul of Franz K. is that of a sacrificial victim. In a symbolic sense Josef K. really is 'like' a dog because the sacrificial human victim is may be a substitute for, or, equally, be substituted with, an animal sacrifice (Wright, 1988). And his 'shame' really does 'outlast him' precisely because he is the human-substitute for 'the goat of the sin offering', which means that he can be replicated an infinite number of times, just as, by the same logic, he is nothing more than one item in an undifferentiated series that long predates him: 'Since sacrifice is always a question of substitution, it is always possible to make a new substitution and henceforth to sacrifice only a substitute of a substitute.'

> Strictly speaking, there is no essential difference between animal sacrifice and human sacrifice, and in many cases one is substituted for the other. Our tendency to insist on differences that have little reality when discussing the institution of sacrifice—our reluctance, for example, to equate animal with human sacrifice—is undoubtedly a factor in the extraordinary misunderstandings that still persist in that area of human culture…all victims, even the animal ones, bear a certain *resemblance* to the object they replace; otherwise the violent impulse would remain unsatisfied. (Girard, 1977: 10–11)

But there is a second, and much more disquieting (meaning less moral) reason why Franz K. is a dog, and, again, it is the 'sin' of metaphysical desire. Although Girard provides us with the reasoning, it is Canetti who offers the clue, which I have already discussed: it is the issue of power and metaphysical desire.

> In a letter to Felice he coins the appalling phrase 'the terror of standing upright'….Standing upright signifies the power of man over beast; but precisely in this most obvious attitude man is exposed, visible, vulnerable. For this power is also guilt, and only on the ground, lying among the animals [dogs], can one see the stars, which free one from this terrifying power of man. (Canetti, 1974: 88)

In a letter to Max Brod, Kafka makes this unsettling confession.

---

[50] See Chap. 9, below.

> We burrow through ourselves like moles and emerge out of our vaults of sand blackened and velvet-haired, with our poor little red feet outstretched for tender sympathy.... While I was out on a walk my dog came upon a mole that was trying to cross the road. He kept leaping at him and wouldn't leave him alone, for he is a young dog, and timid. At first I was amused and liked especially the mole's excitement as he looked for a hole in the hard surface of the road, altogether desperately and ineffectually. But then suddenly, when the dog struck him once more with an outstretched paw, he shrieked *Ks, kss*, just like that. And then I thought—no, I did not think anything. I was simply in a state of delusion, because on that day my head was hanging so heavily that in the evening I noticed with amazement that my chin had grown into my chest. (Canetti, 1974: 90)

And this is Canetti's quite merciless take on the nature of what sin Kafka has accidentally confessed to.

> The dog, let us note, the dog hunting the mole, was Kafka's dog; he was its master. For the mole—who, scared to death, looks for a hole in the hard road, a hole in which to hide—he himself does not exist; the animal is afraid only of the dog, its senses are open only for the latter. But he, Kafka, so exalted above them, by his upright stance, his height, and his ownership of the dog, which could never threaten him, simply laughs at the desperate and ineffectual movements of the mole. The mole does not realize that t could turn to him for help; it has not learned to pray, and is capable of nothing but its small screams. They are the only sounds that touch the god, for here he is the god, the supreme being, the zenith of power, and in this case God is even present. The mole screams *Ks, kss*, and the onlooker, hearing this scream, transforms himself into the mole. Without having to fear his dog, which is his slave, he feels what it is to be a mole. (Canetti, 1974: 91)

This might be a first: Kafkaesque *morality*. Franz does not do the 'natural' thing and assume the position of 'God' (to the mole), which would be therapeutic in a way, allowing him to temporarily suspend the mimetic crisis of metaphysical desire by occupying the Ground of Being and overcoming 'the terror of standing upright'. Instead, he involuntarily assumes the position of the mole, recapitulating the dilemma of his eternal absence of substance while, at the same time, sadistically enjoying the position of the dog; as Canetti remarked, 'Certainly it was his most peculiar gift—the ability to make himself small by transformation' (Canetti, 1974: 52). But transformation requires an act of will, and will always carries within it the possibility of bad faith. So Franz really is a dog in two senses: he is morally low in that he is the extension of the beast that tortures the powerless victim and, at the same time, he assumes the perspective of the innocent victim who is being terrorized by nothing other than—himself. God and victim of God in one. Or, as Kafka described it, "...I am basically a cold, selfish, callous creature, despite my weakness which conceals rather than mitigates these qualities" (Canetti, 1974: 46). Which sounds like his grooming of Felice Bauer. Only it is much worse than that. For Kafka did not groom one woman, he groomed two. And they were the very best of friends.

8.5 At the End There is a Window

I have already had occasion to discuss the law books, which are really the porno books, which are really the law books of the examining magistrate who is a sex pervert; Josef K. 'looked no further but merely opened the second book at the title page. It was a novel called *The Torments Grete Had to Suffer from Her Husband Hans.* 'So these are the law books studied here,' said K. "It's by people like this I'm supposed to be judged"' (Kafka, 1994: 41). I am not aware of any attempts to link the hapless victim of Franz's second calculated attempt at grooming, Grete Bloch, with the almost eponymous merchant. Grete, a dearest friend of Felice Bauer, acts as Felice's 'emissary' in Prague to negotiate with Fran K. concerning the breaking of the engagement (Canetti, 1974: 51): 'Having heard nothing from him, she [Felice] sent her friend Grete Bloch to Prague, with the request that Grete mediate between them. With the entry of a third person, a new and very remarkable phase in the relationship now began' (Canetti, 1974: 49). Franz K. is smitten. A triangle is formed.

> As soon as Grete Bloch enters the scene, Kafka becomes divided. The letters he has been writing to Felice the previous year he now directs to Grete. Now it is she about whom he wishes to know everything, and he asks the same old questions. He wats to be able to picture how she lives, her work, her office, her travels. He wants immediate replies to his letters; and since they sometimes arrive late, though only slightly, he asks her to follow a regular schedule, which of course she refuses to do. He is interested in questions of her health; he wants to know what books she reads. In some respects he has an easier time of it than he had with Felice. Grete Bloch is more flexible, more receptive, more passionate. So she follows his suggestions. Even if she does not read at once the book he recommends, she makes a note of it and comes back to it later. Although her way of life is less conducive to health and less orderly than Felice's, she still gives consideration to his advice in these matters; she discusses them in her letters and thus goads him into making more sharply defined suggestions. He is not allowed to feel that his influence is not having results. In these letters, Kafka is more certain of himself, more overbearing, one might be tempted to say, were not Kafka himself the case in point. Naturally, the abridged form of the earlier correspondence [with Felice] comes to him more easily than the original; it is a keyboard on which he has had ample practice. There is something playful about these letters—a very rare feature in the earlier ones—and quite undisguisedly he is asking for Grete's affection. (Canetti, 1974: 49–50)

The epitome of the catastrophe comes when Felice and Franz make a genuine effort to reconcile and to resume their engagement and Kafka announces that he wants to make it a threesome which is triangulation taken to the most extreme degree; the marriage to Felice 'would only be complete, to his thinking', if Grete was part of it, for 'a marriage which he felt to be a sort of duty, a moral accomplishment, could not succeed without love. Through the presence of Grete Bloch he would have brought into the marriage the love he felt for her' meaning Grete (Canetti, 1974: 55).

Canetti is in no doubt about both the reality and nature of Franz K.'s guilt: 'The question as to guilt or innocence, which is the only possible reason for the court's existence, remains a non-essential one; it even turns out that guilt originates only in the ceaseless endeavour to find out about the court' (Canetti, 1974: 81–82). The attempt to move from exoteric to esoteric knowledge of the Court itself bespeaks an unconscious acknowledgment of bad faith of some kind over some 'thing,' so that the ‘sincere’ quest for enlightenment doubles as a cover for instigating a clandestine but invigorating form of violence.

> To achieve the continuity that he [Kafka] thought indispensable, two things were needed: a very powerful, yet somehow still erroneous shock, like the ‘tribunal,’ [*Gerichtshof*] which mobilized his agonizing passion for precision as a defence against attacks from the outside; and a bond between the external hell of the world and his inner hell. (Canetti, 1974: 60)

Canetti’s final assessment would appear to be borne out by Kafka’s final letter to Felice, 1 October 1917 which suggests a personality not far from the border-line type. A person who is liminal.

> If I closely examine what is my ultimate aim, it turns out that I am *not* really striving to be good and to fulfil the demands of a Supreme Judgment, but rather very much the contrary: I strive to know the whole animal and human community, to recognize their basic predilections, desires, moral ideals, to reduce these to simple rules and as quickly as possible trim my behavior to these rules in order that I may find favor in the whole world’s eyes; and, indeed, (this is the inconsistency), so much favor that in the end I could openly perpetrate the iniquities within me without alienating the universal love in which I am held—the only sinner who won’t be roasted. To sum up, then, my whole concern is the human tribunal, which I wish to deceive, moreover, though without practicing any actual deception. (Kafka, 1976: 387)

Which reads like an expose confessional authored by Job. Deleuze and Guattari powerfully argue for rejecting Kafka’s lingering regard for the ‘transcendence’ of the Law-as-Organism in favor of the devouring immanence of Justice-as-Desire. However, if *The Trial* is an allegory of the mechanism of the emissary victim, then it becomes dramatically impossible to refrain from playing games with the imagery of sacred or divine law, which is always overdetermined, being both present and absent simultaneously. And if this is true, then the most effective form of literary treatment would be to frame the issue in terms of the repetition-inducing properties of sacralization: that which must be endlessly returned to for it is through the act of repeating that the thing which is not there can be invoked for the duration of the sacrificial performance. Hence ‘The End’ that is as controversial as the ‘arrest’ in the beginning.

> He was not to prove his own worth completely, he was not able to relieve the authorities of all work: responsibility for this ultimate defect lay with whoever had denied him the remainder of the requisite strength. His eyes fell on the top storey of the house at the edge of the quarry. The casement window flew open like a light flashing on; a human figure, faint and insubstantial at that distance and height, forced itself far out and stretched its arms even further. Who was it? A friend? A good man? One who sympathized? One who wanted to help? Was it one person? Was it everybody? Was there still help? Were there objections which had been forgotten? Certainly there were. Logic is of course unshakeable, but it cannot hold out against a man who wants to live. Where was the judge he had never seen? Where was the high court he had never reached? He raised his hand and spread his fingers wide. (Kafka, 1994: 178)

Canetti is right to identify the centrality of Kafka’s need for the *Gerichtshof* as a psychic battery to repeatedly re-energize ‘a defence against attacks from the outside’ for it is here that we learn the name of Franz K.’s sin: metaphysical desire. The Son is in an existential life-or-death struggle against his rival the Father for Being itself; the quasi-predatory 'controlling' of both Felice and Grete are the off-shoots of a far more primal struggle, and trauma, that is wholly mimetic in nature. What it suggests, in fact, is that the Son was emulating the Father's tyrannical control of the Mother, as Franz K. implicitly hints at in his infamous letter to his dearest *skandalon*.

> If I wanted to escape you, I would have had to escape the rest of the family too, even Mother. Of course she always gave me protection, but only in relation to you. She loved you too much and was too faithfully devoted to you, for her to be an independent source of moral support in my longer-term struggles as a child. Moreover, my childhood instinct was right, for over the years Mother became even more closely allied to you; where she had once retained some independence in her own affairs, ably and quietly, within the narrowest limits so as to to anger you too much, over the years she began more and more blindly accept the way you judged and condemned your children, more out of emotional sympathy than rational agreement with you .... (Kafka, 2010: 47)

And because his sin is one of mimesis, Franz K. must eternally return to it, so that the religious allegory that he writes for himself must itself imitate the repetitive sacrificial cycle of Leviticus and its goat of the sin offering which is for, or directed at, the Father alone and mortal women be damned. For it is only by becoming the goat of the sin offering itself, the victim who is actually slain, is the Son-as-sacrificial-victim able to achieve an unmediated relationship to Being, replacing, or at least obviating, the profane and capricious fake god who 'did not even have to be at all consistent, and could still never be wrong' (Kafka, 2010: 7).

There is, I admit, a problem here. Sacralization and the sacrificial mechanism is the onto-political ground for cyclical Time, but Kafka invokes a Mosaic sacrificial victim that is embedded within the anti-cyclical Time of the linear, historically progressive, and messianic religion of Judaism (whether actually believed in or not) which is the anti-thesis of a-temporal sacralization. The crucial point, though, is that The Torah is a pre-Christian text so that unmediated communion with the Divine has not yet been realized with the arrival of the Messiah, Davidic or otherwise. Josef K.'s imploring stance vis-a-vis the feminine silhouette in the window (not infrequently identified as his neighbor Fraulein Burstner[51]) is evocative of a messianic expectation, which has proven to be eternally delayed. Both Judaism and Christianity possess linear time but with this vital difference: Christians remember, the *typon* of the future having already been established in the past, while Jews are waiting still, so that the Divine Judgment has not, and perhaps never can be reached and everything is still in play and the Court, along with the law that it represents, can be repeatedly gamed. Metaphysical desire is the key to everything pertaining to the doubles Josef K. and Franz K. Josef K.'s eternal return to the Court and the need to re-initiate combat, just like Franz K.'s condescending but uninterrupted re-engagement with the *Gerichtshof*, truly is his deliberate failure to acknowledge his conscience but which, pace Canetti, would constitute the cataclysmic but a-moral failure of an a-moral metaphysical desire, a Girardian catastrophe of cosmic magnitude. Both Felice and Grete, framed by their suitor as propitiatory surrogates of the dearest Father, are press-ganged into a

[51] Mitchell, 1998: xxiii but perhaps the female silhouette would be better understood as Grete Bloch.

performance of second-rate models for the real object of desire who is the mimetic key to the resolution of the crisis of metaphysical desire, the sin that cannot be expiated in the absence of the arrival of the true end that is voluntarily assumed. And, to pursue take this thought to its bitterest end, would not Franz K.'s metaphysical desire for Being be identical to an *existential envy* of the Father in relation to Mother and her various substitutions? Kafka's desire to victimize surrogates of the model is nothing more than psychic compensation for the sensation of recognition and the fullness of Being that has been eternally denied him through his inability, like Job, to become the true sacrificial victim.

Like a dog.

Leviticus, 16: 1–30

> And the LORD spoke unto Moses, after the death of the two sons of Aaron, when they drew near before the LORD, and died;
>
> And the LORD said unto Moses, Speak unto Aaron thy brother, that he come not at all times into the holy place within the veil, before the mercy-seat which is upon the ark [of the covenant]; that he die not: for I will appear in the cloud upon the mercy-seat...
>
> [Aaron] shall take of the congregation of the children of Israel two he-goats for a sin offering, and one ram for a burnt offering...
>
> And [Aaron] shall take the two goats, and set them before the LORD at the door of the tent of the meeting.
>
> And Aaron shall cast lots upon the two goats; one lot for the LORD, and the other lot for Azazel
>
> And Aaron shall present the goat upon which the lot fell for the LORD, and offer him for a sin offering.
>
> But the goat, on which the lot fell for Azazel, shall be set alive before the LORD, to make atonement for him, to send him away for Azazel into the wilderness...
>
> Then shall [Aaron] kill the goat of the sin offering, that is for the people, and bring his blood within the veil...and sprinkle it upon the mercy-seat, and before the mercy-seat.
>
> And [Aaron] shall make atonement for the holy place, because of the uncleannesses of the children of Israel, and because of their transgressions, even all their sins: and so shall he do for the tent of meeting, that dwelleth with them in the midst of their uncleannesses.
>
> And there shall be no man in the tent of meeting when he goeth in to make atonement in the holy place, until he come out, and have made atonement for himself, and for his household, and for all the assembly of Israel...
>
> And when [Aaron] hath made an end of atoning for the holy place, and the tent of the meeting, and the altar, he shall present the live goat:
>
> And Aaron shall lay both his hands upon the head of the live goat, and confess over him all of the iniquities of the children of Israel, and all their transgressions, even all their sins; and he shall put them upon the head of the goat, and shall send him away by the hand of a man that is in readiness into the wilderness.

And the goat shall bear upon him all their iniquities into a solitary land: and he shall let go the goat into the wilderness...

And he that letteth go the goat for Azazel shall wash his clothes, and bathe his flesh in water, and afterward he shall come into the camp.

And...the goat of the sin offering, whose blood was brought in to make atonement in the holy place, shall be carried forth without the camp; and they shall burn in the fire [its skin], and [its flesh], and [its] dung.

And he that burneth [the sin offering] shall wash his clothes, and bathe his flesh in water, and afterward he shall come into the camp...

And it shall be a statute for ever unto you; in the seventh month, on the tenth day of the month, ye shall afflict your souls...

For on this day shall atonement be made for you, to cleanse you; from all your sins shall ye be clean before the LORD.

References

Primary Sources

Kafka, F. (1952). *Selected short stories of Franz Kafka* (Willa, & E. Muir, Trans.). New York: The Modern Library.
Kafka, F. (1968). *The trial* (Willa, & E. Muir, Trans.). New York: Schocken Books.
Kafka, F. (1976). In M. Brod (Ed.), *Diaries, 1910–1923*. Schocken Books.
Kafka, F. (1994). *The trial*. Trans. Idris Parry. London: Penguin Books.
Kafka, F. (1998). *The trial* (Breon Mitchell, Trans.). New York: Schocken Books.
Kafka, F. (2010). *Dearest father* (Hannah, & R. Stokes, Trans.). Berkshire UK: OneWorld Classics.
The trial (Alpha Video 2003; directed by Orson Welles).
The Thin Blue Line (MGM 2005; directed by Errol Morris).

Secondary Sources

Brod, M. (1995). *Franz Kafka: A Biography*. De Capo Press.
Burkert, W. (1983). *Homo Necans: The anthropology of ancient Greek sacrificial ritual and myth* (P. Bing, Trans.). Berkeley: University of California Press.
Canetti, E. (1974). *Kafka's other trial: The letters to Felice* (C. Middleton, Trans.). New York: Schocken Books.
Cohen, F. S. (1960). *Legal conscience: Selected papers of Felix S. Cohen*. Yale University Press.
Corcos, C. A. (1998). Presuming innocence: Alan Pakula and Scott Thurow take on the Great American legal fiction. *Oklahoma City University Law Review, 22*, 129–166.
Dawson, D. (2013). *Flesh becomes word: A lexicography of the scapegoat or, the history of an idea*. Michigan State University Press.
Deinert, H. (1964). Kafka's Parable before the law. *Germanic Review, 39*(3), 192–200.
Deleuze, G., & Guattari, F. (1986). *Kafka: Toward a minor literature* (D. Polan, Trans.). Minneapolis: University of Minnesota Press.

Dickey, J. (1970). *Deliverance*. New York: Delta.

Eliade, M. (1988). *The sacred and the profane: The nature of religion* (W. R. Trask, Trans.). New York: Harcourt, Inc.

Friedlander, S. (2013). *Franz Kafka: The poet of shame and guilt*. Yale University Press.

Gillet, L. [A Monk of the Eastern Church]. (1980). *The year of grace of the lord. A scriptural and liturgical commentary on the calendar of the orthodox church* (D. Cowen, Trans.). London: Mowbray.

Girard, R. (1977). *Violence and the sacred* (P. Gregory, Trans.). Baltimore: The Johns Hopkins University Press.

Girard, R. (1978). *To double business bound: essays on literature, mimesis, and anthropology*. The Johns Hopkins University Press.

Girard, R. (1986). *The scapegoat* (Y. Freccero, Trans.). Baltimore: Johns Hopkins University Press.

Girard, R. (1987). *Job: The victim and his people* (Y. Freccero, Trans.). London: The Athlone Press.

Girard, R., Oughourlian, J. M., & Lefort, G. (2003). *Things hidden since the foundation of the world* (S. Bann, & M. Metteer, Trans.). London: Continuum.

Leavitt, J. O. (2007). *Esoteric symbols: The tarot in Yeats, Eliot, and Kafka*. University Press of America.

Mack, B. (1987). Introduction: religion and ritual. In R. G. Hamerton-Kelly (Eds.), *Violent origins: Walter Burkert, Rene Girard, and Jonathan Z. Smith on Ritual killing and cultural formation* (pp. 1–72). Stanford University Press.

McKenna, A. J. (1992). *Violence and difference: Girard, Derrida, and deconstruction*. University of Illinois Press.

Mellon, J. (1970). Josef K. and the law. *Texas Studies in Literature and Language 12*(2), 295–302.

Mitchell, B. (1998). Translator's Preface in Franz Kafka. In *The trial* (pp. xv–xxxvi). Schocken Books.

Parry, I. (1994). Introduction. In Franz Kafka, *The trial* (I. Parry, Trans.) (pp. i–xxiv). London: Penguin Books.

Pinker, A. (2008). A goat to go to Azazel. *Journal of Hebrew Scriptures, 7*, 2–25.

Purcell, E. A. (1973). *The crisis of democratic theory: Scientific naturalism and the problem of value*. The University of Kentucky Press.

Ranieri, J. (2008). Modernity and the Jewish question: What Leo Strauss learned from Friedrich Nietzsche. In R. Hamerton-Kelly (Ed.), *Politics and apocalypse* (pp. 139–188). Michigan State University Press.

Sarat, A. (2007). Fathers in law: Violence and reason in 12 angry men. *Chicago-Kent Law Review, 82*(2), 863–886.

Sherwin, R. K. (2000). *When law goes pop: The vanishing line between law and popular culture*. The University of Chicago Press.

Thomson, D. (1996). *Rosebud: The story of Orson Welles*. Vintage Books.

Wright, D. P. (1988). *The disposal of impurity: Elimination rites in the bible and in Hittite and mesopotamian literature*. Scholars Press.

Wright, D. P. (1986). The gesture of hand placement in the Hebrew Bible and in Hittite literature. *Journal of the American Oriental Society, 106*(3), 433–446.

Chapter 9
'...Why do we, All of us, have to Keep Judging and Being Judged?': The Scapegoat and the Scapegoater in Albert Camus' *The Stranger* and *The Fall*

Abstract This chapter continues the approach of the preceding one in discussing a legal, or 'confessional', narrative told from the perspective of the scapegoat-victim: Mersault from Camus' *L'Etranger/The Stranger* (1942). It is then read against a rival confessional text, this one told by a sacrificer of scapegoats, the criminal lawyer Jean-Baptiste Clamence in Camus' *La Chute/The Fall* (1956). Consistent with Camus' own aesthetic concern with Greek tragedy, I argue for Mersault's (secret) status as the *pharmakon*, the sacred bringer of disease into the community whose ritualistic murder releases the occult, or 'magical', power of cure latent within the slain body of the victim. Just as Kakfa's *The Trial* was the diary of a Mosaic scapegoat, so *The Stranger* is the testament of a Sophoclean *pharmakon.* Reading Mersault as *pharmakon* also provides the perfect explanation for the novel's famously ambiguous ending, which an enactment of Aristotle's theory of *katharsis*, the *telos* of Greek tragedy. By contrast, Jean-Baptiste Clamence's verbose and duplicitous confession in *The Fall* is a book length exercise in false consciousness: here, the advocate/comforter/helper/defender (Clamence = clemency = paraclete) is a parasitical figure, a high priest of bad faith, a 'judge-penitent', whose existence can only be justified through his cynical pronouncements of the existence of the 'plague' of reciprocal violence: a perfect twentieth century re-staging of *Oedipus the King*. Reversing the perspective of the sacrificial victim Mersault, Clamence, Camus' second great anti-hero, provides us with the cynical confession' of the ritualistic victimizer: the lawyer-as-judge-penitent as the manufacturer of scapegoats.

Keywords *Pharmakos* · *Pharmakon* · *Katharma* · *Katharsis* · The tragic hero · Absurdity · Chance · Accident · Lucidity

9.1 *L'absurde*: Fate Versus the Accident

By his own reckoning Rene Girard detected the fatal flaw of the great wannabe tragic hero of the twentieth century, French existentialist Albert Camus: an interminable case of romanticism cross-pollinated with juvenile delinquency. Commenting upon

E. M. Wilson, *Rene Girard, Law, Literature, and Cinema*,
https://doi.org/10.1007/978-981-97-1156-7_9

arguably the author's greatest novel, Girard holds forth that *L'Etranger* (1942; translated as either *The Stranger* or, less accurately, as *The Outsider*) was not 'written for pure art's sake, nor was it written to vindicate the victims of persecution everywhere. Camus set out to prove that the hero according to his heart will necessarily be persecuted by society. He set out to prove, in other words, that "the judges are always in the wrong"' (Girard, 1978: 18). One can always recognize a 'romantic hero' because he or she is the one displaying in the most ostentatious manner possible a moral Manicheanism taken to its most extreme form, as does Camus' greatest romantic anti-hero, Mersault: 'The exception is always opposed to the norm as Good is opposed to Evil. Mersault alone is innocent in a sea of guilt; he dies the victim of the Others ... He is the judge of his judges, like all the romantics before him. The hero always escapes the curse which his creator hurls at the rest of mankind' (Girard, 1965: 271). But Girard has Camus' (and Mersault's) number, for the romantic hero is invariably the mask of the equally Manichaean romantic novelist: 'There is always someone who comes out on top of the romantic game unscathed and that someone has to be the *I*, the author, before it is *I*, the reader' (Girard, 1965: 271). We used to call this self-righteousness, the interminable game of holier-than-thou; today we know it as narcissism, a mark of liminality[1] and a sign of the persona of the studied performance of alienation—which Camus, a French cultural superstar for a while, had perfected as an art form.

> Why does Camus crave solitude and society at the same time; why is he both repelled and fascinated by *les autres*? The contradiction is really inherent in the Romantic personality. The Romantic does not want to be alone, but *to be seen alone*. In *Crime and Punishment*, Dostoevski shows that solitary dreams and the 'trial' are the two inseparable facets, the dialectically-related 'moments' of the Romantic consciousness. But this proud consciousness refuses to acknowledge openly the fascination it feels for others (Girard, 1978: 24).

From this quite accurate observation Girard moves to his damning conclusion: the romantic author/persona/anti-hero is a damaged adolescent. 'Observers have pointed out the element of latter-day Romanticism in juvenile delinquency' (Girard, 1978: 21) he informs us, and Camus was ultimately, but predictably, betrayed by his own romanticism[2] which provided the ideological alibi for his aesthetic enrapture with juvenile delinquency as exhibited in *The Stranger*: 'This social aspect can easily be

---

[1] At least until the recent cultural revolution/catastrophe known as 'social media' which has more or less normalized previously neurotic, if not pathological, varieties of emotional disorders.

[2] Although Camus was by no means the only one: 'Romantic individualism becomes so exacerbated with these writers that it verges on a certain type of neurotic behavior' (Girard, 1978: 25). Girard is quite right to advance beyond this point and to accuse Camus of both artistic and psychological solipsism: 'The close analogy between the murder of the Arab and the style of the novel is not difficult to explain; every aspect of the work bears the imprint of a single creative act that stands in the same relation to its own consequence, the book, as Mersault's behavior to his murder. The "innocent murder" is really the image and the crux of the whole creative process' (Girard, 1978: 29). Girard goes on to suggest that 'We feel that someone, on some fine day, handed Camus a pen and a piece of paper and Camus did the natural and mechanical thing to do, in such circumstances, which is to start writing, just as Meursault did the natural and mechanical thing to do, when you receive a gun, which is to start shooting. The book, like the murder, appears to be the result of fortuitous circumstances. The overall impression is that *L'Etranger* was written in the same bored,

reconciled with the ultra-Romantic conception of the self that underlines the novel' (Girard, 1978: 21). In almost criminological fashion, Girard forensically dissects author and text[3] holding that *L'Etranger* 'reflects the world view of the juvenile delinquent with unmatched perfection precisely because it is not aware of reflecting anything, except, of course, the innocence of its hero and the injustice of the judges' (Girard, 1978: 32). And the master-sign that Camus fashioned for himself to impose a semiotic unity upon his delinquent fictional landscape was an all-time favorite adolescent gimmick herein re-worked as high concept: *l'absurde*, or *absurdity*.

> Mersault is the fictional embodiment of the nihilistic individualism expounded in *Le Mythe de Sissyphe* and commonly referred to as *l'absurde*. Mersault is possessed by this *absurd* as others, in a different context, are possessed by religious grace. But the word *absurd* is not really necessary; the author himself ... defines his hero as a man 'who does not play the game.' Mersault 'refuses to lie' and, immediately, 'society feels threatened.' This hero has a positive significance, therefore; he is not an *epave*, a derelict; 'he is a man poor and naked who is in love with the sun' (Girard, 1978: 9).

And the one by whom society comes to feel threatened is, among other things, the one who is most at risk of being declared a scapegoat, whenever mere free-floating anxiety coagulates into full-throttle existential crisis, the mimetic crisis of undifferentiation. Remembering all the while, however, that the One who 'refuses to lie' is the same One who says *non* to *meconnaissance.*

Central to Girard's notion of the sacrificial mechanism, and something which is quite is germane to Camus' literary project, is the clandestine nature of its operations: at all times, the sacrificing community must exhibit a total absence of self-awareness as to what it is 'really doing' when it murders a scapegoat[4]: 'The inaccessible character of the generative event ... is an essential part of that theory, something that it cannot do without. In order to retain its structuring influence the generative violence must remain hidden: misapprehension is indispensable to all religious or post-religious structuring' (Girard, 1977: 310). And the reason why this is so is because generative violence, although the anthropological source of all that there,[5] is inseparable from the notion of the ridiculous, for no matter how counterintuitive this may seem to us at first, 'ridiculousness' is a satirical way of signifying absence, as Kafka labored to show.[6] Sacred violence is, literally, an emptiness.

> Although generative violence is invisible, it can logically be deduced from myths and rituals once their real structures have been perceived. The further one advances along this path and the more transparent the true nature of religious thought appears, the clearer it becomes that there is nothing to suppress or to hide. There is no justification for the idea that religious

absent-minded, and apathetic fashion as the Arab was murdered. We have a crime and no criminal; we have a book and no author' (Girard, 1978: 28–29).

[3] Clearly not realizing that both were already 'dead' in both the medical and the post-structural sense.

[4] Which, as should be obvious, is how Girard reads the famous words of Christ on the cross: 'Father, forgive them, for they do not know what they do' (Luke 23: 34). In anthropological terms this is literally true.

[5] See Chaps. 1 and 2, above.

[6] See Chap. 8, above.

> thought refuses to acknowledge a threatening self-awareness. Such awareness does not yet present any threat to religion. It is we who are threatened by it, we who flee from it (Girard, 1977: 309).

The reasons for this are multitudinous, but one of the most important and surprising is the ineradicable randomness of the selection process: a sacrifice must be found in order to overcome the reciprocal violence of undifferentiation, but the practical efficacy of the procedure is completely neutralized by an understanding of the pivotal role played by *chance*—a difficulty greatly enhanced by the fact that at the time of undifferentiation there is nothing that would clearly mark out the scapegoated One from the scapegoating Many. If the truth be told, that which is random is the enemy of everything that claims the status of the Divine, that which is the opposite of ridiculousness—or absurdity.

> It is natural to assume that the best-concealed aspect of the generative mechanism will be the most crucial element, the one most likely to render the sacrificial system non-functional if it becomes known. This aspect will be the arbitrary selection of the victim, its essential insignificance, which contradicts the meaning accumulated upon its head by the scapegoat projection (Girard, 1977: 311).

The archaic sacrificers were fully aware of this so that Girard is on solid ground when pointing out that any 'close examination' of the scapegoat selection process 'will reveal that even this aspect is not really hidden; it can be readily detected once we know what we must look for. Frequently the rituals themselves are engineered so that they include an element of chance in the choice of the victim, but mythologists have never taken this into account' (Girard, 1977: 311). To-hide-in-plain-sight was the universal ploy settled upon by the first scapegoaters and entire mythological systems were constructed in order to make the mis-recognition work.

> In order to meet the threat of maleficent contagion the community must have recourse to the universal model, to generative violence; it must attend to the advice of the sacred itself.... The community has perceived and retained the role of chance in the liberating decision. If violence is given free play, chance alone is responsible for the ultimate resolution of the process; and the rite tries to force the hand of chance before violence has the opportunity to act. The rite aims at the final result, achieving, as it were, a minimum expenditure of violence (Girard, 1977: 312).

What we get is the near-universal but latently contradictory belief that 'Chance can always be trusted to reveal the truth, for it reflects the will of the divinity' (Girard, 1977: 313) and that the 'sacred nature of Chance is reflected in the practice of the lottery. In some sacrificial rites the choice of victim by means of a lottery serves to underline the relationship between chance and generative violence' (Girard, 1977: 314). To cite just one example, that of the annual festival of Zeus on the island of Cos where

> The choice of the victim was determined by a sort of lottery in which all the cattle, which were originally presented separately by each division of each tribe, were mixed together in a common herd.[7] The animal ultimately selected was executed on the following day, having

---

[7] Predictably, Girard interprets this as a symbolization of the crisis of undifferentiation; 'his deliberate confusion of distinctions, this merger into a communal togetherness, constitutes an obligatory

first been 'introduced to Hestia,'[8] and undergone various rites. Immediately prior to the ritual presentation, Hestia herself receives homage in the form of an animal sacrifice (Girard, 1977: 314).

Sophocles picks up on this and runs with it in the theatrical (and sacrificial) game of Greek Tragedy: 'Oedipus, it will be remembered refers to himself as the son of *Tyche*—that is, Fortune or Chance' (Girard, 1977: 312)[9] and the rhetorical contest among Oedipus, Creon, and Tiresias can be understood to constitute a type of game, or a rule-bound rite, such as an oratorical duel or the (not so) cunning stratagems of adversarial advocacy.[10] Scapegoating, quite literally, is a kind of game, a sports-like competition.

> Sporting contests and games of chance appear to modern man most incongruous as ritual practices.... But, as usual, we have got things reversed. For us, games of chance are a secular activity upon which a religious meaning has been superimposed. The true state of affairs is precisely the opposite: games originate in rites that have been divested, to a greater or lesser degree, of their sacred character (Girard, 1977: 312).

The Stranger, like *The Trial*, is an allegory about ritualistic sacrifice written from the perspective of the scapegoated victim while *The Fall/La Chute* (1956), by contrast, is an allegory written from the perspective of the 'victimizer', or the sacrificer. Despite all of their apparent differences, Kafka and Camus share an over-arching concern with a highly 'existentialist' vision of guilt; 'Camus' work, in its most intimate movement is, like Kafka's, an expiation...In the work of Kafka and Camus alike, the error to be expiated is associated with a feeling of estrangement' (Darzins, 1960: 98, 99) or, we suspect, *ressentiment*. But the different cultural templates that the authors utilize, the Hebraic versus the Hellenic, decisively affect the divergent moral tone of the two novels. Camus, because of his own background and temperament, draws more directly from classical mythology and Greek tragedy than does Kafka; Josef K. is represented as the prospective sacrificial victim, the goat of the sin offering from the Book of Leviticus, whereas *The Stranger*'s Mersault (or Monsieur 'Death-Leap') is the embodiment of the Hellenic form of the sacrificial One, the *pharmakon*, a very different type of creature, now allegorized in secular form as the expellable victim of 'bad faith,' a *meconnaissance* that is at least partly aware of itself. In a complementary manner, the narrator of *The Fall*, Jean-Baptiste Clamence, is the personification of the post-theistic awareness of the absurdity of generative violence, mediated by the pseudo-confessional declamation of the bad faith of the willful but self-knowing persecutor of the innocent victim; in absolute distinction from

---

preamble to the lottery; clearly it was introduced to reproduce the exact order of the original events. The arbitrary and violent resolution that serves as the model for the lottery takes place at the very height of the sacrificial crisis, when the distinctions delegated to the members of society order succumb to the reciprocal violence and are merged into a communal mass' (Girard, 1977: 315).

[8] The goddess of the Hearth, which 'in all probability marked the place where the original act of communal violence was perpetrated' (Girard, 1977: 314).

[9] '...I count myself the son of Chance, the great goddess, giver of all good things—' (Sophocles, 1984: 224). Sometimes. It depends.

[10] See Chap. 1, above.

Mersault, it is Clamence's identity as an extraordinarily 'verbose narrator' (Weisberg, 1984: 123) that marks him as a scapegoater as opposed to the scapegoat. From our perspective, the question concerning Camus is this: why should a mid-twentieth century atheist French existentialist mine Greek Tragedy in order to produce the artistic trope that proved central to his two greatest novels, both of which were in some way concerned with capital punishment? The answer is that Greek Tragedy provided the only available means of re-investing the victim of lawful execution with the requisite degree of meaning necessary to overcome secular existentialism's greatest obstacle: the absurdity of the universe. Today 'All that is left of tragedy is the concept of unmerited guilt, the inevitable defeat and unavoidable mistake. But the absolute has ceased to exist. It has been replaced by the absurdity of the human situation' (Jan Knott qtd. Goodhart, 1978: 62). So that like the Greeks before him Camus had to tortuously revisit the great *skandalon*, or stumbling-block, of chance in order to elevate his anti-heroic alter ego Mersault, to the level of romantic grandeur, or, at the very least, the fever pitch of juvenile delinquency as post-adolescent pseudo-godhood.

Which is how it comes about that the coherence of Camus' aesthetic viewpoint comes to depend upon a very particular interpretation of Greek Tragedy: the systematic de-sacralization of mythological tropes as a way of making traditional Hellenic religion amenable to the political and juridical needs of the newly emergent city-state system (the *polis*) of the Sixth Century B.C.E. It is no coincidence that this occurs at the end of the pre-Socratic era and the cusp of the development of philosophy and logic (Vernant & Vidal-Naquet, 1990).[11]

> Tragedy is born when myth starts to be considered from the point of view of a citizen.... The drama brings to the stage an ancient heroic legend. For the city this legendary world constitutes the past—a past sufficiently distant for the contrasts, between the mythical traditions that it embodies and the new forms of legal and political thought, to be clearly visible; yet a past still close enough for the clash of values still be a painful one and for this clash still to be currently taking place (Vernant & Vidal-Naquet, 1990: 33).

The public spectacle of Tragedy was one of the primary mediums to regulate these theo-political transformations, and the standard account of Tragedy, in terms of both narrative structure and aesthetic effect, was, of course, *The Poetics* of Aristotle who regarded theater as a carefully plotted exercise in mimesis: 'Tragedy...is an imitation...of incidents arousing pity and fear' (Aristotle, 1920: 45).[12] Or, in slightly more complex terms, "Tragedy is an imitation of an action that is serious, complete, and of a certain magnitude... [effecting] through pity and fear...the proper *catharsis*, or purgation, of these emotions" so that from 'this definition it appears first, that the

[11] As is well known, the first philosophers, but especially Plato, were opposed to both Tragedy and Poetry—or alternatively, tragic and poetic 'consciousness'—on the grounds that insofar as Tragedy 'represents "action and life," it conflicts with the truth' (Victor Goldsmith qtd. Vernant & Vidal-Naquet, 1990: 417 n 2).

[12] Girard shares this assessment; even contemporary theater 'relies on imperfectly detected scapegoat processes for its cathartic effects, much attenuated, of course, but structurally identical to the rituals of primitive religion ... and the most efficient strategy of victimage corresponds to the "esthetic rules" defined by Aristotle in his *Poetics*'.

genus of tragedy is Imitation' (Butcher, 1902: 240–241).[13] There are three central elements of the Aristotelian notion of Tragedy properly constituted.[14] The first is the *pharmakos/ katharma*, the generic term for the Hellenic sacrificial victim and the approximate equivalent of the Biblical scapegoat. The second is the *tragic hero*, the protagonist of Greek tragedy, who doubles as a disguised or concealed representation-substitution of the *pharmakos*, meaning that Tragedy is the deliberately occluded mis-remembering of an archaic sacrificial ritual. The third is *katharsis*, the *telos*, or 'purpose', of Greek tragedy, that is achieved through the theatrical enactment of the suffering and/or death of the tragic hero/*pharmakos/ katharma*. In other words, whatever the truth of the scapegoat in objective reality, the phenomenology of the subjective experience of *katharsis* is no lie. Both *katharma* and *katharsis* are derived from the earlier term *katharos*, signifying a generic sacred potency, so that *katharma* is 'not limited to the victim or the surrogate object; it also refers to the supreme efforts of a mythic or tragic hero. Plutarch speaks of the *pontia katharmata*, expulsions that purified the seas, with reference to the labors of Heracles.... "to purge the land of monsters"' (Girard, 1977: 288). There is a subtle doubling of terms here and the 'common denominator appears to be acute suffering destined to assure recovery from an illness or designed to bring about the natural or artificial resolution of a potential crisis' (Girard, 1977: 288). 'Purgation' connotes the medicinal while also denoting the more religious notion of exorcism, which is a form of medicinal-like healing realized through a sacred act of expelling a destructive supernatural force.

> The mutations of meaning from the human *katharma* to the medical katharsis are paralleled by those of the human pharmakos to the medical *pharmakon*, which signifies at once 'poison' and 'remedy'. In both cases we pass from the surrogate victim—or rather, his representative—to a drug that possesses a simultaneous potential for good and bad, one that serves as a physical transposition of sacred duality (Girard, 1977: 288).

The result is a comingling of the profane with the occult that is not lost on Girard: 'Whenever we describe the generative process or its products in terms of expulsion, purgation, or purification, we are attributing natural causes to phenomena that are not in the least natural, because they derive from violence' linked with the other-worldly (Girard, 1977: 289). What matters for the clandestinely arbitrary operations of generative violence is that the one chosen for execution, this as the result of a divine mandate which is neither divine nor mandated, can be performatively reconfigured as both the cause of the solution to the crisis of the community, the 'sacred duality' of the sacrificial victim yet another example of the ambivalent double transference of mimesis.

> In addition to its religious sense .... the word *katharsis* has a specific use in medical language. A cathartic medicine is a powerful drug that induces the evacuation of humors or other substances judged to be noxious. The illness and its cure are often seen as one; or at least, the medicine is considered capable of aggravating the symptoms, bringing about a salutary

---

[13] 'Aristotle notes that tragedy is the imitation of an action, *mimesis praxeos*. It presents characters engaged in action ... And the word 'drama' comes from the Doric *dran* that corresponds to the Attic *prattein*, to act' (Vernant & Vidal-Naquet, 1990: 44).

[14] I discuss each of these in greater detail below.

> crisis that will lead to recovery. In other words, the crisis is provoked by a supplementary dosage of the affliction resulting in the expulsion of the pathogenetic agents along with itself. The operation is the same as that of the human *katharma*, although in medicine the act of purgation is not mythic but real (Girard, 1977: 287–288).

In order to unify these three elements into an aesthetically satisfying and politically efficacious whole, Tragedy rigorously complies with its signature, or stereotypical, plot device: the *fall* of the tragic hero, a calamitous movement from the high to the low, so that Tragedy can only be about aristocrats, for if one is a peasant or a merchant there is, quite literally, nowhere to fall to.[15] Aristotle makes all of this painfully clear.

> We assume that, for the finest form of Tragedy, the Plot must not be simple but complex; and further, that it must imitate actions arousing pity and fear, since that is the distinctive function of this kind of imitation...pity is occasioned by undeserved misfortune, and fear by that of one like ourselves... [Therefore, the tragic hero must be] the intermediate kind of personage, a man not pre-eminently virtuous and just, whose misfortune, however, is brought upon him not by vice and depravity but by some error of judgment, [one of] the number of those in enjoyment of great reputation and prosperity...The perfect Plot, accordingly, must have a single, and not...a double issue; the change in the hero's fortunes must not be from misery to happiness, but on the contrary from happiness to misery; and the cause of it must lie not in any depravity, but in some great error on his part...[the hero having] been involved, as either agents or sufferers, in some deed of horror (Aristotle, 1920: 51).

Girard clearly explicates the implied meaning of this passage: 'Aristotle is discretely vague about which emotions tragedy is meant to purge. But if we see tragedy in terms of fire to combat fire, it is clear that its purpose is to protect the community against its own violence' (Girard, 1977: 292) meaning that the emotions to be purged are those that are attendant upon the psychic contagion, or 'plague', of the universal cause of intra-community violence, undifferentiation.

> On closer inspection, Aristotle's text is something of a manual of sacrificial practices, for the qualities that make a 'good' tragic hero are precisely those required of the sacrificial victim. If the latter is to polarize and purge the emotions of the community, he must at once resemble the members of the community and differ from them; he must be at once insider and outsider, both 'double' and incarnation of 'sacred difference.' He must be neither wholly good nor wholly bad. A certain degree of goodness is required in the tragic hero in order to establish sympathy between him and the audience; yet a certain degree of weakness, a 'tragic flaw' is needed, to neutralize the goodness and permit the audience to tolerate the hero's downfall and death....Having accompanied the hero part of the way, the audience suddenly perceives him as wholly 'other' and abandons him to his fate, his superhuman ignominy and glory. The spectator may shudder with 'pity and fear,' but he must also feel a deep sense of gratitude for his own orderly and relatively secure existence. Every true work of art might be said to partake of the initiatory process in that it forces itself the emotions, offers

[15] Which is why Oedipus is considered the archetype of the tragic hero, being the one who 'falls'; 'Oedipus is "double" ... He is a "savior" king [the destroyer of the sphinx] who, at the beginning of the play, is the object of the prayers of an entire people as if he were a god holding the city's destiny in his hands; but he is also an abominable defilement, a monster of impurity concentrating within himself all the evil and sacrilege in the world, who must be ejected as *pharmakos*, as scapegoat, so that the city can become pure once again and be saved' (Vernant & Vidal-Naquet, 1990: 106). The sacred duality of Oedipus as a tragic hero is conveyed by the dramatic representation of the dual nature of the *pharmakon* as the poison that heals.

> intimations of violence, and instils respect for the power of violence; that is, it promotes prudence [moderation] and discourages hubris [pride; envy] (Girard, 1977: 291–292).

The prevention, or destruction, of arrogant pride, the precondition for the psychic contagion of mimetic envy and the resultant loss of violence-inhibiting differentiation, really does seem to be the primary objective of Tragedy.

> The pain is expelled when the taint of egoism is removed...The tragic *catharsis* requires that suffering shall be exhibited in one of its comprehensive aspects, that the deeds and fortunes of the actors shall attach themselves to larger issues, and the spectator himself be lifted above the special case [of the dramatic plot], and brought face to face with universal law and the divine plan of the world. In order that an emotion may not only be excited but also allayed—that the tumult of the mind be resolved into a pleasurable calm—the emotion, stirred by a fictitious representation, must divest itself of its purely selfish and material elements, and become part of a new order of things (Butcher, 1902: 268, 271).[16]

And to 'become part of a new order of things' signifies voluntary submission to a regenerative process of reconciliation and integration. So it is the *telos* of Tragedy—generative unanimity by way of sacrifice—that explains the defining property (*accidens*) of the tragically flawed tragic hero which is the absence of self-knowledge, for 'does not the basis and origin of his actions lie elsewhere than within himself?' (Vernant & Vidal-Naquet, 1990: 80). Is it not the case that true significance of the options available to him, such as Oedipus' suicidal decision to continue his quest for the facts surrounding his birth parents, invariably

> Remain beyond him right up to the end, because they depend not so much upon his own intentions and plans as upon the general order of the world, presided over by the gods, which alone can give human enterprises their authentic meaning? Only right at the end of his drama does it all become clear to the agent. As he undergoes what he believed he himself has decided, he understands the real meaning of what has in fact been accomplished without either his desire or knowing it. In his purely human dimensions the agent is not the sufficient cause and reason for his actions: On the contrary, it his action, recoiling upon him as the gods have, in their sovereignty, ordered, that reveals him to himself, showing him the true nature of what he is and what he does (Vernant & Vidal-Naquet, 1990: 80).

The '*true nature of what he is*' is the scapegoat and '*what he does*' is to undergo the ritualistic sacrifice that is the salvation of the city. And the key element to secure the production of community-saving *katharsis* for the Socratic-era audiences of Hellas—the imitative reproduction of the release from reciprocal violence that

[16] 'For there to be tragic action [*mimesis praxeos*] it is necessary that a concept of human order with its own characteristics should have already emerged and that the human and divine spheres should have become sufficiently distinct from each other for them to stand in opposition; yet at the same time they must continue to appear as inseparable. The tragic sense of responsibility makes its appearance at the point when, in human action, a place is given to internal debate on the part of the subject, to intention and premeditation, but when this human action has still not acquired enough consistency and autonomy to be entirely self-sufficient [mortals being the 'plaything' of supernatural forces]. The true domain of tragedy lies in the border zone where human actions are hinged together with the divine powers, where—unknown to the agent—they derive their true meaning by becoming an integral part of an order that is beyond man and that eludes him' (Vernant & Vidal-Naquet, 1990: 47). It should be obvious what the tragic flaw of contemporary Tragedy is: how can the 'tragic' actor reconcile herself to a dis-ordered universe, meaning absurd, or, better yet, accidental? See below.

was the *telos* of the pre-historic ritual murder of the scapegoat—was the ability of the tragic hero to conform to the community's expectations of normality, literally 'one of the crowd'. It is the *pharmakon*'s resemblance to everyone else that creates the dramatic space allowing the salvific 'truth' of the sacrificial mechanism to be operate: he-who-appears-the-same is really someone (or something) quite different, enabling the primal difference between sacrifice and sacrificed, victim and victimizer, friend and enemy, to be re-enacted all over again and permitting lost distinctions to be recovered and enforced. And it is the tragedian's ability to poetically entice the audience into perceiving the tragic hero as simultaneously same and different that enables the psychic potency of a transformative empathy to operate, allowing the viewer to affectively respond to the elemental difference that resides within superficial similarity.

> The tragic sufferer is a man like ourselves...and on this inner likeness the effect of tragedy...-mainly hinges. Without it our complete sympathy would not be enlisted. The resemblance on which Aristotle insists is one of moral character. His hero...is not a man of flawless perfection, nor yet one of consummate villainy; by which we must not understand that he has merely average or mediocre qualities. He rises, indeed, above the common level in moral elevation and dignity, but he is not free from frailties and imperfections (Butcher, 1902: 260).

So that instead of physically sacrificing fleshy and bloody scapegoats in real time, the Greek tragedian could induce the regenerative effects of the purgative lynching by leading the audience into partaking as spectators of a virtual simulation of the originating act, now rationalized and rendered culturally safe through the good manners of civic participation, which included going to the theater as proof of citizenship.[17] Camus knew all of this. The challenge that he faced was to find a way of reconciling the sacred tragic of the randomly generated scapegoat with the profane ridiculousness of the *accident*, the ineradicable element of absurdity that, within the secular age God's death, proves to be the spawner of twentieth century scapegoats.

[17] 'Tragedy is not only an art form; it is also a social institution that the city, by establishing competitions in tragedies, set up alongside its political and legal institutions. The city established under the authority of the eponymous archon [the legendary first ruler or 'founding Father'], in the same urban space and in accordance with the same institutional norms as the popular assemblies or courts, a spectacle open to all the citizens, directed, acted, and judged by the qualified representatives of the various tribes [the civic divisions of the non-slave population]. In this way it turned itself into theater. Its subject, in a sense, was itself and it acted itself out before the public' (Vernant & Vidal-Naquet, 1990: 33).

9.2 The Facts of the Strange Case of M. Mersault (a.k.a. 'M. Death-Jump')

Just as Josef K., by Franz K.'s own design, scored extremely high on the index of the Levitical sacrificial goat of the sin offering,[18] so does Mersault rank equally highly on the Aristotelian short-list of the attributes of the tragic hero. Although a 'commoner' in terms of social class, Mersault's tragic 'moral elevation and dignity' resides in his fantastical moral honesty, which Camus quite self-consciously framed as Mersault's *lucidity* in his objective perception and subjective sensation of the absurdity of existence, so that his emotional and affective blankness constituted a form of existential integrity: 'Maman[19] died today. Or yesterday maybe, I don't know (Camus, 1989: 3) …. It occurred to me that anyway one more Sunday was over, that Maman was buried now, that I was going back to work, and that, really, nothing had changed' (Camus, 1989: 24). Girard is fully aware of Mersault's status as an 'icon' of mid-twentieth century existentialism, a very fancy term for bourgeois juvenile delinquency.

> We have always pictured Mersault as a stranger to the sentiments of other men. Love and hatred, ambition and envy, greed and jealousy are equally foreign to him. He attends the funeral of his mother as impassively as he watches, on the following day, a Fernandel[20] movie. Eventually, Mersault kills a man, but how could we feel that he is a real criminal? How could this man have any motive for murder? (Girard, 1978: 9).

For fellow delinquent Jean-Paul Sartre the signature 'Hemingway-esque' nature of Camus' prose owes much to the controlling effect of lucidity, the author's key aesthetic insight, which is the unblinking apperception of ridiculousness conveyed through the compartmentalizing of sense perceptions as unconnected atomistic units.

> *The Stranger* is to be a novel of discrepancy, divorce and disorientation; hence its skillful construction…*The Stranger* gives us a succession of luminously clear views… [Both Camus and Hemingway] write in the same short sentences. Each sentence refuses to exploit the momentum accumulated by preceding ones. Each is a new beginning. Each is like a snapshot of a gesture or object. For each new gesture and word there is a new and corresponding sentence (Sartre, 1962: 114, 116).

But as Aristotle reminds us, the quality that makes the tragic hero high is, once inverted by the dramatic plot, the flaw that brings him low. Which means that there are two apparently serious obstacles in proving Mersault's bona fides as a tragic hero. The first one is that there is a problem with establishing that normality which is required by the sacrificial offering.

> Mostly, I could tell, I made [the examining magistrate] feel uncomfortable. He didn't understand me, and he was sort of holding it against me. I felt the urge to reassure him that I was like everybody else, just like everybody else. But really there wasn't much point, and I gave up the idea out of laziness (Camus, 1989: 66).

---

[18] See Chap. 8, above.

[19] In French, the affectionate form of 'Mother': Mama or Mommy. Which adds to the sting.

[20] A French comedic film actor and vaudevillian from the 1930s to the 1960s, not unlike Jerry Lewis but much funnier.

The second obstacle is that, in direct violation to the theo-dramatic backdrop to Tragedy which, being an allegory of the sacrificial mechanism, must involve the gods in some manner, Mersault appears as a victim of pure randomness. Greek Tragedy, however, operating on the basis of mythology which is the 'lie' that conceals the absurdity/randomness of sacrifice, does not and cannot recognize chance, and replaces the arbitrariness of events with *fate* (*moirai*) in an act of mystification, for 'in a mythico-sacrificial world, what but the anger of a god could be thought to be the cause of any disastrous calamity?' (Bandera, 1989: 220). Once again, we have to face up to the centrality of *meconnaissance* to all aspects of the mythological.

> Modern man flatly rejects the notion that Chance is the reflection of divine will. For him, Chance embodies all the obvious characteristics of the sacred. Now it deals violently with man, now it showers him with gifts. Indeed, what is more capricious in its favors than Chance, more susceptible to those rapid reversals of temper that are invariably associated with the gods? (Girard, 1977: 314).[21]

An element of caution needs to be introduced here, as the Tragedians did, in fact, allow for an at least partial reconciliation between the divine and the random; those events that appear accidental to us may, in fact, have been the results of deities acting in an unconventional manner—'divine caprice,' 'divine anger,' divine intoxication, divine slumber, divine cruelty, or divine madness (e.g., Dionysus) are possible explanations utilized in both Greek Tragedy and *muthos* (Girard, 1986: 81–85). Perhaps the greatest example, though, is not Greek but Judaic, a text very near and dear to the heart of Franz Kafka: the late interpolation of the Prologue to The Book of Job explains that the apparently 'random' disasters that destroy Job's family and estate are the outcome of a wager made between God and Satan so that the entire catastrophe was the by-product of a kind of sacred game, suggesting that the 'Ancient of the Days' and 'the Accuser' are in some sense doubles; 'Believe in God or believe in the Devil, the universe will be no different for it: God as an absolute master ruling all things according to his caprice is indistinguishable from a spirit of mischief' (Christiane Fremont qtd. Bureau, 1989: 37).[22] The result is that

> Chance and destiny have this in common that both escape, by definition, the mastery of men. But men only see the unorganized in chance, while they invoke destiny to account for what they perceive as organized. Therefore if the arbitrary can appear to them as organized, it is because they interpret it as the production of a divinity or some postulated unknown force;

[21] Compare Jean-Pierre Vernant and Pierre Vidal-Naquet with Girard; 'Ancient drama explores the mechanisms through which an individual, however excellent he may be, is brought to his downfall, not as the result of external constraints or of his own perversity or vice, but because of an error, a mistake such as anyone might make. In this way, it lays bare the network of contradictory forces that assail all human beings, given that, not only in Greek society but in all societies and cultures, tensions and conflicts are inevitable. By these means, tragedy prompts the spectator to submit the human condition, limited and necessarily finite as it is, to a general interrogation. The scope of tragedy is such that it carries within itself a kind of knowledge or a theory concerning the illogical logic that governs the order of human activity' (Vernant & Vidal-Naquet, 1990: 247). The point that is missed here is that Tragedy's 'knowledge' of 'illogical logic' of humans is the esoteric truth of the sacrificial mechanism.

[22] See Chap. 8, above.

> even if its meaning escapes them, even if they rebel against the injustice of its decrees. Such is the logic of the sacred (Jean-Pierre Dupuy qtd. McKenna, 1992: 155).

It is absurdity, or the juvenile delinquent's open acknowledgement of it, however, that would seem to render Camus and Sophocles eternal strangers.

> He [Celeste] was asked if I was a customer of his and he said, 'yes, but he was also a friend'; what he thought of me, and he answered that I was a man; what he meant by that, and he stated that everybody knew what that meant; if I had noticed that I was ever withdrawn, and all he would admit was that I didn't speak unless I had something to say…He put his hands on the edge of the box, and you could tell he had something prepared. He said, 'The way I see it, it's bad luck. Everybody knows what bad luck is. It leaves you defenseless. And there it is! The way I see it, it's bad luck' … He again repeated that it was bad luck. And the judge said, 'Yes, fine. But we are here to judge just this sort of bad luck. Thank you' (Camus, 1989: 92).

Jean-Pierre Dupuy has identified the problem with exactitude: whether or not it is ever possible to re-make the accidental occurrence into a truly 'tragic' event.

> Consider Oedipus who kills his father at the fatal crossroads, or Camus' 'stranger,' Mersault, who kills the Arab under the blazing sun in Algiers—these events appear to the Mediterranean mind [sic] both as accidents and as acts of fate, in which *chance and destiny are merged and become one*….Accident, which points to chance, is the opposite of fate, which points to necessity; but without this opposite, fate cannot be realized. A follower of Derrida would say that the accident is the *supplement* of fate, in the sense that it is both its contrary and the condition of its occurring (Dupuy, 2013: 192).

Girard adopts a similar line of reasoning although with a more nuanced anthropological perspective: in social praxis our conscious referencing of fate is an unconscious invocation of the culturally suppressed notion of the supernatural (or the sacred), as Piggy attempted to warn the lost boys of *Lord of the Flies* with his parable of the television set that wouldn't work if ghosts were 'real'.[23]

> The critics [of *The Stranger*] who … have best captured the atmosphere of the murder reject all rational interpretations and attribute this event to the same *Fatum* that presides over the destinies of epic and tragic heroes in ancient and primitive literatures. They point out that the various incidents and objects connected with this episode can be interpreted as symbols of an implacable Nemesis. We still invoke fate today when we do not want to ascribe an event to chance, even though we cannot account for it. This 'explanation' is not meant seriously, however, when we are talking about real happenings taking place in the real world. We feel that this world is essentially rational and that it should be interpreted rationally (Girard, 1978: 15).

But although Sophocles may have no truck or trade with Camus, the real issue is that it is only the latter who is of the twentieth century, an arbitrary fact which encapsulates a wider truth: given the theo-political and onto-political foundations of Tragedy, is it possible, Nietzsche notwithstanding, to resurrect Tragedy, from either the 'spirit of music' or from some other medium?

One way to proceed, albeit an intellectually tortuous one, is to conclude that there is no such thing as randomness; according to Dupuy, the geo-culturally localized

---

[23] See Chap. 2, above.

'Mediterranean mind,' at least, is able to unify the willed and the un-willed at a higher level of synthesis. Obviously, we are free to reject the coherence of probability theory, although a great deal of intellectual labor has to be expended before we are able to arrive at this conclusion, and even if successful would likely to prove highly uneconomical. A more persuasive and cost-effective approach would appear to lie within the domain of aesthetics and the formalities of Art theory. Clearly, tragic art, to be tragic in the correct sense, must bear some sort of necessary relationship to the Dionysian, precisely because the event of collective *katharsis* is the overriding *telos* of the tragic art form.

> Greek tragedy...in its beginnings was but a wild religious excitement, a bacchic ecstasy. This aimless ecstasy was brought under artistic law. It was ennobled by objects worthy of an ideal emotion. The poets found out how the transport of human pity and human fear might, under the excitation of art, be dissolved in joy, and the pain escape in the purified tide of human sympathy (Butcher, 1902: 273).

The solution to the problem of tragedy in the age of de-sacralizing 'Enlightenment' (or the hegemony of the un-heroic middle class) may lie with the appropriation (or 'high-jacking' in the vulgar) of the function of Tragedy—*katharsis* through universal empathy—which is then re-deployed within a strictly contemporary context of an ontologically bereft modernity. A phenomenology of Tragedy, then, the remnant left over following the jettisoning of the metaphysical machinery of the pre-modern. The question now is: for the modern bourgeoisie what is it that is psychically guaranteed to induce a transformative and salvific sensation of 'pity and fear'? We have to return to Aristotle's typically useful set of instructions of 'how to do' tragedy.

> Now pity and fear in their relation to real life are by Aristotle reckoned ... [to be] a form of pain. Fear Aristotle defines to be 'a species of pain or disturbance arising from an impression of impending evil which is destructive or painful in its nature.' Moreover, the evil is near, not remote, and the persons threatened are ourselves. Similarly, pity is 'a sort of pain at an evident evil of a destructive or painful kind in the case of somebody who does not deserve it, the evil being one which we might expect to happen to ourselves or to some of our friends, and this at a time when it is seen to be near at hand.' Pity, however, turns into fear where the object is so nearly related to us that the suffering seems to be our own. Thus pity and fear in Aristotle are strictly correlated feelings. We pity others where under like circumstances we should fear for ourselves. Those who are incapable of fear are incapable also of pity (Butcher, 1902: 255–257).

Accordingly, the

> emotion of fear is profoundly altered when it is transferred from the real to the imaginative world. It is no longer the direct apprehension of misfortune impending over our own life. It is not caused by the actual approach of danger. It is the sympathetic shudder we feel for the hero whose character in its essentials resembles our own (Butcher, 1902: 258–259).

Although Aristotle asserts that the feeling of pity will remain constant, it is also true that at

> different moments of a [tragic] play pity or fear will be uppermost according as the course of the action brings home to us more vividly the undeserved nature of the suffering or the moral resemblance between ourselves and the hero...But the fact that fear is inspired by the

> sufferings of a [tragic hero] indicates that even tragic fear is in the last analysis traced back psychologically to a self-regarding instinct. The awakening of fear as distinct from mere pity depends on the close identification of the hero and ourselves (Butcher, 1902: 259 n 1).

The heightening and conflation of pity and fear through mimesis yields an altered state within the viewer that is empathy, an intensification of the affectivity of a disinterested altruism, one that causes the spectator to temporarily lose her own sense of egoism.

> The true tragic fear becomes an almost impersonal emotion, attaching itself not so much to this or that particular incident, as to the general course of the action, which is for us an image of human destiny...And the reason [for this] is that this fear, unlike the fear of common reality, is based on an imaginative union with another's life. The spectator is lifted out of himself. He becomes one with the tragic sufferer, and through him with humanity at large. One effect of the drama, said Plato, is that through it a man becomes many, instead of one; it makes him lose his proper personality in a pantomimic [mimetic] instinct, and so prove false to himself. Aristotle might reply: True; he passes out of himself, but it is through the enlarging power of sympathy. He forgets his own petty sufferings. He quits the narrow sphere of the individual. He identifies himself with the fate of mankind (Butcher, 1902: 266).

So the way may be cleared for Camus' project of reviving twentieth century Tragedy: the phenomenology of Tragedy is therapeutic in its effect and political in its consequences. Everything else (nobility et al.) is the means to this end or just a set of disposable props, for all that counts is the tragic sensation of the middle-class experiencing 'a feeling of being connected to or affected by something much bigger than one's self'. But in order for the therapy, the profane modern substitute for the sacred *katharsis* of antiquity, to take place, a formidable stumbling-block must be overcome: the ontological meaninglessness of every and all forms of human suffering. To paraphrase both Akira Kurosawa and William Tecumseh Sherman as one: the universe is a vacuum and there is no refining it. How can Camus magically reinvest the utterly profane with the grace of transcendental meaning? Affectivity can only get you so far; one may experience 'pity and fear' reading a tragic novel about an innocent victim being executed, but if, as Marx said, the point of philosophy, and by extension Art, is not to understand the world but to change it, then more solid foundations for long-term political action must be provided. The answer is surprisingly simple: by an act of mimesis. Mersault literally cannot be a *pharmakon* for the pre-modern *nomos* is dead, but he might be able to successfully imitate one and thereby simulate the simulacrum of *katharsis*. The original tragic hero imitated the scapegoat for an audience that believed in Fate and Destiny; the post-tragic hero imitates the tragic hero for a crowd that does not believe in gods. This substitution has all of the efficacy of a medical procedure.

9.2.1 *Katharsis/Pharmakos/Pharmakon/Katharma*

For Aristotle, the 'proper object' of Tragedy is *katharsis*; it is 'a physical stimulus which provides an outlet for religious fervor. Patients[24] who have been subjected to this process, "fall back," to quote Aristotle's phrase, "into their normal state, as if they had undergone a medical or purgative treatment." The emotional result is a "harmless joy"' (Butcher, 1902: 249). Harmless, that is, in opposition to blood-thirsty, which is always a possibility whenever there is a crowd involved. Aristotle highlights the therapeutic nature and function of Art, re-formulating it in expressly medical terms, specifically that of a surgical extraction.

> The original metaphor [of *katharsis*, 'extraction' or 'purgation'] is in itself a guide to the full aesthetic significance of the term. In the medical language of the school of Hippocrates it strictly denotes the removal of a painful and disturbing element from the organism, and hence the purifying of what remains, by the elimination of alien matter (Butcher, 1902: 253).

Katharma in its original sense prior to its more hidden connection with the tragic hero, is a term taken from ancient Greek magical practices in which the victim of an ailment was cured through the supernatural extraction from his/her body of a 'foreign object' that was the source of illness; 'The extracted object had no place in the human organism and no right to be there [it is 'strange']. It was something brought in by outside forces' (Girard, 1977: 287). For its part, *pharmakos* possesses two meanings: (i) originally, the 'strange object' removed from the victim; (ii) a *ritualistic human sacrificial victim* that 'substituted' for the generic 'strange object' that was the cause of suffering; 'The Greek term for an evil object extracted by means of a [dramatic-magical] ritual is *katharma*. This term was also used as a variant of *pharmakos* to designate a sacrificial human victim' (Girard, 1977: 286). So the 'human' *pharmakos* is the occult notion of the 'strange object' applied to an actual person who is scapegoated to both represent and explain the collective illness of the public community.

> The word *katharsis* refers primarily to the mysterious benefits that accrue to the community upon the death of a human *katharma* or *pharmakos*. The process is generally seen as a religious purification and takes the form of cleansing or draining away impurities. Shortly before his execution the *pharmakos* is paraded ceremonially through the streets of the village. It is believed that he will absorb all the noxious influences that may be abroad and that his death will transpose them outside the community (Girard, 1977: 287).

Pharmakos strictly equates with *pharmakon* as an iterable, or liminally migratory, 'poison' and 'remedy': the person or thing that can absorb all of the illnesses of the community (remedy; cure) can also serve as the source of (re-)contamination (poison) if not handled properly (ritual); 'The *pharmakon* is thus a magic drug or volatile elixir, whose administration had best be left by ordinary men in the hands of those who enjoy special knowledge and exceptional powers—priests, magicians, shamans, doctors, and so on' (Girard, 1977: 95)—and tragic play-wrights.

---

[24] Sic. In the alternative, theatre-goers.

Hippocratic medicine provides Aristotle with the necessary intellectual bridge to aesthetics.

> Applying this to tragedy we observe that the feelings of pity and fear in real life contain a morbid and disturbing element. In the process of tragic excitation they find relief, and the morbid element is thrown off. As the tragic action progresses, when the tumult of the mind, first aroused, afterwards subsided, the lower forms of emotion are found to have been transmuted into higher and more refined forms. The painful element in the pity and fear of reality is purged away; the emotions themselves are purged. The curative and tranquillizing influence that tragedy exercises follows as an immediate accompaniment of the transformation of feeling. Tragedy, then, does more than effect the homeopathic cure of certain passions. Its function on this view is not merely to provide an outlet for pity and fear, but to provide for them a distinctively aesthetic satisfaction, to purify and clarify [neutralize?] them by passing them through the medium of art (Butcher, 1902: 253–255).

The question that arises is to what degree can the 'morbid and disturbing' unexpurgated emotions, and their resultant extraction via the suffering of the tragic hero, be understood in terms of violence and ritualistic sacrifice? The answer is that *katharsis*, as the exorcism of destructive or pathological emotions, initiates the violent and traumatic transformation of the emotional basis of intra-group violence into 'peaceful sociability'.

> Aristotle would probably admit that indirectly the drama has a moral influence in enabling the emotional system to throw off some perilous stuff, certain elements of feeling, which, if left to themselves, might develop dangerous energy, and impede the free play of those vital functions on which the exercise of virtue depends (Butcher, 1902: 269).

Which corresponds exactly with the substitution of the conflictual mimesis that unites for the acquisitive mimesis that divides as essayed by Girard.[25] And, provided that we get the phenomenology of Tragedy right, it becomes possible, at least in theory, to reconstruct the scapegoated victim as a suitable post-heroic post-tragic tragic hero.

> 'The unity of a given ritual,' says Victor Turner in *The Drums of Affliction*, 'is a dramatic unity. It is in this sense a work of art.' If we agree with this opinion—and it would be difficult to disagree—the reverse should be true as well: a given dramatic performance constitutes a sort of rite, the shadowy similitude of the religious experience (Girard, 1977: 290–291; Turner, 1969: 269).

So, mimesis once again: Greek Tragedy is in essence the deliberate imitation of an earlier set of religious rites that formed part of the sacrificial mechanism; 'In describing the tragic effect in terms of katharsis [Aristotle] asserts that tragedy can and should assume at least some of the functions assigned to ritual in a world where ritual has almost disappeared' (Girard, 1977: 290).[26] Sophocles, for one, made this clear—but not too clear, lest the nature of the game be given away.

---

[25] See Introduction, above.

[26] Again, this is the by-product of myth being superseded by Tragedy at the very moment that it had reached its aesthetic apogee; 'Tragedy emerged in Greece at the end of the sixth century [B.C.E.]. Within a hundred years the tragic seam had already been exhausted and when Aristotle in the fourth century set out, in his *Poetics*, to establish the theory of tragedy, he no longer understood tragic man who had, so to speak, become a stranger. Tragedy ... faded away as philosophy experienced its

As we have seen, the tragic figure of Oedipus becomes the original *katharma*. Once upon a time a temple and an altar on which the victim was sacrificed were substituted for the original act of collective violence; now there is an amphitheatre and a stage on which the fate of the *katharma*, played out by an actor, will purge the spectators of their passions and provoke a new katharsis, both individual and collective. This katharsis will restore the health and well-being of the community (Girard, 1977: 290).

Girard postulates a strict equivalence, as well as the reversibility, between the *pharmakon* of religious-medical ritual, and the hero of Greek tragedy, who now begins to resemble not only Mersault but his creator as well, Albert Camus the juvenile delinquent celebrity-savant.

If my thesis is correct, the *pharmakos*, like Oedipus himself, has a dual connotation. On the one hand he is a woebegone figure, an object of scorn who is weighed down with guilt; a butt for all sorts of gibes, insults, and of course, outbursts of violence. On the other hand, we find him surrounded by a quasi-religious aura of veneration; he has become a sort of cult object. This duality reflects the metamorphosis the ritual victim is designed to effect; the victim draws to itself all the violence infecting the original victim and through its own death transforms this baneful violence into beneficial violence, into harmony and abundance...The victim is considered a polluted object, whose living presence contaminates everything that comes in contact with it and whose death purges the community of its ills—as the subsequent restoration of public tranquillity clearly testifies. That is why the *pharmakos* was paraded about the city. He was used as a kind of sponge to sop up impurities, and afterward he was expelled from the community or killed in a ceremony that involved the entire population (Girard, 1977: 95).

There is now only last step that needs to be taken in order to complete the circle rendering the archaic-mythic scapegoat a suitable dramatic character for the atheistic twentieth century. If the *pharmakos* was the primitive model of the Aristotelian tragic hero, then the entirety of the sacrificial machinery that manufactured the *pharmakon* would have to have been assimilated into the practices of Greek drama. This appears to have happened with *katharma*, which originally denoted both the 'strange object' along with the dramatic rites enacted to withdraw it from the body of the afflicted; '*Katharma* is not limited to the victim or the surrogate object; it also refers to the supreme efforts of a mythic or tragic hero' that constitute the core of the plot of the tragedy (Girard, 1977: 288). So, a new question: what precisely is 'the supreme effort' of the tragic hero? And the new answer is: his or her voluntary reconciliation with Fate (*moirai*) and acceptance of the will of the gods. Not dissimilar to what Josef K. was attempting to do in *The Trial*.[27]

The artistic unity of plot, binding together the several parts of the play in close inward coherence, reveals the law of human destiny, the causes and effects of suffering. The incidents

---

moment of triumph' (Vernant & Vidal-Naquet, 1990: 29). Tragedy had already effectively disappeared by the late Socratic period (the Romans did not like, preferring comedies, satires, and epics with Seneca being the sole Roman tragedian of which we are aware) and is not resuscitated until the late Renaissance during the beginning of scepticism concerning the 'providential' order of the universe. Macbeth's 'sound and fury, signifying nothing' is tragic drama minus divine agency, the germination of the concept of the accident.

[27] See Chap. 8, above. The difference being that Josef K., the textual double of Franz K. actually wanted to occupy the existential space of God-Father.

> which thrill us are intensified in their effect, when to the shock of surprise is added the discovery that each thing as it happened could not be otherwise; it stands in organic relation to what has gone on before. There is a combination of the inevitable and the unexpected (Butcher, 1902: 266–267).

If we recall two of the essential qualities of Aristotle's 'fear and pity'— the fearful 'evil is near, not remote, and the persons threatened are ourselves' (Butcher, 1902: 257) and that pity 'turns into fear where the object is so nearly related to us that the suffering seems to be our own' (Butcher, 1902: 257)—then, it follows that the only properly 'tragic hero' for the age of post-theistic absurdity is the product of the failure of risk assessment, the victim of an *accident*.[28] Think about it. The 'guilty pleasure' or hidden jouissance of the horror film, that quintessentially modern cinematic appropriation of the mythology of monsters,[29] is the shameful and sadistic pleasure that one is watching a stranger being exposed to extreme danger from the vantage point of absolute safety.[30] And Aristotle directly anticipates this (accidentally) when he highlights one of the signature elements of the tragic plot as 'a combination of the inevitable and the unexpected', which is an antiquated way of saying 'risk assessment'. For us the godless post-tragic post-hero is the aesthetic and phenomenological substitute of an automobile or plane crash victim, with the un-Aristotelian side effect that the 'new order of things' that the properly purged post-modern spectator is supposed to be incorporated into is one of total randomness under the master-sign of the godless accident. With, however, one vital difference: in the case of the Camusian anti-hero, the accident, while truly random, is also deliberately but mis-directedly *willed*. We call it capital punishment.

9.3 Mersault as Tragic Hero, or the Accident Waiting to Happen

The 'updated' scapegoat is the 'dangerous supplement' to the modernity that encompasses all, the 'victim' (a sublime double entendre) of a horrible accident that absolutely anyone can fall prey to. We are all exactly the same in that we are all subject to the omnipotence of randomness, as elucidated by the lucidity of Mersault.

> If we feel, when we are reading the novel, that Mersault lives dangerously, this impression evaporates under examination. The man goes to work regularly, he swims on the beaches of the Mediterranean and he has dates with the girls in the office. He likes the movies but he is not interested in politics. Which of these activities will take him to the police station,

---

[28] Which lends weight to Aristotle's assertion that the fear 'inspired by the sufferings of a [tragic hero] indicates that even tragic fear is in the last analysis traced back psychologically to a self-regarding instinct' (Butcher, 1902: 259 n 1). Because accidents are to be avoided at all costs for they are truly horrible when they happen.

[29] If it is true, as Stephen King opined, every tale of Horror has a monster in it, then it also follows that every myth is a tale of Horror.

[30] See Noel Caroll for a valiant attempt to explain why people appear to extract pleasure from a filmic text that is dedicated to inducing fright (Caroll, 1990).

> let alone the guillotine? ... Mersault has no responsibilities, no family, no personal problems; he feels no sympathy for unpopular causes. Apparently he drinks nothing but *café au lait*. He really lives the prudent and peaceful life of a little bureaucrat anywhere and of a French petit bourgeois in the bargain.... His way of life should constitute a good insurance against nervous breakdowns, mental exhaustion, heart failure, and, *a fortiori*, the guillotine (Girard, 1978: 13, 14).

Even though he would appear to be at the extreme low end of the risk assessment spectrum—'The only real threats to his welfare are those he shares with every other little bureaucrat, or with the human race as a whole' (Girard, 1978: 17)—Mersault still manages to wind up getting lawfully decapitated by the government. Through Camus we have entered into the domain of a uniquely atheistic sense of post-heroic horror: that calculations of normality are no defense against a universe devoid of order.

> When an existence as uneventful as that of Mersault is described in minute detail, without any humor, an atmosphere of tense expectation is automatically created. As I read the novel, my attention is focused upon details that are insignificant in themselves but that come to be regarded as portents of doom just because the writer has seen fit to record them. I sense that Mersault is moving toward a tragedy, and this impression, which has nothing to do with the hero's actions, seems to arise from them (Girard, 1978: 17).

Even murder is worth nothing. Mersault's fatal but apparently unmotivated shooting of 'the Arab' may, at first glance, 'be a pretext, but it is the only one available, and upon this unfortunate event, the whole structure of meaning erected by Camus comes to rest. It is very important, therefore, to understand how the murder comes to pass. How can a man commit murder and not be responsible for it?' (Girard, 1978: 14). In order for the crime of homicide to be made out, the prosecutor must establish beyond a reasonable doubt the evidence of *atcus reus* (the criminal act) combined with *mens rea* (the criminal intent); in the absence of the intent to kill, a criminal (as opposed to a civil) wrongful death is a homicide in the third degree, alternatively a form of manslaughter, which should not ordinarily constitute a capital offence. For Girard this is the most serious weakness of *The Stranger*, for Camus, through his own neo-adolescent romanticism, is unable to come up with a truly tragic narrative: 'The murder of the Arab, in a novel otherwise rational and realistic, is a *deus ex machina*, or rather a *crimen ex machina* that provides the author not with a happy ending but with a tragic one that is really precluded by the character he himself has given to his hero' (Girard, 1978: 19). So, answering his own question, Girard concludes

> The obvious answer is that the murder must be an *accident* ... Mersault is guilty of involuntary manslaughter at worst. How could Mersault premeditate a murder, since he cannot premeditate a successful career in Paris or marriage with his mistress? Involuntary manslaughter, as everyone knows, should not send a man to the guillotine. This interpretation seems to clinch Camus's case against the 'judges' (Girard, 1978: 14).

But there is a catch. If Mersault really did commit a crime of some kind, 'we agree that he must be an involuntary rather than a voluntary criminal, but why should he commit a crime in the first place? Accidents will happen, no doubt, but no general conclusion can be drawn from them, or they cease, quite obviously, to be accidents' (Girard, 1978: 14). Or, what is almost the same thing, Mersault can only be executed if his action against 'the Arab' was formally criminal in some legal manner as opposed to only a moral wrong in a non-legal sense.

> If the murder is an accident, so is the sentence that condemns Mersault, and *L'Etranger* does not prove that people who do not cry at their mother's funerals are likely to be sentenced to death. All the novel proves, then, is that these people will be sentenced to death if they also happen to commit involuntary manslaughter, and this *if*, it will be conceded, is a very big one. The accident theory reduces Mersault's case to the proportions of a pathetic but rather insignificant *fait-divers* (Girard, 1978: 14).

Girard concludes, wrongly I think, that it is 'as difficult to ascribe an "ontological status" of the murder as it is easy to ascertain its function in the story' (Girard, 1978: 16). In fact, the 'function' of the murder, which is as senseless as the world itself, is, in fact, quite easy to understand, Camus' romantic juvenile delinquency notwithstanding: Mersault is not executed because he did not weep during the internment of his Maman; rather, it his absence of filial tears, ordinarily interpreted as a positive demonstration of complete normality that provides exoteric evidence of his esoteric identity as a *pharmakon*. Girard is deeply distrustful of both romanticism and the romantics for perfectly sound reasons,[31] but his somewhat Ahab-like persecution of Camus partially blinds his vision to the novelist's quixotic quest to derive cathartic affectivity from the ridiculous.

> Mersault...could never have been tried, convicted, and sentenced if he had not killed the Arab. But Camus thought otherwise, and he said so in the preface of *L' Etranger*: 'A man who does not cry at the funeral of his mother is likely to be sentenced to death.' Is this an a posteriori judgment deduced from the facts of the story, as everybody has always taken for granted, or is in an a priori principle to which the 'facts' must somehow be fitted? Everything becomes intelligible if we choose the second solution. Camus needs his 'innocent murder' because his a priori principle is blatantly false (Girard, 1978: 16).

Which leads to an outburst of textual hilarity, rare in Girard's work.

> Let a million devotees of *l'absurde* copy Mersault's way of life down to the last dregs of his *café au lait*, let them bury their entire families without shedding a tear, and not one of them will ever die on the guillotine, for the simple reason that their *imitation absurdi* will not and should not include the accidental murder of the Arab; this unfortunate happening, in all probability, will never be duplicated (Girard, 1978: 14).

But this time it may be Girard and not Camus (or Aristotle) who has given the (competitive) game away: the use of the terms *imitation absurdi*, although clearly intended sarcastically, is, in fact, rather illuminative, as it connotes Mersault's passing resemblance to Christ, in the very strict sense of one who is deliberately put to death for knowing, and telling, the truth, although here of a completely atheistic kind.

---

[31] Girard savagely critiqued romanticism and the bourgeois conceit of the romantic (Dostoevskii's parodic 'beautiful soul' in *Notes from the Underground*) throughout his career, but the primary text is *Deceit, Desire & the Novel: Self and Other in Literary Structure* (Girard, 1965). Expressed concisely, Girard detested romanticism's all-too-easy inclination to interpret both personal and political violence as expressive forms of existential authenticity.

The narrative framing of Mersault's juridical murder in terms of scapegoating as an *imitatio Christi* provides the necessary component of Fate/Divinity that 'true' Tragedy requires, the sacrificial machinery of the sacred now allegorically represented as the secular-sacred rites of capital punishment. Mersault is quite literally scapegoated precisely because his tragic flaw (*hamartia*) is lucidity, and Camus makes this clear: 'Mersault "refuses to lie" and, immediately, "society feels threatened"' (Camus qtd. Girard, 1978: 9). By seeing the universe as absurd he dismantles the occluding screens of *meconnaissance* (false consciousness, ideological mystification, and bad faith) that act as the protective barrier of the sacrificial mechanism and the possibility of regenerative violence; therefore, his execution is a silencing that allows the scapegoat process to continue uninterrupted. Furthermore, if lucidity really is the tragic flaw of the anti-hero then, like the *pharmakon*, Mersault is also the signifier of undifferentiation; there can be no stable hierarchy of values or status within a universe of pure randomness. By abolishing the lucidity that itself abolishes distinctions among the humans who are the interchangeable and accidental victims of godlessness, the threat of annihilating sameness, or undifferentiation through absurdity, can be overcome. Girard has got it backward for as he himself admits, 'a given dramatic performance constitutes a sort of rite, the shadowy similitude of the religious experience' (Girard, 1977: 291) and a public execution, if it is nothing else, is a spectacle that borders on religious experience and invokes the fervor of a unifying moral absolutism and violent enmity within the participants. Camus does not evoke the symbols of *Fatum* in order to turn Mersault into a scapegoat; rather, by presenting Mersault to us as a victim of scapegoating through the medium of a prejudicial trial and a public guillotining, the author sub-textually invokes the psychic landscape of divinity, a supernaturally organized universe that is the necessary precondition for generative violence to take place,[32] so as to reproduce the phenomenology of cathartic 'pity and fear', now secularized.

> I wiped away the sweat covering my face, and I had barely become aware of where I was and what I was doing when I heard the director of the [retirement] home being called. He was asked whether Maman ever complained about me, and he said yes but that some of it was just the way the residents all had of complaining about their relatives. The judge had him clarify whether she used to reproach me for having put her in the home, and the director again said yes. But this time he didn't add anything else. To another question he replied that he had been surprised by my calm the day of the funeral. He was asked what he meant by 'calm'. The director then looked down at the tips of his shoes and said that I hadn't wanted to see Maman [in the coffin], that I hadn't cried once, and that I had left right after the funeral without paying my last respects at her grave. And one other thing had surprised him: one of the men who worked for the undertaker had told him I didn't know how old Maman was...[The judge] then asked the prosecutor if he had any questions to put to the witness, and the prosecutor exclaimed, 'Oh no, that is quite sufficient!' with such glee and with such a triumphant look in my direction that for the first time in years I had this stupid urge to cry,

[32] As Girard appears to recognize, albeit in a negative manner: 'If supernatural necessity is present in *L'Etranger*, why should Mersault alone come under its power?' (Girard, 1978: 15). Of course, if Mersault's profane execution is able to bring about *katharsis*, as Camus implies in the novel's final line, then the crowd itself, even if only allegorically, has been brought into the purview of God(s) under the rubric of affectivity and life-restoring generative unanimity has been achieved.

> because I could feel how much all these people hated me…It was then I felt a stirring go through the room and for the first time I realized that I was guilty (Camus, 1989: 89–90).

Aristotle does not yield the point that the *pharmakon* of Tragedy 'must at once resemble the members of the community, and differ from them; he must be at once insider and outsider' (Girard, 1977: 291)[33] and it is in this way that Camus attempts to solve the dilemma faced by Kafka in his not dissimilar disquisition concerning the nature, purpose, and identity of the scapegoat: whereas in *The Trial*, Kafka framed the issue in terms of esoteric knowledge, Camus, in *The Stranger*, opts for the inductive finding of 'deviance' by a quantitative compilation of exoteric knowledge and empirical observation.

> I sat down with the policemen standing on either side of me. It was then I noticed a row of faces in front of me. They were all looking at me: I realized that they were the jury. But I can't say what distinguished one from another.[34] I had just one impression: I was sitting across from a row of seats on a streetcar and all these anonymous passengers were looking over the new arrival to see if they could find something funny about him. I knew it was a silly idea since it wasn't anything funny they were after but a crime. There isn't much difference, though—in any case that was the idea that came to me (Camus, 1989: 83).

The paradox of Mersault as a literary character that is of vital importance to his allegorical identity as *pharmakos* is his perfect fusion of elements of extreme normality and abnormality: normality pertaining to his lack of unique characteristics that makes him a passive coconspirator with the forces of the crisis of undifferentiation, and abnormality signifying an irreducible and unassimilable singularity (strangeness), which makes him the possible cause of the crisis (he signals the inability of everyone else to stand 'outside' the mob) and the one whose sacrificial death will abolish the plague of the crowd.

> If [the proper sacrificial offering] is to become a true representative of the original victim he must first establish some sort of relationship with the group and be made to appear like an

---

[33] Terry Eagleton makes a similar point, explaining that both 'pity and fear, identity and otherness, are at stake' in every goat song. 'The scapegoat must be neither too foreign nor too familiar; it must be Lacan's term *extime*, different enough to dread and loathe, yet enough of a mirror-image to be a credible point of displacement for one's sins. As such, it bears an oblique relation to the Freudian notion of the uncanny, another ambiguous phenomenon caught between life and death, the strange and the familiar' (Eagleton, 2020: 271).

[34] Meaning, of course, that the 'jury' is really a 'crowd', a hostile aggregation suffering from an acute lack of differentiation. A similar scene is invoked when Mersault is participating in the vigil over Maman's body; 'That's when Maman's friends came in. There were about ten in all, and they floated into the blinding light without a sound. They sat down without a single chair creaking. I saw them more clearly than I had ever seen anyone, and not one detail of their faces or clothes escaped me. But I couldn't hear them, and it was hard for me to believe they really existed…. What struck me most about their faces was that I couldn't see their eyes, just a faint glimmer in the wrinkles. When they'd sat down, most of them looked at me and nodded awkwardly, their lips sucked in by their toothless mouths, so that I couldn't tell if they were greeting me or if it was just a nervous tic. It was then that I realized that they were all sitting across from me, nodding their heads, grouped around the caretaker. For a second I had the ridiculous feeling that they were there to judge me' (Camus, 1989: 9–10). Not ridiculous at all; they were there to judge him and both ended up with a verdict of guilt.

> 'insider'—without, however, surrendering the sacred exteriority that remains his essential characteristic.... Through the process of sacrificial preparation the victim acquires a sufficient resemblance to the 'natural,' direct target of violence—that is, the other members of the community—to ensure the transference of their aggressions and to make him an attractive sacrificial object. At the same time, he remains sufficiently foreign for his death not to risk plunging the community into a cycle of revenge (Girard, 1977: 277).

So what is there about Mersault, exactly, that makes him 'strange', and, therefore, eligible to assume the role of the *pharmakos*? Although Girard's preferred, and dismissive, term is juvenile delinquent, a more accurate and clinical description would be 'borderline personality'[35] that is directly suggestive of a liminal person which is a dead giveaway that we are dealing with a scapegoat, or at least one who is statistically far more likely to be singled out as one in the event of a mimetic crisis of sameness.

> He [Mersault's boss] was planning to open an office in Paris which would handle his business with the big companies, on the spot, and he wanted to know how I felt about going there. I'd be able to live in Paris and to travel around for part of the year as well. 'You're young, and it seems to me it's the kind of life that would appeal to you.' Then he asked if I wasn't interested in a change of life. I said that people never change their lives, that in any case one life was as good as another and that I wasn't dissatisfied with mine here at all. He looked upset and told me that I never gave him a straight answer, that I had no ambition, and that was disastrous in business...When I was a student, I had lots of ambitions like that. But when I had to give up my studies I learned very quickly that none of it mattered (Camus, 1989: 41).

A comparison of Kafka and Camus on this point highlights the issue of the identity of the scapegoat as well as the intellectual temperament of the two authors; Kafka's approach is esoteric, so the question for him is '*Who* is Josef K.?' whereas Camus is, predictably, exoteric, so that the game of sacrificial discretion is establishing '*Why* did Mersault do it?' and is practically forensic in his approach. From the perspective of the sacrificer, the death of Mersault's Maman is highly fortuitous for with the extinction of his natural family he is left without an advocate or an avenger—a necessary attribute of the scapegoat because the absence of an avenger precludes the possibility of reciprocal violence following the lynching. Furthermore, Mersault's apparent absence of emotion indicates that he is immune to the process of *katharma*; therefore, his emotions remain unexpurgated and, throughout the text, Mersault is

---

[35] Mersault's status as 'nobody' can be taken as proof that of all of the classic Tragedians the one whom Camus most closely resembled was the Socratic Euripides, who tried to short-circuit the scapegoat mechanism by reducing the presence of divinity to the mere background noise of *deus ex machina*: 'In the plays of Euripides the divine background is toned down, or, at any rate, distanced from the vicissitudes of human life. Here, in the last of the great tragic writers, the spotlight is in preference directed onto the individual characteristics of the protagonists and their mutual relationships. But left in this way to his own devices, to a large extent disentangled from the supernatural and restored to his own human dimensions, the agent is still no more vigorously portrayed. On the contrary, instead of action being depicted as it was in Aeschylus and Sophocles, in Euripides tragedy shifts toward the expression of the pathetic. As J. de Romilly notes, "By no longer being concerned with the divine significance, one is no longer concerned with action: one's attention turns to the sufferings and tricks of human life"' (Vernant & Vidal-Naquet, 1990: 83). There is something undeniably pathetic about Mersault; without the backdrop of the sacred veil, he is literally a no-one.

repeatedly juxtaposed with characters who are highly emotional and demonstrative in their responses:

> Everybody felt sorry for me, and Celeste said, "You only have one mother" (Camus, 1989: 3–4).
>
> A minute later she asked me if I loved her. I told her it didn't mean anything but that I didn't think so. She looked sad. But as we were fixing lunch, and for no apparent reason, she laughed in such a way that I kissed her (Camus, 1989: 35).

But most striking of all are the quiet sufferings inflicted by Mersault upon his alleged 'best Friend' Thomas Perez, who, it might be suggested, is suffering emotional trauma from having accidentally exposed himself to the psychic strangeness of the *pharmakos*: 'Big tears of frustration and exhaustion were streaming down [Perez's] cheeks. But because of all the wrinkles, they weren't dripping off. They spread out and ran together again, leaving a watery film over his ruined face' (Camus, 1989: 18). The high-low point comes when Perez, who had managed to cry at the funeral of the future scapegoat's mother, is questioned by the Court during Mersault's murder trial.

> He was asked how I had acted [on the day of the funeral] and he replied, 'You understand, I was too sad. So I didn't see anything. My sadness made it impossible to see anything. Because for me it was a very great sadness. And I even fainted. So I wasn't able to see monsieur (Camus, 1989: 91)

As I have already discussed, Mersault as a tragic hero must possess a tragic flaw, a character trait that is the basis of his superiority (or 'specialness') but also the cause of his downfall; expressed in sublime terms, it is his lucidity, the capacity that enables him to perceive the absurdity of existence, but in its more banal form, appropriate for the twentieth century, it manifests as the legal concepts of 'diminished capacity' and 'irresistible impulse'; he commits murder for no other reason than the sun gets into his eyes: 'I could feel the blood pounding in my temples' he says (Camus, 1989: 17).

> The sun was starting to burn my cheeks, and I could feel drops of sweat gathering in my eyebrows. The sun was the same as it had been the day I'd buried Maman, and like then, my forehead especially was hurting me, all the veins in it throbbing under the skin. It was this burning, which I couldn't stand anymore, that made me move forward. I knew that it was stupid, that I couldn't get the sun off me by stepping forward. But I took a step, one step, forward. And this time, without getting up, the Arab drew his knife and held it up to the sun. The light shot off the steel and it was like a long flashing blade cutting at my forehead…All I could feel were the cymbals of sunlight crashing on my forehead and, indistinctly, the dazzling spear flying up from the knife in front of me. The scorching blade slashed at my eyelashes and stabbed at my stinging eyes. That's when everything began to reel. The sea carried up a thick, fiery breath. It seemed to me as if the sky split open from one end to the other to rain down fire. My whole being tensed and I squeezed my hand around the revolver. The trigger gave; I felt the smooth underside of the butt; and there, in that noise, sharp and deafening at the same time, is where it all started (Camus, 1989: 58–59).

In terms of substance, this passage deliberately evokes the tragic conceit of both psychological and supernaturally pre-ordained determinism, not just the absence but the impossibility of free-will; the tragic hero is ultimately unable to behave in any other manner other than that which has been prescribed by the gods and which his mortal 'character' inclines him toward (Vernant & Vidal-Naquet, 1990: 49–84). And, on this point, it should be pointed out in fairness to Girard that he not unsympathetic to Camus regarding the artistic challenge of twentieth century literature, at least implicitly: 'As far as we can tell, there is something unique in the ability of modern culture to perceive victimage as such, to interpret scapegoat effects, in other words, as psycho-social phenomena rather than as religious or aesthetic epiphanies'. In terms of form, this passage is written so as to convey a 'dual' reading: (i) Mersault is suffering from diminished capacity, being controlled by the 'mindless' forces of nature, the physical manifestation of *l'absurde* in the form of the universal excuse of 'It just happened'; or (ii) Mersault is being controlled by his hitherto unexpressed emotions which are seeking expression through violence (*katharsis*); 'The blazing sand looked red to me now' (Camus 1989: 53). It is by means of literary style that Camus is able to effect the profane secularization of a religious concept by substituting psychology for the sacred by revealing that Mersault, like the tragic hero, is 'not in himself truly the center and productive cause' of his own agency: 'Because his actions take place within a temporal order over which he has no control and to which he must submit passively [diminished capacity], his actions elude him; they are beyond his understanding'(Vernant & Vidal-Naquet, 1990: 82). Notice the novel's frequent conjunctions of the sun with blood,[36] that compels Mersault to recall the funeral of his mother which, in his account, was governing his state of mind immediately prior to his act of killing. Both the shooting and the execution are linked through references to the funeral of Maman, the site and occasion of the greatest grief at which Mersault does not mourn, or expel his emotions, which makes him dangerous.[37] It also makes him popular with adolescent existentialists everywhere. "In our society, a man who does not cry at the funeral of his mother is likely to be sentenced to death" (Camus qtd. Girard, 1978: 16) Camus famously commented on his own novel, diluting somewhat the profound anthropological insight of his own text and earning this severe rebuke from the anti-romantic Girard.

> The author wants to prove that, in our world, an innocent man is doomed to persecution. But he wants to prove this about an innocent man of a peculiar sort and in a peculiar context inimical to his design. The character of the hero, his lack of ambition, his radical solipsism rule out any possibility of a significant conflict between him and society. That is the problem that is resolved, in appearance, by the involuntary murder of the Arab. To find the mythical model of the first part of *The Stranger*, one must go back to the murder of Laius.[38] Just as Oedipus kills his father 'without knowing it', Mersault kills the Arab 'without meaning it' (Girard, 2004: 16–17).

---

[36] For similar references to the Sun see Camus 1988: 6, 7, 15, 16-17, 47, 52, 53, 55, 56, 58-59, 67, 82; for other examples of blood or the 'pounding' of blood see Camus 1988: 31, 33, 47, 53, 57, 58-59, 67.

[37] The unnerving conversation between Mersault and the director of the retirement home unconsciously suggests that there is a contagion-like effect emanating from the cadaver of the mother of the to-be scapegoated murderer; 'We've moved her to our little mortuary. So as not to upset the others. Whenever one of the residents dies, the others are a bit on edge for the next two to three days. And that makes it difficult to care for them' (Camus, 1989: 5).

[38] See Introduction, above.

And as Girard quite rightly points out, 'Thanks to the involuntary murder, the hero is *guilty enough* for his punishment to be plausible but *innocent enough* to remain the victim of a cruel injustice' (Girard, 2004: 17). As involuntary manslaughter should not result in a capital sentence, Camus is technically cheating by bringing about an utterly unrealistic outcome within a realist novel in order to achieve a suspect romantic objective: the blinding revelation of the absolute moral degeneracy of the judicial system of the bourgeoisie which knows and cares nothing about *l'absurde*, the knowledge of which is the master-sign of the existential[39] superiority of savvy adolescent existentialists.

> From a purely textual standpoint, Mersault's condemnation is almost unrelated to his crime. Every detail of the trial adds up to the conclusion that the judges resent the murderer not for what he did but for what he is. The critic Albert Maquet expressed his truth quite well when he wrote: 'The murder of the Arab is only a pretext; behind the person of the accused, the judges want to destroy the truth he embodies.' Let there be no murder and a good pretext to get rid of Mersault will, indeed, have been lost, but a pretext should be easy to replace, precisely because it does not have to be good. If society is as eager to annihilate Mersault as it is pictured by Maquet, the remarkable existence of this hero should provide more 'pretexts' than will ever be needed to send an innocent to his doom (Girard, 1978: 13).

I can, and will, raise objections to both Camus and Girard on this point. Against Camus, Mersault is not executed because he does not cry at his mother's funeral; rather, his amoral deviance is re-constituted by the Court as exoteric knowledge of his outsider status making him eligible for a scapegoating that serves an entirely different purpose, the regeneration of the community. However, even though Mersault is frequently understood to be 'affectless' (in a very cool juvenile delinquent sort of way), I believe that we obtain a deeper, and more sophisticated, understanding of both the character and the novel by situating both within the context of the parallel mechanisms of sacrifice and *katharsis*. Contra Girard, there really is an explanatory connection between Maman's funeral and the killing of the Arab: because Mersault did not shed, or expel, tears during the time of the first event his violent emotions remain unexpurgated at the time of the second event which, at least in the allegorical terms of the scapegoat, makes his irrational and spontaneous violence intelligible; as was the case with Cain who remained violent because, unlike Abel, he did not shed (expel) blood through his bloodless vegetable offering God.[40] And because Mersault's emotions are not purged, he is the bearer of a latent propensity of violence, which is enacted on the beach with murder of the significantly *nameless* Arab.[41] So, to slightly rework Girard's comment on 'the real function of the murder of the Arab'

---

[39] This for 'spiritual' to use an outdated term.

[40] To perhaps push this connection overly much: Cain sheds blood, Mersault sheds tears, and they both sweat through their brows: 'At the same instant [as the Arab's knife flashed] the sweat in my eyebrows dripped down over my eyelids all at once and covered them with a warm, thick film. My eyes were blinded behind a curtain of tears and salt' (Camus, 1989: 59). Mersault sheds tears when he sheds blood. We do not know whether Cain wept.

[41] At this point I need to address an issue that goes against the thesis of this chapter but which cannot be avoided: colonialist racism. Even though my approach is based on mimetic theory and not post-colonialism, a persuasive alternative reading to the one that I am presenting would explicitly politicize Mersault by reading his scapegoating by the French legal authorities, who are also colonial

(Girard, 2004: 16), we could say that whereas Kafka treated the scapegoat as an esoteric mystery, Camus, in good crime novel fashion, places his forensic report of the sacred outsider in terms of an exoteric 'frame'. Mersault is the site of a 'double' dramatic enactment: he is the strange or outside object to the community and he is the agent of his own private *katharsis*, resulting in the completion of his tragic-heroic *katharma*,[42]that 'something brought in by outside forces' which had 'no right to be there' and must be removed by the most precise legal extraction possible: execution, which precludes the possibility of re-infection. Making matters even worse for the defendant is that under inquisitorial law the examining magistrate has the right to

---

authorities, as a means of appeasing the alienated and outraged 'non-White' population of Algeria as well as falsely demonstrating the enlightened nature of French imperial occupation through a cynically staged display of racial neutrality and the color-blind impartiality of French jurisprudence. The *identity* of both the murderer and his victim is significant: that it was an Arab no-body (meaning a person whose name is unknown) that was killed, in an apparently 'senseless' (unmotivated) manner by a French colonist (a *pied-noir* who possesses an identity) would mean that the only possible rationale for the killing would have been racism; ergo, Mersault is condemned for the crime of murder in an act of expiatory scapegoating as a way of performatively exorcising the contagion of racism and its violence that infects colonial Algeria and of maintaining the *meconnaissance* of French colonialism as a humanitarian enterprise through the 'magical' effects of ideological mystification (i.e., the French cannot really be racists because they killed one of their own for killing one of the native savages). Mersault is revealed to stand even closer to the archetypal scapegoat Oedipus than he is under my mimetic reading; Sophocles raises the possibility that Oedipus is the victim of a 'frame' so that that Mersault is not only a scapegoat, he is a political scapegoat, or scapegoated because of colonial politics. He, like Oedipus is a true *pharmakon* because his death achieves a salvific outcome as a result of his esoteric nature. What motivates the French/ *pied-noir* jury to convict Mersault is his 'strangeness' as both a threat to the simulated 'unified' community of French and Arabs and which marks him as the double bearer of the violence of both psychological abnormality and colonial racism, the cause of a crisis of undifferentiation signified by the namelessness of *all* Arabs, and of its cure, the regeneration of the French empire through the catharsis of an anti-racist public execution. For colonial Algeria in the time of Camus see Fanon (2008), Fanon (1990), Memmi (1991), Memmi (2000).

[42] The less sophisticated precursor of the more theorized *pharmakos*, the *katharma* was the generic term for the unassimilable human refuse of the *polis*. David Dawson provides two illustrative examples; the first is from the classical critical commentary (*scholia*) on Aristophanes' *Plutus*: '"Offscourings" [*katharma*] is abomination. It follows from such a reference [made by the play-wright], that in Athens there was such a custom, that if it happened that the city committed some offence against the gods ... to atone ... for such an offence ... the people separated out ... one man who was the ugliest of everyone. In sum, they sacrificed him ... as a payment ... for all' (Dawson, 2013: 137). The second is taken from the *scholia* on Aristophanes' *The Knights*: 'By *demosius* "those who are public" he [Aristophanes] means those who are called *pharmakoi*. Who cleanse the city by their death. For the Athenians would nourish some who were exceedingly low-born, penniless, and useless ... and when a time of a disaster of some sort came upon the city, I mean a famine or something similar, they would sacrifice these to cleanse the city from pollution and from their evil, and to find a cure [*therapeian*] for the disaster they were enduring. They also gave the *pharmakoi* the name offscourings [*katharmata*]' (Dawson, 2013: 139). The 'rule', if there was one, seems to be that every *pharmakos* was of the *katharma*, but not every one of the *katharma* got to become a ritualistically designated *pharmakos*; the former were the ready-at-hand supply pool for the latter. The boundaries between the two are porous, but we might say that the *pharmakos* was a singled out member of the *katharma* who had been ritualistically sacralized.

investigate the entirety of the private life of the accused rendering facts of moral character or social behavior into admissible evidence.

> I had lived my life one way and I could just as well have lived it another. I had done this and I hadn't done that. I hadn't done this thing but I had done another. And so? It was as if I had waited all this time for this moment and for the first light of this dawn to be vindicated. Nothing, nothing mattered, and I knew why…Throughout the whole absurd life I'd lived, a dark wind had been rising toward me from somewhere deep in my future, across years that were still to come, and as it passed, this wind leveled whatever was offered to me at the time, in years no more real than the ones I was living…What would it matter if [someone] were accused of murder and then executed because he didn't cry at his mother's funeral? (Camus, 1989: 121).

Here, then, and in the face of Girard's critique, is Camus' own version of the necessary sense of *Fatum* which is re-worked as physicalist determinism understood dramatically, a kind of all-encompassing 'organic relation' (Butcher, 1902: 267). Which, to be honest about it, does sound somewhat adolescent, since Camus does rely more than a little on thrill and intensity of effect (Weisberg, 1975–1976). The sub-textual invocation of Fate also underlines the fact that the account of the 'new order of things' that Mersault embraces and reconciles himself with is an absurd one, devoid of the theological imaginary that supported Greek tragedy, but consistent with his flaw that is tragic.

> I was pouring out on him [the priest] everything that was in my heart, cries of anger and cries of joy…I was sure about me, about everything, surer than he could ever be, sure of my life and sure of the death I had waiting for me. Yes, that was all I had. But at least I had as much of a hold on it as it had on me. I had been right, I was still right, I was always right…For the first time in a long time I thought about Maman. I felt as if I understood why at the end of her life she had taken a [fiancée], why she had played at beginning again. Even there, in that home where lives were fading out, evening was a kind of wistful respite. So close to death, Maman must have felt free then and ready to live it all again. Nobody, nobody had the right to cry over her. And I felt ready to live it all again too. As if that blind rage had washed me clean, rid me of hope; for the first time, in that night alive with signs and stars, I opened myself to the gentle indifference of the world. Finding it so much like myself—so like a brother, really[43]—I felt happy and that I was happy again (Camus, 1989: 120–121, 122–123).

And it is the fact that Mersault does qualify as *pharmakos* that the purported 'difficulty' of the concluding sentences of the novel that has troubled interpreters is effectively resolved: 'For everything to be consummated, for me to feel less alone, I had only to wish that there be a large crowd of spectators the day of my execution and that they greet me with cries of hate' (Camus, 1989: 123). It is at this moment, a moment of a double *katharsis*, that the empathetic connection between victim and reader reaches its greatest intensity, moving beyond similitude toward imitation. The apotheosis of Mersault's own cathartic purgation, acted out as the pivotal dramatic action of Camus' atheistic Greek tragedy, is the achievement of his self-awareness as a *pharmakon*, the bearer of the lucidity that is both 'poison' and 'remedy', ritualistically sacrificed to guarantee the survival of the community. Which unfortunately means,

[43] *Imitation absurdi.*

and quite in contrast to the author's humanitarian intentions, we can never be done with judges and judging because we can, as a society, never be done with accusations and executions, physical or symbolic. Camus eventually came to understand this: 'How had I not seen that there was nothing more important than an execution, and that when you come right down to it, it was the only thing a man could be truly interested in?' (Camus, 1989: 110).

It was horror.

9.4 Jean-Baptiste Clamence: The Judge-Penitent as Universal Sacrifice

When discussing the religious dimensions of capital punishment in his paradigmatic *Violence and the Sacred* (1977) Girard relies a great deal on the work of the French anthropologist Louis Gernet.[44]

> The death penalty is a means of eliminating pollution...It purifies the affected group, who are often partly or wholly absolved of responsibility for the newly spilt blood...The violent expulsion, the expulsion unto death of the unworthy or accursed individual, has an ancillary sense: that of *devotion.* Indeed, the killing seems in one sense to be an act of piety. It makes us think of those ancient ordinances which declare that the murder of an outlaw does not cause pollution, or of that prescription of Germanic law that makes such a killing a civic duty...Then, too, the victim himself fills a true religious function, a function parallel to the priest-kings who are also put to death. The religious function can be seen in the Latin term for these victims: *homo sacer*, as well as in the Greek term *pharmakos* (Louis Gernet qtd. Girard, 1977: 298).

The *skandalon* that a purely secular form of capital punishment poses to Girard is one that he openly admits: on the basis of his theory of the scapegoat, the profane nature of state sanctioned murder should be devoid of regenerative power and, therefore, incapable of creating generative unanimity.

> For if it cannot be proven that the penal system owes its origins to generative violence, it might well be maintained that the judicial system is based upon rational agreement, on a sort of social contract, and that men are indeed able to master their social environment in the direct and explicit way that rationalists conceive. Such a conclusion would flatly contradict my line of argument (Girard, 1977: 298).

The rationality of the social contract, meaning its self-validating nature, is something that Girard cannot concede because, like Durkheim, he is committed to the

[44] Gernet also had a decisive influence on the revisionist classicists Jean-Pierre Vernant and Pierre Vidal-Naquet, who adopted his pioneering work on the early evolution of the Hellenic city-state and the juro-political dimensions of Greek Tragedy, 'a moment that occurred in between law as it was about to be born and law as it was already constituted,' that accounts for the paradox of Tragedy's appropriation of mythic narrative in the service of a post-mythic legal order; 'myth was both *in* tragedy and at the same time rejected by it.' It was Gernet 'who first made a precise link between the theme of the tragedy [of Oedipus] and the Athenian ritual of the *pharmakos*' (Vernant & Vidal-Naquet, 1990: 14–15, 128).

view that all social integration mechanisms, no matter how secular in appearance, are, in hidden truth, the mutated descendants of earlier forms of religious practices.

> The theory of the surrogate victim is paradoxical in that it is based on facts whose empirical characteristics are not directly accessible. These facts can be drawn exclusively from texts that invariably offer distorted, fragmentary, or indirect testimony. We can only gain access to the generative event through constant reference to these enigmatic sources, which constitute at once the foreground in which our theory situates itself and the background against which its accuracy must be tested (Girard, 1977: 309).[45]

On this matter, the atheist Camus is in tacit agreement with the theologically inclined but anthropologically savvy Girard; in both *The Stranger* and *The Fall*, Camus is able to resurrect the tragic victim-hero of antiquity as the causality of the post-theistic tragic accident, who, in the case of Mersault, is revealed to be a victim of the statist appropriation of an allegedly demystified ritual, the guillotine. However, in the case of the *The Fall*, the protagonist Jean-Baptiste Clamence testifies to the survival of the sacrificial mechanism and the haunting presence of the scapegoat in another manner: the 'framing' of the criminally accused as the mimetic (and phenomenological) replica of the scapegoat as the means through which an historically uninterrupted universal will-to-sacrifice may continue to operate unabated. Clamence states this clearly and in a manner wholly consistent with Gernet: 'A person who obeys the law is not afraid of judgment: it restores him to a system in which he believes. But the greatest of human torments is to be judged without law. Yet this is the torment in which we find ourselves' (Camus, 2006: 73). And, even more chilling, is that the machinery continues uninterruptedly precisely because, not in spite of, the fact that the sacrificers are actually fully aware of scapegoating being a collective exercise of *meconnaissance*.

> And don't our lies finally put us on the road to truth? And my stories, true or false; don't they tend toward the same aim, don't they have the same meaning? So, does it really matter whether they are true or false, if, in either case, they are indicative of what I've been and of what I am? We sometimes see more clearly into a person who lies than one who tells the truth (Albert Camus qtd. Weisberg, 1984: 126).

For Girard, the Orwellian realization that 'we *are* sacrificers, we have *always* been sacrificers' is the secret history of the twentieth century.

> We have managed to extricate ourselves from the sacred somewhat more successfully than other societies have done, to the point of losing all memory of the generative violence; but we are now about to rediscover it. The essential violence returns to us in a spectacular manner—not only in the form of a violent history but also in the form of subversive knowledge. This crisis invites us, for the very first time, to violate the taboo that neither Heraclitus nor Euripides could ever quite manage to violate, and to expose to the light of reason the role played by violence in human society (Girard, 1977: 318).

Camus' literary objective in *The Fall* jibes well with Girard's insistence upon the deliberately self-occluding nature of ritualistic sacrifice, both being in common agreement that the only essential difference between the pre-modern and modern

---

[45] See Chap. 1, above.

variants is that the latter is subject to a more intense form of mystification than the former. For the moderns subsume their mystifying efforts under the universal exculpation of 'reason of state'; the 'basic function' of generative violence remains exactly the same as it was in pre-modernity, which 'is to get rid of the truth, to transpose it beyond the realm of human activity' (Girard, 1977: 275).

> The mechanism of the surrogate victim is redemptive twice over: by promoting unanimity it quells violence on all fronts, and by preventing an outbreak of bloodshed within the community it keeps the truth about men from becoming known. The mechanism transposes this truth to the realm of the divine, in the form of an inscrutable god....If the modern mind fails to recognize the strongly functional nature of the scapegoat operation and all its sacrificial surrogates, the most basic phenomena of human culture will remain misunderstood and unresolved (Girard, 1977: 276).

But certain knowledge of the lurking presence of this 'gap' in human memory, or even a vague suspicion of a semi-consciously collectively willed act of amnesia, is exactly the message delivered by Clamence, the self-declared 'generous lawyer', who is himself the disguised imitator of the Sophoclean version of Oedipus, the lawyerly combatant who unveils the reality of both the groundlessness and the universality of that will-to-revenge which doubles as the will-to-scapegoat.[46] Which is why, after hearing Clamence's seemingly interminable 'confession,' anything short of the complete abolition of the death penalty can be nothing other than bad faith, the conscious and willful embrace of *meconnaissance.*

In *The Fall*, Camus reverses the perspective put forward in *The Stranger*, substituting the voice of the sacrificing accuser for that of the sacrificial victim. Appropriately, Camus changes the rhetorical tone of the first-person narrative voice from dead-pan irony to insinuating cynicism, for this time it is not the one who is persecuted but the one who persecutes who is speaking.

> The determining of the precise function of the surrogate victim permits us to understand the aim of the sacrificers. They are striving to produce a replica, as faithful as possible in every detail, of a previous crisis that was resolved by means of a spontaneously unanimous victimization. All the dangers, real and imaginary, that threaten the community are subsumed in the most terrible danger that can confront a society: the sacrificial crisis. The rite is therefore a repetition of the original, spontaneous 'lynching' that restored order in the community by re-establishing, around the figure of the surrogate victim, that sentiment of social accord that had been destroyed in the onslaught of reciprocal violence (Girard, 1977: 94–95).

Or as Clamence puts it: 'In any case, we cannot be certain of anyone's innocence, while we can confidently pronounce everyone guilty. Each man bears witness to the crime of all the others: this is my faith and hope' (Camus, 2006: 69). Which sets the tone beautifully: *The Fall* is both a parodic allegory of the French Left and Camus' monumental *J'accuse* of false consciousness. The Left's neo-Stalinist program of class revolution is predicated upon the universalization of guilt—meaning the universalization of persecution—and the novel doubles as the disguised auto-confession of a sacrificer of the innocent while highlighting the self-exculpatory nature of the political discourse of the Left: 'So, in philosophy as in politics, I'm in favor of

---

[46] See Introduction, above.

anything that denies innocence to Man and every practice that treats him as guilty' (Camus, 1989: 82). Clamence is committed to the universalization of guilt precisely so that the entirety of the community may be rendered subject to the 'impersonal' operation of the sacrificial machinery, an outlook that is consistent with Girard's: the implacable logic of mimetic desire and mimetic rivalry endlessly re-cycles the 'collective guilt' of the community, meaning the universality of *ressentiment*, that culminates in the ritualistic sacrifice of the surrogate victim. The result is a surge in the will-to-power of the sacrificer, who becomes the universal judge, who, in the singular case of Clamence as Camus' mouthpiece, assumes the guise of an eternally resentful *judge-penitent* who performatively assumes moral guilt as an instrument of revenge.

> Since one could not condemn others without at the same time judging oneself, one should heap accusations on one's own head, in order to have the right to judge others. Since every judge eventually becomes a penitent, one had to take the opposite route and be a professional penitent in order to become a judge (Camus, 1989: 86).

This is something that Josef K. should have thought of, provided that Franz K. had not, and, if expressed as a secular political program, might read 'We do not kill in order to save; we save in order to kill.'

Girard is fully aware of the mimetic dimension of Clamence as the sacrificing *generous lawyer* and illustrates the obvious parallels between the judge-penitent and Oedipus the Tyrant who was himself a 'sacrificer before being sacrificed' (Girard, 2004: 63).

> On the pretext of defending widows and orphans, the generous lawyer had sought to place the accusers in the position of the accused. In sum, he had forged an Oedipal myth for his own personal use[47] ... Camus reveals implacably the symbolic meaning of his earlier creations. And he defines them as attempts at personal justification. He recognizes his Double in the ferocious judge, the culprit, unknown and known, that he cursed in each of his writings. The generous lawyer is a judge in disguise, a superior judge who sets himself up as a judge of the judges. The Oedipal circle has closed back in on him. *The sentence that you pronounce on others ends up flying straight back into your face, where it manages to do some damage* (Girard, 2004: 17).[48]

Girard's italicized quotation from *The Fall* is Camus' own adaptation from Sophocles' original text where Tiresias responds to Oedipus the allegedly 'guilty' one: 'I pity you, flinging at me the very insults each man will fling at you soon' (Sophocles, 1984: 181), meaning after the Tyrant has been found guilty. Tiresias' counter-thrust is just one moment within a larger triangulated sequence among himself, Oedipus, and Creon, each of the combatants consumed by a mimetic rivalry to establish themselves as the sole arbiter of both truth and guilt,[49] which, as Girard intuits, implies the exclusive possession of a symbolized 'height,' that thing which precedes a fall; ' a natural balcony ...was the place where I felt most at ease, especially if I was alone,

[47] By 'Oedipal myth' does not mean the Freudian theory of incest but the 'lie' (*mythos*) of Oedipus' guilt that, mythically, renders him a scapegoat.

[48] Signifying the potential of scapegoating to escalate into unlimited reciprocal violence.

[49] See Chap. 1, above.

high above the human ants.... I relished my life and my own superiority' Clamence testifies (Camus, 2006: 16). Camus clearly imitates Sophocles here.

> The 'generous lawyer' wants to be *above* everybody else and to sit in judgment over the judges themselves; he is a judge in disguise. Unlike the ordinary judges who judge directly and openly, he judges indirectly and deviously. When anti-Pharisaism is used as a device to crush the Pharisees, it becomes another and more vicious Pharisaism (Girard, 1978: 10).

Girard realizes that Clamence realizes that 'mercy, in his hands, was a secret weapon against the unmerciful, a more complex form of self-righteousness. His real desire was not to save his clients but to prove his moral superiority by discrediting the judges' (Girard, 1978: 10) and thereby implicitly seizing the sole title of judge, a metaphysical desire to supplant the obstacle-model through occupying the space of the real. Clamence, in fact, served as the avatar for Camus himself which Girard discusses at great length, the 'biographical fallacy' be damned.

> The pre-*Chute* Camus[50] is quite different from his hero Clamence, but the two have a common trait in their contempt for the 'judges'. Both of them have built an intellectually complex and socially successful life around this one hallowed principle. The contemporary advocate of literary 'revolt' is perpetually challenging social institutions and values, but his challenge, like that of the lawyer, has become a part of the institutions themselves; far from entailing any personal risk, his activities bring fame and comfort in their wake (Girard, 1978: 11).

Camus not only conformed to the character of the generous lawyer, he was the actual double of the all-damning judge-penitent, the romanticism of the juvenile delinquent now unmasked as the mis-recognized bearer of the most contagious form of *ressentiment* conceivable.

> The only difference [between Clamence and Camus] is that the 'clients' are characters of fiction in the first case and real human beings in the second. From the cynical perspective of Clamence this difference is unimportant. To the generous lawyer, the clients are never quite real since they are not ends in themselves, but they are never quite fictional since they are a means to discredit the judges ... [the generous lawyer] represents only a variation on the theme of 'bad faith,' one of the many forms that a secretly self-seeking dedication to the downtrodden can assume (Girard, 1978: 12).

Camus as a romantic ultimately failed in his quixotic attempt to differentiate himself from the mimetic crowd (in his case, the 'middling' classes), which meant that he himself was the bearer of the contagion of undifferentiation, that is the same of plague of mimesis that felled Oedipus.

> Camus wrote *L'Etranger* against the 'judges' or, in other words, against the middle class who are his sole potential readers. Instead of rejecting the book as the author had half hoped, half feared, these bourgeois readers showered it with praise. The 'judges,' obviously, did not recognize their portrait when they saw it. They, too, cursed the iniquitous judges and howled for clemency. They, too, identified with the innocent victim and they acclaimed Mersault as a Galahad of sun-worshipping 'authenticity.' The public, it turned out, in short, to be made not of judges, as the author mistakenly believed, but of generous lawyers like the author himself (Girard, 1978: 32).

---

[50] The Camus of *L'Etranger*, *La Peste* (*The Plague*, 1947), and *Le Mythe de Sissyphe* (1942).

And Camus was finally able to confess all of this, just as Oedipus was finally able to confess his supposed crimes, which may have been a frame that resulted from his loss in combat against both Cleon and Tiresias and immediately followed by an act of extreme abnegation: Oedipus literally blinded himself and Camus authored a sadistically truthful alter ego.

> In *La Chute*, the author questions his own motives for writing fiction within the framework of this fiction itself. Mersault, as a 'client' of Clamence, has retreated in the background and become anonymous, but he is still a *dramatis persona*, and the structural incoherence of *L'Etranger* must be expressed primarily in terms of *his* personal motivations. In order to denounce what [Camus] now regards as his own moral illusions and creative weakness, Clamence must say, as he does, that *his clients were not so innocent after all*. Their allegedly spontaneous and unmotivated deeds were, in fact, premeditated. If Camus is to abide by the rules of the fictional game initiated in the first novel, he must attribute to the hero the 'bad faith' that really belongs to his creator, and this is precisely what he does. The 'good criminals' killed, not for any of the ordinary reasons, as we are well aware, but because they *wanted* to be tried and sentenced. Clamence tells us that their motives were really the same as his: like so many of our contemporaries, in this anonymous world, they wanted a little publicity (Girard, 1978: 19).

And of course 'publicity' means recognition, the soothing balm of *ressentiment*. Girard approvingly notes that 'Most people ignore the fact that Albert Camus was the first to react against his own cult' (Girard, 1978: 21) and then proceeds to exploit this damningly faint praise for maximal critical effect.

> Clamence really suggests that the author of *L'Etranger* was not really conscious of his own motivation until he experienced his own *chute*. His purpose, which disguised itself as 'generosity', was really identical to egoistical passion.... The author did not consciously try to deceive his audience, but he succeeded all the better because he managed to deceive himself in the first place. The dichotomy between Mersault and his judges represents the dichotomy between the Self and the Others in a world on intersubjective warfare (Girard, 1978: 20).

So that, and this is Girard's real point, the adolescent romantic is really not any different from anyone else at all because she is as contaminated by mimetic desire as everyone else is; it must have truly disturbed Camus that so many of his un-romantic targets, members of the French bourgeoisie, so easily identified with the juvenile delinquent, proving not only that individualism, the belief in the originality of one's own desires, in any form is a cheap illusion but that 'Romanticism' and all that comes in its wake (such as 'world revolution' or 'global emancipation') is really the greatest bourgeois conceit of all.

> The universal need for self-justification haunts all modern trial literature. But there are different levels of awareness. The so-called 'myth' of the trial can be approached from several mutually exclusive perspectives. In *L'Etranger*, the real question is that of the innocence and guilt of the protagonists. The criminal is innocent and the judges are guilty. In the more conventional ego-nourishing fiction, the criminal is usually guilty and the judges innocent. But this difference is really secondary. In both cases, 'good' and 'bad' are rigid concepts; the verdict of the judges is challenged but not their vision. *La Chute* goes higher and deeper. Clamence is still busy proving that he is 'good' and that other people are 'bad,' but his systems of classification keep breaking down. The real question is no longer 'who is innocent, who is guilty?', but 'why do we, all of us, have to keep judging and being judged?' It is a more

> interesting question, the very question of Dostoevski. In *La Chute*, Camus lifts trial literature back to the level of this great predecessor (Girard, 1978: 34).

Although not without an intriguing element of self-irony. Girard argues that 'the right perspective' with which to read the novel is humor: 'The author, tired of his popularity with all the *bien-pensants* of the intellectual elite, found a witty way to deride his quasi-prophetic role without scandalizing the pure at heart among the faithful' (Girard, 1978: 13). Humorous but not too humorous, provocative but not deflating; confession and penitence are intrinsically serious things as they invoke self-sacrifice, and Girard admits that even though 'Allowance must be made for overstatement,' meaning his own, it remains the case at all times that *The Fall* (from the heights) 'cannot be discounted as a joke or safely extolled as art for art's sake' because what Camus is doing is publicly confessing his own post-theistic tragic flaw; 'The confession of Clamence is Camus' own, in a broad literary and spiritual sense' (Girard, 1978: 13), although Clamence, like Oedipus, is 'blind' by the end of the ordeal of self-emptying.

> Why does Clamence point out to us that his new posture is still one of bad faith? He undermines his own position in order to prevent others from undermining it. After deriding the generous lawyer, he mockingly describes himself as a penitent-judge. Slyly anticipating his readers, whom he knows to be adept at gleaning moral comfort from the most sinister parables, he gives a new twist to the now familiar serpent, hoping to keep one step ahead of everybody else in a game of self-justification that has tuned into a game of self-accusation (Girard, 1978: 33).

'A game of self-justification that has tuned into a game of self-accusation' is, of course, an excellent way of summarizing *Oedipus Tyrannus*, but it could never work any better for Camus than it did for Oedipus, really, because Camus/Clamence's stratagem deliberately courted the risk of the all-too-easy appropriation of the post-tragic hero's occupation of the vantage point of higher morality by the undifferentiated mimetic middle class.

> As he questions the authenticity of *L'Etranger* and similar works, Camus questions the question itself. *La Chute*, no less than *L'Etranger*, is directed against all potential readers because it is directed against the lawyers in a world where only lawyers[51] are left. The technique of spiritual aggression has become more subtle but its aim has not changed (Girard, 1978: 33).

A conversion experience, or *metanoia*, may be of central biographical importance to the author but, for the reader, it merely results in the creation of one more commodity—the most recent novel—to be consumed.

> Let the judge repudiate judgment and he becomes a judge in disguise; let the lawyer repudiate the disguise and he becomes a penitent-judge; let the penitent-judge ... We are spiraling down the circles of a particularly nasty hell, but this more and more precipitous *chute* is perhaps not so fatal as it seems. The penitent-judge does not believe in his role half as much as the generous lawyer did. The conclusion of *La Chute* is a final pirouette as well, perhaps, as the image of what may happen to a world entirely given over to the lawyers and the penitent-judges (Girard, 1978: 33).

[51] Meaning accusers, or 'persecuting prosecutors'.

In terms of the universal logic of sacrifice, even the sacrificer is guilty in that he/she will be subject to the same intra-community plague of reciprocal violence. However, whereas one might consider this the breaking point of the mechanism—the eternal recurrence of universal guilt and sacrifice requires a cessation of the process in the face a *Yojimbo*-like murder-suicide of the community[52]—Clamence parasitically feeds off the cycle as a means of exalting his own sense of self, which is bad faith, which eternally repeats, which is endless, striving to fill the emptiness of the metaphysical desire of lack: since the model of the profane judge (as opposed to the divine that Josef K. was striving to reach/become) is false, Clamence the judge-penitent can never be real.

> In sackcloth and ashes, slowly tearing out my hair, my face ploughed with scratches, but sharp eyed, I stand before the whole of humankind, going over my shameful actions, ever-conscious of the effect I am having and saying: 'I was the lowest of the low.' Then, imperceptibly, my speech slips from 'I' to 'we'. When I get to the point of saying: 'This is what we are', the switch has been made and I can tell them some home truths. Of course, I'm like them: we're all in the same boat. But I have one superiority over them, which is that I know, and that gives me the right to speak. You can see the advantage, I'm sure. The more I accuse myself, the more I have the right to judge you. Better still: I incite you to judge yourself, which relieves me by that much more…confessing my sins permit me to start again with a lighter heart and to gratify myself twice, firstly enjoying my nature, and then a delicious repentance (Camus, 1989: 87–89).

When reading this passage, we realize that we have encountered the figure of the judge-penitent before, although under another name, but one that still spells the will-to-revenge.

9.5 Jean-Baptiste Clamence Meets the Anti-Christ

The penitential imagery, coupled with the groveling, self-hating, and deflecting accusatory tone is suggestive not merely of Uriah Heep but, on a more sublime level, that of the patron atheist saint of French existentialism, the self-proclaimed anti-Christ Friedrich Nietzsche, the most radical of all revolutionary prophets because, through his parodic inversion of Christianity he intentionally sought the re-establishment of the sacrificial mechanism and regenerative violence—quite unlike Karl Marx who thought that he could dispense with the need for sacrificial violence until proven wrong by his greatest disciple, Lenin. 'Nietzsche was the first thinker to see clearly that the singularity of Judeo-Christianity was that it rehabilitates victims that myths would regard as justly immolated' (Girard 996: 272). He was also, like Camus/Clamence, highly susceptible to mimetic contagion, in Nietzsche's case to a singularly pathological degree (Fornari, 2013) coupled, as with Clamence, with a neurotic inability to keep his mouth shut.

---

[52] See Chap. 5, above.

> Nietzsche's superiority over his century and ours may well be that he alone pushed the *ressentiment* that he shares with quite a few lesser mortals to such a height that it yielded its most virulent and significant fruit. None of Nietzsche's achievements as a thinker can be divorced from *ressentiment*, whether the subject is Wagner, the divine, or Nietzsche himself ... (Girard, 1996: 246).

As Nietzsche learned from a lifetime of annihilating and unappeasable bitterness, the raw stuff of existence is *ressentiment*:

> Many features of *ressentiment*, as Nietzsche describes them, resemble the consequences of the mimetic process. *Ressentiment* is really a thwarted and traumatized desire. The very word evokes the image of an immovable obstacle against which the initial 'sentiment' did in fact collide and to which it keeps obsessively coming back, only to be frustrated again and again (Girard, 1978: 73).

Skandalon. The single most important thing to know about the anti-Christ-of-self-promotion-as-symbolic-homicide is that the whole of his philosophical oeuvre consists of a series of phantasmagorical encoded love letters to Cosima Wagner, his great unrequited and for good reason, being the spouse of the operatic Titan of the nineteenth century. The tragic farce of Nietzsche's life was the triangulation of mimetic desire: Nietzsche ('Dionysus') was in an unannounced pathological rivalry of metaphysical desire with Richard Wagner ('Theseus') over the sole ownership of the gaze of Cosima ('Ariadne') (Girard, 1978: 61–83). Nietzsche was truly an outstanding figure in many ways but perhaps his greatest claim to genuine uniqueness lay with his having to go through what virtually no other mortal ever had to experience: the physical manifestation of his private *skandalon* in the shape of a world-transformative music festival, the production of Wagner's Ring Cycle at the Bayreuth Festival Theater on August 16, 1876, a day never to be forgotten by those seduced by Wagner.

> Bayreuth is presented by Nietzsche as Wagner's monstrous effort to organize his own cult. Nietzsche may not be completely wrong, but *Ecce Homo*[53] is exactly the same thing. It is Nietzsche's effort to organize his own cult. It is Nietzsche's reply to Bayreuth, an act of retaliation, and, like all such acts it is the same thing as the act against which it retaliates (Girard, 1978: 62).

To prove himself the 'true' anti-Wagner/Theseus to the 'true' Cosima/Ariadne Nietzsche had to make himself into the 'true' Dionysus, the god of Tragedy, the paramount consumer of sacrifices, to the most extreme degree conceivable, which, under his increasingly unsteady hands, turned out to be Dionysus-Nietzsche-as-anti-Christ, the abolisher of He who abolished all sacrifices, the joyful prophet of the restoration of truly orgiastic sacrificial violence, whose alchemical transformative potencies manifest as the uber-intoxicating will-to-power. But all of this will require the return of, and the conscious re-affirmation of, the scapegoating process but this time devoid of the bad conscience of bad faith (or unconfessed *meconnaissance*), self-negating (or 'nihilistic') moral consciousness now superseded by the transmogrifying altered state (ASC) of *ekstasis.*

---

[53] Nietzsche's sort-of autobiography, composed in 1889.

> Already in *The Birth of Tragedy*[54] Nietzsche mentioned the violence that accompanies and often precedes Dionysus everywhere. All epiphanies of the god leave ruins in their wake. 'Mania', after all, means homicidal fury. Unlike many of his followers, Nietzsche did not turn the Dionysian into something idyllic and inconsequential. He was too honest to dissimulate the disturbing sides, the ugly sides of the Dionysian.... He realized that this type of killing, which is reflected in many rituals as well as myths, is often executed by a large number of murderers; it is a collective deed in which an entire human group is involved (Girard, 1996: 247).

Nietzsche provides the classic exposition of this in Note 1052 of his *Nachlass*[55] entitled 'The Two Types: Dionysus and the Crucified'.

> Dionysos versus the 'Crucified One': there you have the opposition. It's *not* a distinction regarding their martyrdom—just that this martyrdom has a different meaning. Life itself, its eternal fruitfulness and recurrence, conditions torment, destruction, the will to annihilation ...in the other case suffering, 'the Crucified as the innocent', counts as an objection to this life, a formula to condemn it. ... 'the God on the cross' is a curse on life, a hunt to deliver oneself from it. Dionysos cut to pieces is a *promise* to life: it will be eternally reborn and come home out of destruction (Nietzsche, 2003: 249–250).

But as I have already shown in my discussion of Kafka,[56] the eternal return demystified is nothing more than the periodic re-staging of the performance of sacrificial murder as the repetitive exorcism of the recurrent will-to-revenge that is *ressentiment*. 'Nietzsche is not satisfied with ignoring the Bible in the sense that his time is beginning to do; he is trying to reverse it and to rehabilitate the violence of Cain' (Girard, 1996: 251), the builder of cities and, therefore, the creator of civilization, including music festivals. This is confirmed by Aphorism 125 of *The Gay Science*.

> God is dead. God remains dead. And we have killed him. How shall we, the murderers of all murderers, comfort ourselves? What was holiest and most powerful of all that the world has yet owned has bled to death under our knives. Who will wipe this blood off us? What water is there for us to clean ourselves? What festivals of atonement, what sacred games shall we have to invent? (Nietzsche qtd. Girard, 1996: 257).

The reverse of this, however, is also true: if the return of scapegoating requires mass violence, then the 'willed' return of mass violence requires an equally 'willed' scapegoating, which, to repeat my earlier point, when expressed as a political program would run as 'We do not kill in order to save; we save in order to kill.' Which takes us straight back to one of Girard's most subversive insights: that civilization was created in order to create the conditions necessary for the staging of a certain kind of murder, that of the scapegoat.[57]

> Gods do not have to exist really in order to be murdered. As a matter of fact, unless they are first murdered they will never exist. Unlike ordinary beings who can exist only if they are

---

[54] His first published work which appeared in 1872. The full title *is On the Birth of Tragedy from the Spirit of Music*; the last fifteen chapters are devoted to Richard Wagner.

[55] The 'Estate' or 'Word', a collection of notebooks, letters, and marginalia misleadingly translated as *The Will to Power*.

[56] See Chap. 8, above.

[57] See Chap. 1, above.

> not murdered, gods begin to exist as gods, at least in the eyes of men, only after they have been murdered (Girard, 1996: 256).

Meaning that a 'god,' the source of all value and meaning, is merely a victim of violence who has been mystified. Which is the will-to-totalitarianism in a nutshell. Lenin knew it. Stalin knew it. Hitler knew it. And Camus knew it too, albeit a posteriori: 'a-theism' is deliberate and self-conscious deicide as a means of paving the way for the (at last!) 'truly' regenerative violence that permits revolution to be *consciously* understood as the return of the sacrificers—which is the only way that we can get rid of the amnesia that has been holding us back for the preceding two thousand years. Nietzsche, increasingly desperate to out-grandstand Wagner, spoke the demystified truth of the matter out loud, prophesizing the coming of the post-human Fourth Industrial Revolution in the process.

> Through Christianity, the individual was made so important, so absolute, that he could no longer be *sacrificed*: but the species endures only through human sacrifice.... Genuine charity demands sacrifice for the good of the species—it is hard, it is full of self-overcoming, because it *needs human sacrifice*. And this pseudo-humaneness called Christianity wants it established that *no one should be sacrificed* (Friedrich Nietzsche qtd. Girard, 2005: 174).

Juvenile delinquency does not even begin to cover it; Nietzsche 'opposes, so he believes, the crowd mentality, but he does not recognize his Dionysian stance as the supreme expression of the mob in its most brutal and its most stupid tendencies' (Girard, 2005: 173) which is the orgiastic. The return to sacrifice will establish the paramountcy of the will-to-power now mediated by those capable of the self-affirmation required to exercise the most 'genuine' form of charity, with one paradoxical twist: if the pagan theistic sacrificers were righteous because there were gods, then the neo-pagan a-theistic sacrificers will be righteous precisely because there are no gods, which makes their un-mediated righteousness, the objective expression of their subjective will-to-power, unlimited in scope, just as metaphysical desire is mimetic rivalry unbounded, as it certainly was in the case of 'Nietzsche Contra Wagner'.

> And the crime is so great that new festivals of atonement,[58] new sacred games will have to be invented. New rituals will undoubtedly appear. The consequences of God's murder are religious, therefore, purely religious. The very deed that seems to put an end to the religious process is really the origin of that process, the sum total of it, really, the religious process par excellence. These new festivals and sacred games will certainly re-enact the collective murder of God. They will be sacrificial rites. The death of God is also his birth (Girard, 1996: 257).

In *The Fall*, Camus deliberately parodies Mersault's 'love of heights' in *The Stranger* (Camus, 1989: 21–24)—which was, intriguingly, a character trait not only of Camus/Clamence himself but also of Nietzsche—by employing it as an outward manifestation of his alter ego's unexpurgated will-to-revenge.

> Let us pause on these lofty peaks. You understand now what I meant when I spoke about aiming higher. I was referring to these high summits, the only place where I can live. Yes, I

[58] Bayreuth with real-life special effects?

> have never felt so much at home as up there, at the top. Even in the minutiae of daily life, I needed to be up above. I preferred the bus to the metro, hansom cabs to taxis and balconies to mezzanines...I was the man of high ridges, at the very least...especially if I was alone, high above the human ants...So at least I relished my life and superiority (Camus, 1989: 16–17).

The peak experience of physical elation induced by height receives its metaphorical expression in the moral and professional heights achieved by Clamence through his success as an advocate/generous lawyer: that is, as a full-time technician of the post-theological, or secularized, machinery of sacrifice.

> Fortunately, my profession satisfied this call to the heights. It relived me of any bitterness towards my fellow man, whom I constantly put under an obligation without ever owing him anything. It set me above the judge, whom I judged in his turn, and above the accused, whom I compelled to feel gratitude. Mark this well, sir: I lived with impunity. No judgment affected me: I was not an actor on the stage of the courtroom, but somewhere in the flies like those gods who are lowered from time to time by mechanical means, so that they can raise the performance to a new level and give it sense (Camus, 1989: 17).

The *deus ex machine* is a mainstay of Greek tragedy, especially in the works of Euripides, a fellow-traveler of the rationalist Socrates and a coconspirator in the murder of the gods; in the event of a deciding dramatic crisis, a deity suddenly appears to resolve the situation, usually by divinely selecting a substitution for the designated victim, and, thereby, ruling out any possibility of the role of chance. So it is natural that Clamence assumes the mockery of a post-divine descent from above as a means of resolving the crisis afflicting the mortals: let each one condemn all of the others. The only twist that Camus adds is a Christian one: Clamence = 'clemency' = the Paraclete (The Holy Spirit), so that Jean-Baptiste Clemency is really John the Baptist, the channeler of the divine Advocate (who is, hopefully, generous), and the bearer of witness to the One who came into the world not in order to judge it but to save it. But the effect is the same as with the pagan Greeks, only this time the bearer of witness announces the coming of the One who is to inaugurate the sacrificial world *nomos* without end.

> Then I grow my dearest fellow, I am on the mountain top with the plain stretching out before my eyes. What intoxication to feel that one is God the Father, handing out definitive testimonials of bad character and behavior. I am enthroned among my bad angels at the peak of the Dutch heavens[59] and watch the multitude of the Last Judgment rise towards me out of the mists and the damp. Slowly, they drift upwards. I can already see the first of them coming. On his distraught features, half hidden by one hand, I read the sadness of our common condition and the despair of being unable to escape it. As for me, I pity without absolving, I understand without forgiving[60] and above all (ah!) at last I feel adored! Yes, I'm getting excited. How do you expect me to stay sensibly in bed? I have to be higher up than you; my thoughts uplift me...And you could lift my newly severed head above the crowd, so they could recognize themselves in it and I would dominate them once more, as an example to them. All would be consummated: unseen, unknown, I should have finished my career as false prophet crying in the desert and refusing to come forth (Camus, 1989: 89, 91).

---

[59] The judge-penitent is currently hiding out in Amsterdam at the time of making his confession being party to a major art theft.

[60] He continues sacrificing.

Note the strict parallelism between the conclusion of both *The Fall* and *The Stranger*: Camus could only undergo conversion, the turning away from romanticism, by rewriting himself not as a unique model for others but as merely another fallen victim of mimetic rivalry that required another's victimization to validate the truth of his own being. Which is not that far from Josef K. other than at 'The End' he more or less embraced the role of the goat of the sin offering in order to resolve the scandal of metaphysical desire.[61]

> As long as the egoistical Manicheism that produced *L'Etranger* held its sway over him, the author could not perceive the structural flaw of his novel. All illusions are one. They stand together and they fall together as soon as their cause, egoistical passion, is perceived. The confession of Clamence does not lead to a new 'interpretation' of *L'Etranger* but to an act of transcendence; the perspective of the first novel is rejected (Girard, 1978: 21).

It is not *The Stranger* but *The Fall* that is Camus' true and truthful complementary reply to Kafka's *The Trial*, because it is only in the latter novel that Camus completely succeeds demystifying both modernity and its jurisprudence by revealing the suppressed continuities of both with ritualistic sacrifice and scapegoating, a continuation by other means of an unbroken history of adverse judgment; 'As I told you, you can't be certain of anything' said Clamence in complete honestly (Camus 988: 80).[62] Girard frames the issue of Camus as being nothing less than authentic *metanoia*, a genuine spiritual, if not formally religious, turning toward the non-sacrificial and away from the generous lawyer's mimetic desire.

> The first Camus did not realize how far-reaching, how pervasive the evil of judgment is. He felt that he was outside judgment because he condemned those who condemn[63] … Mersault viewed evil as something outside of himself, a *problem* that concerned the judges alone, whereas Clamence knows that he himself is involved. Evil is the *mystery* of a pride that, as it condemns others, unwittingly condemns itself. It is the pride of Oedipus, another hero of trial literature,[64] always uttering the curses that result in his own undoing. Reciprocity between the I and the Thou asserts itself in the very efforts I make to deny it: 'The sentence which you pass against your fellow man,' says Clamence, 'is always flung back into your face where it effects quite a bit of damage' (Girard, 1978: 34).

And the figure that merely his characters but that Camus himself came to most perfectly emulate was, appropriately, a fictional (mythic) one: Oedipus the Tyrant, the one who was 'sacrificer before being sacrificed.'

---

[61] See Chap. 8, above.

[62] Another way that Mersault bears a marked resemblance to Oedipus who, as "the one who solves riddles" doubles as a demystifier of a fake reality, suggesting a deeper meaning for both tragic heroes: they work to uncover the disguised nature of the scapegoat mechanism while, for that very reason, remaining unaware of their true nature and purpose until it is too late. 'Oedipus is a double' embodying the duality of the *pharmakon* as destroyer and restorer; 'He is himself a riddle whose meaning he can only guess when he discovers himself to be in every respect the opposite of what he thought he was and appeared to be' (Vernant & Vidal-Naquet, 1990: 116, 105), just as Mersault regenerates the community by voluntarily 'willing' the purgative effects of his execution and rendering his sacrificial death efficacious.

[63] A parallel might be found in the currently all-consuming phenomenon of 'identity politics' on both sides of the ideological spectrum: love is hating the haters.

[64] See Introduction, above.

> Oedipus sits on the throne of Thebes.... The only shadow in the picture is the plague[65] lingering over the city. An unclean creature must be attracting the wrath of the god. Oedipus vows to punish the monster. He begins hunting him after uttering solemn curses against him[66] ... Oedipus' excessive indignation, his zeal to track down the culprit, are revealing.... The shortest path from the non-guilty to the guilty is a straight line, and so our champion of justice marches straight ahead. He does not notice when the path begins to curve—yet it proves to be a circular path in the end.[67] The investigator turns back towards the Self he believes he has left safely in the distance behind him. If, somewhere in the world, evil exists, somebody else must be responsible. At first Oedipus is certain of only one thing: he is not himself implicated in the business. Such is the imperious stance of natural subjectivity. But this imperious stance is secretly undermined. The hero would not condemn the Other if he were not acting for the Self's benefit (Girard, 2004: 13).

'Why do we, all of us, have to keep judging and being judged?' is the hypocritical lament of the judge-penitent who already knew the answer that encapsulates the entirety of Girard's anthropologically informed literary project: the mimetic crises of undifferentiation and generative violence are universal events which are mediated by ritualistic sacrifice. And it is arguably Camus who provided the template for the post-theistic re-sacralization of the formerly sacred victim known as the scapegoat. But whatever his political objectives—always of paramount importance to him—Camus, at the same time, accidentally initiated a new form of secular allegory with his *Outsider*. From now on it will be possible, in the hands of a superior writer, to aesthetically reconfigure as scapegoats those profanely abnormal ones who can be convincingly represented as the victims of the horror of an accident narratively reconstructed as re-sacralizing Fate.

It is no longer human character but the absurdity of crime that is Destiny.

References

Primary Sources

Camus, A. (1989). *The stranger* (M. Ward, Trans.). New York: Vintage International.

Camus, A. (2006). *The fall* (R. Buss, Trans.). London: Penguin Books.

Sophocles. (1984). *The three Theban plays: Antigone, Oedipus the king, Oedipus at colonus* (R. Fagles, Trans.). London: Penguin Books.

Secondary Sources

Aristotle. (1920). *Aristotle on the art of poetry* (I. Bywater, Trans.). Oxford UK: Clarendon Press.

---

[65] The crisis of undifferentiation. See Chaps. 1 and 5, above.

[66] Like a juvenile delinquent.

[67] Suggestive of the turning of the circle of mimetic and sacrificial violence. It also recalls the circularity of the Kafkaesque narrative.

Bandera, C. (1989). From Mythical Bees to Medieval Anti-Semitism. In P. Dumouchel (Ed.), *Paul Dumouchel, violence and truth: On the work of Rene Girard* (pp. 209–226). The Athlone Press.
Bureau, R. (1989). A Gabonese Myth. In P. Dumouchel (Ed.), *Paul Dumouchel, violence and truth: On the work of Rene Girard* (pp. 27–43). The Athlone press.
Butcher, S. H. (1902). *Aristotle's theory of poetry and fine art with a critical text and translation of the poetics*. The Macmillan Company.
Caroll, N. (1990). *The philosophy of horror or paradoxes of the heart*. Routledge.
Darzins, J. (1960). Transparence in Camus and Kafka. *Yale French Studies, 15*, 98–103.
Dawson, D. (2013). *Flesh becomes word: A lexicography of the scapegoat or, the history of an idea*. Michigan State University Press.
Dupuy, J-P. (2013). *The mark of the sacred* (M. B. DeBevoise, Trans.). Stanford: Stanford University Press.
Eagleton, T. (2020). Excerpt from *sweet violence*. In M. R. Anspach (Ed.), *The Oedipus book: Reading Sophocles Oedipus the king* (pp. 269–279). Michigan State University Press.
Fanon, F. (1990). *The wretched of the Earth* (C. Farrington, Trans.). London: Penguin Books.
Fanon, F. (2008). *Black skin, white masks* (C. L. Markmann, Trans.). London: Pluto Books.
Fornari, G. (2013). *A god torn to pieces: The Nietzsche case* (K. Buck, Trans.). East Lansing MI: Michigan State University Press.
Girard, R. (1965). *Deceit, desire, and the novel: Self and other in literary structure* (Y. Freccero, Trans.). Baltimore: The Johns Hopkins University Press.
Girard, R. (1977). *Violence and the sacred* (P. Gregory, Trans.). Baltimore: The Johns Hopkins University Press.
Girard, R. (1978). *To double business bound: Essays on literature, mimesis, and anthropology*. The Johns Hopkins University Press.
Girard, R. (1986). *The scapegoat* (Y. Freccero, Trans.). Baltimore: The Johns Hopkins University Press.
Girard, R. (1996). In J. G. Williams (Ed.), *The Girard reader*. The Crossroad Publishing Company.
Girard, R. (2004). *Oedipus unbound: Selected writings on rivalry and desire* (M. R. Anspach, Trans.). Stanford: Stanford University Press.
Girard, R. (2005). *I see Satan fall like lightning*. Orbis Books.
Goodhart, S. (1978). Oedipus and Lauis' many murderers. *Diacritics, 8*(1), 55–71.
McKenna, A. J. (1992). *Violence and difference: Girard, Derrida, and deconstruction*. University of Illinois Press.
Memmi, A. (1991). *The colonizer and the colonized* (H. Greenfield, Trans.). Boston: Beacon Press.
Memmi, A. (2000). *Racism* (S. Martinot, Trans.). Minneapolis: University of Minnesota Press.
Nietzsche, F. (2003). In R. Bittner (Ed.), *Writings from the late notebooks* (K. Sturge, Trans.). Cambridge UK, Cambridge University Press.
Sartre, J.-P. (1962). An explication of *the stranger*. In G. Bree (Ed.), *Camus: A collection of critical essays* (pp. 108–121). Prentice-Hall Inc.
Turner, V. (1969). *The drums of affliction: A study of religious processes among the Ndembu of Zambia*. Clarendon Press.
Vernant, J. P., & Vidal-Naquet, P. (1990). *Myth and tragedy in Ancient Greece* (J. Lloyd, Trans.). New York: Zone Books.
Weisberg, R. (1975–1976). Comparative law in comparative literature: The figure of the 'examining magistrate' in Dostoevski and Camus. *Rutgers Law Review, 29*, 237–258.
Weisberg, R. H. (1984). *The failure of the word: The protagonist as lawyer in modern fiction*. Yale University Press.

Chapter 10
'Out There': Monstrous Doubles and the *Folie a Deux* in Truman Capote's *In Cold Blood*

Abstract This chapter takes up with arguably the greatest non-fiction novel ever written, Truman Capote's *In Cold Blood* (1966). Not the least notorious of the many contentious aspects of Capote's master work is his fabrication of a totally false ending: in order to provide his 'true' tale with closure, Capote invented a fictional encounter within a Kansas cemetery, one that carries remarkably sacrificial implications. *In Cold Blood* will be subjected to a close Girardian reading, focusing on two key themes. The first is the reversibility, or exchangeability, at work in the scapegoating mechanism: just as the entire Clutter family is the sacrificial victim of the victimizing monstrous doubles of Perry Smith and Dick Hickock, so are the two murderers the scapegoats of the community striving to expel its internal mimetic violence through the public ritual of law and capital punishment. The second is that the personalized violence of the deviant criminals (*folie a deux*) and the impersonal violence of the 'law-abiding community' are both governed by the exact same psychological processes: mimetic desire and mimetic rivalry—the same curse of the boys from another great novel of mis-recognized violence, William Golding's *Lord of the Flies*. The fictitious ending unifies both of these themes beautifully well, suggesting, in an artfully disguised manner, that the youngest murder victim, Nancy Clutter, is herself nothing less than a sacrificial victim, whose violent death and forcible descent into the Underworld bestows a regenerative power upon those around her.

Keywords Truman Capote · *Folie a deux* · Monstrous doubles · The non-fiction novel · Creative reportage · Catharsis · Capital punishment · *Apagoge*

10.1 'The Odor of Windfall Apples Rotting Under the Apple Trees': Ghosts and Monsters

By way of background.

> There was a man living in Babylon whose name was Jo'akim. And he took a wife named Susanna … a very beautiful woman and one who feared the Lord … Jo'akim was very rich, and had a spacious garden adjoining his house; and the Jews used to come to him because he was the most honored of them all. (The Book of Daniel, 13: 1–2, 4 *The Didache Bible*)

E. M. Wilson, *Rene Girard, Law, Literature, and Cinema*,
https://doi.org/10.1007/978-981-97-1156-7_10

One Sunday, not long after the slaughter of the Clutter family, Mrs. Kidwell, 'a fanciful woman' allegedly, had a strange experience: she 'had been standing at a window watching dusk tint the outdoors, the sprawling prairie. And out of the blue she said, "Susan? You know what I keep seeing? Nancy. On Babe. Coming this way"' (Capote, 2000: 29). To portray Nancy Clutter, the daughter of the butchered family, as a horse-riding wandering spirit is to signify her status as a sacred murder victim either because of the circumstances or the meaning of her death as a scapegoat. Within the Horror genre, the signification of trauma, either repressed memory (historical) or repressed desires (erotic), is usually centered upon the return of a dead person, a revenant in Irish folklore. It is worth remembering that Truman Capote wrote the screenplay for *The Innocents* (1961), the film adaptation of *The Turn of the Screw* by Henry James; the 'notion of a threat from within is integral to the terror of *In Cold Blood*' (Fahy, 2012: 61) and, consistent with his general artistic preoccupation with the gothic, Capote encapsulates the imaginary of the 'threat from within' through the presentation of the Clutter home as a pseudo-haunted house: 'the first thread of decay's cobweb ... A gravel rake lay rusting in the driveway; the lawn was parched and shabby ...The Clutter place seemed shadowed, and hushed, and motionless' (Capote, 2000: 206–207). It is a central tenet of psycho-analysis that the house is the premiere symbol of the Self, but Capote makes clear that there is not only something wrong with the Clutter house, there is something wrong with the entire prairie landscape which may be more pagan than Christian.

> The village of Holcomb stands on the high wheat plains of western Kansas, a lonesome area that other Kansans call 'out there' ... The land is flat, and the views are extraordinarily extensive; horses, herds of cattle, a white cluster of grain elevators rising as gracefully as Greek temples are visible long before a traveller reaches them. (Capote, 2000: 1)

And then—the juxtaposition with the horrific rupture of the bucolic scene by an elemental violence.

> Until one morning in mid-November of 1959, few Americans—in fact, few Kansans—had ever heard of Holcomb. Like the waters of the river, like the motorists on the highway, and like the yellow trains streaking down the Santa Fe tracks, drama, in the shape of exceptional happenings, had never stopped there ... But then, in the earliest hours of that morning in November, a Sunday morning,[1] certain foreign sounds impinged on the normal nightly Holcomb noises—on the keening hysteria of coyotes, the dry scrape of scuttling tumbleweed, the racing, receding wail of locomotive whistles. At the time not a soul in sleeping Holcomb heard them—four shotgun blasts that, all told, ended six human lives. But afterwards the townspeople, theretofore sufficiently unfearful of each other to seldom trouble to lock their doors, found fantasy re-creating them over and again—those sombre explosions that stimulated fires of mistrust in the glare of which many old neighbours viewed each other strangely, and as strangers. (Capote, 2000: 16–17)

The weird 'Midnight callers' on the Clutter family are the dual bearers of the collective violence of the entire village, marking the externalized projection 'out there' of a group violence emanating from within. The first clue is the implicit correlation Capote draws between nature and community. Nature first: 'Not far from

[1] Which increases the outrage of the defilement.

River Valley Farm there is a mysterious stretch of countryside known as Sand Hills; it is like a beach without an ocean, and at night coyotes slink among the dunes, assembling in hordes to howl' (Capote, 2000: 50). Then community:

> Actually, I've never known such bedlam. It's noisier than a bomb raid. Train whistles. Coyotes. Monsters *howling* the bloody night long. A horrid racket. And since the murders it seems to bother me more. So many things to do. Our house—what an old creaker it is! Mark you, I'm not complaining. Really, it's quite a serviceable house—has all the mod. cons.[2]—but, oh, how it coughs and grunts! And after dark, when the wind commences, that *hateful* prairie wind, one hears the most *appalling* moans. I mean, if one's a bit nervy, one can't help imaging—silly things. Dear God! That poor family! No, we never met them. I *saw* Mr. Clutter once. In the Federal Building. (Capote, 2000: 122–123)

The essence of monsters, the primary 'objects of art-horror,' is impurity, the product of their anomalous being: 'Obviously, the anomalous nature of these beings is what makes them disturbing, distressing, and disgusting. They are violations of our ways of classifying things and such frustrations of a world-picture are bound to be disturbing' (Carroll, 1990: 188). While at all times pre-representational, monsters do not always have to be supernatural for 'some types of monsters may be explained as "real" ... [in that they] are not remarkable in any physical sense. Their threat to normality is manifested solely through abnormal behavior challenging the rules of social regulation through "monstrous" and transgressive behavior' (David Russell qtd. Fahy, 2012: 60). So that like the scapegoat, the monster may not be wholly transgressive but merely somewhat strange or inconsistent with the nor of normality, the *nomos* of the everyday and undifferentiated. Capote's achievement in short was to write a gothic horror story in form that is a realist text in substance, being populated solely by real things which he makes clear at the beginning of *In Cold Blood* (Wilson, 2020). But if he is to introduce monsters or ghosts symbolically encoded within 'the real' as signifiers of something that dwells within the community but which is mis-recognized, then he inherits along with them all of the cultural baggage in their train, the shadowy presence of religion and the sacred. If he begins the text in a gothic manner, then artistic unity demands that he must end it the same way. But since his concern is with journalistic realism as high literature, he is compelled to provide a fake ending, the gothic subordinated to realism.

10.1.1 Alvin Dewey's Uncanny Encounter in the Graveyard

As Capote acknowledged, 'I was criticized a lot for [the fictional ending]. People thought I should have ended with the hangings, that awful last scene. But I felt that I had to return to the town, to bring everything back full circle, to end with peace' (Capote qtd. Clarke, 2010: 359). The gothic novel demands that if the monster appears at the beginning, the community must be saved by the end. So what is the narrative

[2] A nice touch: the uncanny juxtaposition of the modern and the archaic that foreshadows the approaching union of the scientific-judicial with the archaic-sacrificial.

logic of the fake ending that Capote finally settled upon? The answer lies with the correlation he establishes between death and restoration which he hints at several times: 'Mr. Clutter's orchard of pear and apple trees, the elms shading the lane—were lightly veiled in a haze of virginal green The fine lawn surrounding the Clutter house was also newly green' (Capote, 2000: 270). But this is only foreshadowing; the real artistic triumph comes on the last pages. 'One afternoon the previous May, a month when the fields blaze with the green-gold fire of half-grown wheat,' Kansas Bureau of Investigation (KBI) Special Agent Alvin Dewey attended his Father's grave in Valley View cemetery. He also visited the graves of the Clutters.

> As Dewey approached them, he saw that another visitor was already there: a willowy girl with white-gloved hands, a smooth cap of dark-honey hair, and long, elegant legs. She smiled at him, and he wondered who she was.
>
> 'Have you forgotten me, Mr. Dewey? Susan Kidwell.' Nancy Clutter's best friend.
>
> He laughed; she joined him. 'Sue Kidwell. I'll be darned.' He hadn't seen her since the trial; she had been a child then (Capote, 2000: 342).
>
> They converse.
>
> This is my junior year at K.U.,' she said, meaning the University of Kansas. 'I'm just home a few days.
>
> That's wonderful, Sue. What are you studying?
>
> 'Everything. Art, mostly. I love it. I'm really happy.' She glanced across the prairie. 'Nancy and I planned to go to college together. We were going to be room-mates. I think about it sometimes. Suddenly, when I'm very happy, I think of all the plans we made' (Capote, 2000: 343).
>
> Sue cannot stay.
>
> I've got to run! But it was nice to see you Mr. Dewey.
>
> 'And nice to have seen you, Sue. Good luck,' he called after her as she disappeared down the path, a pretty girl in a hurry, her smooth hair swinging, shining—just such a young woman as Nancy might have been Then, starting home, he walked towards the trees, and under them, leaving behind the big sky, the whisper of wind-voices in the wind-bent wheat. (Capote, 2000: 343)

It was not only Capote and his readers that were troubled by the absence of closure within the true-life story that became the first true crime novel—Alvin Dewey was troubled by it as well. Capote makes clear that Dewey falsely anticipated that the lawful murder of the unlawful murderers would provide him with an emotional release, or catharsis, of some kind (Capote, 2000: 68). Yet the author could not bring himself to end the novel with a nakedly realist depiction of an execution ('that awful last scene').[3] Why? Because the violence that the criminals inflicted and that the victims suffered is inherently meaningless in the absence of some transformational event that redeems the blood spilled as a form of healing and regeneration. Capote, as an artist, is forced to confront the absurdity of History in the absence of a restorative

[3] This, however, did not pose an obstacle to the filmmakers who end the adaptation on a long slow-motion shot of Perry Smith's swinging corpse at the end of a rope *In Cold Blood* (directed by Richard Brooks, Columbia Pictures, 2003). Apart from the undeniably visceral payoff of this final scene, the real reason why movie evades the allegorical resurrection of Nancy Cutter of the novel is the formidable metaphysical baggage that would have had to have been brought onboard.

ritual, in which pain is devoid of value (History is 'just a bunch of stuff that happened' as Homer Simpson once said) unless it is organized into some over-arching system of meaning. Which is a double challenge, for as Victor Turner knew full well, art and religion are, in some subterranean way, doubles: 'The unity of a given ritual is a dramatic unity. It is in this sense a work of art' (Turner, 1968: 269). An observation picked up and run with by Girard: 'a given dramatic performance constitutes a sort of rite, the shadowy similitude of the religious experience' (Girard, 1977: 291).[4] And the surest way to transmogrify a parricide into something transcendent is to narratively re-work it as a sacrificial occurrence, meaning that a dual movement to both *mythos* and tragedy are required: 'If tragedy was to function as a sort of ritual, something similar to a sacrificial killing had to be concealed in the dramatic and literary use of *catharsis*, just as it was concealed in the religious and medical use of the term' (Girard, 1977: 291). The problem for the author, as Camus found out on writing about a fictitious murder in colonial Algeria, is that it is difficult to make America the proper subject of anything tragic in the correct sense of the term precisely because the universalization of internal mediation compels social conscious to eternally move in the direction of the unbounded that is infinite optimism (when it is not apocalyptic). The other impediment is that the society is simply too unreflexively secular to endure contemplation of the power of the invisible over and within the mundane which is all that we have; nevertheless, American society, as with every other, requires, even if only in the form of pure function, a regenerative and cathartic mechanism of some kind. And the name that we give to this generative violence in post-Reality America is the supremely functionalist ritual of capital punishment, so the mechanical portion of Capote's problem is solved: he needs merely to write about the execution in a particular manner, presumably allegorical, as William Golding did in *Lord of the Flies* and James Dickey in *Deliverance*. But although a symmetrically gothic conclusion is necessary (monsters die so world is saved), it is still not clear why, out of all the possible fake endings Capote could have chosen, he decided to have Sue Kidwell standing beside Nancy Clutter's grave in a manner clearly suggestive of a revenant, or a ghost. Classical literary theory holds that the conclusion of a properly constructed novel not only unifies the text but, through its consummating apotheosis, lays bare the textual and sub-textual logic of all that has come before it. It is not pretty.

10.2 The Double-Monstrosity of Hickock-Smith: The Non-fiction Novel and the Techniques of Allegory

As we should expect, although a true crime novel much of the sub-text of *In Cold Blood* is allegory. John Hellman has brilliantly argued that *In Cold Blood* should not be read as a novelistic form of reportage but as a 'post-religious' or secular allegory,

[4] See Chap. 9, above.

the 'fabulist vision' of transcendental meaning conveyed through the realism of journalistic prose (Hellman, 1980: 65).

> Capote's position in *In Cold Blood* … [shows a] predisposition to present landscapes, environments, and objects in repeated patterns. He leaves to the reader the attribution of value and the responsibility of moral interpretation He resists the temptation to impose meaning or to moralize upon fundamentally inexplicable events. Yet, despite Capote's relentless care to present only the facts and his reluctance to impose a too easy moral, his story achieves in the end a kind of mythic significance. The destiny of an archetypal American family crosses paths with warped killers whose vengeance is portrayed more as a result of fate than of human motivation. (Hollowell, 1977: 79)

Hellman suggests that the text should not be read primarily in terms of a highly novelistic form of reportage but as a secular allegory, like *Lord of the Flies*. As discussed in Chap. 2, 'a narrative, whether prose or verse, is allegorical when the agents and actions, and sometimes the setting as well, are contrived by the author to make coherent sense on the "literal", or primary level of signification, and, at the same time to signify a second, correlated order of significance.' There are two types of allegory: the historical or the political ('in which the characters and actions that are signified literally in their turn represent, or "allegorize", historical personages and events'), and the sustained allegory of ideas wherein 'the literal characters represent concepts and the plot allegorizes an abstract doctrine or thesis…the central device is the *personification* of abstract entities such as virtues, vices, states of mind, modes of life, and types of character' (Abrams, 1990: 5). For Hellman *In Cold Blood* would come under the second category, 'the sustained allegory of ideas', specifically the naturalist 'worldview' of social and psychological determinism, and Capote made it clear that the model for his own novel was *An American Tragedy* by Theodore Dreiser (1925), which was itself concerned with allegorizing a Chicago homicide as the microcosmic representation of the totality of urban industrialism. *In Cold Blood* is 'what I really think about America. Desperate, savage, violent America in collision with sane, safe, insular even smug America—people who have every chance, against people who have none' (Truman Capote qtd. Garrett, 1996: 3). Which means that there is a great deal of latent, and not an inconsiderable amount of overt, violence, physical, and symbolic. 'It is significant that Capote at no time renders a judgment about the criminals' (Reed, 1981: 97), and, if there is any doubt that he is imitating Dreiser, Capote casts before us this pearl of naturalistic reductionism.

> About 70 per cent of the letters [from readers] think of the book as a reflection on American life—this collision between the desperate, ruthless, wandering, savage part of American life, and the other, which is insular and safe, more or less. It has struck them because there is something so awfully inevitable about what is going to happen: the people in the book are completely beyond their control. For example, Perry [Smith] wasn't an evil person If he'd had any chance in life, things would have been different. But every illusion he'd ever had, well, they all evaporated, so that on that night [of the Clutter killings] he was so full of self-hatred and self-pity that I think he would have killed *some*body—perhaps not that night, or the next, or the next. You can't get through life without ever getting anything you want, ever. (Capote qtd. Plimpton, 1987: 67)

Which means that Capote occupies a somewhat anomalous place between reportage ('a reflection on American life') and clinical ('there is something so awfully inevitable about what is going to happen … so completely beyond their control') and by 'constructing an allegory which is journalistic in subject matter and realistic in formal method, Capote presents a fabulist vision which has both the credibility of promised fact and the authority of apparent objectivity' (Hellman, 1980: 65). Which is another way of saying that his non-fiction novel is concerned with myth which is the form that *meconnaissance* assumes regarding the sacrificial mechanism. But at the same time, and fully consistent with the aesthetic tropes of literary Modernism, the text is also highly self-reflexive of its own status as a 'work of writing'; in other words, Capote's concern is at least as much with the form of the text and its techniques as with any truth or 'objective meaning' that it may or may not possess. 'I've often thought of the book as being like something reduced to a seed. Instead of presenting the reader with a full plant, with all the foliage, a seed is planted in the soil of his mind' (Capote qtd. Plimpton, 1987: 55) and he is able to square the circle of naturalistic medium with the performative gesture toward 'mythic significance' through the re-staging of allegory as a kind of social and psychology commentary, which, by chance or design, yielded a new literary sub-genre of the *non-fiction novel* in the form of crime reporting. 'Capote never claimed—as many critics thought he did—that he invented narrative journalism or, as *In Cold Blood* came to be labeled, the non-fiction novel. He *did* consider it to be a serious new literary form and he did feel he had made a major contribution toward its establishment. And he also staked a claim to have undertaken the most comprehensive and far-reaching experiment in the medium of reportage' (Grobel, 1985: 99). In brutal fact, Capote had no inherent interest in the murder of the Clutters; his objective was a wholly aesthetic one (*jouissance*), an opportunity to refine and perfect a particular form of writing: journalism, or reportage, infused with formal literary technique.

> I didn't choose that subject because of any great interest in it. It was because I wanted to write what I called a non-fiction novel—a book that would read exactly like a novel except that every word of it would be absolutely true…I settled on this obscure crime in this remote part of Kansas because, I felt, if I followed this from beginning to end it would provide me with the material to really accomplish what was a technical feat. It was a literary experiment where I was choosing a subject not because of a great attraction to the subject, because that was not true, but because it suited my purposes literally speaking. (Grobel, 1985: 112)

As a result, Capote's entire approach was grounded in purely aesthetic concerns rather than moral, legal, or social ones.

> The motivating factor in my choice of material—that is, choosing to write a true account of an actual murder case—was altogether literary. The decision was based on a theory I've harbored since I first began to write professionally…It seemed to me that journalism, reportage, could be forced to yield a serious new art form: the 'non-fiction novel' as I thought of it…on the whole, journalism is the most underestimated, the least explored of literary mediums. (Capote qtd. Plimpton, 1987: 47)

Within this aesthetic frame, the 'reality' of the events become not objectively falsified but strictly subordinated to an over-arching artistic design: an extended, and minutely detailed, journalistic report governed by the concerns of a novel which is that of the 'the *lift*—that final, dreadful thing that it takes. There's a moment in writing when it's either going to really lift or it's not' (Capote qtd. Grobel, 1985: 114). And Capote realized that he had struck gold, as well as 'mythic significance,' the moment that he heard about the butchery of the Clutters.

> But after reading the story [of the Hickock-Smith murders on the back pages of *The New York Times*] it suddenly struck me that a crime, the study of one such, might provide me the broad scope I needed to write the kind of book I wanted to write. Moreover, the human heart being what it is, murder was a theme not likely to darken and yellow with time (Capote qtd. Plimpton, 1987: 51) ...the first essential of the non-fiction novel [is] that there is a timeless quality about the cause and events. That's important. If it's going to date, it can't be a work of art (Capote qtd. Plimpton, 1987: 62) ...Still, the circumstances of the place being altogether unfamiliar, geographically and atmospherically, made it much more tempting. Everything would seem freshly minted—the people, their accents and attitudes, the landscapes, its contours, the weather. All this, it seemed to me, could only sharpen my eye and quicken my ear (Capote qtd. Plimpton, 1987: 51)....above all, the reporter must be able to empathize with personalities outside his usual imaginative range, mentalities unlike his own, kinds of people he would never have written about had he not been forced to by encountering them inside the journalistic situation. This last is what first attracted me to the notion of narrative reportage. (Capote qtd. Plimpton, 1987: 48)

If it is true that the 'essence of this creative reportage is to set down a continuum of factual information in such a way that it carries a fictive quality to its presentation' and if it also true that reportage requires 'the imposing of artistic order and arrangement over a body of information that, while lending itself to systematic narration, nevertheless requires a sense of structure and coherence' (Reed, 1981: 94), then it is certainly true that creative reportage has all of the hallmarks of the mis-recognition of *muthos*. As with the Western,[5] Capote's creative reportage ('the first essential of the non-fiction novel is that there is a timeless quality about the cause and events') complies with Claude Levi-Strauss' admonition that the mythic must represent the attempt to reconcile opposing cosmic forces, in this case the anomalous and the ordinary, or the monstrous and the non-monstrous. And Capote achieves this resonance with the mythological by strictly compartmentalizing the characters and action in parallel narrative universes, each the focus of a contest of dualistic forces that are native to that particular domain; rather than favors any particular allegorical frame, Capote represents his various sets of characters as inhabiting one of them which are then portrayed as being inherently incommensurable.[6]

> Capote has undercut the fictions through which his major characters make up their realities by showing their fatal lack of correspondence to actuality. His dominant unifying device in *In Cold Blood*—irony—constantly announces the failure of the characters to comprehend their fates...Donald Pizer has pointed out that the ironic juxtaposition that pervades *In Cold Blood* 'implies that a shaping destiny controls all life despite our unawareness of that destiny as it fulfils itself'.... (Hellman, 1980: 75)

Which is the condition of *meconnaissance*. In the case of *In Cold Blood*, 'Unawareness,' or mis-recognition, originates not with the invisible nature of the supra-human causality as with religion but is the subjective experience of an objective absence of

[5] See Chap. 4, above.

[6] I will discuss below whether these frames are as hermetically sealed as Hellman makes out.

perception owing to the epistemic compartmentalization of the actors. Outside of the contrapuntal framing of the contending allegorical landscapes Capote presents the reader with not only a secular allegory but, with far greater originality, an actively *secularizing* allegory: the only 'truth' is the incompatibility of the frames that the characters inhabit which, through their containment, afford a pluralistic world of rival but equal world-views.

> Whether presenting victim or murderer [contrapuntal], traumatic event or delicate detail [*le temps fort*], Capote seeks the language and pattern which will point toward universal significance. *In Cold Blood* is as much allegory as it is journalism and realism because Capote has shaped his facts into an aesthetic construct which constantly points toward the realm of mythic truth.[7] Capote's true interest in his material is its symbolic value, but he emphasizes its objective factuality in order to strengthen the power of the symbolism. For if the symbolic meaning seems to be present in undeniable facts, rather than merely the result of philosophically motivated invention, then allegory takes on a new power. (Hellman, 1980: 66)

To achieve this, *In Cold Blood* is centered around the rhythmic juxtapositions (contrapuntal); among three allegorical 'frameworks': the 'Garden of Eden' occupied by the Clutter family ('An inch more of rain and this country would be paradise—Eden on earth,' said Herb Clutter (Capote, 2000: 24)); the 'American Dream,' the tragic struggle between success and failure, inhabited by both the murderers Perry Smith and Dick Hickock and the townsfolk of Holcomb; and the 'Detective Story,' whose primary inhabitant is Alvin Dewey and central to which is the assumption that 'innocence is dangerous, for the classic pattern or formula begins with an inexplicable murder': the crime re-enacts the Fall and 'opens society to chaos and requires' the detective 'to respond in order to reassert the validity of the notions of rationality and justice…Through the rational perspective of cause and effect, the detective restores order and thus meaning to his world' (Hellman, 1980: 69).

Capote, like William Golding in *Lord of the Flies*, presents the reader with characters who without exception inhabit an allegorical landscape but do not know it; they act unconsciously and, quite literally, know not what they do, which is the universal condition of *meconnaissance.* Their 'truth' resides not within their interior self but within their respective frame, each set of characters—Clutters, murderers, townsfolk, detective—the bearers of the allegorical meaning(s) of their respective landscape.

> By portraying factual events in terms of cultural sources [allegory], Capote has repeatedly forced the reader to view events as manifestations of recurrent, timeless patterns. But he does not develop this allegory into a coherent vision of an ordered universe. Narrating the facts in ironic juxtaposition to the expectations of the cultural sources' elements, he continually suggests pattern through his allegory only to reveal blankness. As a result, *In Cold Blood* is an allegory of possible meanings, not meaning. The combination of a journalistic contract and an allegorical form gives *In Cold Blood* a unique tension between the impervious mystery of fact and the human need for meaning. As a fable of fact, it both explores and embodies the need for human consciousness to pattern experience. (Hellman, 1980: 78)

[7] As will become clear, this is a problem for Capote in the end, for the essence of the 'realm of mythic truth' is that mythic truth is a lie. Meaning that whenever anyone recounts a myth they are disseminating mis-recognition, like that of an invented ending attached to a series of realist accounts of true events supposedly.

But as Dewey's allegorical world is of detection which is of restoration, then we have moved away from the myth of Levi-Strauss to the *mythos* of Girard: the sought for reconciliation of the community can only be achieved through some act of killing that is sacrificial in meaning and purpose. And the invocation of the sacrificial, now presented to us in a wholly secular manner, at least at first glance, is achieved by the narrative dexterity employed by Capote in the discursive 'framing' of the acts of multiple killings, for as he has indicated six lives ended when four shots were fired. And six victims, two of whom were the slayers of the other four, requires two sets of sacred executioners. And the masterly interweaving of his secular text with the unifying sub-text of sacrificial killing is achieved through the numerous (and ironic) incidents that foreshadow death littered throughout the novel. Capote's most artful mythic union of allegorical meaning with the realism of both psychological determinism and risk assessment, which is the only form of Destiny that we as a society are prepared to contemplate.[8] And it is undeniable that Capote's sense of the ironic was the determining factor in his selection and highlighting of the myriad of 'significant moments' (*le temps fort*) scattered throughout the text. On the one hand this is merely Capote displaying his credentials as a modernist; 'Like most good writing, *In Cold Blood* is constructed on a series of ironic elements. One of these elements [is]...Capote's steadfast resistance to offering any kind of moral judgment on the Clutter affair. But other ironies of a situational sort are present almost without end in the book' (Reed, 1981: 98). On the other hand is Capote's subliminal importation of the sacrificial sacred into the profane narrative(s) as a means of 'lifting' the sordid mess into the realm of allegory, that which must always signify something 'other' and something 'higher' (or more foundational); the strategic foreshadowing of death transfigures the profane banality of the killer's as agents of Fate (*moirai*) concealed in the form of a 'freak occurrence,' but especially in the case of Perry Smith's, whose psychosis is utilized as a literary invocation of the cultural nostalgia for transcendental meaning through the novel's movie-script like treatment of secular facts as metaphors for supra-worldly significance. And the thing that holds this brilliant literary allegory together in perfect dramatic tension, the unification of the secular with the secular that enables Capote to pull off against all odds, is the framing of the impending convergence between the Clutters and their killers as *inevitable*—which is a choice word. For inevitable bespeaks of fate, and fate bespeaks of tragedy, and tragedy bespeaks of ritualistic sacrifice, and ritualistic sacrifice bespeaks of scapegoat and regeneration, or, in mundane terms, the law's detection of the Other and the assignment of guilt. Here are a few choice examples of Capote's creeping invocation of that invisible otherness that stands behind all things visible in their undifferentiated banality. First the patriarch.

> Just nothing scares you [Herb], [Mrs. Ashida] said, commenting upon a generally recognized quality of Mr. Clutter's: a fearless self-assurance that set him apart, and while it created respect, [it] also limited the affections of others a little. 'I can't imagine you afraid. No matter what happened, you'd talk your way out of it. (Capote, 2000: 47)

And then the matriarch.

---

[8] See Chap. 9, above.

> Now, on this final day of her life, Mrs. Clutter hung in the closet the calico housedress she had been wearing, and put on one of her trailing nightgowns and a fresh set of white socks. Then, before retiring, she exchanged her ordinary glasses for a pair of reading spectacles. Though she subscribed to several periodicals...none of these rested on the bedside table—only a Bible. A bookmark lay between its pages, a stiff piece of watered silk upon which an admonition had been embroidered: 'Take ye heed, watch and pray: for ye know not when the time is'. (Capote, 2000: 41)

And finally the youngest daughter, the 'town darling'[9] Nancy.

> Nancy was invariably the last of the family to retire: as she had once informed her friend and home-economics teacher, Mrs. Polly Stringer, the midnight hours were her 'time to be selfish and vain'...Tonight, having dried and brushed her hair and bound it in a gauzy bandana, set out the clothes that she intended to wear to church the next morning: nylons, black pumps, a red velveteen dress—her prettiest, which she herself had made. It was a dress in which she was to be buried. (Capote, 2000: 67)

Which is then juxtaposed on the next page to the masterly, and unifying, stroke that announces the unpredictable arrival of the monsters: 'The headlights disclosed a lane of Chinese elms; bundles of wind-blown thistle scurried across it. Dick doused the headlights, slowed down, and stopped until his eyes were adjusted to the moon-illuminated night. Presently, the car crept forward' (Capote, 2000: 68). Which is directly suggestive of a Horror film, as Capote knew: 'I think most of the younger writers have learned and borrowed from the visual, structural side of the movie technique. I have' (Hollowell, 1977: 69). For no sooner do we have the hellish car with its nightmarish passengers creep forward than we then jump forward, as if by cinematic editing, 167 pages to 235, which is the beginning of Smith's after the fact ('flashback') first-person narration of the murders (Hollowell, 1977: 235–248). 'Capote's structural method can be called cinematic: he uses intercutting of different story strands, intense close-ups, flashbacks, traveling shots, background detail, all as if he were fleshing out a scenario' (Stanley Kauffman qtd. Hollowell, 1977: 69) and, to repeat an earlier point, it must never be forgotten that Capote's work on the novel took place at the same time that he was hammering out the screenplay for the gothic masterpiece *The Innocents*, which, in a way, is a dark invocation of the murder victims from *In Cold Blood*.

> The structural relationship between film technique and *In Cold Blood* is most apparent in the parallel narratives of the opening sections. Two narratives—one of the Clutter's last day alive, the other of the preparations of Hickock and Smith—are made to appear simultaneous, yet casually unrelated stories...Gradually, Capote tightens the trajectory of two independent narratives until they converge in Holcomb on the night of the murders. (Hollowell, 1977: 69)

'Parallel narratives' or the contrapuntal technique is the thematic equivalent of cinematic editing which 'forms a collage, an assortment of images joined together in a sequence. When images are joined, audiences formulate ideas and derive meanings by comparing the visual details of each shot...Editing can also encourage audiences

[9] There were three daughters in all—Eveanna, Beverly, and Nancy—but only the third was living at home on the night of the unforeseeable weird visitors (Capote, 2000: 18).

to compare and contrast the cinematographic qualities of each shot' (Pramaggiore & Wallis, 2011: 193). Within the novel, the contrapuntal 'cuts,' the markers of the boundaries of the three parallel allegorical worlds, involve

> …the contrasts of short sub-sections within the four main divisions [of the text]. The contrasts themselves can be seen in more than one way, as for example contrasts of light and dark, optimistic and tragic, productive and counter-productive. It is clear enough that the generally positive, successful, productive character of the Clutter family contrasts vividly with the essentially negative, unsuccessful and unproductive lives of Perry Smith and Dick Hickock (Capote, 2000: 203) … In still another contrast, the 'trust in God' that had once 'sustained' Mrs. Clutter is pitted against the moral and philosophical waste land of her executioners. (Reed, 1981: 111)

Consistent with Capote's over-arching artistic concept of the non-fiction novel, the primary instances of contrapuntal juxtaposition are all concerned with the alternating presentation of 'life' and 'art,' a set of differences that are employed to maintain the complex relationship among the parallel allegorical frames of order.

> There is the prevailing assumption that 'life' provides only the raw materials out of which 'art' is fashioned, and that until the artist somehow modifies, proportions, and rearranges these raw materials, there can be no art. Part of the experience of reading *In Cold Blood* is the impression that life has indeed somehow taken on the balance and proportion of art. Capote had managed to orchestrate the story of the Clutter murders, not through the distortion of facts, but by the reordering and proportioning of it. In terms of focus, the book moves between the activities of the victims, the criminals, and the law-enforcement people. In terms of time, [the author] moves without restriction between past and present. Once aware of the crime, the reader moves back in time to follow the course of events that led up to it. But while the reader can depend upon the high degree of accuracy in Capote's documentation, it should be borne in mind that the selectivity of detail and the particular points singled out for emphasis are elements left to the discretion of the artist himself. (Reed, 1981: 112)

And the greater part of the artist's discretion is the strategic deployment of *le temps fort* or 'the significant moments': actual events, usually ordinary factual occurrences, that, depending upon their being 'privileged' by the authorial voice or being tactically placed within the narrative structure, are invested with a high degree of narrative significance, or 'meaning'. French literary critic Jean Mouton

> …compared Capote's selection of scenes and dialogue to that that of a classical dramatist, who chooses only those scenes that contribute cumulatively to his dramatic purposes: 'There is obviously a certain artifice in selecting significant moments, the same artifice as in the classical theater where one only represents a crisis isolated from its antecedents; because of these significant moments with which the dramatist satisfies himself to accomplish his action, numerous events of an interior order, which unfold themselves between the scenes, remain hidden' It is precisely Capote's ability to capitalize on the hidden meanings of these significant moments that contributes to the narrative impact of the book. The conversations of close friends of the Clutters, of the chief detectives, and even of the killers themselves are powerfully rendered. A comment dropped innocently by a neighbour or a casual remark made by an investigator to his wife takes on meanings in the context of the murders that were not apparent in the original context. (Hollowell, 1977: 71)

Which has led to no little criticism of both the narrative design and intent of *In Cold Blood*; 'Capote's ability to capitalize on the hidden meanings of these significant moments,' an event that 'takes on meanings… that were not apparent in the original context'—do these actually exist within the real world, or are they authorial constructions by Capote himself? Tony Tanner has been vocally critical of the novel in this regard.

> I find something just a shade suspicious in this maintained illusion of objective factual presentation Certainly it is in the American grain—'pleads for itself the fact,' said Emerson But facts do not 'sing themselves,' as Emerson maintained. Facts are silent as Conrad said, and any singing they do depends on their orchestration by a human arranger. (Tony Tanner qtd. Hollowell, 1977: 73)

But that facts do not sing themselves meaning that Conrad was right and Emerson was wrong only holds true if it is not the case that the world can be understood as an allegory, which is precisely the notion that Capote is trying to put into play. For if Capote's own project, and clearly not Tanner's, is to author a text of mythic significance then he must, knowingly or unknowingly, reproduce the logic of *mythos* itself, which means that he must come to grips with the narrative urgrund of the sacrificial, which is a lie of mis-recognition. Capote's evocation of 'a timeless quality about the cause and events' signifies Destiny, his deployment of 'the impervious mystery of fact' summons the uncanny specter of the double; through the literary techniques of a supremely aestheticized reportage, Capote has artistically configured a real-world tale of murder into an allegory of mimesis, monstrous doubles, and scapegoating, an allegory about lies that has the added virtue of being 'true'.

10.3 The *Folie a Deux*: Monstrous Doubles or Monsters Who are Brothers

It is a question of *moirai*, brilliantly heralded by the novel's staging of the manifestation of the monsters as doubles, both to their victims as well as to each other, and Capote's account of the primal nature of anomalous beings is a virtual word-for-word replication of Girard's definition: 'Under the heading *monstrous double* we shall group all of the hallucinatory phenomena provoked at the height of the crisis by un-recognized reciprocity. The monstrous double is also to be found wherever we encounter an "I" and an "Other" caught up in a constant interchange of differences' (Girard, 1977: 164). Which is why it is essential to Capote's project that Dick and Perry be represented as failed or un-loving brothers.

> There is no monster who does not tend to duplicate himself or to 'marry' another monster, no double who does not yield a monstrous aspect upon close scrutiny ... The nature of the relationship between monster and double, stubbornly denied by the antagonists, is ultimately imposed on them in the course of the shifting of differences—but it is imposed *in the form of hallucination* The unity and reciprocity that the enemy brothers have rejected in the benign form of brotherly love finally impose themselves, both from without and within, in the form of monstrous duality—the most disquieting and grotesque form imaginable. (Girard, 1977: 160)

If Hickock and Smith can be truthfully established as monstrous doubles then Girard's theory of the sacrificial mechanism can be deployed as the unifying narrative device of Capote's non-fiction novel and, if this has been done successfully, Capote is then able to translate a banal reality into an allegorical truth by way of aestheticized reportage, the drama of the ironic/unconscious re-enactment of the myth/lie of the scapegoat on the plains of western Kansas. The mythic unity of the novel hinges on this: doubling is established by the clear presence of a mimetic envy invisibly directing the slaughter of the Clutter family and the imitative nature of the crime is therapeutically denoted as the *folie a deux*, in which both actors desire the same object and 'feed' off of each other's desire. The author leaves us in absolutely no doubt with this incisive portrait of Hickock: 'Envy was constantly with him; the Enemy was anyone who was someone he wanted to be or who had anything he wanted to have' (Capote, 2000: 200). As Capote explained

> I didn't love either one of them, but I had a great understanding for both of them, and for Perry I had a tremendous amount of sympathy. Dick, I thought, was just a small-time crook who got into water way over his head [which was also the opinion of Alvin Dewey] and was really responsible for this whole murder, which Perry actually committed. But Perry would not have committed it if he hadn't been led on in what the French call a *folie a deux*. (Grobel, 1985: 118)

The sudden appearance of a monster, a recurrent motif of Greek mythology and tragedy, serves as a projection in the form of an hallucination of the pathological intensification of the mimetic conflict of the twins/doubles; a fundamental principle of Hellenic myth 'is that the double and monster are one and the same being … The unity and reciprocity that the enemy brothers [or twins] have rejected in the benign form of brotherly love finally impose themselves, both from without and within, in the form of monstrous duality—the most disquieting and grotesque form imaginable' (Girard, 1977: 160, 160–168). Meaning that the two are ultimately unable to maintain their separate existence as an autonomous one, which is the threshold of the supremely dangerous moment when the Self begins to become unconsciously aware that she is not really herself but the channeler of the being of another, truer self. Capote provides (perhaps unconscious) recognition of this through his extraordinarily poetic depictions of the physical appearances of the two strange ones that suggests that their almost subliminally decomposing bodies are bleeding into a single monstrous construction. This for Dick Hickock.

> But neither Dick's physique nor the inky gallery [tattoos] adorning it made as remarkable impression as his face, which seemed composed of mismatching parts. It was as though his head had been halved like an apple, then put together a fraction off centre. Something of the kind had happened; the imperfectly aligned features were the outcome of a car collision in 1959—an accident that left his long-jawed and narrow face tilted, the left side rather lower than the right, with the results that the lips were slightly aslant, the nose askew, and his eyes not only situated at uneven levels but of uneven size, the left eye being truly serpentine, with a venomous, sickly-blue squint that although it was involuntarily acquired, seemed nevertheless to warn of bitter sediment at the bottom of his nature. But Perry told him, 'The eye doesn't matter. Because you have a wonderful smile. One of those smiles that really work.' It was true that the tightening action of a smile contracted his face into its correct proportions, and made it possible to discern a less unnerving personality—an American-style 'good kid' with an outgrown crew cut, sane enough but not too bright. (Capote, 2000: 42)

And this for Perry Smith.

> Sitting, he had seemed a more than normal-sized man, a powerful man, with the shoulders, the arms, the thick, crouching torso of a weight-lifter—weight-lifting was, in fact, his hobby. But some sections of him were not in proportion to others. His tiny feet, encased in short black boots with steel buckles, would have neatly fitted into a delicate lady's dancing slippers; when he stood up, he was no taller than a twelve-year old child, and suddenly looked, strutting on stunted legs that seemed grotesquely inadequate to the grown-up bulk they supported, not like a well-built truck driver but like a retired jockey, overblown and muscle-bound…Time rarely weighed upon him, for he had many methods of passing it—among them, mirror gazing…his own face enthralled him. Each angle of it induced a different impression It was a changeling's face, and mirror-guided experiments had taught him how to look ominous, now impish, now soulful; a tilt of the head, a twist of the lips, and the corrupt gypsy became the gentle romantic (Capote, 2000: 27)….Perry, too, had been maimed, and his injuries, received in a motorcycle wreck, were severer than Dick's…his chunky, dwarfish legs, broken in five places and pitifully scarred, still pained him so severely that he had become an aspirin addict. While he had fewer tattoos than his companion, they were more elaborate—not the self-inflicted work of an amateur but epics of the art contrived by Honolulu and Yokohama masters…Blue-furred, orange-eyed, red-fanged, a tiger snarled upon his left biceps; a spitting snake, coiled around a dagger, slithered down his arm; and elsewhere skulls gleamed, a tombstone loomed, a chrysanthemum flourished. (Capote, 2000: 43)

In good police procedural style, Capote has an expert explain the nature of the criminal's homicidal desires which turns out to be the raw psychic stuff of pre-representation.

> Dr. Joseph Satten of the Meninger Clinic in Topeka, Kansas…suggests that though the crime would not have occurred except for a certain frictional interplay between the perpetrators, it was essentially the act of Perry Smith who, he feels, represents a type of murderer described by him in an article: 'Murder Without Apparent Murder—A Study in Personality Disorganization'… 'In general, these individuals are predisposed to severe lapses in ego-control which makes possible the open expression of primitive violence, born out of previous, and now unconscious, traumatic experiences (Capote, 2000: 298–299). … Such individuals can be considered to be murder-prone in the sense of either carrying a surcharge of aggressive energy or having an unstable ego-defence system that periodically allows the naked and archaic expression of such energy… a chance acquaintance or even a stranger was easily able to lose his 'real' meaning and assume an identity in the unconscious traumatic configuration [of the killer]. The 'old' conflict was reactivated and aggression swiftly mounted to murderous proportions…. (Capote, 2000: 301)

So that every 'new' victim is, psychically, the mimetic surrogate of an old enemy or persecutor, a 'false' meaning substituted for the 'real' meaning marked by difference. And the technical term that Dr. Satten uses to describe the undifferentiating brothers-in-crime is *folie a deux* wherein 'the crime would not have occurred except for a certain frictional interplay between the perpetrators' (Capote, 2000: 298) which means that differences no longer apply between them, let alone the world. Dick recruits Perry who then becomes the controlling agent during the act of butchery, which is ironic in itself given that it was Dick who mis-recognized himself as the dominant one of the not-two.

> Several murderers, or men who boasted of murder or their willingness to commit it, circulated inside Lansing; but Dick became convinced that Perry was that rarity, 'a natural killer'—absolutely sane, but conscienceless, and capable of dealing, with or without motive, the coldest-blooded deathblows. It was Dick's theory that such a gift could, under his supervision, be profitably exploited (Capote, 2000: 65–66)

But as it turned out: 'Hickock said, "Perry Smith killed the Clutters." He lifted his head, and slowly straightened up in the chair, like a fighter staggering to his feet. "It was Perry. I couldn't stop him. He killed them all"' (Capote, 2000: 232). If not for the fact of Hickock commandeering Smith Perry never would have been exposed to the psychic minefield that was the house of the Clutters[10] triggering the homicidal mania that Dick shared but was unable to project: 'When such senseless murders occur, they are seen to be an end result of a period of increasing tension and disorganization in the murderer starting before the contact with the victim who, by fitting into the unconscious conflicts of the murderer, unwittingly serves to set into motion his homicidal potential' (Capote, 2000: 301). The author concurs.

> Obviously, three of the murders Smith committed *were* logically motivated—Nancy, Kenyon, and their mother had been killed because Mr. Clutter had been killed. But it was Dr. Satten's contention that only the first murder matters psychologically, and that when Smith attacked Mr. Clutter he was under a mental eclipse, deep inside a schizophrenic darkness, for it was not entirely a flesh-and-blood man he 'suddenly discovered' himself destroying, but 'a key figure in some traumatic configuration': his father? The orphanage nuns who had derided and beaten him? The hated Army sergeant? The parole officer who had ordered him to 'stay out of Kansas'? [which symbolized Perry's cruel exile from the 'The American Dream'?] One of them, or all of them…. (Capote, 2000: 302)

Differences no longer mattered for they were no longer real—the sacrificers were as one and all of the victims, both actual and potential, had been rendered undifferentiated. In Greek myth, the form that Capote is drawing upon in his creative true crime reportage, it is a constant that the 'surrogate victim meets his death in the guise of the monstrous double' (Girard, 1977: 251); the Clutters become the 'sacrificial victims' of Hickock-Smith—that is, as emissary victims for Father/Family/Life—but Smith and Hickock were then in turn 'singled out' as the scapegoats for the community.

At this point I would suggest that, contra Hellman, there actually is a unifying pattern among the competing frames: the 'shaping destiny' shared by all of the characters of the Garden of Eden (allegory one) and the American Dream (allegory two) is mimetic desire and everybody acts out the logic of mimetic rivalry; the (almost) sole exception is Alvin Dewey, the detective-restorer, evidenced by his encounter with Susan Kidwell which I will explore later on. For now it is enough that Girard's theory of mimesis as the master-trope of literature is the perfect theoretical foil to Capote's seemingly compartmentalized frames of allegory.

> Rivalry does not arise because of the fortuitous convergence of two desires on a single object; rather, *the subject desires the object because the rival desires it*. In desiring an object the rival alerts the subject to the desirability of the object. The rival, then, serves as the model for the subject, not only in regard to such secondary matters as style and opinions but also, and more essentially, in regard to desires. (Girard, 1977: 145)

For Girard, literature's potential for subversion lies not with mis-recognition or ignorance; at issue is the nature of 'common-sense' reality as a myth that is a lie that occludes a truth that is unspeakable but, once unveiled, explains everything: as with those within the grove in *Rashomon*[11] it is not that the characters do not know

---

[10] Or a psychically 'cluttered' house?

[11] See Chap. 5, above.

themselves, it is that they cannot endure to confess the truth about themselves. Girard argues that all dramatic art is anchored in the presence of a set of doubles,[12] who signify either the external (exoteric) relationship between the protagonist ('The Self') and one or more of the other characters, or the internal (esoteric) relationship among the contending parts of the divided and/or fragmented personality of the protagonist. The overriding motive of the double is mimetic desire that culminates in a destructive mimetic rivalry; the Self will model its relationship to the Other/Double on the basis of imitation (mimetic desire) that will narratively culminate in the Self attempting to either replace and/or destroy the Double (mimetic rivalry). The rivalry that mimetic desire unleashes will, in the end, assume the most extreme and grotesque form of violent monstrous doubles who are the signifiers of the mimetic crisis: as the rivals intensify their struggle, they effectively become identical, triggering a pathological crisis of identity which can only be resolved through an act of extreme violence, whether physical, emotional, or symbolic (Girard, 1977: 143–168).

> As mimetic rivalries are socially proscribed because of their violent consequences, the monstrous doubles must displace, or discharge, their common violence against a convenient surrogate victim that serves as the transference object of the violence— the *scapegoat*, a sacrificial victim infused with the sacred, for once the scapegoat is slain enmity vanishes. (Girard et al., 1978: 93)

Girard explains the seeming magical efficacy of the scapegoat by dividing mimetic desire into two distinct forms: divisive acquisitive mimesis, which leads one or more individuals to desire the exact same object at the same moment in time, and unifying conflictual mimesis, which induces the parties to the conflict to settle upon a common rival, or enemy, whom they all wish to 'strike down' (Girard et al., 1978: 26). Historically, the ritualistic enshrinement of the 'scapegoat mechanism' was the domain of religion (Girard et al., 1978: 48), which is grounded upon the intermediary, or emissary, status of the surrogate victim: the one who must die so that the community may live through being spared the apocalypse of the escalating conflict of the monstrous doubles. But a note of caution must be sounded here, for if we read *In Cold Blood* carefully we realize that Perry/Dick are *not* monstrous doubles in the proper sense as defined by Girard; rather, they are doubles who are monstrous but they do not wage mimetic war against each other because their pathology is not divided but unified by way of the *folie a deux*: they are not trying to occupy the exact same space of the Other because for they are already psychically One. To be paired as a monstrous double (or as a double to a monster) there must be another rival, or *skandalon*, or model-obstacle to the monster Hickock-Smith who is identical to Him/Them in their mimetic desire for the same object, in this case the American Dream, that leads the false one/two to destroy the real one.

So who is it? As elsewhere, the twinned monster is lurking in plain sight all over the place.

[12] See Chap. 1, above.

10.4 'Of All the People in the World, the Clutters Were the Least Likely to Be Murdered': Herb Clutter and the Villagers of Holcomb

Capote provides us with a brilliant description of Herb Clutter—'Always certain of what he wanted from the world, Mr Clutter had in large measure obtained it' (Capote, 2000: 18)—and he uses it to segue into an interesting set of snapshots of the psychic relationship between the Clutter family and the Holcomb community: 'Old friends had suddenly to endure the unique experience of distrusting each other; understandably, they believed that the murderer was among themselves' (Capote, 2000: 85); 'What a terrible thing when neighbors can't look at each other without a kind of wondering!' (Capote, 2000: 70); 'If it wasn't him, maybe it was you. Or somebody across the street' (Capote, 2000: 69); 'There's more to it than that. Wait. Some day they'll get to the bottom, and when they do they'll find the one behind it' (Capote, 2000: 233). Following the arrest of Hickock-Smith 'the majority of Holcomb's population, having lived for seven weeks amid unwholesome rumors, general mistrust, and suspicion, appeared to feel disappointed at being told that the murderer was not someone among themselves' (Capote, 2000: 233). *We should expect as much. T*he scapegoat is always the object of a double transference: not only is the emissary victim chosen to be the bearer of the sins of the community through some inherent stain of its nature, but, through the collective projection of impurity into the helpless victim, the community temporarily releases itself from its capacity for the violence that remains eternally latent, thanks to the repetitive nature of mimetic desire. The psychic price to be paid for this ritualistic transference is high: if sacrifice is the essence of religion and religion is the essence of community then the community must constantly repress its self-awareness not only of the innocence of the scapegoat but also of its own capacity for violence in order for the scapegoat mechanism to work. This self-willed collective act of repression, *meconnaissance*, seeks an outlet through symbolic substitution: 'in those localities where ritual killing no longer occurs, or where there is no evidence of its ever having occurred, its place has been taken by another institution also directly linked to generative violence' (Girard, 1977: 297). Historically, this institution is capital punishment, which, because it purges the community of its pent-up enmity, may, in anthropological terms, be considered to be generative rather than destructive. And, to be both truthful and lawful (and, therefore, effective) it is always administered by the community, not by the mediatory private individual whose personal will-to-revenge is stigmatized as vendetta, vigilantism, or, most commonly, the crime of homicide. Capote understands all of this instinctively and he is masterful in discursively framing the Clutter murders as the externalized re-directing of real but mis-recognized psychosis-inducing mimetic pressures.[13] Capote leaves us in no doubt that Perry's massacre of the Clutter family, which not accidentally commenced with the slaying of the patrician Herb Clutter, was an act of

[13] Which raises the interesting possibility that the most truthful definition of 'sanity' is the absence of sufficient psychosis-inducing 'pressures' that are mimetic. As with morality, mental health may, in the end, prove to be a matter of dumb luck.

scapegoating; what Capote is ever keen to remind us is that Herb was a man who was very easy to envy. Herb was 'the community's most widely known citizen...and his name was everywhere respectfully recognized' (Capote, 2000: 17) and 'Like royalty, he was famous for never carrying cash' (Capote, 2000: 46). *Noblesse oblige* all over the place.

> He was not as rich as the richest man in Holcomb—Mr. Taylor Jones, a neighboring rancher. He was, however, the community's most widely known citizen, prominent both there and in Garden City, the close-by county seat, where he had headed the building committee for the newly completed First Methodist Church, an eight-hundred-thousand-dollar edifice. He was currently chairman of the Kansas Conference of Farm Organizations, and his name was everywhere respectfully recognized among Midwestern agriculturalists, as it was in certain Washington offices, where he had been a member of the Federal Farm Credit Board during the Eisenhower administration. (Capote, 2000: 17–18)

Although Capote's primary concern is with Nancy, the townsfolk seem to be most 'anxious' over the killing of Herb; Mrs. Ashida drives the point home.

> The last thing I said to Herb, I told him how I couldn't imagine his ever being afraid. That no matter what the situation was, he could talk his way out of it ... Funny, but you know, Bess, I'll bet he *wasn't* afraid. I mean, however it happened, I'll bet right up to the last he didn't believe it would. Because it couldn't. Not to him. (Capote, 2000: 124)

With an intuitive understanding of the scapegoat mechanism, Capote foregrounds the liminality underlying ritualistic sacrifice by rendering wholly nebulous the boundaries, both psychic and social, between 'inside' and 'out there', between Self and Other, between Friend and Enemy. For him the village of Holcomb is a microcosm of undifferentiation and pre-representation, the two necessary ingredients for sacrificial violence.

> Imagination, of course, can open any door—turn the key and let terror walk right in Tuesday, at dawn, a carload of pheasant hunters from Colorado—strangers, ignorant of the local disaster—were startled by what they thought they saw as they crossed the prairies and passed through Holcomb: windows ablaze, almost every window in almost every house, and, in the brightly lit rooms, fully clothed people, even entire families, who had sat the whole night awake, watchful, listening. Of what were they frightened? 'It might happen again'. That, with variations, was the customary response...the simplest, the ugliest [reason for this] was that this hitherto peaceful congregation of neighbours and old friends had suddenly to endure the unique experience of distrusting each other; understandably, they believed that the murderer was among themselves. (Capote, 2000: 96)

Because, of course, the infallible means of re-constituting the unidentifiable neighbors as identifiable citizens is to select an outsider of some kind, as the bringer of violence and the loss of distinctions, to the community. Although the novel openly announces envy as the primary motive of the killings, Capote, a near-survivor of a life-long baptism in the polluting waters of *ressentiment*, subtly draws our attention to the status of the Clutter family as the object of both mimetic desire and, therefore, of mimetic rivalry, within the community. 'Without exception, Garden Citians[14] deny that the population of the town can be socially graded ("No sir. Nothing like that here.

---

[14] The citizens of the nearby town of Garden City where the murder trial of Hickock-Smith occurred.

All equal, regardless of wealth, colour, or creed. Everything the way it ought to be in a democracy; that's us")' (Capote, 2000: 45) so that the community rests securely upon a foundation of 'Friendlier people or fresher air or sweeter drinking water...Good neighbors, people who care about each other, that's what counts' (Capote, 2000: 33). And yet it remains the case that in western Kansas '... class divisions are as clearly observed, and as clearly observable, as in any other human hive' (Capote, 2000: 45). Fatally, it turned out, Herb was a merciless judge of others less successful, or more un-equal, than himself.

> The truth was he opposed all stimulants, however gentle. He did not smoke, and of course he did not drink...While he was careful to avoid making a nuisance of his view, to adopt outside his realm an externally uncensoring manner, he enforced them within his family and among the employees at River Valley Farm... [Every applicant had to] sign a work contract containing a clause that declared an agreement instantly void if the employee should be discovered 'harbouring alcohol.' A friend ... had once told him, 'you've got no mercy. I swear, Herb, if you caught a hired man drinking, out he'd go. And you wouldn't care if his family was starving'. (Capote, 2000: 21–22)

Some villagers held that there 'wasn't any other family like them ... Mr. Clutter may have been more strict about some things—religion, and so on—but he never tried to make you feel he was right and you were wrong' (Capote, 2000: 50)— but the verb 'tried' suggests that this is exactly what Clutter did; he may not have wanted to make others feel 'wrong,' but 'the town was completely aware of his moral expectation and judgment' (Fahy, 2012: 66). His slaying, while horrific, is not, when one stops to think about it, surprising.

> I'm not surprised,' Mrs. Clare said. 'When you think how Herb Clutter spent his whole life in a hurry, rushing in here to get his mail with never a minute to say good-morning-and-thank-you-dog, rushing around like a chicken with its head off—joining clubs, running everything, getting jobs maybe other people wanted. And now look—it's all caught up with him. Well, he won't be rushing *any* more. (Capote, 2000: 79)

Myrtle Clare is not surprised but she is herself full of surprises.

> Myrt—don't say things like that. Who shot them?
>
> Without pause in her postmarking activities, Mrs. Clare replied, 'The man in the airplane. The one Herb sued for crashing into his fruit trees. If it wasn't him, maybe it was you. Or somebody across the street. All the neighbors are rattlesnakes. Varmints looking for a chance to slam the door in your face. It's the same the whole world over. You know that'. (Capote, 2000: 79)

'*All the neighbors are rattlesnakes*' is as poetic-folksy metaphor of the crisis of undifferentiation as one could hope for. Mimetic contagion spills across the three allegorical frames, rendering identical the nature of that destiny that controls the denizens of all of them. The unspeakable object of desire of the monstrous doubles is the death of the Clutter family, for the monster possessed by metaphysical desire is cursed by *moirai* to be forever incapable of 'being' them in achieving the American Dream and/or occupying the space of Eden, and Herb Clutter, secure in his Abrahamic-patriarchal realm, knew it and let everyone else know it as well. Hickock-Smith was the symbolic representation of divisive acquisitive mimesis; in turn, their righteous, and lawful, 'lynching' by the legally innocent but mimetically contaminated community acted as the regenerative violence of conflictual mimesis. And if we accept as convincing Hellman's categorization of *In Cold Blood* as a secular allegory, I believe that it is still possible to offer a transcendental meaning to the text that fulfills all of Capote's objectives for the non-fiction novel and complies with the Girard's theory of mimetic rivalry as the interpretive key to literature: Capote's novel is a highly ironic yet true-to-life psycho-drama of doubles acted out through the real-world 'crossed paths' of four sets of actual 'twins'.

10.4.1 Herb Clutter and 'Tex' Smith

Without doubt, the 'main dramatic interest of the book, Capote's greatest accomplishment, is his portrayal of Perry Smith. More than the social critic's indictment of injustice, or the crime writer's concern for a "whodunit" plot, the novelist's concern for character analysis and moral ambiguity dominates *In Cold Blood*. A detailed examination of the portrayal of Perry Smith will reveal…the legitimacy of Capote's claims that *In Cold Blood* should be considered literature rather than journalism' (Algeo, 1996: 75–94; Hollowell, 1977: 75; McAleer, 1972). Therefore, it is essential that most of the mimetic couplings should orbit around Perry Smith whom, we discover, has two Father figures: his biological Father 'Tex' Smith and his mimetic surrogate, Herb Clutter, whom Perry murders as an act of sacrificial substitution What links both of them is their emulation of the cultural norm of patriarchy, each one acting as a model-obstacle to their son. Capote virtually telegraphs this in his portrayal of Herb.

> The master of River Valley Farm, Herbert William Clutter, was forty-eight years old, and as a result of a recent medical examination for an insurance policy [irony], knew himself to be in first-rate condition Though he wore rimless glasses and was of but average height, standing just under five feet ten, Mr. Clutter cut a man's-man figure. His shoulders were broad, his hair had held its dark color, his square-jawed, confident face retained a healthy-hued youthfulness and his teeth, unstained and strong enough to shatter walnuts, were still intact (Capote, 2000: 17). … Always certain of what he wanted from the world, Mr. Clutter had in large measure obtained it. On his left hand, on what remained of a finger once mangled by a piece of farm machinery, he wore a plain gold band, which was the symbol, a quarter-century old, of his marriage to the person he had wished to marry—the sister of a college classmate, a timid, pious, delicate girl named Bonnie Fox, who was three years younger than he. She had given him four children—a trio of daughters, then a son (Capote, 2000: 18). … As an educated man successful in his profession, as an eminent Republican and church leader—even though of the Methodist church—Mr. Clutter was entitled to rank among the local patricians, but just as he had never joined the Garden City Country Club, he had never sought to associate with the reigning coterie. Quite the contrary, for their pleasures were not his; he had no use for card games, golf, cocktails, or buffet suppers served at ten—or, indeed, for any pastime that he felt did not 'accomplish something. (Capote, 2000: 45)

A self-made man, *Clutter Agonistes*, Herb would seem an avatar of internal mediation. But, very much like Herb Clutter, the decidedly blue-collar Tex Smith is also a self-made man and a highly self-reliant, and self-authoring, frontier entrepreneur (Capote, 2000: 137–143). But what most clearly unites them is their shared disdain of over-familiarity with others, a desire to maintain and enforce their difference from the wider community, the will-to-distinction.

> On the whole, [Perry Smith's sister] Mrs. Johnson's attitude toward her father was ambivalent, but one aspect of him she had always respected—his fortitude. She well knew how eccentric he seemed to others; he seemed so to her, for that matter. All the same, he was 'a real man'. He did things, did them easily. He could make a tree fall precisely where he wished. He could skin, repair a watch, build a house, bake a cake, darn a sock, or catch a trout with a bent pin and a piece of string. Once he had survived a winter alone in the Alaska wilderness.
>
> Alone: in Mrs. Johnson's opinion, that was how such men should live. Wives, children, a timid life were not for them. (Capote, 2000: 186)

What mediates Clutter and Smith as doubles is their diametrically opposed relationship to The American Dream: success versus failure, reality versus illusion. It also accounts for a shadowy double-doubling of the respective women of Herb and Tex: Perry's hedonistic and alcoholic mother Flo Buckskin and Herb's spinsterish spouse Bonnie Clutter who, like Mrs Kidwell, is a 'fanciful woman'. Superficially opposites, the two are linked through mental illness, a possible result of emotional abuse and/or neglect within the marriage and indicating an underlying problem of reconciling illusion with what we collectively refer to as reality. This is especially the case with Bonnie, whose precognitions are evocative of the supernatural.

> Her bedroom window overlooked the garden, and now and then, usually when she was 'having a bad spell', Mr. Helm had seen her stand long hours gazing into the garden, as though what she saw bewitched her. ('When I was a girl,' she once had told a friend, 'I was terribly sure trees and flowers were the same as birds or people. That they thought things, and talked among themselves. And we could hear them if we really tried. It was just a matter of emptying your head of all other sounds. Being very quiet and listening very hard. Sometimes I still believe that. But one can never get quiet enough…'). (Capote, 2000: 129)
>
> Capote would call this foreshadowing.

10.4.2 Herb Clutter and Perry Smith

Although Hickock was superficially the more violent of the two, Capote leaves us in no doubt that Perry's massacre of the entire Clutter family, which significantly (*le temps fort*) began with Herb Clutter, was a mimetic action of sacrificial substitution 'With a knife in his hand, he, Dick, had power' (Capote, 2000: 201) Capote writes, echoing Perry's own assessment of Dick: 'the glory of having everybody at his mercy, that's what excited him' (Capote, 2000: 239) which is the veritable embodiment of existential envy and *ressentiment*. Yet it is Perry who actually brings annihilation in his wake. Which makes him his Father's son. As Tex Smith confided in a letter to the Kansas State Parole Board on his son's behalf: 'Rite is Rite[15] [sic] and wrong

[15] Which technically counts as an additional act of ironic foreshadowing of Death if we consider capital punishment as a sacrificial rite of execution.

is wrong. I don't stick up for his wrong doings. He must pay the *Hardway* when he does wrong. Law is Boss he knows that by now…The *law is boss*, he knows that. He loves his Freedom' (Capote, 2000: 135, 137). And Perry demonstrated his love of freedom by using it to attempt patricide.

> My hands got hold of his [Tex's] throat. *My* hands—but I couldn't control them. They wanted to choke him to death. Dad, though, he's slippery, a smart wrestler. He tore loose and ran to get his gun. Came back pointing it at me. He said, 'Look at me, Perry. I'm the last living thing you're ever gonna see. (Capote, 2000: 143)

Perry also wanted to kill his sister: 'He "loathed" Barbara, and just the other day he had told Dick, "The only *real* regret I have, I wish the hell my sister had been in that [the Clutter's] house"' (Capote, 2000: 149). Which means that Perry was also psychically inclined to viewing the Clutter domicile as a place for sacrificial murder before he violated their home. Smith himself implicitly admits to regarding Herb as a sacrificial surrogate.

> In his confession, Smith said, 'I didn't want to harm the man. I thought he was a very nice gentleman. Soft-spoken. I thought so right up to the moment that I cut his throat.' While talking to Donald Cullivan,[16] Smith said, 'They [the Clutters] never hurt me. Like other people. Like people have all my life. Maybe it's just that the Clutters were the ones who had to pay for it'. (Capote, 2000: 302)

10.4.3 Perry Smith and Truman Capote

Although the monsters come in a pair it is obvious that Capote's real interest is with the similarly miniscule Perry. This is taken from the notes and recollections of Alvin Dewey.

> The preceding execution [of Dick] had not disturbed him, he had never had much use for Hickock, who seemed to him to him 'a small-time chiseller who got out of his depth, empty and worthless.' But Smith, though he was the true murderer, aroused another response, for Perry possessed a quality, the aura of an exiled animal, a creature walking wounded, that the detective could not disregard. He remembered his first meeting with Perry in the interrogation room at Police Headquarters in Las Vegas—the dwarfish boy-man seated in the metal chair, his small booted feet not quite brushing the floor. And when Dewey now opened his eyes, that is what he saw: the same childish feet, tilted, dangling. (Capote, 2000: 341)

In Cold Blood may be the first novel in history in which the author was physically in love with one of his 'characters'.

> When Perry sat down in front of the judge to be arraigned, Truman nudged Nelle [Harper Lee]. 'Look, his feet don't touch the floor!' Nelle said nothing, but thought, 'Oh, oh! This is the beginning of a great love affair.' In fact, their relationship was more complicated than a love affair: each looked at the other and saw, or thought he saw, the man he might have been Their shortness was only one of many unsettling similarities. They both had suffered from alcoholic mothers, absent fathers, and foster homes. At the orphanages he had been

[16] Another KBI Agent.

> sent to, Perry had been a target of scorn because he was half-Indian and wet his bed; Truman had been ridiculed because he was effeminate. A psychiatrist could have been speaking of both of them when he said of Perry: 'He seems to have grown-up without direction, without love.' Finally, both had turned to art to compensate for what had been denied them. Perry was convinced that with a little encouragement, he could have made his mark as a painter, a singer, a song-writer. (Clarke, 2010: 326)

Although a real person, physically if not psychically, Perry Smith is the corporeal embodiment of a Truman Capote character; 'All Capote heroes have been cheerful narcissists, this in turn a symbol for richness of imagination and the interior life' (Garrett, 1996: 4). As Capote cheerfully admits: 'Something in the whole material [of the murder of the Clutters] appealed to something that has always been inside me anyway, waiting there. It was Perry that made me decide to do it really. Something about Perry that turned the whole thing, because Perry was a character that was also in my imagination' (Hollowell, 1977: 75). But it goes well beyond this into true mimetic neurosis, for Truman recognizes Perry as his double: 'Perry Smith is perfectly, patly, and in almost every detail a spooky embodiment of Capote's earlier fiction. He has all the right characteristics: a rich and childish imagination, his dreams, including one marvelous recurring dream which is mystical in beauty and implication,[17] his physical deformity, his sensitivity, even his background' (Garrett, 1996: 4). I do not know whether Girard ever read *In Cold* Blood, or anything else by Capote, but we cannot be in any doubt under what he would have filed the Capotean novel: individualism and egoistic romanticism, modernity's primary aesthetic medium for the dissemination of internal mediation and mimetic rivalry. The thematic concerns of the non-fiction text fit seamlessly with the over-arching concerns of Capote's oeuvre which is always confessional in some manner.

> In each of [Capote's] books it is the outsiders and the outcasts who are, by virtue of their disengagement from wordly values, the examples of goodness. Those who seem to get along in the 'real' world, that is the world of practical affairs, are exposed as either deceitful or self-deceived. It is they who work mischief and cause trouble, usually invoking the name of conventional morality; and in the end, thanks to the operation of a whimsical kind of poetic justice, they usually get what's coming to them. 'Safe, sane, insular'…long before that knock-out punch 'smug' comes along, these adjectives glisten like black hats on horse-opera bad guys to anyone who has ever read Truman Capote. (Garrett, 1996: 3–4)

Much of Capote's fiction 'can be seen as an attempt to vindicate the abnormal or unusual person…One of the main purposes of his writing… [has been] to safeguard the unique individual from such slighting classifications as "abnormal"' (William L. Nance qtd. Hollowell, 1977: 75) which should give the reader pause. Although it is true that from 'the first, then, we shiver for the Clutters, fearing their fate, because they are such natural victims' (Garrett, 1996: 4) what really makes us shiver is our dawning realization that the author is really an ally of the murderer who is acting out his (Truman's) own fantasies of retributive *ressentiment*. The genuine aesthetic problem here is the objective limit placed upon the author by the real-world nature of the events, for the Clutters 'were real people, not symbols of anything, and their

[17] I discuss this below.

murder was a matter of brute fact' (Garrett, 1996: 4). But if the typical Capotean 'hero' is actually a marginalized narcissist and Perry Smith is placed firmly within this mold through the representational interventions of Capote, then it may not be implausibly inferred that Smith is performing a high concept literary act of 'heroism, the culmination of the authorial transmutation of Smith and Hickock from "illiterate, cold-blooded murderers" to "literate, psychopathic heroes"' (Hollowell, 1977: 74) in real time and space. So that, in yet another instance of mis-recognition, Perry Smith is really emulating Truman Capote and Smith was as twinned with Capote in fiction as he was twinned with Hickock in fact.

> Perry was always asking me: Why are you writing this book?... So I would say that it didn't have anything to do with changing the reader's opinion about anything, nor did I have any moral reasons worthy of calling them such—it was just that I had a strictly aesthetic theory about creating a book which could result in a work of art. 'That's really the truth, Perry,' I'd tell him, and Perry would say, 'A work of art, a work of art,' and then he'd laugh and say, 'What an irony, what an irony.' I'd ask what he meant, and he'd tell me that all he ever wanted to do in his life was to produce a work of art. 'That's all I ever wanted in my whole life,' he said. 'And now, what has happened? An incredible situation where I kill four people and *you're* going to produce a work of art.' Well, I'd have to agree with him. It was a pretty ironic situation. (Plimpton, 1987: 56–57)

The Capote-Smith brotherhood underlines the author's literary intent to transform the murderer into a 'literate psychopathic hero,' the 'darkling' projection of the author's own person which enables him to arrive at a remarkably amoral assessment of the crime.

> I believe Perry did what he did for the reasons that he himself states—that is life was a constant accumulation of disillusionment and reverses, and he suddenly found himself (in the Clutter house that night) in a psychological cul-de-sac. The Clutters were such a perfect set of symbols for every frustration in his life. (Plimpton, 1987: 55)

Translated, this meant that the Clutters were mimetic obstacles that scandalized him, for contra Capote's romantic egoism, the universal truth is that the mimetic failure desires nothing more than successful normality. Hickock-Smith murdered the Clutters and so may have Capote in the after the fact imaginary. But both of them pale into metaphysical insignificance when we compare them to the second person of the monstrous doubles. Hickock-Smith did it, Capote wrote about it, but it was the townsfolk who willed it. The fourth twinning: the murderer(s) and the citizens.

10.5 'No Chicken-Hearted Jurors, They': The Brothers in the Breed of Cain

The success of Capote's effort to write a secular allegory stands or falls with whether or not the execution of the murderers is able to provide the community with a violence that is truly regenerative, for it is Girard's concept of scapegoat that provides the conceptual link between chance and destiny, absurdity and meaning, the secular and the transcendent. To wrest allegory from profanity Capote has to pull off the same trick using real people that Willian Golding was able to do with pretend people in *Lord of the Flies*: purge the community of its violence through a ritualistic killing.

'...I know there isn't no beast—not with claws and all that, I mean—but I know there isn't no fear, either.'

Piggy paused.

'Unless—'

Ralph moved restlessly.

'Unless what?'

'Unless we get frightened of people'. (Golding, 1954: 90)

And therein lies the catch. This is America that Capote is writing about,[18] the land of endless internal mediation. How can we, as a people, ever stop being afraid of, or distinct from, our neighbors since everyone is a competitor to all?

The chances for a successful exorcism look promising at first: Hickock-Smith fulfills many of the criteria of the scapegoat so that their lawful murder may be counted upon to produce the restorative effect of catharsis. The scapegoat must always be socially marginal in some way; an 'expendable victim, human or animal, whose death will not cause violence to rebound because no one will bother to avenge them' (Girard, 2011: x)—they qualify. The scapegoat mechanism is dependent upon the impurity of the sin-bearing object as with Josef K. in *The Trial* and Mersault in *The Stranger*; both Dick and Perry ooze impurity and reek of pollution. It would appear that capital punishment is tailor-made for them, or they for it.

> The death penalty is a means of eliminating pollution...It purifies the affected group, who are often partly or wholly absolved of responsibility for the newly spilt blood...The violent expulsion, the expulsion unto death of the unworthy or accursed individual, has an ancillary sense: that of *devotio*. Indeed, the killing seems in one sense to be an act of piety. It makes us think of those ancient ordinances which declare that the murder of an outlaw does not cause pollution, or of that prescription of Germanic law that makes such a killing a civic duty...Then, too, the victim himself fills a true religious function, a function parallel to the priest-kings who are also put to death. The religious function can be seen in the Latin term for these victims: *homo sacer*, as well as in the Greek term *pharmakos*. (Louis Gernet qtd. Girard, 1977: 298)

The link between capital punishment and pollution is liminality, not only of people but of spaces, signifying the dual meaning of the phrase with which *In Cold Blood* begins: 'out there.'

> One of the tendencies that manifests itself in religious approaches to punishment is that of elimination, and more particularly—for the word must be taken in its etymological sense—of expulsion beyond the frontiers. The bones of the sacrilegious dead are cast out of the community,[19] and ... the inanimate object that caused a man's death, or the corpse of an

[18] In the same way that Golding was writing about England. See Chap. 2, above.

[19] This is taken from Plato's *The Laws* 855c: 'criminals should be publicly displayed...at the frontiers of the country' (Girard, 1977: 298).

> animal that killed a person, is also subject to expulsion. (George Glotz qtd. Girard, 1977: 298–299)

However, it is the second and historically much later secularized version of execution, *apagoge*, that is the one most well-suited to the fearful citizens of Holcomb—the lynch mob, as

> ...its rough and ready character might remind us of the frontier 'justice' of American Westerns.... it was usually visited on criminals who had been caught in the act, and it was always ratified by the common accord of the community. However ... the public nature of these acts would not have been enough to make the execution of the criminals possible if these criminals had not usually been foreigners; that is, individuals whose death entailed no risk of endless revenge within the community...This latter mode of unanimity gradually evolves into what can perhaps be described as an institutionalized and legalized form of mob violence. (Girard, 1977: 299)

Here, for 'foreigners' we should read outsiders, or perhaps the more generic 'anomalous being'. The scapegoat is always the object of a double transference: not only is the ritualistic victim chosen to be the bearer of the collective sins of the community through some occluded impurity, but, through the collectively misrecognized projection of an invented sin/pollution into the alien object the *demos* temporarily releases itself from its capacity for the violence that remains eternally latent thanks to mimetic desire. *In Cold Blood* clearly frames the Clutter murders as the intrusive irruption of possibly existent but only dimly perceived 'internal tensions' that are the original source of the 'endless revenge within the community'. But this leads directly to the single greatest problem of the non-fiction novel already touched on by Tanner: the incommunicability of the 'real' (the metaphorical black box of facts which do not speak themselves) that must be constantly mediated by the author retelling the events subject to the requisites of literary fiction. Capote confesses this.

> My feeling is that for the non-fiction novel to be entirely successful, the author should not appear in the work. Ideally. Once the narrator does appear, he has to appear throughout, all the way down the line, and the I-I-I intrudes when it really shouldn't. I think the single most difficult thing in my book, technically, was to write it without ever appearing myself, and yet, at the same time, create total credibility. (Plimpton, 1987: 55)

The non-fiction novel must eschew the unreliable narrator of Henry James (*The Turn of the Screw*) and Joseph Conrad (*Lord Jim*) because the medium of non-fiction is reportage, which implies objectivity and impersonality; yet because the author is producing a novel, literary tropes and conceits must necessarily intrude, even if only unintentionally. So does Capote really succeed here? The ostensibly neutral construction of the narrative will transmit to the reader feelings, attitudes, and experiences that will be represented as fact but may truly be unrecoverable and therefore un-representable as art. An outstanding case in point is the lengthy entirety of the death-row sequence in Part Four, 'The Corner' (Capote, 2000: 308–341). The obvious limitation to Capote's artistic-non-fictional reconstruction of the experiences, both physical and mental, of Hickock and Smith imitates the unspeakable nature of the relationship between law and violence. Robert M. Cover[20] persuasively argued that all

> Legal interpretation takes place in a field of pain and death… [During the criminal trial the] 'interpretations' or 'conversations' that are the preconditions for violent [forcible] incarceration are themselves implements of violence…The experience of the prisoner is, from the outset, an experience of being violently dominated, and it is colored from the beginning by the fear of being violently treated, (Cover, 1986: 1601, 1608)

Consistent with the law's preoccupation with legitimacy, the judicial process sanitizes itself most furiously at precisely those junctures, a kind of irruption, where the rootedness of the rule of law in violence appears most visible and least susceptible to mis-recognition; 'whether or not the judge and prisoner share the same philosophy of punishment, they arrive at the particular act of punishment having dominated and having been dominated with violence, respectively' (Cover, 1986: 1609). And a large part of this sanitization process is accomplished through the delegation of violent action through seemingly neutral or objective speech; 'Almost all judicial utterance becomes deed through the acts of others—acts embedded in roles' (Cover, 1986: 1621), as is unforgettably conveyed to us Capote's depiction of specially appointed prosecutor Logan Green's summation to the jury at the end of the trial of the monstrous doubles (Capote, 2000: 302–305).

> Pausing, Green gingerly touched a boil on the back of his neck, a mature inflammation that seemed, like its angry wearer, about to burst. 'So, gentlemen, what are you going to do? Give them the minimum [sentence]? Send them back to the penitentiary, and take the chance of their escaping or being paroled?[21] The next time they go slaughtering it may be *your* family. I say to you,' he solemnly said, staring at the panel in a manner that encompassed and challenged them all, 'some of our enormous crimes only happen because once upon a time a pack of chicken-hearted jurors refused to do their duty. Now, gentlemen, I leave it to you and your consciences'. (Capote, 2000: 305)

According to Cover

> We have done something strange in our system. We have rigidly separated the act of interpretation—of understanding what ought to be done—from the carrying out of this 'ought to be done' through violence. At the same time we have, at least in criminal law, rigidly linked the carrying out of judicial orders to the act of judicial interpretation by relatively inflexible hierarchies of judicial utterances and firm obligations on the part of penal officials to heed them. Judges are both separated from, and inextricably linked to, the acts they authorize. (Cover, 1986: 1627)

But any trace of the paradox that Cover reveals vanishes the moment we appreciate, liberated from the demystifying effects of *meconnaissance*—the absence of awareness of what we are actually doing when we execute—the absolute necessity of the connection between law and violence. Charles Bonaparte has made this plain in his discussions of 'the vigilance/vigilante committees' of 'popular justice'

---

[20] See Chap. 1, above.

[21] Just like Frank Miller was in *High Noon* and we all know what Hell that wrought. See Chap. 4 above.

(*apagoge*), which have proven that mob violence can, under the right circumstances, be properly construed as a special kind of natural justice.

> The underlying purpose in all these cases [of lynching] is not to violate, but to vindicate the law; or, to speak more accurately, the law is violated in form that it may be vindicated in substance, its 'adjective' part (i.e. matter of procedure) is disregarded that its 'substantive' part [justice] may be preserved (Bonaparte, 1890: 336).... Lynching is an attempt to supply within the unquestioned province of the government the government's equally unquestioned deficiency, and its practice constitutes a grave proof of the evil it seeks to remedy. If popular government does not so administer justice as to satisfy the moral sense of the people, then popular government fails to fulfil its duty. (Bonaparte, 1890: 342)

So, in the event of the exceptional state of 'a crisis of judicial legitimacy,' the sort that so preoccupied Carl Schmitt,[22] social consensus may be restored through collective and spontaneous acts of 'popular justice' which invariably involved the violent persecution of an enemy of some sort. Operating under a similar set of assumptions, Jeffrie G. Murphy argues that the institutionalization of both hatred and revenge within the criminal sentencing process through the form of 'victim impact statements' actually serves a productive purpose in terms of law's legitimacy in restoring the generative unanimity of those community standards that are supposed to underlay due process.

> For what is a democracy except a form of government in which the majority gets to have its dominant preferences enacted into law—even if those preferences are condemned by a refined and condescending elite?[23] Thus, if most people want to create a system of criminal law that institutionalizes and expresses the hatreds and desires for revenge that crime victims feel towards those who have wronged them, what principle would allow anyone to say nay to the will of the people thus expressed? (Murphy, 1994: 212)

If law is a ritualistic violence mediated by enmity and revenge then it follows that the essence of punishment is pain; 'Nor must we forget that after all, the end of punishment is to punish. A prison should not be hell,[24] but it fails of its purpose if it is too pleasant for purgatory' (Bonaparte, 1890: 341). However, if punishment is reducible to elemental and pre-representational pain then, like every other form of pain, the penal variety of suffering resists precise and differentiating linguistic expression; it remains inherently inexpressible and, therefore, incommunicable which is Capote's problem all over again as Elaine Scarry makes clear in her magisterial *The Body in Pain: The Making and Unmaking of the World* (1985).

> Whatever pain achieves, it achieves in part through its unshareability, and it ensures this unshareability through its resistance to language. 'English,' writes Virginia Woolf, 'which can express the thoughts of Hamlet and the tragedy of Lear has no words for the shiver or the headache...The merest schoolgirl when she falls in love has Shakespeare or Keats to speak her mind for her, but let a sufferer try to describe a pain in his head to a doctor and language at once runs dry.' True of the headache, Woolf's account is of course more radically true

[22] See Chap. 4, above.

[23] Of course the dissenting minority need not be an 'elite'—it could be impoverished, disempowered, and marginalized.

[24] Why not?

> of the severe and prolonged pain that may accompany cancer or burns or phantom limb or stroke, as well as of the severe and prolonged pain that may occur unaccompanied by any nameable disease. Physical pain does not simply resist language but actively destroys it, bringing about an immediate reversion to a state anterior to language, to the sounds and cries a human being makes before language is learned. (Scarry, 1985: 4)

Which is the state of undifferentiation, the psycho-social morass from which the scapegoat is to be extracted, in order to re-create the condition of the possibility of language, that which is required for differences and distinctions.

> Why pain should so centrally entail, require this shattering of language…may be partially apprehended by noticing the exceptional character of pain when compared to all our other interior states…Our interior states of consciousness are regularly accompanied by objects in the external world, that we do not simply 'have feelings' but have feelings *for* somebody or something…a consistent affirmation of the human being's capacity to move out beyond the boundaries of his or her own body into the external, sharable world…[However, when] moving through the human interior one at last reached physical pain [shareability would cease], for physical pain—unlike any other state of consciousness—has no referential content. It is not *of* or *for* anything. It is precisely because it takes no object that it, more than any other phenomenon, resists objectification in language. (Scarry, 1985: 5)

And this takes us back to the vital issue of catharsis which, as we know, has a very unsteady relationship with truth: Capote's awful panopticon-like gaze, both omniscient and embedded, a conceit of novelistic non-fiction mediated by creative reportage, may ultimately be a fiction but it is also works as a noble lie (like *apagoge*) insofar as it succeeds in inducing within the reader the Aristotelian release of emotions, purifying and conversional, that the high art form of Tragedy requires: 'This strategy offers not only an angle into the criminal mind but a catharsis for an audience that can vent its own destructive energies through interaction with this novel rather than through violent action in the community' and against Charles Bonaparte we do not actually have to go out and riot when the 'obviously' guilty is acquitted in 'clear' violation of universally agreed upon 'communal norms'; the non-fiction novel literally strives to release 'the sorts of pressures that might drive someone into a pathological state if not released' (Hickman, 2005: 465, 472). So the answer may lie with a very particular kind of artistic reconfiguration version of the un-artistic ethical concern of Girard's *metanoia*: the story of Hickock-Smith as it is presented *In Cold Blood* may be false but the experience of catharsis and its relationship to both the scapegoat and the sacrificial mechanism is fatally true.

What is the precise technique that Capote employs to solve the problem of incommunicability while complying with creative reportage thereby saving his non-fiction novel from literary failure? The answer comes on page 341. First is the denouement: 'Dewey shut his eyes; he kept them shut until he heard that thud-snap that announces a rope-broken neck' (Capote, 2000: 341). Then comes the 'lift' that is not one: 'Dewey had imagined that with the deaths of Smith and Hickock, he would experience a sense of climax, release, of a design justly completed' (Capote, 2000: 341) and which, of course, does not happen. Today we call 'a sense of climax, release, of a design justly completed' closure but this also does not happen because for us post-theists Death is irreversible and all things are no-thing in the final instance. Capote's selection of

Dewy as the bearer of an occluded but omniscient authorial voice is pivotal then, for the KBI Special Agent is the main the protagonist of the third allegorical frame, the detective story, which is the fable (*muthos*) of the detective-as-restorer, the one tasked to save the community from itself and the only character save one not evidently poisoned by mimetic rivalry. Because he is the one actor that is most closely identified with a regeneration that is purely secular, narratively he is also the logical choice to receive revelation from the sacred. The solution is simple: *Special Agent Dewey must undergo catharsis*. But how? Everyone is dead and nothing good has come out of anything.

10.6 Mythic Un-Truth: The Sacred Murder of Nancy Clutter

Herb was the first to be killed in the sequence of revenge, but Nancy was the last, for she was the apex of the scale of innocence, signifying the absence of existential envy. Consider the occluded meaning of the following two passages. From this…

> Nancy was a pretty girl, lean and boyishly agile, and the prettiest things about her were her short-bobbed, shining chestnut hair (brushed a hundred strokes each morning, the same number at night) and her soap-polished complexion, still faintly freckled and rose-brown from last summer's sun But it was her eyes, wide apart, darkly translucent, like ale held to the light, that made her immediately likeable, that at once announced her lack of suspicion, her considered and yet so easily triggered kindliness (Capote, 2000: 31).

To that…

> Well, it was pretty bad. That wonderful girl—but you would never have known her. She'd been shot in the back of the head with a shotgun maybe two inches away. She was lying on her side, facing the wall, and the wall was covered with blood. (Capote, 2000: 73)

Capital punishment can never be represented as a mere episodic occurrence of murdering 'in cold blood' if it contains within it a sacralising function: the regeneration of the community through the ritualistic execution-expulsion of the emissary of the monstrous. Capote's problem is that he cannot end his novel because the mobbing lynchers of Holcombe have failed to be regenerated, to differentiate, to learn to recognize the latent crisis that threatens the community and, therefore, are unable to truly contain the contagion of violence. Jean-Pierre Dupuy has offered a useful commentary on Indologist Louis Dumont's understanding of the meaning of 'to contain' that is relevant here.

> It has always seemed surprising to me that [Louis] Dumont … should have seen hierarchy as nothing more than the sign of a stable order, guaranteed by religion. One has only to recognize that the verb 'contain' has another meaning—of blocking, inhibiting, repressing—in order to constitute hierarchy, understood as the encompassing of the contrary, in an entirely different and much more disturbing sense, namely, as a system that is constantly in danger of being overturned. Just so, the most stable social order is the one that contains the threat of its own collapse, in the two senses of the verb 'to contain'. (Dupuy, 2015: 251)

Ever since Leibniz, the 'foundation of modern rationalism' is simply this: 'evil is, at bottom, only a lesser evil, a necessary evil, for it is placed in the service of the good; evil is only apparent, for it is an integral part of the good' (Dupuy, 2015: 252). This is the central myth (lie) of the fantastic and unsustainable construct that we call modernity which, far from being a true presence, is, instead, the annihilating absence of the presence of the all-thing that has been hidden since the foundation of the world: the scapegoat.

> [This] idea can be stated less abstractly if we consider the singular relationship that unites murder and sacrifice in a society where sacrifice constitutes the founding ritual. In that case, sacrifice contains the outbreak and spread of murder; though it is in one sense just another murder, it promises to put an end to violence. Capital punishment performs the same function in certain criminal justice systems. But when the religious order ('hierarchy') is overthrown by disorder and violence,[25] ritual killing can no longer be distinguished from murder. Before the onset of crisis, however, sacrifice was both murder and something other than murder. This 'something other' is the sacred. (Dupuy, 2015: 252)

The indestructible source of the 'disorder and violence' of Holcombe is nothing other than the repressed (contained) recognition that the evil brothers are, in truth, the monstrous doubles of Holcombe, precariously perched upon the liminal frontier of 'out there,' the spaces that are empty for being without differences.[26] And this is why, in order to attain his required gothic ending, Capote had to offer up the daughter of the 'fanciful' Mrs. Kidwell who had earlier seen Nancy Clutter attempting to return home on her horse Babe, the uncanny 'Susan Kidwell' as the revenant/double of the dead girl, slain as the sacred scapegoat of the monstrous doubles of strangers and citizens, the banished children of Eve of the Garden of Eden and the failed heirs of the American Dream.

But really, there was no need for Capote to have done this, for all of us have heard the story of Nancy Clutter before: the lost maiden who is abducted by the servants of the God of the Dead, violently imprisoned in the Underworld, and whose annual return announces the coming of the Spring that resurrects the world, who imparts 'the whisper of wind-voices' to the detective-restorer who is to be restored, her face revealed, if only for a passing instant, 'in the green-gold fire of half-grown wheat.'

Persephone.

Epilogue I

Grobel: 'Do most multiple murderers believe in God, or are they atheists?'.

Capote: 'They all believe in God…'.

---

[25] Or by a generic 'secularization'.

[26] This equates well with Mircea Eliade's notion of an absolute dichotomy between profane and sacred space, the former lacking the ordering structure of the latter: 'The unknown space that extends beyond his world—an uncosmicized because unconsecrated space, a mere amorphous extent into which no orientation has yet been projected, and hence in which no structure has yet arisen—foe religious man, this profane space represents absolute non-being. If, by some evil chance, he strays into it, he feels emptied of his ontic substance, as if he were dissolving in Chaos, and he finally dies' (Eliade, 1987: 64). In the case of the Clutters, the migration took place in reverse: the outsiders journeyed towards the focal point of the central and stabilizing pillar of the sacred.

Grobel: 'Most of them have read *In Cold Blood*?'.
Capote: 'Yes, that's how I get the interviews.'
Grobel: 'How many of them have read your book *before* they killed?'.
Capote: 'I don't know. (*Pauses*). I hadn't thought about that' (Grobel, 1985: 126–127).

Epilogue II

According to both Perry Smith and Dick Hickock as told to Truman Capote the following event happened while both of the outlaws were secreted in Miami Beach at the Somerset Hotel on 335 Ocean Drive.

> [Perry Smith] occupied himself with the Miami *Herald*. Presently he came across an inner-page story that won his entire attention It concerned murder, the slaying of a Florida family, a Mr. and Mrs. Clifford Walker, their four-year-old son and two-year-old daughter. Each of the victims, though not bound or gagged, had been shot through the head with a 0.22 weapon The crime, clueless and apparently motiveless, had taken place Saturday night, 19 December, at the Walker home, on a cattle-raising ranch not far from Tallahassee.
>
> Perry interrupted Dick's athletics to read the story aloud, and said, 'Where were we last Saturday night?'.
>
> Tallahassee?
>
> I'm telling you. (Capote, 2000: 202, 201)

Capote, who sees both of the murderers, but especially his double Perry, as victims of circumstance (or life chances gone badly wrong) takes them at their word. However, J. T. Hunter in his *In Colder Blood: The Walker Family Murder* (2016) provides strong circumstantial evidence that Hickock-Smith were in fact responsible for the murder of the Walker family in Osprey, Florida almost one month after the slaying of the Clutter family on November the 15th. The 'coincidences' between the two parricides are uncanny: Cliff Walker the Father, like Herb Clutter, was 'one of the most wonderful guys you ever met,'[27] Christine Walker, like Mrs. Clutter, was executed after being raped, and the three-year old son Jimmy Walker was shot in the head three times, but the daughter, one year old Debbie, was killed in a singularly anomalous fashion: shot once, but not fatally, and then purposefully drowned in the family's bathtub. And just like the denizens of Holcomb the citizens of Osprey do not know what to make it of it; 'I don't know how a human being could shoot a child and put her in a bathtub,' said Uncle Robe Walker (Hunter, 2016: 32–33). Actually, it's easy to understand if the human being in question is Perry Smith. In September 2007 cold-case detective Kimberly McGath, re-opened the Walker case and soon noticed weird parallels with the Clutter massacre.

> 'Undoing' acts by the killer at the Walker crime scene—pulling the quilt over the bloody pillow on Jimmy's bed, and covering Debbie's head with her brother's cowboy hat before shooting her—were similar to actions taken by Perry Smith during the Clutter killings, such as tucking Nancy Clutter in her bed and placing a pillow under [brother] Kenyon Clutter's head before killing them. (Hunter, 2016: 85–86)

[27] Which sounds a lot like Herb Clutter. Perry and Dick must have had a proclivity for bumping off seemingly good-natured patriarchs (Hunter, 2016: 7).

But what was truly disturbing was the connection that McGath established between the immersive homicide and a background detail provided by Capote in his anti-heroic pseudo-hagiography of Perry Smith.

> McGath recalled that Perry Smith claimed that while he was housed in a children's shelter operated by the Salvation Army, one of the shelter's nurses forced him into a tub of ice-cold water and held him underwater until he turned blue, nearly drowning him. McGath believed that Debbie Walker's drowning by being held face down in the bathtub might have been a case of the psychological condition of Identification with the Aggressor, whereby Perry Smith *identified* with the power figure of the nurse who held him under ice-cold bath water when he was a child. Indeed, during Smith's trial for the Clutter killings, a widely respected psychiatrist [Dr. Joseph Satten] concluded that he [Smith] suffered from schizophrenic episodes in which he was prone to commit violent acts while in a 'trance-like state.' The psychiatrist specifically compared Smith to a similarly disturbed individual who had drowned a young girl by holding her head under water[28]. (Hunter, 2016: 86)

Furthermore, of the four previous cases that Satten used in a comparative study of Smith, in every instance the men themselves were 'puzzled as to why they killed their victims, who were relatively unknown to them, and in each instance the murderer appears to have lapsed into a dreamlike dissociative trance from which he awakened to "suddenly discover" himself assaulting his victim' (Capote, 2000: 299). And, like a lot of dreamlike dissociative trances, there's a mystical giant yellow parrot at the end of it.

> And that Perry could not abide: anyone's ridiculing the parrot, which had first flown into his dreams when he was seven years old, a hated, hating half-breed child living in a California orphanage run by nuns—shrouded disciplinarians who whipped him for wetting his bed. It was after one of those beatings, one he could never forget ('She woke me up. She had a flashlight, and she hit me with it. Hit me and hit me. And when the flashlight broke, she went on hitting me in the dark'), that the parrot appeared, arrived while he slept, a bird 'taller than Jesus, yellow like a sunflower,' a warrior-angel who blinded the nuns with its beak, fed upon their eyes,[29] slaughtered them as they 'pleaded for mercy', then so gently lifted him, enfolded him, winged him away to 'paradise'.
>
> As the years went by, the particular torments from which the bird delivered him altered; others—older children, his father, a faithless girl, a sergeant he'd known in the Army—replaced the nuns, but the parrot remained, a hovering avenger.… And afterwards the blessed ascent! Ascension to a paradise that in one version was merely 'a feeling', a sense of power, of unassailable superiority—sensations that in another version were transposed into 'A real place. Like out of a movie. Maybe that's were I *did* see it—remembered it from a movie …'. (Capote, 2000: 90–91)

The home of the Clutters. Foreshadowing. Unveiling.

> One woman, a schoolteacher, observed, 'Feeling wouldn't run half so high if this had happened to anyone *except* the Clutters. Anyone *less* admired. Prosperous. Secure. But that family represented everything people hereabouts really value and respect, and that such a thing could happen to them—well, it's like being told there is no God'. (Capote, 2000: 96)

---

[28] Specifically, a 'hospital employee who drowned a girl of nine by holding her head under water' (Capote, 2000: 299).

[29] It should be remembered that when Perry held his shotgun only two inches away from the back of Nancy Clutter's head the resulting blast was guaranteed to obliterate her eyes which Capote references as a sign of the girl's innocence and absence of the plague of metaphysical desire.

But the schoolteacher got it all wrong. Backwards, in fact. For Perry's 'hovering avenger' was no ordinary mystical giant yellow parrot: while awaiting eternal oblivion on death row '… Perry undulated between half-awake stupors and sickly, sweat-drenched sleep. Voices roared through his head; one voice persistently asked him, "Where is Jesus? Where?" And once he woke up shouting, "The bird is Jesus! The bird is Jesus!"'. (Capote, 2000: 319)

To quote Girard: 'Desire clings to violence and stalks it like a shadow because violence is the signifier of the cherished being, the signifier of divinity' (Girard, 1977: 151).

To paraphrase Nietzsche: what are the Laws of Man to the Sons of God?

References

Primary Sources

Capote, T. (2000). *In cold blood*. Penguin Books.
In Cold Blood (Columbia Pictures 200; directed by Richard Brooks).

Secondary Sources

Abrams, M. H. (1990). *A glossary of literary terms*. Cornell University Press.
Algeo, A. M. (1996). *The courtroom as a forum: Homicide trials by dreiser, wright, capote, and mailer*. Peter Lang.
Bonaparte, C. J. (1890). Lynch law and its remedy. *The Yale Law Journal, 8*(8), 335–343.
Carroll, N. (1990). *The philosophy of horror or paradoxes of the heart*. Routledge.
Clarke, G. (2010). *Capote*. Simon & Schuster.
Cover, R. (1986). Violence and the Word. *The Yale Law Journal, 95*(8), 1601–1629.
Dupuy, J.-P. (2015). Self-transcendence and tangled hierarchies in Catalhoyuk. In P. Antonello & P. Gifford (Eds.), *How we became human: Mimetic theory and the science of evolutionary origins* (pp. 233–260). Michigan State University Press.
Eliade, M. (1987). *The sacred and the profane: The nature of religion* (W. R. Trask, Trans.). New York: Harcourt, Inc.
Fahy, T. (2012). Hobbes, human nature, and the culture of American violence in Truman Capote's *In Cold Blood*. In T. Fahy (Ed.), *The philosophy of horror* (pp. 51–71). The University Press of Kentucky.
Garrett, G. (1996). Crime and punishment in Kansas: Truman Capote's *In Cold Blood*. *Hollins Critic, 3*(1), 1–12.
Girard, R. (1977). *Violence and the sacred* (P. Gregory, Trans.). Baltimore: The Johns Hopkins University Press.
Girard, R., Oughourlian, J. M. & Lefort, G. (1978). *Things hidden since the foundation of the World* (S. Bann, & M. Metteer, Trans.). New York: Continuum.
Girard, R. (2011). *Sacrifice* (M. Pattillo, & D. Dawson, Trans.). East Lansing MI: Michigan State University Press.
Golding, W. (1954). *Lord of the flies*. Faber and Faber.
Grobel, L. (1985). *Conversations with Capote*. Hutchinson.

Hellman, J. (1980). Death and design in *In Cold Blood*: Capote's 'non-fiction novel' as allegory. *Ball State University Forum, 21*, 65–78.

Hickman, T. (2005). 'The last to see them alive': Panopticism, the supervisory Gaze, and Catharsis in Capote's *In Cold Blood*. *Studies in the Novel, 37*(4), 464–476.

Hollowell, J. (1977). *Fact and fiction: The new journalism and the non-fiction novel*. The University of North Carolina Press.

Hunter, J. T. (2016). *In colder blood: The walker family murder*. RJ Parker Publishing, Inc.

McAleer, J. J. (1972). 'An American Tragedy' and 'In Cold Blood. *Thought, 47*, 569–586.

Murphy, J. G. (1994). Getting even: The role of the victim. *Social Philosophy and Policy, 7*(2), 209–225.

Plimpton, G. (1987). The story behind a non-fiction novel. In M. Thomas Inge (Ed.), *Truman Capote: Conversations* (pp. 47–68). University of Mississippi.

Pramaggiore, M., & Wallis, T. (2011). *Film: A critical introduction* (3rd ed.). Laurence King Publishing.

Reed, K. T. (1981). *Truman Capote*. Twayne Publishers.

Scarry, E. (1985). *The body in pain: The making and unmaking of the World*. Oxford University Press.

Turner, V. (1968). *The drums of affliction*. Clarendon Press.

Wilson, E. (2020). "Something radically wrong over at the clutter place": Mythic truth, monstrous doubles, and the killing of Nancy Clutter. In N. Tredell (Ed.), *Critical insights: In cold blood* (pp. 32–48). Salem House.

Chapter 11
The 'Good Murderer' Gary Gilmore: The Re-sacralization of the Scapegoat in the Age of Public Reason

Abstract If Sister Helen Prejean's anti-death penalty book *Dead Man Walking* (1993) suggests the return of the scapegoat in a narratively light manner, then *The Executioner's Song* (1979) does so with nothing less than bloody vengeance; as Norman Mailer made clear on multiple occasions the sordid tragedy of Gary Gilmore constitutes nothing less than the wholesale refutation of the secularist conceits of liberal America. Gilmore presents us with a remainder so indivisible, an accursed share so unassimilable, a lacuna so perfectly empty, that the legal system lacked the vocabulary to successfully name him: an accused sentenced to death who wages all-out legal warfare against those who were trying to stop his execution. By so adamantly, and so publicly, calling for his death at the hands of the State of Utah out of his own free will, Gilmore had improbably seized for himself the mantle of sacrificial victim within a post-theistic world. Even more noxious to the liberal pluralist was Gilmore's motivation for doing so: religious belief. Mailer accepts in toto Gilmore's professed belief in reincarnation; so compelling was Gilmore that Mailer himself converted to the doctrine of the transmigration of souls. Even more interesting from a Girardian perspective is the astonishing account provided by Gary's brother Mikal in *Shot in the Heart* (1994): Gilmore's seemingly pre-destined pilgrimage toward his mimetic enactment of Mormon blood atonement as a *skandalon* to public reason. On the issue of sacrifice Mikal Gilmore's text vastly supersedes Mailer's otherwise excellent *The Executioner's Song*; with the latter we move into the domain of the uncanny, Gary Gilmore having been literally marked at birth as a sacrificial offering of spilt blood—death by firing squad.

Keywords Blood atonement · *Aesthesis* · Authenticity · Public reason · John Rawls · Reasonable citizens · Just war

E. M. Wilson, *Rene Girard, Law, Literature, and Cinema*,
https://doi.org/10.1007/978-981-97-1156-7_11

11.1 Murder, Sacralization, and Apocalypse

In his discussion of Tim Robbin's cinematic adaptation of *Dead Man Walking*,[1] Sister Helen Prejean's account of capital punishment in the United States (Prejean, 2013), Edmund Arens provocatively labels it a prison film that 'contains some elements of a court room film' (Arens, 1998: 16), meaning that it carries within it, along with the sub-genre archetypal themes (confession, guilt, forgiveness, redemption, execution) a theological surcharge; the '"film presents itself as a mini-apocalypse which confronts the viewer with 'first things' and 'last things'" (Inge Kirsner qtd. Arens, 1998: 16). According to Arens, every cinematic work aspiring to the title of 'Art' must possess three characteristics, and according to him, Robbin's film exhibits all of them. The first is *poesis*: the film text must conform to a formal structure dictated by genre. The second is, as we should expect after Aristotle,[2] is *katharsis*, which Arens defines as 'certain emotional effects on the public that are either purifying or edifying.' *Dead Man Walking* performs admirably on this front, as both movie and book are an extended commentary upon the re-legalization of capital punishment in the United States following the case of *Gregg v. Georgia, Proffitt v Florida, Jureka v. Texas, Woodson v. North Carolina, and Roberts v. Louisiana*, 428 U.S. 153 (July 2 1976). The third, and most interesting for this discussion, is *aesthesis*, which is present whenever 'a work of art deals with perception in a double way: while it implies a certain perception of reality, it also invites the audience to participate in this perception and thus to deepen, alter, or correct the perception that they have experienced' (Arens, 1998: 15). *Aesthesis*, that which pertains to both ambivalence and mis-recognition, may be thought of as an aesthetics of disclosing, which, Arens recognizes, is the equivalent of an aesthetics of unveiling or uncovering, meaning that *Dead Man* Walking is, quite literally, an 'apocalyptic' film of *metanoia*.

> Besides the topic of representation, any kind of art raises the question of perception. Art implies a certain perception and at the same time it offers or invites—in the case of visual art—the audience to perceive reality in a different or deeper manner. In a movie the audience, whether by a manipulative 'aesthetics of overwhelming' or by an aesthetics of disclosing, is moved emotionally and imaginatively, the aim being to direct their attention to the secret of the things shown and thus to direct or redirect their view of reality. (Arens, 1998: 15)

And what is '*the secret of the things shown*' in a courtroom drama, or in any of the iconic films and literary texts of law-and-literature? Sister Prejean provides us with the answer in her discussion of popular support for the death penalty: 'I regret that so many people do not understand, but I know that they have not watched the state imitate the violence they so abhor' (Prejean, 2013: 109). If we were to translate this acute moral perception into the terms of Girardian critique, we would read Prejean's commentary as an admission of *meconnaissance*, specifically the submerged reality of the universality and continuity of the sacrificial mechanism that, when uncovered by *aesthesis*, reveals a second and even greater denied truth: the pre-historic anthropological origins of jurisprudence in primitive religion that renders the victim of capital

[1] *Dead Man Walking* (directed by Tim Robbins, Polygram Film, 1995).

[2] See Chap. 9, above.

punishment a profane modern simulacrum of the sacred and archaic scapegoat. For the thing that truly links the post-modern with the pre-modern is the unifying affective mechanism of the will-to-revenge, which, as Girard has argued so ferociously, has remained remarkably constant throughout human history.[3] The only thing that has changed for us is that we cannot openly admit that revenge is what we desire, or, what comes to the same thing, that we are beings of *ressentiment*; instead we rely upon the self-gratifying gimmick of *meconnaissance* that misleadingly represents capital punishment as sanitized deterrence in civilizational opposition to any purely 'unconscious' or 'primitive' desire for revenge.

> [The] establishment of … the restraint that enables people to live with one another and the ineradicable impulse to retaliate when harm is inflicted has always been one of the essential tasks of civilization. The attainment of such a balance depends in large measure on the confidence of the victimized that someone else will act on their behalf against the victimizers[4] … Stripped of moralizing, law exists not only to restrain retribution but to mete it out … A society that is unable to convince individuals of its ability to exact atonement for injury is a society that runs a constant risk of having its members revert to the wilder forms of [vigilante] justice … (Susan Jacoby qtd. Prejean, 2013: 142)[5]

Not surprisingly Albert Camus is a favorite of Sister Helen and she freely deploys him as a sort of secular theologian of state-sanctioned murder. The French atheist writes this.

> Society proceeds sovereignly to eliminate the evil ones from her midst as if she were virtue itself. Like an honorable man killing his wayward son and remarking: 'Really, I didn't know what to do with him…' To assert, in any case, that a man must be absolutely cut off from society because he is absolutely evil amounts to saying that society is absolutely good, and no one in his right mind will believe this today. (Albert Camus qtd. Prejean, 2013: 21–22)

And the Catholic nun replies in kind: 'And I think of what Camus said, that every murderer, when he kills, feels innocent, that he always feels excused by his particular circumstances' (Prejean, 2013: 148). What links both accounts is the dual notion of the existential, if not legal, 'innocence' of the accused, the formation of the homicidal will being an issue of internal mediation, and the externally mediated mis-recognized scapegoating at the heart of the statist destruction of the accused

---

[3] 'The July 26, 1991, CNN/Gallup public opinion poll indicated that of the 76% who said they were in favour of the death penalty, 13% cited deterrence as a reason, 19% cited protection, and 50%, revenge' (Prejean 271 n 9). Which, given Girard's theory of the scapegoat, is exactly what we should expect—capital punishment, as a mis-recognized scapegoating mechanism, is itself the creation of the will-to-revenge that can be directed away from the universal crisis of undifferentiation towards that of the unique and differential Stranger.

[4] Which is a central premise of Girard's concept of the scapegoat who will usually present in the form of a 'stranger' or a 'foreigner' of some kind, 'that is, individuals whose death entailed no risk of endless revenge within the community' (Girard, 1977: 299).

[5] Prejean notes, however that 'Jacoby holds that the public's desire to see serious punishment consistently meted out for serious crimes is legitimate and that to ignore it encourages "the boundless outrage that generates demands for boundless retribution"' (Susan Jacoby qtd. Prejean, 2013: 143). So, *katharsis* can be considered a 'rational facet' of the law provided that there is complete ignorance of its existential connection with the scapegoat mechanism, the prehistoric form of 'pre-rational' killing.

functioning as the cover for the will-to-revenge. Both Girard and Jean-Pierre Dupuy adopt a similar tack, closing following the argument put forward by Louis Dumont in his seminal anthropological study of the Indian caste system, *Homo Hierarchicus* (1981): every instance of social hierarchy actively encompasses that element which is most antithetical to it, allowing hierarchy to reconstitute itself as a form of theodicy (Dumont, 1981: 66–67), in which the '[G]ood must *contain* evil while still being its contrary' (Louis Dumont qtd. Dupuy 2013: 4).

> Here the verb 'contain' has the sense of encompassing, and the relation it describes is hierarchy, which is to say the encompassing of the contrary…[However] One has only to recognize that the verb 'contain' has another meaning—of blocking, inhibiting, repressing—in order to construe hierarchy, understood as the encompassing of the contrary, in an entirely different and much more disturbing sense, namely as a system that is constantly in danger of being overturned. Just so, the most stable social order is the one that *contains* the threat of its own collapse, in the two senses of the verb 'to contain'. (Dupuy 2013: 4–5)[6]

Cultural hierarchies are akin to theodicy because they provide the mechanism through which external mediation (scapegoating) is enabled to prevail over internal mediation (vigilantism) through multifaceted strategies of assimilation; 'religion *contains* violence, in the compound sense of blocking it while at the same time harbouring it within itself' (Dupuy 2013: 104).[7] Dupuy suggests that the European version of the Indian caste system is the *katechon* of both Pauline and Johannine apocalyptic theology, the occluded but divine 'force' that constrains the satanic/vengeful elements within the social order so that the repetitive drive toward undifferentiation rebounds against themselves, recurrently dissipating until the time of the final crisis, the point where undifferentiation and violence reach an extreme pitch, requiring the termination of History through the perfect and final revelation—the apocalypse that rehabilitates Creation.[8] Creation, 'holding bad violence in check by

---

[6] See Chap. 10, above.

[7] This is mirrored by Girard: 'The system does not supress vengeance; rather, it effectively limits it to a single act of reprisal, enacted y a sovereign authority specializing in this particular function' said authority evolving into the parallel systems of religion and law (Girard, 1977: 15).

[8] The main reference to the *katechon*, the unnamed thing that works to bind Satan, occurs in 2 Thessalonians 2: 6–8: 'And now you know what is restraining [Satan], that he may be revealed in his own time. For the mystery of lawlessness is already at work; only He who now restrains *will do so* until He is taken out of the way. And then the lawless one will be revealed, whom the Lord will consume with the breath of His mouth and destroy with the brightness of his coming.' Under the a-millennial interpretation of the New Testament, which postulates that the Millennium ('The Thousand Years'), or the Rule of Christ, is the era of the Church down until the time of the End Days (no matter how distant in the future), then a second reference to the invisible binding force can also be detected in Revelations 19: 15 and 20: 1–3 respectively: 'Now out of His mouth goes a sharp sword, that with it He should strike the nations. And He Himself will rule them with a rod of iron. He Himself treads the winepress of the fierceness and wrath of Almighty God'; 'Then I saw an angel coming down from heaven, having a key to the bottomless pit and a great chain in his hand. He laid hold of the dragon, that serpent of old, who is *the* Devil and Satan, and bound him for a thousand years; and he cast him into the bottomless pit, and shut him up, and set a seal on him, so that he should deceive the nations no more till the thousand years were finished. But after these things he must be released for a little while.' Girard's approach to the topic is robustly a-millenial; 'The first Christian texts, chronologically speaking, are the Letters to the Thessalonians, and they

good violence, holding society together until the truth could be made known' (Robert Hamerton-Kelly qtd. Cowdell, 2014: 210 n 6).[9] The key text is 2 Thessalonians 2: 6–7: 'And you know what is restraining him [the Man of Lawlessness] now so that he may be revealed in his time. For the mystery of lawlessness is already at work: only he who now restrains it [*katechon*] will do so until he is out of the way.' The *katechon*, who is unidentified (or mis-recognized[10]) uses violence among the nations and peoples to keep them restrained and unable to coalesce thereby pre-empting the crisis-of-undifferentiation (Palaver, 1995).

> Theologically [...] the *katechon* is an ambiguous concept. The *katechon* is both poison and antidote. As a restrainer, it is a means to prevent destruction. At the same time, however, it also uses anarchy or violence to prevent the total outbreak of anarchy or violence. Theologically speaking, it not only postpones the reign of the Antichrist but it also holds back the second coming of Christ. This ambiguity of the concept of the *katechon* is rooted in the pagan sacred. The *katechon* contains violence in both senses of the word "contain". (Palaver, 2007: 85)

On a 'mimetic reading, the man and the mystery of lawlessness' refer to 'the sacrificial crisis of the erasure of distinctions, the chaos of undifferentiation whence violence comes' so that the action 'is controlled by the apocalyptic idea of the "right time," and the restraining historical power is there to keep events from happening prematurely. It does not prevent them from happening at all but serves only to ensure

---

are an answer to the question: why is the world continuing when you [Paul] announced its end? Paul says that there is something holding back the powers, the *katochos* (something that holds back). The most common interpretation is that it is the Roman Empire. The Crucifixion has not yet dissolved all order. If you look at the apocalyptic chapters of Christianity, they describe something like the present chaos, which wasn't there in the beginning of the Roman Empire. How can the world end when it is held so tightly by the forces of order?' (Girard, 2020: 173).

[9] For Girard, this 'force' is thoroughly liminal: 'The *katechon* stands in a Christian world, in a world cleared of Satan's rule, which doesn't want any more of it. At the same time, the *katechon* still retains a little of the old order, without which the door to absolute violence could open. The *katechon* restrains violence—that is to say, that which remains after Satan has been rolled, duped. One must admit that, for preventing violence, we are not able to do without a certain violence. We are therefore obliged to think in terms of the lesser violence. But, in fact, it is difficult to precisely define their difference' (Rene Girard qtd. Cowdell, 2014: 121). God, it appears, cannot do without ambivalence.

[10] 'He' may be the symbol of the rule of law (not just the Mosaic) enforced by the police powers; the *katechon* is of the 'lower domains' as Paul makes clear in *Galatians* 3: 19–25: 'Why then the law? It was added because of transgressions; till the offspring should come to whom the promise had been made; and it was ordained by angels through an intermediary. [...] Now, before faith came, we were confined under the law, kept under restraint until faith should be revealed. [...] But now that faith has come, we are no longer under a custodian.' In Girardian terms, this would seem to indicate that the *katechon* must enforce law and uphold differences until Humanity is able to tolerate the abolition of the sacrifice without regressing into undifferentiation and metaphysical violence; it is a call to radical and uncompromising individualism: anti-mimesis. 'It makes perfect sense that the Law, as the instrument of sacred violence, was given only to contain trespasses for the time being ...; and not directly to God but through the angels, because God is not a God of violence. Nevertheless, it served the negative purpose of holding bad violence in check by good violence, holding society together until the truth could be made known. As a product of the surrogate victim and the double transference, it was an advance on the primordial chaos of unconstrained mimetic rivalry' (Robert G. Hamerton-Kelly qtd. Cerella, 2015: 93 n 83).

that the apocalyptic calendar is kept' (Hamerton-Kelly, 2007: 14). The result is that throughout the entirety of the pre-modern era

> ...one finds the same idea which is the foundation of modern rationalism: evil is, at bottom, only a lesser evil, a necessary evil, for it is placed in the service of the good; evil is only apparent, for it is an integral part of the good. But once a hierarchical order enters into crisis ... a quite different picture emerges. Whereas before good was thought to govern evil, its contrary, now evil seems to have governed itself—by distancing itself, by putting itself outside of itself—with the result that the higher level, having been self-externalized, so to speak, takes on the aspect of the good. (Dupuy 2013: 5)

'Integral' after having been assimilated by and subordinated to the cosmic hierarchy of good and evil, or, alternatively, order and chaos. And if we look closely, we realize that contemporary discourse concerning capital punishment operates within the anthropological traces of the theological imaginary, the foundation stone of which was the scapegoat mechanism.

> This idea can be stated less abstractly if we consider the singular relationship...that unites murder and sacrifice in a society where sacrifice constitutes the founding ritual. In that case sacrifice *contains* the outbreak and spread of murder; though it is in one sense just another murder, it promises to put an end to violence. Capital punishment performs the same function in certain criminal justice systems. But when the religious order ('hierarchy') is overthrown by disorder and violence, when the administration of justice loses its transcendent authority, ritual killing can no longer be distinguished from murder. *Before* the onset of crisis, however, sacrifice was both murder and something other than murder. (Dupuy 2013: 5)

And once again we encounter the eternally recurrent truth of sacrifice: in order for the machinery to function correctly, meaning the production of generative unanimity, the entire process needs to be hidden behind an all-encompassing veil of collective *meconnaissance*, which, in the twenty-first century, is functionally little more than an act of moral deflection.

> If control over the ritual [of secular execution] is suddenly lost—say, because the executioner insults the person about to be hanged, as recently happened in Iraq when Saddam Hussein was put to death—the fragile distinction between a death sentence and an act of vengeance dissolves and it suddenly becomes clear to all that the whole point of the [profane] ritual is to say: 'This is not an act of vengeance!' There is nothing supernatural in any of this. It is human, all too human. (Dupuy 2013: 104)

Girard has grasped the essential point: in order for secular capital punishment to produce the cathartic restorative and re-integrative effects of the archaic human sacrifice of which it is the unacknowledged successor it must be re-conceptualized in the metaphysically undemanding terms of a profane moralism: that execution is 'Something other than murder,' for to fail to do so would be to invite the obvious conclusion that execution is tantamount to revenge which would bring into the blinding light of revelation that the death-row inmate really is a modern surrogate for the scapegoat and that we are all primitives. Which means the modernity is not really modern; not only are 'we' all too human, our greatest collective cultural conceit, the Enlightenment, is all too superstitious. *Aesthesis* in its most perfect form, with the result that

> Vocabulary is perhaps more revealing here than judicial theories … Our penal system operates according to principles of justice that are in no real conflict with the concept of revenge. The same principle is at work in all systems of violent retribution. Either the principle is just, and justice is therefore inherent in the idea of vengeance, or there is no justice to be found anywhere. He who exacts his own justice is said to 'take the law into his own hands.' There is no difference of principle between private and public vengeance; but on the social level, the difference is enormous. Under the public system, an act of vengeance is no longer avenged; the process is terminated, the danger of escalation averted. (Girard, 1977: 15–16)

Dupuy makes it clear that Girard sees contemporary forms of secular execution in terms of the anthropological schemas of self-externalization accomplished through the theodicy of moral hierarchy which has historically been expressed through the theological construct of the *katechon.*

> Girard's hypothesis (as he calls it) asserts that the sacred was produced by a mechanism of self-externalization, so that violence, in projecting itself beyond the domain of human control by means of ritual practices and systems of rules, prohibitions, and obligations, became self-limiting. On this view, the sacred is identified with a 'good' form of institutionalized violence that holds in check 'bad' anarchic violence.[11] The desacralization of the world that modernity brought about is built upon a kind of knowledge, or suspicion perhaps, that gradually insinuated itself in human thinking—the suspicion that good and bad violence are not opposites, but actually one and the same; that is, at bottom, there is no difference between them … we know that evil is capable of self-transcendence, and by virtue of just this, capable of containing itself within limits—and so, too, of averting total destruction. (Dupuy 2013: 15–16)

It is a telling accident that Prejean follows this same logic, her mis-recognized imitation only adding to the theological significance of Girard's insight. Although Sister Helen clearly seeks the spiritual redemption (*metanoia*) of both of the death-row inmates she was entrusted to as their spiritual advisor, *Dead Man Walking* cannot help, it seems, to repeat the biblical dichotomy of the 'Good Thief'—or in this case, the 'Good Murderer'—who undergoes a sacralizing death and whose execution secures an at least partial reconciliation, and a 'Bad Murderer' whose profane killing by the State is marred by the stain of an incomplete conversion. In this case, Elmo Patrick Sonnier is the good murderer who voluntarily accepts sacralization, whereas Robert Lee Willie is the bad murderer who refuses sacralization, as he makes clear: '"I want you to know I got my pride. I'm not grovelin' in front of these people. I don't grovel to nobody," he says' (Prejean, 2013: 163). And just in case

[11] The *katechon* as integrated hierarchy. 'The *katechon* restrains evil by containing it, by keeping it, by holding it within itself. It confronts evil, but from within it, by hosting it and welcoming it, to the point of binding its own necessity to the presence of evil. It limits evil, defers it, but does not eradicate it: because if it did, it would also eliminate itself. We could go so far as to say that the *katechon*—its constitutive juridical principle—opposes the absence of law by taking up inside itself, and thereby, in some way, giving it form, rule, and norm. The *katechon* antinomically assigns a *nomos* [order] to anomie, thus restraining its catastrophic unfolding' (Roberto Esposito qtd. Palaver, 2020: 17). Which paradoxically renders the *katechon* a *pharmakon*, an occult remedy that derives its regenerative force from its power to destroy; 'It is the antibody that protects the Christian body from what threatens it. By containing iniquity, the *katechon* forbids its annihilation, removing it from the final battle: the *katechon* nurtures and is nurtured by iniquity, just as the body is nurtured by the antidote necessary to its survival' (Roberto Esposito qtd. Palaver, 2020: 17).

we miss it, Prejean provides us with this theo-poetic gem: 'Pat died in spring when the flowers and trees and grass were exploding with life. If Robert dies, he will die in winter' (Prejean, 2013: 159). Meaning that since Patrick died with the coming of explosive vegetation,[12] Patrick has symbolically achieved the suspension of the crisis of undifferentiation, neutralized through his sacralization, that manifests as the cosmic regeneration that is the Spring; in contrast, Robert Lee, because he will not fully repent, fails to overcome the crisis of difference and the possibility of authentic restoration remains in doubt.[13]

Which fits perfectly with Arens' account of religious themes as the sub-text to modern secular cinema: all 'high concept' or 'artistic' films carry within them 'potential alien prophecies' which are secularized fragments of religious consciousness (Gerhard Larcher qtd. Arens, 1998: 25 n 12) and he highlights the profane/divine dichotomy utilized in *Dead Man Walking* that bestow upon both book and film a 'prophetic quality': the death-row guard shouts out 'Dead man walking!' while Sister Helen quietly intones Isaiah 43: 2: 'Fear not, for I redeemed you. I called you by your name, for you are Mine.' Arens then correctly goes on to identify this liminal prophetic quality with the apocalyptic sensibility of a transformative unmasking that renders the indistinct everyday into the shockingly distinctive unknown, or the alien.

> The 'prophetic quality' of this film emerges by way of its disclosure or apocalypse of capital punishment as a quasi-religious 'ritual of killing' or a secular liturgy of death; it becomes clear by the representation of proximity as redemptive action: in the unusual proximity which overcomes any kind of professional distance, even a murderer may become the needy and vulnerable 'other,' for whom I am responsible....The prophetic quality of *Dead Man Walking* is further shown by its introduction of a fascinating—although implicit—anthropology and even theology of the 'face' ...it underlines [Emmanuel Levinas'] most important insight, namely that the face of the other discloses his or her vulnerability and commands not to kill him or her. It is the 'epiphany' of the face, specially the 'naked' face in all its humility and misery, that prevents murder, including pubic licensed killing. Does it happen by chance that the face of a convict is hidden before execution? In the epiphany of the face the transcendence of the other becomes visible and 'calling'. At the same time, the face of the other points to the dimension of encompassing transcendence, that is to the 'Other'. (Arens, 1998: 25–26)

The cinematic *Dead Man Walking* 'is a film on public as well as religiously licensed killing' (Arens, 1998: 21); its central trope, like that of the book, is the moral and theological ambivalence of the alien prophecy that is the narrative counterpart to the metaphysical ambivalence of the scapegoat as *pharamakon*, the bringer and expeller of disease: ritualistic death as regenerative sacrifice but now accompanied by a symbolical restitutive payment of the 'debt' incurred by the criminal and owed to the victim's heirs.

---

[12] Which bears more than a passing resemblance to Truman Capote's treatment of Nancy Cutter as Persephone reborn in *In Cold Blood*. See Chap. 10, above.

[13] Prejean signals this in the final sentences of the main text; after a rousing, and seemingly unanswerable, exhortation to abolish capital punishment, she adds, 'Since the publication of this book in 1993 the states of Kansas (1994) and New York (1995) have reinstated the death penalty and Congress has enacted the Violent Crime Control and Law Enforcement Act (1994), which expands federal crimes punishable by death to about 60 offenses' (Prejean, 2013: 245).

> Such killing within a legal framework is viewed from one side as legitimate vengeance which is necessary not only to maintain public order and to deter possible criminals but also to help the families of the victims find psychic relief. This public and religiously licensed killing thus is held up as performing a healing or redemptive function. Knowing that those who raise the sword are killed by the sword should contribute to spiritual peace, particularly for those who are mostly concerned by the loss of their beloved ones; at the same time a public peace, broken by any brutal murder, is restored. (Arens, 1998: 21)

In the end everything leads back to *katharsis* and *meatanoia*, which, for Girard (and Aristotle) is how to should be.

> There is, however, a certain ambivalence that has to be considered here, based on the fact that we, the public, are watching a film in which we become witnesses of an execution. We, who normally have no chance of getting access to this kind of forbidden fare are enabled by the movie to enter the [death chamber's] witness box. This precisely is part of the film's attraction. It allows us to get some voyeuristic satisfaction of watching killing and at the same time gives us the moral permission to do so by making us public witnesses. *Dead Man Walking* indeed enables us to become morally 'justified' spectators of public licensed killing in the electronic age…. By showing an execution, *Dead Man Walking* also mimetically repeats and exploits the 'fascinosum et tremendum' or the sacred morbidity that formerly in Europe attracted crowds to public executions. (Arens, 1998: 27)

For the death-row inmate to provide the necessary element of *katharsis* (for without it execution would literally make no cultural sense), she must correspond to the archaic and collectively repressed model of the scapegoat, which means that she must be invested with an element of metaphysical significance however misunderstood in contemporary culture. Which means that she must possess the characteristics of the *pharmakon*, the pre-modern template of what Arens defines as the bearer of an alien prophecy. Which means that the condemned must possess a requisite element of *authenticity*, a visceral connection with the irreplaceable Real, an objective correspondence with the forgotten thing that is summoned back into being at the same moment that its revenant-like return is being denied. Elmo Patrick Sonnier and Robert Lee Willie may or may not have possessed authenticity; we cannot know. But what we can, and do, know with certainty is that double murderer Gary Gilmore (1940–1977) was the authentic alien prophet, the metaphysical scapegoat as executed criminal literally made flesh, ambivalence personified. His true-life story was the genuine 'aesthetics of overwhelming,' *aesthesis* brought to life and then killed for being so. And because of all of this, Gary Gilmore was American liberalism's most repulsive *anathema.*

11.2 Authenticity as Metaphysical Desire: John Rawls and the Violence of Neutrality

If absolutely everything can be made completely visible, then one no longer knows what one is looking at, which is just another of saying: one can longer distinguish the true from the false (Wilson, 2018). Contrary to popular opinion, the technological foundation of modernity, science, does not optimally perform its world-historical function as mere technology (*Technik*, *techne*), but rather as a *Weltanschaung*, a total(-izing) way of viewing the world, what Martin Heidegger called a 'frame': modern science's method of representing Being 'pursues and entraps nature as a calculable coherence of forces,' ordering its experiments 'precisely for the purpose of asking whether and how nature reports itself when set up in this way' (Heidegger, 1977: 21). The frame of science is premised upon the implicitly nihilistic substitution of teleological causality (the 'end' or 'purpose') with an exclusionary mechanical causality, yielding the de-centering result that causality 'now displays neither the character of that occasioning that brings forth nor the nature of the *causa efficiens* [that 'which brings about the effect that is the finished' object or item], let alone that of the *causa formalis* ['the form, the shape into which the material enters'] (Heidegger, 1977: 23, 6). At the same time, and to the same degree, science as 'enframing', with its plethora of optical imagery, demands an unconditional representation of Reality as transparency that ultimately objectifies the Human Subject: 'Enframing is the gathering together that belongs to that setting-upon which sets upon man [sic] and puts him in position to reveal the real, in the mode of ordering, as standing-reserve.[14] As the one who is challenged forth in this way, man stands within the essential realm of Enframing' (Heidegger, 1977: 24). It is not the case that the 'natural' Self is subsumed or controlled by an external and invasive technology, but rather that science is itself the sole cultural means by which the objective truth of the Self can be rendered known or 'revealed,' thereby precluding in advance the interiority, or 'sensibility,' of the Human Subject, that which historically has been denoted as *authenticity*, romanticism's model-of-desire for Camus.[15]

What do we mean by authenticity? I would provisionally define it this way: that the thing, person, object, or event that inspires within us a sense of unmediated and direct contact with the 'Real' (also known as the 'sublime' or the 'Absolute') that is itself, somehow, identical to the subjective feelings that it generates within us; in other words, there is an assumed correspondence between the objective and the subjective, which is known as the phenomenological conceit. My own very rough definition equates with the far more nuanced one offered by Marshall Berman; 'I have used the word "authenticity" to designate a whole family of aspirations and ideals which are central to the cultural life of our age. … our vocabulary overflows with expressions which express a persistent and intense concern with *being oneself*" (Berman, 2009: xxiii). The concept has an impressive pedigree.

> The search for authenticity, nearly everywhere we find it in modern times, is bound up with a radical rejection of things as they are. It begins with an insistence that the social and political structures men live in are keeping the self stifled, chained down, locked up. It argues that only if the old structure is renovated, or if a new one is built from the ground up—or if the old one is wrecked and nothing put in its place, so that men may live without any structure at all—only then can the self come into its own. It asks what is to be done, and tries to do it. Thus the desire for authenticity has emerged in modern society as one of the most politically explosive of human impulses. (Berman, 2009: xvii)

---

[14] As an abjectly instrumentalized object of exploitation.

[15] See above, Chap. 9.

What we might call the problem of authenticity first arose in the eighteenth century as a means of resolving a fundamental fissure within the world-view of the Enlightenment, namely the apparent breach between Newton's deterministic universe (Berman, 2009: 11) and the cultural and political imperative to preserve the value of the Human, expressed in philosophical terms as Humanism. It is important to note that the resultant cult of authenticity was itself the product of a two-fold religious crisis: the replacement of a personal deity with mechanistic causality engineered by Newton and Laplace and, as there is no longer a clear demarcation between the specifically human and the generic object, a parallel loss of the human soul/psyche. Newtonianism, however, proved itself a rather double-edged sword. While the 'mechanistic argument ... cut boldly through the arcane intricacies of the hierarchic scholastic image of the world and projected sharply and clearly a vision of Nature devoid of all normative content,' it simultaneously 'opened up the way to a heightened sympathy with many forms of human life and action which up to then had been condemned categorically as "contrary to nature": for *nothing* could be contrary to nature now' (Berman, 2009: 11–12). The morally neutral universe called forth the specter of moral relativism and the libertine possibilities of uncensored internal mediation, but it undercut the universalism necessary for effective strategies of political resistance: if the universe is an ethical blank on what basis can we know with certainty the presence of injustice?[16] And if all cultures, and their accompanying moral systems, are relative, how can we formulate a unifying discourse of political resistance to that *nomos* that is 'truly' unjust?

> As long as empiricist attitudes and arguments could contribute to the defence of [the] *status quo*, the liberating force of empiricism was neutralized. The possibilities of human experience might indeed be indefinite, but a repressed humanity—even if happily repressed—was clearly in no position to exploit them. The more the *philosophes* explored and illuminated the world, the more they heightened the contrast between what man could achieve in an ideal world and what men did achieve in the empirical one. In practice men were kept from taking possession of a world which in theory had been declared their own. (Berman, 2009: 15)

The solution hit upon, which Berman locates within Montesquieu's *The Persian Letters* (1721) (Berman, 2009: 3–53) is the formulation of a *right to authenticity*, essentially an attempt to reconcile a reductive empiricism (the 'Is') with a universalist normativity (the 'Ought') via a primitive form of social anthropology: 'The brute fact of human enslavement is a living refutation of the premise of human freedom on which [moral] virtue must rest' (Berman, 2009: 43). As Jean-Jacques Rousseau opined, 'To be something, to be himself, and always at one with himself, a man must act as he speaks; he must always be decisive as to what course he should take, he must take that course vigorously and follow it to the end' (Jean-Jacques Rousseau qtd. Berman, 2009: 189). Human freedom is nothing other than 'being oneself,' an

[16] Berman is unyielding on this point: although 'empiricism had many liberating effects, its consequences for individualism proved to be profoundly ambiguous. For if, on the one hand, it overthrew authoritarian claims to legitimacy through Divine Law, on the other it undercut liberal criticisms of existing authority in the name of Natural Rights' (Berman, 2009: 13). From the perspective of metaphysical Realism, the Age of Enlightenment became ontologically 'unmoored' at the moment of its conception.

inalienable right, natural or otherwise, to practically realize one's individual or unique nature in uncompromising opposition to the false 'universal' nature; no social system 'can provide human happiness, unless it posits, and its government guarantees, a basic human right: the right of every man *to be himself*' (Berman, 2009: 16). Accordingly, it is

> Only when men retain their natural individuality—their authenticity—can they participate in nature as a whole, and enjoy the forms of happiness that nature has made available to man in the world. A man can be happy only if he can be—*himself*. But a society which deprives every man of the primary source of happiness cannot hope to satisfy its members; hence it must inevitably disintegrate from within. (Berman, 2009: 23)

The political right to authenticity—or, expressed in a more radical way, *the authentic as a political right*— provokes a parallel existential shift toward sensibility, the invention of 'a new concept of inwardness' which is a recipe for Girard's crisis of metaphysical desire, the mimetic pathology of 'to be or not to be' taking the form of a political program, a point not lost on Leslie H. Fiedler: 'One is almost tempted to say, by the invention of a new kind of self, a new kind of mind; for what has been happening since the eighteenth century seems more like the development of a new organ than the mere finding of a new way to describe old experience' (Fiedler, 1984: 32–33). The outward expression of this inwardness demands the cultivation of revolt appositional to an externally mediated empirical reality and social consensus. At the same time, sensibility manifests itself through a number of highly ritualistic, almost stereotypical, channels. These include, but are not limited to, intensity (the heightening of the desire for a liberation that is an unveiling, both as the cause and the effect of authenticity); sincerity (the Self is 'real', both as a fact and as a value, the 'highest good'); an assumed enmity between Self and Society (in contemporary terms: the personal is the political); and, most importantly, the privately Promethean effort of self-creation and recovery of alienated essence as constituting of a specifically modern form of desire, which, of course, would be wholly original and, therefore, *anti*-mimetic. Somewhat ominously, this desire for self-transcendence often assumes the form of a longing for self-sacrifice, the voluntary movement toward death (or the voluntary assumption of the risk of death) as the authenticating master-sign of both sincerity and intensity; as Sartre famously expressed it in reference to the French Resistance '"each and every individual choice was authentic because it was made in the presence of death"' (Sartre qtd. Hartman, 2002: 238 n 8).

As Geoffrey Hartman has correctly observed, '"Spirit" and "authenticity" are word concepts that cannot be saved from their own pathos' (Hartman, 2002: 3). Hartman's book *Scars of the Spirit: The Struggle Against Inauthenticity* (2002) is most germane to my purposes precisely because it highlights the post-religious spirituality of sensibility as being central to internal mediation: 'In non-theocratic societies, authenticity now signifies a moral strength *not* based primarily on formal or institutional authority' (Hartman, 2002: viii). From the niche that it has assumed within modern art, especially literature, 'We fantasize a public mode of expression whose truth will make us free' (Hartman, 2002: 51), authenticity demanding a return, if not to religion, then at least to the theological imaginary, an under-appreciated situation compounded by the historical rootedness of literary criticism within theological exegesis (Hartman, 2002: 211). For Hartman—along with all of those who ground the legitimacy of art upon the revelation of the authentic (or the 'the impossible real' as Maurice Blanchot termed it)[17]—religion is understood as inseparable from Messianism; the 'continued presence, and recrudescence, of religious politics aims at a state of ultimate transparency, and stops at nothing, paradoxically not even at dissemblance, to unveil a Manichaean world, an anatomy of reality as stark and judgmental as the Apocalypse' (Hartman, 2002: 51). Although startling this makes perfect sense: authenticity is, paradoxically, the substitute for and the continuation of religion, or, more prosaically, the yearning desire for transcendence and *metanoia*, the elimination of the false 'old' self in favor of the authentic 'new' self. Therefore, the unconditional desire for revolt, replicating the historical logic of its origins, must necessarily yield to the messianic impulse, even if this is self-consciously understood in wholly secular terms. And this, in turn, carries with it an undeniable political message: authenticity is the living negation of the social contract and all contractarian theories of State and Society. But now comes the really big problem and, to no one's surprise, it is a Girardian one, the evolution of the crisis of undifferentiation into its specifically modern form. Jurgen Habermas has intuitively divined this.

> Now, metaphysical or religious worldviews are at the very least permeated with answers to basic ethical questions; they articulate in an exemplary fashion collective identities and guide individual plans of life. Hence, world-views are measured more by the *authenticity* of the life styles they shape than by the truth of the statements they admit. Because such doctrines are 'comprehensive' in precisely the sense that they offer interpretations of the world as a whole, they cannot be expressed completely in sentences that admit of truth and they do not form a symbolic system that can be true or false as such. (Habermas, 1995: 126)

If totalizing, or 'comprehensive,' theories of social formation serve as the basis of cultural identities mediated by sensibility and subjectivity, then the quest for authenticity becomes the spawning ground of modernity's version of metaphysical desire: no one can ever rally be authentic for everyone is trying to be the original or true Self in the manner prescribed by the theories of modernity which is a cultural imperative derived from a collective movement. The expression of this paradox in its simplest terms would be: the desire for authenticity is the response to a directive. Present here is 'a normative resonance' which unconsciously assumes the form of an imperative; insofar as it 'relates to the integral role that religion plays in the life of a person of faith' the specifically modern 'totalizing trait of a mode of believing that infuses the very pores of daily life run counter ... to any flimsy switchover of religiously rooted convictions onto a *different* cognitive basis' (Habermas qtd. Lafont, 2009: 133). Which means that the cultural imperative to be authentic requires the marginalization of any cultural institution that impedes the group's ability to attain true individuality. What we are facing then is a secularist version of religion at war with its double which it mis-recognizes as irrationality but is, in the blinding truth of *aesthesis*, revealed to be the modern variant of the crisis of undifferentiation: one can only verify one's true identity, the authentic Self, through the scapegoating

---

[17] Maurice Blanchot qtd. Hartman, 2002: 25.

of anyone and anything that impedes the realization of a radical subjectivity as truth. The social contract, as Hartman quite rightly observes, requires negotiation which, in turn, requires compromise, and 'compromise is not possible when political strife touches religious and especially messianic convictions' (Hartman, 2002: 51). In Hartman's eschatological re-telling of the story of intensity-within-authenticity, cultural prophesy, 'when imbued with such apocalyptic fervour, is based on an idea of authenticity or spiritual fulfilment that is absolute and brooks neither ambiguity nor critique,' it being notoriously difficult 'to nourish faith by evidence of things not seen.'

> There is a temptation to allow a coercive and purely ideological transparency to compensate for that lack of visibility. The tardiness of the messiah—the unreal presence, or simply the unreality of the spirit, its inadequate human and social embodiment—prompts cycles of rage and frustration[18] that lead to renewed catastrophe. From that perspective, history turns out to be not the story of human liberation but one wounding after another, a narrative of scars left in the wake of spiritual violence. (Hartman, 2002: 51–52)

In the face of so much annihilating authenticity what is the American jurist to do? Fortunately, John Rawls (1921–2002) provides the American jurist with the perfect answer: re-formulate the official discourse of the social contract which is *public reason* in such a way as to render religion, the sincerest and most intense form of authenticity, wholly inoperative as a social force.

11.3 John Rawls and the Problem of Religion or, Isotropic Men of No Qualities

In truth, there is only one truly essential question concerning the origin of politics. Is politics: (i) the structural enabling of cooperation (most commonly understood as 'commerce') which is predicated upon friendship, or the presence of the Friend, or is it (ii) the ritualistic proscription of animosity, which both presupposes and requires the omnipresence of enmity, the existential threat of the Enemy?[19] In the 1960s, with the rise of the new legal criticism that rejected the twin pillars of legal realism—positivism and utilitarianism—things took a remarkable turn, largely under the influence of anti-realist jurisprudence theorist extraordinaire, John Rawls, whose mission in life appeared to be the act as the antithesis of Felix S. Cohen[20]: for Rawls new criticism 'countered a coherence theory of truth coming from a logical positivism that tried to purify ordinary as well as literary language in order to produce a relatively transparent medium' (Rawls, 1999: 13). In animosity, Rawls sought to

[18] In Girard's terms, violence and *ressentiment*.

[19] As Saint Augustine expressed it, 'The human race is, more than any other species, social by nature and quarrelsome by perversion' (Augustine qtd. Palaver, 2013: 37; *City of God*, 508, XII, 28).

[20] See Chap. 6, above.

recover the oft repressed radicality of empiricism as a systematic theory of knowledge and attempted to ground the new form legal reasoning as the maximization of outcomes emanating from the 'correctly' formed system of constitutional order. Rawls formulated his principal maxim in this way: 'I propose that in public reason comprehensive doctrines of truth or right[21] be replaced by an idea of the politically reasonable addressed to citizens as citizens' (Rawls, 1999: 132). Which meant that the 'new' criticism was not really new if we mean that under Rawls legal theory remained bridled by wholly normative considerations, which were now the exoteric outcomes of constitutional governance rather than the esoteric moral biases of legal realism and its social scientific formulae of truth. But not, of course, any form of constitutional governance; rather, the only form of constitutional governance that was adequate to the task of jurisprudence in a profane universe was the one that provided the optimal opportunities to generate the required normative outcomes, which was to say a liberal-pluralist *nomos*. 'In this essay I am concerned with the normative conception of democratic governance' (Rawls, 1999: 131 n 3), Rawls wrote in his ground-breaking piece 'The Idea of Public Reason Revisited,' making no bones about it. The visceral heart of Rawls' enterprise was what he identified as a very particular notion of public reason.

> The idea of public reason ... belongs to a conception of a well-ordered constitutional democratic society. The form and content of this reason—the way it is understood by citizens and how it interprets their political relationship—are part of the idea of democracy itself. This is because a basic feature of democracy is the fact of reasonable pluralism—the fact that a plurality of conflicting reasonable comprehensive doctrines,[22] religious, philosophical, and moral, is the normal result of its culture of free institutions.[23] (Rawls, 1999: 131)

The key innovation that Rawls made was that he took as the cardinal principle of public reason, a pure form of neutrality, or neutralism, that was both substantive and procedural, his corpus forming a vast hermetically enclosed circle in which democracy generates neutrality which generates public reason which generates democracy in a perpetual cycle of mutual re-enforcement. But at the center of this perpetually self-validating neutralism was a mechanism for generating acts of political exclusion.

> Central to the idea of public reason is that it neither criticizes nor attacks any comprehensive doctrine, religious or non-religious, except insofar as that doctrine is incompatible with the essentials of public reason and a democratic polity. The basic requirement is that a reasonable doctrine accepts a constitutional democratic regime and its companion idea of legitimate law. (Rawls, 1999: 132)

And the cardinal principle of the cardinal principle (neutrality) is that absolutely anything can be permitted provided that the 'thing' in question in no way proves to be

---

[21] A not so subtle jab at Cohen, Benjamin N. Cardozo, Louis D. Brandeis and Oliver Wendell Holmes. See Chap. 6, above.

[22] Or 'comprehensive views of all kinds...'.

[23] Alternatively, the 'background culture'; this is Rawlsian shorthand for the 'culture of civil society' (Rawls, 1999: 134, 129–180) which can act as a sort of extra-constitutional supplement to public reason; 'Matters of basic justice relate to the basic structure of society and so would concern questions of basic economic and social justice and other things not covered by a constitution' (Rawls, 1999: 133 n 7).

a stumbling-block to neutrality. From this follows what should come as no surprise to anyone: of all of the constitutional systems in History the one truly universal, and universalizable, order, or *nomos*, is American liberalism. Why? Because American liberalism is the only one (or, at least, the very best) that can create a background culture of public reason that yields a population of *reasonable citizens*. And what are reasonable citizens? The ones who have internalized liberalism and regard it as a body of self-evident truths.

> Citizens are reasonable when, viewing one another as free and equal in a system of social cooperation of generations, they are prepared to offer one another fair terms of cooperation according to what they consider the most reasonable conceptions of political justice[24]; and when they agree to act on these terms, even at the cost of their own interests in particular situations, provided that other citizens also accept those terms. (Rawls, 1999: 136)

Expressed schematically, we would say that public reason equates with reasonable citizens who are committed to political justice which means that the outcome of deliberative decision-making complies with all of the perquisites of political legitimacy which ensures the normative and procedural paramountcy of American liberalism's highest goods, equality and reciprocity, so that in the end everyone will be friends and no one will be an enemy. Or, more precisely, no one shall be permitted to be an enemy by the properly ordered *nomos* that maximizes friendship.

> Hence the idea of political legitimacy based on the criterion of reciprocity says: Our exercise of political power is proper only when we sincerely believe that the reasons we would offer for our political actions—were we to state them as government officials—are sufficient, and we also reasonably think that other citizens might also reasonably accept those reasons. … note that [reciprocity's] role is to specify the nature of the political relation in a constitutional democratic regime as one of civic friendship. (Rawls, 1999: 137)

If, as Rawls would have it, reciprocity equates with civic friendship then it follows that the un-civic/un-friendly liminal citizens constitute both a political and a legal problem. Rawls, to his credit, does not flinch.

> The idea of public reason specifies at the deepest level the basic moral and political values that are to determine a constitutional democratic government's relation to its citizens and their relation to one another. In short, it concerns how the political relation is to be understood. Those who reject constitutional democracy with its criterion of reciprocity will of course reject the very idea of public reason. For them the political relation may be that of friend or foe, to those of a particular religious or secular community or those who are not; or it may be a relentless struggle to win the world for the whole truth. Political liberalism does not engage those who think this way. The zeal to embody the whole truth in politics is incompatible with an idea of public reason that belongs with democratic citizenship. (Rawls, 1999: 132–133)

The implications of this are obvious: a large segment, perhaps in certain instances the majority, of the civic population must be excluded from the political process

---

[24] And of course Rawls maintains the sacrosanct primacy of judicial review, the courts themselves one of the primary channelers of public reason; 'Constitutional essentials concern questions about what political rights and liberties … may reasonably be included in a written constitution, when assuming that the constitution may be interpreted by a supreme court, or some similar body' (Rawls, 1999: 133 n 7).

because their 'thought' can in no way constitute a form of public reason properly defined. Which, in a single misjudged maneuver, gives the entire game of secular and progressive liberalism away as Richard Mailey correctly observes.

> [L]iberalism's key gesture vis-à-vis intra-state politics[25] is its proponent's tendency to portray their preferences as requirements of a binding normative order—a conception of constitutional morality or reason, say—that prevents the contrary preferences of many decent and ultimately reasonable people[26] from having any influence on the course of democratic law-making. (Mailey, 2020: 150–151)

In the final analysis liberalism is far less unique, or epoch making, than its multiple conceits would lead us to believe, for the liberal, no less than the pre-liberal, anti-liberal, or post-liberal, actively requires the presence of a rival to scapegoat.

11.3.1 Objection I: The Un-Civil 'Friend or Foe' Distinction of Carl Schmitt

Unfortunately for Rawls, perhaps, many of the greatest and most effective critiques of liberal politics and jurisprudence have come from those who are aligned with, or have chosen to be the champions of, those poor un-civic persons for whom 'the political relation may be that of friend or foe, to those of a particular religious or secular community or those who are not' or who just happen to be existentially committed to 'a relentless struggle to win the world for the whole truth.' One such is Carl Schmitt[27] of whom, it would be fair to say, is the most anti-Rawlsian legal scholar imaginable, just as Rawls is the most anti-Schmittean legal theorist possible. Whatever the merits of Schmitt's state-of-emergency decisionist constitutionalism, he adroitly avoids one of the most serious pitfalls of Rawls. Whereas the latter adopts a strictly a-historical approach to constitutional governance, the former's thought exhibits a deep and rich historical and anthropological consciousness, articulating a theory of the evolution of the liberal-pluralist *nomos* as a secularized adaptation of the primitive essence of the scapegoat mechanism: the friend-enemy grouping.

> The specific political distinction to which political actions and motives can be reduced is that between friend and enemy (Schmitt, 2007: 260)....The friend and enemy concepts are to be understood in their concrete and existential sense, not as metaphors or symbols...The enemy is not merely any competitor or just any partner of a conflict in general. He is also not the private adversary whom one hates. An enemy exists only when, at least potentially, one fighting collectivity of people confronts a similar collectivity. (Schmitt, 2007: 27–28)

---

[25] And *inter-state* politics as well; see below.

[26] Mailey glides over the self-referential nature of liberal reason: anyone who is not liberal, by definition, cannot be either 'decent' or 'reasonable', for, if they were, how could a liberalism that is identical to both neutralism and public reason sacrifice them? There must be a reason for such an act of exclusion.

[27] See Chap. 4, above.

Contra Aristotle and Kant, 'All law is "situational law"' (Schmitt, 2005: 13) which, if true, would tend to draw the reader toward the intuitive understanding of legal and political rivalry as a form of combat, a surrogate for warfare. In a manner perfectly antithetical to that of Rawls, Schmitt asserts that politics is not fundamentally about rational negotiations among groups of friends but the performative exercise of ritualistically prescribed forms of animosity, an existential equivalent of warfare that attains its sincerest form of authenticity in the state of exception, the apocalyptic moment when the Schmittean 'veil of ignorance' is torn away and the identity of the true friend and the true enemy is revealed in an *aesthesis*-like moment of overwhelming disclosure. A German thinker, Schmitt identifies the existential with the authentic so that the existential intensity of true politics, the friend-enemy division, constitutes authenticity in its most intense form for it is the point when everyone decides who they truly are—albeit as part of a collective,[28] which repeats the paradox of the modern conception of the authentic as an ersatz religious value.

> The 'existential justification' for political violence is for Schmitt an empirical description just as much as it is a normative recommendation. ... For each individual, the conflict is rooted in one or the other opposing group, and this fact is itself normative in the sense that it has consequences on the normative level. Membership in a group imposes duties that constitute the individual as a moral being. To say that the justification for conflicts among groups is existential and that they impose themselves on individuals is to say that, in relation to those conflicts, individuals are bound by moral obligations to help and support those who are their 'friends'. Thus, the existential justification corresponds to a 'meta-norm': that of fulfilling a set obligations. (Dumouchel, 2015: 76)

The notion that the 'political is the most intense and extreme antagonism, and every concrete antagonism becomes that much more political the closer it approaches the most extreme point, that of the friend-enemy grouping' (Schmitt, 2007: 29) where everyone decides upon them and then publicly proclaim their own true, or authentic, subjectivity can be translated into the Rawlsian equivalent of 'reasonable' versus 'unreasonable' citizen, or the 'true' versus the 'false'. And, like Rawls, Schmitt can also be expressed schematically: the state of exception is nothing other than law in its 'purest' form for what 'matters for the reality of legal life is who decides' (Schmitt, 2005: 34). Law is always the result of an historically grounded exercise of some kind of power and the source of the constitutionalist *nomos*, sovereignty, goes to that One person or institution who/that '*decides on the exception*' (Schmitt, 2005: 5). History prevails, not a-contextual axiomatic reasoning, for only this definition of sovereignty can 'do justice' to the sacred thing's liminal nature, for 'a borderline concept is not a vague concept, but one pertaining to the outermost sphere' (Schmitt, 2005: 5) of onto-political existence, the existential intensity of true authenticity which is when all notions of normal or banal politics disintegrate.

> It is precisely the exception that makes relevant the subject of sovereignty, that is, the whole question of sovereignty...The decision on the exception is a decision in the true sense of the word. Because a general norm, as represented by an ordinary legal prescription, can

---

[28] Or a 'crowd' as Girard would have it, that thing that spontaneously forms in order to decide upon the identity of the scapegoat in an act of unifying animosity.

> never encompass a total decision, the decision that a real exception exists cannot therefore be entirely derived from the norm. (Schmitt, 2005: 6)

So that in perfect opposition to Rawls the core notion of political and legal decision-making is based neither on reciprocity nor fairness nor cooperation, but on a deliberately *anti*-consensual approach to public reason, the historically embedded hyper-partisan State the exact and perfect opposite of neutrality. In an even stronger sense, being neutral is the very condition that every State must avoid if it wishes to continue its physical existence.

> If such action[29] is not subject to controls, if it is not hampered in some way by checks and balances, as is the case in a liberal constitution, then it is clear who the sovereign is. *He decides whether there is an extreme emergency as well as what must be done to eliminate it.* Although he stands outside the normally valid legal system, he nevertheless belongs to it, for it is he who must decide whether the constitution [the *nomos*] needs to be suspended in its entirety. (Schmitt, 2005: 7)

Decisionism is the fail-safe mechanism of the Schmittean constitutional order for the decider is the one who is able to judge that normal conditions—the everyday negotiations of the well-ordered liberal citizenry—no longer reflects reality after the announcement of the presence of the enemy.

> The norm requires a homogenous medium...There exists no norm that is applicable to chaos. *For a legal order to make sense, a normal situation must exist, and he is sovereign who definitely decides whether this normal situation actually exists...The decision parts here from the legal norm, and (to formulate it paradoxically) authority proves that to produce law it need not be based on law.* (Schmitt, 2005: 13)

The historical moment at which political violence constitutes a form of un-normal legitimacy is the essence of Schmitt's concept of the political which, unsurprisingly, directly corresponds to the modern cult of subjectivity, the ego attempting to manifest itself as an authentic mode of being. Schmitt, no less than Rawls, is engaged in meta-normative legal reasoning, and, to a degree that is somewhat unnerving, directly anticipates him. As the Friend-Enemy grouping is the essence of politics, then the 'Enemy' must necessarily be a *public actor*; 'The enemy is solely the public enemy, because everything that has a relationship to such a collectivity of men, particularly to a whole nation, becomes public by virtue of such a relationship' (Schmitt, 2007: 28). Throughout his early (pre-1945) work, Schmitt is adamant that authentic, and authenticating, friend-enemy conflict cannot occur within private space but requires the performative display of subjectivity; 'A private person has no political enemies. Such a declaration can at most say that he would like to place himself outside the political community to which he belongs and continue to live as a private individual only' (Schmitt, 2007: 51). This allows two generalizations to be drawn; the first is that Schmitt's concept of authentic politics both universalizes and valorizes warfare, so that genuine politics is not merely a substitute for violence but is the foundation of violence in its most intense and authentic form.

---

[29] The decision on the existence of the exception that is identical to the revelation of the identity of the enemy.

> It would be ludicrous to believe that a defenseless people has nothing but friends, and it would be a deranged calculation that the enemy could perhaps be touched by the absence of a resistance…If a people no longer possesses the energy or the will to maintain itself in the sphere of politics, the latter will not thereby vanish from the world. Only a weak people will disappear. (Schmitt, 2007: 53)

The second, and for Rawls the far more lethal conclusion, is that the norm, or the historical period of relative peace between the periodic explosive irruptions of the politics of authenticity, is actually vital for the survival of ritualistic friend-enemy groupings because it is the temporal space within which the all-important statist activity of propaganda may occur. All 'political concepts, images, and terms have a polemical meaning. They are focused on a specific conflict and are bound to a concrete situation; the result (which manifests itself in war or revolution) is a friend-enemy grouping, and they turn into empty and ghost-like abstractions when this situation disappears' (Schmitt, 2007: 30). The similarity with Thomas Hobbes on this point is striking[30]; Hobbes' twinned notions of both the absolute nature of Sovereignty and the universal nature of war are closely mirrored in Schmitt's concept of the friend-enemy distinction, which also presupposes unconditional obedience to the command of the Sovereign.

> The state as the decisive political entity possesses an enormous power: the possibility of waging war and thereby publicly disposing of the lives of men. The *jus belli* [legal right of war] contains such a disposition. It implies a double possibility: the right to demand from its own members the readiness to die and unhesitatingly to kill enemies. The endeavor of a normal state consists above all in assuring total peace within the state and its territory. To create tranquility, security, and order and thereby establish the normal situation is the prerequisite for legal norms to be valid. Every norm presupposes a normal situation, and no norm can be valid in an entirely abnormal situation.[31] As long as the state is a political entity this requirement for internal peace compels it in critical situations to decide also upon the domestic enemy. (Schmitt, 2007: 46)

Schmitt was therefore committed to rejecting one of the signature concepts of classical liberalism, federalism, and republicanism: pluralism, or the division of the non-unitary State into subordinate groups and communities of social actors invested with inferior or derivative forms of sovereignty and quasi-autonomous self-governance (Wilson, 2006). For the first part of his career (1919–1945), Schmitt somewhat dogmatically argued that

> In reality there exists no political society or association but only one political entity—one political community. The ever-present possibility of a friend-and-enemy grouping suffices to forge a decisive entity which transcends the mere societal-associational groupings. The political entity is something specifically different, and vis-à-vis other associations, something decisive. (Schmitt, 2007: 45)

In his later writings, those following the destruction of the Third Reich and the Allied Occupation of Germany, Schmitt tended to replace the militaristic binary relationship of friend-enemy with the mimetic doubling of Self-Other. In large part this

30 See Chaps. 2 and 3, above.

31 The state of exception.

was a by-product of his emerging awareness of the beginning of the process known as globalization and the beginning of the slow erosion of traditional territorial notions of subjectivity, with the perhaps unintentional result that genuinely internal conflicts began to actively imitate the dynamics of the international relations, that which hitherto had been the sole prerogative of the authentic sovereigns, the deciders of the exception. While Schmitt always remained committed to the notion that 'Political unity is the highest unity—not because it is an omnipotent dictator, or because it levels out all other unities, but because it decides, and has the potential to prevent all other opposing groups from disassociating into a condition of extreme enmity—that is, into civil war' (Schmitt, 1999: 203), he realized that the logic of decisionism, the absolute sovereignty of whoever or whatever could practically decide the exception at any given historical moment, gave way to a radical pluralization of the concept of sovereignty, at least potentially; 'In the background of [the] contractual ethic' of the ostensibly unitary State of the normal, 'an ethic of civil war always lurks' (Schmitt, 1999: 207), which makes perfect sense if the state of exception, the naming of enemies and friends, is the foundational event of politics, just as Girard held scapegoating to be. Schmitt could simply not resist the onto-political significance of the radical contingency of History, forcing him to reverse course on the issue of pluralism: 'The political world is a pluriverse, not a universe' (Schmitt, 2008: 53).

> By virtue of this power over the physical life of men, the political community transcends all other associations or societies. Within the community, however, subordinate groupings of a secondary political nature could exist with their own or transferred rights, even with a limited *jus vitae ac necis* [law of life and needs; 'civil law'] over members of smaller groups. (Schmitt, 2008: 47–48)

Ultimately Schmitt was forced to conclude that, 'The unity of the State has always been a unity of social multiplicity' (Schmitt, 1999: 201).

> Because the political has no substance of its own, the point of the political can be reached from any terrain, and any social group, church, union, combine, nation, becomes political, and thereby of the state, as it approaches the point of highest intensity[32]...All human life, even the highest spiritual spheres, has in its historical realization at least the potential to become a State... (Schmitt, 1999: 203)

Which, in an extraordinarily uncanny way, leads Schmitt to a crypto-Rawlsian conclusion: that the individual dissenting un-reasonable citizen, a religious 'fanatic' if you will, a plurality of one who is authentically committed to 'a relentless struggle to win the world for the whole truth' as a way of expressing her unique subjectivity, can, in principle, be lawfully classified as an enemy of the State of reasonable citizens. The war of all against one. Which means that cultural enmity, no less than vigilantism, can become the private passion of the citizen of public animosity that can give rise to a liminal sort of political identity. Which leads directly to the second great objection to Rawls as formulated by Girardian scholar Paul Doumouchel: 'Justice as fairness is justice amongst those who are indifferent' (Dumouchel, 2003: 159).

---

[32] The naming of the enemy, or scapegoat pace Girard.

11.3.2 Objection II: Paul Dumouchel on the Violent Paradox of 'Those Who Exclude Themselves'

Violence, in all of its forms, is the mid-wife of History, and, by extension, both politics and religion as well as law. Despite its pretensions to the contrary, the secular liberal State is intrinsically violent, precisely because the Rawlsian solidarity of reasonable citizens is based upon a form of rationality that, while appearing axiomatic, is, in fact, wholly groundless, being governed by the historicity of the particular formations of social groupings that identify themselves as 'reasonable' or 'well ordered'. In a universe devoid of transcendental signifiers, how can one identify the reasonable citizen by any other means other than her opposition to the citizen that is unreasonable, or 'illiberal'? This is why, as Dumouchel has argued in a supremely anti-Rawlsian manner, the secular contractual State can never really be done with violence, even if only symbolic, precisely because it can never be done with its need for the Other of the un-citizen for it is only in active opposition against the other that each group is able to ascertain its identity as either the authentic or inauthentic member of the polity. So that, understood as a purely empirical phenomenon, 'Public reason's capacity to resolve disputes through compromise, through recourse to just, equitable solutions, rests on the peace imposed by the sovereign's superior violence' (Dumouchel, 2015: xxv). Liberal-pluralist moral narcissism aside, compliance requires policing which is the threat of violence.

> Heir of the social contract tradition, a theory of justice like that of John Rawls is based on the idea of *conditional* rationality and solidarity, in other words, on the idea of a form of solidarity the only condition of which is the other's disposition to engage in solidarity in return. Conditional solidarity corresponds to the ideal of a community that claims to exclude only *those who exclude themselves* by refusing to engage in solidarity.[33] Yet, this 'universality' can exist only among 'friends' who are the 'same'. This is because, in the last analysis, it is the guarantees and exclusions characteristic of the state holding the monopoly of legitimate violence[34] that establish the 'condition' of conditional reciprocity. (Dumouchel, 2015: xxviii–xxix)

This takes us back to the twinned problems of History and violence; 'Anyone who breaks the equality that has to reign between "friends" is by definition a "foe" and thus a "foreigner"' (Dumouchel, 2015: 66). The States' monopolization of 'legitimate violence,' a wholly contingent event arising out of the Wars of Religion of the sixteenth to seventeenth centuries, is the only thing that can guarantee the necessary material preconditions of conditional rationality and solidarity. If we accept Schmitt's core assumption concerning the authenticity of politics—'If such physical destruction of human life is not motivated by an existential threat to one's own way of life, then it cannot be justified' (Schmitt, 2007: 49)—then the corollary is the indispensability of violence for the formation of political identities; 'Law and force flow into one another. We make war in the shadow of law, and law in the shadow of force'

[33] Meaning those who refuse the identity of the 'friend,' in this context the uniquely Rawlsian 'free' contractor pre-committed to the maximization of 'choice' by means of radical neutrality.

[34] That which is 'freely' consented to because it affords protection from enemies.

(Kennedy, 2006: 165). The purported homogeneity of the liberal State necessarily requires the exclusion of 'those who exclude themselves' which may take the form of either physical or symbolic violence for the elemental fact that

> [T]he unanimity postulated by social contract theories cannot be reduced to an insipid agreement of opinions.[35] It is not based on those highly vaunted common values. It corresponds to the disappearance of groups, to the fact that individuals find themselves alone, isolated, facing the whole power of the state. In truth, the atomization of members of society is equivalent to individual's legal independence. Thanks to it, each is protected by the agreement of all. (Dumouchel, 2015: 59)

It is no coincidence that Schmitt considered Thomas Hobbes the most brilliant theoretician of classical European states, providing the theoretical blueprint for the *nomos* of absolutist states resulting from the wars of the Reformation; thanks to the Hobbesian notion of *eius princep, eius religio* ('To each ruler his own religion'[36]) the 'classical European state had managed to achieve the entirely incredible thing, which was to establish domestic peace and exclude hostility as a concept of law' (Schmitt 2009: 67).

> The absolutist state was born out of the centralization of power in the hands of absolute sovereigns towards the end of the wars of religion. It was from real wars, veritable violent exclusions, the modern state was born. The modern state was created by pacifying the land over which it exercised its authority and confining the relation of enmity to relationships between states. (Dumouchel, 2015: 62–63)

But this secular miracle of bringing a more or less stable peace out of more than a century of sectarian warfare came at a price: the de facto segregation of religion from public policy or *Raison d'etat*, culturally exiling faith to the domain of the private wherein it was free to operate but powerless in affecting the political reasoning or the pursuit of self-interest within the public realm. Hobbes' supremely important historical role was to formulate these thoroughly contingent historical arrangements as formal constitutional principles founded upon the exportation of violence to the exterior, the redirection of sectarian enmity (or friend-enemy combat) away from one's fellow citizens and toward the now true alien, the foreigner, who would always be identified as the enemy-agent of a rival sovereign; 'Once the "friend-foe" division is identified with the difference between the inside and outside of the state, the multiple, complex relations of enmity and aid that used to both divide groups apart and bind them together are replaced by a simple dichotomy that both links and isolates individuals' (Dumouchel, 2015: 63). And here, the essential binding force (or *katechon*) is the notion of 'Territory' that operates as the generic term for State (Dumouchel, 2015: 64–72); 'Properly speaking, there is no territory unless the borders of the state coincide with the "friend-foes" dichotomy, in other words, unless groups have been excluded as political players' (Dumouchel, 2015: 64). So it came to pass, through pure historical happenstance, that, beginning with Hobbes, social contract theory became

---

[35] I discuss this same issue in relation to William Golding's *Lord of the Flies* in Chap. 2.

[36] Meaning 'within his own sovereignty'.

> ...an effort to establish a purely rational political order in order to institute a principle of coexistence in which violence never occurs without reason, is never a pressure valve, never targets anyone but those who 'deserve' being violently attacked. The modern state wants both to entirely exclude violence from relations between 'friends,' and to limit its uses to enmity relationships that justify it. The transformation of members of society into 'citizen-friends' through the social contract is thought of as the result of a rational renunciation of violence and a pact to ensure reciprocal security. (Dumouchel, 2015: 64)

But of course the '*rational renunciation of violence*' formed no part of any of this, for Hobbes placed at the center of his system the very thing that Rawls torturously tries to expel from social consciousness: that the absolute and unconditional neutrality that is existentially indispensable to making all authentic citizens true friends is the direct outcome of the State's use of organized violence in eradicating all possible internal political groupings (associations) that could serve as rivals, not the least of which were organized religions now wholly subjugated to the catch-all phrase 'To each prince his own religion'—which could, of course, include secularism as the absolute good.

> Hobbes transformed into logical truth the elimination of groups from political life. Not only are 'foes' now to be found only outside of national borders, but Hobbes confined violence to the chaos of the state of nature, outside of which political order is established. The presence of the enemy at the borders of the state, which is in fact necessary, tends to disappear from political reflection. The role of enmity in political relations disappears at the same time as that of groups.[37] Politics thus became identified with law, which is the contrary of force. The indispensable coercion designed to enforce compliance with shared rules is seen uniquely as a means of turning us away from violence. Legitimate violence is not considered violence. (Dumouchel, 2015: 63)

Dumouchel's *aesthesis*-like final sentence '*Legitimate violence is not considered violence*' is truly apocalyptic, meaning that it reveals the Thing that explains all things but has been perfectly hidden from the very beginning of culture by *meconnaissance*. 'Political violence is violence that structures and brings people together. It establishes groups. It unites and divides at the same time' Dumouchel, 2015: 91) thereby revealing itself to be eternally unstable and incapable of policing itself, because at all times it is always inclined through its lack of foundation in the authentically 'Real' to collapse into pure political violence, the expression of the will-to-power of a wholly contingent and arbitrary political order that operates in a manner not at all dissimilar to Schmitt's decisionism. In the final analysis the reasonable citizen can only authenticate their civic identity through the State's identifying and isolating all of those who are *un*-reasonable. 'Having the monopoly of legitimate violence is to claim to state, or create, the difference between good and bad violence. Wanting to, or thinking one must, invent the difference between good and evil is so eminently modern that it is almost a definition of modernity' (Dumouchel, 2015: xvii; xxv, 75, 110). This takes us directly back to my discussion of Wes Pue's argument concerning the necessary relationship between social contract theory and the isotropic nature of

[37] As exemplified by Schmitt's later comments on 'associations' as possible candidates for sovereignty, a breathtaking retreat to the pre-absolutist era of robust civic corporations and religious communities as mini-sovereignties.

social, and political, spaces, that I dealt with in my discussion of James Dickey's *Deliverance* (1970).[38]

> In contrast [to the pre-modern], [the] unification of the fields of adversarial relations and identity under the sign of the *universality of law* replaces [the] asymmetrical multimode interlacing with an arrangement that has a unique center. All citizens are united together by their identical membership in the nation and uniquely by that. ... Reducing the [various] spaces of adversarial relations and lineage identity into a single one forces solidarity relations to take the form of a homogenous, isotropic net in the sense that all are equally close and distant from one another, and similarly attached to the nation [the sovereign]. (Dumouchel, 2015: 68)

Law, by being radically de-spatialized, this a particular instance of a much wider process of de-contextualization, becomes an 'anti-geography' within which the 'entire world is transmuted into one vast isotropic surface'.

> 'Law' is ... a profoundly anti-geographical faith. Judges are its high priests, courtrooms its sanctuaries, professional schools its seminaries. Its scriptures are 'authorities' passed down from generation to generation by appointed oracles. Its god is a de-contextualized, highly abstracted, and depersonalized 'rationality'. Contexts of all sorts—gender, class, religious, cultural, political, historical or spatial—are the enemies of Law. Law is the antithesis of region, locality, place, community. (Pue, 1990: 566)

Once it attains true cultural hegemony, legal reasoning transmutes the 'subjects of Law' into undifferentiated and inter-exchangeable components; 'these are the men required by "justice" in John Rawl's original position.[39] Abstracted from social relations, they know not who they are, where they are, from whence they came, or where they are going' (Pue, 1990: 567–568). In short: there is no way to tell them apart. If law really is isotropic, then it exhibits a lack of difference and, in Girardian terms, law would suffer from an apocalyptic crisis of undifferentiation, the war of all against all. And following Hobbes, law, along with secular public reason, subordinates all subjective characteristics of any particular human being to the over-arching and a-contextual standard of the rational and contractual liberal Self. Difference is denied to the degree that it is a stumbling-block for the social contract, and the liberal mutates into 'a Man of no qualities' to the extent that all of his distinguishing characteristics are onto-politically trivial. Rousseau expressed Girard's essential insight beautifully by evoking the demon of metaphysical desire: 'Always in contradiction with himself, always oscillating between his inclinations and his duties, neither man nor citizen, no good to himself or others. Such is the ordinary man of our day, an Englishman, a Frenchman, a bourgeois: he is nothing' (Jean-Jacques Rousseau qtd. Berman, 2009: 309) Literally.

---

[38] See Chap. 3, above.

[39] The cornerstone of Rawls' project and a seminal text in the legal doctrine informally known as 'justice-as-fairness'; basically a re-working of the Hobbesian 'original moment' of the social contract wherein all of the pre-citizens would opt for equality of outcomes rather than guaranteed protection from one's neighbors (Mailey, 2020: 160) demonstrating that the thought experiment (or secular allegory) of the social contract can guarantee a social democratic society if tweaked in the correct manner.

> Freed of the traditional solidarity obligations that used to gather them into distinct groups,[40] agents are transformed into individuals. …[thus] individuals no longer have any (or almost any) specific obligations to anyone in particular, aside from those that are voluntary. … Within the space pacified by the monopoly of legitimate violence, more and more social relations tend to become purely mercantile and utilitarian [or 'contractual'].… [Today the] principle that brings these individuals together is that each owes nothing to anyone except what he or she owes to all the others'. (Dumouchel, 2015: 69)

The fatal flaw of the would-be isotopic *nomos* of citizens-without-authenticity is that its State sanctioned insistence upon the de-individualization of all as the price of citizenship recapitulates the Girardian crisis of undifferentiation on an unprecedented scale, engulfing the totality of that which we misleadingly label the modern. On the relatively banal level of the political, this creates an unsustainable crisis of enemy identification through the mass production of cultural homogeneity (neutralism) as proof of authentic citizenship; the result is that no one can ever really trust anyone else because all of the identifying markers of true sensibility have been vitiated by a radical neutrality, causing the police or surveillance power of the State to be continuously invoked in order to guarantee the conditional rationality and solidarity required by the social contract (Dumouchel, 2015: 70–75, 131–137, 148–156). The paradox is as cruel as it is destructive: 'Nothing requires me to act with solidarity. Everything depends on the other's attitude towards me' (Dumouchel, 2015: 149) and it is this very difficulty that 'shines light on what remains implicit in Rawl's text: the fact that the other may be neither "fair nor reasonable" condemns liberals to inhabit a universe of enemies' (Dumouchel, 2015: 150). Which has a remarkably contemporary sensibility to it. Although Rawls freely admits that his work *utopian* (Rawls, 1999: 11)—and, therefore, is talking about 'Nowhere' in particular[41]—it would be nothing short of disingenuous to presume that Rawls is ever not discussing a highly idealized version of the contemporary United States. But, fortunately for all reasonable people everywhere, Rawls has a solution. There is a sign of the identity of the unreasonable that possesses a universal meaning: he/she/they who is/are authentically unreasonable are all of those who have voluntarily chosen to exclude themselves from the social contract, the ones who have voluntarily turned themselves into 'aliens', or 'religious fanatics,' the ones who base their authenticity on things that are invisible and unprovable and can, therefore, constitute no part of public reason.

---

[40] Those 'associations,' such as churches, that could establish themselves as self-segregating dissenters from the supposedly monsitic sovereignty of the State.

[41] Fully consistent with the radically *isotrophic* nature of this thinking. See below.

11.3.3 The Problem of Religion for Fundamentalist Neutralism

On the one hand, Rawls cleaves to jurisprudential orthodoxy in recognizing *eius princep, eius religio* as the foundational principle of modernity's comparative political stability following the sectarian genocide of the Reformation period.

> A society in which many faiths all share this attitude and assume that for the indefinite future their relative numbers will stay roughly the same might well have a constitution resembling that of the United States, fully protecting the religious liberties of sharply divided religions more or less equal in political power. The constitution is, as it were, honoured as a pact to maintain civil peace. In this society political issues might be discussed in terms of political ideas and values so as not to open religious conflict and arouse sectarian hostility. The role of public reason here serves merely to quiet divisiveness and encourage social stability. (Rawls, 1999: 149–150)

The problem for Rawls comes with the word '*merely*': although the classic 'separation of Church and State,' as *eius princep, eius religio* is often mistaken for,[42] has secured a political and cultural peace, it is woefully inadequate with regards to establishing the authenticity, an uncompromising sensibility, of the citizen as a human being, or conversely, of allowing for the reasonableness of the citizen to act as guarantor of the authenticity of conditional rationality. Once again, Rawls does not flinch, being almost disarming in his directness: '*However, in this case we do not have stability for the right reasons, that is, as secured by a firm allegiance to a democratic society's political (moral) ideals and values*' (Rawls, 1999: 149–150). There's the ticket: the one who bases their political beliefs, whatever their content, on things that not all citizens could accept in principle, are inauthentic citizens, or citizens of the inauthentic: '*Political liberalism views this insistence on the whole truth in politics as incompatible with democratic citizenship and the idea of legitimate law*' (Rawls, 1999: 138, 149–152).[43] And why is a demand for a politics on 'whole truth' so incompatible with citizenship? At this point we must revisit Heidegger's concept of *Technik* as enframing. Is a 'whole truth' grounded upon an appeal to an absolute reality that may be unknowable (mediated), or direct knowledge of such a reality (un-mediated), whereas no such thing can exist a priori? And why can no such thing exist a priori? Because for such a thing to exist everyone would have to give their assent to something which could not, by its very nature, be made subject to negotiation, deliberation, and compromise, the existential lifeblood of democracy, as Schmitt never tired of reminding us but in a completely different way. Science and its offspring technology avoid this problem, however, because scientific knowledge is the product of a very long and wholly collective effort of negotiation, deliberation

[42] Mistaken because the doctrine does not technically separate the government from the church; instead, it permits each sovereign to select the Faith of her citizens as a prerogative of her Sovereignty, which is quite a different proposition, for, in principle, it would allow the monarch to establish a theocracy. One suspects that Rawls is simply offering a secularist version of this same game of 'principled' reasoning.

[43] See above.

and 'compromise'[44] so that it is one of the very few forms of cultural knowledge that really can command universal acceptance, meaning that a commitment to science, or the methodology of science, would be a universal sign of the reasonable citizen who both could and would commit unconditionally (or loyally) to public reason, making them trustworthy. For Heidegger this is the equivalent of establishing the reasonable or well-ordered citizen as the standing-reserve, the one who 'stands within the essential realm of Enframing' (Heidegger, 1977: 24). And the reverse, of course, is equally true: a distrust-inducing reluctance to embrace the totality of the scientific world view and the methodology of scientific-empirical reasoning is the symptom of an irrationality that is the antithesis of public reason and, therefore, true democracy. In the final instance, it comes down to a very ancient problem in philosophy: political and legal values cannot be reduced to moral values. The first two are the things of negotiation; morals, however, are, historically at least, the emanations of a 'whole truth' meaning some kind of appeal, on some level, to the transcendental.

> Political values are not moral doctrines, however available or accessible these may be to our reason and common-sense reflection. Moral doctrines are on a level with religion and first philosophy.[45] By contrast, liberal political principles and values, although intrinsically moral values,[46] are specified by liberal political conceptions of justice and fall under the category of the political. (Rawls, 1999: 143)

Rawls, the anti-Schmitt, stakes the onto-political supremacy of the well-ordered citizen upon the liberal-pluralist conception of the political because it alone is fully compatible with public reason which is the antithesis of any claim to an absolute, the one thing that, by definition, is eternally non-negotiable. But this is where the trap lies for Rawls: neutrality rhetorically operates as a kind of categorical imperative, neutralism itself as kind of 'whole truth,' so that it is able to function as a secular version of foundationalism, giving rise to a total and totalizing political system that is able to operate universally from a series of (now) incontestable axioms and first principles which, for Rawls, is the notion of reciprocity, the first fruit of democracy, being the thing that secures that equality which is the social safeguard of neutrality.

> When political liberalism speaks of a reasonable overlapping consensus of comprehensive doctrines, it means that all of these doctrines, both religious and non-religious, support a political concept of justice underwriting a constitutional democratic society whose principles, ideals, and standards satisfy the criterion of reciprocity. Thus, all reasonable doctrines affirm such a society with its corresponding political institutions; equal basic rights and liberties for all citizens, including liberty of conscience and freedom of religion. On the other hand, comprehensive doctrines that cannot support such a democratic society are not reasonable. Their principles and ideals do not satisfy the criterion of reciprocity, and in various ways they fail to establish the equal basic liberties. As examples, consider the many fundamentalist religious doctrines, the doctrine of the divine right of monarchs and the various forms of aristocracy, and, not to be over-looked, the many instances of autocracy and dictatorship. (Rawls, 1999: 173)

---

[44] In the form of the continuous re-examination of empirical evidence so that any theory can, in principle, be readjusted to accommodate any new set of 'incontestable' facts.

[45] They are ontological and foundational.

[46] They are imbibed with a concept of The Good, both substantive and procedural.

Within the Rawlsian form of enframing, the only way that religion can conform to the unconditional demand for authentic reciprocity is for it to pretend that it does not actually exist; religion, within the age of absolute neutrality must be nothing in particular but all things to all people, provided that none of those things and people defect from public reason. 'Political liberalism specifies the idea of the reasonable (Rawls, 1999: 87),' but, Rawls concedes, 'Political liberalism does not dismiss spiritual questions as unimportant, but to the contrary, because of their importance, it leaves them for each citizen to decide for himself or herself' (Rawls, 1999: 127). Provided, of course, that they decide correctly.

> While a constitutional regime can fully ensure rights and liberties for all permissible doctrines, and therefore protect our freedom and security, a democracy necessarily requires that, as one citizen among others, each of us accept the obligations of legitimate law. While no one is expected to put his or her religious or non-religious doctrine in danger,[47] we must each give up forever the hope of changing the constitution so as to establish our religion's hegemony, or of qualifying our obligations so as to ensure its influence and success. To retain such hopes and aims would be inconsistent with the idea of equal basic liberties for all free and equal citizens. (Rawls, 1999: 150)

One good way of thinking about Rawlsian legal philosophy is to imagine it as an enormously complicated exercise in coming up with a seemingly non-exclusionary 'litmus test' for establishing the citizen-patient's susceptibility to the disease of whole truth. Of course, this is most clearly the case with regards to the terminally religious. 'How is it possible for those holding religious doctrines ... to hold at the same time a reasonable political conception that supports a reasonable constitutional democratic regime?' (Rawls, 1999: 149). Easy. The 'answer lies in the religious or non-religious doctrine's understanding and accepting that, except by endorsing a reasonable constitutional democracy, there is no other way fairly to ensure the liberty of its adherents consistent with the equal liberties of other reasonable free and equal citizens' (Rawls, 1999: 151). Which sounds fine, or at least reassuring to those committed to the classical version of the doctrine of Church and State, until one realizes that this is merely the restatement of a semi-disguised prejudice that Rawls openly admits to with the dreaded *proviso* that public reason is a categorical imperative that only those who are committed to authentic neutrality can truly accept.

> The first [aspect of public political culture] is that reasonable comprehensive doctrines, religious or non-religious, may be introduced in public political discussion at any time, provided that in due course proper political reasons—and not reasons given solely by comprehensive doctrines—are presented that are sufficient to support whatever the comprehensive doctrines introduced are said to support. This injunction to present proper political reasons I refer to as *the proviso*, and it specifies public political culture as distinct from the background culture. (Rawls, 1999: 152)

All of this is tantamount to the historically very specific proposition that religious speech, particularly that of the fundamentalist variety, can form no valid part of public reason and, therefore, of public speech, a *proviso* that only the most fanatical

---

[47] A neat and beautifully disguised form of circular reasoning: does not every prophet, the epitome of the alien, impose upon all some sort of demand that is 'uncompromising'?

among us could disagree with for all of the reasons which Rawls has already given. More interesting is that with the *proviso* Rawls introduces an apparently sociological dichotomy between the 'public' (neutral; general) and 'background' (non-neutral; particular) cultures as a social manifestation of a more fundamental onto-political dualism: two parallel, but literally 'alien' worlds. The Kantian duality between the *noumena* (the thing-in-itself) and the *phenomena* (the thing-for-itself) which works well to maintain of intelligibility of Reality in all of its aspects—we can never know anything about the noumenal other than it operates to maintain the perceptual coherence of the phenomenal—right up until that moment that Schopenhauer warned us about: when the dichotomies begin to collapse and one 'invades' or enters into the domain of the other, when the modern has to endure the existential agony of the return of the repressed archaic. In Rawl's own admission the 'background culture' is a veritable sea of onto-political chaos, for, as Goya reminded us, it is the dream of reason itself that breeds monsters. But not all is lost for the unreasonable citizen, the alien who has migrated into the unconditional domain of public reason. It might not be necessary to completely exclude him after all, provided that he can be saved from himself.

11.4 The Stumbling-Block of Public Reason: The Scandalizing Case of Gary Gilmore

The phenomenal public spectacle of Gary Gilmore presents us with an event that is utterly inconceivable within the terms of pubic reason: in the age of Rawls Gilmore managed to pull off what is tantamount to a miracle of unreason, succeeding in preventing the State of neutralism from stopping him in voluntarily offering himself up as a ritualistic sacrifice. Gilmore's scandal for liberalism is his revelation of the religious justification of capital punishment, but this is the least strange thing about him. For, if we are to take the accounts, both written and oral, of Gilmore's life at face value, then what we are confronted with is a paranormal 'folk tale' tale of the sacred scapegoat attempting to manifest itself within a post-religious domain of intolerant secularism. We are looking at a real-life *pharmakon* that is both passively and actively colluding with Fate (*moirai*) in order to bring about his sacrificial murder, the *telos* of his being, which was to apocalyptically tear away the veil that occluded the truth of execution-as-sacrifice. His brother Mikhal Gilmore openly lamented the spectacle that Gary inaugurated while never losing sight of the sacred implications of the event, the carnivalesque grotesquery of a scapegoating weirdly convergent with the preternatural overtones of Destiny.

> I resented the way this whole event was being viewed—as something that was inevitable, as a horrible fate that could not be refused or altered. I could not understand modern American courts throwing aside the processes, structure, and logic of law simply to meet a challenge of bravado or to appease a suicidal demand. It was as though everybody was caught up in the novelty, the excitement, the vicarious deadliness of the event, and nothing could stop it. (Gilmore, 1994: 329)

And nothing could stop 'it' because the word that is missing here is mimetic contagion: the only way that the isotropic denizens of Rawlsian democracy can prove their authenticity as the authors of their own self is by expelling the one who is the real anathema and therefore the true non-citizen who is the alien. The bearers of public reason cannot demand a scapegoat, but they can joyfully reinstate capital punishment as the mimetic substitution for the original. In what follows, I offer no opinion as to the veracity of the accounts concerning Gilmore and his singular biography of the anomalous; I am merely repeating the various tales as they were told and which became an integral part of his family's history. And as they are of such an uncanny and indescribable nature, I am presenting them as they were written with only a minimal amount of commentary as it is best for what is, or claims to be, the supernatural to convey its own meaning concerning the transcendental identity of a young Mormon man selected at birth to be a victim of human sacrifice and which established his 'difference' to the greatest degree imaginable.

The primary source for the ghostly dimensions of Gilmore's life is Mikal Gilmore's superb *Shot In the Heart* (1994) a series of dream-memories of his lost brother Garry.

> I am the brother of a man who murdered innocent men. His name was Gary Gilmore, and he wound up as one of modern America's more epochal criminal figures. But it wasn't his crimes—the senseless murders of two young Mormon men on consecutive nights in July 1976—that won him his notoriety. Instead, what made Gary famous was his involvement in his own punishment. …When Gary received his death sentence in the fall of 1977, nobody had been executed in America in more than a decade, and despite its new laws,[48] the country still didn't have much taste for legal bloodshed. All that changed with Gary Gilmore. (Gilmore, 1994: xi)

Which reconstitutes Gary as incontrovertible proof, contra Rawls, that the United States is not a post-theistic society of authentic reasonable citizens, but a post-secular society of un-compromising un-reasonable citizens of liminal identities and uncertain allegiances. Mikhal tells us that 'When Gary received his death sentence in the fall of 1977, nobody had been executed in America in more than a decade, and despite its new laws, the country still didn't have much taste for legal bloodshed. All that changed with Gary Gilmore' (Gilmore, 1994: xi). What he does not tell us is why after Gary's ritualistic death by firing squad Americans suddenly acquired, or reacquired, their 'taste for legal bloodshed', as well, we would suppose, bloodshed of the extra-legal kind. Could it be that Gary understood that his paying the Blood Atonement would be the sacrificial slaying necessary to suspend, for a while, the hell of the undifferentiation suffered by the wholly indistinct authentically isotropic citizens of Rawlsian public reason, the ones who are perfectly identical in being no-thing in particular? Although Mikhal refuses such an expansive claim, he clearly insinuates that Gary had the intent of bringing about a transformative effect of some kind.

> On November 1, 1976, Gary refused his right to appeal his sentence and insisted that the state go ahead and meet the date it had set for his death. Immediately he hit a national

[48] *Gregg v. Georgia* (1976), the Supreme Court decision finding for the constitutionality of capital punishment. See above.

> nerve, and nearly every day and night for the next several months he made headline news. There were arguments, delays, and intrigues; there was even a love story. But through it all, Gary remained fierce and unswerving in his determination to die—he tried his own hand at it twice—and he had put the State of Utah and death penalty advocates in a difficult, unexpected spot. He made them not just his allies, but he also transformed them into his servants: men who would kill at his bidding, to suit his own ideals of ruin and redemption. By insisting on his own execution—and in effect directing the legal machinery that would bring that execution about—Gary seemed to be saying: *There's really nothing you can do to punish me, because this is precisely what I want, this is my will. You will help me with my final murder.*
>
> And the nation hated Gary; not for his crimes, but because, in his indominable arrogance, he seemed to have figured out a method to win, a way to escape. (Gilmore, 1994: xi)

And also a way to rip in two the veil separating liberalism from its sacrificial origins while escaping into the Other World. Gary was the visceral antithesis of Rawls and the bloody-minded nemesis of public reason, for he committed the greatest heresy against secularizing liberalism imaginable: he waged war on all efforts to prevent his being executed out of devotion to his religious beliefs.[49] But what truly disturbs us about Gary is the very thing that seems to mark his identity as being authentically sacred: absolutely nothing in his life appeared to be the result of chance. And, as these astounding opening words attest, Gary Gilmore appears to have been literally earmarked to perform the role of the stranger to such perfection that his eventual execution by firing squad could only have been preordained to allow him to perform real-life re-enactment of the scapegoating ritual.

> When we would arrive in the town where we were going to stay, my father would rent an apartment or small house. These accommodations were always in an aging or somewhat forlorn part of town. … We usually rented rooms or suites in old post-Victorian-era houses that were clearly on their last legs. Sometimes we were the only tenants who would occupy rooms in these places. To me, they resembled the moody, ramshackle, haunted houses you saw in a black-and-white ghost thriller, and maybe that's how I got my abiding attachment to horror stories. (Gilmore, 1994: 181)

And, without saying so, Mikal broadly hints at the same thing that I have, insinuating that Gary's life was somehow destined to constitute the fulfillment of some of the most central doctrines of the Mormon Church, a most illiberal institution.

> The Mormons had long possessed a strong and spectacular sense of otherness and unity. They saw themselves not only as God's modern chosen people, but also as a people whose faith and identity had been forged by a long and bloody history, and by outright banishment. They were a people apart—a people with its own myths and purposes, and with a history of astonishing violence. (Gilmore, 1994: 10)

---

[49] Gilmore's scandalizing of public reason is magnified that much more when one recalls that the criminal was a prime candidate for sacrificial murder, the paradigmatic scapegoat, pre-modern (and more than a few modern) communities relying upon 'criminals and criminal law to sustain a direct connection with a sacred from which some individuals would never return' (Van der Walt, 2020: 129; 130, 134).

The central text of the Church, *The Book of Mormon* (1830 first edition[50]) strongly resembles the Jewish Torah in that the unifying narratives seem to coalesce around the recurrence of homicidal rivalries between brothers, a fact made much of by Girard who recast the drama of the Old Testament in terms of mimetic conflict and reiterated by Mikhal.

> Once you strip away all the Book of Mormon's pretenses of scriptural import, what you have is nothing more nor less than a lusty tale of America's favorite subject: families and murder. … At the book's close, there is only the voice of one man, Moroni, the last survivor of the Nephites.[51] He ruminates over the history of his fallen people and their last battles, which began in a city called Desolation. …As Moroni looks at the blood-reddened land around him, and as he reviews the full reach of the history that led to this mass extinction, it is plain that the force behind all these centuries of destruction is none other than God himself. It is God who brought these wandering people to an empty land, and it is God who established the legacies that could only lead to such awful obliteration. God is the hidden architect of all the killing at the heart of America's greatest mystery novel, the angry father who demands that countless offspring pay for his rules and honor, even at the cost of generations of endless ruin.
>
> The single strongest instance of blasphemy in the Book of Mormon occurs when a charismatic atheist and Antichrist named Korihor stands before one of God's judges and kings and proclaims: 'Ye say that this people is a guilty and fallen people, because of the transgression of a parent. Behold, I say that a child is not guilty because of its parents'. (Gilmore, 1994: 11–12)

What is most remarkable about this striking passage is that *The Book of Mormon* holds up as the highest blasphemy the denial of collective or intergenerational guilt, which takes us very close to what Sister Helen Prejean has correctly pointed out as one of the central pillars of the pro-death penalty movement: community outrage. 'Indeed, the decision that capital punishment may be the appropriate sanction in extreme cases is an expression of the community's belief that certain crimes are themselves so grievous an affront to humanity that the only adequate response may be the penalty of death' (Prejean, 2013: 115).[52] But she leaves out what *The Book of Mormon* tantalizingly leaves in: that opposition to such displays of robust community vengeance is properly understood as the work of the anti-Christ, a figure much on Girard's mind precisely because Satan is the personification of the will-to-revenge;

---

[50] The Theology, history, politics, and culture of Mormons and Mormonism is a vast topic, so I can only state the essential truth in a single sentence: it represented an unparalleled attempt to create a white Nativist version of Christianity. 'By evert measurement, the Book of Mormon was meant to Americanize Christianity and reposition the religious narrative westward' (Noconi, 2021: 303). Although operating within the Mormon tradition and imaginary, Gary's own belief system was heterodox and syncretic, based upon a firm conviction in reincarnation (Mailer, 1979).

[51] The 'lost tribe' of Israel that had its own maritime Exodus to North America following the fall of Jerusalem and the destruction of the First Temple by the Babylonians.

[52] No wilting lily, Sister Prejean even manages to throw full-time Tory pundit George Will into the mix of those-seeking-blood-atonement: 'George Will says the American people favour capital punishment, not primarily because they believe it's an effective deterrent, but because it satisfies a deeply felt moral intuition that there are some crimes for which death is the only proportionate punishment [so that] vengeance, far from being shameful, can be noble' (Prejean, 2013: 215).

'What does the word *Antichrist* mean? It means that one will imitate Christ in a parodistic manner. It is an exact description of our own world, in which the most horrible acts of persecution are committed in the name of the fight against persecution.' (Girard qtd. Palaver, 2013: 237).[53] And, quite consistent with Girard's anthropology, at the center of the Mormon religion is the ancient concept of the mandatory 'apology to God' that must be made following the committing of a grave sin: *Blood Atonement*. Mikal deploys it as the trope that provides the narrative unity of his brother's life; it also enables him to tangentially explore the implicit connections between Gary's history and the foreboding elements of predestination.

> Between all the Mormon superstitions and various Indian tales, Provo[54] came to be known as a haunted place. There were stories about ghosts who moved through the hills and around the farms at night: the spirits of men who had lost their land and their lives to the Mormons and their strange new rituals. (Gilmore, 1994: 23)

The 'ghosts' here are clearly the souls of the sacrificial victims of Blood Atonement and Mikal pursues this as a way of embedding both Gary and the entire family within a total environment of supernatural intervention.

> More than most people, the Saints [the Mormons] understood that spirits were real. It had been a spirit, after all, in the form of the Angel Moroni, who had led Joseph Smith to the golden plates at the start of their religion, and in the generations since, spirits had made themselves manifest to the Mormons a thousand times, in a thousand ways. But some spirits ...were like people: troubled and ignoble. They might reach for the living through such means as Ouija boards or seances, but any such occult connection would be the work of Satan. Once such a spirit was in a person's life, it could lead him or her wayward—to unredeemable sins, or even a horrible death. (Gilmore, 1994: 35)

And it made perfect cultural sense that the Mormons understood the reality of spirits for they, at a remarkably late date in western history, openly acknowledged the sacrificial nature of capital punishment as the theological basis of their legal system.

> In the early 1850s, when the Mormon-dominated territorial legislature [of Utah] was drafting a criminal code, it designed a punishment for first-degree murder that would specifically satisfy the doctrine of Blood Atonement. Those who were condemned to death could choose between the options of being shot to death by a firing squad or being beheaded (the latter choice was eliminated in 1888, because—not surprisingly—nobody ever opted for it). (Gilmore, 1994: 20)

It is difficult to conceive of a more un-Rawlsian concept than this, for it proclaims proudly what the reasonable citizen would find wholly scandalous; the notion of atoning to an invisible being through the sacrificial offering of the blood of the condemned on the basis of a stricture motivated by the religious faith of the non-well-ordered people of a small and remote sub-culture of the most obscure part of the background is something that resists translation into the terms of any kind of proposition that could command the free consent of reasonable persons within the public domain of negotiation and compromise. Mikal is fully aware of this.

---

[53] In contemporary America this means that 'love' is the hatred of the haters. See Chap. 12, below.

[54] A very pleasant large town in Utah that is alliterative with *proviso*.

> Aside from the practice of polygamy, no other Mormon teaching has proven as complex or controversial as Blood Atonement. In its most widely understood sense—and in Joseph Smith's original precept—the tenet runs like this: If you take a life, or commit any comparable sin, then your blood must be shed. Hanging or imprisonment would not suffice for punishment or restitution. The manner of death had to be one in which your blood spilled onto the ground, as an apology to God. (Gilmore, 1994: 17)

And what was the sacrificial effect of the ritualistically executed victim's blood emptying onto the ground? Joseph Smith's successor and the guiding force of the Mormon settlement of Utah expressed it in these inimitable words worthy of the Book of Job.[55]

> [T]here are transgressors who, if they knew themselves, and the only condition upon which they can obtain forgiveness, would beg of their brethren to shed their blood,[56] that the smoke thereof might ascend to God as an offering to appease the wrath that is kindled against them, and that the law might have its course. (Brigham Young qtd. Gilmore, 1994: 2)

The offering of the blood is the central rite of the sacrifice of the scapegoat, which is the source of that regenerative violence that defuses the crisis of mimetic conflict and undifferentiation, something which the God of monotheism has very much on 'His' mind.

> According to some observers—including former governors and justices of the Utah territory, and a few confessors and witnesses—Blood Atonement was indeed practiced by the Mormons, and it was applied to a wider range of sins than simple murder. … At midnight, the stories went, a committee of Mormon elders, dressed in black, would visit the offender at his home and would lead him or her to a freshly dug grave. Some prayers would be offered as the condemned kneeled by the grave, and then someone—perhaps the wronged husband or father, or a righteous church leader—would lean over and cut the offender's throat, holding him or her by the head, so that the dying person's blood would empty onto the ground. (Gilmore, 1994: 17–18)[57]

---

[55] See Chap. 8, above.

[56] A striking instance of Girard's discussion of the ritual prescriptions embedded within the discursive sub-text of the 'Dialogue' of Job: that the scapegoat is to willingly accept his fate, substituting an imaginary unanimous victimage for the partisan violence of the crowd. See Chap. 8, above.

[57] It hardly needs mentioning that this account is horrifically and beautifully evocative of Kafka's *The Trial*; see Chap. 8, above. Mikal's elaborations add even greater Kafka-esque ambience to the nocturnally informal nature of Mormon justice. 'Did any acts of Blood Atonement ever really occur in Mormon Utah? Church historians have denied the rumors for over a century now and, indeed, there are no proven cases of Mormon authorities ever having sanctioned any acts of execution or bloodletting under the church's auspices.' But the Mormon authorities would not have needed to if all of the friends knew who the enemies were. 'But it is also true that many Danites—the Mormon's band of secret protectors, police, and avengers—were guilty of a sizable number of shootings and murders in the Utah area, without being tried or apparently even chastised for their deeds' (Gilmore, 1994: 18) …. 'As Wallace Stegner wrote in *Mormon Country*: "It would be bad history to pretend that there were no holy murders in Utah … that there was no saving the souls of sinners by the shedding of blood …, and that there were no mysterious disappearances of apostates and offensive Gentiles"' (Wallace Stegner qtd. Gilmore, 1994: 18). Not surprising given that the Danites, or the tribesmen of Dan, were also known as 'The Avenging Angels,' who did double duty as both a secret police force and as a death squad under the command of the Prophet; according to the testimony of Mormon Elder John D. Lee, 'Punishment by death is the penalty for refusing to obey the orders

And so it was with Gary; when he was shot, the ropes that held him in his chair were loosely tied so that after the bullets struck him, he was able to slump far forwards permitting his sacred life-essence to drip onto the dirt floor of the execution chamber. Which may have been the true, or pre-determined, meaning of his life, the point being lost on no one that the effect of Gary's ritualistic death was to strengthen the movement to restore the death penalty with the caveat that the method of the killing would now be made to conform to the tenets of public reason: humaneness.

> Following my brother's execution, an outcry arose in Utah against what many people (including several death penalty advocates) saw as the unnecessarily bloody and 'old West' aspect of Utah's mode of capital punishment. Why hold on to such gruesome conventions, the reformists argued, when an increasing number of other states were opting for the comparatively 'humane' method of putting the condemned to death by lethal injection? In a fairly brilliant act of legal and moral sleight-of-hand, the Utah legislature managed to accommodate both the traditions of their region and the reformist's pressure for change. As of 1980, hanging—an old West practice if there ever was one—would no longer be an option for execution (nobody ever chose it anyway), and in its place, Utah now offered the alternative of lethal injection. However, under what was rumoured to be a tremendous amount of back-room ecclesiastical pressure, the state also retained the firing squad option, in case the man who was going to die wanted his blood to be shed, as a bid for salvation. In the years since, nobody has opted for the choice of being shot, and it is not likely that many will ever again take that course. Chances are, Gary Gilmore will remain the last man to die before a firing squad in America, as well as the last man to pay the Mormon's rigorous cost of Blood Atonement. (Gilmore, 1994: 350–351)[58]

Gary may have sensed what the outcome was going to be, alien prophet that he was. 'Years later, I would learn what my brother's last words were. They stunned me when I heard them, and they haunt me still. Gary Gilmore's final words, before the life was shot out of him, were these: "There will always be a father"' (Gilmore, 1994: 351).[59] Which is a theological double-entendre; because there will always be God

---

of the Priesthood…. the rule that all enemies of the Prophet Joseph [Smith] should be killed, and I knew of many a man who was quietly put out of the way by the orders of Joseph and his apostles … It has always been a well understood doctrine of the Church that it is right and praiseworthy to kill every person who speaks evil of the Prophet. This doctrine was strictly lived up to in Utah…' (Noconi, 2021: 403, 405).

[58] 'Some scholars argue that Idaho's and Utah's adoption of execution by firing squad, like the now abolished practice of beheading, is based on the Mormon religious principle of "blood atonement." This principle holds that some sins, such as murder, are so heinous that they are not covered by Christ's substitutionary atonement. Instead, such sinners are required literally to spill their own blood in order to receive forgiveness. "The strongest link between blood atonement and mainstream Mormondom exists in the simple fact that to this day [1991] the states of Utah and Idaho, unlike the other forty-eight, provide a condemned prisoner the option of dying by firing squad rather than by lethal injection in order that his or her blood might mix with the soil and become the 'smoking incense' that will 'atone for their sins.'" (James Coates qtd. McBride, 1995: 264 n 5).

[59] Which allows us to consider Gary in terms of martyrdom. As Robert M. Cover has argued, martyrdom, 'for all its strangeness to the secular world of contemporary American Law, is a proper starting place for understanding the nature of legal interpretation. Precisely because it is so extreme a phenomenon, martyrdom helps us see what is present in lesser degree whenever [legal] interpretation is joined with the practice of violent domination. Martyrs insist in the face of overwhelming force that there is to be continuing life, it will not be on the terms of the tyrant's law. Law is the projection of an

the Father, there will always be ritualistic murders, or, more suggestively sinister, because there will always be ritualistic murders there will always be God the Father. Gary never said anything about the Mother. But Mikhal said a great deal about both in his dreams, as was his wont.

I have dreamed a terrible dream.

> In this dream, it is always night. We are in my father's house—an old charred-brown, 1950s-era home. Shingled, two-story, and weather-worn, it is located on the far outskirts of a dead-end American town, pinioned between the night-lights and smoking chimneys of towering industrial factories. In front of the house, forming the border to the forest I am forbidden to trespass, lies a moonlit stretch of railroad track. Throughout the night of the dreams, you can hear the train whistle howling in the distance, heralding the approach of a passenger car from the outside world. For some reason, no train ever follows this signal. There is only the howl.
>
> In the house the people come and go, moving between the darkness outside and the darkness inside. These people are my family, and in the dream, they are all back from the dead. (Gilmore, 1994: ix)

First there is the Mother, Bessie Gilmore, 'who lived a life of bitter losses, who died spitting blood, calling the names of her father and her husband—men who had long before brutalized her hopes of love and loving—crying to them for mercy, for a passage into the darkness that she had so long feared' (Gilmore, 1994: ix). Then there is the Father, Frank Gilmore Sr., 'who died from the ravages and insults of cancer' (Gilmore, 1994: ix). He veritably screams retribution, both as the source and as the object, the liminality of both him and the dreamscape perfectly mirroring the ambivalence of the scapegoat to come who will atone for everyone and everything.

> Of all of the family members, he is in these dreams the least, and when he is there, I end up feeling guilt over his presence: I am always happy to see him, it turns out, but no one else is. That's because, in the dreams, as in life, there is the fear that my father will spread anger and ruin too far for his family to survive, that he will somehow find a way to kill those who have already been killed, who have already paid dearly for his legacy. When he appears, sometimes the point of the dream is to convince him that the only cure for all the bitterness,

---

imagined future upon reality. Martyrs require that any future they possess will not be on the terms of the tyrant's law. Martyrs require that any future they possess will be on the terms of the law to which they are committed (God's law). And the miracle of the suffering of the martyrs is their insistence on the law to which they are committed, even in the face of world-destroying pain. Their triumph—which may well be partly imaginary—is the imagined triumph of the normative universe … over the material world of pain and death. Martyrdom is an extreme form of resistance to domination. As such it reminds us that the normative world-building which constitutes "Law" is never just a mental or spiritual act. A legal world is built only to the extent that there are commitments that place bodies on the line' (Cover, 1986: 1605). Cover's is the most perfect expression of anti-Rawlsian thinking conceivable; not for nothing did he declare that Gary 'provides a powerful example of the use of law for mockery' (Cover, 1983: 8) and brother Mikhal concurs: 'I couldn't believe his audacity, the seemingly dispassionate manner with which he sought a state-sanctioned suicide, an act which seemed no less premeditated than murder' (Gilmore, 1994: 328). But, then again, the Gary Gilmore event could only have happened in the United States which originated as a para-theocracy: the 'sacred beginning always provides the typology for a dangerous return. Revelation and (to a lesser extent) prophecy are the revolutionary challenges to an order founded on revelation' (Cover, 1983: 23).

for all the bad blood, is for him to return to death. Lie down, Father, we say. Let us bury you again. (Gilmore, 1994: ix–x)

Ironically, the real-life Gary has what the fictional Mersault lacks, but which Camus could easily have given him: sacralization by Fate. For Gary is the embodiment of the divine truth of intergenerational guilt. Or, as his brother expressed it, 'the blood flowed from Gary's devastated heart and down his chest, down his legs, staining his white pants scarlet and dripping to the warehouse floor' (Gilmore, 1994: 350).

11.4.1 The Visitations

Admittedly Mikal Gilmore implicitly considers the possibility, or imponderability, of wholly secular chance in the criminal descent of his brother.

> When and how does a murder begin? Or to put it another way: Could I locate one moment where everything went wrong, one moment—or period of time—that might have made all the difference? And if I could find such a moment, would it be one inside Gary's life? Or would it be outside him—one, say, in the darkness of his own father's history? ... You tell yourself you could learn from such a moment, that understanding it would explain all of the destruction and free you from its repetition. But when you start looking at all of the links of the story closely enough, you discover something worse: *Each* moment made a difference, and there were just too damn many of them that were bad. The only way to solve the deathly construction of this man's history would be to toss out all of the moments and build a chain of better links. (Gilmore, 1994: 86)

Or is it an *ascent*? For while on one level Mikal conveys the sense of Gary's catastrophic life as the of a web of accidental occurrences, any of which capable of being avoided or producing a different outcome, the overall effect of *Shot in the Heart* is one of tragedies, a trope that carries with it a sense of both mechanistic determinism and supernatural intervention, the two domains of Being nowise in contradiction with each other. This is reminiscent of S. H. Butcher's authoritative account of Aristotle's theory of tragedy (the *Poetics*) and the notion of 'organic relation' which I have already discussed in relation to Camus' *The Stranger*.[60]

> The artistic unity of plot, binding together the several parts of the play in close inward coherence, reveals the law of human destiny, the causes and effects of suffering. The incidents which thrill us are intensified in their effect, when to the shock of surprise is added the discovery that each thing as it happened could not be otherwise; it stands in organic relation to what has gone on before. There is a combination of the inevitable and the unexpected. (Butcher 1902: 266–267)

On the profane level, Mikal opts for a conventional social form of determinism as does Truman Capote in *In Cold Blood* (at least up to a point),[61] the conditioning

---

[60] See Chap. 9, above.

[61] See Chap. 10, above.

environment of Gary's youth the fruit of the wayward and unpredictable earthly Father of extreme liminality.

> [Many] evenings the family ended up sleeping in vagrant's missions, flophouses, in depots or Salvation Army shelters. Sometimes they had a car of their own, sometimes they rode buses and trains, often they hitchhiked. My brothers grew up around desperate strangers throughout this time—people who had lost everything, people who were mad or drunk or violent, or all three. They saw people stabbed, and they saw people die of hunger and sickness.
>
> Sometimes my father would say he was going to the store and then not come back for weeks. My mother would go to a local church and beg the bus fare to take her and her sons on to the next town, or back to Provo. It was like that day after day, for the better part of a decade.
>
> You might think all of this sounds heart-sickening and damaging, and no doubt it was. (Gilmore, 1994: 99)[62]

In an amazing admission, Mikhal reveals that Gary's identity as 'the stranger' was determined at birth, for, as a result of profound emotional insecurities of both parents, and 'Gary Gilmore' was someone who was literally without a name, which, in terms of the symbolism of the scapegoat, is as alien, and alienating, as is (in)humanly possible; Mother had named 'him' Gary after the actor Gary Cooper, while Father had named 'him' Fay Robert Coffman after his mother Fay and first son Robert. Even Franz Kafka wasn't this mimetically cursed.

> Obviously, this child's life is not off to an auspicious start. He has just been born of two people who carry their own bad legacies and who are presently in flight from certain unknown demons. If a parent's fears can be passed on to a child at its birth, then Gary began life as a bundle of insecurity. One top of that, he has been given two names: one, the name of the woman who could never bring herself to love his father; the other—the name he will he will be known by, that he will become famous by—is the name that reminds his father of a loss that will always invoke his bitterness. There's a horribly ironic twist that comes from all this name switching. What it means is, Gary Gilmore was never born: he would only die. (Years later, in fact, the federal penitentiary system would refuse me access to my brother's files because I could prove that any such person by his name had ever been born, or had ever had an official name change.). (Gilmore, 1994: 86–87)

It seemed as though the battle of what name (or identity) to assign their second son was the outcome of the mimetic crises of both mother and father. Frank Senior was obviously sensitive concerning the nature of his masculinity, a not uncommon occurrence especially with men who suffer from extreme feelings of marginalization, and, not surprisingly, he harbored an envy-spawned *ressentiment* of then masculine cinematic model Gary Cooper, who, perhaps not coincidentally in some cosmic sense of synchronicity, was Marshal Will Kane in *High Noon* (1951).[63]

> "'Like *hell* we're going to call him Gary. No son of mine is ever going to have that name." "And why not?" "The name of the man who stole Robert's mother [Frank's first son] was

[62] When discussing the exceptionally severe beatings that Frank Sr. inflicted on Gary every time that he caught him stealing, Mikal provides us with an interesting aside: 'My brother Frank thinks the whole thing may have scared my father more than Gary. Maybe in that moment he saw something of himself coming alive in his child and he wanted to kill it before it grew' (Gilmore, 1994: 14).

[63] See Chap. 4, above.

Grady. The name 'Grady' has always reminded me of him. I hated that man, and I hated his name. I'm not about to think of him every time I call my son"'. (Gilmore, 1994: 85)

Which does not make complete sense, because 'Grady' is not the same as 'Gary,' but it does not matter because the violence is escalating consistent with the family being awash with pre-representational un-reason. Frank Sr. then reciprocated, drawing Bessie's ire of an equal retaliatory force; '"You've … named your son after your *mother* and another one of your sons—somebody you don't even love. What the hell has gotten into you?"' (Gilmore, 1994: 85). Mikal's observation that *'What it means is Gary Gilmore was never born: he would only die'* is brilliant; not only does it operate on the secular level of a botched series of wholly contingent circumstances that brought an all-determinant chain reaction of banal events into play culminating in a horrific 'accident'—Gilmore's double murders that were psychologically unavoidable, not at all unlike Perry Smith's and Dick murder of the Clutter family[64]–but that, in a way that evokes the transcendental, that 'Gary' was somehow ruled by the forces of death, which is everyone's, and everything's, final destiny that is the fruit of the equally unpredictable will of the Heavenly Father. The result is a minor literary masterpiece in which the criminal landscape of the socially and psychologically determined Garry Gilmore doubles as the preternaturally haunted landscape of the otherworldly scapegoat.

Our new home was on the southern border of Milwaukie…one of the larger cities of Clackamas County—an area considerably more rural than Portland's Multnomah County. … there was something dark at the heart of the place: In Clackamas, it was possible for people and their families to live their lives in utter isolation and disinterest. Anything could come from such conditions—transcendence or destruction—but often what came was not for the better. Multnomah may have had a higher crime rate—robberies, drugs, and such—but there was a deeper natural meanness to be found in the outlands around Milwaukie. Many of Oregon's deadliest men—killers and country-bred gangsters—came from homes in Clackamas County. My brother Gary was one of them. (Gilmore, 1994: 217)

But the poetic ambience of background is at first replaced, and then wholly superseded, by matter-of-fact accounts of events which, when taken literally, are evidence of either the supernatural or the paranormal. Just as with Blood Atonement, occult and spiritual forces both angelic and demonic have historically played a central role in Mormon religious sensibilities. Mikal provides us with a litany of negative spiritual experiences infused with Mormon sensibilities: the Oujia board game played by Bessie's sisters Alta and Wanda that goes hideously awry (Gilmore, 1994: 35–37[65]); the subsequent manifestation of a spectral white horse that pre-figured, or possibly even caused, the hideously violent death of Alta and the permanent paralysis

[64] See Chap. 10, above.

[65] So scandalized was the girls' father by their invocation of occult personages that he took the extreme measure of invoking the Danites; '"Are you conjuring spirits in the middle of the night?" he asked. 'Are you my children, or have you already given yourselves to the devil?" Will picked up an axe. He took the Ouija board from their hands and hacked it to pieces. "If I ever find you worshipping the devil again," he said, "I'll give you to the Danites"' (Gilmore, 1994: 38). As it turned out, there was no need to do so.

Wanda from a freakish horse-sleigh 'accident' (Gilmore, 1994: 38–40); the excessively haunted house in Salt Lake City (Gilmore, 1994: 113–115); Mikal's personal experience of ghostly phenomena in the family residence in Portland (Gilmore, 1994: 178–180); Mikal's repeat personal experience of ghostly phenomena (weird dreams and disembodied voices) in the Milwaukie house, outside of Portland (Gilmore, 1994: 215–223, 262). I cannot discuss all of these accounts in detail, especially as they need to be in the original text in full to appreciate their accumulative 'prophetic quality' as assayed by Edmund Arens.[66] Here, I will simply reproduce the three most significant events from the perspective of Gary Gilmore as the divinely pre-ordained scapegoat. I consider all three occurrences, as they involved extended and complex interactions with a supposedly supernatural entity, to constitute not merely episodic hauntings but actual visitations from an alien personality who either performed an important function or conveyed an ominous message of supernatural implication—or, at least that is the way that Mikhal tells it.

11.4.2 Visitation One: Sacramento, Late 1946

Bessie and her three sons Frank Jr, Gary, and Gaylen are living in Sacramento with her mother-in-law Fay Gilmore who regularly conducts seances when the following unusual series of events took place took place.[67]

> Finally, there came a night when Fay told Bessie that she would be conducting a séance that was a bit unusual. She had a special dispensation, Fay explained, to contact a spirit that had died under the shameful suspicion of a murder, and she told Bessie to take the boys to a movie that night and stay out late.
>
> When my brothers came back in the late hours of the night, she found Fay in her wheelchair in the kitchen, looking paler and shakier than Bessie had seen her look before. It seemed to my mother that there was an air of unease about the place that night, that there was, in fact, a smell of something old and wretched in the air. After putting the boys to bed, Bessie slowly got Fay into bed. As she drew the night covers over the old woman, she said, she saw Fay wearing an expression that she had never shown before: a look of utter fear and helplessness.

[66] See above.

[67] For a discussion of the highly theatrical nature of Fay Gilmore's 'daytime spiritualism' see Gilmore 2009: 75–76. For a concise biography of Fay Gilmore—the grandmother who 'has fascinated and perplexed me as much as anyone in my family's history'—see Gilmore 2009: 69–72. Although clearly a fabulist, Fay did appear to work in vaudeville before 'graduating' (?) to the level of a professional medium. The following tale of the 'ghost night' should be read with her history of theatricality and embellishment in mind. Nonetheless, the psychological import of Fay for her grandchildren cannot be overestimated, according to Mikal. 'Along with the tales of Mormon ancestors and Blood Atonement, Fay's mysteries were an important part of our sense of where we had come from. There were secrets and debts in our past, there were birthrights that had been stripped from our hands, there were ghosts on our heels, there was a darkness in the marrow of our history. A darkness that we could not fully understand, except to know that it was the oldest and truest part of ourselves' (Gilmore, 1994: 69–70). In a word, authenticity.

A few hours later, Bessie Gilmore left that house dragging her three sons behind her, and she never saw Fay alive again.…

Sometime in the hours of midnight, she heard movement in the house.… She fell back asleep, hoping he [Frank Sr.] would leave her alone when he came to bed. A little while later, she awakened again—this time to an intimate touch. At first, she told me later, it was a gentler touch than usual for my father, and still half-asleep in the darkness, she pressed up against him. And then, his hand that had pleased and hurt her in so many ways over the years touched her in a manner that no man had ever touched her before, and she was outraged. She pushed away and opened her eyes—and what she saw, she said, what had tried to caress her so shockingly, was not my father. It did not even look truly human, though it bore a distinctly hungry leer on its face.

Bessie moved fast—faster than she ever moved before. She pulled free and ran into the hallway, calling for Frank and Gary. It was there that she met her second shock. Moving slowly toward my mother, her white hair flowing down her shoulders like a wild horse's mane, was Fay, looking entranced and muttering in a low, frightened voice. Fay—who had been an invalid for all the years my mother had known her—had somehow made her way to the upstairs hallway and was walking toward Bessie. At first, my mother was more furious than shocked. Had Fay been faking her debility all this time? But then Fay's words froze my mother's anger. "Bessie," she said, "you must leave here. You must leave this house now. It knows, Bessie—*it knows who you are.*"[68]

Then, my mother told me, Frankie was in the hallway, grabbing my mother's hand, pulling her toward his bedroom. He was crying and pointing toward the door, saying, 'Mommy; *Gary*, Mommy: *Gary*.' Again, she moved fast. When she entered the bedroom, she saw the same figure that had been in bed with her, bending over Gary, staring into my brother's eyes. Bessie was terrified but she reached over and swept Gary from the bed, and then she grabbed my other brothers and left the house. My mother and the boys spent the night in the bus depot. She was worried about Fay, but there was no way to get her to leave the house. Besides, she figured, Fay knew how to handle the spirits.

…a short while later the family moved to San Diego, where my father took a job as a construction worker. On Christmas Eve 1946, my father received a letter: Fay had been returned to the Sacramento County Hospital—which she had been in and out of for the last few years—and died there on December 15. At seven-thirty that evening, her heart just stopped. Shortly after that, Gary started having nightmares. They were always the same dream: He was being beheaded (Gilmore, 1994: 103–105)[69] …

[Gary] would have bad dreams most nights of the week, and he would wake up, calling for my mother, swearing to her that something had been in the room with him, that he had seen it.

One night, following one of these episodes, Bessie studied Gary as he fell back asleep. Maybe he had spent too much time around Fay and her damn spirits, my mother thought.

---

[68] A sceptical, or materialist, reading of this exchange is that Fay was delivering Bessie a notice of immediate vacation of the premises by spiritualist means.

[69] Throughout the time of the family's residence in San Diego, 'the children would watch [Frank's physical abuse of Bessie] and scream and cry. Frank recalls that Gary, in particular, developed trouble sleeping. My parent's fights got tied in with his other dreams about being executed. He would often wet his bed at night and wake up screaming, sitting in his own sweat and urine.' (Gilmore, 1994: 107). This seems to have been a recurrent pattern in Gary's early youth; 'He would have bad dreams most nights of the week, and he would wake up, calling for my mother, swearing to her that something had been in the room with him, that he had seen it' (Gilmore, 1994: 114). This is not uncommon behavior for a child who is experiencing sexual abuse.

> Maybe that awful ghost that night had somehow gotten inside him … Something about Gary's face, as well as his recent wrongful behaviour, Bessie decided, was inexplicably different.
>
> No question about it. There was now a terrible spirit living inside. (Gilmore, 1994: 114–115)

11.4.3 Visitation Two: January 1, 1952, Salt Lake City

> The next night, January 1, 1952, my family was seated back in the living room in Salt Lake, tired and dispirited from the trip to the Provo.[70] There were odd noises around them during the evening, and everybody seemed a bit on edge. Then a sound came from the attic—a moan that was long and mournful, like the noise of a creature caught in the agony of death. Everybody in the family gathered under the ceiling door to the attic and looked upward. Bessie turned to her husband. She said: 'How would you like to go up there and have a talk with that big mouse?' Frank said nothing. He stood there like the rest of the family, staring at the place where the noise was coming from. But Bessie could see that the dark presence in the house had finally got to him. 'If we don't leave here, Frank,' she said, 'we're going to die under the weight of that evil thing.'
>
> The following day, my father put the Salt Lake City home up for sale. (Gilmore, 1994: 115)

11.4.4 Visitation Three: Nevada, Summer 1946

Frank Sr. abandons his family in a Sacramento diner after being approached by what Bessie interpreted to be a spectral 'stranger'.[71] Bereft of the Father, the Mother and her sons take a bus to Reno and then hitchhike back to Provo.

> Bessy got the boys [Gary, Frank and Gaylen] ready to travel again. There wasn't enough money to make it all the way to Provo. They took a bus as far as Reno, then started hitchhiking from there to Utah and saved what money they had left for food.
>
> A couple of days later, Bessie and her sons were stuck along the highway in Humboldt County, Nevada, trying to thumb a ride. They were miles past the last place to eat and many miles from the next. They were weary, and the kids were crying from all the walking and from hunger. 'Boys,' said Bessie, 'I want you to kneel down with me and we'll pray. God won't let us down.'

---

[70] After the entire Gilmore family had been ostracized at a New Year's Party thrown by Bessie's relatives.

[71] As Mikal artfully puts it, 'All through these years, the mythical *something* stayed on Frank's tail. My mother recalled one of the times she actually the face of one of those who pursued my father' (Gilmore, 1994: 99, 99–100). We never learn what the 'something' actually was, but it may have had to do with something with the alleged 'spirt message' that Bessie's sisters Alta and Wanda received after experimenting with a Ouija board, suicidally as it turned out. Spelled out, the message read: '"I-AM-A-DEAD-INDIAN. I-WAS-KILLED-BECAUSE-I-KILLED-A-MAN. HE-STOLE-FROM-ME. I-WANT-BACK…"' (Gilmore, 1994: 37). If the 'something' was connected in some way with a problem of unexpiated violence, then Gary's selection at birth to publicly perform the sacred role of the scapegoat in the age of public reason makes a great deal of anthropological sense, whatever the 'objective' truth of the matter.

> The four of them knelt by the roadside, and Bessie asked for God to deliver them from their hunger and their plight. When she opened her eyes, she looked down the road and saw a man a few hundred yards away, walking their way. As he approached, my mother saw that he was about medium height, plain-faced, bald on top. Looked almost like a monk. When he got to my family, the man held out a small paper bag to my mother. 'Here, lady,' he said, 'would you like some sandwiches and fruit and cupcakes? Some stranger gave them to me on the highway a while back, but I've already eaten and I'm not hungry.'
>
> 'Oh, thank you, mister,' said Bessie and broke down crying. 'We've been so hungry and so alone.'
>
> The man placed the bag into her hands. He patted her on the shoulder and said: 'Things will be all right, ma'am. You and your boys will be fine.' And then he resumed walking down the road.
>
> Bessie took the sandwiches out of the bag and broke them into small parts for her and her sons. She looked down the road, but she could no longer see the man. She looked the other way, but he wasn't there either. Gone.[72]
>
> She decided then that the man must have been one of the Three Nephites. In the Book of Mormon, there was a story about three of Jesus's American disciples, whom he blessed with the gift of eternal life on Earth, as he had once blessed John the Beloved. These men would remain on the continent forever, as witnesses to Christ's truth, and as ministers to the needy. According to Mormon folklore, these disciples—who were known as the Three Nephites—had been transformed into human angels and still went about in the land, often appearing themselves as the homeless and hungry, in need of care. These angels blessed those Saints who helped them, admonished or cursed those who did not, and gave aid to the lost and desperate of God's children whenever possible.

[72] Sudden appearances and disappearances, usually at moments of some importance in the early history of Mormonism, marked the behaviour of Moroni, the angel that brought prophet and Church founder Joseph Smith (805–1844) to the golden plates that Smith later transcribed as *The Book of Mormon.* Here is one example that took place early in Smith's ministry: prominent Mormon leader 'David Whitmer told … about his wagon trip to Fayette [New York] with Joseph Smith and Oliver Cowdrey. As they travelled across a section of prairie, they came upon a man a man walking along the road, carrying something obviously heavy in a knapsack upon his back. Invited to ride, the man replied, "No, I am going to Cumorah" [the hill near Palmyra, New York where Moroni allegedly revealed the gold plates to Smith]. Puzzled, David looked around inquiringly, but when he turned again, the man was gone. David demanded of Joseph: "What does it mean?" Joseph informed him that the man was Moroni and that the bundle on his back contained the plates which Joseph had delivered to him … and that he was taking them for safety, and would return them when he (Joseph) reached father Whitmer's home' (Noconi, 2021: 188). Moroni also made visitations to Whitmer's mother Mary when her enthusiasm for the transcription of the plates was waning; she 'claimed to have seen the same man on two separate occasions, and on at least one of these was allegedly permitted to view the Gold Plates inside the Whitmer's barn', the angel telling her '"You have been very faithful and diligent in your labors, but you are tired because of the increase of your toil; it is proper therefore that you should receive witness that your faith may be strengthened." Thereupon he showed her the plates' (Noconi, 2021: 188, 194 n 75). The secular commentator Cody Noconi quite reasonably opines that 'Moroni' was really a member of the Ephrata Cloister six miles from the Smith residence, the primary center of the Brotherhood of Zion, a mystical and apocalyptic cult whose theology closely paralleled (or actively influenced) that of Joseph Smith's (Noconi, 2021: 188, 187). It is striking, though, that Bessie Gilmore was herself so struck by the stranger's monkish appearance.

> She was sure: this righteous man had been one of the Nephite angels…. Maybe, as the angel said, things would now be all right.
>
> But if the stranger was an angel, the angel lied. (Gilmore, 1994: 100–101)

Mikal got it wrong. The 'angel' really did make everything 'all right'. He intervened in order to speed Gary on his way and make certain that he did not miss his appointment.

11.5 The Violence of the Exclusion of Those Who Exclude Themselves by Refusing the Gift of Neutrality or, Scapegoating the Scapegoaters

Both Gilmore's *Shot in the Heart* and Norman Mailer's *The Executioner's Song* (1979) serve as the apocalyptic counter-point to Rawl's theory of the social contract: the latter's neutrality is wholly dependent upon a prior, and largely sub-rosa, decision to engage in the censorship of language. The scandal of the boys in William Golding's *Lord of the Flies* (1954) is that they freely re-create themselves as Rawls' 'indecent people' or unreasonable citizens (or 'citizens of unreason') through their rediscovery of the sacred utility of the scapegoat and their subsequent establishment of a sacrificial society, meaning that life can be wasted in the name of something that a reasonable person (like Piggy) would never consent to, as an offering to 'the Beast'.[73] It is frequently forgotten, however, that the boys do not move toward religion because of the pre-representational language employed by juvenile sophists such as Maurice; rather, the boys reinstitute the sacred because the latently pre-representational and sacrificial nature of language leads them inexorably toward the imaginary of the religious, wherein any person or object, through the process of substitution, can be assigned a value that corresponds with the sacred. Both Hobbesian and Rawlsian social contract theory, by way of descent, rest upon a temporally prior act of censorship that replaces the logic of substitution with the logic of representation that effects a rhetorical inversion of Maurice's 'sliding' disquisition; this creates the precondition, within History, for the mimetic substitution of the society of persecution for the society of sacrifice.[74] Whereas before the identification of the 'victim' was a matter of supernatural intervention, for the compulsively secularizing society of profane persecution the 'transgressor' is an objective category, a legal entity that every rational person could freely accept as legitimate on the grounds that the alien is deviating from a statistically verified category of the norm and the normal.[75] It is therefore not difficult to grasp the notion that Rawls is unconsciously advocating the

---

[73] See Chap. 2, above.

[74] See Chap. 2, above.

[75] See Chaps. 7, 8, and 9, above. In Schmittean terms, this would also mean deviation from the ordinary or the everyday, which would require some sort of exceptional action.

at least symbolic persecution of that category of indecent people known as 'authentically religious'[76] through the symbolic violence of exclusion from full citizenship; quite hilariously he is offering up the thoroughly profane (reasonable) persecution society as the mimetic imitator of the society of the scapegoat and then pretending that he isn't. And it must be noted that while the persecution society is formally anti-sacrificial (which is what got Mersault killed in Camus' *L'Etranger*), it does not eschew the act of sacrifice—or execution on the basis of an authentic identity of otherness—per se, provided that an adequate alternative to the religious impulse to ritualistically kill can be found. Such 'reason of State' (but not of 'God') can include nationality, race, sexual orientation, political affiliation, extremis, or militancy of every conceivable kind, but it can also be reason (*ratio*) itself and its technocratic offspring science, for anything that cannot be assimilated by the process of enframing can and should be expelled so as not to impede or scandalize public reason.

If we were to take Girard's legal anthropology seriously, we would point out that the seemingly eternal return of religion has nothing to do with the objective failure of secular reason but, more subversively, to the foundational incompleteness or finitude of secular reason: religion recurs because the scapegoat must recur because the structure of metaphysical desire causes the recurrence of the crisis of undifferentiation which calls forth the recurrence of the *pharmakon* as the emissary sacrifice to neutralize the catastrophic effects of the recurrence of envy and resentment. Unfortunately for the neutralist, Rawls's theory is 'only plausible insofar as it excludes—from its outset—all situations that would necessitate sacrifice' of either the reasonable or the unreasonable (Jean-Pierre Dupuy qtd. Palaver, 2013: 234). Contra-wise, for Girard it is sacrifice that resolves the pathological crises of undifferentiation, 'which reintroduces difference into a situation in which everyone has come to resemble everyone else' (Girard, 2009: 1) which makes the figure of the scapegoat more rather than less relevant for our profane age of public reason, for the victim of sacrifice is really all about signs and signification. The scapegoat as the sign of difference also signifies the modern cult of authenticity as the totality of an imitative identity of citizens-who-can-be-anything; the scapegoat establishes the absolute element of difference between They-who-are-really-the-same from The-alien-who-is-different. If the reintroduction of difference is the key to abolishing (or temporarily suspending) the mimetic cycle, then the irreducible authenticity of the scapegoat as the container of true difference, no less than the scapegoat of mythology, is able to serve as a 'circuit-breaker' for any pathological crisis of mimesis the Rawlsian state of public reason might be undergoing, which should be a daily occurrence,[77] given everyone's uninterrupted focus on their own uniqueness (authenticity) in a social order founded upon the interchangeability of everyone by way of absolute neutrality.

At this point a very brief Christological digression in the manner of Girard may be in order. Although like most French intellectuals Girard began his career as an agnostic, he came to formulate a highly heterodox concept of the uniqueness of Jesus

[76] Meaning, those who express their authentic identity through their adherence to that which is incompatible with public reason.

[77] The 'new' normal.

after re-interpreting the New Testament through the prism of his theory of mimetic crisis: the Nazerene is the one who permanently destroyed sacrifice by revealing the scapegoat mechanism as false consciousness so that collective *meconnaissance* of the true purpose and nature of scapegoating was no longer possible.[78] Christianity's proclaimed revelation is the de-mystification of the sacrificial mechanism; the victim-as-scapegoat (Christ) is *authentically innocent*,[79] unveiling the pattern of collective violence as 'mythic' or that which is false; the 'root of the Greek word for myth, *muthos*, is *mu*, which means "to close" or "keep secret". *Muo* means to close one's eyes or mouth, to mute the voice, or to remain mute' (Bailie, 1995: 33). Because Christ is understood to be the incarnation of the Divine but who is nonetheless subjected to the scapegoat process, his death and subsequent resurrection permanently invalidate the notion that the scapegoat is actually guilty of anything. Which, while salvific on one hand, creates an enormous, possibly lethal, problem on the other, for while the machinery has been disabled we can no longer offer sacrifices to expel the mimetic toxins of undifferentiation, with the result that while 'the empathy for victims—*as victims*—is specifically Western and quintessentially biblical' (Bailie, 1995: 19), it creates an enormous reservoir of unexpurgated *ressentiment* as regenerative *katharsis* can no longer operate. In a certain sense, Christianity's greatest success, the person (or character) of Christ himself, is the cause of its greatest failure, which is the inevitability of the apocalypse of interminal undifferentiation. Christianity stakes everything on Christ being the 'Son of Man' or *Bar Enasha*, which is best translated as 'The Human Being' (Wilson, 2016), the only truly authentic 'person', who has been introduced into History for the very first time for the purpose, according to Girard, of eliminating the illusory sense (or lie/*muthos*) of difference established between the community and the *pharmakon*. From now on true authenticity will be realized not through the collective violence of the crowd but by the efforts by each individual to imitate Christ-as-model of mimetic desire, the *imitatio Christi* the universally true path to true and lasting authenticity.[80] And perhaps 'it is because Jesus transformed *Bar Enasha* through his experiments in a new reality that the meaning of the term has been mystifying scholars ever since' (Douglass, 1992: 39). The theological corollary to the Satanic realm of the Real is the domain, or principality, of the 'Son of Man', understood by peace activist and liberation theologian James S. Douglass in terms of an innovative eschatological reading of Matthew 24: 27: 'The coming (*parousia*) of the Human Being (*Bar Enasha*) will be like lightning striking in the east and flashing far into the west'—in essence, a neat inversion of the second overthrow of Lucifer who falls to the Earth like lightning after Christ confers upon his followers the power

---

[78] It should be pointed out that shortly after his reconsideration of Jesus as the last scapegoat who ends scapegoating Girard underwent his own *metanoia* experience and returned to Roman Catholicism. See Chap. 12, below.

[79] If we read the Gospels under Girard's tutelage, we would say that Christs' authenticity, the unique qualities that make him himself as opposed to another, is his innocence.

[80] The raises one of the most serious criticisms of Girard, his relative failure to consider the positive effects of what could be termed 'good mimesis'. Girard's concept of true, or anti-romantic, authenticity would be the imitation of a model who refuses mimesis, meaning that one is imitating, but in full awareness that one's 'own' desires are really those of another. See Chap. 12, below.

to perform exorcisms.[81] Jesus 'identifies that transforming alternative as a divinely revolutionized humanity, the Human Being' (Douglass, 1992: 3), the substitution of this more suggestive phenomenological concept for the cryptic (and awkward) 'Son of Man' underscoring Douglass' understanding of the Passion as an exercise in divinely ordained political transformation (Wilson, 2016) which is based upon a radical trans-valuation of the nature of violence, the will-to-revenge. Christ came to overthrow Satan (the will-to-retribution) by revealing the scapegoat to be a demonic illusion, but the re-introduction of difference through true authenticity (*Bar Enasha*) works to de-stabilize the mystified and mystifying demarcation between legitimate and illegitimate violence: as the Other who is to be persecuted is revealed as the 'authentic' Self through the alien's resemblance to Christ/Human Being who was himself falsely victimized the convergence of a unanimous collective will of the friends against the Enemy becomes impossible (Bailie, 1995). Which means that *homo sapiens* must become either wholly peaceful or a satisfactory substitute for the de-mystified scapegoat must be found. Douglass is not in doubt what Christ (and Girard) intended. Rawls, however, as the self-proclaimed prophet of absolute neutrality, a reflection of his passion for everyone being authentically identical, has suggested his own alternative: a thoroughly profane version of the Crusades.

11.5.1 The Just War of the Decent Peoples Against the Indecent Peoples of the World

It should come as no surprise that the apotheosis of public reason is a Rawlsian variant of the medieval doctrine of just war, or *iustus belli*; no surprise because embedded at the core of Rawls' social contract is the notion of liberal-pluralism as the central pillar of a universally progressive mode of global governance: 'A main task in extending the Law of Peoples[82] to non-liberal peoples is to specify how far liberal peoples are to tolerate non-liberal peoples' (Rawls, 1999: 59). This is another way of saying that in order for liberalism and democracy to exist anywhere they must, out of necessity, exist everywhere because the rational negotiations among national populations of reasonable citizens cannot indefinitely continue in isolation from non-liberal peoples. At some point interaction between liberal and illiberal peoples will become necessary and Rawls makes this easy for us to grasp: 'Liberal peoples and decent peoples I refer to together as "well-ordered peoples"' (Rawls 1994: 4) equating well-ordered (or fully liberal) people with aspirational but not-quite-there-yet non-liberal (or decent) peoples so that contact between the full versus only partial liberal peoples should be unproblematic.

[81] Luke 10: 17–18: 'Then the seventy returned with joy, saying, "Lord, even the demons are subject to us in Your name." And He said to them, "I saw Satan fall like lightning from heaven."'.

[82] A generic term for the law that governs people who constitute reasonable citizens, the ones who are authentically liberal and who act in strict conformity with public reason. Extrapolating somewhat, we could say that the term is sort hand for 'The authentic Law of authentic Peoples'.

> Liberal societies are to cooperate with and assist all peoples in good standing. We recognize that a liberal society is to respect its citizen's comprehensive doctrines—religious, philosophical, and moral—provided that these doctrines are pursued in ways compatible with a [liberal] conception of justice and public reason. Similarly, we say that, provided a non-liberal society's basic institutions meet certain specified conditions of political right and justice and lead its people to honour a reasonable and just law for the Society of Peoples, a liberal people is to tolerate and accept that society. In the absence of a better name, I call societies that satisfy these conditions *decent* peoples. (Rawls, 1999: 59–60)

However, he then goes on to suggest what name, or identity, should be assigned to the remnant populations of the Earth: henceforth they shall be known as the authentically *indecent people*, a somewhat indelicate appellation directly suggestive of the supposedly archaic *pharmakon.*

The entirety of Part II of his *The Laws of People* (1999), entitled 'The Second Part of Ideal Theory,' is taken up with the criteria used in demarcating the truly liberal ('well-ordered people') from the merely indecent (or 'non-well-ordered' populations) and, then again, from the abjectly 'indecent' (Rawls, 1999: 59–88). Here, Rawls re-invents a quintessential nineteenth century notion of International Law, the hierarchy of nations, one of its most fruitful mythologies for the creation of a multi-tiered international society of groupings of unequal states based upon the criteria of civilizational development. This naturally leads us to Part III of *The Laws of People*, 'Theory: Just War Doctrine: The Right to War' (Rawls, 1999: 120, 105). Rawls is nothing if not consistent; 'justice as fairness can be extended to international law' for the 'limited purpose of judging the aims and limits of just war' the result being that the 'aim of the Law of Peoples would be fully achieved when all societies have been able to establish either a liberal or decent regime, however unlikely that may be' (Rawls, 1999: 4, 5). Although this sounds cold-blooded in its implications, such as the historically disastrous practice of what we in all honesty call 'humanitarian intervention,' it is not, really, because Rawls, the secular prophet of the citizenship of reasonableness, is laboring hard to bring about the one true good of an internationalized variant of public reason that no decent or well-ordered citizen could possibly object to: world peace.

> The crucial fact for the problem of war is that constitutional democratic societies do not go to war with one another. … The crucial fact of peace among democracies rests on the *internal* structure of democratic societies, which are not tempted to go to war except in self-defence or in grave cases of intervention in unjust societies to protect human rights. Since constitutional democratic societies are safe from each other, peace reigns among them. (Rawls, 1999: 8)

It is all beginning to make sense. 'The aim of a just war waged by a just well-ordered people is a just and lasting peace among peoples, especially with the people's present enemy' (Rawls, 1999: 94) so that 'Well-ordered peoples do not wage wars against each other, but only against non-well-ordered states whose expansionist aims threaten the security and free institutions of well-ordered regimes and bring about the war' (Rawls, 1999: 94). Although it is considered outmoded today, what Rawls was proposing was a jurisprudential version of what was at the time known as the theory of liberal democratic peace: 'ideally, well-ordered constitutional democratic societies do not go to war against one another, and they engage war in war only in self-defense, or in an alliance defending other liberal or decent peoples' (Rawls, 1999: 125).[83] Translated into the language of Schmitt, what Rawls is saying is that all well-ordered and most decent peoples constitute an association, 'The Society of Friends,' who authenticate their friendship through their group-based hostility to the indecent peoples who may be formally classified as 'Those-Who-Exclude-Themselves,' meaning the ones who provide as great a scandal for international constitutional order as the not-well-ordered citizens do for national constitutional orders. And, just like the unreasonable un-liberals of the nation-state the international personality of the indecent State must be excluded, in some manner, from full political and legal recognition. Which would make them incredibly easy to 'intervene' against, at least in a legal sense.

The violence of the exclusion suffered by Those-Who-Exclude-Themselves is nothing other than the symbolic (judicial; political) and real (physical; military) violence required by public reason in order to stabilize the 'correct' relationship between legitimate and illegitimate violence. This becomes an even more pressing need in the still very much with us 'War on Terror,' which is the internationalization of political violence; in the absence of a universal sovereign the problem of the legitimacy of the violence employed by all sides can be resolved by no means other than political partisanship, allowing the trans-national 'Society of Friends' to collectively reserve for themselves the right to decide the now planetary state of exception. David Kennedy, one of the world's leading critics of both the legality and the morality of humanitarian intervention makes glaringly obvious what any 'reasonable person' should be able to figure out for themselves: 'How should we feel ... when our political leadership justifies warfare in the language of human rights? We need to remember what it means to say that compliance with international law "legitimates". It means, of course, that killing, maiming, humiliating, wounding people is legally privileged, authorized, permitted, and justified' (Kennedy, 2006: 8). Rawls objection to this would be that it makes a difference whether or not the one who is doing the killing and humiliating is authentically well-ordered, meaning the violent enforcer of public reason. Among the decent people, the humanitarian objective of the violence of the intervention governs the nature of military conduct within international spaces as a sort of *katechon*, binding the violent impulses of the decent States and forcing a robust adherence to that humanitarian law that is the sign of the authenticity of the well-ordered people, which, in turn, validates the decision to intervene and legitimates the violence deployed against the authentically indecent. Which, like so many of Rawls' arguments, may be pleasing to the devotees of public reason but is logically vacuous. It has also been empirically falsified by recent History.

> Putatively, these 'enemies' simply have not yet been fully modernized by the peace-making influence of the secular State, the globalist economy, the World Bank, the National Security Agency (NSA), NATO, the United Nations, Neoconservative-democracy bombs, apartheid against archaic and barbaric peoples, or the blandishments of consumer, virtual, entertainment, and erotic culture. ... Terrorist attacks such as 9/11 are merely the last, violent gasps of a terminally ill, ancient-medieval model that only persists due to the West's anemic tolerance

---

[83] It should be pointed out that Serbia, the subject of a 'special' NATO action utilizing considerable military force, was a democracy, although an 'outlaw' one, as noted by Kennedy (2006: 90).

> of and complacency toward the futile resistance of those few fundamentalists and fanatics who are not yet resigned to modernity's inevitable triumph. And, thus, the occupation and destruction of sovereign countries, drone killings, a domestic police state, SA-spying, and threats of nuclear attack on sovereign and non-aggressive States such as Iran, are only the reasonable measures the secular, peace-making West has undertaken to ensure that this triumph becomes a reality sooner rather than later, for the good of all peoples. (Kozinski, 2016: 117–118)

For the well-ordered peoples what 'allows rationality to be the Other of violence is not a property intrinsic to reason, but the presence of a master of violence, a presence that is equivalent to the expulsion of groups from the land that the state controls' (Dumouchel, 2015: 75) meaning a *katechon* that is grounded in History, the 'history' in question being that of the military development of the modern State. Contra Rawls again, what we call both 'law' and 'reason' exist only a posteriori, not a priori, to the successful application of violence, which, historically has equated to the sacrifice of the excluded Enemy/Other following the establishment of *eius princep, eius religio.* So Rawls has got it backwards again; 'The difference between reason and violence, on which we would like to base the unanimous agreement of members of society, does not precede the action that establishes the political order, but flows from it' (Dumouchel, 2015: xvii) and what flows from the violence of scapegoating is generative unanimity. But this is not the half of it—if Rawls has succeeded in making articulate a kind of fundamentalist neutralism wherein public reason is reconstructed as a categorical imperative that must command universal assent in order to operate—or even to exist at all—then the well-ordered peoples of the world have no option other than to undertake a kind of global crusade of 'moral' warfare, which, according to classic military theory, must culminate in a war of cultural extermination.

11.5.2 Fundamentalist Neutralism and the Universal Crisis of Undifferentiation

As it turns out Carl Schmitt was not the only nemesis that John Rawls possessed; the second, and possibly even greater stumbling-block was the reputed 'father' of the modern philosophy of war, Carl von Clausewitz (1780–1831). And what makes the Prussian military theorist such an implacable foe of Rawls is that the former's entire project is devoted to pre-empting the very thing that the latter implicitly accepts as the necessary and even desirable outcome of the Society of Friends: the wholesale destruction of alien cultures. 'The military profession seeks in law a vocabulary in which war is to be fought… [and the] assurance that their killing is authorized and legitimate' (Kennedy, 2006: 33). Yet once more it is a problem of History.

> As the law of armed conflict has become a vernacular for evaluation of the legitimacy of warfare, however, it has merged with the law of war. And the calculations of military commanders have merged with those of the political leadership. Military professionals find themselves turning increasingly to the law of war—find themselves unable to assess the legitimacy of wartime violence without assessing the legitimacy of the war itself. (Kennedy, 2006: 156, 39–45, 119–20, 121, 140, 143, 147, 157, 166)

How has the legitimacy of war traditionally been established? The short answer is that for a war to be legitimate (as opposed to merely legal for law can justify anything), the war in question must be *limited* in its objectives, *finite* in its duration, *localized* in its area of operations, and at all times conducted in a matter wholly subordinate to a strict correspondence between the means and the ends, so that one can never legitimately liberate a country of indecent people by killing fifty percent of them.[84] The truly horrifying question that arises here is what the law of the members of the Society of Friends would actually look like. For all of Rawls' reliance upon an essentially scientific form of reasoning (the perfection of classifications and taxonomies of identities), the 'Rawlsian State' would be radically anti-Realist in its suppositions, meaning, among other things, anti-Clausewitzian. For Clausewitz, the 'moralization' of war[85] always brings with it the risk of transforming the politically rational 'wars of armed observation' into the politically irrational 'wars of extermination'—that is, moralization breaks the bonds imposed upon the retaliatory escalation of violence through the self-grounded sovereignty of a political rationality: 'War is nothing but a continuation of political intercourse, with a mixture of other means. … the chief lines on which the events of the War progress, and to which they are attached, are only the general features of policy which run through the War until peace takes place' (Clausewitz, 1982: 402).[86] So that wars conducted within the state of the 'norm' should be legitimate because the political definition of victory is one based upon a realist or pragmatic concept of self-interest that carries with it the demand that the violence required will be strictly limited, the 'rational' political interest of the State acting as a *katechon* against its own violence. All that would change, however, if any State (or Society of Friends) decided to become Rawlsian and chose to wage war under the aegis of public reason, which knows no bounds and cannot accept the authentically alien[87]—in short, a war of political and legal morality. 'Contrary to *political wars*, which are limited, *moral wars* are total: they can come to the end only through complete destruction of the enemy. They are wars of annihilation' (Dumouchel, 2015: 80) and Clausewitz does not end his warning there; far worse is yet to come. 'If War belongs to policy, it will naturally take its character from thence. If policy is grand and powerful, so also will be the war, and this may be carried to the point at which war attains to *its absolute form*' (Clausewitz 1982: 403; 367–371). And the absolute form of war is an organized violence that is literally unlimited in Time and Space, totally liberated from the binding forces of the secular *katechon*. The greatest killing joke of all times is this: the wars that are guaranteed to kill the greatest number are those that are fought for purely moral or humanitarian reasons.

[84] The greatest counter-example of this rule that quite intentionally validated it was this comment from an anonymous U.S. Marine captain during the American War in Vietnam (1965–1973): 'We had to destroy the village to save it.' Meaning, of course, saved from the indecent anti-liberal people known as communists who were often nationalists too.

[85] Or the doctrine of 'just war' generally.

[86] Here is an alternative translation: 'The main lines along which military events progress, *and to which they are restricted*, are political lines that continue throughout the war into the subsequent peace' (Clausewitz qtd. Kennedy, 2006: 42).

[87] For after all, who is more authentic (or alien) than a suicide-bomber?

> Wars of extermination are in fact *moral* wars from Clausewitz's point of view.... According to Clausewitz, this 'moralization' removes war from the political arena, which is characterized by rational negotiation for limited objectives.[88] It makes war a clash of ideas,[89] an ideological conflict. In fact, wars of extermination escape politics in yet another way. They tend to become independent of the political objectives that were at the origins of the conflict, and in the end the conflict becomes its own end. A war of extermination quickly stops being the 'continuation of politics by other means' and becomes only pure violence freed from all constraint. It then transforms into an unlimited conflict, a confrontation that is no longer anything but destruction, relentlessness, and the 'escalation to extremes,' driven by the infinite will to conquer. (Dumouchel, 2015: 78–79)

To say this another way: moral wars are wars of undifferentiation for everywhere is the same place and the distinction between limited and total has been lost. Intriguingly, Girard nominates the preeminent 'philosopher of war' Clausewitz as modernity's truest prophet, for it was he who successfully systematized what the moralistic revolutionaries of progress merely affirmed while being blind to its implications: that the revolutionary secular order is the site of escalating violence that is potentially unlimited. 'Clausewitz is all the more upsetting because he formulates the apocalypse without realizing it. He therefore never says it outright (Girard & Chantre, 2010: 107); what he does say outright is that war is "'the most imitative of all human activities'" (Martin van Creveld qtd. Krastev & Holmes, 2019: 89) because it is the most intensely reciprocal of all human activities: 'If one side uses force without compunction, undeterred by the bloodshed it involves, while the other side refrains, the first will gain the upper hand. That side will force the other to follow suit; each will drive its opponent toward extremes, and the only limiting factors are the counterpoises inherent in war' (Clausewitz qtd. Lawtoo, 2015: 162). The mimetic sub-text of this is that 'the two adversaries are mirror images of each other' and 'the duels they fight call for unconscious mimetic reactions' (Lawtoo, 2015: 168). The vital concept is the *duel*; warfare is not merely structurally akin to the duel, it mimetically replicates its logic perfectly, culminating in an absolute and totalizing, or undifferentiated, violence that is identical to the duel's 'pure, unmediated reciprocity' (Gardner, 2013: 4). Clausewitz appears to be in complete accordance with Girard regarding mimesis; 'Reciprocal action and the mimetic principle concern the same reality, even though' as Girard admits, 'Clausewitz, strangely, never spoke of imitation' (Girard & Chantre, 2010: 10).[90] Not only is the duel, the ritualistic form of violence that naturally culminates in an 'escalation to extremes' structured as a

[88] Non-revolutionary.

[89] A clash of civilizations a la Samuel Huntington?

[90] Although Clausewitz does appear to do so obliquely at one point: 'The same political object can elicit differing reactions from different peoples, and even from the same people at different times. [...] Between two peoples and two states there can be such tensions, such a mass of flammable material, that the slightest quarrel can produce a wholly disproportionate effect—a real explosion.' As Girard comments, 'This is why Clausewitz sees the escalation of the duel, the confrontation between two nations that go from hostile intent to hostile feeling, but refuses to take his thought about this trend to its logical conclusion; the pathology of national interest to which it leads. Indeed, the emergence of the duel presupposes the disappearance of differences, the end of all the institutions whose only purpose is to control violence.' What is suggested here is an eventual loss of any sense of distinction that may have been present at an earlier phase of the duel, meaning that the

mimetic process, but the duellists themselves are possessed by (or are neurotically susceptible to being possessed by) mimetic desire, becoming monstrous doubles in the process thanks to the dynamic of contagion: 'Violent imitation, *that which makes adversaries more and more alike* imitates perfectly that which is at the root of all myths and cultures' (Girard & Chantre, 2010: 10). However, to Clausewitz this would be a mis-recognition of the truth of the duel, for he insists that the state of totalizing violence will never actually be realized because of the latent *frictions* of combat, the visceral contours of the 'real' that will invariably compel both parties to intentionally de-escalate in the face of the practical impossibilities of conducting absolute warfare. At one point Girard appears to admit to this.

> It is therefore true that reciprocal action both *provokes and suspends* the trend to extremes. It provokes it when both adversaries behave in the same way, and *respond immediately* by each modelling his tactics, strategy and policy on those of the other. By contrast, if each is speculating on the intentions of the other, advancing, withdrawing, hesitating, taking into account time, space, fog, fatigue and all the constant interactions [frictions] that define real war, reciprocal action then suspends the trend to extremes. (Girard & Chantre, 2010: 13)

But what Girard counters with is a new post-Clausewitzian reality that the original could never have imagined: globalization and the (at least partial) realization of a world without borders which would be a world without friction, the contours and barriers of territorial sovereignties replaced by pure isotropic spaces devoid of identifying features. For simplicity I accept David Held's definition of this nebulous term of globalization or 'globalized political economy'—'complex, accelerated interdependence' (Held et al., 1999: 16)—which equates speed with velocity and identifies both as cardinal features of neo-liberal political economy, a 'process (or set of processes) which embodies a transformation in the spatial organization of social relations and transactions—assessed in terms of their extensity, intensity, velocity and impact—generating transcontinental or interregional flows and networks of activity, interaction, and the exercise of power' (Held et al., 1999: 16). Velocity is the 'growing extensity and intensity of global interconnectedness may also imply a *speeding up* of global interactions and processes as the development of worldwide systems of transport and communication increase the potential velocity of the global diffusion of ideas, goods, information, capital and people' (Held et al., 1999: 15) which directly correlates with globalization theory's notion of the critical variable of 'real time communication,' defined as 'the manner in which globalization appears to shrink geographical time and distance; in a world of instantaneous communication, distance and time no longer seem to be a major constraint on patterns of social organization or interaction' (Held et al., 1999: 15 n 2). Which takes all of us to the brink of the greatest crisis of undifferentiation in History: everyone is occupying a

---

reciprocal nature of the ritual has been subsumed by the 'crisis logic' of undifferentiation; 'What if that was the "World Spirit" that Hegel saw pass under his window in Jena? What if it was less the writing of the universal into history than the twilight of Europe, not a theodicy of the Spirit, but *a formidable undifferentiation in progress.*' Alternatively: 'I always see the duel as the end of mis-leading differentiation' (Girard & Chantre, 2010: 104, 10–11, 103). Which jibes perfectly with Roberto Calasso: the perennial return of the Sissyphean project of interminable scapegoating is always susceptible to infinitely 'different applications' (Calasso, 2017: 69).

'space' that is exactly the same for everyone and at a Time that everyone experiences as identical.

Urban theorist Paul Virilio provides Girard with the phenomenological preconditions necessary for his apocalypse of mimetic crisis: if we relocate both politics and war in a universal space that is purely isotropic, then it will follow that both will operate in complete tandem, negating the possibility of the *katechon*, and creating the eternal possibility of the mutual annihilation of everybody, for the erasure of that mimetic distance necessary for external mediation is the universalization of an instantaneous and accelerated internal mediation. 'We became individualists because of the masses and temporal compression, the mass effect of the globe' says Virilio (Virilio & Richard, 2012: 51) and he brilliantly inverts the globalized imaginary of infinity as the master-sign of a finite world without end.

> [Globalization is] first and foremost, a kind of *journey to the center of the earth*, in the darkening gloom of a temporal compression which closes off the human race's living space once and for all, a thing some utopians have termed the *sixth continent*, though it is simply the hyper-center of our environment. Both origin and end of a world that is now foreclosed, where everyone is unceasingly attracted by this *central region* without spatial or temporal extension, which is simply the culmination, the terminal of that *acceleration of reality* which crushes our five continents and seven seas into each other, but, most importantly, crushes together the nations and peoples of the world. (Virilio, 2003: 87)

Claustrophobia is decomposition which is a form of undifferentiation that is the apocalypse of mimesis. Which justifies Girard's reading of the Clauswitzian duel. Reciprocal action 'both accelerates and suspends the escalation to extremes, which only suspends it in order to further accelerate it later,' not simply because 'violence is a terrible adversary, especially since it always wins' but because we ourselves have politically engineered the eternal victory of an unrestrained violence through our collective acquiescence to the universalization of isotropic 'post-space' where everywhere is sameness, as public reason would have it (Girard & Chantre, 2010: 18, xvii). For the first time a universal immediacy of response is both feasible and, given the now global absence of friction, desirable: the technological suspension of physical and social space is reciprocated by the elimination of mimetic distance which is pure undifferentiation. Since there are no boundaries there can be no friction and, therefore, no limits to the escalation of mimetic retaliation; if 'mimetic pathos is responsible for the pathological escalation of violence characteristic of abstract war, mimetic *distance* is responsible for the […] suspension of the violence of real war' (Lawtoo, 2015: 173). But an even greater cataclysm awaits: post-Clausewitzian frictionless signifies the Schmittean conflation of internal civil war with external international war, meaning that the military praxis of internal counter-insurgency is now the reigning metaphor for political 'combat,' which is now a form of 'war'. Even Girard realizes that it is hopeless and that the apocalypse is our only possible future, for liberal-pluralism's *katechon* of the last resort, law,[91] is powerless to halt

[91] For Cover 'law is that which holds are reality apart from our visions and rescues us from the eschatology that is the collision in this material world of the constructions of our minds' (Cover, 1983: 10) suggesting that the *katechon* function of law is very closely related to the policing of the crisis of undifferentiation in which ideal and reality become hopelessly 'confused'.

the Rawlsian cataclysm of public reason gone global; 'Law itself is finished. It is failing everywhere, and even excellent jurists, whom I know well, no longer believe in it. They see it as collapsing, crumbling.' Most damning of all, 'Pascal already no longer believed in it' with the result that 'we are truly facing nothingness' (Girard & Chantre, 2010: 108).

It is necessary to correct Girard slightly on this point: metaphysical desire does not, by itself, compel the apocalypse; rather a frictionless war of moral purity has eliminated all of the obstacles along Girard's 'royal road to violence' that culminates in a symbolic, and potentially physical, collective destruction. 'Violence can no longer be checked. *From this point of view*, we can say that the apocalypse has begun' (Girard & Chantre, 2010: 210). Meaning that there are no longer any automatic fail-safes (*katechon*) in place against unlimited escalation other than mutually assured destruction, which would explain the seduction of militancy and extremism to all sides of contemporary politics: the commitment to the duel will in itself provide the social bonding and *katharsis* that sacrificial ritual used to supply. The problem, again, is that it cannot work after two thousand years of anti-sacrificial social consciousness; *meconnaissation* is impossible to sustain today for any enterprise that is transparently scapegoating.[92] The real issue here is though: who cares? Contemporary activism both left and right imagines the act of combat itself to provide the unifying force of new friend-enemy groupings. If globalization really does mean eternal undifferentiation, then all bets are off and concern with orthodox political rationality and the rule of law is a meaningless superstition, which means that collectively willed mis-recognition can be reworked, once again, into a political utility. And this leads directly, albeit by a much shorter road, to a Kierkegaardian leap of faith: 'Deprived of sacrifice, we are faced with an inescapable alternative: either we acknowledge the truth of Christianity' which is both the sacred and the profane innocence of the one who is scapegoated and which can be mediated by forgiveness and reconciliation, or 'we contribute to the escalation to extremes by rejecting Revelation' (Girard & Chantre, 2010: 103). At the end of his life, Girard realized that the true ideology of globalization, the state of an interminable undifferentiation, was public reason itself.

> The insight is that the Liberal, secular, humanist model of political order, one in which any conception of the sacred, as well as all religious belief and practice, is normatively privatized, necessarily pluralistic, and publicly non-authoritative, and in which the mechanisms of ritual scape-goating are, and never can be, acknowledged as such is not just admittedly duplicitous, but inherently prone to mass deception. The attacks of 9/11 and the War on Terror constitute a self-evident demonstration that scape-goating has never been renounced by the West, but only masked by the discourse of Enlightenment 'reason'; that *pace* pluralist dogma and the separation of Church and State the sacred is as authoritative and intolerant as ever it was in pre-modern society; and that the Empire is itself a public religious cult that brooks no competitors. (Kozinski, 2016: 123)

Following Girard's reasoning, the resurrection of the universal restorer of differences, the recovery of the cosmic solvent for unmediated mimetic resemblances, must be undertaken. But where can we find such a sacred one within a world of

[92] I question Girard's understanding of the matter in Chap. 12, below.

public reason for no one can truly forgive one's enemies if everything is merely a question of 'rights' that every authentic person must accept; nothing is more alien to the contemporary political landscape than the obsolete (or even 'reactionary') virtue of reconciliation, the fruit of regenerative sacrifice. Staying Gilmore's execution was not meant to save his life; rather, it was intended to invalidate his beliefs, subjecting him to the process of integration into public reason by nullifying his authentic identity as a scapegoat, which, with hindsight, may have been the worst of all possible outcomes. For both Christianity and Rawls might have gotten it wrong in the end, if by 'end' we mean the apocalypse. We must find a way to return the man we must pay no attention to his place behind the curtain.

11.6 Concluding Post-secularist Transcript

The following account of the final visitation is reported by Norman Mailer in his true-crime novel about Gary Gilmore, *The Executioner's Song* (1979).

> All through the night before Gary was executed, Peter Galovan had been working at the city [of Provo] swimming pool. He was very tired when he got home early that morning, and he knelt down and prayed. Asked the Lord to forgive him for some of the harsh feelings he had had against Gary. He didn't want to hate him in any way. He felt concerned about that. In fact, Pete got so concerned he began to cry. Then he felt Gary come into the room.
>
> Pete was there praying on his knees, and Gary came into the room accompanied by two other men. Gary was wearing a white shirt and white pants, and the two men with him were dressed in white suits and wore ties. They might be relatives of some sort from the past or the future. Pete didn't know.
>
> Gary now said to Pete that he did not hold anything against him. He explained that right after his execution, his relatives had been there to receive his spirit. The Lord had sent them. It was very clear to Pete that this was exactly what Gary was saying.
>
> Gary was in a good mood and said he was experiencing all kinds of new sensations. They were really funny. He told Pete he was walking through walls, and it was an experience. He felt like a kid in an amusement park. He would now be able to visit every prison in the world, he said, and he planned to go all over as soon as his ashes were cast from the plane. Then he would come back to Provo from time to time.
>
> Gary now revealed that because he had been full of valiant feeling at the end, the Lord was planning to use him as an example for people who had problems similar to his. At the end of a thousand years of peace, his spirit would come forth. He told Pete he had a very good chance of becoming one of the higher people. He had been told he was a dynamic spiritual person who had made a very deep choice in this life, and that could counteract a lot of bad decisions earlier. If he faced up to things now, the Lord was really going to use him.
>
> Right after Gary left, Pete called Elizabeth, and told her about it, and said that he would slip Gary's name onto the prayer rolls, so that Gary M. Gilmore would be in every Mormon temple in the world, and every day countless people would be praying for him. (Mailer, 1979: 969)

References

Primary Sources

Dickey, J. (1970). *Deliverance*. Delta.
Gilmore, M. (1994). *Shot in the Heart*. Anchor Books.
Mailer, N. (1979). *The Executioner's Song*. Warner Books.
Prejean, H. (2013). *Dead Man Walking: The Eyewitness Account of the Death Penalty that Sparked a National Debate*. Vintage Books.
Dead Man Walking (directed by Tim Robbins, Polygram Film, 1995)
The Executioner's Song (directed by Lawrence Schiller, Paramount, 1982)

Secondary Sources

Arens, E. (1998). Dead man walking: On the cinematic treatment of licensed public killing. *Contagion: Journal of Violence, Mimesis, and Culture, 5*, 14–29.
Bailie, G. (1995). *Violence unveiled: Humanity at the crossroads*. The Crossroad Publishing Company.
Berman, M. (2009). *The politics of authenticity: Radical individualism and the emergence of modern society*. New edition. Verso.
Calasso, R. (2017). *The unnameable present* (R. Dixon, Trans.). Farrar, Straus and Giroux.
Cover, R. M. (1983). The Supreme Court 1982 term foreword: *Nomos* and narrative. *Harvard Law Review, 4*, 4–68.
Cover, R. M. (1986). Violence and the word. *Yale Law Journal, 95*, 1601–1629.
Cowdell, S. (2014). *Rene Girard and secular modernity: Christ, culture, and crisis*. University of Notre Dame Press.
Douglass, J. W. (1992). *The nonviolent coming of god*. Wipf & Stock Publishers.
Dumont, L. (1981). *Homo Hierarchicus. Complete Revised English Edition*. University of Chicago Press.
Dumouchel, P. (2003). Indifference and Envy: The anthropological analysis of modern economy. *Contagion: Journal of Violence, Mimesis, and Culture, 10*, 149–160.
Dumouchel, P. (2015). *The Barren sacrifice: An essay on political violence* (M. Baker, Trans.). Michigan State University Press.
Fiedler, L. H. (1984). *Love and death in the American Novel* (2nd ed.). Penguin Books.
Gardner, S. L. (2013). Modernity as revelation: Rene Girard's imagination of the worst. *Journal of Violence and Religion*, 232–252.
Girard, R. (1977). *Violence and the sacred* (P. Gregory, Trans.). The Johns Hopkins Press.
Girard, R. (2009, August). On war and apocalypse. First Things.
Girard, R., & Chantre, B. (2010). *Battling to the end: Conversations with Benoit Chantre*. (M. Baker, Trans.). Michigan State University Press.
Habermas, J. (1995). Reconciliation through the public use of reason: Remarks on John Rawl's Political Liberalism. *The Journal of Philosophy, 92*(3), 109–131.
Hamerton-Kelly, R. (2007). An introductory essay. In R. Hamerton-Kelly (Ed.), *Politics & apocalypse* (pp. 1–28). Michigan State University Press.
Hartman, G. (2002). *Scars of the spirit: The struggle against inauthenticity*. Palgrave MacMillan.
Heidegger, M. (1977). *The question concerning technology and other essays* (W. Lovitt, Trans.). Harper & Row, Publishers.
Held, D., McGrew, A., Goldblatt, D., & Perraton, J. (1999). *Global transformations: Politics, economics and culture*. Polity Press.
Kennedy, D. (2006). *Of war and law*. Princeton University Press.

Kozinski, T. J. (2016). Rene Girard and modernity's apocalypse. In G. G. Preparata (Ed.), *New directions for Catholic social and political research: Humanity versus hyper-modernity* (pp. 109–126). Palgrave Macmillan.
Krastev, I., & Holmes, S. (2019). *The light that failed: A reckoning*. Allen Lane.
Lafont, C. (2009). Religion and the public sphere: What are the deliberative obligations of democratic citizenship? *Philosophy & Social Criticism, 35*, 127–150.
Lawtoo, N. (2015). Dueling to the end/ending 'the duel.' *Contagion: Journal of Violence, Mimesis, and Culture, 22*, 153–184.
Mailey, R. (2020). Sacrificial liberalism: The politics of zeal and its selective denial in Rawls's political liberalism. In B. W. Nail & J. A. Ellsworth (Eds.), *Law's sacrifice: Approaching the problem of sacrifice in law, literature, and philosophy* (pp. 150–168). Routledge.
McBride, J. (1995). Capital punishment as the unconstitutional establishment of religion: A Girardian reading of the death penalty. *Journal of Church and State, 37*, 263–287.
Noconi, C. (2021). *The psychedelic history of Mormonism, magic, and drugs*.
Palaver, W. (1995). Hobbes and the *Katechon:* The secularization of sacrificial Christianity. *Contagion: Journal of Violence, Mimesis, and Culture, 2*, 57–74.
Palaver, W. (2007). Carl Schmitt's 'apocalyptic' resistance against global civil war. In R. G. Hamerton-Kelly (Ed.), *Politics & apocalypse* (pp. 69–94). Michigan State University Press.
Palaver, W. (2013). *Rene Girard's Mimetic theory* (G. Borrud, Trans.). Michigan State University Press.
Palaver, W. (2020). Sacrifice and the origin of law. In B. W. Nail & J. A. Ellsworth (Eds.), *Law's sacrifice: Approaching the problem of sacrifice in law, literature, and philosophy* (pp. 12–22). Routledge.
Pue, W. (1990). Wrestling with law: (Geographical) specificity versus (Legal) abstraction. *Urban Geography*, 11/6, 566–585.
Rawls, J. (1999). *The law of peoples, with 'the idea of public reason revisited.'* Harvard University Press.
Schmitt, C. (1999). Ethic of state and pluralistic state. In *The challenge of Carl Schmitt* (D. Dyzenhaus, Trans.) C. Mouffe, (Ed.), (pp. 195–208). Verso.
Schmitt, C. (2005). *Political theology: Four chapters on the concept of sovereignty* (G. Schwab, Trans.). The University of Chicago Press.
Schmitt, C. (2007). *The concept of the political: Expanded Edition* (G. Schwab, Trans.). The University of Chicago Press.
Schmitt, C. (2008). *Political theology II: The myth of the closure of any political sovereignty*. Polity Press.
Van der Walt, J. (2020). The gift of time and the hour of sacrifice: A philosophical-anthropological analysis of the deep difference. In B. W. Nail & J. A. Ellsworth (Eds.), *Law's sacrifice: Approaching the problem of sacrifice in law, literature, and philosophy* (pp. 113–149). Routledge.
Virilio, P. (2003). *Unknown quantity*. Thames & Hudson.
Virilio, P., & Richard, B. (2012). *The administration of fear* (A. Hodges, Trans.). semiotext(e).
Wilson, E. (2006). Erasing the corporate sovereign: Inter-textuality and an alternative explanation for the publication of Hugo Grotius' *Mare Liberum* (1609) *Itinerario*, XXX/2: 78–103.
Wilson, E. (2016). Unspeakable: James W. Douglass, non-violence, and political murder. In G. Preparata (Ed.), *New directions for Catholic social and political research: Humanity versus hyper-modernity* (pp. 53–80). Palgrave Macmillan.
Wilson, E. (2018). The whole truth and nothing the whole truth, so help me god: Authenticity, public reason and just war. In P. Branco, N. Hosen, M. Leone, & R. Mohr (Eds.), *Tools of meaning: representation, objects, and agency in the technologies of law and religion* (pp. 131–158). Arace editrice.

Chapter 12
Spare a Thought for the Hangman: The Apocalypse of Rene Girard

Abstract This final chapter offers a critical appraisal of Girard's theory of *meconnaissance*, Christianity, and the apocalypse resulting in a comprehensive demystification of the demystifiers of the scapegoat. It also adopts a more openly speculative approach toward current issues in the rising order of techno-information society. The chapter criticizes Girard's naively realist and wholly unproven assumption that the demystification of the scapegoat will result in the invalidation of the sacrificial mechanism. It argues instead that that a new form of political religion is currently evolving that seeks to resurrect the scapegoating process through the return to the Hellenic practice of double-mindedness, the relativization of knowledge and speech creating an epistemic ambiguity concerning the nature and value of the neo-sacralization of the victim. The inversion of Christianity's inversion of pagan sacrifice underlines the cultural hegemony of a new form of sacrificial reason, victimology, in which the neo-sacred victim will be empowered to persecute a new population of scapegoats—the persecutors of the neo-sacred victims who are now the new persecutors.

Keywords Generative unanimity · Apocalyptic anthropology · Double-mindedness · Political religion · The persecution society · The neo-sacred · Neo-sacralization · Victimology · Good mimesis · Cancel culture

By way of anecdote. From the years 2001 to 2007, I always performed the following thought experiment on my first-year law students. It was the classic 'moral dilemma' exercise intended to underscore the common-sense morality of due process, a 'fundamental precept of our criminal justice system' according to Nancy S. Marder, and the very one that so vexed Sidney Lumet and Henry Fonda in *12 Angry Men*, namely that 'it is preferable to allow a guilty man to go free than to convict an innocent man mistakenly' (Marder, 2006: 166). The only change that I made to this question was to alter the number of the guilty from 1 to 100 as a way of testing the virtue of those students who considered themselves virtuous. One would expect, as History has taught us, that the students would find for the single innocent man (a scapegoat, perhaps, being 'railroaded' somehow in order to secure the release of the one hundred guilty inmates) by an overwhelming margin. It started out that way,

E. M. Wilson, *Rene Girard, Law, Literature, and Cinema*,
https://doi.org/10.1007/978-981-97-1156-7_12

but then I began to notice a perceptible shift over the next few years; in 2001 the vote in favor of the innocent one was close to one hundred percent, but by 2007 the result had become, literally, fifty-fifty, at which time I discontinued the experiment, my hypothesis having been confirmed: 'Demystification is not enough to live on' (Sherwin, 2001: 1543).

12.1 Rene Girard and the Problem of *Meconnaissance*

In the previous chapters of this book I have labored to show that the contemporary legal drama, in both its literary and cinematic form, is the unconscious continuation of Girard's critique of the scapegoat which is itself the self-proclaimed fulfillment of the Christian demystification of the sacrificial machinery of emissary victimage. Rigorously conforming to the imaginary of religious allegory, the dramatic and narrative focus of the fictional legal text is centered upon the rule of law as the *katechon*-like guarantor of the innocence of the accused and the apocalyptic implications of the revelation of the arbitrary nature of sacrifice which is nothing other than the transformation of the secular accused into the archaic scapegoat. Law, literature, and cinema perform this cultural function exceptionally well; what it does not perform exceptionally well—indeed, what it actually has no language to even represent—is the other side of demystification: that the abolition of the scapegoat mechanism is itself the mechanical cause of a wholly secular apocalypse.

> The act of demystification retains a sacrificial quality and remains essentially religious in character for at least as long as it fails to come to a conclusion—as long, that is, as the process purports to be non-violent, or less violent than the system itself. In fact, demystification leads to constantly increasing violence, a violence less 'hypocritical' than the violence it seeks to expose, but more energetic, more virulent, and the harbinger of something far worse—a violence that knows no bounds. (Girard, 1977: 24–25)

Honesty kills. For truth is fatal, and even worse, ugly, as said Nietzsche. Ambiguity haunts the entirety of Girard's project for the logic of reversibility dictates that demystification entails the demystification of the demystifiers, the inevitable and inexorable inquisitorial interrogation of their own *meconnaissance*. Nietzsche (aka the anti-Christ) famously hypothesized that the precursor to the birth of nihilism is the will-to-truth that, historically, is a by-product of nothing other than Christianity itself, which, in an unparalleled world-historical irony, turns out to be itself the one who welcomes with open arms 'the uncanniest of guests'. '*What*, in all strictness, has really *conquered* the Christian God? ... "Christian morality itself, the concept of truthfulness taken more and more strictly, the confessional subtlety of the Christian conscience translated and sublimated into the scientific conscience, into intellectual cleanliness at any price"' (Nietzsche, 1969: 160). Pace two thousand years of Christianity the question is *not* 'What is truth?' The question has *never been* 'What is truth?' The question *is* and *always has been* 'What is the ***value*** of truth?' Jean-Pierre Dupuy has provided us with a spiritually Nietzschean answer to this in his useful observation that *meconnaissance*, prosaically understood as 'lies', is indispensable to the successful operation of 'self-organizing systems': in the twentieth century 'some scientists have developed the theory of the so-called self-organizing system, complex entities in which the principle of disorder are one and the same. As soon as disorder reaches a certain threshold in these systems, the forces of disruption turn into a force for reintegration and reordering' (Girard, 1996: 202). This receives neuro-biological correlation in the Mirror Neuron System (MNS): 'The human subject is radically incomplete, insufficient, for being radically mimetic. The scapegoating mechanism is responsible for the transition from violent disorder to a form of order that is always fragile and bound to collapse; and the victim is surely not in a position to control that process' (Dupuy, 2011: 202).[1] Which is the scapegoat mechanism expressed in the form of an algorithm; even if the mechanism of sacrificial violence as generative unanimity ('the forces of disruption turn into a force for reintegration and reordering') has been officially dismantled, the proliferating machineries of mimetic desire are still fully in place and have continued their nebulous operations uninterrupted. Girard understands this.

> Let me reiterate my main point: when the disorder ... gets worse and worse, it automatically brings back the unanimous victimage that generates a new order or regenerates the old. If this is true, human history, before the Christian revelation, must be an endless alteration of order and disorder in all parts of the world. When one cycle is accomplished, everything returns to the crisis of scandals, or, in mythical terms, to 'primordial chaos,' but then a new collective murder is triggered that initiates a new cycle. (Girard, 1996: 205)

And because Girard understands this, he feels that he is correct in assigning History a 'satanic' or 'diabolical' value.

> Satan, therefore, represents a source of transcendence. From the point of view of the Gospels, this transcendence is false in the sense that it is not really supernatural but it is real in the sense that the power of political and social institutions rooted in pagan religion is quite real. In order to designate these strange combinations of religious[2] illusion and social reality, the Gospels have a number of labels such as 'the powers of this world,' 'celestial powers,' 'thrones,' 'dominations,' 'principalities,' 'rulers of this world,' 'angels,' and, of course, 'Satan'. (Girard, 1996: 202–203)[3]

I do not need to add here that Girard's concept of Satan does not rely upon an actual supernatural personage; rather, it is the development of an allegorical *figura* as a way of assigning an exclusively negative value to certain historical processes (Fornari, 2009).

> Aside from the question whether Satan refers to an objective transcendent reality, in the mimetic scapegoat theory the name refers to the personification of the rivalrous mimesis, the mimesis engendering accusation and violence. But this is also the mimesis that is effective in subduing violence and maintaining order. Satan is thus the *arche*, the 'beginning' in the

---

[1] See Chap. 1, above.

[2] Sic. But does Girard mean *mythic* here?

[3] In the terminology of Saint Paul, this is the *stoicheia*, a sacred hierarchy of astral spirits ('the elementary spirits of the world') that extends downwards until it imperceptibly blends with the profane structures of imperial order through the media of the rites, rituals and prohibitions of pagan religions (Arnold, 1992: 53, 54, 132).

sense of the spirit of rivalry and accusation responsible for the originary murder; and the *archon*, the prince or ruler of this world. (Girard, 1996: 293)

'Satan' must exist because the objective nature of History requires his 'presence,' but it must not be forgotten that, as already mentioned,[4] it is an old joke within literary studies that Girard does not really need God because he already has Emile Durkheim. To illustrate this point, which is really nothing more than the empirical observation that the re-stabilizing forces of generative unanimity require *meconnaissance*, I am reproducing the entirety of the fascinating dialogic exchange between itinerant executioner Oswaldo Mobray (Tim Roth) and liminal nomad/bounty-hunter John Ruth (Kurt Russell) from Quentin Tarantino's remarkable film *The Hateful 8* (2015), the director's solitary excursion into the cinematic genre of the Western.

Oswaldo Mobray: If you're found guilty, the people of Red Rock will hang you in the town square, and, as the hangman, I will perform the execution. And, if all those things end up taking place, that's what civilized society calls justice. However, if the relatives and the loved ones of the person you murdered were outside that door, right now, and after busting down that door they drug you out into the snow and hung you up by the neck, that would be frontier justice. Now, the good part about frontier justice is that it's very thirst quenching. The bad part is, it's apt to be wrong … But what, ultimately, is the real difference between the two? The real difference is me. The hangman. To me, it doesn't matter what you did when I hang you—I'll get no satisfaction from your death. It's my job. I hang you in Red Rock, I move on to the next town, I hang someone else there. The man who pulls the lever that breaks your neck will be a dispassionate man. And that dispassion is the very essence of justice, for justice delivered without dispassion is always in danger of not being justice.

John Ruth: 'Amen.'

Nothing reflects the purity of the democratic spirit more than a lynch-mob because it is the perfect fusion of collective mis-recognition with unanimous self-righteousness expressed through the form of un-mediated physical violence. 'The effectiveness of the [scapegoating] mechanism and the richness of ritual production are inversely proportional to a community's aptitude for perceiving the functioning of this same mechanism …' (Girard et al., 1978: 130) precisely because

The better we grasp the mechanism, then, the less value doing so has for us. As we tighten our grip the object in question diminishes, so that we no longer understand the crucial importance, not of the object itself, but of what it must have been before we were able to take hold of it. (Girard et al., 1978: 129)

True unanimity requires perfect ignorance, according to Girard, because 'As we have said, the only true scapegoats are those we cannot recognize as such' (Girard et al., 1978: 129) so that scapegoating 'dies' the instant that its actors achieve recognition of its true nature. Dupuy takes note of the remarkable degree to which Girard prioritizes self-awareness as the ultimate safeguard against the arbitrary victimage (injustice) of scapegoating; 'the mimetic and sacrificial forms are unable to reflect upon themselves without dissolving into nothing … Any true theory of these forms is therefore knowledge of the self's radical opacity to the self, recognition of this mis-recognition' (Dupuy, 1988: 78). It would not be overstating things to say that

[4] See Preface, above.

for Girard the elimination of *meconnaissance* is nothing less than the revolutionary transformation of History itself.

> From the moment when knowledge of the mechanism begins to spread, there can be no turning back. It is impossible to rehabilitate a sacrificial mechanism in the process of decomposition because growing awareness of these mechanisms is what decomposes them; any effort to interrupt or reverse the process can only be made at the cost of the knowledge being disseminated. (Girard et al., 1978: 128)

And, in essence, this is Girard's definition of the apocalypse: 'When I say that modernity is apocalyptic, I mean that it is revelatory' (Girard, 2020: 39), but he also means that his fundamental anthropology doubles as an *apocalyptic anthropology* as Robert Hamerton-Kelly makes clear.

> As apocalypse entails a universal historiography, so mimetic theory entails a universal anthropology. The analysis by means of mimetic rivalry and the scapegoat leads to the vision of this world as a structure of sacred violence, erected by the three powers of the surrogate victim, namely, ritual, myth and prohibition. Ritual makes institutions, myth makes identity, and prohibition makes law. (Hamerton-Kelly, 2007: 17)

And the apocalyptic nature of this anthropology is that the cornerstone of this system, the thing that has been 'kept secret from the foundation of the world' (Matthew 13:35) is the mis-recognized hegemony of *meconnaissance*: civilization depends on everyone not knowing what they are really doing which is sacrificing innocent victims. 'The murderers murdered their victims ... in order not to perceive their own violence; this is the real significance of the scapegoat effect, which projects the violence of the victim onto the community' (Girard, 2007: 31) but also why civilization as we know it will collapse in the 'twinkling of an eye' the moment that universal mis-recognition is replaced by universal recognition. It is the horrific case that 'All human culture begins and continues with a violent burial of truth' (Girard, 2007: 32) so that if it ever comes to pass that the truth is disinterred culture itself will end. But not gently.

> [Recognition] will always lead to an attempt to stifle this knowledge by violence; there will be an unsuccessful attempt to close the human community in on itself. I believe that this sort of undertaking characterizes all totalitarian movements and the virulent ideologies that have succeeded and battled with one another throughout the twentieth century; they are founded on a kind of monstrous but ineffective rationalization of victimage mechanisms. Entire categories of human beings are distinguished from the rest of humanity and are singled out for annihilation—the Jews, the aristocrats, the bourgeois, the faithful of such and such a religion, and miscreants of all kinds. We are always told that the creation of the perfect city, the way to terrestrial paradise, depends on the prior elimination or forced conversion of the guilty category. (Girard et al., 1978: 128–129)[5]

But this is the exact moment where the critical reader must ask the same question that Dupuy does: 'Is it certain that recognition of misrecognition suffices to destroy the misrecognition?' (Dupuy, 1988: 79). From the perspective of self-organization, or complexity theory, at least, the answer is *no*, for within this epistemology it is decidedly not the case that 'the misrecognition of mechanisms is a necessary condition for

[5] See below.

their functioning' (Dupuy, 1988: 80). It appears to be the case, rather, that 'observing at two different levels the social system of which they are a part, the actors can very well see, from the "exterior," the arbitrariness of the process of social differentiation, while still giving it meaning from the "interior"' (Dupuy, 1988: 80). This means that social actors, even after being disabused of their errors (from the 'exterior'), may still continue to function in exactly the same way provided that their 'illusory knowledge' is essential to the completion of a necessary task (within the 'interior'); what matters in the final instance is the practical outcome of the action not the justificatory rationale for it.[6] The recognition of mis-recognition might even constitute the substitution of cynical recognition for naïve mis-recognition; expressed in pedestrian (or amoral terms) this would be: *being wrong is no objection.* And this 'point is not a purely epistemological one; it commands the whole "prophetic" dimension of the Girardian message' which is a totalizing dichotomy of 'either terminal violence or the Kingdom of Love' (Dupuy, 1988:79), the latter being the religious allegorical version of the secular utopia.

> For religion protects man as long as its ultimate foundations are not revealed. To drive the monster from its secret lair is to risk loosing it on mankind. To remove man's ignorance is only to risk exposing them to an even greater peril. The only barrier against human violence is raised on a misconception. In fact, the sacrificial crisis is simply another form of that knowledge which grows greater as the reciprocal violence grows more intense but which never leads to the whole truth. It is the knowledge of violence, along with the violence itself, that the act of expulsion succeeds in shunting outside the realm of consciousness. (Girard, 1977: 135)

Admittedly 'One may find this conclusion undesirable, in that it takes the form of all theodicies and, for that very reason, seems to leave no place for praxis' (Dupuy, 1988: 80).[7] Although Girard does recognize the 'relative stability of the social forms

---

[6] Giuseppe Fornari has pointed out Girard's naivete concerning the alleged apocalyptic effects of disabling *meconnaissation* is the result of ignoring 'the stunningly resourceful capacity shown by human inventiveness in dire straits'—which, more than a few times, rests upon the voluntary embrace of mis-recognition, classically formulated as Plato's 'noble lie' (Fornari, 2009: 22). 'The lack of any religious, cultural and social adhesive that might provide answers for men and women and hold together their fragile individual and social unity, and the resulting atomization, certainly do cause individuals to turn to any unifying motive that looks strong enough in its absurdity to constitute an alternative, where even the maddest of absurdities ends by appearing to be the only appropriate remedy for a state of collective madness' (Fornari, 2009: 22) which is the scapegoat ('the forces of disruption turn into a force for reintegration and reordering') in a nutshell.

[7] It also directly references the issue of *metanoia*, or conversion, which, ambiguously, both runs the risk and bestows the blessing of private voluntarism in lieu of public, and collective, political action: 'conversion is the only true alternative to scapegoats for the reaching of social consensus, and thus conversion has become essential. Yet, because the hidden mechanism of the old consensus can no longer be covered up—and therefore sustained—and the radically renewed behaviour does not materialize, the possibility of humanity's self-destruction [remains]' (Niewiadomski, 2007: 59). The solution would have lie with a literal *mass conversion*—or the conversion of the masses en masse to conversion—which would be difficult, perhaps impossible, to imagine in the absence of a literal intervention by Providence which would be the temporal realization of the Christian apocalypse. The Gospel revelations concerning the scapegoat 'merely take human contact to its logical conclusion: self-destruction is the end of a humanity robbed of the (sacrificial) means of

invented by modernity which are substituted for the sacred'[8] they are nevertheless pre-destined 'on the scale of his theory (the history of humanity!)' to be 'devoured by the very thing on which they are based: the knowledge, partial but growing, of the mechanisms of violence' (Dupuy, 1988: 259 n 16). And for one of Girard's most robust critics, historian Pierre Manent, this is an absurdity because '"if human 'culture' is essentially founded on violence, then Christianity can bring nothing other than the destruction of humanity in the fallacious guise of non-violence"' (Pierre Manent qtd. Dupuy, 1988: 93). Which, in a sense, is precisely what Girard is saying: the crucifixion is the ultimate cause of the apocalypse.

The question then becomes a narrower one: not what is the value of Truth but what is the *positive* value of the mis-recognition of Truth, or *meconnaissance*? If generative unanimity is the summum bonum of the politics of community, then does not frontier justice pragmatically serve this vital function in a manner superior to that of the hangman whose performative neutrality only formally rather than affectively affirms the 'truth' of the accused's 'guilt'? 'To me, it doesn't matter what you did' is equally applicable to the one who is innocent, literally one who has done nothing, as to the one who is really is guilty of something, for all that matters is the performance of the execution and the paradox of Tarantino's parable is that the hangman does not prove the innocence of the accused as Sister Helen Prejean claimed to reveal—he merely dispatches the accused (the one who would have been scapegoated by the lynch mob if not but for the presence of the hangman) whatever his legal status minus the salvific generative unanimity of *katharsis*. So, a situation that is the worst of both worlds: an innocent person may have been murdered by the State and everyone is still alienated (anomie), meaning dis-united. The selective utility of frontier justice is clear: it may be based on mis-recognition but it works wonders, while the hangman may, and very frequently does, signify both recognition and dis-unity. When regarded in this manner, it is fairly simple to conclude that there is nothing that is self-evidently true about the proposition that *meconnaissance* is an absolute evil. In truth, Girard's own position as demystifier is itself based wholly on his reliance upon a set of historical assumptions which are highly contestable: 'Everything in my research leads to this special revelation[9] which defines the uniqueness of Christianity' (Girard, 2020: 70). Alone among the world's religions, with the clear and unsurprising exception of rabbinical Judaism, the Gospels are "revelatory texts" that 'narrate "what no other text has narrated—the drama of the surrogate victim mechanism"' (Burton Mack qtd. Golsan, 2002: 99).

> What you will not find in myth and in any other religion is the relentless drive to uncover the truth of the victim, which implies an awareness of the purely mimetic nature of the scapegoat

---

covering up and controlling violence yet unwilling to behave in a radically new way (because it is unwilling or unable to do so). The logic of self-destruction is not bound to certain dates; rather it remains a permanent possibility. It shows the full urgency of the question of the apocalyptic dimension of God's actions in history' (Niewiadomski, 2007: 59–60).

[8] Which include the economy and money, which are both supremely sacrificial; see below.

[9] Revelation '"is a key term, for Girard finds in the Bible the revelation or disclosure of a God who does not want victims, a God who is disclosed in the action of those who take the side of victims"' (James Williams qtd. Golsan, 2002: 85 n 2).

> reconciliation experienced by the community.... Buddhism, with all its perceptiveness, is not interested in getting back to uncover the origin of violence. This is exclusively Judaic and this is the engine behind the unique power of our world to desacralize religion. This is what people like Feuerbach, Hegel, and Marx understood, but incompletely. They thought it was the historical role of Christianity to unleash the power of reason that is ultimately self-sufficient and independent, which is not true. (Girard, 2020: 71)

Girard's fundamental anthropology receives it most sublime expression in his 'anthropology of the gospels': 'If you understand the old sacred as a closed system, and if you understand the Gospels as a revelation of how that system works, then the Gospels as a revelation cannot come from within the closure of violence' but must emanate from some external source, which, for Girard, can be nothing other than that of Providence for if it were not delivered to us from the 'exterior' there is no means by which we could have conceived of it within the 'interior' (Girard, 2020: 42). Which is a revisitation of the difficult problem of accounting for the transition from pre-representation to representation but now expressed in theological form.[10]

> The special revelation of Christianity really centers on the claim that Jesus was unjustly put to death. The claim is a denial of the scapegoat's guilt, which is the basis of the scapegoat consensus by the community, the very essence of religion. This vindication of Christ extends to all victims 'since the foundation of the world' and is the source of all genuine demystification in our world. (Girard, 2020: 70)

This is, of course, manna to moralizing literary critics like Andrew J. McKenna[11] for whom 'Girard offers not a theology of revelation, which would be of interest only to believers—and intellectual curiosity seekers—but an anthropology of revelation, which is something else again' (McKenna, 1992: 202). It is the best of both worlds, a binding normative force that, while theological in origin is not religious in substance having been empirically verified by historical truth and, therefore, irrefutable. 'What Scripture reveals in a manner unprecedented and unsurpassed is the foundational role of violence and the mystified role of the human victim as the structuring principle of the sacrificial resolution to human violence' (McKenna, 1992: 203) the vital point being that it destroys any possible justification of the epistemic or moral value of *meconnaissance*, for 'Girard's reading privileges Scripture not for its theological but its theoretic import, not its hieratic but its hermeneutic value. And this novelty emerges above all when he says that the theoretical voice in Scripture is not primarily the word of God in the traditional sense' (McKenna, 1992: 202). Girard is 'safe,' then, for secular but moral literary critics to use, because he 'never writes about inspiration, only of revelation. Moreover, what is revealed does not come from on high, but down from below—indeed, from underfoot. The theoretical voice of Scripture is that of the victim, and is thematically marked as such "since the foundation of the world"' (McKenna, 1992: 202). To prove his point, McKenna offers up as irrefutable proof Genesis 4: 8–11.

> Now Cain talked with Abel his brother; and it came to pass, when they were in the field, that Cain rose up against Abel his brother and killed him. Then God said to Cain, 'Where is

[10] See Chap. 1, below.

[11] See Chap. 1, above.

Abel your brother?' He replied: 'I do not know. Am I my brother's keeper?' Thus God said, 'What have you done? The voice of your brother's blood cries out to Me from the ground. So now you are cursed from the earth, which has opened its mouth to receive your brother's blood from your hand.

But then, as Matthew Arnold pointed out quite some time ago, the 'West' has two axes of origin: Jerusalem and Athens, the rival urban 'doubles' offering very different sentiments and epistemologies concerning not merely the nature but the value of conditional and plural rather than absolute and unitary Truth. And it is in a superb study of the social epistemology of Hellenic religion, Paul Veyne's *Did the Greeks Believe in Their Myths? An Essay on the Constitutive Imagination* (1988) that a compelling alternative to Girard's bias of Truth-as-morality may be found. For the Greeks, in a contrarian spirit to the Hebrews, believed that myths, the symbolic viscera of the pre-historic scapegoat, could not be false, or at least not all of them, because it is factually impossible for someone to lie to the entire world.

The Greeks never admitted that the myth-making process could lie to everyone about everything ... It was impossible to lie gratuitously, or lie about everything to everyone, for knowledge is only a mirror; and the mirror blends with what it reflects, so that the medium is not distinguished from the message. (Veyne, 1988: 57)

It is no coincidence that the people who invented oratory, rhetoric, sophistry, philosophy (the last two being twins as Derrida proved[12]) and, lest we forget, democracy, held fast to the notion that speech is a weapon deployed in order to gain an advantage over an opponent as Sophocles made clear in *Oedipus Tyrannus*[13]; 'truth was defined either as it related to daily experience or in terms of the speaker's character: whether it was loyal or treacherous. Statements foreign to experience were neither true nor false. Nor were they falsehoods, for a lie does not exist when the liar gains nothing from it and does us no harm. A disinterested lie is no deception' (Veyne, 1988: 28). In itself 'Fiction is not an error' (Veyne, 1988: 104) and one 'cannot be lying when speaking more highly of values than one strictly should' in the pursuit of the public good of the community (Veyne, 1988: 79)[14] because oratory is a form of combat and rhetoric a means of persuasion. Within the *polis* where politics, the business of the city, is the highest good, it is 'imagination that rules, not reality' (Veyne, 1988: xii) resulting in 'half-beliefs, hesitations, and contradictions, on the one hand, and, on the other, the possibility of juggling different levels of meaning' (Veyne, 1988: 43) which perfectly accords with Derrida's key notion of the undifferentiated nature of both speech and writing.[15]

A world cannot be inherently fictional; it can be fictional only according to whether one believes in it or not. The difference between fiction and reality is not objective and does not

---

[12] See Chap. 1, above.

[13] See Chap. 1, above.

[14] Expressed in its strongest form, this would be 'a lie does not exist if the liar has no motive for lying,' meaning that an un-truth is not objectionable provided that the speaker is not consciously intending to deceive or manipulate (Veyne, 1988: 79).

[15] See Chap. 1, above.

> pertain to the thing itself; it resides in us, according to whether or not we subjectively see in it a fiction. The object is never unbelievable in itself, and its distance from 'the' reality cannot shock us; for, as truths are always analogical, we do not even see it. (Veyne, 1988: 21)

And it was this undifferentiated 'juggling' of 'different levels of meaning' that the 'rhetorical use of mythology emerged' (Veyne, 1988: 43). Greek mythology, the primeval epistemic excrescence of the scapegoat, 'was basically nothing but a very popular literary genre, a vast realm of literature, mainly oral in character—if, indeed, the term "literature" can be applied when the distinction between fiction and reality had yet to be made and the legendary element was serenely accepted' (Veyne, 1988: 17). These 'legendary worlds were accepted as true in the sense that they were not doubted, but they were not accepted the way that everyday reality is'; instead, mythic events 'took place "earlier," during the heroic generations, when the gods still took part in human affairs.[16] Mythological space and time were secretly different from our own' (Veyne, 1988: 17–18). It is 'precisely because the mythical world is definitely other, inaccessible, different, and remarkable that the problem of authenticity is suspended ...' (Veyne, 1988: 20). And because there is no universal, or commanding, source of authenticity, the Greeks, unlike the Jews, for good or ill found it unproblematic to reside within a mental landscape (interior) that Veyne denotes as *Balkanization* (exterior): multiple but parallel realities that can be maintained within human minds all at the same time and which afford everyone a variety of alternative action ins any given situation. 'The Balkanization of the symbolic field is reflected in each mind' for 'we line up our beliefs in accordance with our words, so that we end up no longer knowing what we truly think' (Veyne, 1988: 56)—which is not nearly as bad as it sounds because 'the value of the truth is useless, it is always double-sided. Truth is the name we give to the choices to which we cling' (Veyne, 1988: 127) which is the sort of thing that a scapegoater might say after the sanguinary deed. The 'capacity to simultaneously believe in incompatible truths'—such as the innocence and the guilt of the accused, the normality and the abnormality of the victim— may well be 'the mark of times of intellectual confusion' but such confusion is hardly irrational, for this very confusion 'corresponds to a sectarian politics of alliance' which was the political and cultural lifeblood of the democratic *polis* (Veyne, 1988: 56). As Veyne summarizes

> One feels more at ease studying beliefs, religious or otherwise, when one understands that truth is plural and analogical. This analogy among the true makes the heterogeneity of the programs go unsuspected. We continue to be within the true when we unwittingly change wavelengths. Our sincerity is complete when we forget the imperatives and usages of the truth of five minutes ago in order to adopt those of the new one. (Veyne, 1988: 87)

This sounds like social media. And, as far as Veyne is concerned, 'Regarding myth, the Greeks lived for a thousand years in this state. The moment an individual wishes to convince and be recognized, he must respect different ideas, if they are

---

[16] This notion does not appear to be essentially different from the 'Dreamtime' of Australian aboriginal cultures during which the boundaries between the sacred and profane worlds were first formed.

forces, and must partake of them a little' (Veyne, 1988: 56) if one is to be a true citizen within the democratic city-state, or the internet. The historical experience of Athens proves that the rational conclusion to be drawn is that

> The number and structure of experiential or imaginary worlds are not an anthropological constant but vary throughout history. The only constant of truth lies in its claim to truth, and this claim is only a formal one. The content of norms it embodies depends on the society or, to put it differently: in the same society there are several truths, which, despite their differences, are each as true as the other. (Veyne, 1988: 88)

In clear distinction from the Hebrews, the Greeks found a way to manage the crisis of undifferentiation with techniques that were similar in form but invested with substantially different meaning. The scapegoat is the product of rhetoric and the scapegoating mechanism is a rhetorical device commensurate with its capacity to act as a 'force' within the polis, something that was 'good to think' even if it was devoid of 'truth'; in short, 'myth had become a rhetorical truth' (Veyne, 1988: 79) and it was both recognized and deployed as such.

> One imagines, then, that what [the Hellenes] felt was less disbelief, strictly speaking, than a feeling of conventionality or derision in response to the fixed character of this mythology. Hence, a special modality of belief: the content of set speeches was perceived not as true or, moreover, as false, but as verbal. The obligations of this 'stock language' devolve not to the side of political power but to an institution peculiar to the period: rhetoric. Nevertheless, interested parties were not against it, for they could distinguish between the letter and the good intention: although it was not true, it was well said. (Veyne, 1988: 79)

In contrast, the absolute demand for truth (or the demand for an absolute truth) is a wholly culturally specific form of moralism, primarily of Hebraic origins as per Girard. It was not the case, then, that the Greeks, like Sophocles, 'knew' that there were scapegoats as the Jews did; rather, their epistemological bias, as revealed in *Oedipus Tyrannus*, was 'We know that those who are responsible for knowing whether or not there are scapegoats know, in fact, that there are scapegoats—or so they say, and we must believe them because in times of crisis, the city, which is the most important thing in the world, requires scapegoats, as the case of Oedipus clearly proved as we choose to believe'. The joke may well be on Girard, then, for the 'essence of a myth is not that everyone knows it but that it is supposed to be known and is worthy of being known by all. Furthermore, it was not generally known' (Veyne, 1988: 45), for in a 'general way the Athenian public were aware of the existence of the mythical world in which tragedies took place, but they did not know the details of the stories' (Veyne, 1988: 45). Which is how Sophocles was able to represent an Oedipal tragedy assembled from elements of the Oedipal myth as a way of making his point about the politically engineered nature of the scapegoat which, while true, did absolutely nothing to lessen its power to bring forth generative unanimity, for in the end tragic Oedipus, who might well be innocent, voluntarily complies with the cultural expectations of the citizens and first blinds and then exiles himself in conformity with the community expectation of unanimous victimage.[17] 'Therefore,

[17] See Chap. 1, above.

it is impossible for a myth to be completely mythical. The Greeks could criticize the details of fables, but they could not disregard the fables themselves. The only debate was to decide whether mythology was truthful only in part or in its entirety' (Veyne, 1988: 62). And to provide another stumbling-block to Girard's project: historically, Christianity did surprisingly little to resolve the 'problem' of the alleged truthfulness of Greek *muthos*. As Veyne forces upon us, Christians 'did not call the myths "vain fables' so much as term them "unworthy conceptions"' which explains why the 'apologetics of ancient Christianity leave such a strange impression. It seems that, to establish God, it was enough to banish the other gods. The desire was not so much to destroy false ideas as to supplant them' (Veyne, 1988: 113–114). The surprising, and somewhat disturbing, truth of the early history of Christian de-paganization is that it largely complied with the polytheistic discursive strategies of rhetoric and oratory.

> It mattered little that the attacks against the god of fable were irrelevant; what was important was to make it understood that no logic of appeasement would be tolerated. The pagan gods were unworthy, and that was that. Their unworthiness undoubtedly implied their falseness, but the implication that carried more weight than this intellectual viewpoint was, above all, that people no longer wished to hear about them. They did not deserve to exist. (Veyne, 1988: 114)

And since to deny the gods was to make an implied argument against supernatural agency as such, in effect a kind of primitive a-theism, Christian apologists adopted a technique worthy of any Gentile orator.

> If some thinking person's scruple makes it necessary to translate this unworthiness into doctrine, one will say … that the pagan gods are not untrue gods but falsified gods: they are demons that have passed themselves off as gods in order to mislead men, particularly by their knowledge of the future. They have impressed men with veracious oracles. (Veyne, 1988: 114)

Which is exactly what Sophocles suggested through tragedy. And it might be the source-point for Girard's implacable moral conviction that sacrifice is satanic: the gods who devoured the offerings of blood and flesh were, in an allegorical sense, 'diabolic,' the result being that while we no longer 'officially' sacrifice, because we know that the 'gods' who demand sacrifice really are not, we do continue to execute criminals for we know that the State is real and demands victims of a different sort. For, if it is possible to be double-minded about Greek myth then it as just as possible to be equally double-minded about the *pharmakos* or the scapegoat: it both is and is-not. And it is double-sided thinking that allowed the persecution of innocent victims to continue and exponentially increase to the level of genocide in the Christian and post-Christian eras. My first-year law students knew this as well although, like the Athenians, they didn't know that they knew it. Or they just pretended that they didn't because everything is all subjective anyway.

12.1.1 'Sacrifice with a Bad Conscience': Modernity and De-sacralization

Louis Gernet, whom Girard often follows quite closely, posited two general forms of capital punishment. The first variant is the purification of the community through the violent, and fatal, elimination of spiritual 'pollution' identified with the ambivalently harmful and benign *pharmakon*.[18] The second variant 'was accomplished with the minimum of formalities and is devoid of religious connotations,' meaning it is purely secular.

> It is an *apagoge*; its rough and ready character might remind us of the frontier 'justice' of American Westerns. According to Gernet, it was usually used on criminals who had been caught in the act, and it was always ratified by the common accord of the community. However, says Gernet, the public nature of these acts would not have been enough to make the execution of the criminals possible if these criminals had not usually been foreigners; that is, individuals whose death entailed no risk of endless revenge within the community. (Girard, 1977: 299)

For Girard, this lack of available avengers to exact retribution for the execution of the accused is in indispensable requirement for the scapegoat, so that every victim of the lynch mob may be formally understood as a sacrificial victim de facto if not de jure.

> The second type of capital punishment is very different from the first in form—or rather, lack of form. Nevertheless, the two are related. If we acknowledge the role of the surrogate victim in the genesis of religious forms, we cannot regard them as independent institutions. Generative unanimity operates in both cases. In the first type it perpetrates capital punishment by means of ritual; in the second type generative unanimity makes an actual appearance—admittedly in diluted and degenerate form (otherwise its appearance would not be possible[19]), but savagely and spontaneously nonetheless. This latter mode of unanimity gradually evolves into what can perhaps be described as an institutionalized and legalized form of mob violence. (Girard, 1977: 299)

'The real question' as Rene Girard puts it in direct imitation of Camus' Jean-Baptiste Clamence[20] is 'why do we, all of us, have to keep judging and being judged?'—which is the question of law itself. The answer, I believe, lies with developing a suggestion that Girard made but did not always fully explicate: the historical transition from the sacrificial society to what might be called the *persecuting society*, exemplified by the preternatural case of the blood atonement of Gary Gilmore.[21] We still demand victims but we understand our violence in terms that are exclusively secular. Herein lies the great *skandalon*, or 'stumbling block', of Girardian theory: the persecution mechanism is a 'profane' (secular) substitution for the sacrificial

---

[18] See Chap. 9, above.

[19] Meaning that its 'truth' could no longer be mis-recognized.

[20] See Chap. 9, above.

[21] See Chap. 11, above.

mechanism, necessitating the *de*-sacralization the 'victim'.[22] Which explains why we no longer believe in revolution but only in catastrophe, or in the apocalypse. As Girard intuited (Girard & Chantre, 2010), the future is the apocalypse,[23] meaning that the post-human will not be post-historical but neo-anthropological with all the forms of praxis (rites, rituals, prohibitions) that were spawned by the scapegoating mechanism returning in full, unrestrained force which is nothing less than the return of a collectively willed *meconnaissance* on a planetary scale. For him, 'History,' the by-product of the pre-historical event of sacrificial violence and of all of the accompanying conditions necessary for sacred murder, is wholly mortal, its absolute finitude calamitously revealed through the expulsion of the sacred, that which sets a limit to the violence of the secular. 'The possibility of history's end makes history itself possible' because History was created by a foundational event that is vulnerable to the most radical reversal conceivable: 'Humanity cannot escape its own history, because there is no history without history's end' which is the abolition of the scapegoat which is inevitable (Gardner, 2013: 251). History, being nothing more than the temporal sequence of a series of violent actions that performatively create and police differences, will die when the *katechon*, the counter-force that binds of infinite violence, no longer operates.[24] At this point, Girard, in the face of the apocalypse, has to mimic Kierkegaard and make a leap of faith. The crucial 'difference' between them was that the Girardian apocalypse is not Biblical but historical (profane), devoid of redemptive power: as it is nothing other than the secular regression of modernity to pre-modernity through the universalization of unmediated metaphysical desire and a corresponding crisis-of-undifferentiation, Girard was able to posit a truly revolutionary version of the secularization thesis. What name do we give to the event that takes place when we have to face the full consequences of our knowledge that the secular order is a metaphysically bereft imitation of a foundational act ontologically saturated with murdered innocent people and false 'gods'[25]? Modernity, in the purest Girardian sense, is the cataclysm of the loss of the sacrificial power of the archaic-sacred victim, flowing on from the earlier disabling of the mis-recognized machinery of scapegoating. Ironically, the bearer of responsibility for the disaster is Christianity itself. For Girard, speaking in the purely theological sense, 'Christianity represents a

---

[22] The defining difference between sacred mythology and profane persecution lies with the 'sacralization of the victim: always present with the former, almost completely absent from the latter' (Girard, 1978: 198 n 11). Once again Girard overestimates the effect of demystification: the sacred can only be held to be completely absent from the one executed (like Gilmore) if we assume that the absence of mis-recognition nullifies affectivity.

[23] Understood in completely 'natural' terms': 'For Girard it pertains especially to the collapse of institutions, the disintegration of order, which he sees in the broadest terms as a "destruction of differences" (or in-differentiation), the process by which cultural distinctions are collapsed.' The apocalypse emerges as what remains after we have de-activated civilization's multitudinous circuit-breakers of differentiation that inhibited an infinitely reciprocating and escalating violence, which may or may not culminate in collective self-destruction (Gardner, 2013: 234). See below.

[24] See below.

[25] Who are themselves nothing more than the personified fruits of the sacrificial blood, skin, and fat. As Girard expressed it with graveyard wit, 'every god, ultimately, conceals a dead man,' (Girard, Oughhourlian and Lefort 2003: 82). Usually flayed.

demystification of the sacred, the unveiling of its violent roots' meaning that 'Christ brought to light what was 'hidden since the foundation of the world,' that is, 'by revealing the victim's innocence, the Passion makes positive what was still negative in myths [*muthoi*]: we now know that victims are never guilty" (Rene Girard qtd. Cerella, 2015: 53).[26] Which is the moment of catastrophe.

12.2 Political Religion: The Failed Substitute for the *Katechon*

The problem, perhaps intractable, is that the sacred and its resultant reconciliations don't sell anymore. Why? Because Christianity itself is the cause of its ultimate failure, for of all of the religions of the world Christianity uniquely 'demystifies religion'; 'Demystification, which is a good in the absolute, has proven bad in the relative, for we were not prepared to shoulder its consequences. We are not Christian enough. The paradox can be put in a different way. Christianity is the only religion that has foreseen its own failure. This prescience is known as the apocalypse' (Girard & Chantre, 2010: 10). But what Scripture, the raw template of Girard's 'anthropology of revelation' also does is to anticipate by two thousand years the fatality of a crisis of undifferentiation that has recently globalized.[27] The result is that 'We are threatened with death. The Judeo-Christian message is that if we do not reconcile with one another, there are no longer sacrificial victims to save our skin. The kingdom of God offers reconciliation or nothing' (Girard, 2020: 128).[28] And the existential bleakness of this choice flows from the moralization of Truth as an absolute value.

> We are aware that the Gospels reject persecution. What we do not realize is that, by doing so, they release its mechanism and demolish the entire human religion and the resulting cultures: we fail to recognize the fruit of the prosecutor's accounts of persecution in the symbolic forces surrounding us. But the very fact that these forms have a diminished hold, and their power of illusion weakened, is due precisely to our increasing ability to identify the underlying scapegoat mechanisms. Once understood, the mechanisms can no longer operate; we believe less and less in the culpability of the victims they demand. Deprived of the food that sustains them, the institutions derived from these mechanisms collapse one after the other about us. Whether we know it or not, the Gospels are responsible for this collapse. (Girard, 1986: 101)

In point of fact, however, the Gospels were not the only ancient texts to call for the wholesale abolition of blood sacrifice; the pre-Socratic mystery religion of the Pythagoreans and the Orpheus cult did likewise (Scubla, 1988; Stroumsa, 2012). Despite all of the evidence to the contrary, Girard is wedded to his Gospel-centric view of global cataclysm; 'For better or worse, the Gospel revelation makes the crisis

[26] He means the 'non-guilt' of victims in the transcendental sense.

[27] See below.

[28] In secular terms this would be a universal reconciliation driven by wholly ethical rather than formally religious motivations.

inevitable. By exposing the secret of the persecutors' representation it prevents the mechanism of the victim from ever functioning and creating, at the height of mimetic disorder, a new order of ritual expulsion that replaces the old' (Girard, 1986: 190–191). The real stumbling-block here is 'prevents .... From ever functioning,' for I believe this to be an untested hypothesis as does Dupuy.

As I have already discussed in Chap. 1, the creation of 'History,' which is 'historical' time, or time understood historically, is an accident of the sacred and the mythic sacrificial: 'The history of humankind is really the history of the "sacred," the communal articulation of sacred and profane by which a society orders itself. [...] Every society no matter how advanced still rests on this primitive distinction, at least to the degree it survives and however sublimated it may be' (Gardner, 2013: 238). But a second paradox is present here: Girard's apocalypse-of-the-secular is not an unveiling of the Truth but a collective failure to re-impose the veil of *meconnaissation* which would seemingly require a cultural regression toward the now defunct transcendental. The dawn of the post-human 'is an epoch that can *literally* be read as apocalyptic provided that one interprets this concept as an un-covering, un-veiling and re-vealing of all those contradictions that, maturing during modernity, end up exploding in the Globality' (Cerella, 2015: 44).[29] From this perspective, 'if we agree to follow Christianity, violence is laid bare,[30] unleashed, and its sterility revealed in the eyes of all. ... Violence now founds nothing; only resentment is constantly growing, in other words, mimetically, faced with the revelation of its own truth' (Girard & Chantre, 2010: 103). Christianity disables the scapegoat mechanism from within through the Passion: the naivete (or 'authentic' *meconnaissation*) of polytheistic religions is made impossible given the stumbling-block (*skandalon*) of the true innocence of the victim of sacralizing violence, who can no longer serve as the grounds of that difference (the sacred) which cures mimetic pathology; 'Scapegoating, the time-tested reflex of social self-defense, no longer works—thanks to the Gospels, which robs us of our sacrificial myths and religious lies. Christianity, *in history*, though, cannot but make things worse' (Gardner, 2011: 6).[31] And the reason why it makes things worse is that the 'Truth' cannot restrain violence but perversely operates to intensify the demand for it. If the lie of sacrificial expiation can no longer compel consent, the only manner in which otherwise unbridled violence can be rendered controllable[32] is through some substitutional and profane mechanism of containment, which, within the Christian apocalyptic literature is the *katechon* (a.k.a. the 'Restrainer'[33]): 'The "restrainer" is the force which takes effect

[29] I discuss 'Globality' in terms of globalization; see below.

[30] Meaning that the scapegoat is innocent, at least insofar as she does not possess the supernatural attributes assigned to her regardless of whatever she did or did not do to attract the unanimous enmity of the crowd.

[31] Which is the basis of Pierre Manent's repudiation of Girard; see above.

[32] See Chap. 11, above.

[33] 'Theologically [...] the *katechon* is an ambiguous concept. The *katechon* is both poison and antidote. As a restrainer, it is a means to prevent destruction. At the same time, however, it also uses anarchy or violence to prevent the total outbreak of anarchy or violence. Theologically speaking, it not only postpones the reign of the Antichrist but it also holds back the second coming of Christ.

within history through God's governance of the world, and which sets due limits to evil. The "restrainer" itself is not God; *it is not without guilt*; but God makes use of it in order to preserve the world from destruction' (Dietrich Bonhoeffer qtd. Palaver, 2007: 86). But the 'restrainer' also acts as yet one more point of intersection between Girard and Carl Schmitt,[34] who follows Thomas Hobbes in following Saint Paul who posits the *katechon* as a type of *pharmakon* (poison = antidote); specifically, the application of the *pharmakos* to the realm of international politics and law. For Schmitt, the apocalyptic agent is a personification of the quiddity of the Friend-Enemy distinction which, like the scapegoat mechanism, limits violence through the introduction of difference.

> The political, correctly understood, is only the degree of intensity of a unity. Political unity can contain and comprehend different concerns. But it always designates the most intense degree of a unity, from which, consequently, the most intensive distinction—the grouping of friend and enemy—is determined. Political unity is the highest unity—not because it is an omnipotent dictator, or because it levels out all other unities, but because it decides, and has the potential to prevent all other opposing groups from disassociating into a state of extreme enmity—that is, into civil war. (Palaver, 2007: 74)

The audacity of Schmitt's suggestion is that the Friend-Enemy distinction mimics the work of the *katechon* because it operates not to maximize violence but to compartmentalize it, to prevent a far greater crisis of the undifferentiation[35] of that most extreme existential enmity known as civil war, or political suicide. So, Schmitt, just like Girard, unveils Christianity as the true engine of modernity: the monotheistic erasure of the originary *meconnaissance* of sacrifice receives its profane double in the form of the Enlightenment's totalitarian de-sacralization. Against all odds, the Age of Reason turns out to be a mimetic copy of the Passion, the very junior partner to Christianity's incomparably more revolutionary de-sacralization of the world and its 'History.'

> The crucifixion [...] would represent the event-advent of modernity. It is only thanks to the unveiling of the mimetic mechanism brought about by the Christian message that humanity could escape the 'sacrificial loop,' so starting a progressive and non-cyclic historical path (i.e. not linked to the sacrificial cycle). Modernity, therefore, should be understood literally as [the] overcoming of a modus, a limit, that is, the scapegoat mechanism. (Brighi & Cerella, 2015: 13–14)

The good news is that scapegoating is longer possible because it can no longer be mis-taken as Truth; the bad news is that beginning with the modernizing process in the eighteenth century the proliferating mimetic crises of unlimited internal mediation

---

This ambiguity of the concept of the *katechon* is rooted in the pagan sacred. The *katechon* contains violence in both senses of the word "contain"' (Palaver, 2007: 85). See Chap. 11, above.

[34] See Chap. 4, above.

[35] 'When Schmitt affirms that the political indicates only the degree of intensity of an association or disassociation, he is not doing the apology of conflict and violence. For the political is not only the breaking of form by the disorder that never vanishes, but also disorder in search of a form.... "The political entity presupposes the real existence of an enemy and therefore coexistence with another political entity". Coexistence is difference' (Cerella, 2015: 48).

fuel a collective demand for a return to the machinery of scapegoating, ensuring that mimetic conflict will remain unmediated and unexpiated. Modernity is like Christianity, Nietzsche slyly winked to us, because it 'loves' the Truth, which means that the secular must, in its own way, slavishly imitate the Christian and unconditionally de-mystify the world, which means de-sacralizing it.

> All order must perforce come into being in violence, and no order can evade the arbitrariness of its origins. [...] Suppose, then, an order based on the morality of truth[36]: The progress of such an order would destroy its foundations, because it would reveal their arbitrariness for what it is. It would be a moral order relentlessly inculpating itself. The decomposition of Western morality shows itself in the mad scramble to claim victimhood, the new 'high ground' of moral authority. (Gardner, 2013: 245–246)

For Girard, any great 'Christian experience is apocalyptic because what one realizes is that after the decomposition of the sacrificial order there is nothing standing between ourselves and our possible destruction' (Girard, Antonello and de Castro Rocha 2008: 235). And this means that 'the Christian ethic, with its emphasis on freedom and free will, would lead to a process of demystification and de-sacralization because 'secularization also entails the end of the sacrificial' (Brighi & Cerella, 2015: 14). But there is no cure without a disease which is the concept of the *pharmakon* stood on its head, meaning that modernity is haunted by a Derridean supplement[37] of its own making, 'a temporality of the sacrificial, and violence [that] is subject to erosion and entropy [...] When, thanks to Christianity, we get rid of the sacred, there is a salvific opening to *agape*, to charity, there is also an opening up to perhaps greater violence' (Pierpaolo Antonello qtd. Brighi & Cerella, 2015: 14). The-will-to-scapegoat intensifies without limit precisely because the metaphysically ungrounded machinery of the Enlightenment provides no decisive or binding resolution; violence is profane and devoid of transcendental signification which renders it limitless. The modern Self's mis-recognition of its own latent capacity for mimetic violence is the guarantor of the eternal return of the sacrificial mechanism but now in a wholly secular form; internal mediation makes the potential for mimetic rivalry universal while the abolition of the supernatural (the sacred) results in the loss of effectiveness of sacrifice, which equals the failure of the *katharsis* (or exorcism) that sets an objective limit to the divine violence of sacrifice. Historically, expiation has proven possible because the will-to-revenge can, in the end, be satiated; but because Christianity operates 'as the force of the sacred, violence proper probably cannot exist prior to the sacred itself.'

> If it is a phenomenon of the sacred, though, in the purest, most arbitrary and destructive sense, violence seems to appear especially when the sacred has broken down, in its aftermath, as a futile attempt to restore it. Scapegoating intensifies as a desperate attempt to restore or revert to sacrifice, after it has lost its religious effectiveness; it is sacrifice with a bad conscience. (Gardner, 2011: 6–7)

And politics itself falls prey to the collectively willed 'victimary inflation' of sacrifice (Fornari, 2009: 25) for it is the case that politics 'is part of violence, not

[36] This, of course, is the vital supposition.

[37] See Chap. 1, above.

violence part of politics' (Girard & Chantre, 2010: 109). The rub, for Girard, is that 'liberalism fails to acknowledge the permanently violent, necessarily sacrificial basis of political order' (Brighi & Cerella, 2015: 16) meaning that the mechanism has been rebuilt, founded upon a wholly secular conception of the scapegoat which is the cornerstone of the modernity's defining achievement: *political religion.*

As with so many other things modern, political religion has something to do with Jean-Jacques Rousseau, about whom it can be rightly said was responsible for modernity's greatest invention: the resurrection of the dead God as the State, or, in his unique parlance, the *general will.* Which is pure mimesis, because it is all about social being as *citizenship,* one of the preeminent guises of metaphysical desire within the post-theistic age of profanity.

> The primitive passions, which all tend directly toward our happiness, focus us only on objects that relate to it, and having only *amour de soi*[38] as a principle, are all loving and gentle in their essence. But when, being *deflected from their object by obstacles, they focus on removing the obstacle rather than on reaching the object,* then their nature changes and they become irascible and hateful. And that is how *amour soi,* which is a good and absolute feeling, becomes *amour-propre,*[39] which is to say a relative feeling by which one makes comparisons; the latter feeling demands preferences, and its enjoyment is purely negative, as it no longer seeks satisfaction in our own benefit but solely in the harm of another. (Jean-Jacques Rousseau qtd. Dupuy, 2015: 74 n 19; Dupuy, 2013: 165–168)

As a result, 'When … men begin to cast their eyes upon their fellows …. their interests cross each other … [and] *amour soi* put into fermentation changes into *amour-propre*' (Jean-Jacques Rousseau qtd. Dupuy, 2013: 166 n 16). As Dupuy has argued, what is 'utterly novel about modernity […] is its egalitarian conception of social relationships—not that equality is fully realized, of course, but it nonetheless furnishes the collective imagination with an ideal' (Dupuy, 2013: 158) which is pre-determined to generate crises of metaphysical desire and the successive re-deployment of sacrificial mechanisms to channel the psychic surpluses of mimetic pathology.

> Rousseau demystified the evil that exists in [Leibniz's] the best of all possible worlds—metaphysical evil—by revealing its anthropological foundation: order is built up on the backs of scapegoats. In the collective process of victimization, each person finds in the hateful regard that others cast upon the scapegoat a sufficient reason to hate the scapegoat himself. (Dupuy, 2015: 36)

The public and private rituals of democratic society are, even if only unconsciously, the means by which the internally mediated society attempts to contain otherwise unbridled mimetic rivalry. The catch is that in order to acquire this perfect unity of manners it is necessary to apply unmediated violence to the incorrigibly violent. Benjamin Constant, who in effect re-named Rousseau's general will 'popular sovereignty,' a totalizing form of majoritarianism, expressed it through a very neat formula: 'offering to the people as a whole the holocaust of the people taken one

[38] Natural feeling; spontaneous 'naïve' egoism.

[39] Public persona; calculated social egoism.

by one' (Benjamin Constant qtd. Dupuy, 2013: 109).[40] 'Legitimacy' (*raison d'etat*), the secular cornerstone of political religion, requires a mechanism of violence to establish itself (or re-insert difference) following the establishment of the general will that is itself the revolutionary event.

> With the Christian era, the ritual of bloodshed disappears; a prelude to the disappearance of ritual itself. The following step demands a secular version of sacrifice: regicide, twice over, with Charles I, then Louis XVI. Here, too, a singular irreversible fact, the killing of *that* victim is enough to herald in an age in which neither have goats to be slaughtered nor have beheaded kings to be commemorated. Then the word *sacrifice* returns in triumph in August 1914. It is no longer a single wretched individual—an entire generation of nameless young men is raised to the nobility of victim and buried in ditches, which are now trenches. (Calasso, 2018: 183–184)

Or as Charles Baudelaire put it, since 'superstition is the depository of all truths,' revolution, 'through sacrifice, confirms superstition'. Ergo, modern persecution is a double 'accident,' the repetition of a superstition (= 'error'). The agony of the (post-sacrificial) political religion of modernity is the absolute and inhuman linearity of irredeemable profane (historical) Time, which is the negation of the restorative cyclical pattern of sacred Time (redemption and renewal through sacrifice) which results in mass killings but bereft of a restorative, or re-stabilizing, 'finality'. For the *pharmakon* is the bearer of a double transference: the poison that kills and the medicine that heals. We moderns may or may not achieve *katharsis* through execution but we can never truly regenerate.

12.3 The Persecution Society: Political Religion as *Skandalon*

Michel Serres expressed political religion's dilemma supremely well.

> [The] truth is that no one ever knew and no one knows how a unanimous agreement is formed among separate individuals. The truth is that this question is still dark, black, in the shadows [...] What is the collective? Politics is the set of theatrical discourses of magicians who want us to believe that they know what it is.
>
> However, there is at least one clear answer to this question. And professional politicians usually know it. For unanimity to appear within a group, sometimes all that is necessary is to bring about general animosity toward the one who will be labelled public enemy. All that is necessary is to find an object of hatred and execration. Best-sellers and landslide elections occur in this way. General will is rare and perhaps only theoretical. General hatred is frequent and is part of the practical world. Not only does Rousseau attest to the formation of a general will, but he also observes, through thick shadows, that it is formed only through animosity, that it is formed only because he is its victim. Why? I don't know; he doesn't know; no one knows; it's not clear; it may never be clear: it is nonetheless so. Union is produced through expulsion. And he is the one who is expelled. (Serres, 2007: 118–119)

[40] 'Hitler came to power by way of elections, and any majority power, in the absence of guarantees of ethical origin, is only lynching, as the Greeks knew' (Fornari, 2009: 35).

The answer to Clamence's question concerning the eternal recurrence of judgment is vital to the success of Girard's entire project, as Roberto Calasso fully understood: 'In this tortuous Enlightenment vision [...] Girard's main weakness becomes apparent; persecution has never, in fact, become so widespread as in the modern West which ignores sacrifice and regards it as a superstition' (Calasso, 2018: 170). This is not quite right for Girard does possess an explanation for modernity's hyperviolence. The correct answer, I believe, lies with developing a suggestion that Girard made but often left implicit: the historical transition to the 'post' sacrificial society of modernity generates a dangerous supplement to political religion: the *persecution society*. Because of the universality of mimetic conflict and *ressentiment* we still demand victims; the vital difference is that we understand our violence in terms that are exclusively profane, which means that post-sacrificial killings need to be mediated through the apparatuses of the secular administrative State so that it can then be represented and experienced as a post-metaphysical form of *meconnaissance*. Here is the great *skandalon* of political religion: the persecution mechanism of the Enlightenment (atheist) State is a profane substitute for the sacrificial mechanism that now actively demands the perpetual de-sacralization the victim as part of the wider cultural project of the exclusion of the transcendental from public space. If the sacrificial victim is the cornerstone of History, then the persecuted victim is the cornerstone of modernity. Persecution society, unlike its pre-modern progenitors, always operates under the full self-awareness of a radical finitude ('sacrifice with a bad conscience'): it knows that it will always fail because the true sacrificial mechanism of the conflictual mimesis of mediation and reconciliation will be unable to successfully replicate itself. In its place, however, we observe the scandal of a self-consciously profaned sacrifice as an exercise in mimetic simulation: execution, mass murder, ethnic cleansing, genocide all as the substitutes for the rites and rituals of expulsion and immolation. To telescope things tremendously: political religion is the 'double-minded' partial or quasi-demystification of the scapegoat mechanism, the abandonment of archaic religion and pagan mythology but the uninterrupted quest for generative unanimity through a secular form of *meconnaissance* that is only partially mis-recognized as such.

Girard's favored examples of this long-term trend are the 'persecutorial' (or inquisitorial) texts of the witchcraft trials of the sixteenth and seventeenth centuries (Girard, 1986) that served as the templates for the later bio-medical texts supporting an entire discursive apparatus concerning the sacrilegious-antisocial-criminal-deviant: the insane, the impaired, the diseased, the sexually 'perverted,' and the criminally insane and which, slightly later on as the mimetic intensity of persecution pathologized, entire populations and peoples (Jews, Gypsies, the bourgeoisie). To take a world-historical example: with the great genocides of the Soviet Union and Germany in the twentieth century we find an amazing convergence of language between the two ostensibly antithetical regimes through their shared medicalization of the murdered in terms of 'extermination' and 'sanitation,' words deliberately employed because 'vermin' can never possess positive value, unlike the ambivalent *pharmakon*. 'The central role played by sacrifice in archaic societies has now been taken over by experiment' (Calasso, 2018: 267) for the defining feature of both 'Medieval and modern persecutors do not worship their victims, they only hate them' (Girard, 1986: 38).[41] Contemporary persecutions reveal their *meconnaissation* of 'the degenerated and half-decomposed' myths of the archaic era of the sacred and because of the enforced disenchantment of the world, persecution can never be perceived in its sacrificial dimensions. It is, rather, compelled to eternally operate under a wholly profane form of *meconnaissance*; whereas ritualistic sacrifice sacralized the victim, bureaucratized persecution normalizes the persecutor[42]: 'If the profane—i.e., the profaner—devours what is sacred, then sacred and profane will merge in an entirely new way that makes it impossible, from then on, to separate them' (Calasso, 2018: 333). Whereas the sacred (purified) sacrificer possessed a unitary consciousness (belief in the victim-as-sacred), the profane (normalized) persecutor possesses a split consciousness, an irrepressible anxiety over the possible 'elevation' of the exterminated vermin to the status of innocent victim which, in the now hopelessly archaic language of humanistic morality, denotes a kind of moral 'righteousness' in lieu of a supernatural sanctity. The un-endurable condition of the pure linearity of profane Time is that desacralization has resulted in the wholesale substitution of meaningless mechanical causality for meaningful teleological outcomes.

The bad faith of the performatively secular persecutor is that she is actually transgressing against a modernity mystified by its own profanity by unconsciously mimicking a sacrificial process that can only be superficially disguised as an act of public safety, as Robespierre expressed it. Since the secular is absolute finitude, knowledge and understanding are inherently fallible, meaning that mistakes can be made and procedures violated, accidents which can never occur with the supernatural rites of the sacrifice, as Kafka endlessly agonized over.[43] In a sense, it is an issue of risk management: persecution carries within it the potential for an unintentional reinvestment of the vermin with a quasi-sacred status through the violation of the (allegedly) inalienable 'human rights' of the accused.[44] And it is precisely this uncertainty, the self-doubt of a hyper-developed but quintessentially modern self-consciousness, that,

[41] The 'reified process of mass persecution implies radical "de-ontologization" of the victims, who will be effective only so far as they are declared to be non-existent, or rather are implicitly understood not to exist' (Fornari, 2009: 25). It would appear that anything that can be made subject to mass-commodification cannot, for that reason alone, be considered truly sacred.

[42] 'Since we no longer believe in the ancient gods, whose transfiguring cloak covered the victims they devoured, the repetition itself, organized technically and transformed into bureaucracy, becomes the serial substitute of concealment, a guarantee to each single member to make him more hopeful that he will not be ground up in the mechanism, devoured by the machine enabling him to devour' (Fornari, 2009: 24).

[43] See Chap. 8, above. 'It is a professional misconception that mythic images or mystic terminology represent indistinct oracles, pliable and submissive to any will, while the scientific language of positivism owns the rights of truth. There can be nothing further removed from reality than this historical preconception' (Taubes, 2013: 15).

[44] A full treatment of this problem, one of the most serious for Girard, would require an entirely separate work. It lies at the heart of the occluded interactions between the text of historical transition from paganism to Christianity to atheism and the sub-text of the broader cultural transformations of sacrifice and persecution. Put simply, I believe that the answer lies in alternative ways of

most of the time, worked to provide some kind of *katechon*-like effect in the absence of Providence.[45] Which raises a godless question: does uncertainty operate to limit doubt, or do we actively encourage uncertainty in order to limit persecution? And what can be more inimical to the (anti-) spirit of post-humanism than the inalienable 'right' of the 'human' to 'be' as such? Which is the natural outcome of investing the trans-human 'meat-that-talks' with the properties and value of the immortal soul. For the equally hideous truth of political religion is that while being wholly intolerant in its totalitarian instincts it creates its own profane version of the cult of the victim, because persecution itself can become proof of innocence. A new paradox is created: we attempt to re-introduce a *katechon*-like effect in limiting the violence of unlimited persecution by neo-sacralizing the profane victim but, in the end, set the stage for a new crisis era of undifferentiation: the universalization of victimage.

12.4 From De-sacralization to the Neo-Sacralized Cult of the Victim

Our contemporary reality of neo-sacralization may be defined as the sacralization of the victim within a wholly secular context bereft of metaphysical meaning but replete with cultural value through a series of substitutions of we are only semi-consciously aware but do not wholly mis-recognize. And it was none other than Jean-Jacques Rousseau who was the probable 'founding father' of this profane imitation of the sacred victimage of Christianity: the 'importance of Rousseau's individualism is that he places the victim at the center of culture, making the unique position of marginality the central question for modern society, where the individual person is elevated to the

---

conceptualizing Church and State as contending but not discontinuous forms of bio-power and bio-politics, something which aligns with Giorgio Agamben's vast project on *ecclesia* and *dominium*. Put crudely, the post-Christian cult of the victim is inseparable from the creation of self-sustaining secular *economies of surplus*; no one should ever have to suffer, so that if one does suffer that is unjust in itself. Put mimetically, to suffer is to be *scandalized*. See below.

[45] Giuseppe Fornari offers the intriguing observation that Girard's dogmatic insistence upon the anti-sacrificial meaning of the Gospels causes him to withhold a positive assessment of the safeguarding role performed by the *katechon*. 'Temporary acceptance of the "powers of this world," in Girard, is not accompanied by a really positive evaluation of human culture and the sacred: recognition of institutions founded on sacrifice both before and after Christ is defined in terms of accepting a state of necessity, not as bringing to light what put man in a position to conceive authentic transcendence. As a consequence of this imbalance Girard leans towards an apocalyptic levelling-down somewhat in the style of the early Christians, obviously from a contemporary standpoint but with a similar reluctance to recognize the sphere of political and historical action as really significant ... this reluctance leaves the impression that the apocalypse is settled by Girard's theory and that subsequently, with its assertion of the centrality of the victim, there is nothing else to worry about' (Fornari, 2009: 14). With Girard, having 'nothing else to worry about' really means having nothing else worth talking about: the demystification of the scapegoat mechanism is the be-all and end-all of political and cultural critique, leaving him open to a variety of criticisms concerning the possibly 'positive' value of both mimesis and sacrificial practices. See below.

rank of an institution' (McKenna, 1992: 82); in other words, 'J.J.' is the harbinger of that internal mediation which is intended to provide the ultimate cure for itself.

I have already discussed McKenna's pioneering work on the relevance of deconstruction to Girard's fundamental anthropology in Chap. 1 where I provide a critical discussion of his account of the overlapping ethical concerns of Girard's and Derrida's respective projects, and, by extension, critical legal scholarship and law-and-literature. It comes as no surprise, then, that McKenna shared Girard's conviction concerning the moral imperative linking the innocence of the victim with the demystification of not only the scapegoat but of *meconnaissance* itself: 'The compelling interest of Girard's sacrificial theory of culture is that it locates a victim at "the foundation of the world,"' constituting a 'very concrete case where the victim provides Derrida's terminology … with both anthropological and historical reference' (McKenna, 1992: 130). While it is the case that positive identification 'with the victim can be perverted, diverted into a further conflictual play' this immoral ploy 'only authenticates the undisputed privilege of the victim as the site from which truth is determined in our era' (McKenna, 1992: 164).

> The truth is the victim, and the condition is in our time universal. The post-age is the victim age. The survivor who identifies with the victim, who adopts victimage as his or her truth, as his or her past and future, is a true survivor, a being in whom truth survives and through whom survival is a truth, a genuine human possibility rather than a contingency, alibi, or accident. (McKenna, 1992: 141)

Girard's objection to the 'victim age' is neither that there are no true victims nor that there are only a very few. Neither of these suppositions possess any validity; the reality of genocide, both historical and current, is alone sufficient to prove this and establishes 'the victim as an irreducible referent' who sets an absolute limit upon deconstruction, so that 'What is indelible is just what cannot be erased, what irrefragably remains' (McKenna, 1992: 129). In fact, the cultural construct of victimology in its current and robustly secular form originated with the Holocaust, wherein the '"limit of the thought of sacrifice, its historical limit … is the experience of the death camps, which is perhaps the ultimate horizon of the whole of the modern thinking of sacrifice"' (Miguel de Beistegui qtd. Chabbert, 2020: 30) which is to abolish in toto any distinction between political murder and sacrifice, opening the floodgates to a potential infinite proliferation of neo-sacrificial[46] acts and neo-sacralized victims for, although 'true'[47] sacrifices might be few 'mere' homicides are commonplace. What is valid, however, is the mimetic dimension of victimage, for, just as a human right is no less necessary to the survival and flourishing of the person than any biologically rooted appetite or need, so may the rights of humans give rise to mimetic desire and rivalry, just as do appetites and needs.[48] And it is this ambiguity of objective need versus mimetic desire that serves as the cornerstone of

[46] Meaning politically motivated acts of 'eliminationist' murder but devoid of metaphysical meaning or value.

[47] In the now obsolete 'traditional' or 'religious' sense of the transcendental sacred.

[48] See Chap. 1, above.

our new sacrificial structure, the scapegoating of the scapegoater: 'unnamed, sacrifice continues to demand its victims; it becomes nomadic and displaces everywhere the sites of its cult' (Robert Calasso qtd. McKenna, 1992: 174). The greatest legal anathema of our secular age, the deliberate and wilful infliction of suffering upon the innocent, equates directly to the moral abomination of scapegoating established during the early phases of the Christian age, at least according to Girard; here, law really does seem to be identical to morality.

> Christianity, according to Girard, rehabilitates the sacrificial victims of history against their persecutors or oppressors, but on condition of forgiveness—a condition no one is prepared to acknowledge. The victimary truth revealed by Christ and played out in Christianity, and its self-destruction and the rise of modernity, provokes the counter-response of victimology, the last stand of sacrificial religion, disguised in the garb of victims. This is the situation of fear and trembling that Girard wants to bring to our attention in the contemporary world—the collapse of all moral self-righteousness in the circular firing squad of victimology. (Gardner, 2013: 236–237)

And if moral conscience is insufficient to compel us, McKenna advocates the pragmatic considerations of enlightened self-interest.

> We cannot believe in monsters, for we know what they are. They are sacred, and like the sacred, they are not. When they threaten us, they are nothing but the form violence takes in its indifference to difference, the form our own violence takes when we disown it ... If we know anything, we know that we do not want to be party to a violence born of (self) ignorance of which we stand as much chance as any of being the arbitrary victim. (McKenna, 1992: 198)

Paradoxically, the scapegoat in the post-religious age 'transcends ritual origins to become a sign of vindication' (Dawson, 2013: 133), the affective foundation of both Human Rights and the 'right side of History,' better known as 'social justice'; the 'scapegoat is no longer just a maledicted surrogate—although he is that, too—but a merely expedient victim, and therefore *innocent*. Far from making him an object of contempt, this bestows on him a sympathetic advantage' (Dawson, 2013: 133). Which was not what McKenna anticipated.

> In our day certain aspects of ... the knowledge of the victim, are too vulgarized not to be sullied and perverted, not to become the paradoxical instrument of a more subtle persecution. The unique character of modern times is revealed in the fact that, in the competition for public opinion, the position of the victim is now the most desirable. It is no longer the ancient posture of a supplicant struggling to arouse pity, but a claim for legal and even extra-legal rights. (Girard, 1987a, 1987b (a): 108)

What Girard is doing here is invoking the *bete noire* of undifferentiation: 'Humanity loses its differentiating principles, its powerful victims.[49] Everyone

[49] Along with its capacity to distinguish between 'true' Friend and 'true' Enemy. As Schmitt noted, the de-sacralization of the opponent as a necessary effect of the suspension of the transcendental can have no other result than that of the contemporary scapegoater/persecutor waging *total war* against the enemy. 'Humanization of war means above all a de-divinization, a reduction to a purely human relation renouncing all balances and beliefs, which result from transcendent forces and powers ... Based on pure humanity, on a pure *homo homini homo*, the humanization of war will not last for long. Man rather becomes the being of all beings; he becomes God and animal, and the enemy has to be treated simply like an animal because he cannot be divinized' (Carl Schmitt qtd. Palaver, 2007: 82–83; 91–92 n 63). See below.

becomes a victim and no victim suffices any longer to produce difference—from which it follows, not that victimary antagonisms lessen but that they become frantically intensified, a circular firing squad of victimology, so to say' (Gardner, 2013: 245–246). *'Everyone becomes a victim'* because everyone is an *actor* (who deploys performative gestures to merely mimic the sign of sacralizing suffering) and, after three hundred years of the internal mediation of the de-sacralizing Enlightenment, everyone unconsciously knows it—hence, the 'revenge of the victim,' along with 'its philosophical expressions in post-modernism, deconstruction, and the like' (Gardner, 2013: 236–237). From Girard's dissident perspective the hallmark of the post-Christian world is that 'Christian principles are prevailing in a caricaturist form, whereby the defence of the victim entails new persecutions! One can persecute today only in the name of being against persecution. One can only persecute persecutors. You have to prove that your opponent is a persecutor in order to justify your own desire to persecute' (Gardner, 2013: 258). What appears at first glance as a linear process of 'moral progress'—four thousand years ago the sacralizing condemnation of the victim, two thousand years ago the sacralizing redemption of the victim, today the *neo-sacralizing* elevation of the victim—is, in truth, the mis-recognized return of the primitive represented to modernity in an atheistic form.

> The truth of the victim returns at the height of modernity with the moral inevitability of an avenging angel of the Lord, but also with Satan's demand for compensation.This, the notion that truth is guilt, lies at the heart of revelation in Christ. The West is destroyed by guilt, working itself out through the self-destruction of morality. The triumph of Western ethics culminates in its implosion. [...] That paradox lies at the center of Girard's notion of apocalypse. Echoing Nietzsche, but with reversed values, the *truth* of Western ethics *destroys* Western cultural order. (Gardner, 2013: 244)

If we were to 'blame' any-one or any-thing for this 'revolting predicament' two of the usual suspects immediately spring to mind. The first one is Hegel.

> The purer the principles, the more indelible the stains. [...] Human history has a logic, just as Hegel thought—just not the Hegelian logic terminating in rational 'reconciliation' or the 'rational state' as the 'end of history'. Instead, the archaic returns to wreak the vengeance of the victims through the disintegration of morality into war of all the victims against each other. The archaic returns in the form of the victim, the returning of the dead, to demand compensation. (Gardner, 2013: 248)

The second one is the archetypal world-historical trauma of the Shoah,[50] which was both a de-sacralizing and a neo-sacralizing sacrificial event on a post-sacrificial

[50] In the context of universal history Auschwitz is the symbolic ground-zero of genocide: '"the memory of Auschwitz, that indelible reference point to the Western imagination, forms an obstacle impossible to evade,"' an obstacle in Girard's sense which 'retains its original force' as *skandalon* to logocentrism, 'a stumbling block, a scandal to rationalization' (Saul Friedlander qtd. McKenna, 1992: 129). McKenna approvingly quotes Maurice Blanchot who contributes to the sacralization of the Holocaust by investing the primary (but by no means exclusive) victims of the death-camps with a pseudo-religious significance: 'Humanity was to have died by the ordeal it underwent in some of its members (those who incarnate life itself, almost the totality of a people promised to a perpetual presence)' (Maurice Blanchot qtd. McKenna, 1992: 127).

'industrial' scale, the last great effort to recover the elemental restorative power (*pharmakos*) of the scapegoat, this time employed with full Nietzschean self-awareness in the service of the political religions of atheism, colonialism, racism, antisemitism, and ultra-extremist nationalism. But even if the Shoah had been successful in murdering all of its intended victims it still would have failed: the sacrificial murder depends upon a mis-recognition of what has taken place which would have been precluded by the occlusion (anti-spectacle) of the crime and the demystification of the occult channels required, the regime's laborious resuscitation of pagan mythology notwithstanding. Which, of course, forces a disturbing reconsideration of the role of paganism in the Third Reich: de-Christianization was not just an attempt to create a new politics of cruelty, it was literally intended to provide the magical pre-conditions necessary for a self-consciously restored sacrificial mechanism. The ironic result is that, post-Auschwitz, 'identification with the victim is renunciation of identification with the persecutor' (McKenna, 1992: 211) and failure to strictly comply with either constitutes the violation of two wholly contemporary neo-sacred taboos, whatever the lingering cultural value of the religious origins of the condemnation of false accusations under the Mosaic prohibition against 'bearing of false witness'.

> The Holocaust inaugurated the age of the victim, the foundational category of contemporary politics, and perhaps of ethics too. Nearly every major political battle since has sought to claim the mantle of victimhood. In the victimary, ethics and politics intersect, quickly degenerating into the victimological, as victimhood itself acquires a coveted aura and offers new disguises for victimization. It is the last refuge of the sacred, nearly the only place today from which one can presume to sit in judgment, or at least get away with it. (Gardner, 2016: 1130)

I would, however, reverse this: today, if one claims the entitlement to sit in judgment then one must act as the advocate of the victim—just like Jean-Baptiste Clamence.

> Enlightenment universalism supplies the noose by which modernity closes the circle and strangles itself in post-modernism. Public discourse, politics, media, entertainment, and educational institutions in the West are consumed litigating past injustices, real and imagined, ever since this threshold was decisively crossed in the Sixties. Politics has disintegrated into 'culture war,' in principle non-negotiable (unlike ordinary politics, where nearly everything is negotiable).[51] Victimary revelation splits modern culture into fraternal enemies, the sacred and the profane, the religious and the secular, the archaic and the progressive. The inherent relativity and indeterminacy of the victim renders it inherently polarizing.[52] No culture can be unified on the basis of respect for victims merely, and the tenuous peace between rivals on which modernity depends goes to pieces. (Gardner, 2016: 1130–1131)

The 'universal claim to victim status as the licence for committing atrocities is a strange fruit of the gospel, proving necessary to justify the worst excesses of modern bloodlust' (Cowdell, 2014: 144). Or as Girard, the eternal contrarian, put it, '"the failure of utopia vindicates God and condemns the world"' (Rene Girard qtd. Gardner, 2016: 1131).

---

[51] Not anymore. It is safe to assume that in American politics *everything* has been translated into a question of identity, which, because it is the ultimate source of authenticity, is non-negotiable.

[52] In that no one can be precluded in advance from claiming victimization.

> The biographies of Hitler and Stalin both document the fact that the totalitarian chief is a victim who has escaped his persecutors and succeeded in taking over the persecutory system … in order to become the principle of vengeance itself. The leader is the supreme embodiment of the victim and of the persecutory system that produces victims, a real Christ stripped of his divine nature and transformed into a living, operative image of Satan. (Fornari, 2009: 30)

The occluded paradox of the scapegoat is that within the terms of *meconnaissance* the sacrificer, as understood by himself, is the 'true' victim, not the sacrificed who has 'trespassed' against him[53]: that is, the one who sacrifices does so as a defensive-retaliatory act against the malign presence of the to-be-sacrificed *non*-citizen. This neat trick of mis-recognition is, of course, indispensable to the overall efficacy of scapegoating in establishing the righteousness of the sacrificer's violence. Claiming the mantle of 'true' victimhood, the one who has been injured by the one whom it is *right* to kill, guarantees redemption and, today, compensation. And it is this profane substitution of compensation for reconciliation that provides the interpretive key to Girard's obsession with all things pertaining to secular victimage.

> As soon as concern for victims is universalized in the abstract and becomes an absolute imperative, it can itself become an instrument of injustice. By a sort of overcompensation, there now exists a tendency to make the mere fact of belonging to a minority group a sort of privilege. […] In its extreme forms the omnipotence of the victim in our world is becoming such that we may be slipping toward the brink of a new totalitarianism. (Rene Girard qtd. Armitage, 2021: 102)

To have 'one's historical injuries acknowledged and rectified is dicier than apologists of Enlightenment equity thought' (Gardner, 2011: 8), especially if the related changes within the legal culture concerning compensation for damages and redistribution of outcomes in the face of historical inequalities has provided the material basis for a political culture that has normalized the expectation for automatic reimbursement for injury, trauma, and loss. Girard is certainly not wrong to observe that in least of terms of jurisprudence

> The specific character of the modern world can be ascribed to the victory of the Cross over Satan in the sense of a growing concern for victims everywhere. This concern remained feeble and highly tentative for a long time, but then it became stronger and more focused. We do not realize how anthropologically unique our modern attitude toward victims is. In no other culture has anything even remotely similar ever existed. (Girard, 1996: 208)

But within the culture of political religion things are far more ambivalent because this is the primary arena where struggles over identity are settled; 'Pure justice does not ensure peace; it makes it impossible. Human freedom—the freedom Girard sees exemplified in Dostoevskii's Christ—demands that one abandon the crutch of victimology and by the same token forego the right of retaliation' (Gardner, 2011: 8). Which no one is prepared or even willing to do. Double-mindedness ensures that the true victim is owed the right to become the new victimizer, which is all to the good because truth is partial at best if not relative.

---

[53] Injured? Insulted?

12.5 Victimology: The Sign of Citizenship in the Time of Globalized Undifferentiation

Victimology, or the cult of the victim, may be interpreted as the inversion of Nietzsche's staggering phenomenological critique of the rule of law, which is itself the inversion of the will-to-revenge by means of *ressentiment*: 'Wherever justice is practised and maintained one sees a stronger power seeking a means of putting an end to the senseless raging of *ressentiment* among the weaker powers that stand under it (whether they be groups or individuals)...' (Nietzsche, 1969: 75). He continues.

> The most decisive act, however, that the supreme power performs and accomplishes against the predominance of grudges and rancor—it always takes this action as soon as it is in any way strong enough to do so—is the institution of *law*, the imperative declaration of what in general counts as permitted, as just, in its eyes, and what counts as forbidden, as unjust: once it has instituted the law, it treats violence and capricious acts on the part of individuals or entire groups as offenses against the law, as rebellion against the supreme power itself, and thus leads the feelings of its subjects away from the direct injury caused by such offences; and in the long run it thus attains the reverse of that revenge that is fastened exclusively to the viewpoint of the person injured: from now on the eye is trained to an ever more *impersonal* evaluation of the deed, and this applies even to the eye of the injured person himself ... (Nietzsche, 1969: 75–76)

Victimology = 'the viewpoint of the person injured' = re-training of the eye = the *personal* 'evaluation of the deed' = revenge = 'rebellion against the supreme power' = the substitution of unlicensed internal mediation for external mediation = the reversal of externally mediated justice and injustice. The result is that the ones who feel victimized 'crave to be *hangmen*'.

> There is among them an abundance of the vengeful disguised as judges, who constantly bear the word 'justice' in their mouths like poisonous spittle, always with pursed lips ... Nor is there lacking among them that most disgusting species of the vain, the mendacious failures whose aim is to appear as 'beautiful souls' and who bring to market their deformed sensuality, wrapped up in verses and other swaddling clothes, as 'purity of heart': the species of moral masturbators and 'self-gratifiers.' (Nietzsche, 1969: 123)

But, how exactly, did we reach this historical point in which this inversion-of-the-inversion-which-is-the-reversion-to-revenge become possible?

The globalization of internal mediation culminates in the universalization of *ressentiment* wherein absolutely everyone can lay claim to victim status: everyone resents because in some manner everyone is scandalized, or stumbles over that which blocks them in their efforts to possess the model which is now victimage. The net result is that 'Our world is schizophrenically split between a growing awareness as to the existence of victims and the effort being made to stray far from any revelation of the real causes leading to their persecution' (Fornari, 2009: 12) lest there be any unwanted clarifications concerning the historical agency of victimization. In Girardian terms, the will-to-universal-victimage is the post-modern lynch mob collectively mis-recognized.[54] Under the classic scapegoat mechanism, the sequence of violence

[54] What 'concerns Girard is the potential systemic and bureaucratic totalitarianism that could arise in the name of the equality of outcome for victims' (Armitage, 2021: 102).

terminated with the transformative death of the victim who was immediately sacralized (we could almost interpret this posthumous deification as an archaic form of restitution to the sacrificed), meaning that any further violence by either the sacrificers or the avengers of the scapegoat was taboo, as the murder was itself the founding act of difference that was the salvation of the community. This is why Girard, 'from his anthropological perspective, states that original sin is vengeance—"never-ending vengeance"—because only this process could trigger the cycle of violence that has led to the first mimetic crisis and, therefore, to the actualization of the scapegoat mechanism' (Brighi & Cerella, 2015: 12). But as we have rendered the transcendental obsolete in toto, the magic of the double transference is made nonsensical; today, the violence of the sacrifice is the very thing that spawns the escalation to extremes precisely because there is no terminus, no 'taking up' of the victim,[55] and any attempt to do so is stigmatized as the disguised cynicism of political reaction (or even worse, the a-political). Instead, the exclusionary logic of the profane translates the suffering of the victim into a 'loss,' investing the victim with an inalienable *right* of retribution, in either a hygienic (compensation) or unhygienic (punishment) form. In a desacralized world the escalation to extremes remains a constant threat, and, not infrequently, a realized crisis, because as the scope of retribution can be infinitely expanded owing to the lack of limit/difference, so too can the parameters of victimage be expanded in a similarly unbounded manner—it is something that everyone can claim but which can always be countered by a rival claimant, two different sets of hands reaching for the same thing at the same time. In the end we face the prospect of a Bakhtian inversion of the scapegoating-of-the-scapegoaters, a spectacle wholly worthy of the carnivalesque of social media[56] but which conforms absolutely to the anti-social dynamic of the crisis of undifferentiation.[57]

---

[55] Most clearly evidenced during the 'golden age' (1880–1930) of the American *apogoge*, the lynch-mob as unlicensed hangman. During this time the scapegoated victim was never sacralized after death and remained a defiled corpse throughout, signifying the collapse of the primitive religious sensibility into the communal natural justice of the anti-statist community. If the sacrifice is no longer sublimely salvific it is just a grotesque murder.

[56] See below.

[57] Post-modern culture 'with its various political (neo-Marxist perhaps) configurations, is now a sort of hybrid between the mythic and the Christian, in that it seeks to defend victims while simultaneously victimizing the victimizers. Now, a critique of the logic of the "victimization of victimizers" only works if one accepts the axioms that *all* victims are innocent and that recourse to violence is never helpful in achieving one's ends, namely the defence of victims.' This issue may very well be undecidable; even the introduction of the theory of human rights does not really help because every definition of a right depends upon an un-recognized reservoir of prior assumptions and value judgments. The best and simplest approach may be to opt for a coldly a-moral intellectual lucidity and clinically regard this will-to-inversion as a form of metaphysical violence, wholly apart from any consideration as to whether it is 'justifiable' or not. 'Regardless of the correct response to the cultural situation, it remains perhaps more important simply to recognize the occurrence of sacred violence within the postmodern political landscape in the form of its incessant need to condemn publicly guilty victimizers, for condemnation is [...] perhaps the only cohesive element left to Western culture' (Armitage, 2021: 103). Whatever Girard's politics this last point is a crucial one, for it means that the only true sources of difference and finitude available to us (and highly unstable ones at that) are the endlessly shifting contours of the mimetically possessed self-proclaimed victims

> Resentment unites the very actors who mutually excommunicate each other. It is on a planetary scale that the game of mimetic rivalry will play itself out, a game that binds the rivals all the more compulsively and tightly together even as they claim to have nothing in common. The image that appears to emerge—in place of the 'clash of civilizations' slogan invoked by those who do not understand the state of the world—is that of a civil war within a single global civilization, which has come into being kicking and screaming. (Jean-Pierre Dupuy qtd. Cowdell, 2014: 154)[58]

Which means that the will-to-revenge has gone global which demands the re-emergence of the scapegoat and reintroduces the collective guilt of the populations of the undifferentiated victims/victimizers. According to Girard, the 'apocalypse is a real threat today on a planetary level because the principle of reciprocity has been unmasked and the abstraction has become concrete'(Girard & Chantre, 2010: 19); for, after all, 'the apocalypse is nothing more than an abstraction made real, reality made consistent with its concept, and we have to have the lucidity to say that humanity itself tends toward annihilation.'

> The problem of every social order is to channel and limit desires so that conflict is kept manageable; this is accomplished (though not consciously intended) by religion and its rituals, and by hierarchy [external mediation]. These are weakened or undone by the rise of democracy or equality. And today, the expansive economic dynamism of the West cannot but bring the whole world into the orbit of what one might call democratic desire, mimetic desire emancipated from traditional moral and religious constraints by the ideological triumph of equality. (Gardner, 2011: 10)

What we might call the hyper-mimeticism of globalization is the universalization of internal mediation, tantamount to the 'end of all external mediations.' Desacralization and the post-theistic onto-political crisis-of-undifferentiation[59] are now planetary phenomena: the early post-human crisis is an endlessly reciprocating denial of difference, as contemporary citizenship, the current object of metaphysical form, has as its object of mimetic desire the profane victim. This toxic combination, in turn, requires absolute and unconditional uniformity as a means of validating its 'authenticity' as the neo-sacralizing sacred.

---

governed by the reciprocal logic of metaphysical desire and metaphysical violence, marking the terminus of liberal political and judicial representation which are the domains of representational language. Beyond this horizon lies pre-representation and undifferentiation.

[58] Girard offered the interesting observation that 'suicide-bombing' can be validly interpreted as a wholly contemporary form of self-sacralization (Cowdell, 2014: 148, 215 n 25).

[59] A major paradox: 'desire for recognition and respect is surging throughout the world. It may seem paradoxical that globalization and economic modernization are breeding political nationalism. But that is only if we view nationalism as a backward ideology, certain to be erased by the onward march of progress' (Troy, 2021: 64–65). The explanation resides with mimesis; increasingly civil war is being replaced by *civic* war in the periphery, as hyper-urbanization is creating underdeveloped super cities that act as portal nodes into the high-velocity world-economy facilitating the unbridled spread of mimetic contagion. 'The democratic dogma of egalitarianism [internal mediation] potentially pushes [peer-group] rivalry to its edges, based on wholesaling the possibility to imitate the desire of others'; hence, the counter-intuitive linkage between development and nationalism wherein the 'relative deprivation of basic living conditions drives the "gap between what people feel rightfully entitled to and what they are capable of achieving under existing circumstances"' (Fareed Zakaria qtd. Troy, 2021: xviii).

> [A] radically Christian appropriation [of the political order] could only be apocalyptic. [...] The gradual loosening of various centers of cultural isolation began in the Middle Ages and has now led into what we call 'globalization,' which in my view is only secondarily an economic phenomenon. The true engine of process is the slow decomposition of the closed worlds rooted in victim mechanisms. This is the force that destroyed archaic societies and henceforth dismantles the one replacing them, the nations we call 'modern'. (Girard, 2005: 165–166)

What Calasso has characterized as 'the unnameable present' with all of the lurking apocalypticism in its train—the self-deification of society, a self-grounding and totalizing *telos* of some-thing wholly without form and, thus, utterly devoid of difference—is a radical and radicalizing *'disintermediation'* that irreparably short-circuits the mechanism of sacrifice which has now been replaced by a *terrorism* that is governed by the instantaneous and the simultaneous: frictionless war on a global scale (Calasso, 2017: 11).

> Terror is founded on the idea that only killing guarantees meaning. All else seems feeble, uncertain, inadequate. On that foundation are built the various motivations used to justify the act of terror. And connected also to that foundation, in an obscure way that involves a metaphysical element, is blood sacrifice. As if, from age to age and in widely different places, there were some compelling and irrepressible need to perform killings that might otherwise seem gratuitous and unreasonable. An ominous mirror-like resemblance between the origins and the present today. A hexed mirror. [...] At one time, the fruit of the sacrifice was invisible. The whole ritual machine was conceived to establish contact and interchange between the visible and the invisible. Now, instead, the fruit of the sacrifice has become visible, measurable, photographable. (Calasso, 2017: 4)

It is the perpetual 'collapsing into' planetary claustrophobia that is to blame: via disintermediation and the logic of pre-representation it is 'now enough to tap in a certain sequence of words and anyone would have the impression of acting for themselves, without resorting to the usual tiresome intermediaries'—which explodes the *meconnaissance* governing the relation between disintermediation and that visceral hatred of mediation and the mediator, a condition that is ultimately 'fatal for thought' (Calasso, 2017: 72–73) but which is the essence of pre-representational speech.

> We don't need to go back to Hegel to realize that not only thought but also perception exists only by means of mediation, therefore through continual adjustments and compromises, which are what mediation is all about. Even the mirage of direct democracy[60] now comes not from political reflection, but from an infatuation with information technology Which, by debasing mediation, ends up also debasing immediacy, attainable only after having crossed the lattice of mediations. (Calasso, 2017: 73)

Girard similarly identifies globalization as the catastrophic 'end of all external mediations'.

> Globalisation, according to Girard, reveals the ultimate secret of political modernity: the fragmentation and increasing impotence of territorial sovereign states in both governing the political process and controlling violence. With the triumph of the principle of equality, enshrined in the liberal democratic ethos and central to the project of secular modernity, the

[60] If disintermediation 'was true for a journey or a hotel booking, why couldn't it also be true for politics?' (Calasso, 2017: 72).

> idolatry of the tyrant as mediator is 'replaced by hatred of a thousand rivals', in a move from external to internal mediation.This move has progressively unleashed a dangerous 'crisis of degree', that is, the escalation of unchecked competition among political subjects—turned individual sovereigns. The age of globalisation brings this process to its climax and appears to be hysterically mimetic, but also tragic and apocalyptic in so far as absolute equality to approximate absolute tyranny. (Brighi, 2015: 153–154)[61]

While it is correct to argue that The War on Terror 'is better understood as a global *civil war* based on the *erasure of difference*' rather than a mere reciprocating exercise in political extremism (Cowdell, 2014: 143), what must not be forgotten is Girard's wholly original contribution to the concept of terrorism which is that the terrorist is a victim who proves her identity as a true citizen (political existent) through the spectacular performance of her victimage: 'The radical openness created by globalisation, with its inescapable mediatic spectacle and its endless reverberations, creates relentless *competitive* rather than cooperative effects and the potential for the rise of disaffection whenever winning or successfully emulating the model becomes impossible. Resentment thus goes global' (Brighi, 2015: 154).[62]

The revolutionary effect of atheistic political religion upon citizenship as an object of metaphysical desire cannot be underestimated; with modernity, the citizen

[61] Raymond Aron, one of Girard's mentors, also understood this: 'with humanity on the way to unification, inequality between peoples takes on the significance that inequality between classes once had' (Raymond Aron qtd. Krastev & Holmes, 2019: 35).

[62] This 'radical openness' is the itself the sacrificial foundation of the capitalist world-economy; 'global capitalism in the present is the precise opposite of a "closed" system of victimization, in which certain people in a certain life-world are systematically targeted for victimization. On the far contrary, global capitalism is radically "open" for victimization to become totalized, for it to be *absolute*—even as it hypocritically attacks closed systems of victimization from the past in its process of self-development' (Culkin, 2021: 74–75 n 1). Along similar lines of reasoning, Brian W. Nail has persuasively argued that the 'neo-liberal subject' should be re-classified as *homo sacrificus* owing to globalization's 'anthropological and ideological intensification of the imperative to economize the costs of individual existence through compliance to administrative regimes of disciplinary-incentivization' (Nail, 2020: 79). With *homo sacrificus* as the model, the mimetically predisposed neo-liberal subject will 'voluntarily' internalize (meaning after having mis-recognized the desires of the other as her own) a hyper-ascetic anxiety-inducing regime of self- and other-sacrificial strategies in order to maximize productivity within a global population of increasingly economically marginal human beings in total accordance with the 'omnipresent industry of global finance' (Nail, 2020: 79) that culminates in a neo-capitalist world-economy of perpetual liquification that supports a transnational elite of sacrificers. 'Neoliberalism's subversion of social solidarity funnels the beneficial outcomes of sacrificial economization upwards, to an increasingly privileged and politically isolated plutocracy. It is this asymmetrical power elation which characterizes neoliberal existence for *homo sacrificus*. Rather than acknowledging the active role that a corporatocracy plays in deferring the costs of neoliberal existence unto a relatively inexhaustible population of sacrificial scapegoats rendered vulnerable due to their economic precarity, neoliberalism continually mystifies its own sacrificial logic through rhetorical appeals to the common project of economic nationalism—the ideological locus of the new "model" citizen' (Nail, 2020: 94). The most obnoxious result of this total and totalizing process is the cultural rehabilitation of 'sacrifice' as a social and moral (and economic) good. Sartre's literary dictum that 'Hell is other people' becomes objective reality with neo-liberalism for it normalizes sacrifice as part of the undifferentiated 'everyday'.

is re-constituted as an object-of-desire for imitation, the model that is the guarantor of secular being. In a similar fashion the resolution of the eternally recurrent crisis-of-undifferentiation assumes a post-theological form within the atheistic polity: it is no longer conflictual mimesis but the divisive acquisitive mimesis that fuels the repetition of secular persecution of wholly profane differences, which is Schmitt's 'grouping of friend and enemy' polarity devoid of redemptive transcendental meaning. But what is still with us is the need to provide an effective mechanism of resolution of mimetic crises when they occur; the default is the periodic recurrence of 'senseless' violence unreliably policed by an open-ended logic of retaliation and escalation. Hence the otherwise difficult to explain weird crimes as the signifiers of citizenship-as-differentiation (serial murder, mass shootings, 'copycat' crimes, 'going postal', stalking (celebrity or otherwise), snuff videos, school shootings, identity theft, the Dark Web, basement-dungeons for suspect daughters, the suicide-bomber, the lone-wolf terrorist) in which the mechanics of the spectacle are intuitively sought out and employed as substitutes for the public performance of ritualistic sacrifice, all of which is mediated by the metaphysical desire for citizenship, or 'model membership' within the community. To put it another way: *modernity's profane scapegoat is the one to whom citizenship must be denied*, creating crises of undifferentiation of unprecedented violence. One of the most intriguing aspects of the academic literature on violent crime is that the 'righteous anger' that so often seems to drive it is the inversion of a 'victimary narrative of humiliation'. This is particularly true in the life-stories of lone-wolf killers/'terrorists' (Brighi, 2015: 155, 158) which display three general characteristics: extreme individualization, the refusal to recognize any form of external mediation, and, most importantly, 'self-radicalization,' usually achieved on the Internet.[63] For the lone-wolf the State is the obstacle of citizenship, so that political power, the property of the State, becomes the object-of-desire for the would-be authentic citizen, the one entitled to persecute her persecutors. Consistent with the mimetically contaminated subject-of-desire, the lone-wolf undergoes a kind of profane double-mediation: the State itself is framed as the 'primary target' and 'flesh-and-blood' victims (usually, but not always, 'non-combatants') are represented as 'secondary targets': secular scapegoats, whose performative/sacrificial death will allow the subject unmediated access to the object, which, in principle, is accessible to anyone who can seize it. 'Terrorism therefore rests on a peculiar triangular relation of perpetrators, targets[64] and victims' (Brighi, 2015: 153) which constitutes its own historically specific form of victimology. Although the victimological—the 'last shall be first' of post-modernity with a vengeance—was

[63] Which provides not only technical 'know-how' but, far more weirdly, narrative support and psychological justification: 'For the current generation of lone-wolf terrorists, the Internet has become particularly instrumental in the construction of individually crafted, highly de-historicized and de-contextualized narratives, which are easy to buttress by "factoids" found online and superimpose on a variety of political and personal grievances' (Brighi, 2015: 158).

[64] It is 'the engine of mimetic rivalry that is responsible for the typical tit-for-tat spiral of imitation that often morphs the methods of terrorism and counter-terrorism and makes them "enemies in the mirror" or mimetic doubles' (Brighi, 2015: 153). Reciprocity unbounded will invariably culminate into the 'escalation to extremes' prophesized by Clausewitz. See Chap. 11, above.

first pioneered by the Left and then ferociously imitated by the Right, both sides were equally deft in deploying the '-ology' of the un-real as the mimetic *affectus* at the foundation of modernity's secular sacred; a 'hardening of differences, an ossification of polities' that 'signals the breakdown of differences' (Brighi, 2015: 143).[65]

12.6 Sacrifice with a Good Conscience: The Super-Victimary Machine

As a species, we may or may not derive pleasure from the physical act of killing. It is, however, indisputable that for everybody the infliction of social death upon another constitutes the purest form of *jouissance*.[66] For Calasso, the 'process of secularization does not, as it is claimed, succeed in exhausting or extinguishing the sacred, but only displaces it. And the power it assumes is all the more devastating and uncontrollable in that it no longer has a name, in that it cannot be recognized for what it is' (Roberto Calasso qtd. McKenna, 1992: 160). But as McKenna points out, 'To sacralize the victim is to sacralize violence' (McKenna, 1992: 203).

However, is the reverse also true: to sacralize violence is to sacralize the victim? For if historical victimage is the sacralizing mark of the highest good, and violence is the bestower of the sacred upon the one who is subjected to it by the persecutors, then the mimetic logic of this inversion must necessarily culminate in the re-direction of violence—now in the sacralized form of a 'divine' retribution within the secular world—against the one who persecuted the victim in the original instance. If we were to follow this line of thought to its end it would lead us to question the moral certainty concerning truth and innocence that is a central pillar of Girard's apocalyptic anthropology: 'The answer lies with the victim—not in any perverted desire to be the victim, but in the eminently traceable fact of victimage, in its uniqueness amidst the play of rival desire, its immunity to desire being its forthright undesirability' (McKenna, 1992:171). The problem with this is that victims *are* real but their meaning—and, therefore, their *value*—is, like every other thing that can be

[65] It is not surprising that Girard identifies the 'classic era' of the western witchcraft trials, or 'craze,' that culminated in the Salem witch-trials (February 1692 to May, 1693) as the paradigmatic example of the purely secularized variant of the crisis of undifferentiation. The invention of the printing press and the resultant contagion of the Reformation—the revolt against the corporate religious systems of public spaces by now internally mediated 'private' religious belief fortified by mass copies of vernacular translations of Scripture—created a fatal crisis for the external mediation of Faith. 'Puritan theocrats must have seen all too well that "immediate revelation" obviated the need for an ordained ministry and that this was tantamount to anarchy. The democratic character of [non-conformist] spirituality brings into focus precisely what is at stake in the climacteric shift, from collective forms of religious life with their dependence on priestly mediation to fully individuated and self-determined expressions of belief and unbelief alike' (Dawson, 2013: 118). As I pointed out in Chap. 1, it was the non-conformist William Tyndale's 1530 vernacular translation of the Bible that introduced the word 'Scape Goate' into the English language (Dawson, 2013: x).

[66] 'Death of any sort seems preferable if it can guarantee moments of elation to be relished before the end' is how Fornari puts it (Fornari, 2009: 24).

commodified, meaning that they can become the object of mimetic desire no matter how 'perverted' the desire to be one. For while the originary victim, the archaic scapegoat, was both 'real' (a mutilated cadaver) and 'fake' (a mutilated cadaver with supernatural power), the post-archaic secular victim is both completely real (a body of some sort) and completely valuable (a body of some sort) precisely because the victim and its sign are no longer differentiated but are one and the same meaning that 'it' can be appropriated (acquisitive desire) and circulated (accumulation) as a potentially infinite source of social capital (surplus), which takes us directly into the realm of metaphysical desire. Consistent with Girard's logic, atheistic political religion must, out of necessity, become apocalyptic.

> [By] Apocalypse I don't mean the end of the world, which is the vulgar interpretation of the term. When I say that modernity is apocalyptic, I mean that it is revelatory… Our epoch is characterized by the ongoing revelation of the *human* origin of violence. I think that there's kind of a systematic logic to it. A world without sacrificial protection will create all sorts of tools, more and more dangerous, which will threaten those that use them. Technology, when applied to destruction functions this way: it reveals or disconceals the human origin of violence. (Girard, 2020: 38)

Any 'society that replaces myth by an awareness of persecution is a society in the process of desacralization' (Girard et al., 1978: 126) so that the 'final solution' to the scapegoating crisis will be attempted through the effort 'to bury the modern concern for victims under millions and millions of corpses' (Girard, 2005: 175).[67] In other words, by making genocide banal.

> One can imagine that human beings …. Will be tempted to restore the lost effectiveness of the traditional remedy by forever increasing the dosage, immolating more and more victims in holocausts that are meant to be sacrificial but that are progressively less so. The always arbitrary but culturally real difference between legitimate and illegitimate violence will weaken. Its power of illusion diminishes, and henceforth there are only enemy brothers to confront one another in its name, which all will claim to embody but which in reality no longer exists; cultural difference will be distinguished less and less from the mimetic crisis to which it returns. Any sense of legality will be lost. (Girard et al., 1978: 128)

What is less consistent, or merely less clear, is that Girard appears to waver on this very point: 'The expulsion of religion may paradoxically be the unitive element of our world—yet one more embodiment of the victimage principle' (Girard, 2020: 36) meaning that there might be something authentically regenerative in this process.

> If human beings refuse the non-sacrificial reconciliation that must be substituted for the now exhausted sacrifices, they will inevitably attempt to suppress the knowledge that is provided to them by the gospels; they will try once more to close human culture upon itself and erect more violent barriers against their own violence. It is unavoidable, therefore, that an attempt to consolidate once more the culture of misunderstood scapegoat phenomena will include a new victimage, and the victim, this time, will not be arbitrary, in the sense that this time, he [sic] must be the One who threatens or seems to threaten the entire system through his untimely revelations of what human culture is really about. Unanimous victimage, in other words, will be re-enacted against the one who has revealed the very existence and function of that unanimous murder. (Girard, 2007: 43)

[67] 'The spiritual goal of Hitler's ideology was to root out of Germany, then all of Europe, that calling that the Christian tradition places upon all of us: the concern for victims' (Girard, 2005: 11).

It is obvious that Girard was fully aware that scapegoating would return, albeit in a wholly inadequate (post-transcendental) manner. But his own analysis does raise the possibility that a certain kind of neo-scapegoating may prove to be culturally viable—that is, capable of providing a generative unity of some kind provided that the correct historical conditions are met. Here is one example, although I am speculating wildly.

> To think religiously is to envision the city's destiny in terms of that violence whose mastery over man increases as man believes he has gained mastery over it. To think religiously (in a primitive sense) is to see violence as something superhuman, to be kept always at a distance and ultimately renounced. When the fearful adoration of this power begins to diminish and all distinctions begin to disappear, the ritual sacrifices lose their force: their potency is no longer recognized by the entire community. (Girard, 1977: 135)

Central to Girard's account is the qualifier '*When the fearful adoration of this power begins to diminish*'. This may have been a truthful description of social being in 1977 but is it in 2023 following the unforeseeable rise of globalization, universal victimage, and terrorism? It is not fiction per se to speculate that the return of scapegoating may be made sustainable thanks to the continuing viability of globalized neo-liberalism: the selection process of victimage may now be mediated by artificial intelligence and social media (algorithms), the digital manufacture and regulation of the ready-at-head reserve pools of *pharmakoi* (membership determined by how they are 'trending'). It is, in fact, relatively easy to stand Girard on his head: the crucial issue is to determine whether or not it is possible to finally construct a self-sustaining form of political religion. Expressed in overtly secular terms, this would entail contemplating the possibility, and efficacy, of a new form of politics for a world that has become thoroughly de-ritualized and that would involve the voluntary assumption of the diverse forms of what Derrida has called 'totalitarian risk'.

> Purification, purge, totalization, reappropriation, homogenization, rapid objectification, good conscience, stereotyping and non-reading, *immediate* politicization or depoliticization (it is always the same thing), immediate historicization or dehistoricization (it is always the same thing), immediate ideologizing moralization (immorality itself) of all of the texts and all of the problems, expedited trials, condemnations, or acquittals, summary executions or sublimations. This is what must be deconstructed ... (Jacques Derrida qtd. McKenna, 1992: 184)

McKenna comments that the 'list of these forms is worth citing; they are but variants of a single persecutory structure, but variants of the sacrificial process' (McKenna, 1992: 184), but we should note how unnervingly contemporary these forms appear to us; even worse, they all reflect the same underlying phenomenon.

> Sacrifice is the only word missing from the list, though it summarizes it all. The notion all but surfaces thematically in Derrida's animadversion 'to the expeditious violence of lapidary judgments, even to a symbolic lapidation'. Lapidation is an exemplarily sacrificial practice, a traditional way of instituting a distance between one's violence and its victim so as to delude oneself about one's distance and difference from violent origins and to deceive oneself about one's immunity to violence, or innocence of it. It is a mechanism intended to avoid contamination by a violence that the destruction of the victim is meant to resolve. Of course, it is commonplace to denounce lapidary judgments, as much as it is to denounce scapegoating. (McKenna, 1992: 185)

And the reason why sacrifice no longer seems so offensive to us is that a type of neo-sacrifice has been enabled by contemporary technology; 'It is a question of dividing, of cutting up. Such is the essence of technocratic practice. Control always proceeds by establishing a network of regulations, of norms, of classifications that aim at carving up the social space' (Orlean, 1988: 111). Which leads to a new contemporary variant of double-mindedess that can be regulated directly by social media in precisely the same way that propaganda, or 'misinformation,' may be. According to Eric Santner the hallmark of all propaganda is that '"evil remains that which intervenes from the outside into an otherwise pure and innocent inside"' (Eric Santner qtd. McKenna, 1992: 113), so that the trick is that 'You have to make your scapegoating more convincing to yourself by displacing it and also by accusing your victims of being the chief victimizers, in order to justify your own victimization of them. This is what political propaganda is mostly about, I am afraid' (Girard, 1987a, 1987b: 140). Nietzsche is the mirror-image, or double, of Girard and may well prove to be the truly prophetic one, the one who observed that 'it is victims themselves that we hurl at each other in our denunciations of violence' becoming in the process 'trajectories in our denunciations of violence' which is intrinsically violent; 'They have become trajectories in a battle of words, an alibi for future violence. As a consequence, they are victimized a second time, for being passed over by a desire on its predestined route to violence' (McKenna, 1992: 99). 'Never before in history' Girard claims, 'have people spent so much time throwing victims at one another's heads as a substitute for other weapons. This can only happen in a world that though far from Christian, to be sure, is totally permeated by the values of the gospel. Nietzsche was correct in saying this' (Girard, 1987a, 1987b: 140). So by Girard's own admission, we need to re-examine both Christianity and Nietzsche operating in tandem once more.[68]

A 'whole primitive apparatus makes its appearance in modern totalitarianism' (Girard, 1987a, 1987b (a): 119) with the result that our 'super-modern utopia looks very much at times like a regression to archaic terror' (Girard, 1996: 278[69]) for disowning 'one's own violence as another's, as being the other's, as originating with the other, is the surest means of its perpetuation. It is the functional, the effective—and not merely formal—equivalent of dissimulating the other's desire as our own, of claiming as one's own the other's desire' (McKenna, 1992: 100). Girard neatly supplements this by helpfully reminding us that, 'You know, there are two forms of totalitarianism.'

[68] It becomes somewhat difficult after reading so many 'Nietzsche themed' passages of this kind that litter Girard's work to doubt that the two of them were doubles of some kind. Luca Di Blasi feels the same way: 'Nietzsche is in many senses the main rival of Girard' the latter's 'distinction between Satan and Christ is the perfect inversion of Nietzsche's distinction between Dionysus and the Crucified' (Di Blasi, 2015: 53 n 24).

[69] Not just a regression but a revolutionary inversion; 'those who manipulate public opinion' are wholly 'persuaded that the "deviations" will end once and for all on the day when the "good" seize power and chase the "evil" away for ever—in short, on the day when the "good" alone will be in charge of the purifying expulsion' (Girard, 1987a, 1987b (a): 119). A healthy dose of Manichaenism does wonders for liberal jurisprudence.

> One tries to destroy the concern for victims openly and directly. Its proponents basically attempt to kill as many victims for as little reason as possible. Then there is insidious totalitarianism. Communism in its many forms was insidious, but it will probably be replaced by ideologies still more insidious which outflank the Gospels on the left, presenting themselves as better than the Gospels, trying to show that the Gospels do not side with the victims, but demonize them. Some of these people see themselves as super-Christians, but they are the heirs of the predecessors of Marx, who thought they could achieve a new humanism. Feuerbach, for example. But they laid the groundwork for a disrespect of the truth. I think that it would be helpful to study Feuerbach, who was the primary agent of the transformation of Christianity into Marxism. (Girard, 1996: 275; Girard, 1987a, 1987b (a): 111–117)

Our collective fate will be the uneventful apocalypse of interminable neo-scapegoating. 'It means that the end times will be very long and monotonous—so mediocre and uneventful from a religious and spiritual standpoint that the danger of dying spiritually … will be very great. This is a harsh lesson but one ultimately of hope rather than despair' (Girard, 2020: 193). But then follows this moralizing assertion seemingly plucked out of thin air: 'We just sit it out. But we must try not to surrender to the spiritual decadence of our time and rise above the world around us' (Girard, 2020: 193). On what does Girard ground this admonishing call for virtuous quietism? The answer lies with his very unevenly developed concept of *good mimesis* which is the opposite of the other kind.

Not surprisingly, Girard, as Nietzsche's double, conceptualizes Christ and Satan in turn as doubles, engaged in a singularly unique form of mimetic rivalry, both sharing the same model, the First Person of the Trinity; 'Not unlike Jesus,[70] Satan says to us: "imitate me" and he, himself, is an imitator. His ultimate model is God the Father, the same model like Jesus has' (Girard, 1996: 197). The association of Satan with mimesis and mimetic desire should be clear to anyone who has read the preceding chapters; what is new, and disquieting, is Christ's linkage with the mimetic that establishes an unforeseen doubling with his dark Other. 'Both Jesus and Satan are teachers of imitation and imitators themselves, imitators of God the Father. This means that human beings always imitate God, either through Jesus or Satan. They seek God indirectly through the human models they imitate' (Girard, 1996: 215) but with one critical difference that separates Christ from the devil: 'Since there is no acquisitive desire in God' The Son's 'imitation cannot cause mimetic rivalry. Mimetic rivalry is not sin but rather a permanent occasion of sin. The sin occurs when our relentlessness makes the rivalry obsessive' (Girard, 1996: 215).[71] Even though

[70] *Exactly* like Jesus? Albeit with diametrically opposed consequences, universal violence versus perfect peace. 'What is the difference between the mimetic desire of Jesus and the mimetic desire of Satan? The difference is that Satan imitates God in a spirit of rivalry. Jesus imitates Gog in a spirit of child-like and innocent obedience and this is what he advises us to do as well. Since there is no acquisitive desire in God, the docile imitation of God cannot generate rivalry' (Girard, 1996: 197–198). An obvious theological criticism of Girard on this point is that it is anti-Trinitarian in implication: Christ, as the Second Person of the Trinity, never imitates God because He Himself is 'God' but in the personality (or *hypostasis*) of the Son. However, He claims to be acting in obedience to the Father, the First Person, so Girard is right that central to the Passion is Christ's mimetic role as an exemplar of the mimetically correct (anti-violent) relationship to Divinity.

[71] Girard helpfully adds that 'Its name is envy, jealousy, pride, anger, despair' (Girard, 1996: 215). He forgot to include lust, gluttony, and greed, mentioned envy twice, and filed sloth under despair.

Girard spent decades warning us about the ambiguous undecidability of the mimetic, we can trust Christ on this front because it is an axiom for the Christian that 'Good is what Jesus does'; The Second Person of the Trinity unfailingly 'imitates his Father in perfect fashion. He shows us the way, and we imitate him in order to be like the Father. This imitation is good because it is non-appropriative and free from rivalry. It generates no *skandalon*…If you can imitate God perfectly, you will be God (Golsan, 2002: 131). In contrast, the 'communion of mimetic rivalry is Satan's work.[72] The word "Satan," originally, signifies the accuser, the one who brings a law suit against someone else. In the Gospels, Satan's power is his ability to make false accusations so convincing that they become the unassailable truth of entire communities' (Girard, 1996: 201). Satan is the 'Father of Lies' and lies, as we know, are the building blocks of *meconnaissance*, the necessary condition for scapegoating. This is made clear in John 8:44.

> Jesus said to them, 'If God were your Father, you would love Me, for I proceeded forth and came from God; nor have I come of Myself, but he sent Me. Why do you not understand My speech? Because you are not able to listen to My word. You are of *your* father the devil, and the desires of your father you want to do. He was a murderer from the beginning,[73] and does not stand in the truth, because there is no truth in him. When he speaks a lie, he speaks from his own *resources*, for he is a liar and the father of it. But because I tell the truth, you do not believe me.[74]

And if Satan is the 'Father of Lies' that means that he is the origin of *meconnaissance* which means that he is the inventor of scapegoating which means that his 'son,' the anti-Christ is the master of scapegoaters which means that Nietzsche is too because Nietzsche identified himself as the 'anti-Christ' in opposition to his Other, Christ, who is linked to Girard, the anti-Nietzsche, through Christianity which is the opposite of the cult of Dionysus. Girard reminds us on numerous occasions that Nietzsche/anti-Christ was 'nostalgic for archaic religion' which means the sacrificial; 'he would like to go back to the eternal return; therefore, he is not really apocalyptic, because he is not waiting for the kingdom of God. He would like to go back, and he hopes that there will be an end of Christianity' (Girard, 2020: 192). So

[72] For Girard Satan is '"the name for the mimetic process as a whole … he is the source not merely of rivalry and disorder but all forms of lying inside which humanity lives"'—the greatest lie being, of course, the sacredness and, therefore, the *necessity* of the scapegoat (Rene Girard qtd. Golsan, 2002: 103). Of course, by that same line of allegorical reasoning, 'God' may also be taken as the personification for a 'mimetic process' of His own: positive, or good, mimesis. See below.

[73] Alternatively, from the beginning there was a murderer, or a sacrificer.

[74] Although John 8:88 is often taken as one of the principal sources of Christian antisemitism, Girard differs on the grounds that that John, along with all of the other Gospel authors, represents mimetic violence as a universal phenomenon. Although the passage refers to Christ's opponents within the Jewish community, '*your* father is the devil' is a generic term for any individual or group that has become possessed by mimetic violence (Girard, 1996: 211–221). 'To say that our human will is to do the desires of our father, the devil, is another way of saying that we cannot really cut loose from the primordial lie, from the effects of the primordial murder. We still cannot acknowledge our dependence on primordial violence. Satan is not merely "the father of lies" but, as some manuscripts have it, "the father of liars," which really means all men, insofar as men still do not understand what Jesus is talking about in the lines we are reading' (Girard, 1996: 204).

Nietzsche is searching for a way to formulate a viable and self-sustaining version of the sacrificial model, one based upon his paramount sacrificial conception of eternal recurrence,[75] or the eternal return of the same, which is equivalent to the 'eternity of the present'. 'You have two conceptions of time to consider' says Girard (Girard, 2020: 192). There is the linear, or 'progressive,' Time of the Cross which, because it has suspended the sacrificial cycle, removes History from the eternal returning back to the originary violence; the other is 'the eternal return, which I think is the founding murder of the scapegoat, and therefore a new religion. The scapegoat phenomenon is so powerful, that a community can organize itself around it' (Girard, 2020: 192). But this implies that the return of the sacrificial mechanism in toto is possible, albeit extraordinarily difficult, for the reasons that Girard has already discussed.

> From a Christian viewpoint, ancient theories of the Eternal Return contain some truth since they know about these cycles, which are the same thing as the 'self-organizing system' of Satan, but they cannot discover the engine that powers the cycles, the foundational power of the mimetic consensus, or victimage mechanism, or generative scapegoating. (Girard, 1996: 205)

And once again, Girard's naïve epistemological realism, coupled with his axiomatic normative evaluation of the positive value of Truth and the negative value of *meconnaissance*, serve as the circuit-breaker necessary to disrupt Nietzsche's diabolic agenda for revolutionizing the substance, form, and meaning of History.

> The end of this circular time, the shift from an eternally recurring world to a time which has a real beginning and a real end is inseparable from the revelation of the [satanic] force that until the Judaic and Christian revelation had powered the cycles but now loses its effectiveness as a result of being revealed. (Girard, 1996: 205)

So in the end it is really quite simple, provided that we are in accordance with the specifically Girardian conception of *meconnaissance.*

> Once we realize that the power of Satan is dependent upon a lie, which will not remain effective unless it is firmly believed by all men, an untruth that is always mistaken for a sacred truth, everything else follows. In order to remain credible, this untruth, this satanic lie must remain hidden. It must be presented from human curiosity. (Girard, 1996: 205)

But this is at variance with the clarion call that Girard sounded near the end of his career, in both *Evolution and Conversion* (2008) and *Battling to the End* (2010): the apocalyptic, and by implication, the neo-totalitarian threat of universal victimage. For although the Shoah was indisputably the secular point of origin for the neo-sacralization of the victim in her profane form, within *la longue duree* of 'western civilization,' the millennial-long transformation of the victim into a sacralized innocent began with Christ Himself and the good form of mimesis that He initiated, specifically the form of good mimesis known as *martyrdom*, the self-sacrificial dying as 'witness to the Truth'[76]; 'All of Western and then world history can be interpreted as a turbulent, chaotic, but constantly accelerating process of de-victimization that is

---

[75] See Chap. 8, above.

[76] See below.

unique in all of world history and it can be traced only to Christianity' (Girard, 1996: 209). Christ as the martyred archetypal innocent (and therefore righteous) victim is the pre-modern *typon* of the secular righteous victim who has, as Girard himself claimed, become the new scapegoater; the righteous victim will become the accuser, and scapegoater, of the persecutor, so that today 'love' means hating the hater; or, as Girard beautifully expressed it, 'Compassion is never a principle but a result. The principle is the hatred of the triumphant wicked. Good is loved in order that Evil be hated more. The oppressed are defended for the sake of overwhelming the oppressors' (Girard, 1965: 189). In the Oresteia Trilogy (458 BCE), his master-work on the scapegoat, the Greek tragedian Aeschylus expressed 'the truth' even more beautifully in the finale of the denouement of the third part, the *Eumenides*.

And the brutal strife,
The civil war devouring men, I pray
That it never rages through our city, no
That the good Greek soil never drinks the blood of Greeks,
Shed in an orgy of reprisal life for life—
That Fury like a beast will never
Rampage through the land.
Give joy in return for joy,
One common will for love,
And hate with one strong heart:
Such union heals a thousand ills of man. (Aeschylus, 1977: 274)

Thus do the Eumenides (formerly the 'Furies' now the reassuringly renamed 'Kindly Ones') channel the un-born spirit of Carl Schmitt 2500 years before the fact.[77] Sacrificial violence, or scapegoating, can and will continue, for it truly is generative; what matters now is that the citizens (or the alliance of the Friends) only scapegoat the one who is the *true* enemy, meaning the foreigner, the member of that tribe which is authentically alien, and no mis-recognition about it; 'This new world will know how to make hatred a force for unity, the *great remedy*, identical to, but other than, the terrible force for division it constitutes *so long as it is not unanimous*. Aeschylus understands the crucial importance of unanimity' (Girard, 1987a, 1987b (a): 149–150). For even if it is true that the 'impossibility of sacrificing innocently engenders various processes of repression, diversion and avoidance' (Domenach, 1988: 269 n 6), it should not prove that difficult to get an entire nation to scapegoat not-so-innocently if it comes to believe that its material (as opposed to its 'moral') survival depends upon doing so, especially when it comes to the foundational moment of

[77] Which was not lost on Leo Strauss, a frequent correspondent with Schmitt before The Third Reich: 'If I have correctly understood your opinion … it leads precisely to the conclusion that there is a *primary* tendency in human nature to form *exclusive groups* … Because man is by nature evil, he therefore needs *dominion*. But dominion can be established, that is men can be unified, only in a unity *against*—against other men. Every association of men is *necessarily* a separation from other men' (Leo Strauss qtd. Ranieri, 2007: 169). But Aeschylus beat them both to the punch.

forming a stable community of 'survivors,' a supremely Schmittean event.[78] Which, in a blatantly anti-Girardian manner, is exactly what the Greek trick of double-mindedness is all about, the *dissoi logoi* of 'double speeches' (Vernant and Vidal-Naquet, 1990: 319). Which raises the same question put by Dupuy: is the recognition of misrecognition, or the awareness of *meconnaissance*, itself *sufficient* to disable the scapegoating mechanism? (Dupuy, 1988). Here is Girard again, but now he is sounding less convincing.

> Scapegoating has never been conceived by anyone as an activity in which he himself participates and may still be participating even as he denounces the scapegoating of others. Such denunciation can even become a precondition of successful scapegoating in a world like ours, where knowledge of the phenomenon is on the rise and makes its grossest and most violent forms obsolete. Scapegoating can continue only if its victims are perceived primarily as scapegoaters. (Girard, 1996: 15)[79]

'*Scapegoating can continue only if its victims are perceived primarily as scapegoaters,*' is, I would suggest, exactly what is currently taking place. And what Aeschylus makes clear with cold-blooded logic is that the people of Athens realize that they can avoid civil war by self-consciously scapegoating foreigners so that the organized sacrificial hostility toward the Other becomes infused with that Hellenic double-mindedness that Veyne describes with such gusto: 'we do not know with certainty whether the foreigner is truly evil but we need to kill him in order that we do not kill each other and forge a unifying compact among ourselves, the happy band of persecutors, which is in the best interests of all of us who are citizens.'[80] And it is Girard who explains this curious inversion of orthodox meanings in our 'new world' of post-Christianity by revealing that 'Those we regard as scapegoat-makers, we are tempted to turn into ... our own scapegoats' (Girard, 1987a, 1987b: 78) who can be construed as the 'new foreigners' depending on how we define the borders of the 'true' community.

---

[78] McKenna, for one, is quite up front about this: 'Nothing unites a community, with all the good fellowship and cooperation once can imagine, like the external threat of a common enemy' but then he dilutes the force of his observation by adding the requisite Girardian supplement that 'the threat is originally internal; it is the violent threat of all against all' (McKenna, 1992: 131) which completely obviates our current on-line digital reality of a potentially infinite proliferation of sub-communities and neo-tribes, all of which exhibit a hyper-unanimity coupled with an ultra-hostility to all differences. What no Girardian can contemplate without fear and trembling is that double-mindedness works. See below.

[79] This 'strategy is all too common in the modern world, where persecutors actually seek out the role of victim to justify *their* persecution of their so-called tormentors' (Golsan, 2002: 54).

[80] By implication this raises the question whether *meconnaissance* can be understood in terms of ideology, not merely as a tool for mystifying but as a positive form of false-consciousness in its own right. Robert M. Cover has usefully pointed out that 'the function of ideology is much more significant in justifying an order [*nomos*] to those who principally benefit from it and who must defend it than it is in hiding the nature of the order from those who are its victims'—which means that mystification is more of and for the ruling classes than the ruled, the sacrificers instead of the sacrificed, the ones who need to put the knife in. (Cover, 1986: 1608). If so, and if vested in the social interest of the persecutors, then the double-mindedness of *meconnaissance* becomes that much easier to explain and its counter-intuitive vitality no longer a mystery.

> It is possible to read the history, first of the Christianized West, then of the Westernized planet,[81] our modern history, as dominated by the consequences of the victory first by Jesus himself, then by Paul and others, a process of vindication and rehabilitation of more and more persecuted victims. New hidden victims of society are continuously being brought to light; the consensus against them always dissolves after a while. First it was the slaves, then the lower classes, then people of different ethnic and religious backgrounds. Today the victimization of ethnic groups, women, of handicapped people, of the very young and the very old, is coming to light. The unveiling of mimetic violence has had a more and more powerful influence on our history and on the entire modern world. (Girard, 1996: 208)

The greatest political challenge of the twenty-first century, the first of the interminable age of Girard's apocalypse of banality, may well be to invent (or reinvent) a stable system of politics that is nothing other than pure double-mindedness so that it does not really matter whether the enemy is really guilty or the cause of anything, merely that she is the bearer of the social negativity of the majority of the moment. For if victimology is our Fate (*moirai*) then the way of solving the problem of a self-sustaining sacrificial civilization (which Rome failed to achieve) is to deliberately engineer a political culture in which everyone voluntarily embraces its underlying apocalyptic logic as the highest good. We are already more than half-way there.

> Another indirect testimony is the very perversion of that concern for victims which is highly visible in our world, the constant effort on the part of many groups and individuals to usurp the now privileged position of the most victimized victim, and thus to turn the concern for victims into an instrument of power and even into a paradoxical tool of persecution. (Girard, 1996: 209)

The future, then, will have to be self-consciously *neo-Nietzschean* which is to say *neo-sacrificial* but with a post-Christian twist for as Girard openly confessed 'the greatness of Nietzsche is that he apprehends the truth of Christianity with incomparable force' (Girard, 1988: 244).

> Nietzsche thought it was wrong for Christianity to speak of the innocence of the victim, not because sacrificial victims are really guilty, but because societies need sacrifice. He saw the central religious issue as no one else did. He understood that the gods and heroes immolated in pagan mythology were similar in form to the killing of Christ. But he thought Christianity's witness to the innocence of Christ was socially harmful and that the world needs the sacrifice of the victim as part of life's eternal return, which includes destruction. Nietzsche was the first to see this problem clearly, but he was perverse in choosing the violent lie instead of the peaceful truth of the victim. (Girard, 1996: 273)

Or in Nietzsche's own words: 'The individual was taken so seriously' by Christianity that 'he was posited as such an absolute principle, that he could no longer be *sacrificed*: but the species only survives thanks to human sacrifices' (Girard, 1988: 244). The anti-Christ must be the model precisely because he deconstructed Christianity—and with it anti-sacrificial culture—to the highest and most complete degree possible, laying bare the revolutionary implications of this act.

> Far from taking Christianity to be just another sacrificial religion, Nietzsche reiterates several times that its great fault is to 'prevent sacrifice,' to render impossible the acts of violence

[81] Also known as globalization.

> necessary to the smooth functioning of society. Nietzsche is very close to seeing the *mechanisms* and the *effects* of the surrogate victim, and above all to seeing that the gospels see them and, seeing them, discredit and derail them. The Gospel reveals 'things hidden since the foundation of the world,' and through the intermediary of Nietzsche this revelation begins to become self-aware. (Girard, 1988: 244)

And a self-awareness of the Nietzschean variety is the very thing that we need for the double-mindedness of a neo-sacrificial political religion. Which confirms our suspicions that the anti-Christ was an avid fan of *The Prince*, arguably the foundational text of modern political philosophy.

> Machiavelli also affirms that the foundation and the preservation of communities are *essentially* violent, and that men live continually on the good effects of this violence that they do not want to look in the eye. But Machiavelli, for his part, knows what he is saying: if what we call humanity is founded on violence, then this active power of violence must be preserved and men must be kept from falling under the influence of a deceptive non-violence—that of Christianity—which tends to destroy the very conditions of humanity ... If human culture is essentially founded on violence, then Christianity can bring nothing other than the destruction of humanity in the fallacious guise of non-violence. (Pierre Manent qtd. Scubla, 1988: 278 n 78)

And because Nietzsche (and, we suspect, Machiavelli) 'was entranced with violent differentiation' (Girard, 1996: 273) it is possible to 'foresee the shape of what the Anti-Christ is going to be in the future: a super-victimary machine that will keep on sacrificing in the name of the victim' (Girard, Antonello and de Costa Rocha 2008:236).[82] Meaning that scapegoating will be truly without end, because we have substituted the historical 'truth' of the righteous victim for the 'myth' of the sacred victim, a perfectly symmetrical exchange of the secular neo-sacred for the religious sacred. Which fits the 'spirit' of modernity very neatly, 'the idea that man [sic] has become totally master of himself, and that he doesn't have to bow in front of powers greater than himself, and he's going to triumph in the end' (Girard, 2020: 192). Which is nothing other than the removal of the *katechon*. Which must needs be replaced—again. But how to do it?

12.7 Demystifying the Demystifiers: The *Skandalon* of Cancel Culture

While discussing the Girardian dimensions of capital punishment James McBride asks 'What purpose does it serve to execute the condemned, regardless of the question of their factual innocence?' (McBride, 1995: 266). The answer is: it serves the highest

---

[82] 'The contemporary antichrist corresponds to the ideological effort being made to show that what is, according to Girard, the principal characteristic of our world, namely the concern for and defence of victims, is performed with infinitely better results by some shared, fashionable ideology, while Christianity is condemned as an essentially intolerant and violent message. Christianity thus functions as a scapegoat for our age, providing it with unstable surrogates for the ancient sacrificial foundations' (Fornari, 2009: 12–13).

double-minded purpose if the victim is intended to serve as a scapegoat and his execution a sacrifice that is not formally recognized as such.

> Indeed, *the very denial of its religious nature,* i.e., its substitutionary dynamic, *is necessary in order for it to effectively exorcise violence from social order*. In other words, the public denial of its religious character *supports* the proposition that the death penalty is, in fact, a religious ritual. It could not be otherwise, for to acknowledge the substitutionary atonement of the surrogate victim for transgressors-at-large would negate the cathartic release infects the body politic. The effectiveness of this social mechanism is predicated on the socio-legal designation of the condemned who … is categorically guilty, whether or not s/he [sic] is factually innocent. (McBride, 1995: 272)

Veyne has compellingly argued that double-mindedness, the 'capacity to simultaneously believe in incompatible truths,' concerning both myth and the scapegoat mechanism which it rationalizes was pivotal to the long-term success of the ancient Greek *demos* which was centered upon 'a sectarian politics of alliance' that was the political and cultural lifeblood of the democratic *polis* (Veyne, 1988: 56). If, for the purposes of establishing a self-stabilizing form of neo-Nietzschean political religion, we were to search for a contemporary example of archaic double-mindedness, or psychic 'Balkanization,' then an outstanding example would be electronic *neo-tribalism* as assayed by Michel Maffesoli in his *The Time of the Tribes* (1996) whose phenomenological cornerstone is that "*experiencing the other* is the basis of the community, even if it leads to conflict" (Maffesoli, 1996: 73), for anyone who is on-line constitutes a potential kind of 'neo-terrorist'. And Maffesoli sees neo-tribalism as the necessary outcome of globalization that managed to eliminate local or national identities as viable sources of external mediation.

> Indeed, the *territory-myth* pair that is the organizing principle[83] of the city is both cause and effect of such a structure. That is, like a nest of Russian dolls, the city reveals other entities of the same type: neighborhoods, ethnic groups, associations, various tribes that will organize themselves around (real or symbolic) territory and common myths. These Hellenistic cities are founded essentially on the double polarity of cosmopolitanism and rootedness (which, as we know, was to produce a specific civilization). What does this say other than that all of these groups, strongly united by common sentiments, will structure a collective memory which in its very diversity is a founding structure. These groups may be of many types (ethnic; social); structurally, it is their very diversity that assures the *unicity* of the city. […] it is the *tension* between these various groups that assures the durability of the whole. (Maffesoli, 1996: 124)

And durability-through-tension is the geo-political recipe for mental Balkanization. It is also a world-system that is structurally homologous to the one that Girard describes in terms of the universalization of undifferentiation that, at the same time, exhibits a profound absence of anxiety about itself.

> Girard claims that triangular desire had invaded all areas of contemporary society, stretching from 'the more intimate depths of the individual soul' to 'countries, races, and continents.' The new triangle [of globalization] resembles the shapes of fractal geometry, where the same pattern is reproduced in an infinitely small and infinitely large scale. The space in which it is inscribed is no longer the nation-state or the metropolis. The entire planet is divided

[83] Schmitt would consider this the telluric. See Chap. 4, above.

> into a center and an extended periphery, which in turn are fragmented into smaller, relative centers and peripheries, until we reach the inner word of the individual's consciousness, also composed of multiple, constantly shifting centripetal and centrifugal tensions. (Mucignat, 2015: 144)

Which is where the durability-creating potential for tension comes into play: although anyone can be electronically attacked by anyone anywhere at any time for every humanly conceivable reason,[84] 'When the rules of proper conduct are respected, there is regulation and organic order, which cannot fail to be beneficial to all'—to those who are in the inside (Maffesoli, 1996: 119). Which may serve as the cornerstone of the new post-Christian political religion.

> Religion, then, is far from 'useless.' It humanizes violence; it protects man from his own violence by taking it out of his hands, transforming it into a transcendent and ever-present danger to be kept in check by the appropriate rites appropriately observed and by a modest and prudent demeanor. Religious misinterpretation is a truly constructive force, for it purges man of the suspicions that would poison his existence if it were to remain conscious of the crisis as it actually took hold. (Girard, 1977: 134–135)

We still require rites, rituals, and prohibitions just as much as before, if not more so, because now the entire planetary population is possessed by *skandalon*, the pathological the stumbling-block of mimesis that is the raw stuff of *ressentiment*: 'The *skandalon* designates a very common inability to walk away from mimetic rivalry which turns it into an addiction' meaning 'anything that attracts us in proportion to the suffering or irritation that it causes us' (Girard, 1996: 198). Which is now 24/7.

> *Skandalon* designates the intersubjective process that results from a very general but not universal human failure to walk away from mimetic rivalry. *Skandalon* is the process through which we are attracted to whatever, or, rather, whoever treats us badly. *Skandalon* is destructive addiction of all kinds: drugs, sex, power, and, above all, morbid competitiveness—professional, political, intellectual, spiritual. *Skandalon* is the aching tooth that we cannot stop testing with our tongue, even though it hurts more. (Girard, 1996: 215)

And perhaps the single greatest empirical example of the manner in which the rites of the emergent political religion of neo-tribalism are beginning to develop is the suggestively neo-totalitarian *cancel culture* which is ultimately nothing less than '*the radical democratization of sacrificial logic through technological means* ... aided and abetted by the combinatory effect of global capitalism and computational power ...' (Culkin, 2022: 55). It is almost possible to express this formulaically. Globalization is the universalization of internal mediation (subject to local realities) as well as the concomitant universalization of scandal. Cancel culture, as one of the indispensable rituals of neo-tribalism, both enables and is enabled by: (i) the transnational channeling of *ressentiment*; (ii) the instantaneous generative unanimity of de-territorialized digital or electron communities known as the neo-tribes, the virtual communities of communal 'virtue'; (iii) the successful resolution of the problem of the sacrificial crisis through speed and acceleration: perpetually nomadic and liminal cybernetic lynch-mobs executing symbolic violence coalesce and act at such great

[84] And very soon every inhumanly conceivable reason once A.I. kicks in for real.

velocity that they temporally exceed the comparatively low-velocity re-formation of undifferentiation. In effect, a kind of 'escape velocity' has been achieved in which a new generative event can be produced before the cathartic and unifying effects of the immediately prior 'mobbing' have dissipated. An added bonus that bodes well for the self-stabilizing nature of the neo-tribalism is that the symbolic sacrificers of cancel culture generate social capital faster than they deplete it, allowing the elite 'influencers' to evolve into a de facto electronic techno-priesthood, the ones who handle and prepare the virtual sacrifice of negative symbolization. Within this schema God is dead but the *victim* remains, so the question becomes to whom is expiation *really* due? The answer to this question reveals the obsolescence of Girard's preoccupation with *meconnaissance* and demystification.

> Victimage is still present among us, of course, but in degenerate forms that do not produce the type of mythical reconciliation and ritual practice exemplified by primitive cults. This lack of efficiency often means that there are more rather than fewer victims. As the case of drugs, consumers of sacrifice tend to increase the doses when the effect becomes more difficult to achieve. (Girard, 1996: 16–17)

Girard's fundamental error is that if we remove his transcendental scaffolding (the 'divine revelation' that scapegoating is normatively impossible to justify because of the true innocence of the scapegoat) then the immorality of the mechanism is reduced to the contingencies of *social consciousness*, which can be deliberately re-engineered to an indeterminate degree. Victimology demonstrates the superiority of a neo-scapegoating process as the temporary but fast-moving neo-*katharsis* of the digital age of virtual reality. And, apart from the rites of online exchange themselves, a minimally sufficient degree of external mediation is provided by the restriction of sacrificial violence to the domain of the symbolic as opposed to the physical. The wholly symbolic nature of 'political correctness'—or the correct politics—of the neo-scapegoaters/neo-victimizers solves the problem of how to re-enact scapegoating while avoiding the chaos of the escalation of reciprocal violence: algorithms can now be used to designate the enemy One of the respective neo-tribes governed by that self-same mathematical modeling. Which is nothing less than the holy grail of the sacrificial decision: we now possess perfect knowledge of the identity of the neo-scapegoat through the substitution of artificial intelligence (A.I.) for the casting of lots or the throwing of dice or the telling of lies. Which would put Josef K. at ease.[85]

While social media is not technically a weapon per se, digital technology more generally can, and has, undergone a universal weaponization within the context of the symbolic 'civil war' of a globalization driven by neo-liberalism; 'on the one hand, the model has an opposite meaning depending on whether it is mimetic or rational ['good'], and, on the other hand, in the era of internal mediation that we have entered, the mimetic model will always prevail over the rational model' (Girard & Chantre, 2010: 132) in accordance with the post-age hegemony of pre-representation and undifferentiation.

> [The] peculiarity is how the line between victim and victimizer has become increasingly porous and unstable. The peculiarity is how the very discourses of cancel culture and woke

[85] See Chap. 8, above.

> ideology—discourses entirely concerned with the protection and elevation of victims—have slowly become integrated into some of the largest multinational corporations, financial institutions, and technological platforms on the planet. The peculiarity is how the very worst of the global victimizers now feign solidarity with the victim class—or even worse, present themselves as victims as well. (Culkin, 2022: 26)

The issue is not the substance (or 'ideological content') of cancel culture; the point is the structurally isomorphic relationship between a digitalized metaphysical desire and sacrificial logic; '*"cancel culture" is a term to express the underlying logic of sacrifice in its contemporary, digitized form*' (Culkin, 2022: 35) meaning that 'the act of cancellation is more like a magic trick than a rational cultural or technological phenomenon in which "social justice" is attempted to be delivered' (Culkin, 2022: 39). In his very valuable meditations on cancel culture Brian Francis Culkin has pursued a clearly Girardian line of inquiry.

> Sacrificial logic, which *is* the base logic of martyr culture, is losing any and all clear social function. Sacrificial logic is spreading like wild fire into all corners of our social being and political life. In the early decades of the 21st century, we are entering into a dangerous era of what I term *absolute victimization.* (Culkin, 2022: 33)

Absolute victimization equates with a total(-izing) *sacrificial crisis* because by becoming universal we have deprived ourselves of the collective means of determining who is a true victim, or, what comes to the same thing in terms of affectivity, who is entitled to have their persecutors persecuted so that absolutely everybody can demand the exact same thing simultaneously on the basis of their claim to an identity that everyone else recognizes as their own—a digitalized undifferentiation.

> A 'sacrificial crisis' for Rene Girard, is the term he developed to describe a scenario in which there is no longer consensus as to who or what should be the victim to discharge the surplus desire circulating within a community. This lack of consensus as to where violence should be specially channelled to cleanse and regenerate the social fabric thus leads to a spiralling crisis in which violence becomes unchecked, thus spilling out into society causing instability and chaos for all. We are undoubtedly in the midst of a gestating sacrificial crisis on the planetary level. (Culkin, 2022: 37–38 n 10)

The point here is 'that the person being cancelled—even if they did say something racist or offensive; even if they did do something wildly inappropriate—still functions as a "victim" in an anthropological sense: as a receptacle for the discharge of the Other's desire' (Culkin, 2022: 40), said desire-of-the-Other being mediated by the mimetic convergence of the crowd, the vicissitudes of that hyper-turbulent 'thing' that is the fleshy foundation of the sacrificial crisis, unbridled but high-velocity internal mediation now acting as a *katechon*-like social force, whereas under the aegis of some mechanism(s) of external mediation 'the cancelling was always performed by the victimizer class against the victim class. The social logic of sacrifice operated *because* it was a contained, unique form of violence kept entirely separate from everyday violence' (Culkin, 2022: 40). Which clearly no longer applies, for is not the catch-phrase '24/7' nothing other than the revolutionary immanentization of undifferentiated everyday life? 'Indeed, the phrase "modern world" seems almost like a synonym for "sacrificial crisis"' (Girard, 1977: 188) and just as with the prehistoric spawning of the sacrificial mechanism the judicial stands at the center of it, only this time in an inverted, negative way.

> It is not law, in any conceivable form, that is responsible for the tensions and alienation besetting modern man; rather, it is the increasing lack of law. The perpetual denunciation of the law arises from a typically modern sense of resentment—a feedback of desire that purports to be directed against the law but one that is actually aimed at the model-obstacle whose dominant position the subject stubbornly refuses to acknowledge. The more frenzied the mimetic process becomes, caught up in the confusion of constantly changing forms, the more unwilling men [sic] are to recognize that they have made an obstacle of the model and a model of the obstacle. Here we encounter a true 'unconscious,' and one that can obviously assume many forms. (Girard, 1977: 188–189)

Translated into the terms of law-and-literature, founded upon the secular liberal political religion of a pseudo-anti-sacrificialism, the political religion of neo-tribalism would represent a complete and perfect inversion: the abolition of the hangman, the sign of the rule of law, due process and objectivity counter-balanced by the unmediated immediacy of *apogoge*, frontier justice as the contagious conductor of mimetic desire, sacrificial logic, affective consciousness, subjectivity, and the absolute subordination of all forms of thought, speech, and writing to pre-representational thought. Similarly, the presumption of innocence and burden of proof will be replaced by the presumption of guilt and the reversal of the burden of proof onto the accused based upon the subjective identity of the status of the accuser as an 'authentic' victim or citizen, one that has been subjected to persecution by the (now) accused—which means that Rusty Staub does not escape on the basis of a technicality and is convicted of the murder that everyone 'knows' that he committed (*Presumption of Innocence*), Juror no. 3 manages to secure the execution of the accused (*12 Angry Men*), and Max Cady gets to slaughter the Bowden family (*Cape Fear*). Making 'a model of the obstacle' is tantamount to a liminal state of absolute victimization for there has been a complete inversion of victimized/victimizer. What we might call 'post truth' *meconnaissance* represents the loss of moral and epistemological differentiation between the sacrificed and the sacrificer creating the wholly contemporary category of 'righteous victimizer' who will replace the now antiquated genre stereotypes of the Westerner or the heroic/anti-heroic lawyer—for if there is only the righteous victimizer there can be no such thing as an innocent accused and the externally mediating anti-sacrificial structures of the rule of law and due process are mere reactionary obstacles to the generation of the new for-now-and-for-ever unified community of the true sacrificers. And if society is becoming more mimetic, and this time in an unprecedently self-conscious manner through the electronic channels of universal and instantaneous communication, a global plague of intensely affective video-clips and sound-bites, then, from the vantage point of social psychology, the collective threshold of psychic resistance to the mimetic doubles of contagion and the will-to-revenge will be proportionately diminished. But, and this is essential, the neo-tribalistic age of lynch-mobs-on-demand should be able to survive indefinitely provided that: (i) the technology is adequate to the task of regulating accelerating high-speed neo-tribal formations; and (ii) we collectively dispense with the moral taboo concerning *meconnaissance* and willingly embrace a specifically anti-Enlightenment form of double-mindedness. And it is victimology that is the key, the mediatory forum within which the inversion of persecutor and persecuted takes place. The neo-sacrificial society does away with the demand of *meconnaissance*; objective certainty is produced by the empirical establishment of the accuser as a righteous victim, now collectively defined as a member of a group (or an algorithmic 'crowd') historically subjected to persecution and, therefore, morally unacceptable acts of scapegoating. For, unlike before and in direct contradiction of Christ, *we will know exactly what we are doing* when we press into our sacrificial service the post-human mediators of algorithms and the proliferating virtual persecutions of social media. The net result is that we will have collectively resurrected the *pharmakoi*, with the 'enemy grouping' of our respective sacrificial gazes serving as the ready-made 'offscourings' of our alliances of friendship, each constituted by the unanimous victimage of a universal victimology.[86]

But if all of this is not 'tragic' enough there is one final turn of the screw of the negative: the final demystification of the demystifiers is that Christianity provides the grounds not only of the sacrificial crisis but the post-Christian solution for it once we are made aware that Christianity itself may be far less of an anti-sacrificial religion than Girard generally supposes and for the very reasons that he himself offers. It comes back to the problem of good mimesis which has received its classic expression in Christian spirituality as both *imitatio Christi* and *imitatio Dei*, both Jesus and God the positive model-attractors of mimetic desire. 'I have come to be more positive about the word "sacrificial,"' Girard informs us very late in life, 'so I would like first of all to make a distinction between sacrifice as murder and sacrifice as renunciation. The latter is a movement toward freedom from mimesis as potentially rivalrous acquisition and rivalry' (Girard, 1996: 272). Which, according to Girard, should guarantee benevolent, or, at least, altruistic outcomes. But this, I think, misses the real point: what Girard has conceded is that it is possible to understand *Christianity as a sacrificial religion*—and this, by what it implies, changes everything. For good mimesis is itself the fruit of the ambivalent double transference that haunts mimesis and all things that are mimetic: mimetic desire can lead to the 'bad' of metaphysical desire and it can lead to 'good' of *metanoia*, since the abjuration of acquisitive mimesis can only be secured through the imitation of another whose true being was nothing other than the rejection of mimetic violence, or the 'casting out of demons'. Good mimesis is Girard's second *metanoia*, a personal

86 Although this borders on science fiction it would not, I feel, be unreasonable to anticipate the utilization of an artificial intelligence capable of designating floating populations of deviant populations suitable for the generative mechanisms of the neo-tribes, a contemporary updating of a state of affairs that prevailed in classical Athens. The following is taken from the *scholia* on Aristophanes' *The Knights*: 'By *demosius* "those who are public" he [Aristophanes] means those who are called *pharmakoi*. Who cleanse the city by their death. For the Athenians would nourish some who were exceedingly low-born, penniless, and useless … and when a time of a disaster of some sort came upon the city, I mean a famine or something similar, they would sacrifice these to cleanse the city from pollution and from their evil, and to find a cure [*therapeian*] for the disaster they were enduring. They also gave the *pharmakoi* the name offscourings [*katharmata*]' (Dawson, 2013: 139).

reckoning with his own mis-recognition of the double transference inherent within mimetic desire itself, so that what was before a thing of pure negativity can now be appreciated under the differentiating sign of ambivalence. And, if my account here is correct, then it has the capacity to undermine the whole of Girard's ethical concept of demystification: if mimetic desire is ambivalent (non-dualistic) then 'good' mimesis is fully exchangeable with the 'bad,' so that sacrifice, and, by extension, the scapegoat itself, can be transformed into its 'opposite'.

I am making a very sweeping statement here but I believe that what marks both Nietzsche's and Girard's approach to Christianity is their mutual failure to adequately comes to terms with the martyr, martyrdom, and martyrology, a weird convergence for the same reason but with diametrically opposed motives: the valorization of auto-sacrifice undermines the notion of the essence of Christianity as anti-sacrificial. Nietzsche may have almost have stumbled upon this and Girard makes much of the fact that his great rival almost did so, the anti-Christ noting in his *Nachlass*.

> Dionysos versus the 'Crucified One': there you have the opposition. It's *not* a distinction regarding their martyrdom—just that this martyrdom has a different meaning. Life itself, its eternal fruitfulness and recurrence, conditions torment, destruction, the will to annihilation …in the other case suffering, 'the Crucified as the innocent', counts as an objection to this life, a formula to condemn it. … 'the God on the cross' is a curse on life, a hunt to deliver oneself from it. Dionysos cut to pieces is a *promise* to life: it will be eternally reborn and come home out of destruction. (Nietzsche, 2003: 249–250)

The phrase '*has a different meaning*' is operative, for it underscores the submerged reality that the antithesis is a false one, insofar as both Dionysos and Christ can be the source of mimetic desire mediated by sacrifice, the first one orgiastic, the second one ascetical but both reversible through the double transference of mimetic desire. And, in fact, on several occasions Girard intimated that Christ's Passion might be properly considered sacrificial because of its actively transformative power (*metanoia*) as opposed to its heuristic, revelatory, and performative dimensions: 'Jesus is the last and greatest of the prophets, the one who sums them up and goes further than all of them …This is the complete elimination of the sacrificial for the first time—the end of divine violence and the explicit revelation of all that has gone before it. It calls for a complete change of emphasis and a spiritual metamorphosis without precedent in the whole history of mankind' (Girard et al., 1978: 200). It also intimates the substitution of the 'aneconomy' of the sacrifice-of-the-self for the 'economy' of the-sacrifice-of-the-other (Chabbert, 2020). Which revolutionizes, but does not wholly supplant, divine violence; it should be remembered that for Islam it is not Jesus but Muhammed who is the 'last and greatest of the prophets.' But the more critical point is that the self-martyring *imitatio Christi* could only take place if Jesus had first willingly undergone the sacrificing of his own self, thereby turning the whole of the Pasion into a heuristic device for good mimesis, a kind of a 'sacred pantomime' that mimics perfectly the false supernatural effect of the scapegoat victim but which, within the context of the Gospels, turns out to be spiritually transformative in truth.[87]

[87] And if I were to express this in terms of the imaginary of Atonement theology it would be something like this: the crucifixion of Christ's body 'releases' the spiritual force (the Paraclete?)

Therefore, Christ does not really demystify the scapegoat mechanism; rather, he subjects himself to the process in order to achieve its inversion that underlines the transition from other to self-sacrifice. Not a repudiation of sacrifice, but the clandestine infiltration and appropriation of it now re-tooled for divine purposes which, not coincidentally, turn out to be the same as Girard's, a 'reactive moralism' or 'theoretical Manichaenism' that are the cause of his 'overlooking the emancipatory and positive aspects of internal mediation' (Antonello & Webb, 2015: xxii) as well as the beneficial aspects of a double-minded *meconnaissance.* And this critical oversight may have originated in Girard's first major publication, *Deceit, Desire, and the Novel* (1961) which doubles as both 'a masterpiece of Christian spirituality' (Palaver, 2015: 69) and as 'an anthropological apology for Christianity' (Palaver, 2015: 75). Girard himself indicates as much: 'Since the beginning of the "novelistic conversion" in *Deceit, Desire, and the Novel,* all of my books have been more or less explicit apologies of Christianity' (Girard 2010: xv) concluding that 'As far as I am concerned the subject of literature and Christianity is literally the story of my whole intellectual and spiritual existence' (Girard, 2015: 281). As I have already discussed in Chap. 1, following his first book Girard 'again and again emphasized the "existential" or "spiritual" form of autobiography that reveals a deeper connection between author and literary work' (Palaver, 2015: 74). But the result is that

> Taken in broader historical terms, the increasing spread of internal mediation as represented in the modern novel could be seen not only in negative terms ... but as the inevitable and, from a political and ethical standpoint, welcome result of the democratic transformation of traditional social structures based on radical social separations, aristocratic elitism, patriarchy, slavery, tribal identity ... (Antonello & Webb, 2015: xxviii)[88]

Focused exclusively upon the negative nature of mimetic desire because of the *metanoia* that he extends to all of the 'great' novelists of literary history, Girard felt the need to establish the difference between his post-conversion 'authentic' desires and his 'sinful' mimetic desires pre-conversion[89]: the novelist's recognition and literary confession of the mimetic nature of his own desires is a mimetic repetition of St Paul's conversion on the road to Damascus, the death of the old self that precludes mediation with the 'Pauline idea of the new man' (Girard, 2015: 284).[90] Complicating matters is

that induces *metanoia,* transforming individual recipients of this supernaturally bestowed mimetic 'grace' into a community of aneconomic martyrs.

[88] Similarly, 'In his discussion of the mimetic nature of desire, Girard has put almost exclusive emphasis on its conflictual and antagonistic aspects (envy, jealousy, rivalry, resentment, blaming, scapegoating, violence, sacrifice), leaving aside the positive and constructive ones (empathy, the pedagogical modelling of desire, reciprocal positive mirroring, non-conflictual love, and the emancipatory role of art)' (Gragnolati & Webb, 2015: 114),

[89] 'One of the problems with *Deceit, Desire, and the Novel* is that it retains the polemical tone ... which went ... against the current interpretation of desire in the constitution of modern subjectivity. This led him to adopt a sort of theoretical "Manichaenism" in his early formulations, which posits an intrinsic polarity between the "positive" mediation of desire by God, and the "negative," idolatrous mediation wielded by the others' (Antonello & Webb, 2015: xxi).

[90] Di Blasi rightly highlights Girard's interminable, and possibly self-serving, ambiguity on this point. The 'clear and arguably initial distinction authentic/mimetic desire seems from the start (after

that Girard began to emulate this very conversionary experience as his own; 'From the age of ten to thirty-eight years, Girard was an agnostic, even siding with left-leaning atheists. He sympathized with the intellectual, revolutionary avant-garde. Girard's intense study of major novelistic authors eventually led him back, after decades of indifference, to the Christian faith and the Catholic Church' (Palaver, 2015: 74). Shortly after his intellectual return to Catholicism following the publication of *Deceit, Desire, and the Novel* Girard underwent his own conversion after a false diagnosis for melanoma: 'I realized that I had just ... had an experience similar to that which I had just wanted to describe' in the case of the novelists; 'The religious symbolism, which in the novelists is there in embryo, began to work in my own case, spontaneously bursting into flame' (Rene Girard qtd. Palaver, 2015: 75).[91] The upshot of this series of exceptional, and highly improbable, series of events is that Girard takes as the cornerstone of his own personalized theory of mimesis the contestable assumption that 'Normally the word "imitation" is reserved to designate what is considered inauthentic' (Girard 2010: 59). But later in his career he rejected the narrowness of this focus and suggested that, all along, it was the 'correct' exercise of the specifically mimetic form of desire that is the basis of the truly human which is adaptability or 'mobility,' making mimetic desire and not the rejection of it the true basis of a universalized hominization. This was made clear in his 1993 interview with Rebecca Adams.

> Adams: 'What you are advocating, actually, is not renunciation but imitation of a positive model.'
>
> Girard: 'The idea that renunciation in all its forms should be renounced once and for all may well be the most flagrant nonsense any human culture has ever devised. But as to whether I am advocating the "renunciation" of mimetic desire, yes and no. Not the renunciation of

---

his conversion) obscured by Girard himself. Decades after *Deceit, Desire and the Novel* [1961], he very strangely switched between negating and admitting the very possibility of an authentic desire. In *Evolution and Conversion* [2007], he even switched between two sentences from the claim that "there is no authentic desire and any is mediated by others" to the claim that "the distinction between an 'authentic' and 'inauthentic' desire is not always groundless"' (Di Blasi, 2015: 45; Girard 2010: 45). Di Blasi opts for a political explanation: Girard wanted to anchor his position within the secure bulwark of the center. 'By obscuring the difference between Christian *imitatio Christi* (or renouncement) and regaining access to an authentic desire, Girard was able to fight against elitist individualism *and* struggles for equality at the same time. Or, to put the paradox as clearly as possible: the acceptance of being part of mimetic desire permits us to overcome an illusionary autonomy and to replace it with a real autonomy, which in turn allows us to overcome mimetic desire' (Di Blasi, 2015: 49). He places great emphasis on this passage from *Deceit, Desire, and the Novel* (1961): 'All these dogmas [subjectivisms and objectivisms, romanticisms and realisms, individualisms and scientisms, idealisms and positivisms] are the aesthetic or philosophic translation of world-views peculiar to internal mediation. They all depend directly or indirectly on the lie of spontaneous desire. They all defend the same illusion of autonomy in which modern man is passionately devoted' (Girard, 1965: 16).

[91] Although this must be qualified somewhat. Even though Girard does recognize both a positive and negative form of mimesis fairly early on, he made clear that 'I do believe that "bad" mimesis needs to be emphasized because its reality remains overlooked, and it has been always neglected or mistaken for non-mimetic behaviour and even denied by most observers' (Girard, 2020: 131). The exemplary statement of "bad" mimesis is Girard et al., 1978: 15–19.

> mimetic desire itself, because what Jesus advocates *is* mimetic desire. Imitate me, and imitate the Father through me, he says, so it's twice mimetic. Jesus seems to say that the only way to avoid violence is to imitate me, and imitate the Father. So the idea that mimetic desire itself is bad makes no sense. It is true, however, that occasionally I say 'mimetic desire' when I really mean only the type of mimetic desire that generates mimetic rivalry and, in turn, is generated by it. (Girard, 2020: 63)

Also known as '"good contagion"' and '"non-violent imitation,"' good mimesis is the self's last-ditch attempt to free itself from annihilating metaphysical desire, a form of 'liberation through the release experienced in love and experience' that serves as the basis for a 'good or conversionary mimesis' (*metanoia*). If non-violent imitation achieves psychic dominance it 'becomes effective in a fundamental change of personality through the imitation of God or Christ…' (Girard, 1996: 290, 291) but what matters more, perhaps, is the flexible nature of formation process of mimetic desire which seems analogous to a form of choice.

> If desire is so fixed, it means that there isn't much difference between desires and instincts. In order to have *mobility* of desire—in relation to both appetites and instincts from one side and social milieu from the other—the relevant difference is *imitation*, that is, the presence of the *model* or models, since everybody has one or more. Only mimetic desire can be *free*, can be *genuine* desire, human desire, because it *must* choose a model more than the object itself. Mimetic desire is what makes us human, what makes possible for us the breakout from routinely animalistic appetites, and constructs our own, albeit invariably unstable, identities. It is this very mobility of desire, its mimetic nature, and this very instability of our identities that makes us capable of *adaptation*, that gives the possibility to learn and to *evolve*. (Girard, Antonello and de Castro Rocha 2008: 58)

But evolve into what? Fortunately, Girard, once again, has the (same) answer at hand: it has something to do with Christianity and its mimetic by-products of *imitatio Christi* and *imitatio Dei*.

> Christianity directs existence toward a vanishing point, either toward God or toward the Other. Choice always involves choosing a model, and true freedom lies in the basic choice between a human or a divine mode. The impulse of the soul toward God is inseparable from a retreat into the Self.[92] Inversely the turning in on itself of pride is inseparable from a movement of panic toward the Other. (Girard, 1965: 58)

And, also once again, Christianity seems to constitute a unique religious phenomenon.

> Christianity acknowledges the ultimate goodness of imitation as well as the goodness and reality of the human person. It teaches that instead of surrendering to mimetic desire, by following the newest fashion and worshipping the latest idol, we should imitate only Christ or Christ-like non-competitive models. (Girard, 2015: 283)

As we should expect, the choice of the human model is the fruit of bad mimesis/contagion and the choice of the divine model is the sign of good mimesis, the contagion of positive imitation. But what exactly causes one to choose one path rather than the other? Girard is coming very close to articulation a theory of *grace* (or

[92] Girard draws an implicit correlation between authenticity and grounded-ness; both are taken as 'the good' but no demonstration of the truth of this hypothesis is provided.

just random 'good luck') to account for the differences, rendering his entire project hostage to the reality of Divine presence, which, although it might be true, can in no way be taken for granted. Girard also appears unaware that his ungrounded commitment to mimesis as 'the good' (as opposed to 'good mimesis') opens the door to the weaponization of mimetic desire, as evidenced by the pseudo-totalitarianism of neo-tribalist globalized neo-liberal hyper-corporatism; for although 'real' scapegoats may have been transcendentally 'suspended' (*aufgehoben*) we continue to remain scandalized. And if the social being of Christians, as opposed to their transcendental significance, is rooted in that of a temporal community, then the diverse *ecclesia* of believers become just another sub-set of neo-tribes along with the rest and, therefore, subject to their own forms of scandalization. The key to Girard's blindness to the violent-generating dimensions of Christian sacrifice may lie in his over-reliance upon 'textual effectivity' wholly consistent with his moralistically Manichaen repudiation of *meconnaissance*.[93]

> If Scripture must be read for the world-intervention [of Providence] to take place,[94] what guarantees that it is read properly and thus that the intervention in the world is the one that the literary critic says it is? And what is the guarantee of its being understood, and not, for instance, misused. Despite the hope that Girard places in Scripture, the agency of the Bible in the world cannot, it seems, be guaranteed; its proper reception also not; and its effectivity is—and has been—wayward, violent, and persecutory. These might be effects of misreadings, misappropriations, and perversions of the revelation of Scripture, but they nonetheless belong to the history of Scripture. The bare presence of the Scripture in our midst seems to provide no guarantee to its effectivity: in other words, there looks to be no risk on this earth of coming to a peaceful end with scapegoating, violence, and rivalry. (Feldman, 2015: 62–63)

The Bible is thoroughly 'complicit with the great collective lynching that is renewed every day to consolidate the community' (Alberto Beretta Anguissola qtd. Antonella & Webb, 2015: 1) for it is itself the ultimate source of the *skandalon* of cancel culture by way of an extraordinarily roundabout path of historical and theological deviations: the substitution of the originary mimetic model (pre-representation) for the allegedly 'anti-mimetic' rational model (representation) through the abolition of differences by way of abolishing the scapegoat. So that the end of modernity, the abolition of the Enlightenment as just one more atrophied superstition, will be the Nietzschean-like return of the scapegoat mechanism as the post-secular solution to the apocalyptic crisis of undifferentiation of which Christianity will finally be revealed as the greatest and last of the *pharmakoi*: the cause and cure of the disease.

Contra Girard, the last and best laugh will be Nietzsche's as the true prophet of the post-civilization of absolute sensibility (a more clinical term for the will-to-power), for the real issue may have been paganism all along and not Christianity or Judaism or Islam. Double-mindedness is the mentalist tool necessary to maintain a belief in polytheism, the plurality of gods, none of whom are absolute and each one representing a partial aspect of an inherently pluralistic *nomos*, natural and cultural. Or,

---

[93] See Chap. 1, above.

[94] Which sounds remarkably like James Boyd White's interpretive community with its constitutive rhetoric and participatory dialogue. See above, Chap. 1.

the reverse might be equally true: a pluralistic universe lacking a unifying monistic substance of any kind would receive its most common-sensical cultural expression in a multitude of limited and limiting divinities, each of whom personifies a powerful but relative variant of truth, eternal through time (perhaps) but limited in space. In either case, monotheism, with its double foundational pillars of absolute truth and absolute morality may be rejuvenating in the short-term of world-history, especially for the disempowered masses of believers who require both of these truths as compensation for their undifferentiated marginality, but may simply be too persecutory and absolutist to survive the *long duree*, especially its current form a globalized digital social consciousness of reality-on-demand. The historical destiny of the peoples of the West may well be neo-paganism, albeit perhaps technically more Schmittean than Nietzschean, for Schmitt was the one who realized more than anyone else that generative unanimity is the alpha and omega of social being, the one true universal constant of History.

> The point to grasp in our world today is that contemporary mass-man can bear to put himself on the cross even less than his fellowmen in earlier times because he is accustomed to arguing in terms of rights and expects to enjoy all the comforts established for him by society and promised by science and a dynamic economy. He is therefore much readier to unload the cross onto someone else, anyone else, as long as they are closest at hand. However, this can only be done by joining a group, since crucifixions require some technical division of labor, and hands and ropes ready to put up the crosses. And so it is the despair of contemporary atomized man that breeds a spontaneous neo-tribalism which only flourishes the more for being systematically ignored by the official culture, aided and abetted by a religious culture that insists on thinking in the moralistic, collective terms of centuries past. The pre-totalitarian and totalitarian movements are thus admirably suited to this purpose, indeed they arise for no other reason. They offer a victimary reorganization built around some category of enemy, among the many on offer in our contemporary disintegration, and in that way the particular enemy once more restores an identity that seemed irretrievably lost. (Fornari, 2009: 24)

And because it is decidedly totalitarian, neo-tribalism 'functions by indicating not just one victim but a whole mass of victims, because the victimary choice has to be in proportion to the mass disintegration that it intends to remedy' (Fornari, 2009: 24). In the end 'Any pretext suffices for becoming the victims of a neo-tribal movement; the more gratuitous and incomprehensible those pretexts are, the more they assert the group's strength and cohesions, its crazy sovereignty' (Fornari, 2009: 24), and it is this Schmittean-sounding 'crazy sovereignty' that serves as the point of interface between the political and orgiastic sacrifice. Decades ago while looking forward toward current reality, Leo Strauss, Carl Schmitt's best friend for a while, made the following comment on Nietzsche: '"Could atheism belong to the free mind as Nietzsche conceives of it while a certain kind of non-atheism belongs to the philosopher of future who will again worship the god Dionysos…?"' (Leo Strauss qtd. Ranieri, 2007: 174). For Strauss recognized what Girard did, the apparent paradox that 'the decay of institutional religion coincides with an increase in religiosity' which, for us, has assumed the form of victimage as metaphysical desire (Ranieri, 2007: 174).

> The religion of the future envisioned by Nietzsche may have some resemblance to Vedanta philosophy, but Strauss argues that Nietzsche anticipates 'a more Western, a sterner, more

> terrible and more invigorating possibility: the sacrificing from cruelty, i.e., from the will to power turning against itself, of God which prepares the worshipping of the [sacrificial] stone, stupidity, heaviness, (gravity), fate, the Nothing. He anticipates in other words that the better among contemporary atheists will come to know what they are doing. (Leo Strauss qtd. Ranieri, 2007: 174)

As opposed to the atheists who came before and did not know what they were doing so that they could do what they did 'innocently. But the atheists of the future cannot be innocent for they no longer mis-recognize their truth. The replacement of the single-minded recognition of mis-recognition by the double-minded mis-recognition of mis-recognition that flows from the eternally self-affirming will-to-power which is the-spirit-of-revenge post-atheistically liberated from the Manichaen moralism of *ressentiment* which is our Fate.

Only a scapegoat can save us.

My pupils were my masters.

References

Primary Sources

Aeschylus. (1977). *The Oresteia: Agamemnon, The Libation Bearers, The Eumenides* (R. Fagles, Trans.). Penguin Books.

The Hateful Eight (directed by Quentin Tarantino, The Weinstein Company, 2015).

Secondary Sources

Antonello, P., & H. Webb (2015). Introduction. In P. Antonello & H. Webb (Eds.), *Mimesis, desire, and the novel: Rene Girard and literary criticism* (pp. ix–liii). Michigan State University Press.

Armitage, D. (2021). *Philosophy's violent sacred: Heidegger and Nietzsche through mimetic theory*. Michigan State University Press.

Arnold, C. E. (1992). *Powers of darkness: Principalities & powers in Paul's letter*. IVP Academic.

Brighi, E. (2015). The mimetic politics of lone-wolf terrorism. *Journal of International Political Theory, 11*(1), 145–164.

Brighi, E., & Cerella, A. (2015). An alternative vision of politics and violence: Introducing mimetic theory in international studies. *Journal of International Political Theory, 11*(1), 3–25.

Calasso, R. (2017). *The unnameable present* (R. Dixon, Trans.). Farrar, Straus and Giroux.

Calasso, R. (2018). *The Ruin of Kasch* (R. Dixon, Trans.). Farrar, Strays and Giroux.

Chabbert, M. (2020). Towards a sacrificial aneconomy? Georges Bataille and the aporia of sacrifice. In B. W. Nail & J. A. Ellsworth (Eds.), *Law's sacrifice: Approaching the problem of sacrifice in law, literature, and philosophy* (pp. 23–43). Routledge.

Cover, R. M. (1986). Violence and the word. *Yale Law Journal, 95*, 1601–1629.

Culkin, B. F. (2021). *Rene Girard and Covid-19: Satan. Capitalism. apocalypse*. Brian Francis Culkin.

Culkin, B. F. (2022). *An essay on cancel culture*. Brian Francis Culkin.

Cerella, A. (2015). Until the end of the world: Girard, Schmitt and the origins of violence. *Journal of International Political Theory, 11*(1), 42–60.

Cowdell, S. (2014). *Rene Girard and secular modernity: Christ, culture, and crisis*. University of Notre Dame Press.

Dawson, D. (2013). *Flesh becomes word: A Lexicography of the scapegoat or, the history of an idea.* Michigan State University Press.
Domenach, J.-M. (1988). Voyage to the end of the sciences of man. In P. Dumouchel (Ed.), *Violence and truth: On the work of Rene Girard* (pp. 152–159). The Athlone Press.
Di Blasi, L. (2015). Within and beyond mimetic desire. In P. Antonello & H. Webb (Eds.), *Mimesis, desire, and the novel: Rene Girard and literary criticism* (pp. ix–liii). Michigan State University Press.
Dupuy, J.-P. (1988). Totalization and misrecognition. In P. Dumouchel, *Violence and truth: On the work of Rene Girard* (pp. 75–100). The Athlone Press.
Dupuy, J.-P. (2011). Naturalizing mimetic theory. In S. R. Garrels (Ed.), *Mimesis and science: Empirical research on imitation and the mimetic theory of culture and religion* (pp. 193–213). Michigan State University Press.
Dupuy, J.-P. (2013). *The mark of the sacred* (M. B. DeBevoise, Trans.). Stanford University Press.
Dupuy, J.-P. (2015). *A short treatise on the metaphysics of tsunamis* (M. B. DeBevoise, Trans.). Michigan State University Press.
Feldman, K. S. (2015). On Girard's biblical realism. In P. Antonello & H. Webb (Eds.), *Mimesis, desire, and the novel: Rene Girard and literary criticism* (pp. 55–68). Michigan State University Press.
Fornari, G. (2009). Figures of Antichrist: The apocalypse and its restraints in contemporary political thought. *Innsbrucker Diskussionspapiere Zu Weltordung, Religion Und Gewalt, 31*, 1–37.
Gardner, S. L. (2011). Rene Girard's apocalyptic critique of historical reason: Limiting politics to make way for faith. *Contagion: Journal of Violence, Mimesis, and Culture, 18*, 1–22.
Gardner, S. L. (2013). Modernity as revelation: Rene Girard's imagination of the worst. *Journal of Violence and Religion, 1*(2), 232–252.
Gardner, S. L. (2016). Rene Girard: Christian apocalypse of modernity, or modern apocalypse of Christianity? In Y. Espira (Ed.), *'Images of Europe: Past, Present, Future Issues' Conference Proceedings*, Porto, Portugal, pp. 1123–1131.
Girard, R. (1965). *Deceit, desire, and the novel: Self and other in literary structure* (Y. Freccero, Trans.). The Johns Hopkins University Press.
Girard, R. (1977). *Violence and the sacred* (P. Gregory, Trans.). The Johns Hopkins Press.
Girard, R. (1978). *To double business bound. Essays on literature, mimesis, and anthropology.* Baltimore: The Johns Hopkins University Press.
Girard, R. (1986). *The scapegoat* (Y. Freccero, Trans.). The Johns Hopkins University Press.
Girard, R. (1987a). Generative Scapegoating. In R. G. Hamerton-Kelly (Ed.), *Violent origins: Walter Burkert, Rene Girard, and Jonathan Z. Smith on ritual killing and cultural formation* (pp. 73–146). Stanford University Press.
Girard, R. (1987b) (a). *Job: The victim and his people* (Y. Freccero, Trans.). The Athlone Press.
Girard, R. (1988). The founding murder in the philosophy of Nietzsche. In P. Dumouchel (Ed.), *Violence and truth: On the work of Rene Girard* (pp. 227–246). The Athlone Press.
Girard, R. (1996). *The Girard reader*. In J. G. Williams (Ed.), The Crossroad Publishing Company.
Girard, R. (2005). *I see Satan fall like lightning* (J. G. Williams, Trans.). Orbis Books.
Girard, R. (2007). The evangelical subversion of myth. In R. Hamerton-Kelly (Ed.), *Politics & apocalypse* (pp. 29–49). Michigan State University Press.
Girard, R. (2015). Literature and Christianity. In P. Antonello & H. Webb (Eds.), *Mimesis, desire, and the novel: Rene Girard and literary criticism* (pp. 279–290). Michigan State University Press.
Girard, R. (2020). *Conversations with Rene Girard: Prophet of Envy*. C. L. Haven (Ed.). Bloomsbury Academic.
Girard, R., & Chantre, B. (2010). *Battling to the end: Conversations with Benoit Chantre* (M. Baker, Trans.). Michigan State University Press.
Girard, R., Antonello, P., & de Castro Rocha, J. C. (2008). *Evolution and conversion: Dialogues on the origins of culture.* Continuum.

Girard, R., Oughourlian, J.-M., & Lefort, G. (1978). *Things hidden since the foundation of the world* (S. Bann & M. Metteer, Trans.). Continuum.
Golsan, R. J. (2002). *Rene Girard and myth. An introduction*. Routledge.
Gragnolati, M. & Webb, H. (2015). *Dubbiosi Sisiri*: Mimetic processes in Dante's *Comedy*. In P. Antonello & H. Webb (Eds.), *Mimesis, desire, and the novel: Rene Girard and literary criticism* (pp. 113–131). Michigan State University Press.
Hamerton-Kelly, R. (2007). An introductory essay. In R. Hamerton-Kelly (Ed.), *Politics & apocalypse* (pp. 1–28). Michigan State University Press.
Krastev, I., & Holmes, S. (2019). *The light that failed: A reckoning*. Allen Lane.
Maffesoli, M. (1996). *The time of the tribes: The decline of individualism in mass society* (D. Smith, Trans.). Sage Publications.
Marder, N. S. (2006). Why *12 Angry* Men? (1957): The transformative power of jury deliberations. In R. Strickland, T. E. Foster, & T. L. Banks (Eds.), *Screening justice—The cinema of law: Significant films of law, order and social justice* (pp. 157–169). William S. Hein & Company.
McBride, J. (1995). Capital punishment as the unconstitutional establishment of religion: A Girardian reading of the death penalty. *Journal of Church and State, 37*, 263–287.
McKenna, A. J. (1992). *Violence and difference: Girard, Derrida, and deconstruction*. University of Illinois Press.
Mucignat, R. (2015). For a comparative topography of desire: Mimetic theory and the world map. In P. Antonello & H. Webb (Eds.), *Mimesis, desire, and the novel: Rene Girard and literary criticism* (pp. 133–146). Michigan State University Press.
Nail, B. W. (2020). Homo sacrificus: Sacrificial economization and neoliberal subjectivity. In B. W. Nail & J. A. Ellsworth (Eds.), *Law's sacrifice: Approaching the problem of sacrifice in law, literature, and philosophy* (pp. 79–101). Routledge.
Nietzsche, F. (1969). *On the genealogy of morals and Ecce Homo* (W. Kaufman & R. J. Hollingdale, Trans.) Vintage Books.
Nietzsche, F. (2003). *Writings from the late notebooks*. In R. Bittner (Ed.), (K. Sturge, Trans.). Cambridge University Press.
Niewiadomski, J. (2007). 'Denial of the apocalypse' versus 'Fascination with the Final Days': Current theological discussion of apocalyptic thinking in the perspective of mimetic theory. In R. Hamerton-Kelly (Ed.), *Politics & apocalypse* (pp. 51–67). Michigan State University Press.
Orlean, A. (1988). Money and Mimetic Speculation. In P. Dumouchel (Ed.), *Violence and truth: On the work of Rene Girard* (pp. 101–112). The Athlone Press.
Palaver, W. (2007). Carl Schmitt's 'apocalyptic' resistance against global civil war. In R. G. Hamerton-Kelly (Ed.), *Politics & apocalypse* (pp. 69–94). Michigan State University Press.
Palaver, W. (2015). Creative renunciation: The spiritual heart of *deceit, desire, and the novel*. In P. Antonello & H. Webb (Eds.), *Mimesis, desire, and the novel: Rene Girard and literary criticism* (pp. 69–77). Michigan State University Press.
Ranieri, J. (2007). Modernity and the Jewish question: What Leo Strauss learned from Friedrich Nietzsche. In R. Hamerton-Kelly (Ed.), *Politics & apocalypse* (pp. 139–187). Michigan State University Press.
Scubla, L. (1988). The Christianity of Rene Girard and the nature of religion. In P. Dumouchel (Ed.), *Violence and truth: On the work of Rene Girard* (pp. 160–178). The Athlone Press.
Serres, M. (2007). *The parasite* (L. R. Schehr, Trans.). University of Minnesota Press.
Sherwin, R. K. (2001). Nomos and cinema. *UCLA Law Review, 48*, 1519–1543.
Stroumsa, G. G. (2012). The afterlife of Orphism: Jewish, Gnostic and Christian perspectives. *Historia Religionum, 4*, 139–157.
Taubes, J. (2013). *To Carl Schmitt: Letters and reflections* (K. Tribe, Trans.). Columbia University Press.
Troy, J. (2021). *Desire and imitation in international politics*. Michigan State University Press.
Vernant, J.-P., & Vidal-Naquet, P. (1990). *Myth and tragedy in ancient Greece* (J. Lloyd, Trans.). Zone Books.
Veyne, P. (1988). *Did the Greeks believe in their myths? An essay on the constitutive imagination* (P. Wissing, Trans.). The University of Chicago Press.

MIX
Papier aus verantwortungsvollen Quellen
Paper from responsible sources
FSC® C105338

If you have any concerns about our products,
you can contact us on
ProductSafety@springernature.com

In case Publisher is established outside the EU,
the EU authorized representative is:
Springer Nature Customer Service Center GmbH
Europaplatz 3, 69115 Heidelberg, Germany

Printed by Libri Plureos GmbH
in Hamburg, Germany